shakespearean criticism

"Thou art a Monument without a tomb,
And art alive still while thy Book doth
 live
And we have wits to read and praise to
give."

*Ben Jonson, from the preface
to the First Folio, 1623.*

Mr. WILLIAM SHAKESPEARES
COMEDIES, HISTORIES, & TRAGEDIES.

Published according to the True Originall Copies.

LONDON
Printed by Isaac Iaggard, and Ed. Blount. 1623.

Frontispiece to the First Folio (1623). By permission of the Folger Shakespeare Library.

Volume 57

shakespearean criticism

Excerpts from the Criticism of
William Shakespeare's Plays and Poetry,
from the First Published Appraisals
to Current Evaluations

Michelle Lee
Editor

Detroit
New York
San Francisco
London
Boston
Woodbridge, CT

STAFF

Lynn M. Spampinato, Janet Witalec, *Managing Editors, Literature Product*
Kathy D. Darrow, *Product Liaison*
Michelle Lee, *Editor*
Mark W. Scott, *Publisher, Literature Product*

Elisabeth Gellert, *Associate Editor*
Mary Ruby, *Technical Training Specialist*
Deborah J. Morad, Kathleen Lopez Nolan, *Managing Editors, Literature Content*
Susan M. Trosky, *Director, Literature Content*

Maria L. Franklin, *Permissions Manager*
Edna Hedblad, *Permissions Specialist*
Margaret Chamberlain, *Permissions Associate*

Victoria B. Cariappa, *Research Manager*
Tracie A. Richardson, *Project Coordinator*
Barbara McNeil, Gary J. Oudersluys, Maureen Richards, Cheryl L. Warnock, *Research Specialists*
Tim Lehnerer, Ron Morelli, *Research Assistants*

Dorothy Maki, *Manufacturing Manager*
Stacy L. Melson, *Buyer*

Mary Beth Trimper, *Composition and Prepress Manager*
Gary Leach, *Composition Specialist*

Randy Bassett, *Image Database Supervisor*
Dan Newell, *Imaging Specialist*
Michael Logusz, *Graphic Artist*
Pamela A. Reed, *Imaging Coordinator*
Kelly A. Quin, *Imaging Editor*

Since this page cannot legibly accommodate all copyright notices, the acknowledgments constitute an extension of the copyright notice.

While every effort has been made to secure permission to reprint material and to ensure the reliability of the information presented in this publication, the Gale Group neither guarantees the accuracy of the data contained herein nor assumes any responsibility for errors, omissions or discrepancies. Gale accepts no payment for listing; and inclusion in the publication of any organization, agency, institution, publication, service, or individual does not imply endorsement of the editors or publisher. Errors brought to the attention of the publisher and verified to the satisfaction of the publisher will be corrected in future editions.

This publication is a creative work fully protected by all applicable copyright laws, as well as by misappropriation, trade secret, unfair competition, and other applicable laws. The authors and editors of this work have added value to the underlying factual material herein through one or more of the following: unique and original selection, coordination, expression, arrangement, and classification of the information.

All rights to this publication will be vigorously defended.

Copyright © 2001 Gale Group, Inc.
27500 Drake Road
Farmington Hills, MI 48331-3535

All rights reserved, including the right of reproduction in whole or in part in any form.

Gale Group and Design is a trademark used herein under license.

Library of Congress Catalog Card Number 86-645085
ISBN 0-7876-4695-4
ISSN 0883-9123
Printed in the United States of America

10 9 8 7 6 5 4 3 2 1

Contents

Preface vii

Acknowledgments ix

List of Plays and Poems Covered in *SC* xi

As You Like It

Introduction	1
Gender Issues	2
History and Philosophy	31
Representation and Identity	40
Sports as Metaphor	64
Further Reading	86

Henry IV, Parts 1 and 2

Introduction	88
Overviews and General Studies	88
Character Studies	116
Language	137
Reformation, Redemption, and The Rejection of Falstaff	147
Unity	181
Further Reading	186

Macbeth

Introduction	188
Overviews and General Studies	189

Ethics and Political Ideology 218

Gender Issues 242

Psychological Approaches 267

Further Reading 275

The Winter's Tale

Introduction 277

Language, Structure, and Plot 278

Sexuality and Authority 294

Sources, Influences, and Ideologies 336

Further Reading 378

Cumulative Character Index 381

Cumulative Topic Index 393

Cumulative Topic Index, by Play 413

Preface

Shakespearean Criticism (*SC*) provides students, educators, theatergoers, and other interested readers with valuable insight into Shakespeare's drama and poetry. A multiplicity of viewpoints documenting the critical reaction of scholars and commentators from the seventeenth century to the present day derives from hundreds of periodicals and books excerpted for the series. Students and teachers at all levels of study will benefit from *SC,* whether they seek information for class discussions and written assignments, new perspectives on traditional issues, or the most noteworthy of analyses of Shakespeare's artistry.

Scope of the Series

Volumes 1 through 10 of the series present a unique historical overview of the critical response to each Shakespearean work, representing a broad range of interpretations.

Volumes 11 through 26 recount the performance history of Shakespeare's plays on the stage and screen through eyewitness reviews and retrospective evaluations of individual productions, comparisons of major interpretations, and discussions of staging issues.

Volumes 27 through 56 in the series focus on criticism published after 1960, with a view to providing the reader with the most significant modern critical approaches. Each volume is ordered around a theme that is central to the study of Shakespeare, such as politics, religion, or sexuality. The topic entry that introduces each volume is comprised of general essays that discuss this theme with reference to all of Shakespeare's works. Following the topic entry are several entries devoted to individual works.

Beginning with volume 57 in the series, *SC* provides a works-based approach; each of the four entries contained in a regular volume focuses on a specific Shakespearean play or poem. The entries will include the most recent criticism available on the works, as well as earlier criticism not previously included in *SC*. In addition to regular works-based volumes, *SC* will provide an annual Topics volume; these volumes will be divided into several Topic entries, which will contain essays that analyze various topics, or themes, found in Shakespeare's works, such as Honor, Jealousy, War and Warfare, and Elizabethan Politics.

Up until volume 48, published in October 1999, *SC* compiled an annual volume of the most noteworthy essays published on Shakespeare during the previous year. The essays, reprinted in their entirety, were recommended to Gale by an international panel of distinguished scholars.

Organization of the Book

An *SC* entry consists of the following elements:

- The **Introduction** contains background information that introduces the reader to the work or topic that is the subject of the entry and outlines modern interpretations of individual Shakespearean topic, plays, and poems.

- Reprinted **Criticism** for each entry consists of essays arranged chronologically under a variety of subheadings to facilitate the study of different aspects of the play, poem, or topic. This provides an overview of the major areas of concern in the analysis of Shakespeare's works, as well as a useful perspective on changes in critical evaluation over recent decades. The critic's name and the date of composition or publication of the critical work are given at the beginning of each piece of criticism. Unsigned criticism is preceded by the title of the source in which it appeared. Footnotes are reprinted at the end of each essay or excerpt. In the case of excerpted criticism, only those footnotes that pertain to the excerpted texts are included.

- A complete **Bibliographical Citation** of the original essay or book precedes each piece of criticism.

- Critical essays are prefaced by **Explanatory Notes** as an aid to students using *SC*. The explanatory notes summarize the criticism that follows.

- Each volume includes such **Illustrations** as reproductions of images from the Shakespearean period, paintings and sketches of eighteenth- and nineteenth-century performers, photographs of modern productions, and stills from film adaptations.

- An annotated bibliography of **Further Reading** appears at the end of each entry and suggests resources for additional study. In some cases, significant essays for which the editors could not obtain reprint rights are included here.

Indexes

A **Cumulative Character Index** identifies the principal characters of discussion in the criticism of each play and non-dramatic poem.

A **Cumulative Topic Index** identifies the principal topics in the criticism and stage history of each work. The topics are arranged alphabetically, by topic.

A **Cumulative Topic Index, by Play** identifies the principal topics in the criticism and stage history of each work. The topics are arranged alphabetically, by play.

Citing *Shakespearean Criticism*

When writing papers, students who quote directly from any volume in the Literary Criticism Series may use the following general format to footnote reprinted criticism. The first example pertains to material drawn from periodicals, the second to material reprinted from books.

Tetsuya Motohashi. "Body Politic and Political Body in *Coriolanus*," in *Forum for Modern Language Studies* XXX, no. 2 (April 1994): 97-112; reprinted in *Shakespearean Criticism,* vol. 50, ed. Kathy D. Darrow (Farmington Hills, Mich.: The Gale Group, 2000), 119-128.

Mary Hamer. "Authority and Violence," in *William Shakespeare: Julius Caesar* (Northcote House, 1998), 12-20; reprinted in *Shakespearean Criticism,* vol. 50, ed. Kathy D. Darrow (Farmington Hills, Mich.: The Gale Group, 2000), 230-34.

Suggestions are Welcome

Readers who wish to suggest new features, topics, or authors to appear in future volumes, or who have other suggestions or comments are cordially invited to call, write, or fax the Managing Editor:

Managing Editor, Literary Criticism Series
The Gale Group
27500 Drake Road
Farmington Hills, MI 48331-3535
1-800-347-4253 (GALE)
Fax: 248-699-8054

Acknowledgments

The editors wish to thank the copyright holders of the excerpted criticism included in this volume and the permissions managers of many book and magazine publishing companies for assisting us in securing reproduction rights. We are also grateful to the staffs of the Detroit Public Library, the Library of Congress, the University of Detroit Mercy Library, Wayne State University Purdy/Kresge Library Complex, and the University of Michigan Libraries for making their resources available to us. Following is a list of the copyright holders who have granted us permission to reproduce material in this volume of *SC*. Every effort has been made to trace copyright, but if omissions have been made, please let us know.

COPYRIGHTED EXCERPTS IN *SC*, VOLUME 57, WERE REPRODUCED FROM THE FOLLOWING PERIODICALS:

AUMLA, n. 70, November, 1988. Reproduced by permission.—*College Literature*, v. XVI, Fall, 1989. Copyright © 1989 by West Chester University. Reproduced by permission.—*Comparative Drama*, v. 26, Winter, 1992-93; v. 27, Summer, 1993; v. 32, Spring, 1998. Copyright © 1993, 1998 by the Editors of *Comparative Drama*. Reproduced by permission.—*Critical Quarterly*, v. 12, 1970 for "Casting off the Old Man: History and St. Paul in *Henry IV*" by D. J. Palmer; v. 28, Spring-Summer, 1986. Reproduced by permission of Blackwell Publishers.—*Criticism*, v. XL, Fall, 1998. Copyright © 1998 Wayne State University Press. Reproduced by permission of the publisher.—*ELH*, v. 58, Summer, 1991. Copyright © 1991 by The Johns Hopkins University Press. Reproduced by permission.—*English Literary Renaissance*, v. 16, Spring, 1986 for "Macbeth's War on Time," by Donald W. Foster. Reproduced by permission of the publisher.—*Essays in Literature*, v. 14, Fall, 1987. Reproduced by permission.—*Essays in Theatre*, v. 9, November, 1990. Reproduced by permission.—*Forum for Modern Language Studies*, v. XXXIV, January, 1998. © Forum for Modern Language Studies 1998. All rights reserved. Reproduced by permission.—*Interpretation*, v. 16, Spring, 1989. © 1989 by *Interpretation*. Reproduced by permission.—*Iowa State Journal of Research*, v. 59, February, 1985. Reproduced by permission.—*The Kentucky Review*, v. 8, Summer, 1988. © copyright 1988, by the Editors of *Comparative Drama*. Reproduced by permission.—*Philosophy and Literature*, v. 19, 1995. Copyright © 1995 by The Johns Hopkins University Press. Reproduced by permission.—*Proceedings of the British Academy*, v. 76, April, 1990. © The British Academy 1991. Reproduced by permission.—*Renaissance Drama*, v. 21, 1990; v. 25, 1994. Reproduced by permission.—*Renaissance Papers*, 1991. Reproduced by permission.—*Renaissance Studies*, v. 11, March, 1997. © 1997 The Society for Renaissance Studies and Oxford University Press. Reproduced by permission.—*Shakespeare Quarterly*, v. 35, 1984; v. 36, 1985 for "Poetry and Plot in *The Winter's Tale*" by Russ McDonald; v. 48, Spring, 1997. Reproduced by permission of the publisher and the authors.—*Shakespeare Studies*, v. 21, 1993. Reproduced by permission.—*The Sixteenth Century Journal*, v. 20, Spring, 1989. Copyright © 1989 by The Sixteenth Century Journal Publishers, Inc. All rights reserved. Reproduced by permission.—*Studies in English Literature, 1500-1900*, v. 31, Spring, 1991; v. 33, Spring 1993. Reproduced by permission.—*Studies in the Literary Imagination*, v. 32, Spring, 1999. Copyright © 1999 Department of English, Georgia State University. Reproduced by permission.—*Texas Studies in Literature and Language*, v. 15, 1974. Reproduced by permission.—*Theatre Journal*, v. 41, May, 1989. Copyright © 1989 by The Johns Hopkins University Press. Reproduced by permission.

COPYRIGHTED EXCERPTS IN *SC*, VOLUME 57, WERE REPRODUCED FROM THE FOLLOWING BOOKS:

Adelman, Janet. From 'Born of Woman': Fantasies of Maternal Power in *Macbeth*," in **Cannibals, Witches, and Divorce: Estranging the Renaissance**. Edited by Marjorie Garber. The Johns Hopkins University Press, 1987. © 1987 The English Institute. All rights reserved. Reproduced by permission.—Berryman, John. From **Berryman's Shakespeare**. Edited by John Haffenden. Farrar, Straus and Giroux, 1999. Copyright © 1999 by Kate Donahue Berryman. All rights reserved. Reproduced by permission of Farrar, Straus and Giroux, Inc.—Bradbrook, M. C. From "King Henry IV," in **Stratford Papers on Shakespeare**. Edited by B. W. Jackson. McMaster University, 1965. Reproduced by permission.—Gay, Penny. From **William Shakespeare's As You Like It**. Northcote House, 1999. © 1999 by Penny Gay. Reproduced by permission.—Hunter, Robert G. From "Shakespeare's Comic Sense as It Strikes Us Today: Falstaff and the Protestant Ethic," in **Shakespeare, Pattern of Excelling Nature**. Edited by David Bevington and Jay L. Halio. Associated University Presses, 1978. Reproduced by permission.—Middleman, Louis I. From "*Henry IV, Part I*: The Two Faces of Revolt," in **In Honor of Austin Wright**. Carnegie-Mellon University, 1972. Copyright © by The Department of English, Carnegie-Mellon University.

Reproduced by permission.—Tayler, Edward W. From *Nature and Art in Renaissance Literature.* Columbia University Press, 1964. Copyright © 1964 by Columbia University Press, New York. All rights reserved. Republished with permission of the Columbia University Press, 562 W. 113th St., New York, NY 10025.—Watson, Robert N. From *Shakespeare and the Hazards of Ambition.* Harvard University Press, 1984. © 1984 by the President and Fellows of Harvard College. Reproduced by permission of the publisher and the author.—Wofford, Susanne L. "'o You I Give Myself, For I Am Yours': Erotic Performance and Theatrical Performatives in *As You Like It*," in **Shakespeare Reread: The Texts in New Contexts.** Edited Russ McDonald. Copyright © 1994 by Cornell University. Used by permission of the publisher, Cornell University Press.

PHOTOGRAPHS APPEARING IN *SC*, VOLUME 57, WERE RECEIVED FROM THE FOLLOWING SOURCES:

Act II, scene iii, from William Shakespeare's *The Winter's Tale,* from Smirke's Illustrations, photograph. Special Collections Library, University of Michigan. Reproduced by permission.—Act V, scene iii, from William Shakespeare's *The Winter's Tale,* from the Boydell-Shakespeare Gallery, photograph. Special Collections Library, University of Michigan. Reproduced by permission.—Balogh, Peter as Henry IV and Jason Marr as Prince Hal in GreenStage's 2000 production of William Shakespeare's *Henry IV, Part One,* photograph by Ken Holmes. © GreenStage. Reproduced by permission.—From William Shakespeare's *The Winter's Tale,* from Gallerie des Personnages … facing p. 27, photograph. Special Collections Library, University of Michigan. Reproduced by permission.—From William Shakespeare's *The Winter's Tale,* from Gallerie des Personnages … facing p. 29, photograph. Special Collections Library, University of Michigan. Reproduced by permission.—Gerussi, Bruno as MacDuff, Christopher Plummer as Macbeth, and members of the Festival Company in background, in the Stratford Festival's 1962 production of William Shakespeare's *Macbeth,* directed by Peter Coe, photograph. Courtesy of Stratford Festival Archives. Reproduced by permission.—Gielgud, Sir John as Macbeth in a 1942 publicity photo, photograph. AP/Wide World Photos. Reproduced by permission.—Gordon, Lewis as Falstaff in the 1979 Stratford Festival's production of William Shakespeare's *Henry IV, Part Two,* directed by Peter Moss, photograph. Courtesy of Stratford Festival Archives. Reproduced by permission.—Hepburn, Katharine as Rosalind in the 1950 Theatre Guild's production of William Shakespeare's *As You Like It,* photograph. AP/Wide World Photos. Reproduced by permission.—Mahaffey, Mike as Touchstone and Lisa Viertel as Audrey in GreenStage's 1997 production of William Shakespeare's *As You Like It,* photograph by Grace Reamer. © GreenStage. Reproduced by permission.—McKenna, Senna as Lady Macbeth in the Stratford Festival's 1995 production of William Shakespeare's *Macbeth,* directed by Marti Maraden, photograph. Courtesy of Stratford Festival Archives. Reproduced by permission.—McQuinn, Mark as Mortimer, Kathleen Ulrich as Lady Mortimer, Kimberly Atkinson as Lady Percy, and Barzin Akhavan as Hotspur in GreenStage's 2000 production of William Shakespeare's *Henry IV, Part One,* photograph by Ken Holmes. © GreenStage. Reproduced by permission.—Paltrow, Gwyneth as Rosalind in a 1999 revival of William Shakespeare's *As You Like It* at the Williamstown Theatre, photograph. AP/Wide World Photos. Reproduced by permission.—Sorenson, Peter as Orlando and Erin Day as Rosalind in GreenStage's 1997 production of William Shakespeare's *As You Like It,* photograph by Grace Reamer. © GreenStage. Reproduced by permission.—Thomas, G. Valmont as Mistress Quickly in William Shakespeare's *Henry IV, Part 2* at the 1999 Oregon Shakespeare Festival, photograph. AP/Wide World Photos. Reproduced by permission.—Taylor, Valerie, April Olrich, and Anita Sharp Bolster as the witches in a 1960 production of *Macbeth,* directed by George Schaefer, photograph. The Kobal Collection. Reproduced by permission..

List of Plays and Poems Covered in *SC*

Volumes 1-10 present a critical overview of each play, including criticism from the seventeenth century to the present. Beginning with Volumes 11, the series focuses on the history of Shakespeare's plays on the stage and in important films. The Yearbooks reprint the most important critical pieces of the year as suggested by an advisory board of Shakespearean scholars. Volumes 1-56 are organized around a theme and focus on criticism published after 1960. Beginning with Volume 57, each entry in a volume focuses on a particular play or poem; annual topics volumes include entries that focus on topics or themes found in Shakespeare's works.

Vol. 1
The Comedy of Errors
Hamlet
Henry IV, Parts 1 and 2
Timon of Athens
Twelfth Night

Vol. 2
Henry VIII
King Lear
Love's Labour's Lost
Measure for Measure
Pericles

Vol. 3
Henry VI, Parts 1, 2, and 3
Macbeth
A Midsummer Night's Dream
Troilus and Cressida

Vol. 4
Cymbeline
The Merchant of Venice
Othello
Titus Andronicus

Vol. 5
As You Like It
Henry V
The Merry Wives of Windsor
Romeo and Juliet

Vol. 6
Antony and Cleopatra
Richard II
The Two Gentlemen of Verona

Vol. 7
All's Well That Ends Well
Julius Caesar
The Winter's Tale

Vol. 8
Much Ado about Nothing
Richard III
The Tempest

Vol. 9
Coriolanus
King John
The Taming of the Shrew
The Two Noble Kinsmen

Vol. 10
The Phoenix and Turtle
The Rape of Lucrece
Sonnets
Venus and Adonis

Vol. 11
King Lear
Othello
Romeo and Juliet

Vol. 12
The Merchant of Venice
A Midsummer Night's Dream
The Taming of the Shrew
The Two Gentlemen of Verona

Vol. 13
1989 Yearbook

Vol. 14
Henry IV, Parts 1 and 2
Henry V
Richard III

Vol. 15
Cymbeline
Pericles
The Tempest
The Winter's Tale

Vol. 16
1990 Yearbook

Vol. 17
Antony and Cleopatra
Coriolanus
Julius Caesar
Titus Andronicus

Vol. 18
The Merry Wives of Windsor
Much Ado about Nothing
Troilus and Cressida

Vol. 19
1991 Yearbook

Vol. 20
Macbeth
Timon of Athens

Vol. 21
Hamlet

Vol. 22
1992 Yearbook

Vol. 23
As You Like It
Love's Labour's Lost
Measure for Measure

Vol. 24
Henry VI, Parts 1, 2, and 3
Henry VIII
King John
Richard II

Vol. 25
1993 Yearbook

Vol. 26
All's Well That Ends Well
The Comedy of Errors
Twelfth Night

Vol. 27
Shakespeare and Classical Civilization
Antony and Cleopatra
Timon of Athens
Titus Andronicus
Troilus and Cressida

Vol. 28
1994 Yearbook

Vol. 29
Magic and the Supernatural
Macbeth
A Midsummer Night's Dream
The Tempest

Vol. 30
Politics
Coriolanus
Henry V
Julius Caesar

Vol. 31
Shakespeare's Representation of Women
Much Ado about Nothing
King Lear
Taming of the Shrew

Vol. 32
1995 Yearbook

Vol. 33
Sexuality in Shakespeare
Measure for Measure
The Rape of Lucrece
Romeo and Juliet
Venus and Adonis

Vol. 34
Appearance versus Reality
The Comedy of Errors
Twelfth Night
As You Like It

Vol. 35
Madness
Hamlet
Othello

Vol. 36
Fathers and Daughters
Cymbeline
Pericles
The Winter's Tale

Vol. 37
1996 Yearbook

Vol. 38
Desire
All's Well That Ends Well
Love's Labour's Lost
The Merry Wives of Windsor
The Phoenix and Turtle

Vol. 39
Kingship
Henry IV Parts 1 and 2
Henry VI Parts 1, 2, and 3
Richard II
Richard III

Vol. 40
Gender Identity
The Merchant of Venice
Sonnets
The Two Gentlemen of Verona

Vol. 41
Authorship Controversy
Henry VIII
King John
The Two Noble Kinsmen

Vol. 42
1997 Yearbook

Vol. 43
Violence
The Rape of Lucrece
Titus Andronicus
Troilus and Cressida

Vol. 44
Psychoanalytic Criticism
Hamlet
Macbeth

Vol. 45
Dreams
A Midsummer Night's Dream
The Tempest
The Winter's Tale

Vol. 46
Clowns and Fools
As You Like It
King Lear
Twelfth Night

Vol. 47
Deception
Antony and Cleopatra
Cymbeline
The Merry Wives of Windsor

Vol. 48
1998 Yearbook

Vol. 49
Law and Justice
Henry IV, 1 and 2
Henry V
Measure for Measure

Vol. 50
Social Class
Coriolanus
Julius Caesar
The Two Noble Kinsmen

Vol. 51
Love and Romance
Pericles
The Phoenix and Turtle
Romeo and Juliet
Sonnets
Venus and Adonis

Vol. 52
Morality
Richard II
Richard III
Timon of Athens

Vol. 53
Race
Othello
The Merchant of Venice

Vol. 54
Beginnings and Endings
The Comedy of Errors
Love's Labour's Lost
The Two Gentlemen of Verona

Vol. 55
Feminist Criticism
All's Well That Ends Well
Much Ado About Nothing
The Taming of the Shrew

Vol. 56
Historical Revision
Henry VI, Parts 1, 2 and 3
Henry VIII
King John

Vol. 57
As You Like It
Henry IV, Parts 1 and 2
Macbeth
The Winter's Tale

Future Volumes

Vol. 58
Antony and Cleopatra
A Midsummer Night's Dream
Richard II
The Two Noble Kinsmen

Vol. 59
Hamlet
The Merry Wives of Windsor
The Rape of Lucrece
Troilus and Cressida

As You Like It

For further information on the critical and stage history of *As You Like It,* see *SC,* Volumes 5, 23, 34, and 46.

INTRODUCTION

As You Like It, most likely written in 1599, is one of Shakespeare's most highly regarded comedies and most frequently performed works. Based on Thomas Lodge's prose romance *Rosalynde* (1590), the play recounts the love story of Rosalind and Orlando. Roughly divided into three parts, the play features a middle section set in the Forest of Arden, where many aspects of Elizabethan social order are turned inside out. This magical place—where gender roles are reversed, social restrictions loosened, and time suspended—has garnered much critical attention throughout the twentieth century. Scholars frequently compare Arden to the setting in *A Midsummer Night's Dream,* and analyze the ways in which Shakespeare used this environment to address the social problems of his day, including sexual inequality and changes in the traditional English agrarian life. *As You Like It* introduces many notable characters, including the clown Touchstone and the insightful, melancholy Jaques—the source of the famous line "All the world's a stage." Rosalind, who disguises herself as the boy Ganymede, raises many interesting debates on homosexuality, gender blending, androgyny, and sexual identity. With the rising influence of feminist studies and the application of new historicism, scholars have applied a previously unexplored set of questions to the play. Chief among them is the nature of gender relations, the role of eroticism, and the degree to which patriarchal ideals are maintained in the play. In addition, emerging historical data about Elizabethan popular culture has given scholars new insight into the significance of sport and the influence of philosophical ideals in the play.

Critics note that Rosalind's double role as a female pretending to be a male provides rich fodder for gender studies. The issues about sexuality are further complicated by Phebe's love for Rosalind's alter ego Ganymede, Orlando's complex relationship with the "boy" whom he treats as a confidante about his love for Rosalind, and, most significantly, the fact that all the female roles were played by boys at the time when Shakespeare was writing. What has resulted is a proliferation of studies on the formation of sexuality, the social construction of gender, the significance of gender blending during the Elizabethan era, the politics of sexuality, and the role of homosexuality and crossdressing in English society. Susan Carlson (1987) provides an overview of how thought has shifted among Shakespearean scholars about the role of women in comedies and the critical debate which has developed around this issue. The first school of thought includes those who have endorsed the theories of H. B. Charlton. Charlton argues that women represent an ideal in the comedy genre, and that they are embodiments of creativity and the keys to happiness. Critics of this school focus on the middle section of *As You Like It* where social norms are suspended and women enjoy unprecedented freedom of speech and power. A second group of literary critics, in contrast, argue that in the end the norm is restored, Rosalind and Celia become powerless and voiceless wives, and any gains of insight are enjoyed by the males alone. Carlson counts herself among the latter group of scholars who view *As You Like It,* not as a radical reform of traditional patriarchal ideals, but as a drama which "offers more limitations than possibilities for the women in the play." She states that while Shakespeare tried to advance ideas on the politics of gender, he was limited by the conventions of his day. Kay Stanton (1989) echoes many of these same views, stating that she believes the juxtaposition between the freedom of the middle scenes and the loss of options in the conclusion was Shakespeare's way of voicing criticism. Furthermore, Stanton examines the epilogue, a scene which has troubled and puzzled modern critics. In this scene, the actor playing Rosalind professes to be both man and woman in a convoluted display of both genders. Stanton posits that it is only in this mixture of genders that men and women can be equal; however, this gender blending only existed in Shakespeare's eyes through magic. Penny Gay (1999) more fully examines the ramifications of boys playing female roles in Elizabethan times. She argues that Shakespeare produced a more interesting drama than Lodge because Shakespeare capitalized on the fact that boys occupied female roles, creating an intriguing situation of ambiguities and possibilities. Gay believes that although the play lacks plot, audiences find it a favorite because of the erotic possibilities of Rosalind's courtship scenes. Susanne L. Wofford (1994) considers the role of language in establishing meanings about gender in the play.

Another area of interest for scholars is the topic of representation and identity. In many ways this topic is closely related to issues of gender, sexual identity, and disguise discussed above. In her essay on transvestism, Anne Herrmann (1989) discusses the difference between the divided self, as represented by Orlando, and the doubled self, depicted in the characters of Celia and Rosalind. The scholar states that transvestism is not a violation of social norms but highlights social contradiction. She states that merely by donning a disguise Rosalind cannot alter her true nature as a female. The disguise does not signify veiled eroticism but serves as a means of pointing out the arbitrary constructions of social relations, or the means by which we represent ourselves. In her 1985 essay, Kay Stanton also discusses the relationship between disguise and representation, concentrating on the prevalent use of the device of disguise by many of the cast. She states that all the characters have to don disguises in order to mask their true feelings, and all misrepresent who they are. In her explanation of the epilogue, Stanton suggests that it is only through disguise that Rosalind can be both male and female, but, in fact, she represents "the spirit of art," a necessary component for humans to understand their own identity. In his article on the nature of theater, P. H. Parry (1998) considers the differences between the role of the characters in *As You Like It* and the audience. He argues that Shakespeare understood the self-conscious nature of theater in the Elizabethan era, which is markedly different from the emphasis on realism in today's dramas. Shakespeare incorporated aspects of his audience into the drama, at times making his characters part of the audience as they observed the actions of other characters on stage. Parry points out that although the epilogue is troublesome to modern casts and audiences, to the Elizabethans it would have made perfect sense.

Emerging historical data about Elizabethan popular culture has given scholars new insights into the significance of sport and the influence of philosophical ideals in the play. For instance, Cynthia Marshall (1993) discusses the role of sport as metaphor, particularly the role of wrestling in *As You Like It*. She posits that in the Elizabethan theater wrestling played a role both as sport and as spectacle; it was a means of exercise and entertainment and aided in the establishment of the moral order. Stating that Shakespeare was illustrating the ways in which "truth" may be socially constructed, she argues that through the wrestling match even violence can be "socially codified." In the same vein, A. Stuart Daley (1993) examines the significance of the hunting scenes which take place in the Forest of Arden. While earlier critics have suggested that the scenes may reflect the social prestige and noble background of Senior Duke, Daley analyzes the scenes in light of what scholars now know about upper class hunts for entertainment versus the woodmen's hunt out of necessity. Applying new knowledge about the cultural and ideological developments of the period, Robert Schwartz (1989) considers the role of Jaques, referred to as a libertine by Duke Senior. Schwartz believes that this term refers to the Familist society, an antinomian sect who believed that man could be freed from natural sin through a spiritual awakening linked to nature. Gene Fendt (1995) juxtaposes audience reaction to the play in Elizabethan and modern times in his study of the cathartic role of the comedy. He focuses specifically on the function of the Forest of Arden scenes which he refers to as "the green world," linking the role of such characters as Jaques and Touchstone with the inspiration of empathy among the audience.

GENDER ISSUES

Susan Carlson (essay date 1987)

SOURCE: "Women in *As You Like It:* Community, Change, and Choice," in *Essays in Literature,* Vol. 14, No. 2, Fall, 1987, pp. 151-69.

[*In the following essay, Carlson refutes earlier critics who claim that* As You Like It *reflects sexual equality. She argues that patriarchal norms persist, especially in the play's ending.*]

At the end of *As You Like It,* when Hymen teases Phebe that she cannot love Ganymede—"You to his [Silvius's] love must accord, / Or have a woman to your Lord" (V.iv.127-28)[1]—he reminds us of the comic mileage Shakespeare has gotten from Rosalind's disguise as Ganymede. Also, less obviously, he reminds us of the most steady love of the play, that between two women, Celia and Rosalind. His mockery of such love and the uncharacteristic silence of the women which accompanies it are two final indications of the way women are treated throughout the play. We have learned to read *As You Like It* as a play about the expansiveness of love, the graciousness of fate, and the inevitability of human foible. But it is also a play about women in the comic world. *Love's Labor's Lost* remains our best evidence of Shakespeare's wariness of the comic form—especially as it affects women—but *As You Like It* is our best model of how Shakespeare's women function as part of a comic tradition.

H. B. Charlton has taught a whole generation of Shakespearean critics to see comic heroines like Rosalind as "poetic," "creative" embodiments of "imagination" with powers "to shape the world towards happiness."[2] It has become commonplace to consider women a key to meaning in Shakespeare's comedies. Along with more standard readings of the comedies, even the recent open-eyed, often feminist, criticism by women like Ruth Nevo, Linda Bamber, and Marilyn French grows out of Charlton's equating Shakespeare's comedy with his women.[3] To find Shakespearean comedy a haven for women, as Charlton and others do, a critic must focus on the festive liberation of the middle of the plays where, as Mikhail Bahktin explains, we enter the utopian "realm of community, freedom, equality, abundance."[4] Northrop Frye's "green world" and C. L. Barber's "release" are two tidy labels for this decidedly untidy mid-play world where sex roles are reversed, wrongs righted, and problems solved.[5] Women characters, who must normally exist in a world where double standards leave them less than equal, fare well in this topsy-turvy world, directing actions and emotions. To emphasize this middle section of the play is, as Charlton, Bahktin, and others make clear, to emphasize a world of female freedom. Shakespearean comedy does not, however, end in this liberated world. The multiple marriages, ritual male-voiced pronouncements, women's silence, and return to order of these plays' endings are signs of a return to a norm suspended during the middle of the play. To emphasize such endings is to emphasize an *end* to female freedom. Clara Claiborne Park, Shirley Nelson Garner, Nicholas Grene, Anne Parten, Peter Erickson, Carol Thomas Neeley, and others have adopted this second emphasis, and study of the comic ending as a construct full of power to defuse the sexual revolution of Shakespeare's comedies.[6] In the analysis that follows, I would like to join this second group of critics, those who qualify Charlton's praise, by showing how *As You Like It* offers more limitations than possibilities for the women in the play. I will conclude my study with a fuller analysis of the play's ending, but will offer, first, a study of the play's middle, where Shakespeare establishes the world in which his women search for communities, choices, and changes.

Beginning with the "Norm"-al

The establishment of a "norm"-al world in *As You Like It* is as basic to Shakespeare's comedy as to others far less daring. We begin in the court of Duke Frederick where, in spite of several evil presences, we have a predictable world governed by civil laws and social mores; we move to a world where those norms are relaxed, often reversed; and we end promised a return to the court world, minus its rankest evils. While critics disagree on the effects of this cycle—do we or do we not reach a new (or better or different) world at play's end?—they generally agree on its presence. The special effect such circular motions have on the women of the play has been most thoroughly studied by Peter Erickson. To reach his conclusion that "*As You Like It* is primarily a defensive action against female power rather than a celebration of it," Erickson compiles an extensive list of the signs of a patriarchy present throughout the play.[7] Most importantly, he shows that the altered world of Arden is only superficially a release from everyday, patriarchal norms and that in being but a reversible *reversal* of the norms it is never a threat to them. Although Erickson never makes the connection explicitly, he bases this reading of *As You Like It*'s persistent "norm"-al world on the presence of a sexual double standard. The sexual double standard in Shakespeare's "norm"-al world is not significant because it grants women less freedom and power than it does men. It is significant because in the middle world of the play, where norms are reversed, the power and freedom women *do* gain is *still* based on the double standard, and is only a reversal of it. In other words, the middle world of the play does not revoke the double standard, but only invokes a temporary criticism of it. While the social criticism of *As You Like It* is not negated by the play's reversals, it is continually undercut by the omnipresence of the play's double standard. Such persistent norms complicate a reading of any aspect of the play, but raise the most perplexing questions about those parts of the play generally acknowledged to be sexually liberating, the play's structural foundation in equality, for example.

While the words "equal" and "equally" each occur only once in the course of the play, they are notations of a pattern present throughout the play. Celia and Rosalind, in I.ii, offer us equality as a desirable goal and a standard of judgment, first when Celia finds that the ideal bestowal of Fortune's gifts must be an equal one—"Let us sit and mock the good housewife Fortune from her wheel, that her gifts may henceforth be bestowed equally" (I.ii.29-31)—and later when she counsels Orlando to "a more equal enterprise" (I.ii.161) than Charles the Wrestler appears to be. Most of the play's equality, however, comes not from such obvious pleas as much as from the standards that equality and symmetry become for actions, characters, and language. For example, a standard of symmetry balances one action against another when a conversation on the killing of deer (II.i) is matched by the actual hunting of deer (IV.ii); when Rosalind's first wooing of Orlando (III.ii) is mated to a second (IV.i); when Orlando's triumphant dialogue with Jaques (III.ii) is repeated in Rosalind's similar victory over the cynic (IV.i). The significance of characters is likewise refined when they are considered in pairs—Jaques's cynicism is tempered by Touchstone's loving parody, Silvius's idealism is braced by Corin's realism, one bad brother (Oliver, Duke Frederick) is paired with one good one (Orlando, Duke Senior), and one unrequited love (Phebe's) is upstaged by another one, less vain (Silvius's). And as critics have shown us countless times, the play's language is a comparable series of delicate balances. Orlando's bad poems come coupled with the reassured, regular rhythms of Rosalind's prose, for example. Rosalind, finally, is the crucible for all such equations, symmetries, and balances, acting as a matchmaker for others even as she is self-conscious of her own vacillations between the realistic and the idealistic. By the end of the play, when Silvius leads his litany of love in V.ii and when Hymen and Jaques parcel out their verbal gifts of love in V.iv, Shakespeare has us, also, seeing the play's four marriages as natural extensions of a play full of equations and balances. In the play's final scene, Celia's word "equal" has become "even"; first when Rosalind disappears "To make these doubts all even" (V.iv.25) and second when Hymen elevates her "even" by rhyming it with heaven: "Then is there mirth in heaven / When earthly things made even / Atone together" (V.iv.102-04). "Even," like the "equal" of I.ii, is meant to assure us that life is orderly and balanced at the end of the play.

While it has been common to link the play's balances to a sexual equality, the play's symmetries are more reflections of the orderly "norm"-al world, double standards and all, than guarantees of an advanced notion of relations between the sexes. The androgyny that critics have praised as the pinnacle of the play's many equalities is not a sign-post of sexual liberation but yet another signal of the play's being founded on norms.

In his study of the androgyny of the play, Erickson points out that a levelling of sexual differences is not possible, even in this play's measured, tolerant world, because the basis for both worlds in the play is patriarchy.[8] This limitation makes androgyny of benefit only to the men returning to power at the play's end, not to the women about to give it up:

> However, the conservative counter-movement built into comic strategy applies exclusively to Rosalind. Her possession of the male costume and the power it symbolizes is only temporary. But Orlando does not have to give up the emotional enlargement he has experienced in the forest. Discussions of androgyny in *As You Like It* usually focus on Rosalind, whereas in fact it is the men rather than the women who are the lasting beneficiaries of androgyny.[9]

Androgyny is not a reality for the women in *As You Like It* in the same measure it is for the men because the women are never equal to the men; the most they gain in the middle of the play is only a reversal of an inequitable situation. The play's reversals ensure that while men learn their weaknesses and women their powers in the inversion of the play's middle world, norms do not change. In studying the issue of sexual difference in the broader scope of the Renaissance, Catherine Besley finds, contrarily, that plays like *As You Like It* offer a "radical challenge to patriarchal values by disrupting sexual difference itself." She offers a dazzling case for the social and sexual instability Shakespeare's comedies threaten in their jockeying of sexual identity. She admits, however, that Rosalind's control of her disguise limits the danger posed by this play's transgressions.[10]

The play's inequitable "norm"-al world is tested by its free, levelling middle, but scarcely altered by it. It seems likely that Shakespeare was aware of the formal tension between his agenda for social change and his generic constraints, for this play abounds in his self-consciousness of the comic genre. It is so full of references to its own form that Ruth Nevo has dubbed it a "meta-comedy," a comedy "so self-assured as not to care whether we notice or not that it is talking about its own mode of being."[11] As I study the conventions of the play's middle and end, then, I do so not to berate Shakespeare for attitudes he never considered, but to expand our understanding of the choices he made among the many attitudes he considered—especially those choices influencing his women. As fiercely as any playwright before or since, Shakespeare writes comedy in which he battles against convention even as he nestles his characters into its comfortable, "norm"-al shelters.

Inverting the "Norm"-al

The testing of the normal that constitutes the liberated middle of this play allows and encourages great power and control in the female characters. But the continuing though inverted presence of the "norm"-al helps explain the patterns discernible in the women's language and friendship.

Rosalind commands the special linguistic world at the center of *As You Like It,* yet her mastery of language is continually undercut. In our introduction to the cousins Rosalind and Celia in I.ii, such contradictions establish the women's linguistic pattern. Most immediately, we are struck with the women's facility with a language flexible enough for them to move from sadness to joy and intimate enough to encourage the trust and love equalled nowhere else in the play. After the straightforward discussion of Rosalind's sadness that introduces us to this direct, though playful, way the women trust one another with their emotions, we are introduced to the strategies the two women have had to develop to protect such linguistic loving and giving. In the sport they make of falling in love we notice, first, their verbal versatility: they banter with the good nature of two who indulge often in such matches (ll. 28-40); they feed questions and lines to Touchstone with the deftness of people used to indulging the verbal performances of others (ll. 41-85); and they badger Le Beau with a humane tolerance for his denseness (ll. 86-134). Only belatedly, we notice that such verbal acuity is tarnished by certain sexist assumptions and indirections built into the banter. As Celia and Rosalind discuss the bestowal of Fortune's and Nature's gifts, for example, they rely on traditional stereotypes of women—the fair are stupid and the honest are ugly. As Celia puts it, "for those that she [Fortune] makes fair she scarce makes honest, and those that she makes honest she makes very ill-favoredly" (I.ii.32-34). They depend on such stereotypes even when alone, and despite the fact that—as the rest of the play makes apparent—neither Rosalind nor Celia lacks either looks or brains. Even Touchstone allows for the breaking of such a type by acknowledging ladies "young and fair" *and* bright (II.vii.37-38). When Touchstone enters, these two non-stereotypical women adopt stereotypical behavior, allowing linguistic control to fall to the male as they feed him the lines he needs to exercise his wit. Later in the scene, as the court witnesses the wrestling entertainment, Rosalind protests she is weak—"The little strength that I have I would it were with you" (I.ii.177-78)—this time directly acknowledging that the world she and Celia inhabit is one where women are seen as less capable than men. While the women take first place with their language skills, they accept second place in society.

In Rosalind, especially, both this female mastery of language and the indirections and inversions it is tied to are traceable through the entire play. While in I.ii Rosalind operates in the familiarity and leisure she and Celia share, in I.iii her language, as well as Celia's, becomes a finely tuned instrument on which she must play the melodies of a range of emotions. First Rosalind matches Celia in playfulness, converting Celia's subject, Rosalind's father, into her own—"my child's father" (I.iii.11). Then she moves beyond playfulness to do verbal battle with her uncle, Duke Frederick. He forewarns her that traitorous acts must be redeemed by more than words, yet is battered by her reply, strong in its repetitions, its sound argument, and its graceful sincerity:

> So was I when your Highness took his dukedom;
> So was I when your Highness banished him.
> Treason is not inherited, my lord,
> Or if we did derive it from our friends,

What's that to me: My father was no traitor.
Then, good my liege, mistake me not so much
To think my poverty is treacherous.

(I.iii.55-61)

Rosalind's language is more convincing to us than to Duke Frederick, of course, and even though Celia follows her with an equally graceful plea to her father, his response shows us he has responded not to the cousins' verbal skill, their reason or their words, but to his distrust of female language. He tells Celia "She [Rosalind] is too subtile for thee" (l. 73) and orders his daughter to silence, "then open not thy lips" (l. 78). These women's language skills carry little weight in the Duke's court.

Yet in III.ii we move to Arden, a world where, without Duke Frederick, the limits Rosalind sets to her language are only her own. Rosalind blossoms enough to recognize the inadequacies of Orlando's verbal celebrations of her, telling Celia of his verses, "some of them had in them more feet than the verses would bear" (III.ii.159-60). She can then banter with Celia over the concrete image of "feet" she calls up. She further displays her versatility by matching witty analogies to nature with Touchstone (ll. 111-15) and by making more learned allusions at her leisure—calling up Pythagoras for example (III.ii.168). But her power and control are most obvious in her first conversation with Orlando. From the exit of Jaques in line 281 to Rosalind and Orlando's joint exit at the scene's end, a simple measure of her command of this conversation is the number of lines both characters speak. Rosalind has ninety-eight lines to Orlando's thirty, but even such lopsided numbers only begin to suggest her mastery of their interaction. Orlando, on the one hand, takes on the role Celia and Rosalind had assumed earlier, in I.ii, and feeds lines and questions to Rosalind. In addition, Orlando has brief speeches (usually one line or less) devoid of imagination or wit. Rosalind, on the other hand, is represented by a hearty prose in which form is matched to content, in which the melodies of the language are the melodies of her love. We have had a taste of Rosalind's prose before we see her in Arden, but only in Arden can she use it for power as well as for pleasure.

There continue to be moments when Rosalind's wit and verbal acuity are everything, as she chides Phebe in III.iv or as she directs the others in the recitations of V.ii. But the extent of her linguistic skills is clearest when her heart is in her language, in III.ii and IV.i especially. Rosalind reaches the height of her powers in IV.i. Here the gymnastic playfulness of III.ii is transformed into heart-felt pronouncements on love and marriage. When Rosalind plays the realist in denying to Orlando that one could die from lack of love, the great love she feels for him softens her harsh statement and gives it its graceful rhythms:

> The poor world is almost six thousand years old, and in all that time there was not any man died in his own person, videlicit, in a love cause. Troilus had his brains dashed out with a Grecian club; yet he did what he could to die before, and he is one of the patterns of love. Leander, he would have lived many a fair year though Hero had turned nun, if it had not been for a hot midsummer night; for, good youth, he went but forth to wash him in the Hellespont, and being taken with the cramp, was drowned; and the foolish chroniclers of that age found it was 'Hero of Sestos.' But these are all lies. Men have died from time to time, and worms have eaten them, but not for love.

(IV.i.85-98)

Her feeling for and use of language in such skillful ways is what we miss so much when Rosalind gives up her language along with her disguise and is silent at the play's end. As the ritual takes prominence in the play's final scene, we experience a falling off in the language. As the emotions and powers of Rosalind's language give way to the comparative shallowness of song and dance, Rosalind takes her silent place in the marriage ritual. Even the Epilogue, in awarding the last words to Rosalind, does not make up for Rosalind's silence. Erickson points out that the Epilogue subverts the woman's world of this play by reminding us of the boy Rosalind-Ganymede and not the woman who has been the linguistic heart of the play.[12] I would suggest, in addition, that Rosalind's return as an actor (whether male *or* female) reinforces the consciousness we have had all along that her power comes only from a suspension of the play's—and the world's—reality. The fact that she still must make her last moment of power depend on her male disguise only increases our suspicion that we must lose the Rosalind of the play's middle because her linguistic command is as dangerous as it is endearing.

The Epilogue and the silence that precedes it are, in fact, only our last indications of the way the women's linguistic powers remain attached to assumptions which undercut them. Let me backtrack through the scenes I have already discussed to suggest how each one of them is burdened with a discrediting of the women's linguistic power. In I.iii, Duke Frederick warns Celia of the deception in Rosalind's language:

> She is too subtile for thee; and the smoothness,
> Her very silence and her patience,
> Speak to the people, and they pity her.

(I.iii.73-75)

His warning we can dismiss, because he is so despicably evil, but only until we hear similar reservations voiced elsewhere *by Rosalind herself*. For example, she prefaces her talk with Orlando in III.ii by asking Celia the self-deprecating question, "Do you not know I am a woman? When I think, I must speak" (III.ii.237-38). She reconfirms her diagnosis of logorrhea by lacing the pyrotechnics of IV.i with similar undercuttings of her skill. Here she warns her future husband Orlando that "certainly a woman's thought runs before her actions" (IV.i.127-28) and counsels him, further, to be wary of his wife's wayward wit:

> Make the doors upon a woman's wit, and it will out at

the casement; shut that, and 'twill out at the keyhold; stop that, 'twill fly with the smoke out at the chimney.

(IV.i.148-51)

Rosalind's comments may be tongue-in-cheek, but they cannot simply be dismissed as comic, for the direct discrediting of female language in these three statements is reinforced by the many indirect and subversive tactics women have adopted as part of their presence in the play.

Even as she is Ganymede and liberated from the restrictions placed on Rosalind the woman, Rosalind accepts limiting stereotypes. One might speculate that Rosalind adopts such deferential behavior to preserve her male disguise, but importantly, she makes the same patriarchal assumptions in I.ii, before she adopts the guise of Ganymede. Of the disguise itself, Rosalind tells us that it will help her hide in her heart "what hidden woman's fear there will" (I.iii.115). Later, while collapsing at the end of the journey into Arden, she blames the weak female in her: "I could find in my heart to disgrace my man's apparel and to cry like a woman; but I must comfort the weaker vessel, as doublet and hose ought to show itself courageous to petticoat" (II.iv.4-7). She disdains the woman in herself as much as the woman, Celia-Aliena, she feels an obligation to comfort. Even in III.ii, so rich in Rosalind's confidence and control, her doubts about her female self loom large; she tells Celia that she retains the impatience of a woman (III.ii.185-89) and later after teasing Orlando with a catalogue of women's faults—"All like one another as halfpence are, every one fault seeming monstrous till his fellow-fault came to match it" (III.ii.334-36)—she paints a giddy picture of the female lover:

> At which time would I, being but a moonish youth, grieve, be effeminate, changeable, long and liking, proud, fantastical, apish, shallow, inconstant, full of tears, full of smiles; for every passion truly anything, as boys and women are for the most part cattle of this color; would now like him, now loathe him; then entertain him, then forswear him; now weep for him, then spit at him; that I drave my suitor from his mad humor of love to a living humor of madness, which was, to forswear the full stream of the world and to live in a nook merely monastic.

(III.ii.384-94)

Rosalind's self-conscious mockery means that we never take such comments at their full value, yet we are inclined to agree with Celia in her charge to Rosalind: "You have simply misused our sex in your loveprate" (IV.i.185-86).

What Celia cannot tell us, however, is that we fail to dismiss Rosalind's comments because so much action in the play validates them. For example, all of the women in the play—Rosalind, Celia, Phebe, and Audrey—do become giddy and rash when in love, just as Rosalind has foretold. Rosalind herself is the most severe case, in IV.i, when she demands a wedding ceremony one moment and warns of cuckolds the next. More numerically overwhelming are the many indirect actions of the women in the play. In her disguise, Rosalind gains strength and control, but her indirect expressions of love pale next to Orlando's direct confessions of being "love-shaked" (III.ii.346). By the end of the play Rosalind has never once told Orlando she loves him. Phebe's description of her love for Ganymede similarly gyrates on its negations and contradictions:

> Think not I love him, though I ask for him;
> 'Tis but a peevish boy; yet he talks well.
> But what care I for words? Yet words do well
> When he that speaks them pleases those that hear.
> It is a pretty youth; not very pretty;
> But sure he's proud; and yet his pride becomes him.
> . . . .
>
> There be some women, Silvius, had they marked him
> In parcels as I did, would have gone near
> To fall in love with him; but, for my part,
> I love him not nor hate him not; and yet
> I have more cause to hate him than to love him.

(III.v.108-13, 123-27)

Audrey's nearly non-verbal reactions operate on the same principles. As we laugh at her gross lack of understanding, we are laughing only at a less practiced indirection than we find in the other women. Celia's love for and relationship with Oliver may be an exception to these female patterns of indirection. But we never have the chance to see Oliver and Celia interact, so speculation about how she may have avoided indirection is useless.

In studying the consequences of such linguistic indirection, Madelon Gohlke and Coppelia Kahn have found the powerful language of comic heroines like Rosalind a reflection of a patriarchal order. Though Gohlke's work focuses primarily on the language of tragedy, she connects the linguistic freedoms of comic heroines to the threat of infidelity the women pose for their mates. Arguing that the indirections of the women's language connote infidelity for the men, she identifies the darkest threat implied in free female language like Rosalind's:

> Whereas "honesty" in relations among men may be perceived primarily as a matter of keeping one's word, in relations with women, it is clearly a sexual concern. For a woman to lie is to be unfaithful. For this reason the attribution of complex speech to female characters in the comedies in the form of lies, riddles, puns and statements made in the context of disguise, often involves sexual matters generally or specifically the threat of infidelity.[13]

While such sexual betrayal remains latent in most comedies, the threat is so real that the linguistic freedom women gain is usually reduced to silence. Touchstone's prolonged digression on lies in V.iv (which not coincidentally coincides with Rosalind's silence) is symbolic of the male recapturing of playful language at the end of *As You Like It*. Discussing *The Taming of the Shrew*, Kahn uncovers similar consequences in the indirection of a comic heroine's language. Kahn notes the power of language in *Shrew* where it serves as Kate's only way of asserting herself in her world and as Shakespeare's only device for calling his male order into question. Yet even so, and despite her ironic reading of Kate's final speech, Kahn finds such language ultimately but one more measure of the patriarchical:

> But on the deepest level, because the play depicts its heroine as outwardly compliant but inwardly independent, it represents possibly the most cherished male fantasy of all—that woman remain *un*tamed, even in her subjection.[14]

I believe, like Gohlke and Kahn, that the language of the women in the play does double duty, acting both as a conduit for female power and an automatic check on it. While through her language Rosalind creates a strong counter universe in *As You Like It*, her power is as temporary as is her stay in Arden.

While Rosalind's most showy source of power in the play is language, a second, less immediately obvious one is her friendship with Celia. Not surprisingly, the friendship between the two women is as much affected by the cyclical patterns of the comedy as is the language.[15]

Initially, both the court and the forest worlds of *As You Like It* seem hospitable to female attachments. Although we first hear of Celia and Rosalind's bond in the hostile environment of I.i, bone-breaker Charles softens while describing what is, even to him, a beautiful, strong, enviable attachment:

> . . . the Duke's daughter her cousin so loves her, being ever from their cradles bred together, that she would have followed her exile, or have died to stay behind her. She is at the court, and no less beloved of her uncle than his own daughter, and never two ladies loved as they do.
>
> (I.i.100-05)

When we first meet Celia and Rosalind in I.ii, we are immediately struck by the chasm between the love, trust, and warmth of their woman's world and the harsh world depicted in I.i. In the second scene as in the first, we are told—this time by Le Beau—how deep is the women's love for one another: "[their] loves / Are dearer than the natural bond of sisters" (I.ii.256-57). But more important, we experience the love in the intimate word games that open the scene; here familiarity produces a conversation with two wits in league against the world, not against each other. Such teamwork characterizes the women's verbal games with Touchstone, Le Beau, and even Orlando. Their pleas to Orlando to abstain from wrestling are best described as choric:

> Rosalind:
> The little strength that I have, I would it were with you.
> Celia:
> And mine to eke out hers.
> Rosalind:
> Fare you well. Pray heaven I be deceived in you!
> Celia:
> Your heart's desires be with you! . . .
>
> Rosalind:
> Now Hercules be thy speed, young man!
> Celia:
> I would I were invisible, to catch the strong fellow by the leg.
> *Wrestle.*
> Rosalind:
> O excellent young man!
> Celia:
> If I had a thunderbolt in mine eye, I can tell who should down.
>
> (I.ii.177-82, 192-97)

The third scene stands as the climax of the play's celebration of women's love. Significantly, the voice of the achievement is Celia, not Rosalind. As the crises of this scene necessitate Celia's eloquent defense of her friendship with Rosalind, the two tributes she makes to their love become the touchstones on which we analyze the actions of the rest of the play. First Celia pleads with her father to respect the women's mutual love:

> If she be a traitor,
> Why, so am I. We still have slept together,
> Rose at an instant, learned, played, eat together;
> And wheresoe'er we went, like Juno's swans,
> Still we went coupled and inseparable.
>
> (I.iii.68-72)

That he cannot understand or will not respect the love is predictable. That Celia must repeat the same plea to Rosalind suggests less the depth of their bond than its precariousness:

> Rosalind lacks then the love
> Which teacheth thee that thou and I am one.
> Shall we be sund'red, shall we part, sweet girl?
> No, let my father seek another heir.
>
> (I.iii.92-95)

The disguises the two women subsequently put on, one the garb of a man, one the skirts of a country woman, are obvious manifestations of the rift developing between the two. This female-female couple must now become a female-male team to survive. The two can no longer appear (literally) "as one," as Celia would wish. Thus when Celia and Rosalind set off "To liberty," they set off without the full strength of the love that has, until now, sustained them. In the next four acts, the chart of their actions shows them moving only further and further apart. They never regain the safe, warm closeness of Act I.

The forces that separate the two women include the stereotypes which account for the undercutting of their language, but most detrimental to their friendship is the assumption in the play that the natural, inevitable pairing is that of woman to man. In II.ii, for example, Duke Frederick assumes either that Celia and Rosalind *must* have run off with a man in their entourage or that a man is the

Katharine Hepburn as Rosalind in the Theatre Guild's 1950 production of As You Like It.

cause of their running off. Yet as wrong as he is in assuming that they are chasing Orlando, he is only making the same assumption they have made in preparing their disguises—two women could not take off on their own. The rest of Act II reinforces such assumptions. Rosalind, dressed as a male, assumes a protective male role as she transacts the women's business with Corin in II.iv. Jaques, in his seven ages of man speech, does women the courtesy of inclusion when he speaks of "The men and women merely players," yet he mentions women again only as supernumeraries—nurses and mistresses. Though Celia and Rosalind temporarily gain power in Arden, they have only entered a different sort of man's world than the one they have left at the court, a world which forces one of them into dress as a man and prods both of them to marriage.

In the rich discussions of Acts III and IV, further impositions on the women's friendship accumulate. In III.ii, our first look at the women now happily settled into Arden, Celia teases Rosalind with her (Celia's) knowledge of Orlando's presence in the forest. In a stressful moment, the two are refreshed and comforted by their well-known patterns of banter. Yet as soon as Rosalind begins to woo Orlando, Celia falls silent. Her silence can be partially accounted for by the dynamics of the situation—it is Rosalind and Orlando who are in love, after all, not Celia. But Celia's presence as silent chaperon serves also as a strong visual reminder of the way her friendship with Rosalind no longer remains Rosalind's primary concern. In III.iv, with the two women once again alone together, familiar patterns of conversation return. Celia provides the support Rosalind needs by echoing agreement to each outrageous statement Rosalind makes (III.iv.1-23). She matches her praise for praise, complaint for complaint. But while Rosalind gets the support she needs, she can make no thankful acknowledgment of it. Her mind is all on Orlando, not Celia.

The two women continue to appear together, apparently

inseparable, in III.v, IV.i, and IV.iii. Yet we never again have linguistic evidence of the comfort and support the women can provide for one another. While Celia participates in these scenes largely as a silent partner, Rosalind acts more and more on her own. In III.v, for example, Rosalind handles Phebe and Silvius without a single word from Celia. In IV.i, at the height of Rosalind's linguistic control, Celia has only six short speeches (and twelve lines total). And finally, IV.iii is evidence that the two women have come to face the world separately. The most convincing proof of Celia's sudden love for Oliver is the revival in her language in IV.iii, the scene in which Oliver first appears in Arden. Earlier, in her six short speeches of IV.i, Celia had demonstrated a playful distaste for Rosalind's actions, charging her with the misuse of "our sex" (IV.i.185), calling Rosalind's affection for Orlando, pejoratively, "bottomless" (IV.i.193), and responding to Rosalind's announcement of her vigil for Orlando with uncharacteristic *un*concern, "And I'll sleep" (IV.i.202). So by IV.iii Celia is well ready to focus her energy and concern elsewhere. While in the early parts of IV.iii Celia has only two short speeches, once Oliver enters, she explodes into speech and it is Rosalind's turn to be the bystander. In addition, IV.iii marks the first time we have seen Celia pay attention to anyone other than Rosalind. Celia and Rosalind's exit with Orlando at the end of the scene also marks the last time we can count on seeing the two women together. When Rosalind re-enters in V.ii, she appears without Celia for the first time in the play. When Celia next appears, at the opening of V.iv, she is similarly without Rosalind, who enters shortly after with Phebe and Silvius. By the end of the play we look for not Rosalind and Celia, but Celia with her love Oliver and Rosalind with her love Orlando. Hymen's amusement at the coupling of women in his comment to Phebe adds a final, godly consent to the separation of the cousins.

Rosalind and Celia, the heart of the play's joyous women-powered Arden, are only half of the female population in the play. While the cousins are inseparable until the very end of the play, Audrey and Phebe live isolated existences throughout the play. Their separate presences further underline the slim possibilities for female community in this world. It is no accident that immediately after Rosalind's first show of power in III.ii, we meet Audrey, an unforgettable reminder that few of the world's women are like Rosalind. We also meet, in Audrey, a woman effectively speechless in response to Touchstone's verbal battering, a woman outnumbered three to one by men telling her what to do. While she is a healthy reminder of sexuality in the play, by V.i she is no more than Touchstone's sexual possession. She provides concrete evidence that the stereotypes Rosalind and Celia joked of in Act I have a reality—here is a woman honest *and* ill-favored. The choice of Audrey and Touchstone as the representatives of a lover and his lass in V.iii is also revealing; instead of celebrating headstrong Rosalind and her lover, the two pages celebrate a safer couple, Audrey and her love. Finally, the ways Audrey fulfills our expectations about conventional stereotypes of women is certified by her isolation. The only time Audrey appears on stage with any other women is in V.iv, by which time the business of marriage assures she will be part not of a female community, but of a married, heterosexual one.

Phebe's journey through the inverted world of Rosalind's rule surpasses Audrey's in showing the play's restrictions on female community. We first meet Phebe in III.v when Rosalind, Celia, and Corin are spying on her conversation with Silvius. For the first time, we have three women on stage, and a further attachment developing in that potential female community as Phebe is attracted to Rosalind-Ganymede. But Rosalind entertains Phebe's affection only as sport, and her decision ensures that Phebe's infatuation is cause for laughter—not for alarm or love. One might speculate, on the basis of her love for Celia, that Rosalind would show sympathy for Phebe. Instead, Rosalind shows disdain for Phebe in III.v and belittles her love whenever possible throughout the rest of the play. In IV.iii, for example, when Silvius carries Phebe's letter to Ganymede, Rosalind-Ganymede puts Phebe's love in the harshest terms, telling Silvius, "Wilt thou love such a woman? What, to make thee an instrument, and play false strains upon thee?" (IV.iii.68-69); and in V.ii, when Phebe tells Ganymede of her love, Phebe's desires become the comic link in Rosalind's love chain. As if in payment for her silly infatuation, Phebe is suitably embarrassed in the couplings of the final scene and forced to find her refuge in the man who has picked her, Silvius. While both Phebe and Silvius are silly in their poses, Silvius, through his doggish sincerity, earns a redemption Phebe cannot. There is no place in the play's final order for Phebe's attachment to Ganymede-Rosalind.

Audrey and Phebe serve double duty in the play. First they expose the isolation of the women in the play as Rosalind and Celia—with their long-standing love—cannot. In this way they defuse the threat of women that Shirley Nelson Garner finds responsible for similar isolations in *A Midsummer Night's Dream;* as Garner puts it, "the male characters think they can keep their women only if they divide and conquer them."[16] Second, Audrey and Phebe serve as a multi-purpose counterpoint to Rosalind and Celia. With the simplistic presences of Phebe and Audrey, the power, language, and love of Rosalind and Celia are undercut. What happens to Audrey and Phebe is especially important because they are women *only* of Arden. They, and not Rosalind and Celia, are the true representatives of Arden's inverted world. Most crucially then, the presence of Phebe and Audrey assures that Rosalind is not the rule, that women can be separated, even in Arden. The women of *As You Like It,* besides being no threat numerically (there are only four women in a cast of at least seventeen men), are also no threat to power and order.

Marjorie Garber and George Gordon read positively the movement of women away from each other in the play, each finding a psychic gain in such separation.[17] Marilyn French and Carole McKewin are still more optimistic, French designating plays like *As You Like It* as rare literary sites where female bondage is transformed to female bonding.[18] Most recently, however, both Janet Adelman and Carol Thomas Neely have accounted for a view, like mine, which finds the play's female friendships ultimately counterproductive for the women.[19] I have limited hope for the women of the play, partly because—as I have shown—the play limits female power and community, partly, and more basically, because in doing so it precludes change. Change does occur in the play; the most obvious and important change comes in Rosalind herself, who matures from a sharp, witty, and probably bored woman into a loving, wise woman ready for the compromises of marriage. Yet her personal change loses its significance in the communal end of the comedy. Rosalind's changes remain hers alone and do not translate into social changes. The world emerging at the end of this comedy is "new" only in that four new couples are forming; the society the eight lovers are being accepted into is as old and predictable as is their acceptance of it. As the actions and cycles of the play have made clear, part of that predictability includes tolerance of traditional sexual stereotypes and acceptance of the double standard. The characters' final acceptance of each other is an acceptance of the limits to women's words, powers, and friendships that the play has enforced. To put it more precisely, in *As You Like It* the kinds of change possible for women are as restricted as are their language and their friendships. In a play headed irrevocably towards marriage, which *As You Like It* is as soon as it begins, women, their changes, and their choices are restricted.[20]

Based on her considerations of the comic genre, Bamber comes to a nearly opposite conclusion—that the dictates of comedy are so flexible that an either-or world is created, that the liberation of this world makes choice unnecessary.[21] But her optimistic conclusions hold true only when we consider the free middle section of the comic world without giving due weight to the reversals of comedy's ending. Clearly, as Bamber and others have seen, Shakespeare wants to demonstrate a need for change along with his plan for it—even plays like *As You Like It* and *Twelfth Night* are full of questioning of the status quo. Yet in choosing comedy, in guiding his characters between comedy's Scylla and Charybdis of the revolutionary and the reactionary, Shakespeare accepts a limited kind of social change.

Return to the "Norm"-al

The middle of Shakespeare's play presents us with possibilities for female linguistic power and community, but only together with a plan, at the end, for disrupting them. That plan, in a word, is marriage.

Shakespearean criticism abounds with recognition of the blessing marriage bestows on the comic conclusion. Charlton's utilitarian description of such marriage—"Marriage is to the comic dramatist the beneficent arrangement through which mankind achieves a maximum of human joy and a minimum of social disability"—is decorated in various ways by scholars who applaud marriage's reconciliation of male and female, its service as the capstone to a woman's maturation, and its joyful promise of the continuation of a society and a world.[22] On the other hand, critics who detect in marriage impositions on comedy's characters remind us that a full consideration of comic marriages must include a study of change.[23] The key issue, be it implicit or explicit, acknowledged or unacknowledged, is the relationship between marriage and social change.

In *As You Like It,* marriage is more an assumption than a visible institution. Although marriage is the goal of at least nine characters in the play (the four couples, plus William), we meet no character in the play who we know is married, though at least Dukes Senior and Frederick can be assumed to have been. Thus marriage exists as an abstract idea with the potential of becoming an ideal. Although the play overflows with critical evaluations of life in the country, life at the court, the age itself, and even love, marriage is rarely spoken of or criticized. In III.ii, as Touchstone's love for Audrey is to be translated into marriage by Sir Oliver Mar-Text, our first image of marriage is one Touchstone embellishes with cuckold's horns (III.iii.42-55). A brief exchange between Touchstone and Jaques adds to this a picture of marriage as a contest of animal desires (III.iii.68-71). Yet when Jaques refuses to let a mockery of a wedding take place, we find, curiously, that the sanctity of the institution is preserved by the biggest cynic in the play. Rosalind is the only other character to fully consider, before play's end, the transformation of love into marriage; her view, like Touchstone's, is mockingly brutal. As she fortells of her life as Orlando's wife in IV.i, her portrait of marriage promises little more than infidelity and animal passions. Orlando's firm response and his love stand as proof against her charges, however, as do Rosalind's own pleas with Celia to "marry" her and Orlando. The play absorbs Rosalind's mockery as it absorbed Touchstone's cynicism. Marriage is rescued once by the realist Jaques, once by the idealist Orlando, and is, in both cases, preserved intact for the play's final scene where the would-be marriages of III.iii and IV.i are transformed into real marriages. Marriage remains an ideal unblemished by example.

The less obvious but more pervasive presence of marriage lies in the long-anticipated happy ending of the play. Familiarity with comic convention has led us to expect an ending in marriage, at least since Rosalind and Orlando fell in love in I.ii, and Shakespeare's only interference with such expectations comes in the teasing of his aborted marriages and his gentle ironies. The drive toward marriage controls much action, as we have seen; friendship between women, for example, must finally take second place to the search for a mate, for the physical possibilities of regeneration. Comic endings in marriage are not simplistically happy—as even Shakespeare's array of comedies shows. And extensive criticism has confirmed that there is no equation between marriage and a happy ending; yet the two remain, even if only ironically, attached and inseparable. The pressing question, however, is what marriage as the ending of comedy symbolizes for the women in *As You Like It*.

Northrop Frye assures us that the new society created in the marriages at the end of comedy is a changed one where a younger generation triumphs and gains the right to assert its fresh answers to life's dilemmas.[24] The joy of the comic ending is affixed to the promise of social change. Both Rosalie Colie and Heather Dubrow agree, noting that because genres like comedy create expectations, writers can use them to question such expectations and create a climate where change is real.[25] Yet even if we accept this brightest of readings for comedy, for the women in the genre these possibilities are different than they are for the men, again because of the double standard at the heart of comedy's reversals. Comedy as a genre exists as a paradox; in its middle world the rules are bent, even reversed; but such reversal is acceptable only because we understand its *extra*-ordinary nature. As we have seen, then, the women who flourish in comedy as they do nowhere else do so only on a temporary basis. And further, the growth which a character like Rosalind does achieve is truncated, both by the isolation of the phenomenon (she may change, but the other women do not) and by the limited choices available to her at the end of the play. What Rosalind learns about love is limited by the fact that she cannot *not* choose marriage. Her choice becomes a lopsided either-or one. Either she has the illusive freedom and power of a Ganymede or she has the love and predictable comfort of a married Rosalind. Comedy does not allow for the possibility of combining Rosalind's linguistic power, her friendship with Celia, *and* her marriage to Orlando; we end the play with her marriage to Orlando, with her silence, and with an awareness of her new distance from Celia. While the promise of social change abounds in *As You Like It*, for Rosalind, Celia, Audrey, and Phebe, participation in that change must be funneled through marriage.

The limitations for female community, change, and choice in *As You Like It* are a small part of the play, of course, and my study of them is not meant to exclude a recognition of its invigorating freedom and its serious consideration of female power and community. Recent productions of Shakespeare have been instrumental in showing how, in spite of their patriarchal bases, Shakespeare's comedies *can* highlight sexual freedom and equality. The 1978 Ashland Festival production of *The Taming of the Shrew*, as Martha Andresen-Thom reports, showed great faith in that play's ability to counteract its own sexism. As Andresen-Thom reports, the action which precedes Kate's final treatise on marriage displays the invention of this production's staging:

> In tone and action she [Kate] conveys to us and to the incredulous audience on stage that her alliance is with Petruchio (Rich Hamilton) who attends to her, subdued and moved, until she starts to kneel so as to place her hand beneath his foot. He then goes to her and kneels too, catching her hand in his. Slowly they rise together, face to face, the bond between them enacted in this public ritual and soon to be consummated in the private domain of their bedchamber.[26]

Such action emphasizes an equality comedy's topsy-turvy world—with its emphasis on inversion—often has difficulty showing. The 1983 Royal Shakespeare Company production of *Much Ado About Nothing* employs a similarly bold ending to announce its refusal wholeheartedly to accept comedy's traditional final couplings.[27] The expected male-female coupling of the festive ending is replaced with a series of circle dances where combinations of men, of women, and of men and women make male-female couples only a minor part of a spectrum. In this broadened context of relationship, the final focus on Beatrice and Benedick can come from a new perspective, with the lovers' relationship retaining its romance not because of traditional assumptions but in defiance of them. Such productions stand in marked contrast to the BBC Time/Life production of *As You Like It*. With its mystical Hymen leading a stodgy, boring, and predictable finale of heterosexual coupling, this production endorses traditional marriage as a cultural centerpiece. What the alternative productions of *The Taming of The Shrew* and *Much Ado About Nothing* offer is a possibility for viewing Shakespeare's comedies—*As You Like It* among the rest—as plays which may provide their own ways of exploding comic sexism. These productions offer a joy and hope that mitigate against the closing in of comic marriage. They demonstrate that Shakespeare's plays, in spite of their encoded sexism, also contain a sensitivity to sex-based roles and conventions. *As You Like It* especially, with its surprising lack of a definition for marriage, leaves ample room for producers (and scholars) to posit their own definitions.

By focusing on the conventions of the comic genre that Shakespeare adapted to his drama, I do not intend to erase his artistic victories, only to qualify them. As I study the women in *As You Like It*, I cannot accept the glorious female presences without also acknowledging the parameters of their glory. The men in Shakespearean comedy are burdened with many of the same restrictions that limit the women, but the patterns they grow into accord them power and prestige. The patterns women like Rosalind grow into accord them a loss of freedom, a loss of choice, and an invitation to indirection. When we first meet her in *The Merchant of Venice*, Portia laments her powerlessness to choose—"O me, the word 'choose'! I may neither choose who I would nor refuse who I dislike . . . Is it not hard, Nerissa, that I cannot choose one, nor refuse none?" (I.ii.21-25). Though Portia is as little a complainer as Rosalind is, she speaks for most comic heroines who find—as she does—lack of choice an overwhelming barrier. As much as Shakespeare attempts to make *As You Like It* transcend generic barriers, it does not. He creates magnificent women in an enviable free world, but cannot prevent us from responding by noting their losses as much as their gains.

Notes

1. All quotations from Shakespeare are taken from *The*

Pelican Shakespeare, ed. Alfred Harbage (Harmondsworth, Middlesex: Penguin, 1969). My thanks to Jenny Spencer, Barbara Hodgdon, and Lee Poague for their helpful responses to this essay.

2. H. B. Charlton, *Shakespearian Comedy* (New York: Barnes and Noble, 1938), pp. 277, 285.

3. See Ruth Nevo, *Comic Transformations in Shakespeare* (London: Methuen, 1980); Linda Bamber, *Comic Women, Tragic Men: A Study of Gender and Genre in Shakespeare* (Stanford: Stanford Univ. Press, 1982); and Marilyn French, *Shakespeare's Division of Experience* (New York: Summit Books, 1981).

4. Mikhail Bahktin, *Rabelais and His World,* trans. Helen Iswolsky (Cambridge: MIT Press, 1978), p. 9.

5. See Northrop Frye, *A Natural Perspective: The Development of Shakespearean Comedy and Romance* (New York: Columbia Univ. Press, 1965); and C. L. Barber, *Shakespeare's Festive Comedy* (Cleveland: World Publishing Co., 1959).

6. See Clara Claiborne Park, "As We Like It: How a Girl can be Smart and Still Popular," in *The Woman's Part: Feminist Criticism of Shakespeare,* eds. Carolyn Ruth Swift Lenz, Gayle Greene, and Carol Thomas Neely (Urbana: Univ. of Illinois Press, 1980), pp. 100-16; Shirley Nelson Garner, "*A Midsummer Night's Dream:* 'Jack Shall have Jill: / Nought Shall Go Ill,'" *Women's Studies,* 9 (1982), 157-76; Nicholas Grene, *Shakespeare, Jonson, Moliere: The Comic Contract* (London: Macmillan, 1980); Ann Parten, "Reestablishing Sexual Order: The Ring Episode in *The Merchant of Venice,*" *Women's Studies* 9 (1982), 145-55; Peter Erickson, "The Failure of Relationship Between Men and Women in *Love's Labor's Lost,*" *Women's Studies,* 9 (1981), 65-81; Peter Erickson, "Sexual Politics and Social Structure in *As You Like It,*" *Massachusetts Review,* 23 (Spring 1982), 65-83; and Carol Thomas Neely, *Broken Nuptials in Shakespeare's Plays* (New Haven: Yale Univ. Press, 1985). Karen Newman has also recently considered the power that does or does not accrue to women in comedy's inversion and she traces out a middle critical ground contending that the inversion is not always "simply a safety mechanism" but can be an effective intrusion on male "structures of exchange." See "Portia's Ring: Unruly Women and Structures of Exchange in *The Merchant of Venice,*" *Shakespeare Quarterly,* 38 (Spring 1987), 29.

7. Erickson, "Sexual Politics," p. 82.

8. Erickson, "Sexual Politics," p. 77. While Robert Kimbrough argues that the play's androgyny is a sign of sexual equality, Lisa Jardine concurs with Erickson that the gender swapping in the play does not necessarily benefit women. See Robert Kimbrough, "Androgyny Seen Through Shakespeare's Plays," *Shakespeare Quarterly,* 33 (Spring 1982), 17-33; and Lisa Jardine, *Still Harping on Daughters: Women and Drama in the Age of Shakespeare* (Sussex: The Harvester Press, 1983), pp. 19-20.

9. Erickson, "Sexual Politics," p. 77. An interesting gloss on Erickson's feminist conclusion is provided by Barber and Grene, both of whom conclude that the reversals of comedy are benign. Barber assures us "it is when the normal is secure that playful aberration is benign," *Shakespeare's Festive Comedies,* p. 245. Grene notes the "inverse proportion between the degree of influence normally associated with a social persona and the degree of influence he or she is accorded in the comic action," *Shakespeare, Jonson, Moliere,* p. 45. Louis Montrose, on the other hand, finds the reversals of comedy a "structure for her [Rosalind's] containment" in his "'The Place of a Brother' in *As You Like It:* Social Process and Comic Form," *Shakespeare Quarterly,* 32 (Spring 1981), 52. For other more general studies of the women in Shakespeare's comedies as affected by reversals see Marjorie Garber, *Coming of Age in Shakespeare* (London: Methuen, 1981); Nancy Hayles, "Sexual Disguise in *As You Like It* and *Twelfth Night,*" *Shakespeare Survey,* 32 (1979), 63-72; Martha Andresen-Thom, "Thinking about Women and Their Prosperous Art: A Reply to Juliet Dusinberre's *Shakespeare and the Nature of Women,*" *Shakespeare Studies,* 11 (1978), 259-76; Bamber, *Comic Women, Tragic Men;* and Neely, *Broken Nuptials in Shakespeare's Plays.*

10. Catherine Belsey, "Disrupting Sexual Difference: Meaning and Gender in the Comedies," in *Alternative Shakespeares,* ed. John Drakakis (London: Methuen, 1985), pp. 180, 184.

11. Nevo, pp. 181-82.

12. Erickson, "Sexual Politics," pp. 79-80.

13. Madelon Gohlke, "'All that is spoke is marred:' Language and Consciousness in *Othello,*" *Women's Studies,* 9 (1982), 167-68.

14. Coppelia Kahn, *Man's Estate: Masculine Identity in Shakespeare* (Berkeley: Univ. of California Press, 1981), p. 117. Garber also writes on the role of language in character development, yet studies language only as it applies to male maturation; see Chapter Four.

15. My study of the women in *As You Like It* has been informed by several recent feminist studies of female friendship and community, most centrally those by Nina Auerbach, *Communities of Women: An Idea in Fiction* (Cambridge: Harvard Univ. Press, 1978), and Elizabeth Abel, "(E)Merging Identities: The Dynamics of Female Friendship in Contemporary Fiction by Women," *Signs,* 6 (Spring 1981), 411-35.

16. Garner, p. 61.

17. See Garber, pp. 140-70; and George Gordon, *Shakespearian Comedy and Other Studies* (London: Oxford Univ. Press, 1944), pp. 31-32.

18. See French, p. 79; and Carole McKewin, "Counsels of Gall and Grace: Intimate Conversations between Women in Shakespeare's Plays," in *The Woman's Part,* pp. 117-32.

19. Adelman summarizes the separation of Celia and Rosalind as she contrasts women's friendships in the play to men's. See her "Male Bonding in Shakespeare's Comedies," in *Shakespeare's "Rough Magic": Renaissance Essays in Honor of C. L. Barber* (Newark: Univ. of Delaware Press, 1985), pp. 82-84. In her study, Neely returns again and again to the conclusion that Shakespeare's plays consistently separate women. For a complementary study of male friendship, see W. Thomas MacCary, *Friends and Lovers: The Phenomenology of Desire in Shakespearean Comedy* (New York: Columbia Univ. Press, 1985).

20. Belsey, p. 188, is optimistic about the subversive possibilities of the play's ending in a way I cannot be.

21. Bamber, pp. 117-29.

22. Charlton, p. 117. See also Frye, pp. 82 and 123; and Garber, Chapter Five.

23. See Kahn; and David Sundelson, "Misogyny and Rule in *Measure for Measure,*" *Women's Studies,* 9 (1981), 83-91. For an encyclopedic background on changing Renaissance attitudes to marriage see Antonia Fraser, *The Weaker Vessel* (New York: Knopf, 1984). On the connection between marriage and equality, Neely provides a useful summary of Renaissance and critical attitudes to conclude that marriage was not as equal as some have wanted to make it seem, pp. 8-21. More specifically, Marianne Novy talks of marriage-bound relationships in *As You Like It* as reflections of mutuality; see *Love's Argument: Gender Relations in Shakespeare* (Chapel Hill: Univ. of North Carolina Press, 1984), p. 25.

24. Frye, p. 130.

25. See Rosalie Colie, *The Resources of Kind: Genre Theory in the Renaissance,* ed. Barbara K. Lewalski (Berkeley: Univ. of California Press, 1973); and Heather Dubrow, *Genre* (London: Methuen, 1982). Leo Salingar, likewise, convincingly notes how the convention of comedy finally limits Shakespeare's options in advocating social change. See his *Shakespeare and the Traditions of Comedy* (Cambridge: Cambridge Univ. Press, 1974), pp. 322-23.

26. Martha Andresen-Thom, "Shrew-taming and other Rituals of Aggression: Baiting and Bonding on the Stage and in the World," *Women's Studies,* 9 (1982), 123.

27. Descriptions are of the performance seen during the summer of 1983 at the Royal Shakespeare Company Barbican Theatre, London.

Susanne L. Wofford (essay date 1994)

SOURCE: "'To You I Give Myself, For I Am Yours': Erotic Performance and Theatrical Performatives in *As You Like It,*" in *Shakespeare Reread: The Texts in New Contexts,* edited by Russ McDonald, Cornell University Press, 1994, pp. 147-69.

[*In the following essay, Wofford considers the role of language in establishing meanings about gender in* As You Like It.]

More than almost any other of Shakespeare's comedies, *As You Like It* is the play of proxies, of actions enacted in or undertaken by an alternative persona. Whereas in *The Comedy of Errors* Shakespeare's Adriana says, "I will attend my husband . . . for it is my office / And will have no attorney but myself" (5.1.98-100),[1] in *As You Like It* one can woo, marry, and even die by attorney—indeed, at least in the case of wooing and marrying one not only can but must, or so the play suggests. This essay explores the effect of using a proxy on the performative language necessary to accomplish deeds such as marriage, considering first the purposes of the erotic performance of Rosalind/Ganymede, especially the question of whether it serves to ward off threats to the comic ending, and if so what those threats may be.

The emphasis in Shakespeare studies of the last decade or so on social structure, and its connection to the sexual politics implicit in *As You Like It,* has led to a concern not only with the attitudes a play may express or represent, but also with the extent to which a play acts as an agent in society (in Shakespeare's own or in ours) either to change beliefs and social possibilities or to reconfirm them. In his 1981 essay "'The Place of a Brother' in *As You Like It:* Social Process and Comic Form," Louis Montrose suggested some avenues by which to pursue the difficult project of discussing how theater as an institution may *act:* by providing "compensation," serving as a "projection," and mediating ideological contradictions, he argues, the play performs valuable psychological and ideological work. Since it both reflects social conflict and provides "a theatrical *source* of social conciliation," the play serves a social function, in this case, to provide apparent resolutions that confirm or strengthen the patriarchal order.[2]

Many political interpretations, however, have tended not to discuss how theatrical language may gain the power ascribed to it. If it indeed has the power to act beyond the boundary of the stage, perhaps that action can be understood better through an examination of those speeches that have such power invested in them linguistically—illocutionary and perlocutionary speech acts in general and, in particular, performative utterances that, by definition, participate in social action such as the performing of a marriage. The question of how marriages should be arranged and who had the right to perform them was, of course, a matter of much argument in early modern England.[3] Plays such as *As You Like It,* with its invocation of the wedding performative ("I take thee Rosalind for wife" [4.1.137]) and its potentially subversive representation of a wedding onstage (a wedding which is not "true"), may in fact be participating in a complex way in a cultural debate about the power of fathers and of the state to control the language that gives such actions a social reality—in other words, that makes the language truly performative. Shakespeare's theater contests the control of the performative utterance by the crown, implicitly claiming for itself the right to do things with words.

These issues can best be addressed through strategies of close reading sometimes sidestepped in criticism that defines its aims as explicitly political or sociological.[4] Without closer attention to the workings of language and to rhetoric, such political readings risk duplicating the older thematic approaches they first set out to correct, except that they place a different set of themes in the critical foreground.[5] To focus on the rhetorical structure and social force of words uttered in a play is, in contrast, to link a concern with the play's assertions about gender and cultural authority to the kinds of power such assertions have. Moreover, close reading is essential to criticism that aims to indicate the participation of a text in its culture's ideological work, or that aims to find those moments of fissure and disruption where the text marks the limits to the culture's attempts to resolve social and moral contradiction.

My use of the terminology of performative utterances comes in part out of a critical engagement with J. L. Austin,[6] whose theories most notably exclude precisely the kind of language under study here: "A performative utterance will, for example, be *in a peculiar way* hollow or void if said by an actor on the stage, or if introduced in a poem, or spoken in soliloquy. . . . All this we are excluding from consideration."[7] Austin excludes such "parasitic" or "etiolated" examples of the performative because they meet neither the first condition for all performatives—that the act be a conventional act understood as such by all parties—nor the condition of sincerity, for performative expressions onstage cannot be thought to be meant seriously by the speakers. It is precisely these conditions, however, that one might interrogate in order to consider the value of the theatrical performative, and, more precisely, in order to find a language to describe how power is appropriated or challenged in a given society. This essay briefly reconsiders not just the felicity conditions Austin lays out for successful performatives but also the ways in which they are ideologically constrained.[8]

The speech acts Austin describes in *How to Do Things with Words* take place in the context of what appears to be a completely static and unchanging society: his is a synchronic analysis (though he makes convincing diachronic arguments elsewhere). Certain people—judges, for instance—are described as possessing the institutional power to perform particular speech acts. Those speech acts are considered more dubious if others try to pronounce them; but Austin is not engaged in describing how one might question the source of that institutional power or the ways in which new institutions might take on such power. Thus, Austin requires for a felicitous performative that "the particular persons and circumstances in a given case must be appropriate for the invocation of the particular procedure invoked" (p. 34), without analyzing the ways in which such people come to be "appropriate." The word he uses to describe inappropriateness is "incapacity," yet he limits his account of this incapacity to stating that the person was not "duly appointed." Austin's concern is to show that there is no such thing as unconstrained intentionality, as he sees whatever power may arise from such utterances as institutionalizations of linguistic commitments, and the power they commit us to. Nonetheless, he is not directly concerned with the ways in which institutions gain power, nor is his theory about the regulation of action by law or by authorities; rather it treats these questions as an extension of linguistic commitments that precede any individual intention. His taxonomy of speech acts thus needs to be extended if one wishes to describe how the power to perform a given speech act is instituted or modified in society. Since Shakespeare's plays are filled with examples of moments when characters either lose or claim for the first time the capacity to perform certain speech acts, they call for some theorizing about the origin of this "capacity."

Austin's first requirement—"There must exist an accepted conventional procedure having a certain conventional effect" (p. 14)—presents similar problems, especially with the question of the meaning of the word "accepted." If it means more than simply "conventional," then it raises the difficult question of the extent to which people affirm a given legal or social custom. The example he picks here is telling: "Consider 'I divorce you,' said to a wife by her husband in a Christian country. . . . In this case it might be said, 'nevertheless he has not (successfully) divorced her. . . . We do not admit any procedure at all for effecting divorce—marriage is indissoluble.' This may be carried so far that we reject what may be called a *whole code* of procedure" (p. 27). It is not surprising that Austin's difficult case comes from the debates about who controls and defines the limits of marriage. His example could be interpreted differently, as describing how social or institutional shaping of meaning may eventually be changed if "we reject . . . a whole code of procedure." The question arises how to adjudicate moments when the linguistic commitments implied in performative utterances conflict with legal or governmental regulation, or when the institutional constraints on meaning conflict with other kinds of conventional constraints, such as moral ones. Austin describes how a performative may fail because of social constraints or law, but he does not explicitly focus in *How to Do Things with Words* on those explosive cultural moments when the felicity conditions of a performative utterance are challenged and perhaps redefined. It is precisely such a moment that *As You Like It* is concerned to dramatize—"There's a girl goes before the priest," as Rosalind will put it in act 4 (4.1.131-32).

The question of what is the "accepted" procedure and who

is the "proper" person to perform it leads into historical obscurity and to a (logically) ever receding origin, for Austin does not discuss who has the power to make the speech act "I appoint you as someone who has the power to use the performative in this case," or "I appoint you as someone who may appoint her as someone duly appointed to use the performative in this case." The moment of empowerment precedes his theory just as the struggle against disempowerment seems to fall beyond its purview. His examples thus consistently evade any explanations that might concern those moments of self-instituting power, or any case in which there may be a contest of power.

Austin's concern is to a large extent with the given, then, and not with the origin of the system, and yet he does seem to imply that the origin of such "capacity" is in language itself and the way people use language, rather than in the codifications that make legal regulation possible. He imagines that institutions determine meanings, and that meanings and successful performatives do not take place as an instance of individual free choice or self-origination. But the range of these institutionalizations of linguistic commitment is large, and the theory leaves open the possibility that differing conventions defining the capacity to utter successful performatives may conflict. Thus, the operative phrase in many of his examples is "it might be said"—but how, one may ask, is it determined whether or not "it might be said"? In this essay I extend Austin's theory in ways that I believe are in sympathy with his project, though not articulated expressly within it.

Austin's exclusion of theatrical language fits well with the way his theory, as worked out in *How to Do Things with Words,* necessarily marginalizes those moments in which cultural conventions and social expectations are being challenged or reshaped, for art defines one of the cultural spaces in which such challenges are stated and such changes are given palpable form. A theatrical performative presumably functions on at least three levels: within the play, a performative utterance is understood to have its conventional force,[9] while the audience understands the staged speech act as a representation of a performative utterance. It does not have a direct power outside the action of the play. The same language, however, pronounces simultaneously a second-order performative, in which the play or the theater as institution claims the right to speak with performative power: "I, the theater, appropriate the power to appoint those who will have the power to say 'I do,'" or "I, the theater, name myself as an institution that has the power to use the performative," or even "I, the theater, appropriate the power to take cultural action." Through its own focus on the kind of validity Rosalind's similar use of the performative may have, *As You Like It* provides an exemplary text for considering the ways in which the play and popular theater more broadly may contest the implicit claim of the crown to be the sole arbiter of who is the "proper person" to pronounce a culturally powerful speech act.

In interpreting the erotic performance of Rosalind, I consider the ways in which acting can effect a cure, or, to put it another way, the extent to which performance itself takes on performative power. Apotropaic signs or gestures and other representations intended to ward off evil themselves fit the felicity conditions for a performative utterance in all but one sense: the immediate addressee cannot be named as a person who could be judged to recognize or to fail to recognize the conventionality of the acts. They indicate, then, why the presence of the audience of those who can understand such conventional and social force is essential to the "success" of protective signs, for the audience is the addressee of the "serious" second-order performative at issue in the case of ritual or of theater. Thus, Austin's assumption that the audience, "overhearing" (as it were) the speeches made onstage, will always remember that these actions are neither "serious" nor "sincere" is belied in the case of apotropaic representation, the function of which is clearly "serious" in Austin's sense, although independent of an individual subject-enunciator and a self-conscious addressee. A study of the social force of theatrical language can thus link the theory of performative utterances, to which I return explicitly in the final section of the essay, to the dialectic of protection and contamination that studies of ritual, as well as the documents of the sixteenth- and seventeenth-century debate about the theater, have led us to see at work on the Shakespearean stage.

Erotic Performance as Cure

In Shakespearean comedy, enacted scenes often serve an apotropaic function: they work to ward off the danger that they represent, the representation itself ostensibly protecting the fictive characters (and by extension the actors and audience) from the dangers that usually give the plot its interest. This is notably true in such plays-within-plays as "Pyramus and Thisbe" in *A Midsummer Night's Dream,* where the latent tragedy in the story of the four lovers is represented in unintentionally comic form, in order that such a tragedy might be averted. It might be said to be a generic characteristic of comedy that it allows this warding-off function to appear successful, but such plays also generate a dialectic of protection and contamination, to the extent that the enacted scene or representation may express an unspoken threat or complication, inadmissible by the plot but significant nonetheless for the play's cultural force. These admissions are acknowledged by critical insights such as that, for *A Midsummer Night's Dream,* the play within the play may express the nightmare or tragic aspects of the main action—aspects ostensibly dismissed by the comic conclusion.

As You Like It speaks of "curing" an "infection" ("Why do you infect yourself with them" [3.2.111-12]) rather than of warding off an evil—an infection associated with the disease of love and manifested in bad love poetry and in the lovers' tendency to literalize Petrarchan conceits—witness the debate between Phebe and Silvius (act 3, scene 5) about whether or not eyes are murderers.[10] The actions of warding off and curing are related but distinct: that which needs to be "cured" cannot be precisely the same as that which needs to be warded off, for in the latter case the threat is only potential, and the play need never openly acknowledge its efforts to protect against it. The need for a displacement from the infection that must be cured to the threat that must be averted is indirectly admitted when Ganymede describes the "cure" s/he has in mind: by playing what s/he considers the woman's part, Ganymede explains, "I drave my suitor from his mad humour of love to a living humour of madness, which was, to forswear the full stream of the world and to live in a nook merely monastic. And thus I cured him" (3.2.405-9). This claim understandably provokes Orlando to say, "I would not be cured," and indeed the play does not intend to lead the principal characters to the monastic cell (or to the cave of the convertite). Since Rosalind, if anything, wants to test Orlando's love, not cure him of it, it can be argued that neither of them is in fact engaged in a curing. Interpretation has emphasized the importance of Rosalind's teachings, and of her weaning of Orlando from his narcissistic love—"as loving yourself than seeming the lover of any other" (3.2.373-74)—but whether Orlando changes very much remains in doubt. Such "curing" of the "infection" of lovers' clichés takes a second seat to the more difficult task of warding off the threatening images that Rosalind enacts in the wooing scenes, images that would truly dispel any possibility of a comic ending. The circularity of such imagery of "curing" is enacted in the chiasmus of "his mad humour of love to a living humour of madness": if this is to be the result of Ganymede's erotic performance, the play wants nothing of it. The pretense that this performance is all a cure for love, then, may serve rather as a figure for the kind of warding off or protecting against contamination that may be under way. The mirroring in the chiastic phrase strengthens the warning conveyed by the words ("to a living humour of madness") that such a "cure" may be more contaminating than beneficial, and figures the dialectic of "curing" and reinfecting which will engage the action in the courtship scenes.

In the case of *As You Like It,* the erotic performance of Rosalind/Ganymede as Rosalind indeed seems to ward off several threats to her promised union with Orlando. Given the allusion to the Ganymede story in her self-naming as male, readers have responded to the not-so-submerged homoerotics of her performance as marking one such threat. The enactment of a homosexual wooing scene—if it works successfully as an apotropaic representation—may thus seem to ward off, by representing it, the danger that either lover might actually be attracted to the "wrong" sex and thus make the comic conclusion of marriage impossible. Indeed, the play does seem concerned to break the close, passionate ties between Rosalind and Celia ("never two ladies loved as they do" [1.1.112]; "whose loves / Are dearer than the natural bond of sisters" [1.2.265-66]; "We still have slept together / . . . And whereso'er we went, like Juno's swans, / Still we went coupled and inseparable" [1.3.69-72]), whereas it favors and advances the apparently homoerotic tie between Orlando and Ganymede, finally concluding in the traditional marriage pattern in which the women's friendship is subordinated while male bonds are reaffirmed (ties between brothers and between suitor and father). Especially given the use of a male actor to boy Rosalind's greatness, critics have seen the play as expressing an unacknowledged but powerful homoerotic aesthetic, if not desire. The breaking of the close bonding of women in the affirmation of a patriarchical order which is itself dependent on an unacknowledged homoerotic bonding between male characters could be described as constitutive of comic closure in Shakespeare—exemplified, again, in *A Midsummer Night's Dream*.[11]

If this model is correct, it applies in a somewhat unusual way to *As You Like It,* where the enactment of what appears to be a homosexual liaison becomes the means to the concluding marriage, as if to literalize and radicalize the pattern. Here homosexuality is denied only at the last moment—or, indeed, made a central component of the resolution—so that the erotic performance seems less to ward off the threat of a homoerotic block to the marriage than to indicate the way in which this marriage system depends precisely on such ties between male and male. The homoerotic performance, then, functions apotropaically at the level of plot—the marriages are not undermined by the homoerotic subtexts thereby engaged—while at the same time it represents the play's unadmitted but (at the level of plot) fundamental allegiance to such ties between men.[12]

The principal threat that is warded off by Rosalind/Ganymede's erotic performance is of a different nature. What Rosalind/Ganymede acts out specifically are the vagaries of a woman being wooed or a woman won: s/he stresses the stereotypical attacks on women that characterize the literature of misogyny.[13] Functioning in an apotropaic manner, then, the play put on by Rosalind/Ganymede could be said to avert the threat that Rosalind herself, once married, will play any of these stereotypical female roles so threatening to men, including most notably that of the scold (the woman who talks too much, who develops a kind of female eloquence in order to extend her power), the flighty, changeable woman with no constancy, and the woman who cheats her husband (especially sexually).[14]

The allusions to what we might call homoerotic subtexts serve rather to define this other female threat more clearly. In describing the attire she will wear as Ganymede, Rosalind somewhat improbably says that she will carry "a boar-spear in [her] hand" (1.3.114). Although this part of her disguise never appears again, the allusion suggests that the boy Ganymede is also the boy boar hunter Adonis, and leaves open to question whether Rosalind/Ganymede will be wounded by the boar or, in a rewriting of the myth, be victorious over it. In Shakespeare's *Venus and Adonis,* in either case, Adonis is clearly a young man who, like the Bertram of *All's Well,* scorns love, especially, by implication, love of women: "Hunting he loved, but love he laughed to scorn" (*Venus and Adonis,* 4). The overpowering, maternal Venus of the poem makes heterosexual seduction into something closer to incest than to love, and female desire into a destructive force that, like the boar, wounds men.

Rosalind/Ganymede's erotic performance may serve, then, to distance or at least contain the threat of this powerful female figure, a threat that is indeed of significance to a play in which a woman takes control over both her own marriage and the resolution of the plot. The unacknowledged force of this female threat also explains in part the many allusions in the play to cuckoldry, which, according to a strict reading of the plot, should not be at issue here. One of the scenes in which Rosalind/Ganymede most explicitly lays out the threat posed by the uncontained, powerful woman begins with a series of exchanges about cuckoldry:

> *Rosalind.*
> I had as lief be wooed of a snail.... For though he comes slowly, he carries his house on his head; a better jointure I think than you make a woman. Besides, he brings his destiny with him
> *Orlando.*
> What's that?
> *Rosalind.*
> Why, horns—which such as you are fain to be beholding to your wives for: but he comes armed in his fortune, and prevents the slander of his wife.
>
> (4.1.50-59)

These lines laugh ironically at the very activity undertaken by Rosalind/Ganymede, for her performance could also be described as arming the participants against their fortune and preventing the slanderous accusations of cuckoldry. The play plays with the possibility that such enactment (including apotropaic replaying through witty analogy) can actually ward off such a fate, and suggests that another way to read the seasons of love correctly ("men are April when they woo, December when they wed" [4.1.139-40]) is to be forearmed against fate by wit—that wit has an apotropaic function.

Wit is indeed the central culprit in Rosalind/Ganymede's pseudo-indictment of women. The discussion of a woman's wit centers on its power to find excuses to cover sexual wandering but serves also to suggest the ways in which the play's own ambiguities are implicated in the discussion of the threat of adultery. Rosalind first presents a woman whose wit (and, by extension, whose self) cannot be contained:

> *Orlando.*
> But will my Rosalind do so?
> *Rosalind.*
> By my life, she will do as I do.
> *Orlando.*
> O but she is wise.
> *Rosalind.*
> Or else she could not have the wit to do this. The wiser, the waywarder. Make the doors upon a woman's wit, and it will out at the casement; shut that, and 'twill out at the keyhole; stop that, 'twill fly with the smoke out at the chimney.
>
> (4.1.149-56)

The double reference at the beginning of Rosalind's speech—"to do this" refers both to the changeable roles that Rosalind/Ganymede claims women perform and to the performance at hand—alerts us to the application of this wafting wit to the play's own status. The description of wit escaping enclosure through any and all available exits reflects uneasily similar descriptions of the deeds of witches, a repressed figure of female power, whose souls were said to leave their houses through the windows or chimneys, spending the night far from their bodies. Here, however, the wit of the passage turns on whether the body is imagined to follow:

> *Orlando.*
> A man that had a wife with such a wit, he might say, "Wit, whither wilt?"
> *Rosalind.*
> Nay, you might keep that check for it, till you met your wife's wit going to your neighbour's bed.
> *Orlando.*
> And what wit could wit have to excuse that?
> *Rosalind.*
> Marry to say she came to seek you there. You shall never take her without her answer, unless you take her without her tongue. O that woman that cannot make her fault her husband's occasion, let her never nurse her child herself, for she will breed it like a fool.
>
> (4.1.157-67)

The excuse that Rosalind puts in this imagined woman's mouth works in two quite contrary ways: the intended joke is evident, but behind it hover several suppressed homosexual scenes. Since neither the husband nor the wife could be imagined to go to the neighbor's bed if both neighbors were in it, the scene must be reimagined twice, producing either the image of two women or of two men in bed—two men if one imagines the wife coming to meet her male neighbor and finding her husband there instead; two women if the wife's wit is not to be at fault ("she came to seek you there" suggests that it must be the neighbor's wife with whom the wife is dallying, or else she herself has imagined a scene of two men). Rosalind/Ganymede's imagined excuse hints, then, at a different waywardness (or wisdom?) from that of the simple sexual betrayal of cuckoldry jokes, and it also comes to serve as a figure for the workings of metaphor (and dramatic figuration), connected here as always with promiscuity, and specifically with the threat of cuckoldry.[15] Wit involves, then, the capacity of one meaning to move from its proper "house" to a neighboring "house," where it makes new combinations that are "improper." But a woman's wit specifically claims to be going after the man, going to the nearby house "to seek [him] there," and thereby leaving no one "at home" in his or her own "proper" house at all—or else the man's efforts to seek out the woman in her improper relation, to contain or control it, itself results in a similar "improper" stance, for again no one is left at home in his or her own bed. The project of control itself leads to impropriety.

If this "waywardness" is to be warded off, then, the play will have to make some fast turns, for the very capacity that allows the woman to escape confinement and that poses the greatest threat to the husband (cuckoldry) is intimately connected to metaphor, and to the imaginative doubleness that characterizes all of the playacting scenes (and, by extension, all theater). By virtue of its wit, the erotic performance of Rosalind/Ganymede is thus threatened by the very figure that it at a different level works to ward off—the figure of the powerful, "improper" woman who will dominate and cuckold her husband. The language points to an unending oscillation between protection and contamination, between apotropaic representation and the return, in imagery that bespeaks a submerged ideological assumption, of that which was averted. If this warding off is fictionally successful, then, it is so only at the cost of implicating the play's symbolic action in a related, "female" metaphoric impropriety.

Rosalind/Ganymede goes on to evoke a rather disturbing image: the only way to control such a woman is "to take her without her tongue." In one sense, this "taking" is precisely what cannot and does not happen here—Rosalind is never to be without her tongue—and yet "Rosalind" only gains her tongue with her disguise, as she becomes Rosalind/Ganymede. She loses her tongue as she relinquishes her disguise: except for the Epilogue, she has no lines after she has given herself to father and husband, and the previously marginal male characters such as the Duke Senior step forward to take command and finish the action. The lines evoke the alternative story of Philomela, a woman who was literally taken without her tongue and who found nonetheless a way to describe her victimization. If her erotic performance wards off the figure of powerful female language by evoking it, it also presents the threat that this enactment will become contaminated with what it represents—that Rosalind will become this dominating woman—at which point the only way to control her would be "to take her without her tongue."[16]

This line also resonates in surprising ways with the cultural ideal of woman, which was, after all, one of silence.[17] Rosalind/Ganymede's joke creates a literalized version of this ideal: women should be without tongues; they should all always be taken without their tongues. The literalization makes evident the way in which this "ideal" depends on a lack or an excision, which might be considered a female version of castration, a cutting off of that defining and "improper" thing ("improper" in being associated with the woman's wit). Rosalind/Ganymede's erotic performance serves to ward off the threat of the excision, for as long as s/he is a man, s/he does not need to fear the loss of her tongue. In this latter case, the performance averts the threat in a paradoxical way, for by becoming a man, s/he becomes a "man" without his sexual parts. The hovering sense of the youth as castrated man is brought out in the allusion to the Adonis story, for the wound that the boar leaves in Adonis' "thigh" can be interpreted as a castration wound. Again, the enactment that wards off this threatening alternative becomes itself contaminated by that which it is designed to avert.

The doubled imagery of excision or of castrating wounds—the excised tongue for the woman, the wound of Adonis for the boy—suggests that the roles of Ganymede and Rosalind have become inseparable. The same threat presents itself in both cases, and the question remains whether Rosalind can succeed at averting it through this performance. The doubled threat of excision suggests, then, that although Rosalind thinks she has freely chosen the role of Ganymede and can drop it at will, she in fact becomes contaminated by what it represents in ways that the play measures. Moreover, women who must act as men to have a voice have effectively lost their tongues as women. The character Rosalind as a woman loses her tongue during the scenes in which she must speak as Ganymede even as she averts the threat of the "roaring" or witty woman. The dialectic of protection and contamination leaves the social actor nowhere to stand in gender terms. Being either one gender or the other would leave one open to this threat, so the only solution—the only performance that can be apotropaic—is to remain both genders at once.[18] Indeed, Rosalind/Ganymede is in many ways both, and she sports a male tongue in a female body. The many unanswerable questions and comments about identity made in the playacting scenes point to the play's uncertainty about Rosalind/Ganymede's gender: "And I am your Rosalind" (4.1.61); "Am I not your Rosalind?" (4.1.84); "By my life, she will do as I do" (4.1.150). The play needs to reaffirm a form of enacted gender undecidability to avert the threats to the desired ending that it itself evokes. The only way for Rosalind not to become the kind of woman s/he enacts is never to be only a woman, while to the extent that she becomes fully a woman in the conclusion, her erotic performance cannot be seen as successfully apotropaic. *As You Like It* can perhaps be distinguished in this way from a tragedy such as *Macbeth,* in which the unspeakable threat, suppressed and repressed in various ways by the protagonists, may well be precisely this undecidability of gender.[19] The comedy seems, in contrast, willing to countenance such a doubleness, or in any case requires it for its erotic performances to have their desired end.[20]

This doubled gender in its turn defines the self as already troped, already a performance. The self protects itself by enacting an "other" that also "infects" it or parasitizes it, gaining and losing a tongue in the same moment. This troped self suggests not only that the "I" can never be neutral in phallocentric discourse—for the woman has no unified position of "I" from which to speak—but indeed that the female "I" always must be double in precisely this way, both and yet neither alone. It also suggests why the stage provides a particularly complex space within which to consider the rhetorical status of the "I," most notably whether and how it takes on the status of a figure, since all identities onstage are proxy identities, and yet the gender of the actor—the actor's body—as well as the gender of the character remain crucial determinants of this proxy self.[21]

"There's a Girl Goes Before the Priest": Theatrical Performatives

The principal performative speech acts of *As You Like It* are the vows taken in the betrothal and wedding ceremonies (though Jaques, too, as we shall see, has his performative moment). The moment in which Rosalind gives herself away both allows the play to end and poses a number of difficulties about what kind of action this troped or doubled self can take. Rosalind reenters the scene with Hymen, and immediately turns to her father and says, "To you I give myself, for I am yours" (5.4.115). This line might not seem problematic, were it not repeated immediately in ritual fashion to Orlando. Giving herself to her husband apparently entails giving herself to her father, and vice versa: although Rosalind earlier had commented, "But what talk we of fathers, when there is such a man as Orlando" (3.4.34-35), now the two seem to imply each other, her relation to each being defined in identical terms. The line conveys something different in each case, something centering on the status of each "I." To what extent "is" Rosalind her father's? The line might be read as meaning "to you I give myself, for I (the possibility of being an I, or being a subject, especially the subject of a performative utterance) am yours," a reading marking the marginal position of the female subject in patriarchal discourse. This position is indicated by a simpler thematic interpretation: the only kind of performative that Rosalind as woman can utter is to give herself away to the men who already possess her. The statement is in effect a kind of tautology: if I am yours, then there is no sense in which I am actually "giving" you something you did not already possess. Rosalind's performative utterance can thus be seen as an affirmation of her father's control of her. The repetition of the line—to father, to husband—might thus seem to emphasize what has already been argued in other contexts, that the marriages at the end of such comedies reinforce a restrictive patriarchal order and reinscribe the otherwise rebellious females within it. The repetition also gives an incestuous cast to the final resolution, pointing to the structural dependence of patriarchy as a system on the incestuous doubling of father/husband.[22]

As we know, however, from research on the capacity of children to decide whom to marry, the power Rosalind appropriates here is certainly significant. Not only does she select her own spouse, using the structure of the drama to ensure that her father will not object, but she gives herself away. The play comments on the unusual nature of this move in the person of Sir Oliver Mar-Text, who, uneasy about the projected marriage of Touchstone and Audrey, reminds Touchstone, "Truly she must be given, or the marriage is not lawful" (3.3.63-64). Agnes Latham, the editor of the New Arden edition, has pointed out that "Christian marriage required no more than the consent of the two persons concerned," though the custom of "giving in mar-

Mike Mahaffey as Touchstone and Lisa Viertel as Audrey in GreenStage's 1997 production of As You Like It.

riage" went back to Saxon times and had its roots in the patriarchal system (p. 134). Rosalind's failure to fulfill this custom seems to go unnoted in the ending of the play, but Mar-Text's comment certainly helps to underline the unusual power exercised by a woman in this final scene—and thereby, perhaps, to emphasize as well the ways in which the comic ending may resemble the structure of wish, dream, or desire. Rosalind's power is real, then, even if it is carefully circumscribed by the fact of male possession and priority.

Moreover, the fictional context gives rise to the question whether the enacted marriage vows of Orlando and Rosalind/Ganymede can be understood to have performative force.[23] Both of the characters know that they are only "playing"—that they are not speaking "seriously" in Austin's sense—yet for both Rosalind and Orlando the scene seems to mark a shift in their relation and an end to their "courtship." In addition, a performance can complicate the scene by raising questions in the audience's mind of whether Orlando has begun to suspect the "true" identity of "Ganymede." If this enacted performative of act 4, scene 1 is only fictional, and does not carry performative force, it undermines Rosalind's concluding performatives, which also are theater, after all, suggesting perhaps a woman can speak only in troped performatives which indicate the secondary nature of her power to accomplish deeds in the world, especially with words (while she still has her tongue). And yet, the play seems to affirm the performative force of such enacted vows, as if to emphasize that troped performatives nonetheless carry cultural force, and may be the only performatives that most subjects can pronounce.

Rosalind "is" Orlando's in another sense too, then, for in act 4, scene 1 the same ceremony that will conclude the play is enacted as part of the erotic performance of Rosalind/Ganymede. Thus Rosalind has already given herself to Orlando:

> *Orlando.*
> I take thee Rosalind for wife.
> *Rosalind.*
> I might ask you for your commission; but I do take thee Orlando for my husband. There's a girl goes before the priest, and certainly a woman's thought runs before her actions.
>
> (4.1.129-34)

These enacted performatives indicate that the performative that closes the play—"To you I give myself, for I am yours"—was already in effect a repetition, at least in the case of Orlando. The line could then be construed as reading: "To you I [Rosalind] give myself, for I [Rosalind/Ganymede] am [already] yours." This reading again suggests that some sort of troping or doubling of the self is effected by the doubly repeated performative.

With the double repetition of the line we are already speaking of a fragmented subject, an "I" that is divided and multiple, a ghostly ironizing of the "I" which generates an "I" that cannot easily serve as the subject of a performative utterance. The repetition itself evokes an ironizing, or at least a questioning, of the value of the performative, for, if one repeats a performative, what status does the first statement have? Is it undone by the repetition or reinforced by it? Sense can be made of this repeated performative only if either the "I"s are different or the act of giving is meant differently in each sense. The necessity of this difference suggests that the subject itself—the "I"—is a trope or figure, marking the space of at least two different subjects, possibly of two different genders. Or, to put it another way, the performative itself may be understood as being already troped (though, as we see in the action of the play, in which Rosalind is successfully "given" to her husband, this does not mean that it lacks performative force).

Beyond the problematic status of a woman's power to make performative utterances, the enacted marriage scene (symmetrical with both man and woman vowing, unlike the final scene) raises the broader question of the theatrical performative. Onstage, within the fiction, the line "To you I give myself, for I am yours" has a performative power: Rosalind is understood fictionally as having "given" herself with these words. From the perspective of the audience, however, this performative utterance is understood as being spoken within quotation marks, just like her earlier statement to Orlando ("I do take thee Orlando for my husband"). The potentially radical nature of the scene may seem to be contained, then, by the understanding that this is a representation, and therefore that no woman has in fact achieved this performative power, that no woman goes before the priest (or before the father's legal right to select the husband and give away his daughter).

The limitation on the more socially innovative gestures of the play established by the containing power of theatrical representation is nonetheless not the final level at which this question can be posed. One might speculate that with these performative utterances onstage the theater as institution also claims for itself a performative power, a power to shape or create social norms simply by performing them. What the theater performs in doing so may conserve social norms—as when Rosalind locates herself so clearly as the object, not the subject, of patriarchal discourse—but it need not, as when Rosalind first takes Orlando as her husband. The theater institutionally preserves the power to say that the girl may go before the priest, and this power itself is potentially more disruptive (the power of theater as social institution, appropriating the king's language) than the specific ending that the play represents. Following this logic, one might argue what, indeed, many viewers may feel about the exchange of vows between Orlando and Rosalind/Ganymede in act 4, scene 1: that it can be taken as in some degree a real action, that their troths are plighted by this enacted performance, that Orlando is in some sense agreeing to marry someone who is partly a man, that performance can indeed be performative.

The words spoken, when directed toward the right person ("I take thee *Rosalind,*" not "Ganymede"), come, then, to serve as tropes of themselves. They are both true and fictional at once, just as Rosalind and Ganymede are the same character but exist separately at the same time. The statements Rosalind/Ganymede makes are simultaneously valid for both, but not as man or woman. Neither, one might add, is fully present or absent as man or woman, a situation that offers a critique of the distinction of presence/absence itself. This staged performative thus returns us to the idea of the contagion of role: the comedy affirms generically that the roles played in a wooing game are freely chosen, that one can play them or drop them at will, but the structure of the exchanges between Rosalind/Ganymede and Orlando suggest that, for the woman at least, this is not the case. (The role Orlando plays is equally contagious and necessary for him, though it remains less evident because it is given the same name, "Orlando.") The prosopopoeia of the subject—the taking of someone else's face or mask—rhetorically reveals itself to result in the contamination of the "I."

The doubling of the wedding performatives suggests, then, a more disruptive cultural statement: that all performatives are staged, pronounced by multiple or troped selves. Embracing this cultural and theatrical contamination of the self need not lead to marginalization or lack, the play argues, but rather to the kinds of empowerment the action seems to present, which, appropriately enough for the institution of theater, draw precisely on those modes of self-presentation (with their accompanying speech acts) that have to do with endorsing and putting into action the capacities of this multiple self.

One final performative utterance deserves a brief, concluding comment, since in fact it concludes the play. As the couples prepare to go happily offstage together, Jaques is left unwilling to join the celebration, and he marks his departure by "bequeathing" to the others his best wishes along with that which, in most cases, they have already attained. His bequest, then, like Rosalind's gift, adds Jaques's best wishes to what is otherwise a tautology. Jaques's statement is odd in that it implies that he possesses these qualities of plot resolutions to bequeath, making him momentarily a figure of the author, who bequeaths the consequences of his plot as a closural gesture. A bequest, moreover, becomes valid only upon death, so Jaques's words suggest that, in turning to the convertite's cave, he "dies" to the social world of the play. From this figuratively soon-to-be-dead Jaques, the plot resolution can be established, as if Jaques takes on himself the costs of the happy ending. Jaques, then, may be said to be the true recipient of Ganymede's cure for love: on him is projected the "intended" ending of the erotic performance of Ganymede and Orlando, that the "cured" person would "forswear the full stream of the world and . . . live in a nook merely monastic" (3.2.407-9). Orlando's fate is thus projected onto Jaques, while Orlando is allowed to remain in love (which, as we have seen, is not only to remain mad but to remain in fiction, or in trope).

Jaques's bequest can also be said to provide the model for the female performative, since, as we have seen, a woman cannot use language performatively without being at least partly a man. The only form in which a woman *as woman* can "give" herself is in a bequest, when she has, as it were, died as a woman and taken on a male tongue. Otherwise she can only return herself to those who already possess her, enacting in her performative the social possibility that preceded her utterance. Indeed the humor of melancholy was thought particularly to typify women, so that, like Hamlet, Jaques can be seen to be overtaken by a female mood. Jaques, then, becomes the closing example of the play's penchant for mixed gender, of its structural reliance on an undecidability of gender to pull off its conclusions and to perform them in society.

Notes

1. Quotations throughout are taken from the Arden editions of Shakespeare's plays, notably the New Arden edition of *As You Like It*, ed. Agnes Latham (London: Methuen, 1975), and are subsequently cited in the text. The title quotation is from *As You Like It* 5.4.115-16.

2. See Louis Montrose, "'The Place of a Brother' in *As You Like It*: Social Process and Comic Form," *Shakespeare Quarterly* 32 (Spring 1981): 28-54; the quotation is from p. 54. Many writers have drawn similar political conclusions about Shakespearean comedy. See Sara Claiborne Park, "As We Like It: How a Girl Can Be Smart and Still Popular," in *The Woman's Part: Feminist Criticism of Shakespeare*, ed. Carolyn Ruth Swift Lenz, Gayle Greene, and Carol Thomas Neely (Urbana: University of Illinois Press, 1980); Peter Erickson, "Sexual Politics and Social Structure in *As You Like It*," *Massachusetts Review* 23 (1982): 65-83, reprinted in Peter Erickson, *Patriarchal Structures in Shakespeare's Drama* (Berkeley: University of California Press, 1985). For feminist studies of the comedies as affirmative of female power or disruptive of the patriarchy imposed in the ending, see Catherine Belsey, "Disrupting Sexual Difference: Meaning and Gender in the Comedies," in *Alternative Shakespeares*, ed. John Drakakis (London: Methuen, 1985), pp. 166-90, and Barbara Bono, "Mixed Gender, Mixed Genre in Shakespeare's *As You Like It*," in *Renaissance Genres: Essays On Theory, History, and Interpretation,* ed. Barbara Kiefer Lewalski (Cambridge: Harvard University Press, 1986). See also Lynda Boose's thoughtful review essay "The Family in Shakespeare Studies; or—Studies in the Family of Shakespeareans; or—The Politics of Politics," *Renaissance Quarterly* 40 (1987): 707-42; and the helpful introduction to Marilyn Williamson, *The Patriarchy of Shakespeare's Comedies* (Detroit: Wayne State University Press, 1986).

3. See Keith Wrightson, *English Society, 1580-1680* (New Brunswick, N.J.: Rutgers University Press, 1982), pp. 71-84, 87-88. See also appendix B of the New Arden edition, in which Agnes Latham summarizes the legal evidence concerning private betrothals to suggest that "I take thee Rosalind for wife" (4.1.137) is a statement that transforms the mock marriage into something "very near to being a real one" (p. 133). She cites F. Pollock and F. W. Maitland, *The History of English Law before the Time of Edward I* (London, 1898), II:364., on the contemporary validity of the "sponsalia per verba de praesenti," which takes place if the man and woman "declare that they take each other as husband and wife now, at this very moment." For an account of the validity of such marriage contracts at the time of *As You Like It,* see Ernest Schanzer, "The Marriage-Contracts of *Measure for Measure*," *Shakespeare Survey* 13 (1960): 81-89, who cites Henry Swinburne's *Treatise of Spousals* as evidence of the way the law was interpreted around 1600. Here is the heart of Latham's conclusions: "Marriage *per verba de praesenti* was still valid in the sixteenth century. The Church disapproved, unless its blessing was subsequently asked, especially if the marriage was consummated before

the couple came to church . . . Nonetheless, the troth-plight marriage, provided the couple were careful about their tenses, was legally valid. They were not free thereafter to divorce or to marry again and the children were legitimate" (p. 134).

4. I have singled out the work of Louis Montrose precisely because it stands out as an exception to this tendency. Catherine Belsey, in "Disrupting Sexual Difference," similarly proves an exception, arguing for the importance of close reading in political criticism: "But I want to propose that a close reading of the texts can generate a more radical challenge to patriarchal values by disrupting sexual difference itself" (p. 180). Also, the work of feminist critics such as Madelon Sprengnether Gohlke and Janet Adelman, drawing on an alternative tradition of psychoanalytic interpretation, provides instructive examples of the value of close reading in feminist criticism.

5. Examples of this more thematic approach can be found in Erickson, "Sexual Politics," and Bono, "Mixed Gender, Mixed Genre." I intend here not an attack on these writers for having identified a project different from my own but rather an articulation of the directions in which their work now points us.

6. I distinguish my project, then, from that of Joseph A. Porter in *The Drama of Speech Acts: Shakespeare's Lancastrian Tetralogy* (Berkeley: University of California Press, 1979) and Mary Louise Pratt, *Toward A Speech Act Theory of Literary Discourse* (Bloomington: Indiana University Press, 1977). See Wolfgang Iser, "The Reality of Fiction: A Functionalist Approach to Literature," *New Literary History* 7 (1975-76): 7-38, for an analysis of the extent to which Austin's conditions for illocutionary speech acts fit literature; and, in response, the criticism by Stanley Fish of such extended applications of Austin in "How to Do Things with Austin and Searle: Speech Act Theory and Literary Criticism," *Modern Language Notes* 91 (1976): 983-1025. Fish criticizes Iser for implying that a speech act can "create" meaning: "The only thing that performative or illocutionary acts produce is recognition on the part of the hearer that the procedures constitutive of a particular act have been invoked. . . . It is simply wrong to think of an illocutionary act as producing meaning in the sense of creating it. Indeed, the meaning the act produces (a better word would be presents, as in presents a compliment) necessarily pre-exists it; or, to put it another way, in Speech Act theory, meaning is prior to utterance" (p. 1003). One could argue about this claim, but it suffices to note that Fish sees the limits of speech act theory as definitive, whereas I use them to indicate ways in which the theory can be challenged and extended.

7. J. L. Austin, *How to Do Things with Words*, 2d ed. (Cambridge: Harvard University Press, 1962), p. 22. Subsequent quotations will be cited in the text.

8. It is noteworthy that the argument in print between Jacques Derrida and John Searle (in *Glyph* 1 and 2) centers in part on precisely this exclusion by Austin of the "non-serious" citation (onstage, in a poem, or in soliloquy). In "Signature Event context," *Glyph* 1 (1977), Derrida argues that "what Austin excludes as anomaly . . . is the determined modification of a general citationality—or rather, a general iterability—without which there would not even be a 'successful' performative" (p. 191). Derrida's focus on the ways in which the citation exemplifies the structure of language more generally, and his study of the problems in Austin's concept of limiting context, tend in a different direction from my essay (toward a general theory of language and meaning), but they nonetheless helpfully indicate how very problematic is Austin's attempt to exclude the kind of language at issue in a Shakespearean play.

9. When it does not have that conventional force within the plot, the loss of royal power thereby indicated leads to tragedy, as we see most notably in *King Lear* and *Richard II*. This is an old argument, expounded most eloquently and persuasively by Sigurd Burckhardt in "*King Lear:* The Quality of Nothing," and "The King's Language: Shakespeare's Drama as Social Discovery," in *Shakespearean Meanings* (Princeton: Princeton University Press, 1968), pp. 237-59 and 260-84. I note in particular the value of Burckhardt's early focus on the importance of the performative power of language in Shakespeare.

10. For an account of the way the play treats romantic love as social sickness, see Thomas McFarland, "'For Other Than for Dancing Measures': The Complications of *As You Like It*," in *Shakespeare's Pastoral Comedy* (Chapel Hill: University of North Carolina Press, 1972). pp. 112-13. The imagery of infection in the play, and the notion put forward playfully that bad poetry is infectious, echoes the language of the antitheatrical tracts which speak of theater itself as spreading its contagion among the audience, adding a metatheatrical dimension to the dialectic of infection and cure.

11. See Shirley Nelson Garner, "*A Midsummer Night's Dream:* 'Jack Shall Have Jill: / Nought Shall Go III,'" *Women's Studies* 9 (1982): 157-76, on the breaking of female bonds in the conclusion of Shakespearean comedy; and Montrose, "'The Place of a Brother,'" on the importance of bonds between men, and on the actions of purging and strengthening them in *As You Like It*.

12. One sees a similar treatment of a homosexual subtext in plays such as Lyly's *Gallathea* and *The Maydes Metamorphosis,* in which love between two women is authorized while the threat of

13. homosexuality is evaded by an actual transformation in the conclusion of one of the lovers into a man.

14. One possible source for Rosalind's love cure, noted by Agnes Latham, is Lyly's play *The Woman in the Moon,* where Pandora cures the shepherds of their love by actually behaving as Rosalind says she will behave (see the New Arden edition, p. lix). This source can help a modern reader remember that Rosalind/Ganymede's claims about women were not so far from what could, in another context, seem an acceptable representation of the behavior of a woman.

14. Thus, this play could be said to protect against the dangers to which Rabelais devoted his third book: whether, when he gets married, Panurge will be beaten, cuckolded, and robbed. In Rabelais, the question of female eloquence does not arise as such, though other kinds of noises become associated with femininity.

15. See Patricia Parker, *Literary Fat Ladies: Rhetoric, Gender, Property* (London: Methuen, 1987), pp. 103-13.

16. The story of Philomela provides an etiological myth for art, suggesting that rape and excision of the tongue can be interpreted as the horror that generates great art, or the beauty in nature (the beauty of the nightingale's song) that becomes a figure for human art. It has been seen as a myth defining the human capacity to create beauty out of suffering, yet such interpretations tend to sidestep the fact that it is a myth of beauty made from female suffering. The suggestion here that women should be taken without their tongues to forestall their wayward wit thus suggests the congruence between the cultural ideal of the silent woman and such myths locating beauty as the aftermath of violence against women. On the Philomela myth, see my essay "The Social Aesthetics of Rape: Closural Violence in Boccaccio and Botticelli," in *Creative Imitation,* ed. David Quint et al. (Binghamton, N. Y.: Medieval and Renaissance Texts and Studies, 1992), pp. 189-238.

17. See Catherine Belsey, *The Subject of Tragedy: Identity and Difference in Renaissance Drama* (London: Methuen, 1985), pp. 149-92, esp. pp. 178-92.

18. This same gender undecidability associated with female loudness can be seen in *The Roaring Girl* by Middleton and Dekker, where the principal character cannot be pinned down by gender and switches roles and costumes throughout the play. As Sir Alexander puts it, "It is a thing / One knows not how to name: her birth began / Ere she was all made. 'Tis woman more than man, / Man more than woman, and—which to none can hap— / The sun gives her two shadows to one shape." Thomas Middleton and Thomas Dekker, *The Roaring Girl,* ed. Paul Mulholland (Manchester: Manchester University Press, 1987), 1.2.128-32. *The Roaring Girl* also provides an example of the problem posed by female eloquence—association of female eloquence with the monstrous and also with the bizarre, the uncategorizable.

19. For gender undecidability in *Macbeth,* see Marjorie Garber, *Shakespeare's Ghost Writers: Literature as Uncanny Causality* (London: Methuen, 1987), pp. 87-123.

20. In *The Roaring Girl* the comic "happy ending" seems also comfortably to depend on the principal character's continuing ambiguity of gender. There too this ambiguity is necessary for the plot resolution, though in a more blatant and less problematic way—less problematic because the roaring girl herself is finally not one of the lovers who gets married off in the end.

21. On the ways in which *As You Like It,* and Shakespearean comedy more generally, call into question the audience's knowledge of sexual difference "by indicating that it is possible, at least in fiction, to speak from a position which is not that of the full, unified, gendered subject" (p. 180), see Belsey, "Disrupting Sexual Difference," pp. 177-89. See also Mark Bracher, "Contrary Notions of Identity in *As You Like It,*" *Studies in English Literature* 24 (1984): 225-40, on the play's promotion of an "inclusiveness" of character in which the self accommodates itself to otherness "so as to include the other as *other*" (p. 225).

22. One might note also the fairy-tale solution to the financial worries and to the inevitable problem for a sixteenth- or seventeenth-century audience: the younger son. On the role of primogeniture and the social and plot difficulties it poses, see Montrose, "'The Place of a Brother.'"

23. As my notes to Latham's edition suggest, she concludes that such lines had performative force legally in sixteenth- and seventeenth-century English society. See appendix B, pp. 133-34, of the New Arden edition. On the father-daughter bond, and the significance of the linking of father and husband in Rosalind's performative, see Lynda E. Boose, "The Father and the Bride in Shakespeare," *PMLA* 97 (1982): 325-47, esp. 326-27.

Penny Gay (essay date 1999)

SOURCE: "Call Me Ganymede," in *William Shakespeare: As You Like It,* Northcote House, 1999, pp. 33-50.

[*In the following essay, Gay analyzes the meaning of gender within the context of Elizabethan theater.*]

Few critical issues in Shakespearean comedy have been discussed more energetically in the last twenty years than the question of what it meant to an Elizabethan audience to see boys playing the roles of women. For modern playgoers it is largely a dead issue . . . ; since the mid-seventeenth century the roles of Rosalind and Celia, Phebe and Audrey, have been claimed as their right by actresses who revel in the richness of Shakespeare's language and the potential for complex explorations of gender and sexuality that the roles allow.

There is an important distinction to be made here in the ideas about what it is that the actor/actress does on stage: do they impersonate the character or do they imitate it, standing apart from it a little so that we can see the gap between the actor and the role? Modern Western actors, for the most part, are locked into an ideology of 'becoming' the character, an ideology based on the dominance of naturalism in twentieth-century theatre, and particularly on the claim of films to represent 'reality' and therefore to demand total immersion of actors in the roles they are performing. This was not the theory in Elizabethan theatre, though throughout the history of Western theatre we find audiences praising actors for their 'natural' representation of characters. (A glance at any fifty-year-old film, however, will demonstrate that the criteria of 'natural' acting change approximately every half-century.)

Elizabethan theatre and acting delighted in the conscious recognition of its own artificiality. Disguise, masks, the performance of plays within plays, and word-play by characters on the notions of acting and theatre, are some of the means by which this consciousness was never allowed to lapse. Moreover, the plays that were performed on Shakespeare's stage almost never purported to represent contemporary life: their worlds were distant in time and place. Further, the characters spoke in blank verse most of the time—an artificially heightened version of the English language that allowed rich use of metaphor and other poetic devices that gave pleasure to audience and readers. (*As You Like It* has Jaques remind the audience of just this convention of artificiality: 'Nay then God buy you, and you talk in blank verse!' (4. 1. 29)—ironically enough, in response to Orlando's natural-sounding 'Good day and happiness, dear Rosalind'.)

Nevertheless, C. L. Barber, in the seminal work *Shakespeare's Festive Comedy* (1959) observed that Shakespeare

> wrote at a moment when the educated part of society was modifying a ceremonial, ritualistic conception of human life to create a historical, psychological conception. His drama, indeed, was an important agency in this transformation: it provided a 'theater' where the failures of ceremony could be looked at in a place apart and understood as history; it provided new ways of representing relations between language and action so as to express personality . . . his comedy presents holiday magic as imagination, games as expressive gestures.[1]

I shall explore the idea of Shakespeare's injection of 'personality' into roles for actors later . . . by comparison with Lodge's originary text *Rosalynd*. Perhaps the vexed notion of 'naturalism' can be laid to rest with the formulation that Shakespeare's lines and scenes—despite their poetic artifice and witty conceits—are rich and complex enough for actors to apply their culture's notion of psychology to the characters. There is enough in the lines that actors can make sense of; they can fill in the missing bits of their narratives to create an illusion for the audience of meaningful human behaviour.

Whereas in the tragedies Shakespeare helps the actor create this illusion by providing him with soliloquies in which he explains himself to the audience (thereby, paradoxically, breaking a simple illusion of naturalism, the 'fourth wall' convention), in *As You Like It* there are no soliloquies. 'What is missing', says Karen Newman,

> is not a sense of [Rosalind's] inner life or personal struggles . . . but rather self-consciousness about that equipoise expressed through soliloquy. Rosalind's inner debates are externalized in her role as Ganymede/Rosalind, and we are correspondingly distanced from her feelings, however much we may appreciate her character. We share the pleasures of flirtations, of transvestism, of shifting roles and playful irony, all of which testify to Rosalind's fascination by giving her dimensions in excess of her function. We are called upon to hold together, in the study or in performance, the multiple aspects of her character, but we never have the sense that she herself recognizes or struggles with that multiplicity.[2]

This seems to me a helpful formulation of a tricky issue. Rosalind, in her highly theatrical role as girl-playing-boy-playing-girl, is clearly a *performative* character: her role is to embody and make available to the audience the performative nature of those 'natural' categories we take for granted, such as gender. And here, if we wish, we can take into consideration the historical fact that this immensely playable and therefore believable character was originally performed by a boy (as were also, of course, Celia, Audrey, and Phebe). Michael Shapiro suggests of the original performances of the play,

> On Shakespeare's stage, these oscillations [between female and male identity] became even more dazzling in the light of the spectators' dual consciousness of the boy actor producing all of these abrupt shifts. These multiple layers of identity and the swift movements from one to another produced a theatrical vibrancy that engaged audiences in the illusion that an amalgam constructed of multiple and discrete layers of identity represented a unified character.[3]

The notion of a 'unified character' might well be an anachronism, as I suggested above, but Shapiro does point to one of the particular pleasures that the play provides: the Elizabethan theatre's liminal space is here utilized to disrupt fixed notions of gender through a safe and pleasurable spectacle: the boy who plays the girl (who, in this play, even more disruptively, plays the boy who plays the girl).

Much recent scholarship has attempted to tease out, through the reading of other contemporary documents, just what were the erotic and sexual politics of this experience for that original audience.[4] Was it a homoerotic stage? that is, was the pleasure of the audience in watching the representation of the heterosexual lovemaking in fact a much more subversive pleasure in watching a man and a boy make love? Undoubtedly in *As You Like It* the audience was aware of the *double entendre* in Rosalind's decision to take as her male name 'no worse a name than Jove's own page, / And therefore look you call me Ganymede' (1. 3. 120-21)—since 'Ganymede' was a slang term for a young male homosexual. But, as Stephen Orgel argues, 'there is no indication whatever that Shakespeare is doing something sexually daring there, skating on thin ice'.[5] He presents evidence that the love of Elizabethan men for boys was generally unproblematic in that culture, rendered acceptable by the many literary models in Ovid and other ancient texts; and, in fact, often thought of as less dangerous than love for women, whose sexuality was thought to be voraciously overwhelming, effeminizing of 'manly' men. Although the puritans fulminated against the theatre in general, the potential for homosexual behaviour was only one aspect of their larger phobia. It was basically 'the universal sexuality evoked by theatre, a lust not distinguished by the gender of its object'[6] which was unacceptable to puritans—especially as it disrupts the specific definitions of gender and sexuality which are the bedrock of the patriarchal system. Even more so when in a play such as *As You Like It* such issues are amusingly foregrounded.

Yet on another level, as Orgel points out, the transvestite theatre simply reproduces the order of patriarchy. For 'boys and women are for the most part cattle of this colour' (3. 2. 402-3). 'Cattle'—Rosalind's slang puns significantly: the word is cognate with 'chattel', household possession. The boys were apprentices (not to theatre guilds, but to any profession convenient):[7] dependant and 'a medium of exchange within the patriarchal structure, and both [women and boys] are (perhaps in consequence) constructed as objects of erotic attraction to adult men'.[8] Orgel's conclusion to the interesting question, 'Why did only boys play women?'—or why the transvestite stage was so unproblematically homoerotic—is that

> eroticized boys appear to be a middle term between men and women, and far from precluding the love of women, they are represented as *enabling* figures, as a way of getting from men to women. . . . In a society that has an investment in seeing women as imperfect men, the danger points will be those at which women reveal that they have an independent essence, an existence that is not, in fact, under male control, a power and authority that either challenges male authority, or, more dangerously, that is not simply a version or parody of maleness, but is specifically female. . . . In this context Rosalind's male disguise would be, in the deepest sense, for Orlando's benefit, not for Rosalind's; it would constitute a way around the dangers of the female libido.[9]

Orgel's scholarly speculations are an exciting insight into certain Elizabethan discursive fields which operate largely at the level of unconscious assumptions. On the other hand, historians such as Kathleen McLuskie and Jean Howard argue that at some level boy actors playing women must simply have been accepted in performance as a convention.[10] Otherwise, there would have been little audience involvement with those aspects of the plays based on the representation of heterosexual desire. Howard goes on to underline the equally discursive nature of this more overt representation:

> The representation of Rosalind's holiday humour has the primary effect, I think, of confirming the gender system and perfecting rather than dismantling it by making a space of mutuality within relations of dominance. . . . Progressively this text has narrowed the range of erotic possibilities the play has mobilized in the direction of heterosexual coupling. For example, it has displaced the same-sex bonds between Rosalind and Celia with heterosexual unions; it has muted the homoerotic implications of Rosalind's assumption of the name Ganymede by having Rosalind and Orlando so firmly committed to the heterosexual other; and, as with Olivia, it has corrected Phebe's 'mistake' in loving a man who is 'really' a woman.[11]

If we take the evidence of the play's *telos*, its drive towards closure, then, we will conclude that the play privileges a heterosexual interpretation of the energy flow between adult male actor and adolescent boy-as-woman. But this is somewhat to oversimplify the experience of the audience in the theatre—that liminal space where anything may happen—particularly its moment-by-moment awareness of the potential for disruption that the cross-dressing generates. (It is also to ignore the astonishing Epilogue to this play, on which I shall comment later.)

Two critics who have opened up the possibilities for discussion of what might have been the phenomenological experience of the audience watching the performance of this story are Valerie Traub and Stephen Greenblatt. Traub argues, incisively:

> Clearly, insofar as gender hierarchies seem to be both temporarily transgressed *and* formally reinstated, the question of subversion versus containment can only be resolved by crediting *either* the expense of dramatic energy or comedic closure. Yet, to do either is also to reproduce the artificial distinction between content and form—a capitulation to the logic of binarism.[12]

Traub's version of 'the homoeroticism of *As You Like It*' identifies it as

> playful in its ability to transcend binary oppositions, to break into a dual mode, a simultaneity, of desire. Insofar as Rosalind/Ganymede is a multiple sexual object (simultaneously heterosexual and homoerotic), Orlando's effusion of desire toward him/her prevents the stable reinstitution of heterosexuality, upon which the marriage plot depends . . .
>
> In excess of the dominant ideology of monogamous heterosexuality, to which Rosalind is symbolically wed

at the end of the play, exist desires unsanctioned by institutional favor. By means of her male improvisation, Rosalind leads the play into a mode of desire neither heterosexual nor homoerotic, but both heterosexual *and* homoerotic. As much as she displays her desire for Orlando, she also enjoys her position as male object of Phebe's desire and, more importantly, of Orlando's.[13]

Traub here, I think, touches on the simple reason for the play's apparent formal weakness. Earlier critics argued that it lacks drive, it lacks plot, its lacks motivation. Nevertheless, it is infinitely delightful because of the charm of Rosalind. But in what does this charm consist? Wit and vitality undoubtedly: but most audience members, when quizzed, would locate the play's charm in the courtship scenes. And these scenes are perpetually delightful because of the 'multiple erotic possibilities and positions' that they offer through a cheekily self-conscious employment of the dramatic 'if'—Touchstone's 'If you said so, then I said so' (5. 4. 100-101): 'The dependence on the conditional structures the possibility of erotic exploration without necessitating a commitment to it'.[14]

Stephen Greenblatt's essay 'Fiction and Friction' offers an analysis of Renaissance theories about sexual anatomy as a way of entering into an understanding of the multiple eroticism of Shakespearean comedy. In brief, the view of these anatomists is that women's sexual organs are the same as men's, only hidden and inverted inside the body. For generation to occur, there must be a pleasant 'chafing', which will cause the hidden female 'penis' to ejaculate. Shakespeare realized, argues Greenblatt,

> that if sexual chafing could not be presented literally onstage, it could be represented figuratively: friction could be fictionalized, chafing chastened and hence made fit for the stage, by transforming it into the witty, erotically charged sparring that is the heart of the lovers' experience.
>
> By means of this transformation Shakespeare invested his comedies with a powerful sexual commotion, a collective excitation, an imaginative heat that the plots promise will be realized offstage, in the marriage beds towards which they gesture . . . the unrepresented consummations of unrepresented marriages call attention to the unmooring of desire, the generalizing of the libidinal, that is the special pleasure of Shakespearean fiction. For the representation of chafing is not restricted to Shakespeare's lovers; it is diffused throughout the comedies as a system of foreplay.

'Moreover,' Greenblatt continues,

> for Shakespeare friction is specifically associated with verbal wit; indeed at moments the plays seem to imply that erotic friction *originates* in the wantonness of language and thus that the body itself is a tissue of metaphors or, conversely, that language is perfectly embodied. . . . Dallying with words is the principal Shakespearean representation of erotic heat.[15]

In the second part . . . I shall explore this insight in relation to the courtship scenes in *As You Like It*, proceeding by comparison with the parallel scenes in the originary text, Thomas Lodge's *Rosalynd*.

DALLYING WITH WORDS

Shakespeare's Act 3 scene 2 and Act 4 scene 1—the courtship scenes in the forest between Rosalind (disguised as Ganymede), Celia, and Orlando—are modelled on two segments of Lodge's 1590 novel. Looking at the Lodge text, it quickly becomes clear that the major change that Shakespeare made was in reducing the 'literariness' of Lodge's writing (Lodge's text is subtitled 'Euphues' Golden Legacy', in deliberate homage to the fashionable work of John Lyly). Lodge's Orlando (confusingly known as Rosader) performs five 'sonnetos' and a shared eclogue in the course of the courtship scenes: in Shakespeare these are represented by a couple of parodic pieces, read by the girls and improvised on by Touchstone. Rosader is generally more eloquent than Orlando—better educated and more consciously genteel. As performer of his own poems, he is given more textual space than Orlando; he is the 'hero' of the narrative much more than Rosalynd is the 'heroine'.

A duetting eclogue is the only moment in Lodge when 'Ganymede' offers to 'represent Rosalynd', her eloquence matching Rosader's in a highly formal versified lovers' debate; there is no offer of a 'cure' through an extended cross-gender game as there is in Shakespeare, though Lodge's Ganymede does offer plenty of advice to Rosader about giving up the self-indulgent pains of love. She is eloquent but not witty in the way that Shakespeare's Rosalind is; her intelligence is displayed more through her performance of florid euphuistic prose and elaborate classical references. (The Silvius and Phebe scenes of Shakespeare are a comic displacement of the earnest pastoral of Lodge's principal characters. . . .) Lodge was apparently not interested in the comic or sexual potential of Rosalynd's cross-dressing; for him, safely in a disembodied novel, the girl-as-page trope is simply a plot device. Celia/Aliena has rather more to say in Lodge than in Shakespeare, though the mock marriage which is the culmination of both 'wooings' is over very quickly in Lodge, with none of the anxiety with which Shakespeare surrounds this doubly transgressive act. . . .

Shakespeare transformed the text he had at his elbow into a brilliantly playable theatre script which built on the expertise (and ambivalence) of his boy-players of female parts. This transformation is of the order of a quantum leap. But the experiment of workshopping the Lodge text[16] indicates that had Shakespeare not decided to work his professional magic on this novel, it could still have made a perfectly respectable popular play of the 1590s, in the pastoral romance mode.

The first scene in Lodge which is closely equivalent to Shakespeare (3. 2) is the one in which we first hear Rosader/Orlando's poems. They are not nearly as dire as 'From the east to western Inde', but they do have the same persistent repetitiveness:

Of all chaste birds the Phoenix doth excel,
Of all strong beasts the lion bears the bell,
Of all sweet flowers the rose doth sweetest smell,
Of all fair maids my Rosalynd is fairest.

Of all pure metals gold is only purest,
Of all high trees the pine hath highest crest,
Of all soft sweets I like my mistress' breast,
Of all chaste thoughts my mistress' thoughts are rarest. (etc.)[17]

The conversation between Rosader, Rosalynd and Aliena which follows this effusion is led by Rosalynd as Ganymede in a style very similar to Shakespeare's Rosalind, a hearty parade of manliness which would not fool anyone less self-absorbed: 'What news, forester? has thou wounded some deer, and lost him in the fall? Care not man for so small a loss' (*R*. 68). And although the scene does not lead to a proposed 'love-cure', it is led by Rosalynd onto not dissimilar erotic ground, as she encourages Rosader thus: 'Much have I heard of thy mistress' excellence, and I know, forester, thou canst describe her at the full, as one that hast surveyed all her parts with a curious eye; then do me that favour, to tell me what her perfections be' (*R*. 69). This is of course a cue for a blazon, a nine-stanza feature-by-feature description of Rosalynd's physical excellences: it includes such amorous fantasies as:

Her paps are centres of delight,
Her paps are orbs of heavenly frame,
Where nature moulds the dew of light,
To feed perfection with the same:

Heigh ho, would she were mine.
With orient pearl, with ruby red,
With marble white, with sapphire blue,
Her body every way is fed;
Yet soft in touch, and sweet in view . . .

(*R*. 70)

It is only after this emphatic reminder of Rosalynd's female body that Lodge toys momentarily with the pleasures provided by the cross-dressing trope: 'It makes me blush', says Rosalynd, 'to hear how women should be so excellent, and pages so unperfect'. Rosader replies that the 'page' 'resembl[es] the shadow' of a woman, to which Rosalynd retorts (after a tart remark by Aliena), 'Who knows not . . . if boys might put on their garments, perhaps they would prove as comely; if not as comely, it may be more courteous' (*R*. 71). Lodge seems to accept the Elizabethan idea that there is little difference between boys and women, and that gender is often simply defined by appearance. The conversation ends with a teasing request from Ganymede for 'more sonnets in commendation of thy mistress', and a promise that Rosader will return tomorrow with more of his literary efforts. The courtship, that is to say, will continue to be conducted through the medium of literature, with Rosader as the male entitled to parade his charms through the use of literary (i.e. educated) forms, and Rosalynd playing the role of the (feminine) respondent, though her male disguise enables her to take on a teasing tone.

For Shakespeare, on the other hand, Orlando's literary affectations are merely a starting point for a much more equal dialogue. It is in fact Rosalind/Ganymede who consciously sets up a display of witty and imaginative verbal facility to Orlando's 'straight man' in their opening dialogue. Orlando feeds the cues to Ganymede: 'Who ambles Time withal? . . . Who doth he gallop withal?' and so on. It's a sort of intellectual flirtation—or friction, to use Greenblatt's term—in which Rosalind/Ganymede claims the ground which is culturally ascribed to the male, abstract reasoning.

Much critical ink has been spent on delving into the significance of Rosalind's disquisition upon Time (3. 2. 302-27): can it be read as a structuring theme of the play? Obviously it has connections with Jaques' 'Seven ages of man' speech (2. 7. 139-66): it reminds us that we all live in Time, and that our perspective on it is dependent on the social role we are playing. But perhaps the most immediately relevant effect is that of subconsciously alerting the audience to the 'time out' or 'holiday' aspect of life in Arden: although it is a place of labour for the shepherds, for the aristocratic visitors it is *not* the 'working-day world' whose 'briers' Rosalind complains about in Act 1. None of the activities and social roles that Rosalind mentions in this dialogue are to be seen in the forest community; as Orlando points out, 'there's no clock in the forest'. Instead a simpler pastoral life, based on broader 'time[s] o' day' (morning, noon, afternoon, night) is to be observed. In due course, the aristocrats who categorize and hierarchize the world of money and status will return to that clock-time.

Modern actors use this sequence, however, for its performative possibilities, not to spell out a sermon to the audience (the same is true of Jaques' famous speech): its function is to charm, even hypnotize, Orlando, so that he will be drawn into the next stage of the courtship—asking for the boy's/girl's address: 'Where dwell you pretty youth?' (3. 2. 328). Rosalind answers in terms that foreground the relation between gender and costume—'here in the skirts of the forest, like fringe upon a petticoat' (this is often accompanied in the theatre with a hastily covered-up gesture towards the non-existent feminine garment). She goes on to introduce a discussion of femininity as an abstract category: 'I thank God I am not a woman, to be touched with so many giddy offences' (3. 2. 340-4)—so that she can then proceed to deconstruct the Petrarchan stereotype of the 'man in love' (3. 2. 360):

ORLANDO
What were his marks?
ROSALIND
A lean cheek, which you have not; a blue eye and sunken, which you have not; an unquestionable spirit, which you have not; a beard neglected, which you have not—but I pardon you for that, for simply your having in beard is a younger brother's revenue. Then your hose should be ungartered, your bonnet unbanded, your sleeves unbuttoned, your shoe untied, and everything about you demonstrating a careless desolation.

(3. 2. 362-71)

Orlando, despite his literary poses, is pre-eminently, as this speech makes clear to us, a healthy and natural-looking young man: he is not caught up in the conventional discourses of courtly love. Rosalind cannot resist teasing him about this—'But you are no such man; you are rather point-device in your accoutrements, as loving yourself than seeming the lover of any other' (371-4). Orlando's vitality and self-confidence are an important aspect of his characterization, if he is not to slip from one stereotype—the aggressive young man who protests with his fists—to another, the effeminized lover, whose improper costuming signals him as being 'careless' of his social role as a male. Like Rosalind, although less obviously to modern audiences, Orlando operates outside the strict gender binaries of his society's official discourse.

This point is made more clear by the willingness with which Orlando enters into the love-cure game that Rosalind/Ganymede proposes at the climax of this first courtship scene. Her long speech about her (invented) previous pretence to be a woman provides the equivalent stereotype to the male lover's behaviour that she has just described. The speech becomes obviously parodic through accumulation and exaggeration:

> I set him every day to woo me: at which time would I, being but a moonish youth, grieve, be effeminate, changeable, longing and liking, proud, fantastical, apish, shallow, inconstant, full of tears, full of smiles, for every passion something and for no passion truly anything, as boys and women are for the most part cattle of this colour . . .
>
> (3. 2. 396-403)

Despite this unattractive image, culminating in 'a nook merely monastic', Orlando hesitates only briefly before agreeing to be thus 'cured'. How can the actor justify this decision? The answer must once again lie in the hypnotic energy of Rosalind's words and presence—Orlando wants more of them, on whatever terms. It is interesting, however, to consider the intonations and emphases possible for the actor in his immediate response to Rosalind's speech: 'I would not be cured, youth'. Varieties of resistance, doubt, and self-confidence can be conveyed in these readings of the line:

> *I* would not be cured, youth.
>
> I *would* not be cured, youth.
>
> I would *not* be cured, youth.
>
> I would not *be* cured, youth.
>
> I would not be *cured,* youth.

Rosalind's response—'I would cure you'—is similarly variable and obviously dependent on the emphasis that Orlando gives his line. But she has an extra weapon up her sleeve, an extra clause, '*if* you would but call me Rosalind and come every day to my cote to woo me'. There is 'much virtue in If', as Touchstone remarks later in the play (5. 4. 102). What Ganymede offers is a new type of imaginative erotics, much more lively and unpredictable than the conventions of literary love-songs; here Orlando can act out his fantasies and perhaps even his frustrated longings through the complex reality created by bodily presence.

The second courtship scene, 4. 1, also has its parallel in Lodge. The changes that Shakespeare made to the text at his elbow are again subtle and significant. This is a much longer scene, culminating in the wooing eclogue and the mock-wedding. It takes place on the following day: Lodge informs us that Ganymede/Rosalynd has had a poor night's sleep, Aliena is feeling very chirpy. The two of them come upon their 'melancholy forester' (who hasn't had a good night's sleep in weeks) and Rosalynd accosts him:

> what makes you so early abroad this morn? In contemplation, no doubt, of your Rosalynd. Take heed, forester; step not too far, the ford may be deep, and you slip over the shoes. . . . 'Tis good, forester, to love, but not to overlove, lest in loving her that likes not thee, thou fold thyself in an endless labyrinth.
>
> (R. 74)

It is an eloquent warning against the excesses of romantic love which bespeaks the good sense of Lodge's Rosalynd, a trait carried over into Shakespeare's character; but Shakespeare's Orlando, as we have already seen, is certainly not one for moping around. In fact he arrives late for his appointment, having been, we assume, occupied with strengthening his bonds with Duke Senior and his merry men. This tardiness spurs Rosalind to another flight of fancy that carries a sting:

> ROSALIND
> Nay, and you be so tardy, come no more in my sight.
> I had as lief be wooed of a snail.
> ORLANDO
> Of a snail?
> ROSALIND
> Ay, of a snail. For though he comes slowly, he carries his house on his head; a better jointure, I think, than you make a woman. Besides, he brings his destiny with him.
> ORLANDO
> What's that?
> ROSALIND
> Why, horns—which such as you are fain to be beholding to your wives for: but he comes armed in his fortune, and prevents the slander of his wife.
>
> (4. 1. 49-59)

A double insult: snails are but lowly (and slimy) creatures hardly to be compared with men, the lords of creation; and yet, they do have something in common with men: 'horns', the sign of cuckoldom. We are reminded subliminally of the play's ongoing deconstruction of the signifiers of masculinity, a theme to be taken up graphically in the following scene, the dance and song of the apparently triumphant hunters.

Lodge, who is not at this point using the Ganymede-as-Rosalynd trope, enables Ganymede to regain her witty defensive control of the situation in a speech in which she seems to want to push Aliena into Rosader's arms ('one bird in the hand is worth two in the wood', *R*. 74). The opportunity being declined, Rosalynd changes the subject in order to hear more of her lover's praise of her idealized self: 'But leaving this prattle, now I'll put you in mind of your promise about those sonnets, which you said were at home in your lodge'.[18] Three more 'sonnets' follow, plus prose protestations from Rosader about the beauty of Rosalynd and the importance of his literary performances in 'fixing' this perfection in his mind. Ganymede is allowed one extended speech in response, a critique of the self-indulgence of this mode of being in love—and, itself, an eloquent verbal display:

> 'I can smile,' quoth Ganymede, 'at the sonnetos, canzones, madrigals, rounds and roundelays, that these pensive patients pour out when their eyes are more full of wantonness, than their hearts of passions. Then, as the fishers put the sweetest bait to the fairest fish, so these Ovidians, holding *Amo* in their tongues, when their thoughts come at haphazard, write that they be wrapt in an endless labyrinth of sorrow, when walking in the large lease of liberty, they only have their humours in their inkpot. . . .'
>
> (*R*. 76)

This speech, of which I have quoted only a third, is emotionally and rhetorically similar to Rosalind's swingeing demolition of the grand icons of romantic love:

> No, faith, die by attorney. The poor world is almost six thousand years old, and in all this time there was not any man died in his own person, videlicit, in a love-cause. Troilus had his brains dashed out with a Grecian club, yet he did what he could to die before, and he is one of the patterns of love. Leander, he would have lived many a fair year though Hero had turned nun, if it had not been for a hot mid summer night; for, good youth, he went but forth to wash him in the Hellespont, and being taken with the cramp, was drowned, and the foolish chroniclers of that age found it was Hero of Sestos. But these are all lies: men have died from time to time and worms have eaten them, but not for love.
>
> (4. 1. 89-103)

In Shakespeare's text, just before this flight of witty eloquence, there is a moment of physical tension when Orlando takes the initiative, 'Rosalind' having signalled that she is 'in a holiday humour and like enough to consent' (4. 1. 65-6). Orlando's answer to the challenge, 'What would you say to me now, and I were your very very Rosalind?' is to shift the action onto the physical plane: 'I would kiss before I spoke'. Stage business—an attempted kiss—is clearly implied here, with Rosalind talking fast (and deliberately coarsely, with her mention of spit?) in order to put him off. This brief moment raises the stakes for the watching audience: the fact that the characters' desires are *embodied* in the actors will not be denied: we expect a kiss, if not now, then—all the more urgently for the delay—later.

Lodge is rarely concerned to imagine bodies enacting his story: the delight that he offers his reading audience is in the mind—particularly via the appeal of classical references to the educated reader—and the mind's ear, in the liberal doses of 'sonnetos' which dot the text. The climax of these is the 'wooing Eclogue', a duet between Rosader and Ganymede, in which Ganymede does play the female role. Whereas Orlando's response to the invitation to 'woo' is to offer to kiss, Rosader abides by the rules of courtly love and obeys his 'lady's' command: 'let me see how thou canst woo: I will represent Rosalynd, and thou shalt be as thou art, Rosader. See in some amorous ecologue, how if Rosalynd were present, how thou couldst court her; and while we sing of love, Aliena shall tune her pipe and play us melody' (*R*. 79). The reader, that is, is to imagine appropriate music accompanying this climactic literary performance.

The eclogue is a 'pastoral dialogue' (*OED*); each long stanza concludes with a variation on 'O Rosalynd, then be thou pitiful, for Rosalynd is only beautiful'. Lodge varies it after three stanzas with the fourth stanza broken into short segments of dialogue as the wooing heats up. 'Rosalynd' gives in, and a triumphant duet follows, 'Oh, gain more great than kingdoms or a crown!' / 'Oh, trust betrayed if Rosader abuse me'. Lodge was no doubt familiar with the popular musical mode of the madrigal-dialogue or *pastourelle*; what this scene irresistibly reminds twentieth-century readers of is full-blown opera (an art-form which was, in fact, just beginning to be established as Lodge and Shakespeare were writing). The analogy of tenor and soprano declaring their love for each other and finally uniting in a rapturous *cabaletta* suggests the formality and potential comedy of this scene in Lodge—a risibleness that Shakespeare avoids in favour of something that creates very much more natural-seeming characters:

> ROSALIND
> But come, now I will be your Rosalind in a more coming-on disposition; and ask me what you will, I will grant it.
> ORLANDO
> Then love me, Rosalind.
> ROSALIND
> Yes, faith, will I, Fridays and Saturdays and all.
> ORLANDO
> And wilt thou have me?
> ROSALIND
> Ay, and twenty such.
> ORLANDO
> What sayest thou?
> ROSALIND
> Are you not good?
> ORLANDO
> I hope so.
> ROSALIND
> Why then, can one desire too much of a good thing?
>
> (4. 1. 106-16)

Both these duetting exchanges—Lodge's high art, Shakespeare's colloquial familiarity—lead to the mock-marriage, a scene in Shakespeare which I want to look at in the context of the play's other 'weddings'. . . . But it is worth noting here that it is Lodge's Aliena who proposes the 'marriage'; she has no hesitation in playing the role of priest. It is Rosalynd/Ganymede whose embarrassed response is recorded: she 'changed as red as a rose. And so with a smile and a blush, they made up this jesting match, that after proved to a marriage in earnest, Rosader full little thinking he had wooed and won his Rosalynd' (*R.* 83). The conversation between the young women after this crucial event illustrates the difference between the two writers' imaginations. Lodge's Aliena, always a more chatty figure than Shakespeare's, begins to 'prattle' with Ganymede, offering the opinion that 'by all probable conjectures, this match will be a marriage'. Ganymede is sceptical: 'Tush . . . there goes more words to a bargain than one', and so on; and Aliena concludes the exchange by remarking that she hopes Rosalynd will pay more attention to their sheep, now that she is assured of Rosader's love (*R.* 84). The girls seem very companionable in this chatter, their friendship undisturbed by the remarkable event that has just taken place, a public enactment of Rosalynd's and Rosader's commitment to one another.

Very different is Shakespeare's coda to the mock-marriage and subsequent 'flyting' between Rosalind and Orlando. Celia seems irritated, feeling betrayed?—'You have simply misused our sex in your love-prate. We must have your doublet and hose plucked over your head, and show the world what the bird hath done to her own nest' (4. 1. 191-94).[19] Despite its proverbial origin, the specific image here of stripping off Rosalind's male gender to show a filthy female nakedness is not pleasant. Rosalind replies with an utterance of equally powerful feeling, though very different emotional reference: 'O coz, coz, coz, my pretty little coz, that thou didst know how many fathom deep I am in love! But it cannot be sounded. My affection hath an unknown bottom, like the Bay of Portugal' (4. 1. 195-8). In response to Celia's tart remark ('Or rather bottomless . . .') she continues to expatiate on her feelings, concluding, 'I'll tell thee Aliena, I cannot be out of sight of Orlando. I'll go find a shadow and sigh till he come.' Rosalind is fully in thrall to love—though she cannot admit or display this feeling to anyone except her more-than-sister friend. It's an emotionally fraught situation, which leaves Celia on her own: no wonder she ends the scene with the weary, or cynical, remark, 'And I'll sleep'. The two women are seen to separate for the first time in the play.

Two patterns of movement suggest themselves here: either Rosalind exits stage left, towards the sheep-cote to wait for Orlando's return, while Celia settles to sleep on stage during the brief huntsmen's scene (4. 2); or Rosalind exits stage right, into the forest, narrowly missing the hunters' entrance from the forest, which happens after Celia's exit stage left towards the cottage for her nap. Whichever way it is played, it leaves the visual image of a situation which is particularly difficult for Celia, since unlike Rosalind she has no anticipation of further pleasurable friction at the next meeting with Orlando. The option taken in Adrian Noble's 1985 RSC production—to leave Celia onstage during the hunters' song—allowed this scene to be presented as invading Celia's unconscious, a dream of defloration, male violence feared yet desired. Noble's psychoanalytic reading created a heightened feeling of sexual frustration and expectation in Celia which was answered by the unexpected arrival of Oliver in the next scene. Significantly, there is much mention of violence and blood in this scene, and Rosalind faints at the sight of the 'bloody napkin', which can be read not only as a symbol of the absent, wounded Orlando, but also as a metonym of her own hidden femininity. Eventually the flirtatious and largely verbal pleasures of 'friction' have to give way to the physical realities of the body, if the play's story is to move out of the artificial world of pastoral into the real world of the audience.

Notes

1. C. L. Barber, *Shakespeare's Festive Comedy* (Princeton: Princeton University Press, 1959), 15.

2. Karen Newman, *Shakespeare's Rhetoric of Comic Character: Dramatic Convention in Classical and Renaissance Comedy* (New York and London: Methuen, 1985), 96.

3. Michael Shapiro, *Gender in Play on the Shakespearean Stage* (Ann Arbor: University of Michigan Press, 1996), 126.

4. These debates are summarized in Shapiro, *Gender in Play,* Introduction; Jean Howard, *The Stage and Social Struggle in Early Modern England* (London and New York: Routledge, 1994), 159-60.

5. Stephen Orgel, *Impersonations: The Performance of Gender in Shakespeare's England* (Cambridge: Cambridge University Press, 1996), 43. See also Bruce R. Smith, *Homosexual Desire in Shakespeare's England: A Cultural Poetics* (Chicago and London: University of Chicago Press, 1991), 147-8.

6. Orgel, *Impersonations,* 28.

7. See Orgel, *Impersonations,* 64-72, for discussion of the boy players' social status.

8. Ibid., 103.

9. Ibid., 63.

10. Kathleen McLuskie, 'The Act, the Role, and the Actor: Boy Actresses on the Elizabethan Stage', *New Theatre Quarterly,* 3 (1987), 120-30; Jean Howard, *The Stage and Social Struggle,* 119-20.

11. Howard, *The Stage and Social Struggle,* 118, 120.

12. Valerie Traub, *Desire and Anxiety: Circulations of Sexuality in Shakespearean Drama* (London and New York: Routledge, 1992), 120.

13. Ibid., 122-4.

14. Ibid., 128.

15. Stephen Greenblatt, *Shakespearean Negotiations* (1998; Oxford: Clarendon Press, 1990), 89-90.
16. This experiment was carried out with professional actors at Sydney University's Centre for Performance Studies in 1996.
17. Thomas Lodge, *Rosalynd*, ed. Brian Nellist (Keele University: Ryburn Publishing, 1995), 67. Further quotations from this edition will be incorporated into the text.
18. *Rosalynd,* 75. One likes to think that the author is consciously punning on 'Lodge' here.
19. Cf. *Rosalynd,* 49: "'And I pray you,' quoth Aliena, "if your robes were off, what mettle are you made that you are so satirical against women? Is it not a foul bird defiles the own nest?'" Shakespeare's borrowing from Lodge is obvious.

HISTORY AND PHILOSOPHY

Robert Schwartz (essay date 1989)

SOURCE: "Rosalynde Among the Familists: *As You Like It* and an Expanded View of Its Sources," in *The Sixteenth Century Journal,* Vol. 20, No. 1, Spring, 1989, pp. 69-76.

[*In the following essay, Schwartz argues that Shakespeare's emphasis on Familist ideology, a sixteenth-century libertine movement, accounts for the variations between* As You Like It *and Lodge's* Rosalynde.]

Geoffrey Bullough, considering the ways in which Shakespeare used Thomas Lodge's *Rosalynde,* observed that *As You Like It* "is more than a pastoral play of escape to an idyllic world; it is rather an inquiry into the different ideas of country life current at the time, and a reconciliation between them." Actually Shakespeare's play is an inquiry into, and a reconciliation of, quite a bit more than this. Nonetheless, Bullough is correct in stressing, as have scholars since, that, while pastoral in its underpinnings, *As You Like It* is more significant for the innovations it works on traditions of pastoral than for its wholesale adoption of much that is more superficially conventional in Lodge.[1]

Beyond the shift in pastoral tone evident both in the reduction in number and importance of 'shepherd' scenes as well as the addition of debates on virtually all aspects of love and life, Shakespeare's play differs significantly from Lodge in other ways. There is the addition of Jaques, Touchstone, Audrey, and Sir Oliver Mar-text. Familial parallels are intensified by making Frederick (Torismond) and the Duke Senior (Gerismond) brothers and characterizing the group of exiled "loving lords" as a brotherhood (i.e., *Duke Senior:* "Now my co-mates and brothers in exile"). Scenes are added which further describe the life of Senior's exiled band (in Lodge merely a "lustie crue," and we do not see them eating, drinking, singing, and commenting on the human condition) and especially in references to their somewhat pantheistic, perfectionistic, loving, and communal existence. The notion of religious conversion is also added.

These innovations have seemed haphazard and designed merely to expand the scope of debate in the play—to open up the play's comic and serious potential and introduce a broader range of character types. In fact, however, all of these major changes take on a striking coherence when seen in relation to a peculiar bit of information Shakespeare gives us about the background of his most important addition to the play, the character of Jaques:

> *Duke Senior:*
> Most mischievous foul sin, in chiding sin.
> For thou thyself has been a libertine,
> As sensual as the brutish sting itself;
> And all th'embossed sores and headed evils
> That thou with license of free foot hast caught,
> Wouldst thou discharge into the general world.
>
> (II, vii, 64-69)[2]

This reference to Jaques' "libertine" past has confused Shakespeareans for a very long time. It has been normal either to see Jaques, in light of this, as "an exhausted epicurean" "long experienced in sin," a "sated voluptary," a "blase roue," one who has had "too intimate acquaintance with the seamier side of life," or simply to discount the Duke's comment on the grounds that what he says is just not true, but merely an attempt to draw Jaques into an argument. As George Kittredge pointed out in defense of the latter view, "*Libertine,* to be sure, meant 'loose liver,' but it had not become so specialized as in modern English."[3] A closer look at what "libertine" *did* mean at the time the play was written allows us not only to question Kittredge's judgment about the insincerity of the Duke's comment, as well as the view that Jaques is merely licentious and dissolute, but gives, also, some coherence to many of the changes that Shakespeare made in his major sources for the play.

The primary meaning of "libertine" in the late sixteenth century, and the one most clearly evoked by the context of the Duke's as well as Jaques' comments on chiding and cleansing sin, was one who was a member of an antinomian sect. Libertines, often also referred to as Seekers, Spirituals, Quakers, and, more often, Familists, were condemned as early as 1545 by Calvin (in his attack *Contre la secte phantastique et furieus des Libertins qui se nomment Spirituelz*) and later very bitterly in England, for example by John Knewstub at Paul's Cross in 1576, by Stephen Batman in 1577, by Lawrence Chaderton in 1578, by John Dyos in 1579, by George Gifford in 1596, and others, well into the seventeenth century.[4] The attack on Familists (the libertine sect known as The Family of Love, The Service of Love, The House [or Household] of Love, or The Family) did not come, furthermore, only from the established church, but also from literary circles. Thomas Nashe "sneered at Familism in his *Return of the Renouwned Caualiero Pasquill* in 1589 and in *Pierce Penilesse* in 1592. Early in the seventeenth century we find the same mocking attitude in Thomas Middleton's *Family of Love* and Ben Jonson's *Eastward Hoe* and *The Alchemist*."[5] The relation between the term "libertine" and the so-called Family of Love was especially close in England toward the end of the sixteenth century. In general, as George Mosse writing about Puritan radicalism tells us, "libertinage . . . had meant, in the sixteenth century, those who were filled with the 'Holy Spirit' and thus thought themselves free from any ecclesiastical discipline." It was later, in the seventeenth century, that "it came to be applied to those deists who seemed to justify moral laxness."[6] But beyond this, as Alastair Hamilton has pointed out,

> The identification between libertines and Familists had been a frequent feature of attacks both Catholic and Protestant throughout the 1560s and 1570s, and the Reformed Protestants, who prided themselves on their moral and political integrity, interpreted all attempts at compromise as the work of this vague, but at the same time ubiquitous, sect . . . 'the libertines are increasing, and with them the true atheists', wrote the Reformed preacher Hendrik van den Corput in November 1579. . . . In a further letter, in March 1581, Corput made it clear that libertines and the Family of Love were one and the same thing, that they were peddling their books openly and that the Reformed Protestants must do something about them.[7]

And other historians agree that, as Jean Dietz Moss says, "Familist eventually became synonymous with libertine."[8]

Certainly the meaning of the term, its connection with Familism in a theatrical context, and the appropriateness of its application to Jaques—the critic of romantic love in *As You Like It*—is nicely glossed in Middleton's bitter and relentless attack on the sect in his 1602 (very close in time to *As You Like It*) play titled *The Family of Love,* where the romantic hero, Gerardine, answers Lipsalve and Gudgeon ("two gallants that only pursue city lechery") as they mock men who wish to marry:

> Profane not thus the sacred name of love,
> You libertines, who never knew the joys
> Nor precious thoughts of two consenting hearts!
>
> (*The Family of Love* I, ii, 15-17)[9]

When the Duke Senior told the Elizabethan audience that Jaques had been a libertine or Familist he was telling them very much indeed. The Family of Love was founded by Henry Niclaes, a German cloth merchant, who, in his travels, left groups of converts all over Europe. His works were translated into English and disseminated by his disciple Christopher Vittels in the 1570s, perhaps after a visit to England by Niclaes around 1560.[10] What is most interesting about the group is that although they seem to have been very well known in their time and almost universally condemned, no one seemed to understand exactly what they believed or stood for. As Alastair Hamilton, the most sophisticated and thorough historian of the sect, has admitted, "the doctrine of the community consisted of a confused, and frequently contradictory, list of tenets." E. Belfort Bax found Niclaes' central statement of Familist doctrine "nothing but a turgid mass of theological maunderings, which drones on page after page without *apparently* coming to any intelligible point, and out of which it is difficult to make any coherent doctrine." While historian Julia G. Ebel adds that "little can be learned about the Family's beliefs, since most of the tangible evidence for their creed comes from defamatory literature."[11]

But considerable effort has been made to judge what the Familist creed held, or was thought to hold; and although sometimes muddled and contradictory, the following points have been stressed by church historians: 1) "Believing in the potential goodness of man, [Niclaes] taught that it was possible for him not to be a sinner in his life." 2) "There was something far more important than the Bible, [Familists] claimed: the Spirit, without whose inspiration the Scriptures would never have been written and whose inspiration continued to function independently of the Scriptures." And that ". . . the spiritual formed a group apart in which human learning was of no account but in which divine wisdom was very much present." 3) "Believing that 'all things are ruled by nature, and not directed by God,' they taught that heaven and hell were in this life and defended pre-Adamism."[12] 4) Niclaes rejected the "Lutheran *sola fide* and [urged] man to achieve righteousness by becoming a 'New Man.' [Henry Niclaes signed himself "H. N.," not for his given name but for *Homo Novus*.] As Luther accepted the fact that the believer continues to sin, but that through faith the righteousness of Christ is imputed to the undeserving sinner as a free gift, Niclaes taught that the believer would, through divine love, experience holiness thus being 'made . . . alive, through Christ,' and being separated from the sinful condition through a sanctification which he described as being 'godded . . . with him [i.e. God].'"[13]

Other beliefs that may have some bearing on our specific interest in the sect for its possible relations to *As You Like It* are: (1) The principle stated in the *Terra Pacis* that the Family "do not vow or bind themselves in the Matrimony of Men, nor-yet suffer themselues to be bound therein; but are like the Angells in Heauen." This alleged doctrinal aversion to marriage, although we know Familists did in fact marry and moreover were pretty orthodox on this point, came to be a popular point of departure for attacks on the Family and the charge of loose moral behavior, a common association with the term "libertine" that explains the literal emphasis on sensual behavior and sexual disease in the Duke's admonition to Jaques and perhaps Touchstone's attitude toward the institution of marriage. (2) Familists followed Niclaes' example of segregating himself from the "impure" and setting out on a journey to the Land of Peace by traveling to spread their beliefs. For instance, Christopher Vittels, it was said, "spent his time 'wandryng uppe and downe the Countrey'" proselytising. And Familism was spread by "such other lyke which by travailyng from place to place, do get their lyuyng." And those who, "using such a romyng kynde of Traffique keepe not commonly anyone certaine abidyng place, but runnyng fiskyng from place to place, stay not for the most part any where long together."[14]

The fundamental Familist belief that man, regenerated in nature by spiritual awakening, was free from the effects of original sin provides us with the most profound background possible for many of the comments by the Duke Senior added to Lodge's story by Shakespeare: "Are not these woods / More free from peril than the envious court?" he asks at the start of Act II, celebrating the regenerative quality and moral purity of nature—"Here feel we not the penalty of Adam." Without the background of the antinomian sects, this statement has always been problematic for critics, who don't know how to take the Duke's view in light of the chilling winter wind. But the real pantheism and optimism of the antinomian libertines is most evident in his elaboration:

> And this our life, exempt from public haunt,
> Finds tongues in trees, books in the running brooks,
> Sermons in stones, and good in everything.

Freed to pursue the spirit of Christian value through nature rather than through scripture or the orthodox rituals of the church, the Duke Senior's band of outlaws find God not in their books, but in themselves and in the world around them. And that such a process is specifically dissociated from the authority of the church is made clear by the Duke Senior's admission to Orlando that "True it is that we have seen better days, / And have with holy bell been knolled to church . . ." (II, vii, 119-20), but that, due to circumstances, this is no longer the case.

As far as such connections may take us in understanding the source of Shakespeare's additions to the story of *Rosalynde,* we must still ask: What does it matter if Jaques was a libertine and the Duke Senior seems, by virtue of his outlaw brotherhood and pantheistic/perfectionistic view, to express, or at least experiment with, Familist ideas?

To begin with, Jaques, once a libertine, is now a thoroughgoing melancholic and a skeptic. Is it because of his past that he continues to value "liberty," to debunk orthodoxy, to travel "with license of free foot," as the Familists did in spreading their views, and to remain somewhat the radical reformer? "Jaques, when he is with Touchstone," Agnes Latham says, "treats him with great courtesy, from which we may deduce that Jaques hits only those his own size."[15] Be that as it may, certainly Jaques' kindness grows more from the fact that he sees his own past in Touchstone, and in fact catches the Fool in his affair with Audrey on the verge of making the same mistake in abusing license under the guise of religiousness (rejecting the orthodox rituals of the church as antinomians were thought to have done) for which the libertines were then being condemned, as Jaques himself has been by the Duke Senior. And like Jaques, Touchstone also makes a practice of chiding 'sin,' or, rather, parodies such practice, as in his exchanges with Corin on the evils of fostering the "copulation of cattle." In fact, almost all of the characters added by Shakespeare—Jaques, Touchstone, Audrey, Sir Oliver Mar-text—help to uncover the basis of antinomian belief and practice past and present against which the Duke Senior, the young lovers, and the newly defined 'pastoral' world of the play in general measure their own spiritual development. That Touchstone's desire for "not being well married" by Sir Oliver as an excuse "hereafter to leave my wife" smacks of the popular and cynical view of Familist ethics, we cannot doubt. But even the character of Sir Oliver himself has strong Familist parallels: in reference to a group of "suspected Familists" who in 1574 "had been meeting in a secret conventicle in Balsham. . . ." it was noted that "the leader of the group appears to have been Robert Sharp, parson of the little village of Strethall. . . . It was reported of Sharp that he married people in the fields using a rite of his own." Further, "the unlikelihood of Robert Sharp being an orthodox Puritan minister is apparent from the fact that he was unable to write and had to make his mark at the foot of the confession."[16]

Jaques *was* a libertine, but now, like all good Puritans of the time, looks for sin not in himself, but in others. Touchstone, in his relations with Audrey and Sir Oliver, represents what Jaques would like to forget about his past. The Duke and his co-mates and brothers in exile (Familists greeted one another with phrases like 'here is a brother in the family') as well as the other inhabitants of the Forest of Arden, represent what is best about Familist thought: its belief in the potential to redeem fallen man and to become *Homo Novus,* the New Man spiritually reborn in nature. This accounts not only for Jaques' fascination with what we may call the 'New Man' that is Frederick the convertite (which in itself mimicks the spiritual rebirth of Oliver), but for his disinclination to return from the forest to the world of civil authority as well.

This view of what Jaques represents, the function served by Touchstone, et. al., the relevance of comments given to the Duke Senior about original sin and the family of man (in fact the play's general intensification of the role of families and its occasional questioning of what constitutes a proper family), all serve to make the total action of the play a brief but invigorating antinomian fling—almost in religious terms what C. L. Barber discussed in social and ceremonial terms as "release" and "clarification."[17] There is generally a rejection of the corrupt rules of the 'civil' world and a simultaneous celebration of the moral purity of nature. The unlimited questioning and testing of values in the forest ends in a reaffirmation of traditional social order and an even more orthodox sense of moral redefinition (a visit to an "old religious" man), the proper ceremony of marriage, and finally the restitution of civil authority.

More so than his source in Lodge (and the less proximate

Tale of Gamelyn) Shakespeare asks the question, "What is a proper family?" In spirit some families, as Le Beau tells Orlando, cannot be said to exist:

> Orlando:
> Which of the two was daughter to the Duke . . . ?
> Le Beau:
> Neither his daughter, if we judge by manners.
>
> (I, ii, 261-66)

Later, Adam, too, questions the nature of family ties:

> Your brother—no, no brother, yet the son—
> Yet not the son, I will not call him son—
> Of him I was about to call his father—

And when his own family loyalty is challenged, Orlando firmly defends it:

> I am more proud to be Sir Rowland's son,
> His youngest son, and would not change that calling
> To be adopted heir to Frederick.
>
> (I, ii, 228-30)

Indeed, as Louis Montrose has demonstrated, "It is precisely in the details of inheritance that Shakespeare makes one of the most significant departures from his source," adding that "Shakespeare alters the terms of the paternal will in Lodge's story so as to alienate Orlando from the status of a landed gentleman. The effect is to intensify the differences between the eldest son and his siblings. . . ."[18]

What is striking about Orlando's need to defend his family loyalty here is the degree to which Shakespeare has deviated from Lodge in this small point; for rather than wishing "I would thou hadst been son to some man else" (I, ii, 220), Torrismond in *Rosalynde* favors Rosader (Orlando) and especially for his parentage: "but when they knew him [Rosader] to be the youngest Sonne of Sir *John of Bordeaux*, the King rose from his seate and imbraced him. . . ."[19]

To Adam's odd questions of Orlando, "Why are you virtuous? Why do people love you?" (II, iii, 5), we may apply Orlando's own observations that although "never schooled and yet learned" (Familists rejected formal education in favor of spiritual illumination), "the spirit of my father grows strong in me . . ." (I, i, 161-62; 68-69).

Indeed, freed from the rules of the civil world, in the benevolent and nurturing laboratory of nature, all men have found the spirit of their 'father'—what Familists called the 'holy spirit'—and thus their social and true Christian selves. That Jaques does not participate in the return to a civil society does not in any way diminish this, since the process of self-discovery is unending and, as he says, "Out of these convertites / There is much matter to be heard and learned" (V, iv, 184-85).

Notes

1. Geoffrey Bullough, ed., *Narrative and Dramatic Sources of Shakespeare*, vol. 2: *The Comedies, 1597-1603* (London: Routledge and Kegan Paul, 1958), 153. Cf. *A New Variorum Edition of Shakespeare: As You Like It*, ed. Richard Knowles (New York: Modern Language Association, 1977), 476, which lists among Shakespeare's innovations on Lodge "reducing the pastoral elements;" and Agnes Latham, ed., *The Arden Edition of the Works of Shakespeare: As You Like It* (London: Methuen, 1975), who notes that "in some ways Lodge is more determinedly pastoral than Shakespeare," and that the tone of the play runs less to the pastoral frame of mind than to an ethos stressing the "natural turn of events" (xvi and xliv).

2. References to the works of Shakespeare are cited from *The Complete Signet Classic Shakespeare*, ed. Sylvan Barnet (New York: Harcourt Brace Jovanovich, repr. 1972).

3. Knowles, ed., 120-21 n. Cf. comments by Gervinus, Fletcher, Skipton, Gray, Kittredge and the editor.

4. See George H. Williams, *The Radical Reformation* (Philadelphia: Westminster, 1962), 788-89: "A distinctive feature of the radical movement in England was the close interrelationship of Libertinism, anti-Trinitarianism, Anabaptism of the Melchiorite strain, and Spiritualism." For English critics of the sect see Alastair Hamilton, *The Family of Love* (Cambridge: James Clarke & Co., 1981), 128, and Jean Dietz Moss, "The Family of Love and English Critics," *Sixteenth Century Journal* 6:1 (1975): 44.

5. Lynnewood F. Martin, "The Family of Love in England: Conforming Millenarians," *Sixteenth Century Journal* 3:2 (1972): 100; Hamilton, *Family of Love*, 134-35.

6. George L. Mosse, "Puritan Radicalism and the Enlightenment," *Church History* 29 (1960): 426.

7. Hamilton, *Family of Love*, 109.

8. Moss, *Family & English Critics*, 35.

9. *The Works of Thomas Middleton*, vol. 3, ed. A. H. Bullen (Boston: Houghton, Mifflin, 1885), 15.

10. For background on Henry Niclaes and The Family of Love see Hamilton, *Family of Love, passim;* Martin, *Family in England*, 78-108; Julia G. Ebel, "The Family of Love: Sources of its History in England," *Huntington Library Quarterly* 30:4 (1967): 331-43; Williams, *Radical Reformation*, esp. 778-90; Moss, *Family & English Critics* 35-52; Wallace Kirsop, "The Family of Love in France," *Journal of Religious History* 3:2 (1965): 103-18; Champlin Burrage, *The Early English Dissenters in Light of Recent Research (1550-1641)*, 2 vols (New York: Russell and Russell, repr. 1967), esp. 1:209-14.

11. Hamilton, *Family of Love*, 118; E. Belfort Bax, *The Rise and Fall of the Anabaptists* (London: Sonnenschein, 1903), 359; Ebel, *Family: Sources*, 332.

the characters enter in the course of the play and within which their humorous excesses are purged so that the personal, interpersonal and social reintegrations can occur in the last scene. The green world is the world of desire; it is, as Northrop Frye says, not a world that judges moral worth, but one that wants to see the unity of desire with desired. "Its opposite is not the villainous but the absurd"[2] and the absurd is (in the world of desire) whatever blocks desire. What happens in the audience in this case, if parallel, might seem to be of questionable worth, perhaps just because of the freedom from moral judgment that the comic play generally creates for itself. The comic world, on this view, aims at satisfaction of Id. That, at least, would go far in explaining the negative view of comedy attributed to Plato and Augustine, among others.

That Platonic view of comedy is a little too simplistically moralizing.[3] Generally moral questions are put off, our moral judgment is, as it were, set aside in comedy by making the "normal" society of the play's beginning highly questionable. The green world, then, is not *just* Id's playground. In *As You Like It* we see a brother plot against his brother's life and limb, and hear that the new Duke has just driven his brother off the throne and out to Arden. In other plays the stupidity of one or another law, usually about marriage, disables our moral judgment from taking the side of the "normal society." And while that may not be enough to make desire's world the world of moral virtue, the ridiculous law or obvious injustice of the normal society is enough to give the green world freedom under a presumption of charity: it cannot be as stupid as the court of that original world.

What goes on in the audience, then, can be much more complex than morally questionable fantasizing about a world operating on laws invented by Id. Comic catharses fall into a range of possibilities, only the first of which seems entirely questionable. First, it is possible that an audience member could go into the green world of the theatre as into a fantasy. And when he comes out, eyes blinking, the real world with all its moral claims and political difficulties slaps him like sunlight across the face. To take up the case of the original audience of *As You Like It*, there is still the law of primogeniture, I am still a younger brother with few property rights, and no hope of fulfilling my desire for a Duke's only daughter; or, I am still an older brother with all these young ones eating up my estate, nickeling and diming me to death with their requests for schooling and funds, etc.[4] Comedy, under this dispensation, has a cathartic effect just as circling a track for an hour does—it's hypnotic, we forget our problems; but then the hypnotic or incantatory effect ends and we wake to the world going on apace. This is the explanation of comic catharsis of all those who think of art as mere entertainment. It may be true; but if it is, there is no reason to study the humanities rather than watch football. Further, far from providing a "vicarious benefit," or "facilitat[ing] pacification and escape" (Montrose, p. 53), it would seem to face the audience of such younger brothers of less than lordly families with the complete inadequacy of their own daylight world, and such comedy is likely to be as socially upsetting as Plato is said to have feared. We might call this version of catharsis the merely physiological catharsis, though whether it discharges itself in the theater (as Freud thinks), or on the body of the older brother (as Plato fears and Marx hopes) is left open.

An advance upon this line is marked by the idea that fantasy is not *mere* fantasy for human beings, that just as we expect the new world that will form outside the forest will be one in which the characters act in accord with what their hearts have learned within it, so too the audience of the comedy can go forth into its world, carrying the green world's heart within them. And so younger and older brothers, knowing their legal rights, and without abrogating such law as society has, will treat each other more in accord with the happy spirit of Arden than the murderous spirit of the original dukedom. The enactment of the personal, interpersonal, and social integration on stage will be imitated so far as possible in the world outside the theatre. This is, I assume, the more usual view of comic catharsis, and it is sufficient, if true, to defend comedy against its cultured despisers, for according to it comedy has a quite beneficent social and moral effect. It begins the practice of charity by its work on the community's moral imagination. Comedy is a vision of dianoia, the significance of which is social. We all experience it together.

What both of these first two views have in common is that in them the world that answers desire, the world of Arden, is seen and felt as absolute, as that-than-which-nothing-greater-can-be-conceived, that which is to be loved with all one's heart and soul and mind. In the first version, that world is mere, or dangerous, fantasy; in the other view, it is a source of "social conciliation."[5]

But there is at least one character in *As You Like It*, who, seeing that world's perfection, leaves it. And so, yet another type of comic catharsis must be possible, one in line with the character of Jaques. It may be, of course, that Jaques, preferring solitude and his melancholy, really never enters the green world (not seeing it as green), or if he does, does not change. Early on he claims that the green society "more usurps" (II.1.27) from the natural good than the normal society from which his Duke is but recently banished. In this he would be even more humorous than Touchstone, who at least takes part in the festive couplings of the country, though he is not much pleased with Arden. Under this reading Jaques is simply an irrecoverable surd in the comic movement, and has to be got off stage before the ritual concluding *komos* can begin.[6]

But it is possible to see and to play Jaques as a character who comes to his own kind of recognition, and changes because of it.[7] If he does so change he will also mark a different kind of catharsis that is possible for an audience member as well. Jaques, at the end, loves the green world and sees its goodness, its happiness, but he loves it not in the way we ordinarily think of that word—as a synonym

12. For this and above, Hamilton, *Family of Love,* 4, 7, 118.

13. Martin, *Family in England,* 100-1.

14. *Terra Pacis. A true testification of the spirituall lande of peace, which is the spirituall lande of promyse* . . . (Cologne, c. 1574) cited in Hamilton, *Family of Love,* 37, 55, 119-21.

15. Latham, *Arden Edition,* lxxvi.

16. N. A. Penrhys-Evans, *The Family of Love in England, 1550-1650* (unpublished MA thesis, University of Kent at Canterbury, September, 1971) 84-86. Cf. Hamilton, *Family of Love,* 121.

17. C. L. Barber, *Shakespeare's Festive Comedy* (Princeton: Princeton University Press, 1959), *passim.*

18. Louis Adrian Montrose, "'The Place of a Brother' in *As You Like It:* Social Process and Comic Form." *Shakespeare Quarterly* 32:1 (1981): 28-54.

19. Bullough, *Sources of Shakespeare,* 172.

Gene Fendt (essay date 1995)

SOURCE: "Resolution, Catharsis, Culture: *As You Like It,*" in *Philosophy and Literature,* Vol. 19, No. 2, 1995, pp. 248-60.

[*In the following essay, Fendt explores the cathartic effects of* As You Like It *on the audience, juxtaposing the views of the characters Jaques and Touchstone.*]

> Happiness does not lie in amusement; indeed it would be strange . . . if one were to take trouble and suffer hardship all one's life in order to amuse oneself. Relaxation, then, is not an end; for it is taken for the sake of activity.
>
> Aristotle (NE 1176b30-35)
>
> Comedy is a vision of *dianoia,* a significance which is ultimately social significance.
>
> Northrop Frye, *Anatomy of Criticism*

As with tragedy and music, it seems that there are several kinds of catharsis that are plausible in a comedy.[1] Let us take the example of *As You Like It,* which would seem to be about as perfect an example of the art form as is possible. Indeed, one of the reasons to think it is so is that it allows, as we shall see, of every type of comic resolution and catharsis. In the last scene, Rosalind, whom we see through most of the play as both being in love (as a woman) and mocking romantic love's excesses (as a man), becomes a unified being, loving and sensible; so there is an intrapersonal integration or resolution which follows from what she experiences and recognizes about love. There is, as well, an interpersonal integration—each member of the pairs of country copulatives is united with what it really desires; and further, there is a larger social *redintigratio in statuum pristinum*—the duke is returned to his lands, Oliver to his, and the whole green world society which has turned around Rosalind and Orlando is set to take its place in the normal world outside of the forest of Arden. So, due to the *recognitions* made in Arden there are three axes of *resolution* within the play. Similarly the audience members, who have gone into the golden world of the theatre, and who may have come to some recognitions of their own, are about to go out into the normal world, which is their true inheritance. If the play has worked, they have suffered at least one kind of catharsis. This essay explores those recognitions, their accompanying resolutions and their plausible resulting catharses, and then turns to some cultural implications.

We have mentioned a parallelism between the audience and the characters of the play; that parallelism no doubt includes a similarity in emotional effect, on the one due to being in Arden (where the effect on the characters is the play's resolution), on the other due to being in the theatre (where the effect on the audience is the comic catharsis). Something like this parallelism probably underlies Aristotle's statement that the final cause of tragedy is a catharsis of the emotions of fear and pity raised by the fearful events in the tragedy, as his comments on those emotions in the *Rhetoric* make clear. Hecuba, for example, not only has fears, what happens to her is fearful, and what she does is fearful too. Those things that we would fear if they threatened us, arouse pity when we see them happen to others (*Rhetoric* 1386a25): the object of pity and fear is the same, the subject's relation to that object (direct in fear, and indirect, or distant, in pity) seems to make up the largest part of the difference between the two emotions. The fearfulness of the tragic events evokes the pity of the spectators, the resolution of the plot provides the catharsis of those emotions. Catharsis is not the same as resolution, but the resolution of the plot helps cause the catharsis in the audience.

To return to *As You Like It*. The characters in the play are embued with eros, desire. I suppose it is not unusual for some members of the audience to become directly embued with that same passion for Rosalind or Orlando, or perhaps Touchstone or Audrey. Less directly—but more obviously and more powerfully—the audience will have sympathy for those erotic characters, for we all know what it is to desire and to be separated from what we desire. It is, of course, most likely that audience members will feel something of both emotions (as we feel both fear and pity in tragedy)—an immediate *attraction* for the hero and heroine, and the more mediated feeling, *sympathy,* for their plight. If the main characters were not attractive at all we would be less likely to feel sympathy. The task of the comedy, then—its final cause—is to bring about a catharsis of the emotions of desire and sympathy. How does it accomplish this?

One kind of story goes like this: like the characters in the play, the audience takes part in and identifies with the green world, the world closer to the heart's desire, which for eros, desire—he loves the world of the heart's desire without desiring it, and so he leaves it, and leaving it, he blesses it:

> You to your former honor I bequeath;
> your patience and your virtue well deserve it.
> You to a love that your true faith doth merit;
> You to your land and love and great allies;
> You to a long and well-deserved bed;
> and you to wrangling, for thy loving voyage
> is but for two months victualed. So, to your pleasures;
> I am for other than dancing measures.
>
> (V.4.178-85)

There is none of his usual melancholic bile in this speech; and of Touchstone, the one person who is not so highly blessed, he seems to be merely speaking the plain truth, one that Touchstone himself would be unlikely to deny or find fault with. Touchstone had, in fact, predicted a similar result before his marriage (III.3.77-83).

So then, in the audience of the comedy, may there not be one or two who, leaving the play, admit that all the heart's desires are satisfied in the green world, and bless that world, but are cured of desiring it? They must have an inkling, as Jaques does, that desire's world is not absolute, even when it is fulfilled. I suppose Schopenhauer would like to say this: we learn, in comedy, and the comic catharsis makes us feel the good of, the resignation of desire. But I think that last speech of Jaques' bespeaks something other than Schopenhauerian resignation, for Schopenhauer could not bless the happy couples of the green world, as Jaques, heartfeltly, does.

The kind of comic catharsis I have in mind does not work just by showing us, and letting us identify with, the satisfaction of desire, or showing it to us and denying our feeling for it. It shows the world of eros as a whole, and, as every whole which we can see *as* a whole, the world of eros is a limited whole, and all its perfected satisfactions are but the figure of something greater than that whole world, to which Jaques goes, at the edge of the forest of Arden. *What* that is he has yet to discover, but *that* it is he must already believe. This we should call a religious or sublime comic catharsis, for it raises us entirely above thralldom to desire since it raises us above even the world of desire satisfied. So, of course, does Schopenhauer, in his fashion.

The first two, worldly, versions of catharsis are the ones most commonly attributed to comedy. Each subtype of that catharsis has its figure in *As You Like It*. The purely physiological catharsis is figured in Touchstone, the "material fool" (III.3.28) who, crowding in amongst all the other country copulatives, gives away the fact that he really thinks all the other marriages are as simply physiological as his. For a taste:

> As the ox hath his bow, sir, the horse his curb, and the falcon her bells, so man hath his desires; and as pigeons bill, so wedlock would be nibbling
>
> (III.3.69-71)

and

> If a hart do lack a hind
> Let him seek out Rosalind
>
> (III.2.95-97)

and similar false gallop of verses.

Touchstone takes his satisfaction as some audience members come to a play—for entertainment or titillation; he comes to his resolution in the last scene—or shortly thereafter. He accomplishes his satisfaction upon the body of Audrey, as a younger brother in the audience might achieve some substitutive satisfaction for his real desires by seeing the play. It is "a poor virgin" (ergo, unfruitful), "an ill favored thing" (because fruitless), but his own (V.4.53-56). No doubt such plays as this will titillate and satisfy such a one for two months or so, but then the wrangling will begin, and Audrey—fantasy fulfillment—will be put away for more suitable meat. Or the usual, now galloping, poverty. So, too, the merely physiological catharsis of art wears thin; one needs more opium, more flowers to hide the chains, or else the very thing that hid the chains makes one become more aware of the chains.[8] In short, it would seem, contra Freud,[9] that art is less likely than religion to provide substitutive satisfaction to the demands of a raging Id, for the satisfactions presented to fantasy in dramatic art are manufactured out of things that some people accomplish in the real world; religion's are not. Id is, in this one regard, a realist: it doesn't want the picture of a cigar, it wants the real cigar. Touchstone becomes an incendiary.[10]

The second subtype of worldly catharsis—which we might call the moral catharsis—is figured variously in the other lovers, who undergo the trials of desire, the recognitions those trials lead to, and the personal, interpersonal and social *redintigratio* which the forest offers, and we, the audience, cheer, happily recognizing ourselves.

The second *kind* of catharsis, which we should perhaps call the religious comic catharsis, also has two forms. They both are recognitions that there is an ideal realm which checks or overcomes the world of desire even when that realm is fulfilled. That ideal realm bounds the world of desire and does not allow Arden to take itself as absolute, even when everyone in that green world may be satisfied. Only one of its two subtypes can be instantiated in this play, however, for both can only be instantiated on stage by Jaques. He may be understood (and played) as a prototype of Schopenhauerian denial of the world of desire—one who begins in melancholy and ends in resignation of action and desire. A Hindu might call such a Jaques a religious hero, and the play might bring such an audience member to a religious catharsis. Or, more likely for Shakespeare, and as I think Jaques's last speech makes clear, Jaques may be understood and played as someone who comes to recognize desire's goodness in Arden, who blesses the green world, but lets it be. He goes out to the edge of the green world of the heart to look for something which eye has not seen, nor ear heard, nor did it enter the mind of Bard to represent. Such a Jaques transfigures the play's beautiful comic resolution into a sublime one, and his recognition may be echoed, and engender its catharsis, in the audience.

This paper could end here, and for a while, it did. But it seems to me that the four kinds of catharsis accomplishable *by* the play, and the kinds of resolution reached *in* the play, figure different kinds of culture *outside* the play. The easiest to see is the society of the material fools, symbolized by T and A,[11] for whom everything is merely physiology. Students of physical education come to mind, for whom work is lifting weights, running laps, lines, patterns, plays, and who build a day around these activities, others (philosophy or literature classes) falling in as they may—or not. What kind of thing can be cathartic for them? Things that relax their bodies from the efforts of the day: sex, drugs, rock and roll, or lounging at a play. The more such a one dedicates himself to the work, the stronger the catharsis needed to achieve a kind of normal state. In such a culture *art* is not only not a necessity, but probably an impossibility: sex, drugs, and rock and roll are more likely candidates for providing the necessary release than Shakespearean comedy, or a flash of T and A. Soon one will begin to demand New Year's Day games in sunny locales. *Sic transit gloria mundi*—the body culture, the materialism of atoms and the void.

A second culture is more genuinely social, and may be called moral culture; it exceeds physical culture as the soul, in medieval philosophy, exceeds the body,[12] or as the marriage of true minds surpasses country copulation. This kind of culture may spend its days just as competitively as the first, though the competitions are for intangibles like love, honor, and perhaps money—which are, after all, bound up with signs. As their competitions and their desires, so must their catharses be, and the catharsis provided by a play *may* serve feelingly to recall the unity underlying and making possible the single-minded pursuits of the daylight world. For neither love, nor honor, nor even money is possible except that we live among others who recognize and support the reality of such "things," for such are not merely things, but signs, and signs are a social reality. In this culture, art is a useful catharsis with socially important results. As Aristotle would say, such music conduces to moral and political virtue, whatever we may consider that to be (*Politics* 1339a21). That is to say, its results will be judged differently depending on how the moralist wishes the society to turn: liberals fancy Marx and expect artistic catharses to motivate social revolution (these days watered down to "change"), while conservatives are on the side of Freud, who expects art to work as a substitutive satisfaction for civilization's endemic discontents. But to judge art according to either standard is to make a political judgment on art, not an artistic or even a moral judgment. It transforms the free and reflective judgment of the beautiful into a determination according to concepts of reason.[13]

The other *kind* of culture[14] let us call it religious, for it posits the world of desire as a completed whole, and *thereby* transcends it. Its vision is of a noncompetitive, infinitely sharable, but intimate and personal good: wisdom, beatific vision, communion of saints, Nirvana. The version of this culture corresponding to Schopenhauer's resigning catharsis is the unarmed society of Lamaism.[15] The culture corresponding to the more sublime resolution, which does not seek to evaporate the principle of individuation—as Schopenhauer, nor curse the world as mere humorous illusion—as Schopenhauer, is the more traditional religious spirit of the west.[16] For such a person a play itself is the mimesis of just that religious ideal, for without dissolving the principle of individuation, *each* person comes to his or her catharsis *along with* everyone else in the theatre. A play is an infinitely sharable, but intimate and personal good thing. Such a comedy is far from mere amusement; it is not only a vision, but a mimesis of ultimate social significance. A comedy not only figures, it enacts the good it figures: at a play the audience mimes the communal good we seek to instantiate in life. It is no wonder that drama was a religious ritual for the Greeks, that species of human being which is a permanent embarrassment to every lower type.

Further, and to the point of *this* particular culture. It is probably about as accidental as the fact that $3 - 2 = 1$ that after the dark political ages of the Pax Romana, and the tiring out of rival football clubs of Vandals, Goths, and Visigoths, schools and universities were refounded not by states, but by monks and religious communities. The idea of a university is not an idea that a state would have: it does not need them. A state, particularly one with a highly mechanized economy, will find it much more useful to keep its citizens under the physiological or directly social understandings of culture and catharsis. Football—I mean physiological catharses—and fantasy fulfillment are its major tools.[17] But the pursuit of wisdom exceeds the pursuit of socially constructed, or socially constructible, desires, for besides being an activity engaged in for its own sake and without a return to practical use, it is one which a finite being can never be finished with, or even imagine being finished with: in contrast to desire it is recognized as not having a termination. The pursuit of wisdom is an infinite task, and someone engaged in such a task needs play, for it brings him down to something accomplishable, before he goes back to the task which can never be finished, and into which even his play is taken up. For such a one art is a *necessity,* since only it can grant the catharsis, and the resolution, the spirit requires.

For a time, persons from all three cultures—physical, moral, religious—can meet at a play like *As You Like It.* It is, of course, unlikely that they are *meeting* in any other sense than that which any material fool could describe and understand. In judging a work of art such as *As You Like It,* then, an audience necessarily judges itself; in what members of the audience cheer for, they show their taste, confess their culture, perhaps even their religion. A material fool judges merely the pleasantness of the sensations of the play, and about this there can be no disputing: some prefer Audrey, some prefer sheep. Their pleasures are incommunicable each to each, though the source may be bought, sold, or, in turn, enjoyed by all. Further, like Touchstone, they cannot help what they feel, and they think no one else can either—as pigeons bill, marriage is nibbling.

The more noble lovers, and their correlative audience, have an ontological commitment to freedom, understood as freedom from determination by a material humor; that freedom allows them to make commitments to each other which we can expect to last longer than the two-month, or two-hour, cure of a humor. For them, judgments of taste are not merely personal caprice, but are tied to something more constant: they are not merely judgments of physiological taste. The third figure, Jaques, has, under either reading of him, an ontological commitment to freedom understood positively: a transcendental reality is the condition for the happy possibilities of lovers in the forest of Arden. Of that reality, on the outer and binding edge of our happiness, he would learn more. He goes to seek it.

One of my dyed-in-the-wool Platonist students, Ryan Nelson, has suggested that since each person has an element which aims at each type of catharsis, all three kinds of catharsis work on *each* member of the audience. That idea is more charitable than mine; therefore, no doubt, truer. Further, if art is capable of improving culture, Ryan's idea must be the basis of the how. Someone whose desires run to T and A goes to the play and, seeing his Touchstone desire run to its conclusion in Audrey, is "feelingly persuaded" that he wants more than that—or something other: something more like Rosalind and Orlando, or Celia and Oliver. His passions have begun their education. So, like the forest of Arden, the play does not just flatter our desires, but feelingly persuades us of what we are (II.1.10). What we are is something more than the humorous Touchstone will admit, though his marriage's failure in two month's time will exhibit it—in case the marriage itself hasn't made it plain.[18]

The culture of Touchstone can be reduced to culture embodied in particular unique empirical artifacts, to which the only valid question is "isn't that interesting?" and the only politically correct answer is "yes." If you don't say yes, your preference for one artifact rather than another is merely humorous, a different physiological taste. Touchstone makes Audrey; isn't that interesting? Corin makes sheep; isn't that interesting?[19] You now know everything you need to know about multicultur-alism except what each culture finds interesting; isn't that interesting? This is culture as a historicist, like Herder, understood it. There are still Herders among us. Isn't that interesting?

The culture of the lovers is one of normative commitments open to moral development. It is a culture which by its very existence asks us "isn't this good?" And in order to answer that question you would have to live in that culture of normative commitments, you would have to put *yourself* into such commitments; and the quality of those commitments would be your answer. The play achieves a brief version of this state in the catharsis it produces in the average audience; but insofar as it is but a two-hour version of moral culture, it is not moral culture, and we must advance from the aesthetic to the actual. That is, like the people in Arden, we must now go back to the real world, taking the green world with us. We have noted in the earlier part of this essay that the play is not merely a symbol of morality, but also begins the construction of a world closer to the moral heart, for it constructs in the audience that unity of feeling and reason which is the comic catharsis. This is culture as Kant understood it. There are still Kantians among us. Perhaps this investigation is a Kantian version of play.

Jaques goes to the very edge of culture, and wonders, "What is it that allows these cultures to be?" That is, he asks, "What are the conditions for the possibility of culture?" And the only proper response is continual wonder. Jaques is nothing if not wondering. This culture, if there were one, would be the culture of philosophy, if there was any.

Notes

I thank Dan Pekarske, with whom I have been discussing these issues for years; part of this is his. I would also like to thank Brenda, Laura, Brett, and Ryan, from the Shakespeare class I recently led, who contributed much to my understanding of the play.

1. Aristotle, for example, argues that the catharsis resulting from sacred songs is different depending on the character of the worshipper, but that some kind of catharsis occurs in all hearers (*Politics* 1342a5-16). Just above that he mentioned three kinds of benefit available from music (the kinds of benefit depending on the capacity of the audience) at 1341b33-40. He leaves the question of tragedy's effect "in the theatre" as "another discourse" in *Poetics* 1449a8. In an article from *Renaissance Drama* (New Series) 2 (1969): 3-22, O. B. Hardison outlined "Three Types of Renaissance Catharsis" as "moral, religious, and literal." He does not mention their differences as relative to the character of the audience.

2. Northrop Frye, *The Anatomy of Criticism* (Princeton: Princeton University Press, 1957), p. 167.

3. This is probably too simplistic even for Plato, who died, so they say, with a copy of Aristophanes under his pillow.

4. For many more details on the social import of the enmities played out in *As You Like It*, see Louis A Montrose, "The Place of a Brother in *As You Like It*: Social process and comic form," in *Shakespeare Quarterly* 32 (1981): 40-54.

5. Montrose uses this phrase (p. 54), but seems to have in mind a rather sanguine physiological account (facilitating pacification and escape), or a

bootstrapping economic one "fostering strength and perseverance" in one's effort to achieve, as Orlando does, what birth denies (p. 53). But those younger brothers (and Montrose mentions some) who can bootstrap out of their oppressed condition in Elizabethan society (or any other) are few, and far between, and very, very lucky.

6. Which *komos* is "the sensible rendering of the moral idea" of the community of mankind (*Critique of Judgement,* translated by James Creed Meredith, Oxford: Clarendon Press, 1952), to foreshadow a point I will pick up later.

7. See Robert B. Bennet, "Reform of a Malcontent: Jaques and the meaning of *As You Like It,*" *Shakespeare Studies* (1976): 201f.

8. Even 276 channels might not be enough. The culminating point of this type of culture, "where devotion to what is superfluous begins to be prejudicial to what is indispensable, is called luxury" (Kant, p. 432).

9. See Sigmund Freud, *The Future of an Illusion,* translated by W. D. Robson-Scott (Garden City: Doubleday, 1964). Chapter two defines art as a substitutive satisfaction.

10. I should add that I do not mean to suggest by this that the catharsis signified by Touchstone is not a catharsis, nor would I deny that the other kinds of catharsis—those symbolized by the lovers and Jaques—are *also* physiological. As that poor mild virgin, Emily Dickinson, said, "When I feel physically as if the top of my head were taken off, I know this is poetry" (quoted by Frye, *Anatomy,* p. 27).

11. Lest some ill-humored reader embed me in a context I do not wish to be bedded in, let me say that what I mean by T and A is just Touchstone and Audrey.

12. See, for example Augustine's little treatise, *De quantitate animae,* J. P. Migne (*Patroligia Latina,* vol. 32, Paris: 1845) cols. 1035-1049.

13. That one can make such judgments on art is as old as political philosophy, though neither Plato nor Aristotle would say that political judgments are the only ones that can be made of art. Of music Aristotle remarks that there are three plausible purposes for having it in a state: "for the sake of amusement and relaxation, like sleep or drinking, [or] . . . music conduces to virtue on the ground that it can form our minds and habituate us to true pleasures, . . . or . . . it contributes to the enjoyment of leisure and mental cultivation, which is a third alternative" (*Politics* 1339a16-26).

14. If any readers begin to feel that they have been climbing up and down a ladder built after a familiar pattern, there is probably something to the thought. For those who are not natural Platonists there is also Aristotle's remark in the *Ethics* that the three main kinds of life are the life of pleasure, the practical, social life aiming at moral virtue, and the contemplative life (*NE* 1095b14-1096a5).

15. See Georges Bataille, *The Accursed Share,* vol. 1, trans. Robert Hurley (New York: Zone Books, 1988).

16. Here we see (despite himself) Nietzsche's cultural debt to Schopenhauer, for he evaporates the principle of individuation. In *The Birth of Tragedy* (trans. Francis Golffing [New York: Doubleday, 1956]), Nietzsche seems to claim that the principle of individuation is dissolved: "the transport of the Dionysiac state . . . carries with it a Lethean element in which everything that has been experienced by the individual is drowned" (§7). See also §18 and §21 where he calls the Apollonian charm of art "illusory," "mere appearance" cast upon the darkness, and "the work of Maya."

17. Aristotle speaks of this culture when he says the bodily pleasures "are pursued because of their violence by those who cannot enjoy other pleasures, . . . for they have nothing else to enjoy, and, besides, a neutral state is painful to many people because of their nature. . . . Similarly, the youthful, . . . or people of an excitable nature always need relief" (NE 1154b3-12). In *Politics* he calls this culture the culture of natural slaves, as in *Ethics* he had said that a constitution that does not aim at virtue is a failure.

18. In less liberated days a critic would say that "spectators are of two kinds—the one free and educated, and the other a vulgar crowd . . . [and] their music will correspond to their minds; for as their minds are perverted from their natural state, so there are perverted modes and highly strung and unnaturally colored melodies" etc. (*Politics* 1342a18-25). These days we know that the difference between cultures is mere difference, and no judgments about whole cultures being vulgar are allowed.

19. Lest some lamb think I am here straying from the folds of Shakespeare's play, recall the interesting discussion between Corin and Touchstone on the differences between the hand-kissing court and the more rural rubbing of sheep (III.2.11-79).

REPRESENTATION AND IDENTITY

Kay Stanton (essay date 1985)

SOURCE: "The Disguises of Shakespeare's *As You Like It,*" in *Iowa State Journal of Research,* Vol. 59, No. 3, February, 1985, pp. 295-305.

[*In the following essay, Stanton argues that many of* As You Like It's *characters disguise their true feelings and nature, a fact which clarifies many of the play's nuances.*]

The physical disguise of Rosalind as the male "Ganymede" is one of the most discussed features of Shakespeare's *As You Like It*.[1] Most commentary, however, either completely neglects or minimally addresses the disguises of Celia as "Aliena" and the Clown as "Touchstone." More than a simple plot device, the disguises of these three characters provide an external manifestation for their internal tensions. Furthermore, several of the other characters disguise themselves in less dramatic ways in response to the image expected of them by those who hold power over them. The use of forms of disguising throughout the play gives Rosalind's physical disguise a context, and the necessity for disguise is one of the play's themes: a variation on the nature/art tension that pervades *As You Like It*.

In the household of Oliver and the court of Duke Frederick, the characters who are without political power are unhappy, depressed, frustrated, or angry. Orlando feels that his true identity as the youngest son of Sir Rowland de Boys is obscured by his older brother Oliver's tyranny and unfairness. Similarly, Rosalind must attempt to generate "more mirth" than she is "mistress of," in order to hide her moroseness over her father's political overthrow. Even the minor characters Charles and Le Beau reveal that their political sympathies are not with Duke Frederick. The court's motley fool (who will become "Touchstone") must worry about being whipped for offering his criticism of the current regime. Because they cannot feel support for the present rulers, all of these characters must disguise their attitudes somewhat in order to survive. For these characters, "natural" life has become "unnatural," so they must resort to the art of seeming to be what they are not.

In the case of Orlando, the youth seems to have reached the breaking point of his disguised self-control at the opening of the play. His complaints to Adam show that, rather than actively trying to be what he is not, he had been passively accepting the "disguising" of his true position as Sir Rowland's son imposed upon him through Oliver's treatment of him. His remarks imply that he has endured for some time this condition that hides his genteel self in an enforced disguise of rusticity. At this point, he is not quite sure how to remove the disguise. He also seems to have some difficulty in perceiving exactly who or what he is underneath the disguise; he continually refers to the spirit of his father within him. He can as yet only understand his own identity in terms of his heritage and the qualities in himself that are like those of his deceased father; he has no clear idea of self without the context provided by Sir Rowland.

The means that Orlando settles on as the way to remove the disgraceful disguise given to him from Oliver is to go to court, disguised, in order to challenge Charles, the court wrestler. The point of the disguise is not made clear, and its success is questionable: Charles knows before Orlando even comes to court that this youngest son of Sir Rowland is the wrestler. Although after he has triumphed over Charles, Orlando proudly asserts his identity as Sir Rowland's son, he seems to "mine" his own "gentility" by at first keeping his name a secret. However, the disguise is probably at first merely a device to allow Orlando access to Duke Frederick's court without being turned away at once simply on the basis of his identity as the son of an enemy to the ruler.

Before and during the wrestling match, both Rosalind and Celia are impressed with Orlando, concerned for his safety, and hopeful for his success. Both definitely also find Orlando attractive. But after the match, when Orlando's identity is revealed, Rosalind takes Orlando to be "hers" because of the friendship between their respective fathers. Significantly, immediately before the match, Rosalind says to Orlando, "Pray heaven I be deceived in you!" (I.ii.186).[2] Her wish is granted. She is deceived in underestimating Orlando's strength, but she is also deceived in thinking Orlando to be only a good-looking, strong, bold young man. As the son of Sir Rowland, her father's beloved friend, Orlando is her political ally, thus more "hers" than Celia's. Rosalind perceives herself and Orlando to have an immediate and strong bond because of their heritages and their true selves that are being repressed.[3]

The events of the meeting of Rosalind and Orlando at court rehearse the events of their relationship in the forest, except that at court it is Orlando who is disguised; in the forest it is Rosalind. At court, the unidentified Orlando inspires warm feelings in Rosalind, who has a potential rival for his affections in Celia until Orlando's true identity is known. In the forest, Orlando has warm feelings for Rosalind as "Ganymede," who is loved by Phebe until "Ganymede"'s true identity is revealed. Thus the use of physical disguise by Rosalind is foreshadowed in the less complicated use of "disguise" of political withholding of identity by Orlando.

In trying to forge Orlando into an unrefined menial, Oliver wishes to make Orlando "disguise" himself as a servant like Adam. Although Orlando rejects the proffered role-model, in his rebellion against Oliver he styles himself in the manner of another character, Charles the wrestler. Some parallels between Charles and Orlando can be noted. Each sees physical strength as his means of making a place for himself in the world. In stressing his physical powers, each diminishes the importance of his other characteristics in the eyes of those who observe him. Charles is often considered to be merely a ruffian by many critics; Rosalind and Celia habitually refer to Orlando as the "wrestler."

By understanding that Charles is himself also making use of a kind of disguise, we can resolve some of the difficulties seen in his character by several commentators. Although often called by critics an "inarticulate brute," Charles actually displays considerable nobility of spirit in the concern for Orlando which he expresses to Oliver.

Furthermore, Charles' description of Duke Senior's forest life, often read as being merely a crude means for exposition in the play, actually shows that Charles admires Duke Senior and his life of (as Charles supposes) romantic freedom. Rather than being "evidence" of Shakespeare's uncorrected revision, the discrepancy between Charles' behavior with Oliver and his behavior at court should be understood as an indication that, in order to provide for himself, Charles must play a part. Wrestling is an approved form of entertainment at court because it is a metaphor for the political overthrow by force through which Duke Frederick gained his power.[4] Seeing that Duke Frederick's court offers a place for someone with his kind of talent, Charles exploits his natural ability and artfully disguises his political antipathy. At court, he acts the brute in order to fulfill the expectations of a brutal ruling class. Orlando sees the same opportunity.[5] He wants to succeed at court in order to free himself from one kind of disguising, but he cannot maintain the disguising of his political sympathy as well as Charles does.

Another minor character at court, Le Beau, also disguises his sympathies in his outward show. During his initial conversation with Rosalind and Celia, Le Beau seems to be merely a longwinded, insensitive fop. However, when he converses with Orlando after the wrestling match, Le Beau gives the youth a succinct and comradely warning, hoping to meet him again "in a better world than this" (I.ii.274). His astute warning to Orlando about Duke Frederick's moods suggests his implicit hope for the tyrant's overthrow. Like Charles, then, Le Beau is playing a part, disguising himself in order to provide a place for himself at court.

If Orlando, Rosalind, Charles, and Le Beau are aware of the need to disguise their attitudes at court, so are the power figures, Oliver and Duke Frederick, extremely sensitive to the strategy of disguise. During and after his conversation with Charles, Oliver reveals to the audience his own use of several levels of disguise. While disguising his true feelings about Orlando, Oliver says that he has tried "by underhand means" (I.i.135) to discourage his brother from wrestling Charles. He lies about Orlando's character, disguising the youth's true good nature in a shroud of supposed villainy. Rather than using "underhand means" to prevent Orlando from wrestling, Oliver underhandedly tries to allow the match to proceed and to provoke Charles into eliminating Orlando for him. In his soliloquy following the conversation, we see not only Oliver's true undisguised attitude, but also that he somehow attributes his own lack of popularity to Orlando.

In Duke Frederick, we see another man who is obsessed with the disguising of attitudes. Because he himself had been disguising his negative feelings about Rosalind for so long, he assumes that she is disguising her treason. Again, because he, like Oliver, fails to perceive that naturalness and uncomplicated goodness make for popularity, he suspects those who seem to be natural and good to be putting on a disguise to cover their subversive aims. His excuse for banishing Rosalind is that she disguises Celia's brightness and virtue in the people's eyes, because their attention is distracted by pity for Rosalind. His real reason, made explicit in Shakespeare's source, Lodge's *Rosalynde,* is that he is worried that Rosalind will marry and that her husband will try to reclaim the power in her name. This reason is implied in *As You Like It,* because Duke Frederick is not provoked to act against Rosalind until after the son of his enemy has appeared and has caught Rosalind's eye. Duke Frederick, then, not only induces the need for disguising in his subjects, but he also disguises his own attitudes and reasons for his actions. The obsession of both Duke Frederick and Oliver with disguised attitudes sets the tone for the court scenes and creates a context for the physical disguises that result when disguised attitudes are no longer sufficient.

The necessity for the assumption of physical disguise by Rosalind and Celia is a direct result of Duke Frederick's banishment of Rosalind on the grounds that she disguises her political motives. He saw Rosalind as being disguised when she was not. By assuming a disguise, in one sense she then embodies his conception of her. She chooses, however, to become "Ganymede," the beloved page of Jove. Ganymede's loyalty and love toward his master could not be questioned. By "becoming" "Ganymede," Rosalind demonstrates that she is a loyal and loving subject. The disguise allows her to be what she is naturally, with the layer of disguise projected upon her by Duke Frederick removed. However, by "becoming" a man, *she-he* could claim the dukedom. In V.iv.28-29, Orlando reveals that when he first saw "Ganymede," he thought that "he" was a brother to Rosalind. As her own "husband" or "brother," Rosalind could become the "traitor" that Duke Frederick suspects her to be: one who could reclaim what her father had lost.

Similarly, Celia's choice of a disguise allows her too to become more fully what she is by nature. At court, she is forced to disguise her alienation from the behavior and attitudes of her father, Duke Frederick. By translating her name from "Celia," which means "heaven," to "Aliena," "the estranged one," she demonstrates her change from her lofty position of power to her chosen position in banishment from "his Grace," her father. In "poor and mean attire" and with an umber-besmirched face, Celia shows her voluntary assumption of poverty and her self-conscious besmirching of herself as daughter. She prefers to be alienated, poor, and colored by disgrace in her father's eyes than to seem to be like him.

By recognizing that the disguising of attitudes leads to physical disguise that releases a character's true identity, we can then understand why the Clown seems to change so much from court to country. The change in the Fool's behavior has been unjustly attributed to Shakespeare's supposed haste in composition, his supposed faulty revision, and even to the fact that Will Kempe left Shakespeare's company at about the time that *As You Like It* was composed. Shakespeare, it is sometimes suggested, had to alter the role to suit the talents of Kempe's replacement, Robert Armin, and the Bard then simply forgot to change the "low" comedy of the Clown at court (composed for Kempe) to match the "high" comedy of Touchstone in the forest.[6]

Critics concerned with these arguments usually forget that the Clown is never referred to by name at court and that introducing his first appearance in the forest (II.iv.1) is the stage direction "Enter Rosalind for Ganymede, Celia for Aliena, and Clown, alias Touchstone." "Touchstone," then, is a newly created identity, just as "Ganymede" and "Aliena" are. The Clown should be granted the liberty to express himself more freely in the forest than in the court which is granted by commentators to Rosalind and Celia.

Although the Clown does not seem to use much, if any, physical disguise (Jaques refers to him as a "motley fool" in II.vii.13), Touchstone is in some respects best equipped for a life of deception. At court, he is sometimes on the brink of being whipped for revealing satirical attitudes toward Duke Frederick's rule; however, we learn after he has departed that the Clown had usually managed to make himself agreeable to the usurper (II.ii.8-9). Also, his speech at court in I.ii.69-70, 72-77 points the way toward the subtleties of disguise that Rosalind will achieve as "Ganymede." After he is asked by Rosalind to "unmuzzle" his "wisdom" or show his undisguised logic, the Clown tells Rosalind and Celia to stroke their chins and swear by their beards that he is a knave. When they do, swearing by what they do not have, the Clown reveals to them that they have just learned the secret of how to lie successfully: "if you swear by what is not, you are not forsworn" (ll. 73-74). Although Rosalind will not assume a beard as part of her disguise, she will incorporate the Clown's lesson into it. Whatever she swears to as "Ganymede," even if it is an expression of her most undisguised feelings as Rosalind, she is always protected against being "forsworn" as a disguised maidenly Rosalind by making her statements on the basis of what she is not, a man.

In Arden, physical disguise is also assumed by Duke Senior and his followers and by Orlando. The stage direction for II.i (the first forest scene) tells us that we meet "Duke Senior, Amiens, and two or three Lords, like Foresters." In II.vii another stage direction reveals that Duke Senior and his Lords enter "like outlaws." Of course, "foresters" and "outlaws" could perhaps have been used almost interchangeably, but as a stage direction only once specifies the disguises of Rosalind, Celia, and the Clown, it is possible that the Duke and party are dressed differently in the two scenes. When dressed as foresters, the Duke and his followers fit Charles' previous description of them as being like Robin Hood and his men. The audience has its conception of how the group should look realized. However, as they are dressed as "outlaws" in II.vii, the scene in which Orlando encounters them, their appearance justifies *his* supposition that he is in an "uncouth" forest in which "all things" are "savage." As the people he comes upon are dressed like outlaws, Orlando acts like an outlaw himself. In III.ii.43 Celia will describe Orlando, as she has just seen him, as being "furnished like a hunter." By this time, some of the audience's romantic illusions about Duke Senior's party will have been discarded. Presumably, being now part of the Duke's group, Orlando will be dressed as they are. The group is seen to be neither primarily innocent, jolly "Robin Hood" followers, nor villainous outlaws. They can, however, definitely be characterized as *hunters*—not only after deer, but also after ways to accommodate themselves to their exiled condition. Orlando will also be hunting for the fulfillment of his love, as noted in Rosalind's symbolic interpretation of his costume: "O ominous! He comes to kill my heart" (III.ii.244). The array of the Duke and his group, then, ultimately represents them according to their role in nature. Orlando, specifically, as a hunter, has now assumed an outward semblance that reflects his inner identity better than had the "disguise" forced upon him by Oliver.

Although Orlando takes up the role of lover in the forest, "Ganymede" tells him in II.ii that he is not properly dressed for the part. He is "rather point-device in [his] accouterments" (l. 375.) According to "Ganymede" 's description of the lover, the "hose should be ungartered . . . bonnet unbanded . . . sleeve unbuttoned . . . shoe untied, and everything . . . demonstrating a careless desolation" (ll. 371-74). Of course, Rosalind plays a role while she describes a role. As "Ganymede," she satirizes the traditional presentation of a lover; as Rosalind, she tells Orlando that his looks more suggest his loving himself "than seeming the lover of any other" (ll. 375-76), in order to call forth protestations of love from him. Orlando's excessiveness in love is revealed in his poetry, not in his costume. He need not "disguise" himself as a lover, because he *is* a lover. Ironically, he instead neatly wears the costume of the hunter, while he is unwittingly being hunted by the disguised Rosalind. Beneath her "Ganymede" disguise, Rosalind is evidently pleased that Orlando is not so foolish as to pose as a lover by means of his disguise, while she grants herself the liberty to exploit her own attire in order to test the depth of Orlando's love.

Although commentators often speculate on the reasons for Rosalind's maintenance of her disguise after she is in the forest and has met Orlando, the explanation is quite simple. When she meets Orlando, she has only been in the forest a short time and has not yet found her father. She may consider that she is still in danger—if not from the forest's residents, then from being found by Duke Frederick's men. When she first hears of Orlando's presence in the forest, she is confused about what to do about her disguise: "What shall I do with my doublet and hose?" (III.ii.217-18). As Orlando appears before she can answer this question, she is thus instantly inspired to "speak to him like a saucy lackey, and under that habit play the knave with him" (ll. 291-92). Early in their encounter, she gives Orlando a definite clue that she actually *is* a woman, by telling him that she dwells "here in the skirts of the forest, like fringe upon a petticoat" (ll. 331-32). She seems to be willing to give up her disguise if Orlando can see through it. As he does not, she then makes full use of it in her complicated role-playing that is to follow.

As has been shown, then, Rosalind's physical disguise is echoed by the disguises of Celia and the Clown, and the disguises have their roots in the disguisings of the true self in the unnatural world of the court. The tyranny of Duke Frederick and Oliver resulted in a masking of the natural personalities of Rosalind, Celia, the Clown, Orlando, and even Charles and Le Beau. The tyrants, however, are not in their power free to express themselves naturally but must also resort to the disguising of their motives. The shift in attire in the Duke Senior group in the forest reveals the characters' seeking after the best outward demonstration of their internal reality, as does Rosalind's disguise as "Ganymede." Orlando undergoes several stages of disguise in his transformations, from being an aristocrat disguised as a menial, to being disguised at court as a wrestler, to being a lover "disguised" as a neatly attired hunter. But it is of course Rosalind who exploits the potentials of disguise most fully. What was undertaken as a necessary response to the false identity imposed upon her became the perfect vehicle for testing and teaching Orlando. While disguised as "Ganymede," Rosalind then poses as "Rosalind," in order to pose further as one who will "cure" Orlando of his lovesickness, and this last pose actually masks her truer identity as one who desires the youth's love above anything. She thus constructs layers of disguises, with some reflecting her "true" self more than others, but with all indicating some of her own characteristics. Through this layering, Shakespeare seems to be indicating the levels of real and disguised feelings that an intelligent woman may have toward her lover. She can simultaneously mock his excessiveness and cherish it. She can "identify" with him through her own "masculine" tendencies (and thus gain a larger perspective of the relationship), while at the same time indulging in her "feminine" feelings of passion. The poses of Rosalind, then, can be seen as being enhanced versions of the poses that many intelligent women take in love, with the manifestations here given outward form through disguise.

The disguises of Rosalind, however, also emanate out into the furthest reaches of identity and creativity. By creating "Ganymede," Rosalind provides herself with a homosexual rival for Orlando's affections, as well as providing Silvius with a homosexual rival for Phebe. Rosalind recreates herself as an actor with parts to play in several pageants, splits herself into a variety of characters. Through her disguises she becomes an artist whose mind shapes several identities. She must then step aside and let her work deliver her meaning, which is why she delegates power to Hymen in the masque that reveals her "true," if diminished, identity.

The masque of Hymen has often been misunderstood, criticized as a superfluous, gratuitous intrusion into the play. Actually, it is integral to the consummation of the play's statement on the relationship between nature and art.[7] The masque simultaneously represents the play's "moment of truth" and its height of artifice. Music, poetry, song, and the unrealistic presence of Hymen compensate for the removal of the artifices of Rosalind and Celia, who become again their "natural" selves through art. In her last moments as "Ganymede," Rosalind promises "to make all this matter even" and again "To make these doubts all even" (V.iv.18, 25). However, it is Hymen who makes things "even" by presenting Rosalind and Celia as their real selves; he adds that it is *he* "must make conclusion / Of these most strange events" (ll. 109, 126-27). By this act he seems to usurp Rosalind's role. He is a "new" character; we are not told whether he is Corin or some other character in disguise, which he may well be. The characters and the audience are to suspend disbelief and accept him as the God of Marriage. Yet the characters are less amazed by his presence than by the simple truth of Rosalind's and Celia's identities. Hymen's recapitulation of Rosalind's statements indicate that he is the last identity created by Rosalind. She began by recreating herself as "Ganymede," the page to a god, and she concludes by creating a god, or at least by making him, or an illusion of him, appear. She gives up artifice after she has finally created a work of art that is larger than herself but that shows her to be a person taking her place in society with others, subject to the laws of nature. The masque epitomizes what the play has suggested throughout: that human beings need art in order to realize their natures fully. It is through art that we are struck by the wonder of nature.

The complexities involved in disguise seem to the "made even," or resolved, in the masque, but still another layer of the problem of the relationship between disguise and truth or art and nature is uncovered in the epilogue.[8] In it Rosalind reveals that "she" actually *is* a male. The audience members who had enjoyed the dramatic irony of characters' thinking "Ganymede" a boy now see the play as having pulled an ironic trick upon them. Of course, contemporary audiences "knew" that boys played female's parts, but the epilogue forces the audience to acknowledge the truth behind the convention, the "disguise." But even this revelation is not allowed to be final, as Rosalind in this last speech is really both sexes. She denies being a woman, but by her curtsey at the end, she again seems to be one. She further makes both a heterosexual and a homosexual advance to the audience in offering to kiss some of the men if she were a woman, which she is and is not by being Rosalind. She can only be male and female, character and actor, through art and its disguises. By stripping off her last layer of disguise, Rosalind shows her ultimate identity as the spirit of art, which must use human nature—the artist, the actor, and the audience—as its medium and its subject. Just as nature and art merge in the disguises of the characters of *As You Like It,* so does the art represented by Rosalind merge with the "nature" of the audience members in her offer of sexual interplay with them.

Notes

1. See F. H. Mares, "Viola and Other Transvestist Heroines in Shakespeare's Comedies," in *Stratford Papers, 1965-1967,* edited by B. A. W. Jackson

(Hamilton: McMaster Univ. Library Press, 1969), pp. 96-109; Kent van den Berg, "Theatrical Fiction and the Reality of Love in *As You Like It*," *PMLA*, 90 (1975), 885-93; Margaret Boerner Beckman, "The Figure of Rosalind in *As You Like It*," *Shakespeare Quarterly*, 29 (1978), 44-51; Nancy K. Hayles, "Sexual Disguise in *As You Like It* and *Twelfth Night*," *Shakespeare Survey*, 32 (1979), 63-72; and Shirley F. Staton, "Female Transvestism in Renaissance Comedy; 'A Natural Perspective, That Is and Is Not,'" *Iowa State Journal of Research*, 56 (1981), 79-89.

2. All quotations from *As You Like It* are from the Signet Classic Edition, edited by Albert Gilman (New York: New American Library, 1963).

3. For speculation on the relationship between Duke Senior and Sir Rowland, see David G. Byrd, "Shakespeare's Familiaritie Between Sir Rowland and Duke Senior in *As You Like It*," *Shakespeare Quarterly*, 26 (1976) 205-06.

4. Ralph Berry interprets the wrestling match to be a strikingly appropriate figure for covert power struggles in the play. See his "No Exit from Arden," *Modern Language Review*, 66 (1971), 11-20.

5. For information on the traditional choices open to Orlando as the youngest son, see John W. Draper, "Orlando, the Younger Brother," *Philological Quarterly*, 13 (1934), 72-77.

6. See, for example, T. W. Baldwin, "Shakespeare's Jester: The Dates of *Much Ado* and *As You Like It*," *Modern Language Notes*, 39 (1924), 447-55; and Charles S. Felver, "Robert Armin, Shakespeare's Source for Touchstone," *Shakespeare Quarterly*, 7 (1956), 135-37.

7. For other views on the meaning of the masque of Hymen, see Sylvan Barnet, "'Strange Events': Improbability in *As You Like It*," *Shakespeare Survey*, 4 (1968), 119-31; Marilyn L. Williamson, "The Masque of Hymen in *As You Like It*," *Comparative Drama*, 2 (1968), 248-58; David A. Griffin, "Deus Ex Machina in *As You Like It*," *American Notes and Queries*, 9 (1970), 23-24; and Alan Brissenden, "The Dance in *As You Like It* and *Twelfth Night*," *Cahiers Elizabéthains*, 13 (April 1978), 25-34.

8. For other analyses of the epiloque, see Alvin Thaler, "Shakespeare and the Unhappy Happy Ending," *PMLA*, 42 (1927), 736-61; and R. Chris Hassel, "Shakespeare's Comic Epilogues: Invitations to Festive Communion," *Shakespeare-Jahrbuch*, 8 (1970), 160-69.

Anne Herrmann (essay date 1989)

SOURCE: "Travesty and Transgression: Transvestism in Shakespeare, Brecht, and Churchill," in *Theatre Journal*, Vol. 41, No. 2, May, 1989, pp. 133-54.

[*In the following essay, Herrmann examines the role of transvestism in* As You Like It, *Bertolt Brecht's* The Good Woman of Setzuan, *and* Cloud Nine *by Caryl Churchill.*]

> The woman shall not wear that which pertaineth unto a man, neither shall a man put on a woman's garment; for all that do so are an abomination unto the Lord thy God.
>
> —Deuteronomy (22:5)
>
> This earth that beareth and nourisheth us, hath been turned into a Stage, and women have come forth acting the parts of men.
>
> —Francis Rous (1624)
>
> We're all born stark naked;
> To dress is bizarre.
> And that's the reason why
> Everybody's in drag.
>
> —"You Are What You Wear," Lynn Lavner (1988)

In Marguerite Duras's *The Lover* (1984), the first person narrator recalls her image at fifteen and a half crossing the Mekong on a ferry that takes her to school in Saigon. She is wearing a silk dress that used to belong to her mother, gold lamé evening shoes, and a "flat-brimmed hat, a brownish-pink fedora with a broad black ribbon." "The crucial ambiguity of the image," she suggests, "lies in the hat." Like the shoes, the hat must have been a discount item:

> But why was it bought? No woman, no girl wore a man's fedora in that colony then. No native woman, either. What must have happened is: I try it on just for fun, look at myself in the shopkeeper's glass, and see that there, beneath the man's hat, the thin awkward shape, the inadequacy of childhood, has turned into something else. Has ceased to be a harsh, inescapable imposition of nature. Has become, on the contrary, a provoking choice of nature, a choice of the mind. Suddenly it's deliberate. Suddenly I see myself as another, as another would be seen, outside myself, available to all, available to all eyes, in circulation for cities, journeys, desire. I take the hat, and am never parted from it. Having got it, this hat that all by itself makes me whole, I wear it all the time. With the shoes it must have been much the same, but after the hat. They contradict the hat, as the hat contradicts the puny body, so they're right for me. I wear them all the time too, go everywhere in these shoes, this hat, out of doors in all weathers, on every occasion. And to town.[1]

The ambiguity of living in a French colony in Indochina, of belonging to the colonizer yet being poor, of spending afternoons with a lover instead of in school, is figured as a gendered contradiction between the excessively feminine shoes and the necessarily masculine hat. The particular style of the hat cannot be attributed to either historical or cultural differences. The narrator's own invention, it simultaneously splits between viewer and viewed, and makes whole. The shoes contradict the hat, but the hat contradicts the wearer; "the puny body," an unwanted act of nature, has become a cultural artifact. By putting on the hat, the narrator deliberately inscribes herself as desiring because she sees herself as desirable. She transgresses the boundaries of age, nationality, and sexual difference signified by a single item of clothing meant for someone else. The result is not an androgynous figure by an anomalous one; the object, for her, is not to resolve the contradictions but to proliferate them.

The three plays I have chosen for comparison, Shakespeare's *As You Like It* (1599-1600), Bertolt Brecht's *The Good Woman of Setzuan* (1938-40), and Caryl Churchill's *Cloud Nine* (1979), use transvestism as a dramatic device to figure historicized forms of social transgression. Such transgression never takes the form of travesty itself; that is, cross-dressing as such is not coded as violation. Rather, the vacillation between masculine and feminine serves as a metaphor for a particular social contradiction, the struggle between the natural and the unnatural, the good and the bad, sexuality as sinful and as political. In its historicized context, the conflict takes the form of two competing social formations: in Shakespeare the court and the forest, in Brecht socialism and capitalism, in Churchill hetero- and homosexuality. Structurally, the transvestite functions as mediator between the symbols of these formations—"father" and son, tobacco store and tobacco factory, Victorian and contemporary England.

In addition to mediating between social contradictions, the use of transvestism coincides with the violation of dramatic conventions: *As You Like It* ends with four comic marriages (instead of the usual one or two) and includes an epilogue which exposes the true sex of the actor. *The Good Woman of Setzuan* and *Cloud Nine* both have two endings, depending on the original place of performance.[2] In Brecht, gods appear on earth and disappear into heaven through a reverse *deus ex machina,* and in Churchill, racial as well as sexual boundaries are crossed when a white actor plays a black. In each case the play ends by foregrounding its own open-endedness—suggesting that if beneath the disguise there is a real self it is a sexed one, not an essential but a desiring, sexual subjectivity.

> "Motley's the only wear"
>
> —Shakespeare

On 25 January 1620, John Chamberlain wrote in a letter to Dudley Carleton:

> Yesterday the bishop of London called together all the Clergie about this towne, and told them he had expressed commaundment from the King to will them to inveigh vehemently and bitterly in theyre sermons, against the insolencie of our women and theyre wearing of *brode brimd hats,* pointed dublets, theyre haire cut short or shorne, and some of them stilettaes or poinards, and such other trinckets of like moment: adding withall that yf pulpit admonitions will not reforme them he would proceed by another course: the truth is the world is very far out of order, but whether this will mende yt God knowes.[3]

Why King James I sought to extinguish a female transvestite movement which began in the 1570s, experienced a revival in 1606-1607 and reached its height in 1620, and which was publicly debated in two anonymous pamphlets, *Hic mulier: or, The Man-Woman; Being a Medecine to cure the Coltish Disease of the Staggers in the Masculine-Feminines of our Times* and *Haec-Vir; or The Womanish Man: Being an Answere to a late Book intituled Hic-Mulier,* will never be known.[4] What is known is that the king turned to the authority of the church, a church whose members at the beginning of the movement had argued in anti-theatrical tracts against male cross-dressing. The most cited of these tracts are Stephen Gossen's *The School of Abuse* (1583) which claims that cross-dressing will "adulterate" gender. Men who play the parts of women become like women; and if men become like women, then clothes constitute rather than signify the sex of the subject, suggesting an inherently unstable sexual identity and/or subjectivity.[5]

In the early 1590s John Rainolds, a learned Puritan, William Gager, the leading writer of academic drama at Oxford, and Alberico Gentili, England's most reknowned jurist, engaged in a debate (in Latin) over whether Deuteronomy 22:5 applied to actors, specifically university actors who played in private theaters. Rainolds argued that it did, Gentili that it did not, and Gager that it was wrong for men to wear women's clothing unless they did so to save their lives or benefit their country.[6] Sex differences were seen by all as "natural," God-ordained. Transgressing natural distinctions meant transgressing social and moral ones. Both women dressing as men (on the streets) and men dressing as women (on the stage) led to unnatural behavior, particularly behavior that was sexually "unnatural." Women became sexually aggressive and socially undesirable, taking on the identity of "roaring girls," that is, pickpockets or ruffians;[7] men became effeminate and sexually aroused the male members of their theater audience. In the Renaissance, the androgyne was "the erotically irresistible effeminate boy."[8] The object, then, was to contain the contradiction between the essential sex and the lack of an essential gender in order to prevent its proliferation. As soon as female cross-dressers appeared on the streets of London, they ceased to appear on the Shakespearean stage. The first professional English actress made her debut in 1660.[9]

In *As You Like It,* even before Rosalind dresses as Ganymede, two forms of doubling without disguise establish gendered subject positions which distinguish between masculine and feminine without relying on sexual stereotypes. Orlando begins the play by lamenting that the unfair treatment he received from his brother Oliver results in a misleading single self which in fact conceals two: the gentleman by birth and the rustic by education. Afraid that the latter will usurp the former, he invokes the natural bond with his father against the unnatural bond between brothers. To Adam, his surrogate father, he says: "the spirit of my father, which I think is within me, begins to mutiny against this servitude,"[10] inflicted by the older brother who has usurped the place of the father. The body of Orlando contains the spirit of the father which begins to rebel against the brother, who insists on containing that spirit in a singularly physical existence: "I, his brother, gain nothing under him but growth, for the which his animals on his dunghills are as much bound to him as I" (1. 1. 13-15). Even though Orlando protests against this purely physical increase, his mutiny takes the form of a wrestling match. His brother then reads Orlando's physical superiority as mental prowess by imagining him as doubly devious, precisely because there is no attempt to disguise his desire to repossess his social position.

In contrast with Orlando, caught between man and beast, Rosalind partakes of an external doubling where two appear as one. Rosalind and Celia, although merely cousins, share a love that (unlike the perverted bond between brothers) is "dearer than the natural bond of sisters" (1. 2. 266). Even though not blood-linked, they have been raised together, creating a bond more "natural" and more permanent than kinship. When Celia's father attempts to separate them by suggesting that the adopted daughter has begun to outshine the "real" one, Celia responds:

> If she be a traitor,
> Why, so am I. We still have slept together,
> Rose at an instant, learned, played, eat together;
> And wheresoe'er we went, like Juno's swans,
> Still we went coupled and inseparable.
>
> [1. 3. 70-74]

While the Duke seeks to turn the two girls into rivals, Celia insists that they are one and the same, and therefore indivisible. Not only has Celia already promised to share her inheritance with Rosalind, but she is willing to relinquish it altogether in order to follow her twice dispossessed "sister" into exile.

Here the difference between the masculine and feminine subject position lies in the difference between the divided and doubled self. The divided self rests on a hierarchy of two terms (like Duke Senior and Duke Frederick, the banished ruler and his usurper) where the disenfranchised term must be restored to its rightful place, the rustic must give way to the gentleman. The doubled self, in contrast, has two parts (or "sisters") which reflect each other and thus become suitable substitutions. In order for the doubled self to enter representation as more than a mimetic repetition, it must divide itself by means of heterosexual difference (thus Ganymede and Aliena). Although both "couples" are banished, the male "couple" requires the restitution of one term, while the female one requires the relinquishment of the bond, figured as the difference between reclaiming and renouncing one's patrimonial inheritance.

For the two women, "falling in love" replaces wrestling as a sport, although, like wrestling, it will divide them since they cannot fall in love with each other. This arrangement is guaranteed by their "naturalized" relationship based on two terms which are not differentiated enough to engage in competition and cannot thus act as complements (except in play or performance in the forest). Instead, Rosalind falls in love with Orlando, prefiguring the verbal match they will have as lovers in Arden. There, the love joust takes place between two men (Orlando and Ganymede as well as two boy players), one of whom plays a woman (Rosalind who dresses as Ganymede in order to play Rosalind). Male homoeroticism, as "unnatural" as the bond between brothers and as "sporty" as the fight between wrestlers, is veiled by the doubled costume of the woman which offers a form of heterosexual legitimation. Rosalind's role as transvestite is likewise prefigured in her dual relationship to "wrestling": she is both wrestler, when Celia encourages her to "wrestle with thy affections" (1. 3. 21) and wrestled, when she says to Orlando:

> Sir, you have wrestled well, and overthrown
> More than your enemies.
>
> [1. 2. 243-44]

Here the other man is portrayed as antagonist (like the brother) in contrast to the "friend" (or lover) Orlando will find in Ganymede. While men function in terms of contradictions, women function as imitations of each other unless they become men.

When Rosalind does put on her male attire (since a woman alone was a woman to be raped), there is division with the aid of disguise. Disguise is less deceptive than duplicity because it relies on visual rather than linguistic signifiers. Unlike the fictions created by Oliver against Orlando and by Duke Frederick against Rosalind—whereby words are used to fabricate lies enforced as truth by the authority of the speaker—visual disguise presents only one view to the viewer at a time. Without deceit, the signs of masculine and feminine take the form of sexual stereotypes. Even though Rosalind says herself that "a swashing and martial outside" (1. 3. 118) provides only the deceptive appearance of manly courage, crying and fainting reveal her as a "true" woman. By suggesting that through her disguise "Rosalind becomes 'brother' to herself,"[11] Joel Fineman not only privileges the familial bond the play constitutes as perverted (even if finally restored), but also creates a distinction between "feminine" as "natural" and therefore susceptible to mimesis, and "masculine" as deceptive (both politically and dramatically) and therefore suitable for performance.[12] It is this distinction that offers a profounder difference between the sexes than the signifiers of social roles, or sexual stereotypes.

In the forest, Rosalind further "naturalizes" the feminine by mimicking the words of the misogynist. In response to Orlando's suggestion that her way of speaking might be too refined for a place so removed from the court, she says:

> I have been told so by many. But indeed an old religious uncle of mine taught me to speak, who was in his youth an inland man; one that knew courtship too well, for there he fell in love. I have heard him read many lectures against it; and I thank God I am not a

woman, to be touched with so many giddy offenses as he hath generally taxed their whole sex withal.

[3. 2. 338-345]

Rosalind seeks to emulate the paternal figure, who in this case is not the displaced ruler but the scorned lover, and does so as disciple. Thus she imitates her model by "reading his many lectures," rather than by performing in his place, as son. In the forest the opponent is not another man but woman, made less threatening by the fact that she is played by a man. Rosalind reinforces her disguise through deception—not only is she not a woman but she thanks God she never was one. And in contrast to "man," who appears as contradiction, whether in love or not, corruption contaminates the entire "weaker sex."

If Rosalind breaks her "sisterly" bond with Celia in order to establish an "unnatural" one (both false and homoerotic) with Orlando, what role does Celia play, once one concludes, as Sue-Ellen Case does, that: "The fictional 'Woman' (the character of Rosalind) simply mediates and enhances the homoerotic flirtation between two males."[13] Celia, the one who relinquishes her inheritance but not her sex, is the one who questions Rosalind's identification with and appropriation of masculinist values. This begins even before Rosalind cross-dresses, when she falls in love with Orlando and justifies her feelings by saying: "The Duke my father loved his father dearly." Celia responds: "Doth it therefore ensue that you should love his son dearly? By this kind of chase, I should hate him, for my father hated his father dearly; yet I hate not Orlando" (1. 3. 29-33). Just as Celia breaks with her father in order to follow her "sister," she suggests breaking bonds of kinship in order to pursue the alternative model provided by female friendship (or love). Celia seeks to distinguish between adopting masculine attributes (for survival) and mimicking the misogynist (for play or prowess). Shortly before Rosalind faints, Celia chastises her for betraying her own sex: "You have simply misused our sex in your love-prate. We must have your doublet and hose plucked over your head, and show the world what the bird hath done to her own nest" (4. 1. 192-195). Becoming a traitor to one's own sex exceeds the treachery perceived by the father—outshining one's sex—which serves as the initial reason for banishment. Celia's defense of her sex, potentially subversive, is contained as conservative because she represents an imitative, same-sex reflection of the cross-dressed heroine who has learned to play with gender distinctions by assuming masculine privilege.

Ultimately it is Touchstone—the fool, not the transvestite—who functions as third term in the form of transgressor, using language to manipulate marriage as that institution which keeps sexual difference in place or at bay. For Wolfgang Iser the fool "is always his own double without ever having to disguise himself"[14] and for Terry Eagleton he "is pure transgression . . . because he appears to lack a body. . . ."[15] It is his "motley coat" (an incongruous mixture of colors and materials) that provides the alternative to male and female dress because the wearer of that coat knows the duplicity of language and can thus manipulate the linguistic performance of the marriage ceremony.[16] He would have it both ways at once, a doubleness based not on disguise, but on the instability of meaning. He knows that every signifier has more than one signified, just as every situation can offer more than one referent. This becomes most apparent when asked whether he likes the life of a shepherd, to which he answers:

Truly, shepherd, in respect of itself, it is a good life; but in respect that it is a shepherd's life, it is naught. In respect that it is solitary, I like it very well; but in respect that it is private, it is a very vile life. Now in respect it is in the fields, it pleaseth me well; but in respect it is not in the court, it is tedious. As it is a spare life, look you, it fits my humor well; but as there is no more plenty in it, it goes much against my stomach.

[3. 2. 13-21]

A single situation is described with a potentially limitless set of oppositions which seem to cancel each other out and thus mean nothing at all. On the one hand, "solitary" and "private" both refer to the separation or isolation of the individual from the community; on the other hand, they are juxtaposed to create a contradiction: is he secluded or is he lonely? What initially appears as nonsense ultimately offers a lesson in linguistics. As long as this word-play remains in the realm of what Touchstone calls "philosophy," it matters little whether meaning is ever stabilized. He nevertheless attempts to transfer this doubleness to the marriage ceremony, the ritual which seeks to arrest sexual indeterminacy by legitimizing the heterosexual couple. Knowing that a whore can become a wife only in name, the fool attempts to arrange an illegal ceremony with Audrey (a country girl) that would pronounce him husband and release him from that pronouncement at the same time. Audrey, no longer a virgin and thus indifferent to whether she is pronounced "wife," sets as little store by the ceremony as Touchstone does. Yet she does so out of a lack of understanding of the figurative: "I do not know what poetical is. Is it honest in deed and word? Is it a true thing?" (3. 3. 16-17) Honesty becomes equated with the "natural" as that which is (hetero)sexually explicit rather than (homosexually) implicit.

Louis Montrose suggests: "Marriage, the social institution at the heart of comedy, serves to ease or eliminate fraternal strife. And fraternity, in turn, serves as a defense against the threat men feel from women."[17] If this is the case, then Rosalind, as "her own 'brother,'" will ease the strife between actors and characters by coordinating the four marriages "to make these doubts all even" (5. 4. 25). Yet the homoeroticism contained by these social roles makes its reappearance in the epilogue, where Rosalind reveals her true sex as masculine: "If I were a woman, I would kiss as many of you as had beards that pleased me, complexions that liked me, and breaths that I defied not; and I am sure, as many as have good beards, or good faces, or sweet breaths, will, for my kind offer, when I make curtsy, bid me farewell" (Epilogue 17-22). The audience knows he is not a woman, that he is a boy actor playing a woman's part. This becomes the most transgressive moment in the play because it suggests that the sport, whether athletic or erotic, takes place, both candidly and confidentially, between men. This is the social contradiction *As You Like It* addresses, placing cross-dressed heroines on the stage at the moment when they ceased to appear on the streets, thereby reinforcing the fact that its point of address was men, not women.

> "Shakespeare never flew in the air."
>
> —Brecht

In Brecht, the transgressive moment when the actor reveals his or her true sex forms the basis for an elaborate dramaturgy.[18] Founded on a deliberate "alienation effect" (*Entfremdung*) or "making the familiar strange," the motivation behind the "A-effect" is not an erotic, but a political one: "The object of the A-effect is to alienate the social gest underlying every incident. By social gest is meant the mimetic and gestural expression of the social relationships prevailing between people of a given period." To achieve this effect, the actor must not become his or her character, but speak it "like a quotation," making it appear strange by looking at it strangely him or herself:

> Because he doesn't identify himself with him he can pick a definite attitude to adopt towards the character whom he portrays, can show what he thinks of him and invite the spectator, who is likewise not asked to identify himself, to criticize the character portrayed. The attitude which he adopts is a socially critical one. . . . In this way his performance becomes a discussion (about social conditions) with the audience he is addressing. He prompts the spectator to justify or abolish these conditions according to what class he belongs to.[19]

The lack of identification between actor and character is neither a function of historical necessity nor an opportunity for veiled eroticism, but rather a conscious attempt to "denaturalize" social formations in order to make their arbitrary constructions more visible. The most obvious device for achieving this effect would be to play a character of the opposite sex.

In *The Good Woman of Setzuan* (originally *Der gute Mensch von Sezuan*, which leaves the sex of the protagonist indeterminable) the good Shen Te becomes her evil cousin Shui Ta in order to preserve the monetary gift from the gods which she has traded for a tobacco store. Because of her generosity, she fails to make a profit and, heeding the advice of her exploiters, not only invokes the authority of the cousin but actually embodies him by appearing as a man. In a lyric entitled "The Song of Defenselessness," which Shen Te sings carrying the mask of Shui Ta, both characters ask why even the gods are defenseless against a world which is so evil that it has become impossible to be good. Not the threat of rape, but the spector of economic insolvency forces a female character to acquire the clothes traditionally reserved for the masculine.

Conceived as a parable, the play portrays Shen Te less as a psychological subject than as a subject position (accentuated by the mask borrowed from Chinese theater[20]), a subject position conceivable only in its relation to the masculine. Initially Shen Te is juxtaposed to Wong, the waterseller, who, like the prostitute, must sell a commodity most people manage to acquire for free—water from floods or rainfall and sex through seduction or marriage. Although Shen Te sells herself for a living, she is still considered good, unlike the waterseller who sells water from a cup with a false bottom. Sexual difference is used to figure an economic difference, while the difference between the sexes is neither economic or sexual, but moral. Morality, although differentiated from the hypocritical sexual standards of the bourgeoisie, is largely predicated on psychological differences that lie at the core of sexual stereotypes. Sexual difference is not determined by the commodity one sells—sex or water—but by one's faith in goodness: Wong disappears thinking that even Shen Te's goodness will fail when it comes to offering the gods a place for the night, while Shen Te would like to be good, although she admits that economic necessity often makes it unfeasible. While Wong fears that the gods will discover Shen Te's true profession, the gods are afraid that someone will misread their monetary compensation for a night's lodging as a sex trade. Brecht privileges prostitution (a financial transaction necessitated by poverty) over marriage, because the latter is founded on deception as the corruption of neither money nor sex, but of (heterosexual) love.

In this play marriage does not "make all this matter even"; rather it makes matters worse because it involves the "deadliest weakness" (a weakness deadlier than goodness)—love. Like Audrey, Shen Te no longer has her virginity to sell and instead exchanges her honesty in the form of material generosity. Vulnerability does not stem from an inability to distinguish between the literal and the figurative, but from Shen Te's willingness to sacrifice her own source of livelihood in order to guarantee her husband's reemployment as flyer. (Like Rosalind, she plays the man in order to restore "true manhood" to her lover). Rather than providing an end to the play, the reward for revealing one's true sex, the wedding ceremony interrupts it in the middle and the play does not even offer one union. Marriage provides the moment when the impossibility of appearing as both sexes at once obstructs the nuptial knot: Yang Sun will not pronounce his vows until the cousin appears with the money which he will use as a bribe to acquire the job of a pilot; Shui Ta will not appear until Yang Sun displays two plane tickets and ensures that he plans to take Shen Te with him, and not his mother. The complexity of these gendered subject positions is once again juxtaposed to the simplicity of sexual stereotypes. Like the "uncle" who teaches Rosalind that all women are guilty of "giddy offenses," Yang Sun represents women from the point of view of the misogynist: "Shen Te is a woman; she *is* devoid of common sense. I only have to lay my hand on her shoulder, and church bells ring."[21] While waiting for the wedding to take place, Yang Sun attempts to determine what kind of wife Shen Te will make by testing her "home economics": can she make five cups of tea with three leaves; can she sleep alone on a mattress the size of a book? Meanwhile, Shen Te tries to explain to Yang Sun that "my cousin can't be coming. . . . My cousin can't be where I am" (93). Unlike Wong, who remains Shen Te's best friend, both Shui Ta and Yang Sun become "her worse enemy" because they prevent her from being a "true" woman, kind and in love, and still surviving economically. Being a woman prohibits marriage from taking place; economics perverts marriage into a form of psychological prostitution.

The disguise prevents the transvestite from mediating between herself and her lover (although both Shen Te and Shui Ta attempt to negotiate with Yang Sun in the name of the other); worse yet, the disguised is accused of being a murderer. Again, it is not the act of cross-dressing which transgresses, but the disappearance of the female subject. First Yang Sun hears someone sobbing in the back room; then Shen Te's clothes are found under the table in Shui Ta's office. Brought to the trial which replaced the wedding as the end of the play, Shui Ta reveals himself as both Shen Te and Shui Ta and defends herself as follows:

> Your injunction
> To be good and yet to live
> Was a thunderbolt:
> It has torn me in two
> I can't tell how it was
> But to be good to others
> And myself at the same time
> I could not do it . . .
>
> [136]

Here the split subject embodies neither a mimetic doubling nor a division which can be restored; rather, it represents divisiveness as the symptom of a capitalist system in which moral goodness and economic survival are mutually exclusive. Like Rosalind, Shen Te abandons her sex, this time by making her disguise permanent. And yet it is the impermanence of the clothes—Shui Ta's trousers hanging on Shen Te's clothesline—that finally gives her away.

The body would seem a more stable signifier than the clothes that simply signify it. Yet even as Shen Te becomes increasingly pregnant, it is not her body that betrays her (Shui Ta simply gets fatter as his wealth grows) but her emotional weakness. Like Rosalind's fainting at the news of Orlando's wounding, Shen Te sobs in the back room when she hears that the father has learned of his illegitimate child. Physical weakness can be hidden behind the bravado of the opposite sex, but emotional weakness reveals the true difference between the sexes. This distinction establishes the "good" mother and "bad" father based on the "natural" difference produced by their respective participation in biological reproduction. Unlike Shakespeare, who blurs the difference in social status between the boy actor and the unmarried woman, Brecht conflates social and sexual differences by relying on biology when he makes Shen Te grow large with child. Shen Te abandons herself to her faithless lover at the very moment she reproduces herself in her child; yet that child, a son, reproduces the father, the former flyer who has risen in the world as tobacco factory foreman.

The third term in Brecht's play are the gods, traditionally invoked to mediate in the disputes between men, here called to preside at the trial of the man who apparently has done away with "the good woman." The ethereal gods represent the bourgeois alternative to earthly contradictions, and are figured as inept, uninformed figures who know less about earth than those who live on it. Not having created it, they are trying to maintain the world as it is through their arbitrary "book of rules." Convinced that if they find the exception to the rule (i.e., a good person) the rules need not be changed, they leave Shen Te crying for help. Unlike Shakespeare's fool, these gods are truly foolish, because they adhere to the literal meaning of the law. The most they can offer is a benevolent reading of the "rules" when Shen Te yells that she needs the help of her evil cousin at least once a week and they respond that once a month should suffice. The contradiction between the sexes is left unresolved and the play ends with the existence of morality in question.

The epilogue (to be spoken by either Shen Te or Wong, but not in character) likewise addresses itself to the audience, although not to "conjure," but to implore. Both epilogues reflect on their own breaks with dramatic convention: Rosalind appears as a woman when the last word should be had by a man, and *The Good Woman of Setzuan* offers no closure when a play should have an ending:

> You're thinking, aren't you, that this is no right
> Conclusion to the play you've seen tonight?
> After a tale, exotic, fabulous,
> A nasty ending was slipped up on us.
> We feel deflated too. We too are nettled
> To see the curtain down and nothing settled.
> How could a better ending be arranged?
> How could one change people? Can the world be changed?
> Would new gods do the trick? Will atheism?
> Moral rearmament? Materialism?
> It is for you to find a way, my friends,
> To help good men arrive at happy ends.
> *You* write the happy ending to the play!
> There must, there must, there's got to be a way!
>
> [141][22]

Unlike the boy player who attempts to seduce the male members of his audience, this actor desperately seeks the audience's assistance. The relationship is not erotic, based on the conditional ("if"), but political, grounded in the interrogative. The solution to the binariness of sexual difference is no longer displaced onto homoeroticism; it lies in dramatic closure as the solution to "naturalized" social relations. If the feminine represents the possibility of a socialist revolution, what then is the connection between Shen Te and the women of that utopian social order?

Considering the historical moment during which Brecht wrote this play, it is apparent that Shen Te as the "eternal feminine" becomes divided between the "masculinized" New Woman and a historically specific exploitation of motherhood. Not only does the play's ending take the form of an admonition as opposed to a seduction, but, as Sue-Ellen Case has pointed out, in Brecht "the mothers are defined by their mothering roles and have no sexual definition."[23] By placing the mother in the female subject position, Brecht not only desexualizes her, but also insists on biological differences as they were used and misused by both the sex reformers of the Weimar Republic (1918-1933) and the Nazis of the Third Reich (1933-1945). Atina Grossman describes the New Woman as she appeared in Germany after World War I:

> The New Woman was not only the intellectual with a Marlene Dietrich-style suit and short mannish haircut or the young white-collar worker in a flapper suit. She was also the young married factory worker who cooked only one warm meal a day, cut her hair short into a practical Bubikopf, and tried with all available means to keep her family small.[24]

As women entered the work force in greater numbers and were required to relocate responsibilities assumed by social services into the private home during the Depression, sex reformers were intent on "rationalizing" women's double burden on the one hand by reducing birth rates through available birth control and legal abortion, and on the other hand by improving women's sex lives.[25] Both approaches were based on biological distinctions between the sexes, on women's unique sensibility, and on their entitlement to a separate "Lebensraum."[26] Sex reform carried with it greater control of sexual deviance; those unfit to marry came "close to the malicious stereotype of the New Woman: short, dark hair; dressed in a unisex shift, distinctly unmaternal—the image not only of the prostitute but also of the Jewess and the lesbian."[27]

When the Nazis came to power they simply turned birth control counseling centers into racial hygiene clinics and carried the sex reform movement's eugenics goals to their unthinkable conclusion. Women were hailed as "mothers of the race" or guilty of "racial degeneration." The Nazis were intent both on raising the rate of childbirth and enforcing the sterilization of "asocials," which included prostitutes, women of "inferior character," and those of "alien race."[28] Even though women acquired the vote in 1918 (as a reward for their war effort, not their suffrage struggle), parties of the right, from the Catholic Center party to the National Socialists, were much more successful at attracting women's votes because they encouraged women to participate in politics in order to preserve and enhance their traditional roles as wife and mother.[29] Neither the Communist nor the Socialist party was able to offer a competing conceptual framework. When it came time to mobilize women for war, propagandistic images of women changed, but not basic beliefs about women's nature, which continued to fuel the extension of the maternal role into the public sphere.[30]

Brecht, who more than other theorists has insisted upon the need to historicize social formations, continues to metaphorize and idealize the mother at the very moment in history when she is most exploited as purely biological function. Sara Lennox has suggested that Brecht's dramaturgy is predicated on an "instrumentalism" which necessarily regards women "as demonstration objects rather than subjects in their own right."[31] If the "A-effect" is meant to afford critical distance so as to imagine a different set of social relations, then those arrangements do not include sexual arrangements, just as "the half-Westernized city of Setzuan" serves to promote geographical distance in the service of parable, not history. Like Shakespeare, who ceased to put cross-dressed heroines on stage once they began to appear on the streets, Brecht used his woman figures to embody Communist Party policy at a particular historical moment.[32] The discrepancy between women on stage and their roles on the stage of history reinforces the role of the cross-dressed heroine as metaphor. Even after women have been allowed onto the theatrical stage and have succeeding in winning the vote, they still appear politically as the "woman question," tangential to the electoral process yet crucial to consolidating the power of (white male) political parties.

> "You can't separate fucking and economics."
>
> —Churchill

The work of Caryl Churchill marks the appearance of a female playwright who identifies herself as a socialist-feminist and uses cross-dressing to question the categories that legitimize not only patriarchy and capitalism, but also colonialism. Since many of her plays do not revolve around a central character, she herself becomes the center of a discourse which figures the "female playwright" as oxymoron, a woman occupying the position of a man. Mel Gussow, in a review in the *New York Times* of her most recent play, *Serious Money,* writes the following:

> Just as her work has its contradictions, Ms. Churchill is herself a paradox. Her plays are outrageous, even scandalous and the language, as in "Serious Money," can be scabrous. The playwright, however, is no wild-eyed weird sister, but a genteel woman with a kind of regal reserve, The British director William Gaskill thinks she has a 'classic English beauty'—with her graying hair and high cheekbones. Married to a lawyer and the mother of three sons (they are 24, 22 and 17), she has a close circle of friends. Outside of that circle, she is so aggressively shy that, next to her, Woody Allen would seem like an ebullient self-promoter.[33]

On the one hand, Churchill has illegitimately appropriated the language of men, language which is "outrageous," "scandalous," "scabrous"; on the other hand she is relegitimized through her association with men: her husband, her sons, a male director, Woody Allen. The unthinkable is "the wild-eyed weird sister" she might either be or be a part of, simply by gender association. Fortunately she is seen as neither politically nor sexually aggressive, but only as "aggressively shy," and if her language is "manly," she at least carries the "graying hair" of male royalty. By taming her physically, by domesticating her socially, the words of the female professional become audible.

This review appears four years after the *The New York Times Magazine* presented a cover story entitled "Women Playwrights: New Voices in the Theater." At that time Mel Gussow wrote: "In order to trace the reasons for the proliferation of plays by women, one must begin with the women's movement itself, which nurtured the belief that there is no profession or artistic discipline—from movie making to monumental sculpture—that should be exclusive of men" and "The increase in number of women playwrights is part of a larger pattern in which women are assuming roles of authority and creativity in all aspects of the theater."[34] As long as women are represented as a group separate from men, democratic liberal politics can provide the impression that one is experiencing and/or witnessing historical progress; as soon as a woman appears alone, she leaves her sex and must be demonized or turned into an honorary man.

Churchill further exploits "Brechtian techniques" by exploring capitalism in its relation to sexism and colonialism,[35] and by encouraging actors to examine not only their characters but also their own sexual identities. *Cloud Nine* was written for the British Joint Stock Theatre Group, where the cast, playwright, and director held three-week workshops during which they read relevant texts, did consciousness-raising exercises, and improvised. One such exercise involved

> a game in which numbers and images (jacks, queens, etc.) on playing cards represented varying degrees of power; red and black respectively represented male and female. Players arbitrarily received cards assigning them numerical power as well as a sexual identity; they were then to improvise situations and interact according to their given power. Repeatedly, actors who received cards identifying them as males would assert more power than those who received cards identifying them as females; assigned gender outweighed off-stage sexual identity as well as numerical scores.[36]

Consciousness-raising exercises have replaced dramatic theory as a way of producing "alienation effects" by making visible the interpenetration of theatrical and social roles. This involves not only assuming roles of the opposite sex or of another race, but also playing two different roles from one act to the next.

The disjuncture between actor and character becomes reinforced by the discontinuity between Act I, which takes place in a British colony in Africa during Queen Victoria's reign, and Act II, which takes place in London in the 1970s. Although Act II takes place one hundred years later, the characters are only twenty-five years older. Not only does Churchill "historicize" racial, sexual, and class oppression, but she puts into question "history" as a coherent, truth-telling narrative. Elin Diamond, in "Refusing the Romanticism of Identity: Narrative Interventions in Churchill, Benmussa, Duras" suggests: "To understand history as narrative is a crucial move for feminists, not only because it demystifies the idea of disinterested authorship, but because the traditionally subordinate role of women in history can be seen as the legacy of narrative itself."[37] Thus it becomes not a question of whether women have been excluded from history or how they might be included, but a question of how history *a priori* inscribes the white male subject through a story of power and legitimation. It is this story that Churchill puts into question (as Diamond argues further) by preventing the spectator from producing a coherent narrative within the boundaries of the play's dramatic structure.

The gendered subject positions encountered in Shakespeare (male division vs. female doubling) and in Brecht (Shen Te's relation to her "best friend" vs. her "worst enemies") take on an even more complex configuration in Churchill. The play begins with Clive, the Victorian father/husband/subject, introducing his wife: "My wife is all I dreamt a wife should be, / And everything she is she owes to me."[38] The referent of this statement is not only the ideology of Victorian sexual arrangements but also the male actor who plays the part of Clive's wife, Betty. Betty responds:

> I live for Clive. The whole aim of my life
> Is to be what he looks for in a wife.
> I am a man's creation as you see,
> And what men want is what I want to be.
>
> [4]

To be "a man's creation" means to conform to masculine expectations not by mimicking the misogynist or murdering the feminine, but by leaving nothing to the woman except the name and the clothes. Like Touchstone's "wife," this "wife" is the product of a linguistic operation which unmasks rather than secures her as masculine/marital construct. The lack of correspondence between actor and character is replaced by the enunciated correlation between "what men want" and "what I want to be." The "alienation effect" produced by this disjuncture reinforces the fact that characters *are* their discourses and that their discourses are often someone else's. Sexual stereotypes are parodied and deception virtually disappears.

For further clarification, I will trace the trajectory of a single actor who plays two characters, and of the two characters who appear first in Act I and then as twenty-five years older in Act II. In the New York production, the same actor plays Edward the son in Act I and Victoria the daughter in Act II. In Act I Edward is played by a woman, while Victoria is played by a doll. Churchill herself attributes this technique not to Shakespeare, but to "the English tradition of women playing boys (e.g. PETER PAN)" (viii). At the same time, Edward is gay; that is, homosexuality becomes an issue for the character, not an issue suppressed in the relation between boy actors or veiled in the relation between actor and audience. Male homosexuality in the Victorian period is of course associated with effeminacy, made explicit in Edward's relationship to the doll of his sister Victoria (played by a doll). The controversy over the doll (since the sister *is* a doll she can do little to enter the controversy) has to do with whether Edward is playing with or minding the doll: if he minds the doll, he is beginning to learn his social role as a man; if he plays with it, then he is adopting a feminine role and must be dealt with accordingly. Gender roles (as in Shakespeare) are represented in terms of specular images: Edward must not play with, that is, identify with the doll, otherwise he will grow up to be a girl, like his sister, while his sister has internalized her role so well (without even having to learn it) that she does not even play with the doll but is one.

Unlike the veiled homoeroticism in Shakespeare and the suppression of sexuality in Brecht, homosexuality appears as explicit content in *Cloud Nine*. It is treated both historically (differently transgressive in the nineteenth century than in the twentieth) and as the form of sexuality that has politicized sexual arrangements in general. In Act I homosexuality is still associated with deception. On the one hand, Harry Bagley (Edward's "uncle"/lover) represents Victorian hypocrisy by pretending to love "woman" while preferring sex with men. On the other hand, lying as a form of justification legitimizes not (Shakesperean) primogeniture but the interpenetration of sexism and racism. Edward accuses Joshua, the Black native, of stealing his mother's necklace when he has actually taken (not stolen) it from his mother in order to give it to Bagley. The impermissibility of a "feminine" gesture from one man to another must be blamed on a social inferior, who in this case is racially other. But since this configuration of gestures and words is attributed to Edward's youth (instead of to a network of sexual and racial oppression), when Joshua destroys the (doll's) doll and Edward rightly accuses him, his father no longer believes him. This results in the death of the father, the end of the Empire and the curtain of Act I.

Act I also ends with a marriage between Bagley, the gay explorer, and Ellen, the lesbian governess. The wedding scene once again bisects rather than ends the play, but this time no longer grounded in the romantic illusion of love. Clive insists that Bagley get married: "Rivers will be named after you, it's unthinkable" (53), in order to hide the "perversion," the "sin," the "disease," he calls "effeminacy." Ellen agrees to the marriage, since she is in love with Betty and will be forced to leave her employer as soon as Edward grows up. Initially Bagley asks Mrs. Saunders, "the woman of spirit" (who lives on in Africa as a widow and plans to return to England to introduce threshing machines) to marry him, but she refuses since the only part of marriage she liked was the sex. The only part of marriage Ellen dislikes is the sex, which Betty in turn explains to her: "You must keep still. . . . Ellen, you're not getting married to enjoy yourself" (57). The choice between Mrs. Saunders and Ellen is reinforced as exclusive by the fact that they are played by the same actress (like Shen Te and Shui Ta) and therefore cannot appear at the wedding together. Even more importantly, as women who are equally uninterested in marriage and might potentially be interested in each other, they can literally never meet.

In Act II, Edward continues to play the "effeminate" part by playing the role of the "wife" in the live-in relationship with first, his lover Gerry (who occasionally prefers anonymous sex) and then with his sister Victoria and Lin (who themselves are involved with each other). The "wife" is no longer a linguistic operation; rather, it involves a role that necessarily must be performed within the family unit (given the present social arrangements), but not by someone of a particular biological sex or an assigned place in a kinship system. Victoria, in contrast, has developed from a doll into a feminist. The figure who had no voice now speaks with the voice of critical commentary. In response to Lin who says "I hate men," Victoria answers: "You have to look at it in a historical perspective in terms of learnt behavior since the industrial revolution" (68). The daughter retains a relation to the patriarch, no longer silenced by him but offering theoretical explanations of his institutions.

Betty, the middle-aged divorcee, offers the third term in a world where the taboos surrounding who can enter a relationship with whom have been almost completely broken. She represents the woman alone, who has severed all old ties and forged no new ones, who has sex with herself and thus eliminates the social constructions which determine all sexual relationships. She is the mother who is totally absent in Shakespeare, who replaces the wife in Brecht, and now appears for the first time as a transgressive figure. Her transgression (masturbation) need not be contained and her contradictions will not be solved outside of her personal history. The relationship she commences with a gay man, Gerry—with whom she enters into conversation at the end of the British version of the play—cannot be coded as transgressive because it is *a priori* not sexual.

The most transgressive moment in the play is finally the most parodic:

> Edward:
> I like women.
> Victoria:
> That should please mother.
> Edward:
> No listen Vicky, I'd rather be a woman. I wish I had breasts like that, I think they're beautiful. Can I touch them?
> Victoria:
> What, pretending they're yours?
> Edward:
> No, I know it's you.
> Victoria:
> I think I should warn you I'm enjoying this.
> Edward:
> I'm sick of men.
> Victoria:
> I'm sick of men.
> Edward:
> I think I'm a lesbian.
>
> [92]

This moment puts the very notion of transgression into question. The scene takes the audience back to the one with the doll: is Edward playing with it or minding it? Here the question becomes, are the breasts his or his sister's (and since the question concerns body parts, the answer should be clearer). Does Edward want to be like his sister or be his sister? Does the fact that they are both "sick of men" make them the same? Can a man be a "lesbian" (as the logical conclusion of his feelings about men) or is being a lesbian instead biological? How can "lesbian" refer to both an "effeminate" man and a "masculine" woman? Should the incest taboo be the only one left unbroken (even between consenting adults)?

In Churchill the actor no longer simply comments on the character, but places the very notion of a character in question. Cross-dressing takes place as the disjuncture between body and text, not on the level of who is permitted on stage nor of how to appear on stage as two characters simultaneously. Rather, the discrepancy between actor and character separates the signifier from the signified, pointing this time to the significance of language in the construction of the sex-gender system.

When the "earth . . . hath been turned into a Stage, and women have come forth acting the parts of men,"[39] then the question is not why women dress as men, but why the metaphor of the stage. "New historicism" rereads the Renaissance theater against the "theater" of Renaissance politics, that is, gender and power relations. "Postmodernism" speaks in terms of performance reality as linguistic impersonation. Nazism provided the most extravagent performance of this century, captured in the films of Leni Riefenstahl. On the one hand, if it is only a performance, then one can leave it and return to the real, the everyday. On the other hand, if the performance is all there is, who will write the parts? Shakespeare, Brecht, and Churchill have all written a part for the cross-dressed heroine, and yet in none of these plays does her cross-dressing alter or reconstruct the female subject. In Shakespeare the female character is assimilated by the boy player; in Brecht the female character is appropriated by her male double; and in Churchill the character becomes a gay man, although the actress goes on to play a middle-class feminist. The transgressive figure nevertheless shifts from the fool to the gods to the middle-aged woman, thereby shifting the site of contradiction from the cross-dressed figure (which will always "be appropriated by the 'masculine'") to the female figure as the product of a particular historical moment.

Eagleton has suggested: "If representation is a lie, then the very structure of the theatrical sign is strangely duplicitous, asserting an identity while manifesting a division, and to this extent it resembles the structure of metaphor."[40] The theater as metaphor, the theatrical sign resembling the structure of metaphor, the feminine as the metaphor for that division, are these all signs of duplicity or of proliferation? The cross-dressed heroine, as metaphor, points to the limits of metaphorical structures that rely on an unexamined assumption of gendered distinctions. As theatrical sign, she points to the disjuncture between body and clothes, between clothes as signifying and/or constituting the subject. In Shakespeare and Brecht she stands in for something else; in Churchill where she stands—whether on her high-heeled shoes or under the broad-rimmed hat—is itself the question.

Notes

1. Marguerite Duras, *The Lover*, trans. Barbara Bray (New York: Random House, 1985), 12-13.

2. In Brecht's case the misunderstandings created by the Viennese premiere of *The Good Woman of Setzuan* led him to add an epilogue; in the case of *Cloud Nine*, the New York production sought for a more pronounced "emotional climax" by ending with Betty's self-discovery instead of the beginning of a new relationship.

3. *The Letters of John Chamberlain*, ed. Norman Egbert McClure (Philadelphia, 1939), II, 287-87. Quoted in Linda T. Fitz, "'What says the Married Woman?': Marriage Theory and Feminism in the English Renaissance," *Mosaic* 13:2 (1980): 15. Emphasis added.

4. See Linda Woodbridge, *Women and the English Renaissance: Literature and the Nature of Womankind, 1540-1620* (Urbana: University of Illinois, 1984), 139-51. See also Sandra Clark, "*Hic Mulier, Haec Vir,* and the Controversy over Masculine Women," *Studies in Philology* 82:2 (1985): 157-83.

5. See Laura Levine, "Men in Women's Clothing: Anti-theatricality and Effeminization from 1579 to 1642," *Criticism* 28:2 (1986): 121-41.

6. J. W. Binns, "Women or Transvestites on the Elizabethan Stage?: An Oxford Controversy," *Sixteenth Century Journal* 5:2 (1974): 100.

7. See Paula S. Bergren, "'A Prodigious Thing': The Jacobean Heroine in Male Disguise," *Philological Quarterly* 62:3 (1983): 383-402; Patrick Cheney, "Moll Cutpurse as Hermphrodite in Dekker and Middleton's *The Roaring Girl*," *Renaissance and Reformation* 7:2 (1983): 120-34; Mary Beth Rose, "Women in Men's Clothing: Apparel and Social Stability in *The Roaring Girl*," *English Literary Renaissance* 14:3 (1984): 367-91.

8. Lisa Jardine, *Still Harping on Daughters: Women and Drama in the Age of Shakespeare* (New Jersey: Barnes and Noble, 1983), 17. See also Phyllis Rackin, "Androgyny, Mimesis, and the Marriage of the Boy Heroine on the English Stage," *PMLA* 102:1 (1987): 29-41.

9. See Katharine Eisaman Maus, "'Playhouse Flesh and Blood': Sexual Ideology and the Restoration Actress," *ELH* 46:4 (1979): 595-617.

10. *As You Like It* (Signet), I, i. 21-22. Subsequent references will appear in the text.

11. Joel Fineman, "Fratricide and Cuckoldry: Shakespeare's Doubles" in Murray M. Schwartz and Coppelia Kahn, eds., *Representing Shakespeare: New Psychoanalytic Essays* (Baltimore: Johns Hopkins, 1980), 79.

12. I am endebted to Wolfgang Iser for proposing this distinction, although he does not consider it in gendered terms: "If representation arises out of bridging difference, it can no longer be conceived of in terms of mimesis, but must be construed in terms of performance, for each act of difference-removal is a form of production, not of imitation. Furthermore, the fact that performance is a means of bringing something about suggests a process of staging, and this endows it with an intangible quality." "The Dramatization of Double Meaning in Shakespeare's *As You Like It*," *Theatre Journal* 35:3 (1983): 330.

13. Sue-Ellen Case, *Feminism and Theatre* (New York: Methuen, 1988), 23.

14. Iser, 316.

15. Terry Eagleton, *William Shakespeare* (Oxford: Basil Blackwell, 1986), 33.

16. For an interesting reading of marriage as a non-referential linguistic operation, see Nelly Furman, "The Politics of Language: Beyond the Gender Principle?" in Gayle Greene and Coppelia Kahn, eds., *Making a Difference: Feminist Literary Criticism* (London: Methuen, 1985), 59-79.

17. Louis Adrian Montrose, "'The Place of a Brother' in *As You Like It*: Social Process and Comic Form," *Shakespeare Quarterly* 32:1 (1981): 51.

18. For a reading of "*The Good Person of Setzuan* as a redaction of *As You Like It*," see Helen M. Whall, "The Case is Altered: Brecht's Use of Shakespeare," *University of Toronto Quarterly* 51:2 (Winter 1981/2): 138-47. See also Margot Heinemann, "How Brecht Read Shakespeare" in Jonathan Dollimore and Alan Sinfield, eds., *Political Shakespeare: New Essays in Cultural Materialism* (Manchester: University of Manchester, 1985), 202-30.

19. "Short Description of a New Technique of Acting" in *Brecht on Theatre: The Development of an Aesthetic,* trans. John Willett (London: Methuen, 1964), 139. See also "The Author as Producer" in Walter Benjamin, *Understanding Brecht,* trans. Anna Bostock (London: NLB, 1973), 100.

20. See "Alienation Effects in Chinese Acting" in *Brecht on Theatre,* 91-99.

21. Bertolt Brecht, *The Good of Setzuan,* revised English version Eric Bentley (New York: Grove, 1965), 80. Subsequent references will appear in the text.

22. It is interesting to note that the following lines were omitted from the English translation:

> Dabei sind wir doch auf Sie angewiesen
> Dass Sie bei uns zu Haus sind und geniessen.
> Wir können es uns leider nicht verhehlen:
> Wir sind bankrott, wenn Sie uns nicht empfehlen!
> Vielleicht fiel uns aus lauter Furcht nichts ein.
> Das kam schon vor. Was könnt die Lösung sein?
> Wir konnten keine finden, nicht einmal für Geld.

Brecht, *Der Gute Mensch von Sezuan* (Berlin: Suhrkamp, 1955), 143. By establishing a greater dependency between actor and audience and thus a greater vulnerability on the part of the cast, the economic metaphors begin to function almost like the sexual ones in Shakespeare.

23. Sue-Ellen Case, "Brecht and Women: Homosexuality and the Mother" in John Fuegi, Gisela Bahr and John Willett, eds., *Brecht: Women and Politics,* Brecht Yearbook 12 (Detroit: Wayne State, 1985), 66.

24. Atina Grossmann, "The New Woman and the Rationalization of Sexuality in Weimar Germany" in Ann Snitow, Christine Stansell, and Sharon Thompson, eds., *Powers of Desire: The Politics of Sexuality* (New York: Monthly Review, 1983), 156. See also Grossmann, "'Satisfaction is Domestic Happiness': Mass Working-Class Sex Reform Organizations in the Weimar Republic" in Michael N. Dobkowski and Isidor Walliman, eds., *Towards the Holocaust: The Social and Economic Collapse of the Weimar Republic* (Westport: Greenwood, 1983), 265-93.

25. See Atina Grossmann, "Abortion and Economic Crisis: The 1931 Campaign Against Paragraph 218" in Renate Bridenthal, Atina Grossmann, and Marion Kaplan, eds., *When Biology Became Destiny: Women in Weimar and Nazi Germany* (New York: Monthly Review, 1984), 66-86.

26. Claudia Koonz, "The Competition for Women's *Lebensraum,* 1928-1934" in Bridenthal, 199-236. See also Koonz, "Some Political Implications of Separatism: German Women Between Democracy and Nazism, 1928-1934," in Judith Freidlander, Blanche Wiesen Cook, Alice Kessler-Harris, and Carroll Smith-Rosenberg, eds., *Women in Culture and Politics: A Century of Change* (Bloomington: Indiana University, 1986), 269-85.

27. Grossmann, "The New Woman," 167.

28. Gisela Bock, "Racism and Sexism in Nazi German: Motherhood, Compulsory Sterilization, and the State" in Bridenthal, 271-96. See also Bock, "'No Children at Any Cost': Perspectives on Compulsory Sterilization, Sexism and Racism in Nazi Germany" in Friedlander, 286-98.

29. See Renate Bridenthal and Claudia Koonz, "Beyond *Kinder, Küche, Kirche:* Weimar Women in Politics and Work" in Bridenthal, 33-65.

30. "Public images, unlike basic beliefs about woman's nature, can change quickly in response to economic need. The economic role and the popular image of

women may change drastically in the course of a modern war, but basic ideas about women's proper sphere, characterized by cultural lag even in the case of long-term economic developments, change little. Of course, the war was too short a span of time to expect fundamental changes in people's attitudes. The German and American cases show that public images can adapt to the need for women in jobs previously reserved for men without challenging traditional assumptions." Leila J. Rupp, *Mobilizing Women for War: German and American Propaganda, 1930-1945* (Princeton: Princeton University, 1978), 174-75.

31. Sara Lennox, "Women in Brecht's Works," *New German Critique* 14 (Spring 1978): 93, 91.

32. See Lennox, 88.

33. Mel Gussow, "Genteel Playwright, Angry Voice," *New York Times,* 22 November 1987, Arts and Leisure section.

34. Mel Gussow, "Women Playwrights: New Voices in the Theater," *New York Times,* 1 May 1983, Magazine. For a history of women's theatre see Case, *Feminism and Theatre* and Michelene Wandor, *Carry on, Understudies: Theatre and Sexual Politics* (London: Routledge and Kegan Paul, 1986).

35. See, for instance, Janelle Reinelt, "Beyond Brecht: Britain's New Feminist Drama," *Theatre Journal* 38:2 (1986): 154-63.

36. Helene Keyssar, *Feminist Theatre* (New York: Grove, 1985), 93-94.

37. Elin Diamond, "Refusing the Romanticism of Identity: Narrative Interventions in Churchill, Benmussa, Duras," *Theatre Journal* 37:3 (1985): 276.

38. Caryl Churchill, *Cloud Nine* (New York: Methuen, 1984), 3-4. Subsequent references will appear in the text.

39. Francis Rous, *Oile of Scorpions* (London, 1624), pp. 173-74. Quoted in Susan C. Shapiro, "Amazons, Hermaphrodites, and Plain Monsters: The 'Masculine' Woman in English Satire and Social Criticism from 1580-1640," *Atlantis* 13:1 (Fall/Autumn, 1987): 73.

40. Eagleton, 3-4.

P. H. Parry (essay date 1998)

SOURCE: "Visible Art and Visible Artists: Reflexivity and Metatheatricality in *As You Like It*," in *Forum for Modern Language Studies,* Vol. XXXIV, No. 1, January, 1998, pp. 1-15.

[*In the following essay, Parry discusses Shakespeare's self-conscious representation of the nature of theater and the role of audience in* As You Like It.]

Theatre is based upon twinned assumptions—that theatre is life-like because life is theatrical—which have survived so many changes in dramaturgical fashion that they may reasonably be thought to be foundational.[1] But critics with a heavy investment in beliefs about the differences between kinds or periods of theatre have often failed to notice or to stress the continuity that persists beneath disparate appearances. Thus, while we are happy to applaud the Renaissance stage's interest in reflexivity and meta-theatrical reflection, we are often anxious to avoid detecting the same in some more recent kinds of theatre.[2] Yet evidence is certainly against such prejudice. Ibsen, like most nineteenth-century dramatists, wrote for large, institutionalised theatres with stages set behind, between, and sometimes partially in front of, elaborately ornamented proscenium arches. Everything that spectators saw on these stages was framed by gigantic and ever-present signs of theatricality that are the dramatic equivalent of quotation marks. But Ibsen's suggested staging for *Hedda Gabler,* far from ignoring such unignorable theatricality, puts quotation marks around quotation marks. The stage is dressed as:

> A large drawing-room, handsomely and tastefully furnished; decorated in dark colours. In the rear wall is a broad open doorway, with curtains drawn back to either side. It leads to a smaller room, decorated in the same style as the drawing-room. [. . .] On either side of the open doorway in the rear wall stand what-nots holding ornaments of terra-cotta and majolica. Against the rear-wall of the smaller room can be seen a sofa, a table and a couple of chairs. Above this sofa hangs the portrait of a handsome old man in general's uniform.[3]

Here we witness theatre's imitation of a life that is in its turn an imitation of a theatre whose image is omnipresent throughout our viewing of the play: for what is this curtained opening if not the transparent fourth wall of an onstage-stage let into the second wall of a realistic box-set whose own fourth wall is framed for us by the proscenium arch? We see Hedda's death framed twice, within doubled marks of its own theatricality, as on this inner-stage—its curtains drawn and to the accompaniment of music—she makes her final exit, her greatest *coup de théâtre.* Ibsen's play, masterpiece of the naturalistic stage though it be, is as theatrically self-aware, self-presenting and self-reflecting as the best Renaissance comedies. Both Ibsen and Shakespeare issue an unembarrassed invitation for spectators to reflect upon theatre's founding insight: that all the world's a stage. But, according to Erving Goffman, Jaques' famous similitude ought to promote further questions: "All the world *is* like a stage, we *do* strut and fret our hour on it, and that is all the time we have. But what's the stage like, and what are those figures that people it?"[4] My contention is that thinking carefully about *As You Like It* involves thinking carefully about theatre and theatricality in general.[5]

A stage is a platform upon which plays are performed. A play is the product of human activity in which *x* impersonates *y* in the presence of *z*. But which parts of this activity require human activity? In a play in performance an *actor* impersonates a *character* (*x* imitates, or pretends to be, or stands in for, or dresses up as *y*) in front of an *audience:* the verbs which name what the actor does, though often used interchangeably, have different valencies.[6] To *impersonate* or *pretend* requires (human) consciousness on the part of the impersonator or pretender; to *stand in for* something requires no consciousness at all (a fork stands in for the Fifth Army in a tablecloth campaign); but to be perceived to be standing in for someone or something requires (human) consciousness on the part of the perceiver. Though actors are likely to be human (since, perhaps, you are only an actor if you know that you are one), their representational function, of making an absence present, does not require a human agent: puppet-shows and shadow-plays are genuine theatre, and there is at least one Dutch play in which all of the "actors" are alsatian dogs. The character impersonated is usually human, but is sometimes a supernatural being or an inanimate object: a god, Mrs McLeavy's corpse, a coffee table, or something odder still. In Howard Brenton's *Epsom Downs* one actor ("festooned with the regalia of the race") impersonates The Derby, while another (who "smokes a cigarette in a long holder, wears a summer suit with two-toned shoes and carries a cut turf in the palm of a hand") impersonates The Derby racecourse.[7] A coffee table that does not talk (even one for whom an actor stands in) is perhaps a species of stage-prop rather than a character, but in *The Gingerbread Man* a saltcellar and a pepper mill sing and dance, and Brenton's racecourse is very voluble and has a definite personality of his (not its) own.[8] But the *z* in this formula—the audience in whose presence the play is performed—is not only fundamental to the theatrical experience but can only consist of real human beings: one cannot substitute puppets or German shepherds or corpses or coffee tables. A play is a human activity not principally because of anything that happens on stage but because stage-plays are events that take place in the presence of human spectators and listeners.

One problem with this performance formula is that its linearity suggests that we come to audiences "last scene of all" (which, of course, mimics the rehearsal and production process); and, indeed, these spectators and listeners who are fundamental to the theatrical experience have been curiously neglected. Literary critics for the most part concern themselves with dramatists, whom they treat as though they are poets or novelists, and those critics whose object of attention is performance have traditionally spent most of their time worrying about actors: it is, thus, significant but not at all surprising that Diderot in his famous *Paradoxe sur le comédien* should say some hotly disputed but nonetheless worthwhile things about actors while accepting uncritically the most arrant nonsense about audiences. He argues that the greatness of great actors resides in their ability to imitate human conduct convincingly. But, since this ability is a skill that is for the most part consciously acquired and developed and displayed, it is an error to suppose that a great performance flows from an actor's spontaneously identifying with his character.

Gwyneth Paltrow as Rosalind in the 1999 Williamstown Theatre production of As You Like It.

Indeed, more usually (because a fundamental part of an actor's awareness is his awareness of himself acting), it is necessary that such identification should not occur. Precisely because the actor's art "consiste non pas à sentir [. . .] mais à rendre si scrupuleusement les signes extérieurs du sentiment", an actor need not feel (and probably does not feel) as his character may have done. Instead "il excelle à simuler, bien qu'il ne sente rien".[9] Nevertheless—and this is where Diderot's controversial but invigorating comment degenerates into twaddle—though the perfection of acting is achieved by actors who are thoroughly aware of what they are doing and are, like good plumbers or dentists, curiously neutral towards the whole procedure ("who, moving others, are themselves as stone"), that perfection consists in the encouraging of spectators to be willing (or even unwilling) victims of an illusion. The actor "n'est pas le personnage, il le joue et le joue si bien que vous le prenez pour tel: *l'illusion n'est que pour vous;* il sait bien, lui, qu'il ne l'est pas [. . .]"[10]— or, in the words of "la favorite" in *Les Bijoux indiscrets:* "Je sais encore que la perfection d'un spectacle consiste dans l'imitation si exacte d'une action, que le spectateur trompé sans interruption, s'imagine assister à l'action même."[11] But whether an actor is deeply moved or utterly unmoved during a performance is irrelevant to the questions of how, how far, and whether, an audience is moved and what it is moved towards. One can agree or disagree with Diderot's anti-emotionalist account of acting without needing to believe that his views on this issue have any consequences for spectators. In this respect William Archer, despite strongly rejecting Diderot's anti-emotionalist argument, is surely right: "If an actor can convincingly represent emotion, the critic [. . .] need not inquire whether [the actor] experiences or mechanically simulates it."[12] But what is involved in the spectator's judgement that an actor is, indeed, convincing? If we are able to claim that an actor has convincingly represented a character in the grip of a powerful emotion, surely our claim is compelling evidence that we are not illuded and have not been "trompés sans interruption"? (We may say that a Van Gogh canvas represents sunflowers convincingly, but we expect to smell paint not pollen.) If we are illuded how can we ever be in a position to say that *an actor* has convinced us? Actors presuppose performance; and our recognition of being in the presence of performance is incompatible with our being illuded.

Diderot was right (probably) about actors, but wrong (certainly) about audiences. Theatre, as is obvious if we synchronise our looking and our thinking, is the art of non-deceptive disguise and of non-duplicitous pretence. Yet the obviousness of this point and of its corollary (that theatre is always theatrical) creates resistance: somehow the rumour has got about that theatre is only convincing when it denatures itself: art needs to *be* artful but *seem* artless. And this rot goes deep. Of *All My Sons*—the eighth or ninth play that he had written, only the second that was produced, and his first theatrical success—Arthur Miller noted:

> My intention in this play was to be as untheatrical as possible. To that end any metaphor, any image, any figure of speech, however creditable to me, was removed if it even slightly brought to consciousness the hand of a writer. So far as was possible nothing was to be permitted to interfere with its artlessness.[13]

It is easy to have a sense of Miller's dilemma: in the late 1940s, in the wake of the failure of so much untruthful and artificial playmaking, he wanted to avoid the merely smart exploitation of theatrical tricks in order that this play at least (which remains an unusually chaste example of his work) could engage directly with social issues and with extra-theatrical reality:

> It began to seem to me that what I had written until then, as well as almost all the plays I had ever seen, had been written for a theatrical performance, when they should have been written as a kind of testimony whose relevance far surpassed theatrics.[14]

But, closet-drama apart, all plays are written for theatrical performance: why should it be thought right (and even natural) that they should seem not to have been? Besides, a certain kind of unnaturalness is permitted: a play may proudly bear the marks of having been written "as a kind of testimony". Miller's plays have always seemed artificial in this sense, his characters speaking words that are palpably written for them rather than firing off their thoughts from the tops of their heads. When, right at the end of *All My Sons,* Chris tells his mother:

> You can be better! Once and for all you can know there's a universe of people outside and you're responsible to it, and unless you know that, you threw away your son because that's why he died [. . .][15]

it is obvious that this is not merely (or at all convincingly) a transcription of the way in which one character speaks to another but is also the kind of speech that characters in plays speak when the playwright wants to address an issue and an audience. Peter Szondi's account of how drama in the modern world operates and should operate both fails to describe twentieth-century theatre accurately and, with magisterial certainty, condemns much of Miller's achievement in terms (and this is the sad part) that Miller himself is anxious to endorse:

> The Drama is not written, it is set. All the lines spoken in the Drama are disclosures. They are spoken in context and remain there. They should in no way be perceived as coming from the author [. . .] the lines in a play are as little an address to the spectator as they are a declaration by the author.
>
> (Szondi, p. 8)

Yet Chris's speech to his mother is both address and declaration.[16] Szondi's dogmatism (his deriving a false *is* from a dubious *ought*) is easily exposed: what radiates from good plays whatever their period of origin is not the art that conceals art (which, were it effective, we should never recognise) but the art that reveals itself: plays are written for theatrical performance, declare themselves to be so frankly, and would be poorer plays were they not to do so. If Miller had indeed avoided all theatricality then how far, in that one respect at least, would *All My Sons* have differed from those "poetic" plays—"whose ultimate thought or meaning is elusive, *a drama which appears not to have been composed or constructed,* but which somehow comes to life on a stage and then flickers away"—that, earlier in his "Introduction to the *Collected Plays*", he dispatches disdainfully?[17] So is it a good or a bad thing for a play, which must in the nature of things be both composed and constructed, to seem "not to have been composed and constructed"? When Jane Austen tells us of the Bertram sisters that "their vanity was in such good order, that they seemed to be quite free from it" has she not got the moral measure of what is vicious whether in life or art or artlessness? Why attach value only to that art that conceals art: what about the art that reveals art and revels in what it reveals?

Shakespeare is not—no dramatist need be and no good one can be—invisible: the critic who wrote of Shakespeare's "apparent invisibility" was wittier than he guessed.[18] More Shakespearean still was the innkeeper in *The Invisible Man* who "showed his dislike" of his strange guest "by concealing it ostentatiously". Far from seeking to hide from us the fundamental structure of the theatrical event, Shakespeare "conceals it ostentatiously" in order that it may parade itself in the forefront of our attention. In his best work he reveals the art that conceals art, treading a fine line between concealment and revelation. Much of the pleasure that a Shakespeare play brings, both to a reader and in performance, comes from our treading that line with him: of our being not so much in two minds as two worlds (of fiction and of performance, of underlying story and its theatrical realisation) which are with us always in performance, and which are by no means so easily separated as simplifying theories—especially semiotic theories—would have us believe. Both worlds (and their complex interaction) are explicitly acknowledged by Shakespeare. In the induction to *The Taming of the Shrew* we see a drunken tinker, Christopher Sly, who falls asleep. While he is unconscious a nobleman discovers him and decides to trick him by having a young servant dress up as Sly's wife. He is confident that the outrageous impersonation will be carried through effectively:[19]

> I know the boy will well usurp the grace,
> Voice, gait, and action of a gentlewoman.

Sly will be deceived (or the trick will fail), but the courtiers are not deceived (or the joke will not have worked). Secondly, in an unrelated incident, a troupe of travelling players appears and performs the story of Kate and Petruchio, for the benefit of the duped Sly, his false wife, and his bogus courtiers. Thus *The Taming of the Shrew* is set up in such a way that when we watch it we are aware that we are watching other people watching a play. Shakespeare's other plays are less explicit, but no less effective, in the way in which they air the linked issues of impersonation (*x* impersonates *y*) and spectatorship (in the presence of *z*).

Let us defy the linearity of our formula and begin, for once, at the receiving end. Shakespeare learned to write for, and to live with, dangerous audiences: his plays are alive with, and are alive because they are alive with, permanent awareness of an audience's potential disruptiveness. Most often the vehicle for such awareness is a play-within-a-play of the sort that we find in *Love's Labour's Lost* or *A Midsummer Night's Dream* or *Hamlet*. These intercalated plays are such frequently used devices because, by stressing the huge element of artificiality that is inseparable from theatrical viewing, they enable audiences to be relaxed about that initial act of artifice without which any dramatic performance cannot get started.[20] And what they show us about Elizabethan audiences is that they were accustomed to inspect performances vigorously and intervene as they saw fit. There is a model, though no doubt an idealised one, of the kind of interchange which seems to have been normal in Elizabethan performances in *As You Like It* (III.ii.222-44) where Ganymede keeps on interrupting Aliena's description of Orlando:

> ROSALIND:
> Looks he as freshly as he did the day he wrestled?
> CELIA:
> It is as easy to count atomies as to resolve the propositions of a lover; but take a taste of my finding him, and relish it with good observance. I found him under a tree, like a dropped acorn—
> ROSALIND:
> It may well be called Jove's tree when it drops forth such fruit.
> CELIA:
> Give me audience, good madam.
> ROSALIND:
> Proceed.
> CELIA:
> There lay he, stretched along like a wounded knight—
> ROSALIND:
> Though it be pity to see such a sight, it well becomes the ground.
> CELIA:
> Cry "holla!" to thy tongue, I prithee: it curvets unseasonably.—He was furnished like a hunter—
> ROSALIND:
> O ominous—he comes to kill my heart.
> CELIA:
> I would sing my song without a burden; thou bringest me out of tune.
> ROSALIND:
> Do you not know I am a woman? When I think, I must speak.—Sweet, say on.[21]

But then Orlando and Jaques enter and Aliena is forced to break off:

> CELIA:
> You bring me out. Soft! comes he not here?
> ROSALIND:
> 'Tis he. Slink by, and note him.

They then move to one side of the stage in order to observe Orlando and Jaques, and in doing so convert themselves into one of the play's many examples of an onstage audience, and thus confer the status of play-within-play on the dialogue which follows (III.ii.245-85).

Similar movements, with identical consequences, are typical of the play: *As You Like It* in performance is stuffed full of interior and subordinate performances, which include a not very impressive wedding masque; five songs (more than in any other Shakespeare play); and also, in much subtler fashion, incident after incident that is shaped up (like the ending of *Hedda Gabler*) to replicate in the theatre an image of the theatre. In II.i Duke Senior claims to be able to find "tongues in trees, books in the running brooks, / Sermons in stones, and good in everything" (16-17) and illustrates his meaning by anthropomorphising deer as "native burghers of this desert city" (23). As an audience we both hear (and by convention *overhear*) what he says, but immediately Shakespeare constructs as a commentary on this passage a situation in which hearing and overhearing are highlighted, for an unnamed First Lord describes how Amiens and he stole up behind Jaques (who had himself stolen up behind a stricken deer) in order to listen to (to overhear) his moralised comments on what, emphasising the theatrical metaphor, Duke Senior terms a "spectacle". And Jaques' moralised comments, which consist of finding human analogies for the animal activity that he is inspecting, in effect convert the deer into actors in a play, since they are made to stand in for the human beings whom they emblematise (52-6):

> FIRST LORD
> Anon a careless herd
> Full of the pasture jumps along by him
> And never stays to greet him. "Ay," quoth Jaques,
> "Sweep on you fat and greasy citizens,
> 'Tis just the fashion."

So the deer are actors in a drama that Jaques witnesses.[22] But he, who is audience of that drama, is a player within the drama that Amiens and the First Lord witness; and they, in telling their story at Duke Senior's rural court, convert him and his courtiers into another audience; and the real-life actors who impersonate these stage-beings do so for the benefit of that ultimate audience which is us. Multiple and gradated acts of audition correspond to that sense of plays within plays within plays that Shakespeare is so careful to foster. Every time that Jaques appears we are made aware of multiplied and interlocking audiences. Here (II.vii.136-9) is how Duke Senior introduces Jaques' most famous speech:

> Thou seest we are not all alone unhappy.
> This wide and universal *theatre*
> Presents more woeful *pageants* than the *scene*
> Wherein we *play* in.

This is directed by the duke out to his companions, but by the actor (acting in his capacity as an actor) out to the audience in explicit allusion to the performance itself. And on the stage of the recently opened Globe theatre, whose motto was *Totus mundus agit histrionem,* Jaques deliberately echoes that motto in his opening words. On the boards of a public stage men who are players represent men and women who are in their turn actors in a greater drama.[23]

Once one is made aware of the basic structure of *As You Like It* one begins to see evidence of it everywhere. At II.iv there is again an inlaid drama. Ganymede, Aliena, and Touchstone begin the scene speaking prose. Ganymede announces the entry of Corin and Silvius in words whose prosodic patterns are compatible with either verse or prose:

> Look you, who comes here,
> A young man and an old in solemn talk.[24]

But this transitional speech serves to introduce two shepherds who speak in verse throughout. When they leave, Ganymede has two lines of verse and then Touchstone reverts to prose. Why this strange pattern of verse and prose? It is absurd to suppose that agricultural workers in Elizabethan England were more prone to speak blank verse than were their social superiors. But it would be equally absurd to suppose that Corin and Silvius are in any respects portraits of real-life shepherds: they are pastoral figures who represent a contrast between youth and age, and they speak of love. Elizabethans—just like us, and just like all human beings (except actors) always and everywhere—spoke prose all their working lives. And so they spoke prose on their way to the theatre, and on their way home again afterwards. But briefly, for the two or three hours of performance, they saw men whom they knew to be actors (often, indeed, actors whom they knew by name) and they heard them speaking verse. Actors did not merely put on strange clothes but also assumed strange speech patterns: those patterns, like the clothes, were a disguise—and, like theatrical disguise in general, they were meant to fool no one. Blank verse was one of the great indices of the theatrical experience: an index that differentiated it from the life that surrounded it. Shakespeare uses prose and verse in this scene so as to emphasise that Ganymede, Aliena, and Touchstone are spectators at a theatrical event: that they are once again an onstage audience. And the ambiguous metrics of Ganymede's introduction to the spectacle and the undoubted verse with which she ends the piece serve to highlight her role here as prologue and epilogue. There is an actor who is Rosalind who is Ganymede who is a prologue; then there are actors who are Corin and Silvius who act out the ageless debate between youth and age; and then the actor who is Rosalind who is Ganymede becomes an epilogue and draws out the moral of the piece (41-2):

> Alas, poor shepherd, searching of thy wound,
> I have by hard adventure found my own.

The answer to Goffman's linked questions (What's the stage like, and what are those figures that people it?) is that the stage is a machine for orientating art towards its audience, and that the figures that people the machine ("We're *actors*—we're the opposite of people!") make sense only when we see them through the eyes of spectatorship.[25] Thus, though every actor is an *x* that impersonates a *y,* it is not the case that every actor is an *x* that is disguised as a *y*. And it is not so, because impersonation—defined as non-duplicitous pretence—is a fundamental of acting whereas disguise or dressing up is not, since *x* may or may not dress up as *y* in order to impersonate *y* effectively. Charles tells Oliver (I.i.117-19): "I am given, sir, secretly to understand that your younger brother, Orlando, hath a disposition to come in disguised against me to try a fall." Orlando's disguise does not consist of altering his appearance or of putting on a costume (indeed in most modern productions he *undresses* for the wrestling match) but rather of his not telling spectators who he really is and of claiming to be some other person. And his disguise is utterly unavailing since, by a mechanism that Shakespeare never reveals, Charles has been "secretly" informed of Orlando's true identity. Because Orlando's disguise is perfunctory, transparent, and very much a matter of his simply asserting that he is someone else, it serves as a model for theatrical impersonation in general. Shakespeare, far from being bothered by the transparency of performance, multiplies and replicates pretence and disguise so that they are insinuated into the very centre of his play, not only refusing to disguise disguise but often making a joke at the expense of its obviousness. When, for example, Duke Senior and Orlando discuss Ganymede (V.iv.26-9):

> DUKE SENIOR
> I do remember in this shepherd boy
> Some lively details of my daughter's favour.
> ORLANDO
> My lord, the first time that I ever saw him,
> Methought he was a brother to your daughter [. . .]

they are not principally engaged in trying to assure a sceptical audience of the plausibility of an inherently implausible bit of plot. Those actors and directors who believe that Orlando knows who Ganymede is from the outset and keeps quiet in order to stay one step ahead of Rosalind might reasonably ask themselves why he fails to capitalise upon the rewards of his cleverness. There are, surely, no grounds for doubting that Rosalind's disguise is thoroughly convincing to those on stage, or that it was—and is—thoroughly unconvincing to an audience, and this perceptual discrepancy (which is at the root of our experience of theatre) is the target of Shakespeare's joke in this bit of dialogue.[26]

What the superabundance of onstage disguise in *As You Like It* serves to highlight or foreground is that underlying activity of non-deceptive disguise that is fundamental to the art of the theatre. In III.ii Rosalind (or rather Rosalind disguised as Ganymede) tells Orlando that she (or rather he) will pretend to be a woman and that Orlando must address him as though he were Rosalind. In order to encourage him to comply with this rather strange suggestion Ganymede tells Orlando that he has worked a similar trick previously and that it has served to cure a love-sick heart (III.ii.385-94):

> GANYMEDE:
> Yet I profess curing it by counsel.
> ORLANDO:
> Did you ever cure any so?
> GANYMEDE:
> Yes, one; and in this manner. He was to imagine me his love, his mistress; and I set him every day to woo me. At which time would I, being but a moonish youth, grieve, be effeminate, changeable, longing and liking, proud, fantastical, apish, shallow, inconstant, full of tears, full of smiles; for every passion something, and for no passion truly anything, as boys and women are for the most part cattle of this colour [. . .].

Here Goffman's question—of what we think stage-people are—resolves itself into the question of who we think speaks Ganymede's lines. Editors who follow the infuriatingly inconvenient practice of the First Folio simply ascribe all words that are spoken by the actor who plays Rosalind to Rosalind herself. But it is important when we *read* the play to have as firm a sense as we have in a modern performance of the difference between Rosalind's speaking *in propria persona* and Rosalind's speaking as Ganymede. In a modern performance we see a woman dressed as a man and we hear that man boast that he can counterfeit the actions of a woman to perfection. But Ganymede's bluff is undercut by Rosalind's counterbluff: Ganymede can act this part so well because, in this matter of impersonating a woman, Rosalind does not have to act at all. We witness, in short, a sophisticated joke.

Yet when we read the play, or watch a modern performance, we get only half the joke. We hear Ganymede speaking, and beneath him we hear Rosalind, but in the performance which Shakespeare sought to construct we hear beneath both of them the boy-actor talking about *his* art, for the task which Ganymede sets himself is the task that the stage conventions of the day set for every boy-actor. In every performance that he gave the boy-actor "being but a moonish youth" would "grieve, be effeminate, changeable, longing and liking, proud, fantastical, apish, shallow, inconstant, full of tears, full of smiles; for every passion something, and for no passion truly anything, as boys and women are for the most part cattle of this colour"—so that, with that explicit linking of boys (the means of representation) and women (the objects of representation) Shakespeare's complex joke is complete. Shakespeare's joke is visual: we *see* the point. But it is also audible: a matter of who speaks the words and of who owns the words that are spoken.

At this point a speech-act theorist would wish to register dissent, since it is plainly inadequate to suggest that we here listen to the *boy-actor* talking about his art. To see the force of this objection we need—bearing in mind that though characters (figures in one world) talk to other characters, it is actors (figures in the other world) who do all the speaking—to ask ourselves a question: Does anyone talk to the audience? If this question seems odd, or even impermissible, it does so because a powerful assumption, widespread in modern mainstream theatre and in much critical (especially literary-critical) writing about drama, is that a play's actions are bounded by the limits of the stage, so that (whatever actors do) characters do not acknowledge the presence of an audience. Szondi puts the point with great clarity: "The actor-role relationship should not be visible. Indeed, the actor and the character should unite to create a single personage" (Szondi 1987: 9). What is the status of speech that is directly addressed to the audience? Recently, modern editors of Shakespeare have become utterly uninhibited, to the point of irresponsibility, about supplying a category of stage direction (indicating the object-of-address) that is entirely absent from the quarto and Folio texts of Shakespeare's plays. Yet they are very unwilling to see the audience as an object that is addressed. To whom is Oliver speaking in the following speech?

> Now will I stir this gamester. I hope I shall see an end of him, for my soul—yet I know not why—hates nothing more than he. Yet he's gentle; never schooled, and yet learned; full of noble device; of all sorts enchantingly beloved; and, indeed, so much in the heart of the world, and especially of my own people, who best know him, that I am altogether misprized. But it shall

not be so long. This wrestler shall clear all. Nothing remains but that I kindle the boy thither, which now I'll go about.

(I.i.153-61)

Granted, as a Folio stage direction makes clear, that Charles has left the stage *before* Oliver reveals his unmotivated malevolence, to whom is his malevolence revealed? Is not the simple answer: the audience? Granted that he speaks on an empty stage, to whom is his speech addressed? Is not the same answer obvious, available and correct? But what a powerful school of dramaturgical theorists would have us believe is that Oliver's monologue is a speech that is tethered to Oliver at one end (its point of origin) but is untethered at the other.[27] Since Oliver speaks upon an empty stage the speech cannot be addressed to anyone; it is a soliloquy, and soliloquies are internal monologues that audiences are by convention privileged to overhear. But this is a great deal of argument to cover an elementary case: why not say, altogether more simply, that Oliver addresses the audience?

In order to answer this question we need to look at Rosalind's epilogue, for that—when properly understood—reflects back upon the entire play and helps to form our understanding of it. Everything that the play is and does is implicit in the strange involuted structure of its epilogue—a speech that is so famous that we often forget what a strange beast it is, for prologues and epilogues, though commonplace in plays of the restoration period, are unusual in the Shakespeare canon. And when they do occur—in *Henry V* or *A Winter's Tale* or *Pericles*—they are generally spoken by a special character who takes no other part in the action. Epilogues spoken by one of a play's characters, who steps forward out of the surrounding action in order to do so, are still more unusual, and the epilogue to *As You Like It* is easily the best known of this kind. It is, moreover, the only epilogue in Shakespeare's works that is delivered by a female character and is the earliest such epilogue in English drama.

The clumsy locution "delivered by a female character" simply serves to remind us that in Shakespeare's lifetime Rosalind would have been impersonated by a man. Who, then, speaks the epilogue and in whose character? In one sense the answer is obvious: there is only one group of people which ever speaks in a performance and that group comprises actors not characters. So we can say, without fear of contradiction, that an actor speaks the epilogue. But, equally (and this is what was wrong with my earlier account of the boy-actor telling us about his art), there is no belief that the actor unloads upon us the spontaneous promptings of his own heart, or makes the words up as he goes along. There is all the difference in the world—in the world of the theatre at any rate—between (to take a very famous theatrical *gaffe*) Michael Redgrave's speaking the words that belong to Macbeth and his breaking down and telling an unappreciative audience of Liverpool schoolchildren that if they don't shut up he will go home.[28] So we say that the actor speaks not in his own person but in character, and we shall probably go on to say—a shade incautiously—that he speaks in the character of Rosalind: which is after all, in common parlance, simply to say that Rosalind speaks the words. Yet it is clear that Rosalind does not speak *all* of the epilogue in her character as Rosalind and thus clear that the boy-actor cannot be said to speak all of it in her character either, any more than (since no one supposes that he merely makes up the words) he can be said to utter *any* of it on his own authority:

> I charge you, O women, for the love you bear to men, to like as much of this play as please you. And I charge you, O men, for the love you bear to women—as I perceive by your simpering none of you hates them—that between you and the women the play may please. *If I were a woman* I would kiss as many of you as had beards that pleased me, complexions that liked me, and breaths that I defied not. And I am sure, as many as have good beards, or good faces, or sweet breaths, will for my kind offer, when I make curtsy, bid me farewell.

But, since Rosalind is certainly a woman, she cannot possibly say the line: "If I were a woman I would kiss as many of you as had beards". And in a modern production, where Rosalind will be represented by an actress, the line makes no sense either, and must be cut or reworded or hurried through in the belief that modern audiences do not need to understand what Shakespeare is saying; or perhaps (though I have no record that this has ever been done) the actress playing Rosalind quickly puts on some reminder of her disguise as Ganymede—a feathered hunting-cap perhaps—in order to speak these words. Yet in an Elizabethan performance the line makes perfect sense as it stands without such elaborate subterfuge: an Elizabethan spectator, if he could be bothered to spell out the obvious, would say without hesitation that Rosalind's epilogue is spoken by an actor *in the character of an actor* who represents Rosalind. It is that extra layer in the representational fabric—the actor acting in the character of the actor who acts in the character of Rosalind—that needs to be borne in mind and which the epilogue highlights, for the epilogue is not an isolated joke but rather gives expression to the sophisticated machinery of theatrical self-awareness that runs, and is seen to run, throughout the play; and which—despite superficial variations that are the product of theatrical fashion—runs, and is seen to run, throughout drama generally.

Notes

1. "The elementary mechanisms of human interaction and the elementary mechanisms of dramatic fiction are the same. [. . .] Social life [. . .] is designed as a continuous performance and, because of this, there is a link between theatre and life": Umberto Eco, "Semiotics of Theatrical Performance", *Drama Review* 21 (1977), 107-17 (p. 113). As Eco points out, Erving Goffman is one of the prime modern developers of this observation: see note 4 below.

2. The classic case of criticism driven by a need to assert a development (towards, in this case, "the

absolute dominance of dialogue") is Peter Szondi's *Theory of the Modern Drama*, edited and translated by Michael Hays (Cambridge, 1987), pp. 8-9. Future references to this work are incorporated into my text. (Szondi, whose book first appeared in German in 1956, takes a long view and by "modern" means post-Renaissance.)

3. *Hedda Gabler*, translated by Michael Meyer, in Henrik Ibsen, *Plays: Two* (London, 1980), p. 243.

4. Erving Goffman, *Frame Analysis: An Essay on the Organization of Experience* (Cambridge Massachusetts, 1974), p. 124.

5. Unless otherwise indicated, references to *As You Like It* are to the Oxford Shakespeare edition, ed. Alan Brissenden, Clarendon Press 1993.

6. J. L. Austin, in an agonisingly nimble dance through the issues involved, says (a) that "mere imitation does not imply dissembling" and (b) that pretending is not what actors do, since their elaborate preparations persuade us rather to use of their activity such words as "impersonation or imposture or disguise": "Pretending", in *Philosophical Papers*, 3rd edition, ed. J. O. Urmson and G. J. Warnock (Oxford, 1979), pp. 253-71 (pp. 265-8). But *imposture*, which always implies moral censure, is lowering the tone of the company it keeps.

7. Howard Brenton, *Plays: One* (London and New York, 1986), p. 231.

8. David Wood, *The Gingerbread Man* (London, 1977).

9. Denis Diderot, *Paradoxe sur le comédien*, ed. Marc Blanquet, Librairie Théâtrale (Paris, 1958), pp. 16, 77.

10. *Paradoxe*, p. 17. Emphasis added.

11. Denis Diderot, (*Œuvres complètes*, Tome III, p. 163 (*Les Bijoux indiscrets*, edited by Jean Macary, Aram Vartanian, and Jean-Louis Leutrat [Paris, 1978], Part II, chapter 5 [chapter 38], "Entretien sur les Lettres").

12. William Archer, *Masks or Faces?* in Denis Diderot, *The Paradox of Acting*, translated by Walter Herries Pollock, and William Archer, *Masks or Faces?* (New York, 1957), p. 79.

13. "Introduction to the *Collected Plays*" (1957), reproduced in *The Theatre Essays of Arthur Miller*, ed. Robert A. Martin (London, 1994), p. 128.

14. *Theatre Essays*, p. 129. Compare a more recent statement about *Death of a Salesman*: "Precisely what I had been after [was a play that] might seem so inevitable and natural that an author was hardly even required" (*Collected Plays*, II, [London, 1981], p. 1).

15. Arthur Miller, *A View from the Bridge/All My Sons* (Harmondsworth, 1961), p. 179. *All My Sons* was published in 1947. In his introduction to *Collected Plays*, II (London, 1981), p. 1, Miller claims to have written *Death of a Salesman* so as to avoid having to introduce "one or more speeches announcing in some overt way its philosophical intention".

16. Indeed, in both manner and in mode of address, it parallels a famous speech from a British play that had appeared in the previous year: "But just remember this. One Eva Smith has gone—but there are millions and millions and millions of Eva Smiths and John Smiths still left with us, with their lives, their hopes and fears, their suffering, and chance of happiness, all intertwined with our lives, with what we think and say and do. We don't live alone. We are members of one body. We are responsible for each other. And I tell you that the time will soon come when, if men will not learn that lesson, then they will be taught it in fire and blood and anguish. Good night." (J. B. Priestley, *An Inspector Calls*, in *Time and the Conways and Other Plays* [Harmondsworth, 1969], p. 207). The status of Priestley's speech as testimony can hardly be doubted, but it is also, and inescapably, a speech written for performance, only at home upon a stage or kindred platform.

17. *Theatre Essays*, p. 123. Emphasis added.

18. Gary Taylor, "Forms of Opposition: Shakespeare and Middleton", *English Literary Renaissance* 24 (1994), 283-314 (p. 314). Taylor, who is assessing evidence of Shakespeare's crypto-Catholicism, seems unaware of his invigorating oxymoron.

19. Ind.i.128-9. *The Taming of the Shrew*, ed. H. J. Oliver, The Oxford Shakespeare, Clarendon Press, 1982.

20. "Every dramatic performance [. . .] is composed of two speech acts. The first one is performed by the actor who is making a performative statement—'I am acting'." (Eco, "Semiotics of Theatrical Performance", p. 115.)

21. The dashes with which some of the lines end are Brissenden's way of signalling Rosalind's interruptions. That they are interruptions is clear from the dialogue.

22. George Steevens, in his "Observations on the plays altered from Shakespeare" (1779) noted that, in eighteenth-century performances, "the celebrated Speech that describes the wounded Stag, and the Behaviour of the humourist Jaques, is taken from one of the Lords, its original Proprietor, and is given to Jaques himself" (*Shakespeare: The Critical Heritage, 6 (1774-1801)*, ed. Brian Vickers (London and Boston, 1981), p. 205. This is such a natural piece of theatre (why report a report?) that one is bound to ask why Shakespeare should have set up his text with such a different performance potential in mind.

23. In terms of the present argument, Alan Rickman (Brissenden, p. 151) was surely right in a 1985

revival to resurrect a traditional bit of stage business by miming each of the seven ages of man in turn, thus once again highlighting that act of acting that Shakespeare never seeks to hide from us.

24. II.iv.17-18. The Arden edition, ed. Agnes Latham (London, 1975), which is here cited, prints the lines in verse formation while Brissenden's Oxford edition (following the Folio arrangement) prints them as prose.

25. Tom Stoppard, *Rosencrantz and Guildenstern are Dead* (London, 1968), p. 47 (spoken by The Player).

26. In *Shakespeare at the Globe 1599-1609* (New York, 1962) Bernard Beckerman says of the Elizabethan disguise convention in general that: "Disguise is signified to the audience. But the completeness of the disguise is insufficient to convince an audience that the character would pass undetected [. . .] it is nominal, a token of disguise" (p. 199). But his argument requires more careful wording: precisely because stage disguise is accepted as "nominal, a token of disguise" it is perceived as being an adequate representation of a degree of disguise sufficient to enable a character to pass undetected. On the caution that we need to exercise when we pass from commenting on the actuality of performance to commenting on that counter-factual interpretation of what we see which is "the story of the play", see J. O. Urmson, "Dramatic Representation", *The Philosophical Quarterly* 22 (1972), 333-43 (p. 337).

27. In *How to do Things with Words,* second edition, ed. J. O. Urmson and Marina Sbisà (Oxford, 1975), Austin says of a speech-act that it is a procedure that "must be executed by all participants both correctly and completely" (p. 15), and completeness ensures that "the performance of an illocutionary act involves the securing of *uptake*" (p. 117). Austin specifically cites speech "spoken in soliloquy" (p. 22) as an example of an etiolation of the moral responsibilities that normally attach to speech-acts. Much later in his lectures (p. 92) he lists the etiolations as occurring when (and whenever) "we use speech in acting, fiction and poetry, quotation and recitation". Soliloquy is suspect because of doubts about uptake (rather as though one were to promise in the privacy of one's own bathroom); the other etiolations occur because of doubts over who *owns*—of who is responsible for originating—the words that are spoken.

28. One of the politer versions of this famous story is given in Richard Huggett, *Binkie Beaumont: Eminence Grise of the West End Theatre 1933-1973* (London and Sydney, 1989), p. 387.

SPORTS AS METAPHOR

A. Stuart Daley (essay date 1993)

SOURCE: "The Idea of Hunting in *As You Like It,*" in *Shakespeare Studies,* Vol. 21, 1993, pp. 72-95.

[*In the following essay, Daley questions the nature of the hunt in* As You Like It, *stating that it indicates the desperation of Duke Senior, and that it functions on an allegorical level as well.*]

Dr. Samuel Johnson counsels us that, "He who will understand Shakespeare must not be content to study him in the closet, he must look for his meaning sometimes among the sports of the field."[1] This good counsel certainly applies to studying *As You Like It,* which is in some respects a hunter's play. We learn in the opening scene that the banished duke has taken refuge in the Forest of Arden, and in Elizabethan parlance forest means a spacious habitat for game. Almost immediately thereafter we learn that the hapless duke and his fellow outlaws live like old Robin Hood of England, that is to say by shooting deer for venison. In keeping with this role they will come on wearing, like Robin Hood, the forester's standard summer coat of camouflage green. We are prepared to see why, "in these woods," the exiles must "go and kill us venison" (2.1.21), and hear them talk at some length about a stag "that from the hunter's aim had ta'en a hurt," and come "to languish" at a sylvan brookside (34-35).[2] Subsequently, the topic appears in three more scenes, culminating in the ancient motif of the princely hero who pits his strength and skill against the royal beast, a lioness. Elsewhere, too, the diction and action of venery supplies symbols, metaphors, and similes for lovers, the jester's shaft of wit, and so on.[3]

The pervasiveness and centrality of the theme can be indicated by the extent to which it attaches to the core character, Rosalind, when she plans to escape to the forest disguised as a boy, no less a one than "Jove's own page," Ganymed. It merits attention here since nothing has been made of its significance. For the long, dangerous tramp to the Forest of Arden, Rosalind dresses like a stripling soldier (many then going to the Irish war) or a boyish hunter. Lodge armed his Rosalynde with only a gentlemanly rapier, but Shakespeare gives Rosalind the formidable armament of a "curtle-ax upon my thigh / A boar spear in my hand" (1.3.117-18). The boar spear introduces a fitting symbolism as a traditional weapon for a champion of virtue against intemperance and, more specifically, lust, both being vices represented sometimes by a boar or sanglier.[4] Rosalind's boar spear, then, betokens her temperance and chastity, qualities she shares with a "goodlie Ladie clad in hunter's weed," Spenser's Belphoebe, of whom he declares that "in her hand a sharpe bore-speare she held" (*Faerie Queene* 2.1.21.7 and 29.1). Spenser's chaste and noble Britomart also yields a puissant spear. Moreover, classical symbolism assigns a spear to the goddess of wisdom and sometimes the virgin goddess of hunting, Diana. On the stage, a trident would have especially suggested the "chaste eyed, thrice-crowned queen of night," later invoked by Orlando when he rightly identifies "the fair, the chaste, the unexpressive" Rosalind as a huntress of Diana,[5] because Rosalind's role, like Belphoebe's, is Dianan as well as Venerean.

In a pleasantly allusive manner, royal Rosalind's hunting spear also relates her to her new namesake, for Ganymed, the *puer regius*, as readers of *Aeneid* V. 251-57 (Loeb Classics edition, pp. 462/463) would recall, was pursuing fleet stags with a javelin in his hand when Jove's eagle swooped to abduct him. Rosalind herself has recourse to the hart-heart pun, and she understands the figurative meaning of hunting the hare, the medieval hunt of Venus (4.3.18).[6] Then, too, in the forest context, with a slyly lewd rhyme and pun (on hind and lined), the Clown likens Rosalind to an estrous hind and hound bitch (2.2.101-2; 105-6). Altogether, this mélange of allusions and symbols drawn from classical and contemporary venery corresponds to the complexities of Rosalind's character and its dramatic tensions with her predicament, making her both the hunted and the huntress, pursued and pursuer, and a Renaissance Venerean-Dianan figure harmonizing in herself virtues both masculine and feminine.

Merely to notice Shakespeare's allusions to hunting, however, no longer assures our understanding of the sixteenth-century facts he designates by them, because to us, the words convey little exact meaning. A production of *A Midsummer Night's Dream* 4.1 that turned the royal couple into bird shooters illustrates the problem. The Amazon Queen came on, fowling piece at the ready, looking like, say, a painting of the Electress of Bavaria in Hunting Costume. She, Duke Theseus, and loaders have pushed into the woods, like Puck, through bog, bush, brake, and brier before sunup on May Day, shooting en route the pheasants draped on their aide. Haply, the shooting has not startled awake the charmed sleepers, like russet-pated choughs "rising and cawing at the gun's report" (3.2.21-22). They need to be aroused by a blast of a deer hunter's horn! The date, time (first light), and place of this astonishing pheasant hunt left the audience unperturbed.

Nor did the audience seem puzzled, much less bewildered, by the totally incongruous conviction of Duke Theseus that he was in the woods to set up a stag hunt. The presence of himself, with his forester, huntsmen and a pack of deerhounds in the woods at daybreak means that they have been harbouring, i.e. searching for, a warrantable stag in the covert. (A "palace wood" [1.2.101] is a deer park.) Duke Theseus wants the report without delay so that the chase can be started, as was usually done, in the "vaward of the day" (4.1.105): "Dispatch, I say, and find the forester" (108). The dialogue reports routine preliminaries of a deer chase. The birdshoot innovators believed, or expected us to believe, that the Duke's pack of basset hounds had been brought along in couples to track down, with tunable thunder, the nesting pheasants.[7] In the woods! With hunting horn calls! As Theseus says in another connection, "Such tricks have strong imagination" (5.1.18). But the lesson is that in this arena actions now speak louder than words; for the audience, the Duke simply uttered high-sounding phatic patter. For both audience and players, the startling, even hilarious, contradiction between what was seen and what was spoken did not exist.

This passage uses technical details (103-11, 182-83) to account plausibly for the presence of Theseus and Hippolyta in the woods before the lovers awake at sunrise. They are keeping the hunt assembly at which the woodmen will describe the harbouring of the deer so that one may be selected. In short, their "observation is perform'd" (104) apparently for the game and for the rites of May simultaneously, and the Duke now sends impatiently for the forester (103, 108, and cf. 3.2.390-93) to come and report the tokens. Meanwhile, the huntsmen with their horns (138) and the coupled deer hounds (107) with their handlers stand by at wood's edge ready to begin "Our purpos'd hunting" (183). The only birds of note are the lark (94), signalling approaching sunrise, and the still sleeping "wood-birds" (140), whose discovery delays the preliminaries of the intended chase beyond resumption.[8]

I think it useful, therefore, to discriminate among the usual kinds of Elizabethan deer hunting so that the means of capture can be recognized and, in consequence, their implications about the conditions, purpose, and mood of the participants clarified. These findings can help to solve several interpretive and critical problems. In *As You Like It*, for example, are the refugees fleeting the time in careless idyllic escape, or eking out their existence in fairly straitened circumstances? Are they killing deer as a noble pastime sport, or are they hunting for survival? Is the Duke the comfortable old humbug invented by Shaw's untutored fancy, or a competent, compassionate, and indeed, ideal figure of the Renaissance governor? Is the hunting an arbitrarily imposed piece of humanistic propaganda against blood sports, or is it, on the contrary, an element artistically organic to the meaning of the play? What is there about the shot the Duke mentions that "irks" him? These and other matters in *As You Like It*, may be elucidated by reviewing the pertinent Elizabethan hunting practice and terminology.[9]

Broadly speaking, the Elizabethans pursued or sought for deer (their only big game) either on horseback or on foot, and killed their prey with, respectively, an *arme blanche* or a missile weapon. For the pursuit on horseback, the two common methods were coursing with greyhounds or chasing with scent-tracking hounds. The present-day British restriction of the word hunt to the use of horses with hounds came in later, but is anticipated as in Beaumont and Fletcher's *Philaster* (1608-10), 4.2, where one woodman declares that the princess will shoot and his fellow denies it, saying, "No, she'll hunt."[10] Both kinds of mounted pursuit may be called the chase, as was also a private game preserve large enough for enjoying them. Only the landed well-to-do could afford the many servants, horses, scores of hounds, hundreds of deer, appertaining facilities, and the extensive hunting rights required by this royal sport. The Queen spent far more on her hunting establishment than on her Office of Revels.

Coursing was the less complicated kind of horse and hound hunting. One or more dog varlets on foot accompanied the courser, each leading a brace or leash of greyhounds, swift, keen-sighted dogs. When a suitable hart or buck was located and started, they slipped the greyhounds, and the courser tried to be on hand to kill the animal when the greyhounds caught it. References to horses and the crossbow—or "bent" bow—indicate coursing. Since the courser usually shot the animal held by his greyhounds, he carried his crossbow "bent," i.e. with the string levered back against the powerful steel bow and cocked, ready to discharge the bolt. In contrast, the English longbow, which was bent only in the act of aiming and shooting, could not be effectively handled by a horseman.

A detail in Benozzo Gozzoli's "The Journey of the Magi to Jerusalem" shows a lance-carrying rider pursuing a large red-deer hind, seasonable at that time of year. The dog varlet has just slipped his leash of three greyhounds. Although it was painted about 1460, the detail gives us an easily looked-up picture of this sport if we imagine for the lance a more likely sword or crossbow.[11] In *As You Like It,* however, only the stag's tears "Cours'd one another down his innocent nose / In piteous chase" (2.1.39-40).

A stereotype of the criticism holds that, as R. P. Draper (1958) puts it, the play is concerned with "an ideally leisured existence which gives men and women the opportunity to enjoy life." Are we, then, to picture the refugees passing the days mindlessly chasing the deer? The commentators have given so little analysis to this question that the New Variorum Edition (1977) has no index entry for hunting. In recent years, Marco Mincoff has announced as if it were self-evident that "the picture develops rather on the background of the Elizabethan chase than on the Robin Hood ballads." Madeleine Doran assures us that Duke Senior's "companions find hunting and rough weather at least temporarily attractive," intimating a party of wealthy sportsmen roughing it in the backwoods. Speaking of Jaques' lament for the wounded deer, Claus Uhlig opines that "In *As You Like It* as a whole this characteristically Shakespearean assimilation of the humanistic *topos* investigated [the cruelty of hunting], serves, especially since hunting belongs to the trifling pastimes of courtiers, to accentuate strongly the criticism of courtly life which pervades the play and is explicitly formulated by the banished duke (2.1.1-8)."[12] For our present purpose, Judy Z. Kronenfeld excellently states this position and some of its interpretative consequences. Along the way, an uneasy sense of an ambiguity amounting to artistic incompatibility reveals itself.

Outside a specifically pastoral setting, hunting is a way to turn a noble's "banishment" into holiday "liberty" (1.3.138). For this reason, the Duke's remarks about hunting, seen in a specifically pastoral context, seem to point to a discrepancy between the social idealism of pastoral (which opposes hunting) and the reality of privilege (which licenses it). It is true that Robin Hood, the hunter who champions the poor, becomes a pastoral figure in Renaissance literature, but his hunting is surely in part a matter of *denying* noble privilege. In Arden hunting seems not clearly a necessity (in which case it might be excused), for fruit and wine are apparently available (2.6[7]. 98; 2.5.32). So it seems quite likely that Shakespeare is mildly questioning the Duke's position. And if this genuine questioning is muted by the self-indulgent sentimentality of Jaques' anti-hunting sentiments, it is still important to remember that hunting is a specifically non-pastoral activity—the prototype of the exploitation of man by man and of war, and unknown in the vegetarian and communal Golden Age. . . . Thus the Duke enters into an exploitative relation with the forest—a relation to which our attention is called—by engaging in the specifically noble leisure-time sport of hunting, which is traditionally opposed to the peaceful activities of shepherds who live in harmony with nature.[13]

This discourse poses the critical points to be examined here. To begin with, the "specifically noble leisure-time sport of hunting" has been understood for centuries as being above all the chase or hunt at force. This is the noble sport that Robert Langham praises for being "incomparable."[14] The author of *Turbervile's Booke of Hunting (1576)* announces that "I thinke meete likewise to instruct (according to my simple skill) the huntsmen on horseback how to *chase and hunte an Harte at force*." (My emphasis.) He several times reminds his reader of this aim. Although a fallow deer (the species described in *As You Like It*) might be chased, it was, the author points out, "the hart, the whiche is the right chace to yeeld pleasure unto Kyngs and Princes."[15] By a hunt at force (French, *à force;* cf. Chaucer, slee with strengthe) Turbervile's readers understood the pursuit of a deer by a party of horsemen and auxiliaries with as many as fifty or more scenting-hounds across, usually, miles of country open enough for their passage.

In his unfinished play, *The Sad Shepherd,* Ben Jonson has Robin Hood's woodmen put on (surprisingly) a hunt at force "to kill him venison" for a June feast. The interest to us here is the compression into the dialogue of Scenes 2 and 6 of Act 1 of an epitome—a useful cram—of the textbook stages and technical vocabulary of such a hunt, from the harboring and rousing of the stag to breaking it up and rewarding the hounds and raven. The game is not only a warrantable stag, a hart of ten, but a big wily one which runs for "five hours and more," a heroic hunt.

It is apparent that this sport partook of elements of a cavalry terrain exercise, and Elizabethans emphasized its value in providing the nobility and gentry with an exciting schooling in cavalry techniques. Indeed, the sport had been considered for centuries as a mimic war, hence a recreation of merit, a duty in fact, for princes and noblemen. Thus Thomas Dekker explains in some detail that "hunting is a noble, a manly, and a healthful exercise; it is a very true picture of warre, nay it is a war in itself."[16]

In 1599, the year that *As You Like It* was perhaps first presented, James VI of Scotland, advising his heir about suitable physical exercises, writes, "I cannot omit heere the hunting, namelye with running houndes; which is the moste honourable and noblest sorte thereof," and he deprecates the rival sport of hawking partly "because it neither resembleth the warres as neere as hunting dothe, in making a man hardy, and skilfully ridden in all groundes."[17] Near the end of the era, Henry Peacham cites the opinion of Eusebius "that wilde beasts were of purpose created by God, that men by chasing and encountring them, might be fitted and enabled for warlike exercises."[18] Not surprisingly it is the logical source of some of Shakespeare's metaphors for the exigencies of battle. His Forest of Arden was good country for the chase and the hunt at force.

In *Poly-Olbion* Michael Drayton describes a hunt at force as a representative feature of the Forest of Arden. He devotes seventy-five lines, "Song 13," 87-161, to a vigorous sketch of a "most princely chase" with its troop of huntsmen, horses, and hounds streaming across the Arden landscapes and raising a bedlam of shouts, horn blasts, and barking as they follow "the noble deer" over pasture and ploughland, through herds and hamlets. Such a hunt began by first light, as noted in the plays, when the lord of the hunt had singled out one of the warrantable stags located by the woodman. Once laid on, the hunt might run across country for many miles before it caught up with the deer; despite his ruses, the animal probably rarely escaped from the "piteous chase" unless night fall intervened. With his "legs then fayling him at length" (140), the beast tried in his simple, instinctive way to find a place favorable for defending himself with his antlers against "The cruell ravenous hounds and bloody hunters neere" (151), e.g., "Some banke or quick-set" (153) to back into, or a pond or river where deep water would hamper the hounds.[19]

"Such," marvels Turberville, "is the benefite of nature to give the dumbe beast understanding which way to help himself . . . and to save its selfe by all meanes possible."[20] As the stag took his forlorn stand "in such a desperate bay of death" (*R3*, 4.4.233), the "bloody hounds with heads of steel" (*1H6*, 4.2.51) closed in clamoring, and he was quickly "bay'd about with many enemies" (*JC*, 4.1.49). Then a hunter dismounted, crept upon the distracted creature and cut its throat, or stabbed it to the heart, the horns winding "the mort o' th' deer" (*WT*, 1.2.118). Beholding dead Caesar, Antony recalls such a scene: "Here wast thou bay'd, brave hart, / Here did thou fall, and here thy hunters stand, / Sign'd in thy spoil, and crimson'd in thy lethe" (*JC*, 3.1.204-6). After that they field-dressed the carcass and awarded the "fees" to hounds and hunters according to longstanding practice.[21]

If Shakespeare had intended the audience to blame Duke Senior's party for an excessive indulgence in the chase for no better excuse than their sport, he could have made it known easily and forcefully. On the contrary, he does nothing of the kind. The dialogue avoids mention of any of the unmistakable features of the chase. The beasts are fallow, not red deer. We hear nothing of huntsmen, horns, horses, or hounds. Terms of the chase such as emboss or bay, which Shakespeare uses elsewhere, appear in this play only in their respective medical and geographic senses. Above all, apart from the argument of silence, the sport is, or was, ruled out by its glaring implausibility.

In this connection, it is to be remembered that a great many Elizabethans from the Queen to the ploughman understood the facts of hunting and shooting. Participation in, not to mention observation of, hunting at force, coursing with greyhounds, and shooting driven deer from stands was common enough for a citizen of London, one like Thomas Lodge the son of a Lord Mayor, to enjoy all three pastimes. In *Letters Written by John Chamberlain During the Reign of Queen Elizabeth*, ed. Sarah Williams, Camden Society ser. 1, no. 79 (1861; rpt New York: Johnson Reprint, 1968), pp. 114 and 150, Chamberlain reports from Ascot, 13 August 1601, that at Beckley Park "we coursed, and killed, and carried nothing away," and at Woodstock "last weeke" had great sport bow shooting, presumably from a stand at driven deer. It must have been a real battue: he likens the volume of shooting to a soldiers' skirmish. Then, a year later, on 2 October, he mentions having been in at the chase of a huge stag "which we hunted at force" over two counties.

The many people familiar with the chase would hardly have imagined that a deposed duke hiding in the woods of a "desert inaccessible" with a few fellow exiles "whose lands and revenues enrich the new Duke" (1.1.102), fugitives who have left their "wealth and ease" (2.5.52) to play in "a woeful pageant" (2.7.138), could have got together the large number of expensive, delicate animals, a retinue of foresters and woodmen, grooms and farriers, stable boys and dog varlets, with carters, butchers, and others, and constructed for them necessary stables, kennels, courts, offices, and lodgings. One did not winter horses on picket lines or bed greyhounds and basset hounds in the rain and snow. In that connection, the Duke would need a number of kennels for the scores of dogs required to enjoy a holiday of several hunts a week, each kennel "a little house or lodge, with a spacious and large chimney in the same, wherein in the wintertime you shal allow fire, before which your dogs returned from hunting may stretch, pick, dry, and trim themselues."[22] The dog varlet lodged on the second floor of his charges' kennel. One does not seriously think that the noble proprietors would have returned from a wintry hunt to crouch in a cave, or that they "endur'd shrewd days and nights" (5.4.173) in woodland hovels. Surely their foresters or dog varlets would have taken them in.

On the grounds of silence and verisimilitude, we may dismiss the speculation of any specific leisure-time indulgence in the chase or hunt at force. The elimination of hunting on horseback now leaves deer shooting to be considered as the method.

Before the different ways of shooting deer are explained, it is useful to understand that they were not classed with the noble form of the chase or hunting at force. In Tudor opinion, the shooting methods had come to be tainted with crass utilitarianism. Elyot writes that, "Killing of deer with bows or greyhounds serveth well for the pot (as is the common saying), and there it must of necessity be sometimes used. But it containeth therein no commendable solace or exercise, in comparison to other forms of hunting, if it be diligently perceived."[23] Turberville simply ignores shooting. In the *Basilikon Doron,* James warns his heir that "it is a thievish forme of hunting to shoote with gunnes and bowes."[24] In Ben Jonson's *The Gipsies Metamorphosed,* Part I, lines 215-18, the Captain compliments James for being one who loves "a horse and a hound," and "hunt[s] the brave stag not so much for your food, / As for the weal of your body and the health of your blood." William Harrison had reported that the sale of venison by aristocrats excited strong popular disapproval, "infinite scoffes and mockes, euen of the poorest pezzants of the countrie, who thinke them as odious matters," being one of "such like affaires as belong not to men of honor."[25] Peacham, in turn, cites for his young gentleman reader the example of ancient kings who hunted "not to purchase Venison and purvey for the belly, but to maintain their strength, and preserve their health" (218).

One form of shooting, as will be seen, was certainly a pastime for princes and noble persons, but evidently not a noble pastime in the same sense as the chase. Today, Americans who kill deer for meat and by-products do not think of their activity as primarily a sport,[26] and apparently neither did the Elizabethans. The realization of this attitude toward pot hunting gives distinctive connotations to Duke Senior's command, "Come, shall we go and kill us venison?" (2.1.21), meanings that help us to understand the significance of the deer shooting in *As You Like It*. It is not a matter of noble sport; the Robin Hood type was not a sportsman but a survivor. He killed to eat.

For investigating the subject of shooting deer, two basic means remain to be considered. In one, stand-and-bow shooting, the shooter took a partially screened position ("stand") in or near a bush where he had unobstructed aim at any animal passing him at close range. The Elizabethans used this arrangement in two very different ways. One I shall explain later, the other provided a fashionable, even spectacular entertainment for grand personages, especially women of high rank and eminent men who had passed their physical prime. In such events, the host's woodmen drove selected deer along a killing ground in front of the stands. Since some of the animals would be wounded rather than killed outright, foresters with greyhounds, and sometimes bloodhounds, stood by to run down and dispatch them. In order to regulate the drive and supervise the shooting, stand-and-bow entertainments took place in a large park, which was by definition enclosed with a "pale" or fence designed to confine herds of deer kept for meat and recreation and managed by the estate forester. The identifying details of such an amusement, put on in a royal park for the visiting Princess of France, are carefully mentioned in *Love's Labors Lost*. An elaborate one had been given for Queen Elizabeth in August, 1591, by Lord Montacute in his park at Cowdray where refreshments were served to the spectators and musicians played while the Queen shot deer with a crossbow presented to her by a Nymph singing a ditty.[27]

Almost exactly one year later, two days of shooting were arranged for the heir to the Duchy of Württemberg, Count Frederick Mompelgard, at Windsor Castle, where, his secretary relates, "there are upwards of sixty parks . . . so contiguous that in order to have a glorious and royal sport the animals can be driven out of one enclosure into another, and so on; all which enclosures are encompassed by fences." While no such shooting occurs in *As You Like It*, it does illustrate matters of interest in the play. The secretary's narrative continues:

> And thus it happened: the huntsmen who had been ordered for the occasion, and who live in splendid separate lodges in these parks, made some capital sport for his Highness. In the first enclosure his Highness shot off the leg of a fallow-deer, and the dogs soon after caught the animal. In the second, they chased a stag for a long time backwards and forwards with particularly good hounds, over an extensive and delightful plain; at length his Highness shot him in front with an English cross-bow, and this deer the dogs finally worried and caught. In the third the greyhounds chased a deer, but much too soon [cf. *1H4,* 1.3. 178, "Before the game is afoot, Thou still let'st slip."] for they caught it directly. . . .
>
> [Two days later], August 21st, . . . his Highness shot two fallow deer, one with a gun, the other with an English cross-bow; the latter deer we were obliged to follow a very long while, until at length a stray track- or blood-hound, as they are called, by its wonderful and peculiar nature, singled out the deer from several hundred others and pursued it so long, till at last the wounded deer was found on one side of a brook [cf. *AYL,* 2.1. 33, 35, "To which place a poor sequest'red stag . . . Did come to languish"] and the dog quite exhausted on the other [cf. *Shr.,* Ind. 1.17, "(Brach Merriman, the poor cur, is emboss'd)"]; and the stag, which could go no further, was taken by the huntsmen, and the hound feasted with its blood.[28]

In passing one notes that this historical example suggests contemporary realities behind some of Shakespeare's hunting images. For example, when Talbot realizes that he and his troops have been trapped by superior French forces, the park hunt metaphor defines his predicament exactly: "How are we park'd and bounded in a pale, / A little herd of England's timorous deer, / Maz'd with a yelping kennel of French curs!" (*1H6,* 4.2.45-47). More particularly, perhaps, we can see what the Princess of France had in mind when, taking her shooting stand, she said, "But come, the bow: now mercy goes to kill . . . Not wounding, pity would not let me do it" (*LLL,* 4.1.24, 26).

More directly to our subject, these examples suggest some of the reasons why it irks the Duke that the deer of "this desert city / should in their own confines, with forked heads / Have their round haunches gored" (*AYL*, 2.1.23-25). First, his "native burghers" are not captive park deer, such as we have just seen, but free wild animals, the ferae naturae that live under God and the sovereign "In their assign'd and native dwelling place" (63) in keeping with the divine dispensation (a text for this concept was Job 39:1-8). Second, a quick, clean kill largely depended on the physical fitness and skill of the archer. The preferred target was, and is, the heart-region seen broadside, but the cervine's slim, narrow conformation makes this small target just behind the foreshoulder difficult to hit. The other vital areas, the neck and the upper part of the head, present a small and restless mark. These well-known facts lie behind shooting exploits in romance and ballad, as well as incidents in the plays. Thus Robyn makes the perfect shot when he and Gandelayn go to the wood to get them meat: "Robyn bent hys joly bowe; / Therein he set a flo [arrow]. / The fattest der of alle / The herte he clef a to." Again, the poacher-poet of the Prologue of *The Parliament of the Three Ages* (ca. 1350) illustrates the well-known fact that even a fatally wounded deer may still run for some distance before it falls, even though the shot had "the herte smote, / And happenyd that I hitt hym by hynde the lefte scholdire" (53-54), i.e., the preferred point of aim.[29]

In Lodge's romance, Rosalynde comforts Rosader with the thought that wounded game sometimes escapes, saying, "What newes Forrester? hast thou wounded some deere, and lost him in the falle? . . . 'Tis hunters lucke, to ayme faire and misse: and a woodmans fortune to strike and yet goe without the game."[30] The shot in the rump that Duke Senior speaks of, however, has not only that but other disturbing consequences. He would be further irked for reasons made clear by William F. Hollister, a wildlife biologist and bowhunter: "A rump or rear end shot is undoubtedly one of the worst that can be taken by an archer. Most modern bowhunters with any ethics and concern for the animal will pass up a rump shot. The likely effect on a deer hit with an arrow in [the] rump would more than likely result in a flesh wound in the 'hams'. If, however, the arrow passes through the 'hams' into the intestines and paunch the chances are that animal will die a lingering death."[31] (Cf. *AYL* 2.1.33-37).

In the dramatic situation, a bad hit resulting in the animal's escape (such as is reported by the First Lord), means the loss of a hundred pounds or more of food, and even if the carcass be recovered, the haunch, which was esteemed to be the choice cut, may be totally spoiled. In *As You Like It*, "to strike and yet goe without the game" means a calamity. Even though hunting for belly cheer may be demeaning and irksome to a nobleman, the refugees in the Forest of Arden face starvation, and therefore in the play's given circumstances hunting is as natural and needful as it had been for millennia of human existence. Moreover, an attentive reading or auditing of the play, especially of Act 2, confutes the opinion that "alfresco meals are abundantly provided . . . and there is no worse hardship than a salubrious winter wind,"[32] or, in the criticism quoted above, that "In Arden hunting seems not clearly a necessity (in which case it might be excused), for fruit and wine are apparently available (2.6.98; 2.5.32)." On the contrary, hardships crowd Act 2, including affliction by unsalubrious winds both winter and summer (2.1.7; 5.8; 6.15; 7.174). Shakespeare stresses afflictions in Act 2, but one above all, and that is hunger. Because of the persistent denial of these dark facts, it seems appropriate to state the record of hunger that colors Act 2.

> 2.1.21. Come, shall we go and kill us venison?
> 2.3.31. What, wouldst thou have me go and beg my food?
> 2.3.43-45. Take that, and He that doth the ravens feed, / Yea, providently caters for the sparrow, / Be comfort to my age! (Biblical allusions; Job 39.3 [Geneva; A.V., 38.41], Ps. 147.9, Matt. 10.29 and Luke 12.6, 24.)
> 2.4.64-66. . . . question yond man, / If he for gold will give us any food; / I faint almost to death. (This distress is Shakespeare's addition; in Lodge, they have food.)
> 2.4.73. Bring us where we may rest ourselves and feed.
> 2.4.80-83. My master is of churlish disposition, / And little reaks to find the way to heaven / By doing deeds of hospitality. (Allusions are seen to 1 Sam. 25, and, of course, to Matt. 25.31ff.)
> 2.4.85-86. . . . there is nothing / That you will feed on; but what is, come see, . . .[33]
> 2.5.31-32. Sirs, cover the while; the Duke will drink under this tree.
> 2.5.39-41. [Who] loves to live i' th' sun, / Seeking the food he eats, / And pleas'd with what he gets. . . .[34]
> 2.5.62. And I'll go seek the Duke; his banket is prepar'd.
> 2.6.1-2. Dear master, I can go no further. O, I die for food!
> 2.6.16-18. . . . thou shalt not die for lack of a dinner if there live anything in this desert. (And more, but no thought of fruit!)
> 2.7.88, 89. Forbear, and eat no more . . . till necessity be serv'd.
> 2.7.105. I almost die for food, and let me have it.
> 2.7.128-29. Whiles, like a doe, I go to find my fawn, / And give it food.[35]
> 2.7.129, 132. There is an old poor man . . . / Oppress'd with two weak evils, age and hunger . . .
> 2.7.171. Welcome, fall to . . .

All but one, then, of the seven scenes of Act 2 feature hunger and food, a dramatic fact quite disregarded by the commentators. Yet, as the Duke makes clear at the outset, in the woods one lives not only in hardship, but also in peril. It may be morally commendable to take refuge there from ambition, but it is a risky place to seek one's food. The Duke's opinion has corroboration.

In a possible source, Anthony Munday's *The Downfall of Robert Earl of Huntington,* The Malone Society Reprints (1601; Oxford: Oxford Univ. Press, 1964), 1. 670, Prince John succinctly describes the outlawed earl as "The banisht, beggerd, bankrupt Huntington." When outlawed Fitzwater, "An aged man . . . Neere pin'd with hunger," happens upon Maid Marian in the forest, she gives him wine, venison, and "a manchet fine." He is welcomed like Adam (ll. 1517-27). Writing from experience, Spenser pictures the fate of the outcast Irish: "Out of every corner of the woods and glens they came creeping forth upon their hands, for their legs could not bear them; they looked like anatomies of death." When Spenser's vagrant Ape and Fox had "long straied . . . / Through everie field and forrest farre and nere," they too "almost sterv'd."[36] The Fox could hardly walk. In a famous scene, *2 Henry VI*, 4.10, Jack Cade too illustrates the fate of one who fled to the woods ("Fie on ambitions"), where he fruitlessly sought meat for five days, when, weak and desperate for food, rather like Orlando, he draws upon Alexander Iden, who kills him.

The great dearth of the late nineties would have made hunger of concern (the noted poor relief statute had passed Parliament in 1597). Furthermore, Elizabethans could respond to the subject with a considerable empirical knowledge of diet—Adam gives a brief example in scene 3. Jaques' simile of the "remainder biscuit" (2.7.39) and his jibe about the marriage "but for two months victuall'd" (5.4.183) were not lost on them. They understood that people living north of fifty degrees latitude like themselves need a high energy intake, and the civil and military authorities and the masters and mistresses of large households and holdings gave feeding frequent attention. The protein-rich field rations prescribed for the Queen's troops represent contemporary thinking.[37]

The commander of an isolated party forced to seek the food they eat would be eager to get protein-rich fresh venison, in Palamon's accurate phrase "lusty meat" (*TNK*, 3.3.27). Moreover, three literary analogues clarify for us the Duke's situation in these respects. In the source, *Rosalynde*, the exiled King of France and his outlaws, "frolikt it with store of wine and venison," with which they feed Rosader and old Adam. Later these two refresh Saladyne with "A peece of red Deere . . . and a bottle of wine. Tis Forresters fare brother, quoth Rosader: and so they sate downe and fell to their cates."[38] The analogue in the source behind *Rosalynde*, the romance of *Gamelyn*, comes closer when Gamelyn tells the outlaw king that he and Adam Spenser are seeking their food "under woode-shawes:"

> He moste needes walke in woode   that may not walke in toune.
> Sire, we walke not heer   noon harm for to do,
> But if we meete with a deer   to sheete thereto
> As men that been hungry   and mow no mete find
> And been harde bistad   under woode-linde.
>
> (Lines 672-76)

They are then bid to sit and eat of the outlaws' repast.[39] Third, *Cymbeline*, a later play (about 1610) yet one which resembles *As You Like It* with its deerhunting cave dwellers, who "are held as outlaws" (4.2.67, 138), a starving fugitive from the court and wilderness setting, presents a Shakespearean analogue with the deer hunting in Arden.

In straitened circumstances similar to those in the Forest of Arden, Belarius and the royal youths can kill deer in two ways only. One is the kind of stand-and-bow shooting that I have not yet described, often called still hunting nowadays, i.e., remaining quietly in concealment in a stand beside a deer run in order to ambush passing game. Sometimes a partner of the shooter tries to drive a deer to within range of the stand. An example occurs in *3 Henry VI*, 3.1 where two keepers discuss the arrangements. The other way is stalking, i.e. working stealthily into close bowshot range without alarming the extremely wary beast; stalking is the demanding art of the "best woodman," the tribute awarded Guiderius. Even after the adoption of the long-range rifle for Highland stalking, a Victorian authority described the successful practitioner as a superior type of man: "The *model* deer-stalker . . . should be of good proportions, moderately tall, narrow-hipped to give speed, and with powerful loins and well-developed chest for giving endurance and wind . . . He . . . should care neither for fatigue, nor cold, nor wet. . . . The bodily powers are not the only ones which should be well developed, for the brain should be as active and energetic as the body itself."[40] And somewhat more. A man who could fence, wrestle, and pull the powerful long bow must have possessed similar physical qualities.

In any case, physical exertion gets attention in *Cymbeline*, which excludes hunting on horseback and mentions no dog. They start out at dawn (3.3.4, 7) when Belarius orders Guiderius and Arviragus, "Now for our mountain sport: up to yond hill, / Your legs are young" (10-11), and they return with their deer (75) "thoroughly weary" and "weak with toil" (3.6.36-37) to cook their "meat" (38-39), i.e. venison. Here, again, hunting means no trifling noble pastime, but an arduous pursuit of food, on foot with the bow and arrow in the usual way of banished men, outlaws, poachers, and others who "live i' th' sun."

With their assumptions of pothunting and feeding on venison, all three analogues assume the hunters' charity. "If that he be heende and come of gentil blood," Gamelyn asserts of the outlaw's king, "He woll yeve us mete and drink and doon us some good" (663-64). Moreover, being of "gentil blood," a true aristocrat, and even more, a prince, was especially inclined to mercy because, unlike a churl, he was graced with a piteous heart, i.e. the capacity for "sacred pity" (2.7.123) which the Duke exemplifies.[41]

A historical analogue occurs in a book that Shakespeare probably had read, *The New Chronicles of England and France* by Robert Fabyan where, in Capitulum Clxxii, Alfred ("Alured") the Great's charity to an old religious man changes his fortunes. Several close parallels between the circumstances of Alfred and Duke Senior are seen.

> Alured, being thus overset in multytude of enemyes, as affermeth Policronica and other, ladde an uncertayne lyfe, and uneasy, with fewe folkes aboute hym, in the

wode countree . . . and had ryght scante to lyve with, but suche as he & his people myght purchase by huntynge and fysshynge. [In whiche mysery, he thus by a certayne of tyme contynuynge, . . . Upon a tyme when his company was from hym departed and besyed in purchasynge of vytayle, . . . a pylgryme . . . requyred his almes in Goddes name . . . Then the kynge anone called his servant, that hadde but one lofe and a lytell whatte of wyne, and bad hym gyve the halfe thereof unto the poore man: . . . Shortly after his company retourned to theyr maister, and brought with theym great plenty of fysshe that they hadde than taken. . . .]

That night, in a vision, St. Cuthbert reveals himself as the pilgrim and promises Alfred victory over the Danes. "Than Alured, after this vysyon, was well comforted, & shewyd hym more at large. So . . . dayly resorted to hym men . . . tyll . . . he was strongly companyed."[42]

The uncertain, uneasy life of King Alfred and his few followers in the wooded country gives a good idea of that of Duke Senior, for he too would have "ryght scante to lyue with, but suche as he & his people myght purchase by huntynge and fysshynge." Shakespeare makes abundantly clear in Acts 1 and 2 the impoverishment of the exiles and Orlando and Rosalind by the tyrants' confiscations and embezzlements (1.1.38-39, 102-4; 2.245-47; 3.65; 2.3.31; 5.52). Like the banished men and other fugitives in the sources and analogues examined here, the Duke's men suffer deprivation which forces them to seek their living in the sun like the outlaws idealized in "old Robin Hood of England." In consequence they give not out of superfluity but out of exiguity.

Presumably the scattered references in 2.7 to the "banket" bill of fare pointed to food-simulating properties to be seen on the stage by the audience. In any case, only fruit is named (98), probably indicating local bush berries. In the circumstances, however, it would be a mistake not to overlook its significance as an attribute of personified Misery, for "His food, for most, was wild fruits of the tree," Thomas Sackville tells us in The Induction of *A Mirror for Magistrates* (line 260).[43] Apart from fruit, the operative words are simply feed, food, and table. The dialogue supports two conclusions about the banket. First, food can hardly be abundant because the suppliant can only be offered "what help we have" (125), i.e., to the extent available to us. This implication is confirmed when the Duke assures Orlando, leaving to bring back Adam, "We will nothing waste till you return" (134). Second, while their food may be scanty, it must be substantial enough to revive the weak old man. "Let him feed," urges their host, and "fall to," expressions that suggest fare more substantial than, say, a bowl of berries. It seems logical that a cut of venison served as the expected pièce de résistance of the outlaws' woodland banket in the play as in the romances and Munday's Robin Hood plays.

We can conclude that they kill venison in *As You Like It* not for pastime but for food, and like woodmen or outlaws do so by shooting with the bow—probably the old-fashioned English longbow. Apart from Rosalind's "Love's keen arrows" (3.5.31), Celia mentions Orlando's bow and arrows (4.3.4) and Duke Senior speaks of wounding deer with the forked-head model (2.1.24). The deer that languishes by the brook has been shot, not chased. Moreover, Duke Senior has game shooting in mind when he remarks that Touchstone "uses his folly like a stalking-horse, and under the presentation of that he shoots his wit" (5.4.106-7). These outlaws shoot not for themselves alone, but for the common table of the band. Because for centuries hunters had shared their venison, they could typify on the stage one of the most distinctive human traits, the sharing of food.[44] The idea underlies Act 4, Scene 2, where the successful hunter's kill will be taken to the base camp to the Duke, who *has not been with the party at all*! Critics who accuse the Duke of indulgence in trifling pastime have not explained his absence from the deer kill.

The idea of hunting in *As You Like It* is to dramatize, first of all, the plight of the noble exiles. The particulars given us prevent our mistakenly supposing that they are carelessly passing the time in a happy, hunting holiday. In contrast, the introduction of the chase as their trifling pastime amidst an idyllic pastoral setting would be to trivialize and even falsify what began as a conflict of the virtuous and the loyal with the worldly unjust and capricious fortune. The first Act solidly establishes the reality of that evil and raises the issue of its remedy. To digress from this challenge into pastoral entertainments and anti-hunting topoi would be an artistically unjustifiable evasion of the dramatic issue that has been posed.

Presenting the deposed Duke and his loving lords as seeking their food with bows and arrows shows them reduced to means of survival that are both primitive and storied. Thus they identify with those outlaws in the analogues who "moste needes walke in woode that may not walke in toune," and so become "hard bistad under woode-linde." In the uncouth forest underneath the shade of melancholy boughs, they exist by their skill at pothunting. In addition to effecting this controlling circumstance, the idea of their hunting is to make clear the altruism of their sharing their scanty fare with Orlando and old Adam.

The idea of hunting makes other contributions to the play, of course, one being its rich allusiveness and symbolism.[45] But perhaps the essential idea flowers in Act 2, Scene 7 in the stage image of banished men, like outlaws and foresters, who, far from good men's feasts and where all things seem savage, welcome to their table two fellow players in this world's woeful pageant.

Notes

1. "Preface 1763," in *Johnson on Shakespeare,* ed. Arthur Sherbo, The Yale Edition of the Works of Samuel Johnson, vol. 7 (New Haven: Yale Univ. Press, 1968), 86.

2. My citations of Shakespeare are to *The Riverside Shakespeare,* gen. ed. G. Blakemore Evans (Boston: Houghton Mifflin, 1947).

3. I discuss the pattern of hunting language in 2.1 (which determines the time of year and the species of deer) in "The Midsummer Deer of *As You Like It,* 2.1," *Philological Quarterly,* 58 (1979), 103-7.

4. With reference to Rosalind's "martial outside," cf. *Faerie Queene,* 4.2.42.9, "But speare and curtaxe both used Priamond in field." Her weapons suggest a strong, tall girl. For the spear as an attribute see Adolf Katzenellenbogen, *Allegories of the Virtues and Vices in Medieval Art,* trans. Alan J. P. Crick (1939; rpt New York: W. W. Norton, 1964), 55. For boar and spear, James Hall, *Dictionary of Subjects and Symbols in Art* (New York: Harper & Row, 1974), 49, 247, 288; Guy de Tervarent, *Attributs et Symboles dans l'art profane 1450-1600* (Geneva: Libraire E. Droz, 1958): Minerva carries a *hallbarde,* col. 208, or a *javelot,* col. 224, as does Philosophy and, col. 225, Diana; also see *lance,* col. 230; and, col. 335, *Sanglier,* "Symbole ou Attribut de la Luxure." Cf. Spenser's Sir Sanglier, the "wild boar." Also, on boar symbolism, Beryl Rowland, *Animals with Human Faces* (Knoxville: Univ. of Tennessee, 1973), 38, and Marcelle Thiébaux, "The Mouth of the Boar as a Symbol in Medieval Literature," *Romance Philology,* 22 (1969), 296-98. Ovid's Salmacis, a type of narcissistic lethargy, takes no hunting spear nor does she vary her ease with the hardships of the hunt. Hunting found approval as an antidote to sinful idleness.

5. Furthermore, Diana has a proprietary connection with the Forest of Arden; she and Apollo were patron deities of Britain (cf. the oaths by Apollo, *Lr.* 1.1.160). As Diana Nemorensis, or surnamed Arden, the huntress goddess presides over the Forest of Arden, which is above all not a pastoral but a hunting ground. These associations duly appear in Michael Drayton's *Poly-Olbion,* where a nymph with a bow and arrows adorns the map of Warwickshire.

6. The *chace du connin* provided a classical hunting metaphor. Thus in the thirteenth century, with Ovid in mind, Jean de Meun speaks of his narrative as a "rabbit hunt" (ch. 81); see John V. Fleming, *The Roman de la Rose: A Study in Allegory and Iconography* (Princeton: Princeton Univ. Press, 1969), 186. D. W. Robertson, Jr., *A Preface to Chaucer* (Princeton: Princeton Univ. Press, 1970) explains this familiar medieval "hunt of Venus," 113, 263-64, and passim. Rosalind, in character, prefers the virtuous hunt of Diana. B. G. Koonce, *Chaucer and the Tradition of Fame* (Princeton: Princeton Univ. Press, 1966), 111, n. 46, cites references including the Ovidian source. Marta Powell Harley, "Rosalind, the Hare, and the Hyena in Shakespeare's *As You Like It,*" *Shakespeare Quarterly,* 36 (1985), 335-37, arguing in part belief in the bisexuality of hares, relates the allusion to a latent "theme of homosexuality" (337) in the play. Actual hare hunting, coursing on horseback with greyhounds, was a popular upper-class recreation recommended for gentlewomen.

7. For the Duke's tracking hounds, slow goers with a true nose and a musical voice, see Henry L. Savage, "Hunting in the Middle Ages," *Speculum,* 8 (1933), 36 (the Old Southern Hound or an allied type); C. P. Onions, ed., *Shakespeare's England* (Oxford: Clarendon Press, 1917), II, 347 (bassets); Sacheverell Sitwell, *The Hunters and the Hunted* (New York: Macmillan, 1948), 74 (bassets); and D. H. Madden, *The Diary of Master William Silence,* new ed. (London: Longmans, Green, 1907), 47, 59, 78.

8. An early morning start adapts to the animal's habits; it often enabled the hunt to avoid the fatigues caused by the heat of the day. (Late hunts were shortened by being confined, as to a park.) The foresters first located one or more warrantable stags in their covert ("harbouring") and presented the "tokens" of the animals' age and size to the assembled hunt: then, one being selected, it was roused from cover, the scenting hounds loosed on its trail, and the hunt was off. *Turbervile's Booke of Hunting 1576,* Tudor & Stuart Library (Oxford: Clarendon Press, 1908) devotes much attention to these preliminaries. Also, *Shakespeare's England,* II, 335-36; Madden, ch. 2 and 3; Marcelle Thiébaux, *The Stag of Love: The Chase in Medieval Literature* (Ithaca: Cornell Univ. Press, 1974), 28-32. The early rising of foresters and hunters earned them admiring notice. On present-day practice, G. Kenneth Whitehead, *Hunting and Stalking Deer Throughout the World* (New York: St. Martin's Press, 1982), 16-17, reports that when deer are in open country and can be easily located, "the stalk and shot can be taken during the middle part of the day, even though most of the deer will probably be resting. In dense woodland habitat, however, the shot normally has to be taken when the deer are at feed or on the move, and this is only possible at dawn and dusk." Tudor bowmen would have followed much the same schedule, with a thought to saving daylight for the slow, arduous task of bringing in a heavy carcass unless they had a cart or pony for the purpose.

9. Michael Drayton gives an Elizabethan's impression of "that wondrous sport" of chasing the deer in the Forest of Arden in "Song 13" of his *Poly-Olbion,* and describes the occupation of a forester and the tools of his trade in *The Sixth Nymphal.* Edward, Second Duke of York, *The Master of Game,* ed. William A. and F. Baillie-Grohman (London: Chatto & Windus, 1909), apart from five original chapters, is York's translation (1406-1413) of Gaston de Foix, Comte de Foix, *Livre de Chasse* of which Savage says it "still remains unsupersded in its knowledge of the habits of European game and its insight into the nature of hounds" (31). Much information about deer hunting ca. 1500 can be found in Margaret B. Freeman, *The Unicorn Tapestries* (New York: E. P.

Dutton, 1976). Robert Langham (or Laneham) gives eye-witness accounts of the hunts put on for the Queen at the Kenilworth entertainments, 9-27 July 1575 in *A Letter,* ed. R. J. P. Kuin (Leiden: E. J. Brill, 1983). John Manwood, *A Treatise and Discourse of the Lawes of the Forrest* (London: Thomas Wight and Bonham Norton, 1598) deals with legal and managerial aspects contemporary with the play. T. R. Henn, *The Living Image* (London: Methuen, 1972) has useful background information, and G. Kenneth Whitehead surveys the subject in *Hunting and Stalking Deer in Britain Through the Ages* (London: B. T. Batsford, 1980). *Turbervile's Booke of Hunting 1576,* already cited, reprints the 1576 black-letter edition of George Turberville's *Noble Arte of Venerie or Hunting.* Although a study of German procedures, a valuable reference is David Dalby, *Lexicon of the Mediaeval German Hunt* (Berlin: Walter De Gruyter, 1965). Tudor writers emphasize the recreational and warlike benefits of pursuing deer with hounds and profess disdain for utilitarian pothunting—a distinction not always pragmatically evident.

10. Of modern usage Whitehead, *World,* 13, says, "In the United States of America and in many other countries, shooting—whether it be deer or birds—is generally referred to as 'hunting.' In Great Britain, however, the word 'hunting' is reserved for any sport that entails the use of hounds." Sixteenth-century English usage was less restrictive, yet hunting with horses and hounds is virtually the only subject of the early treatises, with regard to deer.

11. Coursers are seen in the foreground of a painting of the great hunting estate of Nonesuch Palace by David Vinckboens in the Fitzwilliam Museum, Cambridge.

12. Draper, Mincoff, and Doran are quoted from extracts of their criticism in *A New Variorum Edition of Shakespeare: As You Like It,* ed. Richard Knowles (New York: The Modern Language Association of America, 1977), 523, 524, and 525 respectively. This edition is cited hereafter as The New Variorum. Uhlig, "'The Sobbing Deer': *As You Like It,* 2.1.21-66 and the Historical Context," *Renaissance Drama,* NS 3 (1970), 103.

13. Judy Z. Kronenfeld, "Social Rank and the Pastoral Ideals of *As You Like It,*" *Shakespeare Quarterly,* 29, (1978), 338-39.

14. Robert Langham, 44-45, describes "the hunting of the Hart of fors," and asserts that "in mine opinion thear can be none [pastime] ony wey comparabl to this." For the Queen's ease that particular affair took place late in the day.

15. *Turbervile,* 109-10 and 9.

16. Thomas Dekker, *Lanthorne and Candlelight,* ch. 4, in *The Guls Hornbook and the Belman of London* (London: J. M. Dent & Sons, 1905), 209, and 210; the noblest hunters are those who chase the deer.

17. ΒΑΣΙΛΙΚΟΝ ΔΩΡΟΝ. *or His Majesties instructions to his Dearest Sonne, Henry the Prince* (1599; rpt. London, 1603), 121-22.

18. Henry Peacham, *Peacham's Compleat Gentleman 1634,* Tudor & Stuart Library (Oxford: Clarendon Press, 1906), 218.

19. Present-day versions of this sport exist in England and France. In his letter of 10 June 1986, Peter Atkinson, British Field Sports Society, informs me that, "Deer are still hunted with hounds in England as they have been for many centuries. There are three packs of staghounds all centred in and around Exmoor in the counties of Devon and Somerset, and they hunt the red deer. Bucks (male fallow) are hunted by the New Forest Buckhounds." He adds that, "The coursing of deer is no longer carried out in any form of organized way . . ." Whitehead, *World,* reports, "Hunting deer with horse and hound—*chasse á courre*—is still a very popular sport in France and more than eighty packs are actively hunting either stag or Roe buck—or both—throughout the country" (45).

20. The Tudor kill and that of the present-day English hunt seem to be significantly different. Atkinson states that, "The hunting of deer ends when the animal stands at bay. It is then shot either with a specifically adapted shotgun or a humane killer. The deer does not stand at bay when it is exhausted. It stands at bay when it discovers that [it cannot] escape the hounds. The hounds know that the deer is capable of putting up a robust defense and stand clear of it . . ." Drayton's huntsmen, however, run the animal to a standstill, when, like Actaeon's, their hounds lay "their cruell fangs on his harsh skin." Such an attack may be seen in sixteenth- and seventeenth-century paintings.

21. The ceremony of "breaking up" the deer and awarding customary portions to particular members of the hunting party, and the hounds, varied from place to place. *Turbervile,* 127ff, distinguishes between an English and a French procedure.

22. G[ervase] M[arkham], *Countrey Contentments* (1615), 14. Cf. *Shr.* Ind. I, 16, 28-29, where, after a severe run, the Lord gives orders for the recuperation of his pack—but the pack probably ought not to be run again "tomorrow."

23. Sir Thomas Elyot, *The Book Named the Governor,* ed. S. E. Lehmberg (London: Dent, 1962), 68.

24. The King's aversion (121) resembles that expressed by [Charles] Estienne and [Jean] Liebault, *Maison Rustique, or, The Countrey Farme,* trans. Thomas Surflet (1600), 837, i.e., "The hunting of fower footed beasts . . . is performed principally with dogs, horses, and strength of bodie," but the use of ropes, nets, and toils is "more fit for holidaie men,

milke sops, and cowards, then for men of valour, which delight more in the taking of such beastes, in respecte of the exercise of their bodie and pleasure, then for the filling of the bellie."

25. *Holinshed's Chronicles* (1807-1808; rpt. New York: AMS Press, 1965), I, 344.

26. On this attitude, see *White-tailed Deer Ecology and Management,* ed. Lowell K. Halls (Harrisburg, PA: Stackpole Books, 1984), 710. The Tudor upper-class feeling that for a gentleman pothunting is unbecoming contrasts with their ancestors' uninhibited slaughter of game for food, e.g. the drives cited in *Sir Gawain and the Green Knight* and *The Ballad of Chevy Chase.* In fact, the Elizabethans appear to have eaten the deer they killed, whatever the means. The nine hundred or so English game forests and parks had long been a major source of meat.

27. R. Warwick Bond, ed., *The Complete Works of John Lyly* (1902; rpt. Oxford: Vivien Ridler, 1967), I, 421-30. Also, E. K. Chambers, *The Elizabethan Stage* (Oxford: Clarendon Press, 1923), IV, 65. Madden somewhat digressively discusses the shooting from a stand, 226, 229-36. In Anthony Munday's *The Death of Robert Earl of Huntington,* the Queen Mother shoots "Mounted in a stand. / Six fallowe deere have dyed by her hand." See the Malone Society Reprint (Oxford: Univ. Press, 1965 [1967]), 11. 41-42. The men, with crossbows (13, 68-69), are coursing the stags and bucks.

28. Geoffrey Bullough, ed., *Narrative and Dramatic Sources of Shakespeare,* II, The Comedies 1597-1603 (London: Routledge and Kegan Paul, 1958), 47-48. The state of Württemberg had and continued to have good hunting; as late as 1914 grand-veneur was a Court post there as it still was in several royal households of Europe. Details in Lucas Cranach's painting, ca. 1529, "The Stag Hunt of the Elector Frederick the Wise" in the Kunsthistorisches Museum, Vienna, though on a lavish scale, might suggest typical features in the Count's hunting. The activities of the three potentates and their loaders, seen in the foreground, illustrate stand-and-bow shooting of the organized kind that Shakespeare presents in *LLL,* 4.1.

29. "Robyn and Gandelyn," *Middle English Literature,* ed. Charles W. Dunn and Edward T. Byrnes (New York: Harcourt, Brace, Jovanovich, 1973), 519, lines 20-23. Likewise, *The Parliament of the Three Ages,* 240.

30. *Rosalynde, Euphues Golden Legacie,* in Bullough, II, 200. Later, 215, Rosader shoots a deer "that but lightly hurt fled through the thicket." Also, in The New Variorum, 422, 437.

31. Principal Fish and Wildlife Biologist, Division of Fish & Wildlife, New York State Department of Environmental Conservation, letter to the author, 7 January 1986. In *Aeneid 7,* Ascanius looses exactly this "worse" shot, striking Silvia's pet stag through the paunch and the flank: perque uterum sonitu perque ilia venit harundo (499). The stricken deer flees and reaches its wonted shelter with fateful results. The Princess of France stresses the need to strike home, "Not wounding, pity would not let me do 't" (*LLL,* 4.1.27), and mutilated Lavinia, "Straying in the park, / Seeking to hide herself" is like "the deer / That hath receiv'd some unrecuring wound" (*Tit.* 3.1.88-90).

32. Harold Jenkins, "As You Like It," *Shakespeare Survey 8* (Cambridge: Univ. Press, 1968), 43. Since then, two editors who recognize the need to hunt food are Agnes Latham, *The Arden Shakespeare* (1975), lxix, and Roma Gill, *Oxford School Shakespeare* (1977). The latter observes that the duke "makes us aware that this life is not . . . the pastoral existence imagined by poets; in real life, men must eat meat, and they cannot do this without slaughtering the animals" (xvi). Whether Stoic storm or Adam's penalty, wind and winter are ancient symbols of human afflictions; they teach us to know ourselves.

33. Caroline Spurgeon, *Shakespeare's Imagery* (1935; rpt. Cambridge: Univ. Press, 1965), 119, finds that, "The number of food and taste similes in *As You Like It* is remarkable." Corin's apology reminds the audience of the laborer's unpalatable diet of black bread, bacon, beans, and peas with milk or whey and cheese, a fact behind Orlando's sarcasm, "He lets me feed with his hinds" (1.1.19). In the hungry years from 1595 to about 1599, it could have been worse. See Andrew B. Appleby, *Famine in Tudor and Stuart England* (Stanford: Stanford Univ. Press, 1978), 5-7, and J. C. Drummond and Anne Wilbraham, *The Englishman's Food,* rev. ed. (1939; rpt. London: Jonathan Cape, 1957), 48-54 and passim. The use of fruit and vegetables was negligible; scorbutic ailments were common. The dramatic point is that Corin, the good shepherd, represents charity here ("I pity her"). In contrast, Corin's absent master ignores the Queen's order of 2 November 1596 "to stay all good householders in their countries, there in charitable sort to keep hospitality" for relief of the poor; see Paul L. Hughes and James F. Larkin, *Tudor Royal Proclamations,* III (New Haven: Yale Univ. Press, 1969), 172.

34. New Cambridge Shakespeare (1926), 180-81, interprets "to live i' th' sun" to mean "to live the life of an outlaw." The Arden (1975) editor aptly notes "a covert and paradoxical allusion to the distinction between living easily, under a roof, and living roughly exposed to all weather. Cf. the proverb 'Out of God's blessing into the warm sun'" (43-44). Unsurprisingly we are told at the end that they "have endur'd shrewd days and nights" (5.4.172). The New Variorum does not report these

senses which also seem implicit in Amiens' concern that the "stanzo" will depress Jaques (10), and his own reluctance to sing it. Furthermore, Jaques already has his own "verse to this note," one which ridicules it. He who is "pleas'd with what he gets" makes a virtue of necessity.

35. The simile fits a period of a fortnight or so either side of Old Midsummer Day (5 July N.S.), and is consistent with Corin's "still handling our ewes" (2.2.53), the bucks being in velvet (1.1.50), and Jaques' charge that his companions "fright the animals" (2.1.62). Fawn habitat was supposed to be left undisturbed at this time, i.e. the "Fence Month."

36. As late as 1598, the Stratford district required relief from famine; see my, "The Dispraise of the Country in *As You Like It*," *Shakespeare Quarterly*, 36 (1985), 310, n. 25. Shakespeare was required to report his holdings of corn and malt at New Place, 4 February 1598. The shortage of food cereals had seriously affected north Arden from 1596. According to V. H. T. Skipp's study of five parishes above Stratford, *Crisis and Development: An Ecological Case Study of the Forest of Arden* (Cambridge: Cambridge Univ. Press, 1978), 37, the crisis there was "characterized by a steady build-up in the number of pauper burials, while after two or three years the deaths of wanderers, strangers and beggars are recorded: unfortunate people whose lives had been unhinged by the severities of the times, leaving them no alternative but to take to the road and ultimately to die on it."

37. See C. G. Cruickshank, *Elizabeth's Army*, 2nd ed. (Oxford: Oxford Univ. Press, 1966), ch. 5, "Rations," esp. 82, and 88-89, where an issue of 1598 is given as a typical ration. Entries in the State Papers are numerous. On the necessity of adequate rations, Cruickshank points out that, "Although the bow weighed little, only a strong man could get the best out of it" (86), a fact relevant to the play. Also T. R. Henn, 78, 83. With respect to large households, even the minor landed gentry might feed a score or more of workers and dependents.

38. *Rosalynde*, 196 and 220 (New Variorum, 418, 441).

39. "Gamelyn," *Middle English Verse Romances*, ed. Donald B. Sands (New York: Holt, Rinehart and Winston, 1966), 174.

40. Stonehenge (John Henry Walsh), *British Rural Sports*, 13th ed. (London: Frederick Warne, 1877), 132. A diet of fruit and wine would soon render even this paragon of stalkers unfit.

41. Of interest here is J. D. Burnely, *Chaucer's Language and the Philosopher's Tradition* (Cambridge: D. S. Brewer, 1979), where the medieval concept of the association of *pitee* with *gentilesse* and the identification of the villain or churl with hardheartedness is explored. Traits of such psychological and moral types, including the tyrant, identify antagonists in the play.

42. Robert Fabyan, *The New Chronicles of England and France*, ed. Henry Ellis, rpt. from Pynson's ed. of 1516 (London, 1811), 167. The editions of 1542 and 1559 omitted the bracketed text for partisan reasons.

43. *Sackville's Induction, A Mirror for Magistrates*, ed. Lily B. Campbell (1938; rpt. New York: Barnes & Noble, 1960), 307, lines 260-62. Fruit sometimes suggests charity, and the angels brought fruit to Jesus in the wilderness (Hall, 134, 298). If Jaques' "reasons" (2.7.100) punningly (reasons = raisins) signifies grapes, as some believe, they might possibly recall Hosea 9.10: "I founde Israel like grapes in the wilderness."

44. Glynn Isaac, "The Food-Sharing Behavior of Protohuman Hominoids," *Scientific American*, 238:4 (April 1978), 90, writes, "Evidence for food-sharing by early manlike animals suggest it is the essence of being human," and, 92, "Among members of human social groupings of various sizes the active sharing of food is a characteristic form of behavior." In Elizabethan terms, sharing food obeys the natural law; in the play's opening scene the "unnatural" brother, Oliver, had denied Orlando a rightful place at his table. The green of the hunters' jackets visually signalled the play's appeal to love, hope, and regeneration, as well as the deer hunter's folklore-hero's role.

45. For some of the allusions and symbols, secular and religious, associated with stricken deer and the careless herd, see my, "To Moralize a Spectacle: *As You Like It*, Act 2, Scene 1," *Philological Quarterly*, 65 (1986), 147-70.

Cynthia Marshall (essay date 1993)

SOURCE: "Wrestling as Play and Game in *As You Like It*," in *Studies in English Literature*, Vol. 33, No. 2, Spring, 1993, pp. 265-87.

[*In the following essay, Marshall explores the way in which wrestling is used as a metaphor for socially constructed emotion.*]

As You Like It, long considered among the happiest and most refined of Shakespearean comedies, has lately been seen as shadowed by various social tensions. Critics have traced the difficulties of "fraternal enmity" and hostilities over primogeniture,[1] the bitter implications of a changing agricultural economy,[2] and the ambiguous resistances that were enacted against an oppressive sex and gender system.[3] The shift from an idealizing critical tendency to a focus on dark implications enacts the general movement of responses to Shakespeare's comedies, which have appeared far more serious under the gazes of feminism and new historicism than an earlier aesthetic would have dreamed. Yet because what was traditionally admired about *As You Like It* was precisely its ability to manage conflict—as

C.L. Barber put it, the "power to express conflict and order it in art"[4]—, the critical shift in this case raises specific questions about representation and about the relation of social tensions to the comic realm, which are overlooked if we simply ascribe to an inevitable rotation of tastes and interests this movement from "enchanted world" to "inchoate energies."[5] The complexity of "express[ing] conflict" is showcased in the staged wrestling match in I.ii, which functions formally in *As You Like It* to channel and exorcise physical aggressions, but functions theatrically to unsettle various oppositions between art and life. Situated on the structural boundaries differentiating fight, sport, and theater, the match offers a conspicuous avowal of physical presence and conflict, even as it calls into question our modes for recognizing and understanding them. Building on the work of critics who have inquired into the troubled codes of gender in *As You Like It*, this essay will address the play's acknowledgement of the textuality of physical presence through its incorporation of wrestling. I will also consider the implications such textuality has for an understanding of performative violence.

The absolute physicality of wrestling, the perfect identification between the wrestler and his body, led Roland Barthes to define it in a classic essay as "not a sport" but "a spectacle." The "obviousness of the roles," together with the purity of the gestures (Suffering, Defeat, and Justice are all on display), portray "an ideal understanding of things," the "image of the perfect intelligibility of reality."[6] Despite the historical distance between the forms of wrestling known to Shakespeare in late sixteenth- and early seventeenth-century England and those observable in twentieth-century France, Barthes's perception of the sport's performative truth applies to *As You Like It* on several levels. Within the fictional world of the play, the match at Duke Frederick's court is at once entertainment and an attempt to order reality in a morally intelligible way: either Charles will preserve his status (and his employer's) as preeminent, or Orlando will demonstrate his heroic ascendancy. And in the theater, an audience delighting with Celia and Rosalind in the triumph of the underdog ordinarily finds Orlando's victory a memorable display of morally ordered plot. Yet because of its intertextuality—the performance embedded in a highly mannered drama—this spectacle is by no means pure: rules necessary to define the game, its players, the play space, and the audience are all brought into question. As a result, although the emphatic physicality of the wrestling match provides the theater audience with an easily comprehensible display of athletic skill and channeled violence, the episode also interrogates the boundaries of its own game and of social codes more generally. Not least among the codes thus questioned are those ordering the complex layers of theatricality separating the bodies of the performing actors from those of the observing audience.

Barthes's essay suggests that despite its obvious physicality, wrestling as a spectacle is astonishingly flat, teasing in its presentation of ordered reality. Obvious roles, pure gestures, strictly physical identities—none of this can offer assurance that the "image of the perfect intelligibility of reality" is reality itself. Discussions of wrestling in Tudor and Stuart social discourse convey a similar distrust, although Shakespeare's contemporaries are suspicious of wrestling less for its teasing simplicity than for its shifting significations. They see wrestling as a form of play uneasily situated on the margin between sport (ordered and rule-bound) and uncontrolled violence. Thus it offers a spectacle that paradoxically requires interpretation; it demands to be "read," to have judgment rendered as to who plays fairly (wrestles as game) and who transgresses the boundaries of sport (wrestles truly violently). These issues are further complicated by the frequent collapse of the line separating players from audience; in the sixteenth century, as today, a wrestling match could incite violence among its spectators.

The importance of its relation to the audience indicates that wrestling, in itself, is closer to theater than spectacle. Of course the theatrical situation of *As You Like It*'s wrestling match complicates any such distinction mightily. While the presence of wrestlers ordinarily tantalizes with the purported "reality" of violence, the representation of wrestling in the theater underscores the receding quality of any such physical truth. Mimesis deprives the spectacle of exactly that form of validity—physical violence—it would claim for itself. Here we face the redoubled truth of Derrida's insight that "play is the disruption of presence."[7] The wrestlers' violence is mediated by the "play" of both sport and spectacle; their bodies are ambiguously present, problematically known. For if violence can be represented or "played," it can be faked; so too with love, so too with gender. Each of these seemingly simple human truths is shown by *As You Like It* to be constructed, chosen, presented, and represented. By foregrounding wrestling, *As You Like It* shows how even the most simple—some would say crude—forms of human interaction are socially codified.

The play's inquiry into the shifting realities of physical presence begins abruptly, with the skirmish that breaks out between Orlando and Oliver in the first moments of *As You Like It*. An audience is challenged immediately to take sides in the conflict, and since violence signifies differently to these two brothers, our choice carries implications beyond the characterological. Modern productions typically exaggerate Oliver's menacing appearance and unscrupulous behavior, although the text does not make clear who instigates the initial attack: Oliver's "What, boy!" (I.i.52) may announce his attack on Orlando, or it may accompany a threatening gesture.[8] But with Orlando's reply—"Come, come, elder brother, you are too young in this" (I.i.53-54)—actual violence evidently surfaces, as announced by Oliver's response, "Wilt thou lay hands on me villain?" (I.i.55).[9] Orlando uses his position of physical dominance to assert his identity: "I am no villain. I am the youngest son of Sir Rowland de Boys" (I.i.56-57). Affirming identity through the patriarchy, Orlando defends his father's name rather than merely his own:

> he is thrice a villain that says such a father begot villains. Wert thou not my brother, I would not take this

hand from thy throat till this other had pulled out thy tongue for saying so. Thou hast railed on thyself.

(I.i.57-62)[10]

References to "this hand" and "this other," to "thy throat" and "thy tongue," focus and ground the conflict in an opposition between two individuals, but it is precisely this opposition and separability that the blood bond denies. Oliver has insulted not, or not only, the mutual father, but "railed on [him]self" (I.i.62). "Wert thou *not* my brother" (emphasis added), Orlando's violence would be unconstrained; as things are, family ties efface enmity's distinctions. Somewhere in the course of demanding "such exercises as may become a gentleman" or "the poor allottery [his] father left" him (I.i. 72-73), Orlando releases Oliver from his grip.

While the emotions fueling this skirmish are evidently of long duration, the encounter itself seems spontaneous, unpremeditated. Indecorously coming to blows with his brother, Orlando demonstrates the depth and intensity of his outrage; violence for him is the sign of validity. In his opening lines Orlando has set up the play's central thematic contrast, that between nature ("the something that nature gave me" [I.i.17]) and culture ("call you that keeping for a gentleman of my birth" [I.i.8-9]; "I am not taught to make anything" [I.i.301]. The outbreak of violence, a sudden rupturing of cultivated prohibitions on physical resolution of differences, seems to stem from the "nature" side of this antithesis. Oliver's threat to "physic" his brother's "rankness" (I.i.86) may further a sense that Orlando, however sympathetic he is as a character, has restored to violence because he is overgrown and under-educated.

Wrestling, however, was on Oliver's mind before he met his brother and incited him to violence. As soon becomes apparent, Oliver not only knew that Charles the wrestler was on hand (I.i.89-90), but with his elliptical remark "'Twill be a good way. And tomorrow the wrestling is" (I.i.93-94), he reveals prior formation of a plan to sacrifice and dispose of Orlando in a match with Charles. What had seemed a moment earlier the spontaneous expression of Orlando's frustrated pride of place now appears a deliberate attempt by a scheming Oliver to mark Orlando as a wrestler, and thereby to confirm and strengthen the younger brother's resolve (already "secretly" [I.i.122] communicated to Charles) to answer the general challenge issued by the duke's wrestler.[11] Orlando's visceral anger has impressed his sincerity on the audience, but the revelation of Oliver's manipulation shows physical violence to be an unreliable gauge of sincerity.

The immediate arrival of Charles, with his talk of wrestling for "credit" and "for prize" (I.i.125, 159), complicates even further any initial impression of physical violence as pure and unmediated. Oliver's attempt to entice Charles with treacherous instruction—"I had as lief thou didst break his neck as his finger" (I.i.144-45)—reiterates the visceral hatred evidenced in his skirmish with Orlando,

but Oliver fails to infect Charles with his feeling of outrage. Promising to "give [Orlando] his payment" (I.i.158), Charles betrays with his metaphor his own attitude toward wrestling—it is a game played "for prize." His mannered speech reveals the gamesome character of this cultivated wrestler:

> Your brother is but young and tender, and for your love I would be loath to foil him, as I must for my own honour if he come in. Therefore out of my love to you, I came hither to acquaint you withal, that either you might stay him from his intendment, or brook such disgrace well as he shall run into.

(I.i.127-33)

Although he confidently assumes his own physical ascendancy, Charles is clearly no mere natural; he wrestles for "honour," anticipating social and financial outcomes from the match.

Orlando uses physical violence in an expressive manner, both when he confronts his brother and when he appears, possibly disguised (see I.i.124), at Duke Senior's wrestling match. Oliver, more sinister in his calculations, sees the formal violence of the wrestling match as open to manipulation. The sport's propensity to dissolve into direct aggression signifies, for him, the opportunity to cloak homicide in gaming clothes (in a metaphorical sense—wrestlers in Shakespeare's time, as today, typically wore the briefest of trunks). Charles, employed as "the Duke's wrestler" (I.i.89), seems to be keenly aware of the nuances of his professional activity, its sliding signification. On the one hand, by seeking permission from Oliver to "foil" his brother, and by receiving direction to harm Orlando, Charles functions as a courtly hit man. On the other, his references to "credit," "honor," and "prize," together with the attitudes expressed by the audience of the match, suggest that Charles's purpose is primarily to provide entertainment. For an audience backing Orlando or for anyone attuned to the rhythms of myth and fairy tale,[12] the match in I.ii. may seem to offer "an ideal understanding of things," but the presentation early in the play of widely variable attitudes toward wrestling works to erode any firm sense that such an understanding corresponds with reality.

Charles's appearance heralds not only the imminent match, but the sporting attitude glimpsed at Duke Frederick's palace. Despite the machinations of the duke himself, Frederick's palace affords the leisure for games, foolery, and court wrestling. Celia's and Rosalind's genteel practice of "devis[ing] sports" (I.ii.23) contrasts markedly with the "unkept" Orlando's passionate "mutiny against [his] servitude" (I.i.8, 23). Rosalind suggests "sports" by way of following Celia's command to "be merry"; entertainments such as "falling in love" or "mock[ing] the good hussif Fortune from her wheel" (I.ii.22, 24, 30-31) are proposed as a means of passing time, of escaping the burdensome worries Rosalind feels because of her father's banishment. Sport is seen, in a word, as recreation. The ladies, moreover, understand a firm distinction between such gamesome activities and behaving "in good earnest" (I.ii.26); the boundaries marking the safe limits of the game of love must be respected. Their brief exercise in mocking Fortune (I.ii.30-53) demonstrates a prerehearsed quality that suggests the game's familiarity. This is borne out later by Jaques's observation of Touchstone railing "on Lady Fortune in good terms" (II.vii.16) and by his proposing a similar version of the game to Orlando (III.ii.272-74).

The wrestling match is placed within the sporting context by Le Beau's announcement—"Fair Princess, you have lost much good sport" (I.ii.92). But whereas the ladies have proposed games in which they can actively participate, Le Beau announces a spectator sport: "they are coming to perform it" (I.ii.106-107). Le Beau seems to equate the coming of the wrestlers with the arrival of a band of itinerant players, for while "perform" might suggest the skilled execution of a deed, the word's theatrical connotations are also obvious in this context. His fictionalizing narration of "the manner of the wrestling," so stylized that Celia likens it to "the beginning" of "an old tale" (I.ii.110), further distances the event from the putative reality of court. Indeed, Le Beau's explicit attentions to "the beginning" and "the end" (I.ii.104, 105) of the event serve to frame it, to mark in a narrative fashion the boundaries of the wrestling match.[13]

Articulating boundaries through narrative chronology serves a particularly important function here, since the playing space lacks obvious physical definition. The playing space of the wrestling match, while evidently a closed field that has been previously designated, is decidedly portable. Le Beau tells the ladies that "here where you are they are coming to perform it"; "here is the place appointed for the wrestling" (I.ii.106-107, 134-35). Keir Elam, examining the way the dramatic world creates its own context, remarks how "the absent other place—the scene of the wrestling—becomes . . . the here and now of the dialogue not because the present speakers, or the audience, are taken to it, but because *it* is brought, mountain-to-Mohammed- or Birnam Wood-to-Dunsinane-like, to them, in order to be duly subjected to the ladies' commentary."[14] The playing space is evidently temporary as well as portable—before Le Beau's announcement the ladies did not know and apparently could not tell that they occupied "the place appointed for the wrestling."

Rules defining the audience are crucial in marking any game or playing space. While Le Beau is too "full of news" (I.ii.86) to acknowledge propriety, Touchstone raises an objection to the ladies' presence: "It is the first time that ever I heard breaking of ribs was sport for ladies" (I.ii.127-29). The clown must, by profession, pay keen attention to social conventions. Moreover, Touchstone is characteristically alert to physical discomfort, and implicitly objects to the violence of the "sport"; after hearing Le Beau's account of the three challengers left "with little hope of life," he asks with mock innocence, "But

Peter Sorensen as Orlando and Erin Day as Rosalind in GreenStage's 1997 production of As You Like It.

what is the sport monsieur, that the ladies have lost?" (I.ii.118, 124-25). While the normal audience for wrestling is evidently male, this rule would appear to be one that may be broken with impunity, at least by ladies of such important social position, since Duke Frederick acknowledges the presence of Celia and Rosalind "crept hither to see the wrestling" and implicitly grants the "leave" (I.ii.144-45, 146) to watch that Rosalind requests. Rosalind's desire to break the code—and her urging Celia to join her—sets in motion the pattern of transgressing gender boundaries that later provides much of the play's interest. But as audience to the wrestling match, both ladies respect its frame. Rosalind's prayerful reference to Hercules and Celia's wish to be "invisible" or to have a "thunderbolt" in her eye (I.ii.198, 199, 202) attest to the real impermeability of the boundary separating them from the wrestlers: only a superhuman agent could break through to aid Orlando.

Orlando's participation in the match—his very presence at Frederick's court—is also transgressive, but in other ways. Although nobly born, Orlando confesses himself "rustically" kept "at home"; he claims to be less skilled even than his brother's horses, who are "taught their manage" (I.i.7, 12). Le Beau's approving reference to the "three proper young men" (I.ii.111) who have been vanquished, together with the court setting and Charles's speech and general bearing, create a hint of elitism about the match. Clearly it is conceived as a disciplined and entertaining sport—not a skirmish between village thugs. As "the Duke's wrestler" (I.i.89), Charles occupies a position somewhere between an entertainer and a defensive champion. Orlando, however, carries with him into the match the same aura of sincerity that characterized his earlier bout with Oliver. The event signifies for him a "trial" (I.ii.176) in which he might prove himself, and despite attempts by Duke Frederick, Celia, and Rosalind to dissuade him, "he will not be entreated" (I.ii.149-50).

One can begin to sense before the match ever begins that the court party may be protesting too much about the prowess of its champion—that Charles's reputation may properly exist in the same realm as the self-announcing fiction of Le Beau's "old tale." In the theater this will depend on Charles's portrayal. What seems clear, at any rate, is that while Charles wrestles according to custom and in a performative way, Orlando wrestles to prove his identity and self-worth. Orlando, moreover, displaces onto Charles the aggression he has partially controlled in the earlier bout with Oliver. Defining the match differently may in fact result in separate sets of rules for Charles and Orlando, although there is no indication that the match is construed as unfair.

Success at wrestling, as Sir Thomas Elyot noted in 1531, need not necessarily depend on brute strength. Elyot wrote: "it hath ben sene that the waiker persone, by the sleight of wrastlyng, hath ouerthrowen the strenger, almost or he coulde fasten on the other any violent stroke."[15] Orlando evidently uses some such "sleight" in his encounter with Charles, but the Folio stage directions instruct simply "Wrestle" and a few lines later "Shout" (I.ii.200sd, 203sd), when Charles is thrown. The Duke then intervenes and inquires about Charles, who "cannot speak" (I.ii.208) and is, at the Duke's command, borne away. No more is heard of Charles—a change from *Rosalynde,* in which Lodge specifies both how the Norman champion "yielded nature her due" and how "the death of this champion" gains greater admiration for Rosader (the figure corresponding to Orlando).[16]

While it silences Charles, Orlando's victory wins for him the opportunity to announce himself publicly. Having previously been kept "rustically at home" (I.i.7) and "not taught to make anything" (I.i.30), Orlando's announcement of his name and his father's marks a passage into society and a concurrent entry into Duke Frederick's avowed enmity (I.ii.213-19). Clearly Orlando's descent from Sir Rowland de Boys validates Rosalind's budding attraction (I.ii.224-28). These responses signal the immediate access of social forms in the process of interpreting or responding to the wrestling match. Even if it were possible for Orlando and Charles to wrestle "man to man," without intrusions from past, present, and future influences, the match can be understood only through the varied lenses produced by the spectators' desires and expectations. Moreover, the wrestling bout is transmuted into metaphor directly upon its completion. At I.ii.239-45, Orlando and Rosalind "fall in love in wrestling terms"[17] and the trope continues in the next scene when Celia urges Rosalind to "wrestle with thy affections" (I.iii.20). According to Raymond B. Waddington, the lovers' adoption of the wrestling metaphor "establish[es] the precedent of reading stage actions emblematically."[18] Audience as well as critics read stage actions in this way. The ease with which wrestling becomes an emblem shows how violence and conflict flow into the tissue of language.

For an early seventeenth-century audience, wrestling's associative meanings would not have been limited to the emblematic. The shifting attitudes toward wrestling in the first act of *As You Like It* correspond to a similar valency in contemporary references to the sport. Conduct manuals for young gentlemen of the late sixteenth and early seventeenth centuries frequently include wrestling in their recommendations for physical activities. Castiglione "deem[ed] it highly important" for the ideal courtier "to know how to wrestle, because this frequently accompanies the use of weapons on foot."[19] Wrestling was also granted a particular English pedigree by Holinshed's account of how the giant Gogmagog was subdued at Dover.[20] Though it was in the first order a militaristic skill, English writers of the period emphasize how the gentlemanly practice of wrestling can promote strength and provide recreation. Nevertheless, their reiterated stipulations on practicing the sport indicate its potential danger. Sir Thomas Elyot, for instance, implicitly acknowledges the violence of the activity when he specifies that it be undertaken "with one that is equall in strengthe, or some what under, and that the place be softe, that in fallinge theyr bodies be nat brused."[21] In *The Castel of Health* (1541) as in *The Boke Named the Governor* (1531), Elyot mentions the development capabilities of wrestling; he recommends such exercise "only for yonge men, which be inclined, or be apte to the warres."[22] King James, however, is somewhat freer in his recommendations. In *Basilikon Doron* (1598), although he disallows "all rough and violent exercises, as the footeball," he includes wrestling in his list of "exercises of the bodie most commendable to be vsed by a young Prince."[23] James Cleland (1611) and Henry Osborne (1656) also reiterate the potential usefulness of being skilled in wrestling, but Henry Peacham (1622) condemns wrestling, along with "throwing," as "exercises not so well beseeming nobility, but rather soldiers in a camp or a prince's guard."[24] Robert Burton (1621) also acknowledges the lowliness of wrestling when he lists it among "the common recreations of the country folks," although Burton offers a general endorsement of exercises that might preserve the health of a gentry class he sees as dangerously idle.[25]

Orlando might be understood as one whose physical vitality and skill in single combat have been won at the price of social acceptability. Orlando views wrestling as something more than a form of exercise; it offers him, in the confrontation with his brother, a means of expressing anger and, in the match, a chance of winning renown. Conscious that his habits are less than gentlemanly, Orlando complains to his brother:

> My father charged you in his will to give me good education: you have trained me like a peasant, obscuring and hiding from me all gentleman-like qualities.
>
> (I.i.66-70)

Orlando, one might say (or at least *he* might say), wrestles "like a peasant." Contemporary references acknowledge clear class distinctions in the matter and manner of wrestling. While authors of conduct manuals generally allow wrestling for the cultivation of individual skills and capacities among the gentry, other writers make clear the dangers associated with lower-class practice of the sport.

The chronicler John Stow (1603), for instance, was attuned to the social disturbances wrestling occasionally unleashed. Stow's account of the casual activities of London youths, who "in the Holy dayes in Sommer . . . exercised themselves, in leaping, dauncing, shooting, wrestling, casting of the stone or ball, etc." is closely conflated with references to civic disturbances occurring at the annual matches at Clerkenwell.[26] Stow reports that in a match in 1222 between Londoners and wrestlers from Westminster, the "Citizens . . . had the mastrie of the men in the suburbs"[27] although he does not specify, as other sources do, that a number of people were severely wounded or killed in the ensuing riots, which continued for several days.[28] Stow also reports that at the annual matches in 1453 a "tumult [was] made agaynst the Maior,"[29] and though he again provides no further details, simply noting the "tumult" 150 years after its occurrence is enough to suggest its magnitude.

Something of the danger associated with wrestling is also suggested by the description German traveler Paul Hentzner supplies of the annual St. Bartholomew's Day match, as it was practiced during Elizabeth's time.

> [I]t is usual for the mayor, attended by the twelve principal aldermen, to walk in a neighbouring field, dressed in his scarlet gown, and about his neck a golden chain, to which is hung a golden fleece, and besides, that particular ornament, which distinguishes the most noble order of the garter . . . upon their arrival at a place appointed for that purpose, where a tent is pitched, the mob begin to wrestle before them, two at a time; the conquerors receive rewards from the magistrates.[30]

Clearly Hentzner was impressed by the ceremonial quality of "this show," not least because a member of his company had "his pocket picked of his purse" while he was intently watching the spectacle.[31] In Hentzner's account, as implicitly in Stow's, the placement of these matches outside the city demonstrates their liminal quality. However validated by ritual occurrence and the official presence of mayor and aldermen, the wrestling matches were potentially dangerous events, where the violence designated for "a place appointed for that purpose" threatened to spill over into lawless behavior among the assembled crowd.

Wrestling's feigned aggression could incite actual violence, for the "play" of wrestling occurred on the border with reality. For young gentlemen, wrestling was allowed because it prepared one for future duties as courtier or soldier; the practice required regulation, however, because of its structural proximity to such destructive combat. The chroniclers were more concerned that the spectacle of wrestling could provoke violence among its audience. Perhaps because of this spectacular quality, Richard Carew understood wrestling in theatrical terms. Describing in 1602 the wrestling of boys in Cornwall, Carew attributes to both the participants and the audience a self-conscious theatricality.

> For performing this play, the beholders cast themselves in a ring, which they call, Making a place: into the empty middle space whereof, the two champion wrestlers step forth, stripped into their dublets and hosen, and untrussed, that they may so the better commaund the use of their lymmes, and first shaking hands in token of friendship, they fall presently to the effects of anger: for each striveth how to take hold of other, with his best advantage, and to beare his adverse party downe.[32]

The delineation of "a place" is crucial, since play is defined through its difference from the ordinary order of things. As Johann Huizinga points out, "limitation as to space" is especially "striking": "All play moves and has its being within a playground marked off beforehand either materially or ideally, deliberately or as a matter of course."[33] Marking the playground by arranging themselves in a circle, the Cornish youths simultaneously become an audience for the performance. Adopting "the effects of anger," the champions function as performers. So too at Duke Frederick's court, the wrestling match depends upon the willing participation of champion and challenger, but also on the attention of the court party: this sport requires an audience. Yet oddly enough, the theatricality that would seem to belie wrestling's validity—not its proximity to unregulated violence—is what enables Oliver to proceed with his plot against Orlando's life. At Frederick's court, in other words, wrestling might inflict real damage not in spite of but because of its vulnerability to being faked; it is not securely fixed in either a mimetic or a ludic realm. Carew's description of "making a place" perfectly exemplifies the simultaneity of Renaissance concepts of game and play, and shows how "play" comprehended both ludic and mimetic activities.[34] Wrestling, at once sport and spectacle, functioned analogously to theatrical plays conceived and presented in this bivalent manner. The breakdown of this largely inclusive notion of play in modern American culture is evidenced by typical complaints about the falseness of professional wrestling and a corresponding distrust of nonillusionistic theater.

In the case of *As You Like It,* the wrestling match is not merely analogous to but embedded within a theatrical framework. In performance, the various codes revealed by discourse analysis are at least partially subsumed by the patent fact of physical presence. Here, the firmest distinction between the "game" or "spectacle" of the wrestling match and the "drama" of the surrounding action will also be the most obvious one: wrestling is an affair of bodies and not words. Le Beau's announcement of Charles's defeat—"He cannot speak" (I.ii.208)—illustrates perfectly the established priority of deed over word, the capacity of pure spectacle or of violence (and in wrestling the two are coterminous) to destroy language.[35] The ludic interval, because it presents violent physical action of a sort that is anterior to language, would seem to possess greater "reality" than the surrounding text of *As You Like It.* The wrestling match proclaims its truth, as Barthes would have it, by the "emptying out of interiority to the benefit of its exterior signs," the "exhaustion of the content by the

form." Suffering, Defeat, and Justice are perfectly realized: "the wrestler's gesture needs no anecdote, no decor, in short no transference in order to appear true."[36]

But in the theater, if not before the wrestling ring, we suspect that appearance is almost paradigmatically *not* truth. For while any wrestling match depends upon and insists upon the reality of physical presence, the audience of *As You Like It* can scarcely avoid noticing the theatricality of the staged match, which, no matter how naturalistic its presentation, has been choreographed, rule-bound, and carefully rehearsed, to avoid the very injuries it claims to announce. It also matters that the wrestling match has been triply staged—by the theatrical company, by Orlando and Charles, and by Oliver. The effect recalls the "closure of representation" Derrida associates with Artaud's theater of cruelty: in the theatrical "labor of total representation . . . the affirmation of life lets itself be doubled and emptied by negation."[37] Purporting to distill the threatened aggression, frustration, and violence of the play into pure form, to manifest conflict and, through its expression, to allow its release, the wrestling match instead offers only more theater.[38] Promising the clear and emphatic spectacle of physical violence, it betrays its own conventionalized origins.

Herbert Blau names "theater's most compelling power" to be "the precipitating moment when . . . it identifies or reveals or betrays itself as theater. At that moment, we become aware of the role of the audience in the enfabled pursuit of an absence."[39] So here, the supposed purity of physical interaction collapses in the face of an awareness of its theatricality. The wrestling match functions as a marker for what is otherwise largely absent from the comic world of *As You Like It*—an acknowledgement of the body's intractability. But though the match foregrounds the matter of the body, it effectively camouflages physicality in the codes of sport and spectacle, thus necessarily foreclosing any approach to the body proper.

Writ small in the relation of the spectacular wrestling match to the dramatic text in which it is embedded is the age-old debate about Shakespearean plays as performance or text. Those who, like Coleridge, consider Shakespeare's words too pure for the stage would want to limit the significance of the wrestling match to its plotted outcome and its metaphorical capacities. They would consider the match pure performance, "spectacular" in the pejorative sense. In the other court, those more viscerally involved with theater may find the match a compelling focus of the play's initial action, the clearest and most memorable display of Orlando's heroic stance, as well as a stunning preview of the structuring of those games and contests that figure so centrally in the play's development. The lines of this particular debate appear to be clearly drawn, yet as W. B. Worthen points out, it is all too easy to ignore "the institutional practices already inscribed in the theatre, in gesture and intonation, in the body and its behaviors, the 'textualizing' formalities that render theatre significant."[40] So powerful is this theatrical rhetoric that any performance of the wrestling match can more accurately be said to reveal a production's adherence to traditional conceptions of conflict and physical presence than to display the body itself. Theatrical presentation of wrestling in *As You Like It* reiterates rather than resolves the tension between body and text, performance and script; it reveals their mutual and ongoing dependency. As Barthes puts it, expanding the notion of play so that it might include even a highly rhetoricized wrestling match, "the signifier's *infinitude* does not refer back to some idea of the ineffable (of an unnamable signified) but to the idea of *play*."[41] In the absence of "the ineffable" or an absolute truth of the body, the construction of "play" becomes deadly serious, as various responses to the match indicate. Orlando and Charles are caught in the tension between wrestling as sport and wrestling as demonstrative violence. The onstage audience, for whom the match is also an entertainment, enters a triple bond of signifiers: wrestling as sport, as violence, as spectacle. For the theater audience, each of these layers of interpretation is further refracted: wrestling appears as mimetic sport, mimetic violence, mimetic spectacle. The customary temptation has been to resolve the play of meaning set into motion by the wrestling match through reference to the comic frame of *As You Like It,* which supposedly guarantees the simpler meanings of sport and spectacle while banishing the more complex resonances of play and mimetic violence. But would Shakespeare have risked staging an event so ambiguously significant as wrestling without exploiting its potential to question the boundaries of coded violence?

The theatrical presentation of wrestling requires an audience to consider when, how, and why violence becomes real. A similar point about the performability of violence is reiterated late in the play by Touchstone's witty excursus on dueling "by the book" (V.iv.89). As Agnes Latham remarks of the contemporary manuals on dueling etiquette that Touchstone parodies, it can "seem ridiculous to teach people how to kill one another politely."[42] Yet the changing styles people employ in killing one another affirm the constructed quality of expressions of human aggression and suggest the importance of attending to the ways a spectacle of violence is framed and understood. For violence is always a spectacle, performed for an audience, even if that audience plays the simultaneous role of victim.

Of course we expect actors to be self-conscious in their theatricality; we may even expect the same of wrestlers (as Carew did in 1602). Most will assume, however, that violent activity in certain spheres (rampages, for instance) is unmediated, essentially beyond culture. Such an assumption grants a self-authenticating privilege to actions in those zones, a privilege expressive of a dualistic world view in which bodies are considered more real than ideas. Yet, as the discourse on wrestling testifies, what people do with their physical selves is subtly and extensively codified. As a result of this codification, it is difficult to think of a form of violence that lacks at least a potentially performative element; someone must see, suffer, lament, or deride the act—and the perpetrator, at some level, must know it. If the theatrical performance of *As You Like It*'s wrestling match erases the distinction between real and fake wrestling, it should also make us question such distinctions more widely.

In *As You Like It,* wrestling necessitates a constantly shifting focus, since it functions variously as mimetic violence, as game, as spectacle, and, eventually, as metaphor. The changeable rules marking playspace, audience, and participants—the constant transformations undergone by a form supposedly so simple and unaccommodated—suggest the arbitrariness of social convention, and they connect the wrestling match with the play's other interrogations of human illusion, its inquiries into pastoral, melancholy, romantic love, and gender. The match offers an emphatic instance of the way physical existence is construed according to forms and conventions which may be, like the boundary marking the wrestlers' ring, largely invisible.

For instance, the classically pastoral debate between Corin and Touchstone on the relative merits of country and court manners leads Harold Jenkins to the universalizing perception that "in city or country, *all* ways of life are at bottom the same."[43] But this is to privilege one side of the debate, which in fact ends inconclusively. Corin's sensibly relativistic awareness of how "Those that are good manners at the court are as ridiculous in the country as the behaviour of the country is most mockable at the court" (III.ii.44-47) accurately predicts Touchstone's response. The court fool mocks the country man by denying the bases of separate customs in the two realms. Throughout their skirmish of wits, however, Corin insists on the priority of material existence—"he that wants money, means, and content is without three good friends" (III.ii.24-25); "the greatest of my pride is to see my ewes graze and my lambs suck" (III.ii.74-75). Corin's attention is riveted to the ways "the sheep matter," as Ralph Berry succinctly puts it.[44] Touchstone only pretends, in a mock-salacious manner ("That is another simple sin in you, to bring the ewes and rams together" [III.ii.76-77]), to share this concern with the body and physical reality.[45] Corin, the self-described "true labourer" (III.ii.71), can scarcely compete with Touchstone's "too courtly" (III.ii.68) wit, and recognizing this, wishes to end the debate several speeches before the entry of Ganymede finally affords him respite. This encounter, like the one inside the wrestling ring, follows a prescribed form, has an apparent victor, and delights its (theatrical) audience; it seems, moreover, just as little able to reveal anything qualifying as a stable truth about human existence, since Corin sides firmly with his sheep and Touchstone with his wit.

Custom and expectation, the play affirms, shape perception. As Duke Senior, who has been given sufficient cause to be unhappy, remarks, "old custom" makes life in exile "more sweet" (II.i.2) than life at court. Jaques too, though unvariable in his own approach to life, acknowledges the multiplicity of ways in which the world may be construed. His prideful description of his melancholy as "mine own, compounded of many simples, extracted from many objects, and indeed the sundry contemplation of my travels" (IV.i.15-18), makes what seems an unremarkable point to a modern audience, who typically are rather keenly aware of the diverse influences contributing to mood or personality. Yet by labeling his manner "melancholy," Jaques distinguishes it and himself from the merely natural, the unnoticed. His determining characteristics have been "compounded."

Jaques's disgust with Orlando's courtship techniques (III.ii.248-89) and his intolerance for the mutual presence of Rosalind and Orlando (IV.i.29-30) demonstrate the incompatibility between his constructionist view of human identity and the innocent idea of romantic love. The love-play between Orlando and Ganymede pretending to be Rosalind has often been seen to turn on an audience's awareness of the "real" Rosalind lurking beneath two layers of assumed personas. Players as well as critics differentiate between speeches attributable to Ganymede's assumed Rosalind and to Rosalind herself.[46] Following this line of reasoning, Ganymede's faint at IV.iii.157 serves as a token of Rosalind's feminine nature,[47] the betrayal of the male persona by the "reality" of a female consciousness (and in most modern productions, a female body). But Orlando's own swoon (IV.iii.148) calls such a reading into question. Of course Ganymede's faint delivers greater theatrical impact, since it actually occurs on stage while Oliver only reports that Orlando fainted, presumably from loss of blood. Still, the typical response, which fixes on Ganymede's faint as revelatory (of gender) but overlooks Orlando's identical physiological action, reascribes swooning as a feminine behavior. The swoon renders Ganymede's unconscious body the site of an audience's wish to normalize sexual relations in the play. However much they may delight in Rosalind's transvestite performance, audiences inclined toward a happily heterosexual conclusion to the Orlando-Rosalind-Ganymede affair are relieved to see Rosalind's "feminine" nature assert itself in the swoon. But of course in the Elizabethan theater, a reading of the unconscious body of Rosalind/Ganymede as female would be mistaken. Elizabethan casting practices make sex differences a poor base for constructing identity.[48] While the unstable gendering of Rosalind/Ganymede is sometimes supposed to be controlled and regularized by the swoon, this episode offers another example of the body's truth being anything but simple. Instead, the player's artificially unconscious body provides a text that audiences read according to preestablished themes.

Late in the play, Orlando exclaims "I can live no longer by thinking" (V.ii.50). In a mimetic sense he is "venting the constrained libido of Elizabethan youth,"[49] but in theatrical terms he is breaking the courtship game with Ganymede. The irony here, as Joseph Westlund points out, is that Orlando "*can* 'live by thinking' . . . he can imagine Ganymede to be 'Rosalind.'"[50] And of course the audience has been engaged in just such an imaginative act all along; "just as Orlando pretends that Ganymede is Rosalind, so do the spectators pretend that another boy, the actor, is Rosalind."[51] So while Orlando may "los[e] interest in make-believe" upon hearing how "his brother and Celia are betrothed without fussing about such preliminaries as courtship,"[52] the audience is aware of the proximity between the planned nuptials of Oliver and Celia, and the mock-marriage of Ganymede and Orlando in IV.i.[53] Attending to the theatrical dynamic suggests that both events are "merely" playing. Like the wrestling match, the wooing game between Orlando and Ganymede serves as a model for the way human interactions are constructed. Rather than suggesting differences between a real and a pretend Rosalind, or between real and pretend violence, these paradigms show even spontaneous behaviors to be amalgams of learned activities, living "by thinking," or more generally still, merely playing.[54]

Commentaries on *As You Like It* have often involved some set of clearly defined contrasts—between court and country, or reality and illusion, or nature and nurture. Yet with its illustration of the difficulty—or even the impossibility—of confronting a fundamental physical reality, the play dissolves these distinctions. Current attention has centered on the challenge issued to the audience's ordering sensibility by the ambiguous gender of Rosalind/Ganymede. As a number of commentators have suggested, Rosalind's epilogue may enable a seamless transition between theatrical illusion and post-performance reality, but it does so by appropriating and unsettling the ordained constructions of gender and desire. Appearing simultaneously as actor and as Rosalind, speaking from both male and female personae, Rosalind in this final appearance superimposes play and reality, rendering them indivisible.[55] My point is that the wrestling match offers the play's earliest and most spectacular challenge to the modes of bodily interaction presupposed by mimetic theater. Further, the match shows the potential threat of social codes: some forms of violence (here one might include patriarchy, primogeniture, and privatization of property) can become so well coded as to be invisible. By exposing the theatricality of physical conflict, the match explodes the myth of a place in society where one could avoid living "by thinking," where one could ever escape the texts through which people appear to one another and mediate their relations. Just as Orlando's alternative to the wish thus stated is unclear, the audience is denied recourse to a world outside the theater where the boundaries between reality and illusion will be any more consistently drawn.

As You Like It redoubles the sort of ambiguity Castiglione fears from a prince masquerading in his own role: "If he were to perform in play what he must really do when the need arises, he would deprive what is real of its due authority and it might appear that the reality were mere play."[56] When Rosalind, disguised as Ganymede, masquerades her own role with Orlando, the flexible, contiguous, and collapsible boundaries of play and reality are displayed. Celia's reluctance to "say the words" (IV.i.121) of the wedding ceremony indicates her awareness of the danger that the love-play will (to reverse Castiglione's terms) lose its authenticity as pure masquerade and become "mere" reality. For without a clear opposite in play or fiction, reality becomes a more dubious proposition. As Louis Montrose remarks, troping on Jaques's famous theatrical dictum, "To say that all the men and women are *merely* players is to say that they are wholly, entirely players—'without admixture or qualification.'"[57]

When Orlando, rewarded by Rosalind after the match with a token, finds himself unable to speak, he calls himself "a quintain, a mere lifeless block" (I.ii.241). Whereas Orlando's prowess at wrestling deprived Charles of speech, his own verbal ability is "overthrown" (I.ii.244) by Rosalind's attentions. The reference to a "lifeless block" seems facile, perhaps sensationalistic, but it nevertheless suggests how distant an idea of human essence is from this play. Without power to speak, Orlando would be lifeless.[58] Ironically, however, at the very moment Orlando professes himself mute and therefore "lifeless," Rosalind imagines or pretends that "He calls us back" (I.ii.242). Responding to a call not uttered, Rosalind invents an interchange with Orlando that is anything but straightforward communication; like Carew's wrestlers, she is "making a place." So throughout *As You Like It,* speech and the elaborate social coding it performs are revealed to be often false and frequently precarious. Yet since no alternative presents itself to living "by thinking," the play seems to reject any notion of escaping a linguistically ordered world for one somehow more pure. Rather than subverting the fiction's formal order, the presence of the wrestling match in *As You Like It* demonstrates how social codes are continually being made, broken, and remade. The wrestling match advertises a glimpse of "unaccommodated man," but shows instead, in the constant framing and reframing of its spectacle of violence, the ongoing process we call culture.[59]

Notes

1. "Fraternal enmity" is one focus of Joel Fineman's "Fratricide and Cuckoldry: Shakespeare's Doubles," *The Psychoanalytic Review* 64 (Fall 1977), rprt. in *Representing Shakespeare: New Psychoanalytic Essays,* ed. Murray M. Schwartz and Coppélia Kahn (Baltimore: Johns Hopkins Univ. Press, 1980), pp. 70-109, 75. Louis Adrian Montrose examines family polities in "'The Place of a Brother' in *As You Like It:* Social Process and Comic Form," *SQ* 32, 1 (Spring 1981): 28-54.

2. Richard Wilson, "'Like the old Robin Hood': *As You Like It* and the Enclosure Riots," *SQ* 43, 1 (Spring 1992): 1-19.

3. Catherine Belsey, "Disrupting Sexual Difference: Meaning and Gender in the Comedies," in *Alternative Shakespeares,* ed. John Drakakis (New York: Methuen, 1985), pp. 166-90; Barbara J. Bono, "Mixed Gender, Mixed Genre in Shakespeare's *As You Like It,*" in *Renaissance Genres: Essays on Theory, History, and Interpretation,* ed. Barbara Kiefer Lewalski, Harvard English Studies 14 (Cambridge, MA and London: Harvard Univ. Press, 1986), pp. 189-212; Jean Howard, "Crossdressing, The Theatre, and Gender Struggle in Early Modern

England," *SQ* 39, 4 (Winter 1988): 418-40; and Phyllis Rackin, "Androgyny, Mimesis, and the Marriage of the Boy Heroine on the English Renaissance Stage," *PMLA* 102, 1 (January 1987): 29-41.

4. C.L. Barber, *Shakespeare's Festive Comedy: A Study of Dramatic Form and Its Relation to Social Custom* (Princeton: Princeton Univ. Press, 1959), p. 238. Similarly, Harold Jenkins notes how Arden's "illusions" are tested in the play "against reality," although ultimately "ideals, though always on the point of dissolving, are for ever recreating themselves" in the play ("As You Like It," *ShS* 8 [1955]: 40-51, 51). Anne Barton also stresses *As You Like It*'s balance: although aware of "reminders of mortality flicker[ing] everywhere," she believes it retains "classical equilibrium" ("*As You Like It* and *Twelfth Night*: Shakespeare's Sense of an Ending," *Shakespearean Comedy*, Stratford-upon-Avon-Studies 14 [London: Edward Arnold, 1972], pp. 160-80, 166).

5. "Enchanted world" is Jenkins's phrase (p. 51). Bono refers to "inchoate energies" (p. 206).

6. Roland Barthes, "The World of Wrestling," *Mythologies*, 1957, trans. Annette Lavers (New York: Farrar, Straus and Giroux-Noonday, 1972), pp. 15-25, 15, 17, 25.

7. Jacques Derrida, "Structure, Sign, and Play in the Discourse of the Human Sciences," *Writing and Difference*, trans. Alan Bass (Chicago: Univ. of Chicago Press, 1978), pp. 278-93, 292.

8. There is no stage direction in the First Folio text. The stage directions inserted by editors indicate uncertainty about reading Oliver's act of aggression: Agnes Latham puts "striking him" in the New Arden edition (London: Methuen, 1975). Alfred Harbage has "strikes him" in the Pelican (*William Shakespeare: The Complete Works* [New York: Viking, 1969]); but Samuel Johnson's more sedate direction is "menacing with his hand" (qtd. in Latham, p. 5). I have used Latham's edition for quotations from *As You Like It*.

9. Johnson's stage direction here is "collaring him." Grant White's is "Takes him by the throat." Latham makes the action even bolder and more formally consistent: "putting a wrestler's grip on him" (p. 5).

10. As Montrose points out, "Orlando's assertions of filial piety are actually self-assertions, directed against his father's eldest son." Though Oliver, as eldest son, is legal heir to the father's estates and authority, Orlando claims "spiritual inheritance" that obligates him to defend his father's name ("Brother," pp. 36, 37).

11. Oliver falsely tells Charles just the opposite, that he has "laboured to dissuade" Orlando from wrestling (I.i.138).

12. See Jenkins, p. 41.

13. For discussion of artistic framing techniques, see Susan Stewart, *Nonsense: Aspects of Intertextuality in Folklore and Literature* (Baltimore and London: Johns Hopkins Univ. Press, 1979), p. 23.

14. Keir Elam, *Shakespeare's Universe of Discourse: Language-Games in the Comedies* (Cambridge: Cambridge Univ. Press, 1984), p. 75.

15. Sir Thomas Elyot, *The Boke Named the Governour*, ed. Ernest Rhys (London: J. M. Dent and Co., 1907), 1:74.

16. Thomas Lodge, *Lodge's "Rosalynde" Being the Original of Shakespeare's "As You Like It,"* ed. W. W. Greg (London: Chatto, 1907), p. 20.

17. D. J. Palmer, "*As You Like It* and the Idea of the Play," *CritQ* 13, 3 (Autumn 1971): 234-45, 239.

18. Raymond B. Waddington, "Moralizing the Spectacle: Dramatic Emblems in *As You Like It*," *SQ* 33, 2 (Summer 1982): 155-63, 158.

19. Baldesar Castiglione, *The Book of the Courtier*, 1528, trans. Charles S. Singleton (New York: Doubleday-Anchor, 1959), Bk. 1, Sect. 21 (p. 37).

20. Raphael Holinshed, *The Firste Volume of the Chronicles of England, Scotlande, and Irelande* (London: 1577), p. 15.

21. Elyot, *Governour*, p. 73.

22. Sir Thomas Elyot, *The Castel of Helth*, 1541 (New York: Scholars' Facsimiles and Reprints, n.d.), p. 46.

23. James I, King of Great Britain, *Basilikon Doron*, 1599, in *The Political Works of James I*, introd. Charles Howard McIlwain (Cambridge, MA: Harvard Univ. Press, 1918), pp. 3-52, 48.

24. James Cleland, *The Institution of a Young Noble Man*, 1611 (New York: Scholars' Facsimiles and Reprints, 1948), p. 220; Francis Osborne, *Advice to a Son*, 1656, ed. Edward Abbott Parry (London: 1896), p. 23; Henry Peacham, *The Complete Gentleman*, 1622, in *The Complete Gentleman, The Truth of Our Times, and The Art of Living in London*, ed. Virgil B. Heltzel, Folger Documents of Tudor and Stuart Civilization (Ithaca: Cornell Univ. Press, 1962), p. 137.

25. Robert Burton, *The Anatomy of Melancholy*, 1621, ed. Holbrook Jackson, 3 vols. in 1 (New York: Random-Vintage, 1977), Pt. 2, Sec. 2, Memb. 4 (2:74, 2:70-71).

26. John Stow, *A Survay of London* (London: 1603), p. 95.

27. Stow, p. 95.

28. See Christina Hole, *English Sports and Pastimes* (London: B. T. Batsford, 1949), p. 30; Teresa

McLean, *The English at Play in the Middle Ages* (Windsor Forest, Berks.: Kensal Press, [1983?]), pp. 9-10.

29. Stow, p. 95.

30. Paul Hentzner, *Travels in England,* 1588, trans. Horace, Earl of Orford [sic], Strawberry Hill edn. (London: 1797), p. 25.

31. Hentzner, pp. 25, 26.

32. Richard Carew, *The Survey of Cornwall* (London: 1602), 75^v-76^r.

33. J[ohann] Huizinga, *Homo Ludens: A Study of the Play-Element in Culture,* 1944, trans. R. F. C. Hull (London: Routledge, 1949), p. 10; cited in Stewart, p. 171.

34. See Louis Adrian Montrose, "The Purpose of Playing: Reflections on a Shakespearean Anthropology," *Helios* n.s. 7, 2 (Winter 1980): 51-74; and Douglas L. Peterson, "Lyly, Greene, and Shakespeare and the Recreations of Princes," *ShakS* 20 (1988): 67-88.

35. On the conflict between physical pain and language, see Elaine Scarry, *The Body in Pain: The Making and Unmaking of the World* (New York: Oxford Univ. Press, 1985), pp. 3-11, 54, 172.

36. Roland Barthes, "The World of Wrestling," pp. 18, 19.

37. Jacques Derrida, "The Theater of Cruelty and the Closure of Representation," in *Writing and Difference,* trans. Alan Bass (Chicago: Univ. of Chicago Press, 1978), pp. 232-50, 234.

38. Staging of the wrestling match will inevitably reflect current theatrical and recreational styles. In an "improved" production at Drury Lane in 1723, Charles Johnson chose to replace the match with "a duel with rapiers, which he considered more appropriate to the dignity and social status of Orlando" (Oscar James Campbell, ed., *The Reader's Encyclopedia of Shakespeare* [New York: Crowell, 1966], pp. 43-44). Horace Howard Furness remarked in 1890 that "our stage Orlandos and Charleses are generally such feeble adepts in [wrestling], that this match, as it is usually seen, is far from thrilling" (*As You Like It,* ed. Horace Howard Furness, New Variorum Edition, 1890 [New York: American Scholar, 1965], p. 40 n. John Doebler's claim in 1973 that the "stage image of the wrestling match is always a memorable part of the current theater experience of the play" can be supported by the growth in recent years in America of wrestling's popularity as a mostly lower-class spectacle (John Doebler, "Orlando: Athlete of Virtue," *ShS* 26 [1973]: 111-17, 111).

39. Herbert Blau, *The Audience* (Baltimore and London: Johns Hopkins Univ. Press, 1990), p. 197.

40. W. B. Worthen, "Deeper Meanings and Theatrical Technique: The Rhetoric of Performance Criticism," *SQ* 40, 4 (Winter 1989): 441-55, 452.

41. Roland Barthes, "From Work to Text," in *Textual Strategies: Perspectives in Post-Structuralist Criticism,* ed. Josué V. Harari (Ithaca: Cornell Univ. Press, 1979), pp. 73-81, 76.

42. Latham, pp. 125-26 n.

43. Jenkins, p. 48.

44. Ralph Berry, *Shakespeare and Social Class* (Atlantic Highlands, NJ: Humanities Press International, 1988), p. 62.

45. Jenkins believes Touchstone is present in Arden "to remind us of the indispensable flesh" (p. 48). While I also see Touchstone as concerned with creature comforts, his "preoccupation with the physical" (Jenkins, p. 48) seems to me frequently feigned, and fundamentally different from Corin's concern with material survival. See Berry, pp. 61-67 on Corin's general sense that "real estate is always *real*" (p. 63) and its contrast to the idealizing perceptions of the court refugees.

46. See, for example, Carol Rutter et al., *Clamorous Voices: Shakespeare's Women Today,* ed. Faith Evans (London: Women's Press, 1988), pp. 106-14; Joseph Westlund, *Shakespeare's Reparative Comedies: A Psychoanalytic View of the Middle Plays* (Chicago: Univ. of Chicago Press, 1984), p. 83; D. J. Palmer, "Art and Nature in *As You Like It,*" *PQ* 49, 1 (January 1970): 30-40, 38.

47. Palmer, "Art," p. 34; Rutter, p. 117.

48. For a classic discussion of the "erotic androgyny" created by the boy actor playing a female character who masquerades as a boy, see Lisa Jardine, *Still Harping on Daughters: Women and Drama in the Age of Shakespeare,* 2nd edn. (New York: Columbia Univ. Press, 1989), pp. 9-36, esp. 19. Juliet Stevenson nicely summarizes the skeptical view of the illusions of gender in the play when she observes that within *As You Like It* resides "a much more dangerous" and "subversive play, one that challenges notions of gender, that asks questions about the boundaries and qualities of our 'male' and 'female' natures" (Rutter, p. 97).

49. Montrose, "Brother," p. 39.

50. Westlund, p. 82.

51. Kent Talbot van den Berg, "Theatrical Fiction and the Reality of Love in *As You Like It,*" *PMLA* 90, 5 (October 1975): 885-93, 887.

52. Palmer, "Idea," p. 243.

53. Valerie Traub, who sees the "'mock' marriage [as] . . . a deconstruction of the ritual by which two are made one" remarks that "as the distance between Rosalind and Ganymede collapses, distinctions between homoerotic and heterosexual collapse as well" ("Desire and the Differences It Makes," in *The Matter of Difference: Materialist Feminist Criticism*

of *Shakespeare,* ed. Valerie Wayne [Ithaca: Cornell Univ. Press, 1991], pp. 81-114, 104, 103).

54. Palmer's sense of "the idea of play" in *As You Like It* comes close to my own, in that he sees "equivocal relations between fiction and reality, game and earnest, folly and wisdom" ("Idea," p. 235). But in lamenting "Touchstone's inability to do anything except in play" ("Idea," p. 244) and in remarks about play's recreative purposes, he suggests a fundamental opposition between play and reality. Van den Berg affirms this distinction even more emphatically, concluding that "fiction and reality, like true lovers, preserve their separate identities so that they can mutually enhance each other" (p. 892). Montrose, in "The Purpose of Playing," develops a general view of the London playhouse as affording "a material realization of the *theatrum mundi* metaphor" (p. 71).

55. For a fundamentally different view of the epilogue, one which finds in it a late distinction between reality and illusion, see Fineman:

> when . . . in the epilogue the actor who *plays* Rosalind shows himself a boy, he accomplishes with the nakedness of his masculinity a final unmasking, pointing thereby to the play's last disguise and to the conditional that is the premise of the play itself.
>
> (p. 92)

However Fineman may imagine that the actor "shows himself a boy," masculinity (and femininity) have been shown in the course of the play to be anything but naked—gender is "put on" by the actor.

56. Castiglione, Bk. 2, Sec. 11 (p. 103), cited in Thomas M. Greene, "*Il Cortegiano* and the Choice of a Game," in *Castiglione: The Ideal and the Real in Renaissance Culture,* ed. Robert W. Hanning and David Rosand (New Haven: Yale Univ. Press, 1983), pp. 1-15, 6.

57. Montrose, "Purpose," p. 51. Montrose quotes the phrase "without admixture or qualification" from the OED.

58. Cf. the exchange at IV.i.8-9: "*Jaques.* Why, 'tis good to be sad and say nothing. / *Ros.* Why then 'tis good to be a post."

59. This essay originated in a seminar led by Douglas Peterson at the Shakespeare Association of America meeting in Philadelphia, April 1990. My work was supported by a Faculty Development Endowment grant from Rhodes College. I would like to acknowledge the helpful comments and advice of Bruce Boehrer, Jennifer Brady, Robert Entzminger, Joan Hartwig, Naomi Liebler, and several anonymous readers.

FURTHER READING

Criticism

Dusinberre, Juliet. "As *Who* Liked It?" *Shakespeare Survey* 46 (1993): 9-21.

   Discusses the influence of Elizabethan politics on the depiction of Rosalind and the presentation of gender roles.

Harley, Marta Powell. "Rosalind, the Hare, and the Hyena in Shakespeare's *As You Like It.*" *Shakespeare Quarterly* 36, No. 3 (Autumn 1985): 335-37.

   Argues that Rosalind establishes her complex sexual nature partially through the use of animal imagery.

Kott, Jan, "The Gender of Rosalind." *New Theatre Quarterly* 7, No. 26 (May 1991): 113-25.

   Compares Shakespeare's portrayal of gender in *As You Like It* and *Twelfth Night* with other works of literature.

Lifson, Martha Ronk. "Learning by Talking: Conversation in *As You Like It.*" *Shakespeare Survey* 40 (1988): 91-105.

   Considers Shakespeare's use of suppositions in an analysis of the complexities of conversation and sexuality between the play's principal characters.

Marshall, Cynthia. "The Doubled Jaques and Constructions of Negation in *As You Like It.*" *Shakespeare Quarterly* 49, No. 4 (Winter 1998): 375-92.

   Examines the play's structure using the psychoanalytic concept of negation.

Schleiner, Louise. "Voice, Ideology, and Gendered Subjects: The Case of *As You Like It* and *Two Gentlemen.*" *Shakespeare Quarterly* 50, No. 3 (Fall 1999): 285-309.

   Proposes a relationship between gender and ideology in Shakespeare's *As You Like It* and *Two Gentlemen.*

Shapiro, Michael. "Layers of Disguise: *As You Like It.*" In *Gender in Play on the Shakespearean Stage: Boy Heroines and Female Pages,* pp. 119-42. Ann Arbor: University of Michigan Press, 1996.

   Compares Shakespeare's use of cross-gender disguise in *As You Like It* with the use of similar techniques in plays by Heywood, Chapman, and Middleton.

Soule, Lesley Anne. 'Subverting Rosalind: Cocky Ros in the Forest of Arden." *New Theatre Quarterly* 7, No. 26 (May 1991): 126-36.

   Considers the influence of Elizabethan popular theater on Shakespeare's treatment of androgyny and gender.

Stanton, Kay. "Remembering Patriarchy in *As You Like It.*" In *Shakespeare: Text, Subtext, and Context,* edited by Ronald Dotterer, pp. 139-49. Cranbury, NJ: Associated University Presses, 1989.

Studies the relationship between power, gender, and memory in *As You Like It*.

Stirm, Jan. "'For solace a twinne-like sister': Teaching Themes of Sisterhood in *As You Like It* and Beyond." *Shakespeare Quarterly* 47, No. 4, (Winter 1996): 374-86.

Argues that focusing on sisterhood enables students to consider the lives of women apart from their relationships to men and to question assumptions about social and family relationships.

Tiffany, Grace. "'That Reason Wonder May Diminish': *As You Like It*, Androgyny, and the Theater Wars." *Huntington Library Quarterly* 57, No. 3 (Summer 1994): 213-39.

Considers unique elements in Shakespeare's vision of the comedy genre in the context of the *"Poet Wars"* of 1600.

Wilson, Richard. "'Like the Old Robin Hood': *As You Like It* and the Enclosure Riots." *Shakespeare Quarterly* 43, No. 1 (Spring 1992): 1-19.

Considers Shakespeare's condemnation of the Enclosure Act.

Henry IV, Parts 1 and 2

For further information on the critical and stage history of *Henry IV, Parts 1 and 2*, see *SC*, Volumes 1, 14, 39, and 49.

INTRODUCTION

Henry IV, Parts 1 and 2, the second and third plays in Shakespeare's second historical tetralogy, cover the end of Richard II's reign through the beginning of Henry V's reign. Critics have often noted that other characters in the play, most notably the king's son Prince Hal, Sir John Falstaff, and the headstrong rebel Hotspur, overshadow the importance of King Henry IV. This has led many scholars to theorize that it is not so much the king's reign as it is the education of Prince Hal that is the focus of both the plays. In this regard, many comparisons have been drawn between Hal and Hotspur, comparing the fitness of each as the potential ruler of England. Also of interest to critics has been the nature of Hal's relationship with both his father and Falstaff, as well as the reformation of Hal and the rejection of Falstaff. In addition to the study of characters, more recent analyses of the plays have focused on the unity of the plays, and whether or not they present a balanced whole.

While both parts of *Henry IV* are separate and independent plays, and in Shakespeare's time were performed as such, the question of the aesthetic unity of both plays as a whole has been a topic of abiding interest among scholars studying Shakespeare's history plays. Discussing this issue in his 1972 essay, Louis I. Middleman suggests that while a notation at the beginning of the plays suggests a disunity of conception that is hard to ignore, both parts of *Henry IV* ultimately present a balanced whole. According to Middleman, this unity is achieved through Hal's emergence as a complete character, learning from the superabundant spirit of Hotspur and the exuberant spirit of Falstaff. In contrast, in an essay comparing both parts of *Henry IV*, John Berryman (1970) takes issue with critics who see the two plays as a whole. M. C. Bradbrook (1965) also examines the question of unity and continuity between the two parts of *Henry IV*, suggesting that Shakespeare uses *Part I* to create and distinguish each of the main characters, while in *Part II* the role taking becomes more subtle. Bradbrook suggests that this evolution of character between the two parts of *Henry IV* displays Shakespeare's maturity as a playwright, allowing him to explore the emergence of the concept of secular sovereignty versus traditional judgments of right and wrong.

Prince Hal's character has also been an area of critical interest, particularly his transformation from one self to another. Many critics have debated the realism of his reformation; however, Matthew H. Wikander (1992) notes that Hal's earliest speeches prepare the audience for his reformation at the end of the play. Wikander contends that in a political context, this change is absolutely necessary in order to prove his ability to inherit the throne of England. Paul A. Gottschalk (1974) agrees when he notes that the tavern scene in *Henry IV, Part I*, as well as Hal's first soliloquy, predicts the impending change in his character later in the play. In addition to Hal, one of the most significant characters in these plays is Sir John Falstaff. Widely acclaimed as one of Shakespeare's most enduring and beloved characters, Falstaff provides a foil and comic relief to the seriousness embodied in Hotspur, serving as both companion and mentor to the young Prince as he prepares for the assumption of his rightful place as King of England. While much discussion of Falstaff's character has focused on his relationship with and ultimate denouncement by Prince Hal, more recent criticism has begun focusing on the character of Falstaff as a significant dramatic device. Barbara Everett (1990) explores the origin and development of Falstaff's character in Shakespeare's history plays, with an emphasis on the political significance of his appearance in *Henry IV*.

In addition to analyses of character and unity in *Henry IV*, the treatment of the reformation and redemption of Prince Hal and the rejection of Falstaff also have been featured prominently in many critical discussions of the play. Many studies have noted that in contrast to earlier critical interpretations of Hal's redemption and Falstaff's rejection, Falstaff and Hal conspire from the very beginning to build towards the rejection scene. This is so because the future king needs a public occasion, almost a ritual exorcism, to help display his reformation. Noting the sequential nature of both plays, Jonathan Crewe (1990) proposes that Hal's reformation is ultimately an ongoing process that begins in *Henry IV, Part I* and continues through *Henry V*, reflecting Shakespeare's preoccupation with issues of legitimate change and succession.

OVERVIEWS AND GENERAL STUDIES

M. C. Bradbrook (essay date 1965)

SOURCE: "King Henry IV," in *Muriel Bradbrook on Shakespeare*, The Harvester Press, 1984, pp. 72-83.

[*In the following essay, originally published in 1965, Bradbrook offers an overview of* Henry IV, Parts I and II, *contending that they are political plays that address contemporary political issues.*]

There was once a summer school at the other Stratford where, in two successive hours, a first speaker said that anyone who doubted the unity of the great continuous ten-act play was disqualified to understand Shakespeare; while a second said that anyone who thought 2 *Henry IV* more than a feeble 'encore' must be illiterate. The link that I would see is that of adaptability, the imaginative ability to create a part and to play it. In Part 1, this playful, heroic, or sometimes merely crafty capacity distinguishes each of the main characters. In Part 2, the role-taking (to use familiar jargon) is subtle, Machiavellian and by no means subjected to plain ethical judgments of right and wrong. In dismissing Falstaff, Henry V appears both kingly *and* treacherous—because his two roles can no longer be played by the same man; the King cannot be true to the reveller of Eastcheap. In the play as a whole, the width of reference and ambiguity of response shows Shakespeare's full maturity. 'The solution to the problem of life is seen in the vanishing of this problem', said the philosopher Wittgenstein; and Machiavelli's contribution to political thought consisted in dropping theories of political government and observing the facts of behaviour, in all their awkward complexity. 'We are much beholden to Machiavel', said Bacon, 'who openly and unfeignedly declares . . . what men do, and not what they ought to do'. A famous book on princely education, Elyot's *Book of the Governor*, had aimed in the early sixteenth century at producing a traditionally good, well-equipped and high-principled ruler. Machiavelli perceived the emergence of secular sovereignty; and the rest of the world was horrified at what he saw. It had already arrived when Warwick the Kingmaker, in Henry VI's reign, putting pressure on the Vatican to back his policy, manoeuvred in a way any modern student of politics would readily define; but the next century still had no words for it. Behaviour was ahead of statement; for it is the artist that first catches the implications of behaviour. 2 *Henry IV* came out shortly after the first edition of Bacon's essays; these men, however different their minds, were observing the same phenomenon. Shakespeare gave it imaginative form, Bacon gave it definition.

As an actor, Shakespeare was gifted with a special insight into the quick-change aspects of political life; Protean variety, which was the outstanding quality of Elizabethan acting, elicits exactly what the new politics demanded of the ruler. Many have noted that Richard III is a natural actor in his wooing of Anne, his scenes with Clarence, with Edward. However, he is drawn as conventionally wicked; for 'men should be what they seem'. In *Henry IV* Shakespeare is questioning the popular frame of assumptions more radically; yet he had to avoid shocking his audience.

The uncertainties, the troubles, the doubtful roles, the lack of any suitable heir—these issues were calculated to touch powerfully the feelings and engage the interest of any audience in the late 1590s. And the glorious resolution of all doubts in the triumphant coronation of Henry V was exactly what the country was momentarily to feel when James I peaceably succeeded in 1603. Alas! James was no Plantagenet—but instead of leading his people to war against France, he at least united them with Scotland.

Shakespeare was not writing a political treatise or constructing an allegory, but he was playing variations on a live political issue; in these plays the whole of society enters into the conflict. The colourless citizens of *Richard III*, the symbolic gardeners, Welsh tribesmen, the groom of the stable who appear in *Richard II* play minor roles. But here the life of London, and Gloucestershire, and the north is fully drawn into the play; while Shakespeare presents, in ever varying forms, a generous and yet sceptical questioning of that traditional principle which his earlier plays assume. This is political drama in a far profounder way than its dynastic interests would suggest, for the psychology of political life is here developed; the most successful man is he who can adapt himself most flexibly while retaining a clear sense of direction and purpose. This was exactly what the apparently changeable but really determined Elizabeth had done. Unlike her successor, she did not theorize; but she was a superb practitioner.

The Queen *was* the government; so throughout her reign the question of what would happen if she died untimely had troubled her subjects. A disputed succession meant the possibility of civil war—the ultimate worst thing for the sixteenth century (as perhaps it still is). This was a topic which no writer would dare directly to treat on the stage, for the consequences would have been extremely serious; but in the mirror of history it had been reflected ever since the young lawyers in 1561 put on *Gorboduc*—a play written by one of the Queen's gravest counsellors. This play enjoyed a great and continuing success; it is about the wickedness of dividing a kingdom—as Hotspur and the conspirators propose to do. Other plays dealt with similar subjects—*Horestes, Locrine, The Misfortunes of Arthur*. These are now little more than names in a textbook; but then they were the means by which the warnings and counsels of her subjects might be tendered to the Queen herself. They were played before her; when later still in 1601 Essex and his friends wanted to raise the city of London, they put on the old play of *Richard II*.[1] We see this use of history today in such plays as Brecht's *Galileo*, Eliot's *Murder in the Cathedral,* Sartre's *Lucifer and the Lord.*

Within *Henry IV*, each character plays several roles, and the leading characters often substitute for each other. Falstaff is the father of Hal's wit, the King father of his chivalry; Harry Monmouth is the son of Henry's loins, but Harry Hotspur the son of his wishes.[2]

Falstaff plays any and every part. His imagination devises ever-fresh fancies for himself and his followers, which are taken up and discarded as fast as they are conceived. He describes Hal and himself as thieves, in gorgeously poetic terms; he next promotes himself to judge—but is ready to turn hangman; he then becomes melancholy and repents. In the heat of exploit Falstaff is a 'young man' that 'must live', and the victim of Hal's love charm; in the next scene he is 'poor old Jack'. Having justified himself for robbery on the grounds of a vocation for it, he raises a tempest of rage when his pocket is picked, and takes the opportunity to repudiate all his debts. Playing the knight of chivalry, he asks Hal to bestride him if he is down, and boasts that his deeds surpass Turk Gregory's. He rises in fact from his mummer's sham death to claim the spoils of victory.

Against Falstaff's instinctive mobility, Hal's role-taking looks deliberate. He early casts himself for the role of Percy, playing it in a mixture of admiration and irony; in his revels, he plays the part of Prodigal Prince, with Falstaff as his father; and then, assuming the King, deposes and banishes Falstaff as later he will do in earnest. But he can play the potboy in a leather apron, equally well. The fantasy life of Eastcheap (even the robbery is a jest), playing at capital crime, at exhortation, at soldiering, is sharply dismissed by the Prince, even while he enjoys it. It is Idleness—according to Puritan opponents, the capital sin of all players. Idleness and Vanity are keywords in Part 1; both were favourite terms of abuse for the players, but Shakespeare draws their sting. It is in the comedy of Gadshill, sweeping along through the first two acts, that the grand genial theme of Robbery is stated. Thief . . . hangman . . . gallows . . . : the sinister possibilities are suggested only to be brushed aside, for the thieves are in company with 'nobility and tranquility, burgomasters and great oneyers'. In the older plays, it is the King's own money which is taken. Later the note is graver; the rebels carve up the commonwealth and use her as their booty; the King himself is confessedly one who stole the diadem and put it in his pocket; the tussle with Hotspur over the prisoners is an attempt at Gadshill measures. According to Holinshed, Hotspur said of Mortimer, 'Behold the heir of the realm is robbed of his right, and yet the robber with his own will not redeem him.'

Falstaff of Gadshill is succeeded by Captain Falstaff, robbing under royal warrant by his misuse of the King's press. At Shrewsbury the Prince robs Hotspur of all his honours, and finally, most shameless of all, Falstaff robs the Prince of the glory of killing Percy, and staggers off, a porter of the 'luggage' that once was the fiery Hotspur. The Prince, with an indifference more telling than contempt, offers to 'gild' what he at the same time labels as a 'lie'.

Falstaff's chief weapon is neither his sword nor his bottle of sack, but his jests; his power to defend the indefensible springs partly from nimble wits and partly from that innocent and unstudied shamelessness which breeds lies gross, open and palpable as the fantasies of childhood. Somewhere in Falstaff lurks the small boy who boasts that he has just killed a lion. Only by degrees does he penetrate from his Castle of Misrule, the Boar's Head Tavern, to the world of heroic action in which Percy moves; only in Part 2 to the world of judgment, organization, political theory which surrounds the King. He is an Actor, not in the calculating fashion of Richard III, but with the instinctive, ductile mobility of a jester who takes up any position you throw him, and holds it.

Henry IV, as in the play of *Richard II*, stands for the life of judgment against that of the fantasy and imagination; it is his superior skill in deploying his forces that defeats the dash and fire of Hotspur.

Percy's scornful mimicry of the popinjay lord reveals that he, like Hal and Falstaff, lives in the life of the imagination. To think of a plot is enough for him; he can feed on his motto *Esperance;* mappery and closet-war are quite alien to him. Yet when he meets the more primitive imagination of Glendower with its cressets and fiery shapes, its prophecies out of the common lore, Hotspur baits Glendower mercilessly. Glendower is Hotspur's Falstaff.

Before Shakespeare wrote, Hotspur was already a potent name in such common lore. Every member of the audience would have known that old ballad of Douglas and Percy by which Sir Philip Sidney had confessed himself stirred more than with the sound of the trumpet. Hotspur's contempt for balladmongers is ill-deserved; for they were to keep his fame alive. In *The Battle of Otterburn* a single combat, such as the Prince offers at Shrewsbury, is offered by Douglas to Percy, and the conqueror salutes his gallant foe, as the Prince, laying his royal favours on the mangled face, salutes the dead Hotspur. In the ballad, it is Percy himself who

> leaned on his brand
> And saw the Douglas dee:
> He took the dead man by the hand,
> Saying, Woe is me for thee;
>
> To have saved thy life, I would have parted with
> My lands for years three;
> For a better man, of heart, nor of hand
> Was not in all the north country.

The resurrection of Douglas to join the conspirators in this play adds greatly to their potency. Hotspur could so easily have won at Shrewsbury; the battle against odds is a true foretaste of Agincourt—the little troop with its Welsh and Scots contingent, led by one man's courage. Harry learns his role at Agincourt from Hotspur's at Shrewsbury.

Harry Monmouth, the changeling prince, born in the enchanted west, publicly takes up the role of chivalrous knight in Vernon's splendid description of his mounting his horse; and Hotspur cries:

> Come, let me taste my horse,
> Who is to bear me like a thunderbolt
> Against the bosom of the Prince of Wales.
>
> (IV.i. 119-21)

The essence of chivalry is the mounted charge: knights must have horses—and rivals to encounter. The images are cosmic, grand. As Harry says 'Two stars keep not their motion in one sphere'. The image of the rising sun dispelling clouds, which the Prince uses in his opening soliloquy, is inevitably parodied by Falstaff: 'Shall the blessed sun of heaven prove a micher and eat blackberries? a question not to be ask'd. Shall the son of England prove a thief and take purses? a question to be ask'd' (II. iv. 394-7).

Harry of Monmouth and Hal of Eastcheap are different roles for the same young man, who had learnt manysidedness among the pots of ale, where Hotspur contemptuously places him. The opening soliloquy shows the Prince as a passionless manipulator of events, whereas Hotspur is carried away by rage, ardour or mockery. In his presence, calculation fails; his uncle Worcester, the supreme Machiavel, gives up schooling him and at the last dupes him. (In his source, Shakespeare could have found that Worcester had in fact been tutor to Hal; a suitable appointment, had he cared to develop it.)

Hal's many parts, however, do not cohere as naturally as do Falstaff's. In Falstaff the contradictions spring from a great natural vitality; they are the fruit of abundance; in his presence, jests alone are plotted. The Prince is nimbly versatile, witty in a biting style and noble in a restrained one; irony and control are his modes, as lustiness and shamelessness are Falstaff's. In wit they are evenly matched; but Hal dispenses patronage, and a follower can never be quite a friend. The mixture of apparent intimacy and real insecurity which Falstaff develops at the Boar's Head is like that attained by players with such noble patrons as Southampton or Pembroke; and the real Boar's Head Tavern was one of the players' winter houses. Falstaff harps constantly on Hal's position as heir apparent, and though he may dare to call him 'cuckoo' and ask, 'Help me to my horse, good king's son', there is behind the Prince's retort, 'What, shall I be your ostler?' something of the sting that appears in 'I know you all', with its later, more dramatic sequel, 'I know thee not, old man'.

Falstaff's gross body, his constant and clamorous needs, for sack, for wenches, for a hand to his horse (the Prince can vault into the saddle), makes him helpless at times with the helplessness of the flesh and of old age, which raises its voice in the shrill reproaches of the long-suffering Mistress Quickly. Falstaff needs his wits to live; Hal needs his only to jest, and is an extraordinarily ascetic Rioter. In the old plays of the Prodigal Son, an addiction to harlots always characterized the Rioter. In Part 1 Falstaff represents misrule and good cheer rather than riotous life. Dover Wilson noted the many images of food which are applied to him—the most frequent is 'butter'; he 'lards the earth' and is 'as vigilant as a cat to take cream'. Though gross, these images are rich, nourishing, festive.

It is because he inhabits such a mountain of flesh that his wit 'strikes fiery off'. He uses his bulk as a shield to turn reproaches into a jest, and in his extraordinary union of the child, the animal and the criminal, never pursues any single aim, so that all his disabilities serve only to illustrate his freedom. The dexterity with which he extricates himself from danger is a quick and natural response; when he hacks his sword or attempts to cozen, he is always exposed. His confidence in himself is deep, animal, instinctive; in this, he resembles Hotspur. They represent the nobility of instinct, a feckless, unthrifty splendour of living which is unknown to the prudent court. Coarseness and violence, the stench of the battlefield and the smell of the stable, cling to Hotspur, who would have his Kate swear like a mosstrooper, and leave modest oaths to citizens' wives. The praise of instinct which Falstaff bestows on himself has some truth in it. He swears commonly and most properly by himself, for out of himself a whole world of living roles is created for himself and others to play.

Henry IV has only one role to play—that of the King. He has shown courage, and a disregard for conventional restraint and for all the sacred taboos in assuming the crown; as L. C. Knights has observed, he remains the embodiment of the guilt that is inseparable from getting and keeping power. His vision of a united England sets him above his enemies; but against his deep repentance, and that of the Prince in face of his father's 'dear and deep rebuke', is set the mock repentance of Falstaff, couched in the canting whine of the sectaries. Falstaff thus protects himself against the uncou' guid by stealing their thunder.

Interplay of character, exchange of roles, melting of mood into mood, and free range combine to give Part 1 its 'divine fluidity'. All is lucent, untrammelled in the consequence. The consequences are presented in Part 2.

II

Here the characters are sharper, clearer, more definite; they do not blend but contrast. Instead of lambent interplay, division or fusion of roles is provided, with clear separation of man and office. There is more oration and less action; the action belongs to the common people, while the King utters his great soliloquies and Falstaff talks directly to the audience on the virtues of sherris sack.

The embodiment of some of the leading themes appears in the Prologue Rumour, and I was sorry that this Prologue was cut in your production. Morally, Rumour embodies the Lie; socially, she represents 'rotten Opinion' or Seeming; politically, the unstable and troublesome times. The rebels are first shown a false image of victory, then a false peace which is prelude to a new conspiracy, and finally a false show of war, when the true grief lies in the King's death. She addresses the audience as her 'household'; it is a slightly malicious opening jest.

The last abortive rebellion of Henry IV's reign is led by the two symbolic figures of Mowbray and York; Mowbray, the son of Bolingbroke's first public challenger, and York, the prince of the church who echoes Rumour on the 'still discordant wavering multitude':

> The commonwealth is sick of their own choice; . . .
> An habitation giddy and unsure
> Hath he that buildeth on the vulgar heart.
>
> (I. iii. 87,89-90)

A religious rising in the north was the only rebellion of Elizabeth's reign: as a boy of five, Shakespeare might have seen the levies marching up against the Catholic earls, the Nevilles and Percies. Perhaps some of his London audience had marched too.

To his King's anxious calculations of his enemies' strength, Warwick, who is Shakespeare's countryman and speaks always with the voice of Truth, replies:

> Rumour doth double, like the voice and echo,
> The numbers of the feared.
>
> (III. i. 97-8)

Like voice and echo, opposed rulers of church and state recall the deposition and death of Richard II, the Archbishop dwelling on the treachery of the multitude who then denounced and would now worship him, Henry dwelling on the treachery of Northumberland, once Richard's friend, then his, and now his sworn foe.

The connection between ecclesiastical and temporal rule is debated when the armies meet. Lancaster says the Archbishop is misusing his position as God's deputy to take up arms against God's temporal substitute, the anointed King.

> You have ta'en up,
> Under the counterfeited zeal of God,
> The subjects of his substitute, my father,
> And both against the peace of heaven and him
> Have here up-swarm'd them.
>
> (IV. ii. 26-30)

But the treachery of John of Lancaster's ruse is hardly excused by his neat explanation that wrongs will be redressed, while traitors will suffer; and a final blasphemy is not lacking:

> Strike up our drums, pursue the scatter'd stray:
> God, and not we, hath safely fought today.
>
> (IV. ii. 120-1)

Comment is provided in the last scene of this act by Henry himself:

> God knows, my son,
> By what by-paths, and indirect crook'd ways
> I met this crown.
>
> (IV. iv. 184-5)

No one, least of all Bolingbroke, denies the guilt of usurpation or the conflicts it brings. Treachery in the political sphere replaces the mock robberies of Part 1; the presiding Genius is not Valour, but Wit, not Chivalry but Statecraft.

God send us His peace, but not the Duke of Lancaster's, the commons might exclaim.

The lament of Hotspur's widow is immediately followed by the appearance of Falstaff's whore; it is one of the telling silent strokes. Doll hangs on Falstaff's neck and tells him whether she sees him again there is nobody cares. The life of the play resides in these common parts, the roles of his followers who do not think of Hal as their future governor. He himself plays the prentice's part: this was a shrewd touch to endear him to all the prentices in Shakespeare's original audience—an important playgoing group. The action of Falstaff's own followers is largely parody. Pistol presents a great parody of the imaginative life; he outgoes even Falstaff's soaring inventions, a wild impossible creature who talks in scraps of playspeech, and feeds on his own mad imagination. If the ghost of Hotspur walks in Part 2, he is named Pistol. It has been said that we always fundamentally talk about ourselves, or aspects of ourselves; so, if Falstaff represents something of Shakespeare's own assessment of himself, may not Pistol be a player's nightmare? A parody of Ned Alleyn's rant, perhaps, but also an embodiment of Shakespeare's deepest fear—a wild tatterdemalion spouter of crazy verses, hopelessly mistaken in all he says and does, thrown off even by Falstaff. Pistol embodies the life of dream, of playmaking at its most distorted and absurd. It is fitting that he brings the deceptive good news of Hal's succession to Falstaff. When the King wakens from his dream of Eastcheap mirth, both Falstaff and Pistol are jailed. Pistol roaring his defiant Spanish tag as he is carried off, in cruel parody of Hotspur's motto, *Esperance:* 'Si fortuna me tormenta, spero me contenta.'

The great mythological popular scene of the stolen crown is haunted not by an explicit recollection of Richard II, but an echo of his fate, the sad ceremony by which Bolingbroke unkings himself. Giving shape to his imaginary fears, Henry mockingly hails his son by the new title which for all the audience evoked the 'star of England', victor of Agincourt.

> Harry the Fifth is crown'd! Up, vanity;
> Down, royal state! . . .
> O my poor kingdom, sick with civil blows.
>
> (IV. iv. 120-1,134)

Behind the dying king, the anxious father peers out, as death bores through his castle wall. The man fenced in by office, the body fretted by care, bequeath themselves to dust. Bolingbroke admits that even his expiatory crusade had not been without its prudential aspect; he had known only a 'supposed Peace', but he prays for 'true peace' at home in his own son's time. And pat to the catastrophe comes the old prophecy's fulfilment—he is to die in Jerusalem, if not quite the Jerusalem his rather stumbling piety expected.

The transmission of office, the demise of the crown as distinct from the death of Henry Bolingbroke, involves

Prince Henry in the last death-pangs of his old self. In his brief appearance before the King's last sickness, the Prince is shown with Poins, who, unlike Falstaff, is bluntly honest. The Prince must mock his own greatness, gird at Poins, but half confide in him. Hal of Eastcheap has no right to weep for a father's sickness, and is well aware of it. He takes up the prentice's part and surveys from this vantage Falstaff's descent 'from a god to a bull'. The encounter is momentary: there is a revival momentarily of the old manner ('Why, thou globe of sinful continents') a recollection of Gadshill; and a carefully casual goodbye, whose finality was beautifully suggested in the playing: 'Falstaff, good night'. This is the Prince at his most sensitive, subtle and inconsistent. When he finally takes up the poisoned gold of the crown and receives absolution from his natural father, he becomes warmly and simply a tearful son in the closet; but in public, wearing the 'new and gorgeous garment, majesty', he stands as father to his brothers, son to the Lord Chief Justice, and to Falstaff an image of the Last Judgment itself (the Exhortation of the York Judgment Play might serve as parallel to the rejection speech).

In his fears Henry Bolingbroke had given a 'character' of his son, in which sharp changes of mood and irreversible decisions are the leading traits. A strong personality, when its deeps are broken up by an internal earthquake, shows a new and unrecognizable landscape. The 'noble change' so coolly predicted in Part 1 is painfully accomplished in Part 2. The Lord Chief Justice, like the Archbishop a symbol of office, represents the better side of the last reign, all that was true in its 'supposed Peace'. This is how he justified the jailing of the unreformed Prince:

> I then did use the person of your father
> The image of his power lay then in me.
>
> (V. ii. 73-4)

He suggests that Henry should imagine a future son of his own spurning his own image; and the King allows the argument as 'bold, just and impartial'. He is no longer an individual, but a power whose image may by delegation reside in other bodies than his own, such as those of Judge or Prelate. The shadows of past and future kings melt away as the Sun of England mounts with measured confidence an uncontested throne.

Yet he sets himself under the law: 'You shall be as a father to my youth'. Henry, who had played so many parts, now accepts only one. Complete identification of man and office closes the visor of his golden armour upon him, and he becomes the centre of the group of brothers, an impersonal Lancastrian King. Henceforth he has an uncontrollable tendency to speak like a royal proclamation. However, in one jest dexterously combining religious reproof and a recollection of old times, Falstaff is symbolically buried:

> Leave gormandizing; know the grave doth gape
> For thee thrice wider than for other men.
>
> (V. v. 54-5)

In a metaphor derived perhaps from the parable of the tares, the Archbishop of York had seen the fourth Henry's friends and foes growing so inextricably together that he might not pluck up the one without destroying the other. This is not Henry V's problem in weeding his garden now. Falstaff, and that old father antic the law, Justice Shallow, are swept off to prison by Henry's new father and his colder self, John of Lancaster, who, fresh from the beheading of an Archbishop, can hardly see Falstaff's banishment as anything but a 'fair proceeding'.[3] It is a highly conventional scene, the traditional judgment scene for a bitter or moralist comedy, so that even Doll and Mistress Quickly are swept into the net. Rumour is confounded, Seeming is cast off, and Order restored.

At the height of his second military triumph, the capture of Colville, Falstaff boasts, 'I have a whole school of tongues in this belly of mine, and not a tongue of them all speaks any word but my name'. This elaborate way of saying that 'Everyone that sees me, knows me', by its metaphor suddenly clothes Falstaff in the robe which Rumour had worn in the prologue. Within the play, he is her chief representative; as indeed he admits by implication in a self revealing comment on Shallow: 'Lord, lord, how subject we old men are to this vice of lying'.

The delights of the Boar's Head and of Gloucestershire, with their undertones of death and old age sounding through the revelry, like the coming of winter in a harvest play, depict the wide commonwealth, the unthinking multitude of common folk about whom Bolingbroke and the Archbishop have been so loftily eloquent. Among the least of the rout, a little tailor with the 'only man-sized voice in Gloucestershire', suddenly echoes one of Prince Harry's proverbs from Shrewsbury: 'We owe God a death'. Feeble, who outbuys a whole army of Pistols, serves to link the multitude and the throne, as in earlier comical histories such local heroes as George-a-Greene had done.

The audience feels no compulsion to take the side of law and order; indeed the tragic themes predominate in reading, but on the stage this is Falstaff's play. The imaginative life of the action lies less in the sick fancies, the recollections and foreshadowing of Bolingbroke than in the daydreams and old wives' tales of Mistress Quickly and Justice Shallow. Neither Hal nor Falstaff daff the world aside with quite the carelessness they had shown before. More wit and less fun, more dominance and less zest, more shrewdness and less banter belong to these two; humour and gaiety have split off into the life of common men and women. Falstaff's mistaken dream of greatness is shattered and he hears himself reduced to a shadow of the King's imagination; for Henry V stands where his father had stood, for the life of reason and judgment against the life of fantasy.

> I have long dreamt of such a kind of man,
> So surfeit-swell'd, so old, and so profane;
> But being awak'd, I do despise my dream.
>
> (V. v. 50-3)

This was the formula by which the sovereign arose from a play—'Think all is but a poet's dream', as Lyly had urged Elizabeth. But against the voice of reason and judgment may be set a feminine voice, which was to be heard again pronouncing Falstaff's epitaph:

> Well, fare thee well. I have known thee these twenty-nine years, come peascod-time; but an honester and truer-hearted man—well, fare thee well.
>
> (II. iv. 369-71)

Truth resides officially with Henry V, yet in spite of his double triumph (honour, that 'word', has been snatched from Hotspur as if it were a boxer's belt, and now the lie and opinion are banished), Kate Percy and Mistress Quickly remain unconverted; while the incorrigible Pistol produces a line which is both a theological definition of Truth or Constancy and a parody of the motto of Queen Elizabeth herself: 'Semper idem: for obsque hoc nihil est'.

Henry sweeps all the nation behind him, except two women and a few fools. Such exceptions, however, are not to be despised in the world of Shakespeare's England. The uncertainty of the public view of Truth has been demonstrated. 'Thou art a blessed fellow', says Truth's champion, Prince Hal, to Poins, 'to think as every man thinks; never a man's thought in the world keeps the roadway better than thine'. There is no need for an unconditional identification with Falstaff; indeed there is no possibility of it; for the virtue of Shakespeare is to present many incompatibles not reconciled, but harmonized.

Notes

1. The deposition scene was left out of the first printed version.
2. 'Hal' a more vulgar abbreviation may be used only in Eastcheap: 'Young Harry' is the familiar form at court. Compare Falstaff's description of himself, 'Jack Falstaff with my familiars, John with my brothers and sisters, and Sir John with all Europe'.
3. No one would dream of calling John of Lancaster 'Jack'.

Robert N. Watson (essay date 1984)

SOURCE: "The *Henry IV* Plays," in *Henry the Fourth Parts I and II: Critical Essays*, edited by David Bevington, Garland Publishing, 1986, 387-422.

[*In the following essay, originally published in 1984, Watson proposes that the* Henry IV *plays, in addition to being morality plays, also allow Shakespeare to present an analysis of ambition in the private and public arenas.*]

At the end of *Richard II*, Shakespeare's ambitious figures become versions of primal criminals such as Oedipus and Cronus, whose myths associate father/son rivalry with political rebellion. The Henry IV plays use this association to study the evolution of filial identity, the individual's imperative and dangerous growth toward sovereignty. Here, even more elaborately than in *The Tempest*, Shakespeare offers a sort of morality play about an individual's moral and psychological development; but while it may be helpful to make that allegory explicit in a systematic, Freudian way, it is crucial to remember that the playwright uses it as a merely subliminal resonance to his analysis of ambition. Shakespeare exploits his deterministic power over his play-world to simulate a divinely determined world in which ambition is limited by the constitution of the individual as well as the universe. The psychoanalytic allegory which seems to arise naturally from the narrative events is one more way in which Shakespeare makes us feel that there are deep moral imperatives, not only in the universe but also in its human microcosm, for ambition's rise and fall. A coherent pattern attaches to ambition, which may be experienced in similar ways by an individual psyche at one phase in its development, and by English society at a crisis in its historical evolution. In the Henry IV plays, the private and public experiences of ambition are not only congruent, they are simultaneous, and mutually causal.

The rebels in the Henry IV plays suffer their own versions of the ambitious syndrome when they try to replace the reigning king. In *1 Henry IV*, Hotspur and Worcester discuss in suggestive terms the news that Northumberland will not appear for the battle. Hotspur argues that his father will therefore provide

> A rendezvous, a home to fly unto,
> If that the devil and mischance look big
> Upon the maidenhead of our affairs.
> *Worcester.* But yet I would your father had been here.
> The quality and hair of our attempt
> Brooks no division.
>
> (4.1.57-62)

Worcester's fear makes practical sense, but it also reminds us that Northumberland's absence constitutes the sort of bodily division that generally disables Shakespeare's rebels: It is "a very limb lopp'd off" (4.1.43), as Hotspur momentarily admits. When Hotspur subsequently boasts that "our joints are whole," and Douglas rejoins, "As heart can think," the statement is as self-contradictory as Douglas's restatement of the idea: "There is not such a word / Spoke of in Scotland as this term of fear" (4.1.83-85). The Scot has just spoken the word, and the notion of joints as whole as heart can think suggests an unhealthy jumbling of limbs, breast, and brains. The threat to this rebellion's birth is all the greater because Northumberland is figuratively the father of rebellion in these plays, and literally the father of Hotspur, who embodies the rebellious spirit. Without the father's presence at "the maiden-head," the insurrection seems doomed to a sinister, unnatural sort of birth.

In *2 Henry IV*, the implication that rebellion is born only through a dangerous distortion of the procreative process becomes more explicit. Lord Bardolph worries that unless Northumberland's forces arrive, the rebellion will resemble a man's "part-created" construction that must be left "A naked subject to the weeping clouds" of "churlish winter's tyranny." Though the analogy is to the building of an over-ambitious house, the lines immediately following encourage us to recognize the suggestion, on a secondary level, of an infant exposed to the winter by a paternal tyrant, as Oedipus was by Laius, or Perdita by Leontes. Hastings answers:

> Grant that our hopes (yet likely of fair birth)
> Should be still-born, and that we now possess'd
> The utmost man of expectation,
> I think we are so a body strong enough,
> Even as we are, to equal with the King.
>
> (1.3.60-67)

In the same speech, Lord Bardolph also worries about the empty naming and the vegetative death that often accompany rebellion: an insurrection that uses "the names of men in stead of men," he argues,

> Lives so in hope, as in an early spring
> We see th' appearing buds, which to prove fruit
> Hope gives not so much warrant, as despair
> That frosts will bite them.
>
> (1.3.57, 38-41)

The abnormal and premature birth of this uprising generates a nemesis consisting of stillbirth, paternal vengeance, diseased nature, disconnected names, and discordant bodies.

In *1 Henry IV* Gendower portrays his birth as another archetypal perversion of procreation. The archetype here is not a bodily rivalry with the father that must end in stillbirth or infant exposure, but rather the self-induced Caesarean birth by which the father may be overcome. Such a birth—though, significantly, it is merely a boast in Glendower's case—sometimes signals a classical or Renaissance hero's determination to conquer his natural limitations, to surpass his hereditary constraints. When Glendower claims that various disturbances of nature "mark'd me extraordinary" and above "the common roll of men" at his birth, Hotspur replies with a sarcastic, degraded version of Glendower's personal myth:

> Diseased nature oftentimes breaks forth
> In strange eruptions; oft the teeming earth
> Is with a kind of colic pinch'd and vex'd
> By the imprisoning of unruly wind
> Within her womb, which, for enlargement striving,
> Shakes the old beldame earth, and topples down
> Steeples and moss-grown towers. At your birth
> Our grandam earth, having this distemp'rature,
> In passion shook.
>
> (3.1.26-34)

Hotspur has twisted Glendower's analogy between his mother's labor and the world's eruptions, which carries with it an implicit claim to autochthonic birth, into its least appealing form—a form which also allows Hotspur to dismiss Glendower's boast, by metaphor as well as tone, as merely hot air, of a particularly unattractive sort.

Figures in English Renaissance literature whose ambitions compel them to claim autogenous or autochthonic status often claim this sort of birth: they carve their own way out of mother-earth in an eruption of air, and in doing so they topple down the old towers or trees of paternal sexual authority. Such births, or rebirths, are in both senses Caesarean.[1] Tamburlaine makes a new self by martial assertion, disdaining his "parentage" in order to command a thunderous army who "make the mountains quake, / Even as when windy exhalations, / Fighting for passage, tilt within the earth."[2] Spenser's autochthonic giant Orgoglio, the embodiment of pride and partner of the sexually sinister Duessa, performs a figuratively Oedipal attack to permit his own Caesarean rebirth:

> The greatest Earth his uncouth mother was,
> And blustring Aeolus his boasted sire,
> Who with his breath, which through the world doth pas,
> Her hollow womb did secretly inspire,
> And fild her hidden caves with stormie yre,
> That she conceiv'd.

This derivation makes it all the more suggestive that "all the earth for terrour seemd to shake, / And trees did tremble" when Orgoglio advances on Redcrosse. The giant tears "a snaggy Oke . . . Out of his mothers bowelles," and swings it so hard that he could strike down "a stony towre"; the wind from that "thundring" swing, clearly analogous to the force that originally conceived him, strikes down his rival for Duessa (I.vii.7-14)[3] When "his dreadful club" reaches his mother-earth, he seems to be planting himself to reenact his birth by his own power:

> The idle stroke, enforcing furious way,
> . . . . .
> So deeply dinted in the driven clay,
> That three yardes deepe a furrow up did throw:
> The sad earth wounded with so sore assay,
> Did grone full grievous underneath the blow,
> And trembling with strange feare, did like an earthquake show.
>
> (I.viii.8)

The next stanza compares this blow to Jove's lightning—an impregnating force in myth—which "making way, / Both loftie towres and highest trees hath rent, / And all that might his angrie passage stay, / And shooting in the earth, casts up a mound of clay." But Orgoglio's club becomes stuck there, permitting Redcrosse to cut off the arm of the giant, whose resulting howls suggest sexual suffering (I.viii.10-11). Toppled towers and severed arms are still towers and arms in the poem, of course, as cigars in dreams may represent cigars. But the close coincidence of these Oedipal and Caesarean motifs strikes me as significant, particularly because it occurs so consistently in the context of ambitious quests for heroic rebirth.

Milton's Satan is evidence that this archetype survives through Shakespeare's lifetime, and again the creature boasting of rebirth is a creature determined to claim that his own energies have conquered the derivativeness, and hence the fatedness, that limited his aspirations. By his incestuous conspiracy with the parthenogenetic Sin, and with their son Death who so resembles his father, Satan has made an open highway in the windy space beneath the earth, where he himself

> Toil'd out my uncouth passage, forc't to ride
> Th' untractable Abyss, plung'd in the womb
> Of unoriginal *Night* and *Chaos* wild,
> That jealous of thir secrets fiercely oppos'd
> My journey strange, with clamorous uproar
> Protesting Fate supreme.
>
> (Book X, 475-80)[4]

The birth of the rebel Glendower, which Shakespeare revises from Holinshed's account toward this archetype, associates him with a tradition of windy, ambitious, and self-induced rebirths; the efforts of Richard III, Henry IV, Macbeth, and Coriolanus to carve out their own passages to glory may be associated with, and moralized by, the same sexually fraught tradition.

Other symptoms of the ambitious ailment afflict these rebels. When he hears of his son's death in the failed insurrection, Northumberland himself becomes a furious rebel, calling for an end to natural order, individual identity, and family harmony, in a world that has become merely a stage (*2 Henry IV*, 1.1.153-59). His allies urge him to eradicate rather than exaggerate those characteristic ailments of their cause. If he will join forces with the Archbishop of York, the instinct against rebellion that rendered his son's troops divided creatures and lifeless shadows can be reversed:

> *Morton.*
> My lord your son had only but the corpse,
> But shadows and the shows of men, to fight;
> For that same word, rebellion, did divide
> The action of their bodies from their souls.
>
> (1.1.192-95)

The archbishop would prefer to blame the ambitious syndrome—the disruption of time's normal order and humanity's normal form—on Henry's bad fatherhood. In repressing his subjects' pleas, Henry has bred a multi-headed and sleepless son in their place:

> The time misord'red doth, in common sense,
> Crowd us and crush us to this monstrous form
> To hold our safety up. I sent your Grace
> The parcels and particulars of our grief,
> The which hath been with scorn shov'd from the court,
> Whereon his Hydra son of war is born,
> Whose dangerous eyes may well be charm'd asleep
> With grant of our most just and right desires.
>
> (4.2.32-40)

Unless the bad son Henry becomes the good father Henry by such concessions, Hastings adds, this unnatural procreation of Hydras through death will permanently replace England's lifegiving process of generational succession: "And so success of mischief shall be born, / And heir from heir shall hold his quarrel up / Whiles England shall have generation" (4.2.47-49). Inheritance thus becomes a blight on birth, a doubling and redoubling of miscarriages.

The rebels revealingly describe Henry's violation of his own heritage and Richard's as an archetypal parricide, with themselves in the role of abused parent rather than abusive child:

> *Worcester.*
> . . . being fed by us you us'd us so
> As that ungentle gull, the cuckoo's bird,
> Useth the sparrow; did oppress our nest,
> Grew by our feeding to so great a bulk
> That even our love durst not come near your sight
> For fear of swallowing.
>
> (*1 Henry IV*, 5.1.59-64)

The simile uses Henry's warlike approach to confirm his identity as an unlineal child, and even implies that he acts this way precisely because he knows he is not a natural heir. Worcester concludes by telling Henry that he and his fellow-rebels "stand opposed by such means / As you yourself have forg'd against yourself," and when Henry compares himself to a father-bee murdered by the child (Prince Hal) he has fed to strength, we recognize that Worcester was speaking more wisely than he was aware of.

Henry answers by dismissing these accusations as merely "the garment of rebellion" and the "water-colors" that "impaint" their excuse for insurrection; he thus locates the rebellion in the realms of costuming and painting that so often characterize ambitious identity in Shakespeare. This accusation, too, rebounds on Henry, without losing its validity as an accusation, when the king becomes a thing of costumes and colors at Shrewsbury:

> *Hotspur.*
> A gallant knight he was, his name was Blunt,
> Semblably furnish'd like the King himself.
> *Douglas.*
> A fool go with thy soul, whither it goes!
> A borrowed title hast thou bought too dear.
> Why didst thou tell me that thou wert a king?
> *Hotspur.*
> The King hath many marching in his coats.
> *Douglas.*
> Now, by my sword, I will kill all his coats;
> I'll murder all his wardrop, piece by piece,
> Until I meet the King.
>
> (5.3.20-28)

Douglas's remarks carry several unpleasant implications for Henry: first, that his own "borrowed title" of king may prove as costly an acquisition as it was for Blunt, and second, that the kingship may itself be only a wardrobe, clothes with no emperor, since his own act of usurpation has made the royal identity so easy to transfer and divide. When Douglas finally discovers King Henry beneath the colors that have become a disguise rather than a proclamation of identity, he finds him only by a process of elimination that is easily mistaken for a process of multiplication:

> *Douglas.*
> Another king? they grow like Hydra's heads.
> I am the Douglas, fatal to all those
> That wear those colors on them. What art thou
> That counterfeit'st the person of a king?
> *King.*
> The King himself, who, Douglas, grieves at heart
> So many of his shadows thou hast met
> And not the very King.
>
> (5.4.25-31)

Again Douglas raises troubling questions for King Henry. Is there actually any "very King" to be met, in the aftermath of a usurpation, or is there merely an assemblage of borrowed robes, painted colors, and two-dimensional shadows? Is "The King himself" yet one more ordinary mortal "That counterfeit'st the person of a king," as Henry's answer can be taken to imply?

Douglas alludes to Hydra merely to express his exasperation at the fact that each time he beheads a king, two new kings seem to appear. But this allusion may also serve to remind us that Henry has pitted himself against the same sort of unbeatable foe. By causing the assassination of the one rightful king, he has created two heads (as the factions are often called) that are vying for the throne; if the kingship has Hydra's heads, it is because Henry has initiated a splitting of identity that his counterfeits at Shrewsbury nicely symbolize. The myth of Hydra, at least in the Henry IV plays, seems to be a cautionary myth about inheritance: Hydra resembles a gruesome family tree, and the monster that must be quelled is the fraternal strife that would arise over the division of property each time a person died, were there no system of legacies. Civilization successfully represses this monster until Richard and Henry unleash it by violating that system, leaving each legacy open to deadly contention. Shakespeare reveals an England resembling the primal societies described in Freud's *Totem and Taboo* and Girard's *Violence and the Sacred,* societies whose rituals are essential to prevent an endless competition for patrimonies and an endless reciprocity of violence.[5] Some seventy lines before the archbishop blames Henry's misdeeds for generating "this Hydra son of war," Shakespeare prepares us to understand the allusion's larger implications by having the archbishop argue that Henry will not dare to execute the rebels after a negotiated peace, "For he hath found to end one doubt by death / Revives two greater in the heirs of life" (4.1.197-98). As Henry's "buried fear . . . Richard of Burdeaux" (*Richard II,* 5.6.31-33) produces the warring heads of Henry and Mortimer, and as Henry's death is expected to produce a war between Hal and some rival, so will the heirs of the archbishop's rebels second their fathers' rebellion, and their heirs will second the seconding, and so on through eternity (4.2.45-49). That is precisely what we see in Shakespeare's version of the War of the Roses, until Richmond cauterizes the wound in God's order (as Hercules cauterized Hydra's severed neck), and thus turns the two heads—the two Houses—miraculously into one.

Henry V's succession provides an interim solution by setting legacies back on a lineal track. That may help explain why Shakespeare has Canterbury describe the miraculous transmigration of Henry IV's solemn virtue into his son, concurrent with the transfer of the royal body politic, as a glorious conquest of "Hydra-headed willfulness" (*Henry V,* 1.1.24-37). Until his glorious transformation, though, Hal is the unnatural "Hydra son" who threatens to become simultaneously the royal heir and the enemy of royal heritage at his father's death. Hal vacillates repeatedly between his disobedient Eastcheap identity and a noble filial identity. When Hal inherits the unlineal crown, he faces the Herculean task of uniting those conflicting identities, as good and bad son, and as subject and monarch, into a single natural successor. Two crucial scenes, in which Henry's conflict with Hal parallels Hal's conflict with himself, prepare us to recognize the ethical imperatives of that task.

Act three, scene two, of *1 Henry IV* begins with Henry's interpreting Hal's misbehavior as a divine punishment for his own misdeeds. Though Henry, as usual, pretends to be slightly uncertain what his own crime might have been, a son's rebellious refusal to rise to the level of his royal blood would be an entirely appropriate rebuke to his father's rebellious insistence on rising to claim that royal heritage. The psychoanalytic maxim that the bad son has bad sons, and the physical maxim that what goes up must come down, both work to subvert Henry's hopes for a royal heir:

> I know not whether God will have it so
> For some displeasing service I have done,
> That in his secret doom, out of my blood,
> He'll breed revengement and a scourge for me;
> But thou dost in thy passages of life
> Make me believe that thou art only mark'd
> For the hot vengeance, and the rod of heaven,
> To punish my mistreadings. Tell me else,
> Could such inordinate and low desires,
> Such poor, such bare, such lewd, such mean attempts,
> Such barren pleasures, rude society,
> As thou art match'd withal and grafted to,
> Accompany the greatness of thy blood,
> And hold their level with thy princely heart?
>
> (3.2.4-17)

This insistence on blood finding its own level may be Henry's effort to bluster away the fact that "his blood was poor" until he stepped "a little higher than his vow" and usurped Richard's throne (4.3.75-76). Hal's "affections" may indeed "hold a wing / Quite from the flight of all thy ancestors," making him "almost an alien to the hearts / Of all the court and princes of my blood" (3.2.29-35), but Henry is also on an errant flight from his hereditary place. The system rights itself from within: in the very act of being a punitively bad son to Henry, Hal is said to resemble Richard, to stand "in that very line" of the man whose right it was to place his likeness on the throne (3.2.85-94).[6]

As Henry becomes caught up in the excitement of scolding his son, his language reveals a recognition that this throne is actually founded on such externalities as costume rather than such internalities as blood. He boasts of clothing himself in the simulation of an inward virtue, and of maintaining his person as if it were a borrowed garment: he won the people's affection when he "dress'd myself in such humility / That I did pluck allegiance from men's hearts," yet retained their respect by keeping "my person fresh and new, / My presence like a robe pontifical . . ." (3.2.51-56).[7] Marvell's warning to Cromwell in the "Horatian Ode" that "The same arts that did gain / A power must it maintain" (lines 119-20) seems applicable to Henry here: he discovers that the kingship gained by replacing a natural identity with an artificial one, replacing a person with a garment, can only be maintained by his remaining a polished costume rather than an authentic human being.

The redefinition of kingship implicit in Henry's usurpation is inextricably linked to a redefinition of identity, and one result is that not only Hal, but Sir Walter Blunt, and even Jack Falstaff, can play the role of King Henry IV with some success (2.4, 5.3). If Hal is what his father here calls him abusively, "the shadow of succession," there is good reason for it (3.2.99). Even Hal's promise that he "shall hereafter . . . / Be more myself" (3.2.93) has ironic overtones as a response to his father's criticisms, since Henry has just finished arguing that he won the throne by retaining an artificial self, or at least an artificial distance from himself. Whether it is Hal's irony or Shakespeare's, Henry's effort to define a true heir is trapped in a contradiction of his own making.

Finally the king manages to express his ultimate fear, the fear that uncivil disobedience (such as defying a banishment) will become outright murderous rebellion (such as killing a king). The way Henry expresses this fear suggests that he is projecting his own guilty deeds onto Hal, and thus conflating the roles of bad son and bad subject:

> But wherefore do I tell these news to thee?
> Why, Harry, do I tell thee of my foes,
> Which art my nearest and dearest enemy?
> Thou that art like enough, through vassal fear,
> Base inclination, and the start of spleen,
> To fight against me under Percy's pay,
> To dog his heels and curtsy at his frowns,
> To show how much thou art degenerate.
>
> (3.2.121-28)

One of the psychoanalytic tenets about this play is that "Hotspur's rebellion represents also Prince Hal's unconscious parricidal impulses. Hotspur is the Prince's double."[8] If this is so, then Hal's denial of his father's accusation represents a classic Freudian compensation-mechanism: the son's avowed wish to protect the father is really a

Peter Balogh as Henry IV and Jason Marr as Prince Hal in GreenStage's 2000 production of Henry IV, Part One.

response to his forbidden desire to destroy that father.[9] But whether events at Shrewsbury simply demonstrate Hal's filial loyalty, or whether they allegorically anatomize the psychological struggle that precedes and permits such loyalty, the crucial fact is that Hal re-establishes his identity as a true son by defeating Hotspur. He does so, on the figurative level, by retreating with that patricidal alter ego to an earlier developmental phase. There they both struggle for Caesarean rebirth with their swords, both seeking glory, but seeking opposite sorts of glory. Separated from his father, rebelling, "this Hotspur, Mars in swathling clothes, / This infant warrior" (3.2.112-13), is doomed to stillbirth in his own blood with his noble name revoked. Hal, in contrast, reverses the usual dangerous pattern of Caesarean rebirth, since his rebirth entails reclaiming, not evading, his lineage:

> I will redeem all this on Percy's head,
> And in the closing of some glorious day
> Be bold to tell you that I am your son,

> When I will wear a garment all of blood,
> And stain my favors in a bloody mask,
> Which wash'd away shall scour my shame with it.
>
> (3.2.132-37)

The king is right to take this as a complete answer to the indictment at hand. Hal has discovered a way to prove his royal merit while reconciling blood with garments, and the hereditary self with the adopted self. By drawing the battle back to that quasi-infantile stage, Hal can undo his status as an inferior changeling for "this same child of honor and renown, / This gallant Hotspur" (3.2.139-40). Now it is Hotspur who is abandoned by his father, and Hal who has recovered a healthy lineal identity. The son who was, in several senses, "degenerate," is now, in the same senses, regenerate.

The same pair of intermingled confrontations—Henry against Hal, and Hal's loyalty against a representation of his rebelliousness—appears again in *2 Henry IV*, during the crown-stealing sequence (4.5). Shakespeare's willingness to resurrect the doubts that were apparently put to rest by the end of Part One, and to retain so many elements of the first confrontation, suggests that he considered the psycho-symbolic situation very fruitful for exploring his theme. Again the Oedipal threat arises to punish Henry's usurpation, and again the suppression of that threat, by re-enlisting Hal in a healthy filial role, prepares for the martial victory that will affirm the new royal family's place on the throne.

Through most of Part Two, Hal's filial identity is badly in doubt. He is right, both on a personal and a symbolic level, to break Falstaff's head "for liking his father to a singing-man of Windsor" (2.1.89-90): the comparison implies that Henry is a eunuch,[10] his procreative powers ruined like those of Shakespeare's other usurpers, and that Hal therefore cannot be his authentic son or a legitimate successor. In the next scene Hal is reminded that the world still thinks his ambitions and rebelliousness preclude his mourning his father's illness (2.2.39-57). This observation grows out of banter about the ways "kindreds are mightily strengthen'd" by illegitimate births, and leads into two discussions about the ambitious ways people distort their kinship. First, Poins mocks people who seize every conceivable occasion to mention some distant consanguinity with the royal family (2.2.110-18); then Hal mocks Poins for his rumored plan to marry Hal to Poins's sister (2.2.127-41). These ambitious claims to royal kinship are recognizable versions, and hence recognizably symptoms, of Henry's unlineal usurpation and the national disease it caused. Hal, in Eastcheap, is trying to cure that disease by actions precisely opposite to the ambitious claims: he evades his close kinship with Henry, and avoids close contact with the seat of royal power. Naturally his father is unable to recognize the corrective character of this conduct, and the misunderstanding over this paradox sets the stage for the crown-stealing confrontation.

As the scene begins, Henry's visage reveals the ambitious man's emptiness and mutability: "His eye is hollow, and he changes much" (4.5.6). Hal is greeted with the information that "The King your father is dispos'd to sleep," but he soon reminds his father that sleep is forbidden to the ambitious, and reminds us why it is forbidden. Slumber in an unnaturally elevated position—whether literally, as a boy on a masthead (3.1.18-20; cf. *Richard III*, 3.4.99), or figuratively, as a man wrongfully on a throne—is both difficult and dangerous. As soon as Henry lets go, yields to that natural urge to relax, he also implicitly yields to his natural self, and the crown is taken from him. Hal describes the crown as "so troublesome a bedfellow" (4.5.22), as if it were a restless spouse in the king's bed, then steals that spouse from the king's pillow where it was supposed to remain until death did them part. Again the Oedipal overtones are clear, and again they serve a broader purpose than providing a fragmentary psychoanalysis of a character. The fact that Hal must steal his father's "bedfellow" in order to create his royal new self is the most incisive condemnation of his self-promoting impulse.[11]

Henry's response when he awakens sharpens our awareness of an Oedipal pattern, adding to the hint of mother-son incest a clear accusation of patricidal impulses (4.5.63-79) and the suggestion that these impulses have been abetted by a subconsciously chosen error of recognition: "Is he so hasty that he doth suppose / My sleep my death?" (4.5.60-61). The patricidal implications would doubtless have been strengthened for much of the audience by the precedent of *The Famous Victories of Henry V*, in which Hal comes to the brink of actually murdering his father for the crown. Henry's first words to his returning son verify that the mechanisms described in Freud's theories about errors and about the Oedipal impulse are both at work here:

> *Hal.*
> I never thought to hear you speak again.
> *Henry.*
> Thy wish was father, Harry, to that thought:
> I stay too long by thee, I weary thee.
> Dost thou so hunger for mine empty chair
> That thou wilt needs invest thee with my honors
> Before thy hour be ripe? O foolish youth,
> Thou seek'st the greatness that will overwhelm thee.
>
> (4.5.91-97)

The wording of this reproach points to all the symptoms of overreaching in Shakespeare, and as Henry points out, Hal's overhasty seizure of the crown would indeed convert what could be a natural inheritance into another usurpation. Hal would, in taking the bedfellow-crown, be fathering his own wishes into substance; he would therefore, like his father, be a sort of ghost or void while seated in that royal place, as a secondary reading of line 94 suggests. He might eventually have to ask, as Richard III does after battling and seducing his way to the throne, "is the chair empty?" (4.4.469). Hal's acquisition of these honors under such circumstances would be, again like his father's, a mere investiture, an act of costuming; and it would preclude Hal's ever becoming fully "ripe" for the throne, since Shakespeare generally suggests that a life forcibly cut off from its source cannot be given vital growth again (see *Othello*, 5.2.13-15; *King Lear*, 4.2.34-36). Whether Shakespeare is merely using Henry's speech to remind us of these hazards, or whether he intends us to believe that Henry is at least subliminally aware and expressive of them, the cluster of suggestive wordings at such a crucial moment in the transfer of identities seems significant.

Hal, for his part, hastens to re-establish his position as a natural successor, combining his answer to the charge of ambition with an answer to the charge of patricidal intentions:

> Accusing it, I put it on my head,
> To try with it, as with an enemy
> That had before my face murdered my father,
> The quarrel of a true inheritor.
>
> (4.5.165-68)

Again, a Freudian might argue that the son who imagines avenging his father's murder derives his pleasure from the premise of the fantasy, and adds the vengeance as a compensatory cover. But Henry is well satisfied with this answer, and asserts that Hal, because he is "a true inheritor," will be spared the unrest and mere theatricality of his father's reign:

> All these bold fears
> Thou seest with peril I have answered;
> For all my reign hath been but as a scene
> Acting that argument. And now my death
> Changes the mood, for what in me was purchas'd
> Falls upon thee in a more fairer sort;
> So thou the garland wear'st successively.
>
> (4.5.195-201)

Even this formulation, of course, depicts kingship as a garment, rather than an immanence, to be inherited; and Hal enjoys only a partial immunity to the ambitious disease as a lineal heir to an unlineal throne. His very first lines as king indicate that, as in Macbeth (5.2.20-22), the giant robes of majesty hang incongruously on a successor of questionable legitimacy: "This new and gorgeous garment, majesty, / Sits not so easy on me as you think" (5.2.44-45). Even his heart and its inmost filial sorrow are tainted by the theatrical world his father's role as player-king created:

> Yet be sad, good brothers,
> For by my faith it very well becomes you.
> Sorrow so royally in you appears
> That I will deeply put the fashion on
> And wear it in my heart.
>
> (5.2.49-53)

The difficulty in discerning what is sincere feeling here and what is acting alerts us to the fact that this world has only been partly redeemed from its artificialities, and that it will be virtually impossible to return it to a Golden Age. The nation's loss of innocence about identity, like the ambitious man's loss of self that often causes it in Shakespeare, is extremely difficult to reverse.

Perhaps the terrible difficulties that critics have in agreeing on who Hal really is provide a good measure of Shakespeare's success in portraying a world where moral distinctions and distinct identities have clouded simultaneously.[12] Is Hal entirely a cynical manipulator of his Eastcheap companions, or does he truly enjoy their kind of life and their version of friendship until the time comes when he must abandon them? Is he a ruthless king, or merely a king who must avoid thinking sentimentally about individuals so that he can be kind to his kingdom as a whole? Significantly, these questions about Hal's personality are intimately connected with questions about his legitimacy as a king (over France as well as England) and as a son (to Falstaff as well as Henry). The problems of kingship and kinship remain as deeply interwoven as they were in *Richard III*.

One index to the elusiveness of Hal's identity is the number of different names he is given; one indication of his peculiar genius is the way he converts this multiplicity, which shatters Richard II, Henry IV, and Macbeth, into a political advantage.[13] From his famous first soliloquy onward (*1 Henry IV*, 1.2.195-217), Hal seems conscious of an opportunity that his father grasps only sporadically. Henry makes use of theatrical identity in wooing the common people (3.2.39-59) and in sending counterfeits into the field at Shrewsbury, but nearly all of Hal's actions are based on the theory that, if identity must be merely role-playing, he should make the most of it. He wins a new set of adherents to his reign by befriending "a leash of drawers" who "take it already upon their salvation, that though I be but Prince of Wales, yet I am the king of courtesy, and tell me flatly I am no proud Jack like Falstaff, but a Corinthian, a lad of mettle, a good boy (by the Lord, so they call me!)" (2.4.6-13). By letting them choose his names, he becomes their master. In France, he uses the name Harry le Roy for another strategic incursion into the lower ranks of his subjects.

In his confrontation with Hotspur, Hal's quest for an ideal name becomes deeply interwoven with his quest for a filial identity. Hal fights Hotspur to regain his good name—we may think of Edgar whose "name is lost" until he proves himself a loyal rather than a patricidal son (*King Lear*, 5.3.121)—and wins "proud titles" by defeating him (5.4.79). But the process of winning back those noble names involves not only a superficial act of loyalty to the father, but also a deep, quasi-allegorical acceptance of the father's role in forming Hal's selfhood. Hal's encounter with Hotspur—like the returning Henry's first encounter with Richard's lieutenants (*Richard II*, 2.3.69-75)—begins with a dispute over names:

> *Hotspur.*
> If I mistake not, thou art Harry Monmouth.
> *Hal.*
> Thou speak'st as if I would deny my name.
> *Hotspur.*

> My name is Harry Percy.
>
> *Hal.*
> Why then I see
> A very valiant rebel of the name.
> I am the Prince of Wales.
>
> (5.4.59-63)

There is something archetypal in this combat, where "Harry to Harry shall, hot horse to horse, / Meet and ne'er part till one drop down a corse" (4.1.122-23): it recalls the symmetrical mythic combats, the desperately serious shadow-boxing between the hero and his Doppelgänger, in which the hero's survival is rewarded with a name.[14] England cannot "brook a double reign," as Hal here tells Hotspur, and a name cannot brook a double occupant; only one of them can be Harry the Fourth's royal heir. In seeking to win the "name in arms" that Hotspur acknowledges is at stake (5.4.70), Hal is actually trying to recapture the names Harry Monmouth and Prince of Wales—in other words, the identities as his father's son and his king's rightful heir. Both were nearly forfeit to Hotspur, as King Henry warned: Hal's relative dishonor left his political succession uncertain, and made his father wish,

> that it could be prov'd
> That some night-tripping fairy had exchang'd
> In cradle-clothes our children where they lay,
> And call'd mine Percy, his Plantagenet!
> Then would I have his Harry and he mine.
>
> (1.1.86-90)

Hal's roles as bad prince and bad son, by jeopardizing his name, have nearly dislodged him from his political and familial patrimonies; to retrieve them he must retrieve the name along with his royal father's love, and become the Harry who succeeds a Harry (*2 Henry IV,* 5.2.48-49).

Shakespeare emphasizes that Hal's victory over Hotspur is essentially an incorporation rather than an obliteration of the vanquished man's identity. Hal promised to "make this northren youth exchange / His glorious deeds for my indignities" (3.2.145-46), and that is what he has done; Hotspur, like Henry IV later, must have "gone wild into his grave" (*2 Henry IV,* 5.2.123), because all Hal's faults went with him, while his glories revert to Hal. Those glories consist of all the noble public virtues, all the things Hal knows his society and his father admire and expect him to embrace—in Freudian terms, they are the superego. The argument by analogy, especially an anachronistic analogy, is very risky, but in this case it suggests some intriguing possibilities, some deep resonances to Shakespeare's study of a conflict over filial identity. Freud argues that the superego is shaped in the renunciation of the Oedipal desires, and consists essentially of the father's censorious will within the son's psyche; the construction of the superego is at base the son's incorporation of the father.[15] Such a superego triumphs on several complementary levels at once when Hal promises to become the glorious Hotspur of the world and simultaneously vows not to rebel murderously against his father.

The standard psychoanalytic interpretation that makes Hotspur the embodiment of Hal's patricidal impulses therefore needs revision. Until Shrewsbury, only Shakespeare, and not Hal, could create such a displaced self; but the battle allows Hal to alienate his own rebellious spirit by both destroying and incorporating the opponent who is both rebel and noble son. When he retreats to a figuratively infantile level to compete with Hotspur for his filial identity, Hal may be retreating to a point prior to the Oedipal struggle and its shaping of the superego. In taking over Hotspur's glories while defending his father, what Hal really appropriates is a loyal filial posture. The fact that Hal can fully incorporate his father's nominal identity only by seizing Hotspur's glories corresponds strikingly to Freud's suggestion that the acquisition of a superego and the incorporation of the father are inseparable transactions.

In *1 Henry IV* Hal must defeat Hotspur for possession of his names and the accompanying hereditary roles; to reclaim his hereditary identity in *2 Henry IV,* Hal must similarly overcome his base rebellious impulses in order to reject the names Falstaff offers him. Hal accepts the many playful epithets his Eastcheap companions apply to him in place of his actual name, but only in the way that he accepts their clouding of his royal light in general: temporarily, strategically. A king's name, to twist Richard II's phrase, must not be twenty thousand names, and when Falstaff renews the epithets after the coronation, Hal rejects them and him simultaneously (5.5.41-47).

Several critics have observed that the repudiation of Falstaff is the repudiation of an alternative father.[16] The names that Falstaff bestows on Hal compromise his transformation into Henry's heir. Rejecting them is a forceful and fitting way of rejecting Falstaff's claim to paternity, which was already rendered dubious by procreative powers so badly abused that Falstaff, not Henry, deserves to be slandered as a eunuch. He spends those powers on prostitutes and "begets" only "lies" (*1 Henry IV,* 2.4.225). Even the children that his pillow-stuffed whore claims to be carrying are mocked or willed to miscarriage from all sides (*2 Henry IV,* 5.4.7-15). He taints Hal with a degrading patrimony, claiming credit for making Hal somehow no longer consanguineous with his father or his brother, Prince John:

> Good faith, this same young sober-blooded boy doth not love me, nor a man cannot make him laugh, but that's no marvel, he drinks no wine . . . . Hereof comes it that Prince Henry is valiant, for the cold blood he did naturally inherit of his father, he hath, like lean, sterile, and bare land, manur'd, husbanded, and till'd with excellent endeavor of drinking good and good store of fertile sherris, that he is become very hot and valiant. If I had a thousand sons, the first humane principle I would teach them should be, to forswear thin potations and to addict themselves to sack.
>
> (*2 Henry IV,* 4.3.87-125)

We are invited to recognize that Falstaff does indeed have thousands of such sons, all of whom have belatedly become consanguineous with him. They are what they drink. He is the father of the appetitive id, and those who give themselves over to that force incorporate him and become his more-than-adopted children. With the filial id as with the filial superego, the father is in the son as the son was in the father.

Of course, in claiming that Hotspur and Falstaff correspond suggestively to Freud's superego and id, I do not mean to imply that Shakespeare set out to write a psychoanalytic allegory in the Henry IV plays. Several critics have become understandably testy about the tendency to read literature as if it were secretly a series of morality plays that have lain inert awaiting a Freudian key to the characters.[17] But the history these plays describe was made by complex human minds, and the plays themselves were made by and for such minds. Characters who exist as words on a page do not have a superego and an id, but the historical person they are designed to evoke presumably did, and the reader or listener presumably does too. What would be absurd to attribute to Shakespeare's characters may nonetheless be relevant to the responses of his audience. As we watch Hal struggle with his alter egos, "we are made to experience a kind of psychomachia or internal civil war."[18]

If Falstaff bears a strong resemblance to what we call the id, then we may legitimately ask what deep associations he might have aroused in Shakespeare's mind and might be capable, whether Shakespeare was conscious of it or not, of arousing in ours. Several of the play's eminent critics have flirted with this issue. Jonas Barish argues that "To banish plump Jack is to banish what is free and vital and pleasurable in life, as well as much that is selfish and unruly," and that there is therefore an "element of *self-rejection* in the new king's action."[19] Franz Alexander calls Falstaff a "pleasure-seeking principle" that "the prince must master in himself."[20] W. H. Auden makes it more explicit: "Once upon a time we were all Falstaffs: then we became social beings with superegos."[21] Most other readings of Falstaff's allegorical identity are compatible with the idea that he represents the id. E. M. W. Tillyard lists several such readings: Satan's assistant since the Fall, youthful vitality, incorrigibility, the fool, the adventurer, the Vice, the epitome of the Seven Deadly Sins, the lord of misrule, and "a perpetual and accepted human principle" resembling Orwell's "principle of man's perpetual revolt against both his moral self and the official forces of law and order" which we may love but must banish from within ourselves.[22] If we accept the contention of J. Dover Wilson and Bernard Spivack that Falstaff is a version of the medieval Vice, we may still inquire what the medieval Vice was supposed to represent, and how it was intended to engage and rebalance the audience's psychic forces.[23] The combination of universality and elusiveness in Falstaff's character invites us to anachronism: we may call him the id if that is the name by which we most effectively understand the force he represents. When some new system for explaining the human psyche emerges, critics will doubtless find another name for Falstaff within it, and another reading of the Henry IV plays arising from it.

The identification of Falstaff with the id provides its most valuable insights at the moment when Hal banishes him, just as the identification of Hotspur with the superego became most valuable at the moment when Hal defeated him. Hal's visible act of loyalty to his father in defeating the rebel Hotspur complements the psychological transaction implicit in that conquest, namely the incorporation of the paternal superego. In the same way, Hal's actual banishment of Falstaff is an act of obedience to, and imitation of, his father, as its precedent in the tavern suggested (*1 Henry IV*, 2.4.481); simultaneously, on the level of the psychological allegory, Hal is banishing his own id, which urges him to resist the demands of his father and of his social role. The outward and the inward transactions in Hal's moments of crisis are equally real; they are absolutely necessary concomitants to each other under the circumstances. Shakespeare has again shaped a situation where the political and the psycho-symbolic imperatives coincide, giving us the impression of a deep moral truth in a morally resonant universe.

This striking coincidence also encourages us to accept one of the stranger implications in Shakespeare's treatment of ambition: the notion that refashioning one's identity constitutes an Oedipal crime. The theft of Hotspur's honor and the banishment of Falstaff establish Hal as a loyal son and a rightful heir; they represent at the same time his incorporation of the paternal superego and his willingness to suppress his id in accepting the hereditary royal role. The establishment of the superego, according to Freud, is necessary to intercept the Oedipal desires put forward by the boy's id, which might lead to castration or death if they were obeyed.[24] The correspondence in Hal between granting the superego power to repress the id, and accepting the hereditary identity, may suggest that an Oedipal desire has been forestalled in both cases, whether it is the literal desire to kill the father and sleep with the mother, or its figurative counterpart in the desire to suppress the self the father made and to let one's deepest wishes conceive a replacement, perhaps in some version of the original womb.

What interests me especially about the banishment of Falstaff, in terms of the psychological allegory, is Hal's use of the Lord Chief Justice as the enforcer of that edict. The notion that this corresponds to the superego's assignment of suppressing the id has been suggested, but its implications have not been fully explored.[25] In *1 Henry IV* Hal faces the ego's usual problems in dealing with the id and the superego. He must conceal the criminal Falstaff from the sheriff in the tavern, worrying at the same time about the political rebellion taking place in the nation as a whole (2.4.500-45); this recalls Freud's description of the ego as "a poor creature owing service to three masters and consequently menaced by three dangers: from the external world, from the libido of the id, and from the severity of the super-ego."[26] When Hal stands between the dead Hotspur and the supposedly dead Falstaff at Shrewsbury, he has apparently solved that ego's problems. Unfortunately for him, fortunately for admirers of *2 Henry IV*, Falstaff simply rises back up from its latency, as the id tends to do, and the superego must be reinvigorated to deal with him. The Lord Chief Justice is essentially a reincarnation of the paternal conscience, and his confrontations with Falstaff early in *2 Henry IV* resemble the evasions and encounters of the psyche's mighty opposites. Falstaff declares himself blind and deaf to the Justice's existence, and the Justice replies that Falstaff is indeed insensible or uncomprehending of any moral consideration (1.2.55-69). In their next encounter, the Justice tells Falstaff that "You should have been well on your way to York," and that he should "Pay [Hostess Quickly] the debt you owe her, and unpay the villainy you have done with her" (2.1.67, 118-20). He tells Falstaff, in other words, to meet his unpleasant social obligations in war, money, and marriage—the standard message of the superego.

Falstaff expects to be fully indulged when Hal becomes king, and Henry IV fears that Hal's id will know no restraint once he acquires the power to indulge it:

> For when his headstrong riot hath no curb,
> When rage and hot blood are his counsellors,
> When means and lavish manners meet together,
> O, with what wings shall his affections fly
> Towards fronting peril and oppos'd decay!
>
> (4.4.62-66)

The metaphor portrays Hal as an unruly horse, which is a symbol of the id from Plato's *Phaedrus* up through Freud himself, and which here associates Hal with Phaethon, the Renaissance archetype of the disastrously disobedient son.[27] Falstaff's response, on hearing that Hal has gained such power, is "woe to my Lord Chief Justice" (5.3.138). But Hal refuses to accept either the name or the role of Falstaff's "sweet boy" (5.5.43); he turns instead to the father of the superego, or more accurately, the superego of his father, embodied in the Justice. We may not enjoy watching this choice, but no one says the suppression of instinctual desires is a pleasant, generous act, only that it becomes a necessary one at maturity. When Hal, feigning indignation, asks how the Lord Chief Justice earlier dared arrest and imprison "Th' immediate heir of England," the man replies that he dared as the one who gave the heritage:

> I then did use the person of your father,
> The image of his power lay then in me,
> . . . . .
> Your Highness pleased to forget my place,
> The majesty and power of law and justice,
> The image of the King whom I presented,
> And strook me in the very seat of judgment;
> Whereon (as an offender to your father)
> I gave bold way to my authority.
>
> (5.2.70-82)

The emphasis on the Oedipal overtones of Hal's deed could hardly be stronger; but the surrogate father against whom he has done violence also offers himself as a surrogate father to whom Hal may submissively return. The Lord Chief Justice warns quite clearly what the consequences might be of not submitting. In this confrontation as in all of Hal's dealings with his actual father, Shakespeare's cautionary pattern looms ominously. The son who disdains his father, the subject who disdains his sovereign, invite similarly violent disobedience from their own sons or subjects:

> Be you contented, now you wear the garland,
> To have a son set your decrees at nought?
> . . . . .
> Nay more, to spurn at your most royal image,
> And mock your workings in a second body?
> Question your royal thoughts, make the case yours:
> Be now the father and propose a son,
> Hear your own dignity so much profan'd,
> See your most dreadful laws so loosely slighted,
> Behold yourself so by a son disdained;
> And then imagine me taking your part.
>
> (5.2.84-96)

This exchange, it seems to me, looks all the way back to the birth of civilization. This decisive moment in the reformation of English society involves the same forces and choices that, according to Freud's furthest-reaching speculations, led to the formation of the first human society: we are watching the superego evolve its authority from the compelling need to prevent endless strife. According to *Civilization and Its Discontents*, the sons in the Primal Horde suffered an ambivalence much like Hal's, and with like consequences. Their hatred yielded guiltily to love, whether or not they actually committed the patricide they fantasized, when they saw their wish fulfilled by their father's death. That love "set up the super-ego by identification with the father; it gave that agency the father's power, as though as a punishment for the deed of aggression they had carried out against him, and it created the restrictions which were intended to prevent a repetition of the deed."[28] The description of this transaction in *Totem and Taboo* bears an equally suggestive resemblance to Hal's submission to the Lord Chief Justice. As penance for a patricidal impulse, even one that was never acted on, the son bows in worship to the dead father's surrogate: "Totemic religion arose from the filial sense of guilt, in an attempt to allay that feeling and to appease the father by deferred obedience to him. . . . They revoked their deed by forbidding the killing of the totem, the substitute for their father."[29] The superego originates from this totemic conversion, Freud argues, and always takes the form of a surrogate father,[30] as the Lord Chief Justice does here: Hal urges him to "be as a father to my youth," then calls him simply "father" (5.2.118, 140).

Freud adds that we re-enact such a transaction in each of our lives: we form the superego by incorporating idealized versions of the self that have been lost as external objects—a dead rival, or, especially, a dead father.[31] Hal announces:

> My father is gone wild into his grave;
> For in his tomb lie my affections,
> And with his spirits sadly I survive,
> To mock the expectation of the world.
>
> (5.2.123-26)

This is an unnatural sort of succession, more the transmigration of a soul than the procreation of a body; but as at Hotspur's death, Hal becomes ideally filial by absorbing the ideal father in his superego. The opportunistic revival of the appetitive impulses embodied by Falstaff has, as I suggested, compelled a reincarnation of the conscience to cope with those impulses. The best part of Henry lives on in his repressive actions, which the Lord Chief Justice both symbolizes and performs; this new father becomes a part of the royal Hal, becomes the new king's censorious agent against Falstaff's pleas, the id's pleas, for special consideration. "The first requisite of civilization," Freud writes, "is that of justice—that is, the assurance that a law once made will not be broken in favour of an individual."[32] The laws of England are not at Falstaff's commandment, as he claims (5.3.136-37), because Hal has installed a new father within his own sovereignty. Such a substitution is possible, however, here as in Freud's analysis, only when the threatening real father is dead, and a surrogate, understood as protective rather than repressive, has taken his place by the son's own will. The Lord Chief Justice says he will now protect Hal (5.2.96), rather than restrain him on behalf of the previous royal father; the same shift occurs from the repressive father in the horde to the protective totem-animal that takes his place, a shift on which Freud comments extensively.

This intricate correspondence between Hal's psychological events and his nation's political events helps to justify the notion that both correspond to the events of human society as a whole. The psychomachia allows Hal's struggle to resemble the struggle of every human mind; its political counterpart may therefore allow us to generalize to the struggle of every human society. Freud argues repeatedly that the individual psyche relives metaphorically the experience of the sons in the Primal Horde, as if phylogeny were recapitulating ontogeny in psychological development, as it was once supposed to do in physical development.[33] Societies established throughout history, he also argues, have all experienced their own versions of the Primal Horde's formative trauma.[34] Nor is the notion wholly anachronistic. In medieval morality plays, the central figure in psychomachia of the sort Hal clearly undergoes was *Humanam Genus;* "Mankynde" is the name of an entire species. Shakespeare himself, in the Prologue to *Henry V,* asks us to "Into a thousand parts divide one man," and freely to jump

> o'er times,
> Turning th' accomplishment of many years
> Into an hour-glass: for the which supply,
> Admit me Chorus to this history.
>
> (lines 24, 29-32)

At the end of *2 Henry IV,* Shakespeare has already tacitly requested admission as such a Chorus.

What the Lord Chief Justice offers to Hal is precisely what the institutionalization of the superego offered to the liberated sons in Freud's Primal Horde: prophylaxis against an eternal cycle of rebellion. Without a surrender of the id to the totemic father-surrogate, the result in virtually any society would be "an ever-recurring violent succession to the solitary paternal tyrant, by sons whose patricidal hands were so soon again clenched in fratricidal strife."[35] The only solution is a law, embodied in the totemic father-surrogate, that distributes rights fairly among the brothers and becomes internalized by each of them as the superego; both this creation of the surrogate, and its internalization, are clearly outlined in Hal's submission to the Justice who promises to end rebellion by even-handedness. Hal has learned the bitter lesson of his father's usurpation, which loosed "this Hydra son of war" not only by the violent precedent it set, but also by Henry's refusal to share the royal privileges among those who helped him overthrow the previous tyrant (*2 Henry IV,* 4.2.35-40). The Percies resemble the younger brothers in the Primal Horde, who, having assisted in killing the repressive father, find they have no choice (and no qualms) about attacking the repressive new father-figure as well. The dying Henry IV seems to recognize the problem, urging Hal's favorite brother Thomas to nurture their affection so that "noble offices thou mayst effect / Of mediation, after I am dead, / Between his greatness and thy other brethren," and thereby provide, as if he were an Anglo-Saxon ring-giver,

> A hoop of gold to bind thy brothers in,
> That the united vessel of their blood,
> Mingled with venom of suggestion
> (As, force perforce, the age will pour it in),
> Shall never leak.
>
> (4.4.19-47)

Three scenes later, when Hal actually succeeds his father, his first words to his brothers are a defense against this danger: he encourages them to continue in their communal mourning for the dead father, but assures them that "Not Amurath an Amurath succeeds," that he will not be like the man who murdered all his brothers when he took power (5.2.46-50). Instead, he has taken into himself the protective (and therefore protected) qualities of the totemic father whom the brothers now mourn and reverence unitedly. For England, as (Freud argues) for societies in all times and places, this is the only way to break the violent cycle. Shakespeare has again grounded his English history in the history of all human societies.

Hal thus becomes a sort of St. George, or perhaps a sort of Beowulf, defending England against the monster of fratricide that his predecessors have awakened, whether that primal dragon takes the name of Hydra or Amurath or Cain. Bullingbrook first appears before Richard II to avenge the spilt blood of the Duke of Gloucester, "Which blood, like sacrificing Abel's, cries, / Even from the tongueless caverns of the earth, / To me for justice and rough chastisement" (1.1.98-106). The lurking accusation, apparently well founded, is that Richard (through Mowbray) played the role of Cain against his kinsman; this accusation starts in motion the horrible fratricidal struggle that dominates both of Shakespeare's tetralogies.

Perhaps the worst thing about this moral ailment is that it is contagious, and that it is paradoxically congenital to any *unlineal* inheritance of the throne. When Henry completes the promised vengeance by an indirect murder of his own, he desperately tries to displace his primal culpability onto his agent Exton, whom he sends to wander through the dark world "With Cain" (5.6.43). But the circle cannot so easily be broken. Henry must war with Northumberland, his son Hal with Northumberland's son Hotspur, and when the word of Hotspur's death arrives, Northumberland states the danger only too plainly in bitterly endorsing it:

> But let one spirit of the first-born Cain
> Reign in all bosoms, that each heart being set
> On bloody courses, the rude scene may end,
> And darkness be the burier of the dead!
>
> (*2 Henry IV*, 1.1.157-60)[36]

The crime that "hath the primal eldest curse upon't," in the Henry IV plays as in *Hamlet* (3.3.37), combines patricide, fratricide, and usurpation, in an invitation to endless bloodshed. The same sort of conflation appears in *Gorboduc,* and in the Elizabethan "Homily against Disobedience and wilful Rebellion," which warns that insurrection can only lead "the brother to seek and often to work the death of his brother, the son of the father."[37] Half a century after Shakespeare wrote the Henry IV plays, Thomas Hobbes expressed similar fears in terms that anticipate Freud's interpretation of the primal murder.[38] So the danger Freud perceived was at least partly visible to Shakespeare's contemporaries, and therefore a plausible subject for Shakespeare's stage.

In forbidding Falstaff (and therefore his own id) from using royal power to gratify his appetites at the expense of others, Hal is reenacting society's first triumph over the force that threatened to destroy it, and renewing English society's will to resist that force. It is natural enough, given the respective occupations of Falstaff and the Lord Chief Justice and the relations between the two men, that accepting one as a surrogate father would entail excluding the other; but that natural situation carries a sharp allegorical import. On a realistic level, Hal's suppression of his own unruly impulses allows him to accept the Lord Chief Justice, and that acceptance leads to the rejection of Falstaff. On the level of the psychomachia, the rejection of Falstaff is merely the acting-out of the suppression of the id that we have seen moments earlier in the acceptance of the Justice. We are on shifting levels of allegory that disguise themselves as chronological sequence, as for example when the Redcrosse Knight's battle with Error is essentially an acting-out of a battle he has already fought in traveling through the Wood of Error with Una to reach that dragon, or when Christian and his companions fall into the net of Flatterer only after being coaxed out of the rightful path by flattery and led some distance, in *The Pilgrim's Progress*.[39] Hal's embrace of the Justice and his casting-out of Falstaff can be viewed as a single psychological moment. Time yields to allegory in that archetypal situation, even as that moment in the history of English society becomes suddenly synchronous with the formative moment of all human societies.

The psychomachia lends metaphorical richness to Hal's comparison of his experience of Falstaff to the experience of a wicked dream, in which the appetites of the id run rampant. The self-transformation Hal claims to have accomplished in the rejection speech becomes a slightly presumptuous exclusion of one side of his human heritage, one half of his divided father-figure. The speech shows clear traces of the self-alienation and the wakefulness that characterize the ambitious syndrome, but this is an alienation only from the id, and an awakening only from the dreams of the id:

> I have long dreamt of such a kind of man,
> So surfeit-swell'd, so old, and so profane;
> But, being awak'd, I do despise my dream.
> . . . . .
> Reply not to me with a fool-born jest,
> Presume not that I am the thing I was,
> For God doth know, so shall the world perceive,
> That I have turn'd away my former self;
> So will I those that kept me company.
> When thou dost hear I am as I have been,
> Approach me, and thou shalt be as thou wast,
> The tutor and the feeder of my riots.
>
> (5.5.49-62)

The precedents of this announcement are not promising: other Shakespearean characters who use such phrases are unhealthily at war with their own natures and with nature itself. Richard III asks Queen Elizabeth to "Plead what I will be, not what I have been; / Not my deserts, but what I will deserve" (4.4.414-15); Richard II struggles to "forget what I have been! / Or not remember what I must be now!" (3.3.138-39). Hal's proclamation may even anticipate Iago's "I am not what I am" (1.1.65). From these moments through his last plays, Shakespeare persistently asks whether we can leave a degrading but natural part of ourselves behind, kill the heart of its father, without inviting a devastating nemesis. He refuses to adopt the notion, offered by most of his sources, that Hal simply underwent a miraculous transformation at his coronation; the problems of identity are too important and too complex for him to accept such an evasion.[40] The psychomachia invites us to recognize Hal's self-*askesis,* his amputation of the facets of his identity that do not fit with his royal role. What I am raising again, from a different perspective, is the vexed question of whether Hal's humanity survives the task of assuming a kingship that is only partly lineal, only partly legitimate in its birth.

If *Richard II* ends with Henry being brought "Thy buried fear" (5.6.41), *2 Henry IV* ends with Hal confronting his buried id; and both cases invite our fear that the triumph may prove Pyrrhic, that the king may have buried an essential part of himself in burying his supposed enemy and assuming the crown. Hal's manipulation of his former companions and his wording of grief for his father seem to lack human grace, and may betoken a lack of human feeling. But this apparent heartlessness, and his bloodless mode of inheritance, unattractive and unhealthy as they may be, represent a plausible way for Hal to fulfill his role as the nemesis generated by Henry's violations, without incurring a similar nemesis of his own. Shakespeare and Hal virtually conspire to find an escape from the vicious cycle of Oedipal justice. Hal's political strategy of imitating the sun by hiding his glory temporarily in Eastcheap corresponds, in timing and symbolic form, to the psychological strategy whereby he merely imitates the rebellious son. He plays the disobedient and potentially patricidal part long enough to punish his father and fulfill the general expectation, meanwhile retaining an identity as a temporarily loyal son to Falstaff, against whom he can later carry out the patricidal violence that Shakespeare's pattern insists he must have inherited. Falstaff, like Richard III, becomes a scapegoat in his dramatic creator's system of poetic justice. Like the Lords of Misrule to whom he is often compared, Falstaff is placed in his exalted role only to allow an outlet for hostilities that would be dangerous to express against the actual sovereign. Then, at Henry's death, Hal reclaims his lineal virtues metempsychotically, with the Lord Chief Justice as the visible father of this immaculately conceived new royal self. Hal proves himself his father's natural son by coming to the royal identity as unnaturally as his father had, without committing his father's crimes against lineage in the process.

But if Hal's genius is his ability to live constantly in the familial and political roles his world demands of him, that is also his torment. The unity of his character must always be its capacity for multiplicity, including an unappealing talent (like his brother John's) for duplicity. His innermost self may be so difficult for critics to locate and define because it is equally elusive for Hal himself. The difference between Hal and other victims of the ambitious pattern is not that he retains a vital inner self—it is not clear that he does—but rather that his theatrical self is hereditary, and that he has the *sprezzatura*, the art of disguising his artfulness, to make it viable. To inherit his father's role as king, as Henry had warned him (*1 Henry IV*, 3.2.46-59), he must inherit first his father's theatrical use of his "person," the arm's-length manipulation of the self. Hal learns this lesson and betters the instruction.

Notes

1. The analogy between births such as Glendower's and Tamburlaine's, and eruptions of trapped air, recalls Lucan's description of Julius Caesar's martial energies: "As lightning by the wind forc'd from a cloud / Breakes through the wounded aire with thunder loud." James M. Swan, "History, Pastoral, and Desire: A Psychoanalytic Study of English Renaissance Literature and Society" (Ph.D. diss. Stanford University, 1974), pp. 300-302, has interpreted this passage as the source for images of self-induced Caesarean birth in Philemon Holland's *Historie of the World* (translated from Pliny in 1601) and in Marvell's "The Unfortunate Lover"; he also confirms my longstanding suspicion that the much-debated lines 13-24 of Marvell's "Horatian Ode" allude to a similar action, complete with a pun on Caesar's name. See also C. A. Patrides, "'Till Prepared for Longer Flight,'" in *Approaches to Marvell* (London: Routledge and Kegan Paul, 1978), p. 35.

2. Christopher Marlowe, *Tamburlaine, Part One*, in *The Complete Plays of Christopher Marlowe*, ed. J. B. Steane (Harmondsworth, Middlesex: Penguin, 1969), 1.2.49-51.

3. Edmund Spenser, *The Faerie Queene*, in *Spenser: Poetical Works*, ed. J. C. Smith and E. De Selincourt (New York: Oxford University Press, 1970). For the impregnating power of Jove's lightning, see Plutarch, *Lives of the Noble Grecians and Romans*, trans. Thomas North (1579), ed. W. E. Henley (London, 1895), IV, 299, 330-331; here again such a conception generates a suggestively Oedipal hero.

4. John Milton, *Paradise Lost*, ed. Merritt Y. Hughes (Indianapolis, Ind.: Odyssey-Bobbs Merrill, 1962); subsequent citations are from this edition.

5. Sigmund Freud, *Totem and Taboo*, trans. James Strachey (New York: Norton, 1950), pp. 142-144. In chapter 6 of his *Violence and the Sacred*, Girard examines the Hydra-like threat presented by twins or doubles, which raise the danger of fraternal rivalry over legacies and even identity.

6. Norman Sanders, "The True Prince and the False Thief: Prince Hal and the Shift of Identity," *Shakespeare Survey* 30 (1977), 30, remarks on the propriety of this resemblance.

7. Ronald Berman, "The Nature of Guilt in the Henry IV Plays," *Shakespeare Studies* 1 (1965), 27, discusses Henry's use of disguise to gain the throne. See also Righter, *Shakespeare and Idea of Play*, pp. 126-127.

8. Ernst Kris, "Prince Hal's Conflict," in Faber, *Design Within*, p. 395.

9. Dreams of saving the father from an assailant, however one wishes to interpret them, are apparently common among young men. Freud, in *Totem and Taboo* (p. 72), speculates about a mechanism whereby "the original *wish* that the loved person may die is replaced by a *fear* that he may die. So that when the neurosis appears to be so tenderly altruistic, it is merely *compensating* for an underlying contrary attitude of brutal egoism."

10. Derek Traversi, *Shakespeare from Richard II to Henry V* (Stanford: Stanford University Press, 1957), p. 125.

11. The parallel is of course imperfect: marrying one's mother does not become appropriate at one's father's death, as inheriting his title might. John W. Blanpied, "'Unfathered heirs and loathly births of nature': Bringing History to Crisis in *2 Henry IV*,"

English Literary Renaissance 5 (1975), 228-229, discusses the displacement of the parricide into the crown; Freud argues that the Oedipal impulse is often displaced into the mother, who is here equated with the crown.

12. Norman Rabkin, *Shakespeare and the Problem of Meaning* (Chicago: University of Chicago Press, 1981), pp. 33-62, argues eloquently and convincingly that our ambivalence toward Hal is not only permissible, it is essential to understanding Shakespeare's sort of meaning.

13. Warren J. Macisaac, "'A Commodity of Good Names' in the *Henry IV* Plays," *Shakespeare Quarterly* 29 (1978), 417-419, comments on the meaningful modulations of Hal's name.

14. George Steiner, in a conversation in 1978, reported finding such stories in many mythologies, stories of a hero battling through the night against a Doppelgänger, and receiving a name from him in the morning.

15. Sigmund Freud, *The Ego and the Id*, trans. Joan Riviere, rev. and ed. James Strachey (New York: Norton, 1962), pp. 21-29; in *Totem and Taboo*, this incorporation of the father takes the literal form of a ritual meal in which the patricidal sons consume the father or his totem-surrogate as part of a penitential renunciation of their common deed (p. 142). See similarly Freud's *Civilization and Its Discontents*, trans. James Strachey (New York: Norton, 1961), p. 76. An interesting sidelight here is Jacques Lacan's theory that the Oedipal conflict resides essentially in a boy's relation to the name (*nom*, with a pun on *non*) of the father; see Monique David-Menard, "Lacanians Against Lacan," trans. Brian Massumi, in *Social Text* (Fall 1982), p. 90.

16. Kris, "Prince Hal," in Faber, *Design Within*, p. 399, is an early example; see also Faber, pp. 421-422.

17. Meredith Skura, *The Literary Use of the Psychoanalytic Process* (New Haven: Yale University Press, 1981), p. 16, cites several such objections.

18. Edward Pechter, "Falsifying Men's Hopes: The Ending of *1 Henry IV*," *Modern Language Quarterly* 41 (1980), 216.

19. Jonas Barish, "The Turning Away of Prince Hal," *Shakespeare Studies* 1 (1965), 15 and 10.

20. Franz Alexander, "A Note on Falstaff," *Psychoanalytic Quarterly* 2 (1933), 592-606; cited by Barish, *Shakespeare Studies* 1:16 n. 5.

21. W. H. Auden, *The Dyer's Hand and Other Essays* (New York: Random House, 1948; rpt. 1962), p. 195.

22. Tillyard, *Shakespeare's History Plays*, pp. 285-291; the quotations are from p. 289. S. C. Sen Gupta, *Shakespeare's History Plays* (London: Oxford University Press, 1964), p. 127, calls Falstaff "a symbol of the unrepressed instincts of humanity, which thirst for fulfillment, rebel against repression"; cited by Sidney Shanker, *Shakespeare and the Uses of Ideology*, Studies in English Literature, vol. 105 (The Hague: Mouton, 1975), p. 65 n. 19. We may add to Tillyard's list the figure of the *picaro*, cited as an element of Falstaff by H. B. Rothschild Jr., "Falstaff and the Picaresque Tradition," *Modern Language Review* 68 (1972), 14-21.

23. J. Dover Wilson, *The Fortunes of Falstaff* (New York: Macmillan, 1944), pp. 18-28; Bernard Spivack, *Shakespeare and the Allegory of Evil* (New York: Columbia University Press, 1958), pp. 87-91.

24. Freud, *Ego and Id*, p. 26, is one of many statements of this theory.

25. Skura, *Literary Use*, p. 36, mentions "the obvious psychomachia in the triple world of *Henry IV, Part Two*, where Hal has to choose between the id (Falstaff) and the superego (the Lord Chief Justice)." Danby, *Doctrine of Nature*, p. 95, asserts that "In the rejection scene Hal and my Lord Chief Justice stand for Authority; Falstaff is Appetite." Traversi, *Richard II to Henry V*, p. 108, sees Hal in *2 Henry IV* as "engaged in the more arduous and sober pursuit of self-conquest, externally manifested in his submission to the Lord Chief-Justice"; but on p. 158 he doubts that the Justice is "a sufficient counterpart to the 'riot' incarnated in Falstaff."

26. Freud, *Ego and Id*, p. 46.

27. Sigmund Freud, "The Anatomy of the Mental Personality," in *New Introductory Lectures on Psychoanalysis*, trans. W. J. H. Sprott (New York: Norton, 1933), p. 108.

28. Freud, *Civilization*, p. 79. For the sufficiency of a fantasy patricide, see *Totem*, p. 160, and "Moses and Monotheism" in the Standard Edition of Freud's *Works*, trans. James Strachey, XXIII (London: Hogarth, 1964), 87.

29. Freud, *Totem*, p. 145 and p. 143.

30. Freud, *Ego and Id*, p. 28 and p. 38.

31. Freud, *Ego and Id*, pp. 18-21; see also p. 44, and his "Mourning and Melancholia," passim, in *Works*, XIV (London: Hogarth, 1957); see also Hans Loewald, *Papers on Psychoanalysis* (New Haven: Yale University Press, 1980), pp. 270-271.

32. Freud, *Civilization*, p. 42.

33. Ibid., p. 44: "At this point we cannot fail to be struck by the similarity between the process of civilization and the libidinal development of the individual," and goes on, pp. 44-45, to suggest "that the development of civilization is a special process, comparable to the normal maturation of the individual." Further, "The analogy between the process of civilization and the path of individual development may be extended . . . The super-ego

of an epoch of civilization has an origin similar to that of an individual" (p. 88). However, we must also heed Freud's warning, on p. 91, that "we are only dealing with analogies and that it is dangerous, not only with men but also with concepts, to tear them from the sphere in which they have originated and been evolved."

34. Freud, "The Group and the Primal Horde," in *Works,* XVIII (London: Hogarth, 1955) 123.

35. J. J. Atkinson, *Primal Law* (London, 1903), p. 228; quoted by Freud, *Totem,* p. 142 n. 1, as the characteristic problem that the totemic law must solve. See also Freud's "Postscript" in *Works,* XVIII, 135, on the necessity of this fraternal pact as a preventative to civil war.

36. For another perspective on these Cain allusions, see Berman, in *Shakespeare Studies* 1:20.

37. Thomas Sackville and Thomas Norton, *Gorboduc* or *Ferrex and Porrex,* Regents Renaissance Drama Series, ed. Irby B. Cauthen, Jr. (Lincoln: University of Nebraska Press, 1970), 2.1.172-75, 5.2.212-14, and passim, shows this combination of crimes plunging the nation out of civilization and into a welter of bloodshed. Intriguingly, these themes are combined here, as they are in Shakespeare, with occasional suggestions of unnatural birth and the dangers of a usurper's sleep: see 4.1.65-75 and 4.2.181-90. The Homily is quoted by Tillyard, *Shakespeare's History Plays,* p. 70.

38. In *Leviathan,* part I, chapter 13, Hobbes, discusses the difficulty of holding any sort of sovereign privileges in a world where "the weakest has strength enough to kill the strongest, either by secret machination, or by confederacy with others, that are in the same danger with himself." This parallels Freud's observation that the brothers, though individually weaker, manage to overthrow the father and seize his privileges by conspiring together. A few paragraphs later Hobbes points out the same danger that Freud saw arising from such a conspiracy. In the absence of the father, or a just totemic law that takes his place, the brothers will inevitably continue to battle each other to their deaths: "Hereby it is manifest, that during the time men live without a common power to keep them all in awe, they are in that condition which is called war; and such a war, as is of every man, against every man."

39. Edmund Spenser, *The Faerie Queene,* I.i; John Bunyan, *The Pilgrim's Progress,* ed. Roger Sharrock (Harmondsworth, Middlesex: Penguin, 1965), pp. 172-173.

40. Tillyard, *Shakespeare's History Plays,* p. 305, makes note of this deviation from Walsingham and the *Famous Victories of Henry V.*

Paul Dean (essay date 1993)

SOURCE: "Shakespeare's Historical Imagination," in *Renaissance Studies,* Vol. 11, No. 1, March, 1997, pp. 27-40.

[*In the following essay, Dean compares Shakespeare's treatment of historical fact and politics in his history plays, focusing on* Henry IV, Parts 1 and 2.]

If there is one view about Shakespeare which can be said to be shared by most of the critics of the last ten years, it is that he is—and not just in the history plays—a *political* writer. But in this, it is argued, he has no choice: *all* literature is political, and all criticism, in consequence, ideological. A glance at the editor's introduction to the 1992 'New Casebook' on *Shakespeare's History Plays: 'Richard II' to 'Henry IV',* aimed at an undergraduate readership, reveals how embedded such assumptions have become: in New Historicism, we read, 'literature can be seen to enact a type of political discourse', criticism being a 'verbal and structural investigation of a range of rhetorical strategies' aimed at laying bare 'the conditions of cultural, ideological and political power'. Even this, however, has been felt to be insufficiently *engagé* by Cultural Materialism in its various forms, especially feminism, in which 'a politics of culture operates in more or less direct relationship with a committed politics of social and economic action'. At the same time, thanks to the cross-fertilization of literary theory with the work of history theorists such as Hayden White, belief in the possibility of historical objectivity, of the distinction between fact and interpretation, and of historical narrative as a validly autonomous category of writing, has been shattered: 'All writing is equally historical.' Fortunately, as it turns out, Shakespeare foresaw all these developments, with the happy result that 'Shakespeare's history plays are about history in the same way as post-modern thought is about history'.[1]

Tom McAlindon has recently protested against such an approach, on the grounds that it:

> seems at times to participate in the prevalent blurring of all generic distinctions to the extent of dissolving immensely complex artistic structures and consigning them to an amorphous continuum of ideology and discourse. Thus it is apt to evade a question of perennially absorbing interest: what constitutes the unique quality or singular greatness of this particular play?[2]

We should, I think, heed this caution—without denying that, from the beginning, Shakespeare's history plays show an awareness of a variety of ideological stances. There is a sense in which he *is* a postmodern historian, at least as such a figure was presented by Gertrude Himmelfarb in a *Times Literary Supplement* article in 1992:

> Formerly, when historians invoked the role of imagination, they meant the exercise of imagination required to transcend the present and immerse oneself in the past. Today, it more often means the opposite: the imagina-

tion to create a past in the image of the present and in accord with the judgement of the historian.[3]

This seems to me a false antithesis. 'Has justice ever been done to the power of his historical imagination?' asks Blair Worden of Shakespeare in a recent essay.[4] Shakespeare seems to me to combine both kinds of imagination distinguished by Professor Himmelfarb, and to think about time like a philosopher. Mindful, however, of the fact that Shakespeare the Philosopher may be as much of a falsifying abstraction as Shakespeare the Political Ideologue, I shall be taking the *Henry IV* plays and, to a lesser extent, *Henry V* and their theatrical political context as a test case, trying to work from particular details.

Another thing I find puzzling about Professor Himmelfarb's remarks is her assumption that 'the imagination to create a past in the image of the present' is a specifically modernist ploy. Those words describe historiography as practised by many classical, medieval, and Renaissance historians. Moreover, in the view of the greatest British philosopher of history in the twentieth century (who, however, underrated the sixteenth century's contribution to that discipline)—R. G. Collingwood—the ambition to 'transcend the present' is futile: the historian lives and thinks in the present, inescapably, and the life of history is in the historian's mind here and now. To imagine now a past which is our past, so as to make it alive for us now, would hardly have seemed aberrant to Virgil, Ovid, Boethius, Chaucer, Spenser—or Shakespeare. What we have in his work are neither events nor non-events but 'counterevents', events as the alchemical imagination has transformed them.[5] He is engaged on nothing so banal as dramatizing the past, but on something more heroic and more awesomely difficult: on what Michael Dummett brilliantly calls 'bringing about the past'.[6]

I

Of course, in the sense in which politics is about the organization of human beings into communities, hardly any of Shakespeare's plays lacks a political dimension; yet when everything is political nothing is; there must be distinctions. I cannot go to the other extreme, however, and agree with David Womersley that 'the political interpretations we offer of Elizabethan literature ought to [. . .] be reducible to, or re-statable as, narratives of potential or accomplished moves made by actual Elizabethan politicians'.[7] Such austere rigour would leave hardly anything in the category of political literature. Shakespeare's history plays existed, of course, in a political context in their own day, and have been appropriated repeatedly for political—even, if we must use the word, ideological—purposes ever since. But the politics *of* the plays are not identical with the politics *in* them. Graham Holderness's contention that political interpretation only becomes meaningful when one takes sides, and hence that 'a political criticism should then be a question of judging the political meanings literature generates, evaluating the political potentialities of specific works, and discriminat-

ing between reactionary and progressive forms of criticism',[8] misplaces the emphasis because it relegates criticism to the status of propaganda, a matter of *partis pris* rather than understanding, which is surely foreign to Shakespeare's methods of work. He was committed, not to this or that political position, but to the exploration of what it might mean to have—or to lack—a political position.

Let us consider a familiar set of circumstances. In 1599 a prohibition was issued against the printing of any more English histories without the permission of the Privy Council. Some authors, such as Grenville and Raleigh, reacted by self-censorship, while others, such as Jonson and Hayward, got into trouble, for *Sejanus* and *The Life and Raigne of Henrie IIII* respectively. Shakespeare's *Richard II* was famously hijacked by the Essex faction just before the ban was imposed. Shakespeare, who had acted in *Sejanus,* no doubt wryly recalled the scene in which Cremutius Cordus is condemned to death by the Senate for writing the wrong kind of history, adulating Brutus and Cassius who are non-persons in Tiberius' Rome. One of Tiberius' toadies, Afer, alleges that Cordus is making a veiled attack on Tiberius. In vain does Cordus plead that discussion of a remote period of history cannot reasonably be construed as a commentary on contemporary events: the Senate is as unconvinced by him as the Council was by Jonson. Cordus, like some modern innocent surrounded by literary theorists, discovers that he is simply not *allowed* to be apolitical, and that his apparently straightforward historical narrative is perceived to have a subversive ideological subtext. Such paranoia was a living force in Renaissance English society. It was, after all, a play on Antony and Cleopatra, not on an English historical subject, which its author Greville burned out of fear that it was 'apt enough to be construed, or strained to a personating of vices in the present Governors, and government';[9] Raleigh, languishing in the Tower, reflected ruefully that 'whosoever, in writing a modern history, shall follow truth too near the heel, it may happily strike out his teeth';[10] while the second part of Hayward's *History of Henrie IIII* remained unpublished until 1991.[11]

By 1599, the new school of 'politique history', which grew up following the publication in 1591 of Sir Henry Savile's translation of Tacitus, was well established and had superseded the earlier Tudor—really late medieval—view of history as a storehouse of universal moral exempla. Tacitus and Machiavelli had replaced Cicero and Livy as the models to imitate. (We may see a parallel in the development of Shakespeare scholarship itself in recent years, with a reading of the Histories as Ciceronian 'mirrors for princes' replaced by the radical-political approach I have already mentioned.[12]) This replacement entailed an important change in the understanding of causation. History was still referred to the Divine Will, but was more often scrutinized in terms of purely human agents; God remained the First Cause, but there were now also Second Causes. Plotting is to playwrights what causation is to philosophers,[13] and to the history playwright this shift in the causal concept obviously has supreme importance.

It was also in 1599, of course, that *Henry V* was acted, and in that play Shakespeare presents a concept of historical imagination explicitly, through the chorus. This too has its context, for the role of imagination in history had received attention during the movement from early to late Tudor thought. A world of intellectual development separates the statement, in the Henrician translation of Polydore Vergil's *Anglia Historia,* that 'an Historie is a full rehearsall and declaration of things don, not a gesse or divination',[14] from Raleigh's devotion of a chapter of his *History of the World* (bk. I, ch. 21: 6) to a plea for the 'liberty of using conjecture in Histories', and Raleigh's conception of the role of imagination in historiography has been compared to that of Collingwood.[15] Blair Worden makes effectively the same point in remarking how the careers of Jonson, Greville, and Daniel 'remind us of how far historical insight rested [. . .] on a historian's doing what a dramatist does: ask himself how a given character would have thought and acted in a given situation'.[16] By 1599 the creative artist's interpretative freedom with historical materials hardly needed defending. Shakespeare's Henry V is a notoriously difficult character to interpret, but this difficulty is built into the play; it is an aspect of our task as well as Shakespeare's, for the Histories typically, as Phyllis Rackin puts it, 'cast their audiences in the roles of historians'.[17] Repeatedly the Chorus implores us to supplement what we see (the historical events dramatized) with our own creative powers, to produce not a synthesis but a complementarity:

> Piece out our imperfections with your thoughts:
> Into a thousand parts divide one man,
> And make imaginary puissance.
> Think, when we talk of horses, that you see them . . .
>
> (Prologue, 23-6)
>
> Work, work your thoughts, and therein see a siege . . .
>
> (Act III, 0, 25)
>
> Yet sit and see,
> Minding true things by what their mock'ries be.
>
> (Act IV, 0, 52-3)
>
> But now behold,
> In the quick forge and working-house of thought . . .
>
> (Act V, 0, 22-3)

Notice how these passages insist upon the imagination as a *visual* faculty: we see physically and with our mind's eye, and the two visions—the representation and the truth it figures—together *are* the act of imagining. The Chorus, in fact, exhorts us to do what Shakespeare had to do as he worked on his source materials, altering, supplementing, reordering, and filling out—performing acts of imagining which *were* acts of interpretation.

Not that Shakespeare, in enlisting our co-operation, abnegates his responsibility or licenses any subjective fantasy; what is on the stage is really there. Yet 'really' is a slippery word here: it is really the case that certain actors are speaking certain words and performing certain physical movements; but it is not really the case that we are witnessing the battle of Agincourt. We are witnessing an attempt to represent that battle, and the attempt is real: but it is in the nature of an attempt that it must succeed or fail, and must therefore be supplemented by someone's being convinced or not convinced by it. The reality of the attempt (its 'truth' if I dare use another slippery word) is not enough: our acceptance or rejection of it is needed before it can be evaluated. This is the logic behind the speeches of the Chorus. I am, of course, aware that widely differing accounts have been given of the function of these speeches,[18] but in a sense their ambivalence is the point; the work of historical imagining is like that, a matter of contradictions, elusive, tricky, baffling. Shakespeare would have recognized much in Collingwood's celebrated chapter on 'The historical imagination' in *The Idea of History*—as when, for instance, Collingwood says that 'The historical imagination [. . .] is properly not ornamental but structural', or that 'the imaginary, simply as such, is neither real nor unreal', or that the historical imagination is an active heuristic force, 'a self-dependent, self-determining, and self-justifying form of thought'.[19]

II

Henry IV is a natural choice for testing the hypothesis that Shakespeare's imagination transcends party ideology while encompassing what it is to have such an ideology, since, manifestly, it was shaped by political considerations in more than one sense of the term. Designed as in some way a response to the earlier play *The Famous Victories of Henry V,* its portrayal of Sir John Oldcastle as Prince Hal's disreputable companion led to protests from the Oldcastle family, the substitution of 'Falstaff' for 'Oldcastle' as the character's name, and a counter-play, *Sir John Oldcastle,* in two parts, of which the second is lost.[20] The relationship between these three plays depends on an amalgam of topical satire, political censorship, and religious polemic (the historical Oldcastle was a leading Protestant martyr). Oldcastle in *The Famous Victories* is so called only once, on his first appearance; he is not a major character, and, as Gary Taylor has pointed out, Shakespeare took some trouble to align the characteristics of *his* Oldcastle more closely with those of the historical figure, so that 'the parallels demonstrate that the name of the character, his historical identity, forms a part of the meaning of the extant text'.[21] In *Sir John Oldcastle* itself the Prologue is careful to distinguish the protagonist from a certain 'aged counsellor to youthful sins' (line 7). With a striking irony, the name 'Falstaff' in *Sir John Oldcastle* has become the name of a 'historical' person separate from Oldcastle: King Henry V, walking abroad disguised, as his namesake had done in Shakespeare's play, muses, 'Where the devil are all my old thieves that were wont to keep this walk? Falstaff, the villain, is so fat he cannot get on's horse' (x. 53-5) while the criminal priest he encounters, called Sir John (but nothing can be made of that—it was a conventional name for a priest),[22] grumbles that the King, when Prince of Wales, once robbed him, 'when that foul villainous guts, that led him to all that roguery, was in's company there, that Falstaff' (x. 82-3). Recurring to the point about 'reality' I made in the previous section, we can say that, just as the reality of the historical Oldcastle must be distinguished from that of his stage representation, so the reality of Falstaff as a character in Shakespeare's play must be distinguished from the reality of 'Falstaff' as a referent in *Sir John Oldcastle,* a character external to the play but assumed to have a corresponding reality in the minds of the audience.

It could be argued without undue paradox that both *The Famous Victories* and *Sir John Oldcastle* are more entitled to be called historical plays than Shakespeare's,[23] for they both stick quite closely to what were thought to be the historical facts of the personal development and public career of Henry V—so closely, indeed, that Shakespeare had to omit direct treatment of what they had dramatized if he was not to fall into repetitiousness. The network of relationships between these plays again shows the intricacy with which drama, politics, and history interact in the Elizabethan period. However, Shakespeare is exceptional, not only in his remodelling of the facts into a more complex structure, but also in his interest in history as an abstract process as well as a repository of plot material. The other two plays have a political-theological interest: Shakespeare alone, it would seem, seized the implications of the fact that a history play is an event *in* time which is also an event *about* time, and hence has a philosophical dimension which we apprehend through the dramatic structure. This is one of the marks of his historical imagination, a quality none of his contemporaries possesses in the same way. I shall lead up to a fuller definition of it by way of an apparently minor bibliographical puzzle, which I hope to show has far-reaching consequences.

III

Two Quartos of *2 Henry IV* were printed in 1600, and the first one does not contain what is in modern editions Act III, scene i, the soliloquy of the insomniac King and his conversation with Warwick. Several explanations for this omission have been offered. Until recently it was assumed to be due to compositorial oversight, but in 1987 John Jowett and Gary Taylor argued that the scene was an afterthought on Shakespeare's part.[24] Two subsequent editors of the play have disagreed. Giorgio Melchiori argues that the scene was part of what he called the 'ur-*Henry IV*', the original single play which, in his view, Shakespeare expanded into two: while Thomas L. Berger finds this over-speculative, and believes that the scene must have been part of the original conception because, without it, two comic scenes would succeed one another, and this is contrary to Shakespeare's usual practice.[25] Several different issues are involved here, but the one which most interests me is the clues to the workings of Shakespeare's historical imagination provided by the debate—the debate in the scene, that is, as well as the one about it. It can hardly be denied that the scene in question raises the discussion of history to a plane of abstraction hardly paralleled elsewhere in Shakespeare's work, and nowhere in Elizabethan historical drama outside it. It is no overstatement to say that Henry and Warwick discuss questions now associated with the philosophy of history.[26] Warwick articulates a Neoplatonic idea of time as a 'necessary form' whose archetypal nature enables us to 'create' the future in our imaginations, to 'guess' but to guess perfectly. The King's question 'Are these things then necessities?' is unanswered; all we can do is to act as if they were. As Westmorland later advises Mowbray, we must 'construe the times to their necessities' (*2 Henry IV,* IV. i. 102). Such historical imagining produces, not 'the truth', whatever that may be, but a balance of probability, a reasonable conjecture, issuing in political decisions which are also acts of faith.

As noted above on the *Henry V* choruses, there are instructive parallels, I believe, between the historical imagining in the scene and the historical imagining of its author as he felt his way into the material.[27] Jowett, Taylors and Melchiori point out that, without III. i, the end of what is now II. iv and the beginning of what is now III. ii would echo each other verbally:

> Come—She comes blubbered,—Yea, will you come Doll?
> Come on, come on, come on, sir

This, they suggest, supports their view that III. i was not present in the original scheme of the play. But the final words of II. iv are themselves in dispute, since they occur in Q but not in F; and, even if we allow them, III. i opens, 'Go, call the Earls of Surrey and of Warwick, / And ere they *come* . . .', which also picks them up, and it ends, 'where these inward wars once out of *hand,* / We would, dear lords, unto the Holy Land', which is in turn picked up by III. ii, 'Come on, come on, come on, sir, give me your *hand,* sir, give me your hand, sir'. If we are going to go by verbal echoes there is no reason why the scene should not have stood where it is from the beginning. Moreover, on a larger scale, its depiction of a monarch plagued by insomnia comes between Falstaff's 'the undeserver may sleep, when the man of action is called on' (II. iv. 378f) and Shallow's 'An early stirrer, by the Rood!' (III. ii. 2f). Whether the scene was an afterthought or not, these echoes indicate the workings of an imagination which could pass apparently instinctively from verbal to conceptual interconnections as it brooded over what the prose chronicles called 'the unquiet time' of Henry IV.

'Are these things then necessities?' Perhaps we make them so, by our choices. Shakespeare seems to show, in the Histories, and above all in the figure of Prince Hal in *Henry IV* and *Henry V,* something contrary to the determinism of contemporary theory: that it is what we do and wish to be which shapes the universe we live in. The time which people experience is, in a weird way, like the people who experience it. Hal is such an uncomfortable figure to many people, both other characters and modern readers, because he is a man who embodies the principle of teleology in a world which is otherwise dominated by contingency. That becomes plain in the 'I know you all' speech in Part 1, I. ii. Professor Melchiori wants this to be a later insertion too: he says, on no evidence at all, that it 'has the air of being an after-thought'.[28] But why should it not have the air of being a forethought? It is where it is for a purpose, in order to affect the whole balance of our subsequent relationship with Hal and his relationship with other characters.

Nor is this sense of interconnectedness confined to individual scenes. It can occur between quite disparate scenes. Consider, alongside the scene just discussed, the beginning of II. i in Part 1, the conversation between the two Carriers. In dramatic terms the exchange is redundant, but it serves to establish atmosphere and, in its attention to apparent trivia, conveys a sense of the quotidian occupations of the insignificant people of England: we hear of the 'new chimney' of the inn, of the enfeebled condition of one of the horses, of the chaos that has come to the management of the inn 'since Robin [Ostler] died', of the flea-bites the Carriers have suffered, of the lack of a chamber-pot and the consequent inconveniences, and so on. In its beautiful inconsequentiality the dialogue looks forward to the greater achievement of the Gloucestershire scenes in Part 2, which have been justly compared to Chekhov[29] and which revel in *reminiscence* where the King is troubled by painful *memory*. Scenes like these, which are the polar opposites of that between the King and Warwick, are essential in creating the illusion of a three-dimensional 'ordinary' world in which political action takes place. Yet the Carriers, Shallow and Silence, Henry and Warwick also represent complementarities, and no account of Shakespeare's historical imagination can be fruitful which does not hold both types of scene in mind. We are not helped to appreciate this by occasional failures of imagination on the part of editors. The First Carrier tells us that Robin Ostler 'never joyed since the price of oats rose; it was the death of him' (II. i. 12f). Professor Bevington is ready with his note: 'This ostler [. . .] was ruined by an inflation in costs that outpaced his revenue. The price of oats more than doubled between 1593 and 1596-7, after which it again fell.' But this is the kind of information we both need and do not need to know. It explains the allusion of the remark while leaving its mysterious poetry completely untouched. People like the Carriers live in a world where time can be measured fairly precisely—'an it be not four by the day, I'll be hanged'—but also by things like the installation of new chimneys or by changes in the prices of things which affect them. The King's method in Part 2 is different: within the space of a few lines we have "Tis not ten years gone [. . .] and in two year after [. . .] It is but eight years since' (III. i. 52, 54, 55). It is beside the point for Professor Melchiori in *his* note to correct the arithmetic with the comment 'Shakespeare is deliberately manipulating historical time'. Yes indeed, but more profoundly he is asking what 'historical' time *is*, and is returning two answers: it is the external framework of chronology and it is time as internally experienced. Silence knows that it is 'fifty-five year ago' that Shallow arrived at Clement's Inn; but when Falstaff says that he and Shallow 'have heard the chimes at midnight' (*2 Henry IV,* III. ii. 207, 211f) he is not evoking a particular passing from one day to another day, but savouring a generalized memory of revelry and youthful energy that lives now only in his memory—and also, perhaps unconsciously, thinking ahead to death (compare Falstaff's mysteriously evocative 'I shall be sent for soon at night', V. iv. 87f). This is both beautiful and unbearably sad, but it is inevitable and at least evidence of the persistent reality and continuity of experience. Every act of remembering and recreating, Shakespeare's included, is an exercise of the historical imagination which is the act of fitting, to echo a celebrated distinction of Collingwood's, the insides of events to their outsides.[30]

Sooner or later, writers on the *Henry IV* plays have to consider the question of their genesis. I do not find this question a particularly gripping one insofar as it retreats from understanding the plays we have to trying to reconstruct hypothetically plays we do not have. Modern discussions of the matter derive from Harold Jenkins's lecture *The Structural Problem in Shakespeare's 'Henry IV'* (1956) and very few of them add much to his conclusions. The most innovatory theory has come from Professor Melchiori in a number of studies now collected and extended in his book *Shakespeare's Garter Plays,* which develops, sometimes in a boldly conjectural way, Jenkins's original proposals.[31] I accept Jenkins's conclusion that Shakespeare did indeed intend to write a single play in which the dual victory of Hal over Hotspur and Falstaff would be shown, but that this schematic plan was jettisoned, probably during the writing of Act IV, and a new ending devised which would make a self-contained play while still leaving open the possibility of a sequel if the piece proved popular. When it did, Shakespeare incorporated the remaining chronicle material, which was less than had been available for Part 1, obliging him to expand the comic episodes. No one can seriously maintain that the result is a single ten-act play, and the arguments urged in support of that view by Tillyard and Dover Wilson seem to me simply untenable. The structural parallels between the two parts, as Jenkins shows, make an artful compromise between crude repetition and developed variation. In his words, 'The two parts are complementary; they are also independent and even incompatible.'[32] What needs emphasizing is that, whether or not there may be a 'structural problem' for us, there certainly was one for Shakespeare, and that the concept of overlapping was his solution. He had to fit Part 2 to Part 1 to some degree, and this imposed a number of constraints upon him. Like Hal, he was working within a teleological frame in which the end was known, and in which details had to be organized to lead up to that end. I like to think that he reflected upon the ways in which his own freedom of creative action had been shaped by his previous decisions; and if I were really going to speculate I should make a connection between this and that midnight conversation with which I began this section. For, of course, Shakespeare employed the

liberty of conjecturing counterevents as well as the Sidneian 'bare was' of historical record.[33] He not only altered historical facts in *Henry IV* (by making Hal and Hotspur the same age, for example); he invented Falstaff. And when, in Act V, scene iv of Part 1, 'Sir John riseth up', the freedom to counterfeit (a key word in that scene) in its etymological sense, creating something opposed to something else, rises with him. 'Fact' and 'fiction' share a common root, in Shakespeare's imagination as in etymology: something done, something made about what was done, reflect upon each other ceaselessly. The references to Henry V at the beginning of *1 Henry VI*, and to Henry VI at the end of *Henry V*, make of Shakespeare's career as a history playwright what they make of history itself: a *perpetuum mobile* between glory and chaos.

IV

Where, it may be asked, does this leave Shakespeare the political thinker, the dramatist of ideology? Before addressing that question we ought to acknowledge that our understanding of Renaissance politics is still being formed and cannot be predicated upon the politics of our own time. I referred at the beginning of this article to David Womersley's work on political readings of sixteenth- and seventeenth-century texts. He has made a formidable case against assuming that modern understanding of political transactions and preoccupations can simply be read back into the writings of Renaissance scholars: we need to recognize the alien character of their thought-processes rather than to acclaim them as familiar and anticipatory of our own.[34] Working from the Folio categories, G. K. Hunter proposed to define a history play as 'a play about English dynastic politics of the feudal and immediately post-feudal period'.[35] 'About', of course, is a relative term. I think a valid distinction may be drawn between the kinds of political exploration we see in the two tetralogies. It does make sense to talk about the *Henry VI* trilogy as 'about' dynastic politics, as Michael Hattaway has shown in his New Cambridge editions. He is absolutely right to stress the plays' secular vision of political behaviour, their demystification of monarchy, their opposition of dated chivalry to 'modern' feudalism, and their preference for efficient to final causes, and to characterize their 'radicalism' etymologically as 'an ability to root out the causes of political dilemmas, to demonstrate the partiality of contesting explanations of particular events'.[36] As he also points out, their scepticism about teleology or providence (tellingly given an exceptionally ineffectual champion in the person of Henry VI himself) leads to a rich multiplicity of causalities and representational modes, with allegory, mythography, emblem, and carnival prominent aspects of the dramatic technique. They move only gradually towards psychological inwardness and then (even in Richard of Gloucester) in a way which looks primitive when set against the second tetralogy, where the distribution of emphasis is so different. There are one or two places where I cannot share Professor Hattaway's views, notably when he writes that Shakespeare's art in the *Henry VI* plays is one of 'demonstration, rather than, as it had been in the hands of medieval chroniclers, an art of interpretation'.[37] I find this very surprising given the care with which he has shown the resourcefulness and scope of Shakespeare's interpretative skills, and conversely his rejection of any reading of the plays which makes them doctrinaire. They are as much products of historical imagination as any other plays by Shakespeare. Nor can I accept his parallel between the Cade and Falstaff scenes as offering a 'vision both of the limits of government and of the consequences of aristocratic factionalism'.[38] Cade, while more complex than is sometimes allowed, can never move or disturb us as Falstaff can, nor can we ever warm to him. By the time Shakespeare created Falstaff he had left such relative simplifications behind.

Structural differences between the two tetralogies are a significant pointer to their varying outlooks on political behaviour. The *Henry VI* trilogy, as Professor Hattaway says, has a processional character which looks back to the medieval mystery cycles,[39] while 'the *liaison des scènes* is figurative rather than causal'.[40] The *Henry IV* plays do not regress to providential explanations (*Henry V* does, but not unironically), but their structural sophistication is remarkable[41] and, in my view, connected to a new direction in Shakespeare's thinking about imagination. Politics ceases to be a matter of factions or class divisions and becomes rooted in individual psychology. If David Womersley is right to claim that 'political transactions in the reign of Elizabeth seem in the first instance to have been transactions between individuals' and to conclude that 'in England in the late sixteenth century there was no public domain of politics',[42] one has to say that Shakespeare had reached a similar conclusion. Politics, a gestural activity in his early work, is a mental activity in his later. I have tried to make the case for him as an inclusive thinker whose historical imagination works by overlapping units of construction large and small, playing off opposites against each other until the whole of *Henry IV* resembles a spectrum in which continuity and differentiation are simultaneously perceptible.

Shakespeare had understood what A. N. Whitehead was to perceive early in this century: that time as we experience it is not a mechanical framework but a continuum of durations. When I visit, say, York Minster, my experience occupies a certain amount of clock-time but it overlaps with the experiences of other visitors, with my own experiences of earlier visits, and, on the theological plane, with the experiences of thousands of visitors down the centuries. Time, as Marjorie Grene puts it in her exposition of Whitehead, 'is not one dimension, but a host of them' which 'overlap in an undetermined and, for any single knower, non-determinable number of ways'; and she adds that in any one event there may be 'thousands of intricately interlacing temporal rhythms'.[43] This reverberant phrase might well be applied to Shakespeare's history plays. The concept of process familiar to him from *The Faerie Queene* (it goes back, of course, much further than that) was of nature as at once a stable order and as a kaleidoscope of change, and he seems to have conceived of time in a similar way. Consider two moments in which his monarchs reflect upon time. In *3 Henry VI,* II. v. he shows Henry longing for the security of a completely mechanistic system of reckoning time, individual minutes aggregating into a whole life, and, conversely, dreaming of dividing up a single day into so many hours for its appointed tasks. 'So minutes, hours, days, weeks, months, and years, / Pass'd over to the end they were created, / Would bring white hairs unto a quiet grave' (lines 38-40). Now consider *Richard II,* V. v. Richard moves from time as musical rhythm to time as the rhythm of 'the music of men's lives', a music he has turned into discord: 'I wasted time, and now doth time waste me, / For now hath time made me his numb'ring clock' (lines 41-50). The clock is no longer a machine, it is Richard's physical body, his emotional distress figured as the tolling of the bell. To pass from *Henry VI* to *Richard II* is to pass from time as external mechanism to time as felt experience—Richard does not experience just time but 'my time' (line 58).[44] The *Henry VI* plays, and their interest in overlapping, are the fruit of that realization of time as process.

Marjorie Grene concludes her discussion of Whitehead with the observation that 'time itself, as lived time, is telic'—as it is for Hal. We are the creatures of our past, so far determined but also free to create, building on that past, the future which beckons us but which we also draw toward ourselves by what Grene finely calls 'the protensive pull of our transcendence which is the core of conscious life'.[45] That, I think, is how Shakespeare went about creating the political world of his history plays and it is also the most important thing he shows in them.

Notes

This article is a revised version of a paper given to the Renaissance Graduate Seminar at York University in February 1993 at the kind invitation of Professor Jacques Berthoud. I am most grateful to him and to Dr John Roe for their comments on that occasion.

All Shakespeare quotations are from the one-volume Oxford *Complete Works,* general editors Stanley Wells and Gary Taylor (Oxford, 1988).

1. Graham Holderness (ed.), *Shakespeare's History Plays: 'Richard II' to 'Henry V'* (London, 1992), 11, 13, 10, and 22.
2. Tom McAlindon, 'Tragedy, *King Lear* and the politics of the heart', *Shakes Surv,* 44 (1992), 85-90.
3. Gertrude Himmelfarb, 'Telling it as you like it: postmodernist history and the flight from fact', *TLS,* 16 October 1992, 14. Mary Warnock makes analogous criticisms of postmodernists from a philosophical point of view in her *Imagination and Time* (Oxford, 1994), 95-6.
4. Blair Worden, 'Shakespeare and politics', *Shakes Surv,* 44 (1992), 8.
5. I borrow the term 'counterevent' from Paola Pugliatti, '"More than history can pattern": the Jack Cade rebellion in Shakespeare's *Henry VI, 2*', *J of Med and Renaiss Stud,* 22 (1992), 455. Sec, further, her book *Shakespeare the Historian* (London, 1996), which appeared after my own paper was completed.
6. Michael Dummett, 'Bringing about the past', *Philos Rev,* 73 (1964), 338-59, reprinted in Robin Le Poidevin and Murray MacBeath (ed.), *The Philosophy of Time* (Oxford, 1993), 117-33.
7. David Womersley, 'Sir Henry Savile's translation of Tacitus and the political interpretation of Elizabethan texts', *Rev Engl St,* NS 42 no. 167 (1991), 340.
8. Graham Holderness, *Shakespeare Recycled: The Making of Historical Drama* (London, 1992), 43.
9. Quoted by Joan Rees, *Fulke Greville, Lord Brooke, 1554-1628: A Critical Biography* (London, 1971), 30.
10. Raleigh, *Selected Writings,* ed. Gerald Hammond (Manchester, 1984), 149.
11. *The First and Second Parts of John Hayward's 'The Life and Raigne of King Henrie IIII'*, ed. John J. Manning (Camden Fourth Series, vol. 42; London, 1991). The editor's introduction gives a detailed and illuminating account of the Privy Council's treatment of Hayward and other suspected partisans of Essex. See further David Womersley, 'Sir John Hayward's tacitism', *Renaiss Stud,* 6 (1991), 46-59.
12. This point is made by Phyllis Rackin, *Stages of History: Shakespeare's English Chronicles* (London, 1991), 35. Her first chapter (pp. 1-39) is an outstanding discussion of the development of historical thought in Renaissance England, with full reference to previous work. See also Manning's edition of Hayward, pp. 34-42.
13. I have discussed this matter more generally in 'Shakespeare's causes', *Cahiers Elis,* 36 (1989), 25-35.
14. *Polydore Vergil's English History,* ed. Henry Ellis (London, 1844), 26.
15. Stephen Greenblatt, *Sir Walter Raleigh: The Renaissance Man and his Roles* (Yale, 1973), 135-6. Collingwood is also invoked by Wilbur Sanders in his excellent chapter 'Literature as history: with some questions about "historical imagination"', in *The Dramatist and the Received Idea: Studies in the Plays of Marlowe and Shakespeare* (Cambridge, 1968), 1-19. Pugliatti, *Shakespeare the Historian,* 31, notes Hayward's interest in narrative technique and his apparent acceptance, with Raleigh, of the historian's interpretative liberty in the cause of art.
16. Worden, 'Shakespeare and politics', 8.
17. Rackin, *Stages of History,* 28.
18. For a recent discussion, taking in earlier views, see Andrew Gurr's edition of *Henry V* (Cambridge, 1992), 6-16.

19. R. G. Collingwood, *The Idea of History* (Oxford, 1946), 241, 249.

20. *The Famous Victories* and *Sir John Oldcastle* are now conveniently available in Peter Corbin and Douglas Sedge (eds), *The Oldcastle Controversy* (Manchester, 1991), from which I quote.

21. Gary Taylor, 'The fortunes of Oldcastle', *Shakes Surv*, 38 (1985), 96. That Shakespeare's character was intended to evoke precise historical resonances is also argued by E. A. J. Honigmann, 'Sir John Oldcastle: Shakespeare's martyr', in John W. Mahon and Thomas A. Pendleton (eds), *'Fanned and Winnowed Opinions': Shakespearean Essays Presented to Harold Jenkins* (London, 1987), 118-32.

22. Corbin and Sedge (eds), *The Oldcastle Controversy*, 17, argue that this Sir John is 'a surrogate "Oldcastle/Falstaff" vice-figure'. Richard Helgerson, in *Forms of Nationhood: The Elizabethan Writing of England* (Chicago, 1992), 236, seeks to distinguish between Falstaff as surrogate father to Hal, and Oldcastle and Wrotham as victims of monarchy: but Falstaff is ultimately a victim too.

23. A comparable conclusion emerges from Helgerson's brilliant discussion of the Elizabethan history play, which makes clear the divergence between Shakespeare's preoccupations and those of the authors of *The Famous Victories, Sir John Oldcastle,* and other 'populist' dramas: *Forms of Nationhood*, 195-245.

24. John Jowett and Gary Taylor, 'The three texts of 2 Henry IV', *Stud in Biblio*, 40 (1987), 36.

25. *The Second Part of King Henry the Fourth*, ed. Giorgio Melchiori (Cambridge, 1989), 3, 5, 9-12, 201; *The Second Part of King Henry the Fourth, 1600*, ed. Thomas L. Berger (Oxford, 1991), xiii-xiv.

26. I repeat here some remarks from my essay 'Forms of time: some Elizabethan two-part history plays', *Renaiss Stud*, 4 (1990), 428.

27. The same suggestion is made by Pugliatti, *Shakespeare the Historian*, 126-30, whose discussion of the whole episode is excellent.

28. *King Henry the Fourth*, ed. Melchiori, 12.

29. Alexander Leggatt, *Shakespeare's Political Drama* (London, 1988), 106; Barbara Everett, 'The fatness of Falstaff: Shakespeare and character', *Pr Br Acad*, 76 (1991 for 1990), 127.

30. Collingwood, *The Idea of History*, 213. Warnock, *Imagination and Time*, has some pertinent remarks on Proust's distinction between 'the artificial meaning we give to the past when we deliberately attempt to recall it' and 'the significance it has when we relieve the past through spontaneous memory. Then and only then, according to Proust, the meaning of the past comes with our recollection and shows us the truth' (pp. 137-8).

31. Giorgio Melchiori, *Shakespeare's Garter Plays: 'Edward III' to 'Merry Wives of Windsor'* (Newark, N.J., 1994), 21-73.

32. Harold Jenkins, 'Structural problem', reprinted in G. K. Hunter (ed.), *'King Henry IV, Parts 1 and 2': A Casebook* (London, 1970), 171.

33. Sir Philip Sidney, *An Apology for Poetry*, ed. Geoffrey Shepherd (London, 1965), 110.

34. Besides Womersley's articles cited above, notes 7 and 11, one should also note his 'Sir Thomas More's *History of King Richard III*: a new theory of the English texts', *Renaiss Stud*, 7 (1993), 272-90, with its reservations about the 'reductive and distorting influence' of some recent scholarship on sixteenth-century historiography in 'its tendency to distract scholars from the study of historical writing to the study of that beguiling abstraction, "historical thought"' (289 n. 61).

35. G. K. Hunter, 'Truth and Art in History Plays', *Shakes Surv*, 42 (1990), 15.

36. *The Second Part of King Henry VI*, ed. Michael Hattaway (Cambridge, 1991), 7.

37. *Ibid*. 7.

38. *Ibid*. 20.

39. *The First Part of King Henry VI*, ed. Michael Hattaway (Cambridge, 1990), 9; see also Emrys Jones, *The Origins of Shakespeare* (Oxford, 1977), 31-56.

40. *First Part of Henry VI*, ed. Hattaway, 8.

41. See the fuller account in Dean, 'Forms of time', 426-30.

42. Womersley, 'Sir Henry Savile's Tacitus', 335.

43. Marjorie Grene, *The Knower and the Known* (Calif. 1966), 246. This inspirational work first suggested to me the importance of overlapping as a concept. Once again, my argument complements that of Paola Pugliatti, who calls attention to the importance of the image of the *border*—and of its transgressions—in the narrative and construction of the *Henry IV* plays (*Shakespeare the Historian*, 108-9).

44. Compare the extraordinary scene in *Woodstock*, ed. A. P. Rossiter (London, 1946), in which Richard discovers that he has reached the age of majority when he hears his own birthdate read out of the 'English Chronicles' as 1365: 'KING: 1365 . . . What year is this? GREEN: ''Tis now, my lord, 1387.' (II. i. 109-10). If the author was not joking, this is an embarrassing piece of clumsiness, almost Hollywood standard, which makes an instructive contrast with Shakespeare's Richard's internalized growth to maturity.

45. Grene, *The Knower and the Known*, 245, 252.

CHARACTER STUDIES

Paul A. Gottschalk (essay date 1974)

SOURCE: "Hal and the 'Play Extempore' in *I Henry IV*," in *Henry the Fourth Parts I and II: Critical Essays,* edited by David Bevington, Garland Publishing, 1986, 337-48.

[*In the following essay, originally published in 1974, Gottschalk presents an analysis of Prince Hal's character by examining the tavern scene in* Henry IV, Part I, *noting that this scene is crucial to Hal's development as a hero.*]

The great tavern scene of *I Henry IV* (II.iv) is the longest of the play and the most elaborate, ranging over five hundred lines from the gulling of Francis and the attempted showing-up of Falstaff to the Sheriff's sudden entry and Hal's imminent departure for court. Understandably, the scene has attracted a number of critical studies relating its parts to one another or to the play as a whole,[1] and certainly its richness and complexity warrant any attempt to clarify the aesthetic unity that lies beneath. Yet for all this complexity, the scene progresses smoothly enough, looking back toward Gadshill in its first half and forward to the royal palace in the second, back toward Hal's disgrace and forward to his redemption. This shift coincides with what, in view of the impending confrontation of Hal with his father, is clearly the crisis of the scene: the staging of the "play extempore," in which first Falstaff and then Hal assumes the role of King Henry lecturing his truant son. The importance of this episode has already been underlined in Richard L. McGuire's "The Play-within-the-Play in *I Henry IV*" (*Shakespeare Quarterly,* 18 [1967], 47-52), where it is treated, indeed, as the crisis in Hal's development as hero. Dealing with the play extempore as an example of the Elizabethan play within a play, McGuire states that Hal attains "discovery of self through pretense" (p. 52), that, in acting out his role of King, he comes to realize it is time for the change he had predicted in his soliloquy of I.ii and thus time at last to reject Falstaff. In response to Falstaff's mock plea against banishment, Hal's final words in the episode—"I do, I will"—are spoken "as Prince *and* King" (p. 50). "This short reply after much rhetoric and repetition," says McGuire, "underlines the change in character and the finality of the renunciation" (p. 50).

Despite its humor, then, the play episode is highly serious drama, and McGuire's study is important in showing how this may be so. Yet this study is itself somewhat distortive. The play episode is not technically a play within a play at all; for that reason, we shall see, it cannot lead to "discovery of self through pretense" and thus is not crucial in the way that McGuire suggests.[2] Both the nature of the play episode as play and its function as Hal's crisis need to be reexamined.

Indeed, the very notion of Hal's crisis in this play is problematic. McGuire's interpretation becomes puzzling the moment we apply the principle that change of character onstage can be indicated only by change in the personage's avowed attitude, by change in his actions, or by comments from other characters. The last we do not find until the King's praise of Hal in Act III and Vernon's in Act IV. As to change in attitude, Hal's "I will" is no more than a summary of his soliloquy at the end of I.ii, in which he first reveals his intention to renounce Falstaff and his companions. Finally, if Hal's words "I do" promise a present change in his actions, as at first they seem to do, the promise remains unfulfilled. When, moments later, the Sheriff enters seeking Falstaff, Hal lies to protect his friend.[3] As soon as his interview with his father is over, Hal returns to the tavern, and his exploits there merely perpetuate the humor of earlier scenes. And when at the end of the play Falstaff claims credit for killing Hotspur, Hal acquiesces in the deceit:

> For my part, if a lie may do thee grace,
> I'll gild it with the happiest terms I have.
>
> (V.iv.161-162)[4]

Hal has not renounced Falstaff in the play episode. Falstaff continues to woo Hal, Hal to contemn Falstaff (as he did in his first lines of the play) but also to sport with him and, when the chips are down, to help him. In short, nothing has happened—and nothing does happen subsequently in the play that would not have occurred had the play scene never taken place. The play episode is not a "discovery of self through pretense," because Hal has discovered nothing that he did not already know in I.ii. It is not a crisis in character because his character shows no change.

In the play scene, nothing really happens. Indeed, we might ask ourselves, what *could* happen? Hal has already made his crucial commitment to regality in Act I; he carries it out in Act V and again in Act V of Part 2. Between the moment of decision and the moment of action, what is there to dramatize? Shakespeare was to work again at that problem in *Hamlet,* but Hal is not like Hamlet. If we analyze dramatic character into *potential* to perform a given action and *probability* of performing it, we see that in Hamlet the discrepancy between these two is enormous. The horizons of Hamlet's character are so vast, his potential for a wide variety of actions so broad, that the probability of his committing any one action is proportionately nebulous. In Hal, however, potential and probability are virtually identical. While Hamlet's character doesn't organize around his task, Hal's does. His time, too, is out of joint, but on the whole he seems quite pleased that he was born to set it right.

Therefore, *I Henry IV* is a play without a normal climax.[5] Shrewsbury is at once its moment of crisis and its moment of resolution. Hal's royal identity and his merely provisional relationship with Falstaff are announced in the soliloquy of I.ii, not as a grasping towards identity, as in Hamlet's soliloquies, but as a moral *fait accompli.* But this identity is latent. Throughout almost all of both parts of

Henry IV it remains in solution, invisible to Hal's companions, but not manifest until, first at Shrewsbury and then in the final rejection of Falstaff, it crystallizes openly and irrevocably.

Shakespeare's strategy in the play is to hide the inevitable fulfillment of Hal's character from Hal's contemporaries while revealing it to us. It is the same technique he had used shortly before in *Richard III*. Richard, however, must overcome a long series of obstacles on his way to success, while Hal faces only one crucial act in each part of *Henry IV:* the battle with Hotspur and the rejection of Falstaff. So although the basic problem of plot is much the same in *Richard III, Henry IV,* and *Hamlet,* the solutions differ, for Hal's character is simpler than Hamlet's and his goal closer than Richard's. Shakespeare's solution in *1 Henry IV* is to provide Hal with three analogous episodes of promise, episodes that seem to build toward the ultimate fulfillment of Shrewsbury while in fact doing little or nothing to bring it about. Each episode is followed by an apparent moral relapse to further maintain the suspense. First comes Hal's promise to himself in the soliloquy of I.ii, followed by the robbery at Gadshill; then the play episode, a promise to Falstaff, followed by Hal's protecting Falstaff from the Sheriff; and finally the throne room scene, in which Hal promises allegiance to his father—and then procures Falstaff his commission in the royal army.

To further the illusion of progress, these episodes are climactically arranged. The soliloquy is mere statement, completely hidden from all other characters in the play, and represents Hal's potential at its most latent. In the play episode Hal's regality becomes more overt, but only in the apparent context of play and only in the world of the tavern. In the throne room scene, however, the early promise of the soliloquy becomes a solemn oath to the King: it is both overt and totally serious. Finally, at Shrewsbury, the promise is fulfilled in action. When, therefore, McGuire says, "we never again see Falstaff and Hal together as they were before the play-within-the-play" (p. 50), he is right, but the stress must be laid on the "we never see": although the relationship of Hal and Falstaff is consistent throughout, the point of view from which it is shown us systematically shifts.[6] Thus, these promissory episodes do not simply mark time until Shrewsbury. If they are not crises, they are moments of heightened definition in the developing portrait of the young man who will be King.

The play episode begins its contribution to this portrait by bringing the immediately antecedent action into new focus, just as the soliloquy of I.ii refocuses the action of that scene. There, however, the effect is quite clear: Hal simply detaches himself morally from his companions ("I know you all . . ."). But here Hal must ultimately detach himself not only from Falstaff, the embodiment of amoral irresponsibility, but also from Francis and Hotspur, each in his own way an embodiment of loyalty so blind that it becomes irresponsibility too, of a different sort from Falstaff's but no less dangerous.[7] Yet, as in the earlier scene,

Hal at first seems to be moving further and further away from commitment as the scene progresses, as he transposes the many-faceted world of *1 Henry IV* into play. First, he plays at being a tapster, a Francis. Then, as Francis's single-minded simplicity reminds him of Hotspur's, he prepares to play that worthy: "I prithee call in Falstaff. I'll play Percy, and that damn'd brawn shall play Dame Mortimer his wife" (II.iv.122-124). There follows the attempted trapping of Falstaff, in which the reality of thievery becomes play (Falstaff's disguise of valor, complete with costume: the bloodied garments and hacked swords) within play (Poins and Hal having robbed the robbers—and with their own costumes of buckram) within play ("By the Lord, I knew ye as well as he that made ye"), the momentary butt of which is Hal himself, ironically most out of touch with the hopes of the theater audience just when Falstaff claims to have recognized the true Prince by instinct. The playfulness of the scene culminates in Falstaff's proposal, "What, shall we be merry? Shall we have a play extempore?" There is a momentary jockeying for position as Hal answers, "Content—and the argument shall be thy running away," and Falstaff retorts, "Ah, no more of that, Hal, an thou lovest me!" (ll. 308-313). We scarcely have time to ponder Falstaff's conditional before the Hostess bursts in to announce that a nobleman has just arrived from the court. Falstaff is sent out to speak with him, returns with word that Hal is to go to court in the morning, and begs Hal to "practise an answer" for the King (l. 412). Hal's reply seems to revive the momentarily interrupted atmosphere of play and, finally, to bring into it the two chief remaining figures from the world of *Henry IV:* Hal as Prince, and the King himself. "Do thou stand for my father," Hal tells Falstaff, "and examine me upon the particulars of my life" (ll. 413-414). A skit of some sort has been in the offing throughout the entire scene—first one on Hotspur and Lady Percy, then on Falstaff's running away, now on an event that has yet to occur: the confrontation of Henry IV and Prince Hal.

What makes this skit unusual among Elizabethan and Jacobean plays within plays is precisely that it is a "play extempore": both characters create their own roles as they go along. What is more, we see with increasing clarity that what the roles—and role-playing itself—mean to each is quite different.

For the chief temptation that Falstaff poses as a vice-figure is to reduce all things to play. The humor of the "men in buckram" episode stems from the very havoc that Falstaff's narration plays with reality as he creates a world where honor, valor, and mathematical identity itself are mere shadows, a world that denies the earnestness, practicality, and logic that are the forte of the two Henrys. Now in the play extempore Falstaff, sensing impending danger, begins to move the King himself into this unreal world; he makes Henry speak "in King Cambyses' vein," and in Euphues's as well.[8] McGuire suggests that the style is Falstaff's conception of kingly speech, that he is trying to be realistic,[9] but Falstaff has a very precise, self-conscious awareness of the rhetorical figure he is cutting:

he is not imitating kingly speech, he is parodying it, reducing kingship to literary convention, making reality a fiction. Thus, King Henry's agony over Hal's truancy becomes, in Falstaff's hands, a ludicrous exercise in euphuism. And that is precisely Falstaff's point. Falstaff's rhetoric picks up some dignity only when he turns to his own praises, and then changes again as he breaks off and addresses Hal more directly: "And tell me now, thou naughty varlet, tell me where hast thou been this month?" (ll. 473-475). The shift is deliberate and effective. Its friendly, teasing informality places Hal's offense precisely in the light in which Falstaff wants it to be considered.

Finally, Falstaff's reaction when Hal "deposes" him takes his dangerous lack of earnestness a step further. If, as McGuire suggests (p. 50), his chief concern is to maintain his position by having Hal "practise an answer," he might reasonably be concerned that Hal has not done so. But his reaction to the "deposition" indicates that that is not what is on his mind at all: "Depose me? If thou dost it half so gravely, so majestically, both in word and matter, hang me up by the heels for a rabbit-sucker or a poulter's hare" (ll. 478-481). His concern is for the pure virtuosity with which he has played his role. He does not even embrace the opportunity to show Hal how the Prince should speak to the King but here again, as with the men in buckram, abdicates prudence and gives himself to the jest of the moment: Hal as king speaks of grievous complaints against the Prince, and "'Sblood, my lord," replies Falstaff indecorously, "they are false! Nay, I'll tickle ye for a young prince, i' faith" (ll. 488-489). Role-play becomes his world, its practical implications forgotten. The game, to borrow from Dr. Johnson, is the Cleopatra for which he loses the world and is content to lose it. If Falstaff's hope lies in maintaining the verisimilitude of the play, he has undermined his hope. But if his hope—and the chief temptation he presents to the Prince—is to reduce the serious to play, the real to unreal, we see him here in a moment of triumph, and the Prince, if he does not counteract this temptation, in a moment of extreme moral danger.

When Hal "deposes" Falstaff, the crisis of the scene has arrived: "Dost thou speak like a king? Do thou stand for me, and I'll play my father" (ll. 476-477). First Falstaff acts the king, and now Hal will. But whose king will he act? If Falstaff's—that is, if he turns kingship into play—then the play world dominates political reality for Hal, and Falstaff wins.

But Shakespeare has already indicated that Hal will mean something radically different when *he* acts the king. We begin to see the difference at the very moment that the world of the skit first begins to separate itself from the reality of Eastcheap, the moment that real objects become props. "This chair shall be my state, this dagger my sceptre, and this cushion my crown," proclaims Falstaff. "Thy state," replies Hal, "is taken for a join'd-stool, thy golden sceptre for a leaden dagger, and thy precious rich crown for a pitiful bald crown" (ll. 415-420). Dr. Johnson wished that Hal's reply had been omitted, in that "it contains only a repetition of Falstaff's mock-royalty."[10] But Hal is repeating the lines with a difference. Falstaff is more interested in the props than in what they symbolize ("This chair . . . this dagger . . . this cushion") while to Hal the props as such are remote and what they represent foremost in his mind: not only does he reverse Falstaff's syntactic order, citing the royal object before its stage symbol, but he refers to the object specifically ("*thy* state") and to the symbol indefinitely ("*a* join'd stool"), while his adjectives build up into an eloquent climax ("Thy state . . . thy golden sceptre . . . thy precious rich crown"). Falstaff transforms the crown into a cushion; Hal sees the cushion but thinks of the actual state, scepter, and crown of England.[11] In these two apparently similar speeches of Falstaff and Hal, the throne and the Falstaff world are implicitly debating the issue shortly to be raised in greater earnest: the relative reality of each to the other.

The second intimation that Hal will play the king with a difference comes when Falstaff concludes his king speech: "And tell me now, thou naughty varlet, tell me where hast thou been this month?" and Hal makes no answer. Indeed, what sort of an answer might he make? Falstaff presumably hopes for the sort he himself would give, one that would reduce the whole problem to felicitous jest. But Hal does not reply in the role Falstaff has assigned him; he will not mock himself. Instead, deposing Falstaff, he himself becomes king,[12] and his first words indicate in their terseness and sobriety the seriousness of the confrontation that is to occur in III.ii:

> Now, Harry, whence come you?
> . . . . .
> The complaints I hear of thee are grievous.
>
> (ll. 484, 486-487)

And when Falstaff breaks his role to heighten the jest—"Nay, I'll tickle ye for a young prince, i' faith"—Hal turns the jest back to seriousness: "Swearest thou, ungracious boy? Henceforth ne'er look on me" (ll. 488-491).

In the lines that follow, one could debate whether Hal is speaking as the king or as himself. McGuire observes that Hal's tirade against Falstaff, though it is rant, is what Hal conceives to be kingly rant (p. 49); yet it is also reminiscent of the contempt that Hal has shown for Falstaff earlier in the scene:

> Call in ribs, call in tallow.
>
> (l. 125)
>
> These lies are like their father that begets them—gross as a mountain, open, palpable. Why, thou clay-brain'd guts, thou knotty-pated fool, thou whoreson obscene greasy tallow-catch—
>
> (ll. 249-253)

The tone is darker, but the style remains much the same. The ambiguity is resolved, of course, in the epiphanic moment when Falstaff pleads "banish not him thy Harry's company" and Hal replies, "I do, I will" (ll. 526, 528).

McGuire says that here Hal is speaking "as Prince *and* King," but, we have seen, Hal as prince never rejects Falstaff. Rather, he is speaking first as player-king and then in his actual role of future king, and we see that the two roles are continuous, that, in fact, Hal hasn't been acting at all. And that is his response to Falstaff's transformation of the serious into play: he has transformed play back into reality. This reality comes bursting in on them in the form of the Sheriff, and Falstaff, falling asleep behind the curtain, hides from it both in deed and in spirit. Meanwhile, the Prince has the last word on the thievery game—which he cancels by returning the money—and moves on to his encounter with his father, an encounter that will take place as predicted.

There is not, then, a single play extempore in *I Henry IV*: there are two, Falstaff's and Hal's, each moving away from the actual present, but one toward the unreal, the other toward the future. This ambivalence is possible precisely because the play is extemporaneous, without script or predetermined action. In genuine plays within plays, as in any regular play, the action is presented as autonomous, the events portrayed as beyond the control of either actor or spectator. A play creates its own world; whatever its relevance to the real world, there can be no question of identity. The actor, as Antonin Artaud puts it, is "entirely penetrated by feelings that do not benefit or even relate to his real condition."[13] and so is the actor-analogue of a play within a play. But neither actor in the play within *I Henry IV* possesses such autonomy. There is no script, no mimetic *a priori*, and both must shape their roles from whole cloth out of their own characters, their own penchant for involvement in the action that they portray. By its very nature, the play cannot be seen as separate from them.

Falstaff becomes absorbed in the play; as we watch him, the dimension of the actor behind the role sometimes fades away. "Play out the play," he cries, with the sheriff at the door. "I have much to say in the behalf of that Falstaff" (ll. 531-532). And indeed we cannot define Falstaff solely as the shrewd, ambitious parasite that he would appear without the roles that he continually plays. It is the whole-heartedness with which he plays them, the enthusiasm with which he invests his whole personality in the unreal and the impossible, that sets him aside from the other vice characters and eirons that inhabit the world of drama. But in the world of *Henry IV* he is dangerous precisely because he testifies to the primacy of the play world and thus to the unreality of the political.

Hal, on the other hand, is ultimately not playing at all. The fictional world he creates is, in fact, not fictional. It is separated from actuality not as an object of the imagination but as an object of prediction. The poet, as Sidney observes, does not affirm, but Hal's half of the skit ends on a mimetic affirmation which he immediately extends into the reality of the future: "I do, I will." It has often been suggested that the play scene parodies the encounter of King and Prince in III.ii,[14] but that, in effect, is merely what Falstaff wants it to do, since the end of parody is to undermine the serious; Falstaff wants the tavern to define the throne room. Hal brings about the precise opposite. The destiny that defines his character transmutes play into sudden prophecy: the duties of the throne define this moment in the tavern. For the second time, and through the very medium that threatens it the most, Hal's latent regality becomes manifest.

If the play episode does not mark a major shift in Hal's character, it does mark a major shift in the point of view of the play itself. The skit begins by showing us Hal's duties under the aspect of Falstaff; it concludes by showing Falstaff under the aspect of royalty. And it is thus that we shall see Falstaff henceforth, for England is not playing his game, and his actions as he carries a bottle of sack into battle, leads his men to slaughter, and stabs the dead Hotspur, justify the Prince's disgust. From now on, and throughout Part 2 as well, Falstaff stands in the shadow of royalty until at last, fulfilling his prophecy of the play extempore, King Henry V banishes him and commits himself, as he knew all along that he must, to an action in which Falstaff can play no part.

Notes

1. See Fredson Bowers, "Hal and Francis in *King Henry IV*, Part 1," *Renaissance Papers, 1965*, publication of Southeastern Renaissance Conference (Durham, N.C., 1966), pp. 15-20; Waldo F. McNeir, "Structure and Theme in the First Tavern Scene of *Henry IV, Part One*," *Essays on Shakespeare*, ed. Gordon Ross Smith (University Park, Pa., 1965), pp. 67-83; and S. P. Zitner, "Anon, Anon: or, a Mirror for a Magistrate," *SQ*, 19 (1968), 63-70. An ambiguously entitled essay is F. M. Salter's "The Play within the Play of *First Henry IV*," *Transactions of the Royal Society of Canada*, 3rd ser., vol. 40, sec. 2 (May, 1946), 209-223, which deals with the relation of the comic to the historical plot.

2. McGuire is disputing Dieter Mehl's point that plays staged by protagonists and involving "startling shifts of identities" are "a distinctly Jacobean feature" ("Forms and Functions of the Play within a Play," *RenD*, 7 [1965], 41-61, at p. 50). But Mehl seems to mean shifts from role-playing to actuality in such a way that one "may sometimes wonder whether the characters are still acting their parts or speaking in person" (Mehl, p. 50), rather than shifts in the character itself. As we shall see, neither situation applies to *I Henry IV*, though the latter comes close.

3. McGuire takes issue with McNeir (p. 79), who says that "the whole world of Falstaff hangs in the balance" pending Hal's words to the Sheriff, McGuire maintaining that Hal has already in effect made up his mind in the play episode (p. 50 and n.). But that this moment is in fact tense on the stage and that Hal does not resolve the tension by renouncing Falstaff here and now calls precisely into question what he means by "I do, I will."

4. The word "grace" marks the shift between these lines and Falstaff's final rejection: "Make less thy body, hence, and more thy grace . . ." (Part 2, V.v.56). Here, as throughout, I follow the argument of G. K. Hunter, "*Henry IV* and the Elizabethan Two-Part Play," *RES*, n.s. 5 (1954), 236-248, that Shakespeare took responsibility for the thematic coherence of the two parts of *Henry IV* even if he did not originally plan for the second; certainly, Hal's rejection of Falstaff is predicated in Part 1: see Harold Jenkins, *The Structural Problem in Shakespeare's Henry the Fourth* (London, 1956), reprinted in R. J. Dorius, ed., *Discussions of Shakespeare's Histories* (Boston, 1964), pp. 41-55.

5. See Fredson Bowers, "Shakespeare's Art: The Point of View," in *Literary Views,* ed. Carroll Camden (Chicago, 1964), pp. 45-58.

6. Note that whereas Hal's encounter with his father (III.ii) seems *to us* to mark a major estrangement of Hal from Falstaff, in fact Falstaff's position is consolidated once the interview is gotten over: "I am good friends with my father, and may do anything. . . . I have procured thee, Jack, a charge of foot" (III.iii.203-204, 208-209).

7. For a development of this point, see Bowers, "Hal and Francis in *King Henry IV,* Part 1," pp. 18-20.

8. See notes in the New Variorum edition of *I Henry IV,* ed. Samuel Burdett Hemingway (Philadelphia, 1936), pp. 161-164. Arnold Davenport sees an additional parallel in both substance and style to the dialogue on love vs. kingship in II.ii of Lyly's *Campaspe,* where Hephestion upbraids Alexander for wishing to relinquish his royal station and duties over the love of an unworthy captive girl ("Notes on Lyly's 'Campaspe' and Shakespeare," *Notes and Queries,* 199 [n.s. 1, 1954], 19-20), while G. B. Harrison sees a parody of the style and repertory of the Admiral's Men ("Shakespeare's Actors," in *A Series of Papers on Shakespeare and the Theater,* Shakespeare Association [London, 1927], pp. 62-87, esp. pp. 76-79). All three arguments suggest a reduction—for those in Shakespeare's audience who detect the allusions—of the serious to play.

9. Thus, when the Hostess interrupts, "he must silence her, the symbol of his bawdy-house, tavern-frequenting aspect of character, before he may imitate Henry Bolingbroke and speak to Hal" (p. 49).

10. Cited in Hemingway, ed., New Variorum edition, p. 159.

11. See Richard Farmer's observation (cited in New Variorum, p. 160): "This is an apostrophe of the prince to his absent father, not an answer to Falstaff," which is a necessary complement to McNeir's comment that "the signs of Falstaff's assumed royalty in throne, sceptre, and crown are reduced by Hal's literal directness to what they are—a joined-stool, a leaden dagger, and a bald crown" (McNeir, p. 77).

12. For the dramatic effectiveness of this visual stage metaphor, see McGuire, p. 49.

13. "The Theater and the Plague," in *The Theater and Its Double,* tr. Mary Caroline Richards (New York, 1958), p. 24. Even in such an extreme case as *The Spanish Tragedy,* this general principle holds true for the play within the play insofar as we see Hieronimo *as playing* Soliman: the role is analogous to reality and will erupt into reality, but it is not identical to it. If it were, there would be no suspense in the play within *The Spanish Tragedy.*

14. For an able counterargument to this view, see McGuire, pp. 49-52.

Barbara Everett (essay date 1990)

SOURCE: "The Fatness of Falstaff: Shakespeare and Character," in *Proceedings of the British Academy,* Volume 76, 1990, pp. 109-28.

[*In the following essay, Everett explores the origin and development of Falstaff's character in Shakespeare's history plays, with an emphasis on the political significance of his appearance in* Henry IV.]

One day early in the 1590s a clown came on to a London stage, holding a piece of string. At the end of the piece of string there was a dog. It's hard not to think that some in this first audience, realizing what an extraordinary thing was happening, put down their oranges and concentrated.

The dog, possibly the first on the Elizabethan stage, I want to leave where it is for a moment. My main subject in this lecture isn't Launce and his dog (for this is, of course, the first entry of the clown in *The Two Gentlemen of Verona*): but the much more complicated character who, charged by the Lord Chief Justice with having led astray the Prince of Wales, answers: 'The yong Prince hath misled me. I am the Fellow with the great belly, and he my Dogge'. No one now quite follows this joke, which may be an airy reference (to distract attention) to the Man in the Moon. What is more interesting than Falstaff's ancient joke is his capacity to make us listen to him while he tells it. We concentrate.

Falstaff can get away with this debate as to who precisely, as between him and the future King of England, is whose dog, because the *Henry IV* plays give him peculiar authority. This is an authority that works not only inside the plays but outside them as well. One of the few early stories, rare but trustworthy, that come straight from Shakespeare's own theatre-world, reports that when Falstaff walked out on to the stage the groundlings stopped cracking their nuts so that they could hear him better. From the time of this well-known anecdote up to the beginning of our own critical period, some 60 or 70 years ago now, Falstaff was widely agreed to be the dramatist's greatest character.

We now tend not to believe in Character in general, or in Falstaff in particular. The time-span of this disbelief can probably be synchronized with the full professionalizing of literary studies into the academic: the process by which the thing worth knowing was standardized into the thing capable of proof. The Shakespeare industry has brought into a kind of perfection something begun perhaps as early as the First Folio's categories, which made the Falstaff plays Histories and Launce's play a Comedy.

Those decades during which Shakespeare studies have matured in our own time have been governed by a concept of History primarily political and constitutional. The King is dead; long live the King. As a result, certain inflexible presuppositions are lodged in even the best of the earlier academic work on Shakespeare's Histories: and I am thinking here of basic studies of the 1940s and 1950s, like Dover Wilson's *The Fortunes of Falstaff*, or useful popular books like Tillyard's on *Shakespeare's History Plays*, both still with a certain influence.

These early studies, with their monarchical interests, tended to be strongly conservative in their attitudes. They worked to defend the rejection of Falstaff. In the course of time, they generated in opposition a series of essays implicitly radical in their attitudes. Looking back to Bradley's very fine, and essentially liberal, praise of Falstaff, Auden's and Empson's essays (for instance), like Orson Welles's film, *Chimes at Midnight,* make a brilliant case, in different ways, for the old Knight's generous, even loving, even saintly cast of character. Yet these remarkable studies, like more recent writing with a radical stance (Greenblatt's powerful essay 'Paper Bullets' would be a case in point) do little to dislodge the intellectual bases of more conventional criticism: they merely reverse them. Stress on the whole Tudor Myth, concern with the source-materials which Shakespeare took from contemporary historians, whether primarily 'for' the Prince or 'for' Falstaff, prejudges the actual form and substance of these plays.

Scholarly criticism of the *Henry IV* plays is haunted by an interesting problem of structure. There is marked difference of opinion as to whether they constitute one or two dramas, whether the second is separate, a continuation, or a sequel—whether envisaged from the beginning or enforced by the success of what became Part One. These questions appear to depend on a decision to define plot in political terms. Both parts of *Henry IV* are commonly described as working in terms of what is called its main plot—which is to say, the story about how Henry IV overcomes rebellion in his kingdom. The sub-plot describes how Henry's son Hal, on his way to becoming the great and good Henry V, at once helps his father and also defeats riotous impulses in his own character and in his companions, the chief of them Falstaff.

Lewis Gordon as Falstaff in the 1979 Stratford Festival production of Henry IV, Part Two.

The trouble with this main plot is that it leaves much of the actual and fascinating substance of both plays to be known as the sub-plot, which merely entertains by its account of the adventures of the Prince's riotous group. Even those most firmly appreciative of the *Henry IV* plays often display not only the anxiety about structure I have mentioned, but a tendency to praise in terms which have a tell-tale imprecision, a sheer inaccuracy: words like 'epic' and 'panoramic' recur disturbingly. Both are attempts, I suspect, to categorize what is always thought of as the realism of these plays—a realism made synonymous with randomness and used to explain how the greatest character in Shakespeare, or one so considered for centuries, comes to be lurking in a sub-plot.

Other odd circumstances attend Falstaff's connexion with the political. It is now generally accepted that the character was invented under the name of Oldcastle, but that Shakespeare's acting company was forced to alter this name after protest from powerful descendants of the original or historical Oldcastle. Yet political incaution of this kind hardly characterized Shakespeare in general: he was a writer with a prudent tendency to keep his hands clean. Moreover, and odder still, Shakespeare took his name, 'Oldcastle', from a major source for the comic side of his play, the rambling and formless but not lifeless chronicle drama called *The Famous Victories of Henry V,* where the knight Oldcastle is one of the small group of companions of the wild young Prince. The interesting thing is that Shakespeare borrowed the apparently dangerous name, while taking no other attribute whatever from the character. The people in *The Famous Victories* after all have no attributes. They do not rise, strictly speaking, to the level of the characterized.

Shakespeare created Falstaff; and the role had no real sources except a name. The name I shall return to. The character's chief attributes are startling in their apparent incompatibility. He has an extreme, wittily fantastic and talkatively humorous intelligence. And this free mind is—paradoxically, according to the stock physiology of the age—united to an enormous body. That Hal's Vice-like and riotous tempter, the ever-thirsty if in practice rarely gluttonous Falstaff, should be a 'whoreson round man' of course makes sense. But I want to record an impression that, just as the character becomes preposterous as the offspring of a subplot, so is his fatness something more than an incidental attribute. Falstaff is fat necessarily. Certainly we may say that the groundlings fell silent because of his superlative free-wheeling play of wit, enthrallingly dangerous in a political milieu. But perhaps they also fell silent when he first walked on to the stage: entranced to find the simple individual body (and so much of it!) given a star part in the drama of History.

Here I want to turn back to Launce's dog, still there on the stage of the early 1590s. There aren't, so far as I know, many other acting dogs in the considerable amount of Renaissance drama in English that has come down to us. There is one—and it doesn't seem likely that Ben Jonson was uninfluenced by Shakespeare when, in *Every Man Out of His Humour,* only a few years after the earlier comedy, he gave a dog to his foolish country Knight. Jonson's Knight doesn't just have a dog—he totes around a cat as well, though we never see her because she isn't let out of her bag. And the dog too might have been better off in a bag, because before very long he is poisoned off. So much (Jonson may have felt) for Shakespeare.

Despite the cat at home—'wringing her hands', Launce the fool tells us, for grief of the parting—there is no invisible cat on stage to challenge the solitary splendour of Shakespeare's dog. Moreover, he survives. In fact, he triumphs. Launce does everything for the creature he calls his 'servant'. 'I have', he says crossly, 'sat in the stockes, for puddings he hath stolne'; he has 'stood on the Pillorie for Geese he hath kil'd'. And lastly, the dog has a name. He's called Crab, presumably short for crab-apple, for his Petrarchan-mistress-like hardness and bitterness of heart: he is, reports Launce regretfully but still dotingly, 'the sowrest-natured dogge that lives . . . this cruell-hearted Curre'.

The Two Gentlemen illustrates through its pair of gentlemen and their ladies the crazy if beautiful things romantic love can make human beings do; and its plot is merely a dazzle of love's permutations and possibilities. The perplexed and innocent feeling of the clown for his dog is the matching shadow of that dazzle. Both more and less than 'gentlemanly', his experience limited to an acquaintance 'with the smell before' and yet given (as in the remark about the stolen puddings) thought-provokingly Scriptural verbal cadences, the fool is without argument a fool, and hardly a holy one; yet he is happy, and we are glad he is happy, a man who gets what he wanted.

This early comedy, full of weaknesses as it is, is none the less decidedly agreeable on the stage: and its intrinsic affectionateness focuses on Launce and his dog. All the play's Elizabethan paradoxes of love shimmer round the clown and finally embody themselves in the entirely original figure of the dog. We have to say 'figure' rather than 'character'. In the first place, Crab can't talk. Talked-at, his silence promises the huge capacity to contain meaning which is common to all true theatrical presences. He *is,* beyond analysis: to be is as much the dog's function as it is Hamlet's. He is character as an end more than a means, the thing in itself: a dog (Gertrude Stein might have said) is a dog is a dog. Or, as Shakespeare himself put it with some desperation in a Sonnet, 'You alone are you'. Opaque, incurable and absolute, the beloved is.

Dogs can't talk; and they can't act, either. *Qua* dogs, they aren't gentlemen, aren't civilized, don't tell lies and don't betray. It's this pleasant lack of the complicit that makes animals amusing in their domestic relations. To quote another and finer Modernist, about another and subtler animal, one of T. S. Eliot's 'Practical Cats', 'He will do / As he do do / And there's no doing anything about it!' The basic joke about the Petrarchan 'cruell-hearted Curre' depends on a shared understanding of writer and reader, or actor and audience. The first onstage dog, like all his successors, must have been the kind of reliable creature that can be counted on to do little worse than sit on the boards and smile and pant and thump his tail. If the dog's silence says something about his own nature, then his simple recalcitrance—his inability to be either good or bad to order—says something about ours, as loving beings and as audiences. Our loves are not meaningless, but we do imagine things.

The clown seems almost to perceive this when he acts out his departure from home, casting himself and the dog: 'I am the dogge: no, the dogge is himselfe, and I am the dogge: oh, the dogge is me, and I am myselfe'. He can try in this way to rationalize and mutualize their relation, despite his protest that, unlike the compassionate cat, the dog did not 'shedde one teare: he is a stone, a very pibble stone, and has no more pitty in him then a dog'. The circularity is instructive. The clown is thinking through things more than philosophically difficult. The animal gains our and the fool's feeling by natural sympathy, and holds it by equally natural (natural to him) resistance to sympathy: 'No, the dogge is himselfe'. Like the future Cleopatra's superbly theatrical hold on the heart, Crab's opacity is of the essence. He is real enough to attract and compel startled attention, but obdurately bodily or thingy enough never to bore the imagination by satisfying it.

In his 'I am the dogge', the clown is wrestling, in words of one syllable, with the issues that give the Sonnets all their love-metaphysics. But his words also help any critic in the effort to analyse what we mean by 'character' in Shakespeare's plays: a factor inimitably itself and thingy ('No, the dogge is himselfe') yet also boundlessly giving to the imagination ('Oh, the dogge is me, and I am my selfe'). *The Two Gentlemen of Verona* is a mild, small play, not much revered (it seems) by any critic; but every time it is performed, an audience will be riveted by a character which is also a non-character—an actuality, life itself standing at the centre of the comedy, wagging its tail. Dr Johnson, who praised Shakespeare because there was always a way out from his fictions 'to nature', may have included among his meanings something like this.

I want to suggest that Shakespearean character-creation is from the beginning an exemplifying of this unique process: that a character in his work is less a person than an insight, but an insight embodied into brilliant forms of the real. The dramatist's characters, that is to say, are supremely observed. But they are observed in a special way: they are not merely social, but recognizably opaque, essentially thingy. They are poetically embodied into forms which oddly compel our dreaming loyalty, whatever decisions of morality may seem to intervene—'I am the dogge'.

The most splendid case of this in Shakespeare's early drama is of course the King known as Richard Crookback. The chronology of the early writing being as vexed as it is, it's hard to say whether *Richard III* precedes *The Two Gentlemen of Verona*. But the character has all the compelling, attention-focusing quality I am trying to define, and it derives from more than the glittering eye which holds the theatre from the beginning, the index of a mental force unmatched in these early Histories. Richard's real power surely emanates—as the sinister wooing of Anne will at once make plain—from what is crookedly yet straightforwardly physical in him, from the symbolic (though of course historical) crookback in itself: from the oddly undeceptive, doggish body that humps and thumps its way forward to the dead centre of the stage, saying first by its sheer presence what it thinks at last aloud: 'Richard loves Richard, that is, I am I'.

A sweeter proposition altogether, Bottom too has something in him of this heroic physicality. The idea of Bottom as a character is hampered by the problem of his name—which didn't mean what we think it means until two centuries later. The word 'Bottom' for our lower parts was an 18th-century euphemism. Yet *A Midsummer Night's Dream*, which layers together our night-time with our daytime selves, has a place in it for euphemisms: the gentle, decent, arty artisans who are Bottom's companions agree that 'You must say, Paragon. A Paramour, God bless us, is a thing of naught'.

Poor Bottom, an innocently dreaming egoist, a would-be artist, becomes in the wood by night what we would now call a donkey. But that word is another 18th-century euphemism. Elizabethans would have said roundly that Bottom was an ass. And they pronounced that word exactly as they said the word *arse*, one of their two current terms for what we call the bottom. The other term, Shakespeare was to use later on (he clearly wasn't incapable of it) for the name of one mean and degraded as Bottom never is, in a far darker, more realistic comedy, *Measure for Measure:* where the servant to the Bawd is named Pompey Bum. The word itself Shakespeare certainly introduces into the earlier comedy, where, after Bottom has just left the stage at his first appearance, Puck is made, with a degree of firmly stated earthiness, to introduce the word into the first of the fairy scenes, in his story of the old woman falling off her stool. The poetic effect of the clash of worlds is marked.

The evidence suggests that Shakespeare did think of Bottom in these not unfriendly terms, giving him, from all sorts of propriety, dramatic and otherwise, a decent euphemism, decided on because of its first and last letters (the profession of weaver would obviously follow). And he did so, surely, because he saw the euphemized, civilized Bottom as tender and funny, with the Queen of the Fairies draped adoringly round his stupidity, in a way that the character's own refined self would have been shocked by if he could ever have conceived it, but which the poet's own even more refined self saw as a good, human (which is, creaturely) truth about love.

I don't want to work through all the dramatist's earlier characters: the most brilliant of them all, Shylock, has subtleties that can't and shouldn't be cut down to a sentence or two. But the fastidious and intellectual money-lender isn't an exception to the physicality I'm talking about here: Shylock focuses this hardest and most Marlovianly bejewelled of all Shakespeare's comedis in his incantatory, ironic, highly personal utterance, extreme in its hatred and speaking of human brotherhood: 'Hath not a *Jew* eyes? hath not a *Jew* hands, organs, dimentions? . . . if you pricke us, do we not bleede?' There is a Shakespearean depth of meaning in the way this most abstract and conceptual drama of money is at the same time peculiarly physical, directed towards acts of love, its plot turning on a pound of flesh.

The pound of flesh brings us in sight of that 'Tunne of Man', Sir John Falstaff. I've been arguing that throughout Shakespeare's developing power of characterization, the physical has a special place: from Crab the dog to Richard Crookback, then to Bottom, then to the magnificently delineated yet isolated Shylock, and then the 'fat old man' himself. I have made a deliberate decision hardly to quote from or to illustrate Falstaff's fatness in this lecture, only to try to explain it—and this, for a specific reason. The brief phrases I've already quoted come, of course, from Hal in the Tavern Scene of *1 Henry IV*, before he goes on to detail 'that Trunke of Humors, that Boulting-Hutch of Beastlinesse, that swolne Parcell of Dropsies, that huge Bombard of Sacke' and the rest.

It's striking that this flyting of Hal's is no more (or less) vivid than Falstaff's own winningly modest, 'plumpe *Jacke*'. Earlier in this same scene, recalling his thinness at Hal's age ('I could have crept into any Aldermans Thumbe Ring'), Falstaff has lamented, 'A plague of sighing and griefe, it blowes a man up like a Bladder'. This is ridiculous, of course. And yet the fact is that the character does indeed seem to do a good deal of waxing and waning. Like the 'Jet Ring Sent' by the poet John Donne, there is 'nothing more endless, nothing sooner broke' than our sense of Falstaff's fatness. The brilliance of these plays, in short, is that they give a kind of metaphysical witty status to Falstaff's fatness—at once all human solidity, and yet as subject to Shakespeare's magical conjuring skills as a vanishing rabbit. The character is absolutely large and ultimately present, the whole round world in person—the Globe. But he is best evoked in the theatre by an actor's illusion, and elsewhere, by the individual reading imagination.

Explanations are probably easier than illusions. There are sixteenth-century intellectual movements in terms of which we should perhaps see Shakespeare's art of bodies. On many fronts, as in some revival of the ancient skill in bas-relief, figures begin to solidify, and to grow out of their backgrounds. The whole humanistic period, as recent studies of Rabelais have shown, counterpoises its abstraction by an immersion in the physical. Aesthetic Mannerism in Europe inaugurated a vision intoxicated with relativities, and at ease in a world of giants and dwarfs. But to these large mental contexts, imagining a newly material universe, there needs to be added one simpler factor. Shakespeare's discoveries would probably not have been perfected by a writer who had not acted for years on the public stage: a process which induces awareness of the body as few others can. On stage, the visible public self can seem to the inner consciousness of the actor or speaker to grow, like Falstaff, 'gross as a mountain', to become a 'huge hill of flesh'. It is a notable fact that Richard, Bottom and Falstaff are all natural actors; the reserved Shylock mimics others; even Crab the dog is a kind of joke about what T. S. Eliot might have called, 'acting and not-acting'. In a memorable autobiographical study, an actor—Simon Callow—has described the long discipline of learning to act as a 're-inventing' of the physical self, an actual 're-birthing'. This is the context from which Falstaff was 'borne about three of the clock in the afternoon, with a white head, and something a round belly'.

It may be possible to go further than this, and to give some details of (so to speak) the character's birth certificate, under the name Oldcastle. I've already mentioned the dramatist's major source for the Falstaffian incidents in the three later Histories, the raw but not unentertaining *Famous Victories of Henry V*: a work which strikes many scholars as so bad as to lead them to argue that Shakespeare must have had to hand a text fuller than that which has come down to us. This is theoretical, however. On the evidence that we have, Falstaff took nothing but his original name, Oldcastle, from the source play. The change of name proceeded from (or so we now assume) the forceful if foolish protest by descendants of the original Oldcastle. This whole political incident now attracts a good part of the interest of scholars and critics in the second cycle of Histories. But none seems to have asked why Shakespeare bothered to retain the name of a personage from whom he took so little. Nor does any apparently go on to wonder why so generally cautious a man as the dramatist now seems could have got himself into trouble by dabbling in a political scene he was at most other times so careful to avoid.

One simple answer offers itself, which may solve the second problem in meeting the first. The name, Oldcastle, was suggestive and important enough for it to be stated as early in the play as possible, hence Hal's 'My old lad of the Castle'. But it doesn't seem to have mattered that the writer dropped it for *2 Henry IV* and after. Efforts on the part of editors to replace the name in editions may be a waste of energy: all its virtue (as we say in cooking) has gone into the character. Therefore the name and the character are consonant with each other.

Shakespeare incautiously failed to observe the political bearings of the name because its literal and metaphorical sense excited him more: it may even for a while have served as some kind of poetic guideline. The name's resonances, I would suggest, were a matter of a whole late-medieval iconology of the Castle in itself. As fortification, the Castle was central to the entire militaristic feudal culture. But over the centuries, the fortress gradually changed its function. By the sixteenth century, many were ruinous, and others had been transformed into palaces, mansions or just ordinary large houses. (It's perhaps instructive that in Shakespeare's period the words 'castle', 'mansion' and 'house' approximate and grow near to synonymous: a fact which permitted the witty apophthegm of the great Elizabethan jurist, Sir Edward Coke, who seems first to have coined the axiom, 'A man's house is his castle', *et domus sua cuique est tutissimum refugium*). As the old castles were altered in their uses, so too the symbolic meanings of the Castle grew different. Once a symbol of power, of the mailed fist, the image of the Castle was internalizing itself, even representing the battle for virtue on the part of the human spirit, castled within and conscious of its own body.

Some glimpse of this context, both linguistic and cultural, can be seen in Shakespeare's Sonnet 146, 'Poore soule, the center of my sinful earth'. In this poem, the soul inhabits the body as a medieval Lord might have done an embattled castle, struggling with 'these rebell powres that thee array', and 'Painting thy outward walls so costlie gay'. With a rapid transition the castle becomes a short-leased house: 'Why so large cost having so short a lease / Dost thou upon thy fading mansion spend?' The sestet of the poem welcomes ruin: the spirit needs death, the death of the body.

Though there are some fine and touching things in it, Sonnet 146 is not the poet's best: its conventional images are unhandily played with, and unsuccess makes the whole curiously unconvincing. It's hard for a reader to reach the end without feeling some impulse to answer as old Falstaff does Dol in Part Two of *Henry IV*: 'Peace (good *Dol*) doe not speake like a Deathshead: doe not bid me remember mine end'. Dol has been recommending that he should 'leave fighting on dayes, and foining on nights, and begin to patch up thine old Body for Heaven'. Variable and human as both characters are, this moment of quiet in a scene of sometimes savage, always wonderfully funny farce is extraordinarily compelling as the sonnet perhaps is not. The comparison of play and poem says something simple about the nature of Shakespeare's genius. It needs to embody, to build the contradictions of existence into people and moments as richly ambiguous as this one. The poet isn't most at home sorting out the iconology of the Castle in religious sentiments. Falstaff needs to be fat.

One touching phrase in the poem, the 'fading mansion', is revealing, because it has (I suspect) a word-play on the first syllable of its noun. The fading *man*sion is *man*hood, the ruinous castle where men live all their lives: those who live by the sword, dying by the sword. These resonances are a living part of Shakespeare's dramatic vision in his Histories. In the *Henry IV* plays, a royal usurper, even a Cain-like brother-murderer, spends his troubled reign thinking of Jerusalem. In short, the name Oldcastle in his source perhaps suddenly articulated for the poet all the meanings of History—of men alive and embodied in what we call 'History'—that he wanted to bring together. At their centre was a magnificent old reprobate, Sir John Oldcastle/Falstaff, who is also one of the names of Everyman.

I have used here the phrase, 'What we call "History"', in recognition of the fact that we can mean different things by it. The history Shakespeare took from his sources has been called 'the Tudor Myth'. What he did with it is a large question. History plays may be the dramatist's first work. Indeed, he probably invented the form, planning his first tetralogy (the *Henry VI*'s and *Richard III*) with immense ambition and originality. The ecclesiastical and political censorship of the time lending distance a certain enchantment, he took his historical subjects from the years before the ascent to the throne of his own Queen's grandfather, Henry VII. And, as is well-known, he deals with the chronologically later kings in his earlier sequence. The *Richard II-Henry IV-Henry V* sequence, written towards the end of the 1590s, takes him back historically into the further past, Henry V being of course the father of Henry VI.

This reversal has interesting effects. It intensifies that play of memory and irony which all retrospective art brings into play. The triumphant story of Henry V is acted out in the knowledge that Henry V's son Henry VI has already—in the past of the audience and in the work of this dramatist—thrown away the spoils of his father's victories, and with his mixture of uncertainty and good principle submerged his kingdom in civil war. As a result, Shakespeare's own sense of History is always, and increasingly, circular, individual and ironic. It says that nothing is final; it says that—as the sub-title of *Henry VIII* would finally have it—*All Is True*.

It is commonly agreed that the *Henry IV* plays are the poet's finest Histories. It is also commonly agreed that they are the least historic—they depend least on historical sources. We need perhaps to put these agreements together. These are Shakespeare's best Histories because the least historical. I spent a good deal of time at the beginning of this lecture stressing the importance to Shakespeare's developing art of characterization of a non-character: a dog. The academic, even the professional literary intellect can impose its own categories on Shakespeare's work, confusing the vital with the important and the important with the large. The poet's genius is an intrinsic and effortlessly intelligent sureness with symbols and the other media of his art: media not always explicitly recognizable as having the status of the political and historical.

The central presence of the historically factual in these plays ought not to deflect us from seeing what is special in them—their strangeness, their originality, their identity as imagined works. Falstaff's fatness matters in them; there is a substantive point to the character's challenge of the Prince's authority, with his 'I am the Fellow with the great belly, and he my Dogge'. I will give one example of the plays' originality from outside these two characters. Scholarly commentators have done excellent work on the dramatist's adaptations and alterations. Most mention for instance that Shakespeare radically changes the age of Hotspur, historically twenty-three years older, to make him of Hal's generation. He therefore becomes the young man's rival, his mirror-image or alter ego.

But it is interesting to go further than this. When the heroic Harry Hotspur is dead, his grieving young widow (a marvellously vivid character in both parts, and essentially invented by Shakespeare) describes the husband she loved as having had an intensely real physical identity:

> speaking thicke (which Nature made his blemish)
> Became the accents of the valiant.

Whether this means stammering, or lisping, or merely fiercely rapid stumbling speech, everyone did it (says Lady Hotspur) just to be like him. In Shakespeare's hands, through Lady Hotspur's desolate words, a dead History comes alive. Like a haunting literary presence, the historical Hotspur has turned into a living and wholly human stutter.

One simple way of explaining the splendour of these plays is to say that they are full of Falstaff's fatness—they are full of people, newly defined as Falstaff is defined. In terms of stored resources suddenly and fully utilized, Shakespeare seems to have travelled a startling distance in *1 Henry IV* from *Richard II*, that exquisite unpeopled verse exercise, a thin play in the sense that the *Henry IV*'s are fat. It is of course relevant that *Richard II* is written wholly in verse, while the *Henry IV* plays invent a new and magnificent prose, widespread in the plays and different with every character who uses it. Particularly in a raffish urban milieu, it is a prose that characterizes, identifies, realizes.

Many critics react appreciatively to what they feel as an intense reality and variety in the *Henry IV* plays. But they may be driven by a deference to what is in appearance historical and political in them to speak with a puzzled generality of what is called 'epic' or 'panoramic' breadth of life. It is perhaps worth recalling that these are dramatic worlds with specific lineaments. The two *Henry IV* plays, like *Henry V*, are in fact so little panoramic as to omit those major elements of their audiences, both Elizabethan and modern, the middle classes—from which the dramatist himself came. Sociologically these dramas concern themselves only with the Court and the Tavern; they are about power and the lack of it. Their world is of the Castle: medieval, militaristic and male. In this last respect they are actually less 'panoramic' than the earlier Histories. Hugely-peopled, with more characters in each than *Hamlet*, the two parts of *Henry IV* hold only a quartet of brilliant female cameos, Ladies Percy and Mortimer, Mistress Quickly and Dol Tearsheet, all powerless either in high or in low life. Loved by her husband, Lady Percy can't influence his life, and Lady Mortimer can't even be understood by hers.

Certainly the Falstaff plays give an image of the real hardly achieved elsewhere in Shakespeare's first decade. Indeed, the very nature, intensity yet elusiveness of this sense of the real earns them the title of (perhaps) his first and best early tragicomedies, the two parts of *Henry IV* seeming actually to explore the possibilities of a mode first (Part One) comic, then (Part Two) tragic. A condition of this truthfulness is an expressiveness within laws almost ruthlessly maintained. The fine experience of randomness in these plays, so exhilarating and absorbing, at the same time proceeds from considered decisions and exclusions. The superb dawn scene before Gadshill (*1 Henry IV*, II.i), with its '*Charles waine . . .* over the new Chimney', its country dankness and its fleas, its smell of urine, its gammon of bacon and its roots of ginger, is where it is to serve as a quizzical alternative to 'Gadshill' itself, juxtaposing to the systematic thieveries of high life the mere fleabites of the low.

With this mention of Gadshill I want to pause briefly to give some sense of what I mean by the peculiar decisions and exclusions of the *Henry IV* plays: for the Gadshill incident, essentially invented by the poet and given elaborate treatment, throws a surprisingly clear light on to the historical in this First Part. It's first necessary to say that perhaps the most initiatory of the academic studies of these plays, and for a long time the most influential, Dover Wilson's *The Fortunes of Falstaff*, is an admirable piece of scholarship spoiled by those innocent snobberies, those deferences to politics believed to characterize Shakespeare's Histories, which were formerly too often found in English studies. Supporting his case for the severe loyalism of *1 Henry IV*, Dover Wilson quotes with approval an earlier scholar's description of Prince Hal as 'a man among animals', only preferring to the word 'animals' (which he finds 'too modern') the term 'pack of scurvy rascals, inhabiting a sphere altogether remote from that to which Hal rightly belongs'. (Falstaff he incidentally downgrades by proposing that as the Fool he was played by Kempe—a judgment possibly shaky: *Much Ado*'s Beatrice too would perform many of the functions of the Fool, but would hardly be likely to be played by Kempe.)

The phrase 'a man among animals' mixes social snobbery with a speciesism Crab the dog would have been amused by. It seems to me wrong in other ways as well. Shakespeare worked with intensity in *1 Henry IV* to locate the Prince as a 'man among men'. This has both private and public interlocking meanings, of which the public most directly affects Gadshill: but because they do interlock, it is worth remembering the private as well. I mentioned earlier the monosexuality of the plays' world. By confining female companionship to Mistress Quickly, and by excluding any hint of that homosexuality suggested in (for instance) *Troilus and Cressida*, this throws into a more brilliant light the relation of Falstaff and Hal, and the conditions in which friendship survives or dies in the world at large.

Innumerable studies have quoted Falstaff's opening question, 'Now *Hal*, what time of day is it Lad?', with an interesting discussion of his and the Prince's different notions of time and its proper use. None as far as I know bothers with the word, '*Lad*'—a word which Housman's usage has of course made largely unhandleable now, even apart from the passing of Edwardian and earlier social conditions. '*Lad*' was, like '*fellow*', in Shakespeare's time a word of kindly contempt, used to those younger or lower in the social scale than oneself. In using it to the Prince—whose irritation sparks the wit of his response—Falstaff is manifesting from the first his cheerfully arrogant resistance to social hierarchy. That this might amount to more than what Dover Wilson calls his 'sauciness' is made plain by the odd but functional scene at II.iv, where Hal teases Francis the naïve tavern drawer. Poor Francis has the helpless corruptibility of the wholly powerless; he is spellbound in an instant by the Prince's mere murmur of 'a thousand pound', that talismanic ghost- or dream-fortune which haunts these two plays. Francis simply can't forget the Prince's rank and status, and think of him as a person. It takes a Falstaff, tough enough to exist, at least for the moment, in the free kingdom of his own fatness, to maintain something like real feeling for this prodigal prince.

But Hal is a man among men in a public sense as well as a private one. At least in the only text in which we have it, the source-play, *The Famous Victories,* notably lacks Shakespeare's value of human feeling, the world of relationship and its terms and treacheries. And it opens only *after* the Gadshill incident, which we hear about at some distance. This incident Shakespeare chose to bring into the foreground and to make the basis of his Falstaff's character in action, giving four whole scenes to it—it becomes, indeed, something almost like a play-within-the-play.

Why did Shakespeare like it so much, this story of thieves who rob rich travellers, and of a prince who robs the thieves? Hal comes well out of it: he sends the money back and protects Falstaff. But the incident, playful escapade as it is, shows Hal a thief, all the same. Like Hamlet (who also found friends among 'thieves of mercy', pirates), Hal could, quoting the Book of Common Prayer, call his hands 'these pickers and stealers', recognizing a guilt both largely human and specifically royal. The Histories are haunted by the figure of Cain, thief and brother-murderer; and Hal is after all the son of the usurper who 'seized the crown' from Richard.

His soliloquy at I.ii, beginning with the words 'I know', endows the Prince with responsibility, almost with guilt: sooner or later he will enter the world of power natural to him and win virtue by making 'offence a skill'. At the battle of Shrewsbury, the play's climax, he articulates his relationship with the near-fraternal Hotspur:

> All the budding Honors of thy Crest
> Ile crop, to make a Garland for my head.

He has done what he promised his father earlier, made Percy 'but my factor . . . / To engross up glorious deeds on my behalf'. And Hotspur, dying, understands what has been done: 'O Harry, thou hast rob'd me of my youth'.

Yet Hotspur is of course essentially no different in his politics: he is merely given the beauty of the historical loser. The historians used by Shakespeare called the reign of Henry IV 'troubled', one of 'unrest'. In the drama, that trouble and unrest internalize, changing from the accidentality of data to the necessity of vision. Henry the King himself, politician and usurper, dreaming of Jerusalem, generates the ambiguities reigning everywhere in these plays. In this First Part, the poet has invented Gadshill as an ironic mirror of the great world of power which Henry rules over, and which the political rebels envy, pursue, but won't defer to. Prince, rebel and Fool; reticent Hal, heroic Hotspur and wise Falstaff, all alike and equally make 'offence a skill'. We may call Hal's honour true, Hotspur's a dream and Falstaff's non-existent, but the only honour the play knows is Honour Among Thieves.

Wholly characteristically, Falstaff knows this: 'A plague upon't, when theeves cannot be true one to another' (II.iv). These profoundly sceptical conditions release the play's stereotyped hierarchies; conventions are shaken free into a glitter of relativities. *1 Henry IV* is as fine as it is because of the depth with which it shows Hal as no other than a man among men. These are the terms on which he must learn his fidelities, infidelities, and historical survivals. And this is a world in which a man's supremacy is as individual to him as is Falstaff's massive body, his rapid mind.

I earlier made the suggestion that Falstaff's original name, Oldcastle, may have held in itself a certain potency for the poet. It carried with it, perhaps, to an Elizabethan imagination alive to language, something of the late-medieval and chivalrically militant world of this play, a world—as Shakespeare's own was still—of 'fading mansions', ruinous castles. An architectural historian, conceding that the psychic image of the Castle must be predominantly one of terror and aggression, has suggested that there may still be an aesthetic beauty in castles: that these fortifications may now, from their aspect of security, their defensive function, reveal to the mind an image of what he calls (in a fine phrase) 'stored energy'.

The debates on the structural problems of Parts One and Two of *Henry IV* may reflect difficulties in coming to terms with their great originality of form. They possess what Coleridge called 'form as proceeding', as against 'shape as superinduced': a form which has some relationship to Falstaff's massive, natural and always (theoretically) waxing and waning body. Though the Second Part is, if anything, even more original than the First in its loose expressive deliquescence of form, the First Part has always given more pleasure. And the enjoyment it gives might be glossed by the historian's aesthetic image of the Castle. Part One of *Henry IV* has above all a 'stored energy', a beautiful weighing of violent and indeed aggressive forces against each other. The play is everywhere in a state of active self-balance: Kings and subjects, fathers and sons, robbers and robbed, usurpers and rebels, exchanging roles but never out of true.

The political ambiguities of *1 Henry IV* allow no escape, but they do afford what might be called suspension. 'Time, that takes survey of all the world / Must have a stop'— and both stop and survey are the play. When the brisk but adoring Lady Percy asks her husband what carries him away, he answers laughing, 'Why my horse my love my horse'. This hint on the play's part about the natural, unarguable Crab-the-dog-like energies of youth is balanced by the very different but equally unarguable detachment in the historical memory of reader or audience: a detachment suddenly explicit in the Second Part of the play, when the tired old King says that life is so terrible to the eyes of experience that it can't be thought about, there is nothing to do but 'shut the book, and sit him down and die'. Such vitality and such sadness work together in a fashion more like music than politics.

The actor's autobiography I mentioned earlier happens to remark that 'There is nothing in a play *but* the characters', and though this is an actor's reaction, he is quite right: but he might not have said it about *The Famous Victories,* or many other scores of plays of the period. The *Henry IV* plays, and especially the First Part, enthrall because their actors are all characters: Falstaff may be greater than Glendower, or Mistress Quickly, or Cousin Silence, or Feeble, the woman's tailor, but they are hardly less intensely realized. In these plays, something rare and Shakespearean and hugely important to the literary tradition that followed was being achieved.

Moreover, this full translation of drama into character seems dependent on a quality of vision more than dramaturgical. *1 Henry IV* is a world of men of action, acting upon each other, struggling throughout for mastery, yet in the process each man becomes less destructive than autonomous. The world of action has become, in its way, purely contemplative. Concomitantly, and in simpler terms of behaviour, the play's combatants battle (to borrow another phrase from Coleridge) 'as in a war-embrace'. Lovers quarrel laughing, or talk different languages to each other; fathers and sons fall out from sheer affection; rivals imitate each other. Centrally, of course, there are Hal and Falstaff, fighting and flyting and planning betrayal, perhaps the richest, the most human, but also the most worldly portrayal of friendship in Shakespeare's works. And always, playing off against the powerful, cool and withdrawn royal boy, is the man Falstaff, perpetually making a kind of grumbling, smiling peace within himself, between the cumbersome body and the incomparable mind.

Part One of *Henry IV* brilliantly succeeds by turning History into a tension of relationships, which we may think of, as we wish, as private or public: the sort of political history the dramatist was handling made these interchangeable—among the rebels, for instance, Lady Percy is Mortimer's sister, and Lady Mortimer is Glendower's daughter. Such a world permits the play to celebrate love and friendship snatched, like Hotspur's flower, 'Out of this Nettle, Danger'. The terms of the feeling which unites the characters are a vivid disinterest or dissociation combined with alert attention to the other. It is this element of dissociation that makes arguments about Falstaff curiously irrelevant. Moral criteria only obtain as conditions are laid down; a person may flee from the plague without being a coward, nor is a soldier necessarily cowardly who takes part in an orderly military retreat. Falstaff is no more a coward at Gadshill than Crab the dog is hard-hearted.

But at Shrewsbury there is a change. Throughout this First Part, Shakespeare has naturalized history and politics into a living world in which Falstaff's fatness has its place. Success and succession are all about growth, about movement upward, with the thrusting energy of Hotspur's flowering nettle. The play sets us in that world envisaged by the poet's fifteenth Sonnet, where 'every thing that grows / Holds in perfection but a little moment / . . . Men as plants increase / . . . at height decrease, / And were [wear] their brave state out of memory'. Part One is a kind of historical comedy, in which everyone gets as near as may be to having what he wants (the idealistic Hotspur would have found life horrifying, had he survived). But it is comic only because the clock stops, the action is suspended, the sheriff is shut out, the fighters are 'Cheared and chekt even by the self-same skie'.

In Part Two, naturally enough for a second part, the clock starts again. It has often been pointed out how far this almost tragic Second Part is dominated by the power of Time. Age and disease darken the scene. Hotspur is gone, Hal little on stage. There begins here that 'rejection' of Falstaff which is the climax the whole Second Part moves towards, in which the newly crowned Henry V rebukes and dismisses his old companion. Even Bradley, in what may be the best essay ever written on the *Henry IV* plays, sorrowfully assumes that the dramatist has willed and even rigged this rejection, has degraded his character through this play and on into the diminished and different (though still enjoyable) horseplay of *The Merry Wives*. There may be something that qualifies this. I have suggested the effect of the autonomous in the characterization of these plays: and the Falstaffian decline is surely similarly powered from the inside, like an illness that proceeds from his great bulk.

The turning-point is that obscurely disturbing moment at Shrewsbury, at the end of Part One, in which Falstaff stabs the dead Hotspur, his 'new wound in your thigh' bringing an odd erotic shame to the incident: some fleshing has taken place. Devoid as these plays are of any homosexual feeling, the sheer fatness of Falstaff, most male of men, allows him some of the soft freedoms of the female role; and now, some of its betrayals, too. It's a striking minor fact that at the very beginning of this play Shakespeare has remembered from the chronicles the detail of the Welshwomen's emasculation of the enemy dead in battle.

Early in Part One, the old Knight had turned on the Prince an ironic reversal of his own role as tempter: 'Before I knew thee, Hal, I knew nothing: and now I am (if a man should speake truly) little better then one of the wicked'. There is always a lurking truth in these floating ironies Falstaff is expert in. The shadow of their friendship is a double corruption. However much Sir John chooses—from some point of view that is anarchic or democratic or Elizabethanly aristocratic—to feel himself outside or even above Hal's royalty, he depends on it, just as he does on the Prince's youth. As Hal is involved and committed at Shrewsbury, so for the first time is Falstaff too. The battle that kills Hotspur and brings alive Hal does both to the old Knight. He dies in some part of his intellectual detachment, and rises from that death a survivor, to lose Hal's friendship by stealing his glory: 'Ile follow as they say, for Reward. Hee that rewards me, heaven reward him. If I do grow great again, Ile grow lesse. For Ile purge, and leave Sacke, and live cleanly, as a Nobelman shold do'.

The quarrelling friendship of Hal and Falstaff is, like other relationships in Part One, in its tension a high-wire on which both safely run and somersault. Falstaff's last-act stabbing of Hotspur is also a tragicomic betrayal of the Prince which cuts the wire. In Part Two neither he nor his circumstances are ever quite the same again. There are subtle adjustments of tone: the old Knight, now decisively poorer yet grander, grows faintly but pervasively ambitious, snobbish, with an eye to the main chance, talking Court talk in a manner never quite certainly enough ironic. His fatness loses its easy airy poise, its grace of imagination, and begins to solidify, greasily, into unnerving realisms of social class and gender. For the first time in this always dangerous territory, the old man's bulk begins to be touched by the queasily androgynous: as when, self-mockingly boasting about his wit, Sir John 'walks before' his new Page, 'like a Sow, that hath o'erwhelmed all her litter, but one'.

The stagger in the rhythm of that line is telling. The change in Falstaff is more than tonal, it is situational; and it is dictated by his new separation from the Prince, who growing up towards his royalty, is often a felt absence, a silence here. When he does appear, Hal is colder, Falstaff more demanding; Hal withdraws, Falstaff presumes. The entire play is more erotic than Part One, and there is a trace of the erotic in the power-game of relationship the two have started to play.

The action of Part Two, while we wait for the rejection that we know must come, is anything but boring. But it possesses a marked rhythm of entropy or running-down, a centrifugal loss of energy. The contrast with Part One is obvious. The world is one where, as in the Sonnet, men 'were [wear] their brave state out of memory'—or even that 'great world' of *King Lear* which 'wears out to naught'. Everywhere in this Second Part of *Henry IV,* we sense imbalances. No longer made brilliant by the Prince's bright hostilities, Falstaff has to talk to his own minimal Page; to a faceless, unindividuated and unshakeable old man, the Lord Chief Justice; to the coarsely savage Tearsheet and the wonderfully dizzy Quickly, whose human weight of farce and pathos almost upstages the Knight; and Shallow and Silence, the two country cousins.

These last two inhabit a Gloucestershire estate that grounds in itself much of what the closing phase of the play is saying, a back-of-beyond at once sad and preposterous, hilarious and charming. Both true and fantastic (not even Elizabethans saw Gloucestershire as on the main road North from London), their estate, with Davy's wistful hope 'to see London once ere I die', achieves a provinciality that is suddenly Chekhovian. This is not a place merely satirized by the dramatist, as it is patronized by Falstaff. It has its own ludicrous, deathly beauty, a mildewed richness: the strength of a Feeble who disturbingly achieves the heroic, telling the ruinous Falstaff that he owes God a death, and the surprise of a Silence, flowering through wine into an unstoppable music.

As at the end of the play Falstaff stands waiting for Hal, the new King, he talks troublingly of 'new Liveries' and of a borrowed 'thousand pound', of his travel-stained clothes, 'this poore shew doth better'—acting out a love: 'thinking of nothing else, putting all affayres in oblivion, as if there were nothing els to bee done, but to see him'. Stirring as it is, this is all hypothetical, a rhetoric—'Painting thy outward walls so costlie gay'. In the course of the Second Part, Falstaff's fatness might even be said to have gone into such shows, becoming an outer man only. Its true spirit has, in some way not easy to articulate, flowed out of him into the London tavern's noise and fury of 'Swaggerers', and the gone-to-seed energies of a country estate, where Feeble is hero and Silence sings: all the vagrant forms of life which almost mimic, in reverse, those 'by-paths and indirect crookt ways' by which, Bolingbroke has said, he 'met his crown'. Power is leaving Falstaff by the same routes. Part Two begins with Rumour bringing 'smooth-Comforts-false', and it may be that it ends, for fat Falstaff, in nothing but words.

There is, of course, life in the old dog yet, though some of his admirers find his third translation, into the sharp caricature of *The Merry Wives,* so disheartening as to make them prefer the fourth: the death-bed Falstaff of *Henry V.* That the old Knight died of a broken heart I don't find it altogether easy to believe; it's less difficult to accept Shakespeare's genius in hiding whatever happened to be the truth—and death-beds should be reticent—behind the lush sentimentality of the small group of crooks who talk about it in *Henry V.* Yet they are marvellous crooks, and the involvement of the hard with the soft in the narration brings back that recognizable tension that reigns in *Henry IV.*

Everything in Falstaff's reported death-scene is supreme and ambiguous. More than one scholar has pointed out that the poet seems clearly to be recalling an account of the death of Socrates. But that grave and noble demise of a philosopher is so rendered by Quickly as to keep straying into quibbles obscurely sexual: 'A bad me lay more clothes on his feet: I put my hand into the Bed, and felt them, and they were as cold as any stone: then I felt to his knees, and so upward, and upward, and all was as cold as any stone'.

This inimitable mix of the Socratic with the farcical-erotic is a poetry entirely right for the tragicomic passing of the brilliant fat Falstaff. And it is echoed in the pride with which Mistress Quickly locates the old Knight in '*Arthurs Bosome,* if ever man went to *Arthurs Bosome*'. The more orthodox would have sent him to Abraham. But Arthur was the founder of knighthood; he was moreover to Elizabethans the King of Romance. This made him, in the view of hard-headed classicists of the time, the representative of that whole realm of archaic folly which (they thought) goes along with love. This hint of Romance, and the Socratic, and the helplessly physical jokes coming through the tenderly lamenting babble of Mistress Quickly about *stones,* make us look back, in fact, down a great decade of invention to a clown holding a dog on a piece of string, and complaining that as to heart, he is a 'stone, a very pibble stone, and has no more pitty in him then a dogge'.

In the Tudor Myth of History, Prince Hal has the authority and the moral right on becoming King to reject Falstaff. It is probably good that he does so, for History's sake. But with a gesture new at every re-playing of these later Histories, Mistress Quickly hands Falstaff over to the feeling of reader or audience, on whose imagination, after all, this whole hearsay death-bed depends. The old dog stands up, shakes itself, and wags its tail in the air of reality.

Matthew H. Wikander (1992-93)

SOURCE: "The Protean Prince Hal," in *Comparative Drama*, Vol. 26, Number 4, Winter, 1992-93, pp. 295-311.

[*In the following essay, Wikander discusses the ambiguity surrounding Prince Hal's character as it is portrayed in the* Henry IV *plays. The critic observes that Hal is fully prepared to assume his place as rightful king from the beginning, and that his ultimate transformation at the end is revealed to the audience in his earliest speeches.*]

"Presume not that I am the thing I was," King Henry V, no longer the familiar Prince Hal, tells Falstaff. "For God doth know, so shall the world perceive, / That I have turn'd away my former self" (*2 Henry IV* V.v.56-58).[1] Many critics have been vexed about the nature of the "former self" that he tells Falstaff he has turned away. The bald declaration of Hal's agenda in the soliloquy in *Part 1*, certainly, makes it clear that Hal has never been *really* in thrall to Falstaff, never really a member of the criminal rout at the tavern. In *Part 2* he wearily wastes his time with them. When he "please[s] again to be himself," he tells us, he will "imitate the sun" (*1 Henry IV* I.ii.197, 200): but if he has not been himself in the tavern, who has he been? What was he doing?

"Go, you thing, go!" Falstaff dismisses the hostess in *Part 1*. "Say, what thing? what thing?" she cries, and when Sir John calls her a beast, she pursues the issue: "Say, what beast, thou knave, thou?" "What beast? Why, an otter." "An otter, Sir John," Prince Hal interrupts, "why an otter?" "Why? she's neither fish nor flesh, a man knows not where to have her" (III.iii.115-16, 124-28). Yet it is not the hostess but Hal who has been the amphibian in the play. Here in III.iii, he has just returned from convincing his father of his loyalty and zeal. He is flourishing in both of his environments, the tavern and the court.

The amphibian has its own complex range of suggestion. "[P]oor monster," Viola pronounces herself, neither man nor woman; her brother, lost at sea, was last glimpsed "like [Arion] on the dolphin's back," in amphibious linkage (*Twelfth Night* II.ii.34, I.ii.15). Sir Dauphine Eugenie finds himself among a riot of amphibians in the list of persons in Ben Jonson's *Epicoene,* along with Madame Centaure and Sir Thomas Otter, "a land and sea captain." Mistress Quickly, vigorously repudiating the name of otter in *1 Henry IV,* falls into Falstaff's trap: "Thou or any man knows where to have me, thou knave, thou!" (III.iii.129-30). Viola, in a more homiletic vein, blames her attractive outside, her masculine garb: "Disguise, I see thou art a wickedness / Wherein the pregnant enemy does much" (II.ii.27-28). Viola's sentiment here is in sympathy with the antitheatrical writings of the period, with their rejection of disguise and repudiation of the amphibious boy actors of the public stage. More vigorously aligned with that tradition of antitheatrical thinking is Jonson's representation of Morose's house of babble, a cacophonous theater in which the key revelation turns on the person of the boy actor himself. On the other hand, Hal, until he repudiates "the thing I was," seems content to be an otter; like Francis the apprentice shuttling from one room to another, he is continually promising "Anon, anon" while shuttling between his two worlds.

The linkage between the otter, the "thing" that Hal was, and the boy actor points towards an indeterminacy in Hal. Like the boy actor or the apprentice, he is at a liminal phase of his development, neither fish nor flesh. As such, he joins the ranks of dubious creatures that Jonas Barish has grouped together in his important book *The Antitheatrical Prejudice:* Proteans and Chameleons, common seventeenth-century vilifications for actors.[2] Proteus figures frequently in antitheatrical writings in the seventeenth century; Barish quotes, for example, Robert Burton's *Anatomy of Melancholy.* It is all too common, Burton tells us,

> To see a man turn himself into all shapes like a Chameleon, or as Proteus transform himself into all that is monstrous; to act twenty parts & persons at once for his advantage, to temporize and vary like Mercury the Planet, good with good, bad with bad; having a several face, garb, & character, for every one he meets; of all religions, humours, inclinations; to fawn like a spaniel, with lying and feigned obsequiousness, rage like a lion, bark like a cur, fight like a dragon, sting like a serpent, as meek as a lamb, & yet again grin like a tiger, weep like a crocodile, insult over some, & yet others domineer over him, here command, there crouch, tyrannize in one place, be baffled in another, a wise man at home, a fool abroad to make others merry![3]

Such hatred of the indeterminate, the ambiguous, and the improvisatory epitomizes the antitheatrical tradition in Western philosophy. Its exponents, Barish reminds us, are not only "hard-shelled, mole-eyed fanatics," but also "giants like Plato, Saint Augustine, Rousseau, and Nietzsche." Following Plato, antitheatrical writers in the seventeenth and eighteenth centuries celebrated simplicity and integrity: "Simplicity means purity, stability, and health," in Barish's words: "Complexity spells impurity, instability, distemper." "Perhaps," Barish concludes, "the antitheatrical prejudice reflects a form of self-disgust": "Human existence can hardly avoid resembling in basic ways the experience of actors in the theater, and human consciousness can hardly escape the tinge of bad faith this introduces into our actions, the incitement it gives us to wish to be admired, stared at, made much of, attended to."[4] While Barish's study is limited to philosophers who have written explicitly against the institution of theater, he does find antitheatrical theater in some of the latest experiments of the postmodern stage.

Expressions of distaste for theater and challenges to traditional mimetic modes, though, are common in the Renaissance and neoclassical drama as well as in the late modern drama. Hal's repudiation of the "thing" he was, of his festive or amphibious other self, postulates an unknowable real self, a true self, that has been concealed throughout his two plays and that may, indeed, remain unknowable in Henry V. Hamlet, rejecting the "actions that a man might play" and insisting upon "that within which passes show," pushes antitheatricalism further (*Hamlet* I.ii.84-85). He refuses to be known theatrically—by his actions, his cloak, his sighs, his tears. "Theatre has mimesis, not as its method, but as its subject matter," David Cole has argued.[5] Building on Barish and Cole, it is possible to argue that expressions of antitheatrical sentiments by characters in plays constitute a playwright's critique of theatrical mimesis. The unease we feel about the Protean Hal is an unease about theatrical mimesis, written into the plays. To the extent that Hal is a kind of otter, a cipher like Viola into whom significances can be all too easily read, criticism of Hal and of his reformation has tended to reveal rather the critics' attitudes toward mimesis than to pin down Hal's elusive essence.

While Prince Hamlet rejects utterly the proposition that a true self, an own self, can be publicly known, Prince Hal wants to be known most fully in his public self. "I do; I will," Hal announces in the Boar's Head tavern when Falstaff urges him that to "banish plump Jack" is to "banish all the world" (*1 Henry IV* II.iv.479-80). There is nothing of Hamlet's riddling uncertainty in the expression of this resolve. Hal has fully prepared the audience in the theater (as opposed to his drunken onstage audience) for his resolution in his famous first-act soliloquy:

> I know you all, and will a while uphold
> The unyok'd humor of your idleness.
> Yet herein will I imitate the sun,
> Who doth permit the base contagious clouds
> To smother up his beauty from the world,
> That when he please again to be himself,
> Being wanted, he may be more wond'red at,
> By breaking through the foul and ugly mists
> Of vapors that did seem to strangle him.
>
> (I.ii.195-203)

Hamlet envisions self-revelation as impossible, but Prince Hal sees it as a cosmic *coup-de-théâtre* in which he will reveal himself to be at one with his iconic image, as the blessed sun of heaven, the son of England, the prodigal son returned—as, in short, the resolution of that impossible paradox, a Christian king. In his first soliloquy he proposes a narrative, a way of seeing his career, that transforms him into the answer to history's desire for fully legitimate authority.

Legitimation, Hayden White has argued, is specifically the task of history in the theory of Hegel. "Only in a State cognizant of laws," Hegel wrote, "can distinct transactions take place, accompanied by such clear consciousness of them as supplies the ability and suggests the necessity of an enduring record." As White paraphrases it, "the reality that lends itself to narrative representation is the conflict between desire and the law." Historical studies, by Hegel's definition, have a specific subject matter: "those momentous collisions between existing, acknowledged duties, laws, and rights, and those contingencies that are adverse to this fixed system."[6] In Hegelian terms, the project of historical narrative is the legitimizing of authority, the self-definition of the state.

But Hal is not Hegel, and historical narrative and popular drama are different genres. His method, we note (and not for the first time, for critics like Anne Righter and James Calderwood have led the way here), is theatrical.[7] Upholding the unyoked humor of idleness is what professional actors do: Hal will present himself as a surprise not only to his erstwhile companions, but also to the audience. "I'll so offend, to make offense a skill," he promises, "Redeeming time when men think least I will" (I.ii.216-17). The skillful acting of offensive behavior is what attracts the audience's eyes to the public stage. When Hal says, "I know you all," the actor speaks through the character directly to us. Hal knows what we want—a fully fledged vision of a triumphant, true prince—and he knows how to give it to us. "By how much better than my word I am, / By so much shall I falsify men's hopes" (I.ii.210-11): we may feel ourselves caught short by this description of Hal's strategy, because it suggests an element of fraud. The hopes he will falsify, of course, are those of his criminal friends (we can hear, if we listen, Falstaff's name in the line itself). But he will also surprise and dazzle his audience, falsifying their expectations to the extent that the expectations themselves fall short in imagining their consummation.

Hal achieves his objective of appearing in iconographic or emblematic triumph in a surprising way. It is in the rebel camp that we see his first convert. Hotspur asks Vernon, who has just returned from a parley with the royal forces, about Hal: "the nimble-footed madcap Prince of Wales, / And his comrades, that daff'd the world aside / And bid it pass." Much to his surprise, what he gets in reply is a mannerist painting, a highly decorated emblem (or impresa) of the true prince. "All furnish'd, all in arms," reports Vernon (although we in the theater know that none of the Eastcheap gang has reformed along with Hal):

> All plum'd like estridges, that with the wind
> Bated like eagles having lately bath'd,
> Glittering in golden coats like images,
> As full of spirit as the month of May,
> And gorgeous as the sun at midsummer;
> Wanton as youthful goats, wild as young bulls.
> I saw young Harry with his beaver on,
> His cushes on his thighs, gallantly arm'd,
> Rise from the ground like feathered Mercury,
> And vaulted with such ease into his seat,
> As if an angel [dropp'd] down from the clouds
> To turn and wind a fiery Pegasus,
> And witch the world with noble horsemanship.
>
> (IV.i.95-110)

"No more, no more!" Hotspur cries out. The images pile together here, with a range of reference from the heraldic (the estridge, or ostrich, is special to the Prince of Wales) to the mythological (the taming of Pegasus was considered in Renaissance iconography to be an allegory of self-mastery, triumph over the appetites, and statesmanship). That the witness who testifies to the transformation of the madcap Hal into a gallant feathered Mercury is a member of the rebel forces only adds to its potency. Hal is amphibious here, but he inhabits now the elements of air and fire.

Hal presents himself as master of his situation, both as prince and as actor. But there are moments in the play when the richly ambiguous world of seeming appears to confound him. At the end of *1 Henry IV,* Prince Hal seems actually to be taken in by Falstaff's sham death. He is baffled upon returning with his brother John to find the fat man up and Hotspur over his shoulder. But he gilds the story with a lie, and as a result loses sufficient credibility to make *Part 2* necessary. And in *Part 2,* looking at his sleeping father, the Prince makes the same mistake. Like the funeral orations over Hotspur and Falstaff, his speech as he takes the crown is undercut by Hal's inability to tell false death from real. "This sleep is sound indeed," Hal pronounces,

> this is a sleep
> That from this golden rigol hath divorc'd
> So many English kings. Thy due from me
> Is tears and heavy sorrows of the blood,
> Which nature, love, and filial tenderness
> Shall, O dear father, pay thee plenteously.
> My due from thee is this imperial crown,
> Which, as immediate from thy place and blood,
> Derives itself to me.
>
> (*2 Henry IV* IV.v.35-43)

Hal's leaping to a conclusion here is especially revealing of the moral historiography of his agenda. As he staged his victory in *1 Henry IV* to conform to our expectation that the prodigal prince should triumph over both Hotspur and Falstaff in an instant, so here Hal scripts his succession. "Place and blood" and, later on, "lineal honor" are the keynotes here. For Hal's plan to succeed, he must inherit the crown, not earn it; the transaction must be as private and mysterious as conception itself. It is not for the legitimate prince to "study deserving" like the bastard Edmund. By claiming the crown through right of blood alone, and by doing so secretly, with none but the dead king by, Hal replaces his father's crime of usurpation with a mystic rite that proclaims the king's two bodies to be one.

In the process, he attempts to satisfy the craving for narrative, historiographical coherence that he aroused in the audience with the soliloquy. More to the point, an audience to the play has desired this consummation more devoutly perhaps than he has, especially an audience that has experienced the frustrations of *Richard II* and *1 Henry IV*. For Hal has been England's sweetest hope in two special senses: first, he can resolve the dilemma proposed in *Richard II,* where the blood of Edward III is wasted by both the lineal successor, Richard, and the usurper, Henry. Hal's succession will not be parricidal. Second, Hal figures not simply a dynastic but a historiographical hope. He can move us from a kind of history that is cyclical and (finally) nihilistic in its vision to a kind of history that is linear and leads to a coherent moral ending, the crowning of Henry V and the banishment of Falstaff. But the sense we get in the whole of *2 Henry IV* that we have seen all this before threatens a linear narrative line, and Hal's secret rite, to his revived father's eyes, seems an utterly Bullingbrookian maneuver.

Just as Falstaff refuses to be dead and permit the prince's reformation to glitter untarnished, so too the deathbed scene in *2 Henry IV* does not fit the prince's plan. Not only are we reminded of Falstaff's revival as King Henry awakes, but we notice that somehow the play has coerced Hal into re-enacting his father's highly significant gesture in the abdication scene in *Richard II*. "Here, cousin, seize the crown," Richard prompts there, and Bullingbrook, unhappily, must theatrically act out his crime (*Richard II* IV.i.181-82). "Where is the crown?" cries Henry when he awakes. "The Prince hath ta'en it hence" (*2 Henry IV* IV.v.57, 59). Like father, like son, the third play in the sequence suggests. An inheritance has changed hands, legitimized by the family gesture of seizing and taking.

Hal has set himself a task of legitimation, and Vernon, at least, cannot see the young man without seeing the true prince. Yet the moments in which he most triumphantly enacts his legitimation, as he transcends the vanity of Falstaff and Hotspur at the end of *Part 1* and as he succeeds to his father's crown in *Part 2,* take place without witnesses and in error. Hal promises a transformation that will be sudden, devastating, miraculous. But what is most surprising about his triumph in *Part 1* is his reversion into idleness.

A common answer to Hal's disappointing performance has been to side with Warwick's assessment in *Part 2* that Hal was maturing, growing up, going to school:

> The Prince but studies his companions
> Like a strange tongue, wherein, to gain the language,
> 'Tis needful that the most immodest word
> Be look'd upon and learnt, which once attain'd,
> Your Highness knows, comes to no further use
> But to be known and hated. So, like gross terms,
> The Prince will in the perfectness of time
> Cast off his followers, and their memory
> Shall as a pattern or a measure live,
> By which his Grace must mete the lives of other,
> Turning past evils to advantages.
>
> (IV.iv.68-78)

Warwick's interpretation of Hal's conduct is reminiscent of Renaissance defenses of theater, which tend to be similarly reductive and homiletic. But to accept it, curiously, is to adopt an antitheatrical stance towards Hal's agenda in the play. To the extent that Hal's own agenda is narrative, not theatrical, and that it has its greatest successes offstage, such a stance is appropriate. Hal is not, in this view, a true amphibian, but merely a visiting swimmer.

For Thomas Van Laan, for example, only Falstaff can be allowed the fluidity, the liminality, of the actor:

> Falstaff's is a world for playing roles for pleasure, as many as possible, and the more innovative the better; the emphasis falls on the role of the playwright-actor. In the heroic world, however, such role-playing would be unequivocally evil. There the ideal consists of finding one's proper role from an approved list of existing possibilities and striving to fulfil it satisfactorily by obeying its dictates. In Falstaff's world, all roles are possible because none is crucial. In the heroic world, only certain roles can be tolerated, and one of them, that of king, matters more than all the others.[8]

Van Laan's distinction between a "heroic world" and "Falstaff's world" of play is well-taken, but what are we to make of "unequivocally evil?" The main tenet of Plato's antitheatricalism is that the proliferation of roles identifiable with the actor is socially destabilizing. Is the antitheatricality here Van Laan's, or Hal's? To condemn Hal for merely playing, not being, the true prince is to miss the complex engagement of theatrical and iconic conventions in Hal's playing.

James Calderwood finds a more subtle distinction in dramatic modes: Falstaff is a "rebel" to the "realism" of the play's genre of history play, bringing into it the rules of his own brand of festive comedy, threatening "a secession of the theatrical from the mimetic aspects of the play."[9] The distinction between "theatrical" and "mimetic aspects" of what is after all a play suggests that somehow the theater itself can be reduced to the status of improvisatory clowning and banished in favor of serious business. The strongest exponent of this hard-nosed approach, though, is not Calderwood but Richard Levin, who rejects Falstaff as though his own soul were at risk. Falstaff is dangerously immature, he argues, because "Falstaff does want to make all the year one continuous saturnalia, this being the ritual corollary of his perennial childishness and obliviousness of time which is brought out most forcefully in his parallel attempts to extend his misrule into the serious climaxes of both parts of *Henry IV,* and in the Prince's parallel rebukes." For Falstaff's "timeless, static world," Hal must learn to substitute a world of real time.[10]

Certainly *Hal* has a right to complain about Falstaff's festive irruptions into the serious parts of his plays. Hal's project is making moral sense of himself, staging his reform so that it is maximally surprising. To be fully known, for Hal, is to be known as a true prince, casting off his followers as the sun dissolves the mists "in the perfectness of time." His problems with corpses that refuse to stay dead suggest that Hal is so successful in making others see him iconically, as prodigal son or ideal prince, that he has a tendency to read others iconically as well.

They are also, of course, problems with timing: as long as King Henry lives, Hal cannot be allowed to be fully seen as England's sweetest hope. The theater complicates the promulgation of his image, but in the end it is the medium in which his image can be most luminous.

Subscribing wholly to this luminousness is an older tradition, and it tends to do so without reference to the worlds of the stage at all. Tillyard, of course, celebrates Hal as a true prince without irony; for Joseph A. Porter, Warwick's analogy to a language-lesson is the key to Henry V's emergence from Hal as a "many-tongued monarch who, using a wide range of language purposefully and responsibly, initiates a reign of 'high . . . parliament'."[11] Porter seems to adopt in a quite literal way a "Whig view of history" as Henry V becomes a parliamentarian. If revisionist history does not permit us in the antitheatrical Puritans of the early seventeenth-century to glimpse the later parliamentary forces, Porter, by focusing so exclusively on language as speech and eschewing talk of spectacle, reveals a different kind of antitheatrical bias. "Many-tongued" is not quite the same as Protean: this Hal has an ethical, sincere self, which he can fluently express.

There is division, too, among those critics who believe that Hal has a sincere self and those who believe he does not, especially in the way in which the prince works with readily recognizable iconography. Robert B. Pierce describes the royal interview (*1 Henry IV* III.ii) as richly satisfying in this way: "In the parable, the Prodigal Son restored to his father is man restored to God, and in the Elizabethan system of correspondences the king is to his kingdom as God is to the universe. Hal's reconciliation with his father symbolizes a larger commitment to all that is good and orderly in the world."[12] Striking a more cynical pose is John Wilders, who argues that in III.ii the prince is only acting: "The winner in this game of deception is Hal, who deliberately impersonates the prodigal son and feigns the false impression he knows his subjects have formed of him in order that, eventually, they will be convinced by his equally contrived reformation."[13] More positive in his attitude towards theater (and less eager to appear naively sucked in than Pierce) is John Blanpied, who sees Hal as having the nature of "an 'actor,' with all the doubleness the term implies"; his "dramatic genius lies in his coolly playing the prodigal son."[14]

Hal has played more than the parabolic role of the prodigal son. He has also arrogated to himself a large number of exclusively theatrical models, especially as drawn from morality plays. "Hal may be Lusty Juventus, counseled by Vices and Virtues, gradually learning to be the true prince and the savior of the commonwealth," muses Alvin Kernan, "but Vices and Virtues like Falstaff and Hotspur speak with such ambiguous voices that it is difficult to tell which is which, and 'the mirror of all Christian kings' is so complex a character, and the nature of rule so mixed a business, that we are left wondering whether the restoration of the kingdom represents a triumph of morality or of Machiavellian politics."[15] The evocation of old morality patterns in the rejection of Falstaff is, for John Cox, a mimetic enactment of real, historical use of those patterns in Elizabethan image-management. "Whatever the truth about the relationship, the most important thing for Hal is that it be defined in the categories of morality drama, because those conventions are such effective conveyors of the broad generalizations about his supposed moral development that Hal wishes his people to believe about him as he proceeds in securing his power." Hal is as scrupulous about his image as Elizabeth and as Essex: as he comes to power, "the heroic king is exactly like the chivalric heroes Shakespeare really knew: utterly opaque in his ability to charge his single-minded quest for political dominance with the compelling vision of a social ideal."[16] Here Hal's virtuosity is seen to intersect with real-life Renaissance self-fashioning.

For Frank Whigham as for Cox, the issue of sincerity is beside the point. Protean virtuosity, Whigham reminds us, was necessary for courtiers; George Puttenham's "numbing catalog of deceits suggests that the smallest daily acts of courtly life have an infinitely varied symbolic weight (and hence are vulnerable to differing interpretations)." Whigham points, in his analysis of Puttenham's *Arte of English Poesie*, to a theatrical—tragic—dimension: "Who would not pity and fear this our chameleon?"[17] Whigham's attention, like that of the courtesy tracts he studies, is upon the courtier; the courtier's attention is upon the prince, and the adaptability and suppleness that courtiers must cultivate is irrelevant to the prince himself. That is, the more closely Prince Hal can be seen to recall "chivalric heroes" like Essex, the more he appears to be a competitor for power, the less he can lambently appear to be a true prince. The tragic competitor for power in the *Henry IV* plays is Hotspur, and he is less chameleon than parrot, an inflexible but loquacious "paraquito," as his wife puts it (*1 Henry IV* II.iii.85).

By reminding us of the theatricality of daily life, Cox and Whigham help to collapse the distinctions between theater and life that troubled earlier critics. But this new historicist claim can become exaggerated. David Kastan asserts that theater itself "enacts, not necessarily on stage, but in its fundamental transaction with the audience, the exact shift in the conception of authority that brings a king to trial and ultimately locates sovereignty in the common will of its subjects."[18] By showing that kings are like actors playing roles, in other words, the seventeenth-century English theater legitimized the seventeenth-century English regicide. Kastan's article is a corrective to the totalizing language of Stephen Greenblatt's famous invisible bullets; he reclaims for the English theater subversion without containment. But in the process he accepts the word of the antitheatrical writers of the age for what theater could do, what theater could make people do. "New historicist and cultural materialist critics of Renaissance drama tend to share with Phillip Stubbes and Thomas Nashe the assumption that the theater mattered to the shape and direction of English society," Paul Yachnin has recently observed.[19]

Whigham's sense of the pathos of the courtly climber and Cox's insistence on *Realpolitik* signal a more moderate engagement of the theater's confusion of realms. Blurring of distinctions, confusion of realms, as the antitheatrical argument runs, is endemic to the theater, and Kastan reveals the power of this argument as he transforms it into historical narrative. The ambivalence that many critics feel about Hal's acting is similar to the ambivalence they must feel about Shakespeare's institution. The problem is first and foremost historical: the peculiar institution of the early-modern English theater is a phenomenon that we cannot grasp phenomenologically. "Between a drama and its meaning," Herbert Blau puts it, ". . . particularly an older drama, there is always the distance of history, which moves fast in the space of perception between the desire for meaning and the currency of any play." Blau imagines "some contribution to scholarship from science fiction" that could actually take us back to seventeenth-century London, so we "could see what 'they' saw." "It should be obvious that to have been there is, in some definitive approach to meaning, a rather dubious privilege."[20] By insisting upon the complexity of plays in performance and by stressing the dubious quality of extracting meaning from performance, Blau puts us in much the same dilemma as does Prince Hal.

To extract a moral meaning from his glittering reformation, we have to endorse Vernon's narration (in the face of our own witnessing of Hal's continued sponsorship of Falstaff); to ratify the eulogy over the panting and, to us, obviously undead fat man; to approve of snatching the crown away from the sleeping king. It is the fact of performance itself that blurs the contours of Hal's performances. Hal's agenda, the historical narrative in which he reveals himself like the sun, is in conflict with the theatrical means of its production. Approaching meaning is indeed a dubious activity, when the desire for meaning that Hal provokes and indulges is so often, like Vernon's vision, set before our inner eyes as wishful seeing.

Attempting to make sense out of Hal's acting embroils both scholars and audiences. The plays do not help by identifying acting, through Falstaff, with fraud and deceit. The rejection of Falstaff could be a rejection of bad, fraudulent acting (or excessive, festive overacting); but then we are forced to endorse the Protean skills of Hal. And it is his kind of acting—the kind that the other inhabitants of his world (and a number of critics) can read iconically, accept, be convinced by—that antitheatrical thinkers would see as by far the more dangerous kind of acting, the kind of acting that leaches into real life.

"If we seriously consider the very forme of acting Playes," William Prynne argues, "we must needes acknowledge it to be nought but grosse hypocrisie." Quoting "sundry Authors and Grammarians," Prynne forges the etymological link to *"stile Stage-players, hypocrites; Hypocrites, Stage-players, as being one and the same in substance; there being nothing more familiar with them, then to describe an hypocrite by a Stage-player; and a Stage-player by an hypocrite."* Prynne sticks to "Latine Authors";

had he turned to the Greeks, he would have discovered a closer connection.[21] On the ancient Greek stage, as Gerald Else has pointed out, the professional actor—the actor who was not the tragedian, the actor who was only an actor—was dubbed the answerer, or *hypokritês*.[22] "Let the end try the man," Prince Hal declares cryptically to Poins, refusing "all ostentation of sorrow" despite the fact that his "heart bleeds inwardly" at the fact of his father's illness. "What wouldst thou think of me if I should weep?" "I would think thee a most princely hypocrite," Poins rejoins, and the prince ruefully agrees: "It would be every man's thought, and thou are a blessed fellow to think as every man thinks" (*2 Henry IV* II.ii.47-57). So the prince is in a sense doomed to act the part of indifference to his father's sickness lest his true feelings be interpreted as feigned. "Behold how like a maid she blushes here!" Claudio exclaims against Hero in *Much Ado About Nothing*; "Would you not swear, / All you that see her, that she were a maid, / By these exterior shows?" (IV.i.34, 38-40). That Hero looks modest becomes an index of her immodesty; for Hal to appear saddened by his father's sickness would be similar proof of his inward joy. Every man would think so—just as every man thinks he knows the truth about Hero.

Theatrical mimesis itself is misleading, the antitheatrical thinkers tell us. Students, laboriously rehearsing the conflict of appearance *versus* reality, seem to agree. The problem, of course, is that sometimes things *are* as they appear. The basic assumption of theater is that appearances somehow do reveal realities, and it corresponds to the assumption in the Anglo-American legal system that the degree of doubt be reasonable. To consider appearances as always misleading is to consider too curiously much of the time. The difficulty is knowing when to trust an appearance and when not to trust it. As Poins confidently declares what he knows every man knows, and what the audience knows to be at least simplistic, if not dead wrong, we face a vortex of theatrical antitheatricality. The choruses of approval or disapproval about Hal's behavior cannot avoid the language of antitheatricality, for to judge Hal ethically is to judge him as a real person, and as the interlude with Poins points out, every man confronts a hall of mirrors here.

This is true even when the attempt is to offer a balanced perspective. "[N]ot quite the paragon some would have him nor the heartless prig others see," Robert Ornstein says, staking out a middle ground: "Like a clever Elizabethan shopkeeper, Hal knows how to display the merchandise of his behavior in such a light that it appears richer than it is."[23] Tarring the theater with the brush of commercialism, Ornstein is able to accept Hal without embracing him. So, too, according to Jean-Christophe Agnew, did the Stuart courtiers dodge the contagious commerciality of professional players by sealing them off in the world of the antimasque.[24]

The new historicist blurring of the boundaries between theater and life allows us to see broad ramifications in the problem of Hal's acting as it branches away from Falstaff's towards Essex's, Queen Elizabeth's, and our own. Drawing from Erving Goffman's *The Presentation of Self in Everyday Life,* we can assert that we are always acting, always playing roles, managing our images.[25] As Bruce Wilshire has argued, however, Goffman's notion of role-playing is nominalist: "He construes as manifest appearance, as one real thing, the character played by the actor, whereas the actor himself must be another particular thing, just momentarily hidden by the character he plays." This sounds like Hal, imitating the sun behind the base contagious clouds. Wilshire sees Goffman as antitheatrical: given his nominalist premises, Goffman "must see the actor's artistry as a kind of deceit. Inevitably, then, he must construe role-like activity offstage as a kind of deceit."[26] Acting in everyday life becomes hypocrisy, and, as we have seen, critics who praise Hal's acting skills, like Blanpied or Wilder or Greenblatt, tend to see him as Machiavellian, although not to agree on the moral weight this should bear.

"Theatre reveals, but does not reveal at all clearly the limits of its ability to reveal," Wilshire says. "Does theatre reveal what is the case or only what we would like to be the case? The distinction enshrined by the question is grossly misleading. For what could be more actual than the dreams and desires we do have? How can we know ourselves unless we know what these are? Theatre is peculiarly apt to reveal them."[27] Again we can find Hal, teasing the audience's desire for a true prince, its dream of a prodigal son, lurking in the general statement of the problem. The plays dramatize a powerful ambivalence about what theater can reveal about our dreams and desires. What further complicates the problem is that the dreams and desires revolve around the problem of kingship.

The *Henry IV* plays are ambivalent about theater insofar as they are ambivalent about kingship, and they are ambivalent about kingship insofar as kingship is theatrical. (We can say the same about the criticism of the plays, too.) Prince Hal presents his transformation from prince to king as a miraculous change, planned from the outset and well worth waiting for. The premature self-coronations (over Falstaff and over the sleeping Henry) merely whet our appetite. As king, Hal becomes Shakespeare's most successful public man, Henry V. Critics who argue the issue of King Henry V's sincerity or opportunism miss the point. Kings are ambiguous beings, unavailable to public knowledge: this is the truth ensconced in the doctrine of the king's two bodies, one of which is a body physical and visible to the eye, one of which is a body politic, visible everywhere but by no means a mortal body like ours.

In a different sense, actors also have two bodies, one of which belongs to them personally as ours do, and one of which belongs to the role. "No, that's certain, I am not a double man," says Falstaff with Hotspur slung over his shoulder; "but if I be not Jack Falstaff, then am I a Jack" (*1 Henry IV* V.iv.138-39). Here the true prince confronts a parody of his own plan to use Percy as a factor, engrossing up glorious deeds on his behalf. Falstaff has taken the true prince's heroic part (just as—"Depose me?"—the prince took away Falstaff's royal role in the tavern scene.) He embodies theatrical vitality, the theater's resistance to the moral scheme of Hal's narrative of legitimation.[28] But he goes further. Falstaff here, as in the tavern scene, plays Hal and shows Hal himself reduced to the most ridiculous level, to the "thing" he has become.

Antitheatricalism, Barish argues, tends to find its fullest expression in times when the theater is prosperous, "when it counts for something in the emotional and intellectual life of the community."[29] Theater counts for little nowadays, except in the emotional and intellectual life of its practitioners and its scholars. Critics' and audiences' struggles to make sense of Prince Hal mirror his struggle to make moral, historical sense of himself in the ambiguous world of his plays. This is appropriate to the myth of Proteus: once you have grasped and held on to him, the truth he tells you is about yourself.

Notes

1. *2 Henry IV*, quoted from *The Riverside Shakespeare*, ed. G. Blakemore Evans *et al* (Boston: Houghton Mifflin, 1974). All subsequent quotations from this and other Shakespeare plays are incorporated in the text.

2. Jonas Barish, *The Antitheatrical Prejudice* (Berkeley and Los Angeles: Univ. of California Press, 1981), pp. 99-126. Here we might also reflect upon the *dorado,* or dolphin-fish, "celebrated for its beautiful colours, which, when it is taken out of water, or is dying, undergo rapid changes of hue" (*OED,* s.v. 'Dolphin,' 2).

3. Robert Burton, *The Anatomy of Melancholy,* ed. Floyd Dell and Paul Jordan-Smith (New York, 1927), p. 53, as quoted by Barish, *The Antitheatrical Prejudice,* p. 102.

4. Barish, *The Antitheatrical Prejudice,* pp. 2, 25, 476-77.

5. David Cole, *The Theatrical Event: A Mythos, a Vocabulary, a Perspective* (Middletown, Conn.: Wesleyan Univ. Press, 1975), p. 161.

6. Hayden White, *The Content of the Form: Narrative Discourse and Historical Representation* (Baltimore: Johns Hopkins Univ. Press, 1990), pp. 12, 30.

7. Ann Righter, *Shakespeare and the Idea of the Play* (London: Chatto and Windus, 1962); James Calderwood, *Metadrama in Shakespeare's Henriad: 'Richard II' to 'Henry V'* (Berkeley and Los Angeles: Univ. of California Press, 1979).

8. Thomas F. Van Laan, *Role-Playing in Shakespeare* (Toronto: Univ. of Toronto Press, 1978), p. 150.

9. Calderwood, *Metadrama in Shakespeare's Henriad,* p. 88.

10. Richard Levin, *The Multiple Plot in English Renaissance Drama* (Chicago: Univ. of Chicago Press, 1971), pp. 143, 146.

11. Joseph A. Porter, *The Drama of Speech Acts: Shakespeare's Lancastrian Tetralogy* (Berkeley and Los Angeles: Univ. of California Press, 1979), p. 115.

12. Robert B. Pierce, *Shakespeare's History Plays: The Family and the State* (Columbus: Ohio State Univ. Press, 1971), p. 174.

13. John Wilders, *The Lost Garden: A View of Shakespeare's English and Roman History Plays* (London: Macmillan, 1978), p. 90.

14. John W. Blanpied, *Time and the Artist in Shakespeare's English Histories* (Newark: Univ. of Delaware Press, 1983), p. 163.

15. Alvin B. Kernan, *The Playwright as Magician* (New Haven: Yale Univ. Press, 1979), p. 116.

16. John D. Cox, *Shakespeare and the Dramaturgy of Power* (Princeton: Princeton Univ. Press, 1989), pp. 120, 127.

17. Frank Whigham, *Ambition and Privilege: The Social Tropes of Elizabethan Courtesy Theory* (Berkeley and Los Angeles: Univ. of California Press, 1984), p. 130.

18. David Scott Kastan, "Proud Majesty Made a Subject: Shakespeare and the Spectacle of Rule," *Shakespeare Quarterly,* 37 (1986), 474.

19. Paul Yachnin, "The Powerless Theater," *English Literary Renaissance,* 21 (1991), 51.

20. Herbert Blau, *The Audience* (Baltimore: Johns Hopkins Univ. Press, 1990), pp. 48-49.

21. William Prynne, *Histriomastix* (1633; rpt. New York: Garland Publishing, 1974), pp. 156, 158-59.

22. Gerald Else, *The Origin and Early Form of Greek Tragedy* (New York: Norton, 1972), p. 59.

23. Robert Ornstein, *A Kingdom for a Stage: The Achievement of Shakespeare's History Plays* (Cambridge, Mass.: Harvard Univ. Press, 1972), p. 138.

24. Jean-Christophe Agnew, *Worlds Apart: The Market and the Theater in Anglo-American Thought, 1550-1750* (Cambridge: Cambridge Univ. Press, 1986), p. 148.

25. Erving Goffman, *The Presentation of Self in Everyday Life* (Garden City, N.Y.: Doubleday, 1959).

26. See Bruce Wilshire, *Role Playing and Identity: The Limits of Theatre as Metaphor,* Studies in Phenomenology and Existential Philosophy (Bloomington: Indiana Univ. Press, 1982), pp. 274-81, for his critique of Goffman; my quotation is from p. 275.

27. Ibid., p. 252.

28. Phyllis Rackin, in *Stages of History: Shakespeare's English Chronicles* (Ithaca: Cornell Univ. Press, 1990), concentrates on the way the actor's bodily presence on stage works to undercut the historical record's determination to separate "past from present, writing from speech, fact from fiction, nobles from commoners" (p. 222).

29. Barish, *The Antitheatrical Prejudice,* p. 191.

LANGUAGE

Ronald R. Macdonald (essay date 1984)

SOURCE: "Uneasy Lies: Language and History in Shakespeare's Lancastrian Tetralogy," in *Henry the Fourth Parts I and II: Critical Essays,* edited by David Bevington, Garland Publishing, 1986, 359-85.

[*In the following essay, originally published in 1984, Macdonald traces the development and use of language in Shakespeare's history plays, focusing on* Henry IV, Parts I and II, *and examines the linguistic conventions that sustain and govern the vision of kingship as portrayed in these plays.*]

There has always been uncertainty about what we call Shakespeare's "histories." The genre (if it is a genre) seems inherently unstable under critical scrutiny, always threatening to become something else, to slide over into other generic modes about which there is firmer agreement, to become simply tragedy (*Richard II*) or comedy (*1 Henry IV*), or dramatic satire (*2 Henry IV*). Yet, with the possible exception of early work like *The Comedy of Errors,* Shakespeare seems never to have been willing to accept the traditional genres quite as he found them, and the evidence of impurity, even in the lighthearted romantic comedies, is well known. We will never find in the Shakespearean canon the kind of generic purity that a more strictly classical temperament would consider indispensable.

Yet something does distinguish Shakespeare's histories, particularly the mature work of the second tetralogy here to be considered. I hope I will not be accused of tautology in saying that the "something" is a scrupulous concern for history, for by "history" I do not mean a narrative of events, the "story" of the past, but a concern with processes and the inner necessities of historical change, the mechanisms of transition, the deep and nearly invisible shifts in thinking and assumptions that form the basis of what we call in retrospect, and partly for interpretive convenience, "epochs." History in this sense was, for Shakespeare, not a compilation of events (set down in the chronicles in apple-pie order), on which he could hang a series of brilliantly conceived (if fundamentally ahistorical) dramatic characters. It was, rather, an extra-personal—if not quite impersonal—phenomenon, playing itself out in different registers in the huge cast of characters that peoples the tetralogy. I am aware that it is not usual to credit Shakespeare with this kind of sophisticated historical understanding; indeed, it is only in our century that it has become usual to credit him with sophistication at all.[1] Yet I do so, for once we have abandoned the "native woodnotes wild" hypothesis, rich and complex vistas are open to us. Protests about over-reading often mask a nostalgia for a simple and "natural" Shakespeare, whose small Latin and less Greek are part of his charm. I believe that no reading which makes sense can fairly be called an over-reading.

Because I have said roughly what I mean by history, and because I will refer to "myths" in what follows, I had better say roughly what I mean by myths. I mean neither those colorful tales of gods and goddesses in ancient times, nor "archetypal" patterns in the plays themselves, but, quite simply, the stories men tell one another to achieve political order and consensus. Let me begin by proposing a theory, itself perhaps a myth of origins, which suggests why it is that men speak of kings as "anointed," as deputies elected by the Lord, and what they hope to accomplish by speaking in this by no means inevitable fashion.

Say that the language of sacred kingship arises in response to a fundamental contradiction in the feudal system as Shakespeare understood it. That contradiction may be brought to the surface by wondering why a feudal system should have a king at all, for feudal society is marked by the formation of *many* centers of power, independent families with bands of retainers, each internally bound together by blood ties and *comitatus* loyalty. To speak of a centralized monarchy in a situation which yields, in effect, a number of private armies verges on paradox. I make no attempt to explain (for I really do not know) why it is that monarchies arise in the first place. Perhaps the explanation implicit in 1 Samuel.viii, that the presence of a common enemy leads a pluralistic tribal society to seek centralized leadership, is as good as any. My subject is not, in any case, the origin of monarchy, but the linguistic conventions that sustain it, the conventions that attempt to manage certain fundamental contradictions which threaten disruption.

It seems clear that in a feudal system the language of sacred kingship does not begin by naming those powers and perquisites that are naturally present in the person of the king and in the monarchic institution, but by naming precisely those that are not naturally present. The king is not called "God's anointed," one does not speak of the divinity that hedges a king because the king really *is* supreme and untouchable, but because he is patently vulnerable, because in many ways his position is the shakiest one in the pluralistic feudal world. If there is something shrilly hysterical about Richard's manic swing from the extreme position that sees the king as inviolate and inviolable, to the equally extreme position that sees him as the quintessential victim (kings may be deposed, slain in war, poisoned by their wives, killed as they sleep—"all murthered," says Richard), there is yet the force of insight in his extremity. And we remember that the phrase about the divinity that hedges a king comes from the fratricidal Claudius of Denmark, the most unanointed, so to speak, of Shakespearean monarchs. We may admire (some may even envy) the cool arrogance it must take for one in his position to use the phrase, but we will scarcely accept it from him without protest.

The vocabulary is thus deployed in an attempt to patch up a contradiction, to redress an imbalance, to achieve political consensus. As long as the achieved consensus remains virtually unanimous, as long as it is taught early on to the young, like the very language on which it depends for transmission, it can continue to masquerade, however uneasily, as a description of the nature of things. Thanks to an apparently incorrigible tendency of the human mind to confound culture and nature,[2] it will be understood not as a collective fabrication of the social order with discernible historical origins, but as a part of the metaphysical order handed down from on high at the creation.

But such consensuses are notoriously fragile. Any essentially secular and social construct, which has managed to get itself promoted to the status of the nature of things, so that it is viewed as the original creation of God and an expression of His will, is liable to be asked for its credentials, to prove that its origin lies in the mind of God, and not, as it seems to do as a matter of fact, in the minds of men. The initiative may well come from a child, who has as yet to master the language of the social order to the point where it is part of his unconscious stock-in-trade. In fact, as we shall see, it is more accurate to say that such a child has not yet allowed that language to master him. "The emperor has no clothes," the candid child observes in Andersen's tale. He has not yet come under the sway of the bizarre notion that the emperor's word is as good as the fact; and, not being subject to this mastering assumption, he will not be surprised to learn that the insane project of appearing in public stark naked originated with an unscrupulous tailor in possession of a bright idea. In what follows, we will encounter the emperor in the slender person of King Richard II, the child in the more robust person of Henry Bullingbrook, and the tailor in the huge bulk of Jack Falstaff.

What follows also falls into three parts, corresponding roughly to the dialectical moments of thesis, antithesis, and synthesis. The first part ends with Richard, whose thesis has collided with the antithetical Bullingbrook and his fellow conspirators, including Hotspur. The second ends with Hotspur, who has now become the antithesis of an antithesis in that he is engaged in conspiracy against the very Lancastrian throne he has previously helped to establish. His veering about expresses what will happen to Bullingbrook as Henry IV, and it is on the complex figure of the new king, traversed by contradiction, yet attempting a reluctant and uneasy synthesis, that the third part comes to rest. The triadic structure of my argument thus seeks to reveal some unsuspected similarities among three heterogeneous and apparently ill-sorted figures, and to plot those figures as three points converging.

I

Briefly, what the emperor learns from the child and what Richard learns from Bullingbrook is that you don't need any water at all (let alone all the water in the rough, rude sea) to wash the balm off an anointed king. The usurpation brings to awareness the essentially secular, *fabricated* character of the political order. The awareness arrives with the force of Platonic anamnesis, the unforgetting of what we knew all along; in contemporary terms it effects what Freud called the return of the repressed. Amidst the wreckage of the institution of sacred kingship, Richard must learn, somewhat in the manner of Molière's bourgeois gentleman, that he has actually been speaking prose all his life. His words have no privileged efficacy, certainly not the magical force that the old consensus seemed to confer upon them. Perhaps even more important, his power to silence others depends solely on their acquiescing in being silenced. Here is Thomas Mowbray responding to Richard's sentence of banishment:

> A heavy sentence, my most sovereign liege,
> And all unlook'd for from your Highness' mouth.
> A dearer merit, not so deep a maim
> As to be cast forth in the common air,
> Have I deserved at your Highness' hands.
> The language I have learnt these forty years,
> My native English, now I must forgo,
> And now my tongue's use is to me no more
> Than an unstringed viol or a harp,
> . . . . .
> Within my mouth you have enjail'd my tongue,
> Doubly portcullis'd with my teeth and lips, . . .
> 			(I.iii.154-62, 166-67)[3]

These are the words of an old loyalist, assenting to the underlying assumption that the king's speech (his sentence in a number of senses) has force. But even in this apparently unproblematic, ritualistic tribute to the king's verbal efficacy, there lurk certain troubling hints of what has been repressed, and now fairly clamors for expression. For in saying that he deserves a better fate at Richard's hands, Mowbray must allude, whether he intends to or not, to his loyal silence concerning Richard's conniving in the murder of Thomas of Woodstock, a very real silence that precedes any ritualistic sentence of banishment and the merely metaphorical silence attendant upon it. Richard has "enjail'd" Mowbray's tongue in the perfectly ordinary sense that he has gotten him to promise to keep quiet about the murder of Woodstock. That Mowbray now abides by this promise is not the result of some mysterious power inhering in the words of the king, but the result of his loyalty and sense of personal honor. And it is precisely on this prior silence, the product of the give and take of political conspiracy, that such power as Richard has very materially rests.

It is remarkable that Shakespeare nowhere passes moral judgment on the murder of Woodstock. It may, indeed, and for all we are told, have been the smartest thing to do in the circumstances. Perhaps it has been Richard's only means of consolidating his power, hard won from the Lords Appellant in the previous decade. But what really interested Shakespeare was that the move, whatever its merits, was *truly* political, a matter of agreements, trade-offs, the give and take of bargains. Whatever the circumstances of Woodstock's death, and whoever is implicated, Richard has not brought it about by a magical decree. But in banishing Mowbray, Richard attempts to take refuge in the notion of the king's magical and ritual power. In so doing he becomes embroiled in enormous difficulty, for he attempts to solve a real problem by imaginary means.

This is not to deny, of course, that there will be plenty of occasions when it will be expedient and shrewd for the king to speak as if he had not only magical powers, but a virtual monopoly of divine vengeance. Henry IV will do this repeatedly, usually with an eye for contingencies, and very much alive to the possibility that no one will believe him. But this is still to speak politically, to use the vocabulary of sacred kingship as a special language aimed at bringing about secular solutions. It is not to embrace as truths those things the special language enables you to say.

But Richard does not use the language of sacred kingship: he allows it to use him. In surrendering himself entirely to the assumptions inherent in the system, he represses the altogether pertinent fact that the divinity that hedges a king is an ambiguous concept. If there really is such a divinity, it hedges a king in two senses: it hedges him in, and it hedges him off; it at once protects him, and sets real limits to his power. It is surely the second meaning that Richard has forgotten in his attempt to cover political action with ritualistic and magical means, to deny the palpable contradiction of a divinely anointed king engaging in political maneuvering.

This is perhaps Richard's real abdication, that in insisting on his role as *rex,* he forgets he must also be *dux,*[4] and the scene later on (IV.i), where he actually gives Bullingbrook the crown, is but the seal and capstone to it. Richard's attempt to deny the historical and political character of his world is no more successful than most attempts at repression, though it is only in the heightened vision of drama that the repressed returns with the signal clarity with which Henry Bullingbrook returns to England. But there is much that is deeply and humanly moving about Richard's failure, and it is certainly a mistake to read his tragedy simply as a tragedy of character, the collapse of a shrill and rather precious neurotic in a situation that could have been successfully managed by a different personality. Shakespeare certainly differentiated Richard's personality profoundly, he certainly succeeded in creating a compelling and complex dramatic person, but this should not obscure the fact that it is Richard's distinct and unenviable role to enact and clarify certain paradoxes that do not stem from his idiosyncrasies, but are latent in the political order.[5] He must live those paradoxes for all to see, and not the least of these is the fact that the more he insists on his power as the anointed king, the less real power he wields.

Richard is abetted in contradiction by his friends quite as much as by his enemies. There is much talk of flatterers and flattery in *Richard II,* and the Lancastrian faction is fond of conjuring the bogey of hypocritical and ill-intentioned friends, who are leading the king astray for self-serving reasons. But a careful search of the play will fail to turn up any clear-cut examples of such friends. It is as if the Lancastrians, in speaking of evil flatterers, were trying to evoke the world of the first tetralogy with its stage villains and quasi-devils, as well as its saviors. Such talk has ultimately the effect of reminding us of the altogether different world we have entered with the second tetralogy. That world is too stubbornly concrete to yield to the simple moral patterns that men try to impose on it.

Evidence of this concreteness is partly furnished by the inadequacy of the existing idiom to manage the complexities of the actual, historical situation. Those critical of Richard are, willy-nilly, his flatterers quite as much as those who remain loyally silent. Here is Gaunt, for instance, advising Richard from his deathbed:

> Now He that made me knows I see thee ill,
> Ill in myself to see, and in thee, seeing ill.
> Thy death-bed is no lesser than thy land,
> Wherein thou liest in reputation sick,
> And thou, too careless patient as thou art,
> Commit'st thy anointed body to the cure
> Of those physicians that first wounded thee.
> A thousand flatterers sit within thy crown,
> Whose compass is no bigger than thy head,
> And yet, [incaged] in so small a verge,
> The waste is no whit lesser than thy land.
>
> (II.i.93-103)

In the very act of denouncing flatterers, Gaunt is constrained to use the language of sacred kingship, to speak of the king's anointed body, and to suggest the analogy between the health of that body and the health of the land as a whole. It is not that Gaunt wishes to flatter Richard (quite the opposite), but that the only language available to him contains and supports the contradictions and confusions in the system of sacred kingship that are emerging with the return of Bullingbrook. Gaunt's deathbed speech is in reality a tissue of proverbs and homilies, all a good deal too neat to manage the concrete complexities of the historical moment:

> Methinks I am a prophet new inspir'd,
> And thus expiring do foretell of him:
> His rash fierce blaze of riot cannot last,
> For violent fires soon burn out themselves;
> Small show'rs last long, but sudden storms are short;
> He tires betimes that spurs too fast betimes;
> With eager feeding food doth choke the feeder;
> Light vanity, insatiate cormorant,
> Consuming means, soon preys upon itself.
>
> (II.i.31-39)

It is not that Gaunt's string of proverbs does not contain some truth, but that it is not prophetic in any useful sense. His speech becomes, with its iterations and heavy emphases, an attempt to conjure an England which, if it ever existed at all, is now certainly dying along with Gaunt himself:

> This blessed plot, this earth, this realm, this England,
> This nurse, this teeming womb of royal kings.
>
> . . . . .
>
> This land of such dear souls, this dear dear land,
> Dear for her reputation through the world,
> Is now leas'd out—I die pronouncing it—
> Like to a tenement or pelting farm.
> England, bound in with the triumphant sea,
> Whose rocky shore beats back the envious siege
> Of wat'ry Neptune, is now bound in with shame,
> With inky blots and rotten parchment bonds;
> That England, that was wont to conquer others,
> Hath made a shameful conquest of itself.
> Ah, would the scandal vanish with my life,
> How happy then were my ensuing death!
>
> (II.i.50-51, 57-68)

We will meet this relatively flat-footed repetitiveness in the discourse of others: it is always an indication that the speaker is in the presence of a concrete circumstance he has no real power to control. Gaunt's concluding wish that his death might be a sacrifice to relieve England of scandal contains the residue of magical thinking. If there is a way out of difficulty, it lies not in magical expiation, but in facing language and the ambiguities it generates, perhaps in working through those "inky blots and rotten parchment bonds" that Gaunt simply wishes away in contempt.

The homiletic idiom is bankrupt in the world of *Richard II*, for it has no power to govern the ways in which men really behave. Bullingbrook significantly ignores it. Not for him the consolations of philosophy:

> Teach thy necessity to reason thus:
> There is no virtue like necessity.
> Think not the King did banish thee,
> But thou the King. Woe doth the heavier sit
> Where it perceives it is but faintly borne.
> Go, say I sent thee forth to purchase honor,
> And not the King exil'd thee.
>
> (I.iii.277-83)

This begins to anticipate Polonius, and it has about the same success in restraining Bullingbrook as Polonius' wise saws have in restraining Laertes. Bullingbrook will not pretend that he has banished the king: he will, indeed, banish him. My point is simply that Richard is not the only one in the play who unreflectingly allows the established idiom to speak in him, rather than using that idiom in all self-consciousness as a means to a political end. Richard's volatile personality drives him to extreme positions, to be sure, but those positions do have the merit of exposing the contradictions inherent in the established idiom that everyone else is willing to leave unexamined. Thus to Aumerle's and Carlisle's gentle promptings to action, Richard characteristically responds with a metaphor that he does not quite recognize as a metaphor:

> So when this thief, this traitor Bullingbrook,
> Who all this while hath revell'd in the night,
> Whilst we were wand'ring with the antipodes,
> Shall see us rising in our throne, the east,
> His treasons will sit blushing in his face,
> Not able to endure the sight of day,
> But self-affrighted tremble at his sin.
>
> (III.ii.47-53)

Richard takes the extreme position that, if what the language of sacred kingship seems to be saying is really true, if he really is God's anointed, then he should not have to lift a finger to retain his kingdom. Battles are, of course, not won with glorious angels in heavenly pay, but Richard's uncompromising stand, by taking the established idiom at its word, at least tests that idiom, ultimately finding it inadequate to the real and historical facts of the matter. Having wrung from the idiom a confession of its real inadequacy, Richard will go on to remake a poetic language which, if impotent, is still in touch with a tangible world:

> In winter's tedious nights sit by the fire
> With good old folks and let them tell [thee] tales
> Of woeful ages long ago betid;
> And ere thou bid good night, to quite their griefs,
> Tell thou the lamentable tale of me,
> And send the hearers weeping to their beds.
> For why, the senseless brands will sympathize
> The heavy accent of thy moving tongue,
> And in compassion weep the fire out,
> And some will mourn in ashes, some coal-black,
> For the deposing of a rightful king.
>
> (V.i.40-50)

This is in many ways the discourse we have known all along, and Richard's characteristic extravagance, his narcissism, his tendency to see himself as a character in a story ("For God's sake, let us sit upon the ground / And tell sad stories of the death of kings," III.ii.155-56) are fully in evidence. But what is in some respects the most extravagant image of his farewell to his queen, the image of the firelogs weeping at his fate, is grounded in observation of the concrete. Anyone who has ever watched a green log burn will know what he is talking about, and anyone who has built a fire with green wood will know that it can "weep" a fire out. This is a fundamentally sounder metaphor (and Richard treats it *as* a metaphor, and nothing more) than talk of angels in heavenly pay. Green logs are real. Angels must remain a supposition.

It is not, of course, that Richard achieves an idiom adequate to political realities, though he does achieve an authentic idiom. He rises to a self-conscious mastery of language that no one else in this play approaches. Richard perhaps glimpses the fact that language, like magic, must be discounted before it can become effective. The man who invokes divine vengeance and expects a prompt bolt of lightning may have a long wait in store for him. He hasn't, after all, completed the trick, for though he may well and truly have sawed the lady in half, he hasn't put her back together again. To insist on what is ultimately fictional power ends up in exposing real weakness. But real weakness, properly managed, may result in real power. It is certainly possible, for instance, to invoke divine vengeance, and all the while be perfectly clear in your mind that divine vengeance has a reputation for unreliability, that it frequently fails to materialize, and, that when it does, it has a notorious tendency to miss its mark. The question here will be the expediency of invoking divine vengeance in the first place. If the truculent and fractious persons with whom you have to deal happen also to be superstitious, you might well murmur something about heavenly retribution. And if something fairly momentous has *already* happened, a decisive battle, say, the victor may choose to call his victory divine vengeance with relative impunity. He invokes it, in effect, after the fact.

But these are matters for the precocious child and the unscrupulous tailor. The emperor, for all his achievement of an authentic poetic idiom, turns his back on history. Who is to say that he does this out of a neurosis the like of which we will never know? For it is not just that Richard fears history: history really *is* a fearful thing. It tells us, not only that actions and events are irreversible, but that we initiate those actions and events, and must bear their consequences. We are all of us at times aware of having all too much power, aware that our words really do make a difference, though it is assuredly not by magical means that they do. It may be futile to work magic, but, given the continuous pain of historical consciousness, it may not be altogether inexplicable that one in Richard's position should try.

II

It would be in some ways convenient to say that we have done with the emperor and are now at liberty to concentrate on the child and the tailor. But the dialectical process in which the past is continually reassumed in the present, the veering about which so often accompanies political upheaval, makes it a difficult matter to forget the emperor entirely. The name of Richard becomes a rallying cry for faction in the vigorous world of the two parts of *Henry IV*, and the memory of the old order, now at enough of a distance that it may be readily sentimentalized, will continue to fascinate even those who have been most materially involved in pulling it down.

To be sure, the discoveries effected by the usurpation are experienced at first as an enormous liberation. So much energy is, in fact, set loose that the man responsible for its liberation, now Henry IV, seems in certain private moments overwhelmed as he contemplates the huge and unruly rabbit he has plucked from what looked like an ordinary-sized hat. He is a man, and in this he is like most of us, not entirely happy about bearing the consequences of his irreversible historical actions. A king who is in the curious position of having denied that the king's words have any privileged efficacy, who has rightly seen that the power of the word lies in its context and not in itself, will be hard pressed to keep his discovery a secret. Certain implications of the usurpation are not lost on John Falstaff, for instance, and he will not fail to point out some embarrassing correspondences in the scheme of the new order. Here he is, trading lines with Prince Hal, admitting quite frankly that he is a thief; in fact, as he says, thievery is his vocation, and "'tis no sin for a man to labor in his vocation" (*1 Henry IV*, I.ii.104-5). Under other circumstances we would not allow this outrageous extension of the word's reference; we would argue that the criteria in virtue of which we apply the word "vocation" are simply not present in the area of thievery. But if the man now sitting on the throne has, indeed, stolen his crown, has he not in some sense sanctioned the extension of reference that we would otherwise be prone to disallow? If the king resents being called a thief (and he surely does), must he not buy the silence of thieves by allowing them to call their thievery a vocation? Here is Richard's old problem with Mowbray fantastically compounded, for presumably Richard had a choice about entering into conspiracy with Mowbray, though, as we have seen, once in conspiracy he was powerless to get out again. But in a very real sense, Henry, in choosing to steal the crown, has relinquished his freedom to choose his confederates, for he depends on the silence of all who speak English and have the wit to understand the situation he has created. This is perhaps a historical consequence of the usurpation that he has not foreseen.

As Henry enters, willy-nilly, into uneasy alliance with pick-pockets, footpads, and similar unsavory types, he must notice not only the presence of unforeseen consequences, but also the absence of certain institutions of convenience generated by the old order that he has swept away with such apparent ease. Consider, for instance, the oath, that locutionary act by means of which men bind themselves, on pain of personal discomfiture, to carry out specific performances. Here is a sampling of oaths, selected not quite at random from the literally hundreds that stuff the language of *1 Henry IV*:

1. By the Lord, and I do not, I am a villain.

(I.ii.96)

2. I'll make one, an' I do not, call me villain and baffle me.

(I.ii.100-101)

3. By God, he shall not have a Scot of them,
   No, if a Scot would save his soul, he shall not!

(I.iii.214-15)

4. An' it be not four by the day, I'll be hang'd.

(II.i.1-2)

I choose these because they represent a situation, not at all uncommon in the play, where an oath is given and then immediately contravened. The first two, and the clearest examples, are Falstaff's. With the first he swears to reform his wicked ways; with the second, a mere five lines later, he swears to join Hal in stealing a purse. Falstaff makes the outrageous contradiction highly visible by invoking the same penalty (being reduced to the rank of villain) on two incompatible performances. We should be exceedingly wary of believing (as Hal seems to do here) that Falstaff has been caught out, that the contradiction is inadvertent. He *displays* the contradiction, invites our attention to it, precisely in the way he will later underscore a patent fabrication by multiplying men in buckram suits (II.iv.191 ff.). In that later instance Hal will accuse him with some heat of lying about his exploits. The accusation imprudently overlooks the fact that Falstaff's exaggerations are clearly designed to be seen through. He isn't lying, he claims implicitly, but spinning a yarn, and to accuse a yarn-spinner of lying is to make yourself look something of a sore-headed spoilsport. One of the weakest kinds of triumph is to think you have caught a man in a lie, and then have him show that he was only trying to entertain you. The stakes are perhaps somewhat lower in the matter of Falstaff's contradictory oaths, but the principles are similar: catch him out, and you become a killjoy; let the contradiction pass unremarked, and you seem to connive in degrading the whole institution of promising. This real dilemma, conjured up with a couple of apparently casual oaths, suggests that Falstaff's verbal skill is of a very high order.

Not so with the next oath in our sample, which belongs to Hotspur. He is denying his Scottish prisoners to King Henry, and doing this with some force; but fifty lines later, when Worcester has broached the conspiracy against the King, he agrees without demur to deliver them up unransomed. He is by no means aware of the contradiction; he has simply forgotten, in his characteristically hare-brained way, that he has promised anything at all.

The shrewd man may very well break a promise: this is the case with our last oath, which belongs to the unnamed carrier in II.i. He swears that it is four o'clock in the morning (if it is not, he will be hanged); he even offers supporting astronomical evidence: "Charles' wain is over the new chimney" (l. 1-2). Yet when the thief Gadshill, about whom the carrier has every reason to be suspicious, asks him the time, he says "I think it be two a' clock" (l. 33). He is very wisely denying a potential highjacker information about a time when he may expect to find portable property on the road. This is clearly more important in the circumstances than the very remote possibility that anyone will actually offer to hang him for contravening his initial oath. Perhaps the worst that can happen is that Gadshill will glance at Charles's wain over the new chimney and conclude that the carrier is lying. But that risk is certainly worth taking: if it succeeds, the advantage gained is real; if it fails, the consequences are trivial.

But no such careful calculation informs the promises that Hotspur makes and breaks. It may be argued that genuinely to forget a promise is not the same as to break it, and that the forgetful man enjoys a certain moral superiority over the consciously duplicitous one. But there is, for all that, a very high price to be paid for this moral superiority, for you deliver yourself over, body and soul, to those with a deeper understanding of the institution of promising, to those who are more than willing to suffer your old-fashioned talk about honor and justice and right, and then let you pay, for an hour or so of chivalric masquerading at Shrewsbury, with your life. The day belongs, even as it did in Richard's time, to the man who thinks in and through the language he speaks, and not to the man who allows that language to think in him.

The day belongs, in short, at least in the world of *1 Henry IV,* to Falstaff. He has fully mastered one of the lessons that Richard has to teach, that weakness, properly managed, may result in real power. Another characteristic locutionary act in the play, one closely related to the oath, is the boast, an assertion of personal power peculiarly vulnerable to deflation:

> *Gadshill.*
> We steal as in a castle, cock-sure; we have the receipt of fern-seed, we walk invisible.
> *Chamberlain.*
> Nay, by my faith, I think you are more beholding to the night than to fern-seed for your walking invisible.
>
> (II.i.85-90)

> *Glendower.*
> I can call spirits from the vasty deep.
> *Hotspur.*
> Why, so can I, or so can any man,
> But will they come when you do call for them?
>
> (III.i.52-54)

> *Falstaff.*
> But, as the devil would have it, three misbegotten knaves in Kendal green came at my back and let drive at me, for it was so dark, Hal, that thou couldest not see thy hand.
> *Prince.*
> These lies are like their father that begets them, gross as a mountain, open, palpable.
>
> (II.iv.221-26)

The difference between Falstaff's boast and those of Gadshill and Glendower is simply that Falstaff offers his in full awareness of the way in which it renders him vulnerable. Indeed, his vulnerability is so obvious that the prudent man will be wary of it, and suspect that it conceals a trap.

In *2 Henry IV,* Falstaff will speak of turning "diseases to commodity": "'Tis no matter if I do halt, I have the wars for my color, and my pension shall seem the more reasonable. A good wit will make use of any thing" (I.ii.245-48). It is a good description of Falstaff's strategy in general, for he is continually presenting himself as weak and vulnerable in order to gain advantage. Asked to impersonate the king in a play *ex tempore* (and much of Falstaff's behavior elsewhere might be described as a play *ex tempore,* for he is above all a brilliant improviser), he elects to do the part "in King Cambyses' vein," that is, in the patently artificial and old-fashioned ranting style of Thomas Preston. Falstaff embraces incompetence (and King Cambyses' vein turns out to sound oddly like the euphuistic prose of John Lyly) in order to play what is in fact a deep and complicated game. For in presenting himself as a clumsy actor, Falstaff manages to insinuate with utter impunity the very disloyal suggestion not only that the real king is a player-king (because he has no lineal title to the office of anointed king which he now fills), but that his monarchical impersonation is transparent and unconvincing. The style of Thomas Preston (or John Lyly) is the appropriate one for the part of King Henry precisely because it *is* artificial and obvious:

> That thou art my son I have partly thy mother's word, partly my own opinion, but chiefly a villainous trick of thine eye, and a foolish hanging of thy nether lip, that doth warrant me. If then thou be son to me, here lies the point: why being son to me, art thou so pointed at? Shall the blessed sun of heaven prove a micher and eat blackberries? a question not to be ask'd. Shall the son of England prove a thief and take purses? a question to be ask'd.
>
> (*1 Henry IV,* II.iv.403-10)

Falstaff avoids any unseemly explicitness, but the nimble play with the homophones "sun" and "son" is rather dazzling. To the ear, the phrase "son of England" is indistinguishable from "sun of England," a well-known locution for the reigning monarch. It is a question to be asked, since the present sun of England has, indeed, proved a thief, and not of paltry purses, but of a throne. Falstaff's pretended vulnerability reveals Henry's very real vulnerability at a deeper level.

To speak effectively in the new world created by the usurpation requires the exploitation of all the figurative resources of language, of irony, of understatement, of wary hyperbole and deft paronomasia. The days are gone when simple grandiloquence of the "This land of such dear souls, this dear dear land" kind will do. When in the deposition scene of *Richard II* Bullingbrook asks Richard if he is contented to resign the crown, Richard's riddling reply; "Ay, no, no ay" (IV.i.201), is something more than idle play with the homophones "ay" and "I." Richard has come to realize that a language that can only speak of either/or, that can generate no discourse governing the in-between, is inadequate to cover the complex of feelings he is now experiencing. His equivocation is the true expression of his inability to answer Bullingbrook's bald question with anything like the clarity Bullingbrook seems to require.

The changes of history demand changes of language, and to survive in the world of the two parts of *Henry IV* is to learn to speak in ways that are adequate to the occasion. Much of Hal's "education" in the course of the plays, if that is what it is, may be described as his attempt to master new languages, to be able to "drink with any tinker in his own language" (II.iv.19); to be able to speak like Hotspur ("'Give my roan horse a drench,' says he, and answers, 'Some fourteen,' an hour after; 'a trifle, a trifle,'" II.iv.106-8); to speak like a king; or to speak like himself:

> I know you all, and will a while uphold
> The unyok'd humor of your idleness,
> Yet herein will I imitate the sun.
>
> (*1 Henry IV,* I.ii.195-97)

The homophonic play (which at this early stage, when Hal tends to sound a bit smug, may not be fully conscious) suggests "imitate the son." The real task, in the shifting and ambiguous world created by the usurpation, is to be yourself. This is not a matter of the "naturalness" of manner tirelessly recommended in books of etiquette and treatises on how to succeed. It is a rigorous process of learning the languages of others and inventing a language of your own. When in the first reconciliation scene, Hal replies to his father's long sermon on the proper behavior exemplified by his aristocratic ancestors, his reply is anything but casual: "I shall hereafter, my thrice-gracious lord, / *Be more myself*" (III.ii.92-93). And we will not be surprised to find him at the very end of *Henry V* learning yet another language, this time the French of his affianced Kate.

It is those who do not grow in language, who do not submit themselves to its shifting substance and stubborn materiality, who are defeated by history in the world of the Henry IV plays. Hotspur is first in this group, because, for all his eloquence, he has a thoroughly naïve relation to the language he speaks. There is so much in him to remind us of the new order that it is easy to underestimate the extent to which he abandons himself to the aristocratic myths of the old order. Yet his gaze is basically retrospective, and it is in his casualness with language, and particularly in his unreflective relation to the institution of promising, that we can discover his allegiances most clearly. Here is Hotspur in soliloquy, congratulating himself warmly on the excellence of the anti-Lancastrian conspiracy:

> By the Lord, our plot is a good plot as ever was laid, our friends true and constant: a good plot, good friends, and full of expectation; an excellent plot, very good friends. . . . Is there not my father, my uncle, and myself? Lord Edmund Mortimer, my Lord of York, and Owen Glendower? is there not besides the Douglas? have I not all their letters to meet me in arms by the ninth of the next month?
>
> (*1 Henry IV,* II.iii.15-19, 23-28)

We should be suspicious of Hotspur's way of upping the verbal ante here ("a good plot, good friends. . . . an excellent plot, very good friends"), for, as the example of Richard made clear, you can't make a thing so by saying it, nor a friend true by heaping him with honorific adjectives. Wishes are not horses, they are words, and that is why beggars have to walk. Hotspur's touching faith in the written promises of his fellow conspirators, in the letters he has in hand, is rather cruelly rewarded when, of the good friends he mentions here, all but two fail to show up and do battle.

III

I do not want to leave the impression that in Richard's day (or any other) no one broke promises. We have seen that a man's word is never in fact a magical guarantee of anything, and that men keep promises because, for whatever reasons, they choose to keep them. We have been concerned with the institution of promising, a matter of consensus, not a matter of some mysterious power actually present in words. It is doubtful that any society can securely maintain for long the collective fiction that words bind when men choose not to be bound. Too much happens to contradict it: divine vengeance invoked will fail to materialize, men under oath will continue to renege after consulting private interest. But this sensible and hardheaded view should not obscure the fact that there are in every society a few people who believe the myth of verbal magic some of the time, and still others who would like to believe it. There is often a very fine line between wishing something were so and believing you can bring it about by wishing. We are all liable at times to confuse imagination with power, which is one reason why words must be discounted if they are to have any real power at all. Perhaps kings are particularly vulnerable, since they tend to be surrounded by flatterers, by men who see it as their job to support the confusion. If the king does not smell them out, as Lear finally does on the heath, he may come to believe that he really is everything. But we know that this is a lie; the king is not ague-proof.

King Henry, shrewd man of the new order that he is, is yet not immune to this danger. He is certainly capable of wishing, and his wishes are revealing. He wishes, for instance, that his eldest son would behave better, be an old-fashioned gentleman like Northumberland's son Hotspur:

> O that it could be prov'd
> That some night-tripping fairy had exchang'd
> In cradle-clothes our children where they lay,
> And call'd mine Percy, his Plantagenet!
>
> (*1 Henry IV*, I.i.86-89)

Henry is perfectly in possession of himself here, and we shall hardly credit him with a belief in fairies on the basis of these lines. They hint, however, at a genuinely dialectical phenomenon in which a process begins to veer back on itself, in which the man who succeeded in pulling down the old consensus now looks back on its ruins in search of those consolations mere history refuses to provide. In his first reconciliation with Hal, Henry will speak a language which on one level is designed to scold a wayward boy, but which is nonetheless obliquely eloquent of Henry's own longings for order and clarity, for an unambiguous world where good and evil are readily identifiable and rewards and punishments are symmetrically distributed. There is a conundrum implicit in the lines that follow, which turns out to be as pertinent to the relationship between kings and their subjects as it is to the relationship between parents and their children: who will scold the scolder?

> I know not whether God will have it so
> For some displeasing service I have done,
> That in his secret doom, out of my blood
> He'll breed revengement and a scourge for me;
> But thou dost in thy passages of life
> Make me believe that thou art only mark'd
> For the hot vengeance, and the rod of heaven,
> To punish my mistreadings. Tell me else,
> Could such inordinate and low desires,
> Such poor, such bare, such lewd, such mean attempts,
> Such barren pleasures, rude society,
> As thou art match'd withal and grafted to,
> Accompany the greatness of thy blood,
> And hold their level with thy princely heart?
>
> (*1 Henry IV*, III.ii.4-17)

This language, on careful examination, proves to be full of odd displacements and skewed emphases. Henry calls his own misdoings "mistreadings"; he speaks vaguely of "some displeasing service" for which God must be angry with him. But these misdoings he so evasively names were once called usurpation and regicide, and still would be if some were empowered to speak freely. Henry's language thus reduces what are (by some standards) enormities to mere misdemeanors, at the same time that it takes Hal's misdemeanors (which amount, after all, to some youthful pranks and a couple of drinks with the boys) and promotes them to enormities—"such poor, such bare, such lewd, such mean attempts." We recognize in Henry's catalogue the same technique of repetition and adjectival onslaught that we remarked in Gaunt's deathbed speech and in Hotspur's soliloquy. And those features are here, as elsewhere, the surest sign that words are at odds with a reality the speaker has no *real* power to control.

In the heady days of the usurpation, Henry certainly did not behave like a man who believed that transgression would be punished swiftly by the efficient operation of the cosmic machine. Yet here he speaks of God breeding "revengement and a scourge," of "hot vengeance, and the rod of heaven," terms which are, by the way, oddly out of proportion to the kinds of sins one can legitimately call "mistreadings." The return of the repressed, which no political revolution ever succeeds in doing away with, operates with full force in these lines, for even as Henry struggles to mitigate his sense of sinfulness by calling usurpation and regicide "mistreadings," his conviction of guilt is bound upon him afresh with the inflated terms he chooses for divine vengeance. It is further remarkable that not once does Henry suggest that God might punish *Hal* for Hal's misdoings—remarkable because, after all, Hal is the one who incurs blame for his own actions, whether we choose to call them sins or the youthful sowing of wild oats. The reasonable expectation that Henry is warning *Hal* of divine displeasure is so powerful that it is something of a struggle for us to see what Henry's lines

G. Valmont Thomas as Mistress Quickly in the 1999 Oregon Shakespeare Festival production of Henry IV, Part Two, *featuring an all-male cast.*

are really saying. Henry speaks of his own punishment, and in so doing betrays a wish for the moral order he has in another sense denied.

It is understandable that a man who begins by discovering an intoxicating freedom—even *thrones* are there for the taking—should come to long, deep in his soul, for the very sanctions he has daffed aside. Historical consciousness is painful precisely because it cannot generate a stable and symmetrical world. In the new order Henry is nominally the most powerful man in the land, yet he can not even control the behavior of his own flesh and blood. Meanwhile, he has relinquished the consolations of the old order, among them a language that seemed to enable men to speak with authority and conviction about a symmetry of crime and punishment. Henry is perhaps not the only man who would—even at the price of his *own* punishment—buy back that symmetry if only the balefulness of history would allow.

The tinge of nostalgia in Henry's speech, which becomes much more than a tinge as he sickens throughout the second part of *Henry IV*, is indicative of a general inertia in language. On account of this inertia, language tends to lag behind the rapid changes of historical movement; it tends to continue to be governed, in the face of massive upheaval, by a previous harmony. This retrograde character of language is particularly in evidence in the second part of *Henry IV*, where it afflicts even the verbally nimble Falstaff. It puts visible strain on certain words whose meanings are beginning to be placed in doubt by history, words so common that they seem, without question, to designate a readily distinguishable segment of reality. "Gentleman" is such a word, and when the Lord Bardolph arrives at Northumberland's castle with a glowing report of rebel victory, he does not hesitate to guarantee the truth of his report by invoking the breeding of the gentleman from whom he has had it:

> I spake with one, my lord, who came from thence,
> A gentleman well bred and of good name,
> That freely rend'red me these news for true.
>
> (I.i.25-27)

That the good news proves utterly false is an early indication that the word "gentleman" is no longer the powerful guarantee that it once was.

The second part of *Henry IV,* even more than the first, shows us a world in which the old aristocrat no longer finds himself alone. There is an extremely vital and energetic underclass in the plays, and it makes itself increasingly known to the higher orders. The petit bourgeois merchant, the tradesman, the seller of various commodities (a word very much in the process of changing its meaning in this historical watershed) are all jostling for position and asserting their rights.[6] This cast of characters is largely invisible, hardly more than a succession of names and occupations cropping up here and there in the speeches of the main characters, yet they are somehow more real than the country folk with label-names (Mouldy, Wart, Shadow, Feeble) who actually appear on stage. There is, for instance, the witty physician who says of Falstaff's urine sample that "the water itself was a good healthy water, but for the party that ow'd it, he might have moe diseases than he knew for" (I.ii.3-5). There is Master Tisick, the deputy, and Master Dumbe, the minister, impressive men in the eyes of the Hostess. There is, above all, Master Dommelton, the independent mercer, who refuses Falstaff credit:

> Let him be damn'd like the glutton! Pray God his tongue be hotter! A whoreson Achitophel! a [rascally] yea-forsooth knave, to bear a gentleman in hand, and then stand upon security! The whoreson smoothy-pates do now wear nothing but high shoes, and bunches of keys at their girdles, and if a man is through with them in honest taking up, then they must stand upon security. I had as live they would put ratsbane in my mouth as offer to stop it with security. I look'd 'a should have sent me two and twenty yards of satin (as I am a true knight), and he sends me security!
>
> (I.ii.34-45)

Falstaff encounters here a stubborn reality, which refuses to credit an older language (the words "gentleman" and "true knight") with the power to guarantee that it once had. Falstaff encounters increasing difficulty, even with the gullible Hostess:

> *Falstaff.*
> As I am a gentleman!
> *Hostess.*
> Faith, you said so before.
> *Falstaff.*
> As I am a gentleman! Come, no more words of it.
>
> (II.i.136-38)

It is not a little ironic that Falstaff should find himself using a language that has become partly obsolete, for he has been active in discrediting it. Not only have his escapades put the integrity of knighthood in doubt; his profound playing with language has suggested the very transformations that here inconvenience him. When, as in the first part, "squires of the knight's body" become "squires of the night's body" (I.ii.24), it is not certain whether thieves shall be taken for knights, or knights for thieves. In some sense Falstaff's attempt to give thievery a good name has gone awry in the second part, and succeeded only in giving knighthood a bad one. But what is of real interest is the extent to which Falstaff clings to an idiom whose power has been substantially reduced in the face of historical change. The world of the first part is concerned with a transitional period in between two consolidated orders, a time when the vocabulary of the vanished order still has a certain power, even though the system on which it rested has been virtually dismantled. But such a situation must be inherently unstable. The old appraisive terms are increasingly met with a healthy skepticism on the part of the newly independent underclass, and are in the process of being discarded or redefined. The period when the man skilled in language can seem to rule the world is necessarily short-lived. Language cannot be appropriated permanently, because it is not, finally, property. It is "vulgar" in the literal sense, held in common, and Falstaff's dwindling power in the second part is largely due to the public's decreasing willingness to credit his vocabulary with the power conferred upon it by the vanished order.

We see the tendency to cling to the idiom of the old order nowhere more clearly than in the private moments of Henry IV himself, the very man who has been most practically involved in bringing the old order down. In his first reconciliation with Hal in the first part (III.ii), the fact that he invokes the old standard of aristocratic blood and speaks of Hal's "affections, which hold a wing / Quite from the flight of all thy ancestors" (l. 30-31) is remarkable, but not ultimately surprising. The king's nostalgia for the very order that his actions have so profoundly denied is simply a measure of the historically generated divisions within the man, divisions that are close to the surface in his famous soliloquy in the second part:

> How many thousands of my poorest subjects
> Are at this hour asleep! O sleep! O gentle sleep!
> Nature's soft nurse, how have I frighted thee,
> That thou no more wilt weigh my eyelids down,
> And steep my senses in forgetfulness?
> Why rather, sleep, liest thou in smoky cribs,
> Upon uneasy pallets stretching thee,
> And hush'd with buzzing night-flies to thy slumber,
> Than in the perfum'd chambers of the great,
> Under the canopies of costly state,
> And lull'd with sound of sweetest melody?
> O thou dull god, why li'st thou with the vile
> In loathsome beds, and leavest the kingly couch
> A watch-case or a common 'larum bell?
>
> (III.i.4-17)

We detect here a rather sentimental portrayal of the lower orders, some members of which we have just seen in anything but peaceful repose. The thrust behind Henry's speech is a pastoral longing, and we suspect that his emergent "nostalgia for the bottom" comes not from his sense of the responsibilities attendant upon high station, but from the guilt of having acquired that high station in

the first place. Envying the lower orders is a pastoral alibi for the guilt of continuing to possess things got by doubtful means. Pastoral is an aristocratic myth aimed at covering up the real character of a longing for the bottom, and the surest sign of this is that pastoral always wants to have it both ways: it wills a simple life *and* the perquisites that go with high station. Shakespeare elsewhere pokes a good deal of fun at this willed contradiction in pastoral,[7] but here Henry's embracing of the contradiction is simply the sign of his divided allegiance. He would like to go on speaking the language of the old order, while enjoying the advantages of the new.

"Uneasy lies the head that wears a crown": this familiar, sententious utterance contains a telling pun, one that we have already seen Falstaff exploiting adeptly at Shrewsbury in part one: "Lord, Lord, how this world is given to lying! I grant you I was down and out of breath, and so was he, but we rose both at an instant and fought a long hour by Shrewsbury clock" (V.iv.145-48). In the world after the usurpation, the head that wears a crown will always lie, however uneasily, for possession of the crown depends upon a fabrication. That this has always been the case is made clear by the example of Richard, but in the old order perhaps the lie of anointed kingship was not always an uneasy one. At least it had the tacit support of a consensus. In sweeping away that consensus, Henry acquires an uneasiness that will hereafter be part of the business of ruling.

Notes

1. At the outset I should like to make clear my debt to Sigurd Burckhardt in much of what follows. His "Swoll'n with Some Other Grief: Shakespeare's Prince Hal Trilogy" in *Shakespearean Meanings* (Princeton: Princeton Univ. Press, 1968), pp. 144-205, takes much the same view of history as the one propounded here. Joseph Porter's *The Drama of Speech Acts: Shakespeare's Lancastrian Tetralogy* (Berkeley: University of California Press, 1979) came to my attention after I had written this article, but I note that we agree about a number of points about speech acts in the Lancastrian plays.

2. Mircea Eliade remarked, "In this total adherence, on the part of archaic man, to archetypes and repetition, modern man would be justified in seeing not only the primitives' amazement at their own first spontaneous and creative free gestures and their veneration, repeated *ad infinitum,* but also a feeling of guilt on the part of man hardly emerged from the paradise of animality (i.e., from nature), a feeling that urges him to reidentify with nature's eternal repetition the few primordial, creative, and spontaneous gestures that had signalized the appearance of freedom." See *The Myth of the Eternal Return, or Cosmos and History* (1949), tr. Willard R. Trask, Bollingen Series XLVI (Princeton: Princeton Univ. Press, 1971), p. 155.

3. *The Riverside Shakespeare,* ed. G. Blakemore Evans, et al. (Boston: Houghton Mifflin, 1974). All subsequent quotations from Shakespeare's plays are taken from this edition.

4. For a succinct statement of this duality in monarchy see Otto Gierke, *Political Theories of the Middle Age,* tr. Frederic William Maitland (Boston: Beacon Press, 1958), pp. 30-37.

5. One such paradox is the doctrine of the king's two bodies, thoroughly discussed by Ernst Kantorowicz in *The King's Two Bodies: A Study in Mediaeval Political Theology* (Princeton: Princeton Univ. Press, 1957). See especially chap. 2, "Shakespeare: King Richard II," pp. 24-41.

6. For an excellent discussion of the shifting meanings of words in history, and specifically of the word "commodity," see Quentin Skinner, "Language and Social Change" in *The State of the Language,* ed. Leonard Michaels and Christopher Ricks (Berkeley: Univ. of California Press, 1980), pp. 562-78.

7. C. L. Barber remarked in discussing *As You Like It* that Touchstone's discussion of the shepherd's life (III.ii.13-22) "mocks the contradictory nature of the desires ideally resolved by pastoral life, to be at once in the court and in the fields, to enjoy both the fat advantages of rank and the spare advantages of the mean and sure estate." See *Shakespeare's Festive Comedy: A Study of Dramatic Form and Its Relation to Social Custom* (1959; rpt. Princeton: Princeton Univ. Press, 1972), p. 227.

REFORMATION, REDEMPTION, AND THE REJECTION OF FALSTAFF

D. J. Palmer (essay date 1970)

SOURCE: "Casting off the Old Man: History and St. Paul in *Henry IV,*" in *Henry the Fourth Parts I and II: Critical Essays,* edited by David Bevington, Garland Publishing, 1986, 315-36.

[*In the following essay, originally published in 1970, Palmer points to several instances in the* Henry IV *plays that anticipate Prince Hal's reformation at the end of Part II, drawing parallels between the words of the apostle St. Paul and those of the Prince.*]

I

Biblical quotations abound in Shakespeare's two *Henry IV* plays, and most of them are made by Falstaff, whose allusions, as Richmond Noble says, "are the aptest in the whole of the plays."[1] They are also, of course, singularly profane in Falstaff's mouth, and his "damnable interation" of Scripture, we may suspect, is a relic of his former identity as Sir John Oldcastle, the name of Prince Hal's riotous companion in that execrable play, *The Famous Victories of Henry the Fifth*. It seems that after borrowing the name of his fat knight from the older play, Shakespeare subsequently rechristened him as Falstaff out of deference to the family feelings of Oldcastle's Elizabethan descendant, Lord Cobham.[2] For the historical Oldcastle, as the Epilogue in Part Two tells us, "died a martyr, and this is not the man." He was in fact a Lollard burned at the stake for his faith during the reign of Henry V, and honoured by the more zealous Protestants of Shakespeare's day as one of the early heroes of their cause. A familiarity with the Bible was therefore particularly, if scurrilously, appropriate to the first Sir John, and no doubt this irreverent representation of his ancestor as a pseudo-puritan offended Lord Cobham as much as the imputation of cowardice.

Prince Hal, however, knows his Bible at least as well as Falstaff, and in the concluding couplet of his soliloquy at the end of the first tavern scene,

> I'll so offend to make offence a skill,
> Redeeming time when men think least I will,
>
> (1.2.209-10)[3]

editors have noted the echo of St. Paul's *Epistle to the Ephesians*:

> Take hede therefore that ye walke circumspectly, not as fooles but as wise,
> Redeeming the time: for the days are evil.
>
> (5:15-16)[4]

The aptness and full significance of this allusion, however, remain to be explored. Preserving an essential distinction between the fool and the wise man, Hal's resolve "to make offence a skill" parallels Falstaff's virtuosity in avoiding reproof by turning offence into an ingenious and apparently harmless display of wit, while Hal's promise to redeem the time follows Falstaff's mock-determination, "I must give over this life, and I will give it over" (1.2.92). The soliloquy clearly has an important dramatic function: it distinguishes the Prince at the beginning of the play from the wild youth that others, including Falstaff and the King, suppose him to be, and in so doing it puts an entirely new complexion upon the traditional legends of the riotous Prince, such as those represented on the stage in *The Famous Victories*.

As Falstaff says, but in two senses that he is not aware of, "the true prince may, for recreation sake, prove a false thief" (1.2.149). Behind Falstaff's back, Poins and Hal plot the Gadshill robbery as a "jest," "for recreation sake," to prove Falstaff himself "a false thief," that is, a liar and no thief at all. But at a deeper level in the play, the "recreation" signifies that "reformation" which Hal promises in his soliloquy at the end of this scene. The soliloquy therefore states the central business of both plays, to show us the process by which Hal is to redeem the time; it also insists that Hal's "reformation" will be not so much an amendment of life, as a "recreation" of his true identity in men's eyes. "Never call a true piece of gold a counterfeit," Falstaff tells him at the abrupt end of the "play extempore," "thou art essentially made without seeming so" (2.4.476). Moreover, this "recreation" of the true Prince also reflects Shakespeare's artistic and historical purpose in the two plays, which are themselves presented to us "for recreation sake."

Hal's allusion to the words of St. Paul is thus at the heart of the dramatic structure. It is no accident that the Eastcheap community is described to Hal in Part Two as "Ephesians, my lord, of the old church" (2.2.143), for when Hal's promise to redeem the time is eventually fulfilled at the end of Part Two, his rejection of Falstaff ("I know thee not, old man")[5] again recalls the Apostle's injunctions to the Ephesians:

> That is, that ye cast of, concerning the conversation in the time past, the olde man, which is corrupt through the deceivable lustes,
> And be renewed in the spirit of your minde,
> And put on the new man, which after God is created in righteousnes, and true holines.
> Wherefore cast of lying, & speake everie man trueth unto his neighbour: for we are members one of another.
>
> (4:22-5)

Paul speaks of a metaphorical "olde man," the unregenerate Adam in the self, and Hal addresses an all too substantial counterpart, but one surely well qualified to recognise the appropriateness of the text. If we can suppose so, Shakespeare's old man must have found the Biblical context as a whole particularly galling:

> Let no man deceive you with vaine wordes: for suche things commeth the wrath of God upon the children of disobedience.
> Be not therefore companions with them.
>
> (5:6-7)

> And be not drunke with wine, wherein is excess.
>
> (5:18)

The page in the Geneva Bible which Hal seems to have had particularly in mind bears the heading over its double columns, "Put on the new man . . . Awake from slepe," words which must have struck a responsive chord in the imagination of the author of *A Midsummer Night's Dream* (where Bottom himself, in his garbled fashion, has occasion to recall the Apostle on the subject of dreams and visions):[6]

> Wherefore he saith, Awake thou that slepest, and stand up from the dead, & Christ shal give thee light.
>
> (5:14)

So Hal says in his rejection speech:

> I long have dreamt of such a kind of man,
> So surfeit swell'd, so old, and so profane;
> But, being awak'd, I do despise my dream.
>
> (5.4.50-2)

If there is an ironic echo of this image of awakening and standing up from the dead at the end of Part One when Falstaff arises from the dead on the battlefield ("Counterfeit? I lie, I am no counterfeit: to die is to be a counterfeit," 5.4.114), then it is also remembered in Hal's last interview with his dying father in Part Two, when he mistakes sleep for death and prematurely removes the crown to the distress of his waking father. "Ye were once of darkenes," says Paul (5:8), and it is true that Hal was formerly one of the "squires of the night's body" (Part One, 1.2.23), but when he assumes the crown, he will "have no fellowship with the unfruteful workes of darkenes, but even reprove them rather" (5:11). Finally, Hal stands up from the dead, not only as his father's rightful successor, but in his renewed existence on Shakespeare's stage.[7] The history play itself is redeeming time.

Henry IV therefore owes considerably more to St. Paul's *Epistle to the Ephesians* than the passing reference noted by the commentators. The use of these allusions to relate the beginning of Part One to the end of Part Two reinforces the arguments of those who regard the two plays as structurally unified although individually self-contained. The theme of time's redemption and the renewal of life also links the two plays with the comedies. In addition, it does not seem likely, as some have suggested, that Hal's soliloquy in the second scene of Part One is an interpolation inserted when Shakespeare was revising the play, since the very phrase which carries such a burden of dramatic significance, "redeeming time," is integrated with the language of Part One as a whole, as well as being carried through to Part Two.

II

The influence of the earlier Tudor morality drama upon the structure of the *Henry IV* plays has often been observed. In treating the theme of Hal's "reformation," Shakespeare naturally turned to the "prodigal son" motif of the interludes, and Falstaff is actually referred to in terms of the leading comic character of the morality plays, as "that reverend vice." More specifically, Paul A. Jorgensen[8] has pointed out that one such interlude, *Lusty Juventus* (c. 1550), anticipates Shakespeare in making the same allusion to St. Paul:

> Saint Paul unto the Ephesians giveth good exhortation,
> Saying, walk circumspectly, redeeming the time,
> That is, to spend it well, and not to wickedness incline.

Jorgensen also notes that this text was introduced into the Homily for Rogation Week, where many in Shakespeare's audience must have become familiar with it. But his explanation of the text "as meaning to take full advantage of the time that man is given here on earth for salvation," however theologically correct, falls a long way short of its significance in relation to Hal's situation and purpose, because it overlooks the primary importance of the etymological association with buying and selling. Even the lines from *Lusty Juventus* paraphrase "redeeming the time" as "to spend it well." Strictly the word means "buying back," as in redeeming a debt: in the language of the pawnshop, even today, it has no theological overtones.

The marginal glosses to the text in the Geneva Bible explain the word in these terms:

> Selling all worldlie pleasures to bye time . . . In these perilous dayes & crafte of the adversaries, take hede how to bye again the occasions of godlines, which the worlde hathe taken from you.

So in his soliloquy Hal says he will "pay the debt I never promised" (1.2.202), and the language of settling debts is heard throughout Part One.

The days of Henry IV are indeed evil and perilous, as the King's speech opening the play makes clear. The disastrous consequences of the deposition of Richard are felt throughout the land, in "the intestine shock And furious close of civil butchery." In an attempt to redeem his guilt, the King has vowed a crusade to the Holy Land,

> Over whose acres walk'd those blessed feet
> Which fourteen hundred years ago were nail'd
> For our advantage on the bitter cross.
>
> (1.1.25-7)

To walk circumspectly (or rather to march "in mutual well-be-seeming ranks") in the path of his Redeemer is the vow that Bolingbroke will never redeem; the very act of usurpation was that of an oath-breaker, and the rebels know him as a man who will not pay the debt he promised.

After the succeeding tavern scene and Hal's soliloquy, the rebels are introduced, and Hotspur exhorts his companions to purge the dishonour of their complicity in the usurpation:

> Yet time serves wherein you may redeem
> Your banish'd honours, and restore yourselves
> Into the good thoughts of the world again.
>
> (1.3.180-2)

In their very different context, Hotspur's words echo those of Hal's resolve in the soliloquy of the previous scene. Worcester finds another motive for rebellion, in self-defence rather than high principle, but he also uses the language of redemption:

> To save our heads by raising of a head:
> For bear ourselves as even as we can,
> The King will always think him in our debt,
> And think we think ourselves unsatisfied,
> Till he hath found a time to pay us home.
>
> (1.3.284-8)

The first three scenes of Part One therefore establish the theme of "redeeming time" in relation to each of the play's three worlds: the court, the tavern, and the rebel camp. The talk of dues and payment heard in the tavern scenes must also be related to the major preoccupations of the play. Falstaff, for instance, "will give the devil his due," but his other accounts must be settled by Hal on his behalf:

> *Prince.*
> Why, what a pox have I to do with my hostess of the tavern?
> *Falstaff.*
> Well, thou hast call'd her to a reckoning many a time and oft.
> *Prince.*
> Did I ever call thee to pay thy part?
> *Falstaff.*
> No; I'll give thee thy due, thou hast paid all there.
>
> (1.2.46-51)

At the end of the second tavern scene, when Hal discovers in the pocket of the sleeping Falstaff the outstanding account for that "intolerable deal of sack," he also speaks of the money taken at Gadshill, which "shall be paid back again with advantage" (2.4.528).

Thus, when Hal promises his father in the interview scene of Part One to "redeem all this on Percy's head," the appropriateness of his analogy has by this point been well established in the play:

> Percy is but my factor, good my lord,
> To engross up glorious deeds on my behalf;
> And I will call him to so strict account
> That he shall render every glory up,
> Yea, even the slightest worship of his time,
> Or I will tear the reckoning from his heart.
>
> (3.2.147-52)

The interview scene closes with the King's line, "Advantage feeds him fat while men delay," which is Falstaff's cue to begin the following scene with a reference to his fancied loss of weight ("Do I not dwindle?") suggesting also the dwindling of his role in the increasing imminence of more urgent affairs. He makes another vow of amendment, echoing that we have just heard from Hal: "Well, I'll repent, and that suddenly, while I am in some liking" (3.3.5). He was, he says, virtuous once, and "paid money that I borrowed—three or four times." So too before the battle of Shrewsbury, Falstaff confides his fear to the Prince before launching upon his "catechism" of honour:

> *Falstaff.*
> I would 'twere bed-time, Hal, and all well.
> *Prince.*
> Why, thou owest God a death. (*Exit*)
> *Falstaff.*
> 'Tis not due yet; I would be loath to pay him before his day. What need I be so forward with him that calls not on me? . . . What is honour? A word. What is that word? Honour. What is that honour? Air? A trim reckoning!
>
> (5.1.125-40)

These illustrations demonstrate how central is that Pauline phrase, "redeeming time," to the play's concern with the proper time for settling debts of one kind or another. The very language of the play is coloured by this Biblical allusion, which in its sense of redeeming a promise relates to the many oaths that are sworn and foresworn in the course of the action, and so to the idea of honour, (honour is "a word," but a word that should be kept), while the phrase also expresses that sense of time as a commodity spent well or ill in the play. When the days are evil, and the time is out of joint ("Find we a time for frighted peace to pant," sighs the King in the play's opening lines), the idleness of the tavern life with its "play extempore" ("What a devil hast thou to do with the time of the day?" as Hal demands of Falstaff), is contrasted with the hasty impatience of Hotspur:

> O gentlemen, the time of life is short!
> To spend that shortness basely were too long
> If life did ride upon a dial's point,
> Still ending at the arrival of an hour.
>
> (5.2.82-5)

"The time will come," Hal promises his father, and with a sense of mounting urgency in the play, the hour arrives at Shrewsbury: "What, is it a time to jest and dally now?" For the dying Hotspur, "life, time's fool, And time, that takes survey of all the world, Must have a stop," but for Hal in his triumph, "the day is ours" at the end of Part One and his father acknowledges, "Thou hast redeem'd thy lost opinion."

III

"Redeeming time when men think least I will," Hal speaks not of being renewed in the spirit of his mind, but rather of renewing his reputation in the minds of others. He intends to "falsify men's hopes," to "show more goodly and attract more eyes." Hotspur has a similar understanding of honour, as being restored "into the good thoughts of the world again," though of course he has a misplaced conception of how this is to be achieved. What men think, both collectively as the world at large, and as particular individuals, is of crucial concern throughout both plays. Facing his father's suspicion that he is even in collusion with the rebels, Hal replies,

> Do not think so; you shall not find it so:
> And God forgive them that so much have sway'd
> Your Majesty's good thoughts away from me!
> I will redeem all this on Percy's head.
>
> (3.2.129-32)

Such a sustained association with men's thoughts suggests that for Shakespeare the word "redeem" not only bore its etymological sense of settling a debt, but also, through a species of pun, attached itself to the meaning of "deem." To be restored from disgrace into men's good thoughts is thus to be "re-deemed."

"I would to God thou and I knew where a commodity of good names were to be bought," says Falstaff to Hal

(1.2.80), and honour and reputation in Part One have had as much to do with what men call one as with what they think of one. A man is known by his name, and Falstaff is a master of giving good names to bad things:

> Marry, then, sweet wag, when thou art King, let not us that are squires of the night's body be called thieves of the day's beauty; let us be Diana's foresters, gentlemen of the shade, minions of the moon; and let men say we be men of good government, being governed, as the sea is, by our noble and chaste mistress the moon, under whose countenance we steal.
>
> (1.2.22-8)

The Ephesians were worshippers of Diana, and so Falstaff can argue, "'tis no sin for a man to labour in his vocation" (1.2.102). Does not St. Paul exhort the Ephesians to "walke worthie of the vocation whereunto ye are called" (4:1)?

Talk of being "called" to a reckoning, to a "strict account" (e.g., 1.2.48, 3.2.49, 5.1.128, all quoted above) is thus related to the importance of names and titles in the play. What a man is called by, and what he is called to, are, in the strict meaning of the word, his "vocation," and to be worthy of his vocation as Prince is Hal's chief concern in Part One. When he reappears in the tavern after the Gadshill robbery, he shows a wry sensitivity to the names he is called by the potboys:

> I have sounded the very base-string of humility. Sirrah, I am sworn brother to a leash of drawers and can call them all by their christen names, as Tom, Dick, and Francis. They take it already upon their salvation that though I be but Prince of Wales yet I am the king of courtesy; and tell me flatly I am no proud Jack, like Falstaff, but a Corinthian, a lad of mettle, a good boy—by the Lord, so they call me—and when I am King of England I shall command all the good lads of East cheap. They call drinking deep, dyeing scarlet; and when you breathe in your watering, they cry "hem!" and bid you play it off. To conclude, I am so good a proficient in one quarter of an hour that I can drink with any tinker in his own language during my life.
>
> (2.4.3-16)

There follows the jest with Poins at Francis' expense, an episode that seems to have baffled satisfactory interpretation. But to understand the point of Hal's joke, we should note his reference to being called "a Corinthian," for the Corinthians, like the Ephesians, were exhorted by Paul to mend their ways, and offered advice on vocation:

> Let every man abide in the same vocation wherein he was called.
> Art thou called being a servant? Care not for it; but if yet thou maist be free use it rather.
>
> (I Corinthians, 7:20-21)

So in stage-managing his play extempore with Francis, Hal plays upon the multiple meanings of "vocation," calling his name, and talking of his calling, while Poins calls him to a reckoning:

> *Prince.*
> Come hither, Francis.
> *Francis.*
> My lord?
> *Prince.*
> How long hast thou to serve, Francis?
> *Francis.*
> Forsooth, five years, and as much as to—
> *Poins*
> (within). Francis!
> *Francis.*
> Anon, anon, sir.
> *Prince.*
> Five year! by'r lady, a long lease for the clinking of pewter. But Francis, darest thou be so valiant as to play the coward with thy indenture and show it a fair pair of heels and run from it?
>
> (2.4.37-47)

In Francis, Hal is parodying himself as a fellow-Corinthian and a fellow-apprentice, and the repetition of "Anon, anon, sir," like the stage-direction at the end of the joke, *Here they both call him: Francis stands amazed, not knowing which way to go,* dramatises Hal's critical reflection upon his own neglect of his vocation: "Away, you rogue! Dost thou not hear them call?" It is certainly Hal's private joke as far as both Francis and Poins are concerned, and one that expresses a very different mood from the confident, even complacent, tone of the soliloquy at the end of the first tavern scene. He is close here to the mood of Hamlet's "O what a rogue and peasant slave am I!"

Hal's problem is to seem what he is, to be given his due, and to be called by his proper name ("Prince Hal" itself reflects an indecorous mixture of formality and familiarity). He is, in Falstaff's words, "essentially made without seeming so," a peculiar irony for one whose title is "heir apparent." It is small comfort to hear from Falstaff in jest what he would claim from all men in earnest:

> By the Lord, I knew ye as well as he that made ye. Why hear you, my masters: was it for me to kill the heir apparent?
>
> (2.4.258-9)

Unfortunately, it is only too true that Falstaff knows the Prince no better than "he that made ye," his own father. But the "open and apparent shame" which the Gadshill adventure was intended to fix upon Falstaff is thus turned instead upon the Prince himself.

In the self-assured vein of his soliloquy, Hal compared himself to the sun,

> That when he please again to be himself,
> Being wanted, he may be more wondered at.
>
> (1.2.193-4)

Ironically, this "policy" of withholding oneself from the public eye to be the more admired is the very same argument which his father uses to reproach Hal for keeping low company (and the irony is doubled when we recall that in *Richard II* it was this Bolingbroke who courted popular favour in an undignified fashion: "Off went his bonnet to an oyster wench"). The premises of Hal's self-justification are thus invalidated in the interview scene, and it is a much chastened Prince who now promises in the plainest terms,

> I shall hereafter, my thrice-gracious lord,
> Be more myself.
>
> (3.2.92-3)

On Shrewsbury field, the King shamefully lends his name and identity to others to protect himself in battle, and when Douglas encounters him and supposes he is addressing yet another decoy,

> What art thou
> That counterfeit'st the person of a king?
>
> (5.3.27-8)

the question cuts deeply into Bolingbroke's dubious claim to the title. By contrast, Hal's decisive encounter with his namesake begins with a declaration of his true identity:

> *Hotspur.*
> If I mistake not, thou art Harry Monmouth.
> *Prince.*
> Thou speak'st as if I would deny my name.
> *Hotspur.*
> My name is Harry Percy.
> *Prince.*
> Why then I see
> A very valiant rebel of the name.
> I am the Prince of Wales.
>
> (5.3.59-63)

Seen on the stage, Hal is quite literally now in his true colours, bearing over his armour the heraldic insignia of the heir apparent. This transformation was earlier described in what are surely the play's most magnificent lines, spoken by Vernon in answer to Hotspur's scornful enquiry about "the nimble-footed madcap Prince of Wales, And his comrades that daff'd the world aside And bid it pass":

> All furnish'd, all in arms;
> All plum'd like estridges, that with the wind
> Bated like eagles having lately bath'd;
> Glittering in golden coats, like images;
> As full of spirit as the month of May,
> As gorgeous as the sun at midsummer;
> Wanton as youthful goats, wild as young bulls.
> I saw young Harry with his beaver on,
> His cushes on his thighs, gallantly arm'd,
> Rise from the ground like feathered Mercury,
> And vaulted with such ease into his seat
> As if an angel dropp'd down from the clouds
> To turn and wind a fiery Pegasus,
> And witch the world with noble horsemanship.
>
> (4.1.97-110)

All the "wild" and "wanton" energies of youth, associated in legend with the "madcap Prince," are here beautifully assimilated to the imagery of natural vitality, and transcended by the picture of the rider on his horse, the traditional emblem of disciplined energy and good government. Hal has "put on the new man."

IV

Hal's tribute to Hotspur, also reported by Vernon,

> He gave you all the duties of a man,
> Trimm'd up your praises with a princely tongue;
> Spoke your deservings like a chronicle,
>
> (5.2.56-8)

reminds us that the chronicle, the record of history, is the final arbiter of reputation. The chronicler himself, "redeeming time," gives honourable men their due, restoring them into the good thoughts of the world again. Shakespeare's treatment of Hal's "reformation" in terms of men's judgements of him rather than any sudden moral conversion on his part reflects his attitude to the stories of the Prince's reprobate youth as unauthoritative material, distinct from the authentic matter of historical record. The very existence of these stories must have demonstrated to Shakespeare how prone are men's minds to invent and credit fiction and to entertain conjecture—a phenomenon which as poet and dramatist he naturally exploited, and which throughout his work was obviously one of his deepest and most abiding interests.

As Vernon says, the Prince is "So much misconstrued in his wantonness" (5.2.69). The lines in which Hal protests to his father,

> in reproof of many tales devis'd,
> Which oft the ear of greatness needs must hear,
> By smiling pick-thanks and base newsmongers,
>
> (3.2.23-5)

follows Holinshed's account of the supposedly riotous youth as a fabrication, so many "tales" and "slanderous reports":

> Whilest these things were a dooing in France, the lord Henrie prince of Wales, eldest sonne to king Henrie, got knowledge that certeine of his fathers servants were busie to give informations against him, whereby discord might arise betwixt him and his father: for they put into the kings head, not onelie what evil rule (according to the course of youth) the prince kept to the offense of manie: but also what great resort of people came to his house, so that the court was nothing furnished with such a traine as dailie followed the prince. These tales brought no small suspicion into the kings head, least his sonne would presume to usurpe the crowne, he being yet alive, through which suspicious gelousie, it was perceived that he favoured not his sonne, as in times past he had doone.
>
> The Prince sore offended with such persons, as by slanderous reports, sought not onelie to spot his good

name abrode in the realme, but to sowe discord also betwixt him and his father, wrote his letters into everie part of the realme, to reproove all such slanderous devises of those that sought his discredit.[9]

Even the word "pick-thanks" is taken from Holinshed: "Thus were the father and sonne reconciled, betwixt whome the said pick-thanks had sowne division."[10]

"Let no man deceive you with vain words": it is certainly appropriate that in the tavern world, which has attached itself to history by "slanderous report," Falstaff should be the embodiment of lies, "gross as a mountain, open, palpable." In his account of the men in buckram, we see the very process by which history is translated into fiction, and his "play extempore" bears the same relationship to Shakespeare's history play as the unlicensed tales of the wild Prince do to the authentic versions of the chronicle. Falstaff habitually takes the Lord's name in vain; he also takes in vain all titles of honour: they are "a word," no more.

It is supremely ironical, but presumably a sheer coincidence, that a play so deeply concerned with the "commodity of good names" and "vocation" should have run into difficulties over the name and reputation of its chief slanderer. When Shakespeare redeemed Oldcastle from the posthumous ignominy of his stage identity, he baptised the fat knight after the cowardly figure of Sir John Fastolfe, who had made a brief début in the poet's first history play, and was there condemned as one who

> Doth but usurp the sacred name of knight,
> Profaning this most honourable order.
>
> (*The First Part of King Henry VI*, 4.1.42-3)

Even this reincarnation was to provoke some complaint that Shakespeare had taken another good name in vain, and later in the seventeenth century Thomas Fuller tried to do for Sir John Fastolfe what Shakespeare had done for the Prince, to rescue him from ill-fame:

> Now as I am glad that *Sir John Oldcastle* is *put out*, so I am sorry that *Sir John Fastolfe* is *put in*, to relieve his memory in this base service, to be the *anvil* for every *dull wit* to strike upon. Nor is our Comedian excusable, by some alteration of his name, writing him *Sir John Falstafe* (and making him the *property* of *pleasure* for King *Henry* the fifth, to abuse) seeing the *vicinity* of sounds intrench on the memory of *that worthy Knight*, and few do heed the *inconsiderable difference* in spelling of their name.
>
> (*The Worthies of England*, 1662)[11]

The difference in spelling, however, is sufficient to achieve a certain propriety in the first syllable of Falstaff's name.

Hal keeps his promise to call Hotspur to "so strict account That he shall render every glory up," and in his defeat Hotspur surrenders his "proud titles" to the Prince. But what is the nature of the honour so won by Hal at the end of Part One? There is little glorification of Hal's victory; it is rather the hollowness of Hotspur's conception of honour that is stressed. Hal's generosity to his dead enemy is certainly noble:

> Thy ignominy sleep with thee in the grave
> But not remembered in thy epitaph.
>
> (5.3.100-1)

But far from coveting the admiration of men's thoughts at the end of the play, Hal is contemptuously acquiescent in Falstaff's demand to be given the official credit for Hotspur's fall:

> For my part, if a lie may do thee grace,
> I'll gild it with the happiest terms I have.
>
> (5.3.156-7)

The Prince, one feels, is more genuinely concerned about his personal relationship with his father, and more deeply affected by the pointless death of the young Hotspur; he is content to let the rest go, just as he orders Douglas to be set free without claiming ransom. Hal has come a long way since the desire of the soliloquy to "show more goodly and attract more eyes."

In the eyes of true judgement (and in the theatre Shakespeare flatters us with this vantage point), such a refusal to court public esteem will commend itself all the more favourably. "Nothing confutes me but eyes, and nobody sees me," says Falstaff, even as we watch him desecrate the body of Hotspur. If honour lives only in men's eyes and opinions, it is a very ambiguous and unstable commodity, as Hal has now learned:

> An habitation giddy and unsure
> Hath he that buildeth on the vulgar heart
>
> (Part Two, 1.3.89-90)

When the days are evil, where does true judgement of honour reside? This, however, is where Part Two takes up the story.

V

Lord Cobham, and Thomas Fuller too, might well have turned against the poet himself Rumour's words in the Prologue to Part Two:

> Upon my tongues continual slanders ride,
> The which in every language I pronounce,
> Stuffing the ears of men with false reports.
>
> (6-8)

Indeed, with an aggressive swipe worthy of Ben Jonson, and striking the discomfiting note which is characteristic of this play, Rumour identifies "the still-discordant wavering multitude" with his present theatre-audience:

> But what need I thus
> My well-known body to anatomize
> Among my household?
>
> (20-2)

Here in the theatre Rumour recognizes his home, the place where men's judgements and imaginations are exercised upon the illusions they see and hear. Rumour is the presiding spirit of Part Two, and Falstaff is his Apostle: "Lord, Lord, how subject we old men are to this vice of lying" (3.2.294). But the course of the play is to fulfil the words of that other Apostle, "that ye cast of, concerning the conversation in time past, the olde man, which is corrupt through the deceivable lusts . . . and put on the new man":

> Wherefore cast of lying, & speake everie man trueth unto his neighbour: for we are members one of another.
>
> (*Ephesians*, 4:22-5)

With Hotspur gone, the prevailing mood of Part Two is set by its old men: Northumberland, Falstaff, the Lord Chief Justice, that other Justice, Shallow, and of course the King himself. There is much talk of sickness and death, and the time is burdened with memories of the past and anticipations of things to come. As the Archbishop of York says, "The commonwealth is sick of their own choice . . . What trust is in these times? . . . Past and to come seems best; things present worst" (1.3.86-108). Even more than was the case in Part One, the days are evil, and "we are time's subjects" (1.3.110).

Hal's reappearance in the tavern, after his personal triumph at the end of Part One, is a reversion that defeats our expectations, in a play full of false anticipation. The "weary" Prince who makes his entrance in 2.2. is a very different figure from the buoyant confident youth who promised to redeem the time in Part One, and who there seemed about to "witch the world with noble horsemanship." He now appears oppressed, in accord with the disenchantment of this old men's world, and bitter in his self-reproach. "What a disgrace is it to me to remember thy name," he says unflatteringly to Poins, whose equally bald rejoinder raises the very question in our minds concerning Hal's apparent relapse after his achievement on Shrewsbury field:

> How ill it follows, after you have laboured so hard, you should talk so idly! Tell me, how many good young princes would do so, their fathers being so sick as yours at this time is?
>
> (2.2.27-30)

Stung by the reproof coming from such a quarter, Hal's reply goes to the heart of the play's concern with slanderous rumour, opinion, and men's judgements:

> *Prince.*
> Marry, I tell thee it is not meet that I should be sad, now my father is sick; albeit I could tell to thee—as to one it pleases me, for fault of a better to call my friend—I could be sad and sad indeed too.
> *Poins.*
> Very hardly upon such a subject.
> *Prince.*
> By this hand, thou thinkest me as far in the devil's book as thou and Falstaff for obduracy and persistency: let the end try the man. But I tell thee my heart bleeds inwardly that my father is so sick; and keeping such vile company as thou art hath in reason taken from me all ostentation of sorrow.
> *Poins.*
> The reason?
> *Prince.*
> What wouldst thou think of me if I should weep?
> *Poins.*
> I would think thee a most princely hypocrite.
> *Prince.*
> It would be every man's thought; and thou art a blessed fellow to think as every man thinks.
>
> (2.2.37-54)

With the death of the King imminent, a sudden display of grief from his successor would be construed as hollow indeed, particularly in one whose former estrangement from the court was on every tongue of Rumour. The very depth of Hal's genuine feelings for his father, far more than a mere politic concern of the Prince for his reputation, cannot tolerate the prospect of such an imputation being put upon the most intimate relationship of his life. But this is indeed what happens later in the play, when Hal's misprision of his father's sleep leads to the King's misprision of Hal's motives for removing the crown:

> *Prince.*
> I never thought to hear you speak again.
> *King.*
> Thy wish was father, Harry, to that thought.
> I stay too long by thee, I weary thee.
> Dost thou so hunger for mine empty chair
> That thou wilt needs invest thee with my honours
> Before thy hour be ripe?
>
> (4.5.92-7)

In Part One, Hal's vow to redeem the time signified the need to recover an essentially personal esteem, to be recognised for what he is, "heir apparent." In this sequel, the course of time is to lead him, not to his true name and vocation, but to a new name and vocation as King. Now "redeeming time" signifies a duty to the nation as a whole, for the time is out of joint, and the sick commonwealth must be rejuvenated, the divided realm reunited as "members one of another":

> *King.*
> Then you perceive the body of our kingdom
> How foul it is; what rank diseases grow,
> And with what danger, near the heart of it.
> *Warwick.*
> It is but as a body yet distempered
> Which to his former strength may be restored
> With good advice and little medicine.
>
> (3.1.38-43)

The Hal of Part One fulfilled his vow by defeating young Hotspur; in Part Two, it is the old man who must be cast off, though not in the sense that the King suspects.

"You that are old consider not the capacities of us that are young," as Falstaff says (1.2.165). The old indeed totally misjudge the young, and in harbouring very similar expectations of Hal, one in fear and the other in hope, both the King and Falstaff misconstrue the times to come:

> The blood weeps from my heart when I do shape
> In forms imaginary, th' ungirded days
> And rotten times that you shall look upon
> When I am sleeping with my ancestors.
> For when his headstrong riot hath no curb,
> When rage and hot blood are his counsellors,
> When means and lavish manners meet together,
> O, with what wings shall his affections fly
> Towards fronting peril and oppos'd decay!
>
> (4.4.58-66)

But Hal's youth has no more "headstrong riot" in it than the youth of Justice Shallow: "Jesu, Jesu, the mad days that I have spent! and to see how many of my old acquaintance are dead!" (3.2.32-3). Time past and future lives in "forms imaginary," and Shallow's wonderful reminiscences ("every third word a lie," says Falstaff) exemplify how natural it is to turn history into mythology and legend.

The consciousness of time in Part Two is developed into the idea of history itself, as the play looks both before and after, through the long memories of old men and through their anticipations of the future. In this respect the dialogue between the King and his wise counseller Warwick in 3.1. is of central significance. Reflecting ruefully upon the former allegiances of Richard's time between men now bitter enemies, the King sees "the revolution of the times" as merely the flux and mutability of Nature, in which man is helplessly and unpredictably tossed and turned by "necessity":

> how chances mock,
> And changes fill the cup of alteration
> With divers liquors! O, if this were seen,
> The happiest youth, viewing his progress through,
> What perils past, what crosses to ensue,
> Would shut the book and sit him down and die.
>
> (3.1.51-6)

In his reply Warwick advances a different conception of history, not as some impersonal, inscrutable decree in "the book of fate," but as an essentially human process, analogous to Nature's laws of organic growth rather than to lawless mutability:

> There is a history in all men's lives,
> Figuring the natures of the times deceas'd;
> The which observ'd a man may prophesy,
> With a near aim, of the main chance of things
> As yet not come to life, who in their seeds
> And weak beginning lie intreasured.
> Such things become the hatch and brood of time;
> And by the necessary form of this . . .
>
> (3.1.80-7)

Warwick's point of view lends quite a different significance to the idea of historical "necessity"; instead of being mere victims of blind circumstance, as the King supposes, men can and must direct their lives by reaping advantage from experience. It is Warwick who later correctly prophesies that

> The Prince will, in the perfectness of time,
> Cast off his followers; and their memory
> Shall as a pattern or a measure live,
> By which his Grace must mete the lives of other,
> Turning past evils to advantages.
>
> (4.4.74-8)

Hal's progress through both plays demonstrates that life is not "time's fool," as Hotspur believed, but a meaningful and purposeful relationship between past and future. What will appear to Hal's contemporaries (and to legend) as a sudden and unpredictable "revolution of the times" has been presented to us a wise use of time on Hal's part, and also a process of developing wisdom and insight from the moment of that over-simplified, over-confident view of things expressed in the soliloquy at the beginning of Part One. Hal is to inherit a usurped crown and its attendant evils, that have driven his father into his grave, and he is to succeed, not by "indirect crook'd ways" but by the "plain and right" inheritance of the "hatch and brood of time" from "the times deceas'd." Youth does not usurp age, although age may often suppose so, and feel itself cast off. In the larger design of the play, and of Nature, time is redeemed as youth matures, and assumes the burdens which age can carry no more. Shakespeare's reading of history in Part Two, like that of Warwick, is related to the wider perspectives of natural processes.

When at his father's death Hal puts on the new man with "this new and gorgeous garment, majesty," he is royally proclaimed by a stage-direction which indicates his change of name, habit, and company: "*Enter* KING HENRY THE FIFTH, *attended.*" In losing his father he has also cast off the old man:

> And, Princes all, believe me, I beseech you,
> My father is gone wild into his grave,
> For in his tomb lie my affections;
> And with his spirits sadly I survive,
> To mock the expectation of the world,
> To frustrate prophecies, and to raze out
> Rotten opinion, who hath writ me down
> After my seeming.
>
> (5.2.122-9)

Such sad mockery of expectation is seen in the rejection of Falstaff, which we have been led to anticipate from the very start, but which we actually witness with a feeling of regret, for in banishing the old man, as in burying his father, Hal has also cast off his youth.

Notes

1. Richmond Noble, *Shakespeare's Biblical Knowledge* (1935), p. 169. An indispensable but far from complete treatment of the subject.

2. See Introduction to *The First Part of King Henry IV* (new Arden Shakespeare), edited by A. R. Humphreys (1960), pp. xxxix-xlii.

3. Quotations of Shakespeare's text are from *The Complete Works*, edited by Peter Alexander (1951).

4. Quotations from the Bible are from *The Geneva Bible: A Facsimile of the 1560 Edition* (Madison, Milwaukee, and London, 1969).

5. "I know you not" is also the Bridegroom's reply to the foolish virgins (*Matthew*, 25:12).

6. "The eye of man hath not heard, the ear of man hath not seen, man's hand is not able to taste, his tongue to conceive, nor his heart to report, what my dream was" (4.1.20-2). Cf. *I Corinthians*, 2:9.

7. A well-known Elizabethan tribute to the power of the history play to restore the dead to life and so to redeem the time is Thomas Nashe's allusion to Shakespeare's *Henry VI Part One* in *Pierce Penilesse His Supplication to the Divell* (1592):

> How would it have ioyed braue *Talbot* (the terror of the French) to thinke that after he had lyne two hundred yeares in his Tombe, hee should triumphe againe on the Stage, and haue his bones new embalmed with the teares of ten thousand spectators at least, (at seuerall times) who, in the Tragedian that represents his person, imagine they behold him fresh bleeding?

Quoted in E. K. Chambers, *William Shakespeare: A Study of Facts and Problems* (2 vols., 1930), II.188.

8. Paul A. Jorgensen, *Redeeming Shakespeare's Words* (Berkeley and Los Angeles, 1962), pp. 52-69.

9. Humphreys, *ed. cit.,* p. 177.

10. *ibid*, p. 179.

11. Quoted in Chambers, II.244.

Robert G. Hunter (essay date 1978)

SOURCE: "Shakespeare's Comic Sense as It Strikes Us Today: Falstaff and the Protestant Ethic," in *Henry the Fourth Parts I and II: Critical Essays,* edited by David Bevington, Garland Publishing, 1986, 349-58.

[*In the following essay, originally published in 1978, Hunter theorizes that the rejection of Falstaff in the* Henry IV *plays dramatizes the victory of the Protestant ethic, presenting the evolution of Prince Hal as a triumph of the principles represented by this moral code.*]

If there are such things as antibodies (and I am told that there are), then let there be such things as antiembodiments and let Falstaff be one. Let him also be an embodiment (there is plenty of room), for Falstaff embodies a large part of my subject, Shakespeare's comic sense. Simultaneously he antiembodies the Protestant ethic. What he is, it is not. What it is, he is not. Did Shakespeare's comic sense serve the body politic by generating Falstaff in an attempt to immunize comparatively Merrie England against those foreign organisms, the Puritan Saints? If so, the attempt failed, and Shakespeare knew it would. The Henriad, I will maintain but not demonstrate, dramatizes, in the rejection of Falstaff, the victory of the Protestant ethic, presenting that social triumph as a psychological event, the decision of Henry the Fifth to labor in his vocation, to do his duty in that royal station to which it pleased God to call him.

Thus Falstaff came into being, almost four centuries ago, during the first insurgency of the Protestant ethic and, perhaps, in response to it. Today we are celebrating the bicentennial of one of that ethic's more elaborate offspring. And do we not sense today that we are living through the decadence and disappearance of the ethic, that we watch going down the great drain of history what Shakespeare saw coming up it? What will take the ethic's place? That seems to me one of today's more nagging questions, and I haven't the vaguest notion of its answer. But we might explore the question by consulting the comic sense of our particular oracle. Let us have a look first at the ethic and then at Falstaff as antiembodiment of it.

The phenomenon that I claim Falstaff antiembodies is authoritatively described and accounted for by Max Weber in *The Protestant Ethic and the Spirit of Capitalism.* Weber identifies the main characteristic of that ethic as "worldly asceticism . . . a fundamental antagonism to sensuous culture of all kinds." He sees the ethic as the result of two theological causes, one Lutheran and one Calvinist. The Lutheran cause is the "conception of the calling." In reacting against the monastic ideal Luther did not entirely repudiate the worthiness of ascetic self-denial. What he did was to replace the insistence upon withdrawal from the world with a "valuation of fulfilment of duty in worldly affairs as the highest form which the moral activity of the individual could assume." To this exaltation of the importance of laboring in one's vocation was added the Calvinist notion of absolute predestination. If you believe that humanity has been irretrievably divided into the elect and the reprobate, then it becomes a matter of some importance to convince yourself that you are a member of the right group. "In order to attain that confidence intense worldly activity is recommended as the most suitable means. It and it alone disperses religious doubts and gives certainty of grace." As a paradoxical result, Protestantism, which proclaims that works are useless as a means of gaining salvation, ends by finding them "indispensable as a means . . . of getting rid of the fear of damnation." "Getting rid of fear" is a key phrase for an understanding of the psychological power of the Protestant ethic and of Falstaff as a compendious alternative to that ethic. Hope of eternal life gets rid of the fear of death. Faith in our election gets rid of the fear of eternal damnation, and contemplating the success of our worldly activity ratifies our faith in election. Success is evidence of salvation. The Protestant ethic is a superb strategy for getting rid of those fears which are inherent in the human condition, fears of time, of death, and of damnation. It is one of the greatest in what Freud calls "the great series of methods devised by the mind of man for evading the compulsion to suffer."

Falstaff is an anthology of such methods. I count and will try to define five, taking them in the order Shakespeare presents them to us. The first I label "living within appetite," the second "play," the third "success," the fourth "carnival," and the last, "hope." Of these the first, second, and fourth are in direct opposition to the ideals and practices of the Protestant ethic. The third and the last are distorted imitations of Protestant ethic methods and I will call them serious parodies, though it makes me uneasy to claim that anything about Falstaff is serious.

The first of Falstaff's methods is the most effective and also the most difficult to sustain. It is common to all of us, originates in infancy, and antedates the fear of time itself. Our first clock is appetite, and time first presents itself to us as that which intervenes between appetite and its satisfaction, and its rebirth. The time we thus perceive through appetite is circular in nature, a time of eternal return. A day is that which separates breakfast from breakfast. There is nothing to fear in time thus perceived as circular, as the element in which pleasure, the satisfaction of appetite, takes place. And much in the reality we begin to perceive outside our bodies appears to confirm the truth of time's circularity. The sun also ariseth, and the sun goeth down and hasteth to the place where he arose. Spring, summer, autumn, winter—spring. Not much of this appetitive, circular time has passed, however, before its passing forces upon us the knowledge that our understanding of time is incomplete. The bodies whose appetites we have satisfied change permanently. Today is not yesterday despite the similarity in breakfasts. Summer returns but last summer will never return. Time, we find, is rectilinear, the shortest possible distance between birth and death. With that discovery our fear of time is born, and our minds must devise methods for evading the suffering in that fear. The method of the Protestant ethic is to glorify time's rectilinearity, to proclaim time the element not of pleasure, but of duty, of the worldly achievement that ratifies faith in our election. This, however, is not Falstaff's way.

Henry IV, Part One opens with the King doing desperate battle against the implacability of rectilinear time. "Find we a time" is his plea. A time for peace, for the establishment of order, for the crusade, the achievement that will expiate Richard's murder and convince the King that his soul is saved after all. The second scene begins when Falstaff first waddles into our consciousness on the line, "Now, Hal, what time of day is it, lad?" a question whose total banality inspires Hal to a rather wonderful tirade on the question: "What a devil hast thou to do with the time of the day?", a question that Hal himself proceeds to answer: "Unless hours were cups of sack, and minutes capons, and clocks the tongues of bawds, and dials the signs of leaping-houses . . ." Hal's conditional answers his interrogative. Falstaff's clock is Falstaff's paunch and the time it tells is circular, revolving from thirst to sack to thirst to sack. From hunger to capon to hunger to capon. From lust to wench to lust to fair, hot wench. Falstaff copes with the fact of time's linearity by stoutly denying it, by doing his best to live his life within the circular time of appetite. Such a life would be a life without fear of time, but of course no moderately conscious life can be so lived. It's not just that capons, sack, and wenches refuse to arrive on schedule—though that is annoying enough. The rectilinearity of time is constantly being forced upon our unwilling minds. Even our best friends are in the habit of saying things like "gallows," and when we try tactfully to change the subject to something pleasant like "a most sweet wench," they refuse to cooperate and we end up depressed, "as melancholy as a gib cat, or a lugged bear."

When this happens to Falstaff, he moves to his second strategy. He answers the reproaches of his superego with the exhilarating language of play—purely verbal play at first. Falstaff copes with melancholy by playing with Hal at finding similes for it: a gib cat, a lugged bear, an old lion, a lover's lute, the drone of a Lincolnshire bagpipe, a hare, the melancholy of Moor-ditch. Having thus put the forces of his conscience on the defensive, he proceeds to polish them off by employing his favorite play method, role-playing. Falstaff has the ability to make anything appear ridiculous by pretending to be it. Here he represses his own tendencies to contrition by pretending to be contrite: "But Hal, I prithee trouble me no more with vanity . . . thou hast done much harm upon me, Hal, God forgive thee for it: before I knew thee, Hal, I knew nothing, and now am I, if a man should speak truly, little better than one of the wicked." What Poins calls "Monsieur Remorse" is Falstaff's first and in some ways best role. Nowhere does Shakespeare make it clearer how the humorous man copes with the certainty of death and the possibility of damnation. By parodying his own fears, Falstaff answers the challenge Hamlet gives the skull of Yorick: he makes us laugh at that. But of course it is not just himself that Falstaff is mocking here. Monsieur Remorse is pretty clearly a Puritan gentleman. He is one of the Protestant Saints whom the Prince of Wales has so far misled as to make him doubt his own election and fear that his conduct indicts him as little better than one of the reprobate. Not only does Falstaff's role-playing purge him of his own melancholy, it accuses the Protestant ethic of being a role that the Puritan thinks (or pretends to think) he is playing in earnest. But it is not only the specific mockery, the parochial satire that the Protestant ethic would find offensive. Falstaff's roles release him from the depressing confines of reality and that, unless done religiously, will not do. Play in all its forms, from morris-dancing to the great Globe itself, is an inadmissible alternative to laboring soberly in one's vocation. But Falstaff, *homo ludens*, goes on playing. On Gadshill and in the tavern his roles increase and multiply: the young desperado ripping off the fat chuffs who batten on the commonwealth ("They hate us youth"); the battered survivor of a better time who sees a virile world of courage and honor among thieves degenerating, disintegrating around him: "Go thy ways, old Jack, die when thou wilt—if manhood, good manhood, be not forgot upon the face of the earth, then am I a shotten herring . . ."; and Sir John Fairbanks, Sr., driving before him two, four, seven, nine, eleven men in buckram; and finally, of course, the King, the Prince, himself. So Falstaff's Protean mind copes with itself, represses and escapes its fears by becoming not dying Jack Falstaff but anything and everything, turning all things to laughter.

But again this is not enough. On the morning after the night before the body whose appetites have been so assiduously satisfied informs the Protean mind that time is rectilinear and he is but Falstaff and a man: "Do I not bate? Do I not dwindle? Why, my skin hangs about me like an old lady's loose gown. I am withered like an old apple-john." And we get a reprise of Monsieur Remorse, rather more Romanist in his second version, I think. Clearly, sterner measures than play are called for. Living in appetite is the strategy of the infant. Play is the strategy of the child. Falstaff is never such a fool as to put away childish things. He knows he needs all the strategies he can get. While retaining the two I have already identified, he moves to those of the mature man and specifically to an antiversion of the Protestant ethic itself. Having parodied the remorse of the Puritan, he now more seriously parodies its results: the determination to labor in one's vocation.

When, in their first scene, Hal interrupts the finer flights of Monsieur Remorse to ask Jack Falstaff where they should take a purse tomorrow, he gets the reply, "'Zounds, where thou wilt, lad, I'll make one." Upon which the prince observes, "I see a good amendment of life in thee, from praying to purse-taking." Monsieur Remorse's rejoinder is a model of Christian forbearance: "Why, Hal, 'tis my vocation, Hal, 'tis no sin for a man to labor in his vocation." If one wished to be unfair to the Protestant ethic (and I do), one could say that Weber's description of the shift in Christian morality from the medieval exaltation of the monastic ideal to the seventeenth-century Puritan enshrinement of capitalist worldly asceticism is encapsulated in Hal's phrase "from praying to purse-taking." Falstaff's methods in purse-taking are not commercial and therefore his calling is not lawful. But he is not really a highwayman either. The night's exploits on Gadshill are closer to play than to vocation, an especially exciting game of cops-and-robbers. Ordinarily and whenever possible, Falstaff combines the crafts of the professional soldier and the confidenceman. He combines them very successfully. The £300 that he extorts from reluctant draftees compares favorably with the £250 Shakespeare is estimated to have made in a good year and very favorably indeed with the £20 annual salary of the Stratford schoolmaster. And Falstaff is a success on the battlefield as well. He does his duty by leading or somehow chivvying his soldiers into a position where they can be thoroughly peppered, and then he distinguishes himself by stabbing the corpse of Hotspur in the thigh. Does he expect anyone to believe that he and not Hal has killed Harry Percy? It doesn't matter, for there are distinct orders of success in lying. A liar may succeed because he is believed or because he cannot be contradicted. Falstaff is content with the more modest degree, and thus he achieves one of those reputations, common enough in fields other than the military, for having done something or other at some time or other.

The result of these successful labors is the Sir John Falstaff of *Henry the Fourth, Part Two:* Jack Falstaff with his familiars, John with his brothers and sisters, and Sir John with all Europe. Such are the secular rewards of laboring in one's vocation—self-fulfillment and a sense of one's identity confirmed by the respect of the community. And there is no strategy more successful than success for concealing from us our participation in the common human condition. For the Puritan, of course, the rewards of such laboring also include the conviction of one's election and a consequent faith in one's eternal salvation. Falstaff does not go that far, not by some distance. Indeed, his profession is an extension of his play. He has added a new dimension to his role-playing and has begun to pretend really to be what he is pretending to be. To what extent that makes him different from the rest of us, including the ethical Protestants, I must leave it to the subtler masters of the dramaturgical school of social psychology to decide. My point is that as a technique for dealing with our fears of time and death, becoming Sir John with all Europe works very well. Monsieur Remorse is no longer needed to repress the natterings of the superego. Being Sir John is enough.

Or almost enough, for again the body reminds us of our inevitable predicament. The owner of Sir John's urine may have more diseases than he knows for, but Sir John is aware of a good number of them: "A pox of this gout! or a gout of this pox! for the one or the other plays the rogue with my great toe." That great toe, long invisible to its owner's eye, is transmitting the body's tedious message: you cannot conquer time. Falstaff's fourth method for jamming that communication is related to all of the previous three. Carnival is an attempt to regain occasionally and temporarily the bliss of living within appetitive time. It is that period which society sets aside for sanctioned play, for humor, wit, and role-playing. It is the necessary holiday in which we may rest from doing our duties in that station to which it has pleased God to call us. Except, of course, that the Puritans recognized no such necessity. They were opposed to Carnival, but they were equally opposed to Lent—not because they found its lugubrious self-denials distasteful (though they knew there was no merit in them) but because they thought it should be Lent all the year round. Once more, Sir John embodies a different point of view. After a hard day's labor devoted to evading the Lord Chief Justice, placating Mistress Quickly, devising methods for bilking Master Dommelton the slops-maker, and avoiding the importunities of a dozen sweating captains—after such a day, the warrior deserves his repose. Wine, women, and song, sack and canary, Doll Tearsheet and Sneak's noise—all the components of an ideal saturnalia are present in the great festive scene of *Henry IV,*

Part Two. But Shakespeare is here aiming to present us with the real as well as the ideal, and real saturnalia has indecorous results: vomit, urine, syphilis, and violence. Our women enter talking of wine and its effects and when asked how she is doing now, Doll replies, "Better than I was—hem!" That "hem," I suspect, is Shakespeare's suggestion to his boy-actor that he should indicate audibly but nonverbally why Doll is doing better than she was. Sir John enters with song: "When Arthur first in court," and urine: "Empty the jordan." A bout of wit follows between Doll and Falstaff on the subject of who is responsible for whose venereal disease. The episode with Pistol brings us to violence and Sir John's valor inspires Doll to ask her little, tidy, Bartholomew boar-pig when he will leave fighting a-days and foining a-nights and begin to patch up his old body for heaven. *Carpe diem* is a motto of carnival, but one of the things we ask of saturnalia is that it make us forget why it is that we want to seize the day. Doll's comment is malapropos and her most flattering busses cannot make Falstaff forget the consequences of linear time: "I am old. I am old." And finally, in spite of the fun and games with Hal and Poins, it looks as if Shakespeare were going to let Falstaff be frustrated by age and time and by the demands of his vocation, for "The man of action is called on" and must leave the sweetest morsel of the night unplucked. Farewells must be said: "Well, fare thee well. I have known thee these twenty-nine years, come peascod-time, but an honester and truer-hearted man. . . ." I thoroughly agree with the Arden editor's note on peascod-time: "The precision with which Mistress Quickly dates a 29-year-old meeting is entirely touching." Just how entirely that is, however, can be understood only if one apprehends the bawdy of "peascod," and to do that one must reverse the syllables. Doing so emphasizes that the time that finally triumphs here is appetitive and circular. Bardolph reenters with a command: "Bid Mistress Tearsheet come to my master." Poins was wrong: desire has not outlived performance. Codpiece time comes round again and Plump Jack lives!

This is a heartening conclusion to a brilliant scene and yet we suspect Shakespeare of suggesting that Falstaff is coming to the end of his strategies. This suspicion is strengthened by the King's magnificent speeches in the next scene on the book of fate, the revolution of the times, and the necessity of meeting one's necessities. The scene that follows informs us that old Double is dead and John of Gaunt, who loved him well, is dead and death is certain, very sure, all shall die, and that the one way left of coping with that perception seems to be to let one's shallow mind wander quickly to the price of a good yoke of bullocks at Stamford Fair. Yet Falstaff continues to labor cheerfully in his fraudulent vocation, and it is not until act 5, scene 3 that we discover that he has been doing battle with time and the prospect of death by employing one strategy more than the four we have already examined. Pistol interrupts senility's saturnalia in Gloucestershire with news of yet another death: the old king is dead as nail in door. Falstaff, whom Shallow and Silence have kept quietly amused to this point, now explodes with excitement: "I am Fortune's steward . . . I know the young King is sick for me . . . the laws of England are at my commandment . . . woe to my Lord Chief Justice!" This is the revelation of a life illusion. Since the first time we saw him in the second scene of the Henriad, Falstaff has never repeated to Hal or us his speculations on what will happen when the Prince becomes the King. We realize that he much overestimates Hal's devotion to sack and laughter, but we have small reason to know, until we find out, that Falstaff thinks Hal's accession will put the laws of England at Sir John's commandment. What here stands revealed is Falstaff's last strategy, his secular, temporal version of a religious faith in one's election to eternal salvation. Falstaff copes with his condition by living in hope, as which of us does not. We must cling to our faith in that intervening event (the doctorate, tenure, the professorship, retirement) which will with millennial effect transform the quality of our existence. Delusive hope was included in Pandora's box lest we should despair and destroy ourselves. What kills Sir John is the destruction of his delusive hope and the consequent knowledge that his future does not exist.

He would have died anyway. Falstaff, like everybody else, is killed by death. But that death is designed by Shakespeare to show us something. The King kills Falstaff's heart, but what impels the King to do so is the desire to do his royal duty by laboring in his vocation. I lack the time to demonstrate why I think Henry of Monmouth stands for the Protestant ethic but I believe that, consciously or not, Shakespeare has transposed into his early-fifteenth-century action the uncompleted spiritual and political struggles of the 1590s. Hal's psychomachia is a battle between Carnival and Lent, and Falstaff is on the losing side. Hal and the Protestant Ethic reject Falstaff, but Shakespeare does not reject Falstaff nor does he reject Hal for rejecting Falstaff.

Falstaff defines the Protestant Ethic by being what it isn't, but also by being a different variety of what it is: a means of coping with the fears engendered by the realities of the human condition. The ethic defeats Falstaff because of the superior strength that derives from the religious faith on which it is based—a faith that enables it to cope with our fears by denying that the realities that inspire them are ultimately real, by asserting that linear time will give way to eternity and that death is a transition to eternal life. Falstaff's being what he is, however, poses a great question to the ethic's answer: may not the ethic's faith be as illusory a strategy as any of Falstaff's, finally a form of delusive hope itself? Hal, in accepting his necessary form, must reject Falstaff because the Protestant ethical form cannot encompass the question Falstaff poses. But Shakespeare's art can and does. It encompasses, as always, question and answer and the questioning of the answer. And the questioning of the questioning, for what is the Falstaff action but a demonstration of the inevitable inadequacy of the strategies of which his character is composed? Shakespeare's sense, whether comical or tragical or tragical-comical-historical-pastoral, seems to me to be always interrogative. For me the great thing about Shakespeare's art is its ability simultaneously to reveal and accept our inadequacies, above all the inadequacy of our answers. The motto carved on the temple of our particular oracle is, "Your answers questioned here."

Jonathan Crewe (essay date 1990)

SOURCE: "Reforming Prince Hal: The Sovereign Inheritor in *2 Henry IV*," in *Renaissance Drama*, Vol. 21, 1990, pp. 225-42.

[*In the following essay, Crewe disputes critical thinking that denies substantive reformation in Prince Hal's character. Instead, Crewe proposes, the subject of reform is continuously revisited in both parts of* Henry IV, *making it difficult to define successful reformation in the political context of the plays.*]

The "matter of Hal's redemption," as A. R. Humphreys, the Arden editor of *2 Henry IV,* calls it, may now seem too stale or tainted for further consideration.[1] It has certainly been discussed at length, and to go on talking about it now is to risk the charge of reviving the ideological discourse of the centered, sovereign, masculine subject. Resisting this possibility is in fact one imperative of a developing critique in Shakespeare studies, the stakes of which are declared to be high.[2] This risk aside, the notion of Hal's reform may still seem question-begging. The most influential current arguments deny that there is any substantive reform of Prince Hal's character. These are the arguments, associated mainly with Stephen Greenblatt, which insist on Hal's role-playing, and hence on the theatricality of his madcap character and of the metamorphosis he effects in *1 Henry IV*.[3]

Instead of confronting these arguments directly, I shall simply point out that, for better or worse, their privileged text is *1*, not *2, Henry IV*.[4] The definitiveness of this theatrical reading of Prince Hal, based on *1 Henry IV,* is implicitly challenged by *2 Henry IV*, and then again by *Henry V.* In each of these plays the matter of Prince Hal's reform is reinvestigated, while the reform itself is reattempted, either by Hal in his own person or—interpretively—by others on his behalf.[5] Yet the *repetition* of the reform-attempt begins to call for its own accounting. Its apparent compulsiveness (or sociopolitical compulsoriness) implies that a good deal is invested in it, not just by Hal, but by those in the plays who expect it of him—and then also by Shakespeare, by subsequent interpreters, and perhaps by a political imperative of "reform" that Shakespeare receives and transmits. At the same time, the sheer fact of repetition makes it increasingly difficult to imagine in what successful reform would consist.

In fact, *2 Henry IV* confronts us with just those issues. As already noted by the Arden editor, the play proceeds as if the reformation effected (or enacted) by Prince Hal in *1 Henry IV* had never happened. In his own eyes, in his father's eyes, and evidently in the eyes of the world, Prince Hal is still the unreformed scapegrace prince.[6] This seemingly burdened prince keeps anticipating—or is it desperately resisting?—his own reform right up to the moment of his father's death:

> O, let me in my present wildness die,
> And never live to show th'incredulous world
> The noble change that I have purposed!
>
> (4.5.152-54)

What is implied by such deferral, resistance or incapacity? What is at stake *in* reform? What is to be understood by the noble change Hal claims to purpose—and with which he is credited by his father at the moment in which the crown changes hands?[7]

These questions will lead on to further questions if, as I believe, *2 Henry IV* reveals a deepening Shakespearean preoccupation with mechanisms of "legitimate" change and succession, not just in the historical narrative of the Henry plays, but at every level including that of his own textual composition.[8] What I suggest, in effect, is that the fluid, somewhat facile, theatrical and/or metamorphic dynamics of reform invoked in *1 Henry IV,* enabling Hal as "Renaissance prince" to effect his own spectacular transformation at Shrewsbury, come into question in *2 Henry IV*. On one hand, mysterious resistances to reform surface in the latter play, while on the other hand the ever-questionable attainment of reform is staged in such a way as to pose more fundamentally than in *1 Henry IV* the question of Hal's legitimizing transformation: in what does it consist, or how, *faute de mieux,* is it managed? While no simple counter-model to that of spectacular metamorphosis necessarily emerges, *2 Henry IV* reopens the question of change-as-reformation; in doing so, it calls upon us to discover new interpretive resources or at least adapt existing ones to deal with the important as well as time-honored question of this reform.

To begin with a sidelong glance at some interpretive leads that I shall not pursue, it could be argued that the inconclusive repetition of Hal's reform in *2 Henry IV* skeptically exposes the emptiness or *un*thinkability of the historical reform-scripts Shakespeare inherits, or even of the Prince Hal character he inherits from earlier texts. Enough Pyrrhonism is in the air Shakespeare breathes—and in the Rumor prologue to *2 Henry IV*—for this to be entirely possible. Shakespeare's apparent derealization of reform in *2 Henry IV* could also be an effect of its displacement. The failure of "reform" to materialize where one is looking for it, for example in the life of Prince Hal, does not mean that it simply fails to materialize. Indeed, Greenblatt implies that a displacement of reform *is* effected in the Henry plays. Prince Hal's onstage reform may be empty in the sense of being merely played, yet "reforming" Prince Hal also becomes the one who, occupying the inside/outside position of the master-anthropologist in relation to the realm, will learn all its languages before substantively re-forming it as Henry V.[9] The reform, in other words, will not be the interior one that Prince Hal undergoes as a character, but the one he effectively imposes as a centralizing, homogenizing, and nationalizing ruler, appropriating and transmuting all the wild, polyglot diversity of an unreformed Britain. Yet this critical displacement of reform, which is also a strong, conservative reclamation of it, again relies primarily on *1 Henry IV*, and confirms the tendency in Shakespeare criticism to read *2 Henry IV* as a straightforward narrative and logical extension (if not a diminished repetition) of *1 Henry IV*. The surprising annulment, however, of the previous play's reform action in *2 Henry IV* constitutes a virtual starting over. Implicit in this curious new beginning is the suggestion that the reform-mechanisms of *1 Henry IV*, which Prince Hal has exploited with a certain opportunistic brilliance, are no longer effectual—or were so only in appearance. These seemingly discounted mechanisms of "reform" will include theatrical metamorphosis, in which Hal has certainly been adept, but also various equivalent forms of facile change or exchange troped in *1 Henry IV* and consciously manipulated by Hal. It is he, after all, who appropriates and reverses his father's thesis that he is a misbegotten changeling while Hotspur is the real princely son. It is he who thinks that characters can be "reformed" by positional changes since they are not real in the first place. It is he, finally, who thinks that the commodity-form of character enables one to be exchanged for another (Harry Percy for Harry Monmouth), or enables a good composite character to be acquired through the appropriation of others' desirable properties, including, as Hotspur complains, their "stolen" youth. Yet if none of this has really worked, we may have to conclude that reform doesn't mean change or exchange, nor does it mean the staged appearance of change. What then, to repeat the question, does or could it mean in *2 Henry IV*? How are we to construe it?

Let us briefly recall some of the data concerning the young Henry V that Shakespeare incorporates and revises. Various chronicle accounts of the young Henry V, including near-contemporary ones, mention not just that the unconstrained prince was a reveller, but that he gathered a formidable popular following which included gentry and commoners. Most Tudor accounts of Henry V, including those in Elyot's *Boke of the Gouernor* (1531), Redmayne's *Vita Henrici Quinti* (1540), Holinshed's *Chronicles* (1587), and Stow's *Annales* (1592) mention Henry's having given the Chief Justice a box on the ear, but also mention punishments that include the young Henry's imprisonment and dismissal from the Privy Council (Humphreys xxix-xlii). The assault on the Chief Justice was, in other words, taken seriously as the political gesture of a popular usurper-manqué threatening to repeat his father's history. In *The Famous Victories* the young Henry behaves, as Humphreys puts it, like a hooligan, though this so-called hooliganism can also be read as a legitimate popular politics of festive (and theatrical) revolt. Recognizing here a difficulty of critical description, but perhaps also of dramatic characterization, we might say that Shakespeare produces a disconcertingly censored and/or agreeably refined version of the young Henry V of folklore, chronicle, and *The Famous Victories of Henry V*. At all events the Arden editor describes Hal's alleged madcap revelling in *1 Henry IV* as harmless, and as essentially nonexistent in *2 Henry IV* (Humphreys xli). This is a marked departure from the sources on Shakespeare's part—or, to put it differently, it is a conspicuous rewriting of the young Henry. Insofar as Shakespeare renders the wild prince surprisingly tame or inactive—and apparently less political—he may appear self-defeatingly to void the dramatic action of reform by removing in advance any real need or occasion for it.

Despite this apparent voiding, a persistent "need" for reform as well as an action supposedly effecting it continues to be inscribed in *2 Henry IV*. As external or objective conditions giving rise to this need vanish, however, the need itself may increasingly seem to belong to an order of shared psychic compulsion rather than political or moral obligation. Indeed, the tame, passive, and increasingly ironized Prince Hal who finds himself subject to the widespread demand that he reform begins to resemble his chronological near-twin in the Shakespearean canon, namely Prince Hamlet, an "inward" protagonist oppressed and divided by a troublesome demand.

Such an interior shift, in which psychic (in)action is "substituted" for physical and/or overtly political action, is by no means unusual in Shakespeare. Yet it is not necessarily a shift *from* the political to the psychological. Rather, it is a move in which, characteristically, the psychic interior is politicized while the political exterior is correspondingly psychologized—that is, subjected to psychic "laws."[10] This crossing isn't one in which the differentiated and *prima facie* opposed realms of the political and the psychological are simply deconstructed, but rather one in which a certain reciprocal reconstruction is effected between these orders without the difference between them ever being effaced. A proposal simply to shift *from* political to psychoanalytic reading of *2 Henry IV* would accordingly be misplaced; what is required, I believe, is a reading that takes account of this putative crossover. Whether we want to speak in the final analysis of a psychologized politics or a politicized psychology, it is in such hybrid terms that the reform action of *2 Henry IV* takes on whatever degree of intelligibility can be claimed for it. That, at least, is the proposition according to which I shall now proceed.[11]

* * *

Whatever initial effect of unintelligibility may be produced by the reform-action(s) of the Henry plays does not arise from any shortage of models and contexts, historical and otherwise, for Prince Hal's reform. Well-recognized models, which are neither fully discrete nor fully successive, include those of a New Testament theology of the "new man," of medieval psychomachia, of disciplinary humanist pedagogy, and even of ego-psychology. Coercive vectors of reform include those of Renaissance subject-formation, of censorship and "courtly" refinement in the public theater, and—broadly speaking—of what Norbert

Elias has called the civilizing process.[12] The dominant model that has been applied to Hal's reform is also, however, one that renders it less rather than more intelligible: this is the model of the prodigal son.[13] The prodigal-model is a tellingly *failed* one partly because it is not a narrative of primogeniture—of the scapegrace *eldest* son who is nevertheless to be the sovereign inheritor—but if anything a narrative somewhat subversive of that rigorously "unjust" principle. It is above all a model that acknowledges no parricidal impulse or dynamic in the process of reform and hence of "legitimate" or "authentic" succession. If anything, once again, that dynamic is forestalled, or displaced into sibling rivalry and reconciliation, in the prodigal son story. This refusal in any sense to license parricide is the condition on which patriarchal law and order properly so called can be maintained.

The action (or inaction) of reform in the Henry plays conspicuously does take account of the parricidal moment in the process of sovereign succession. So, implicitly, do the chronicles in presenting the young Henry as a usurper-manqué who raises his hand against the paternal lawgiver in the person of the Chief Justice. So does *The Famous Victories,* in which Hal's impatience for his father's death is an explicit motif, assimilated to his general wildness.[14] This parricidal recognition is accompanied in *2 Henry IV* by an increased emphasis, rising to the pitch of apocalyptic hysteria in a late speech by Henry IV, on Hal's "wildness" as covert murderous savagery rather than mere youthful excess. In the eyes of Henry, the ailing, threatened father, the son's wildness constitutes an unreformed interior that must always be socially dissimulated. Correspondingly, any innocuous revelling or even show of reform on the part of Prince Hal will be taken as dissimulation, the hidden content of which can be expected to emerge once he has succeeded to the throne. Thus Henry IV prophesies a wild apocalypse brought on by the unreformed, and perhaps unreformable, prince:

> Harry the fifth is crown'd! Up, vanity!
> Down, royal state! All you sage counsellors, hence!
> And to the English court assemble now
> From every region, apes of idleness!
> Now, neighbour confines, purge you of your scum!
> Have you a ruffian that will swear, drink, dance,
> Revel the night, rob, murder, and commit
> The oldest sins the newest kind of ways?
> . . . . .
> . . . the fifth Harry from curb'd licence plucks
> The muzzle of restraint, and the wild dog
> Shall flesh his tooth of every innocent.
> . . . . .
> O, thou wilt be a wilderness again,
> Peopled with wolves, thy old inhabitants!
>
> (4.5.119-37)

Despite its prophetic hysteria, Henry's vision isn't wholly inconsistent with the expanded *potentiality* given in *2 Henry IV* to resistant wildness and the "need" to reform. Nor is it inconsistent with the threatened tragic declension of wildness from relatively harmless masquing and revelling in *1 Henry IV* to savagery in *2 Henry IV*. In other words, it is not just the issue of parricidal succession, but of a corresponding predatory "wildness" resistant to any transformation—a wildness anterior and *interior* to civility, to the process of lawful inheritance, and to legitimized political rule—that *2 Henry IV* appears to take more seriously than does its predecessor. As this issue surfaces, the historical contingencies of Bolingbroke's "parricidal" usurpation and Hal's wildness may seem increasingly to belong to an order of necessity—in which case Henry IV's prophecy may also begin to sound like hysterical denial.

Insofar as succession is conceived to be wild in *2 Henry IV,* and to be so of necessity, its dynamic may seem to originate or inhere in the male character or specifically male *agency,* not as a natural fact but as the consequence of what I have already referred to as a politicized psychology or psychologized politics of sovereign succession. It is this agency that is "missing" in *1 Henry IV,* and from the reform that would, in effect, make Hal the inheritor in a theater-state. Under the "post-theatrical" regime of *2 Henry IV,* the sovereign inheritor will be required to reform in order to legitimize himself, but will also (contradictorily) be required not to reform in order to succeed. Moreover, the paternal demand for reform will seem like an effort to forestall rather than facilitate succession by taming—emasculating—the sovereign inheritor. Under these circumstances, Hal's constant anticipation and *deferral* of reform become intelligible, as do his curious paralysis and avoidance of his father. Yet it is not through Prince Hal and his father alone that the difficulties or even contradictions of reform are precipitated out in the play. Falstaff is exultantly unreformed and unreformable; he and his cronies, fond recallers of their wild youth, help at least as much as do Prince Hal and his father to unpack reform in the play.

At one level, the Falstaff-Shallow-Silence episodes function as a wickedly satirical exposure of "original" male deficiency rather than wild excess. There is no need to belabor the point that the wild youth of Shallow and Silence is a nostalgically recalled condition, denied by their contemporary, Falstaff. Their wild youth as unreformed students belongs to a commonplace nostalgic script, beloved of the law-abiding elderly. No need either to belabor the point that, insofar as Falstaff has claims to be the real wild man of the play, he is a wild *old* man. If anything, wildness is more plausibly the social condition of the old man than the young one, and it is more plausibly a function of social denial, marginalization, and conscious impotence than of any supposedly untamed or untamable excess in the "true" male character. In this satirically reductive setting, the name of Fall-staff speaks him no less than do those of Shallow and Silence.

The genuinely funny satirical comedy, as distinct from festive heartiness, of the Falstaff-Shallow-Silence episodes may thus seem to contest the "wild" male character and its ontological violence of agency as well as the process of succession in which it is justifyingly subsumed. Yet the zero-point of final reduction is one at which we never quite arrive. Or, more accurately, the satirical vanishing-point of "wild" maleness turns out to be indistinguishable from its mythic origin, glimpsed in and through Falstaff's alleged recall of the young Shallow:

> I do remember him at Clement's Inn, like a man made after supper of a cheese-paring. When a was naked, he was for all the world like a forked radish, with a head fantastically carved upon it with a knife. A was so forlorn, that his dimensions to any thick sight were invisible; a was the very genius of famine, yet lecherous as a monkey, and the whores called him mandrake.
>
> (3.2.302-09)

What this strange "recall" produces is a subhuman or inhuman grotesque of indeterminable sex, or of no sex at all, like the bare, forked animal Lear thinks he sees on the heath. (The apparition here is fully in keeping with Elizabethan folklore regarding the mandrake root: it can look male, female, or androgynous; human or non-human.) Apparently open to any construction—or to no determinate one—the root-like apparition of the young Shallow may all too literally mock any aspiration to get to the root of the matter of reform in terms of gendered character. What we find at the end of the line is literally a root.

At the critical moment, however, the interposition of a "thick-sighted" observer relativizes and equivocates any ontological determination. Furthermore, while the stark-naked Shallow is seen from the start as a remainder—a cheese-paring—rather than a bodily totality, and while he is always and already subsumed in an order of figurative likeness—he is cheese-like, radish-like—this characterization through deficiency is tantamount to masculine *re*characterization in terms of insatiable appetite rather than substance or "matter." Appropriately, it is Falstaff who effects this particular recharacterization. He assimilates any male sexual deficiency to a psychic and bodily economy of "prior" starvation, while, as characteristically, he recalls Shallow in the guise of an edible vegetable—a garden radish—and thus as an object as well as subject of insatiable appetite. It is left to the whores to translate this garden radish (ironically?) into the exotic and erotically mythologized mandrake root. Exotic sexual desire is thus superinduced upon domestic appetite in a novel etiology of the ontologically violent male character. It is evidently in terms of this prior "deprivation" and consequent appetite that greedy Falstaff not only resists reform, but considers himself entitled (and driven) by "law of nature" (3.2.326) to make a regal mouthful of such dace as Shallow—or Prince Hal as inheritor of the kingdom. If it were to be suggested that Falstaff fails in his more extravagant ambitions because he is captive to a dysfunctional conception of ontological necessity and empowerment, it should be recalled that an intuition of the same drive may inform Henry IV's prophecy that Hal's reign will be one of unbridled appetite: "fleshing the tooth on every innocent."

The point to be made here is that the "need" to reform as well as the sources of resistance to it remain curiously undetermined *and* overdetermined in *2 Henry IV* without ceasing to be invoked as crucial to the play's action(s) and outcome(s). I have already suggested that this situation gains a certain intelligibility if it is critically linked to what I have called a psychologized politics or politicized psychology of masculine sovereignty; this linking does not constitute an explanation so much as an attempt to (re)situate the problem where it belongs. At a minimum, the "return" of an ontological violence seemingly displaced from *1 Henry IV* is at issue in *2 Henry IV,* as it is in *Julius Caesar* and *Hamlet*. That this attempt to resituate isn't wholly misplaced is suggested by the terms in which Hal's "reform" and the royal succession are finally staged—or perhaps, *faute de mieux,* stage-managed. This event transpires in the complicated bedroom scene between Hal and his father.

Briefly to reprise, Prince Hal's reform in *1 Henry IV,* climactically staged on the battlefield of Shrewsbury, may seem, in the extended perspective offered by *2 Henry IV,* like a dress rehearsal. There, Prince Hal stages his own spectacular apotheosis for such wondering "choral" onlookers as Vernon, but also kills his rival-twin Hotspur in an act of virtual *Brudermord, unbestraft* in this case. (Falstaff finishes off the job but also decodes it, as the saying goes, by wounding Hotspur in the groin.) Hal then gives full credit for the deed to Falstaff in a way that conveniently masks the doer from most of those onstage if not from the audience. It is as if Henry IV sees through just *this* dissimulation of savagery; his deathlike sleep in *2 Henry IV* accordingly seems like a device of entrapment designed to make Prince Hal show his murderous hand—as Henry believes Hal has done when he seizes the crown and tries it on.

Furthermore, as Henry IV approaches his end, he increasingly sees Prince Hal not just as the feral harbinger of universal wildness/wilderness (wild-boy as wolf-boy) but, in a totalizing projection of sovereign male appetite and desire, as the original totemic despot reborn: a savage "Amurath" rather than a gentle Harry. (Though this is not what Warwick understands to be happening, his observation that the Shakespearean Prince Hal is studying his companions to "gain the language" [4.4.69]—to engross *all* language?—is consistent with this dread.)[15] As if confirming this anticipation, toward the end of the play as well as Henry's life, Hal is suddenly everywhere onstage in the guise of sibling-delegates including the notoriously "cold" Prince John; in Henry's view, however, he also threatens to consume those sibling-agents along with everyone else in the kingdom. This feared outcome is what Henry attempts to forestall by belatedly imploring his son Clarence to become Prince Hal's civilizing mediator while sentimentally fabricating a more humane (if still disturbingly "mixed") character for Prince Hal:

> For he is gracious, if he be observ'd,
> He hath a tear for pity, and a hand
> Open as day for melting charity:
> Yet notwithstanding, being incens'd, he's flint,

> As humorous as winter, and as sudden
> As flaws congealed in the spring of day.
>
> (4.4.30-35)

These scarcely tractable anxieties, which threaten to bedevil any smooth or consensual transfer of power between a threatened father and a supposedly unreformable son, are, however, mitigated by a certain identification on Henry's part with Prince Hal: identification in the sense both of sympathetic recognition and recognition of likeness. Indeed, Henry's dread is also the projection of an unsatisfied appetite upon Prince Hal: specifically, an appetite for the power that he has desired but conspicuously failed to concentrate in himself during his troubled reign. The differences between himself and Prince Hal on which he keeps harping are thus undercut, even in his own mind, by the perception of likeness:

> Most subject is the fattest soil to weeds,
> And he, the noble image of my youth,
> Is overspread with them.
>
> (4.4.54-56)

> This part of his conjoins with my disease,
> And helps to end me.
>
> (4.5.63-64)

It is partly Henry's recognition of likeness that allows a political settlement of the parricidal succession to transpire between him and Hal. It allows Henry to be reconciled to his own deep mortification, and to displacement by one who can be a surrogate-success as well as a rival. It allows Hal's reform to be effected in a mode of vertical rather than horizontal exchange, Harry for Harry again. It allows Henry's own putative hunger and wished-for engorgement to be glimpsed, even as it does Hal's putatively corresponding insatiable appetite:

> How quickly nature falls into revolt
> When gold becomes her object!
> . . . . .
> For this [fathers] have engrossed and pil'd up
> The canker'd heaps of strange-achieved gold.
>
> (4.5.65-71)

Finally, since the "wildness" to be reformed does not constitute a category of absolute difference, or definitively characterize anyone in particular, its putative form and location can be shifted around in the process of settlement.

Briefly, what this situation allows is that wildness in its various aspects as criminality, natural excess, inordinate appetite, and even fulminating disease can *consensually* be transferred from the scapegrace son to the father as original usurper, on one hand allowing it to be buried with the corpse and on the other permitting the instantly reformed son to become the legitimate heir. Hal can then ostentatiously place himself under the paternal law, embodied in the Chief Justice, and begin laying down the law himself. As soon as Henry "confesses," the reforming and legitimating bargain is sealed:

> For all the soil of the achievement goes
> With me into the earth. It seem'd in me
> But as an honour snatch'd with boist'rous hand.
>
> (4.5.189-91)

The sole acknowledgment of this parricidal "boisterousness" will not only be in the past tense, but will occur in the moment in which the violent hand is being transferred for burial from son to father.

This relatively diplomatic transaction does, however, have a price. It is paid by neither party to the transaction, and the payment exacted is such as to suggest that the dynamics of the play do indeed belong to a psychologized politics or politicized psychology of specifically masculine sovereignty. In the complicated transfer we witness, the Oedipal scenario is conspicuously reconstructed as one of exclusively male agency, empowerment and succession. It is Prince Hal as inheritor who, in a state of sublime innocence or Machiavellian callousness, reads the Oedipal situation as one in which the woman is always and already displaced by the crown as substitute-object, which is to say as object substituted for her, but also as object constituted in her likeness:

> Why doth the crown lie there upon his pillow,
> Being so troublesome a bedfellow?
> O polish'd perturbation! golden care!
>
> (4.5.20-22)

Syntactically, as Hal presumably doesn't register, it remains undetermined which bedfellow is troublesome to which, yet the woman has been displaced by the crown as the pursued and piously denied object of appetite, while the void figure of the feminine (*res nulla*) has been appropriated and transmuted into the substantial figure of masculine sovereignty.[16] If this displacement and transmutation of the woman can't be effected without a remainder of "feminine" meretriciousness or troublesomeness, that remainder can in turn be identified as the cause of any violent disturbance, not just in men but between them. Indeed, it enables the *crown* to be incriminated as the real parricidal agent, threatening and coming between generations of men, but also, once identified as the source of the trouble, facilitating their diplomatic reconciliation:

> Accusing it, I put it on my head,
> To try with it, as with an enemy
> That had before my face murder'd my father,
> The quarrel of a true inheritor.
>
> (4.5.165-68)

"The quarrel of a true inheritor"—the bad yet still seemingly "necessary" parricidal one—is realigned to become the good quarrel of the inheritor with the intermediate parricidal agent/object, while this object can in turn be reclaimed as the sullied/solid currency of a benign transaction between father and son. What is *sacrificed* to the settlement of parricidal succession is evidently the woman; what is appropriated for it is women's agency. Political Shakespeare with a vengeance.[17]

This version of reform as parricidal transfer and place-changing, in which the parricide is also backdated to Henry's usurpation of Richard II, is of course no more absolute or final than the theatrical metamorphosis enacted in *1 Henry IV*. It is undone again in *Henry V*, while the brutal exclusionary reduction of the woman is "liberalized" inasmuch as Henry V's legitimation turns out to depend on the lawfulness of female inclusion in the royal line. Henry V must also eventually confront a French Catherine as potentially troublesome and usurping bedfellow, whose language he is far from having engrossed, and in relation to whom his provincial tongue seems disabled. Moreover, in the process of translation during the courtship, language is punningly "engrossed" again in the sense of being resexualized; this dirty talk isn't Henry V's *forté*.[18]

Inconclusiveness notwithstanding, what I should like to suggest in conclusion is that our critical tendency to elide or "forget" *2 Henry IV* in this tetralogy, at the same time critically and affectively privileging *1 Henry IV*, is related to an apparent displacement of ontological violence and corresponding, agreeable theatrical facilitation in *1 Henry IV*. This tendency to overlook *2 Henry IV* is heightened by a certain critical tradition in which its disillusioning traits, including the waning, sickening, or fading in it of the bright stars of *1 Henry IV*, are emphasized, as is the devaluation of the royal currency. Yet in addition to getting down to some *Realpolitik* glossed over in *1 Henry IV*, *2 Henry IV* marks the "return" of an ontological violence neither fully locatable nor fully erasable in the contexts of Shakespeare's production. It is the critique of such violence, which cannot be regarded as fully performed even if it is desired in our own political and professional contexts, that recalling *2 Henry IV* facilitates.

Notes

1. By "matter" Humphreys means primarily the extensive chronicle materials on which Shakespeare draws in the Henry plays (as in the traditional phrase "the matter of Britain"), but the term resonates beyond that denotation (xix). His term "redemption" appropriately invokes the religious and morality-drama context(s) of Hal's putative betterment. My choice of the term "reform" emphasizes secular contexts, including that of a disciplinary, character-forming humanism. Mention of Hal's "reformation" will, however, recall the Protestant epoch in which the play was written. See also Dickinson 33-46.

2. This critique is widely implied in radical new historicism and/or feminism, partly in response to the reading of Prince Hal in Stephen Greenblatt's "Invisible Bullets: Renaissance Authority and Its Subversion." Traditional readings subject to this critique would include all ego-psychological ones as well as C. L. Barber's festive-political reading, in which Prince Hal progressively manifests his "sovereign nature" (192-221).

3. "Invisible Bullets" is the *locus classicus* for this argument. It does envisage some changes in Prince Hal in *2 Henry IV*, but not of the positive kind associated with self-improvement.

4. The theatrical reading depends partly on Hal's self-unmasking in the "I know you all" soliloquy in *1 Henry IV* (1.1.192-214). The revisions effected in *2 Henry IV* suggest that this speech embodies the young prince's fantasy of masterful knowledge as theatrical knowledge, soon to be dispelled.

5. Interpretively by various interested characters in the Henry plays, including the politic archbishop of Canterbury in *Henry V*, who finds that, at the moment of Henry IV's death, Hal's "wildness, mortified in him / Seem'd to die too . . . consideration like an angel came / And whipp'd th' offending Adam out of him / Leaving his body as a paradise" (1.1.27-31). Quite soon, however, the clerics get down to postlapsarian business, which consists in making a preemptively large contribution to Henry's military budget.

6. This peculiarity is extensively discussed by Humphreys, who properly relates it to the problem of the relationship between *1* and *2 Henry IV*. While questionably accepting that "redemptions" do occur in both plays, he concludes that "naturalistically speaking these twin-redemptions are an incoherence, [yet] dramatically and by folktale or morality canons they are acceptable" (xxviii). Humphreys concludes, moreover, that the two versions of Hal's "redemption" are radically incompatible: while the playful version in *1 Henry IV* comes from Daniel and *The Famous Victories*, the serious, father's-deathbed version comes from Holinshed.

7. "Noble change" is a peculiarly resonant phrase. While the change effected in *1 Henry IV* hardly merits the description "noble," the phrase invokes such change in the field of the play's representation but also in contexts such as those of Elizabethan upward mobility, of disciplinary humanism, of ruling-class appropriation of popular culture and theater, and even of self-sacrificial assumption of the burden of kingship. It is understandable, then, that the process of noble change may seem at once bafflingly complex, compulsory, and subject to endless resistance. I shall deal with the question largely in terms of the play's representation rather than of its implied contexts.

8. Jonathan Goldberg's *Writing Matter* enables us to conceive of this particular displacement of the reform-action. It could be said that the action is displaced to the level of Shakespeare's "reforming" authorship and textual revision, to which considerations similar to those of Hal's reform may apply. Under this assumption, questions regarding Shakespeare's authorial "character" and the notoriously troublesome *text* of *2 Henry IV* take on paramount importance. The process of "theatrical legitimation" that Timothy Murray sees being pursued by Jonson as author and editor is also, *mutatis mutandis*, pursued by Shakespeare.

9. The republication of Greenblatt's "Invisible Bullets" in *Shakespearean Negotiations: The Circulation of Social Energy in Renaissance England* brings it under the purview of new categories of displacement, circulation, etc.

10. The apparent phenomenon of the interior shift generally results in a critical shift toward psychological (psychoanalytic) reading of Shakespeare. What can easily be overlooked is the simultaneous shift in the other direction in Shakespeare, such that the represented political world seems increasingly governed by psychological "laws."

11. I take it that implicit recognition of psychologized politics and/or politicized psychology has been widespread during the past decade, notably in politically conscious Freudian (often feminist) criticism. This is the critical recognition which, without necessarily crystallizing into a fully coherent model, informs my discussion. An essay that importantly embodies this recognition with reference to Shakespeare is Jacqueline Rose, "Sexuality in the Reading of Shakespeare: *Hamlet* and *Measure for Measure*."

12. The pertinence of courtesy literature and conduct books need hardly be insisted upon. Part of Hal's "reforming" consists in his "fashioning" (self-fashioning?) as a courtier and a gentleman. However, see Elias for the most sweeping contextualization of this process.

13. We have been taught to recognize the sophisticated refinement, allegorization, and economic transcription of the prodigal reform-model during the English sixteenth century by critics, notably including Helgerson and Hutson. Nonetheless, my point stands.

14. I don't assume that "wildness" is mere code for parricide in the play; rather, parricide appears to inhere in a more diffuse wildness. It is around parricide, nevertheless, that diffuse wildness seems to become centripetally organized toward the end of the reform-action in *2 Henry IV*. Harold Jenkins notes that the young Henry V is not just a historic figure but a folkloristic wild-boy, hence some of the "trickiness" of his reform in the Henry plays (Humphreys xxvi-xxvii). A pervasively invoked "wildness" in the Henry plays can sometimes be construed as that of the wild sign in an otherwise stable signifying system, or of the wild card—the joker—in a pack otherwise stably denominated. If Hal is the character most often associated with these forms of wildness, perhaps especially as the changeling-figure in *1 Henry IV*, he is by no mean exclusively so. Part of the difficulty in staging any reform-action is the elusive, bound ary-crossing character of this "wildness"; however, the "solution" in *2 Henry IV* depends on this mobility.

15. Here it is pertinent to recall that "engrossing" means writing in the sixteenth century—Shakespeare's all-engrossing mastery of the language clearly makes him a threatening figure for the paranoid or even just anxious interpreter.

16. Some of my locutions here are indebted to Eve Kosofsky Sedgwick, *Between Men: English Literature and Male Homosocial Desire*. It would appear that the transactions she identifies "between men" can occur vertically between father and son as well as horizontally between sibling-like rivals. See also Berger and Holland.

17. The atrocities ascribed to the Welshwomen at the beginning of *1 Henry IV* include mutilation of men's corpses on the battlefield. Sure enough, this "unmanly" power will be appropriated and re-gendered by Falstaff-Hal in the killing of Hotspur. The falling-silent and disappearance of women in the course of the so-called Henriad (the English epic-manqué constructed by modern critics) is conspicuous.

18. Some of the oddity of Prince Hal's character comes from his overt sexual apathy idle Falstaffian talk of his sexual adventures notwithstanding. The repression of an indeterminate sexuality, which will include at least a homosexual component, is inevitably to be suspected. The word "wild" could be applied to homosexuality, though not exclusively to it as a sexual practice, in the sixteenth century (Bray 25-27).

Works Cited

Barber, C. L. "Rule and Misrule in *Henry IV*." In his *Shakespeare's Festive Comedy A Study of Dramatic Form and Its Relation to Social Custom*. Princeton: Princeton UP, 1959. 192-221.

Berger, Harry, Jr. "Psychoanalyzing the Shakespearean Text: The First Three Scenes of the *Henriad*." Parker and Hartman 210-29.

Bray, Alan. *Homosexuality in Renaissance England*. London: Gay Men's Press, 1982.

Cohen, Walter, "Political Criticism of Shakespeare." Howard and O'Connor 18-46.

Dickinson, Hugh. "The Reformation of Prince Hal." *Shakespeare Quarterly* 12 (1961) 33-46.

Dollimore, Jonathan, and Alan Sinfield, eds. *Political Shakespeare: New Essays In Cultural Materialism*. Ithaca: Cornell UP, 1985.

Drakakis, John, ed. *Alternative Shakespeares*. London: Methuen, 1985.

Elias, Norbert. *The Civilizing Process: The Development of Manners*. Trans. Edmund Jephcott. New York: Urizen, 1978.

Faber, M. D., ed. *The Design Within: Psychoanalytic Approaches to Shakespeare*. New York: Science House, 1970.

Goldberg, Jonathan. *Writing Matter: From the Hands of the English Renaissance.* Stanford: Stanford UP, 1990.

Greenblatt, Stephen. "Invisible Bullets: Renaissance Authority and Its Subversion, *Henry IV* and *Henry V.*" Dollimore and Sinfield 18-47.

———. *Shakespearean Negotiations: The Circulation of Social Energy in Renaissance England.* Berkeley: U of California P, 1988.

Helgerson, Richard. *The Elizabethan Prodigals.* Berkeley: U of California P, 1976.

Holland, Norman. "Introduction to *Henry IV, Part 2.*" Faber 411-28.

Howard, Jean E., and Marion F. O'Connor, eds. *Shakespeare Reproduced: The Text in History and Ideology.* New York: Methuen, 1987.

Humphreys, A. R. "Introduction." *2 Henry IV.* Shakespeare xi-xci.

Hutson, Lorna. *Thomas Nashe in Context.* Oxford: Clarendon, 1989.

Murray, Timothy. *Theatrical Legitimation: Allegories of Genius in Seventeenth-Century England and France.* New York: Oxford UP, 1987.

Parker, Patricia, and Geoffrey Hartman, eds. *Shakespeare and the Question of Theory.* New York, Methuen, 1985.

Rose, Jacqueline. "Sexuality in the Reading of Shakespeare: *Hamlet* and *Measure for Measure.*" Drakakis 95-118.

Sedgwick, Eve Kosofsky. *Between Men: English Literature and Male Homosocial Desire.* New York: Columbia UP, 1985.

Shakespeare, William. *The Second Part of King Henry IV.* Ed. A. R. Humphreys. The Arden Shakespeare. New York: Vintage, 1967.

Maurice Hunt (essay date 1998)

SOURCE: "The Hybrid Reformations of Shakespeare's Second Henriad," in *Comparative Drama,* Vol. 32, No. 1, Spring, 1998, pp. 176-206.

[*In the following essay, Hunt offers an account of the coexisting Catholic and Protestant elements characterized in Falstaff, King Henry IV, and Prince Hal, arguing that this mixture of traits does not impede any of these characters' attempts to reform themselves.*]

Granted the late-medieval, early fifteenth-century settings of Shakespeare's *1* and *2 Henry IV* and *Henry V,* theater audiences are not surprised by the large number of references in these plays to Catholic practices and beliefs.[1] What has proved problematic for commentators is the coexistence of Catholic elements with explicitly Protestant traits in Shakespeare's characterizations of Falstaff, Henry IV, and Prince Hal/Henry V. In what follows, I argue that different forms of this mixture either impede or undermine these characters' attempts during the Second Henriad to reform themselves ethically and spiritually, at least until a noteworthy blend of Catholic and Protestant traits enables King Henry V in the aftermath of Agincourt to achieve a relatively successful transformation of character. Many plays of Shakespeare are syncretic in matters of religion: *Othello,* for example, reflects a mixture of Protestant predestinarian and Catholic voluntaristic theologies.[2] Having apparently committed himself in his portrait of Falstaff to satirizing the proto-Protestantism of his character's Lollard namesake Oldcastle, Shakespeare at the same time resolved to give the plays of the Second Henriad a late-medieval air, and hence perhaps found characterizations built upon a mixture of Catholic and Protestant components inevitable. What does not appear inevitable in the Second Henriad, however, is the sustained, thoughtful manner of the many critiques of Catholicism, Protestantism, and the Protestant Reformation entailed by the blend of antithetical religious traits within characters trying to reform themselves. Whether by accident or design, this dramatic phenomenon poses a question: how can individuals reform themselves in societies—like Shakespeare's—wherein Catholicism remained a strong threat to Protestantism by positing a contradictory route to reformation?[3] An answer to this question emerges from Henry's third and most successful attempt at reformation. Getting to that end involves starting with Falstaff.

Falstaff's name in original performances of *1 Henry IV* was Sir John Oldcastle, a conjuration of the Lollard martyr of the late fourteenth century. Shakespeare's apology concerning Falstaff in the Epilogue of *2 Henry IV*—"for Oldcastle died a martyr, and this is not the man" (29-30)—clinches the earlier proto-Protestant allusion in Hal's calling Falstaff "my old lad of the castle" in *1 Henry IV* (1.2.41).[4] Elizabethan godly Protestants thought of the Lollard Oldcastle, executed for his purported attempts to purify English Catholicism and make the Word of God more meaningful to the masses, as a saint.[5] Falstaff at one point tells Hal that the Prince is "indeed able to corrupt a saint" (1.2.90), ironically subverting the memory of the saint Oldcastle by reference to his namesake's tavern vices. Shakespeare's apology apparently grew out of objections that Oldcastle's Elizabethan heirs Sir William Brooke and his son Sir Henry Brooke raised over Falstaff's travesty of the Lollard's memory, including Falstaff's proto-Protestantism.[6] A detail strengthening Falstaff/Oldcastle's mock Protestantism involves his implication that men and women are to be saved by faith rather than merit (based on works): "O, if men were to be saved by merit," Falstaff comically says in an age when men *were* thought to be saved by merit, "what hole in hell were hot enough for [Gadshill]" (1.2.105-06). By Shakespeare's time, the dictum that Protestants primarily relied upon faith rather than merit acquired through spiritual good deeds had become a cliché.[7] Falstaff, skeptical about being saved by merit, seems to rely upon his self-serving belief—a Lutheran tenet attributed by Elizabethan Protestants to the Lollards—that undemonstrated faith alone can save him near the end of a hedonistic life void of good deeds.

This reading suggests that Falstaff's Protestantism occasionally mocks central tenets or practices of Reformation Protestants. Falstaff's Reformation Protestantism is implied by his pronouncement that "'Tis no sin for a man to labor in his vocation" (1.2. 102-03). However, the "vocation" in which Falstaff "labors" is thievery. Falstaff misapplies Matthew 12:33 when he says of himself, during his playlet with Hal, "If then the tree may be known by the fruit, as the fruit by the tree, then peremptorily I speak it, there is virtue in that Falstaff" (2.4.423-25). If Falstaff were known by his fruits, he would be known by his deeds of theft. Gadshill tells the Chamberlain that the thieves, including Falstaff, "pray continually to their saint, the commonwealth, or rather not pray to her but prey on her, for they ride up and down on her and make her their boots [booty]" (2.1.80-83). Latent in this punning judgment lies a criticism of Reformation Protestants' rape of a sainted Catholic commonwealth, their plunder of its material wealth. The critique of Protestantism deepens when mention is made of these thieves' plan to waylay "pilgrims going to Canterbury with rich offerings" (1.2.123-24).

Finally, Falstaff could be any one of a number of Protestants walking the streets of Shakespeare's London when he says, "I would I were a weaver; I could sing psalms or anything" (2.4.130-31). (Concerning this utterance, David Bevington notes that "many psalm-singing Protestant immigrants from the Low Countries were weavers,"[8] and Clifford Davidson notes that the practice had caught on among craftsmen such as weavers in England.[9]) Falstaff's "Elizabethan" Protestantism unequivocally surfaces in his hypocritical condemnation of "whoreson smoothy-pates [who] do now wear nothing but high shoes and bunches of keys at their girdles" (*2 Henry IV* 1.2.37-39)—in other words, of short-haired Puritan tradesmen of the later sixteenth century who have bartered their faith for commercial success (something that Falstaff would doubtless be willing to do). Shakespeare's playing fast and loose with Falstaff's stage Protestantism, his making it of several ages and thus no age, makes it vaguely generic.[10] A combination of Oldcastle and the Elizabethan Puritan, Falstaff is both old-fashioned and progressive. On the one hand, the Falstaff constructed by Reformation allusions is too late to be a character actually involved in the events of Henry IV's late-medieval England. On the other, the Lollard Falstaff/Oldcastle comes too early to profit spiritually (even if he sincerely wanted to) from the godly Reformation of religion occurring in later Tudor times.

The paradox is evident in the play's dialogue. The first dialogue involving Falstaff that auditors hear in *1 Henry IV* stresses his out-of-dateness, his not knowing the time of day, his being out of sync with the natural sequence of day-night activities (1.2.1-12). He quotes the old-fashioned fustian tragedy, popular in the 1570s and 1580s but dated by the time of *Henry IV*'s production. And he styles himself as one of "Diana's foresters," a minion "of the moon" (1.2.25-26): epithets that link him with Queen Elizabeth, and thus tie him to an era which, in 1596-97, when *1 Henry IV* was first performed, was clearly drawing to a close. Told by Hal to hide behind the arras from the sheriff, Falstaff laments that he once had "a true face and good conscience . . . but their date is out" (2.4.496-98). All these lines emphasize Falstaff's belatedness, which will hinder his attempts to reform.[11]

Evidence exists that Falstaff's weak faith, usually deferred, at moments kindles a genuine desire to repent and reform himself. "Do I not bate? Do I not dwindle?" he asks Bardolph: "Why, my skin hangs about me like an old lady's loose gown. . . . Well, I'll repent, and that suddenly, while I am in some liking. I shall be out of heart shortly, and then I shall have no strength to repent. An I have not forgotten what the inside of a church is made of, I am a peppercorn, a brewer's horse" (3.3.2-9). These lines suggest that Falstaff's proto-Protestant faith is not nearly strong enough to overcome ignorance and vices that Elizabethan Protestants typically thought of as Catholic. Like any proto-Protestant before the advent of the sixteenth-century Reformation, which made the Bible available in national languages, Falstaff has imperfectly learned much of his religion from biblical tableaux woven into wall hangings hung in taverns and other buildings. Moreover, on the battlefield at Shrewsbury he misuses the Catechism to rationalize cowardice, a dramatic fact made easier by the inability of late-medieval men to read it in English in an accessible book of devotions. Falstaff is a thief because he is idle, afflicted by a slothful, hedonistic temperament. If he in some minds represents merry Old England, it is a dissolute late-medieval Catholic England of Elizabethan Protestant imagination. Its dissolution is evident when Falstaff tells Prince Hal that "An old lord of the council rated me the other day in the street about you, sir, but I marked him not; and yet he talked very wisely, but I regarded him not; and yet he talked wisely, and in the street too" (1.2.82-86). Commentators on *1 Henry IV* have long recognized Shakespeare's ironic allusion here to Proverbs 1:20-24, to Wisdom which cries out in the streets but to deaf ears. If Falstaff is deaf to biblical wisdom, or if he misapplies it, the fault lies not wholly in his character but partly in his historical date. As a liar, thief, drunkard, and wencher, Falstaff stands in need of the personal spiritual reformation that Shakespeare's countrymen dated from the Protestant Reformation beginning in the first half of the sixteenth century. And yet, as noted above, Shakespeare problematically identifies Reformation Protestantism with thievery, with plundering the riches of a "sainted" commonwealth.[12] So portrayed, this flawed Protestantism does not promise his successful reformation of stereotypical Catholic vices, simply because it seems to participate in them.

It is difficult to overstimate Falstaff's need for spiritual reformation. The bankruptcy of Falstaff's saving faith symbolically reveals itself in *1 Henry IV* in the gross disproportion of his notorious debt—only "one halfpennyworth of bread" to two gallons of sack in the itemized tavern bill (2.4.529-36), only a symbolized bit of the transubstantiated body of Christ in relation to an excess of his blood. This grotesquerie underscores the enormity of Falstaff's addiction to pleasure at the expense of life-sustaining nourishment (that scrap of bread), an obsession that apparently keeps him from the true nourishment of the redemptive bread and wine served in church. By several devices, Shakespeare underscores Falstaff's great need of reformation for salvation. Falstaff perjures himself by claiming his lies about the Gadshill robbery are true, "or I am a Jew else, an Hebrew Jew" (2.4.177). Falstaff says that Bardolph's red nose constitutes his unconventional *memento mori*: "I never see thy face but I think upon hellfire and Dives that lived in purple; for there he is in his robes, burning, burning" (3.3.31-33). Yet in fact the postulated light in Bardolph's face serves Falstaff's vices, as a beacon at night between taverns (3.3.40-48). "God reward me for it!" (3.3.48), Falstaff blasphemously exclaims regarding the sack that he has bought Bardolph, and that he fancies fuels the nasal torch lighting his drunken way. "But thou art altogether given over," Falstaff pronounces of his crony, "and wert indeed, but for the light in thy face, the son of utter darkness" (3.3.35-38). A godly Protestant auditor, however, might object that the flame in Bardolph's face signifies that Bardolph is a "son of utter darkness."

Throughout the Second Henriad, Shakespeare offers no evidence for Falstaff's conclusive repentance and reformation. In *2 Henry IV*, Poins states that "the immortal part [of Falstaff] needs a physician, but that moves not him" (2.2.98-99). The Page touches on Falstaff's "Catholic" dissoluteness when with tongue-in-cheek he tells Hal that the company which Falstaff keeps in the tavern consists of members "of the old church" (2.2.142)—that is to say, "good fellows of the usual, disreputable fellowship."[13] Playgoers might think that the process of Falstaff's authentic reformation begins with his inclusion of himself in his condemnation of old men's addiction to the vice of lying, made as a preface to his clear-sighted correction of Shallow's history of his youth (*2 Henry IV* 3.2.302-26, esp. 302-03); but this apparently honest basis for personal reformation dissolves with his declaration that he will bilk Shallow out of his "land and beefs" (3.2.326-31). "If the young dace be a bait for the old pike, I see no reason in the law of nature but I may snap at him" (3.2.328-30), Falstaff concludes in proto-Darwinian fashion.[14]

The Hostess's memorable account of Falstaff's death confirms audiences' impression that this character never does get around to reforming himself until it is too late. On his deathbed, Falstaff may babble of green fields (*Henry V* 2.3.16-17), evidently his musings on Psalm 23; but the fact that he "babbles" suggests that his meditation is incoherent, directionless. He may cry out "'God, God, God!' three or four times" (2.3.18-19), but the Hostess urges him not to think on God (as though he will live). Falstaff may cry out against sack and women in his last hours (2.3.26-35), and, feverish ("rheumatic"), he may talk of the "Whore of Babylon" (2.3.37-38) (as though he seeks to die a proto-Protestant condemning a personification of the Church of Rome);[15] but all playgoers hear is evidence of his guilt, and nothing of his reformation. An upwardly progressive chill takes hold of Falstaff's body, and he dies before he can genuinely repent.[16] Thus the Hostess's blackly comic malapropism in her uttered conviction that dead Falstaff lies in "Arthur's bosom, if ever man went to Arthur's bosom" (2.3.9-10) aptly suggests the lack of Christian salvation in Falstaff's end.[17] Rather than to Abraham's salvific bosom, Falstaff in the Hostess's confused mind goes to that of a patron of secular chivalry.[18]

Shakespeare's characterizations of Prince Hal and later Henry V include and develop a critique of Protestant and Catholic traits working at cross purposes in the matter of personal reformation. As he formulates it, Hal's intended reformation appears mainly politico-ethical in nature. But Elizabethan playgoers would also have considered it spiritual, for Hal's misbehavior has consisted of those vices of the flesh that Reformers especially thought required amendment for the sinner's Christian salvation. This statement holds true even if a calculated Machiavellian program for personal political advancement wholly motivates Hal's performance of the sins of the tavern and brothel (a vexed question in the play), for the wages of sin are death, regardless of a person's reasons for sinning.[19]

Hal presents his calculated scheme for political advancement in *1 Henry IV* in his notorious soliloquy in act 1. In this speech, playgoers hear a stereotypical Protestant distrust of sloth, valuing of work, and curtailment of holiday:[20]

> I know you all, and will awhile uphold
> The unyoked humor of your idleness.
> . . . . .
> If all the year were playing holidays,
> To sport would be as tedious as to work;
> But when they seldom come, they wished-for come.
> (1.2.189-90, 198-201)

Hal's employment in his soliloquy of the pointedly Protestant word "reformation" (1.2.207) for his planned conversion strengthens the identification in his case of Protestantism and the distrust of sloth, valuing of work, and curtailment of holiday.[21] Hal intends his projected reformation of idleness and vice into a strict moral life to play its part in "Redeeming time" (1.2.211)—not simply the wasted time of the prince's life thus far but that of the exhausted, dissipated age of Henry IV's England as well.[22] Redeeming lost or wasted time by hours and days strictly regulated by religious meditation but mainly by serious productive work for the benefit of one's material life and soul as well as for the commonwealth became a hallmark of Tudor Protestantism.[23]

But even as stereotypical vices of Catholicism mingled with Falstaff's proto-Protestantism and could be said to undermine it, so a similar medley taints Hal's expression of his intention to reform and calls the authenticity of his resolution into question. "And like bright metal on a sullen ground," Hal states,

> My reformation, glittering o'er my fault,
> Shall show more goodly and attract more eyes
> Than that which hath no foil to set it off.
>
> (1.2.206-09)

With this language Hal conceives of his future reformation as mostly show with little substance, as something that, "glittering," superficially hides faults but dazzles beholders' eyes. Superficially, the metaphor makes Hal's purposed reformation a jewel glittering the better for the foil/fault set under it, enhancing it by contrast. But granted this primary meaning, playgoers can also hear the phrase "glittering o'er my fault," applied to Hal's intended reformation, as signifying that it will amount to golden, dazzling show deceptively covering his fault beneath it. Interpreted this way and considered within the matrix of the Second Henriad's Protestant critique of Catholicism, Hal's reformation conjures the image of those golden glittering icons of Catholicism, which by Elizabethan times had been smashed by reforming Protestants and condemned by their Elizabethan sons and daughters because their visual splendor once deceived gullible Christians.[24] Thus Shakespeare implicitly criticizes the idol worship latent in Hal's conception of his reformation. The taint of stereotypical Catholicism emanates as much from the articulated details of Hal's planned reformation as it does from the characterization of the degenerate idle holiday life that he expects to amend.

Shakespeare further undermines the Protestantism of Hal's intended reformation by involving him in Falstaff's and his cronies' thievery. Their robbery concerns—to repeat and slightly revise Gadshill's words—"pray[ing] continually to their saint, the commonwealth, or rather not pray[ing] to her but prey[ing] on her, for they ride up and down on her and make her their boots [booty]" (2.1.80-83). Hal joins the flawed Protestant Falstaff to pillage a "sainted" commonwealth, which was the later activity of Henry VIII, Cromwell, and their confederates, who sacked the Catholic monasteries.[25] The phrasing indicts Hal's projected reformation and its Protestant overtones.

As previously stated, Reformation Protestantism had by Elizabethan times made itself a religion of salvation by faith versus salvation by stereotypical Catholic deeds. Henry IV's planned medieval crusade against infidels in the Holy Land not only would divert armed aggression from himself to enemies outside England; leading troops there would also amount to a Catholic deed of penance for his part in Richard II's death. A different and more Protestant and modern kind of penitential deed constitutes Prince Hal's vehicle for his scripted reformation (at least in his account to his father of the projected process). Hal wishes that Hotspur's honors "were multitudes" (3.2.143), so that during calculated single combat with him he might

> make this northern youth exchange
> His glorious deeds for my indignities.

> Percy is but my factor, good my lord,
> To engross up glorious deeds on my behalf;
> And I will call him to so strict account
> That he shall render every glory up,
> Yea, even the slightest worship of his time,
> Or I will tear the reckoning from his heart.
> This in the name of God I promise here.[26]
>
> (3.2.145-53)

By means of these savage deeds, Prince Hal "will wear a garment all of blood / And stain [his] favors in a bloody mask, / Which, washed away, shall scour [his] shame with it" (3.2.135-37). Hal's words certainly ring with vindictive anger, traceable no doubt to his intense frustration over hearing his father and others praise Hotspur at his expense. But his notion that washing slain Hotspur's blood from his face shall scour shame from his countenance suggests that this deed of combat represents an act of personal penance.

But this method of redemption gets called into question by the negative overtones that it acquires in act 4 of *1 Henry IV*. Hal's chosen war-like vehicle of reformation possesses overtones of Catholic iconolatry. Vernon tells Hotspur that armed Hal and his comrades appear

> All plumed like estridges, that with the wind
> Bated like eagles having lately bathed,
> Glittering in golden coats, like images. . . .
>
> (4.1.98-100)

Resembling "gilded statues" (Bevington's gloss of "images"),[27] Prince Hal and his followers appear like those Catholic icons hated by Reformers, gilt images of all show and no worth that encourage idolatry.[28] Hal's pronouncement near the end of *1 Henry IV* firmly clinches the association in the Second Henriad between a glittering exterior and falsehood. "For my part," he tells Falstaff, who claims single-handedly to have killed Hotspur, "if a lie may do thee grace, / I'll gild it with the happiest terms I have" (5.4.155-56). The Chorus of *Henry V* makes explicit a pun latent in Shakespeare's use of the word "gilt" throughout *1* and *2 Henry IV*. Richard Earl of Cambridge, Henry Lord Scroop, and Sir Thomas Grey of Northumberland—all three traitors to Henry V—have, according to the Chorus, "for the gilt of France—O, guilt indeed!— / Confirmed conspiracy with fearful France" (2.Chorus.26-27). Playgoers can read this identification of guilty falsehood and glittering gold back into most of the distinctive appearances of the Catholic-icon imagery of the Henry IV plays.[29] Idol-worship, regarded from a Reformation Protestant viewpoint, convicted worshipers of guilt by misleading them into a false faith.[30]

In part 1, Hal's projected reformation of character becomes convincing for King Henry IV not through any evidence of his son's saving faith but through Hal's chivalric deed of rescuing the king from Douglas's assault (5.4.39-58), which becomes Hal's unlooked-for act of filial atonement. Furthermore, once Hal has killed Hotspur and captured Douglas, he sets his prisoner free, ransomless, rather than executing him because

His valors shown upon our crests today,
Have taught us how to cherish such high deeds
Even in the bosom of our adversaries.

(5.5.29-31)

Bloody deeds rather than evidence of inner faith or morality save an ethically questionable man's life in a case of double-standard justice (other traitors such as Worcester and Vernon are quickly put to death). Hal perhaps favors Douglas out of gratitude for the effect that his capture has had on the Prince's relationship with his father.

Granted the several ways by which Shakespeare invites auditors to question the nature of Hal's reformation in *1 Henry IV*, theater audiences are not surprised by his lapsing in *2 Henry IV* into his former, dissolute life of the street and tavern.[31] Disguising himself as a tavern waiter, sneaking back to the Boar's Head (thus violating a promise made to his father) simply to observe Falstaff ridiculously in love, Hal is interrupted, once he discloses himself to argue with Falstaff, by Peto, who tells him that Henry IV needs the reputed slayer of Hotspur, Falstaff, to quell the remaining rebels. "By heavens, Poins, I feel me much to blame," Hal confesses,

So idly to profane the precious time
When tempest of commotion, like the south
Borne with black vapor, doth begin to melt
And drop upon our bare unarmèd heads.
Give me my sword and cloak. Falstaff, good night.

(2.4.360-65)

Prince Hal has fallen into his former prodigal way of living partly because Falstaff cleverly wrested from him the credit for killing Hotspur, the deed upon which Hal's scripted reformation depended for its long-term credibility.

If early fifteenth-century England, rent by rebellion and relatively hard economic times, is ever to become a nation reformed, then the reformation of its monarch would seem to be a necessary precondition or corollary of the event.[32] This precondition initially concerns the character of Henry IV rather than that of his son. That Henry IV wants to be known as a reformer king becomes apparent in part 1 when Hotspur admits that this monarch "takes on him to reform / Some certain edicts and some strait decrees / That lie too heavy on the commonwealth" (4.3.80-82). The specter of a morally unreformed Henry VIII haunted Tudor Reformers in their efforts to purify their national religion.[33] Henry VIII's lapses were particularly egregious, since in himself he had married the pope and monarch into a prototype of the Reformer king. King Henry IV foreshadows this prototype when he says of his calculated absences from the public eye, "Thus did I keep my person fresh and new, / My presence, like a robe pontifical, / Ne'er seen but wondered at" (3.2.55-57). When Prince Hal begs pardon of his father for his prodigal youth, Henry IV's weighty response, "God pardon thee!" (3.2.29), is simultaneously a totalitarian monarch's pronouncement and a priestly absolution from God the Father.

Nevertheless, in Henry IV's case the blend of spiritual and secular power in the monarch proves unstable. This king vacillates between playing the parts of God's ordained agent and God's victim, the latter a wretched man who suspects that God has bred his scourge out of his own blood in the form of a prodigal son who indirectly punishes him for crimes against Richard II (3.2.4-11). The man who would be a priestly monarch yearns to atone for his sins by means of a pilgrimage to the holy city of Jerusalem, and yet he dies in the Jerusalem room of Westminster Abbey, as though a punster deity were mocking him.[34] Certain episodes of *1* and *2 Henry IV* predictively rehearse the Reformation scenario of the absolutist monarch and pontiff confronting each other. Act 4, scene 4, of *1 Henry IV* shows Richard Scroop, Archbishop of York, busily planning to muster allies to defend himself from Henry IV should the other rebels fail at Shrewsbury. Like Popes Clement VII and Paul III as they faced Henry VIII, Shakespeare's Archbishop of York becomes an adversary of the English nation so that he might purge the realm of the moral diseases incurred by the ambitions of an absolutist monarch who would appropriate pontifical roles for himself (*2 Henry IV* 4.1.41-87).

Thus Shakespeare gives playgoers the impression that, if Prince Hal is to become in some sense a Reformation monarch, he ought not to follow his father's example. Hal's personal reformation seems to occur authentically when he becomes king and accepts the Lord Chief Justice as his father. "The tide of blood in me / Hath proudly flowed in vanity till now," newly crowned King Henry V announces:

Now doth it turn and ebb back to the sea,
Where it shall mingle with the state of floods
And flow henceforth in formal majesty.

(*2 Henry IV* 5.2.129-33)

When Henry V coolly rejects the bloated image of his own former vices, Falstaff, he does so in language that suggests a just-completed personal reformation. "Presume not that I am the thing I was," he tells Falstaff, "For God doth know, so shall the world perceive, / That I have turned away my former self" (*2 Henry IV* 5.5.56-58). In this reforming vein, Henry V has banished his tavern companions from his presence "till their conversations [their behavior] / Appear more wise and modest to the world" (*2 Henry IV* 5.5.101-02). This personal reformation of Henry V appears to be the basis for claims that he is "a Christian king, / Unto whose grace our passion is as subject / As is our wretches fettered in our prisons" (*Henry V* 1.2.241-43). He is a ruler who, in the Chorus's estimation, invites his subjects to imitate the actions of "the mirror of all Christian kings" (*Henry V* 2.Chorus. 6).[35]

A stereotyped Catholic foil accentuates the Protestant nature of Henry V's second reformation of character in an apparently conclusive way. Ely marvels that Henry V could have quickly developed integrity while living dissolutely, but he finds precedence for the possibility in Nature:

> The strawberry grows underneath the nettle,
> And wholesome berries thrive and ripen best
> Neighbored by fruit of baser quality;
> And so the Prince obscured his contemplation
> Under the veil of wildness, which, no doubt,
> Grew like the summer grass, fastest by night,
> Unseen, yet crescive in his faculty.
>
> (*Henry V* 1.1.61-67)

"It must be so," Canterbury agrees, "for miracles are ceased. And therefore we must needs admit the means / How things are perfected" (1.1.68-70).[36] It was a Reformation Protestant—not a late-medieval Catholic Archbishop—who believed that "no miracles occurred after the revelation of Christ."[37] By the late sixteenth-century, belief in the continued occurrences of religious miracles had, in Protestant opinion, become a stigmal badge of Catholicism. With the Protestant subscription to the ceasing of miracles came a corresponding opportunity for self-fashioning, for the godly life of relative self-perfection. That this is Henry V's new life is the burden of the Archbishop's slightly earlier speech:

> Consideration like an angel came
> And whipped th' offending Adam out of him,
> Leaving his body as a paradise
> T'envelop and contain celestial spirits.
>
> (1.1.29-32)

Archbishop Canterbury's memorable metaphor of the functioning beehive (1.2.183-206) is no metaphor if such self-fashioning is possible, but a likely reality, for this self-perfection, even if relative, among a large portion of the citizenry and their magistrates, including their "emperor," would realize obedience in a harmoniously working commonwealth.[38] According to the Archbishop, honeybees

> have a king, and officers of sorts,
> Where some, like magistrates, correct at home;
> Others, like merchants, venture trade abroad;
> Others, like soldiers, armèd in their stings,
> Make boot upon the summer's velvet buds,
> Which pillage they with merry march bring home
> To the tent royal of their emperor,
> Who, busied in his majesty, surveys
> The singing masons building roofs of gold,
> The civil citizens kneading up the honey,
> The poor mechanic porters crowding in
> Their heavy burdens at his narrow gate,
> The sad-eyed justice with his surly hum
> Delivering o'er to executors pale
> The lazy yawning drone.
>
> (1.2.190-204)

A Reformation Protestant commonwealth could identify with this society, mainly because it celebrates the individually and socially redemptive benefits of proper work. The soldiers' war-work finds its justification in the "singing masons'" and "civil citizens'" transformations of their plunder into the commonwealth's food-stuffs and architecture. And while auditors might feel sorry for the plight of the heavy-burdened porters, reconsideration suggests that even this painful work, necessary to society, saves the laborers, for those who do not work die. By framing his picture of a commonwealth with "magistrates, correct[ing] at home" and a sober judge ordering a drone's execution, Canterbury underscores the justice of this world of work, wherein the emperor especially is "busy" in his majesty. Elizabethan Protestants would thus have found understandable the efficiency of the Archbishop's ruler, Henry V, by means of the Archbishop's flattering implication.

Despite these positive portrayals of Henry V's second, more authoritative reformation, troubling undercurrents swirl through it. For one thing, it—as previously mentioned—is crafted partly on the rejection of his former Falstaffian self: the Prodigal within him (*2 Henry IV* 5.5.56-59). The father in the biblical parable of the prodigal son (Luke 15:11-32) accepts the formerly profligate but now reformed younger son and blesses him. Since the prodigal Falstaff and Prince Hal's low-life companions have not reformed themselves, King Henry cannot be blamed for rejecting them until they give evidence of character reformation (5.5.66-71). But he can be blamed for the hypocrisy of terming Falstaff and his cronies the "misleaders" of his youth (5.5.64), for audiences of the Second Henriad know that, from the beginning, Hal cleverly allowed himself to be "misled" by Falstaff so that his purposed reformation would look better. Traces of an old, ethically troubling duplicity in Henry V's rejection of Falstaff beg the question of the complete honesty (or authenticity) of his second reformation.[39] If as a "model" Christian king Henry V controls his passions, the effect produced occasionally suggests an unpleasantly cold man.

Moreover, Shakespeare evokes aspects of the Tudor Reformation at the beginning of *Henry V* in order ironically to show King Henry subverting one of the Reformation's principal benefits. Appreciating this claim involves initially grasping certain correspondences between the life and times of Henry VIII and those of Shakespeare's Henry V. Shakespeare's countrymen could consider these parallels stronger than those between Henry IV and the great Tudor monarch. Both Henry V and Henry VIII were fond of disguising themselves to trick others. In 1540, Henry VIII disguised himself, traveled to Rochester, met the newly arrived Anne of Cleves, embraced and kissed her, talked with her, and then later, undisguised, returned to her.[40] Both kings warred against the French. "In 1513, as part of the propaganda campaign to justify his invasion of France, Henry VIII commissioned an English translation of Tito Livio's *Vita Henrici Quinti*. . . . Henry VIII took his model sufficiently to heart to ride about his rain-drenched camp in France, encouraging his soliders on the night before they set out to engage the French."[41] Both personally participated in the siege of a French city (Henry V at Harfleur, Henry VIII at Boulogne). Like Henry V, Henry VIII mercifully killed no one after the besieged city had surrendered (4,000 Boulognese departed unharmed). Like Henry V at Agincourt, Henry VIII at Boulogne achieved a miraculous victory. In the first French attempt to retake Boulogne, which pitted 14,000 Frenchmen against 5,000 Englishmen, many French troops died with little English loss of life. Like Shakespeare's Henry V, Henry VIII thanked God for this apparent martial miracle and ordered a *Te Deum* to be sung.[42] Both kings were reformers of religion who executed men for corrupting it (Shakespeare's Henry V executes Bardolph for stealing a *pax*). Both kings had to contend with northern rebels, including the Percies (Henry VIII was confronted by the Pilgrimage of Grace in 1536-37). Finally, both Henry VIII and Henry V shared the same name: "To his people [Henry VIII] remained to the end 'Bluff King Hal'."[43]

Dramatic similarities in Shakespeare's portraits of Henry V and Henry VIII suggest that the playwright intellectually linked these monarchs and their reigns. Even as Shakespeare shows Henry V disguising himself in false identities to his advantage, so in the playwright's later *King Henry VIII* he shows this monarch entering "*habited*" as a shepherd in a masque to dance with an unsuspecting Anne Bullen and with impunity savor her physical beauty (1.4.65-109 and *s.d.*). Like Shakespeare's King Henry VIII, Henry V enjoys the privilege of uncannily knowing his enemies' plots against him. Concerning the imminent treason of Scroop, Cambridge, and Grey, Bedford says that "The King hath note of all that they intend, / By interception which they dream not of" (*Henry V* 2.2.6-7). This mysterious political foresight anticipates and resembles Shakespeare's Henry VIII's, when the later ruler with the assistance of Dr. Butts, from a superior hidden vantage point, sees Gardiner and members of the Privy Council mistreating the king's agent, Cranmer. Even as Henry VIII later providentially detects his favorite Wolsey's treachery, so Henry V's prescience discovers the homicidal plot of Scroop, "the man that was his bedfellow, / Whom he hath dulled and cloyed with gracious favors" (2.2.8-9). The association of the two Henrys in Shakespeare's mind accounts for the resemblance between Henry V's formulation of Scroop's Judas-like betrayal and Henry VIII's angry conception of Wolsey's sin. "What shall I say to thee, Lord Scroop," Henry V begins,

> thou cruel,
> Ingrateful, savage, and inhuman creature?
> Thou that didst bear the key of all my counsels,
> That knew'st the very bottom of my soul,
> That almost mightst have coined me into gold,
> Wouldst thou have practiced on me for thy use.
>
> (2.2.94-99)

Nowhere else in the Shakespeare canon but in *King Henry VIII* 3.2 does the betrayal of the most trusted, rewarded inner counselor of a king acquire these archetypal Luciferian connotations. Having read Wolsey's missent inventory of his wealth secretly acquired, often at the king's expense, and the Cardinal's letters to the Pope, wherein he promotes his own ambition, a disillusioned Henry rejects the man he had "kept . . . next [to his] heart" and leaves Wolsey to—in his own words—fall "like Lucifer" (3.2. 158, 372).

The relevance of events in the reign of Henry VIII for those in Henry V's memorably materializes after the Archbishop of Canterbury actually uses the historically charged word "reformation" to convey Henry V's revolution of character:

> Never was such a sudden scholar made;
> Never came reformation in a flood
> With such a heady currance, scouring faults;
> Nor never Hydra-headed willfulness
> So soon did lose his seat, and all at once,
> As in this king.
>
> (1.1.33-38)

In the dialogue that follows this reconstruction, Shakespeare begs the question of the relationship between Henry V's acknowledged reformation and the fifteenth-century analogue of a defining event of the English Protestant Reformation: Henry VIII's appropriation of the Catholic Church's immense, mainly dormant wealth. In the play, Canterbury refers to the fact that Parliament currently considers passing a bill originally introduced during Henry IV's reign. Under it, Henry V would become the beneficiary of the largest part of more than one-half of the Church's English possessions. In Canterbury's words,

> all the temporal lands which men devout
> By testament have given to the Church
> Would they strip from us, being valued thus:
> As much as would maintain, to the King's honor,
> Full fifteen earls and fifteen hundred knights,
> Six thousand and two hundred good esquires,
> And, to relief of lazars and weak age
> Of indigent faint souls past corporal toil,
> A hundred almshouses right well supplied;
> And to the coffers of the King besides
> A thousand pounds by th' year. Thus runs the bill.
>
> (1.1.9-19)

Henry V, like Henry VIII after him, would profit personally from the conversion of Catholic wealth into thousands of new aristocratic entitlements that he could bequeath to secure loyalty as well as into an additional one-thousand pounds annually for the royal coffers. More important, the proposed dispossession of the Church will be justly beneficial, for a hundred new almshouses will be built from the proceeds of the rechanneled wealth (as though the Church has hoarded riches uncharitably). By promoting passage of the bill, Henry V can genuinely be styled a Christian king.

But the Bishop of Ely expects that King Henry will block the legislation, simply because he is "a true lover of the holy Church" (1.1.24). Concerning "this bill / Urged by the Commons" (1.1.71-72), Canterbury asserts that the new king "seems indifferent, / Or rather swaying more upon our part / Than cherishing th'exhibiters against us" (1.1.73-75). Essentially Canterbury bribes Henry V by privately offering him a sum of money greater than the Church ever at one time gave an English monarch (but certainly less than the wealth diverted to the king by the provisions of the pending bill) if he will wage war in

France to reestablish the English claim to that throne (which Canterbury attempts to justify through a murky explanation of the Salic law).[44] (Actually, embedded in the Archbishop's earlier allegory of the beehive is the subtle argument that the emperor wages "foreign" war to plunder the enemy ["velvet buds"] for domestic foodstuffs and building materials. Were Henry V to hear this veiled rationale and respond to it by pillaging the French, the Church would need to give even less money to the monarch for domestic use.) Whatever the case, both Henry and Canterbury tacitly understand that the king's acceptance of the Archbishop's private offer effectively kills the Parliament bill. Thus Henry V neglects a great spiritual good—the hundred new almshouses that his championing the parliamentary reform might accomplish. In this respect, his behavior does not testify to the profound spiritual dimension of his personal reformation as reported by Canterbury and others. Like Henry VIII after him, Henry V opens himself to the criticism that Catholic wealth redirected to his own and other noble strongboxes mainly serves the ends of militant personal glory and material gain, acquired under the jingoistic aegis of public good.[45]

Nevertheless, in the latter acts of *Henry V,* identifiably Reformation Protestant traits surface in the king that more than compensate for (or supersede) earlier troubling behavior. King Henry abandons his questionable practice of Machiavellian policy to tell the Dauphin's herald Montjoy humbly that he has resigned himself and his cause to God, and he does so in words that eschew bragging for a repentant plain idiom:

> For, to say the sooth,
> Though 'tis no wisdom to confess so much
> Unto an enemy of craft and vantage,
> My people are with sickness much enfeebled,
> My numbers lessened, and those few I have
> Almost no better than so many French,
> Who when they were in health, I tell thee, herald,
> I thought upon one pair of English legs
> Did march three Frenchmen. Yet, forgive me, God,
> That I do brag thus! This your air of France
> Hath blown that vice in me. I must repent.
> Go, therefore, tell thy master here I am;
> My ransom is this frail and worthless trunk,
> My army but a weak and sickly guard.
> Yet, God before, tell him we will come on,
> Though France himself and such another neighbor
> Stand in our way.
>
> (3.6.142-58)

A spirit of Protestant Calvinism informs King Henry's repentance of vain speech and his conception of his earthly being as a "frail and worthless trunk." Regarded in this context, the following utterance from his later St. Crispin's Day speech rings authentically:

> By Jove, I am not covetous for gold,
> Nor care I who doth feed upon my cost;
> It yearns me not if men my garments wear;
> Such outward things dwell not in my desires.
>
> (4.3.24-27)

The adversity of suffering hardships in France has begun to refine Henry's character into figurative gold.

Moreover, Henry V's conviction that "Every subject's duty is the King's; but every subject's soul is his own" (4.1.176-77) squares with the historically later Protestant greater emphasis upon the Christian's individual responsibility for confirming his or her salvation by daily charities and godly behavior unmediated by either a priest or religious ritual. (Catholic doctrine admitted some penitential deeds unmediated by a priest or ritual, such as penitential combat, but their number was far fewer than the total possible under Protestantism.) In a Protestant spirit, Henry implies that no outside authority such as a monarch or an institutionalized Church can vouch for the purity or sin of a person's soul. Henry V's non-Catholic notion of individual responsibility for the health of one's soul derives from his recently matured sense of personal accountability for his soldiers' lives and the welfare of English citizens. Henry disguised as a common soldier has told Bates that the king's "ceremonies laid by, in his nakedness he appears but a man" (4.1.105-06). When Henry thus vigorously forswears worship of the idol Ceremony, his denunciation acquires the value of a Protestant vilification of a stereotypical Catholic trait:

> And what have kings that privates have not too,
> Save ceremony, save general ceremony?
> And what art thou, thou idol ceremony?
> What kind of god art thou, that suffer'st more
> Of mortal griefs than do thy worshipers?
> What are thy rents? What are thy comings-in?
> O ceremony, show me but thy worth!
>
> (4.1.236-42)

Henry V goes on to say that the idol Ceremony is basically a hollow god, attractive only in its superficial trappings.

Still, Henry's proto-Protestant reformation of character does not satisfy his anxious belief that he stands in need of certain Catholic rituals of penance. The night before the Battle of Agincourt, a worried King Henry V prays,

> Not today, O Lord,
> O, not today, think not upon the fault
> My father made in compassing the crown!
> I Richard's body have interrèd new,
> And on it have bestowed more contrite tears
> Than from it issued forcèd drops of blood.
> Five hundred poor I have in yearly pay
> Who twice a day their withered hands hold up
> Toward heaven, to pardon blood; and I have built
> Two chantries, where the sad and solemn priests
> Sing still for Richard's soul. More will I do;
> Though all that I can do is nothing worth,
> Since that my penitence comes after all,
> Imploring pardon.
>
> (4.1.290-303)

Despite this and one other vestige of Catholicism (see below), a distinctly Protestant spirit animates Henry V's

St. Crispin's Day oration/sermon, inspiring his outnumbered troops to perform Herculean feats of arms at Agincourt. The inspiration of Christians chiefly by means of a central sermon-like speech became identified with Reformation Protestantism. Understanding the proto-Protestantism of Henry V's "sermon" to his soldiers involves appreciating its non-Catholic message of a democratic leveling of hierarchical privilege delivered via Christian language and ritual. His speech can be considered a sermon partly because it is delivered on the feast day of St. Crispin and is focused on the two saints Crispin and Crispinian. It amounts to a sermon designed, through brilliant rhetorical means, figuratively to put the spirit of Christian martyrs into enervated, apprehensive English soldiers. (By contrast "Saint" Oldcastle's spirit never did inhabit and purify the mountain of flesh, Falstaff.) In keeping with this day of martyrdom, Henry urges English survivors of Agincourt to show later generations their scars (as though they were those of near-martyrs). Superficially, this behavior resembles Catholic relic-veneration. Nevertheless, the names of the "host"—the English soldiers (4.3.34)—shall then be "Familiar in [their] mouth[s]" (4.3.52), as though they formed a symbolic rather than transubstantiated salvific body that auditors will ingest (through the story of Agincourt retold).[46] In this context, the Communion chalice is recalled by the "flowing cups" in which the "host"—"Harry the King, Bedford and Exeter, / Warwick and Talbot, Salisbury and Gloucester" (4.3.53-55)—is "freshly remembered." Like the regularly repeated Last Supper-Communion story of salvation through Christ, the immortalizing narrative of English St. Crispin's Day shall, according to Henry, recur "From this day to the ending of the world" (4.3.58).[47] And like the story of Christ's redemption commemorated by the Host and cup of wine, Henry's celebrated miracle of St. Crispin's Day gains its authority and transmits it through the original shedding of blood. "For he today that sheds his blood with me / Shall be my brother" (4.3.61-62), Henry V asserts: "be he ne'er so vile, / This day shall gentle his condition" (4.3.62-63). Henry's words vaguely evoke both the language of Christ to the thieves on either side of the cross and the details of the Last Supper. Imitating the life and death of Christ/Henry radically transforms and elevates a devotee's identity.[48]

Certainly Henry V's extravagant imitation of Christ puts him at risk for the charge of blasphemy.[49] In fact, he could be accused of inviting his troops to idolize him. Nevertheless, the Protestant insistence that the process of salvation applies equally to the foot soldier as to the king, if each is elect, surfaces in Henry's willingness to shed his royalty to stoop and join soldiers who spiritually distinguish themselves through their martyr-like willingness to shed their own blood for England. A warmth has replaced within Henry V a certain coldness he displayed during earlier moments of extreme self-control, such as that of Falstaff's banishment. The St. Crispin's Day's "sermon's" leveling of aristocrats to make all men plain brothers becomes a Protestant feature of *Henry V* when Shakespeare artfully makes its opposite a Catholic practice: the Catholic French warriors' blood in the Constable's words may be "spirited with wine" (3.5.21), but that wine never gets figuratively transformed into an immortal brotherhood of blood because the French embody an aristocratic hauteur. This icy attitude informs the King of France's battle oration, the complementary antithesis of Henry V's St. Crispin's Day exhortation. His oration fails to invigorate because it is little more than a mechanical, snobbish catalogue of pedigrees:

> Up, princes, and with spirit of honor edged
> More sharper than your swords, hie to the field!
> Charles Delabreth, High Constable of France,
> You Dukes of Orleans, Bourbon, and of Berri,
> Alençon, Brabant, Bar, and Burgundy,
> Jaques Chatillion, Rambures, Vaudemont,
> Beaumont, Grandpré, Roussi, and Faulconbridge,
> Foix, Lestrelles, Boucicault, and Charolais,
> High dukes, great princes, barons, lords, and knights,
> For your great seats now quit you of great shames.
> Bar Harry England, that sweeps through our land
> With pennons painted in the blood of Harfleur.
> Rush on his host, as doth the melted snow
> Upon the valleys, whose low vassal seat
> The Alps doth spit and void his rheum upon.
> Go down upon him—you have power enough—
> And in a captive chariot into Rouen
> Bring him our prisoner.
>
> (3.5.38-55)

One might object that King Henry, despite his rhetoric of brotherhood, reveals a trace of the French king's class-consciousness when he reads the Agincourt English casualty-list:

> Edward the Duke of York, the Earl of Suffolk,
> Sir Richard Keighley, Davy Gam, esquire;
> None else of name, and of all other men
> But five-and-twenty.
>
> (4.8.103-06)

But before we accuse him of hypocrisy, we need to realize that he is reading a list of English dead prepared formulaically by someone else. The fact that Henry just before he reads the English casualty-list recites a note of French dead (4.8.80-102)—a note which begins with princes and nobles and descends through "knights, esquires, and gallant gentlemen" and that includes a catalogue of most of the aristocrats chanted by the French King—reinforces the impression that too much should not be made of his manner of naming English dead.

Henry V's possession of two qualities the French king lacks further suggests his more generous attitude toward slain English troops. The French king's image of his aristocrat warriors hurtling down upon Henry's army like alpine snow, burying valleys beneath, betrays two characteristics of the speaker fatal to his cause—his lack of empathy with his common mercenaries and French gentry (much of that "melted snow") and an extreme disdain for simple folk (the French aristocratic avalanche will "spit and void [its] rheum upon" a "low vassal seat").

Never uniting with the rank and file of his army, the late-medieval, feudalistic Catholic King of France goes down to defeat.

Henry's St. Crispin's Day speech thus becomes more Protestant through comparison with its Catholic complement. Furthermore, Henry's address to his troops gets associated with Protestant labor in the implicit contrast of Protestant work with Catholic idleness when Westmorland prefaces the speech by exclaiming, "O, that we now had here / But one ten thousand of those men in England / That do no work today!" (4.3.16-18). For the English, Agincourt's "feats" of war (4.3.51) will amount to work of a kind far different from the Catholic saying of beads or lighting of candles. Henry V echoes Westmorland's word "work" in a proto-Protestant spirit when he says, "We are but warriors for the working day. / Our gayness and our gilt are all besmirched / With rainy marching in the painful field" (4.3.109-11). Once again Shakespeare evokes the stage Catholic imagery of a glittering ("gilt") outside only to deny it; Henry's troops are muddied, appropriate for a Protestant "working day." Beginning with his act 1 soliloquy in *1 Henry IV* (1.2.198-201), Henry has from time to time characterized fighting as a holiday game; but on the eve of Agincourt the odds against the English, their weakened, unreinforced state, and the monumental significance of the impending battle make work rather than game combat's appropriate referent. Finally, unlike the precious bones in an often-sold Catholic reliquary, Henry's bones, if he is killed in battle, shall in his estimation yield the French little if they try to sell them (4.3.123-25); for since he clearly intends to die fighting rather than risk capture (4.3.124), they will be shattered by warfare and unsuitable for enshrinement.

Henry V's St. Crispin's Day "sermon," charged with Protestant overtones, works a miracle, the English victory at Agincourt with only twenty-nine English dead (three of whom are noblemen) to ten-thousand French dead (of whom sixteen hundred are mercenaries and the rest French nobility, knights, and "gentlemen of blood and quality" [4.8.80-106]). This miraculous preservation of English lives prompts Henry to exclaim, "O God, thy arm was here! / And not to us, but to thy arm alone, / Ascribe we all" (4.8.106-08). "Take it, God," he concludes, "For it is none but thine" (4.8.111-12).[50] "For miracles are ceased," the Archbishop of Canterbury proclaimed at the beginning of the play, "And therefore we must needs admit the means / How things are perfected" (1.1.68-70). As noted earlier, the belief that miracles ceased after the revelation of Christ was a major tenet of Reformation Protestantism. The miniscule loss of English life at Agincourt, incredible to reason, suggests that the age of miracles extends to encompass the fifteenth century. The paradoxical implication in the play *Henry V* is that leading a proto-Protestant life of faith and service can result in a "Catholic" miracle. In typically syncretic fashion, Shakespeare melds aspects of two religious systems held to be antithetical during the later sixteenth century. In *All's Well That Ends Well*, Lafew, commenting on Helena's wondrous cure of the King of France's fistula, states, "They say miracles are past, and we have our philosophical persons to make modern and familiar things supernatural and causeless. Hence is it that we make trifles of terrors, ensconcing ourselves into seeming knowledge when we should submit ourselves to an unknown fear" (2.3.1-6). If we are to judge by this passage, Shakespeare, around the turn of the sixteenth century, became interested in a doctrine of miracle in which the hand of heaven could be seen, a doctrine that—by Lafew's logic—deserved admiration rather than intellectual inquiry into its causation.

Henry V's awareness that he has been the recipient of a divine miracle completes an arguably authentic personal reformation. The unprecedented difference between the English and French loss of life at Agincourt, rationally incomprehensible, by itself resolves Henry's long-harbored doubts about God's blessing upon him and his monarchy and completes the character revolution attempted previously but unsuccessfully. Concerning the English victory with so little loss of life, Henry commands,

> And be it death proclaimèd through our host
> To boast of this or take that praise from God
> Which is his only.
>
> (4.8.114-16)

Henry's accomplished reformation can be detected in his humble response to his lords' desire "to have borne / His bruisèd helmet and his bended sword / Before him through" London:

> He forbids it,
> Being free from vainness and self-glorious pride,
> Giving full trophy, signal, and ostent
> Quite from himself to God.
>
> (5.Chorus.17-22)

Nevertheless, playgoers must reconcile certain ungodly behaviors of Henry's during the Battle of Agincourt with his definitive reformation. Henry indicated then that at moments of group violence he could still become passion's slave. In the heat of conflict, he cruelly orders every English soldier to kill his prisoners because "the French have reinforced their scattered men" (4.6.36-38). Gower believes that Henry gives this savage order in retaliation for the French killing of the English boys guarding the luggage (4.7.1-10). But Henry in the text of the play gives his bloody order before he learns of this fact (thus making it appear prior), and he does so simply because French reinforcements suddenly threaten the English position. After Henry becomes aware of the slaughter of the helpless English boys, he snarls, "I was not angry since I came to France / Until this instant" (4.7.54-55). "Besides, we'll cut the throats of those we have," he ominously pronounces regarding the French prisoners in his entourage, "And not a man of them that we shall take / Shall taste our mercy" (4.7.62-64).[51] But in Shakespeare's staging these prisoners never are killed, for the French capitulate before the deed can be done.

Significantly, the above-described vestiges of the Old Adam surface in Henry *before* his learning of the miracle of Agincourt refines the remaining dross of sadism and pride into golden humility. King Henry V manifests this ultimately refined humility in his fifth-act wooing of Princess Katharine. An attractive directness and modest plainness of speech color his courtship.[52] "Thou wouldst find me such a plain king," he tells Katharine, "that thou wouldst think I had sold my farm to buy my crown. I know no ways to mince it in love, but directly to say, 'I love you'" (5.2.126-29). Henry forswears bragging (5.2.140); he at last admits to having a "saving faith" within him (5.2.204). Henry V's reformation is as complete as it could ever get in the short time remaining to this "star of England" (Epilogue, 6). One senses that Henry V will rarely—if ever—again be Machiavellian in quite the same cold way that he was, but rather will be a sincere, plain-speaking man who constitutes the implicit ideal of Elizabethan Shakespeare comedies such as *Love's Labor's Lost*.[53] Admittedly, a trace of the calculating Henry appears in his having made Katharine his "capital demand, comprised / Within the fore-rank of [the peace] articles" (5.2.96-97). Certainly the word "capital" carries economic overtones, the notion being that Henry has commodified his future queen. A political expediency, however, does not preclude, on the level of the heart, his sincere love-suit. The "good heart" (5.2.163) that Henry has purified within himself might be a model for Protestants sitting or standing in the Globe Theater. The Catholic "miracle" that at a decisive moment helps to cleanse this heart is Shakespeare's subtle argument for Protestant tolerance of Catholics and their dogma in a darkening world of religious division.[54]

Notes

1. Shakespeare takes considerable pains to imbue the late medieval setting of *1 Henry IV* with the spirit of Catholicism. King Henry's reference to the Crucifixion "fourteen hundred years ago" (1.1.26) and his desire to be Christ's soldier in a crusade to wrest the Jerusalem sepulcher from pagan hands date the events of the play in the Catholic early fifteenth century. In this context, the speech's thirty-three verses evoke Christ's apocryphal age at his martyrdom, a fitting allusion in light of Henry's latent wish to atone for his guilt for Richard II's murder. The Catholic atmosphere of *1 Henry IV* thickens with Westmorland's mention of "Holy Rood Day" (1.1.52), references to pilgrims going to Canterbury, repeated oaths such as Prince Hal's "By'r Lady" (2.4.295), and Falstaff's phrase "*ecce signum!*" ("behold the proof!")—familiar words from the Mass—spoken with reference to the miracle of his claim of escape from a dozen enemies (2.4.162-67). The Catholic elements of *Henry V* are strongly emphasized by Stephen M. Buhler, "'By the Mass, our hearts are in the trim': Catholicism and British Identity in Olivier's *Henry V*," *Cahiers Élisabéthains* 47 (April 1995): 55-70.

   All quotations of Shakespeare's plays in the present article are from *The Complete Works of Shakespeare,* ed. David Bevington, 4th ed. (New York: Longman, 1997).

2. See Maurice Hunt, "Predestination and the Heresy of Merit in *Othello*," *Comparative Drama* 30 (1996): 346-76, esp. 367-69.

3. Huston Diehl, in *Staging Reform, Reforming the Stage: Protestantism and Popular Theater in Early Modern England* (Ithaca: Cornell University Press, 1997), demonstrates through a fine analysis of selected Shakespeare and early modern English plays (she omits the plays of the Second Henriad) that Elizabethan and Stuart playwrights subtly used "the theater to dramatize the divisive conflicts and explore the central religious controversies of the Reformation" (64).

4. For an exhaustive study of the *Henry IV* plays as an exploration of the Oldcastle issue, see Alice-Lyle Scoufos, *Shakespeare's Typological Satire* (Athens: Ohio University Press, 1979). Also see Gary Taylor, "The Fortunes of Oldcastle," *Shakespeare Survey* 38 (1985): 85-100; E. A. J. Honigmann, "Sir John Oldcastle: Shakespeare's Martyr," *"Fanned and Winnowed Opinions": Shakespearean Essays Presented to Harold Jenkins,* ed. John W. Mahon and Thomas A. Pendleton (London: Methuen, 1987), 118-32; and Kristen Poole, "Saints Alive! Falstaff, Martin Marprelate, and the Staging of Puritanism," *Shakespeare Quarterly* 46 (1995): 47-75, esp. 48-53. Taylor's argument that editors ought to substitute Oldcastle's name for Falstaff's in the texts of the Second Henriad has been effectively rebutted by Jonathan Goldberg, "The Commodity of Names: 'Falstaff' and 'Oldcastle' in *1 Henry IV*," in *Reconfiguring the Renaissance: Essays in Critical Materialism,* ed. Jonathan Crewe (Lewisburg: Bucknell University Press, 1992), 76-88.

5. For the story of Sir John Oldcastle as it was told and retold throughout the sixteenth century, "with different ideological emphases," see Annabel Patterson, *Reading Holinshed's "Chronicles"* (Chicago: University of Chicago Press, 1994), 130-53.

6. Summaries of Falstaff's "Puritanical" traits of character and speech appear in J. Dover Wilson, *The Fortunes of Falstaff* (Cambridge: Cambridge University Press, 1943), 15-35; Poole, "Saints Alive! Falstaff, Martin Marprelate, and the Staging of Puritanism," 65-69; and especially in Grace Tiffany, "Puritanism in Comic History: Exposing Royalty in the Henry Plays," forthcoming in *Shakespeare Studies* 26 (1998). Generally critics such as Poole who notice these traits endorse the opinion that "the person of Falstaff is in and of himself a parody of the sixteenth-century puritan" (54). See, for example, Harold Bloom, *Ruin the Sacred Truths: Poetry and Belief from the Bible to the Present* (Cambridge: Harvard University Press, 1989), 84.

Usually critics regard this purported parody of Puritanism in Falstaff as Shakespeare's jibe at the Protestantism of the Lollard Oldcastle's late Elizabethan heirs William and Henry Brooke; See, for example, Robert J. Fehrenbach, "When Lord Cobham and Tilney 'were at odds': Oldcastle, Falstaff, and the Date of *1 Henry IV*," *Shakespeare Studies* 18 (1986): 87-101. Poole, however, regards the supposed Puritan satire generated by Falstaff's character as "perfectly in keeping with the tenor of the anti-Puritan literature of the late sixteenth century, especially the anti-Marprelate tracts and the burlesque stage performances of the Marprelate controversy, which frequently depicted Puritans as grotesque individuals living in carnivalesque communities" (54). Tiffany's article offers a stimulating alternative interpretation of the relevance of the Marprelate controversy to Falstaff's characterization.

7. See Christopher Hill, "Protestantism and the Rise of Capitalism," *Change and Continuity in Seventeenth-Century England* (Cambridge: Harvard University Press, 1975), 81-102, esp. 82-83.

8. Bevington, *The Complete Works of Shakespeare*, 779.

9. Davidson made this comment in response to an earlier version of my present essay.

10. Phyllis Rackin, in *Stages of History: Shakespeare's English Chronicles* (Ithaca: Cornell University Press, 1990), points out that "[t]he recognition of anachronism, in fact, was a basic premise of Reformation thought. No longer seen as an institution unchanged from its beginnings, the contemporary church was contrasted with the church as it had been before centuries of Roman Catholic corruption had polluted it" (10). Playgoers' recognition of anachronisms in Falstaff's stage Protestantism, by this logic, would betray the fact that they lived in the sixteenth century.

11. This specific linkage of Falstaff and Queen Elizabeth has been noted by Barbara Hodgdon, *The End Crowns All: Closure and Contradiction in Shakespeare's History* (Princeton: Princeton University Press, 1991), 156.

12. Despite Gadshill's claim that "There's money of the King's coming down the hill; 'tis going to the King's Exchequer" (*1 Henry IV* 2.2.53-54), Shakespeare nevertheless suggests that Falstaff and his cronies rob not the agents or officers of Henry IV's treasury but certain members of a commonwealth (one "sainted" because "preyed/prayed" upon). The persons plundered are termed "Travelers" (2.2.78 s.d.), apparently the Canterbury pilgrims and "traders riding to London with fat purses" (1.2.122-25) whom Poins first specified as the subjects of the robbery.

13. Bevington, *The Complete Works of Shakespeare*, 819.

14. This is essentially the interpretation of Edward I. Berry, "The Rejection Scene in *2 Henry IV*," *Studies in English Literature* 17 (1977): 201-18, esp. 202.

15. This is the reading of both Roy Battenhouse, "Falstaff as Parodist and Perhaps Holy Fool," *PMLA* 90 (1975): 32-52, esp. 46-47; and Paul M. Cubeta, "Falstaff and the Art of Dying," *Studies in English Literature* 27 (1987): 197-211, esp. 206.

16. By the logic of his symbolic role, Falstaff cannot reform himself. "I know thee not, old man," King Henry V says near the end of *2 Henry IV*, "Fall to thy prayers" (5.5.47). As the Old Man, the Old Adam, Falstaff's typology precludes his reformation. See D. J. Palmer, "Casting off the Old Man: History and St. Paul in *Henry V*," *Critical Quarterly* 12 (1970): 267-83, esp. 268-69.

17. Falstaff's successful death-bed reformation is argued—unconvincingly, I believe—by J. Dover Wilson in his edition of *Henry V* (Cambridge: Cambridge University Press, 1947), 142; and by Christopher Baker, "The Christian Context of Falstaff's 'Finer End'," *Explorations in Renaissance Culture* 12 (1986): 68-86, esp. 81-83. Also see Michael Platt, "Falstaff in the Valley of the Shadow of Death," *Interpretations: Journal of Political Philosophy* 8, no. 1 (1979): 5-24.

18. Concerning the Hostess's "Arthurian" judgment (2.3.9-10), Baker claims that Falstaff's "final end, resting in 'Arthur's bosom,' is the return of a comic prodigal to the father he sought to escape" ("The Christian Context of Falstaff's 'Finer End'," 70-71).

19. For decades, a critical debate has focused upon the question of whether Prince Hal is truly debauched and thus genuinely in need of reformation or whether he play-acts the debauchee and so needs not actual reformation. An overview of the debate is provided by Kristian Smidt, *Unconformities in Shakespeare's History Plays* (Atlantic Highlands, N. J.: Humanities Press, 1982), 107-10, who joins those critics who think Hal is debauched and needs reformation (108). The critic to focus most recently the question of Hal's reformation, Jonathan Crewe ("Reforming Prince Hal: The Sovereign Inheritor in *2 Henry IV*," *Renaissance Drama* 21 [1990]: 225-42), concludes: "The most influential current arguments deny that there is any substantive reform of Prince Hal's character. These are the arguments, associated mainly with Stephen Greenblatt, which insist on Hal's role-playing, and hence on the theatricality of his madcap character and of the metamorphosis he effects in *1 Henry IV*" (225). (The reference to Greenblatt concerns "Invisible Bullets," *Shakespearean Negotiations: The Circulation of Social Energy in Renaissance England* [Berkeley and Los Angeles: University of California Press, 1988], 21-65, esp. 40-65.) My claim that accomplished vice taints the actor of it even when the sin is play-acted nevertheless entails

some kind of true reformation of the subject. More important, my demonstration that Hal/Henry V possesses several faults that are not play-acted more conclusively argues for the refinement of his character and represents an alternative to Crewe's thesis concerning Hal's reformation of parricidal (oedipal) feelings.

20. An excellent analysis of this soliloquy different from mine appears in Harold Toliver, "Workable Fictions in the Henry IV Plays," *University of Toronto Quarterly* 53 (1983): 53-71, esp. 59.

21. Unquestionably Shakespeare's contemporaries used the modern term "reformation" for not only the Protestant revolution of purified manners but also for the cultural upheaval identified with King Henry VIII, his ministers, and the Church of England's displacement of Roman Catholicism. Subsection 3b under the noun 'Reformation' in the *OED* includes this illustrative usage taken from Fregeville's *Reformed Politicke*: "To the end to ship the Clergy in the League, they wer perswaded, that within six moneths the Reformation should be vtterly extinguished." In 1544, John Bale concluded that Sir John Oldcastle "dyed at the importune sute of the clergye, for callynge vpon a Christen reformacyon in that Romyshe church of theyrs . . ." (*Brefe Chronycle concernynge the Examinacyon and death of the blessed martyr of Christ syr Johan Oldecastell the lorde Cobham* [Antwerp, 1544], fol. 53ʳ, as quoted in Poole, "Saints Alive! Falstaff, Martin Marprelate, and the Staging of Puritanism," 48).

22. See J. A. Bryant, Jr., "Prince Hal and the Ephesians," *Sewanee Review* 67 (1959): 204-19; and Paul A. Jorgensen, "'Redeeming Time' in Shakespeare's *Henry IV*," *Tennessee Studies in Literature* 5 (1960): 101-09.

23. See Maurice Hunt, *Shakespeare's Labored Art* (New York: Peter Lang, 1995), 6.

24. For excellent histories of the Protestant iconoclastic impulse during the English sixteenth century, see John Phillips, *The Reformation of Images: Destruction of Art in England, 1535-1660* (Berkeley and Los Angeles: University of California Press, 1973), 1-156; Margaret Aston, *England's Iconoclasts* (Oxford: Clarendon Press, 1988), vol. 1; *Iconoclasm vs. Art and Drama*, ed. Clifford Davidson and Ann Eljenholm Nichols, Early Drama, Art, and Music Monograph Series, 11 (Kalamazoo: Medieval Institute Publications, 1989); James R. Siemon, *Shakespearean Iconoclasm* (Berkeley and Los Angeles: University of California Press, 1985), 30-75; and Diehl, *Staging Reform, Reforming the Stage*, 9-39. Also see John N. King, *English Reformation Literature: The Tudor Origins of the Protestant Tradition* (Princeton: Princeton University Press, 1982), 144-60.

25. See, for example, John Stow, *The Annales of England* (London: Ralph Newbery, 1592), 965-66. Stow, after composing the grim list of priests and citizens executed by Henry VIII in 1535 for resisting edicts of the Reformation, and after remarking that the king seized 376 religious houses, £32,000 worth of Church land, and more than £100,000 of church moveables in 1536 alone, indicts Henry VIII by writing: "It was (saith mine author) a pitifull thing to heare the lamentation that the people in the countrie made for [the expelled priests, monks, and nuns]: for there was great hospitalitie kept among them, and as it was thought more than ten thousand persons, masters and seruants had lost their liuings by the putting downe of those houses at that time" (966). For a commentary that applies to Henry VIII's and Edward VI's theft of moveable church property, see Eamon Duffy, *The Stripping of the Altars* (New Haven: Yale University Press, 1992), 379-503.

26. Alexander Leggatt, in *Shakespeare's Political Drama: The History Plays and the Roman Plays* (London: Routledge, 1988), remarks that Prince Hal's language of commerce in this speech undercuts the honor he would win by killing Hotspur (94). It thus serves to suggest that this deed will ultimately fail as a vehicle for Hal's reformation.

27. The idea of images "Glittering in golden coats" could possibly involve auditors' recollections of painted figures on tombs or even silhouettes in memorial brasses, which when polished look golden. Nevertheless, the next verse of the passage—"As full of spirit as the month of May" (4.1.101)—would discourage funereal evocations, a likelihood that would allow the play's late-medieval setting and its accumulating Catholic allusions to suggest to Elizabethans the notion of Catholic icons.

28. Siemon demonstrates that "certain features of Shakespearean drama can be profitably understood as refracting the struggles over imagery and likeness that vexed post-Reformation England and found their most obvious expression in the various phenomena of iconoclasm" (*Shakespearean Iconoclasm*, 30). This critic posits in Shakespeare's *Henry V* "an iconic counterforce to the 'iconic tableaux' that the play repeatedly forms" (101).

29. In a similar vein, David Scott Kastan makes this comment on *Richard II* 2.1.294 ("Wipe off the dust that hides our scepter's gilt"): "The homonymic pun on 'gilt' signals that the symbols of rule in Bolingbroke's usurping hand have been 'derogated,' we might say, tainted and diminished by the process of their attainment. 'Gilt' has been tarnished by Henry's guilt" ("Proud Majesty Made a Subject: Shakespeare and the Spectacle of Rule," *Shakespeare Quarterly* 37 [1986]: 471).

30. The overtones of idol-worship inherent in Vernon's portrait of Hal and his comrades "Glittering in golden coats, like images" reappear more strongly

when Falstaff at the end of *2 Henry IV* falls to his knees before recently crowned Henry V and exclaims, "My King! My Jove! I speak to thee, my heart" (5.5.46). Nevertheless, Falstaff's motives of flattering Hal at this moment to gain preferment render these overtones doubtful.

31. A different explanation of Hal's backsliding, one that involves his progressively "wise" unlearning of certain of his own and other characters' ideas, is given by F. Nick Clary, "Reformation and Its Counterfeit: The Recovery of Meaning in *Henry IV, Part One,*" *Ambiguities in Literature and Film,* ed. Hans P. Braendlin (Tallahassee: Florida State University Press, 1988), 76-94, esp. 80-84.

32. The relatively hard economic times depicted at times in the Second Henriad (e.g., *1 Henry IV* 2.1.1-32) may have been a misleading fabrication of Shakespeare's. Fifteenth-century England appears to have been more prosperous than the preceding century and, in many ways, more so than the following one. See Charles Phythian-Adams, *Desolation of a City: Coventry and the Urban Crisis of the Late Middle Ages* (Cambridge: Cambridge University Press, 1979).

33. Stories of Henry VIII's repeated fornication and adultery, for example, accentuated the harshness of the 1539 Parliamentary enactment that priests were to have no wives and that priests with wives were to divorce them, or else they were to forfeit their goods and benefices and after a second warning suffer death (Charles Wriothesley, *A Chronicle of England During the Reigns of the Tudors,* 2 vols. [Westminster: J. B. Nichols, 1875], 1:102-03). Cf., however, Stephen Gardiner's treatise *On True Obedience* and Richard Rex's commentary on its portrait of a reformed Henry VIII in *Henry VIII and the English Reformation* (New York: St. Martin's Press, 1993), 24-25. Nevertheless, Henry VIII forfeited forever among European kings and princes his reputation of being a humane prince when he beheaded Sir Thomas More and Bishop John Fisher. His savagery during the spoilage of Thomas Becket's shrine—he had the saint's bones burnt, the ashes mingled with earth, and the composite shot from a cannon—shocked Europeans even more than his notorious beheadings (H. Maynard Smith, *Henry VIII and the Reformation* [London: Macmillan, 1962], 101-02).

34. See Robert J. Fehrenbach, "The Characterization of the King in *1 Henry IV,*" *Shakespeare Quarterly* 30 (1979): 43-50, esp. 44.

35. Harold Jenkins, in *The Structural Problem in Shakespeare's "Henry the Fourth"* (London: Methuen, 1955), 24-25, set a precedent by maintaining that "in the two parts of *Henry IV* . . . there are not two princely reformations but two versions of a single reformation. And they are mutually exclusive." Jenkins resolved this contradiction by claiming that it is typical of folkloric narrative and that Shakespeare's method in this instance is theological allegory (and thus folkloric). Nevertheless, Edward I. Berry, in *Patterns of Decay: Shakespeare's Early Histories* (Charlottesville: University Press of Virginia, 1975), articulates "the inconsistencies in Hal's double reformation" (109). By positing three main attempts at personal reformation on Hal's part, I necessarily subscribe to Berry's qualifier.

36. Moody E. Prior, in *The Drama of Power: Studies in Shakespeare's History Plays* (Evanston: Northwestern University Press, 1973), 321-24, understands King Henry V's apparent reformation as described by Ely and Canterbury as a doffing of the Old Man and a putting on of the New Man according to descriptions in Ephesians 4:22-24, John 3:6-7, and certain passages in the *Book of Common Prayer.*

37. The quotation represents Bevington's gloss. For documentation of the idea, see Keith Thomas, *Religion and the Decline of Magic* (New York: Charles Scribner's Sons, 1971), 80, 107-8, 124-25, 128, 203, 256, 479, 485, 490, 577-78, 643. Samuel Harsnett's *A Declaration of Egregious Popish Impostures* (1603), a text informing Edgar's bogus miracle in act 4, scene 4, of Shakespeare's *King Lear,* amounts to a contemporary endorsement of the Protestant position concerning ceased miracles.

38. Jonathan Dollimore and Alan Sinfield, however, argue for the metaphorical status of the notorious beehive of *Henry V* by asserting that it is the construct of a part of society claiming to be the whole ("History and Ideology: The Instance of *Henry V,*" in *Alternative Shakespeares,* ed. John Drakakis [London: Methuen, 1985], 212-13).

39. Jonas A. Barish, in "The Turning Away of Prince Hal," *Shakespeare Studies* 1 (1965): 9-17, argues that Henry V's rejection of Falstaff amounts to a self-rejection, a turning away a more honest compassionate self. In the king's casting off Falstaff, "we find the exigencies of the history play leading to a 'reformation' that we can only feel as a dehumanization" (14).

40. Wriothesley, *A Chronicle of England,* 1:109-10.

41. Peter C. Herman, "'O 'tis a gallant king': Shakespeare's *Henry V* and the Crisis of the 1590s," in *Tudor Political Culture,* ed. Dale Hoak (Cambridge: Cambridge University Press, 1995), 204-25, esp. 220.

42. Wriothesley, *A Chronicle of England,* 1:149-52.

43. Smith, *Henry VIII and the Reformation,* 16.

44. Dollimore and Sinfield note that during the latter part of Queen Elizabeth's reign, "[t]he Church resented the fact that it was expected to help finance foreign wars, but in 1588 Archbishop Whitgift

encouraged his colleagues to contribute generously towards resistance to the Armada on the grounds—just as in *Henry V*—that it would head off criticism of the Church's wealth" ("History and Ideology: The Instance of *Henry* V," 216). For the text of the Archbishop's opinion, see his May 1588 circular letter to England's Bishops quoted by John Strype, *The Life and Acts of John Whitgift,* 3 vols. (Oxford: Clarendon Press, 1822), 1:525.

45. Jeffrey Knapp, in "Preachers and Players in Shakespeare's England," *Representations* 44 (Fall 1993): 29-59, places the conniving of the Bishop of Ely and the Archbishop of Canterbury at the beginning of *Henry V* within the context of Shakespeare's career-long negative depiction of episcopal militarism and claims that in this episode King Henry V disturbingly absorbs "both the bishops' money and their piety" (39).

46. See Joel B. Altman, in "'Vile Participation': The Amplification of Violence in the Theater of *Henry V*," *Shakespeare Quarterly* 42 (1991): 16, for the observation that "Shakespeare enables the audience of *Henry V* to participate Harry the King just as the drawers, companions, and—more distantly—the people of England participated the Prince in the two parts of *Henry IV*. Which is to say that now they share him in both a sacramental and a poetic—and most needfully, a political—way. In partaking him—to conflate Hooker and Jonson—in digesting him, turning him to nourishment, and growing 'very Hee'," Shakespeare's audience assimilates Henry's aggression, bravado, and savagery.

47. Remarking that *Henry V* "has strong affinities with mainstream English Protestant conceptions of the eucharist" (33), Knapp investigates the broad symbolic function of the eucharistic *pax* in the play ("Preachers and Players in Shakespeare's England," 41).

48. For other analyses of the St. Crispin's Day speech, see Norman Rabkin, *Shakespeare and the Problem of Meaning* (Chicago: University of Chicago Press, 1981), 45-46; and Lawrence Danson, "*Henry V:* King, Chorus, and Critics," *Shakespeare Quarterly* 34 (1983): 34-35, 42.

49. Knapp comments that "Harry's gift to his soldiers . . . is to liberate a holy-seeming communion from the confines of the church to the open battlefield" ("Preachers and Players in Shakespeare's England," 41). There, physical violence and secular chivalry, rather than a godly ritual, become King Henry V's vehicle for his communion of brotherhood.

50. Hodgdon states that "through Henry's pious insistence that God won the battle [of Agincourt], he reconnects himself to the mystifying force of divine right that was Richard II's special province" (*The End Crowns All,* 188).

51. The dramatic problem of King Henry V's double, apparently inconsistent order to cut French prisoners' throats has been well focused and analyzed by Joanne Altieri, "Romance in *Henry V,*" *Studies in English Literature* 21 (1981): 223-40, esp. 223-24, 236; by Berry, *Patterns of Decay,* 109; and by John W. Blanpied, *Time and the Artist in Shakespeare's English Histories* (Newark: University of Delaware Press, 1983), 267.

52. Cf., however, Paola Pugliatti, "The Strange Tongues of *Henry V,*" *The Yearbook of English Studies* 23 (1993): 235-53, esp. 243.

53. Maintaining that all the aspects of Henry V's character form an integrated whole, Carol M. Sicherman, on the other hand, in "'King Hal': The Integrity of Shakespeare's Portrait," *Texas Studies in Literature and Language* 21 (1979): 503-21, argues that Hal's maturation in the use of formal language, from prose to progressively more controlled and formal verse, charts his reformation (508).

54. Knapp concludes that "the anticlericalism of the history plays may suggest Shakespeare's longing for a religion that would be inclusive and pacifist rather than elitist and bellicose; but the last of these plays [*Henry V*] seems to leave us with the image of a communion broadened from clergy to congregation, from paxes to peace, only when first sanctified by violence" ("Preachers and Players in Shakespeare's England," 41-42).

UNITY

John Berryman (essay date 1970)

SOURCE: "Shakespeare's Poor Relation: *2 Henry IV,*" in *Berryman's Shakespeare,* edited by John Haffenden, Farrar, Straus and Giroux, 1999, pp. 335-39.

[*In the following unfinished essay, originally composed in 1970, Berryman presents a comparison between the two parts of* Henry IV, *stressing that he does not agree with those who see the two plays as a whole.*]

Producers, critics, and mere readers have not been kind to *Part II, Henry IV.* In thirty-five years of playgoing I have seen it performed only once. The single quarto of 1600 was never reprinted, so far as we know, and one may doubt whether one in fifty readers of *Part I* go on to *Part II.* As for critics, they have mostly considered the two plays together, with very little said about the second. But it happens that in recent years half a dozen of them have bestirred themselves on its behalf, some on the unity of the giant double play considered as a whole, some on the unity of *Part II* taken alone as a sequel to the immensely successful *Part I.* It forms no part of my present purpose to canvas these views, though of course I shall refer to them now and again. My purpose is to account for the relative inferiority of *Part II* and then to make some remarks in mitigation of that argument: that is, to try to say why spectators and readers who do push on to it find themselves disappointed, in spite of the obviously great self-confidence and competence of the play and its occasional glories. Let me say first, though, that I cannot agree with those who see the two plays as a whole, and I feel no affinity with those who are surprised and depressed by the final rejection of Falstaff.

Shakespeare faced two problems. Hotspur was gone, and the relations between Prince Henry and Falstaff clearly had to deteriorate if the rejection was not to chill the reader wholly. The greatest dramatist the world has ever known took steps.

He kept the *spirit* of Hotspur going with two fine elegiac scenes. And in an attempt to replace him with some character *inward* among the nobles, he took special pains with poor ill old Northumberland—well done, but hardly a substitute for the vaulting Harry Percy. One critic, Clifford Leech, remarks that this is a play about *old* men; to this may be added that there is no fighting—the faith breech at Gaultree Forest compares miserably with Shrewsbury. The world where Hotspur flourished is gone, and his father Northumberland's betrayal bears on one less than his betrayal in *Part I*. Everything is cheapened and darkened in the play. One sees this in the women, in what we may call the love interest. Kate Percy being now merely a widow (a splendidly articulate one), it is Doll Tearsheet who replaces her, with Falstaff ("I am old, I am old"), and Doll is no chicken. The love scenes in the two parts are correlated: both begin with abuse and wind up in reconciliation. But what a world of difference there is between

> *Fal.*
> . . . the rogue fled from me like quicksilver.
> *Doll.*
> Yfaith, and thou followedst him like a church, thou horson little tydee Bartholomew borepigge, when wilt thou leave fighting a daies and foyning a nights, and begin to patch up thine old body for heauen.
> *Fal.*
> Peace good Doll, do not speake like a deaths head, do not bid me remember mine end.

and Lady Percy's "I faith, I'll break thy little finger, Harry." Both passages delight, but one also with sadness (church, heaven), the other purely with young love's mockery. One can hardly imagine the Welsh lady and her song and her "lap" (so attractive to Hotspur) in *2 Henry IV*. The loves here are remembered loves, Justice Shallow's senile exploration with Falstaff of their early exploits imaginary and unsatisfactory. Falstaff despises Shallow (though with a grand gesture Shakespeare gives him one enlarged acknowledgement: "We haue heard the chimes at midnight, M. Shallow") and has a horrid description of him. No one in this play likes anyone else very much.

Names matter, for instance. Prince Hal of *Part I* is not "Hal" through four long acts (this is Shakespeare's longest play so far except *Richard III*, 3,180 lines in Hart's count, suggesting his deep interest in its themes): he only becomes so in Falstaff's mouth in the final scene of entreaty and rebuke and loss. Prince Henry's intimate in this play is, surprisingly, Poinz, and the nearest one gets to the old *Part I* is their disguised overspying of Falstaff at the Boar's Head. Exploits like the Gadshill robbery are out of the question. In fact, Prince Henry does not figure largely in this play, except for the scene with his dying father and the chastisement, after his coronation, of Falstaff. It takes place in the world that he will transform—another play about him is promised by the Epilogue—after his change. This observation leads us in two directions. First, the failure to develop Henry in an intimate way, before his explanation to his father about the taking away of the crown, is certainly one of its author's gravest omissions. Shakespeare even takes the trouble to darken the stain on the whole royal family, by altering Holinshed to make Prince John of Lancaster responsible for the ghastly, Machiavellian business at Gaultree Forest.

Second, both D. A. Traversi ("Henry IV—Part II," *Scrutiny,* XV:2 [Spring 1948], pp. 117-27) and Leech (*Shakespeare Survey,* 1953) connect this play with *Troilus and Cressida* and other later works of profound disillusion, with images of sickness and so on, and raise the question of whether a *personal* reorientation towards the world and towards human nature distinguishes *Part II* from *Part I*—in short, whether we are not looking partly forward to the tragic period beginning with *Hamlet* two years hence in 1600.

Surely there is some truth in this view, just as surely as it is exaggerated. In Chamber's chronology, *Much Ado, As You Like It,* and *Twelfth Night* shine at us between *2 Henry IV* and the tragic period. (I may remark in passing that Chambers's classical chronology of 1930 and J. McManaway's remarks about it in *Shakespeare Survey* are strictly out of date, as I hope to demonstrate in later papers.) But certain meannesses there are which claim notice here. The worst is the hideous little scene where Mistress Quickly and Doll are dragged off to gaol, just before Falstaff's downfall and consequent inability to help them—indeed, he is arrested himself, and no spectator or reader likes this—surely the new King's tirade was enough punishment for—for what?—for whatever his sins may have been. What are his sins, anyway? Certainly he has been a highway robber. Certainly, in this play, a poor comedown, he allows Bardolph to allow two men to buy their way out of the draft. But really it is for his *way of life* that he is banished and then arrested.

He has run away from armed combat. He has gloriously lied about it. He seeks credit (at Shrewsbury) for what he has not done in the way of battle. He is prepared to steal horses in order to get to his friend's coronation. He looks on companions as prey: of Shallow he says: "If the yong Dace be a baite for the old Pike, I see no reason in the law of nature but I may snap at him." The very sharp word "snap" defeats any Huckleberry Finn view of Falstaff. And yet does all this misdoing amount to much? Is it worth punishment? One feels a certain coldness in the young King's speech, put there by Shakespeare to swerve part of the audience's sympathy away from the King to Falstaff:

> I haue long dreampt of such a kind of man,
> So surfet-sweld, so old, and so prophane:
> But being awakt, I do despise my dreame,
> Make lesse thy body (hence) and more thy grace.

From a partaker in these riots, this is *good,* or seems so to us; I doubt that an Elizabethan playgoer would feel any sanctimoniousness here, being committed to monarchism (and nervous already about the succession to Elizabeth's throne). One might argue, even, that this word "grace" is too often at Shakespeare's disposal for this kind of situation—Caliban you remember promises to be wiser thereafter and "seek for grace."

I have put the case against the play as strongly as I could. Let me now argue that a play containing the line "My father is gone wild into his graue" (V.ii.128) cannot be negligible. This is Prince Henry speaking to the Lord Chief Justice, and it might as well be Dylan Thomas three and a half centuries later. Less remarkable but valuable are some lines cut from the quarto, appearing only in the folio:

> It was your presurmize,
> That in the dole of blowes, your Son might drop . . .

(anything like this is inconceivable in the early histories), and

> Thou (beastly Feeder) art so full of him,
> That thou prouok'st thy selfe to cast him vp

(the Archbishop about Henry IV) and "Their eyes of fire, sparkling through sights of Steele."

But the argument from style will concentrate rightly upon prose, and in fact upon Falstaff's second speech: "Men of all sorts take a pride to gird at me: the braine of this foolish compounded clay-man is not able to inuent any thing that intends to laughter, more than I inuent, or is inuented on me, I am not only witty in my selfe, but the cause that wit is in other men." This really does have the tone of *Hamlet,* and since Shakespeare's prose developed much more slowly than his verse, it is remarkable. As in *Part I* he was merciless on Honour, so now he bandies back and forth "securities," which he detests (having no credit rating), and his dialogue with the Justice is so funny that it has to be read to be believed.

> I cannot tell, vertue is of so little regard in these costarmongers times, that true valour is turn Berod [bearherd]. Pregnancie is made a Tapster, & his quick wit wasted in giuing reckonings, all the other giftes appertinent to man, as the malice of his age shapes them, are not worth a goosebery, you that are old consider not the capacities of vs that are yong, you doe measure the heate of our liuers with the bitternesse of your galles, and we that are in the vaward of our youth, I must confesse are wagges too.

Only Thomas Nashe could have replied to this.

> I would I might neuer spit white again: there is not a dangerous action can peepe out his head, but I am thrust vpon it. Wel, I cannot last euer, but it was always yet the tricke of our English nation, if they haue a good thing, to make it too common.
>
> (I.ii.236)

To pass from style to incident: the little passage of Colevile of the Dale has always interested me. Falstaff on the battlefield recognizes this gentleman as a worthy foe, but on being recognized himself, Colevile yields without a blow. Falstaff shepherds him to where the leaders are, and not only does he receive no reward or thanks from Prince John, but John orders Colevile and others to "present execution." Shakespeare is full of instruction and I suppose we are bound to interpret. Falstaff *was* once such a warrior that his name suffices to convict; in short, his braggardism is diminished for us. Now the world is such that he receives for his exploit: nothing; hence his frequent complaints against the world have some foundation in fact. Third, Colevile having so nobly (to our hero) surrendered that it strikes one as an extreme of butchery that he should immediately be slain or murdered; a sympathy from his association with Falstaff—and his testimony, as it were, to Falstaff's valour—well his death hurts us, and our feelings about Lancaster (no one has ever liked Lancaster) harden.

To pass from incident to motive. Falstaff somewhere contends [*Unfinished*]

Louis I. Middleman (essay date 1972)

SOURCE: "*Henry IV, Part I:* The Two Faces of Revolt," in *In Honor of Austin Wright,* Carnegie-Mellon University, 1972, pp. 63-68.

[*In the following essay, Middleman discusses the apparent disunity of conception in* Henry IV, Part I, *noting that the action focuses equally on the political rebellion confronting* Henry IV *and the private struggle that Prince Hal contends with throughout the play.*]

Looking at the first part of *Henry IV,* we are struck by an apparent disunity of conception. The title in the quartos suggests a division between the history and the comedy: "The Historie of Henrie the Fourth; With the battell at Shrewsburie, betweene the King and Lord Henry Percy, surnamed Henry Hotspur of the North. With the humorous conceits of Sir John Falstalffe." While it is true that Falstaff, that "huge hill of flesh," will in production clearly be the heaviest thing on stage and could, were Hal or Hotspur inadequate, carry away the show, Shakespeare's text proves to be a wonderfully balanced whole. The drama is structured around a series of contrasts and correspondences between high life and low, responsibility and self-indulgence, moderation and intemperateness, and, most important and inclusive, between seriousness and jest.

Tillyard has remarked (*Shakespeare's History Plays,* p. 301) that Prince Hal represents a kind of Aristotelian mean between Hotspur's superabundant military spirit and Falstaff's utter lack of it. Falstaff's unadulterated lust for life makes him archetypal, but it also limits him, as immoderate valor limits Hotspur. Hal learns from both, and becomes complete. How he achieves this is the subject of the play: the heir-apparent contending with overt rebellion and private riot, with the grimace and the grin, the two faces of revolt.

The play opens with King Henry, "shaken" and "wan with care" trying, ultimately without success, to recover from *Richard II.* Past, present, and future are all at issue here, and the emphasis is on public, military action. Then, when Falstaff asks Hal, "What time of day is it, lad?" (1.2.1) we move into what appears a timeless present, with the emphasis on private sport. But the timeless world lasts only sixteen lines, shattered in the seventeenth with Falstaff's "when thou art king," a phrase he repeats four times in this initial conversation. If Hal is concerned with growing up to ascend the throne, Falstaff senses, if distantly, the precariousness of his safety as a sweet hulk of disorder, and worries lest the true prince, turned king, no longer protect a false thief. Falstaff wants to identify Hal with the moon, but Hal identifies himself instead with the sun, symbol of royalty. Yet, if we can trust Hal in his soliloquy, he will be like the moon, merely seeming to change, while actually remaining the same. In any case, Falstaff is just one of his "phases."

Falstaff exits to Eastcheap, whereupon Poins informs the Prince, "I have a jest to execute that I cannot manage alone. Falstaff, Bardolph, Peto, and Gadshill shall rob those men that we have already waylaid. Yourself and I will not be there" (1.2.180-83). Now, the "treachery" of Hal and Poins is conceived purely in fun, but it exactly mirrors, in an unserious dimension, the revolt of the Percies and, within the revolting faction, the defection of Northumberland and Glendower. The Percies' motive is also robbery—stealing the crown they helped bestow, and the parallel between comic and serious treason continues as Poins explains, "we will set forth before or after them, and appoint them a place of meeting, wherein it is at our pleasure to fail, and then will they adventure upon the exploit themselves . . ." (1.2.189-92). During the execution of the jest, we hear Falstaff unknowingly sounding the death-knell of the northern rebellion: "A plague upon it when thieves cannot be true one to another" (2.2.29-30). And shortly after the Prince and Poins steal the money back, Hal speaks tellingly of both the game at hand and the abortive revolt to come: "The thieves are all scattered and possessed with fear / So strongly that they dare not meet each other" (2.2.112-13).

Since the theme of the two faces is developed linearly, the discussion from this point on will follow the movement of

Mark McQuinn as Mortimer, Kathleen Ulrich as Lady Mortimer, Kimberly Atkinson as Lady Percy, and Barzin Akhavan as Hotspur in GreenStage's 2000 production of Henry IV, Part One.

the play, so that we may not be liable to Falstaff's indictment of the hostess, that "a man knows not where to have her." In the parley among the Percies the reference to Mortimer, Earl of March, provides a connection with the situation of Hal who, like the rebels, "in the world's wide mouth / Live[s] scandalized and foully spoken of" (1.3.153-54). Hotspur's reply to Worcester and Northumberland could be Hal talking to himself: ". . . yet time serves wherein you may redeem / Your banished honors, and restore yoursel[f] / Into the good thoughts of the world again" (1.3.180-82). The parallel is appropriate, for if Mortimer is the supposed heir to the crown, Hal will be heir in fact, and prove himself worthy of it.

Hotspur's "Oh, let the hours be short, / Till fields and blows and groans applaud our sport" (1.3.301-02) is echoed, contrapuntally, by preparations for analogous sport on a different level. Gadshill's reply to the chamberlain, whose use of the word "hangman" betrays a lamentable want of tact, provides the link: "Tut! There are other Trojans that thou dreamest not of, the which for sport sake are content to do the profession some grace; that would, if matters should be looked into, for their own credit sake, make all whole" (2.1.76-80). There is a fine irony in these last words. Hal, the "Trojan," will "make all whole" by seeming to countenance the robbery, but also 1) by giving the money back (ultimately to himself, since it was headed for the King's Exchequer, and hence we see a pun on "credit"), and 2) by establishing law and order once he is king. Not for long will Gadshill be able to say to his confederates, "We steal as in a castle, cocksure" (2.1.95).

With the jest carried out and the rebellion hatched, the butt of the former and the spur of the latter are juxtaposed for our attention. Shakespeare contrasts them via references to strength and horsemanship. Whereas Hotspur is anxious about his mount because he yearns for gallant action, Falstaff's need for his is weakness: "Eight yards of uneven ground is threescore and ten miles afoot with me" (2.2.26-27). The "beads of sweat" (2.3.61) on Hotspur's eager brow sharply differentiate him from weary Falstaff "sweat[ing] to death, / . . . lard[ing] the lean earth as he walks along" (2.2.115-16). More significant is the comparison between the two, tying together the serious and mock revolts. Hotspur reads a letter suggesting that the rebels' plan is "dangerous; the friends . . . uncertain . . . and your whole plot too light for the counterpoise of so great an opposition" (2.3.10-13). His reaction to the pessimistic unidentified source sounds like something Falstaff might have said, echoing Gadshill's confidence, had anyone warned him of danger: "By the Lord, our plot is a good plot as ever was laid; our friends true and constant—a good plot, good friends, and full of expectation. An excellent plot, very good friends. What a frosty-spirited rogue is this!" (2.3.16-21) The language itself is Falstaffian, linking these two men who can see the present very clearly but are blind to the consequences of their actions. The juxtaposition of these scenes accurately hints that the Percy robbery will go as badly as did the one at Gadshill.

And there are other hints, not about the traitors' weaknesses, but about Hal's maturing strength. Hal emerges from the Boar's Head's wine cellar where, "with three or four loggerheads, amongst three or fourscore hogsheads" he has "sounded the very base string of humility" (2.4.4-6). That is, he has been humble with the lowest class of persons, but also, and more importantly, he has found the essence of humanity in these men, and has, himself, reverberated with that harmony. He is "king of courtesy," and will continue to be so even when he is also king of honor. Hal is a good mixer, a man of the people, motivated not by public policy, as his father would be, but by natural impulse. "They . . . tell me flatly," he says, "when I am King of England, I shall command all the good lads in Eastcheap" (2.4.11-15). Hal enjoys playing with the literal tautology, yet we realize that under Henry it is no tautology, that at present England and Eastcheap are distinct and separate. Hal wants to be king of a people, not of a piece of a map. His drinking bout with the drawers is proof of his mettle among the commoners, endearing them to him, just as his prowess at Shrewsbury will reconcile him with those in high life. "I tell thee, Ned," he continues to Poins, "thou hast lost much honor that thou wert not with me in this action" (2.4.21-23), and the words "action" and "honor" seem to make this a jest. But not merely that: they reinforce the correspondence between this private victory and the public one to come.

As yet, however, for Hal, time is to be wasted, to be "drive[n] away . . . till Falstaff come" (2.4.30-31), while Hotspur is dashing to Bangor. Unaware of threatened treachery, Hal, the killer of time, is "not yet of Percy's mind, the Hotspur of the North, he that kills me some six or seven dozen of Scots at a breakfast, washes his hands, and says to his wife, 'Fie upon this quiet life! I want work'" (2.4.113-117). That "yet" is Shakespeare's, not Hal's, since, uninformed as he is, Hal has no reason to foresee any swift burst through the clouds. "I'll play Percy" (2.4.121-22) he says, but never does. This is no oversight on the dramatist's part; Hal will play himself and the King later, but these are actual and potential selves. Hal's excessive zeal is not his.

Falstaff enters, and the fun begins. The buckram episode is to be read, not written of, but the palpable lies of a man who "said he would swear truth out of England" (2.4.336-37) remain palpable lies. Sir John is *Fal*staff, not the historical Fastolfe, and even his confederate Bardolph admits, "I blushed to hear his monstrous devices" (2.4.343-44). But if the fat knight can lie magnificently about the little rebellion, Shakespeare makes him messenger of the truth about the big one. This is consummate artistry: all the information is there to forward the plot, but everything is made to seem less serious, and the comic tone of the delivery and reception of the news doesn't seem to call for immediate action. Thus Hal can remain in the tavern for the "play extempore." Falstaff asks, "Art thou not horribly afraid?" and the reply is, "Not a whit, i' faith. I lack some of thy instinct" (2.4.408-09). The contrast with Hotspur is fine here: Hal comes off as sufficiently master of the situation that he can proceed coolly, with ease and deliberateness, like a glacier.

Hotspur's haste and impetuosity (he misplaces the map almost as soon as he picks it up) contrasts with Hal's ease. Hotspur lets go the large matter in hand in favor of a nearer contention, when he determines to change the course of the River Trent, a relatively paltry consideration, and not even warranted, since Mortimer says that the kingdom was divided "very equally" (3.1.73). And Hotspur's cavilling with Glendower over the latter's boasts is another trivial matter, foreshadowing the dissension among the rebels. Hal can enjoy the deceptions and exaggerations of Falstaff; Hotspur can't stomach the same things from his Welsh ally. He is afraid of having his own powers eclipsed, even in theory, by someone else. But Hal, when Falstaff later claims to have killed Hotspur, pledges to uphold the lie.

An earlier pledge is more significant, for by the time Hal and his father are reconciled, he has promised to uphold the realm. Henry is again ready for action, with a better perspective on the two Harry's. We, too, have had a good look at the new Hal, and the old Falstaff suffers by comparison. Perhaps he has "bated" and "dwindled" since the "action" at Gadshill, but not in units of weight. Falstaff jests with himself, while Hal has done with jesting. Hal has made a solemn oath to change—"I shall hereafter, my thrice gracious lord, / Be more myself" (3.2.92-93)—whereas nothing comes of Falstaff's "desire" to repent, which is cancelled as soon as spoken. It is not Falstaff's nature to change: "Do thou amend thy face, and I'll amend my life" (3.3.27-28), he tells Bardolph, and the latter is as impossible as the former. In a word, if we are given the promise of Hal's salvation, we are also given the complementary and necessary promise of Falstaff's damnation.

When Sir John says to Bardolph, "I never see thy face but I think upon Hell-fire" (3.3.35-36), this is funny, but also warranted.

Such a warrant gains currency as the tavern conversation over pocket picking turns to Falstaff's £24 debt to the hostess. True to his thieving ways, Falstaff answers flatly, "I'll not pay a denier" (3.3.91). Contrast this behavior with that of Hal, who owes his father and country a more significant debt, and is ready, finally, to "make all whole." Hal in fact expressed his determination in business metaphors:

> . . . I shall make this Northern youth *exchange*
> His glorious deeds for my indignities.
> Percy is but my *factor*, good my lord,
> To *engross up* glorious deeds on my behalf.
> And I will call him to so strict *account*
> That he shall *render* every glory *up*—
> Yea, even the slightest worship of his time—
> Or I will tear the *reckoning* from his heart.
>
> (3.2.145-52; emphasis mine)

Later he will greet Hotspur, "It is the Prince of Wales that threatens thee, / Who never promiseth but he means to pay" (5.4.42-43). The time when Hal permitted himself to sport with stealing is past. "To horse, to horse" he cries to Peto, by now somewhat closer to being "of Percy's mind."

The overall movement of Hal's development from jest to earnest is apparent as he silences Falstaff's jibe at Worcester, "Rebellion lay in his way, and he found it" with "Peace, chewet, peace!" (5.1.29). Such a reaction looks forward to the time when Hal, having lost his weapon and desiring Falstaff's pistol, asks him to remove it from its case. Falstaff produces a bottle and exclaims, "There's that will sack a city" (5.3.55-56). To this pun Hal responds by throwing the bottle at him and demanding, "What, is it a time to jest and dally now?" (5.3.57).

Finally Hal and Hotspur meet, for the first and last time. Shakespeare has deliberately kept them apart, and the resolution of dramatic tension is satisfyingly climactic. Falstaff's cheering Hal on, then playing dead, provide a final contrast between young chivalry and old "discretion." Falstaff's next act, however, is difficult to pardon. Although he does it while wittily excusing himself, the stabbing of the dead Hotspur, over whom Hal has just spoken so movingly, must, if momentarily, qualify our love for the fat knight.

Our respect for Hal in the final scenes needs no such qualification. He is ideally heroic and magnanimous. He doesn't stop to rest, though badly wounded. Self-effacing, he praises his brother John as one who "lends mettle to us all" (5.4.24). After killing Hotspur he asks for Douglas' pardon, giving John the honor of the delivery. Lancaster's response, "I thank your Grace for this high courtesy" (5.5.32) is perfect. "Grace thou wilt have none," Falstaff had said. He was mistaken. Hal, now "king of honor," is also "king of courtesy" high and low, on the battlefield as well as in the wine cellar at Eastcheap.

FURTHER READING

Criticism

Abrams, Richard. "Rumor's Reign in *2 Henry IV:* The Scope of a Personification." *English Literary Renaissance* 16, No. 3 (Autumn 1986): 467-95.

> Expounds on the role of rumor and hearsay in the two *Henry IV* plays.

Barish, Jonas A. "The Turning Away of Prince Hal." *Shakespeare Studies* 1 (1965): pp. 9-17.

> Analyzes the rejection of Falstaff.

Bennett, Robert B. "The Golden Age in the Cycles of History: Analogous Visions of Shakespeare and Chekhov." *Comparative Literature Studies* 28, No. 2 (Spring 1991): 156-77.

> Compares the supper scene in Justice Shallow's orchard in *Henry IV, Part II* and Chekhov's *Cherry Orchard,* characterizing both scenes as similar in their innovative use of the tradition of the Golden Age.

Burelbach, Frederick M. "Name-Calling as Power Play in Shakespeare's *1 Henry IV.*" *Literary Onomastics Studies* 16 (1989): 17-20.

> Analyzes the impact of name-calling in *Henry IV, Part I,* labeling it as a form of authorship and as an instrument that maintains social norms.

Findlay, Heather. "Renaissance Pederasty and Pedagogy: The 'Case' of Shakespeare's Falstaff." *The Yale Journal of Criticism: Interpretation in the Humanities* 3, No. 1 (Fall 1989): 229-38.

> Theorizes that Falstaff's character is representative of the development of early modes of the capitalist economy.

Hoegberg, David E. "*Master Harold* and the Bard: Education and Succession in Fugard and Shakespeare." *Comparative Drama* 29, No. 4, (Winter 1995-96): 415-35.

> Compares Fugard's *Master Harold* and *Henry IV* as political plays that trace the attempts of two new regimes to solidify their power, while also focusing on the development of their leaders.

Kastan, David Scott. "Killed with Hard Opinions: Oldcastle, Falstaff, and the Reformed Text of *1 Henry IV.*" In *Textual Formations and Reformations,* edited by Laurie E. Maguire and Thomas L. Berger, pp. 211-27. Newark: University of Delaware Press, 1998.

> Traces the historical origins of Falstaff's name and character as represented in *Henry IV, Part I.*

Krims, Marvin B. "Hotspur's Antifeminine Prejudice in Shakespeare's *Henry IV.*" *Literature and Psychology* 40, Nos. 1-2 (1994): 118-32.

> Discusses Hotspur's phallocentric attitudes in the play.

Reid, Robert L. "Humoral Psychology in Shakespeare's *Henriad.*" *Comparative Drama* 30, No. 4 (Winter 1996): 471-502.

> Chronicles Shakespeare's use of the four humors in the *Henry IV* plays.

States, Bert O. "Hamlet's Older Brother." *Hudson Review* 39, No. 4 (Winter 1987): 537-52.

> Compares and contrasts the characters of Prince Hal and Hamlet, noting the similarities in their temperament and tempo.

West, Gillian. "Falstaff's Punning." *English Studies: A Journal of English Language and Literature* 69, No. 2 (December 1988): 541-58.

> Presents an analysis of Falstaff's puns in both *Henry IV* plays, and contends that Falstaff's use of language is more complicated than he is given credit for.

Willems, Michèle. "Misconstruction in *Henry IV.*" *Cahiers Elisabethains* 37 (April 1990): 43-57.

> Analyzes misunderstandings and misconstructions of events and characters in Shakespeare's plays, characterizing these as common devices that allow the dramatist to engineer complicated plots and character depictions.

Wood, Nigel. Introduction to *Henry IV, Parts One and Two,* by William Shakespeare, edited by Nigel Wood, pp. 1-34. Buckingham: Open University Press, 1995.

> Offers a detailed overview of *Henry IV, Parts I and II.*

Macbeth

For further information on the critical and stage history of *Macbeth,* see *SC,* Volumes 3, 20, 29, and 44.

INTRODUCTION

Most likely written in 1606 and based on Raphael Holinshed's *Chronicles of England, Scotland, and Ireland* (1577), *Macbeth* is one of Shakespeare's shortest plays. Many critics have speculated that Shakespeare compressed the action and time frames of the tragedy for increased dramatic shock. *Macbeth* has often been praised for its artistic coherence and the intense economy of its dramatic action, which is replete with vivid scenes of violence and treachery. Although many critics have remarked on the overwhelming nature of the violent action in the play, it has received almost universal acclaim as one of Shakespeare's most profound and mature visions of evil. Early critical scholarship of the play focused mainly on comparative analyses of *Macbeth* with traditional medieval morality plays, as well as Shakespeare's treatment of topical and political issues. Many of these analyses focused their attention on examining *Macbeth* as primarily a political play that focused on and was written expressly to commemorate the accession of James I to the throne of England. While interest in studying the play as a political allegory continues to interest critics, it is the contrast of opinions between critics who perceive Macbeth as a tragic hero and critics who see him merely as an evil and egotistical character that has evolved into one of the most enduring themes of modern critical scholarship regarding the play. Other areas of critical interest include the study of ethics, political ideology, and gender issues in the play, as well as psychological approaches to Macbeth's character.

Many scholars suspect that some of the scenes in *Macbeth* were added and other scenes were modified by someone other than Shakespeare. David Lowenthal (1989) proposes that despite this possibility, all the disparate scenes combine to present a unified vision of human life. According to Lowenthal, Macduff and his family present a Christian contrast to Macbeth and the supernatural elements in the play, relying on natural order and God for their own preservation. In the end, the play divulges that the world is not the dark or unintelligible place it seems, and that although there are contrasts and evil in the world, the forces of good are more fundamental and lasting and eventually overcome the chaos to reestablish a coherent human existence. Joseph A. Bryant (1988) takes issue with critics who maintain that *Macbeth* is more of a melodrama or morality play than a tragedy due to Macbeth's wicked and malicious character. Bryant maintains that whether wicked or noble, "the epiphany that tragedy brings . . . is available to all alike . . . the unjust as well as the just."

Much of the twentieth-century scholarship of *Macbeth* has focused on both the political ideology and ethical considerations of the play. In an essay discussing these issues, Alan Sinfield (1986) stresses that the play focuses on the distinction between violence that the state considers legitimate and violence that it considers evil. For example, Macbeth's victory over Duncan's enemies in the beginning of the play is violent, yet it is not considered evil because it is in the service of the prevailing power. However, Macbeth's later actions, especially Duncan's murder, represent evil because it disrupts established power. In England, at the time *Macbeth* was written, this would have been an extremely topical matter because of such contemporary events as the Essex rebellion in 1599 and the Gunpowder Plot of 1605, both of which had resulted in many years of state violence. Barbara Riebling (1991) also discusses *Macbeth* as a political play and feels that while most scholarship has focused on the contextual ideologies prevalent at the time it was written, it can also be read as a discourse in civic humanism. Riebling feels that in *Macbeth,* Shakespeare studies the consequences of misrule in a Machiavellian context rather than a Christian one. Therefore, though Duncan is a Christian ruler, it is his very Christianity that invites disaster in the Machiavellian world.

Recent scholarship has also increasingly focused on Shakespeare's depiction of women in his plays, and *Macbeth* has been central to this analysis for many scholars. Joost Daalder (1988) contends that although Shakespeare did not portray men more favorably than women, he did have a strong sense of which traits and actions were "male" and which were "female," and believed that women should not attempt to cross over into the male domain. The critic points to Lady Macbeth's attempt to adopt a male role and deny her womanhood, which proves disastrous and harms both herself and others. Similarly, William T. Liston (1989) maintains that the play presents a conflation of sex roles and gender, where, if men and women step outside their roles, they lose their humanity. In Liston's opinion, it is the liberation from their defined roles which destroys both Macbeth and Lady Macbeth. In contrast, Janet Adelman (1987) theorizes that *Macbeth* presents a powerful fantasy of escape from an absolute and destructive maternal power. According to Adelman, maternal power permeates the play via the figures of Lady Macbeth, the witches, and Macbeth's relationship to both, and that his relationships to these women represent primitive fears about the loss of male identity and autonomy. Adelman stresses that the issue of male autonomy was a common thread in many other Shakespearean plays, including *King Lear* and *Henry IV,* and that *Macbeth* presents his most powerful introduction to the realm of maternal malevolence unleashed in the absence of paternal protection.

The level of violence and chaos that permeates the play has led to numerous psychological interpretations of the characters and action in *Macbeth*. Pierre Janton explores the theory that the fear of assuming manhood is Macbeth's tragic flaw. The critic contends that it is this flaw that leads him to annihilate all the potential and virtual father figures in the play. Robert L. Reid (1992) proposes that the play is fundamentally concerned with showing the horrific consequences of a truly heroic spirit embracing evil. From Reid's perspective, the three murders in the play denote the three stages of the evolution of evil in Macbeth's psyche. According to Reid, Macbeth's victims ultimately represent the human bonds he breaks, and his degeneration into evil is deliberately worked into the psychological and dramatic design of the play.

OVERVIEWS AND GENERAL STUDIES

Joseph A. Bryant, Jr. (essay date 1987)

SOURCE: "*Macbeth* and the Meaning of Tragedy," in *Kentucky Review*, Vol. 8, No. 2, Summer, 1988, pp. 3-17.

[*In the following essay, originally delivered as a lecture in 1987, Bryant takes issue with critics who maintain that* Macbeth *is more of a melodrama or morality play than a tragedy.*]

For years the one tragedy that almost all Americans read, or at least encountered, was Shakespeare's *Macbeth*. High schools regularly included it in the curriculum for the senior year, perhaps preferring it to the other major tragedies of Shakespeare because of its brevity, its simple plot line, and its melodramatic appeal. Among professional critics, however, enthusiasm for the play has never been high. Robert P. Heilman in a 1966 essay, revealingly entitled "The Criminal as Tragic Hero," set forth the principal reason for that.[1] Tragedy, he argued, echoing centuries-old opinion, presents a "noble enterprise," one of uncommon dignity and ethical sophistication, which fails, not because the protagonist is wicked or malicious but because he is afflicted by some recognizable human frailty that causes him or her to err. The reasoning has usually been that we who participate vicariously in that enterprise contemplate the protagonist's downfall with pity and terror but in the process achieve emancipation from the crippling effects which those emotions normally produce.

This, according to Heilman, is where the problem with the play *Macbeth* lies. After Act II the hero is an habituated criminal who in the end is destined to meet an appropriate punishment. Thus we cannot comfortably participate with Macbeth throughout his enterprise. At some point after Act II moral revulsion compels us to detach ourselves from his action and sit in judgment on it; and at that point our sympathies necessarily shift from Macbeth to Macbeth's victims. Even if we do not switch allegiances entirely, we look thereafter at the spectacle as if it were a melodrama (the alternative, by the way, that Roman Polanski exploited in his movie version) or at best a morality play. "This," Heilman concluded, "is not the best that tragedy can offer"; and in view of the ontological and ethical assumptions that most of us, knowingly or unknowingly, have inherited from Greek philosophy and our Judaeo-Christian religion, we can hardly afford to disagree. In any case, today's scholar-critics, presumably in an effort to redeem for tragedy Shakespeare's most conspicuous hero-villains, have increasingly tended to look favorably on the view that Macbeth and his spouse were demonically possessed and therefore to some extent themselves victims.[2] Following a similar line of reasoning, they have excused Hamlet for committing himself to an unholy and unethical vengeance by arguing that he was misled by a demon disguised as his father's ghost.[3] Such evasions as these may preserve temporarily the principle that many modern readers mistakenly identify with tragedy, but they distort our perception of Shakespeare's text and confirm the repudiation of tragic vision that began when our ancient forebears abandoned Heraclitus in favor of Parmenides.

Genuine tragedy is a Western phenomenon, and since the time of Euripides it has been relatively rare. True comedy is much more common; for comedy is the appropriate literary mode for expressing that view of the universe which we in the West, whether Christian, Jew, or agnostic, seem to prefer. Most of the things that have gone by the name of tragedy, at least from Seneca to Arthur Miller, have been pale substitutes, sometimes more comic in essence than tragic: heroic plays, sentimental domestic fables, problem plays, moralities, or melodramas. Had it not been for the haven provided by the novel during the past two centuries, tragedy might have vanished altogether.

The seeds for genuine comedy and tragedy were both present in the perceptions of primitive man, who saw, first, that some things in this world recur and, second, that some things do not. As hunter first and later as agriculturalist he recognized that a regular recurrence of the seasons and their attendant phenomena was necessary to his survival; and as time went on, he developed gestures designed to signify, support, and perhaps even precipitate such recurrence. These gestures, we are told, hardened into ritual, and ritual gave rise to literary forms as we know them, all celebrating in various fashions the happy mystery of recurrence and renewal. The second perception of primitive man was less happy, since among the things that do not recur he inescapably saw himself and his wife and children. Moreover in time it prompted the reflection that annihilation is the destiny of all individuals in the universe, whether animal, vegetable, or mineral. In some quarters of the globe, advancing mankind took that soberer perception and developed compelling expressions of it in symbolic ritual and corresponding art forms. In others, including our own, the fear of individual death prevailed over acceptance; and in these quarters men placed their faith, as I have already noted, in recurrence. More important, they placed it in the dream of permanence that an uncritical faith in recurrence engenders. The attitude we in the West call tragic appears whenever that faith, for whatever reason, ceases to be strong enough to obscure the perception of irreversible change that our senses will never let us absolutely deny.

By the time of Plato, however, faith in permanence had come to seem almost unchallengeable. Change or flux had become the mischievous illusion which human beings were enjoined to avoid either by exercising rational discipline or by expressing their confidence in some remote god of permanence. After Plato, the Stoicism which dominated much of Roman thought and then went on to achieve a second currency in Renaissance humanism reaffirmed for generations of intellectuals the view that "the eternal course of the universe is cyclical . . . [and] all change is imminent in [an unchanging] God."[4] Formal comedy automatically found support in such views, as did political and ecclesiastical establishments; and so long as nothing happened to shake popular confidence in the institutions that counseled people about eternal verities, writers who might be inclined to explore alternative views could do little. The pragmatic Machiavelli was vilified soon after his treatise on practical politics appeared, and the voice of a skeptical Montaigne went largely unheeded except by a handful of intelligentsia.

Of the Shakespeare was surely one. Near the end of his last play, he put what was most likely his own conviction about humanity's involvement in eternal change into the mouth of an aging and disillusioned but still unembittered Prospero. The old gentleman, having just dismissed abruptly the spirits who had been performing a prenuptial masque for his daughter and her spouse-to-be, dismissed the young people's disappointment with an unforgettable speech:

> These our actors
> (As I foretold you) were all spirits, and
> Are melted into air, into thin air,
> And like the baseless fabric of this vision,
> The cloud-capp'd towers, the gorgeous palaces,
> The solemn temples, the great globe itself,
> Yea, all which it inherit, shall dissolve
> And like this insubstantial pageant faded
> Leave not a rack behind. We are such stuff
> As dreams are made on; and our little life
> Is rounded with a sleep.
>
> (*The Tempest,* IV.1.148-58)[5]

Heraclitus could not have put it better, but nothing could have been more inconsonant with the implications of the presumably formal comedy in which those words appeared. What Shakespeare had done in this play was to unite the two fundamental perceptions of primitive man in a single comprehensive view, thereby transcending the limitations of comedy and bringing that genre into harmony with the vision of his major tragedies, *Hamlet, Lear, Othello,* and *Macbeth.* In these masterpieces of midcareer he had emulated his predecessor Euripides by dramatizing for his countrymen situations which discredited their confidence in a stable universe, moral or otherwise, and made plain the reality of perpetual change for all but the most naive to see.

Changing attitudes rather than naiveté have tended to obscure Shakespeare's presentation of that perception in the play *Macbeth*. Obsessed by dreams of order, we resist the vision of flux that is fundamental to tragedy and, when confronted by a character like Macbeth, look for causes, external or internal, to explain the changes that time alone is responsible for bringing to him. Macbeth to Shakespeare's audiences was not necessarily the criminal that modern sensibility often makes him out to be. We in the twentieth century need to be reminded that seventeenth-century Englishmen—the presence of a Scottish Stuart on their throne notwithstanding—habitually thought of their cousins to the north as uncivilized barbarians and so were prepared to see Macbeth's savagery as an example of cultural labeling and not as evidence of latent criminality. They could not forget that James's mother was supposed to have conspired with her lover to dispatch James's father by means of a well-placed charge of gunpowder; and Sir Christopher Piggott, member of Parliament from Buckinghamshire, who made a public allusion to what he believed to be the general Scottish practice of removing sovereigns by assassination, spent time in the Tower for his indiscretion.[6] Shakespeare in dealing with Scottish material tactfully dramatized a subject set six hundred years in the past, when most peoples in that part of the world, English as well as Scots, were to some extent barbaric, and assassination was fairly common as a mode of achieving succession. For all that, however, Shakespeare's Macbeth was a Scot and, in English eyes, behaved like one.

The attempt to salvage something of Macbeth's character by declaring him demonically possessed derives from a similar aversion to a view of the universe indifferent to our notions of order. It usually involves interpreting the women on the heath as either devils or the devils' agents and thus the primary motives for Macbeth's behavior—a view that Shakespeare's contemporaries might have considered questionable, to say the least. Shakespeare found the three hags in Holinshed, and his retention of them in the play may have been prompted in part by a wish to flatter the King. James, it is said, liked to trace his ancestry to the murdered Banquo, who, those same hags had promised, should be father to a line of kings. We note that Shakespeare included in Act IV a reference to Edward the Confessor's practice of touching for the scrofula, something James had revived, reportedly with fair success; and this royal sanction of what amounted to faith healing had probably reinforced the popular belief, dubious but still prevalent, that James also believed in witches.[7] Yet Holinshed himself never characterized the women as devils or witches. Initially he referred to them simply as "three women in strange and wild apparell, resembling creatures of an elder world"[8] and then, after explaining that no one at first took their prophecies seriously, went on to say:

> Afterwards the common opinion was, that these women were either the weird sisters, that is (as ye would say;

the goddesses of destiny, or else some nymphs or feiries, indued with knowledge or prophesie by their necromanticall science, bicause everie thing came to passe as they has spoken.[9]

He referred to them once more, in passing, as "the three fairies or weird sisters"; but the important point is that Holinshed, who adapted the story from a source of his own (specifically the account by Hector Boece) avoided responsibility for saying that they were supernatural in any sense. He merely allowed "the common opinion was" that the hags were supernatural and let it stand that they were "three women in strange and wild apparell, resembling creatures of an elder world." Kenneth Muir, a current student of Shakespeare's sources, is willing to let it stand there too;[10] and thus Muir joins the company of A. C. Bradley, who, regardless of what one may think of his criticism, was one of the closest readers Shakespeare has ever had. Bradley had written of these creatures:

> The Witches . . . are not goddesses or fates, or, in any way whatever, supernatural beings. They are old women, poor and ragged, skinny and hideous, full of vulgar spite, occupied in killing their neighbours' swine or revenging themselves on sailors' wives who have refused them chestnuts. If Banquo considers their beards a proof that they are not women, that only shows his ignorance. . . . There is not a syllable in *Macbeth* to imply they are anything but women.[11]

Bradley has more to say on this score, but this is the general drift of his argument. He notes that Shakespeare culled from books like Reginald Scot's enlightened *The Discoverie of Witchcraft* (1584) (writing today Scot probably would have called his book *The Exposure of Witchcraft*) popular notions that might serve as atmospheric enhancement, but he gave his hags no power to influence the action.

Ironically the one undeniably metaphysical detail in the play is probably not of Shakespeare's doing. This is the unexpected appearance of Hecate, the Greek goddess of sorcery and witchcraft, at two points in the play (III.v. and IV.i). Scholars, virtually without exception, agree that her language and meter are incompatible with the rest of the play; and, noting that the two songs she calls for appear in full in Thomas Middleton's *The Witch* (1614), assume that Middleton, who continued to write plays for the company after Shakespeare left it, was the interpolator. The point of interest here, however, is the probability that someone in Shakespeare's company recognized a need to provide supernatural reinforcement for three characters who otherwise would have come across to Jacobean audiences as they did later to A. C. Bradley: that is, as nothing more than skinny hags who fortuitously provided material for the superstitious minds of two ambitious Scottish warriors to feed upon. As Shakespeare originally wrote the play, Macbeth's initial encounter with those creatures was nothing more mysterious than encounters modern travellers have had in some third-world countries, where pathetic beggars still emerge from ditches or the underbrush to demand gifts in return for fortunes.

Thus the prophecies of Macbeth's hags were beggars' clichés, directed at the bounty of their famous hero, Macbeth, Thane of Glamis, who had crossed their path on his return to the King's palace, to hear that he was already Thane of Cawdor and would someday be king (I.iii.49-50). Their prophecy to the less well-known Banquo was also a cliché, second best perhaps but the best they could do under the circumstances (Macbeth having already received their prize promises). Like scavengers on battlefields the world over they were in a position to see things that would escape the notice of those preoccupied with fighting, and they could easily have known, as obviously Macbeth did not, of the defection and disgrace of the Thane of Cawdor. Hence, they promised Macbeth a prize which, knowing of its availability, he might have reached for on his own initiative, without any prompting. As for the crown, Macbeth was now clearly the strong man in the realm, regardless of his title; and this realm, after all, was Scotland. Thus kingship for Scotsman Macbeth was not beyond the expectation of a trio of beggars any more than it was beyond the expectation of Macbeth himself.

With all his valor, strength, and accompanying ambition, however, Shakespeare's Macbeth, as we have already noted, was superstitious—to Englishmen, simply another predictable Scottish characteristic. He was prepared, as sophisticated Englishmen would not have been, to see signs of the supernatural in old hags with fortunes on their lips. As they begin to slip away, he bids them stay; and when minutes later word of Cawdor's treachery reaches him, he immediately thinks of the second prophecy ("the swelling act / Of the imperial theme") and confidently expects confirmation of that as well. Admittedly he pauses momentarily to reflect, "If chance will have me king, why, chance may crown me / Without my stir" (I.iii.143-44); but even here he is already assuming that some divine, or diabolical, intelligence has determined to make him King of Scotland. Thus when Duncan back in his comfortable palace at Forres names young Malcolm immediate heir to the throne, Macbeth automatically begins to think of ways to remove what he takes to be a patent impediment to destiny. Of course, destiny, as ambitious Macbeth is prone to understand it, has nothing to do with any of these events, though with his first assumption to the contrary, the possibility of a tragic action begins to emerge. Macbeth's real destiny is simply the combination of ambition, superstition, and a hand accustomed to letting blood, all of which have now coalesced to direct his course.

What we see in the first act of Shakespeare's *Macbeth,* in short, is the inchoate tragic hero, the man who suddenly is able to believe that he has reached through the mists of circumstance to touch the hard rock of reality and for the moment does not dream that he can err seriously in feeling his way forward along what he takes to be a reliable surface. Macbeth's epiphany will come when he realizes that his solid rock is only one more illusion, when he begins to understand that there is no hidden agenda for him, perhaps no such agenda for anyone, that nothing on earth is determined, that in the end crowns go either to the strong or to the lucky, and that killing, however glorious the cause, is never anything more or less than simple killing.

Some may argue that the later prophecies in the play must surely be meant to suggest that a supernatural design of some sort lies behind that joke that the three hags play upon the gullible Scot. Actually Shakespeare gives no hint of such a design. The apparitions that deliver the prophecies on Macbeth's second visit are, like the dagger and the Ghost of Banquo, seen only by Macbeth. Unlike the ghost in *Hamlet* they are not confirmed by a second viewer, and they tell him nothing that he could not have known already. He hardly needed witches to tell him to beware of Macduff, who even on the night of Duncan's Scottish style murder was clearly the one who would in time go after Macbeth. Unknown to him the second prophecy, that "none of woman born / Shall harm Macbeth," also points to Macduff; but it makes use of information that would have been common knowledge among old wives in the countryside. It is the kind of gossip that a warrior chieftain would not have been likely to recall even if he had ever possessed it. Thus Macbeth took a midwife's conundrum for prophecy and went on to swallow a third pseudo-prediction, the meaning of which should have been clear to anyone whose sense of strategy had not been beclouded by a morbid concern for signs and portents:

> Macbeth shall never vanquish'd be until
> Great Birnam wood to high Dunsinane hill
> Shall come against him.
>
> (IV.i.92-94)

Dunsinane, supposedly an impregnable fortress built on the highest hill in the region, provided an elevation well above the tree line and thus gave the possessor an advantage over any enemy who might seek to approach. The obvious strategy for such an enemy was to take advantage of the resources of the wooded flatlands below in precisely the way that even the inexperienced Malcolm thinks of and proceeds to implement with great success. Thus the wood moves, as it had to do, and Macbeth quickly falls before the superior forces of England, Northumberland, and such Scottish defectors as Macduff and Malcolm between them have managed to muster. In the end he is a victim of nothing more mysterious than a retribution that he himself has provoked in his repeated attempt to implement a force of destiny that exists only in his own superstitious (and Jacobean viewers might have added) Scottish mind.

Removing the possibility that the fate of Shakespeare's Macbeth is determined in some way should make it possible for most readers to consider the play a tragedy. The widespread objection about the protagonist's villainy will probably remain for those who find it difficult to see the play in its original context, but even that presents no real impediment. Aristotle expressed a preference for a hero who is "highly renowned and prosperous" and who, though not "eminently good and just," meets his reversal because of some error or simple frailty rather than because of "vice or depravity"; but this should not be taken as evidence that the essence of tragedy resides in its ethical implications. Tragedy in the last analysis deals primarily with Western humanity's recurring need to be reassured that eventually a manifestation of universal order will somehow remove, at least for men of good will, the threat of indiscriminate annihilation. The characters that Shakespeare sets before us in his tragedies all seek in varying ways to satisfy that need. Like Samuel Beckett's clowns they tolerate the absurdity of their lives in the expectation that in time a Godot or his equivalent will appear and fit the pieces together; and the prelude to any enlightenment that Shakespeare may give them is the realization that the resolution they anticipate will never come—that, in fact, such a resolution may never have even been possible.

A character who experiences this dispiriting prelude and never goes beyond it is Lady Macbeth, who near the beginning of her last scene (V.i) declares chillingly, "Hell is murky!" Custom has often interpreted what follows as the presentation of a guilty soul morbidly contemplating its own damnation, but what Lady Macbeth is really contemplating is the involvement she shares with all humanity in the interminable process of existence, the Heraclitean flux, which simply goes on without reference to any pattern or plan that human beings may ascribe to it and like the rain in the Gospel (Matt. 5:45) affects just and unjust alike. The terror that makes chaos of her final moments is something she derives from her recognition that time is a continuum and refuses to divide into meaningful discrete units, a nightmare in which the dead king will never stop bleeding and the stained hand never return to sweetness, in which all the subsequent murderous activities can never, for her, entirely pass away, and in which friend Banquo and the innocent Lady Macduff must abide as perpetual memories, conditioning her every thought and action for the rest of her time on earth.

Macbeth, we may recall, contemplated briefly in Act I the possibility that a similar nightmare might be his, but he thrust the spectre of that aside to initiate a course which he hoped would enable him to escape into a future secure from the troubled past he was on the brink of creating for himself:

> If it were done, when 'tis done, then 'twere well
> It were done quickly. If th' assassination
> Could trammel up the consequence, and catch
> With his surcease success; that but this blow
> Might be the be-all and the end-all—here,
> But here, upon this bank and shoal of time,
> We'ld jump the life to come.
>
> (I.vii.1-7)

The expectation which temporarily deflects Macbeth's thinking at this point, as we later learn, consists of the "honor, love, obedience, and troops of friends" that he will wistfully speak of in Act V as blessings that have eluded him (V.iii.25). Here at the outset of his course he can easily imagine that such things as these are the normal consequence of the kingship that he thinks is destined to be his: once the crown is securely on his head, he believes, he will be able to live indefinitely in his hard-won comedy, "jumping," at least for the time being, the thought of death and whatever else may follow. To do Macbeth credit, one must acknowledge that he has also begun to contemplate the unsavory consequences of his intended action when Lady Macbeth intervenes to redirect him to the murder; but he never quite recognizes that taking the crown, by whatever means, must involve living for a time in the fear of his friend Banquo's ambition, then, Banquo dead, in the fear of Banquo's children, and thereafter in the fear of challenger after challenger, until at last he will have no choice but to accept the joyless, sleepless existence awaiting a death he has spent the best part of his life avoiding. When at last Macbeth begins to realize that this is what kingship really means, he will cry out in a weariness that approaches despair:

> I am in blood
> Stepp'd in so far that, should I wade no more,
> Returning were as tedious as go o'er.
>
> (III.iv.135-37)

What Macbeth wishes for desperately here at midcourse is a place to stop, and that is what he seeks and thinks he has found after his second visit to the old women.

Even at the beginning of Act V Macbeth still clings to his dream of a universe of absolutes inhabited by supernatural powers which can, and on occasion may, make those absolutes known. When told that his thanes have begun to defect, he reviews the latest prophecies for all within hearing concluding with the boast, "The mind I sway by, and the heart I bear, / Shall never sag with doubt, nor shake with fear" (V.iii.9-10). Yet the fear that Macbeth still cannot acknowledge has already stolen away any lingering taste of sweetness that life may have had for him. When an unidentifiable shriek within the castle proves to have signalled the death of his wife, that fear emerges in the twelve lines critics have sometimes read as marking the nadir from which Macbeth will recover triumphantly in his final moments:

> She should have died hereafter;
> There would have been a time for such a word.
> To-morrow, and to-morrow, and to-morrow,
> Creeps in this petty pace from day to day,
> To the last syllable of recorded time;
> And all our yesterdays have lighted fools
> The way to dusty death. Out, out, brief candle!
> Life's but a walking shadow, a poor player,
> That struts and frets his hour upon the stage,
> And then is heard no more. It is a tale
> Told by an idiot, full of sound and fury,
> Signifying nothing.
>
> (V.v.17-28)

The nadir, however, is bedrock; and the fear that brings Macbeth to it becomes the agent of his salvation. The vision he confronts in these lines that have sometimes terrified western audiences is nothing more than the long view which for many people of older cultures is the beginning of wisdom. Macbeth has put his faith in a veil of dreams, partly his heritage and partly fabric of his own devising. What saves him when circumstances rip that veil from his eyes is his ability to resist averting his gaze from a world that makes no promises and gives no guarantees and to accept, in the last minutes of his life, that world at face value.

Two details in the play, one early and one late, prepare us to see the conclusion of *Macbeth* in this light. In Act I Shakespeare goes out of his way to have young Malcolm report the last moments of the first Thane of Cawdor, who, like Macbeth, had betrayed King Duncan and was to pay for that defection with his life:

> Nothing in his life
> Became him like the leaving it. He died
> As one that had been studied in his death.
> To throw away the dearest thing he ow'd,
> As 'twere a careless trifle.
>
> (I.iv.7-11)

This is the model of spiritual courage which Macbeth, whose physical courage had already proved itself in his confrontation with the "merciless Macdonwald," will eventually be called upon to emulate. In addition to courage, however, tragic stature will require also achievement of that indifferent death which negates anxiety and can come only as the result of seeing that the human life by which we set so much store has all the glitter and all the transitoriness of a bubble in a stream.

To reinforce this brief image of a tragic Cawdor Shakespeare in the closing moments of the play gives us a compelling reminder. In Act V, Scene vii, Macbeth meets young Siward, son of the Earl of Northumberland, exults that the boy was born of woman, and promptly kills him. Later, in Scene ix, after the battle is over and Macbeth has been killed, the old man receives the news that his son is among the slain. At first he seems incredulous. "Then is he dead?" he asks; and the answer comes from nobleman Ross, a steadfast opponent of tyranny: "Ay, and brought off the field. Your cause of sorrow / Must not be measur'd by his worth, for then / It hath no end." "Had he his hurts before?" old Siward asks; and Ross's answer comes, "Ay, on the front." "Why then," says Siward, "God's soldier be he! / Had I as many sons as I have hairs, / I would not wish them to a fairer death. / And so, his knell is knoll'd." Malcolm, still the callous youth, interrupts: "He's worth more sorrow, / And that I'll spend for him." But Siward quietly continues, "he's worth no more; / They say he parted well, and paid his score, / And so, God be with him!" Undoubtedly for Siward and Cawdor, as for Macbeth, the universe remains a mystery, and Macbeth's comprehension of it at the end, is still best characterized as "a tale told by an idiot, signifying nothing," words that the play never contradicts. The death that he has feared and avoided for so long has turned out to be nothing more than the dusty conclusion to what must eventually become, for all human beings, a wearisome parade of tomorrows. The question that remains for those of us who watch this spectacle is this: Can one ever hope to achieve, much less retain, something resembling dignity in a universe that requires us to live and act in the face of certain dissolution but gives no unequivocal signs of controlling deities or of moral or even natural law to provide meaning either for our lives as a whole or for the single activities within it?

Tragedy's answer to this question (and tragedy is not required to give more than an implicit answer) has always been a qualified affirmative. From the beginning it has enjoined its Western audiences to emulate those millions in the Eastern half of the world, to say nothing of humbler sentient creatures worldwide, and accept gracefully the dissolution that was never the nightmarish annihilation we imagine it to be but simply part of the necessary accommodation of all life to existence in an unlimited continuum. To paraphrase an American author of this century, it has advised us to touch vicariously the great death and learn that it is, after all, only the great death.

Moreover, tragedy continually reminds all who see or read that human beings, whether they know it or not, whether they be saints or sinners, monks with begging bowl or world conquerors, achieve meaning for their lives existentially. This is true, tragedy says, whether one takes sword in hand or simply bows to the inevitable. What matters is the exercise of the will. Thus Macbeth, rising to tragic stature moments before the avenging Macduff kills him, abandons his delusion about a providence that would determine his course—whether diabolical or divine is not important—and lays down his life in awareness, for him newly achieved, that no life is more than a passing incident in the cosmic process:

> I will not yield
> To kiss the ground before young Malcolm's feet
> And to be baited with the rabble's curse.
> Though Birnam wood be come to Dunsinane,
> And thou oppos'd, being of no woman born,
> Yet I will try the last. Before my body
> I throw my warlike shield. Lay on, Macduff,
> And damn'd be him that first cries, "Hold, enough!"
>
> (V.viii.27-34)

So saying, Macbeth stands as a knowledgeable human being, fully if only briefly master of his destiny because he has at last recognized the nature of that destiny and accepted it. In this gesture he joins not only Cawdor and young Siward but Hamlet before him and Cleopatra and Coriolanus, who will come after in the succession of Shakespeare's tragedies. We Westerners who tend to stand in fear and embarrassment before the prospect of dissolution in the indifferent universe that gave us our fragile identities may still ask whether this is the best that tragedy has to offer. One must answer that if it offered better, it would be less than tragedy. In any case, this is what all the best tragedies have offered since tragedy was first invented to enlighten, console, and strengthen human beings frustrated at the collapse of their attempts to maintain a spurious dream of immortality. For those of us who have been led to think of the good death of tragedy as being contingent upon the elevated status of the protagonist and the nobility of his enterprise, it may be at least mildly comforting to think that good death has never been a respecter of persons and that the epiphany that tragedy brings, in poetry and in life, is available to all alike, young and old, woman as well as man, the unjust as well as the just.

Notes

1. In *Shakespeare Survey*, ed. Kenneth Muir, 19 (1966):12-24.

2. The best statement of this view is that by W. C. Curry, *Shakespeare's Philosophical Patterns*, 2d ed. (Baton Rouge: Louisiana State University Press, 1959), 53-93.

3. For example, Roy Battenhouse, *Shakespearean Tragedy, Its Art and Its Christian Premises* (Bloomington, Indiana: Indiana University Press, 1971) and Eleanor Prosser, *Hamlet and Revenge*, 2d ed. (Palo Alto, California: Stanford University Press; London: Oxford University Press, 1971).

4. Philip Hallie, "Stoicism," *The Encyclopedia of Philosophy* (New York: Macmillan, 1967), 8:21.

5. Quotations from Shakespeare are from *The Riverside Shakespeare*, ed. G. Blakemore Evans (Boston: Houghton Mifflin, 1974).

6. See Geoffrey Bullough, *Narrative and Dramatic Sources of Shakespeare* (London: Routledge & Kegan Paul; New York: Columbia University Press, 1973), 7:428-29.

7. For an account of James's changing attitude on witchcraft see Henry N. Paul, *The Royal Play of "Macbeth"* (New York: Macmillan, 1950), 90-130.

8. Bullough, 494-95.

9. Bullough, 495.

10. "Folklore and Shakespeare," in *Shakespeare, Contrasts and Controversies* (Norman, Oklahoma: University of Oklahoma Press, 1985), 39, 47-49.

11. *Shakespearean Tragedy* (London: Macmillan, 1905), 341.

David Lowenthal (essay date 1989)

SOURCE: "*Macbeth*: Shakespeare Mystery Play," in *Interpretation: A Journal of Political Philology*, Spring, 1989, pp. 311-57.

[*In the following essay, Lowenthal examines the mysteries in* Macbeth—*including character reversals and questions of fact and motivation—and concludes that the play "mixes pessimism with a more fundamental optimism."*]

PRELIMINARY VIEW OF THE SUBJECT

In its date of composition, *Macbeth* falls about midway between *Julius Caesar* and *The Tempest,* and like them is known only from the First Folio. Its condition, however, seems not to be as good as theirs, or so say the editors, some of whom find it too short—it is one of the shortest of the plays—and suspect paring by hands other than Shakespeare's. All the editors are sure there have been additions by another hand in at least one or two scenes (see K. Muir's Arden edition, pp. xii-xiii, xxiii-xxxiii). Despite such scholarly uncertainties, *Macbeth,* along with *Caesar,* and some of the history plays, is popularly considered one of Shakespeare's most political plays, as well as one of his best. To Abraham Lincoln it *was* the best: "Nothing," he said, "equals *Macbeth.*" How simple and moral is its story! Led on by the prophecy of witches, Macbeth and his Lady succeed in secretly murdering King Duncan and gaining Scotland's throne. Yet they never enjoy the happiness they anticipated from this cruel regicide. Macbeth becomes engrossed in a series of additional murders, one worse than the other, until opposition to him mounts. When Malcolm, Duncan's elder son, returns to Scotland at the head of an English army, he is joined by those suffering under Macbeth's tyrannies, and together they lay siege to his castle. Shortly afterward, Lady Macbeth commits suicide, and Macbeth himself dies in face-to-face combat with Macduff, leaving Malcolm as Scotland's next king.

This is the obvious dramatic action of the play, but there are also signs of a deeper philosophical subject. In a play better known for memorable lines or phrases than speeches, no doubt the most memorable speech is one of Macbeth's last, just after the queen's death. Launching into a very abstract reflection on life, with its endless and aimless "tomorrow, and tomorrow, and tomorrow," Macbeth cries

> . . . Out, out brief candle
> Life's but a walking shadow, a poor player
> That struts and frets his hour upon the stage,
> And then is heard no more. It is a tale
> Told by an idiot, full of sound and fury,
> Signifying nothing.

According to this "atheistic" speech, as it has been called, Macbeth finds that life itself, like a tale told by an idiot, is completely unintelligible. Now he could not mean by this simply that life has no moral plan or purpose, for he thinks of himself as deeply immoral, and might easily have concluded, from his wife's fate and his own imminent downfall, that injustice is always punished, that the world is indeed moral—which is the conclusion usually drawn by the audience. But Macbeth has something else in mind when he calls life a "tale told by an idiot," something very radical, and going far beyond the atheism often attributed to him at this point. For an idiot cannot tell a tale: his words do not hang together, or, better, are not words at all, but only noises, only fury. When an idiot "speaks," one noise follows another unpredictably, and so, Macbeth seems to think, is it with life. Life too has no connections among things, no intelligible sequences of cause and effect. What made Lady Macbeth sick? Why is she now dead? Why is he about to be overcome? Why have they both failed? Macbeth finds himself completely unable to explain this turn of events. To him it is simply unintelligible.

In fact, the play does contain a real and great puzzle of causality, for, knowing what Macbeth and Lady Macbeth were like when they planned Duncan's murder, could we have predicted their ultimate fate? No one has stated the problem better than Sigmund Freud, who found it inexplicable that, over so short a span of time, the remorseless Lady Macbeth should be suicidally "borne down" by remorse, while the fearful Macbeth ends up "all defiance." Freud criticizes Shakespeare because he finds these apparent reversals of character unintelligible; quite rightly he refuses to allow the dramatist any leeway that "breaks the causal connection" (*Macbeth Casebook,* pp. 132, 136-37). If Freud is correct in his diagnosis, Shakespeare seems to have constructed an unintelligible play, almost as if to corroborate Macbeth's view of life's unintelligibility.

Freud may well be correct on one point: the changes Shakespeare depicts in his protagonists could not naturally have occurred over a brief span of time—certainly not if Freud has accurately gauged the time involved (he thinks it a mere matter of days). But it is possible Shakespeare has consciously sought a kind of compression in the play—that what by nature would take much longer he has caused to occur within not only a relatively short period of time but in a very small number of pages as well. If he could do this while providing the thread of intelligibility—of cause and effect in the seeming reversal of the main characters—better than Freud thinks he does, he will have engineered a special kind of dramatic shock, and a special goad to searching out these causes and effects, much as would a scientist or philosopher like Freud himself. The cause of *Macbeth*'s oft-noted brevity would then lie not in paring by others but in Shakespeare's dramatic and philosophical intentions combined. If we can prove, further, that the scenes thought to be superfluously added by someone else are also intrinsic to Shakespeare's overall plan, the play will be completely freed from the kind of editorial censure it has received.

But there is more. What would life be like if it is *not* a "tale told by an idiot"? In what sense is life a "tale" or story at all? If it is a tale told by a non-idiot, a normal man, life must be intelligible and capable of being understood in terms of cause and effect. But does its being a tale suggest an overall purpose or meaning to life? Is life intelligible in the higher sense of being what reason or wisdom would choose? Is it conclusively moral, directed by a providential supreme power working for the just and the good and guaranteeing their triumph? Certainly this would be the case if the God Christians believe in ruled

Valerie Taylor, April Olrich, and Anita Sharp Bolster as the witches in the 1960 film adaptation of Macbeth, *directed by George Schaefer.*

the world. *Macbeth* does have a number of minor characters who seem to be the very embodiment of Christian belief and conduct, and who trust in a universe where good inevitably triumphs over evil. Duncan (and earlier, his queen as well) is said to have been like that; at first Lady Macduff is, and also the English king, who miraculously cures men of a disease known as the Evil (IV, 3: 108-11, 146-60; IV, 2: 73-79). In fact, there is a strong element of this belief in Macbeth and Lady Macbeth as well: Macbeth fears what will happen to him in the life to come, and knows he has lost his "eternal jewel"; Lady Macbeth, sleepwalking, thinks she is in hell. Yet the witches opening the play, and giving it its essential atmosphere, seem to personify evil rather than good, and it is they, rather than any invisible good God, that, by arranging Macbeth's doom, seem to triumph in the play.

Macbeth is a mystery play—like a mystery story or novel—in more ways than one, and not simply in the sense that all Shakespearean plays are mysteries. Beyond the mystery of its character reversals and of imposing elements like the witches, it is filled with mysteries of fact left to the reader's notice and investigation. To mention only the most prominent: to whom does Ross refer (toward the beginning) by the term "Bellona's bridegroom"? What makes Macbeth decide to slay the sleeping guards when he goes up to see the dead Duncan (since it was not part of his plan)? To whom does Banquo so insistently travel the day of Macbeth's banquet, and who is the third murderer involved in his slaying? Why does Ross turn up at Lady Macduff's castle shortly before her murder, and who sends the messenger to warn her? What brings Ross to England? These questions of fact and motivation are essential to the understanding of life—of human affairs—and we must not be willing to notice an unexplained gap in the sequence without trying to pursue it. We cannot remain satisfied with the chaotic surface of things, or with superficial and apparent motivations. In ways small as well as large, we are given incentives to observe and think, to search for cause and effect, and thus to confirm life's intelligibility in at least this sense. We are also given sufficient information to decide upon its intelligibility in the higher sense of rational or moral order.

The Witches from Beginning to End

More than any Shakespearean play that is neither English history nor Roman, *Macbeth* derives its content from historical narratives. It is amazing to find how much of the characters, and of their speech and action, Shakespeare drew from Holinshed's *Chronicles* and like sources. It is even more amazing, and instructive, to discover the changes he made, using certain features but not others, inventing new ones, and putting them all together in a manner conducive to his own purpose. The general outlines of the story of Macbeth are followed, but many of the details of Duncan's murder come from Donwald's earlier murder of King Duff. Various witches and wizards are already in the story, waiting to be congealed into three witches, to whom Shakespeare, defiantly anachronistic, adds Hecate. Most of Macbeth is already there, and even Macduff. But Lady Macbeth had to be constructed out of a few lines referring to her ambition and her inciting Macbeth to murder Duncan. And while Ross and Lady Macduff are present in the story, their character and role had to be wholly invented. (See the Furness edition (Dover), pp. 379-95, and *Shakespeare's Holinshed* (Dover), pp. 18-45.) Let us begin by examining those eerie yet contemptible witches.

The play opens with a brief appearance of the three witches and then a much longer one two scenes later. Their meeting with Hecate, so universally spurned by the editors, occurs at the end of Act III and the beginning of Act IV. There, after a reproving lecture from Hecate, the witches are directed to prepare for a final glorious deception of Macbeth, which all four then consummate together. The details of word and deed provided in all these scenes are more than "atmospherics," though they certainly create a most particular atmosphere and mood. The reader is intended to think seriously about the witches: What kind of beings are they? Are they real? What is their significance? Who is Hecate, and why is she needed? In their very first lines, the witches show a predilection for bad weather ("thunder, lightning or in rain"), a taste for paradox ("when the battle's lost and won"), and a gift of prophecy (knowing that the battle will be finished "ere the set of sun"). Their "fair is foul, and foul is fair" seems to reek of moral as well as meteorological paradox; their answering the call of little spirits ("I come, Graymalkin!", "Paddock calls") propounds an equally perplexing metaphysical paradox—that of the greater being seeming to serve the lesser, like a pet owner his pet. And, of course, why they are intent on meeting Macbeth is never discussed or divulged.

When they have convened again a little later to meet Macbeth, the witches begin a rather lengthy conversation, asking each other what they had just been doing in the interim. They address each other as "sister," indicating a kinship either of blood or kind, but they use no first names, and give the impression that they may lack such names, even though their petlike spirits have them. And since they must ask about each other's doings, some drastic limits to their foreknowledge are indicated: perhaps it extends only to the doings of men, or to the things receiving their attention. Their answers are equally interesting. One has been killing swine—evidently an activity needing no further explanation. The other begs for chestnuts from a sailor's wife, who interrupts her chewing only to dismiss the witch quite airily, fully aware she is a witch. Out of what looks like a desire for revenge, this one—knowing the wife's husband is the master of a ship at sea—will pursue him in a sieve and "do" something to him. One thing she will clearly do is use the wind she commands, and the winds offered by her two sisters, to blow his ship about for "nine times nine" (that is, eighty-one) weeks, tossing it in a tempest, but unable to destroy it. Suddenly, she interrupts this train of thought to show her sister, childishly eager to see it, the thumb of a wrecked pilot. Hearing, then, a drum, they dance around three-times-three times to make up nine, and set the charm for Macbeth's appearance before them, apparently not knowing, or caring, that Banquo will be with him.

What, so far, has Shakespeare told us with these witches? Remembering Macbeth's later claim that "life is a tale told by an idiot, full of sound and fury, signifying nothing," it cannot quite be said that the witches talk like idiots, since their conversation makes some sense. But it makes very little sense, and what strikes us most of all is their childishness, combined with a singular inclination to relish acts (or relics) of human harming, even while exhibiting kindness toward each other. We do not know what they look like yet, but they seem to have certain human needs (for example, the desire for food) and therefore bodies. They have command of the winds and can travel anywhere swiftly, but their powers of destruction seem oddly restricted—swine yes, but the master of the Tiger, no. The net impression overall remains one of unintelligibility and hence impossibility: their powers or traits seem inconsistent with each other. Above all, we do not perceive—nor would it be at all consistent with what we do perceive—any link between these witches and the devil. Satanically bent on evil, in defiance of God's commands, these witches are not. There is nothing Christian about them.

What the witches look like we must wait to learn from Banquo, the first to see them. They are withered, wild in their attire, female yet bearded, standing on the earth yet looking not like its "inhabitants." They can understand Banquo's "Live you? or are you aught that man may question?" though by placing wrinkled fingers on their thin lips they apparently signal him to remain silent. Only when Macbeth, both commanding and asking, says "Speak, if you can. What are you?" do they break their own silence and give him the famous "hails." To Banquo they say nothing, but at his subsequent urging also address their hails to him, prophesying his destiny, and making comparisons between it and Macbeth's. With their final "Banquo and Macbeth, all hail," they refuse to answer Macbeth's further questioning and disappear.

Why the witches seem originally concerned with Macbeth alone, and why they accede to Banquo's demands, cannot be known, nor even whether they anticipated those demands—which seems unlikely. The "hails" given Macbeth mention three heights of place and power, two of them—the thanedoms—already achieved, one—the kingdom—to be gotten in the future. Since we have just witnessed (in the previous scene) the bestowal of Cawdor's title on Macbeth, in his absence, by King Duncan, and learn from Macbeth himself that he is already Thane of Glamis due to his father's death, two-thirds of what the witches tell him are not prophecies at all, though the power of the witches to know even these seems beyond any human power. Only Macbeth's becoming king can be considered a prophecy, which, as the story unfolds, turns out to be true. But the "hails" to Macbeth contain utterly no reference to any evils he may encounter along the way, or to any defects in his greatness. These emerge only with the prophecy given to Banquo, which is actually stated in terms of comparison with Macbeth. Banquo will be lesser or greater, not so happy, yet much happier, a begetter of kings but not a king himself. These too are largely confirmed by the further action of the play, but the evil Banquo will encounter along the way—being murdered with twenty gashes in his head and thrown in a ditch, all by command of his friend, Macbeth—could hardly be gathered directly from what the witches say.

At this point in the play, we have no idea whether it is the purpose of the witches to praise and please the great humans they single out for their attention, or—as it turns out—to tempt them by the promise of great good into actions that lead to a doom concealed from them. We have no idea whether the witches form part of a large organized group or are out there uncoordinated, in unknown numbers, perhaps even working at cross-purposes to each other, in a kind of chaos. To clarify the larger framework of their operations, Shakespeare later arranges for them to meet with Hecate, in the scene (penultimate in Act III) that most editors seem intent on extruding as spurious. Duncan has already been murdered and replaced by the Macbeths. Banquo (but not his son, Fleance) has also been murdered, and Macbeth, still shuddering after seeing Banquo's ghost at the banquet, and anticipating his need for still further murders, has just declared his intent to visit the "weird sisters." He is "bent on knowing, by the worst means, the worst"—and this we only learn indirectly when the visit takes place. He wants to learn what will happen to him now that he has again waded, and will continue to wade, in blood.

When the witches meet Hecate, Macbeth has already indicated to Lady Macbeth his intent to visit him, and Hecate is aware of it. The first witch has the first and last lines of the scene: all the rest are Hecate's. Told by the first witch that she looks angry, Hecate begins by explaining and justifying her anger, which is directed at them. She takes command of their further operations, indicates her own general principle and the one underlying their future strategy regarding Macbeth, and concludes by responding to the call of her "little spirit." Of these three parts of Hecate speech, the first has caused the most trouble:

> Have I not reason, beldams as you are,
> Saucy, and overbold? How did you dare
> To trade and traffic with Macbeth,
> In riddles, and affairs of death;
> And I, the mistress of your charms,
> The close contriver of all harms,
> Was never call'd to bear my part,
> Or show the glory of our art?
> And, which is worse, all you have done
> Hath been but for a wayward son,
> Spiteful and wrathful; who, as others do,
> Loves for his own ends, not for you.

An earlier American editor named W. A. Rolfe presented one of the strongest attacks on the authenticity of this scene. To begin with, Rolfe notes that Hecate speaks in iambics, whereas "the eight-syllable lines that Shakespeare puts into the mouth of supernatural beings are regularly trochaic." Furthermore, in what sense could the witches have been said to "trade and traffic" with Macbeth, since no bargain or exchange has transpired between them? What were the "gains" in which they were all to share, according to Hecate (said a little later, at IV, 1:43)? And how has Macbeth proved a "wayward son, spiteful and wrathful"? These and similar considerations lead Rolfe to conclude that the part of Hecate is the work of some "hack writer in the theater" (Furness, pp. 232-33).

Rolfe's criticisms are sensible, and deserve an adequate response. In accusing the witches of "trading" ("trafficking" emphasizes the same idea), Hecate seems to look upon their presentation to Macbeth as something like a rational exchange, where the trading partners both have in view an end or benefit to themselves. But the gravamen of her complaint comes in the next lines: You failed, Hecate says, to bring me into the action; I, who both control your charms and secretly contrive all harms; I, who alone can show the full "glory" of our art. In short, you set up shop on your own, so to speak, and were therefore "saucy, and overbold." And the complaint has a second even stronger component, for, "which is worse," you have done this for a "wayward," not a loving or devoted "son," who loves selfishly, "for his own ends" (but not different from others in this respect), rather than "for you." In this part, the image of commerce or rational exchange is dropped, and replaced by that of love, with Hecate picturing the witches as Macbeth's mother, who loves her son and expects both love and devotion from him. In both cases, Hecate seems, rather paradoxically, to presume that the witches are bestowing a benefit, not inflicting a harm, on Macbeth—a benefit they expect to result in some good to themselves, either in the form of a benefit rationally exchanged or one bestowed through love.

What can possibly be the reason for such complications? Shakespeare has Hecate call herself the "close contriver of all harms," almost along the way, not unproudly, yet matter-of-factly. What she means is that all the harm—at least the human harm, and perhaps harm to all beings capable of being harmed—is under her control. Hecate is not Satan—she is very unlike Satan—but she affords

Shakespeare something like a substitute for Satan through whom he can raise, more guardedly, the questions that ought to be directed at Satan himself. Satan had to be brought into existence to help explain the persistence, gravity, and frequent success (short of domination) of evil in a universe completely created by a good God. Since he could not create himself, he must have been created by God, as a good being that somehow manages to derange itself, thus leaving God without responsibility for evil. Satan must, to oppose God completely, represent evil loved for itself. Hecate demonstrates the impossibility of this idea. Once one postulates beings that bring evil into the world, and contrive all harms, they do so for the sake of either harming or benefiting. But a being that wants only to harm must want to harm itself, and such a being contradicts the very notion of being. Every being must therefore want to benefit at least itself. This is also why Hecate can later say to the witches, "O, well done! I commend your pains, and everyone shall share i' the gains" (IV, 1:42-43)—leaving us wondering what possible gains they can obtain either from this successful performance before Macbeth or from his ultimate downfall. Will Macbeth become something like that wrecked "pilot's thumb" the first witch carries around in her pocket? What needs of Hecate and the witches—and how must they be constructed to have such needs—are satisfied by the contriving of harm?

While Hecate may look "angerly," and is clearly angered, it is surprising how little of the punitive or vindictive she manifests toward her "saucy" minions. On the contrary, all she asks is that they "make amends now" by following her directions. She plans a great display of their art, in all its glory, and is engrossed in the thought of it—but not as a malevolent Satan, anticipating with joy the pain, suffering, and destruction to be brought about. Hecate is, above all, an artisan—or, better still, an artist who must create all the elements necessary to a successful charming of Macbeth. And the shortness, lightness, and rhyme of her lines are perfectly in keeping with this approach to her job as "chief contriver of harms." We never learn whether there is a "chief contriver of benefits," or by whom—other than themselves—the "glory of our art" is to be appreciated. Nevertheless, she gives the impression that bringing about harm is a difficult and complicated thing, and hence in need of a complex and glorious art. She is therefore characterized by something like the human love of excellence—an excellence which in her eyes remains untarnished because harms, presumably, are a necessary part of the nature of things. The witches seem to do, by impulse, what Hecate does out of a sense of rational necessity, and by art. They can therefore be pictured as childlike, she as a mature adult.

Yet Shakespeare wants us to see an essential kinship between them as well, and therefore makes her leave in response to the call of her "little spirit," just as they had in the very first scene. Not only must one wonder how a devotion to harming is consistent with this love of pets, but also how the higher and greater being can seek to serve the lower. This touch is meant to draw even more sharply the contrast between Hecate and these witches, on the one hand, and Satan and his witches—viewed in the context of Christianity—on the other. Satan is all evil, from top to toe, but Hecate and her witches are peculiar combinations of good and evil, and hardly reek of malevolence in their evildoing. Their peculiarity provokes our interest not only in their motive for doing harm but in their motive for doing good. Is there a counterpart to Hecate responsible for causing good, and if so, what is the relation between the two? Or is evil subservient to good—somehow more difficult to bring about than good? Applied in the context of Christianity, what causes God to do good? What possible want or desire in Him could make Him create a world, and then suffer for one of His creatures?

Rolfe is quite right in his criticism of Hecate's speech, so long as one considers it a set of charges against the witches that, in a literal and simply factual sense, are either true or false. In this sense they are false, and seem entirely wide of the mark—hence the work of some hack writer. But the sheer poetry should have told him better than that, and if one thinks of Hecate's lines primarily as a vehicle for exposing the general problem of the relation between good and evil in the universe, Rolfe's objections disappear. That Shakespeare wants to confront this problem is shown, much more graphically than ever before, in the next witches' scene, set, as Hecate had told us, at the "pit of Acheron," where Macbeth will soon come. Here we find the witches boiling in a cauldron a stew made of things that would utterly and instinctively repel the audience as evil: hideous animals that crawl and fly, run and swim, poisoned entrails, poisonous plants, parts of Jews, infidels, and the strangled offspring of prostitutes.

These ingredients are not selected in accordance with the strictest of principles, however. Some—like toads, snakes, bats, sharks—may be considered clearly repellent by nature, but others—Jews, Turks, and Tartars—only by divine law, or from a Christian point of view, and still others—poisoned entrails and prostitutes' strangled offspring—at least partly by human intervention. None are simply characteristic of a universe evil by nature or in itself. In fact, as if to remind us faintly of those parts of the universe that do not repel, or that even attract, Shakespeare has the witches include in their stew items of questionable repugnance, like "toe of frog" and "tongue of dog." Later, as if to make sure the mood of the horrid is sustained, the witches throw into the cauldron the blood of a sow that has devoured her nine farrow, and grease from the noose of a murderer's gibbet, reminding us, with the last, of the most repellent spectacle in the play—that of the murderous Macbeth and Lady Macbeth themselves.

Macbeth insists on being answered by the witches concerning the future even if all things must be destroyed by the winds they command. But even before he can frame his question, the First Apparition knows how to answer it. The spectacle now presented to Macbeth—evidently Hecate's masterful contrivance—is in fact much more complicated than what the witches had originally presented on their own. In each of three cases, an unnamed and puzzling apparition explicitly tells him how to act, practically calling for injustice, and apparently promising him impunity. Finally, at his own insistence, he is given shattering confirmation of the earlier prediction that Banquo's issue will reign in this kingdom, which leads him to call for this "pernicious hour" to "stand aye accursed in the calendar!" But Hecate has done her job well, and, true to her word, led him on "to his confusion" by assuring him security for his crimes. This she has done not through outright lies but through equivocation, using words that in their ordinary meaning give guarantees, while in some unusual meaning withdrawing them.

Toward the play's end, on discovering these extraordinary meanings, Macbeth senses the "equivocation of the fiend that lies like truth," and exclaims against these "juggling fiends" that "palter with us in a double sense" (V, 5:50; V, 8:25-28). He ends up dead and headless, after the wife concerning whose destiny he had never inquired has already committed suicide. But his last meeting with the witches, at the pit of Acheron, concludes in their effort to cheer him up with music and dancing, as he stands distracted. Their spell is now complete, and its ultimate consequences guaranteed, without any necessity on their part to check later. Hecate and her helpers—beings whose function and good it is to do harm, without malice—must be satisfied with their success. And Shakespeare must have been satisfied with his. For by this point he has clearly distinguished the witches in *Macbeth* from Christian witches, and plainly entitled them to be headed by Hecate rather than Satan. At the same time, he has deepened our interest in the problem of evil in the universe. How is it to be accounted for? Why are so many things in nature repellent to man? Why is evil so important a feature of all human affairs? What causes evil in people like Macbeth and Lady Macbeth?

Clearly the perspective from which Shakespeare views these matters, in the play, is not Christian, although the protagonists are. With the help of his witches, Shakespeare can illuminate the problem of intelligible being (to help us decide whether life is a tale told by an idiot), using as a specimen case the nature of beings supposedly dedicated to the contrivance of harm. At the same time—allowing the witches to tempt men by promising security for injustice—Shakespeare can study, as if under artificial laboratory conditions, the rapid amplification and intensification of tyrannical evildoing, and the state of soul motivating and accompanying it. He will have recourse to important elements of Christian expectation—the porter as hell's gatekeeper, Lady Macbeth thinking hell murky—but only to show the natural hell, the hell on this earth, to which wickedness can lead. And he will have his little joke: a character named Seyton is suddenly introduced toward the end (and as suddenly disappears) to serve simultaneously as a bringer of bad news and Macbeth's assistant, in the process showing a supernatural ability that makes it impossible to identify him as a mere man (see M. Levith, *What's in Shakespeare's Names?* pp. 20, 56).

Good Plan, Bad Plan

We must now turn to two bold plans of which we learn early in the play. The Macbeths' plan to murder Duncan, while paraded before our eyes, is poorly planned and executed, but successful. On the other hand, Duncan's plan to frustrate Macbeth's ambition is almost invisible, well planned, and well executed—but unsuccessful. We must begin with Duncan's plan, since it shows itself almost at once, in Act 1, scene 2. Duncan has always struck the careless reader as even less capable of forethought than King Lear, who had at least constructed a plan for the succession in Britain. Duncan seems old, weak, impetuous, too trusting, and too ready to distrust. We first see him in the midst of a combined revolt and invasion, relying not on his own efforts in battle but on Macbeth, Banquo, and his older son, Malcolm. Looks can be deceiving, however, for Duncan's support among the thanes is amazingly solid: only Cawdor has joined the rebel, Macdonwald. The chief problem facing Duncan, once we put all the facts together, has to do not with the invasion or the rebellion, as might first appear, but with the succession. Scotland was not then a strict hereditary monarchy, and, with its feudal aristocracy, obviously needed a mature soldier at its helm. Not only was Malcolm young for this task, but his military ineptitude has just shown itself for all to see: only the efforts of the bleeding sergeant keep him from being captured in this battle. At the same time, the sergeant's story testifies to the unrivaled military prowess of Macbeth, who proves himself to be the kingdom's salvation against the rebels.

This predicament accounts for a series of apparently disparate actions on Duncan's part that, taken together, display the coherence of a plan—and a good plan. Duncan had not yet made his son Malcolm the Prince of Cumberland—that is, he had not yet publicly made him his heir. Since hereditary succession (as shown by this very fact) was still not automatic, the king had perhaps delayed to keep from seeming selfish for his family and insufficiently devoted to the public good, hoping for some impressive military accomplishment from Malcolm that might justify his choice. But the king's own advanced age, Malcolm's youthfulness and incapacity as a soldier, and Macbeth's recent successes on the battlefield make Macbeth rather than Malcolm the all but irresistible choice for the throne. In these circumstances, what can Duncan do, and do instantly? We do not know for sure whether Duncan, like Macduff and others we learn about later, was already suspicious of Macbeth's moral character (for example, Macduff at II, 4: 88, Banquo at I, 3: 121-24 and III, 1: 1-3; even Banquo's prospective murderers at III, 1: 76-79). It is quite likely that he was, or he may have simply favored his own sons. In any case, he must quickly proclaim Malcolm Prince of Cumberland, and thus his heir, but in such a way as to prevent violent dissidence and opposition from Macbeth.

Already Duncan had tried to dilute Macbeth's influence by the unusual step of making him and Banquo co-captains in the war: we can see this motive in his question, after hearing of Macbeth's prowess alone, as to what effect the entrance of the Norwegian force into battle had on "our captains, Macbeth and Banquo"—thus bringing Banquo to the center of attention along with Macbeth. But the presumed treason of the thane of Cawdor gives Duncan a new and much more substantial opportunity, for Macbeth can instantly be invested with his title and lands just at the time the announcement about Malcolm is made. It strikes the reader as most precipitate on Duncan's part to call for Cawdor's death, especially on a mere verbal report of his treason by Ross. But the action had to be calculated, and Duncan speaks truly—of himself if not of Cawdor—when he says, "There's no art to find the mind's construction in the face." His plan, as we must reconstruct it, is to make Macbeth obligated and grateful to him publicly—to double his thanedom—at the very moment that his own son, Malcolm, is openly and legally set in line for the throne.

These conjectures can be confirmed by scrutinizing the events immediately surrounding Duncan's proclamation of the succession in scene 4. He has already sent Ross and Angus to greet Macbeth, on the way to Forres, where the king is staying, with the title "thane of Cawdor." When Macbeth enters, the king calls him "O worthiest cousin," thus indicating a family kinship later confirmed by Macbeth himself, and of course all the more dangerous in light of the succession problem. Duncan then talks of how much he owes Macbeth, without going into details, and ends with "More is thy due than more than all can pay." Notice no mention yet of the title of Cawdor, amid large but vague promises of reward. Macbeth responds dutifully, expressing—to excess, it seems—the obligations generally owed not only to Duncan's "throne and state" and his children but to his *servants* as well! "Welcome hither!" responds Duncan. "I have begun to plant thee, and will labour to make thee full of growing." Again, large but vague promises, this time permitting the inference that until then he has *not* "planted" Macbeth. In short, Macbeth—and we can understand why—had not been one of his favorites hitherto.

Then Duncan addresses Banquo as of equal deserving, and he embraces him, leading the reader to wonder whether anything he had just said to Macbeth indicated an embrace for him as well. By this point Duncan seems to have tears of joy in his eyes. Suddenly, without warning, he launches into the announcement naming Malcolm Prince of Cumberland and heir to his estate and, without saying so explicitly, his throne. The nobility of others shall also be honored. Then, with suddenness again, and striking brevity: "From hence to Inverness." What this means is that he has just invited himself to Macbeth's castle! Probably as surprised as anyone, Macbeth says he will ride ahead and bring the good news of Duncan's coming to his wife, and only then does Duncan say: "My worthy Cawdor!" That is, only after receiving Macbeth's earlier public commitment of duty, and now his acquiescence in receiving him as a guest in his castle, does Duncan publicly confirm by his own words the honor he had had Ross bestow on Macbeth. Once at Inverness, Duncan's plan culminates in his sending Banquo to Lady Macbeth with the gift of a diamond that night, just before going to sleep. Nor has he been without protective care for himself, even then, for his grooms are just outside his bedchamber, and he has asked *Macduff* to call upon him early that morning (II, 1: 13-16; II, 3: 50-51). So there is the plan in full: another high honor for Macbeth, a bauble for his wife, the appointment of the next king (so killing Duncan, as Macbeth realizes at once, still leaves an equally large obstacle in the way), and then arranging to become Macbeth's guest, taking some precaution nonetheless. It is an excellent plan and would have worked, even in spite of the witches' favorable prophecies, had it not been for the extraordinary ambition and persuasiveness of Lady Macbeth, coupled with her and her husband's stupidity, and one other unanticipated factor, to be discussed below.

This is the well-conceived plan that did not work. Now let us see the ill-conceived one that did. If one examines carefully Macbeth's written and oral communications to his wife, one will discover that he never reveals to her two important facts—the prophecy the witches made for Banquo, and the naming of Malcolm as Prince of Cumberland. Had he done so, their task in usurping the throne would have looked at least doubly difficult and far less promising. This is why they make no overt plan for killing Malcolm, though both he and Donalbain, his younger brother, are at Inverness with their father that night. And it is also why—after luck, not brains, catapults them into the throne—Macbeth plans Banquo's murder alone, without the queen's help. In the case of Duncan's murder, Lady Macbeth must first persuade Macbeth to do a deed they both acknowledge to be deeply immoral, and also convince him it can be done with impunity. To prove the latter, she suggests that by plying the two chamberlains with alcohol she can put them into a deep sleep, leaving Duncan at their mercy. Macbeth adds a touch of his own: they will use the chamberlains' daggers for the dead, and then spread blood on their bodies as well. In the ensuing clamor, their guilt will be accepted by all.

As it turns out, although her plan called for their doing the deed together, it ends up wholly in Macbeth's hands. And some improvisations are made. From Lady Macbeth the audience learns that she has drugged the grooms' wine and only then done her part in laying out their daggers for Macbeth's use immediately thereafter. But, stricken with terror after committing the murder, Macbeth forgets to smear the grooms with blood and leave the bloody daggers with them—a task that must then be undertaken by Lady Macbeth, whose hands are bloodied in the process, like Macbeth's. And a final improvisation, wholly uncalled for in the perfected plan, occurs when Macbeth goes up to see the king after the murder has been discovered and on his own kills the grooms. This is the real reason why Lady Macbeth, upon hearing Macbeth blurt out his account to those assembled in the castle, faints straightway.

How good is this plan, both in its original and its improvised variations? The weak point of the former was its blaming the chamberlains, who, if they had any motive for killing the king, would not be so obliging as to lie down immediately in the very spot where they were expected to stay for the night and fall asleep there, defiled with blood. And, of course, once awake the chamberlains would stoutly deny they had such a motive, would tell of being plied with liquor by the queen, and might receive support from those in the king's trust (see Lennox's allusion at III, 6: 11-16). Now, for some reason we never learn from Macbeth's own lips, he quickly decides to kill the guards when he goes up to see the dead king. From Lenox, who accompanied him, we learn that the guards "star'd, and were distracted." Macbeth must have observed this himself, and perhaps thought it unnatural that they were not simply asleep (the drug applied by Lady Macbeth may have caused this unusual condition). What, he might have wondered, would happen if they were shaken and still would not awaken from their drunken stupor? Did he guess that they had been drugged—a fact of which he was not informed by Lady Macbeth? Did he fear that an inquiry into their condition might lead back to Lady Macbeth and himself?

By killing the guards, Macbeth does something exceedingly strange, and hardly justifiable on the grounds of the righteous indignation to which he pretends. But he takes this risk, and Lady Macbeth—not seeing what it can accomplish for them—swoons. At this point, a huge piece of unanticipated luck falls their way: Malcolm and Donalbain, fearing for their own lives after their father's murder, flee, which, as Macduff later tells Ross, "puts upon them suspicion of the deed," it being thought—no doubt with much urging from the Macbeths—that the chamberlains were suborned by them to murder their father. The story is still highly improbable, but another accident helps make it accepted. It was Macduff who demanded that Macbeth explain why he killed the grooms; after he does, Lady Macbeth's apparent fainting spell may have kept him from pursuing the matter further. That Macduff did indeed harbor suspicions is shown by his later refusal to be present at Macbeth's coronation. But there was one person in the castle that morning who had much more solid grounds than Macduff for suspecting Macbeth, and who had actually concluded the murder was done by him. This, of course, was Banquo. Just after Lady Macbeth's collapse, Banquo calls for everyone to get dressed and return "to question this most bloody piece of work, to know it further." But we can easily guess why he never gives voice to his suspicions (explicitly admitted at the beginning of Act III): he must have thought the witches' prophecy about the future kingship of his sons would be realized after their prediction about Macbeth's gaining the throne is. We can therefore imagine that the Macbeths unexpectedly found in Banquo a strong supporter for their effort to condemn the king's sons and then install Macbeth in Duncan's place. This, too, was how the Macbeth overcame the obstacle Lady Macbeth had never been told about—that of Malcolm's being named Prince of Cumberland. In other words, by one and the same piece of luck, wholly unanticipated, Malcolm could be blamed for Duncan's murder and removed from the line of succession! His flight became the key to Macbeth's success.

Why all this emphasis on plans? For one thing, it tells us something about Duncan and about the Macbeths—about their mental stature. It permits us to distinguish further between a tyrannical usurper like the Duke of Gloucester (in *Richard III*) and the Macbeths, the latter being more superstitious, more moral, and a good deal less intelligent than the former. But there is a general purpose as well, for it refines the reader's perception and understanding of human affairs generally, and moves him closer to being able to say whether life is a tale told by an idiot or not. To the extent that intelligent purpose, human or nonhuman, directs life, it is not such a tale—in fact it is the precise opposite of such a tale. In *The Tempest* we see the wise, premeditated plan of its hero, Prospero, determine the action of practically the whole play. In *Macbeth* we learn how one serious bit of miscalculation or ignorance (of Lady Macbeth's character by Duncan) can thwart an otherwise excellent plan, and how chance can make a very poor one succeed. These are important features of human life, but in neither case does life lose its causal intelligibility. In other words, we can see just what it is that makes the two plans develop and eventuate as they do, showing that no part of life is a tale told by an idiot. And the part of life least deserving that description is the perfectly designed work of art—the philosophical drama—which allows no part of itself to bear any but a necessary relationship to all other parts and the whole. The play *Macbeth* itself is an entirely sufficient proof that life is not unintelligible sound and fury!

Macduff and Ross

Macduff and Ross are cousins, but they are very unlike each other. Much of Macduff's character was already available to Shakespeare in Holinshed's *Chronicles,* whereas Ross was barely named and had to be built up from scratch. We see Ross before we see Macduff. With Angus, he comes riding in from Fife. There, according to the account he gives King Duncan, the traitor Cawdor and the King of Norway himself were defeated in battle by someone Ross refers to as "Bellona's bridegroom." Bellona was the goddess of war, and most commentators take this hero to be Macbeth again. But Fife is a great distance from the area near Forres where the first battle has just taken place—the battle involving the bleeding sergeant, Malcolm, Macbeth, Banquo, Macdonwald, and the Norwegian lord. For that simple reason Macbeth could not also have been the hero of Fife—a conclusion fortified by the fact that Macbeth knows nothing of Cawdor's disloyalty (I, 4: 11-12). And who a more likely candidate for this role than that other great warrior, the thane of Fife himself? For reasons unknown to us, Ross' strange reference to "Bellona's bridegroom" seems to have had the purpose of concealing from Duncan's view the heroic deeds of that other thane and Ross' own cousin, Macduff.

Macduff himself has not yet arrived at Forres, nor is he present when Duncan makes his announcement about the succession. But he must have ridden in from the battle at Fife before the king's party leaves for Inverness, because he is with that party as it arrives there. Within the castle, he and Lennox have been quartered in a kind of annex, and we first hear Macduff speak in the famous porter scene early the next morning, when he and Lennox knock at the gate to be admitted into the main part of the castle. Minutes before, both Macbeths had heard the knocking just as Lady Macbeth leaves to return the chamberlains' daggers. Macbeth goes to the gate and is greeted rather coolly by Macduff: "Is the king stirring, worthy thane?" He adds that the king had commanded him "to call timely on him. I have almost slipp'd the hour." Hearing this the reader once again senses the importance of accident: a few minutes earlier, and the Macbeths might have been caught red-handed, literally.

Calling alone on the king, Macduff is the first to find him murdered, and from his exclamation we learn that he is a very pious man: "Most sacrilegious murder hath broke ope the Lord's anointed temple"—the last phrase combining elements from the Old and New Testaments. He rouses the whole house, calling by name Banquo, Donalbain, and Malcolm, but not Ross or Lady Macbeth. It is Macduff who asks Macbeth why he had just killed the guards, and who then seconds Banquo's proclaimed opposition to the "undivulged pretense . . . of treasonous malice." The next we see of him is at a meeting with Ross, apparently as he emerges from Macbeth's castle. For some reason Ross must have left the castle quickly after the murder, for he asks Macduff what happened there. Macduff tells him that the flight of Malcolm and Donalbain cast suspicion of their father's murder on them, that Macbeth had already been named king (presumably by a council of the thanes, unattended by Ross, in the castle) and that he has already left for Scone to be invested. Asked by Ross whether he will go to Scone, Macduff says he will go instead to Fife, his own castle. And to Ross' declaring his own intention to follow Macbeth to Scone, Macduff bids him see that things are well done there, "Lest our old robes sit easier than our new!" Either suspecting Macbeth of murder, or knowing of his character otherwise, Macduff is clearly uneasy, and is courageous—or imprudent—enough to reveal his state of mind by absenting himself from the coronation.

In Act III Macbeth has Banquo murdered, and in Act IV, the family of Macduff. The editors are never able to make out where Banquo and Fleance are riding the afternoon of their murder, and think it unimportant to boot. A guess could be hazarded rather easily, had they not followed one of the earliest editors (Capell) in locating Macbeth's palace at Forres, not far from Cawdor and Inverness in northern Scotland. In all likelihood, they do so not because of any stage directions, of which there are none, but because they assume Macbeth's second visit to the witches (at the end of Act III) takes place where he originally met them—a heath near Forres. From Inverness (near Forres), however, he had gone to Scone to be crowned, and no direction of any sort ever has him coming away from there (historically, the Scottish kings were likely to reside in Perth, close to Scone). If one also realizes that the final action of the play, in Act V, plainly takes place in or near the castle he had been busy fortifying at Dunsinane—close to both Scone and Perth—one will not have Macbeth spend all his time in Acts III and IV one hundred or more miles to the north at Forres. Moreover, he seeks out the witches not at the heath near Forres but at something called "the pit of Acheron"—a fictitious location derived from the Bible (2 Kings i, 2-7). Like its Biblical archetype, this pit seems to be known for its supernatural clientele. Nor should we forget that the three witches in the play are associated with the various winds and can therefore meet anywhere with one who seeks them—all the more if they are, so to speak, hovering over him and watching his destiny, as they are with Macbeth.

If Macbeth's castle in Act III is actually located at either Scone or Dunsinane, it is also within twenty or thirty miles of wherever it was in Fife that Macduff had his castle. Could this have been Banquo and Fleance's destination, so mysteriously left unidentified when Macbeth questions Banquo about their ride the day of the banquet? The reason for Banquo's reserve is perfectly clear: Macduff had refused to attend Macbeth's coronation and was already under suspicion. No doubt Banquo had worries to share with a close friend—only Banquo calls him "Dear Duff" the morning of Duncan's murder—and therefore, despite being Macbeth's chief guest, and despite Macbeth's strong and repeated urgings that he stay, Banquo insists on departing for several hours, perhaps until the early evening. This, and possibly the news of Banquo's murder as well, may have contributed to Macduff's decision to rebuff Macbeth's messenger and flee to England—a decision of which we learn very shortly afterward (II, 3: 94; III, 6: 39-43).

On his visit to the witches, Macbeth is told both that he should beware the thane of Fife and that (as he interprets it) he can be harmed or defeated by no human hand. Despite this last guarantee, he decides to kill Macduff, just to make sure. Discovering Macduff's flight to England, however, he decides immediately, and without any reason, to slaughter his wife and babes instead. The next scene is as mystifying as it is pathetic. Last present at the banquet, Ross is suddenly found in conversation with his cousin Lady Macbeth (and her son) in her castle, hearing her castigate her husband for leaving his wife, babes, mansion, and titles "in a place from whence himself does fly. . . ." Ross says he will return before long, hints he would burst into tears at their plight if he stays longer, and then departs—leaving the reader, as well, in complete ignorance as to the purpose of his visit. A moment later an unidentified messenger enters, warning Lady Macbeth to flee with her children, and in another moment the murderers themselves appear to kill her and the boy.

Let us try to explain these puzzles. The murderers, of course, were sent by Macbeth, and the messenger could only have been sent by Lennox, whom we know to be in

Macbeth's confidence, yet opposed to him. But why Ross? Why has he come to Macduff's castle? He offers his cousin no assistance, gives her no warning, tells her nothing of Macbeth's hostility and tyranny. Only one possibility remains: Ross had to be sent by Macbeth, for Macbeth could not know in advance how Macduff had left his castle guarded, and only someone Lady Macduff trusted—in this case a cousin of hers—could easily gain access and find out. Of course, this casts Ross in the worst possible light as a tool of the tyrant and a traitor to his relatives and friends. (Furness cites M. F. Libby's old suspicions of Ross in *Some New Notes on Macbeth* [1893].) Whether he actually returned (per his promise) as one of the murderers is hard to say, though not impossible, since they may be masked, and only one of them speaks. But startling as this deduction is, one fact is even more startling: Macduff had left his castle entirely unprotected! No army, no guards, no servants at the gates or door, as shown by the fact that both the messenger and the murderers are able to enter without the slightest interposition, obstruction, or disturbance. There is no one else around, so that Lady Macduff hardly exaggerates when she pictures her situation as one of complete and unnatural abandonment, and her husband as a traitor to his family.

Before trying to explain this, let us examine the last scene coupling Ross and Macduff, at the very end of Act IV. Macduff is already with Malcolm in England, and has passed the test of his loyalty to which he has been subjected by a suspicious young Malcolm, who explains to the older but rather simpleminded and naive man that "Devlish Macbeth by many of these trains hath sought to win me into his power, and modest wisdom plucks me from over-credulous haste." Suddenly Ross appears and is greeted by Macduff as his "ever-gentle cousin." Ross speaks of their poor country, Scotland, groaning in oppression and suffering, and is then asked directly by Macduff: "How does my wife?" Answer: "Why, well." Question: "And all my children?" Answer: "Well, too." Question: "The tyrant has not batter'd at their peace?" Answer: "No; they were well at peace when I did leave 'em."

Only with this last answer does Ross indicate—though Macduff does not seem to notice—his earlier presence at Macduff's castle. But that answer has one or more of three possible defects: either it is politically naive, or much less cognizant of Macbeth's intentions toward the Macduffs than Ross should have been, even as an innocent; or it is technically true, since when he left them they had not yet been assailed; or it is only metaphorically true—wickedly true—since their being "well at peace" would be consistent with their being dead, if he left them a second time as one of their murderers, or immediately afterward. In any case, it seems entirely odd that Ross should not know of, and report upon, the horrible fate of Macduff's family.

Very shortly afterward, this last peculiarity is shown to be such by an astonishing reversal. In line 178, Ross had just spoken of Macduff's family as "well at peace." In line 201 he prepares Macduff for hearing the worst possible news, which he then delivers, full force, in 204: "Your castle is surprised; your wife and babes savagely slaughtered. To relate this manner, were, on the quarry of these murder'd deer, to add the death of you." Incredulous, Macduff asks, "My children too?" Answer: "Wife, children, servants, all that could be found." Macduff: "And I must be from thence! My wife kill'd too?" And finally:

> Did Heaven look on,
> And would not take their part? Sinful Macduff!
> They were all struck for thee. Naught that I am,
> Not for their own demerits, but for mine,
> Fell slaughter on their souls: Heaven rest them now!

By this point, we have learned quite a bit about both Macduff and Ross. First, Ross knows about the complete extermination of Macduff's household, down to the last detail. He speaks as if he could even "relate the manner" of it, though he is never pressed to do so. Since he himself makes no claim to have learned this from others, after he left the Macduff castle, he must have learned it while he was there, at the time of the murders themselves.

As for Macduff, notice that he and Ross both confirm our suspicion that he had left no soldiery, no guards to defend the castle. How could this possibly happen, particularly since Macduff is not without suspicion that the "tyrant" might have "batter'd at their peace." Only one explanation seems possible, and it may be seen in the line "Did heaven look on, and would not take their part?" Macduff is portrayed as having trusted to heaven to defend his family—trusted, that is, to the God of Christianity, the "gentle heavens" he even now begs to let him confront Macbeth in personal combat. That God, Macduff's lines suggest, could be expected to defend innocent people against attack, and only failed to do so not because of any sins of theirs, which were nil, but because of *his*, Macduff's, sins! In short, Macduff takes it to follow from his Christian belief that God permits harms, or at least injustices, only to those who have sinned against Him, or to those for whom a sinner cares. Nor does it strike him that some question about God's justness is raised by the latter case—the case he takes to apply to his own family.

If one responds to this conjecture that it is entirely unrealistic to suppose a man like Macduff so fanatically given to such beliefs as to take no precautions for his family, one would be correct—on the level of real psychological probability. But Shakespeare frequently makes a motive unrealistically extreme in order to display it, to bring it to our attention, even at the risk of a certain unrealism. Or better, he gives up a more superficial realism for a deeper one. Many examples can be cited to show this. In real life, would a Jew (Shylock) really try to cut a pound of flesh out of a Christian (Antonio)? Would a friar be likely to give Juliet an apparently fatal potion? Could there be a girl so naive as Miranda? Would Enobarbus, after deserting Antony, drop dead out of a sense of guilt? Or, from *Macbeth* itself, would Lady Macbeth never have complained to Macbeth of her increasing isolation from him? Is it realistically possible, in the superficial sense (as

Freud, taking this to be the only sense, denied it was), for Macbeth to have changed so rapidly after becoming king? Still a murderer by premeditation, as he showed with Banquo, he knowingly becomes, only a short time later, a murderer by impulse with Macduff's family, announcing that "From this moment, the very firstlings of my heart shall be the firstlings of my hand."

The exaggeration in Macduff's motivation must have some relation to the subject of the play as a whole, which is the extent to which human life, and the universe, are intelligible, reasonable, moral. Christianity represents one pole among the possible conceptions, for, whatever place it allows to evil and sin, it insists on the supremacy of good, and of good manifested more through love than through justice, though both must be combined in the ultimate divine dispensation and governance. The primacy Christianity gives to love, and thus to "gentleness" (again, as in Macduff's appeal to "gentle heaven"), is an element closer to the feminine than the masculine; it results in excessive trust, excessive confidence that a good God will come to our rescue, so that we need not make sure we ourselves are stronger than, and smarter than, the human forces of evil.

This problem is explicitly brought to our attention in Macduff's castle just before the murders. Lady Macduff is talking to her cousin Ross, whom Macduff later addresses as "my ever-gentle cousin," but who—we now know—intends, in but a moment, to have her murdered. She complains bitterly that her husband has acted unnaturally in leaving his family unprotected. Her example is that of the mother wren, most diminutive of birds, that will fight to protect her young against attack. Ross, of course, tells her to have confidence in her husband's judgment—just as his actions are about to confirm hers. After Ross leaves, a conversation occurs between Lady Macduff and her small son, in which she talks as if his father is dead and asks how he will survive. He says, like the birds she has just been talking about—that is, by foraging on his own, by nature. But what about the traps men have laid for birds, she asks. He responds that such traps are laid not for "poor" birds but (by implication) for rich ones, and he has become a poor bird. What she means, of course, is that children cannot take care of themselves, nor can good people generally, and he—naively—thinks that only the wealthy must protect themselves against attack, since the poor offer no temptation to would-be attackers.

Asked what he will do for a father, the son asks, in turn, what she will do for a husband. Her joking reply that she can buy twenty (and his, that she could then equally sell them) tells us something about the inner core of human life, which is founded, necessarily, on ties far stronger than those of commercial advantage and exchange. The family, the root of society, is based on love and loyalty, on mutual devotion and protection. Otherwise it cannot last, children will receive neither proper nurture, nourishment, or protection, and all will fall asunder. To strengthen this loyalty, men take vows, and are held to them by a moral sense they themselves heighten, supported by the most drastic sanctions. This is why Lady Macduff can tell her son that his father was a traitor, one who swore and lied. She is thinking of his loyalty to her and the children, not to Macbeth, of whose relations to Macduff she seems entirely ignorant. A traitor must be hung—though, as the boy shrewdly reports, this will require that there be more honest men than wicked ones. And when she says, "Now God help thee, poor monkey!" we realize that their discussion of human affairs, up to that point, had included no reference to and shown no need for, an almighty Being, a God or gods. But the inherent instability, and insecurity, of human affairs seems—as her prayerful remark shows—to require the belief in some supreme and stable power that can be appealed to when all else fails, that can strengthen the dedication of human society itself to its necessary bonds and institutions. Society requires religion—and Christianity seems to be the main example here—but religion can also make men too dependent on God, and insufficiently dependent on themselves.

After the mysterious messenger comes in to warn her of grave danger, Lady Macduff asks why she should fly if she has done no harm, and immediately corrects herself by acknowledging what "this earthly world" is like, suggesting a distinction between it and the afterworld. It was a "womanly defence," she says, to have thought that because she has done no harm, she would not be harmed. No, this earthly world is not like that, for here "to do harm is often laudable, to do good sometime accounted dangerous folly." In a moment, she and her son will be subjected to the most blameable harm of murder—to deter or repel which it would have been most proper, most laudable to harm the would-be attackers. Similarly, to do good to enemies is not only accounted but *is* most dangerous folly—Lady Macduff does not speak strongly enough. She too remains under the influence of her Christian upbringing, which asks that evil not be resisted and that all men be loved, thus making it hard for her to acknowledge the crucial political distinction between friends and enemies, the former to be benefited, the latter harmed. This accounts for her hoping her husband is in "no place so unsanctified" that murderers such as these could find him. This is the same thought Macduff himself must have had when he left his family unprotected, thinking it a place sanctified by their innocence. But of course there is no place which by any sanctification whatsoever could keep men like the murderers from committing their crimes.

The scene's end shows not only the immoral strong slaying the moral weak, but gives us another view of the problem of treason. Like Lady Macduff before, the murderers accuse Macduff of treason. She, of course, had in mind his apparent disloyalty to his family, but the murderers his supposed (by them) disloyalty to Macbeth. Disloyalty is sometimes merited, however, as the latter case shows: it may be necessary to averting, or expelling, great evil. The moral laws, which society necessarily thinks of as absolute—and which are stated most absolutely, if unpolitically, by Christianity—must bow to a larger understanding of justice, looking to the real benefits and harms of society. The spirited loyalty of Macduff's son is necessary, but not enough; his mother's affection and moral demands are necessary, but not enough: both must be directed by a wisdom capable of suppressing the wicked and advancing the good. In this play, Malcolm, young as he is, represents such a wisdom.

Ross

By its outcome, *Macbeth* gives the impression of being an extremely moral play—a play in which two murdering usurpers at first succeed but ultimately, and by some kind of cosmic necessity (or so its appears) come to horrible ends, the one killing herself, the other meeting a violent death in battle, with both utterly miserable in the final period of their lives. Why then Ross? What does he stand for in this play? Having come to know Ross for what he is in the two last acts, we are anxious to return to the earlier parts of the play and reexamine his entire career. This Ross is perhaps the most successful scoundrel in all of Shakespeare, and never, from beginning to end, does he suffer misfortune or defeat. Not only is he never discovered: at the very end he even reaps the rewards of the thanes who opposed the tyrant, being elevated, with them, to an earldom!

Let us see whether Shakespeare provides any sign of Ross' true colors early in the play. If he did not, would he be Shakespeare? But we must look with eagle eyes, for men like Ross are most difficult to penetrate. After all, he is, to simple eyes like Macduff's, the "ever-gentle" Ross—a tribute to his powers of deception. When he first arrives at Forres, in Act I, scene 2, Duncan does not recognize him, but Malcolm does. Ross and Angus seem to have just ridden up, and Duncan asks him from where, again not knowing. It is at this point that Ross tells about the battle at Fife—a battle editors often place Macbeth at both because Ross names no one but "Bellona's bridegroom" as its hero and because they have not consulted a map. We have conjectured earlier that Ross uses this rhetorical invention to keep from naming Macduff—the logical person to be fighting at Fife—but we do not know why. He certainly has no hesitation to go to greet Macbeth, coming from a battle scene not too far from Forres, as the new thane of Cawdor. He says, "I'll see it done," but when it is done, Angus is there again accompanying Ross.

The words Ross first addresses to Macbeth, when they meet, are peculiar. He mentions the king's "reading" of Macbeth's personal success in the fight against the rebels, and finding him responsible for many deaths among the Norwegians. "As thick as hail came post after post" praising Macbeth's defense of Duncan's kingdom—but this is queer, for Ross was not in the scene when the bleeding sergeant spoke, since he seems to have entered with Angus just afterward. Yet he never mentions the sergeant, speaks as if only written messages appeared, and exaggerates the number of them ("post after post"). This leads us to think that Ross may have at least overheard the bleeding sergeant but does not wish to mention it, and then flatters Macbeth by overstating the number of messengers. In that case, perhaps Ross, from the beginning, wanted to see Macbeth elevated, and had no wish to see Macduff—his own cousin—elevated. This inclination (his flattery of Macbeth, and his playing on his ambition) even shows itself at the beginning of Ross' speech to Macbeth, where he says the king did not know whether he should be praising Macbeth or himself (as the one Macbeth serves)—something the king certainly never expressed, but bound to have a subtle effect on Macbeth. And the same tendency shows itself in Ross' last words on that occasion, when he says that "for an earnest of a greater honour, he [the king] bade me, from him, call thee thane of Cawdor. . . ." This "earnest" or promise is certainly a bald invention by Ross, meant to play upon Macbeth's ambition, and flatter—the opposite of Angus' intention, which was to reduce, rather than to add to, the king's words.

It is interesting that when Macbeth, Banquo, Ross, and Angus enter the king's presence together, the king speaks to both Macbeth and Banquo, makes his crucial announcement about Malcolm (as we have already seen), but says nothing at all to Ross and Angus, who simply stand there without a word. We shall see the importance of this in a moment. The next time Ross' name is mentioned, he is simply numbered among those nobles who accompany the king into Macbeth's castle, and the time after that is one some overbold editors want to undo. Here is why. We must realize that the king's chamber was in a hall of the castle that had several adjoining rooms, and that was probably approached by mounting a staircase. When Macduff and Lennox come in from the annex early in the morning, Macduff is shown to the king's chamber by Macbeth, who must then be presumed to return to the central area at the foot of the staircase (off of which, incidentally, must be his own bedroom). When Macduff comes out, he must run at least to the head of the staircase, if not to the floor below, and shout out about the murder. Macbeth and Lennox then go running up and Macbeth kills the guards, but, according to the stage direction in the folio, they come down with one other person—our old friend Ross. Ross says nothing, and, throughout the excitement, still says nothing. Rub him out, say some editors and critics: what purpose does he serve? How could he appear out of nowhere and then say nothing? In the Arden edition he is expunged, without a word of explanation.

We can turn this apparent chaos into an intelligible pattern by thinking along with Shakespeare, instead of presuming ourselves superior to him. In the two previous scenes where Ross was present (because named in the stage directions there too), he also said nothing. Here he surprises us by his very appearance even more than his silence. Looking ahead, we know that in the next scene he has quite a bit to say, telling Macduff he will follow Macbeth to Scone, despite Macduff's veiled warning. But he lets us infer that he had been mysteriously absent from the castle when the discussion of Duncan's murder took place and the other thanes decided upon Macbeth as his successor.

Now, in the castle, just after the discovery of the murder, he does not go up with Macbeth and Lennox, but he does come down with them. What does this suggest? In the rooms in the hall before the king's, we had already been rather curiously told there was a second chamber Macbeth had to pass on his way to, and back from, the king's. We learn from the queen, responding to Macbeth's inquiry, that in it were Donalbain and someone else—the second person is not named by the queen. Editors who suppose that Malcolm and Donalbain were lodged together, since they are shown together after the clamor, ask why Lady Macbeth mentions only Donalbain (Arden edition, p. 53, note 25). But let us assume she knew what she was saying. This means Malcolm was in still another room—a third chamber, probably beyond the king's, either alone, or, like his brother, with someone else. In one of those chambers was probably Angus, and in the other, Ross.

Given the attention Donalbain and his unnamed partner get from Shakespeare, through Macbeth's narration, we would have to say that Ross is more likely to have been Donalbain's than Malcolm's chambermate. Why such apparently irrelevant details, as telling us what Macbeth heard outside the door of the second chamber? It is, I suspect, to cause us to put two things together: the problem Malcolm posed for Macbeth (without his wife's knowing it), and the character of Ross, which we have begun to suspect, and which later on becomes as clear as Shakespeare can allow in such a case. Macbeth understood that the Prince of Cumberland would inherit the title from his murdered father, yet he could not dispose of Malcolm the same night without giving himself away. What he could do is begin a relationship that at some point would lead to Malcolm's undoing, and Ross, already so useful, might be glad to associate with the young men, preferring Donalbain, perhaps, because it seemed less direct, and because of his youth, but really with Malcolm in mind from the outset. It is then interesting to speculate which of the two men Macbeth heard was Ross and which Donalbain. In any case, Ross would not be told of Duncan's intended murder—he was hardly enough of an intimate for that—and so, when the clamor broke out, might be expected to bolt, as a person whose sense of self-interest was peculiarly keen. That is why he comes flying down the stairs with Macbeth and Lennox!

Why did Ross absent himself from the ensuing meeting of thanes by which Macbeth's fate was decided? He could not know in advance, for sure, how that meeting would go—after all, the possibility that suspicion would be directed at Macbeth himself could hardly be ruled out. Nor could he be sure just how he himself was perceived, just then, by others—that is, whether the group headed by Macduff would sense his recently having favored Macbeth over his own cousin. As it turns out, he need not have feared. In response to his inquiry, Macduff tells him that Macbeth has already left for Scone—but Ross, somewhat nervous up to the point of decision, and outside the castle, might already have observed Macbeth's departure himself. And if anyone doubts Ross' capacity as a most thoroughgoing liar and deceiver, let him look at the cruel way he talks to the superstitious old man in that very scene. First he assures the old man that Duncan's horses broke out of their stalls that night, an apparent omen of the disobedience soon to be demonstrated in the murder. Then, hearing the old man report, from hearsay, that those horses ate each other, Ross—no doubt enjoying himself immensely—extends his lie quite a bit further, saying: "They did so, to th'amazement of mine eyes that look'd upon't." After this, no word of Ross' should be viewed without suspicion by the reader, and, as we soon learn, there is much more to be suspicious of.

True to his word to Macduff, Ross follows Macbeth to Scone, and is next seen at the banquet Macbeth has prepared in his palace for Banquo, and just after Banquo's murder some distance from the palace. Throughout that banquet scene, Ross shows himself to be a most serviceable courtier, almost always saying just the sort of thing Macbeth would want him to (a possible exception is his asking about the strange sights Macbeth reports seeing). But by that point another flagrant mystery has been waved before us, like a bloody flag, and that is the identity of the Third Murderer. Without going into all the details, Macbeth has been shown directly talking to two men, convincing them to murder Banquo, and Fleance as well. He tells them he will advise them of where to stay and the exact time for the deed. This he actually does, at least in part, through the Third Murderer, with whom he is never shown talking, and who comes independently of the other two to the scene of the crime. Why so much mystery about this man? The first two murderers are from some other part of the country than the palace area, and have been chosen because Macbeth placed greater trust in the reliability of revenge as a motive, rather than profit. These men think they have been wronged by Macbeth, but he persuades them that Banquo was responsible, not himself. It is the Third Murderer who knows his way around the palace and knows the habits of visitors, such as the strange one of leaving their horses a mile from the palace and walking the rest of the way. He must also make sure Fleance does not escape. As it turns out, all three set on Banquo, whose denunciation of one of them as a "slave" suggests that he was known to him. Perhaps not unintentionally, the First Murderer puts out the torch Fleance was carrying, allowing his escape into the night, unpursued.

Even Macbeth has been suspected of being the Third Murderer, so great has been the urge to solve this mystery. But Macbeth will not do for more reasons than one, the foremost being that he seems spontaneously surprised at hearing the First Murderer's report about what happened, particularly in connection with Fleance. On the other hand, it is entirely possible that Macbeth would have arranged for independent reports from both the First and the Third Murderer—and that the Third Murderer was able to find his way back to the palace before the First, who knew little of the area. This might account for a certain jocular quality in Macbeth when the banquet scene opens, though his good humor also suggests that the Third Murderer could not have told him the whole truth, that he reported Banquo's death, but perhaps said of Fleance only that one of the others was in pursuit of him. It is also possible, however, that the Third Murderer did not get a chance to report to Macbeth, or perhaps preferred not to, knowing that Fleance had escaped. Macbeth's good spirits at the banquet could have been based on expectation rather than report. In either case, Ross might well have been the Third Murderer. His aptitude for such concealment we learn shortly afterward, when he visits the Macduff castle for hidden and murderous reasons. Whether, or what, he reported to Macbeth before the banquet—and before the First Murderer reports—is much less certain.

We need not recapitulate the role Ross must have played in the Macduff murders, nor the deft but striking change in his story about that tragedy when, again mysteriously, he shows up in England. Let us try to explain the reason for that change, between lines 178 and 193, growing to a climax at 204, where Ross had first denied, and then admitted, what in fact happened to Macduff's family. To begin with, why is he in England at all? His reason is given in line 186: "now is the time of help; your eye in Scotland would create soldiers, make our women fight, to doff their dire distresses." But we must realize that by "your eye" Ross means Macduff's eye, not Malcolm's: Ross has come to win Macduff's return. Why? So that Macbeth can kill him. Ross thus turns out to be precisely the kind of person Malcolm feared Macduff might be, that is, someone sent by Macbeth to trick him into returning. Why Macbeth took such interest in Macduff can easily be guessed: Macduff was a potent soldier, and the only living person against whom the witches had warned him.

At this point, the conversation—as Ross must have viewed it—takes an unexpected turn, for Malcolm, not Macduff, responds: "Be't their comfort we're coming thither. Gracious England hath lent us good Siward and ten thousand men; and older and a better soldier none that Christendom gives out." And in the very next lines, Ross begins his shift. Having just learned that he will not be able to separate Macduff from Malcolm, and that both are about to invade Scotland with a very powerful English army, it is "Goodbye Macbeth, hello Malcolm!" From this point onward, in the course of the last act, Ross' history is all told in stage directions. Scene 4 shows that he is absent from Malcolm's invading army, but in the final scene (scene 8) he appears out of the blue, alongside Malcolm and Old Siward, flattering the latter and his son, receiving—along with the other thanes—the title of earl, and avoiding being classified among the "cruel ministers of this dead butcher and his fiend-like queen"—in short, apparently crowned with success.

Ross is the consummate opportunist, always looking out for himself, content to remain in the shadow of great men, and completely unscrupulous in their service, willing to do anything, however foul, that they require of him, yet so good at appearing otherwise, and deceiving everybody, that he is never detected and never punished. Whatever the forces in human nature or the world at large that are working for justice, they are not so powerful as to prevent the coming into existence, and even the flourishing, of men without a speck of justice in them. Ross is also important because he makes us even more aware of the hidden motive, the secret action in human affairs, linking together and making intelligible a whole series of events. These events, stretching from the very beginning to the very end of the play, would have to be considered unintelligible mysteries were it not for the clues, carefully left by Shakespeare, pointing to a solution in the character and deeds of Ross. Thus understood, Ross is not a mere superfluity, or of merely marginal interest in the play, but an essential element, staking out one pole of evil in human affairs that must never be forgotten, either by political practitioners—statesmen—or moral and political philosophers. As for the judgment to be placed on this apparently happy scoundrel, we would have to consider not only the evil done to others, so manifest in the play, but the state of his soul in itself, the full deformity of which Shakespeare was compelled to leave to the reader's surmise. Alone, without friends, caring for no one, willing to kill anyone, never in open command of events, completely dependent on the rise and fall of the great, always calculating, never at ease, exulting only in the success of his machinations—here is not a whole man but a narrow part of a man, worked to a peak of efficiency within that narrow range, and sacrificing all else to it.

The Fate of the Macbeths

The central focus of the play is on Macbeth and his wife—not only on their words and actions, but on the state of soul from which these emanate. Of all the mysteries in the play, the chief, by far, is how their internal condition at the beginning can develop into what it becomes by the end. The paradox was well stated by Freud: their conditions seem to interchange, with Lady Macbeth becoming much more like what Macbeth had been, and Macbeth becoming much more like what she had been: "She becomes all remorse, he all defiance." Freud does not regard such a transformation as psychologically impossible in itself, but he does think it impossible within the very compressed time frame of the play (one week, he says), and on the basis of the motives explicitly suggested there. For psychological plausibility, Freud prefers the historical account in Holinshed, where Macbeth, after his usurpation, rules justly for ten years, and only then begins the murders of Banquo and others. That chronology would be consistent with Macbeth's increasing desperation as the childless condition of his marriage persists.

Freud is mistaken about the *actual* time frame of the play, but he is correct about its *felt* duration, which certainly seems exceedingly short, with actions swiftly succeeding each other from beginning to end (see Furness, pp. 504-07 for a time analysis and some of its complications). In either case, his charge of lapsed causality against Shakespeare would be devastating, because the states of mind of the protagonists are so obviously at the center of Shakespeare's attention, and the general problem of the intelligibility of human affairs so particularly important in this play. A gap or void in causal explanation would, in fact, be fatal, despite the play's dramatic effectiveness. But let us remember Lincoln's praise: "I think nothing equals *Macbeth*. It is wonderful." Given Lincoln's inclination to search deeply for causes, he must have found in the play all the connections necessary to explaining its outcome. Let us see.

Both Macbeths want the crown badly, and immediately think of murder as the means of getting it. Clearly this is the case with Macbeth once he receives his prediction from the witches, and with his wife once she receives word of it by letter from him. In fact, it seems they had spoken of assassination even before the action of the play begins, and that he had then been the author of "this enterprise," not she (I, 7: 47-48). Clearly also their present views of the enterprise are sharply divergent. She is absolutely determined to do everything required for the purpose, tarrying for no moral or religious compunctions. On the other hand, the thought of murdering Duncan makes Macbeth's very soul tremble with fear and foreboding. While his conscience tells him that the act is immoral and irreligious, he would risk the life to come (I, 7: 1-28; I, 3: 130-42) were it not for the likely consequences of the assassination here on earth. To kill such a king as Duncan, under such circumstances, would make Macbeth himself hated and the likely victim of a second assassination.

Until that point Macbeth had evidently not considered concocting a plan both to keep from becoming known as the murderer and to lay the guilt on someone else. We can also see from his great "If it were done . . ." speech that he partly conceals direct moral considerations, as such, from himself by trying to think of them as merely prudential: thus all he says about being Duncan's kinsman, subject, host (he omits beneficiary here), and about Duncan's virtues is taken up under this head. Yet, Macbeth *does* seem to be "too full of the milk of human kindness," as Lady Macbeth had told herself earlier. These decent moral sentiments, and his wish to enjoy the "golden opinions" coming from his recent accomplishments and honors, do not win out. They succumb to a combination of his own "vaulting ambition," Lady Macbeth's attack on his manliness (through relentless accusations of cowardice), and her suggesting a way of pinning guilt for the murder on others (the guards). He is made ready to do what both religion and reason tell him is deeply wrong by her appeal to ambition, pursued with courage, as the most profound element of his nature as a man. No longer fearing detection or failure, they lose the last restraint on immoral conduct, and the process of murder begins (I, 7: 30-82).

Yet it would be wrong to think of Lady Macbeth, even then, as wholly without conscience. Someone wholly without conscience would not have to think of conscience—of the "compunctious visitings of nature"; someone utterly lacking in the gentleness of her sex would not have to ask to be "unsexed," and for the milk in her breasts to be replaced by gall; someone unashamed of her deed would be willing to look upon it herself, and would not ask that it be hidden in night, darkened further by the smoke of hell, so that her "keen knife will not see the wound it makes," nor heaven be able to see the act and call a stop to it. This impression is strengthened by small facts strewn along the way by Shakespeare. Watched with care, Lady Macbeth is first shown saying that the whole murder should be left to her, then that the two of them will do it, and finally arranging for Macbeth to do it alone, with only auxiliary help from her. As further extensions of the same pattern, we learn that she had to strengthen herself with some of the same wine she gave the guards, and that she would have killed Duncan herself when she went up to prepare the daggers for Macbeth "had he not resembled my father as he slept." So all of Lady Macbeth's coldness before and immediately after the murder, her pedestrian literalness, her apparent firmness of purpose, hide another kind of element in her—gentler, weaker, conscious that the murder is a horrible deed, believing in the afterlife. Viewed in this light, her swooning at Macbeth's improvised slaying of the guards is much more likely to have been involuntary than deliberate. For a moment, after all the keyed-up effort and tension, it looked like the whole plan they had concerted would come crashing down. The swoon, rather than a sign of rational strength, is a small indication pointing in the direction of her later sleepwalking and suicide (I, 5: 53; I, 7: 69; II, 2: 1, 13-14).

We are not told what made Lady Macbeth so ambitious, but we do get some idea of what she and Macbeth looked forward to. Macbeth thinks about "the imperial theme" when he thinks of the kingship; his letter to his wife calls her "his dearest partner in greatness," and speaks of the "greatness" promised her by the witches' prophecy, even though it can only be indirectly, since her name was never mentioned. As she sees it, the murder that night "shall to all our nights and days to come give solely sovereign sway and masterdom." When Lady Macbeth persuades Macbeth to surrender his compunctions, she does not do so by magnifying his vision of what ruling would bring, but by castigating his inconsistency, his weakness in wanting it—which she simply takes for granted—yet not being willing to do what is necessary to get it. Along the way, they say nothing about their children enjoying the succession, even though there are other allusions to children. Macbeth has asked Banquo, "Do you not hope your children shall be kings . . . ?" Lady Macbeth says, "I have given suck, and know how tender 'tis to love the babe that milks me" (another sign she is gentler than she makes out). Macbeth tells her to "Bring forth men-children only." But if any children have already come from this union, they have not survived, and others are not consciously anticipated or discussed by these peculiar would-be parents. The ambition motivating both Macbeths therefore seems primarily for themselves, and of very moderate, even ordinary, scope. They want to be king and queen in the way Duncan and his predecessors have been, want the power and the honor (not any increase in wealth), want to be the commanding force at the top—but that is all. They have no plans for conquest, or for domestic political changes; they have no past injustices or even slights to avenge. They certainly do not anticipate being involved in a series of grizzly murders: on the contrary, their notion seems to be that they will simply step into Duncan's shoes and rule in a most ordinary way—so weak are their powers of understanding and foresight (I, 3: 86, 117; I, 7: 54-55, 73-75. See also V, 2: 22-28).

We have no reason to believe Macbeth and Lady Macbeth to be anything but a loving couple, and, despite certain appearances, even to the end. The puzzle, however, is to explain their mutual attraction. Coriolanus was also an outstanding soldier, also a spirited and ambitious man, but his wife, Virgilia, was utterly unlike Lady Macbeth. She was the soul of gentleness, and meant to be quite different, in this respect, from the only other woman in Coriolanus' life, his mother Volumnia. Macbeth's marriage would be comparable to Coriolanus' choosing a mate modelled on his mother. This suggests a peculiar weakness in Macbeth, who too readily thinks of greatness as something that must be shared equally with his wife, perhaps because she possesses some element lacking in him. He may think of her as more realistic, of greater resolve, more daring, steadier. He certainly does not regard her as bringing to political rule the typically feminine virtues: on the contrary, he senses in her more of what he considers manliness—the manly virtues—than he possesses. This coincides with her conception of herself, as necessary to suppressing his weaker elements, only thereby enabling him to realize his potential for greatness. What he admires in her is strength in areas where he is weak, and vice versa: he could not rise to the heights without her, nor she without him.

We can only speculate whether Lady Macbeth became lividly ambitious because of not having children, or whether not having children—children who survived and grew up—was due to (or symbolic of) a masculinity in her that was already there, and that would have given any children of hers two fathers, rather than a father and a mother. Coriolanus and Virgilia have a small son. In *Macbeth,* Banquo has a son of some years, the Macduffs a small son and other children as well, and Duncan two older boys. The Macbeths' lack of issue is therefore far from accidental. Whatever its cause, it certainly helps to explain their capacity for subsequent acts of inhumanity. Duncan reminded Lady Macbeth of her father, which made it impossible to kill him. And, as Macduff later exclaims upon learning the fate of his family: "He has no children"—which, if it is a reference to Macbeth, probably means that Macbeth was able to kill mere children only because he had none himself (IV, 3: 216). Being a child tended by parents, and tending children of one's own, seem to strengthen the sense of moral limits or the natural conscience. In further support of this, Ross is portrayed as utterly without family—without father, mother, wife, children. And the witches, also without progenitors or progeny, have what moral feelings they possess only because they are, or regard themselves as, sisters.

While the Macbeths are very close—perhaps too close—prior to murdering Duncan, their paths immediately start to diverge once they are king and queen. Macbeth's thoughts are all on Banquo: "There's none but he whose being I do fear," both because of his "royalty of nature" and the witches' prophecy. That prophecy left Macbeth only "a barren sceptre" and therefore made his murder of Duncan, his sacrifice of "mine eternal jewel"—his soul—serve only "Banquo's issue." After this reflection Macbeth consults and incites the two men he has chosen for murdering Banquo and Fleance. No longer is his conduct at least consonant with the prophecies, as in the case of Duncan's murder: he now tries to defy the prophecy for Banquo by making its fruition impossible. All this is done secretly, and without any prior discussion with Lady Macbeth. He had not been frank with her about the prophecies originally, narrating only the favorable ones applying to him (and hence to her) while withholding Banquo's, which was unfavorable to them in the longer run. Tempted by the favorable good prospect, he might have thought he could overcome the unfavorable evil one. He would grasp the former first, and worry about the latter afterward.

Here we see him doing just that. But his separation from his wife involves more than simply planning an important operation without her: he becomes physically less available to her, compelling her practically to make an appointment to speak with him. Already, by this separation, and his giving himself (as she thinks) to fearful solitude, worrying still about the murder of Duncan, she begins to sense the happiness they both thought easily within their grasp slipping away:

> Nought's had, all's spent,
> Where our desire is got without content.
> 'Tis safer to be that which we destroy
> Than by destruction dwell in doubtful joy
>
> (III, 2: 4-8).

Her ensuing interview with Macbeth reads queerly. He speaks as if they are still in danger, as if they cannot eat without fear or sleep without "terrible dreams," as if he is preoccupied not with Banquo's murder but with those who might be conspiring against the throne now, and as if the whole frame of things in this and the other life may need to be "disjointed" in order to free them from these fears. Nothing he says, of course, could possibly strike Lady Macbeth as being directed against Banquo. No names are named—he must speak vaguely—and if anything his remarks seem directed against Duncan's sons, Malcolm and Donalbain.

She tells him to be "bright and jovial among your guests tonight"; he tells her to give "eminence" with eye and tongue to Banquo, and then seems to return to the theme of their needing to flatter and disguise out of a fear for their safety. "You must leave this," she says, probably not comprehending the drift of his remarks. Then: "O, full of scorpions is my mind, dear wife!"—but the scorpions are horrible things that might kill others as well as fill Macbeth himself with loathing and fear. His addition, "Thou know'st that Banquo and his Fleance lives," must have struck Lady Macbeth as quite irrelevant, and her reply, "But in them nature's copy's not eterne," should not be read as extending to Macbeth a license to have them killed—certainly not now. Impressed, perhaps, by a strong note of concern in his voice, she may have wished to calm him, as if to say: "If ever they become worrisome to us, we know that they are not immortal, that things can happen to them." Macbeth's rejoinder—that "they are assailable"—might have comforted him but certainly not her. His words start to become the poetry of death, and at her inquiry, "What's to be done?", he tells her to be "innocent of the knowledge, dearest chuck," and continues to talk with funereal but poetic expectation.

The last times we see Lady Macbeth, prior to hearing about and then seeing her plight in Act V, are at and just after the banquet scene. Macbeth's vision of Banquo's ghost sitting in his place is the last such vision he will have. The scene starts off quietly enough, with Macbeth apparently in a good mood—probably because he expected good news about Banquo and Fleance, and perhaps also because he thought he had received some sign of acquiescence from the queen. The First Murderer reports: Banquo is dead, Fleance escaped. Suddenly, he sees Banquo sitting in his seat and is completely unnerved and terror-stricken: the murdered no longer stay put, as they had both before and after human laws were instituted to protect the common good. Lady Macbeth, of course, thinks his visions cowardly and womanly. She tells him to act like a man, which he says he would do in the face of any natural challenge from beast or man. After his guests leave, he shows what deeply worries him—that the universe is so made that it reveals, one way or another, the identity of secret murderers. The universe is on the side of the just! All the more startling, then, Macbeth's next thought, which concerns Macduff. Banquo's ghost has just scared the living daylights out of him, but his mind moves, by some spontaneous inner force, to the next possible source of opposition. He will send for Macduff and visit the "weird sisters" to learn—what, he does not say. As we can now guess, and later discover, it is whether any evils will occur to him (that is, whether, unlike Duncan, he will die a natural death), and whether the prophecy about Banquo's sons still holds. He will do anything now "for mine own good," including murder after murder, so steeped in blood is he already (he does not mention again his lost soul). He has in mind "strange things" that will be acted upon without delay, without even being "scann'd." He expects his strange "self-abuse" to cease as he grows inured to the doing of evil. This, not the sleep Lady Macbeth says he lacks and needs, will do away with his visions (III, 4: 128-44).

Lady Macbeth seems utterly unaware of their need to protect themselves; she simply wants to relax and enjoy sovereignty. Macbeth, on the other hand, is gripped by excessive insecurity. Having killed his own king, he seems deeply convinced that murderers cannot get away with their deeds, not only in the afterlife but in this life as well. He now engages in a struggle against this moral power of the universe, refusing to bow to it, and striking out against all he thinks might oppose him. His very courage leads him to rashness and cruelty, whereas less impulsiveness and greater understanding of the world would have made him solidify his position by acts of beneficence and justice. Macbeth is hardly a politic man. His successful and secret usurpation leads into tyranny, but he differs from the tyrant Socrates describes in *The Republic*. Macbeth is not dominated by erotic and other appetites aimed at uninhibited pleasure or gain. There is no riotous living. Only in ambition and fear does he seem excessive, and these, unguided by superior intellect, lead him to actions that make his ultimate success increasingly unlikely. By apparently guaranteeing him impunity, the witches only accelerate a tendency that was plainly in him before his second visit, just as their very first message to him only intensified an ambition that was already there.

Now for the end of this amazing and mystifying story. After her absence from all of Act IV, Lady Macbeth sweeps back into our purview most dramatically. Only her nighttime activity is disclosed, all of it done unconsciously, in sleep. Either she silently writes and seals a letter, or she walks with a light in her hand—a light she always has next to her. She is trying to rub out a spot on her hands, just as she had said a little water would wash off Duncan's blood from her hands and Macbeth's. But this blood will not wash off—and it is literally a "damned spot," since it has helped land her in hell. The candle is meant to help her see through the murkiness of hell. And each utterance, in this marvellous reconstruction of her consciousness, is tied to a particular point in her experience, from the time Duncan was killed up to the recent past, when Macbeth was still fearing Banquo had emerged from his grave, and news of Lady Macduff's murder had come to her ears. Quite properly, the doctor fears she may do harm to herself, and the next thing we hear is a wail of women, signifying the queen's death.

The letter she writes in her sleep can only be to Macbeth, who has now undertaken the murder of Banquo and the Macduff family on his own, in a headlong rush he explains to no one. Would the letter simply ask to see him? Would it in any way express her deep confusion? The reason why Lady Macbeth thinks in unconnected pieces is that she believes herself lost and damned, yet without being able to understand how it has all happened. She is in utter misery and can only recollect points along the way. But, having importuned Macbeth to murder Duncan against his will, and having so often told him what to do in the course of that great action, she is in no position to criticize now. Nor will she complain of being left alone. Strong in the midst of her unhappiness, convinced it will not diminish, she will take the one way out available to her: suicide. At her own urging, Macbeth did indeed murder sleep, the "season of all natures"—her sleep.

That Macbeth still loves his wife is shown in his conversation with the doctor he has called in to observe her. He knows she has a "mind diseased," and asks whether "physic" or medicine can, with physical remedies, cure such a condition. Clearly he wishes deeply for her cure, but he is also preoccupied with the English forces coming to defeat him and place Malcolm on the throne. He has told himself the prophecies keep him secure and free of fear, but he is shaking inwardly with fear as he humiliates the messenger who comes to report the approach of the English army. And he admits to being entirely "sick at heart," convinced that

> My way of life
> Is fallen into the sear, the yellow leaf;
> And that which should accompany old age;
> As honour, love, obedience, troops of friends,
> I must not look to have; but, in their stead,
> Curses, not loud, but deep, mouth-honour, breath
> Which the poor heart would fain deny, and dare not
>
> (V, 2: 22-28).

This is the most pathetic passage in the play. It shows how decent and ordinary were the ends Macbeth had sought to achieve through ambition, all unattainable because he had pursued his ambition through murder. It is amid this fear that he puts on his armor and takes it off again, and gives orders to "Hang those that talk of fear."

A moment later, Macbeth hears a dreadful cry, and remarks that "I have almost forgot the taste of fears," remembering how easily set off his fears used to be, and thinking he has gotten so used to plotting horrible murders that such cries can no longer startle him. Informed that it was the cry of women at the death of the queen, Macbeth says "She should have died hereafter; there would have been a time for such a word." And this leads him into "Tomorrow and tomorrow and tomorrow"—the most memorable speech in the play by far. Macbeth has not forgotten the taste of fears: the cry fails to startle him because he is already brimming over with fear, a fear with a more obvious and pressing claim on his attention. His speech, it is true, says nothing directly about his wife, but this does not mean he feels nothing, or would not have had more to say (and think) had she died "hereafter"—that is, at a less frantic moment. But neither does he dwell upon himself or his present preoccupations. Instead, he gives voice to a reflection that covers them both, and all other men as well—or so his thinks. Tired, desperate, concealing both his sorrow and his fear, he seeks a vantage point external and superior to life's strivings.

Still, it is surprising that in a great speech at this point Macbeth does not reaffirm the moral nature of the universe—its finally detecting his wife and himself, gravely criminal, and meting out condign punishment. This would correspond to that deep strand in him that used to regard the world in this fashion. And we must also admit to something peculiar in the manner of his delivery, with its air of a set declamation. Macbeth's greatest stupidity, his greatest self-deception, one is tempted to say, comes in his finding the world, not his wife and himself, to blame. Life may be like a brief candle, but our tomorrows, todays, and yesterdays do not constitute a patternless sequence with no end but death. Just like his wife, Macbeth seems not to understand how what happened to them both could possibly happen. As several critics have remarked, his speech is to be read with the counterpart of the Bible in mind. It charges the Bible—the book that more than any other affirms the moral nature of the universe—with error. Replacing the Bible is an almost equally apodictic statement deposing the perfect God, and enthroning aimless idiocy as the ruling principle of the universe.

Those who find this great speech unsuitably pronounced by Macbeth, at this moment, are not entirely wrong. We should bear in mind, however, that the one person before whom it is delivered—Seyton—has certain unique characteristics. Seyton appears in only two scenes (3 and 5 of Act V) in the entire play. Before the former, no one knew Macbeth had an attendant or assistant by that name; in the latter, after announcing the death of the queen, he is heard from no more: following the "Tomorrow" speech, spoken, apparently, in his speechless presence, he completely disappears. When Macbeth first calls Seyton, he repeats his name three times within one speech, making sure the audience catches it. When he finally appears, he confirms the bad news about the coming of Malcolm and his English army. When Macbeth asks him for his armour—as if Seyton were also a kind of armour-bearer, a protector of the body—he asserts, rather pertly and knowingly: "'Tis not needed yet." In scene 5, when Macbeth hears what the stage direction calls "a cry of women within" and asks what that "noise" was, Seyton presently tells him: "The Queen, my lord, is dead."

At this point the editors run into an obvious difficulty, for in the text no call is made for Seyton to go out, discover the queen to be dead, and return. Nor is he asked to do so by Macbeth, who, lost in a reverie about himself lasting seven lines, only then asks "Wherefore was that cry?" and receives Seyton's answer immediately. To make this answer physically possible, the editors add stage directions to the text calling for Seyton's exit after he says "It is the cry of women" and his reentrance just before Macbeth's "Wherefore was that cry?" But tinkering with the folio is always dangerous, as we have already seen with the character of Hecate, whom so many editors consider spurious and expendable. Here we must go by Shakespeare's mischievous indications and try to make sense of them. Seyton would not have to leave if he is Satan in disguise—a character with supernatural capacities, whose primary function in the play is witnessing and confirming the coming of evils. Without taking a step away, Satan knows the queen is dead. And after he hears the "Tomorrow" speech, he is gone—his function in the play ended. As something like an extension of Hecate and the witches, he is there to make sure that all—that is, all harm-doing—is going well.

Because of the presence of this unusual being, the "Tomorrow" speech may have to be interpreted in a special way.

It is almost as if the view of life expressed in the speech must please Satan—as if the forces of harm and evil have no desire to make the world wholly evil, but are content if they can keep it from being understood as a moral place, directed by a good God. In reality, however, to convince men that "Life is a tale told by an idiot" is to disarm them utterly, and to make life itself impossible. It is, in fact, the view the forces of evil, by a stroke of genius, might have hit upon to harm men the most! So when Macbeth expresses this general conception, it is almost as if a mind not given to philosophizing suddenly sets forth a profound alternative to all religious and rational views of life. Considered from the standpoint of Macbeth's psychology, this view could only be the consequence of a mind fearing the existence of a good God, yet still unable to understand how two such criminals as himself and his wife come to the end they do. And the end comes soon enough for Macbeth. Sensing that he is doomed in body as well as soul, and despite learning of the witches' equivocation, earlier working in his favor but now against him, he fights on, lifting himself, by this courage, above the execrable and pathetic. Even when all is lost he refuses to bend or break.

Let us return to Freud's observation about the reversal of roles in *Macbeth*: Lady Macbeth goes from initial remorselessness to becoming "all remorse," whereas Macbeth, who became "all defiance," had earlier been filled with compunctions and fear. But does Lady Macbeth show remorse at the end? Keeping a light by her side is not remorse but fear. And when she is rubbing out the "damned" blood spots on her hand, or rueing the smell of blood on her "little" hand, what does she have in mind? At that point, her sigh—"oh, oh, oh!"—is taken by the doctor to mean that "the heart is sorely charged," but, again, is it regret at actions that have led to deep disappointment and misery, or is it repentance, remorse at having done unjust and evil things? Her reference to her hand and her sigh may be evidence of femininity, gentleness, and moral conscience trying to express themselves, but such is the pride Lady Macbeth still takes in her masculinity, and in the hardness of her ambition, that she cannot openly acknowledge them. What she does is relive some of her own words and actions, particularly in connection with Duncan's murder, but all the while she senses herself damned in hell, undergoing punishment for her part in the murder, and trying desperately to undo the signs and symbols of her part in it. She undoubtedly connects her suffering with her crime, but of direct remorse, direct contrition, she gives no sign.

It is particularly remarkable how little of Macbeth's recent conduct, or of their recent relationship, is at the forefront of her mind. A word here about Lady Macduff, and there about Banquo, is all. Her present misery, the rupture in their closeness, are never mentioned directly. Her mind returns, again and again, to the past, to the words and deeds that set the awful train of events in motion. Nor can we presume that her daylight hours are free from care. After all, she keeps light by her continually—that is, day and night—and her suicide itself occurs during the day.

But we learn directly of her nocturnal life alone. We gather from her gentlewoman's remarks that her nocturnal movements are repeated again and again, indicating that she is completely unable, on her own, to find a way out of her misery. Nor does her literal or pedestrian cast of mind alter at the end: the audience is aware of the symbolic importance of what she remembers, much of it having to do with how easily involvement in a grave crime can be cleansed and forgotten. Still, her own awareness of this is at best subconscious, and her mind does not expand into ramifications of what she remembers: there are no reverberations of belief or sentiment even in the stricken Lady Macbeth.

Macbeth is quite different. Initially he experiences both compunctions and extravagantly fearful visions at the thought of murdering Duncan, and during the murder. But with Banquo and Macduff's family there are no compunctions, and his visions of the former's ghost is not repeated with the latter. Originally, Macbeth's fears, and to some extent his compunctions, were based on his religious belief—on the deep sense that the good God of the Bible protects the good and punishes the evil, and that the world as a whole hunts down murderers. As he moves successfully from murder to murder, with apparent impunity, he does become hardened. Considering himself irretrievably destined for hell, his compunctions disappear as his fear for his earthly security mounts. Nevertheless, we cannot say with Freud that he is "all defiance." At the end, he is sick at heart about what his life has turned into, and while he does not complain of being separated from his wife, he remains deeply concerned about her health. Nor does his remark at learning of her death, and the ensuing "Tomorrow" speech, breathe defiance but, rather, an awareness of hopeless and contemptible unintelligibility. Only at the very end, when he knows he must die, is he defiant, spurning suicide and choosing to die in battle.

Christianity and Its Opposite

It is disconcerting to realize that Macbeth's Christian belief helps worsen his tyranny. Thinking himself already damned beyond redemption for murdering Duncan, fearing punishment here as well as in the afterlife, he plunges into a series of heinous murders he did not foresee originally. Having grown somewhat hardened to these crimes, he finds no security in them. Judging by the fears that continually agitate him during the day, his nights must be as miserable as his wife's: together they had indeed murdered their own sleep. And while she thinks of herself as already undergoing divine punishment in hell, he never ceases to anticipate a similar destiny for himself. Recognizing this, Macduff, at the very end, addresses him as "hell-bound," and refers to the angel he has served—meaning the fallen angel, Satan. Jose Benardete argues that Macbeth's last words "Lay on, Macduff, and damn'd be him who first cries, 'Hold, enough!'" imply that Macbeth did not think of himself as necessarily damned by his murders, or at least thought that acts of courage or cowardice on his part could still be decisive in determining his eternal fate.

While the words are subject to this interpretation, it does not jibe with Macbeth's actual outlook that day. He is filled with fear and foreboding, and neither speaks nor acts with the optimism this view of bravery and victory should instill in Scotland's greatest warrior. (See "Macbeth's Last Words" in *Interpretation,* Summer 1970, pp. 63-64.)

The importance of hell to the play had been prefigured in a very humorous scene some editors have also thought un-Shakespearean and sought to delete. It involves the famous knocking-at-the-gate, the dramatic effect of which De Quincey so admired. The scene occurs just after Duncan's murder, as Macduff and Lennox seek to enter the main part of the castle early that morning. The porter imagines himself the "porter of hell-gate," and fancies himself answering, in the name of Beezlebub (and Lucifer), the knocks of those who deserve to sweat in hell. He finally gives up the task, exclaiming:

> But this place is too cold for hell. I'll devil-porter it no further. I had thought to let in some of all professions that go the primrose way to th' everlasting bonfire.

The castle is too cold for hell, says the porter, but frigidity would not prevent it from being considered part of hell, as every reader of Dante's *Inferno* knows. There, in the ninth and deepest circle of hell, held by a frozen sea of ice, Lucifer is eternally fixed for his treason against God, and Judas, Brutus, and Cassius for like sins. Of course, what has just occurred in Macbeth's castle is an act of treasonous murder. The hell begun with that act in the castle may be said, in fact, to constitute one of the play's main themes, closely linked to its central issue of the intelligibility of life. But the hell Shakespeare describes is the natural hell to which these simpleminded murderers unknowingly bring themselves: their suffering, fear, and sleeplessness is their hell.

By all appearances, an equally irrelevant episode dealing with a related religious theme occurs toward the end of Act IV, and some editors retain it for reasons that, were they the only ones, would hardly suffice. Macduff had just tried to persuade Malcolm to return to Scotland and save it from Macbeth's tyranny. Testing him, Malcolm claims to be a very vicious man himself—lecherous, avaricious, with none of the virtues, and eager to

> Pour the sweet milk of concord into hell,
> Uproar the universal peace, confound
> All unity on earth.

Somewhat strangely, Macduff is willing to accommodate the first two of these vices, but he gives vent to anger and despair at the rest, and perhaps particularly at the last. Finding Malcolm so "accurs'd," he compares him with his parents:

> Thy royal father
> Was a most sainted king; the queen that bore thee,
> Oftener upon her knees than on her feet,
> Died every day that she liv'd. Fare thee well!

> These evils thou repeat'st upon thyself
> Hath banish'd me from Scotland.

That Macduff is a deeply Christian man is again shown by these lines. Concord, universal peace, the unity of mankind are living ideals for him—however little realized in practical political life. And the queen's spending her days on her knees, and dying every day, the thane of Fife considers great virtues. His despair comes from thinking that the evils of Macbeth have counterpart evils in Malcolm, and that Scotland is doomed to suffer on interminably.

This induces Malcolm to reveal that he spoke as he did to test Macduff and make sure he had not been sent by Macbeth. No doubt with some exaggeration, Malcolm now denies he has the vices to which he had so vehemently confessed and lays claim instead to their opposite virtues. He adds that Siward was on the point of leading ten thousand Englishmen against Macbeth, but now they will all return together, hoping "the chance of goodness" being achieved is as great as their quarrel with Macbeth is warranted. At this point in the final scene of Act IV a doctor enters—the first to show himself in the play, and very soon to be succeeded, at the beginning of Act V, by the doctor in attendance on Lady Macbeth. After the brief incident with the English doctor is concluded, none other than the ever-gentle (the ever-evil) Ross arrives. What happens during this brief interlude with the doctor? Malcolm asks whether the English king will come forth, once he is finished curing a "crew of wretched souls," whose malady defeats the medical art, but quickly amends at his touch—"Such sanctity hath Heaven given his hand."

We are not told, of course, what a doctor was doing there if the king's touch had such efficacy: perhaps the testimony of a doctor to the superiority of supernatural (to natural) capacities serves as the most effective of all testimonies. The doctor departs, leaving Malcolm to explain to Macduff that the disease the king cures is called "the evil," and that he has seen the king work these miracles with his own eyes. Malcolm does not know how the king gets heaven's help, but he cures people with sickly and deformed bodies by "hanging a golden stamp about their necks" and pronouncing certain "holy prayers." This "healing benediction," says Malcolm, is rumored to be a legacy the king will leave to his successors. He also has a "gift of prophecy," and is shown to be "full of grace" by "sundry blessings" that "hang about his throne." Toward the very end of the scene, after the exchange with Ross, Malcolm is still intent on seeing the English king, but not to ask for his "healing benediction," or to solicit his "gift of prophecy." It is to bid farewell and then march on Macbeth with the help of the English army the king has provided.

Nothing in a Shakespearean play is irrelevant to its central theme, and here the relevancy lies almost at the surface. How is human evil (symbolized by a disease called "the evil") to be cured? By his actions, Malcolm makes it clear that he will not depend on Christian prayers, love, or miracles. The evil of Macbeth must be fought against, outsmarted, overpowered, and only in this way can it be eradicated and the good established in its place. Another variation on the same theme occurs later when the besieged Macbeth asks his doctor "What rhubarb, senna, or what purgative drug, would scour these English hence?" (V, 3: 54-55) Just as it is absurd to purge military evils by medical drugs, so is it absurd to purge political evils by either medical drugs or religious rites. Politics may benefit from widespread religious belief, but only if that belief permits the political art to cope with political evils as part of the natural world in the broad sense of the term. Macduff is pictured by Shakespeare as having false and dangerous confidence in God's interventions, much in the spirit of Malcolm's mother. But Malcolm himself is wary, distrustful, sober. He directly asks Macduff, "Why in that rawness left you wife and child, those precious motives, those strong knots of love, without leave-taking?"—referring to his having hurriedly abandoned them to the "rawness" of Macbeth (IV, 3: 24-28). Yet while Malcolm will not solicit secret prayers and amulets from the English king, and sees the political danger of Macduff's piety, he is not above playing on that piety. He adroitly makes himself seem, in Macduff's eyes, to be a wholehearted believer in the practices of the English king, and therefore a fit successor to his own "sainted" father and kneeling mother.

After the final scene in England, at the end of Act IV, we are shown Malcolm in Scotland four brief times. Three of these are in battlefield scenes, the fourth in the finale. In the first, he orders the army to deceive the enemy about its numbers by camouflaging themselves with branches cut from Birnam Wood. In the second, he sends Old and Young Siward into the vanguard of the battle, keeping back with his fellow Scotsman, Macduff. The third occurs after Macduff goes off hunting for Macbeth, with Malcolm learning from Old Siward that the castle has been surrendered, and that they have been assisted by the thanes and many of Macbeth's own people. At no point is there any sign that Malcolm himself entered the battle: he seems to have remembered full well the occasion with which the play began, when he was almost captured by the enemy. So Malcolm's contribution to Scotland will not consist in abilities of the sort Macbeth and Macduff preeminently possess. He will be a smarter, less superstitious leader than them both. He will need all his wariness, since his first act—one of beneficence as compared to Macbeth's murder of Banquo—is to reward his thanes by making them all earls, including Ross. Yet Ross may not have escaped completely, for Malcolm intends not only to call home exiled friends (he does not mention his brother by name) but also to find and punish the "cruel ministers" of Macbeth and Lady Macbeth. And in a final contrast to Macbeth and Macduff again, he vows that, whatever else is needful, "by the grace of Grace"—that is, apparently by God but in fact by his own resources, his own acumen—he will perform "in measure, time, and place." The firstlings of his heart will not, like Macbeth's, be the firstlings of his hand, and he will not be as impetuous and trusting as he knows Macduff to have been.

Macbeth may be said to be a play about two defective extremes of evil, one "masculine," one "feminine," and its setting is most suitable to this purpose. Eleventh-century Scotland contains two powerful and mutually antagonistic elements: a feudal aristocracy, devoted to the virtues of courage and manliness, best shown in war, and the Christianity in which the nobles believe, with its absolute demand for love and peace. As a practical matter it might seem that the former needed the restraint of the latter—that warlike thanes would be constantly in revolt against their king, and in contention with themselves, were it not for the influence of Christianity. It was Christianity that made them regard their king as the vicar of God, and themselves as fellow believers in Christ. In the play, obedience to Duncan is plainly strengthened by the Christian belief of men like Macduff, who refers to the murdered king as "the Lord's anointed temple."

Macbeth, who begins by killing the rebel, Macdonwald, and then himself rebels against Duncan, is moved to this act by Lady Macbeth's appeal to his valor and manliness, traits on which she prides herself above all. The question as to whether this manliness—connected to war, ambition, mastery, the love of superiority and honor—is the highest good, or is itself subordinate to the virtue of justice, keeps animating events in the play. Excessive manliness occurs when the ends and qualities of manliness are made to rise superior to all. Not only does it show itself in the Macbeths, but also in Old Siward, who is perfectly happy to lose a son who has died bravely, and even in Macduff, who refuses to cry at the news of his family's murder, and whom Malcolm somewhat unsympathetically tries to goad into manly action against Macbeth.

Almost equally dangerous to human life is the opposite extreme, which denies the difference between friends and enemies, and exhorts men to love all men as they love and trust the good God. Warned about her imminent murder, Lady Macduff first asks why she should flee if she has done no harm, and then berates herself for having used this false "womanly defence." But it is her husband, Macduff, who much more than she embodies trust in God for the protection of good human beings. Neither Macbeth's excessive manliness, nor Macduff's excessive womanliness, can form the basis of human society (compare Jose Benardete's account of these opposites, *op. cit.*, p. 68). The former turns everyone into enemies and leaves no room for friendship—for the concord of good people in a body politic. The latter turns everyone into friends and offers no protection against enemies, internal or external, again subverting the body politic.

In the play these defective views of human life seem to be associated with opposite views of the universe at large. One is expressed by Macbeth in the form of "Life is a tale told by an idiot, full of sound and fury, signifying nothing," but it is also related to an older view, first formulated by the pre-Socratic philosopher, Heracleitus, according to which "War is the father of all things." Heracleitus generalizes into the first cause of everything the contention and vying for mastery that are characteristic of warring men. Nothing is simply at rest or in harmony. All states of seeming concord and rest are only temporary phases—the resultants of clash themselves—in a never-ending sea of change. The difficulties with Heracleitus' view, so much at odds with the rule of mind in Anaxagoras, and the self-sufficiency of being in Parmenides, received much attention from Plato and Aristotle. It cannot account for the coherence of individuals or species, for the causal interconnection of things, for the existence of human knowledge, or for the range of beings in the universe. Even while granting the existence of individuals, it cannot allow for their holding together, for the persistence of any classes, unities, or wholes, or for any transcendence of the flux whatsoever. Its defect comes from its very simplicity. It says war is the father of all things, not the partial cause of all or some things. Its whole intention is to make war the cause of things it does not seem to be the cause of—to make it the supreme and sole cause. And not the least of its weaknesses is its inability to account for itself as an eternally true and universal thought about flux in a world of flux.

By having Macbeth compare life to the unintelligible sound and fury of an idiot, Shakespeare takes Heracleitus' thought to its logical conclusion. He seems to have realized that the very idea of nature—of kinds of things and their necessary developments—could not be sustained on the basis of a philosophy of total flux: Heracleitus' natural philosophy destroys nature. In this respect, Christianity may at first seem to be the very opposite of Heracleitus. It considers the universe an essential harmony and even unity founded in the good will of God. But if nothing happens without God's active will and its imperative for ultimate good, Christianity and Heracleitus may in fact have something in common. Heracleitus' view, taken full strength, would deprive human life of its nature and render it unintelligible sound and fury: nothing makes life exist or change in ascertainable ways; nothing holds it together. But from the Christian view as well the world, constantly subject to God's exercise of his will and miraculous power, is undetermined by anything like the independent natures of things. Both views make nature in its original and proper sense impossible.

Everything in *Macbeth is* bound by the natures of things (and by chance). Even Hecate and the witches have a nature they are bound by—a nature filled, perhaps, with mutually inconsistent elements and therefore physically impossible, but a nature imagined, nonetheless. Not that the working out of the natures, particularly in the case of man, is simple. Over and above the general, sexual, and individual parts of our nature, we are affected by life in society, and particularly by the high commanding voices of politics and religion. To such causes must be added the range of invention and choice available to each of us, along with the mind's unique ability to control its face and hide its purpose. The consequence is an amazing complexity of human affairs, where motives, actions, and plans are frequently concealed, and where idiotic chaos might appear to rule rather than intelligible causes of any kind. This is why the play is filled with mysteries of fact and cause, and the hovering presence of the witches almost prepares us for such a world. Nevertheless, on closer scrutiny, the mysteries vanish. We can discover Duncan's good plan and see why it failed; we see why the unsound plan to kill him happened to succeed. We can guess why Banquo had to take his trip. We are no longer mystified by Ross' descent from the level of the royal bedchambers, by his remaining outside the castle, by his appearance at Lady Macbeth's castle and soon afterward in England, by his return with the invading forces, his disappearance in the subsequent battle, and his reappearance among the thanes at their final elevation to earldoms.

Shakespeare is also interested in determining the place of reason within human nature, and the extent to which it guides human conduct. This is why the play gives much more prominence to involuntary visions, incoherent sleep-talking, impulses, and passions that reason does not master than it does to deliberate planning. By having Macbeth degenerate to the point where his impulses become the basis for action, untested and undirected by reflection, he brings life as close as it can get to the behavior of an idiot. The witches at the outset prefigured much of this irrational impulsiveness, and no better symbol of the return to a more completely human life can be found than Malcolm's accession to the throne. With him comes not only an avoidance of the extremes of both masculinity and femininity but a restoration of rational calculation and deliberateness dedicated to the common good—in short, of justice under the direction of prudence. Malcolm will not make the mistake made by the obviously Christian "Old Man" when he says to the departing Ross, "God's benison go with you; and with those that would make good of bad, and friend of foes!" (II, 4, at the end)—a lesson in benignity that can only feed the malignity of the morally worst character in the play. Malcolm will not follow excessive masculinity in making foes of friends, nor excessive femininity in making friends of foes.

Of course Shakespeare is particularly anxious to trace the causal lines that bring Macbeth and Lady Macbeth to their surprising fates. Quite clearly the witches do not put ambition into these would-be murderers but play upon an ambition already there, promising it success, and later assuring Macbeth that he cannot be conquered or killed. As a general matter, they facilitate courses of action already prepared for in the souls of men by removing obstacles to their success, and in this respect function very much like the ring of Gyges in Plato's *Republic* (Book II, 359-61). But all the while, hidden from their own eyes, the characters and circumstances of Macbeth and his wife are at work, leading them to their peculiar and separate dooms. And it all happens within a span of time compressed even further by Shakespeare's dramatic art, with indications given in speeches that unnaturally accelerate a process already unnaturally accelerated by the witches' guarantees of success and security. It would be easy to conclude that this is what happens to murderers: God catches up with them and punishes their crimes. And the confidence that such is the case may be politically salutary. But the real fate of the Macbeths is entirely natural, just like that of the Macduffs. It stems from the fixed nature of things, and not essentially from accident or external supernatural intervention of any sort, demonic or divine.

Good and Evil

Despite the optimism associated with Malcolm's final accession to the throne, the atmosphere of *Macbeth* is generally dark, repellent, threatening. This effect is achieved by an unnatural poetic exaggeration, emphasizing those elements of reality most in keeping with the problem of the play, and omitting those that would point in other directions. The sunlight, summer, flowers, plain enjoyment of life, jocularity, even the use of moonlight for romantic associations that color so many other plays are for the most part absent from this one. Instead, we have fog, darkness, blood, and foreboding. The witches embody the subject by their visible ugliness and their proclivity to harm. They also combine unnaturally, and therefore confuse, not only masculinity and femininity but old age and childishness, purpose and purposelessness, even a kind of wisdom and folly. When they receive Macbeth's visit much later in the play, a palpable magnification of their connection with the humanly repellent occurs. Hecate is certainly quite matter-of-fact in her approach to their art, but once she steps in the results are much more powerful than in Act I. And as the witches add to their cauldron the parts of so many abhorrent things, we can see the kinship these things have with the Macbeths themselves, whose distortion of their own nature makes them frightful and horrifying to behold.

What bearing does the existence of so much that is abhorrent have on the nature of the universe? Why are abhorrent human beings possible? Clearly, the universe is not simply the theater or home of human happiness, and many beings exist despite the fact that man fears and detests them. Nevertheless, like man's potential for good, the many splendid things in the universe—the ones understated in this play—may not be available without allowing for those that repel as well. In a material world, a world of separate beings and classes of beings, the possibility of harm and evil derives inevitably from the presence of benefit and good, and the good of some things will be the harm of others. To ask for a world in which all men are always rational, always in control of their passions and appetites, never errant, is to ask for a world that is physically impossible. To ask for a world filled only with things attractive and beneficial to man—for cows and dogs but not rats, for health but not disease, for growth but not decay—is also to ask the impossible. Moreover, man has a natural place in this world. While sharing characteristics, moral and physical, with various parts and gradations of the world, he also adds something necessary to its completion. Without him the world would lie there unknown, uncelebrated, unrhymed; and poets, like philosophers, would never be called upon (with Hecate) "to show the glory of our art."

That the Macbeths meet with such bad endings seems to prove the world emphatically moral, but it does not. If the world were good in a simple and unqualified way, the Macbeths could not have gone wrong in the first place. And while it may be said that Banquo's conniving in Macbeth's crime made him deserve a punishment almost as serious as the harm he receives from Macbeth, the same cannot be said of Lady Macduff and her children. They prove that some good people perish solely through the evil of others, and the example of Ross shows that some evil people are never punished for their evil. So evil—human evil—is a permanent feature of the human world. Nor is an abhorrence of even the worst evil-doing—a conscience—to be found in all human beings, though it is most unusual to find it completely lacking. Shakespeare seems to associate the growth of conscience in us with family upbringing—Lady Macbeth finds she cannot kill Duncan because he reminds her of her father. Macbeth and Lady Macbeth both do what they do despite their consciences: the former knows murder is a crime that God and human societies have always condemned most strongly, and the latter refers to ambition's need for such instruments as an "illness." Only Ross is the kind of man likely to have no conscience or contrition, and we know less about him than we do about Richard III and Iago, his greater but less successful peers in evil-doing.

But what is this evil of which we speak? Do evil men have a conscious will to do evil for its own sake? Are they lovers of harm rather than good? In the case of the Macbeths, evil is not sought for itself. They commit murder not because they enjoy slaughter but because they are willing to do something wrong in order to achieve something they know to be good. The goods they seek are all too ordinary: to rule, to be admired and loved. Even in the case of Macbeth's most irrational undertaking—the Macduff family murders—his motives, while far from clear, do not include any kind of sadism. He expresses no reasons, not even any wish to strike at Macduff in some way, or to warn others against deserting to Malcolm. From his failing to act instantly against Macduff he has concluded that he must in the future act on impulse rather than on slower-moving reflection if he is to prevail. We must imagine that Ross himself probably enjoys his superior ability to deceive and defeat more than the pain of those he hurts: in short, human evil is primarily the consequence of seeking some good at the cost of harming others, whether the good is sovereignty, superiority, or any of many other goals that entice men. What defects of upbringing or nature could bring a Ross to be what he is we can only guess. Nor does this play contain any direct evidence (as *The Tempest* does, for example) of a way of life—philosophical or poetical—rising superior to politics per se and making the soul essentially gentle rather than rough. The closest to this, in the play, is Hecate's devotion to the excellence of her craft—the craft of contriving harm. Hecate speaks in rhymed couplets, as if to remind us of the kinship between her mastery of "charms"—using combinations of words and apparitions—and the poetic art. (See III, 5, and IV, I, where the witches do Hecate's bidding and receive her praise.)

This dependence of harm on good accounts for the peculiar work and character of Hecate and her witches, for there is nothing satanic about them, not even the slightest sign of an urge to do evil for the sake of evil. Is arranging Macbeth's doom on a par for the witches with cherishing a pilot's thumb? Hecate's motive seems to be her art or craft itself: paradoxically, it is only her love of excellence that makes her enjoy the contrivance of harm, for no other motive for her activity is ever given. Shakespeare never ascribes either to her or the witches any need of their own nature requiring them to bring harm to others. It is false, moreover, to consider harm an independent and separate element in the universe. By nature men seek only good, and it is their limited intelligence and their passions that cause them to do harm. They rarely understand what is really good in general or for themselves in particular, and often miscalculate the actual consequences of their actions. They are not so solicitous of the well-being of others as to avoid harming them if an important benefit to themselves is at stake. These characteristics often cause men to engage in acts of grave injustice that bring grave harm to themselves as well. Exaggerated, magnified, and compressed for dramatic effect, this is certainly the most obvious moral lesson of *Macbeth*.

If we put together what the play divulges directly with what it consciously keeps from our view, the world is not the dark place it seems, and certainly not unintelligible. It is intelligible because the natures of the things in it are, and must be, intelligible. With its amazing array of beings, culminating in man, it is even the kind of world reason would choose, given what is possible. It contains ugliness because it also contains beauty, baseness because it also contains nobility, evil because it also contains good. But it is far from a moral order in the simple sense, where forces internal or external to it guarantee the flourishing of good and the failure of evil. Life is not a tale told by an idiot, but neither is it a parable told by a perfectly good and all-powerful God. It is a dangerous place for men, who are subject not only to natural perils but to those deriving from themselves. All too readily tempted into distortions of their nature and harboring false or imperfect notions of good, they are the source of their own greatest misery. Political, religious, and social institutions can do much for them, but they may also do harm, and, like all other things, are subject to decay. Human happiness is therefore very difficult to achieve, and even modest contentment may not easily be within man's grasp. At the end of the play Malcolm returns to a wise and just course, but we are never told what it is in Malcolm that will resist temptations and hold him to this course.

The darker side of life does not seem to have embittered Shakespeare, despite his having had as full a view of it as anyone can have. He seems to have concluded, as a general matter, that good is more fundamental than evil in the world, whatever the practical difficulties in the way of realizing it, and however great the actual predominance of evil. From this came the composure making it possible for him to write both tragedy and comedy, and even to commingle them appropriately. And his confidence in the good must have been confirmed, or given its highest expression, in his own philosophizing and poetry, which perhaps more than anything else show man's connection with the divine. If Macbeth's great "Tomorrow" speech expresses the deepest pessimism, the conclusion to which Shakespeare himself points in this play mixes pessimism with a more fundamental optimism.

ETHICS AND POLITICAL IDEOLOGY

Donald W. Foster (essay date 1986)

SOURCE: "*Macbeth*'s War on Time," in *English Literary Renaissance,* Vol. 16, No. 2, Spring, 1986, pp. 319-42.

[*In the following essay, Foster offers an account of* Macbeth *in the context of Jacobean politics and history.*]

James I, in his preface to the *Basilikon Doron* (1603), notes that men must "be very warie in all their secretest actions, and whatsoeuer middesses they vse for attaining to their most wished ends." This is especially true, he says, in the affairs of kings:

> for Kings being publike persons, by reason of their office and authority, are as it were set (as it was said of old) vpon a publike stage, in the sight of all the people; where all the beholders eyes are attentiuely bent to looke and pry in the least circumstance of their secretest drifts: Which should make Kings the more careful not to harbour the secretest thought in their minde . . . assuring themselues that Time the mother of Veritie, will in the due season bring her owne daughter to perfection.[1]

We have no record of James's critical response to *Macbeth,* but there are many who would applaud his meditation on the old figure of the "player-king" as a commentary on Shakespeare's Scottish tragedy: Truth, the daughter of Time, has at last a coming-out party in Act V, as riddling prophecies are unravelled, and as King Macbeth, "the secretest man of blood," is shown to his countrymen for what he is, a fiendlike butcher, so unlike his spiritual opposite, that most sainted prince, young Malcolm.[2] The sin, disease, chaos, and falsehood of Macbeth find their answer in Malcolm's piety, medicine, order, and truth. *Macbeth,* like those nineteenth-century French narratives discussed by Roland Barthes, raises "the question as if it were a subject which one delays predicating; and when the predicate (truth) arrives, the sentence, the narrative, are over, the world is adjectivized (after we had feared it would not be)." In short, Shakespeare in his Scottish play poses a problem and solves it, producing thereby a drama which follows Barthes' "classic" narrative pattern: "Truth, these narratives tell us, is what is *at the end* of expectation. This design brings narrative very close to the rite of initiation (a long path marked with pitfalls, obscurities, stops, suddenly comes out in the light); it implies a return to order, for expectation is a disorder."[3] This, some would say, is no less true of the disorder in Macbeth's Scotland than of the narrative's own "disorder" of expectation. In fact, the expectation of order is so strong at the close of *Macbeth* that critics for years have out-Malcolm'd Malcolm in their expressions of a beatific future. "Blood will cease to flow," writes one, "movement will recommence, fear will be forgotten, sleep will season every life, and the seeds of life will blossom in due order." "Virtue and justice are restored," exclaims another. "The time is free, the 'weal' once more made 'gentle.'" "The true cosmic playwright"—God—"now controls the world stage," writes a third, "and is prepared to create pattern out of the chaos and significance out of Malcolm's victory. . . ." "No longer will innocent flowers shelter serpents," writes a fourth. "Appearances will be attuned again with reality. . . . Macbeth's reign becomes the memory of a nightmare, scarcely disturbing Scotland's serene future."[4] All will be performed in measure, time, and place.

I

What interests me is not so much whether these critics are right or wrong in their unequivocal prophecies of bliss, but that such prophecies are made at all. It is not that I fault them for speaking of Malcolm and Macduff and company as "real" people with a "real" future, for insofar as the text comments on a past or future beyond the confines of narrative time, it is our business to discuss it as part of the fiction, as an inherent part of what defines the world of *Macbeth*. But it is curious that the criticism, until very recently, has been so unanimous in its expectation of a return to order after Macbeth's demise. For how can we know, finally, what sort of world it is that Malcolm's Scotland has inherited? We have, of course, the testimony of Macduff that the "time is free," which is perhaps the most oft-quoted line from the play outside Macbeth's "tomorrow" soliloquy; and most have taken his word as gospel, assuming either that Macduff is a man of astute judgment, or else that his words have a kind of magical efficacy in defining his world's future. Yet Macduff is the man who fled to England to escape Macbeth's bloody sword, while trusting his wife and children to the power of positive thinking; and though he declares that the time is free, he does so in a play in which the "good" characters are marked by their signal inability to learn from their mistakes. His declaration carries no greater freight of truth than Duncan's announcement in 1.2 that the Thane of Cawdor shall never more deceive his bosom interest.

From the play's opening line, the text glances repeatedly at Scotland's troubled future, as the natural harvest and inevitable repetition of a troubled past. In Malcolm we are presented with a future king whose speech—beginning with his self-impeachment (the only lie ever told by this "weak, poor, innocent lamb"), or perhaps even with his odd response to the news of his father's murder ("O, by whom?")—displays nothing but an empty bosom, a cunning mind, and a ready tongue. And though we are not told which of the two princes laughed in his sleep as Duncan bled, in the end it makes no difference, for at the close revenges still burn in men, and it is "certain" that Donalbain is not with his brother (5.2.7-8). In fact, his conspicuous and pointed absence in the fifth act (by which Shakespeare refers his audience to Holinshed's familiar chronicles) might well prompt Malcolm to say of Donalbain what Macbeth once said of Fleance: his absence is material. Holinshed reports that Malcolm eventually died a gruesome death, his head skewered through the eye upon the spear of an English knight; after which Donalbain returned from Ireland, slew Malcolm's eldest son, and usurped the throne. Moreover, during Malcolm's reign, "all the laws that Makbeth had ordeined were abrogated"; the whole realm was given over to "intestine rebellion," "slaughter in all parts," "more crueltie than euer had beene heard of before," "discommoditie and decaie," "outragious riot," "licorous desires," "corrupted abuses," "riotous manners," and "superfluous gormandizing."[5] If art in this case imitates a life, Malcolm's crafty false-speaking against himself is only too true.

Nor can there be a "return" to order when there was none to begin with. We are given no hint in Shakespeare that Duncan's reign was ever anything but bloody and chaotic. Indeed, the King's opening question, "What bloody man is that," might well be answered, "a *Scotsman*." Word of rebellion, treason, betrayal, and killing come post with post, without so much as breathing space between. An ineffectual king, Duncan can do nothing but inquire after "the newest state" of a broil which seems to have no beginning or end. And insofar as the three weird sisters represent the forces of darkness, the first line of the play—"Where shall we three meet *again*"—suggests already that what we shall see on the heath, or stage, is a repetition, more of the same.

That *Macbeth* follows a narrative curve from order/goodness/truth to chaos/badness/falsehood and back again is the illusion of those who would have their drama serve, not as a metaphor for life (in which our search for a first cause or grammatical subject drives us ever into the dark backward and abysm of time), but rather as a metaphor for some fictive or dream reality that has, in fact, a beginning, middle, and end: that is, a neatly contained world without causality or transience. In this respect, the reader's demand for a narrative based on the diad of subject and predicate, noun and verb, on expectation and desire for its imminent closure, is kin to the old cry for "poetic justice," for it demands that the poet belie his world in the interest of the reader's metaphysical comfort. In the end, of course, all poets, all tests, do belie life; but the old demand for hermeneutic narrative, in which "truth" predicates an incomplete subject, is the demand for a *conventional* lie, the *expected* lie, linked, as Barthes would say, "to the kerygmatic civilization of meaning and truth, appeal and fulfillment."[6]

In Macbeth the predicate, as truth, never arrives; nor is the world adjectivized, except by characters within the fiction, all of whom are partial to the action, and hence, unreliable judges. Shakespeare never essays to articulate the truth of Macbeth's history, nor even offers us a sum of perspectives which, when viewed holistically, comprise the truth. What we get instead is a variety of conflicting interpretations expressed by figures who themselves exist (until our imagination amends them) only *as* interpretation, as words in a text. "Some say he's mad; others, that lesser hate him, / Do call it valiant fury" (5.2.13-14). It is impossible to say, finally, whether Macbeth is aptly named "coward" or "brave," "Bellona's bridegroom" or "bloody villain," "royal lord" or "dwarfish thief," "Majesty" or "monster," "something wicked" or "angry god," "noble partner" or "abhorréd tyrant." Even the adjectives most frequently used to describe him—"good" (ten times) and "worthy" (nine times)—are neither true nor false, for all such words refer us not to any external reality but only to the figures who voice them, even as Macduff's "time is free" directs us not to truth, but to an interpretation, that is, to Macduff's own vision of a redeemed future, and to his sense that time past has been chained, hampered, enthralled by that cruel tyrant whose head is now mounted on a stick. Were the detached head able to speak in the final scene, it would, no doubt, say it was the other way around, that time was the tyrant, Macbeth time's fool and slave.

But if the passage of time in *Macbeth* fails to bring truth to perfection, the language of time may at least serve as a vantage from which to gain a new perspective: for time, in *Macbeth,* is the mother of many words. Nearly everyone is heard to "pay his breath to time" (4.1.99), from the lordly Malcolm to the lowly porter. Predictably, all this talk of time has generated a good deal of critical discussion as well; but according to the orthodox consensus (in essays by Stephen Spender, Roy Walker, Barbara Parker, Fred Turner, Ricardo Quinones, Francois Maguin, and Wylie Sypher, among others), this textual preoccupation with time and time's laws only serves to confirm *Macbeth* as a "closed" play (Sypher's term) in which the untimely Macbeths knock the time out of joint only to have the Malcolm-Macduff-Nature team knock it back in.[7] As articulated by Frank Kermode, "The suffering of the Macbeths may be thought of as caused by the pressure of the world of order slowly resuming its true shape and crushing them. This is the work of time; as usual in Shakespeare, evil, however great, burns itself out, and time is the servant of providence. Nowhere is this clearer than in *Macbeth.* The damnation of the principal characters involves murder and destruction, outrage not only upon the state but upon the whole cosmos; but the balance is restored." Kermode goes on to survey the numerous references in *Macbeth* to time and time's laws, and concludes, "As in Spenser, Time, apparently the destroyer, is the redeemer; yet it is itself redeemed. It seems very characteristic . . . of Shakespeare that there should be, in the greatest of the plays about human guilt, these semantic complexities concerning time, the element in which human life succeeds or fails, in which virtue is tested and evil brought to good."[8] Thus Macbeth's true history, which begins with a capital crime, ends (to use a figure from Othello), in a "bloody period." Be sure your disorders will find you out.

But when hermetic abstractions of Time-as-redeemer are set aside long enough for us to look at the actual language used, we find that Macbeth is plagued by a persistent though largely unconscious impulse to take revenge on *time itself,* as the chief obstacle to the human will, as the very devil from which man must be redeemed. Perhaps the most famous (though by no means original) formulation of his dilemma is that expressed by Nietzsche's Zarathustra:

> 'It was'—that is the name of the will's teeth-gnashing and most lonely affliction. Impotent against what is transpired, the will is a resentful spectator of all that has passed.
>
> The will cannot will backwards; that it cannot break time and time's covetousness—that is the will's loneliest affliction.[9]

But this passage is often misunderstood. The human will does not resent simply the "what was" of time, or the past. Time exists as past, present, and future, and contains not only an "it was" but an "it is" and an "it shall be." By stressing the "it was" as the object of the will's resentment, Nietzsche is concerned not merely with time *past,* but with time *passing,* with transience. The past bears the brunt of the will's resentment only because the past most obviously is ground whereon the will cannot operate. That which has come before cannot be changed or recreated in any literal sense. Therefore, having stumbled over this immovable rock, the will yields to a counter-will, a willing-against, an impulse to "get even." All sentiment becomes *ressentiment.* Seeking to liberate itself from its chains, the resentful will lashes out against time and time's laws, sometimes in foolish ways:

> Alas, every prisoner becomes a fool! The imprisoned will, too, releases itself in a foolish way.
>
> It is resentful that time does not run back. . . . And so, out of rage and ill-temper, the will rolls stones about, taking revenge on him who does not, like it, feel rage and ill-temper.
>
> Thus the liberating will becomes a felon, and upon all that can suffer it wreaks revenge for its inability to go backwards.
>
> This, yea, this alone is *revenge* itself: the will's aversion to time and time's "It was."[10]

Shakespeare's Troilus, in speaking of love, observes "that the will is infinite and the execution confined, that the desire is boundless and the act a slave to limit" (*T&C,* 3.2.80-82). Substitute the will to power for the sex drive, and we have the problem of *Macbeth.* Here is the figure of an infinite will trapped in a finite, transient body. The driving force behind Macbeth is not just a petty ambition to be named King of Scotland, but a far more radical impulse to be King over life itself, as indicated by his verbal obsession with time, causality, and transience. Macbeth would "entreat an hour to serve" his will, rather than vice versa (2.1.22). But for time's inexorable laws, his will "had else been perfect, / Whole as marble, founded as the rock. / As broad and general as the casing air." Instead he finds his will "cabined, cribbed, confined, bound in," (3.4.25), "the servant to defect, / Which else should free have wrought" (2.1.17-18). Unable to stem the flow of time, or to clip the chains of causality, unable to alter or recover that which time has established as the order of accomplished fact, Macbeth feels compelled to express his resentment in acts of bloody execution.

Macbeth's rage against time, like his impulse to murder Duncan, lies hidden until that fateful meeting with the weird sisters on the road to Forres. Heretofore his resentment has been repressed, denied, locked away in the unconscious. Since present fears are less than horrible imaginings, this Thane of Glamis has cast himself into the thick of every fray, "Nothing afeard of what [him]self didst make, / Strange images of death" (1.3.96-97); he has preferred to blot out the inner impulse, or "horrible imagining," with an external sign, or "image of death." Therefore, when it comes to protecting Duncan from the daggers of ambitious men, Macbeth is the nonpareil. The bloody man who brings report "of the revolt / The newest state" (1.2.1-2) cannot imagine what has possessed the Thane of Glamis to fight so relentlessly against overwhelming odds, unless perhaps he "meant to bathe in reeking wounds, / Or memorize another Golgotha" (1.2.39-40). But there is an element here of psychological realism, for according to Freud, *drive* (whether it be the will to power, sex drive, death drive, or poetic will) employs various mechanisms to defend itself against its own completeness, against its own need to look at what cannot be seen. Thus Macbeth's zeal in slaying the King's foes may be understood as a reaction formation by which he seeks to secure his ego against the return of bloody, repressed impulses from within.

The net effect of the witches' visit is that Macbeth is stripped forever of his ability to defend himself against his own black desires—which is why he "starts" when the weird sisters name him "King hereafter." Their prophetic greeting is at once a fresh beginning and a cause of terror, for the suggestion that he may yet be King brings to mind, involuntarily, the repressed image of a bloody corse, a horrid vision of slain royalty which unfixes his hair and makes his seated heart to knock against his ribs, "against the use of nature." He therefore attempts to dismiss the matter, and murder his murderous thought, with a chopped couplet, a failed attempt at closure: "Come what come may," he says, "Time and the hour runs through the roughest day" (1.3.147-48). That his words are spoken not in resignation, but with an edge of resentment, is made apparent not only in the potentially bloody verb, "runs through," but in the swelling act which follows. Were he resigned, there would be no assassination, and no play.

By referring him to "the coming on of time, with a 'Hail, King that shalt be!'" the weird sisters legitimize, as it were, Macbeth's claim to a kingly title. But every title—whether it be the name of king, father, god, or Thane of Cawdor—is a "former title" (1.2.65). We always arrive too late: someone else has always come first. Macbeth, likewise, feels a vague resentment that he has not come first, that another should be already that which he wishes himself to be. Like many of his contemporaries, he would like to be King, and he is nearer than most to the crown. Unfortunately, Duncan exists already as the thing itself. Macbeth has been deprived of the kingship, as it were, by his own "belatedness." Since Duncan holds a prior claim to the title, having come first in time, Macbeth must wait on time, as time's slave, for that which is "rightfully" his. It is an injury to his will, and Duncan will suffer for it.

It is here on the road to Forres that Macbeth's conscious assumptions about time are first called into question, as the play begins to probe the nature of man's relationship to time and causality. For example, there is in Banquo's phrase, "the seeds of time," a genitive, and generative, ambiguity. If the "of" signifies composition or content (box of alabaster, bag of groceries), if the seeds of time exist as sprouts of future time *in potentia,* the implication is that the future is not yet determined: men are the gardeners of their world, and as willful creators with "free hearts" they may cultivate this or that seed of time, causing it to flourish. That this is Duncan's view is made apparent in his words to Macbeth: "I have begun to plant thee," he says, "and will labor / To make thee full of growing" (1.4.28-29). If, on the other hand, the "of" is possessive, and time itself is the gardener, then it is left to the goddesses of destiny to say which grain will grow and which will not. The future then is fixed, contained in the present, and though man's seated, or "seeded," heart may knock against the use of nature, time shall have its pleasure. This is Banquo's assumption, which is why he neither begs nor fears the witches' favors nor their hate.

Banquo's organic perception of time and stoic indifference to the chains of causality are foreign to Macbeth's mind. Macbeth advises men to plant *themselves* (3.1.129), and holds that man may be the master of his time (3.1.40). He therefore recoils before the witches' strange intelligence, for their words, their "shalt be" instead of "mayst be," or even a "shalt be—if," implies that all growth is foreordained. In this more than mortal knowledge the Thane of Glamis "seems rapt withal," and wrapped as well, perceiving himself as, perhaps, a mere seed cast by time and fortune—a fearful meditation. Ironically, it is at precisely this moment, in which he hears himself named King hereafter, that the chilling thought first occurs to Macbeth that he may, in fact, be no more than time's slave.

That Macbeth cannot command transience is illustrated for him, as for us, in his command to the weird sisters: "Stay, you imperfect speakers," he says, "tell me more / . . . Speak, I charge you" (1.3.70, 78). But the women promptly vanish, like the inhabitants of the earth, "Into the air, and what seemed corporal melted / As breath into the wind" (1.3.81-82). Macbeth's cry—"Would they had stayed!"—

should, I think, be spoken on stage not wistfully, but with sudden and unexpected anger. Here was a vision of that earthly transience before which the self is nullified, and the assertive "will" reduced to "would." Banquo and Macbeth, no less than these three old women, are among earth's "bubbles" (1.3.79), to be burst, sooner or later, by antic Death's little pin.

Lost in his contemplation of time's "it was," Macbeth is overcome with a temporal vertigo that dizzies his speech. For example, when he learns that he has been named Thane of Cawdor, he says, "The greatest is behind" (1.3.117). Macbeth's conscious meaning is that the greatest is "to follow," is yet to come, but the odd phrasing, which curiously conflates past and future, contains a suspicion that the greatest is irredeemably "behind him," has come and gone.

Again, when he turns to those who stay upon his leisure, Macbeth excuses himself, saying, "My dull brain was wrought / With things forgotten" (1.3.149-50). The sentence itself is an attempt to murder the thought of killing Duncan. We might expect Macbeth to say, "My dull brain was wrought with matters that I will forget about for now. Let us toward the King." Rather, his use of the past participle seems an attempt, in mid-sentence, to pronounce himself free of that horrible imagining which continues to shake him. Thus his lie to Banquo and company is a lie also to himself, for his mind is wrought with deeds, names, and men that are all *but* forgotten.

Having been referred to the coming on of time, Macbeth can see only time's "it was." That which is great to be, is only a mirroring repetition of that greatness which lies behind. "Kind gentlemen," he says, "your pains / Are registered where every day I turn / The leaf to read them" (1.4.150-52). But which way are the pages turning, forward or backward? He seems to mean, "Each day you perform new favors to be recorded," but his words demand another reading as well: every day of his life he turns a new leaf, looking for a blank page on which to inscribe his name, only to find, *already recorded* there, the pains of kind (like-minded) gentlemen. As he speaks to his friends, Macbeth sees nothing before him but the spectres of the past. Every dread exploit, every heroic deed, every great name, is anticipated by time. Moreover, even if he does succeed in carving out a name and passage, his life will only fall into the sear, the yellow leaf of a tedious chronicle (5.3.22-23)—so that nothing is, but what is not.

In considering what motivates Macbeth, our vision has been too easily clouded by our own conventional goodness and perhaps, too, by the timidity of our evil. The traditional view of Macbeth as a man torn between his black desires on the one hand and Christian virtue on the other is too simple. For example, the thought occurs to Macbeth, "If chance will have me king, why chance may crown me, / Without my stir" (1.3.143-44). According to the customary reading of these lines, Macbeth has, then, good cause not to murder Duncan: if the weird sisters speak true, he need only wait, and the crown will fall into his lap—and that, perhaps, is Macbeth's conscious meaning. But we may perceive also in this short aside a spur to regicide: for if chance crowns him without his stir, what will he have gained? Only that which was foretold, a fruitless crown and barren sceptre. But he will have lost much. It is essential to Macbeth that he create *himself* as King, that he be crowned not passively by the hands of time and chance, but actively, by his own mortal hands. To be made King without his stir will not answer for him the question of whether or not he is simply time's slave, subject to experience whatever time has in store. Macbeth's question is not, Dare I do a wicked deed to gain the Scottish crown, but rather, Do I dare disturb the universe? Shall I resign myself as the slave of limit, or shall I seek to liberate myself, by jumping the life to come and seizing the future now, on my own terms? Lady Macbeth, therefore, says more than she knows when she chides her husband, saying that when neither time nor place adheres, he "would make both," but when "they have made themselves," their very fitness doth "unmake him" (1.7.51-54). The paradox of willful self-creation could not be more succinctly stated. Macbeth is nothing afeard of what he makes himself (1.3.96), but only of what makes *him*.

Macbeth's answer to his humiliation at the hands of the clock is to take a literal revenge: he will attack time with a dagger, will break time's laws, will take the future now in the ignorant present, seizing forcibly that which he has come already to perceive as his—the name and all the addition to a king. But the name of king, in Macbeth's mind, is no ordinary name, and his deed shall be no ordinary deed. Macbeth, like Cleopatra, wills "To do that thing that ends all other deeds, / Which shackles accidents and bolts up change"; but he is far from sharing Cleopatra's opinion that "'Tis paltry to be Caesar," nor perceives that a king, "not being Fortune," is but "Fortune's knave" (*A&C*, 5.2.2-6). Cleopatra wills to defeat time by transforming herself into an everlasting legend. Macbeth cares nothing for legend. He'll defeat time literally, by creating himself King of the empirical realm whether or not Fortune wills to have it so. He'll have a name greater than any name named under Heaven.

Harold Bloom, in his essay on poetry as a mode of lying against time, has followed the Gnostic Valentinius in noting that mortal man, desiring to transcend time and flesh and death, may fashion images, in the name of a god, which in turn become objects of fear to him, as for example, the idolator with his stone idol, or the terrified speaker of Blake's "Tyger." This fear may be identified as the fear of a name, whether it be the artist's fear of a daemonic name (in having fashioned the *unheimlich*, or "uncanny"), or the pagan's creation of a god with a name greater than his own.[11] Macbeth likewise, perceiving himself to be a slave of time, quakes not so much at the thought of mere killing as at the image, fashioned by himself, of "King" Macbeth, a being which seems, in his mind's eye, to transcend time. The name of King, pre-existent and immortal, and endowed with a power and

John Gielgud as Macbeth in a 1942 publicity photo.

freedom not available to Macbeth as subject, seems to offer the promise of a new temporality in which time and death become subject to the self. Macbeth, like the sublime poet, like the savage idolator, thus creates an image before which he may bow the knee, populating the empty vault with a god after his own fashion. If he trembles before the image of a fallen King Duncan, he trembles also before the image of King Macbeth, a being shaped not by time but by his own devices, a sublime creation, greater than himself, a King of kings, and killer of kings. It is this doubly frightening thought which makes his heart knock against his ribs, for having once fashioned in his mind the image of King Macbeth, that identity alone seems authentic. To be a self-made King is to be sublime. To be less is nothing.

It now becomes clear why Macbeth's mind is given to such marvellous soliloquies regarding the horror of the deed he is about to perform: Macbeth *needs* these images, as it were, to convince himself of the sublimity of his crime. His fecund imagination would rescue the intended act from time's abyss, and endow it with meaning. While "pity, like a naked newborn babe, / Striding the blast" and "heaven's cherubin horsed / Upon the sightless couriers of the air" appear strong against the deed, it is precisely such images that allow Macbeth to continue believing that a knife in Duncan will indeed break the bands of transience. Pale Hecate's offerings, images of withered murder alarumed by the wolf, Tarquin's ghostly presence, all help to reassure Macbeth's heat-oppressed brain that his crime will surely be a deed horrid and grand enough to free his will from its chains. For most men, such visions were enough to sickly o'er the native hue of resolution, but Macbeth's bloody dagger, a false creation, only marshalls him the way that he was going. He must allow nothing to "take the present horror from the time" (1.7.58). I do not suppose, of course, that Macbeth knows all this. Maybe Shakespeare knew it, in his own way, but the argument is not, finally, a "psychological" one, for it takes place in the interstice of a continuing textual preoccupation with time and causality.

Ironically, Macbeth's deed, crucifixion of sorts, does seem to shock time into a momentary stasis: "By th'clock tis day," says Ross, "And yet dark night strangles the traveling lamp" (2.4.6-7). It is a critical commonplace to note that the shock is only momentary; but the reaction is not, as in DeQuincey's formulation, a matter of the "human" making its reflux upon the "fiendish." Rather, *time* and *transience* reassert themselves, as Macduff calls "timely" upon the King. Nor was time or the "natural order" ever really assaulted, though many Scotsmen would interpret it so. 'Twas a rough night, but the regicide, no less than Macdonwald's rebellion, Norway's invasion, the earthquake and storm, is a confused event "New hatched to th'woeful time" (2.3.53). There is no causal link between Macbeth's deed and the storm, any more than between Macdonwald's rebellion and the "contending 'gainst obedience" of Duncan's horses (2.4.17). Brutal violence, whether by man or beast, is very much a part of the so-called "natural order," both before and after Duncan's death.

To seize the kingship had seemed to Macbeth a deed to stop "the spring, the head, the fountain," the "very source" of natural succession, while halting also the flow of kingly blood (2.3.100-01). It is neither. If one man may seize the crown by violence without an apocalypse, so then may another. The sun has not yet come full circle before King Macbeth realizes that his fears in Banquo stick deep. Banquo, who in his sleep is given to cursed thoughts (2.1.7-9), has confessed that he, too, dreams at night of the weird sisters (2.1.20); and Macbeth notes that he "chid the sisters, / When *first* they put the name of King upon *me*"—an observation which suggests that Banquo resents Macbeth's priority, resents that the sisters did not first put the name of King upon *him* (3.1.58). Macbeth had hoped that his deed without a name would trammel up consequence. Finding it otherwise, he is vexed by every minute of Banquo's being (3.1.117), and resolves that it "must be done tonight" (3.1.131). If the assassination of Duncan proved nothing, the murder of Banquo and Fleance will, for the seeds of Banquo then will never grow as prophesied. Just two more murders will "Cancel and tear to pieces that great bond" which keeps him pale, the bond of causality, or "fate," which subjects him as time's debtor, captive, and slave (3.2.49-50).

When he has come to terms with the killers, Macbeth exclaims happily, "It is concluded!" (3.1.141)—only to find, once again, that nothing is concluded. Lady Macbeth, for her part, would like to think that "Things without all remedy / Should be without regard: what's done is done" (3.2.11-12). But she soon finds herself asking her lord, "What's to be done?" (3.2.44)—as if to say, What's yet to be done? What shall be done? What ought to be done? What can or does it mean—"to be done?"

When the murderers return and tell the King "how much is done" (3.3.22), his fit comes again, in the figure of Banquo's ghost; although "when all's done," he looks but on a stool. The vision only hardens his resolve: "It will have blood, they say: blood will have blood. / Stones have been known to move and trees to speak"—or stones to speak and trees to move—"Augures and understood relations have by maggot-pies and choughs and rooks brought forth / The secret'st man of blood" (3.4.123-27). Here again, the usual error is to hear in these words only the voice of fear, when there is, in fact, some metaphysical comfort (for Macbeth, as for us) in the thought that the natural order has risen up against him—else the sublimity of his crime threatens to vanish into a futile insignificance, as mere death and emptiness. Nature's supposed opposition will not, therefore, discourage Macbeth from doing his will: ". . . I will . . . / . . . I will . . . / . . . I will . . . / . . . For mine own good / All causes shall give way." In other words, "All considerations shall be forgot as I take my revenge on all causation." It will be a bloody, tedious business: for "I am in blood / Stepped so far that, should I wade no more, / Returning were as tedious as go o'er" (3.4.131-41). There is now only a "going o'er" (and over and over), and no "o'erleaping." In the landscape of Macbeth's imagination there is a swift river of time, a tide of blood having as its source time's "it was" and all that has gone before. He once conceived himself as outside time, on the bank and shoal, seeking to o'erleap transience to reach the golden shore of a timeless present. But having once pricked the sides of his intent and spurred vaulting ambition, Macbeth has jumped the life to come, and—fallen in! If he makes it now to that other shore, it will only be by slogging through blood up to his ears.

The Thane of Fife is next to bleed. When Macbeth learns, from the apparition of the armed head, that he should "Beware Macduff," he vows to "make assurance double sure / And take a bond of fate" (4.1.71, 83-84) to make fate prisoner and debtor to *himself*. Best to force the apparition to keep its word of promise: he will kill Macduff, and have done. But once again, Macbeth arrives too late, for the Thane of Fife is fled to England. "Time," exclaims the King, "thou anticipat'st my dread exploits" (4.1.144). From now on, it will be an open battle. If Macbeth cannot make his time stand still, he will make it run:

> The flighty purpose never is o'ertook
> Unless the deed go with it. From this moment
> The very firstlings of my heart shall be
> The firstlings of my hand. And even now,
> To crown my thoughts with acts, be it thought and done.
>
> (4.1.145-49)

And "Thus," in Zarathustra's words, "the liberating will becomes a felon, and upon all that can suffer it wreaks revenge for its inability to go backwards."[12] Have I arrived too late to kill Macduff? Very well, I'll kill "His wife, his babes, and all unfortunate souls / That trace him in his line" (4.1.152-53). This is a key moment in the history of Macbeth's reactivity, as we go from Macdonwald to Duncan to Banquo to the Macduffs. Macbeth turns again to frantic killing, as if on a battlefield, as a means of erasing the temporal interval *between* acts, by constantly acting, allowing time no interval for *re*-action, and no chance to anticipate him, like a boxer who flails his opponent against the ropes. His brandished steel will smoke in bloody execution until such time as he can say, "It is done." Thus "Each new morn / New widows howl, new orphans cry, new sorrows / Strike heaven on the face" (4.3.5-6). What's the newest grief? "Each minute teems a new one," for each minute is itself a grief, a ceasing to be, an injury to the will that must be avenged with the sword (5.3.174-76). Yet Macbeth finds that with each bloody revenge, time will "close and be herserlf, whilst our poor malice / Remains in danger of her *former* tooth," her "it was" (3.2.14-15).

Too late, Macbeth realizes that "He cannot buckle his distempered cause / Within the belt of rule" (5.2.15-16). Having willed himself to be a causeless man, a self-made king, he learns that causation resists the will as surely as "being" resists "being done." There is stasis only in death. This recognition that being exists only as transience proves too great a burden for his will to bear. The formula, "Nothing is, but what is not," turns upon itself: What is, is nothing, for all that is, is transient, a vanishing into the abyss:

> Tomorrow, and tomorrow, and tomorrow
> Creeps in this petty pace from day to day,
> To the last syllable of recorded time;
> And all our yesterdays have lighted fools
> The way to dusty death.
>
> (5.5.19-23)

Macbeth has always favored "tomorrow" as the blessed ground whereon the will may appear to operate freely: "We'll take tomorrow" (3.1.22); "But of that tomorrow" (3.1.32); "Tomorrow / We'll hear ourselves again" (3.4.32-33); "I will tomorrow, / And betimes I will, to the weïrd sisters" (3.4.133-34). But now his will seems extinguished by the stuttering repetition of a million deadly tomorrows endlessly the same. It does not matter, in the end, what history's "last syllable" is. Macbeth knows it only as a "like syllable of dolor," a sound that signifies nothing. Three, or four, or a billion tomorrows cannot finally be distinguished from the plural yesterday which led like-minded gentlemen to their inevitable, and redundant, conclusion.

Thus Macbeth comes at last to cast off the sublimity of self-creation *in spite of* time, as he embraces the sublime necessity of dying *in* time. "Out, out, brief candle!" If a man cannot have, cannot be, the be-all and the end-all, better then not to be, better that no man should be, that earthly existence itself should cease to be. Thus spake Zarathustra: "Because the willer must suffer, because he cannot will backwards—thus willing itself and all life has been perceived as—punishment! . . . until at last madness preached: 'Everything passes away; therefore everything *deserves* to pass away!'"[13] "What's done cannot be undone" (5.1.71)—which is precisely *why* Macbeth wishes that "th'estate o' th' world were now undone" (5.6.50). He'd have "nature's germens tumble all together, / Even till destruction sicken" (4.1.59-60).

It is his weariness of time's petty procession which allows Macbeth finally to embrace his fate: "Blow wind, come wrack!" he cries. "There is nor flying hence nor tarrying here" (5.5.51, 48), no afterlife or permanence, nothing but death and transience, a passing away. He therefore leaves the safety of Dunsinane, a castle which might indeed have laughed a siege to scorn, and marches forth to meet his fate, come what come may, motivated no longer by "poor malice" and a will to revenge but by a profound acceptance of death—of his own and every man's.

Yet, as a man bound to Fortune's wheel, Macbeth has come around, at least, to perceive the futility of brandished steel and smoking execution, unlike those "good" men in his world who still look to revenge as the answer to their ills: "Be comforted," says the future King. "Let's make us med'cines of our great revenge, / To cure this deadly grief" (4.3.213-15). Caithness likewise sees in Malcolm's burning revenge "the med'cine of the sickly weal" (5.2.27), with an unintended pun on "wheel," for he fails to apprehend that literal revenges lead inevitably to revenges in kind. Revenge cannot, in fact, cure deadly grief, for it is revenge itself which makes grief deadly. Time's "it was" cannot be remedied in the empirical realm. Therefore, says Macbeth, "Throw physic to the dogs, I'll none of it" (5.3.47). Having acknowledged his fate as time's fool, he is determined only to fight the course, to see the dismal story out, to meet his enemy on the field beard to beard, and let the gashes fall where they may; for though revenge as a physic may comfort the dogs that bait the bear-like king (5.7.1-2), Macbeth for his part has come to perceive it rather as a poisoned chalice which men raise to their own lips, a sickly wheel which returns to plague the inventor—though there is, of course, no "inventor," no author, no prime mover. That was his illusion in Act I. *All* revenges are revenges in kind, more of the same, and every deed has a pre-existent name, including *regicide*.

Resolved still that he "must not yield / To one of woman born," King Macbeth learns, too late, that his adversary was "from his mother's womb / Untimely ripped" (5.8.12-16). Macduff, the living consequence of Macbeth's revenges of the past, appears as the outcome of an untimely breach in nature. Macbeth must face him and perish, or yield, and live to be the literal fool of time, "the show and gaze o'th'time," a poor player on a tether to be baited with the rabble's curse. "I will not yield," he vows, "To kiss the ground before young Malcolm's feet" (5.8.27-28). The ground before young Malcolm's feet is Scotland's future, a dusty path which Macbeth has no will to see. Rather, he will continue to carve his own passage till he finds himself concluded on the bloody point of Macduff's sword: "Yet I will try the last . . . / And damned be him that first cries, 'Hold, enough!'" (5.8.32-34).

When Macduff enters with "King" Macbeth's severed head fixed upon a spear, he greets Malcolm, saying, "Hail, King! for so thou art: behold, where stands / Th'usurper's cursed head. The time is free" (5.8.54-55). Macduff means, of course, that Malcolm may now be called "King," since the world has been liberated from the tyrant Macbeth. But the ambiguous "so" suggests a second, ironic, meaning: "O 'King,' behold this pitiful scarecrow, this death's head upon a stick: *for so thou art*. The man who would be king is a poor usurper, cursed by time; for time, in fact, is king, and time is free to work his will on all his human slaves." Fortune thus has granted to Macbeth his wish that he "memorize another Golgotha": for when his robes have been removed, we, like Malcolm, may behold Shakespeare's macabre caricature of the human potentate, "a new Gorgon," the King of kings, in a grotesque crucifixion, "as our rarer monsters are, / Painted upon a pole, and underwrit, / 'Here you may see the tyrant'" (5.8.25-27).

If indeed the late King's bodiless head may serve the usurping Malcolm as a mirror by which to view his own figure and fate (even as Macdonwald's might have done for Macbeth), then King Malcolm—Macbeth's first cousin once removed—is next in line to tread the dusty path to Calvary, as in the *Chronicles*. He has been revenged on his foes, and in his final speech vows to make himself "even" with his thanes and kinsmen in exchange for their several loves (5.8.62). But Malcolm will not be "even" with his subjects until he, too, lies like Macbeth, "planted newly with the time," six feet beneath the earth, that another seed may grow. His revenge on Macbeth and time, his succession to the throne of Scotland, is not a redemption but another belated repetition, for in the world of *Macbeth*, all such literal revenges, unlike the poet's figurative revenge, in the end yield only death.

John Irwin has noted that this phenomenon, this impulse to take revenge on time and its inevitable failure, seems to be "the very essence of tragedy": "for I take it that all tragedies are in a sense revenger's tragedies—actions in which the central figure (or the audience observing him) comes to the tragic awareness that, because of the irreversibility of time, man in time can never get even, indeed, comes to understand that the whole process of getting even is incompatible with time."[14] There is no better play to illustrate Irwin's point than Shakespeare's *Macbeth*. Having lashed out at time and failed, Macbeth's frustrated will gradually turns against itself, and yields finally to the nihilistic conclusion that all life is punishment, all existence incoherent gibberish to the last petty syllable of recorded time.

II

The will must be delivered from its aversion to time and transience if ever it is to be delivered from the impulse to degrade what is transient. But to deliver itself from *all* willing requires a plunge into the abyss, a deliverance from all earthly existence. Rather, the will must find a way to say "yes" to life, a "yes" that would have transience abide, and would not have it degraded to nothingness; a "yes," not to *being* as *being done,* but to *being* as *becoming.* But to say "yes" to transience the will must no longer be limited in its temporality by the necessity of an irreversible and immovable past. One answer, then, is to seek a figurative triumph over time. Only through poetry and art—in a different sense, the syllables of recorded time—is the will able to transform "it was" into "it is," and "thus did it happen" into "thus have I willed it!"

Harold Toliver, in his essay on "Shakespeare and the Abyss of Time," has said that "Perhaps the central paradox of the play is that the most depraved of Shakespeare's tragic heroes should have become also the most poetic."[15] For "depraved" let us read "degraded," and for "paradox," "irony": the central irony of the play is that Macbeth, degraded by time, *should* have become also the most poetic, for Macbeth fails to realize his own powers of figuration. Though masterful in his use of figurative language, he neglects language as an alternate means of transcending time's inexorability. Although his imagination spawns timeless metaphors, his dull brain is, nevertheless, all too literalistic. Macbeth, in waging a literal war on the natural order, "chokes [his] art," impressing language into the service of a literal revenge. (1.2.9).

What Harold Bloom says about sado-masochistic poets may be applied also to Macbeth, Shakespeare's poetic sado-masochist; to wit, when figuration and sadism are identified, "then we find always the obsession with . . . *belatedness* risen to a terrible intensity that plays out the poet's revenge against time by the unhappy substitution of the body, another body or one's own, *for* time. Raging against time, forgetting that only Eros or figuration is a true revenge against time, the sadomasochist overliteralizes and so yields to the death drive."[16] Bloom goes on to say that "Sadism and masochism are overliteralizations of meaning," a "failure in the possibilities of figurative language."[17] As "a furious literalism," sadism "denies the figurative representation of essence by act. . . . Lacking poetry, the sado-masochist yields to the literalism of the death drive precisely out of a rage against literal meaning."[18] Macbeth wills to degrade all that is, because he has failed to recognize in his own mythopoeic imagination the tool by which he may redeem actuality and say "yes" to life; he has not perceived that the only revenge on time's "it was" is figurative and poetic; to seek a literal revenge is to yield to the abyss. Thus, when his literal revenges on time have failed, he accepts literal death.

Against the literalism and compulsive repetition of Macbeth's death drive, Shakespeare has set his own sublime poetic will. In *Macbeth* the impotence of kings before time is contrasted with the dramatist's power to recover the past, and to impose upon it his own order, by means of poetic figuration. This is not, of course, peculiar to *Macbeth*. As Irwin has noted, "One might say that the purpose and point of . . . all narration is to use the temporal medium of narration to take revenge against time, to use narration to get even with the very mode of narration's existence in a daemonic attempt to prove that through the process of substitution and repetition, time is not really irreversible."[19] Historical narrative is, in its very essence, an argument against time, a willful recovery and revision of the past, a revengeful substitution of "it is" for "it was." Moreover, Bloom's point is well taken that this argument inevitably splits in two, for after displacing time's "it was," the poetic will "needs to make another outrageous substitution of 'I am' for 'It is.' Both parts of the argument are quests for priority."[20] The poetic will's revenge on time, no less than the empirical power thrust, is taken to avenge one's own sense of belatedness.

But what's to be done, then, when time's "it was" is already recomposed by another? Shakespeare, in following Holinshed, is faced with a double perplexity, for he is preceded not only by time, but by recorded time. Shakespeare, therefore, in his dramatic narrative, must assert his priority over both history and "history," transforming time past, and past narrative, into the timeless presence of an acted text. Doubly redoubling the strokes of his pen, he performs marvels of temporal dexterity throughout the drama, demonstrating that he is not, like his predecessor Holinshed, limited by time. For example: the script of Macbeth's performance against Norway and Macdonwald which King Duncan "reads" is, in fact, a tale told by a dramatist some 550 years later (1.3.90, 97). Again, when "Two truths are told / As happy prologues to the swelling act / Of the imperial theme" (1.3.127-29), the act is at once a self-aggrandizing, bloody deed in the dramatic future, and the present grand dramatic performance of an historical deed already done. Macbeth, who has in his head "strange things . . . / Which must be acted ere they may be scanned" (3.4.140-41), alludes unwittingly to the day in which his thoughts shall be set to lines of blank verse, having been acted by him ere scanned by a player, and acted by a player ere scanned by the world at large. Again, the heavens which, "troubled with man's act, / Threatens his bloody stage" (2.4.5-6), are at once the "real" heavens over Macbeth's Scotland and the imaginary "heavens" over Shakespeare's bloody stage, some six centuries after the fact. Time and again we find that the dramatist need not be bound by terrestrial *or* by narrative time. Past, present, and future may be captured in an instant.

Any well-crafted play is, of course, bound to be more immediate, more "present," than an equally well-crafted prose narrative of those same events. If dramatist and historian alike are friends that lie like truth, if both tell lies against time, at least the dramatist's "it is" recalls the past in a way that the historian's "what was" can never hope to match. But Raphael Holinshed tells many a sad story of the deaths of kings, some deposed, some slain in war, some haunted by the ghosts that they deposed, some sleeping killed, all murdered by time. What, then, was there, given the six long volumes of the Chronicles, about the tale of King Makbeth that alone captured Shakespeare's imagination? Almost any story therein might have served as a vehicle by which to displace time's "it was" with the dramatic present. But what in Makbeth's life story suggested to Shakespeare a possibility to assert his own "I am?" The answer is not immediately apparent. His selection of Makbeth, at first glance, seems rather arbitrary, for as Holinshed tells the story, it would appear to have little in the way of dramatic potential: "To be briefe, such were the woorthie and princely acts of this Makbeth in the administration of the realme, that if he had atteined thervnto by rightfull means, and continued in vprightness of iustice as he began, till the end of his reigne, he might well haue been numbred amongest the most noble princes that anie where had reigned."[21] There was, of course, the murder of Duncan, the portents in earth and sky, and the attendant prophecy of witches to lend interest to the story, but regicides, omens, and prophecies are all but commonplace in Holinshed. If anything, the Makbeth of the Chronicles is distinguished not by his evil, but by his goodness, specifically by his "manie holesome laws and statutes." Holinshed lists in all twenty laws enacted by King Makbeth for "the publike weale of his subiects." But the statute which seems most to have intrigued Shakespeare is the King's decree that poor players should be heard no more: for Holinshed reports that Makbeth was the first Scottish king to outlaw such vain and foolish entertainments: "Counterfeit fooles, minstrels, iesters, and these kind of iuglers, with such like idle persons, that range abroad in the countrie, hauing no speciall license of the king, shall be compelled to learne some science or craft to get their liuing; if they refuse so to doo, they shall be drawen like horsses in the plough and harrows."[22]

King Makbeth's hubris in asserting his supremacy over players, in licensing the few and demeaning the rest, thus lends to the "Tomorrow" soliloquy of Shakespeare's *Macbeth* a wonderful irony: we may see now why it should be especially galling to this great usurper that his life in retrospect should appear so like the antics of a poor player strutting and fretting upon a stage. The King is forced to turn to the player for a metaphor by which to express the meaning of his own meaninglessness—thereby giving to the player a possibility for value and meaning which he himself cannot seem to find. Holinshed, for his part, wholly approves of King Makbeth's diligence in having protected the commonwealth from such theatrical knaves.[23] But it is here that Shakespeare makes his figurative revenge on time complete, for we find in *Macbeth* that the tables are turned. Counterfeit kings, with such like idle persons, may not range abroad without special license of the playwright, but are compelled to learn the art of playing to get their living. Macbeth, the man who begins the play as "Bellona's bridegroom lapped in proof," the minion of his race, thus must die "with harness on [his] back," not only as time's fool, but as time's jade, carving his bloody furrow at the crack of the dramatist's whip (1.2.19, 54; 5.5.52).

In their moment of defeat, most earthly kings, like the King of Norway, crave composition (1.2.59). Their fate, thereafter, lies in the hands of fiends who lie like truth. It is not the sort of immortality sought by King Macbeth. Unlike Hamlet or Cleopatra, Macbeth expresses no desire to have his story told, for it seems a tale told by an idiot. He would not have the moment of his greatness reduced to a flickering shadowshow for generations to come. Indeed, his aversion to Banquo's ghost appears to be, at least in part, the unspeakable horror of one day being pulled from his tomb by "these juggling fiends" (5.8.19), by players "and these kind of iuglers" (Holinshed), whom the historical Makbeth once outlawed; it is a fate which Macbeth cannot endure to think on. "Hence, horrible shadow!" he cries. "Unreal mock'ry, hence!" (3.4.107-08). Such imitations of immortality are not to his liking.

Seeing Banquo resurrected upon the stage, Macbeth cries out,

> If charnel houses and our graves must send
> Those that we bury back, our monuments
> Shall be the maws of kites.
>
> (3.4.72-74)

Macbeth is thinking here of his own dusty death; when he passes, better that his flesh should be hacked and fed to birds than to be resurrected thus. If, in the false creations of heat-oppressed brains, men may rise again with twenty mortal murders on their crowns, it will surely push kings from their stools (3.4.80-83); therefore, Macbeth will none of it. He feels his secret murders sticking on his hands, and the intuition that such murders, too terrible for the ear, may be "performed," leaves him sick and trembling—so that, when the vision passes, he is left only with the desperate hope that no one should "muse" at him (3.4.78, 86). The worst fate that Macbeth can imagine is to survive in time only as a display of "unreal mock'ry," or as an illustration for an underwrit text which says, "Here you may see the tyrant."

Macbeth's wish is not granted, for it was ordained otherwise. This once and future king, whose brain the playwright wrought with things not to be forgotten, is to be cast forever as a slave of time, his life transformed into a timeless act. In his hour upon the stage, he will speak the same lines, hear the same prophetic greeting, make the same futile gestures. Each time he is ushered forth, he will waver in his determination to kill the King, wondering if his will is truly free. His secret murders shall be performed not just once, but o'er and o'er, so long as men can breathe, or eyes can see. And, full of sound and fury, he'll proceed to his own smoking execution, only to be heard no more—until the next performance.

If there is a lesson to be learned in all this, it is not the moral didacticism of a narrative which seeks to demonstrate the wickedness and chaotic consequences of ambition or regicide, but rather a living illustration of how far superior the poet is to the king, and the figurative to the literal revenge on time. Kings may like to think themselves the harbingers of the life to come, but when the hurlyburly's done, when kings and subjects are dead and rotten, it is the verbal jugglers, the poets and playwrights, who "give them all breath, / Those clamorous harbingers of blood and death" (5.6.9-10). In this regard, it is worth noting Shakespeare's final salute to his own magnificence, for *Macbeth*, having begun with one prediction, closes with another. Malcolm promises to use his time wisely:

> Producing forth the cruel ministers
> Of this dead butcher and his fiendlike queen,
> . . . —this, and what needful else
> That calls upon us, by the grace of Grace
> We will perform in measure, time, and place.
>
> (5.8.68-73)

It is on this note that the play draws to a close, while drawing us, at the same time, to the play's beginning. Shakespeare asserts his priority one last time, pointing in advance to his own masterful triumph over temporality. When all's done, someone *shall* "muse" at Macbeth. Malcolm unwittingly looks ahead to the day in which the King's Men will produce forth Macbeth and his fiendlike queen and all their cruel ministers, performing the story in measured verse, at Hampton Court, in 1606, by the grace of his Grace, the King—and by the conjurations of a wizard poet, whose redemptive time is the timeless present of that measure itself.

Notes

1. James I, "To the Reader," preface to *Basilikon Doron*, in *The Political Works of James I* (New York, N.Y., 1965), 5.
2. Quotations are from the *Signet Classic Shakespeare*, ed. Sylvan Barnet (New York, 1972).
3. Roland Barthes, *S/Z*, tr. Richard Miller (New York, 1974), p. 76.
4. Mark Van Doren, "Macbeth," in *Shakespeare* (New York, 1939), p. 230; Frank Kermode, "Macbeth," in *The Riverside Shakespeare* (Boston, 1974), p. 1307; Richard S. Ide, "The Theatre of the Mind," in *ELH* 42 (1975), 359; and Herbert R. Coursen, Jr., *Christian Ritual and the World of Shakespeare's Tragedies* (Lewisburg, Pa., 1976), p. 369. What makes these quotations the more remarkable is that I took them at random from the few sources available on my own desktop. A host of more egregious examples may be found elsewhere.
5. Raphael Holinshed, *Holinshed's Chronicles of England, Scotland, and Ireland: in six volumes,* rev. John Hooker et. al. (1587; rpt. London, 1807-08), V, 289-94.
6. Barthes, p. 76.
7. Stephen Spender, "Time, Violence, and *Macbeth*," *Penguin New Writing,* III (New York, 1946), pp. 115-26; Roy Walker, *The Time is Free* (London, 1949); Barbara L. Parker, "*Macbeth*: The Great Illusion," *Sewanee Review* 78 (1970), 476-87; Frederick Turner, *Shakespeare and the Nature of Time* (Oxford, 1971); Ricardo Quninones, *The Renaissance Discovery of Time* (Cambridge, Mass., 1972), pp. 351-60; Francois Maguin, "The Breaking of Time: *Richard II, Hamlet, King Lear, Macbeth*," *Cahiers Elisabethains* 7 (1975), 25-41; Wylie Sypher, *The Ethic of Time* (New York, 1976).
8. Kermode, p. 1310.
9. Friedrich Nietzsche, "Von der Erlösung" in *Nietzsches Werke* 2 vols., ed. Gerhard Stenzel (Salzburg, 1952), II, p. 421. (My translation of Nietzsche.)
10. Nietzsche, II, p. 421.
11. Harold Bloom, "Lying against Time: Gnosis, Poetry Criticism," in *Agon* (Oxford, 1982), p. 53.
12. Nietzsche, II, p. 421.
13. Nietzsche, II, p. 421.
14. John Irwin, *Doubling and Incest/Repetition and Revenge: A Speculative Reading of Faulkner* (Baltimore, Md., 1975), p. 4.
15. Harold Toliver, "Shakespeare and the Abyss of Time," *JEGP* 64 (1965), 250.
16. Bloom, "Freud's Concepts of Defense and Poetic Will," in *Agon* (1982), p. 140.
17. Bloom, *Agon,* p. 139.
18. Bloom, *Agon,* p. 140.
19. Irwin, p. 4.
20. Bloom, *Agon,* p. 124.
21. Holinshed, V, p. 270.
22. Holinshed, pp. 270-71.
23. Holinshed, p. 271.

Alan Sinfield (essay date 1986)

SOURCE: "*Macbeth*: History, Ideology and Intellectuals," in *Critical Quarterly,* Vol. 28, Nos. 1-2, Spring-Summer, 1986, pp. 63-77.

[*In the following essay, Sinfield contends that* Macbeth *is a political play that centers on the distinction between violence that the state considers legitimate and violence that it considers evil.*]

It is often said that *Macbeth* is about 'evil', but we might draw a more careful distinction: between the violence which the State considers legitimate and that which it does not. Macbeth, we may agree, is a dreadful murderer when he kills Duncan. But when he kills Macdonwald—'a rebel' (I.ii.10)—he has Duncan's approval:

> For brave Macbeth (well he deserves that name),
> Disdaining Fortune, with his brandish'd steel,
> Which smok'd with bloody execution,
> Like Valour's minion, carv'd out his passage,
> Till he fac'd the slave;
> which ne'er shook hands, nor bade farewell to him,
> Till he unseam'd him from the nave to th' chops,
> And fix'd his head upon our battlements.
> *Duncan.* O valiant cousin! worthy gentleman!
>
> (I.ii.16-24)[1]

Violence is good, in this view, when it is in the service of the prevailing dispositions of power; when it disrupts them it is evil. A claim to a monopoly of legitimate violence is fundamental in the development of the modern State; when that claim is successful, most citizens learn to regard State violence as qualitatively different from other violence and perhaps they don't think of State violence as violence at all (consider the actions of police, army and judiciary as opposed to those of pickets, protesters, criminals and terrorists). *Macbeth* focusses major strategies by which the State asserted its claim at one conjuncture.

Generally in Europe in the sixteenth century the development was from Feudalism to the Absolutist State.[2] Under Feudalism, the king held authority among his peers, his equals, and his power was often little more than nominal; authority was distributed also among overlapping non-national institutions such as the church, estates, assemblies, regions and towns. In the Absolutist State, power became centralised in the figure of the monarch, the exclusive source of legitimacy. The movement from one to the other was of course contested, not only by the aristocracy and the peasantry, whose traditional rights were threatened, but also by the gentry and urban bourgeoisie, who found new space for power and influence within more elaborate economic and governmental structures. Because of these latter factors especially, the Absolutist State was never fully established in England. Probably the peak of the monarch's personal power was reached by Henry VIII; the attempt of Charles I to reassert that power led to the English Revolution. In between, Elizabeth and James I, and those who believed their interests to lie in the same direction, sought to sustain royal power and to suppress dissidents. The latter category was broad; it comprised aristocrats like the Earls of Northumberland and Westmorland who led the Northern Rising of 1569 and the Duke of Norfolk who plotted to replace Elizabeth with Mary Queen of Scots in 1571, clergy who refused the State religion, gentry who supported them and who tried to raise awkward matters in Parliament, writers and printers who published criticism of State policy, the populace when it complained about food prices, enclosures, or anything.

The exercise of State violence against such dissidents depended upon the achievement of a degree of legitimation—upon the acceptance by many people that State power was, at least, the lesser of two evils. A principal means by which this was effected was the propagation of an ideology of Absolutism, which represented the English State as a pyramid, any disturbance of which would produce general disaster, and which insisted increasingly on the 'divine right' of the monarch. This system was said to be 'natural' and ordained by 'God'; it was 'good' and disruptions of it 'evil'. This is what some Shakespeareans have celebrated as a just and harmonious 'world picture'. Compare Perry Anderson's summary: 'Absolutism was essentially just this: *a redeployed and recharged apparatus of feudal domination,* designed to clamp the peasant masses back into their traditional social position.'[3]

The reason why the State needed violence and propaganda was that the system was subject to persistent structural difficulties. *Macbeth,* like very many plays of the period, handles anxieties about the violence exercised under the aegis of Absolutist ideology. Two main issues come into focus. The first is the threat of a split between legitimacy and actual power—when the monarch is not the strongest person in the State. Such a split was altogether likely during the transition from Feudalism to the Absolutist State; hence the infighting within the dominant group in most European countries. In England the matter was topical because of the Essex rebellion in 1599: it was easy for the charismatic earl, who had shown at Cadiz that Englishmen could defeat Spaniards, to suppose that he would make a better ruler than the aging and indecisive Elizabeth, for all her legitimacy. So Shakespeare's Richard II warns Northumberland, the kingmaker, that he is bound, structurally, to disturb the rule of Bolingbroke:

> thou shalt think,
> Though he [Bolingbroke] divide the realm and give thee half,
> It is too little, helping him to all.[4]

Jonathan Dollimore and I have argued elsewhere that the potency of the myth of Henry V in Shakespeare's play, written at the time of Essex's ascendancy, derives from the striking combination in that monarch of legitimacy and actual power.[5] At the start of *Macbeth* the manifest dependency of Duncan's State upon its best fighter sets up a dangerous instability (this is explicit in the sources). In the opening soliloquy of Act I scene vii Macbeth freely accords to Duncan entire legitimacy: he is Duncan's kinsman, subject and host, the king has been 'clear in his great office', and the idea of his deposition evokes religious imagery of angels, damnation and cherubins. But that is all the power the king has that does not depend upon Macbeth; against it is ranged 'Vaulting ambition', Macbeth's impetus to convert his actual power into full regal authority.

The split between legitimacy and actual power was always a potential malfunction in the developing Absolutist State. A second problem was less dramatic but more persistent. It was this: what is the difference between Absolutism and tyranny?—having in mind contemporary occurrences like the Massacre of St Bartholomew's in France in 1572, the arrest of more than a hundred witches and the torturing and killing of many of them in Scotland in 1590-91, and the suppression of the Irish by English armies. The immediate reference for questions of legitimate violence in relation to *Macbeth* is the Gunpowder Plot of 1605. This attempted violence against the State followed upon many years of State violence against Roman Catholics: the Absolutist State sought to draw religious institutions entirely within its control, and Catholics who actively refused were subjected to fines, imprisonment, torture and execution. Consider the sentence passed upon Jane Wiseman in 1598:

> The sentence is that the said Jane Wiseman shall be led to the prison of the Marshalsea of the Queen's Bench, and there naked, except for a linen cloth about the lower part of her body, be laid upon the ground, lying directly on her back: and a hollow shall be made under her head and her head placed in the same; and upon her body in every part let there be placed as much of stones and iron as she can bear and more; and as long as she shall live, she shall have of the worst bread and water of the prison next her; and on the day she eats, she shall not drink, and on the day she drinks she shall not eat, so living until she die.[6]

This was for 'receiving, comforting, helping and maintaining priests', and refusing to reveal, under torture, who else was doing the same thing, and for refusing to plead. There is nothing abstract or theoretical about the State violence to which the present essay refers. Putting the issue succinctly in relation to Shakespeare's play, what is the difference between Macbeth's rule and that of contemporary European monarchs?

In *Basilikon Doron* (1599) King James tried to protect the Absolutist State from such pertinent questions by asserting an utter distinction between 'a lawfull good King' and 'an usurping Tyran':

> The one acknowledgeth himselfe ordained for his people, having received from God a burthen of government, whereof he must be countable: the other thinketh his people ordeined for him, a prey to his passions and inordinate appetites, as the fruites of his magnanimitie: And therefore, as their ends are directly contrarie, so are their whole actions, as meanes, whereby they preasse to attaine to their endes.[7]

Evidently James means to deny that the Absolutist monarch has anything significant in common with someone like Macbeth. Three aspects of James's strategy in this passage are particularly revealing. First, he depends upon an utter polarisation between the two kinds of ruler. Such antitheses are characteristic of the ideology of Absolutism: they were called upon to tidy the uneven apparatus of Feudal power into a far neater structure of the monarch versus the rest, and protestantism tended to see 'spiritual' identities in similarly polarised terms. James himself explained the function of demons like this: 'since the Devill is the verie contrarie opposite to God, there can be no better way to know God, then by the contrarie'.[8] So it is with the two kinds of rulers: the badness of one seems to guarantee the goodness of the other. Second, by defining the lawful good king against the usurping tyrant, James refuses to admit the possibility that a ruler who has *not* usurped will be tyrannical. Thus he seems to cope with potential splits between legitimacy and actual power by insisting on the unique status of the lawful good king, and to head off questions about the violence committed by such a ruler by suggesting that all his actions will be uniquely legitimate. Third, we may notice that the whole distinction, as James develops it, is in terms not of the *behaviour* of the lawful good king and the usurping tyrant, respectively, but in terms of their *motives*. This seems to render vain any assessment of the actual manner of rule of the Absolute monarch. On these arguments, any disturbance of the current structure of power relations is against God and the people, and consequently any violence in the interest of the status quo is acceptable. Hence the legitimate killing of Jane Wiseman. (In fact, the distinction between lawful and tyrannical rule eventually breaks down even in James's analysis, as his commitment to the State leads him to justify even tyrannical behaviour in established monarchs.)[9]

It is often assumed that *Macbeth* is engaged in the same project as King James: attempting to render coherent and persuasive the ideology of the Absolutist State. The grounds for a Jamesian reading are plain enough—to the point where it is often claimed that the play was designed specially for the king. At every opportunity Macbeth is disqualified ideologically and his opponents ratified. An entire antithetical apparatus of nature and supernature—the concepts through which a dominant ideology most commonly seeks to establish itself—is called upon to witness against him as usurping tyrant. 'Nature' protests against Macbeth (II.iv), Lady Macbeth welcomes 'Nature's mischief' (I.v.50) and Macbeth will have 'Nature's germens tumble all together, / Even till destruction sicken' (IV.i.59-60). Good and evil are personified absolutely by Edward the Confessor and the Witches, and the language of heaven and hell runs through the play; Lady Macbeth conjures up 'murth'ring ministers' (I.v.48) and Macbeth acknowledges 'The deep damnation of his [Duncan's] taking-off' (I.vii.20). It all seems organised to validate James's contention, that there is all the difference in this world and the next between a usurping tyrant and a lawful good king. The whole strategy is epitomised in the account of Edward's alleged curing of 'the Evil'—actually scrofula—'A most miraculous work in this good King' (IV.iii.146-7). James himself knew that this was a superstitious practice, and he refused to undertake it until his advisers persuaded him that it would strengthen his claim to the throne in the public eye.[10] As Francis Bacon observed, notions of the supernatural help to keep people acquiescent (e.g. the man in pursuit of power will do well to attribute his success 'rather to divine Providence and felicity, than to his own virtue or policy').[11] *Macbeth* draws upon such notions more than any other play by Shakespeare. It all suggests that Macbeth is an extraordinary eruption in a good State—obscuring the thought that there might be any pronity to structural malfunctioning in the system. It suggests that Macbeth's violence is wholly bad, whereas State violence committed by legitimate monarchs is quite different.

Such manoeuvres are even more necessary to a Jamesian reading of the play in respect of the deposition and killing of Macbeth. Absolutist ideology declared that even tyrannical monarchs must not be resisted, yet Macbeth could hardly be allowed to triumph. Here the play offers two moves. First, the fall of Macbeth seems to result more from (super)natural than human agency: it seems like an effect of the opposition of good and evil ('Macbeth / Is ripe for shaking, and the Powers above / Put on their instruments'—IV.iii.237-9). Most cunningly, although there are material explanations for the moving of Birnam Wood and the unusual birth of Macduff, the audience is allowed to believe, at the same time, that these are (super)natural effects (thus the play works upon us almost as the Witches work upon Macbeth). Second, in so far as Macbeth's fall is accomplished by human agency, the play is careful to suggest that he is hardly in office before he is overthrown. The years of successful rule specified in the chronicles are erased and, as Paul points out, neither Macduff nor Malcolm has tendered any allegiance to Macbeth.[12] The action rushes along, he is swept away as if he had never truly been king. *Even so,* the contradiction can hardly vanish altogether. For the Jamesian reading it is necessary for Macbeth to be a complete usurping tyrant in order that he shall set off the lawful good king, and also, at the same time, for him not to be a ruler at all in order that he may properly be deposed and killed. Macbeth kills two people at the start of the play: a rebel and the king, and these are apparently utterly different acts of violence. That is the ideology of Absolutism. Macduff also, killing Macbeth, is killing both a rebel and a king, but now the two are apparently the same person. The ultimate intractability of this kind of contradiction disturbs the Jamesian reading of the play.

Criticism has often supposed, all too easily, that the Jamesian reading of *Macbeth* is necessary on historical grounds—that other views of State ideology were impossible for Shakespeare and his contemporaries. But this was far from being so: there was a well-developed theory allowing for resistance by the nobility,[13] and the Gunpowder Plotters were manifestly unconvinced by the king's arguments. Even more pertinent is the theory of the Scotsman George Buchanan, as we may deduce from the fact that James tried to suppress Buchanan's writings in 1584 after his assumption of personal rule; in *Basilikon Doron* he advises his son to 'use the Law upon the keepers' of 'such infamous invectives' (p. 40). With any case so strenuously overstated and manipulative as James's, we should ask what alternative position it is trying to put down. Arguments in favour of Absolutism constitute one part of *Macbeth*'s ideological field—the range of ideas and attitudes brought into play by the text; another main part may be represented by Buchanan's *De jure regni* (1579) and *History of Scotland* (1582). In Buchanan's view sovereignty derives from and remains with the people; the king who exercises power against their will is a tyrant and should be deposed.[14] The problem in Scotland is not unruly subjects, but unruly monarchs: 'Rebellions there spring less from the people than from the rulers, when they try to reduce a kingdom which from earliest times had always been ruled by law to an absolute and lawless despotism'.[15] Buchanan's theory is the virtual antithesis of James's; it was used eventually to justify the deposition of James's son.

Buchanan's *History of Scotland* is usually reckoned to be one of the sources of *Macbeth*. It was written to illustrate his theory of sovereignty and to justify the overthrow of Mary Queen of Scots in 1567. In it the dichotomy of true lawful king and usurping tyrant collapses, for Mary is the lawful ruler *and* the tyrant, and her deposers are usurpers *and yet* lawful also. To her are attributed many of the traits of Macbeth: she is said to hate integrity in others, to appeal to the predictions of witches, to use foreign mercenaries, to place spies in the households of opponents and to threaten the lives of the nobility; after her surrender she is humiliated in the streets of Edinburgh as Macbeth fears to be. It is alleged that she would not have shrunk from the murder of her son if she could have reached him.[16] This account of Mary as arch-tyrant embarrassed James, and that is perhaps why just eight kings are shown to Macbeth by the Witches (IV.i.119). Nevertheless, it was well established in protestant propaganda and in Spenser's *Faerie Queene,* and the Gunpowder Plot would tend to revivify it. Any recollection of the alleged tyranny of Mary, the lawful ruler, prompts awareness of the contradictions in Absolutist ideology, disturbing the customary interpretation of *Macbeth.* Once we are alert to this disturbance, the Jamesian reading of the play begins to leak at every joint.

One set of difficulties is associated with the theology of good, evil and divine ordination which purports to discriminate Macbeth's violence from that legitimately deployed by the State. I have written elsewhere of the distinctive attempt of Reformation Christianity to cope with the paradoxical conjunction in one deity of total power and goodness, and will here only indicate the scope of the problem. *Macbeth,* in the manner of Absolutist ideology and Reformation Christianity, strongly polarises 'good' and 'evil', but, at the same time, also like the prevailing doctrine, it insists on complete divine control of all human events. This twin determination produces a deity that sponsors the 'evil' it condemns and punishes. Orthodox doctrine, which was Calvinist in general orientation, hardly flinched from this conclusion (for example, James said in his *Daemonologie* that fallen angels are 'Gods hang-men, to execute such turnes as he employes them in').[17] Nevertheless, fictional reworkings of it often seem to point up its awkwardness, suggesting an unresolvable anxiety. Traditional criticism registers this factor in *Macbeth* in its inconclusive debates about how far the Witches make Macbeth more or less excusable or in charge of his own destiny. The projection of political issues onto supposedly (super)natural dimensions seems to ratify the Absolutist State but threatens also to open up another range of difficulties in contemporary ideology.

Macbeth also reveals a range of directly political problems to the reader rendered wary by Buchanan's analysis. They tend to break down the antithesis, upon which James relied, between the usurping tyrant and the legitimately violent ruler. Many of them have been noted by critics, though most commonly with the idea of getting them to fit into a single, coherent reading of the play. For a start, Duncan's status is in doubt: it is unclear how far his authority runs, he is imperceptive, and his State is in chaos well before Macbeth's violence against it (G. K. Hunter in the introduction to his Penguin edition (1967) registers unease at the 'violence and bloodthirstiness' of Macbeth's killing of Macdonwald (pp. 9-10)). Nor is Malcolm's title altogether clear, since Duncan's declaration of him as 'Prince of Cumberland' (I.iv.35-42) suggests what the chronicles indicate, namely that the succession was not necessarily hereditary; Macbeth seems to be elected by the thanes (II.iv.29-32).

I have suggested that *Macbeth* may be read as working to justify the overthrow of the usurping tyrant. Nevertheless, the *awkwardness* of the issue is brought to the surface by the uncertain behaviour of Banquo. In the sources he collaborates with Macbeth, but to allow that in the play would taint King James's line and blur the idea of the one monstrous eruption. Shakespeare compromises and makes Banquo do nothing at all. He fears Macbeth played 'most foully for't' (III.i.3) but does not even communicate his knowledge of the Witches' prophecies. Instead he wonders if they may 'set me up in hope' (III.i.10). If it is right for Malcolm and Macduff, eventually, to overthrow Macbeth, then it would surely be right for Banquo to take a clearer line.

Furthermore, the final position of Macduff appears quite disconcerting, once we read it with Buchanan's more realistic, political analysis in mind: Macduff at the end stands in the same relation to Malcolm as Macbeth did to Duncan in the beginning. He is now the king-maker on whom the legitimate monarch depends, and the recurrence of the whole sequence may be anticipated (in production this might be suggested by a final meeting of Macduff and the Witches).[18] For the Jamesian reading it is necessary to feel that Macbeth is a distinctively 'evil' eruption in a 'good' system; awareness of the role of Macduff in Malcolm's State alerts us to the fundamental instability of power relations during the transition to Absolutism, and consequently to the uncertain validity of the claim of the State to the legitimate use of violence. Certainly Macbeth is a murderer and an oppressive ruler, but he is one version of the Absolutist ruler, not the polar opposite.

Malcolm himself raises very relevant issues in the conversation in which he tests Macduff: specifically tyrannical qualities are invoked. At one point, according to Buchanan, the Scottish lords 'give the benefit of the doubt' to Mary and her husband, following the thought that 'more secret faults' may be tolerated 'so long as these do not involve a threat to the welfare of the state' (*Tyrannous Reign*, p. 88). Macduff is prepared to accept considerable threats to the welfare of Scotland:

> Boundless intemperance
> In nature is a tyranny; it hath been
> Th' untimely emptying of the happy throne,
> And fall of many kings. But fear not yet
> To take upon you what is yours: you may
> Convey your pleasures in a spacious plenty,
> And yet seem cold—the time you may so hoodwink:
> We have willing dames enough; there cannot be
> That vulture in you, to devour so many
> As will to greatness dedicate themselves,
> Finding it so inclin'd.
>
> (IV.iii.66-76)

Tyranny in nature means disturbance in the metaphorical kingdom of a person's nature but, in the present context, one is likely to think of the effects of the monarch's intemperance on the literal kingdom. Macduff suggests that such behaviour has caused the fall not just of usurpers but of kings, occupants of 'the happy throne'. Despite this danger, he encourages Malcolm 'To take upon you what is yours'—a sinister way of putting it, implying either Malcolm's title to the State in general or his rights over the women he wants to seduce or assault. Fortunately the latter will not be necessary, there are 'willing dames enough': Macduff is ready to mortgage both the bodies and (within the ideology invoked in the play) the souls of women to the monster envisaged as lawful good king. It will be all right, apparently, because people can be hoodwinked: Macduff allows us to see that the virtues James tries to identify with the Absolutist monarch are an ideological strategy, and that the illusion of them will probably be sufficient to keep the system going.

Nor is this the worst: Malcolm claims more faults, and according to Macduff 'avarice / Sticks deeper' (lines 84-5): Malcolm may corrupt not merely people but property relations. Yet this too is to be condoned. Of course, Malcolm is not actually like this, but the point is that he well could be, as Macduff says many kings have been, and that would all be acceptable. And even Malcolm's eventual protestation of innocence cannot get round the fact that he has been lying. He says 'my first false speaking / Was this upon myself' (lines 130-1) and that may indeed be true, but it nevertheless indicates the circumspection that will prove useful to the lawful good king, as much as to the tyrant. In Holinshed the culminating vice claimed by Malcolm is lying, but Shakespeare replaces it with a general and rather desperate evocation of utter tyranny (lines 91-100); was the original self-accusation perhaps too pointed? The whole conversation takes off from the specific and incomparable tyranny of Macbeth, but in the process succeeds in suggesting that there may be considerable overlap between the qualities of the tyrant and the true king.

Macbeth allows space for two quite different interpretive organizations: against a Jamesian illustration of the virtues of Absolutism we may produce a disturbance of that reading, illuminated by Buchanan. This latter makes visible the way religion is used to underpin State ideology, and undermines notions that established monarchs must not be challenged or removed and that State violence is utterly distinctive and legitimate. It is commonly assumed that the function of criticism is to resolve such questions of interpretation—to go through the text with an eye to sources, other plays, theatrical convention, historical context and so on, deciding on which side the play comes down and explaining away contrary evidence. However, this is neither an adequate programme nor an adequate account of what generally happens.

Let us suppose, to keep the argument moving along, that the Jamesian reading fits better with *Macbeth* and its Jacobean context, as we understand them at present. Two questions then present themselves: what is the status of the disturbance of that reading, which I have produced by bringing Buchanan into view? And what are the consequences of customary critical insistence upon the Jamesian reading?

On the first question, I would make three points. First, the Buchanan disturbance *is in the play,* and inevitably so. Even if we believe that Shakespeare was trying to smooth over difficulties in Absolutist ideology, to do this significantly he must deal with the issues which resist convenient inclusion. Those issues must be brought into visibility in order that they can be handled, and once exposed they are available for the reader or audience to seize and focus upon, as an alternative to the more complacent reading. A position tends to suppose an *op*position. Even James's writings are vulnerable to such analysis, for instance when he brings up the awkward fact that the prophet Samuel urgently warns the people of Israel against choosing a king because he will tyrannize over them. This prominent biblical instance could hardly be ignored, so James quotes it and says that Samuel was preparing the Israelites to be obedient and patient.[19] Yet once James has brought Samuel's pronouncement into visibility, the reader is at liberty to doubt the king's tendentious interpretation of it. It is hardly possible to deny the reader this scope: even the most strenuous closure can be repudiated as inadequate. We are led to think of the text not as propounding a unitary and coherent meaning which is to be discovered, but as handling a range of issues (probably intractable issues, for they make the best stories), and as unable to control the development of radically divergent interpretations.

Second, the Buchanan disturbance has been activated, in the present essay, as a consequence of the writer's scepticism about Jamesian ideological strategies and his concern with current political issues. It is conceivable that many readers of *Macbeth* will come to share this outlook. Whether this happens or not, the theoretical implication may be taken: if such a situation should come about, the terms in which *Macbeth* is customarily discussed would shift, and eventually the Buchanan disturbance would come to seem an obvious, natural way to consider the play. That is how notions of appropriate approaches to a text get established. We may observe the process, briefly, in the career of the Witches. For many members of Jacobean audiences, Witches were a social and spiritual reality: they were as real as Edward the Confessor, perhaps more so. As belief in the physical manifestation of supernatural powers, and especially demonic powers, weakened, the Witches were turned into an operatic display, with new scenes, singing and dancing, fine costumes and flying machines. In an adaptation by Sir William Davenant, this was the only stage form of the play from 1674 to 1744, and even after Davenant's version was abandoned the Witches' divertissements were stagged, until 1888.[20] Latterly we have adopted other ways with the Witches—being still unable, of course, to contemplate them, as most of Shakespeare's audience probably did, as phenomena one might encounter on a heath. Kenneth Muir comments: 'with the fading of belief in the objective existence of devils, they and their operations can yet symbolize the workings of evil in the hearts of men' (New Arden *Macbeth,* p. lxx). Recent critical accounts and theatrical productions have developed all kinds of strategies to make the Witches 'work' for our time. These successive accommodations of one aspect of the play to prevailing attitudes are blatant, but they illustrate the extent to which critical orthodoxy is not the mere response to the text which it claims to be: it is *remaking* it within currently acceptable parameters.[21] The Buchanan disturbance may not always remain a marginal gloss to the Jamesian reading.

Third, we may assume that the Buchanan disturbance was part of the response of some among the play's initial audiences. It is in the nature of the matter that it is impossible to assess how many people inclined towards Buchanan's analysis of royal power. That there were such may be supposed from the multifarious challenges to State authority—culminating, of course, in the Civil War. *Macbeth* was almost certainly read against James by some Jacobeans. This destroys the claim to privilege of the Jamesian reading on the ground that it is historically valid: we must envisage diverse original audiences, activating diverse implications in the text. And we may demand comparable interpretive license for ourselves. Initially the play occupied a complex position in its ideological field, and we should expect no less today.

With these considerations about the status of the Buchanan disturbance in mind, the question about the customary insistence on the Jamesian reading appears as a question about the politics of criticism. Like other kinds of cultural production, literary criticism helps to influence the way people think about the world; that is why the present essay seeks to make space for an oppositional understanding of the text and the State. It is plain that most criticism has not only reproduced but endorsed Jamesian ideology, so discouraging scrutiny, which *Macbeth* can promote, of the legitimacy of State violence. That we are dealing with live issues is shown by the almost uncanny resemblances between the Gunpowder Plot and the 1984 Brighton Bombing, and in the comparable questions about State and other violence which they raise. My concluding thoughts are about the politics of the prevailing readings of *Macbeth*. I distinguish conservative and liberal positions; both tend to dignify their accounts with the honorific term 'tragedy'.

The conservative position insists that the play is about 'evil'. Kenneth Muir offers a string of quotations to this effect: it is 'Shakespeare's "most profound and mature vision of evil"; "the whole play may be writ down as a wrestling of destruction with creation"; it is "a statement of evil"; "it is a picture of a special battle in a universal war . . ."; and it "contains the decisive orientation of Shakespearean good and evil"'.[22] This is little more than Jamesian ideology writ large: killing Macdonwald is 'good' and killing Duncan is 'evil', and the hierarchical society envisaged in Absolutist ideology is identified with the requirements of nature, supernature and the 'human condition'. Often this view is elaborated as a socio-political programme, allegedly expounded by Shakespeare and implicitly endorsed by the critic. So Muir writes of 'an orderly and closely-knit society, in contrast to the disorder consequent upon Macbeth's initial crime [i.e. killing Duncan, not Macdonwald]. The naturalness of that order, and the unnaturalness of its violation by Macbeth, is emphasized . . .' (New Arden *Macbeth*, p. li). Irving Ribner says Fleance is 'symbolic of a future rooted in the acceptance of natural law, which inevitably must return to reassert God's harmonious order when evil has worked itself out'.[23]

This conservative endorsement of Jamesian ideology is not intended to ratify the Modern State. Rather, like much twentieth-century literary criticism, it is backward-looking, appealing to an earlier and preferable supposed condition of society. Roger Scruton comments: 'If a conservative is also a restorationist, this is because he lives close to society, and feels in himself the sickness which infects the common order. How, then, can he fail to direct his eyes towards that state of health from which things have declined?'[24] This quotation is close to the terms in which many critics write of *Macbeth*, and their evocation of the Jamesian order which is allegedly restored at the end of the play constitutes a wistful gesture towards what they would regard as a happy ending for our troubled society. However, because this conservative approach is based on an inadequate analysis of political and social process, it gains no purchase on the main determinants of State power.

A liberal position hesitates to endorse any State power so directly, finding some saving virtue in Macbeth: 'To the end he never totally loses our sympathy'; 'we must still not lose our sympathy for the criminal'.[25] In this view there is a flaw in the State, it fails to accommodate the particular consciousness of the refined individual. Macbeth's imagination is set against the blandness of normative convention and for all his transgressions, perhaps because of them, Macbeth transcends the laws he breaks. In John Bayley's version: 'His superiority consists in a passionate sense for ordinary life, its seasons and priorities, a sense which his fellows in the play ignore in themselves or take for granted. Through the deed which tragedy requires of him he comes to know not only himself, but what life is all about.'[26] I call this 'liberal' because it is anxious about a State, Absolutist or Modern, which can hardly take cognizance of the individual sensibility, and it is prepared to validate to some degree the recalcitrant individual. But it will not undertake the political analysis which would press the case. Hence there is always in such criticism a reservation about Macbeth's revolt and a sense of relief that it ends in defeat: nothing could have been done anyway, it was all inevitable, written in the human condition. This retreat from the possibility of political analysis and action leaves the State virtually unquestioned, almost as fully as the conservative interpretation.

Shakespeare, notoriously, has a way of anticipating all possibilities. The idea of literary intellectuals identifying their own deepest intuitions of the universe in the experience of the 'great' tragic hero who defies the limits of the human condition is surely a little absurd; we may sense delusions of grandeur. *Macbeth* includes much more likely models for its conservative and liberal critics in the characters of the two doctors. The English Doctor has just four and a half lines (IV.iii.141-5) in which he says King Edward is coming and that sick people whose malady conquers the greatest efforts of medical skill await him, expecting a heavenly cure for 'evil'. Malcolm, the king to be, says 'I thank you, Doctor'. This doctor is the equivalent of conservative intellectuals who encourage respect for mystificatory images of ideal hierarchy which have served the State in the past, and who invoke 'evil', 'tragedy' and 'the human condition' to produce, in effect, acquiescence in State power.

The Scottish Doctor, in V.i and V.iii, is actually invited to cure the sickness of the rulers and by implication the State: 'If thou couldst, Doctor, cast / The water of my land, find her disease . . .' (V.iii.50-1). But this doctor, like the liberal intellectual, hesitates to press an analysis. He says: 'This disease is beyond my practice' (V.i.56), 'I think, but dare not speak' (V.i.76), 'Therein the patient / Must minister to himself' (V.iii.45-6), 'Were I from Dunsinane away and clear, / Profit again should hardly draw me here' (V.iii.61-2). He wrings his hands at the evidence of State violence and protects his conscience with asides. This is like the liberal intellectual who knows there is something wrong at the heart of the system but will not envisage a radical alternative and, to ratify this attitude, discovers in Shakespeare's plays 'tragedy' and 'the human condition' as explanations of the supposedly inevitable defeat of the person who steps out of line.

By conventional standards, the present essay is perverse. But an oppositional criticism is bound to appear thus: its task is to work across the grain of customary assumptions and, if necessary, across the grain of the text, as it is customarily perceived. Of course, literary intellectuals don't have much influence over State violence, their therapeutic power is very limited. Nevertheless, writing, teaching, and other modes of communicating all contribute to the steady, long-term formation of opinion, to the establishment of legitimacy. This contribution King James himself did not neglect. An oppositional analysis of texts like *Macbeth* will read them to expose, rather than promote, State ideologies.

Notes

1. *Macbeth* is quoted from the New Arden Shakespeare, 9th edn., ed. Kenneth Muir (London: Methuen, 1962).

2. See Nicos Poulantzas, *Political Power and Social Classes,* translation editor Timothy O'Hagan (London: New Left Books, 1973), pp. 157-68; Perry Anderson, *Lineages of the Absolute State* (London: New Left Books, 1974).

3. Anderson, *Lineages of the Absolute State,* p. 18. For further studies of the scope of Absolutist ideology in England see V. G. Kiernan, 'State and nation in Western Europe', *Past and Present,* 31 (1965), 20-38; W. T. MacCaffrey, 'England: the Crown and the new aristocracy, 1540-1600', *Past and Present,* 30 (1965), 52-64; Alan Sinfield, 'Power and ideology: an outline theory and Sidney's *Arcadia*', *English Literary History,* 52 (1985), 259-77. On attitudes to government and *Macbeth* see Michael Hawkins, 'History, politics and *Macbeth*' in *Focus on 'Macbeth',* ed. John Russell Brown (London: Routledge, 1982).

4. *King Richard II,* ed. Peter Ure, New Arden edn. (London: Methuen, 1956), V.i.59-61.

5. Jonathan Dollimore and Alan Sinfield, 'History and ideology: the instance of *Henry V*', in *Alternative Shakespeares,* ed. John Drakakis (London: Methuen, 1985).

6. John Gerard, *The Autobiography of an Elizabethan,* trans. Philip Caraman (London: Longman, 1951), pp. 52-3.

7. *The Political Works of James I,* ed. Charles Howard McIlwain (New York: Russell and Russell, 1965), p. 18.

8. King James the First, *Daemonologie (1597), Newes from Scotland (1591)* (London: Bodley Head, 1924), p. 55.

9. See James, *The Trew Law of Free Monarchies,* in *Political Works,* ed. McIlwain, pp. 56-61, 66.

10. Henry Paul, *The Royal Play of 'Macbeth'* (New York: Octagon Books, 1978), p. 373.

11. Francis Bacon, *Essays,* introduction by Michael J. Hawkins (London: Dent, 1972). See further Jonathan Dollimore, *Radical Tragedy* (Brighton: Harvester, 1984), specially ch. 5; Alan Sinfield, *Literature in Protestant England 1560-1660* (London: Croom Helm, 1983), ch. 7.

12. Paul, *The Royal Play of 'Macbeth',* p. 196.

13. See W. D. Briggs, 'Political ideas in Sidney's *Arcadia*', *Studies in Philology,* 28 (1931) 137-61, and 'Philip Sidney's political ideas', *ibid.,* 29 (1932), 534-42.

14. See *The Tyrannous Reign of Mary Stewart, George Buchanan's Account,* trans. and ed. W. A. Gatherer (Edinburgh University Press, 1958), pp. 12-3; James E. Phillips, 'George Buchanan and the Sidney circle', *Huntington Library Quarterly,* 12 (1948/9), 23-55; I. D. McFarlane, *Buchanan* (London: Duckworth, 1981), pp. 392-440.

15. *The Tyrannous Reign of Mary Stewart,* p. 49; see also p. 99.

16. *The Tyrannous Reign of Mary Stewart,* pp. 72, 86, 91, 111, 119, 145, 153; cf. *Macbeth,* III.i.48-56; V.vii.17-8; III.v.130-1; V.viii.27-9.

17. King James, *Daemonologie,* p. 20. See further Sinfield, *Literature in Protestant England,* specially chapters 2, 6.

18. However, as Jim McLaverty points out to me, the play has arranged that Macduff will not experience temptation from his wife. In the chronicles Malcolm's son is overthrown by Donalbain; in Polanski's film of *Macbeth* Donalbain is made to meet the Witches.

19. *The Trew Law of Free Monarchies,* in *Political Works,* ed. McIlwain, pp. 56-61; referring to I Sam. 8:9-20.

20. See Hunter, *Macbeth,* Penguin edition, pp. 33-4; Dennis Bartholomeusz, *'Macbeth' and the Players* (Cambridge University Press, 1969). On the Witches and the ideological roles of women in the play see Peter Stallybrass, '*Macbeth* and witchcraft', in Brown, ed., *Focus on 'Macbeth'.*

21. See further Jonathan Dollimore and Alan Sinfield, eds., *Political Shakespeare* (Manchester University Press, 1985), chs. 7, 9, 10.

22. Muir in the New Arden *Macbeth,* p. xlix, quoting G. Wilson Knight, L. C. Knights, F. C. Kolbe, Derek Traversi. See also Irving Ribner, *Patterns in Shakespearean Tragedy* (London: Methuen, 1960), p. 153; Robert Ornstein, *The Moral Vision of Jacobean Tragedy* (University of Wisconsin, 1965), p. 230; Hunter, Penguin edition, p. 7.

23. Ribner, *Patterns in Shakespearean Tragedy,* p. 159.

24. Roger Scruton, *The Meaning of Conservatism* (Harmondsworth: Penguin, 1980), p. 21.

25. A. C. Bradley, *Shakespearean Tragedy,* 2nd edn. (London: Macmillan, 1965), p. 305; Wayne Booth, '*Macbeth* as tragic hero', *Journal of General Education,* 6 (1951), revised for *Shakespeare's Tragedies,* ed. Laurence Lerner (Harmondsworth: Penguin, 1963), p. 186. See also Hunter, Penguin edition, pp. 26-9; Wilbur Sanders, *The Dramatist*

and the Received Idea (Cambridge University Press, 1968), pp. 282-307.

26. John Bayley, *Shakespeare and Tragedy* (London: Routledge, 1981), p. 199; see also p. 193. I am grateful for the stimulating comments of Russell Jackson, Tony Inglis, Peter Holland and Jonathan Dollimore.

Barbara Riebling (essay date 1991)

SOURCE: "Virtue's Sacrifice: A Machiavellian Reading of *Macbeth*," in *Studies in English Literature 1500-1900,* Vol. 31, No. 2, Spring, 1991, pp. 273-86.

[*In the following essay, Riebling analyzes* Macbeth *as a discourse in civic humanism, contrasting the principles of Machiavellian governance to those of Christianity.*]

"I love my city more than I love my soul," Machiavelli wrote in a letter to a friend. If we take him at his word—including the belief that he has a soul—Machiavelli is describing the ultimate patriotic sacrifice. In both of his major theoretical works, *The Prince* and *The Discourses,* he presents this sacrifice as more likely the deeper one ventures into politics, and as virtually unavoidable for the prince. Machiavelli's works shocked sixteenth-century audiences, who were accustomed to seeing Christian and civic virtue as interchangeable; in his version of truth, "la verità effettuale," political *virtù* is ineluctably at odds with religion and its rules. The English were particularly appalled by Machiavelli's ideas; hence the enormous popularity in the late sixteenth century of the villainous "stage Machiavel." For centuries medieval and Renaissance citizens had been assured of an essential harmony between religious and political truths—any apparent conflicts were resolved either by a rejection of worldly values or their procrustean fit to the Decalogue. English audiences by Shakespeare's time would have been familiar with a number of traditional religio-political models: the *de casibus* theme carried forward from Boccaccio through writers like Lydgate, that valorizes the contemplative life and presents earthly power and glory as transitory vanities; the providential view of political history in works like *Mirror for Magistrates* or the play *Cambises,* that sees divine justice acted out in the political realm; the picture of virtuous statecraft drawn by Christian humanists like Thomas Elyot and Erasmus, who equate effective rule with upright behavior and advise the prince to be nothing more nor less than a good Christian. In sharp contrast, Machiavelli boldly states that any prince who would take such advice and let go of what *is* done for what *should* be done studies his own ruin (*The Prince,* 15). In *The Discourses* he even goes so far as to blame Christianity for the triumph of evil in contemporary politics.[1] Clearly, Machiavelli's views are not in harmony with the religious beliefs of his time. After his advent, Renaissance audiences are confronted by two antipathetic philosophies of state. Political life is played out either in a world bound to Christian rules of conduct or a delegitimized world cut loose from any rule but survival. The question I would like to raise is: which world does *Macbeth* inhabit?

For many years *Macbeth* was read as one of Shakespeare's most unambiguous works and analyzed as if it were a political-moral fable.[2] More recent scholarship has attempted to place *Macbeth* within the context of conflicting ideologies of early seventeenth-century England and Scotland—as a response, for instance, to the clash of absolutism and resistance theory.[3] I would like to suggest another context for the politics of the play, the discourse of civic humanism. In this context, *Macbeth* can be read specifically as a response to Machiavelli's most controversial models for effective rule. By the beginning of the seventeenth century in England, the real Machiavelli started to replace the "Machiavel," opening the way for both the republicanism of *The Discourses* and the "ragione di stato" arguments in *The Prince.*[4] An analysis of the portraits of kingship in *Macbeth* suggests that the play participates in this shift in political consciousness, reflecting standards of conduct that are far more Machiavellian than Christian.

Political tragedy studies the consequences of misrule, and *Macbeth* is no exception, censuring two extremes in civic malpractice. Although the majority of the play is taken up with Macbeth's criminal reign—a regime at odds with both Machiavellian and Christian precepts—*Macbeth* begins its exploration of tragic politics in Duncan's chaotic realm, presenting a brief but succinct portrait of the consequences of political innocence. Measured by traditional Christian values, Duncan's behavior is impeccable. By Machiavellian standards, it is a menace to himself and his people. Because Duncan's kingship can be admired from one perspective and condemned from the other, it serves as a locus for uncovering the play's ideological sympathies, particularly since *Macbeth* provides an alternative model of political virtue in Malcolm. At the beginning of the play, Duncan "rules" by the rules; later his son will "rule" by breaking them. These opposing images of the good king frame the portrait of Macbeth and his criminal regime, and it is Malcolm's politic practice that emerges as the normative standard against which both Duncan and Macbeth are measured.

The rebellion that almost destroys Duncan's kingdom is set in a Machiavellian context. A central theme of *The Prince* is Machiavelli's new take on the classic opposition of fortune and virtue. In late medieval philosophy Christian virtue could defeat the goddess Fortune by making a man indifferent to her blows. Machiavelli, however, argues that although a private individual can afford to hold the world in contempt, a prince has aggressively to impose his will upon it. He inverts the standard virtue-fortune model, stating that a man with sufficient *virtù* can violently conquer Fortuna (*The Prince,* 25). In the first act of *Macbeth,* the goddess Fortune is a battle prize tossed back and forth among virile warriors. Initially, Fortune is the "rebel's whore" who aids the traitorous Thanes (I.ii.15).[5] But she is finally conquered by Macbeth, who "Disdaining" her, prefers instead to be "Valor's minion," "Bellona's bridegroom" (I.ii.17, 54). Significantly, Duncan is left on the sidelines; in the delegitimized world of power struggle, his Christian virtue cannot come into play. In order to conquer Fortune he needs the *virtù* of men like Macbeth. However, according to Machiavelli, a prince cannot maintain his power by relying on the *virtù* of another; like the goddess, the state belongs to the man who wins her by force. It is for this reason Machiavelli advises that every prince should be his own best general and "never lift his thoughts from the exercise of war" (*The Prince*, 14). In Machiavelli's view, Duncan's delegation of the violent arts of war would be consistent with both Christian values and the eventual loss of his kingdom.

Machiavelli does not dismiss Christian virtues; he understands their appeal and acknowledges their prestige. In *The Prince* he instructs the ruler in the proper "use" of traditional virtues. If the times are peaceful and all men trustworthy, the prince can afford the luxury of moral practice. If, however, his state is insecure, he must cultivate an appearance of virtue while being willing to practice its opposite. In chapter 18 Machiavelli explains why it is dangerous for the prince to possess in actuality the virtues that he must always project:

> Nay, I dare say this, that by having them [virtues] and always observing them, they are harmful; and by appearing to have them, they are useful, as it is to appear merciful, faithful, humane, honest, and religious, and to be so; but to remain with a spirit built so that, if you need not to be those things, you are able to know how to change to the contrary. This has to be understood: that a prince, and especially a new prince, cannot observe all those things for which men are held good, since he is often under the necessity, to maintain his state, of acting against faith, against charity, against humanity, against religion.

As this passage makes clear, Duncan, however admirable a man, is by Machiavellian standards a dangerous king—a ruler whose gentle and trusting character has invited treason, civil war, and foreign invasion. By being a perfect Christian, Duncan succeeds in becoming a perfect lamb—a sacrificial offering on the altar of real-world politics.

Given the potentially deadly environment a prince must inhabit, Machiavelli recommends that his nature should combine two less endearing animals, the lion and the fox: "Thus, since a prince is compelled of necessity how to use the beast, he should pick the fox and the lion . . . one needs to be a fox to recognize snares and a lion to frighten wolves" (*The Prince*, 18). Because he sees survival as a prince's first duty, Machiavelli selects for emulation animals known for their survival skills rather than their service to others. Although this advice may seem to be nothing more than the glorification of self-interest,[6] it can be argued that altruistic virtues will be of little value to the prince or his kingdom if they open the way to his destruction and die with him, along with countless subjects. At the beginning of *Macbeth* Duncan displays the kind of fatal naïveté characteristic of a prince who possesses virtue rather than *virtù*. Mystified by Cawdor's treason, he states,

> There's no art
> To find the mind's construction in the face:
> He was a gentleman on whom I built
> An absolute trust.
>
> (I.iv.12-15)

Duncan admits that he cannot penetrate appearances, yet he tries to build his kingdom on relationships of "absolute trust." The Machiavellian prince, on the other hand, has mastered the art of seeing into others while remaining a mystery himself, and he is utterly self-reliant. In chapter 17 of *The Prince*, Machiavelli warns against depending on the love and loyalty of one's followers. He calls the generality of men "ungrateful, fickle, pretenders and dissemblers," and urges the prince to build his kingdom on fear rather than love since love is "held by a chain of obligation, which, because men are wicked, is broken at every opportunity for their own utility, but fear is held by a dread of punishment that never forsakes you" (*The Prince*, 17).[7]

Duncan's faith and trust cost him his life. But it is through his death that his son Malcolm learns the art of survival. Machiavelli considered the prince fortunate to found his state in adversity since the struggle instructs him in the ways of maintaining power (*The Prince*, 20). Indeed, by the end of the play, Malcolm's fortunes seem to have transformed him into a total Machiavellian. Immediately following his father's murder, Malcolm wishes to speak his heart, but his brother stops him, considering it more prudent to run than to stay and protest against a hidden and deadly enemy (II.iii.118-25). By Act IV, scene iii, Malcolm has acquired *virtù*, which is above all else the art of prudence.[8] He tells Macduff, who has come from Scotland to offer his services to the prince in exile, that he cannot depend on a mere verbal assurance of Macduff's virtuous intent. After all, as Malcolm points out, "This tyrant whose sole name blisters our tongue / Was once thought honest" (IV.iii.11-12). He suspects that Macduff may be trying to ingratiate himself with Macbeth by offering him up "a weak, poor, innocent lamb / T'appease an angry god" (IV.iii.16-17). However, unlike his father, Malcolm is more fox than lamb, and although he maintains that he cannot know what is in a man's heart, he has learned to attain some measure of control over a world of deception by turning dissimulation itself into a tool.[9] In other words, he has learned to "rule" by breaking the rules of Christian conduct. He tests Macduff's virtue by pretending to every vice a tyrant proverbially possessed.[10] In this Machiavellian test, a virtuous man dissimulates (a non-virtuous act) that he *is not* virtuous in order to prove that the object of his test *is* virtuous. And it is not until Macduff violently rejects him ("Fit to govern? / No, not to live") that he can accept Macduff. Malcolm has put into practice what Machiavelli recommends in chapter 18 of *The Prince*: "How laudable it is for a prince to keep his faith, and live with honesty and not by astuteness, everyone understands. Nonetheless one sees by experience in our times that the princes who have done great things are those who have taken little account of faith and have known how to get around men's brains with their astuteness; and in the end they have overcome those who have founded themselves on loyalty."

The exchange between Malcolm and Macduff is not only interesting as a Machiavellian demonstration of "how to get around men's brains," it also reveals the extent to which conventional rule-bound notions of ethical conduct have yielded to moral concepts that are prudential or ends-oriented. In the area of religious practice, late sixteenth and early seventeenth-century England is witness to a growing adiaphorism which relegates to the realm of things indifferent all matters that do not directly affect salvation. At the same time, James I asserts a political adiaphora which contains any royal vice that does not directly affect the state.[11] These developments in English religious and political ideology harmonize with Machiavellian notions of civic virtue that subordinate personal morality to considerations of political consequence. Thus during the testing scene, Macduff can promise that Scotland will accommodate a series of personal vices—deceit, lust, avarice—but he rejects Malcolm as a king when his vices turn political:[12]

> Nay, had I pow'r, I should
> Pour the sweet milk of concord into hell,
> Uproar the universal peace, confound
> All unity on earth.
>
> (IV.iii.97-100)

The scene between Malcolm and Macduff not only illustrates concepts of virtue that subordinate traditional rules of Christian conduct to the pressing needs of troubled times; it also succeeds in cloaking Malcolm's true nature in an impenetrable veil. When Malcolm "unspeaks" the crimes he has just laid upon himself, claiming that he is a virgin who has never before lied or broken faith, Macduff is struck dumb with confusion. Malcolm's claims of perfect innocence and honesty are incredible under any circumstances but particularly since they are belied by the speech that asserts them. After this *virtù*oso display of politic dissimulation, it becomes impossible for Macduff, or the audience, to get a precise fix on Malcolm. He has successfully cultivated the "mystery of state" that is characteristic of both Machiavellian theory and absolutist practice.[13]

Before Malcolm tests Macduff's honesty by lying, the breakdown of an easy equivalence between being "true" literally and politically has been introduced in a conversation where the subject is also Macduff's loyalty—the exchange between Lady Macduff and her son moments before their murder. The boy asks if his father is really a traitor, and when his mother replies that he is, he wants a definition of treason:

> *Son.* What is a traitor?
> *L. Macd.* Why, one that swears and lies.
> *Son.* And be all traitors that do so?
> *L. Macd.* Every one that does so is a traitor, and must be hang'd.
> *Son.* And must they all be hang'd that swear and lie?
> *L. Macd.* Every one.
> *Son.* Who must hang them?
> *L. Macd.* Why, the honest men.
> *Son.* Then the liars and swearers are fools; for there are liars and swearers enow to beat the honest men and hang up them.
>
> (IV.ii.46-58)

Lady Macduff's definition of treason is never meant to be taken seriously, quickly collapsing in the face of her son's simple "reality test." However, her explanation of the supreme crime against the state echoes the political writings of Christian humanists, who insist that political evil is identical to religious sin. Lady Macduff's equating treason with breaking the second and ninth commandments has serious philosophical precedent, and the ease with which that equation is dismissed by her son is a reflection of the erosion these views have undergone by the early seventeenth century. Thus Shakespeare's domestic exchange illustrates that by this time even a child knows what political writers from Cicero to Suarez vigorously deny—lying is not treason; as the world goes, it is a ubiquitous tool of survival.

Given his strength, courage, and willingness to commit evil, Macbeth might seem to be Machiavelli's ideal prince. Actually, he manages to fall short in several regards, not the least of which is his inability to dissimulate. From the moment he hears the witches' prediction, his ambition becomes transparent. He attracts Banquo's suspicion early on, and he has to be instructed by Lady Macbeth to hide his feelings from the first moment she sees him:

> Your face, my thane, is as a book, where men
> May read strange matters. To beguile the time,
> Look like the time; bear welcome in your eye,
> Your hand, your tongue; look like th' innocent flower,
> But be the serpent under't.
>
> (I.v.62-66)

His acting abilities hardly improve once he becomes king. The play is filled with references to Macbeth's ill-fitting costumes (I.iii.144-46; V.ii.20-23), references which are usually read as symbols of Macbeth's inability to "fill Duncan's shoes." I would like to suggest that these costumes which never seem to fit may also refer to Macbeth's incompetence at maintaining illusion. The mask of the "mystery of state" keeps slipping, revealing Macbeth's naked face—filled with ambition, fear, hatred—for anyone to read. He reveals fear and guilt in the banquet scene in front of the assembled lords of Scotland, and Macduff senses danger in time to escape his grasp. The sarcastic exchange between Lennox and another lord in Act III, scene vi, reveals that not one of his attempts to shift the blame for his crimes has succeeded. One tactic for which Machiavelli praises Borgia is his use of Rimirro de Orca; Rimirro commits all of the crimes necessary to pacify the

Romagna, and once the people begin to hate him for his cruelty, he is killed, leaving Borgia both secure and popular. Unlike Borgia, Macbeth carries the personal stigma of every crime in his realm.

However, by Machiavellian standards Macbeth's greatest sin would probably be not his inability to dissimulate but his initial reluctance to commit totally to the course of wrongdoing that his position as usurping prince has made essential. In *The Discourses* Machiavelli praises the wisdom of those who prefer to live as private citizens rather than suffer the guilt all kings must incur. He goes on to warn against the greatest danger, the desire to have it all—the clean conscience of a private man and the power of a prince. Having just described the means by which Philip of Macedon made himself prince of Greece, Machiavelli states:

> Such methods are exceedingly cruel, and are repugnant to any community, not only a Christian one, but to any composed of men. It behoves, therefore, every man to shun them, and to prefer rather to live as a private citizen than as a king with such ruination of men to his score. None the less, for the sort of man who is unwilling to take up this first course of well doing, it is expedient, should he wish to hold what he has, to enter on the path of wrong doing. Actually, however, most men prefer to steer a middle course, which is very harmful; for they know not how to be wholly good nor yet wholly bad.
>
> (Bk. 1, chap. 26)

Machiavelli's complaint about men's longing to attain power without sacrificing personal virtue sounds very much like Lady Macbeth's fears concerning her husband's double desire:

> Thou wouldst be great,
> Art not without ambition, but without
> The illness should attend it. What thou wouldst highly,
> That wouldst thou holily; wouldst not play false,
> And yet wouldst wrongly win.
>
> (I.v.18-22)

One can see Macbeth's deep desire to be "holy" and yet "wrongly win" in Act II, scene ii, where, incredibly, he seeks a blessing by trying to join his own "Amen" to the prayer of two sleeping innocents seconds after he has murdered Duncan; it seems genuinely to surprise him that the "Amen" sticks in his throat (II.ii.24-31). Macbeth is like the Porter's "equivocator," a man who wants it all and "could swear in both the scales against either scale, who committed treason enough for God's sake, yet could not equivocate to heaven" (II.iii.8-11).

It is a delicate issue to argue that Scotland would have been better off had Macbeth been more thoroughly evil—especially since Macbeth becomes evil incarnate by the end of the play. What Machiavelli would argue is that Macbeth's conversion comes too late for himself and for the kingdom. In Act I Macbeth wants his murder of Duncan to be a single, limited crime, and he alternates between fantasizing an assassination that "Could trammel up the consequences," and the realization that he may not be able to control what will follow.[14] By murdering Duncan, and Duncan alone, Macbeth's worst fears come true. He unleashes a flood of events that so outrace his efforts at containment that he finally resorts to a reign of terror. In what must be the most troubling passages in *The Prince*, chapters 7 and 8 on Borgia and Agathocles, Machiavelli distinguishes between cruelties that are well or badly used:

> Someone could question how it happened that Agathocles and anyone like him, after infinite betrayals and cruelties, could live for a long time secure in his fatherland, defend himself against external enemies, and never be conspired against by his citizens, inasmuch as many others have not been able to maintain their states through cruelty even in peaceful times, not to mention uncertain times of war. I believe that this comes from cruelties badly used or well used. Those can be called well used (if it is permissible to speak well of evil) that are done at a stroke, out of the necessity to secure oneself, and then are not persisted in but are turned to as much utility for the subjects as one can. Those cruelties are badly used which, though few in the beginning, rather grow with time than are eliminated. Those who observe the first mode can have some remedy for their state with God and with men, as had Agathocles.

Machiavelli's condemnation of "cruelties badly used" could easily serve as a gloss to *Macbeth*, where the crimes are few in the beginning but do indeed grow with time. It is particularly interesting to note that Machiavelli brings in the judgment of God as well as men; both distinguish between these two cruelties and both find only the latter beyond remedy. Machiavelli can praise Borgia and Agathocles, and even offer them a kind of divine dispensation, because his perspective is "of the people" (*The Prince*, dedicatory letter). He is not interested in the personal virtue of the prince, only in the effect of his actions on the kingdom. Since the civil chaos and terror that follow innocent blunders and half-hearted crimes are more deadly to the people than the quick and ruthless pacification of a kingdom, Machiavelli saves his condemnation for those princes whose actions cost the most lives.

Machiavelli warns against the dangers of traveling the "middle course" throughout his works. He states in *The Prince* that men should either be "caressed or eliminated" (3). In both *The Prince* and *The Discourses,* he particularly emphasizes the importance of eliminating the blood line of the former ruler when founding a new kingdom (*The Prince*, 3; *The Discourses,* Bk. 3, chap. 4). Macbeth's failures in this regard are obvious. He lets Malcolm and Donalbain escape after having done them the gravest injuries. And because he feels insecure from the moment he seizes power, he continues to murder in order to feel safe: "to be thus is nothing / But to be safely thus" (III.i.48-49). When he speaks to Lady Macbeth about his fears, he illustrates the escalation of violence that follows from half-hearted measures:

We have scorch'd the snake, not kill'd it;
She'll close and be herself, whilst our poor malice
Remains in danger of her former tooth.
But let the frame of things disjoint, both the worlds suffer,
Ere we will eat our meal in fear.

(III.ii.13-17)

He ends the scene with a reiteration of the same concept—increased evil to secure their shaky position: "Thou marvel'st at my words, but hold thee still: / Things bad begun make strong themselves by ill" (III.ii.54-55). But after his initial crime, no matter how willingly or quickly he kills, it never seems to be enough. Having begun his crimes by killing Duncan while allowing his heirs to escape, he will crown them by killing all of Macduff's heirs after allowing Macduff to escape. The violence increases exponentially, but its efficacy decreases at an even higher rate.

Machiavelli never praises brutality for its own sake; he advocates its politic use as a necessary evil, a prophylactic against widespread and indiscriminate violence. He is particularly critical of the kinds of cruel actions that breed mayhem; and more than any other political writer, he understands the destructive power of vengeance. When in chapter 17 of *The Prince* he advises that it is better to be feared than to be loved, he adds an important caveat—one should be feared but never hated. In chapter 20 he discusses fortifications and concludes, "the best fortress there is, is not to be hated by the people, because although you may have fortresses, if the people hold you in hatred fortresses do not save you; for to people who have taken up arms foreigners will never be lacking to come to their aid." By committing acts like the massacre of Macduff's family, Macbeth has become universally hated. He faces an avenging army, aided by a foreign king, with nothing at his back but a fortress, soldiers in revolt, and "Curses, not loud but deep, mouth-honor, breath / Which the poor heart would fain deny, and dare not" (V.iii.27-28). Shortly after this speech, Macbeth will be defeated and decapitated. Machiavelli would have predicted his violent end, but not on providential grounds. He would have seen Macbeth's destruction as no more or less inevitable than Duncan's—both of Shakespeare's portraits in political disaster could have found a place among his vast collection of object lessons in *virtù* and the art of survival.

Notes

1. In *The Discourses* Niccolò Machiavelli rails against Christianity's effect on political life. Unlike the state religion of the Romans, Christianity holds the world and its glories in contempt:

   > Our religion has glorified humble and contemplative men, rather than men of action. It has assigned as man's highest good humility, abnegation, and contempt for mundane things [cosi umane], whereas the other identified it with magnanimity, bodily strength, and everything else that conduces to make men very bold. And, if our religion demands that in you there be strength, what it asks for is the strength to suffer rather than the strength to do bold things.
   >
   > This pattern of life, therefore, appears to have made the world weak, and to have handed it over as prey to the wicked, who run it successfully and securely since they are well aware that the generality of men, with paradise for their goal, consider how best to bear, rather than how best to avenge, their injuries.
   >
   > (Bk. 2, chap. 2)

   (All citations from *The Discourses* are from Leslie J. Walker's translation, New York: Penguin, 1970; all citations from *The Prince* are from Harvey C. Mansfield, Jr.'s translation, cited by chapter. Chicago: Univ. of Chicago Press, 1985).

2. See among others L. C. Knights, "How Many Children Had Lady Macbeth," in *Explorations: Essays in Criticism Mainly on the Literature of the Seventeenth Century* (London: Chatto and Windus, 1963), pp. 1-39, and Maynard Mack, Jr., *Killing the King: Three Studies in Shakespeare's Tragic Structure* (New Haven: Yale Univ. Press, 1973).

3. See David Norbrook's "*Macbeth* and the Politics of Historiography," in *Politics of Discourse: The Literature and History of Seventeenth-Century England,* ed. Kevin Sharpe and Steven N. Zwicker (Berkeley: Univ. of California Press, 1987), pp. 78-116.

4. The reception of Machiavelli in England in the sixteenth and seventeenth centuries was a welter of contradictions; however, it is clear that by the seventeenth century his philosophy was beginning to gain respectability. For detailed accounts of the extent and levels of Machiavellianism, open and covert, see Felix Raab, *The English Face of Machiavelli* (London: Routledge, 1964), and the recent study by Peter S. Donaldson, *Machiavelli and the Mystery of State* (New York: Cambridge Univ. Press, 1988). As Donaldson's investigations have confirmed, there were a number of avid followers of Machiavelli in the early Tudor courts—among others, William Thomas, who wrote a secret work of royal pedagogy based on Machiavelli's works for the young prince Edward VI, and Bishop Stephen Gardiner, who wrote a Machiavellian treatise for Mary's consort, Philip of Spain.

   By the late sixteenth century many of Machiavelli's most controversial ideas were also gaining ground in public political discourse, although authors often avoided defending him by name. For instance, in an English translation of *The Six Bookes of Politickes or Civil Doctrine* (trans. William Jones, London, 1594), Justus Lipsius, a writer noted for his piety, praises the politic use of deception and actively defends Machiavelli (identified in a marginal note):

   > Surely when one is not strong enough to debate in the matter, it is not amisse secretly to intrappe. And as the King of Sparta teacheth us, where we

cannot prevaile by the Lions skinne, we must put on the Foxes. . . . Of such a person we shall easily obtaine this; neither will he so strictly condemne the Italian fault-writer, (who poore soule is layde at of all hands) and as a holy person sayth, that there is a certaine honest and laudable deceipt.

(p. 114)

For seventeenth-century adoption of Machiavelli's republican theories, see Zera S. Fink, *The Classical Republicans: An Essay in the Recovery of a Pattern of Thought in Seventeenth-Century England* (Evanston: Northwestern Univ. Press, 1945).

5. All quotations are from *The Riverside Shakespeare*, ed. G. Blakemore Evans (Boston: Houghton Mifflin, 1974).

6. Machiavelli's attitude towards self-interest is clearly expressed in one of his poems, "Tercets on Ambition" in *Machiavelli: The Chief Works and Others,* 3 vols., trans. Allan Gilbert (Durham: Duke Univ. Press, 1965), 2: 735-39. He sees personal ambition as a great evil unless it is harnessed by the state and its energies turned against her enemies. If it is allowed to rage unchecked within a kingdom the results are reminiscent of Macbeth's Scotland: "Wherever you turn your eyes, you see the earth wet with tears / and blood, and the air full of screams, sobs, and sighs" (lines 157-58).

7. It has long been noted that Machiavelli has a very "Protestant" conception of human nature. See for example, Hiram Haydn's *The Counter-Renaissance* (New York: Scribner's, 1950) for a discussion of Calvin and the Florentine school. One can also see an affinity with Luther, whose bleak view of humanity is the basis on which he justifies the need for coercive government: without rule by force, "seeing that the whole world is evil and that among thousands there is scarcely one true Christian, men would devour one another, and no one could preserve wife and child, support himself and serve God; and thus the world would be reduced to chaos." *Martin Luther: Selections from his Writings,* ed. John Dillenberger (New York: Doubleday, 1961), p. 370. These views of man's nature, along with the antinomianism inherent in the doctrine of election (which does not contain a rule-bound view of virtue), contribute to a world-view receptive to both absolutism and civic humanism. Thus as England became more Protestant and more absolutist, it became more hospitable to Machiavelli.

8. For a detailed discussion of the relationship between Machiavellian *virtù* and prudence see Eugene Garver's *Machiavelli and the History of Prudence* (Madison: Univ. of Wisconsin Press, 1987). Garver states: "Machiavelli 'empties' virtù of its conventional semantic, moral, and intellectual associations in order to substitute a prudential structure for understanding it" (p. 31).

9. See Victoria Kahn's article, "*Virtù* and the Example of Agathocles in Machiavelli's *Prince*," *Representations* 13 (Winter 1986): 63-83, for a discussion of the breakdown of the Ciceronian equation of *honestas* and *utilitas* (if a statement is true it will be effective) subscribed to by Christian humanists. Kahn points out Machiavelli's adoption of an ironic mode of discourse that achieves its ends by seeming to speak against them.

10. See Rebecca W. Bushnell's *Tragedies of Tyrants: Political Thought and Theater in the English Renaissance* (Ithaca: Cornell Univ. Press, 1990) for a detailed discussion of the character of the tyrant in classical and Renaissance political theory and theater. He was conventionally conceived as a slave to desire and therefore subject to any number of appetitive vices.

11. In *Basilikon Doron,* James I separates the King's personal conduct from the rest of the work in a book labeled, "Of a King's Behaviour in Indifferent Things." Earlier in the work he admits every king has his faults, but insists that they are to be kept between him and God and "should not be a matter of discourse to others whatsoever." *The Political Works of James I,* 1616, intro. Charles Howard McIlwain (New York: Russell and Russell, 1965), p. 21.

12. Bushnell notes the relationship between absolutist notions that relegate personal sins to the adiaphora and this turn in Macduff's attitude (pp. 140-42).

13. See especially Donaldson's *Machiavelli and the Mystery of State* for an exhaustive study of the role of mystery in both Machiavelli's political theory and his reception and use in England. See also the treatment of the *arcana imperii* in Jonathan Goldberg's *James I and the Politics of Literature* (Baltimore: Johns Hopkins Univ. Press, 1983), and Stephen Orgel's connection of Machiavellian illusion with the celebration of power in the Jacobean masque in *The Illusion of Power: Political Theater in the English Renaissance* (Berkeley: Univ. of California Press, 1975).

14. In *The Machiavellian Moment: Florentine Political Thought and the Atlantic Republican Tradition* (Princeton: Princeton Univ. Press, 1975), J. G. A. Pocock notes the mixed nature of *virtù;* its cardinal characteristic, innovation, can easily turn against its practitioner:

On the one hand *virtù* is that by which we innovate, and so let loose sequences of contingency beyond our prediction or control so that we become prey to *fortuna;* on the other hand, *virtù* is that internal to ourselves by which we resist *fortuna* and impose upon her patterns of order, which may even become patterns of moral order. This seems to be at the heart of Machiavellian ambiguities. It explains why innovation is supremely difficult, being formally self-destructive; and it explains why there is incompatibility between action—and so between politics defined in terms of action rather than tradition—and moral order.

(p. 167)

GENDER ISSUES

Janet Adelman (essay date 1985)

SOURCE: "'Born of Woman': Fantasies of Maternal Power in *Macbeth*," in *Cannibals, Witches, and Divorce: Estranging the Renaissance,* edited by Marjorie Garber, The Johns Hopkins University Press, 1987, pp. 90-121.

[*In the following essay, originally presented in 1985, Adelman suggests that* Macbeth *represents a powerful fantasy of escape from an absolute and destructive maternal power.*]

In the last moments of any production of *Macbeth,* as Macbeth feels himself increasingly hemmed in by enemies, the stage will resonate hauntingly with variants of his repeated question, "What's he / That was not born of woman?" (5.7.2-3; for variants, see 5.3.4, 6; 5.7.11, 13; 5.8.13, 31).[1] Repeated seven times, Macbeth's allusion to the witches' prophecy—"none of woman born / Shall harm Macbeth" (4.1.80-81)—becomes virtually a talisman to ward off danger; even after he has begun to doubt the equivocation of the fiend (5.5.43), mere repetition of the phrase seems to Macbeth to guarantee his invulnerability. I want in this essay to explore the power of these resonances, particularly to explore how Macbeth's assurance seems to turn itself inside out, becoming dependent not on the fact that all men are, after all, born of woman but on the fantasy of escape from this universal condition. The duplicity of Macbeth's repeated question—its capacity to mean both itself and its opposite—carries such weight at the end of the play, I think, because the whole of the play represents in very powerful form both the fantasy of a virtually absolute and destructive maternal power and the fantasy of absolute escape from this power; I shall argue in fact that the peculiar texture of the end of the play is generated partly by the tension between these two fantasies.

Maternal power in *Macbeth* is not embodied in the figure of a particular mother (as it is, for example, in *Coriolanus*); it is instead diffused throughout the play, evoked primarily by the figures of the witches and Lady Macbeth. Largely through Macbeth's relationship to them, the play becomes (like *Coriolanus*) a representation of primitive fears about male identity and autonomy itself,[2] about those looming female presences who threaten to control one's actions and one's mind, to constitute one's very self, even at a distance. When Macbeth's first words echo those we have already heard the witches speak—"So fair and foul a day I have not seen" (1.3.38); "Fair is foul, and foul is fair" (1.1.11)—we are in a realm that questions the very possibility of autonomous identity. The play will finally reimagine autonomous male identity, but only through the ruthless excision of all female presence, its own peculiar satisfaction of the witches' prophecy.

In 1600, after the Earl of Gowrie's failed attempt to kill James VI, one James Weimis of Bogy, testifying about the earl's recourse to necromancy, reported that the earl thought it "possible that the seed of man and woman might be brought to perfection otherwise then by the *matrix* of the woman."[3] Whether or not Shakespeare deliberately recalled Gowrie in his portrayal of the murderer of James's ancestor,[4] the connection is haunting: the account of the conspiracy hints that, for Gowrie at least, recourse to necromancy seemed to promise at once invulnerability and escape from the maternal matrix.[5] The fantasy of such escape in fact haunts Shakespeare's plays. A few years after Macbeth, Posthumus will make the fantasy explicit: attributing all ills in man to the "woman's part," he will ask, "Is there no way for men to be, but women / Must be half-workers?" (*Cymbeline,* 2.5.1-2).[6] The strikingly motherless world of *The Tempest* and its potent image of absolute male control answers Posthumus' questions affirmatively: there at least, on that bare island, mothers and witches are banished and creation belongs to the male alone.

Even in one of Shakespeare's earliest plays, male autonomy is ambivalently portrayed as the capacity to escape the maternal matrix that has misshaped the infant man.[7] The man who will become Richard III emerges strikingly as a character for the first time as he watches his brother Edward's sexual success with the Lady Grey. After wishing syphilis on him so that he will have no issue (a concern that anticipates Macbeth's), Richard constructs his own desire for the crown specifically as compensation for his failure at the sexual game. Unable to "make [his] heaven in a lady's lap," he will "make [his] heaven to dream upon the crown" (*3 Henry VI,* 3.2.148,169). But his failure to make his heaven in a lady's lap is itself understood as the consequence of his subjection to another lady's lap, to the misshaping power of his mother's womb:

> Why, love forswore me in my Mother's womb;
> And, for I should not deal in her soft laws,
> She did corrupt frail nature with some bribe
> To shrink mine arm up like a withered shrub;
> To make an envious mountain on my back.
>
> [3.2.153-57]

Richard blames his deformity on a triad of female powers: Mother, Love, and Nature all fuse, conspiring to deform him as he is being formed in his mother's womb. Given this image of female power, it is no wonder that he turns to the compensatory heaven of the crown. But the crown turns out to be an unstable compensation. Even as he shifts from the image of the misshaping womb to the image of the crown, the terrifying enclosure of the womb recurs, shaping his attempt to imagine the very political project that should free him from dependence on ladies' laps:

I'll make my heaven to dream upon the crown
And, whiles I live, t'account this world but hell
Until my misshaped trunk that bears this head
Be round impalèd with a glorious crown.
And yet I know not how to get the crown,
For many lives stand between me and home;
And I—like one lost in a thorny wood,
That rents the thorns and is rent with the thorns,
Seeking a way and straying from the way,
Not knowing how to find the open air
But toiling desperately to find it out—
Torment myself to catch the English crown;
And from that torment I will free myself
Or hew my way out with a bloody axe.

[3.2.168-81]

The crown for him is "home," the safe haven. But through the shifting meaning of "impalèd," the crown as safe haven is itself transformed into the dangerous enclosure: the stakes that enclose him protectively turn into the thorns that threaten to impale him.[8] Strikingly, it is not his head but the trunk that bears his head that is so impaled by crown and thorns: the crown compensatory for ladies' laps fuses with the image of the dangerous womb in an imagistic nightmare in which the lap/womb/home/crown become the thorny wood from which he desperately seeks escape into the open air. Through this imagistic transformation, these lines take on the configuration of a birth fantasy, or more precisely a fantasy of impeded birth, a birth that the man-child himself must manage by hewing his way out with a bloody axe.[9] Escape from the dangerous female is here achieved by recourse to the exaggeratedly masculine bloody axe. This, I will argue, is precisely the psychological configuration of *Macbeth,* where dangerous female presences like Love, Nature, Mother are given embodiment in Lady Macbeth and the witches, and where Macbeth wields the bloody axe in an attempt to escape their dominion over him.

At first glance, Macbeth seems to wield the bloody axe to comply with, not to escape, the dominion of women. The play constructs Macbeth as terrifyingly pawn to female figures. Whether or not he is rapt by the witches' prophecies because the horrid image of Duncan's murder has already occurred to him, their role as gleeful prophets constructs Macbeth's actions in part as the enactments of their will. And he is impelled toward murder by Lady Macbeth's equation of masculinity and murder: in his case, the bloody axe seems not an escape route but the tool of a man driven to enact the ferociously masculine strivings of his wife.[10] Nonetheless, the weight given the image of the man not born of woman at the end suggests that the underlying fantasy is the same as in Richard's defensive construction of his masculinity: even while enacting the wills of women, Macbeth's bloody masculinity enables an escape from them in fantasy—an escape that the play itself embodies in dramatic form at the end. I will discuss first the unleashing of female power and Macbeth's compliance with that power, and then the fantasy of escape.

In the figures of Macbeth, Lady Macbeth, and the witches, the play gives us images of a masculinity and a femininity that are terribly disturbed; this disturbance seems to me both the cause and the consequence of the murder of Duncan. In *Hamlet,* Shakespeare had reconstructed the Fall as the death of the ideal father; here, he constructs a revised version in which the Fall is the death of the ideally androgynous parent. For Duncan combines in himself the attributes of both father and mother: he is the center of authority, the source of lineage and honor, the giver of name and gift; but he is also the source of all nurturance, planting the children to his throne and making them grow. He is the father as androgynous parent from whom, singly, all good can be imagined to flow, the source of a benign and empowering nurturance the opposite of that imaged in the witches' poisonous cauldron and lady Macbeth's gall-filled breasts. Such a father does away with any need for a mother: he is the image of both parents in one, threatening aspects of each controlled by the presence of the other.[11] When he is gone, "The wine of life is drawn, and the mere less / Is left this vault to brag of" (2.3.93-94): nurturance itself is spoiled, as all the play's imagery of poisoned chalices and interrupted feasts implies. In his absence male and female break apart, the female becoming merely helpless or merely poisonous and the male merely bloodthirsty; the harmonious relation of the genders imaged in Duncan fails.

In *Hamlet,* the absence of the ideal protecting father brings the son face to face with maternal power. The absence of Duncan similarly unleashes the power of the play's malevolent mothers. But this father-king seems strikingly absent even before his murder. Heavily idealized, he is nonetheless largely ineffectual: even while he is alive, he is unable to hold his kingdom together, reliant on a series of bloody men to suppress an increasingly successful series of rebellions.[12] The witches are already abroad in his realm; they in fact constitute our introduction to that realm. Duncan, not Macbeth, is the first person to echo them ("When the battle's lost and won" [1.1.4]; "What he hath lost, noble Macbeth hath won" [1.2.69]). The witches' sexual ambiguity terrifies: Banquo says of them, "You should be women, / And yet your beards forbid me to interpret / That you are so" (1.3.45-47). Is their androgyny the shadow-side of the King's, enabled perhaps by his failure to maintain a protective masculine authority? Is their strength a consequence of his weakness? (This is the configuration of *Cymbeline,* where the power of the witch-queen-stepmother is so dependent on the failure of Cymbeline's masculine authority that she obligingly dies when that authority returns to him.) Banquo's question to the witches may ask us to hear a counterquestion about Duncan, who should be man. For Duncan's androgyny is the object of enormous ambivalence: idealized for his nurturing paternity, he is nonetheless killed for his womanish softness, his childish trust, his inability to read men's minds in their faces, his reliance on the fighting of sons who can rebel against him. Macbeth's description of the dead Duncan—"his silver skin lac'd with his golden blood" (2.3.110)—makes him into a virtual icon of kingly worth; but other images surrounding his death make him into an emblem not of masculine authority, but of female vulnerability. As he moves toward the murder, Macbeth first imagines himself the allegorical figure of murder, as though to absolve himself of the responsibility of choice. But the figure of murder then fuses with that of Tarquin:

> wither'd Murther,
> . . . thus with his stealthy pace,
> With Tarquin's ravishing strides, towards his design
> Moves like a ghost.
>
> [2.1.52-56]

These lines figure the murder as a display of male sexual aggression against a passive female victim: murder here becomes rape; Macbeth's victim becomes not the powerful male figure of the king, but the helpless Lucrece.[13] Hardened by Lady Macbeth to regard maleness and violence as equivalent, that is, Macbeth responds to Duncan's idealized milky gentleness as though it were evidence of his femaleness. The horror of this gender transformation, as well as the horror of the murder, is implicit in Macduff's identification of the king's body as a new Gorgon ("Approach the chamber, and destroy your sight / With a new Gorgon" [2.3.70-71]). The power of this image lies partly in its suggestion that Duncan's bloodied body, with its multiple wounds, has been revealed as female and hence blinding to his sons: as if the threat all along was that Duncan would be revealed as female and that this revelation would rob his sons of his masculine protection and hence of their own masculinity.[14]

In *King Lear*, the abdication of protective paternal power seems to release the destructive power of a female chaos imaged not only in Goneril and Regan, but also in the storm on the heath. Macbeth virtually alludes to Lear's storm as he approaches the witches in act 4, conjuring them to answer though they "untie the winds, and let them fight / Against the Churches," though the "waves / Confound and swallow navigation up," though "the treasure / Of Nature's germens tumble all together / Even till destruction sicken" (4.1.52-60; see *King Lear*, 3.2.1-9). The witches merely implicit on Lear's heath have become in *Macbeth* embodied agents of storm and disorder,[15] and they are there from the start. Their presence suggests that the absence of the father that unleashes female chaos (as in *Lear*) has already happened at the beginning of *Macbeth*; that absence is merely made literal in Macbeth's murder of Duncan at the instigation of female forces. For this father-king cannot protect his sons from powerful mothers, and it is the son's—and the play's—revenge to kill him, or, more precisely, to kill him first and love him after, paying him back for his excessively "womanish" trust and then memorializing him as the ideal androgynous parent.[16] The reconstitution of manhood becomes a central problem of the play in part, I think, because the vision of manhood embodied in Duncan has already failed at the play's beginning.

The witches constitute our introduction to the realm of maternal malevolence unleashed by the loss of paternal protection; as soon as Macbeth meets them, he becomes (in Hecate's probably non-Shakespearean words) their "wayward son" (3.5.11). This maternal malevolence is given its most horrifying expression in Shakespeare in the image through which Lady Macbeth secures her control over Macbeth:

> I have given suck, and know
> How tender 'tis to love the babe that milks me:
> I would, while it was smiling in my face,
> Have pluck'd my nipple from his boneless gums,
> And dash'd the brains out, had I so sworn
> As you have done to this.
>
> [1.7.54-59]

This image of murderously disrupted nurturance is the psychic equivalence of the witches' poisonous cauldron; both function to subject Macbeth's will to female forces.[17] For the play strikingly constructs the fantasy of subjection to maternal malevolence in two parts, in the witches and in Lady Macbeth, and then persistently identifies the two parts as one. Through this identification, Shakespeare in effect locates the source of his culture's fear of witchcraft in individual human history, in the infant's long dependence on female figures felt as all-powerful: what the witches suggest about the vulnerability of men to female power on the cosmic plane, Lady Macbeth doubles on the psychological plane.

Lady Macbeth's power as a female temptress allies her in a general way with the witches as soon as we see her. The specifics of that implied alliance begin to emerge as she attempts to harden herself in preparation for hardening her husband: the disturbance of gender that Banquo registers when he first meets the witches is played out in psychological terms in Lady Macbeth's attempt to unsex herself. Calling on spirits ambiguously allied with the witches themselves, she phrases this unsexing as the undoing of her own bodily maternal function:

> Come, you Spirits
> That tend on mortal thoughts, unsex me here,
> And fill me, from the crown to the toe, top-full
> Of direst cruelty! make thick my blood,
> Stop up th'access and passage to remorse;
> That no compunctious visitings of Nature
> Shake my fell purpose, nor keep peace between
> Th'effect and it! Come to my woman's breasts,
> And take my milk for gall, you murth'ring ministers.
>
> [1.5.40-48]

In the play's context of unnatural births, the thickening of the blood and the stopping up of access and passage to remorse begin to sound like attempts to undo reproductive functioning and perhaps to stop the menstrual blood that is the sign of its potential.[18] The metaphors in which Lady Macbeth frames the stopping up of remorse, that is, suggest that she imagines an attack on the reproductive passages of her own body, on what makes her specifically female. And as she invites the spirits to her breasts, she reiterates the centrality of the attack specifically on maternal function: needing to undo the "milk of human kindness" (1.5.18) in Macbeth, she imagines an attack on her own literal milk, its transformation into gall. This imagery locates the horror of the scene in Lady Macbeth's unnatural abrogation of her maternal function. But latent within this image of unsexing is the horror of the maternal function itself. Most modern editors follow Johnson in glossing "take my milk for gall" as "take my milk in exchange for gall," imagining in effect that the spirits empty out the natural maternal fluid and replace it with the unnatural and poisonous one.[19] But perhaps Lady Macbeth is asking the spirits to take her milk *as* gall, to nurse from her breast and find in her milk their sustaining poison. Here the milk itself is the gall; no transformation is necessary. In these lines Lady Macbeth focuses the culture's fear of maternal nursery—a fear reflected, for example, in the common worries about the various ills (including female blood itself) that could be transmitted through nursing and in the sometime identification of colostrum as witch's milk.[20] Insofar as her milk itself nurtures the evil spirits, Lady Macbeth localizes the image of maternal danger, inviting the identification of her maternal function itself with that of the witch. For she here invites precisely that nursing of devil-imps so central to the current understanding of witchcraft that the presence of supernumerary teats alone was often taken as sufficient evidence that one was a witch.[21] Lady Macbeth and the witches fuse at this moment, and they fuse through the image of perverse nursery.

It is characteristic of the play's division of labor between Lady Macbeth and the witches that she, rather than they, is given the imagery of perverse nursery traditionally attributed to the witches. The often noted alliance between Lady Macbeth and the witches constructs malignant female power both in the cosmos and in the family; it in effect adds the whole weight of the spiritual order to the condemnation of Lady Macbeth's insurrection.[22] But despite the superior cosmic status of the witches, Lady Macbeth seems to me finally the more frightening figure. For Shakespeare's witches are an odd mixture of the terrifying and the near comic. Even without consideration of the Hecate scene (3.5) with its distinct lightening of tone and its incipient comedy of discord among the witches, we may begin to feel a shift toward the comic in the presentation of the witches: the specificity and predictability of the ingredients in their dire recipe pass over toward grotesque comedy even while they create a (partly pleasurable) shiver of horror.[23] There is a distinct weakening of their power after their first appearances: only halfway through the play, in 4.1, do we hear that they themselves have masters (4.1.63). The more Macbeth claims for them, the less their actual power seems: by the time Macbeth evokes the cosmic damage they can wreak (4.1.50-60), we have already felt the presence of such damage, and felt it moreover not as issuing from the witches but as a divinely sanctioned nature's expressions of outrage at the disruption of patriarchal order. The witches' displays of thunder and lightning, like their apparitions, are mere theatrics compared to what we have already heard; and the serious disruptions of natural order—the storm that toppled the chimneys and made the earth shake (2.3.53-60), the unnatural darkness in day (2.4.5-10), the cannibalism of Duncan's horses (2.4.14-18)—seem the horrifying but reassuringly familiar signs of God's displeasure, firmly under His—not their—control. Partly because their power is thus circumscribed, nothing the witches say or do conveys the presence of awesome and unexplained malevolence in the way that Lear's storm does. Even the process of dramatic representation itself may diminish their power: embodied, perhaps, they lack full power to terrify: "Present fears"— even of witches—"are less than horrible imaginings" (1.3.137-38). They tend thus to become as much containers for as expressions of nightmare; to a certain extent, they help to exorcise the terror of female malevolence by localizing it.

The witches may of course have lost some of their power to terrify through the general decline in witchcraft belief. Nonetheless, even when that belief was in full force, these witches would have been less frightening than their Continental sisters, their crimes less sensational. For despite their numinous and infinitely suggestive indefinability,[24] insofar as they are witches, they are distinctly English witches; and most commentators on English witchcraft note how tame an affair it was in comparison with witchcraft belief on the Continent.[25] The most sensational staples of Continental belief from the *Malleus Maleficarum* (1486) on—the ritual murder and eating of infants, the attacks specifically on the male genitals, the perverse sexual relationship with demons—are missing or greatly muted in English witchcraft belief, replaced largely by a simpler concern with retaliatory wrongdoing of exactly the order Shakespeare points to when one of his witches announces her retaliation for the sailor's wife's refusal to share her chestnuts.[26] We may hear an echo of some of the Continental beliefs in the hint of their quasi-sexual attack on the sailor with the uncooperative wife (the witches promise to "do and do and do," leaving him drained "dry as hay") and in the infanticidal contents of the cauldron, especially the "finger of birth-strangled babe" and the blood of the sow "that hath eaten / Her nine farrow." The cannibalism that is a staple of Continental belief may be implicit in the contents of that grim cauldron; and the various eyes, toes, tongues, legs, teeth, livers, and noses (indiscriminately human and animal) may evoke primitive fears of dismemberment close to the center of witchcraft belief. But these terrors remain largely implicit. For Shakespeare's witches are both smaller and greater than their Continental sisters: on the one hand, more the representation of English homebodies with relatively small concerns; on the other, more the incarnation of literary or mythic fates or sybils, given the power not only to predict but to enforce the future. But the staples of Continental witchcraft belief are not altogether missing from the play: for the most part, they are transferred away from the witches and recur as the psychological issues evoked by Lady Macbeth in her relation to Macbeth. She becomes the inheritor of the realm of primitive relational and bodily disturbance: of infantile vulnerability to maternal power, of dismemberment and its developmentally later equivalent, castration. Lady Macbeth brings the witches' power home: they get the cosmic apparatus, she gets the psychic force. That Lady Macbeth is the more frightening figure—and was so, I suspect, even before belief in witchcraft had declined—suggests the firmly domestic and psychological basis of Shakespeare's imagination.[27]

The fears of female coercion, female definition of the male, that are initially located cosmically in the witches thus find their ultimate locus in the figure of Lady Macbeth, whose attack on Macbeth's virility is the source of her strength over him and who acquires that strength, I shall argue, partly because she can make him imagine himself as an infant vulnerable to her. In the figure of Lady Macbeth, that is, Shakespeare rephrases the power of the witches as the wife/mother's power to poison human relatedness at its source; in her, their power of cosmic coercion is rewritten as the power of the mother to misshape or destroy the child. The attack on infants and on the genitals characteristic of Continental witchcraft belief is thus in her returned to its psychological source: in the play these beliefs are localized not in the witches but in the great central scene in which Lady Macbeth persuades Macbeth to the murder of Duncan. In this scene, Lady Macbeth notoriously makes the murder of Duncan the test of Macbeth's virility; if he cannot perform the murder, he is in effect reduced to the helplessness of an infant subject to her rage. She begins by attacking his manhood, making her love for him contingent on the murder that she identifies as equivalent to his male potency: "From this time / Such I account thy love" (1.7.38-39); "When you durst do it, then you were a man" (1.7.49). Insofar as his drunk hope is now "green and pale" (1.7.37), he is identified as emasculated, exhibiting the symptoms not only of hangover, but also of the green-sickness, the typical disease of timid young virgin women. Lady Macbeth's argument is, in effect, that any signs of the "milk of human kindness" (1.5.17) mark him as more womanly than she; she proceeds to enforce his masculinity by demonstrating her willingness to dry up that milk in herself, specifically by destroying her nursing infant in fantasy: "I would, while it was smiling in my face, / Have pluck'd my nipple from his boneless gums, / And dash'd the brains out" (1.7.56-58). That this image has no place in the plot, where the Macbeths are strikingly childless, gives some indication of the inner necessity through which it appears. For Lady Macbeth expresses here not only the hardness she imagines to be male, not only her willingness to unmake the most essential maternal relationship; she expresses also a deep fantasy of Macbeth's utter vulnerability to her. As she progresses from questioning Macbeth's masculinity to imagining herself dashing out the brains of her infant son,[28] she articulates a fantasy in which to be less than a man is to become interchangeably a woman or a baby,[29] terribly subject to the wife/mother's destructive rage.

By evoking this vulnerability, Lady Macbeth acquires a power over Macbeth more absolute than any the witches can achieve. The play's central fantasy of escape from woman seems to me to unfold from this moment; we can see its beginnings in Macbeth's response to Lady Macbeth's evocation of absolute maternal power. Macbeth first responds by questioning the possibility of failure ("If we should fail?" [1.7.59]). Lady Macbeth counters this fear by inviting Macbeth to share in her fantasy of omnipotent malevolence: "What cannot you and I perform upon / Th'unguarded Duncan?" (1.7.70-71). The satiated and sleeping Duncan takes on the vulnerability that Lady Macbeth has just invoked in the image of the feeding, trusting infant;[30] Macbeth releases himself from the image of this vulnerability by sharing in the murder of this innocent. In his elation at this transfer of vulnerability from himself to Duncan, Macbeth imagines Lady Macbeth the mother to infants sharing her hardness, born in effect without vulnerability; in effect, he imagines her as male and then reconstitutes himself as the invulnerable male child of such a mother:

> Bring forth men-children only!
> For thy undaunted mettle should compose
> Nothing but males.
>
> [1.7.73-75]

Through the double pun on *mettle/metal* and *male/mail*, Lady Macbeth herself becomes virtually male, composed of the hard metal of which the armored male is made.[31] Her children would necessarily be men, composed of her male mettle, armored by her mettle, lacking the female inheritance from the mother that would make them vulnerable. The man-child thus brought forth would be no trusting infant; the very phrase *men-children* suggests the presence of the adult man even at birth, hence the undoing of childish vulnerability.[32] The mobility of the imagery—from male infant with his brains dashed out to Macbeth and Lady Macbeth triumphing over the sleeping, trusting Duncan, to the all-male invulnerable man-child, suggests the logic of the fantasy: only the child of an all-male mother is safe. We see here the creation of a defensive fantasy of exemption from the woman's part: as infantile vulnerability is shifted to Duncan, Macbeth creates in himself the image of Lady Macbeth's hardened all-male man-child; in committing the murder, he thus becomes like Richard III, using the bloody axe to free himself in fantasy from the dominion of women, even while apparently carrying out their will.

Macbeth's temporary solution to the infantile vulnerability and maternal malevolence revealed by Lady Macbeth is to imagine Lady Macbeth the all-male mother of invulnerable infants. The final solution, both for Macbeth and for the play itself, though in differing ways, is an even more radical excision of the female: it is to imagine a birth entirely exempt from women, to imagine in effect an all-male family, composed of nothing but males, in which the father is fully restored to power. Overtly, of course, the play denies the possibility of this fantasy: Macduff carries the power of the man not born of woman only through the equivocation of the fiends, their obstetrical joke that quibbles with the meaning of *born* and thus confirms circuitously that all men come from women after all. Even

Macbeth, in whom, I think, the fantasy is centrally invested, knows its impossibility: his false security depends exactly on his commonsense assumption that everyone is born of woman. Nonetheless, I shall argue, the play curiously enacts the fantasy that it seems to deny: punishing Macbeth for his participation in a fantasy of escape from the maternal matrix, it nonetheless allows the audience the partial satisfaction of a dramatic equivalent to it. The dual process of repudiation and enactment of the fantasy seems to me to shape the ending of *Macbeth* decisively; I will attempt to trace this process in the rest of this essay.

The witches' prophecy has the immediate force of psychic relevance for Macbeth partly because of the fantasy constructions central to 1.7:

> Be bloody, bold, and resolute: laugh to scorn
> The power of man, for none of woman born
> Shall harm Macbeth.
>
> [4.1.79-81]

The witches here invite Macbeth to make himself into the bloody and invulnerable man-child he has created as a defense against maternal malevolence in 1.7: the man-child ambivalently recalled by the accompanying apparition of the Bloody Child. For the apparition alludes at once to the bloody vulnerability of the infant destroyed by Lady Macbeth and to the bloodthirsty masculinity that seems to promise escape from this vulnerability, the bloodiness the witches urge Macbeth to take on. The doubleness of the image epitomizes exactly the doubleness of the prophecy itself: the prophecy constructs Macbeth's invulnerability in effect from the vulnerability of all other men, a vulnerability dependent on their having been born of woman. Macbeth does not question this prophecy, even after the experience of Birnam Wood should have taught him better, partly because it so perfectly meets his needs: in encouraging him to "laugh to scorn / The power of men," the prophecy seems to grant him exemption from the condition of all men, who bring with them the liabilities inherent in their birth. As Macbeth carries the prophecy as a shield onto the battlefield, his confidence in his own invulnerability increasingly reveals his sense of his own exemption from the universal human condition. Repeated seven times, the phrase *born to woman* with its variants begins to carry for Macbeth the meaning "vulnerable," as though vulnerability itself is the taint deriving from woman; his own invulnerability comes therefore to stand as evidence for his exemption from that taint. This is the subterranean logic of Macbeth's words to Young Siward immediately after Macbeth has killed him:

> Thou wast born of woman:—
> But swords I smile at, weapons laugh to scorn,
> Brandish'd by man that's of a woman born.
>
> [5.7.11-13]

Young Siward's death becomes in effect proof that he was born of woman; in the logic of Macbeth's psyche, Macbeth's invulnerability is the proof that he was not. The *but* records this fantasied distinction: it constructs the sentence "You, born of woman, are vulnerable; but I, not born of woman, am not."[33]

Insofar as this is the fantasy embodied in Macbeth at the play's end, it is punished by the equivocation of the fiends: the revelation that Macduff derives from woman, though by unusual means, musters against Macbeth all the values of ordinary family and community that Macduff carries with him. Macbeth, "cow'd" by the revelation (5.8.18),[34] is forced to take on the taint of vulnerability; the fantasy of escape from the maternal matrix seems to die with him. But although this fantasy is punished in Macbeth, it does not quite die with him; it continues to have a curious life of its own in the play, apart from its embodiment in him. Even from the beginning of the play, the fantasy has not been Macbeth's alone: as the play's most striking bloody man, he is in the beginning the bearer of this fantasy for the all-male community that depends on his bloody prowess. The opening scenes strikingly construct male and female as realms apart; and the initial descriptions of Macbeth's battles construe his prowess as a consequence of his exemption from the taint of woman.

In the description of his battle with Macdonwald, what looks initially like a battle between loyal and disloyal sons to establish primacy in the father's eyes is oddly transposed into a battle of male against female:

> Doubtful it stood;
> As two spent swimmers, that do cling together
> And choke their art. The merciless Macdonwald
> (Worthy to be a rebel, for to that
> The multiplying villainies of nature
> Do swarm upon him) from the western isles
> Of Kernes and Gallowglasses is supplied;
> And Fortune, on his damned quarrel smiling,
> Show'd like a rebel's whore: but all's too weak;
> For brave Macbeth (well he deserves that name),
> Disdaining Fortune, with his brandish'd steel,
> Which smok'd with bloody execution,
> Like Valour's minion, carv'd out his passage,
> Till he fac'd the slave;
> Which ne'er shook hands, nor bade farewell to him,
> Till he unseam'd him from the nave to th' chops,
> And fix'd his head upon our battlements.
>
> [1.2.7-23]

The two initially indistinguishable figures metaphorized as the swimmers eventually sort themselves out into victor and victim, but only by first sorting themselves out into male and female, as though Macbeth can be distinguished from Macdonwald only by making Macdonwald functionally female. The "merciless Macdonwald" is initially firmly identified; but by the time Macbeth appears, Macdonwald has temporarily disappeared, replaced by the female figure of Fortune, against whom Macbeth seems to fight ("brave Macbeth, . . . Disdaining Fortune, with his brandish'd steel"). The metaphorical substitution of Fortune for Macdonwald transforms the battle into a contest between male and female; it makes Macbeth's deserving of his name contingent on his victory over the female. We are prepared for this transformation by Macdonwald's sexual alliance with the tainting female, the whore Fortune;[35] Macbeth's identification as valor's minion redefines the battle as a contest between the half-female couple Fortune/Macdonwald and the all-male couple Valor/Macbeth. Metaphorically, Macdonwald and Macbeth take on the qualities of the unreliable female and the heroic male; Macbeth's battle against Fortune turns out to be his battle against Macdonwald because the two are functionally the same. Macdonwald, tainted by the female, becomes an easy mark for Macbeth, who demonstrates his own untainted manhood by unseaming Macdonwald from the nave to the chops. Through its allusions both to castration and to Caesarian section, this unseaming furthermore remakes Macdonwald's body as female, revealing what his alliance with Fortune has suggested all along.

In effect, then, the battle that supports the father's kingdom plays out the creation of a conquering all-male erotics that marks its conquest by its triumph over a feminized body, simultaneously that of Fortune and Macdonwald. Hence, in the double action of the passage, the victorious unseaming happens twice: first on the body of Fortune and then on the body of Macdonwald. The lines descriptive of Macbeth's approach to Macdonwald—"brave Macbeth . . . Disdaining Fortune, with his brandish'd steel . . . carved out his passage"—make that approach contingent on Macbeth's first carving his passage through a female body, hewing his way out. The language here perfectly anticipates Macduff's birth by Caesarian section, revealed at the end of the play: if Macduff is ripped untimely from his mother's womb, Macbeth here manages in fantasy his own Caesarian section,[36] carving his passage out from the unreliable female to achieve heroic male action, in effect carving up the female to arrive at the male. Only after this rite of passage can Macbeth meet Macdonwald: the act of aggression toward the female body, the fantasy of self-birth, marks his passage to the contest that will be definitive of his maleness partly insofar as it is definitive of Macdonwald's tainted femaleness. For the all-male community surrounding Duncan, then, Macbeth's victory is allied with his triumph over femaleness; for them, he becomes invulnerable, "lapp'd in proof" (1.2.55) like one of Lady Macbeth's armored men-children.[37] Even before his entry into the play, that is, Macbeth is the bearer of the shared fantasy that secure male community depends on the prowess of the man in effect not born of woman, the man who can carve his own passage out, the man whose very maleness is the mark of his exemption from female power.[38]

Ostensibly, the play rejects the version of manhood implicit in the shared fantasy of the beginning. Macbeth himself is well aware that his capitulation to Lady Macbeth's definition of manhood entails his abandonment of his own more inclusive definition of what becomes a man (1.7.46); and Macduff's response to the news of his family's destruction insists that humane feeling is central to the definition of manhood (4.3.221). Moreover, the revelation that even Macduff had a mother sets a limiting condition on the

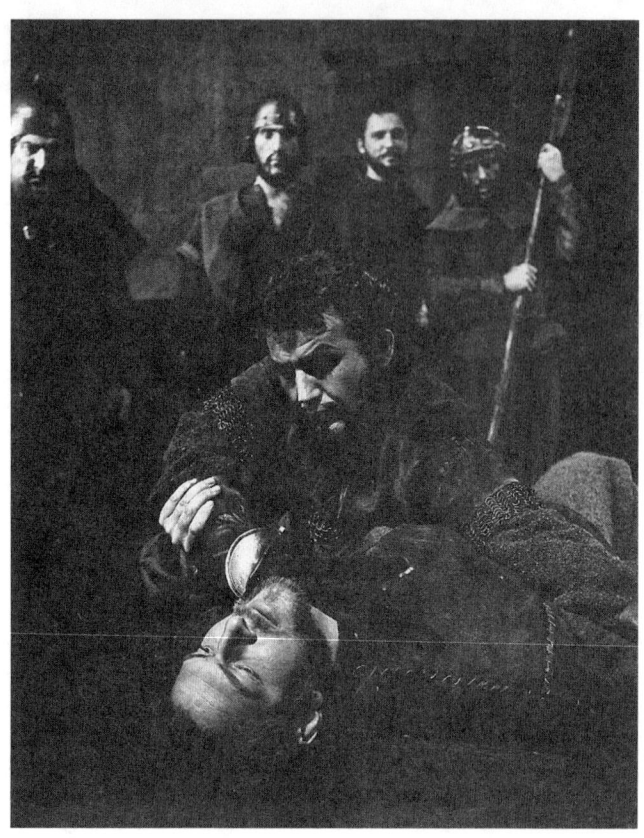

Bruno Gerussi as MacDuff and Christopher Plummer as Macbeth in the Stratford Festival's 1962 production of Macbeth.

fantasy of a bloody masculine escape from the female and hence on the kind of manhood defined by that escape. Nonetheless, even at the end, the play enables one version of the fantasy that heroic manhood is exemption from the female even while it punishes that fantasy in Macbeth. The key figure in whom this double movement is vested in the end of the play is Macduff; the unresolved contradictions that surround him are, I think, marks of ambivalence toward the fantasy itself. In insisting that mourning for his family is his right as a man, he presents family feeling as central to the definition of manhood; and yet he conspicuously leaves his family vulnerable to destruction when he goes off to offer his services to Malcolm. The play moreover insists on reminding us that he has inexplicably abandoned his family: both Lady Macduff and Malcolm question the necessity of this abandonment (4.2.6-14; 4.3.26-28); and the play never allows Macduff to explain himself. This unexplained abandonment severely qualifies Macduff's force as the play's central exemplar of a healthy manhood that can include the possibility of relationship to women: the play seems to vest diseased familial relations in Macbeth and the possibility of healthy ones in Macduff; and yet we discover dramatically that Macduff has a family only when we hear that he has abandoned it. Dramatically and psychologically, he takes on full masculine power only as he loses his family and becomes energized by the loss, converting his grief into the more "manly" tune of vengeance (4.3.235); the loss of his family here enables his accession to full masculine action even while his response to that loss insists on a more humane definition of manhood.[39] The play here pulls in two directions. It reiterates this doubleness by vesting in Macduff its final fantasy of exemption from woman. The ambivalence that shapes the portrayal of Macduff is evident even as he reveals to Macbeth that he "was from his mother's womb / Untimely ripp'd" (5.8.15-16): the emphasis on untimeliness and the violence of the image suggest that he has been prematurely deprived of a nurturing maternal presence; but the prophecy construes just this deprivation as the source of Macduff's strength.[40] The prophecy itself both denies and affirms the fantasy of exemption from women: in affirming that Macduff has indeed had a mother, it denies the fantasy of male self-generation; but in attributing his power to his having been untimely ripped from that mother, it sustains the sense that violent separation from the mother is the mark of the successful male. The final battle between Macbeth and Macduff thus replays the initial battle between Macbeth and Macdonwald. But Macduff has now taken the place of Macbeth: he carries with him the male power given him by the Caesarian solution, and Macbeth is retrospectively revealed as Macdonwald, the woman's man.

The doubleness of the prophecy is less the equivocation of the fiends than Shakespeare's own equivocation about the figure of Macduff and about the fantasy vested in him in the end. For Macduff carries with him simultaneously all the values of family and the claim that masculine power derives from the unnatural abrogation of family, including escape from the conditions of one's birth. Moreover, the ambivalence that shapes the figure of Macduff similarly shapes the dramatic structure of the play itself. Ostensibly concerned to restore natural order at the end,[41] the play bases that order upon the radical exclusion of the female. Initially construed as all-powerful, the women virtually disappear at the end, Lady Macbeth becoming so diminished a character that we scarcely trouble to ask ourselves whether the report of her suicide is accurate or not, the witches literally gone from the stage and so diminished in psychic power that Macbeth never mentions them and blames his defeat only on the equivocation of their male masters, the fiends; even Lady Macduff exists only to disappear. The bogus fulfillment of the Birnam Wood prophecy suggests the extent to which the natural order of the end depends on the exclusion of the female. Critics sometimes see in the march of Malcolm's soldiers bearing their green branches an allusion to the Maying festivals in which participants returned from the woods bearing branches, or to the ritual scourging of a hibernal figure by the forces of the oncoming spring.[42] The allusion seems to me clearly present; but it serves, I think, to mark precisely what the moving of Birnam Wood is not. Malcolm's use of Birnam Wood is a military maneuver. His drily worded command (5.4.4-7) leaves little room for suggestions of natural fertility or for the deep sense of the generative world rising up to expel its winter king; nor does the play later enable these associations except in a scattered and partly ironic way.[43] These trees have little resemblance to those in the Forest of Arden; their branches, like those carried by the apparition of the "child crowned, with a tree in his hand" (4.1.86), are little more than the emblems of a strictly patriarchal family tree.[44] This family tree, like the march of Birnam Wood itself, is relentlessly male: Duncan and sons, Banquo and son, Siward and son. There are no daughters and scarcely any mention of mothers in these family trees. We are brought as close as possible here to the fantasy of family without women.[45] In that sense, Birnam Wood is the perfect emblem of the nature that triumphs at the end of the play: nature without generative possibility, nature without women. Malcolm tells his men to carry the branches to obscure themselves, and that is exactly their function: insofar as they seem to allude to the rising of the natural order against Macbeth, they obscure the operations of male power, disguising them as a natural force; and they simultaneously obscure the extent to which natural order itself is here reconceived as purely male.[46]

If we can see the fantasy of escape from the female in the play's fulfillment of the witches' prophecies—in Macduff's birth by Caesarian section and in Malcolm's appropriation of Birnam Wood—we can see it also in the play's psychological geography. The shift from Scotland to England is strikingly the shift from the mother's to the father's terrain.[47] Scotland "cannot / Be call'd our mother, but our grave" (4.3.165-66), in Rosse's words to Macduff: it is the realm of Lady Macbeth and the witches, the realm in which the mother *is* the grave, the realm appropriately ruled by their bad son Macbeth. The escape to England is an escape from their power into the realm of the good father-king and his surrogate son Malcolm, "unknown to woman" (4.3.126). The magical power of this father to cure clearly balances the magical power of the witches to harm, as Malcolm (the father's son) balances Macbeth (the mother's son). That Macduff can cross from one realm into the other only by abandoning his family suggests the rigidity of the psychic geography separating England from Scotland. At the end of the play, Malcolm returns to Scotland mantled in the power England gives him, in effect bringing the power of the fathers with him: bearer of his father's line, unknown to woman, supported by his agent Macduff (empowered by his own special immunity from birth), Malcolm embodies utter separation from women and as such triumphs easily over Macbeth, the mother's son.

The play that begins by unleashing the terrible threat of destructive maternal power and demonstrates the helplessness of its central male figure before that power thus ends by consolidating male power, in effect solving the problem of masculinity by eliminating the female. In the psychological fantasies that I am tracing, the play portrays the failure of the androgynous parent to protect his son, that son's consequent fall into the dominion of the bad mothers, and the final victory of a masculine order in which mothers no longer threaten because they no longer exist.

In that sense, *Macbeth* is a recuperative consolidation of male power, a consolidation in the face of the threat unleashed in *Hamlet* and especially in *King Lear* and never fully contained in those plays. In *Macbeth,* maternal power is given its most virulent sway and then abolished; at the end of the play we are in a purely male realm. We will not be in so absolute a male realm again until we are in Prospero's island-kingdom, similarly based firmly on the exiling of the witch Sycorax.

Notes

1. All references to *Macbeth* are to the new Arden edition, edited by Kenneth Muir, (London: Methuen, 1972).

2. I have written elsewhere about Coriolanus' doomed attempts to create a self that is independent of his mother's will; see my "Anger's My Meat': Feeding, Dependency, and Aggression in *Coriolanus*," in *Representing Shakespeare: New Psychoanalytic Essays,* ed. Murray M. Schwartz and Coppélia Kahn (Baltimore: Johns Hopkins University Press, 1980), 129-49. Others have noted the extent to which both *Macbeth* and *Coriolanus* deal with the construction of a rigid male identity felt as a defense against overwhelming maternal power; see particularly Coppélia Kahn, *Man's Estate: Masculine Identity in Shakespeare* (Berkeley & Los Angeles: University of California Press, 1981), 151-92, whose chapter title—"The Milking Babe and the Bloody Man in *Coriolanus* and *Macbeth*"—indicates the similarity of our concerns. Linda Bamber argues, however, that the absence of a feminine Other in *Macbeth* and *Coriolanus* prevents the development of manliness in the heroes, since true manliness "involves a detachment from the feminine" (*Comic Women, Tragic Men: A Study of Gender and Genre in Shakespeare* [Stanford: Stanford University Press, 1982], 20, 91-107).

3. "Gowries Conspiracie: A Discoverie of the unnaturall and vyle Conspiracie, attempted against the Kings Maiesties Person at Sanct-Iohnstoun, upon Twysday the Fifth of August, 1600," in *A Selection from the Hadeian Miscellany* (London: C. & G. Kearsley, 1793), 196.

4. Stanley J. Kozikowski argues strenuously that Shakespeare knew either the pamphlet cited above ("Gowries Conspiracie," printed in Scotland and London in 1600) or the abortive play on the conspiracy, apparently performed twice by the King's Men and then canceled in 1604 ("The Gowrie Conspiracy against James VI: A New Source for Shakespeare's *Macbeth*," *Shakespeare Studies* 13 [1980]: 197-211). Although I do not find his arguments entirely persuasive, it seems likely that Shakespeare knew at least the central facts of the conspiracy, given both James's annual celebration of his escape from it and the apparent involvement of the King's Men in a play on the subject. See also Steven Mullaney's suggestive use of the Gowrie material as an analogue for *Macbeth* in its link between treason and magical riddle ("Lying Like Truth: Riddle, Representation and Treason in Renaissance England," *ELH* 47 [1980]: 32, 38).

5. After the failure of the conspiracy, James searched the dead earl's pockets, finding nothing in them "but a little close parchment bag, full of magicall characters, and words of inchantment, wherin, it seemed, that he had put his confidence, thinking him selfe never safe without them, and therfore ever carried them about with him; beeing also observed, that, while they were uppon him, his wound whereof he died, bled not, but, incontinent after the taking of them away, the blood gushed out in great aboundance, to the great admiration of al the beholders" ("Gowries Conspiracie," 196). The magical stopping up of the blood and the sudden return of its natural flow seem to me potent images for the progress of Macbeth as he is first seduced and then abandoned by the witches' prophecies; that Gowrie's necromancer, like the witches, seemed to dabble in alternate modes of generation increases the suggestiveness of this association for *Macbeth.*

6. All references to Shakespeare's plays other than *Macbeth* are to the revised Pelican edition, *William Shakespeare: The Complete Works,* ed. Alfred Harbage (Baltimore, Penguin Books, 1969).

7. Richard Wheeler, Michael Neill, and Coppélia Kahn similarly understand Richard III's self-divided and theatrical masculinity as a defensive response to real or imagined maternal deprivation. See Wheeler, "History, Character and Conscience in *Richard III*," *Comparative Drama* 5 (1971-72): 301-21, esp. 314-15; Neill, "Shakespeare's Halle of Mirrors: Play, Politics, and Psychology in *Richard III*," *Shakespeare Studies* 8 (1975): 99-129, esp. 104-6; and Kahn, *Man's Estate,* 63-66.

8. *Impale* in the sense of "to enclose with pales, stakes or posts; to surround with a pallisade" (*OED*'s first meaning) is of course the dominant usage contemporary with *Macbeth*. But the word was in the process of change. *OED*'s meaning 4, "to thrust a pointed stake through the body of, as a form of torture or capital punishment," although cited first in 1613, clearly seems to stand behind the imagistic transformation here. The shift in meaning perfectly catches Richard's psychological process, in which any protective enclosure is ambivalently desired and threatens to turn into a torturing impalement.

9. Robert N. Watson notes the imagery of Caesarian birth here and in *Macbeth* (*Shakespeare and the Hazards of Ambition* [Cambridge, Mass.: Harvard University Press, 1984], esp. 19-20, 99-105); the metaphors of Caesarian section and Oedipal rape are central to his understanding of ambitious self-creation insofar as both imagine a usurpation of the defining parental acts of generation (see, for

example, pp. 3-5). Though it is frequently very suggestive, Watson's account tends too easily to blur the distinction between matricide and patricide: in fantasies of rebirth, the hero may symbolically replace the father to re-create himself, but he does so by means of an attack specifically on the maternal body. In Shakespeare's images of Caesarian birth, the father tends to be conspicuously absent; indeed, I shall argue, precisely his absence—not his defining presence—creates the fear of the engulfing maternal body to which the fantasy of Caesarian section is a response. This body tends to be missing in Watson's account, as it is missing in his discussion of Richard's Caesarian fantasy here.

10. In an early essay that has become a classic, Eugene Waith established the centrality of definitions of manhood and Lady Macbeth's role in enforcing Macbeth's particularly bloodthirsty version, a theme that has since become a major topos of *Macbeth* criticism ("Manhood and Valor in Two Shakespearean Tragedies," *ELH* 17 [1950]: 262-73). Among the ensuing legions, see, for example, Matthew N. Proser, *The Heroic Image in Five Shakespearean Tragedies* (Princeton: Princeton University Press, 1965), 51-91; Michael Taylor, "Ideals of Manhood in *Macbeth*," *Etudes Anglaises* 21 (1968): 337-48 (unusual in its early emphasis on the extent to which the culture is complicit in defining masculinity as aggression); D. W. Harding, "Women's Fantasy of Manhood: A Shakespearean Theme," *Shakespeare Quarterly* 20 (1969): 245-53 (significant especially in its stress on women's responsibility for committing men to their false fantasy of manhood); Paul A. Jorgensen, *Our Naked Frailties: Sensational Art and Meaning in "Macbeth"* (Berkeley & Los Angeles: University of California Press, 1971), esp. 147ff.; Jarold Ramsey, "The Perversion of Manliness in *Macbeth*," *SEL* 13 (1973): 285-300; Carolyn Asp, "'Be bloody, bold, and resolute': Tragic Action and Sexual Stereotyping in *Macbeth*," *Studies in Philology* 25 (1981): 153-69 (significant especially for associating Macbeth's pursuit of masculinity with his pursuit of omnipotence); Harry Berger, Jr., "Text Against Performance in Shakespeare: The Example of *Macbeth*," in *The Forms of Power and the Power of Forms in the Renaissance*, ed. Stephen Greenblatt, special issue of *Genre* (15 [1982]), esp. 67-75; and Robert Kimbrough, "Macbeth: The Prisoner of Gender," *Shakespeare Studies* 16 (1983): 175-90. Virtually all these essays recount the centrality of 1.7 to this theme; most see Macbeth's willingness to murder as his response to Lady Macbeth's nearly explicit attack on his male potency. Dennis Biggins and James J. Greene note particularly the extent to which the murder itself is imagined as a sexual act through which the union of Macbeth and Lady Macbeth is consummated; see Biggins, "Sexuality, Witchcraft, and Violence in *Macbeth*," *Shakespeare Studies* 8 (1975): 255-77; Greene, "Macbeth: Masculinity as Murder," *American Imago* 41 (1984): 155-80; see also Watson, *Shakespeare and the Hazards of Ambition*, 90. My account differs from most of these largely in stressing the infantile components of Macbeth's susceptibility to Lady Macbeth. The classic account of these pre-Oedipal components in the play is David B. Barron's brilliant early essay "The Babe That Milks: An Organic Study of *Macbeth*," originally published in 1960 and reprinted in *The Design Within*, ed. M. D. Faber (New York: Science House, 1970), 253-79. For similar readings, see Marvin Rosenberg, *The Masks of Macbeth* (Berkeley & Los Angeles: University of California Press, 1978), 81-82, 270-72, and especially Kahn, *Man's Estate*, 151-55, 172-92, and Richard P. Wheeler, *Shakespeare's Development and the Problem Comedies* (Berkeley & Los Angeles: University of California Press, 1981), 144-49; as always, I am deeply and minutely indebted to the two last named.

11. Harry Berger, Jr., associates both Duncan's vulnerability and his role in legitimizing the bloody masculinity of his thanes with his status as the androgynous supplier of blood and milk ("The Early Scenes of *Macbeth*: Preface to a New Interpretation," *ELH* 47 [1980]: 26-28). Murray M. Schwartz and Richard Wheeler note specifically the extent to which the male claim to androgynous possession of nurturant power reflects a fear of maternal power outside male control (Schwartz, "Shakespeare through Contemporary Psychoanalysis," in *Representing Shakespeare*, 29. Wheeler, *Shakespeare's Development*, 146. My discussion of Duncan's androgyny is partly a consequence of my having heard Peter Erickson's rich account of the Duke's taking on of nurturant function in *As You Like It* at MLA in 1979; this account is now part of his *Patriarchal Structures in Shakespeare's Drama* (Berkeley & Los Angeles: University of California Press, 1985); see esp. pp. 27-37.

12. Many commentators note that Shakespeare's Duncan is less ineffectual than Holingshed's; others note the continuing signs of his weakness. See especially Harry Berger's brilliant account of the structural effect of Duncan's weakness in defining his (and Macbeth's) society ("The Early Scenes," 1-31).

13. Many note the appropriateness of Macbeth's conflation of himself with Tarquin, given the play's alliance of sexuality and murder. See, for example, Ian Robinson, "The Witches and Macbeth," *Critical Review* 11 (1968): 104; Biggins, "Sexuality, Witchcraft, and Violence," 269; and Watson, *Shakespeare and the Hazards of Ambition*, 100. Arthur Kirsch works extensively with the analogy, seeing the Tarquin of *The Rape of Lucrece* as a model for Macbeth's ambitious desire ("Macbeth's Suicide," *ELH* 51 [1984]: 269-96). Commentators

on the analogy do not in general note that it transforms Macbeth's kingly victim into a woman; Norman Rabkin is the exception (*Shakespeare and the Problem of Meaning* [Chicago: Chicago University Press, 1981], 107).

14. Wheeler sees the simultaneously castrated and castrating Gorgon-like body of Duncan as the emblem of the world Macbeth brings into being (*Shakespeare's Development,* 145); I see it as the emblem of a potentially castrating femaleness that Macbeth's act of violence reveals but does not create.

15. The witches' power to raise storms was conventional; see, for example, Reginald Scot, *The Discoverie of Witchcraft* (London 1584; reprint, with an introduction by Hugh Ross Williamson, Carbondale: Southern Illinois University Press, 1964), 31; King James's *Daemonologie* (London, 1603), 46; and the failure of the witches to raise a storm in Jonson's *Masque of Queens.* Jonson's learned note on their attempt to disturb nature gives his classical sources for their association with chaos: see *Masque,* 11.134-37, 209-20, and Jonson's note to l.134, in *Ben Jonson: The Complete Masques,* ed. Stephen Orgel (New Haven: Yale University Press, 1969), 531-32.

16. Many commentators, following Freud, find the murder of Duncan "little else than parricide" ("Those Wrecked by Success," in *The Standard Edition of the Complete Psychological Works of Sigmund Freud,* trans. and ed. James Strachey [London, Hogarth Press, 1957], 14: 321); see, for example, Rabkin, *Shakespeare and the Problem of Meaning,* 106-9, Kirsch, "Macbeth's Suicide," 276-80, 286, and Watson, *Shakespeare and the Hazards of Ambition,* esp. 85-88, 98-99 (the last two are particularly interesting in understanding parricide as an ambitious attempt to redefine the self as omnipotently free from limits). In standard Oedipal readings of the play, the mother is less the object of desire than "the 'demon-woman,' who creates the abyss between father and son" by inciting the son to parricide (Ludwig Jekels, "The Riddle of Shakespeare's *Macbeth,*" in *The Design Within,* 240). See also, for example, L. Veszy-Wagner, "*Macbeth:* 'Fair Is Foul and Foul Is Fair,'" *American Imago* 25 (1968): 242-57; Norman N. Holland, *Psychoanalysis and Shakespeare* (New York: Octagon Books, 1979), 229; and Patrick Colm Hogan's very suggestive account of the Oedipal narrative structure, "*Macbeth:* Authority and Progenitorship," *American Imago* 40 (1983): 385-95. My reading differs from these Oedipal readings mainly in suggesting that the play's mothers acquire their power because the father's protective masculine authority is already significantly absent; in my reading, female power over Macbeth becomes the sign (rather than the cause) of that absence.

17. For those recent commentators who follow Barron in seeing pre-Oedipal rather than Oedipal issues as central to the play, the images of disrupted nurturance define the primary area of disturbance; see, for example, Barron, "The Babe That Milks," 255; Schwartz, "Shakespeare through Psychoanalysis," 29; Berger, "The Early Scenes," 27-28; Joan M. Byles, "Macbeth: Imagery of Destruction," *American Imago* 39 (1982): 149-64; Wheeler, *Shakespeare's Development,* 147-48; and Kirsch, "Macbeth's Suicide," 291-92. Although Madelon Gohlke (now Sprengnether) does not specifically discuss the rupture of maternal nurturance in *Macbeth,* my understanding of the play is very much indebted to her classic essay, "'I wooed thee with my sword': Shakespeare's Tragic Paradigms," in which she establishes the extent to which masculinity in Shakespeare's heroes entails a defensive denial of the female (in *Representing Shakespeare:* 170-87); in an unfortunately unpublished essay, she discusses the traumatic failure of maternal protection imaged by Lady Macbeth here. In his brilliant essay "Phantasmagoric *Macbeth*" (forthcoming in *ELR*), David Willbern locates in Lady Macbeth's image the psychological point of origin for the failure of potential space that Macbeth enacts. Erickson, noting that patriarchal bounty in *Macbeth* has gone awry, suggestively locates the dependence of that bounty on the maternal nurturance that is here disturbed (*Patriarchal Structures,* 116-21). Several critics see in Macbeth's susceptibility to female influence evidence of his failure to differentiate from a maternal figure, a failure psychologically the consequence of the abrupt and bloody weaning imaged by Lady Macbeth; see, for example, Susan Bachmann, "'Daggers in Men's Smiles'—The 'Truest Issue' in *Macbeth,*" *International Review of Psycho-Analysis* 5 (1978): 97-104; and particularly the full and very suggestive accounts of Barron, "The Babe That Milks," 263-68, and Kahn, *Man's Estate,* 172-78. In the readings of all these critics, as in mine, Lady Macbeth and the witches variously embody the destructive maternal force that overwhelms Macbeth and in relation to whom he is imagined as an infant. Rosenberg notes intriguingly that *Macbeth* has twice been performed with a mother and son in the chief roles (*Masks of Macbeth,* 196).

18. Despite some overliteral interpretation, Alice Fox and particularly Jenijoy La Belle usefully demonstrate the specifically gynecological references of "passage" and "visitings of nature," using contemporary gynecological treatises. (See Fox, "Obstetrics and Gynecology in *Macbeth,*" *Shakespeare Studies* 12 [1979]: 129; and La Belle, "'A Strange Infirmity': Lady Macbeth's Amenorrhea," *Shakespeare Quarterly* 31 [1980]: 382, for the identification of *visitings of nature* as a term for menstruation; see La Belle, 383, for the identification of *passage* as a term for the neck of

19. *For* is glossed as "in exchange for" in the following editions, for example: *The Complete Signet Classic Shakespeare,* ed. Sylvan Barnet (New York: Harcourt, Brace, Jovanovich, 1972); *The Complete Works of Shakespeare,* ed. Hardin Craig (Chicago: Scott, Foresman, 1951), rev. ed. edited by David Bevinton (Chicago: Scott, Foresman, 1973); *The Riverside Shakespeare,* ed. G. Blakemore Evans (Boston: Houghton Mifflin, 1974); *William Shakespeare: The Complete Works,* ed. Alfred Harbage (Baltimore: Penguin, 1969); *The Complete Works of Shakespeare,* ed. George Lyman Kittredge (Boston: Ginn, 1936), rev. ed. edited by Irving Ribner (Boston: Ginn, 1971). Muir demurs, preferring Keightley's understanding of *take* as "infect" (see the Arden edition, p. 30).

(Note: the womb. See also Barron, who associates Lady Macbeth's language here with contraception ["The Babe That Milks," 267].)

20. Insofar as syphilis was known to be transmitted through the nursing process, there was some reason to worry; see, for example, William Clowes's frightening account, "A brief and necessary Treatise touching the cure of the disease called Morbus Gallicus" (London, 1585, 1596), 151. But Leontes' words to Hermione as he removes Mamillius from her ("I am glad you did not nurse him. / Though he does bear some signs of me, yet you / Have too much blood in him" [*The Winter's Tale,* 2.1.56-58]) suggest that the worry was not fundamentally about epidemiology. Worry that the nurse's milk determined morals was, of course, common; see, for example, Thomas Phaire, *The Boke of Chyldren* (1545; reprint, Edinburgh: E. & S. Livingstone, 1955), 18. The topic was of interest to King James, who claimed to have sucked his Protestantism from his nurse's milk; his drunkenness was also attributed to her. See Henry N. Paul, *The Royal Play of "Macbeth"* (New York: Macmillan Co., 1950), 387-88. For the identification of colostrum with witch's milk, see Samuel X. Radbill, "Pediatrics," in *Medicine in Seventeenth-Century England,* ed. Allen G. Debus (Berkeley & Los Angeles, University of California Press, 1974), 249. The fear of maternal functioning itself, not simply of its perversions, is central to most readings of the play in pre-Oedipal terms; see the critics cited in note 17 above.

21. Many commentators on English witchcraft note the unusual prominence given to the presence of the witch's mark and the nursing of familiars; see, for example, Barbara Rosen's introduction to the collection of witchcraft documents she edited (*Witchcraft* [London: Edward Arnold, 1969], 29-30). She cites contemporary documents on the nursing of familiars, for example, pp. 187-88, 315; the testimony of Joan Prentice, one of the convicted witches of Chelmsford in 1589, is particularly suggestive: "at what time soever she would have her ferret do anything for her, she used the words 'Bid, Bid, Bid, come Bid, come Bid, come Bid, come suck, come suck, come suck'" (p. 188). Katharine Mary Briggs quotes a contemporary (1613) story about the finding of a witch's teat (*Pale Hecate's Team* [New York: Arno Press, 1977], 250); see also Wallace Notestein, *A History of Witchcraft in England from 1558 to 1718* (Washington: American Historical Association, 1911), 36; and George Lyman Kittredge, *Witchcraft in Old and New England* (New York: Russell & Russell, 1956), 179. Though he does not refer to the suckling of familiars, King James believed in the significance of the witch's mark, at least when he wrote the *Daemonologie* (see p. 33). M. C. Bradbrook notes that Lady Macbeth's invitation to the spirits is "as much as any witch could do by way of self-dedication" ("The Sources of *Macbeth*," *Shakespeare Survey* 4 [1951]: 43).

22. In a brilliant essay, Peter Stallybrass associates the move from the cosmic to the secular realm with the ideological shoring up of a patriarchal state founded on the model of the family ("*Macbeth* and Witchcraft," in *Focus on "Macbeth,"* ed. John Russell Brown [London: Routledge & Kegan Paul, 1982], esp. 196-98).

23. Wilbur Sanders notes the extent to which "terror is mediated through absurdity" in the witches (*The Dramatist and the Received Idea* [Cambridge: Cambridge University Press, 1968], 277); see also Berger's fine account of the scapegoating reduction of the witches to a comic and grotesque triviality ("Text Against Performance," 67-68). Harold C. Goddard (*The Meaning of Shakespeare* [Chicago: University of Chicago Press, 1951], 512-13), Robinson ("The Witches and Macbeth," 100-103), and Stallybrass, ("*Macbeth* and Witchcraft," 199) note the witches' change from potent and mysterious to more diminished figures in act 4.

24. After years of trying fruitlessly to pin down a precise identity for the witches, critics are increasingly finding their dramatic power precisely in their indefinability. The most powerful statements of this relatively new critical topos are those by Sanders (*The Dramatist and the Received Idea,* 277-79), Robert H. West (*Shakespeare and the Outer Mystery* [Lexington: University of Kentucky Press, 1968], 78-79), and Stephen Booth ("*King Lear,*" "*Macbeth,*" *Indefinition, and Tragedy* [New Haven: Yale University Press, 1983], 101-3).

25. For their "Englishness", see Stallybrass, "*Macbeth* and Witchcraft," 195. Alan Macfarlane's important study of English witchcraft, *Witchcraft in Tudor and Stuart England* (New York: Harper & Row, 1970), frequently notes the absence of the Continental staples: if the witches of Essex are typical, English witches do not fly, do not hold Sabbaths, do not commit sexual perversions or attack male potency, do not kill babies (see pp. 6, 160, 180, for example).

26. Macfarlane finds the failure of neighborliness reflected in the retaliatory acts of the witch the key to the social function of witchcraft in England; see ibid., 168-76 for accounts of the failures of neighborliness—very similar to the refusal to share chestnuts—that provoked the witch to act. James Sprenger and Heinrich Kramer, *Malleus Maleficarum,* trans. Montague Summers (New York: Benjamin Blom, 1970), is the *locus classicus* for Continental witchcraft beliefs: for the murder and eating of infants, see pp. 21, 66, 99, 100-101; for attacks on the genitals, see pp. 47, 55-60, 117-19; for sexual relations with demons, see pp. 21, 112-14. Or see Scot's convenient summary of these beliefs (*Discoverie,* 31).

27. The relationship between cosmology and domestic psychology is similar in *King Lear*; even as Shakespeare casts doubt on the authenticity of demonic possession by his use of Harsnett's *Declaration of Egregious Popish Impostures,* Edgar/Poor Tom's identification of his father as "the foul Flibbertigibbet" (3.4.108) manifests the psychic reality and source of his demons. Characteristically in Shakespeare, the site of blessing and of cursedness is the family, their processes psychological.

28. Although *his* was a common form for the as yet unfamiliar possessive *its,* Lady Macbeth's move from "while it was smiling" to "his boneless gums" nonetheless seems to register the metamorphosis of an ungendered to a gendered infant exactly at the moment of vulnerability, making her attack specifically on a male child. That she uses the ungendered *the* a moment later ("the brains out") suggests one alternative open to Shakespeare had he wished to avoid the implication that the fantasied infant was male; Antony's crocodile, who "moves with it own organs" (*Antony and Cleopatra,* 2.7.42), suggests another. (*OED* notes that, although *its* occurs in the Folio, it does not occur in any work of Shakespeare published while he was alive; it also notes the various strategies by which authors attempted to avoid the inappropriate use of *his.*)

29. Lady Macbeth maintains her control over Macbeth through 3.4 by manipulating these categories: see 2.2.53-54 ("'tis the eye of childhood / That fears a painted devil") and 3.4.57-65 ("Are you a man? . . . these flaws and starts . . . would well become / A woman's story"). In his response to Banquo's ghost, Macbeth invokes the same categories and suggests their interchangeability: he dares what man dares (3.4.98); if he feared Banquo alive, he could rightly be called "the baby of a girl" (l. 105).

30. In "Phantasmagoric *Macbeth,*" David Willbern notes the extent to which the regicide is reimagined as a "symbolic infanticide" so that the image of Duncan fuses with the image of Lady Macbeth's child murdered in fantasy. Macbeth's earlier association of Duncan's power with the power of the "naked new-born babe, / Striding the blast" (1.7.21-22) prepares for this fusion. Despite their symbolic power, the literal babies of this play and those adults who sleep and trust like infants are hideously vulnerable.

31. See Kahn, *Man's Estate,* 173, for a very similar account of this passage.

32. Shakespeare's only other use of *man-child* is in a strikingly similar context: Volumnia, reporting her pleasure in Coriolanus' martial success, tells Virgilia, "I sprang not more in joy at first hearing he was a man-child than now in first seeing he had proved himself a man" (*Coriolanus,* 1.3.15-17).

33. De Quincy seems to have understood this process: "The murderers are taken out of the region of human things, human purposes, human desires. They are transfigured: Lady Macbeth is 'unsexed'; Macbeth has forgot that he was born of woman" ("On the Knocking at the Gate in 'Macbeth,'" in *Shakespeare Criticism: A Selection, 1623-1840,* ed. D. Nichol Smith [London: Oxford University Press, 1946], 335). Critics who consider gender relations central to this play generally note the importance of the witches' prophecy for the figure of Macduff; they do not usually note its application to Macbeth. But see Kahn's suggestion that the prophecy sets Macbeth "apart from women as well as from men" (*Man's Estate,* 187) and Gohlke's central perception that, "to be born of woman, as [Macbeth] reads the witches' prophecy, is to be mortal" ("I wooed thee," 176).

34. See Kahn's rich understanding of the function of the term *cow'd* (*Man's Estate,* 191).

35. Many comment on this contamination; see, for example, Berger, "The Early Scenes of *Macbeth,*" 7-8; Hogan, "Macbeth," 387; Rosenberg, *The Masks of Macbeth,* 45; Biggins, "Sexuality, Witches, and Violence," 265.

36. Watson notes the suggestion of Caesarian section here, through not its aggression toward the female. Barron does not comment specifically on this passage but notes breaking and cutting imagery throughout and relates it to Macbeth's attempt to "cut his way out of the female environment which chokes and smothers him" ("The Babe That Milks," 269). I am indebted to Willbern's "Phantasmagoric *Macbeth*" specifically for the Caesarian implications of the unseaming from nave to chops.

37. The reference to Macbeth as "Bellona's bridegroom" anticipates his interaction with Lady Macbeth in 1.7: only the murderous man-child is fit mate for either of these unsexed, quasi-male figures.

38. To the extent that ferocious maleness is the creation of the male community, not of Lady Macbeth or the witches, the women are scapegoats who exist partly to obscure the failures of male community. For

fuller accounts of this process, see Veszy-Wagner, "Macbeth," 244, Bamber, *Comic Women,* 19-20, and especially Berger, "Text Against Performance," 68-75. But whether or not the women are scapegoats insofar as they are (falsely) held responsible for Macbeth's murderous maleness, fear of the female power they represent remains primary (not secondary and obscurantist) insofar as the male community and, to some extent, the play itself define maleness as violent differentiation from the female.

39. A great many critics, following Waith ("Manhood and Valor," 266-67), find the play's embodiment of healthy masculinity in Macduff. They often register some uneasiness about his leaving his family, but they rarely allow this uneasiness to complicate their view of him as exemplary. But critics interested in the play's construction of masculinity as a defense against the fear of femaleness tend to see in Macduff's removal from family a replication of the central fear of women that is more fully played out in Macbeth. See, for example, Wheeler, *Shakespeare's Development,* 146; and Berger, "Text Against Performance," 70. For these critics, Macduff's flight is of a piece with his status as the man not born of woman.

40. Critics interested in gender issues almost invariably comment on the centrality of Macduff's fulfillment of this prophecy, finding his strength here in his freedom from contamination by or regressive dependency on women: see, for example, Harding, "Women's Fantasy," 250; Barron, "The Babe That Milks," 272; Berger, "The Early Scenes," 28; Bachmann, "Daggers," 101; Kirsch, "Macbeth's Suicide," 293; Kahn, *Man's Estate,* 172-73; Wheeler, *Shakespeare's Development,* 146; and Victor Calef, "Lady Macbeth and Infanticide or 'How Many Children Had Lady Macbeth Murdered?'" *Journal of the American Psychoanalytic Association* 17 (1969): 537. For Barron and Harding, Macduff's status as the bearer of this fantasy positively enhances his manhood; but for many of these critics, it qualifies his status as the exemplar of healthy manhood. Perhaps because ambivalence toward Macduff is built so deeply into the play, several very astute critics see the fantasy embedded in Macduff here and nonetheless continue to find in him an ideal manhood that includes the possibility of relatedness to the feminine. See, for example, Kahn, *Man's Estate,* 191; and Kirsch, "Macbeth's Suicide," 294.

41. The triumph of the natural order has of course been a commonplace of criticism since the classic essay by G. Wilson Knight, "The Milk of Concord: An Essay on Life-Themes in *Macbeth,*" in his *Imperial Theme* (London: Methuen, 1965), esp. 140-53. The topos is so powerful that it can cause even critics interested in gender issues to praise the triumph of nature and natural sexuality at the end without noting the exclusion of the female; see, for example, Greene, "Macbeth," 172. But Rosenberg, for example, notes the qualifying effect of this exclusion (*Masks of Macbeth,* 654).

42. See, for example, Goddard, *Meaning of Shakespeare,* 520-21; Jekels, "Riddle," 238; John Holloway, *The Story of the Night* (London: Routledge & Kegan Paul, 1961), 66; Rosenberg, *Masks of Macbeth,* 626; and Watson, *Shakespeare and the Hazards of Ambition,* 89, 106-16. Even without sensing the covert presence of a vegetation myth, critics often associate the coming of Birnam Wood with the restoration of spring and fertility; see, for example, Knight, "Milk of Concord," 144-45; and Greene, "Macbeth," 169. Only Bamber demurs: in her account Birnam Wood rises up in aid of a male alliance, not the Saturnalian disorder of the Maying rituals (*Comic Women,* 106). My view coincides with hers.

43. When Malcolm refers to planting (5.9.31) at the play's end, for example, his comment serves partly to reinforce our sense of his distance from his father's generative power.

44. Paul attributes Shakespeare's use of the imagery of the family tree here to his familiarity with the cut of the Banquo tree in Leslie's *De Origine, Moribus, et Rebus Gestis Scotorum* (*Royal Play,* 175). But the image is too familiar to call for such explanation; see, for example, the tree described in *Richard II* (1.2.12-21).

45. As Wheeler notes, the description of Malcolm's saintly mother makes him "symbolically the child of something approximating virgin birth" (*Shakespeare's Development,* 146)—in effect another version of the man not quite born of woman. Berger comments on the aspiration to be "a nation of bachelor Adams, of no woman born and unknown to women" ("Text Against Performance," 72) without noting the extent to which this fantasy is enacted in the play; Stallybrass calls attention to this configuration and describes the structure of antithesis through which "(virtuous) families of men" are distinguished from "antifamilies of women" ("*Macbeth* and Witchcraft," 198). The fantasy of escape from maternal birth and the creation of all-male lineage would probably have been of interest to King James, whose problematic derivation from Mary, Queen of Scots must occasionally have made him wish himself not born of (that particular) woman, no matter how much he was concerned publicly to rehabilitate her image. See Jonathan Goldberg's account of James's complex attitude toward Mary and especially his attempt to claim the Virgin Queen, Elizabeth, rather than Mary as his mother as he moved toward the English throne (*James I and the Politics of Literature* [Baltimore: Johns Hopkins University Press, 1983], 11-17, 25-26, 119); see also

Goldberg's very suggestive discussions of James's poetic attacks on women (ibid., 24-25) and his imaging himself as a man taking control of a woman in becoming king of England (ibid., 30-31, 46). Stephen Orgel speculates brilliantly about the ways in which James's concerns about his own lineage and hence about the derivation of his royal authority are reflected in *The Tempest*: James "conceived himself as the head of a single-parent family," as a paternal figure who has "incorporated the maternal," in effect as a Prospero; the alternative model is Caliban, who derives his authority from his mother ("Prospero's Wife," *Representations* 8 [1984]: 8-9). Perhaps *Macbeth* indirectly serves a cultural need to free James from entanglement with the problematic memory of his witch-mother (portrayed thus, for example, by Spenser in book 5 of *The Faerie Queene*), tracing his lineage instead from a safely distanced and safely male forefather, Banquo.

46. Although neither Berger nor Stallybrass discusses the function of Birnam Wood specifically, I am indebted here to their discussions of the ideological function of the play's appeal to cosmology in the service of patriarchy, Berger seeing it as "a collective project of mystification" ("Text Against Performance," 64), Stallybrass as "a returning of the disputed ground of politics to the undisputed ground of Nature" ("*Macbeth* and Witchcraft," 205-6). If, as Bradbrook suggests, witches were thought able to move trees ("Sources," 42), then we have in Malcolm's gesture a literal appropriation of female power, an act of making the unnatural natural by making it serve patriarchal needs.

47. See Erickson's fine discussion of this geographic distinction (*Patriarchal Structures*, 121-22).

Joost Daalder (essay date 1988)

SOURCE: "Shakespeare's Attitude to Gender in *Macbeth*," in *Australasian Universities Language and Literature Association Journal (AUMLA)*, No. 70, November, 1988, pp. 366-85.

[*In the following essay, Daalder examines Shakespeare's attitude toward women as portrayed in* Macbeth.]

With the new interest in 'women's studies' there has been a whole flurry of works devoted to the question whether Shakespeare in any significant way discriminated against—or in favour of—women.[1]

In my view, discussion of this issue is much clarified if we remember what Ruth Kelso wrote some thirty years ago concerning the debate about the matter which was conducted during the Renaissance itself:

> Four attitudes can be distinguished in this confused debate. Some thought woman at best a necessary evil, some admitted her good in a limited and humble way but of inferior value compared to men, some took her as good and necessary equally with men, and some claimed superiority for her over men.[2]

I think that Kelso is amply supported by relevant evidence from the Renaissance (which we must carefully distinguish from the assertions of twentieth century commentators), and that her useful statement for one thing makes it very difficult to generalize about a supposedly universal 'Renaissance attitude to women'. And, in view of that fact, we must also be cautious about accepting any argument based on the assumption that there actually was such an attitude, to which—it is then also often maintained—Shakespeare must surely have subscribed, or which he was peculiarly individualistic in resisting.

Of course, if there had been some universally accepted view, it would indeed be tempting to see Shakespeare as automatically conditioned by it, or as heroically—and Romantically—opposing it. Either conclusion would not necessarily have been justified at all, of course; but it is much easier to reject modern simplifications when we can point to complexity in the past.

I think that fortunately those who are not ideologically committed to any particular view of the world, and who are acquainted with both the Renaissance and recent studies of the period, are less and less inclined to think that it is fruitful to speak of what scholars like E. M. W. Tillyard and others who wrote several decades ago saw as 'the Elizabethan world picture'. Even on a purely theoretical basis it surely is not likely that all Elizabethans would have felt and thought the same about everything, but the evidence is, even in very broad terms, conspicuously against such an assumption: the Renaissance was, in fact, a period of profound chance in just about every aspect of life.

Those of us who, like myself, were brought up on the thinking of such scholars as Tillyard, and who have only recently come to concern themselves with attitudes to women in the Renaissance, may well have gone through the following pattern of development in their beliefs. The first stage, in my own case, was that I accepted that 'the' world picture of the Elizabethans was hierarchical. This did not mean that I thought that Shakespeare felt that men were so superior to women that the latter should be seen as 'a necessary evil', to use Kelso's phrase. But I did consider it likely (without really probing the matter) that Shakespeare thought women were sufficiently inferior to men to deserve no more than a subservient role in what he saw as essentially a male world. In fact, then, I imputed to Shakespeare something like the second view mentioned by Kelso, according to which in principle women were 'good in a limited and humble way but of inferior value compared to men'. The notion that Shakespeare's world picture was hierarchical was so firmly implanted in me that I never contemplated the possibility that Shakespeare saw men and women as equals before I moved on to my own second stage (Kelso's fourth view) and came to believe that Shakespeare saw women as superior over men. In these matters, it is difficult to develop a totally dispassionate view, and I must admit that my enthusiasm was in no small measure sparked by irritation with those who believed that Shakespeare was contemptuously 'sexist' in his attitude to women. More importantly, though, I felt I was really led by the evidence in Shakespeare's own works.

As I held this view for some years with real conviction, and have only very recently abandoned it, I should just briefly like to mention some of the evidence in favour of it. It does seem, to speak sweepingly, that whenever one thinks of a character in Shakespeare who is both morally good and intellectually formidable the example that comes to mind is a woman. For instance, in *The Tempest* the most admirable character, in all respects, is Miranda, and it is surely no accident that Shakespeare presents her as willing to carry logs for Ferdinand and able to catch him out when he cheats at chess: obviously, Shakespeare wishes to shatter any stereotyped view of her as possibly inferior to Ferdinand, and, on the contrary, sets her up as at once superior and his own ideal of what, at our best, we humans can be like. In several plays, Shakespeare seems to go out of his way to suggest that women are totally capable of such things as are conventionally often thought to be above their reach. Rosalind in *As You Like It* is a perfect instance. To indicate that she combines the best 'male' and 'female' qualities, Shakespeare presents her as a woman in a man's clothes who retains, by implication, everything positive that she was able to show when presenting herself as a woman, while yet she demonstrates that, given the chance, she can fully hold her own, as a 'man', in a male-dominated world. There are several such characters, of course, and their existence always appears to suggest this same message.

It is possible that Shakespeare was personally fascinated with the image of a male-female hybrid because he idealized the young man in the *Sonnets* as having both male and female characteristics. Sonnet 20 provides the most telling evidence in this regard, and if we believe that Shakespeare was bi-sexual, we will find it the easier to persuade ourselves that to him the perfect human being—if such a creature could be created—would be both male and female. At all events, Shakespeare's interest in a male-female being was intense and persistent.

Intriguingly, however, there is a contrast between Shakespeare's attitude in the *Sonnets* and that in the plays. In the *Sonnets,* it is the young man who is described as a hermaphrodite. It would thus be possible to believe that Shakespeare's main preference is for a male, and indeed his feeling for the dark lady could well be described as misogynist. On the other hand, in the plays the hermaphrodites are invariably female, suggesting that Shakespeare admires women more than men. Or are we to believe that his attitude is, after all, consistent?

I think we can, and that the seeming inconsistency is not real. The young man of the *Sonnets,* we must remember, lets Shakespeare down, and in the end does not live up at all to the ideal of sonnet 20. Assuming—not unreasonably, I think—that the *Sonnets* describe events more or less chronologically, this early sonnet would indicate that one reason why Shakespeare was so attracted to the young man was that that person was so much like a woman. But, not being a woman, the young man cannot sustain the level of people like Miranda and Rosalind. I do not suggest that Shakespeare disapproves of all men, or approves of all women. But I do contend that his preference is for women, and not so much sexually but because he views them as superior creatures.

That, to speak rather crudely and generally, would make Shakespeare 'sexist', of course. And I still think that the argument which I have outlined has merit, but I have now come to believe that it needs to be severely modified.

My change of mind has been brought about by my former student Pauline Carter and her recently completed M.A. thesis, *Between Two Spheres of Authority: The Interregna of Shakespearean Heroines.*[3] Carter has extensively studied the way Shakespeare presents young women during the period which intervenes between the time when they were under the control of their fathers and the new stage when they will be under the authority of their husbands. Rosalind is merely one of several such women. Carter does not deny that Shakespeare sees these women as superior during their interregna. What she does refute, though, is the thought that Shakespeare therefore allows them *general* superiority. I may perhaps legitimately quote the following passage as illustrative of Carter's thesis:

> Shakespeare's obedient Renaissance daughters become, after a short interval, obedient Renaissance wives. The freedom he allows them through the medium of their interregna, and the superiority he claims for them, place Shakespeare amongst the progressive thinkers in relation to the position of women in Renaissance society, but such progressive thinking is modified when his heroines approach marriage. In their submission to their husbands they conform to the ideal advocated by Church and State and supported by the orthodox.
>
> (p. 50)

Upon reflection, the submission of the heroines to their husbands is indeed striking. One reason for it, as Carter argues, is no doubt that Shakespeare felt that women with independent means, like Portia and Olivia, could afford not to submit to the authority of a man, but that their position was exceptional. We may add, though, that even they are keen to get married, and to submit, at least outwardly, to the authority of their husbands. Portia, admittedly, will no doubt rule the roost. But, in general, the meekness with which women in Shakespeare accept marriage and the authority of husbands which the institution will bring with it is disconcerting to a feminist, and contrasts most oddly with the independence of mind which Shakespeare grants so many heroines during their interregna.

At the outset, I expressed my approval of Kelso's view that there were essentially four different attitudes held by

Renaissance thinkers concerned with the status of women. My chief reason for satisfaction is that I think she is right. But that fact also helps me greatly in other ways. It enables me to see that, if attitudes in the Renaissance were so varied, we should not be at all surprised to find them varied now. Furthermore, it is of course not at all unlikely that a critic with a particular ideological commitment may well wish to find that reflected in Shakespeare. But, especially, where several views existed, it would not seem at all unrealistic to expect that Shakespeare's own view is complex rather than simplistic. To say that it is complex (as I believe it is) is not, however, to suggest that it is confused, or that it is indecisive. Shakespeare seems to be very clear in his mind that, although it is desirable for a woman to develop 'male' qualities as well as female ones, ultimately the role of a woman is quite distinct from that of a man. And this is not something we can confidently ascribe to conditioning by society: Shakespeare's women actively *want* to get married, and, normally, to play the part traditionally associated with being a wife. We have no reason for supposing that he sees this desire as something other than internal and innate. As far as we can tell, Shakespeare does not believe that women and men are psychologically identical, or should be.

I must therefore reluctantly part company from Robert Kimbrough, who has written some very interesting and valuable articles on androgyny, the most relevant for my present purpose being the one which he called 'Macbeth: The Prisoner of Gender', *Shakespeare Studies* (1983), pp. 175-90.[4]

I use the word 'reluctantly' because Kimbrough's view of what life should be is appealing, as Shakespeare's would be if he agreed with Kimbrough. The latter's outlook is androgynous, and he believes Shakespeare's is too. Kimbrough holds that 'female and male differences are, for the most part, matters of mind', and that 'through all of Shakespeare there runs the theme that both male and female must be liberated from the restrictions inherent in the concept of the two genders' (p. 175).

Kimbrough emphasizes the importance of the fact that Lady Macbeth is afraid that her husband's nature will not allow him to kill Duncan:

> Yet I do fear thy nature:
> It is too full o' th' milk of human kindness
> To catch the nearest way.
>
> (I.v.13-15)[5]

Kimbrough comments:

> The phrase makes us pause, ring in our ears: 'The milk of human kindness'. No other expression better reveals Shakespeare's basically optimistic vision of the nature of humankind (except possibly Miranda's speeches). 'Human kindness' was still a redundancy in Shakespeare's day because to be kind was to be human. Kindness is humanness; mankind is humankind. *Mensch.*
>
> (p. 179)

As it seems to me, Kimbrough is too optimistic about Shakespeare's optimism. Certainly characters like Lear and Gloucester believe that it is natural to be kind; Edmund's vision of what is natural, however, is quite different, and *Lear* does not present us with a world in which kindness wins out. But, in the context of this essay, I object yet more strongly to Kimbrough's blurring of the distinction between the two sexes, and in particular of the physical difference which lies at the root of that distinction. Lady Macbeth is afraid that Macbeth is too full of the *milk* of human kindness. Throughout his article, Kimbrough in effect ignores the importance of the word 'milk', and the fact that the speaker is a woman.

My concern, by contrast, is not to show that Shakespeare thought women superior to men, or vice versa, but that he considered that there are vital physical differences between them which in turn make for important psychological distinctions. A man may well have the upper hand in certain spheres (e.g. the battlefield) and a woman in others (e.g. the home), but, while this is significant, it does not mean that *in sum* one of the two genders is superior to the other.

Let us be clear that it is Lady Macbeth who sees the milk of human kindness as something undesirable, not her husband. This is not because her husband is less sensitive than she, but because Shakespeare wants us to understand that it would be, in principle and ideally, natural for a *woman* to associate human kindness with milk. Significantly, and inevitably, Lady Macbeth does associate the two, and her perversion is the greater in rejecting her own natural feeling and projecting it onto Macbeth as though it is something perverse. Of course, she has a shallow rhetorical point: it would indeed be inappropriate for Macbeth to be too full of the *milk* of human kindness, because he is a man.

Lady Macbeth's attitude, therefore, is not just anti-human, as Kimbrough would make us believe, but violates essential concepts of manhood and womanhood that we should have. A little later, she says:

> Come, you spirits
> That tend on mortal thoughts, unsex me here:
> And fill me, from the crown to the toe, top-full
> Of direst cruelty.
>
> (I.v.37-40)

As Shakespeare sees things, for a woman to be unsexed automatically carries with it loss of good. We cannot distinguish, in this respect, between 'sex' and 'gender'. As many readers have noted, the spirits invoked by Lady Macbeth may well be those which make witches what they are. They are, obviously, devilish. When those 'women' are first met in the play, Banquo says to them:

> You should be women,
> And yet your beards forbid me to interpret
> That you are so.
>
> (I.iii.45-46)

The word 'should' here is interesting. No doubt there is some physical evidence that the witches are not men, but presumably Banquo also means that they *ought* to be female: he reacts to what is unnatural and wrong about them. (Significantly, Macbeth does not.) Shakespeare is far removed from any androgynous vision. If he were really interested in obscuring distinctions, and believed that essentially men and women are/should be the same, he would not stress that the beards are a major physical oddity. One—perhaps *the*—reason why these women are evil is that they deny their female nature.

I think that Shakespeare implies that there is a real choice involved. The women *ought* to be female: if they were, they would not have beards. I believe that this is what Shakespeare intends because of his attitude to the unsexing of Lady Macbeth. In this connection, we ought to consider the curious matter of Lady Macbeth's offspring.

Ever since the time that L. C. Knights made a mockery of the question 'How many children had Lady Macbeth?', critics have been timid about tackling the very real problem in interpretation that arises from Lady Macbeth saying 'I have given suck' (I.vii.54), whereas Macbeth himself complains about his 'barren sceptre' (III.i.61).

Certainly no naturalistic reading is likely to make sense of this strange discrepancy. Shakespeare apparently does not ask us to postulate (for he provides no hint to that effect) about a child which Lady Macbeth had before her marriage to Macbeth, about a child which was theirs but which has meanwhile died, etc. One might feel inclined to read something into the fact that Macbeth considers his sceptre barren because no *son* of his will succeed (III.i.63), but he does not put any emphasis on the gender of the child himself, and we have absolutely no evidence for believing that the Macbeths have a daughter.

Often, and naturally enough, critics suggest in cases like this that there are times when Homer, or Shakespeare, nods, and that there is some untidiness in the writing. And again and again we are reminded that Shakespeare's drama is not 'realistic', so that we should not look into this kind of inconsistency too closely.

I would agree that Shakespeare is probably not 'realistic' in a case like this, but that is not to say that we must not pay close attention to the oddity that apparently at one time Lady Macbeth had, according to her own admission, a child while no such child occurs in the action of the play, anywhere.

What *symbolic* significance is the discrepancy likely to have, supposing that it is deliberate on Shakespeare's part? I think there is an obvious explanation which fits in well with Shakespeare's general intention in the play. We probably are asked to believe that by nature Lady Macbeth was fertile, and indeed the sort of woman who wishes to have children, in one part of her mind. For she not only claims that she has 'given suck', but that she knows 'How tender 'tis to love the babe that milks me' (I.vii.55). Her natural inclination is, therefore, maternal, if only she followed her instinct. But, in her conscious mind, she rejects this inclination. It is not as though her society has taught her to be 'male' in any sense. Rather, she does not accept the role which her nature would assign to her, but, of her own volition, denies her deepest instincts to herself. She opts not to act on her physical and mental womanhood, but to turn herself into a 'man' instead. The consequence, thus Shakespeare implies, is loss of womanhood to the extent that she makes herself infertile. Thus, whether she ever had a child or not, she certainly cannot have one when once she adopts the mentality which the play shows her as having chosen for herself. Thus inevitably Macbeth's sceptre is indeed 'barren'.

Traditionally, we perhaps associate the wish to have children with women rather than men. Men, it is often felt, can manage without offspring in that, at any rate prior to the time when women began to look for work outside the home, their mind is filled with concern about their career, while to women children are essential if they are to have faith in the value of their existence. It is worth remembering, in this respect, that on the whole, in Shakespeare's time, a woman's 'place', to use the modern expression, was, in fact, 'in the home'. It therefore would not be illogical to suppose that, however enlightened Shakespeare may have been in principle, it would have been difficult for him to imagine a situation in which women could find fulfilment by working outside the home and not having children, or by having children as well as a job. This is not to say that Shakespeare could not understand Lady Macbeth's wish to be like a man—to be successful in a non-domestic sphere. But, clearly, in adopting that goal, Lady Macbeth sacrifices her womanhood. And this is the more so because her idea of what it means to be a man is absurdly restricted in its 'macho' emphasis: to be a man, she feels, one has to be prepared to kill, and not just on the battlefield, but also in one's own home (a major irony, here) and in the criminal cause of satisfying one's ambition against all considerations of what is proper when one entertains one's king and one's kinsman, as well as one's guest and someone who has borne his faculties so meek, has been so clear in his great office, etc., etc. (cf. Macbeth's 'If it were done when 'tis done', I.vii.1-27).

It is one of the more interesting features of this play that Shakespeare does not present Macbeth as a man who wishes to have no children. On the contrary, he clearly would like to have them, and it is his being without them which is one of the driving forces in his destructive course of action.

The main force, of course, is his ambition. In this respect, we must not forget that, typically, it is Macbeth himself, not his wife, who initiates the idea of killing Duncan. His guilty conscience is obvious the moment the witches, very early in the play, hail him as a future king, and Banquo says:

> Good sir, why do you start, and seem to fear
> Things that do sound so fair?
>
> (I.iii.51-52)

And again a little later, when he has just been made Thane of Cawdor, and he reflects in an aside:

> Glamis, and Thane of Cawdor!
> The greatest is behind.
>
> (I.iii.116-17)

Still in this scene, when he is found to be absentminded, he excuses himself by saying that his 'dull brain was wrought / With things forgotten' (lines 149-50). But perhaps the most conclusive proof of his initiative comes in I.vii, when Macbeth says 'I dare do all that may become a man; / Who dares do more is none', and his wife replies:

> What beast was't then
> That made you break this enterprise to me?
>
> (lines 46-48)

Prior to this scene, there is no evidence *within the play* of Macbeth breaking the enterprise to her, and we are clearly asked to believe that he mentioned it to her at some stage well into the past. This should come as no surprise to us. As a man, Macbeth can be expected—presumably for what are essentially biological/psychological reasons—to wish to advance his career.

But once he has killed Duncan and is king, he does not stop murdering. And it is at this stage that Macbeth's preoccupation with children becomes obvious. Again, I do not think that the play in any sense leads us to consider it unnatural for him to want to be a father. Such a desire is not at all incompatible with manhood. But this wish is one of the most important things to set Macbeth apart from his wife. Later in the play, the Macduffs are shown as both caring for children. Lady Macbeth, however, has no children because she wishes to kill; Macbeth kills because he has no children, and cannot stand those who have. While I have no wish to defend Macbeth, I think that Shakespeare sees him as perverting his manhood less than Lady Macbeth does her womanhood. It is, indeed, a contrast between them that Macbeth is more closely in touch with both his own deepest wishes and the workings of society. The two are no doubt connected, possibly because as a man he is more exposed to contact with other members of society than his wife is, and therefore, understanding the reality around him more, is also more likely to understand himself better.

The chief reason which Macbeth offers (in the soliloquy 'To be thus is nothing') for murdering Banquo is that he fears his being. But he is not at all specific about what Banquo might undertake against him, and it soon becomes clear that in fact he is jealous of Banquo because Banquo does have a son, and the witches have prophesied that his children will be kings:

> They hail'd him father to a line of kings.
> Upon my head they plac'd a fruitless crown
> And put a barren sceptre in my gripe,
> Thence to be wrench'd with an unlineal hand,
> No son of mine succeeding. If't be so,
> For Banquo's issue have I fil'd my mind;
> For them the gracious Duncan have I murder'd.
>
> (III.i.59-65)

Macbeth has considerable understanding of what tortures him about the existence of Banquo and his son. It is part of his manhood, however, that he seeks the resolution of his problem in violence. I think we have little reason for believing that Shakespeare does not see violence as much more characteristic of men than of women. The sergeant who at the beginning of the play gives an account of the way in which Macbeth kills Macdonwald, one of the rebels against King Duncan, comments how Macbeth fought

> Till he unseam'd him from the nave to th'chaps,
> And fix'd his head upon our battlements.
>
> (I.ii.22-23)

We may well want to question Duncan's immediate response: 'O valiant cousin! worthy gentleman!' But it is not evident that Shakespeare disapproves of Macbeth's action, or Duncan's comment; and in any case, whether or not he does, he appears to be in no doubt that this is how men behave. Thus, in principle, the action of killing is more congenial to Macbeth than to his wife—not because of individual differences between them, but because it is part of the role of a man to engage in violence. Therefore, despite Lady Macbeth's 'macho' talk it is Macbeth who is the murderer in the play.

The play shows how his character deteriorates as he moves from lawful killing to increasingly evil butchery. At first, he is presented very much as a courageous soldier (Duncan's 'valiant cousin'). When he kills Duncan, the thought of progeny is not yet important to him, though it is not absent. In I.vii, Macbeth firmly resolves upon the murder of Duncan. His wife has rejected offspring:

> I have given suck, and know
> How tender 'tis to love the babe that milks me—
> I would, while it was smiling in my face,
> Have pluck'd my nipple from his boneless gums,
> And dash'd the brains out . . .
>
> (lines 54-58)

Macbeth does not respond to this terrifying denial of motherhood, but, when his wife later persuades him that there is no danger of failure, Macbeth says:

> Bring forth men-children only;
> For thy undaunted mettle should compose
> Nothing but males.
>
> (lines 72-74)

We may dislike the fact that he praises his wife for being like a male, as well as his wish for 'men-children'; but he is quite unlike his wife in that he does not reject fatherhood.

Even so, at this stage it is Duncan's death only which he has in mind, not that of children which he cannot have. This changes when he plans the murder of Fleance, and especially when Fleance escapes. Yet even then Macbeth's attitude is less bizarre than when he decides to have Macduff's wife and children killed. Fleance, after all, may wish to take his crown away from him ('the worm that's fled / Hath nature that in time will venom breed'—III.iii.29-30). But he has absolutely nothing to fear from Macduff's family; yet he decides:

> The castle of Macduff I will surprise,
> Seize upon Fife, give to the edge o' th' sword
> His wife, his babes, and all unfortunate souls
> That trace him in his line.
>
> (IV.i.150-53)

Obviously, in a crazy way, his fear that others may oust him from his throne is connected with his wish to kill their children even if those cannot harm him, and a yet more potent reason for that wish, even if unconsciously, must be that he has no children of his own to succeed him.

Macduff, I think, understands this factor in Macbeth's psychology. Critics are often puzzled by Macduff's remark, upon hearing that his wife and children are dead: 'He has no children' (IV.iii.216). Indeed, in the context 'He' might seem to be Malcolm. But it is much more likely to be Macbeth, and to mean: 'He, Macbeth, has no children—and that is why he has killed mine.'

Shakespeare thus sees a wish for fatherhood as a perfectly normal thing in a man, and he explains that, in Macbeth's case at least, that wish is in fact a desire to continue one's own existence into the future. Presumably, Lady Macbeth finds it easier to deny her maternal instinct because she does not share Macbeth's typically male preoccupation with such a continued existence. Indeed, it is one of the most important elements of her mental make-up that she lives for the moment, for the immediate here-and-now, rather than for anything larger, in time or place. I believe that Shakespeare sees this tendency in her character as typically female. I do not mean that he shows himself misogynist in this. Rather, he appears to imply throughout the play that it is inevitable, given their role in society and possibly the way they are made, that women have a more restricted vision than men. Neither should we see it as admirable in Macbeth that he can look further; as a male, he has simply been equipped to do so.

Examples of Lady Macbeth's curious shortsightedness are abundant in the play. She herself would like to overcome it. When we first see the Macbeths discussing the possibility of murdering Duncan, in I.iv, Lady Macbeth declares that she will herself take charge of it: 'you shall put / This night's great business into my dispatch' (lines 64-65). Yet, in the event, she is not up the task she has set herself, as the instinct which she tries to ignore asserts itself: 'Had he not resembled / My father as he slept, I had done't' (II.ii.12-13). It appears to be typical of her, as a woman, to try and cast herself into a role which she thinks she should assume. Therefore, she sets herself goals of which she has no real understanding. Shakespeare seems to believe that a woman is more prone to make this mistake than a man as she is only superficially in touch with the world outside the home: things are done for the sake of appearance without real thought as to the consequences. Thus, for example, after the murder of Duncan Lady Macbeth says to her husband: 'A little water clears us of this deed' (II.ii.67). She not only thinks (foolishly) that she can wash off her sin in the eyes of God, but also that it will be far from difficult to hide their crime from the view of others (her next words are 'How easy is it then!'). But the people around her are far more suspicious than she thinks. Although she tries to bury her fears in her unconscious, she does not succeed in keeping them there. It would appear that Shakespeare considers that this situation is more likely to occur in the case of a woman than a man. A man is less likely to hide things from himself for two reasons: he is in closer contact with the outside world, and he is less sensitive to other human beings (Lady Macbeth does know, in a way that no man can, how tender 'tis to love the babe that milks her). Thus, despite her attempt to be more 'macho' than her husband, Lady Macbeth ends up with her unconscious asserting itself. When she walks in her sleep (V.i), she expresses her surprise that Duncan had so much blood in him, and raises the possibility that her hands will never be clean.

Macbeth is often seen as someone who has more imagination than his wife. I do not think that is quite the point: rather, he is more directly in contact with the reality of things, and therefore his unconscious sends its messages to him more quickly, no matter whether the message is one of desire or of fear. That is why he so readily sees a dagger, or Banquo's ghost. I think it is a mistake to believe that he has better knowledge of right and wrong than his wife and acts more on his conscience. Let us for example examine some of his reasoning in his famous soliloquy before the murder of Duncan, 'If it were done when 'tis done' (I.vii.1-27):

> If th'assassination
> Could trammel up the consequence, and catch,
> With his surcease, success; that but this blow
> Might be the be-all and the end-all here—
> But here upon this bank and shoal of time—
> We'd jump the life to come. But in these cases
> We still have judgment here, that we but teach
> Bloody instructions, which being taught return
> To plague th'inventor.

This is not the talk of someone who cares about right and wrong, but who is speculating on the consequences of his deed. He first wonders whether he can escape unhurt here on earth; if so, he'd 'jump the life to come'. Punishment in the after-life, in other words, is hardly of concern to him; his mind is on his mortal existence. The lack of regard for metaphysics is not, as it would be in the case of his wife, due to a restricted vision: he rejects what he is aware of, but he is aware of it nonetheless. He is similarly aware of the fact that it will be very difficult to gain what he wants 'here' in this life. He realizes that his action may serve as an example to others, so that it may rebound on him. He is not in any sense *morally* superior to his wife, but merely has a different, more 'male' kind of insight.

But, we may wonder, does he not show similar confusion in allowing himself to be swayed by the witches? I do not think so. Lady Macbeth psychologically does not *need* the witches, as she is fully capable of engendering her own evil and believing in it as something she can get away with. Macbeth is no less evil, but worries more about the consequences of his actions. Hence the witches, like his wife, serve the function of strengthening him in his evil inclinations, of providing a reality (as it seems) in which he can believe. We must note that they do not actually lie: it is true, for example, that Macduff is not 'of woman born'. We may think that the witches trick him, and so indeed they do, for they are evil, but they can only make Macbeth believe what he wishes to believe anyway. We may well once again see Shakespeare making an important comment on gender in this. The man is more doubtful than the woman (Lady Macbeth) about the results of his actions because he knows the ways of the world better. But, unlike Lady Macbeth, he is incapable of coming to conclusions independently: he needs female comforting, from both his wife and the witches.

Lady Macbeth is not, however, herself a witch, and hence she comes to a very bad end. It would be wrong to say that Macbeth was able to predict at all completely what their life would be like after the murder of Duncan. Even so, he had a better notion, and indeed understands the misery of his situation fairly clearly immediately after the murder: 'from this instant, / There's nothing serious in mortality' (II.iii.90-91). Lady Macbeth, however, has more suffering in store for her exactly because she has tried to repress all female feeling which, therefore, will inevitably create havoc in her unconscious and finally seek a violent way out. Thus she must die. Her tragedy is the greater because of her loneliness. Shakespeare implies that after the murder of Duncan Macbeth treats her with typically male disdain. Planning Banquo's murder, he will not tell her about it: 'Be innocent of the knowledge, dearest chuck, / Till thou applaud the deed' (III.iii.45-46). It is probably significant that Macbeth is now king and that this new murder is to be committed outside the domestic sphere; as he judges, this leaves no place for his wife.

Healthier notions of manhood and womanhood exist in the case of the Macduffs. The first thing we may notice about them as setting them apart from the Macbeths is that they have children, and deeply care about them. This appears to make for a less violent outlook, although it is to be observed that this is a far more pronounced phenomenon in the case of the women than in that of the men. Lady Macbeth's violence seems to be strongly connected with her infertility; presumably Shakespeare wishes us to believe that her violence was always a feature of her character, that it caused infertility after initial fertility, and that her barrenness then in turn further increased her violence. Lady Macduff is both fertile and non-aggressive. In fact, while Lady Macbeth has an unnatural desire to mingle in men's affairs, Lady Macduff does not understand them. When Macduff leaves for England, Lady Macduff reacts with puzzlement and indignation:

> *Lady Macd.* What had he done to make him fly the land?
> Ross. You must have patience, madam.
> *L. Macd.* He had none;
> His flight was madness. When our actions do not,
> Our fears do make us traitors.
>
> (IV.ii.1-4)

Superficially, Lady Macduff may have a point about her husband's fear. In truth, however, she does not know what world she is living in. Shortly afterwards, a messenger warns her that she is in danger; but she stays where she is, and gets killed, with her children. Macduff's flight should thus be seen as, for one thing, an act of caution. The realm would not have been served if he had been killed. For, and this is a second major point that his wife fails to grasp, his wellbeing is essential to that of Scotland. It is his male responsibility to establish contact with Malcolm so that the two of them can restore order in the kingdom, a process in which Macduff plays a vital part by not only assisting Malcolm generally—as the future and lawful king—but also by killing Macbeth.

It is possible to make a good deal of Macduff's sensitivity to his wife and children when he hears of their death. Certainly, his attitude is contrasted with Macbeth's when the latter says about his wife, 'She should have died hereafter' (V.v.17). Macduff, when informed of the loss of his family, is admonished by Malcolm:

> Dispute it like a man.
>
> (IV.iii.220)

Engagingly, he replies:

> I shall do so;
> But I must also feel it as a man.

To be male does not mean that one cannot and should not feel human grief. In an instance like this, Shakespeare rejects the 'macho' stereotype. However, there is time for momentary grief only, as his male duty calls Macduff. Malcolm encourages him to turn his grief into anger, which Macduff does proceed to do, whereupon Malcolm can say with satisfaction:

> This tune goes manly.
>
> (IV.iii.235)

At the end of the play, we become strongly aware that Shakespeare's world is male-dominated. If Macduff had to lose his wife and children that was a serious matter, but one for private grief; and private grief is less important than his role as a warrior who must secure a harmonious state of affairs in Scotland. I do not think that Shakespeare leaves us in doubt that Macduff *must* do what he does.

Lady Macbeth, who so much tried to live up to an extreme 'macho' image, has failed miserably. She has perverted her womanhood, and shown that she could not successfully maintain herself in a male-dominated world. Her death is, we must surely concede, less glamorous than her husband's. I do not, of course, mean that Shakespeare idealizes Macbeth's violence. Nevertheless, violence is more appropriate in him than in his wife, and it is difficult to avoid some admiration for his bravery (against all logical odds) at the end of the play.

My case is not that Shakespeare offers us a 'sexist' view which amounts to a simple preference for men. Obviously, we are not asked to view Macbeth more positively than Lady Macduff; the latter may well be wrong in her assessment of her husband's motives, but this is a pardonable misjudgment which is far less serious than Macbeth's set of crimes. But, even though Shakespeare is anxious to avoid anything like blunt stereotyping (so that, for example, he stresses that Macduff must feel his grief as a man), he appears to have a very strong sense of certain traits of mind and actions as 'male' and others as 'female'. It would not do, of course, to suggest that Shakespeare's view as developed in this play is necessarily identical to his attitude as embodied elsewhere in his work. But even the joyous comedies, which might temporarily give us the feeling that women like Rosalind or Viola are really not unlike men, must be read with an awareness of the fact that *in the end* Shakespeare does not allow them a role similar to that of a man.

Macbeth is crucially important, in our context, for enabling us to see that Shakespeare above all relates the differences between male and female roles to the significant fact that women are childbearers and men are not. But he does not stop there. He also appears to emphasize that there are certain spheres of activity in which it is disastrous for a woman to interfere, not only in that such an adoption of a 'male' role harms others, but also in that it injures the woman herself: Lady Macbeth possibly hurts herself more than anyone else.

Shakespeare sees it as a distinct disadvantage that our male-dominated society is inclined towards violence—a tendency which good women like Lady Macduff do not share. Nevertheless, order in such a society can only be maintained by men, and, although they should not be unfeeling, and fight in the right cause, they must be prepared to secure peace by engaging in battle and bloodshed. There is no evidence that Shakespeare can imagine a society in which women would be, and do, much the same as men.

Notes

1. See, as examples of recent studies, especially: Juliet Dusinberre, *Shakespeare and the Nature of Woman* (London: Macmillan, 1975); Lawrence Stone: *The Family, Sex and Marriage in England, 1500-1800* (London: Weidenfeld and Nicolson, 1977); Carol J. Carlisle, 'The Critics Discover Shakespeare's Women', *Renaissance Papers* (1979), pp. 59-73; Carolyn Ruth Swift Lenz, ed., *The Woman's Part: Feminist Criticism of Shakespeare* (Urbana: Univ. of Illinois, 1980); Ian Maclean, *The Renaissance Notion of Women* (Cambridge: Univ. Press, 1980); Irene G. Dash, *Wooing, Wedding, and Power: Women in Shakespeare's Plays* (New York: Columbia Univ. Press, 1981); Linda Bamber, *Comic Women, Tragic Men: A Study of Gender and Genre in Shakespeare* (Stanford: Univ. Press, 1982); Marilyn French, *Shakespeare's Division of Experience* (London: Jonathan Cape, 1982); Lisa Jardine, *Still Harping on Daughters: Women and Drama in the Age of Shakespeare* (Brighton: Harvester Press, 1983); Linda Woodbridge, *Women and the English Renaissance* (Brighton: Harvester Press, 1984).

2. Ruth Kelso, *Doctrine for the Lady of the Renaissance* (Urbana: Univ. of Illinois Press, 1956), p. 10.

3. Flinders University of South Australia (South Australia 5042), 1987. At the time of writing, the thesis had been awarded an M.A., but not yet been accepted for publication. It certainly is to be hoped that it will be. I am much indebted to Ms Carter for what I have learned from her during the last two years or so.

4. His other important studies in this area (at the time of writing) are: 'Androgyny, Old and New', *The Western Humanities Review* (1981), pp. 197-215, and 'Androgyny Seen Through Shakespeare's Disguise', *Shakespeare Quarterly* (1982), pp. 17-33.

5. I quote from Peter Alexander, ed., *William Shakespeare: The Complete Works* (London and Glasgow: Collins, 1951), which still seems very satisfactory. I have not yet been able to make a thorough investigation of what will no doubt prove an important text: Stanley Wells and Gary Taylor, gen. eds., *William Shakespeare: The Complete Works* (Oxford: Clarendon Press, 1986).

William T. Liston (essay date 1989)

SOURCE: "'Male and Female Created He Them': Sex and Gender in *Macbeth*," in *College Literature*, Vol. XVI, No. 3, Fall, 1989, pp. 232-39.

[*In the following essay, Liston examines gender issues and sex roles in* Macbeth, *and theorizes that when men and women step out of their defined roles they lose their humanity.*]

Probably none of Shakespeare's plays is so explicit in demarcating man from woman as is *Macbeth*. Man (including the plural and such obvious derivatives as *manly, manhood,* and *unmanned*) appears more than 40 times, almost always with a conscious sense of defining the term—or rather, of defining a person by the term. *Woman* (including similar formations) appears about a third as frequently, with a similar sense of precise definition.

The most obvious examples of this defining process appear in the preparations for the murder of Duncan and in the discovery of it (1.7 and 2.3); in the preparations for the murder of Banquo and the Banquet scene (3.1 and 3.4); and in the scene in which Malcolm tests Macduff's loyalty (4.3). In all of these scenes, what is at issue is a definition of human nature. (*Nature* and derivatives appear 27 times; and *kind,* with similar meaning, as in the "milk of human kindness," appears a few times also.) In several instances the words take on a highly sexual meaning, as when Lady Macbeth challenges Macbeth's manhood prior to the murder of Duncan and questions it during his apparent hallucinations in the Banquet scene. Similarly, she is highly conscious of her own sexuality when she speaks of her "woman's breasts" while calling on the "spirits / That tend on mortal thoughts" to "unsex me here" so that she will not be impeded in her plan by "compunctious visitings of nature" (1.5).[1] What presents itself here is a conflation of sex roles and of gender, and a demonstration that human beings are by nature sexual beings. When men and women step outside these sex and gender roles, they lose their humanity. Their liberation from definition destroys them; paradoxically, in fact, it confines them. After their great crime, Macbeth feels "cabin'd, cribb'd, confin'd, bound in / To saucy doubts and fears" (3.4.23-24), and Lady Macbeth is imprisoned within her own sick mind.

After the witches' short opening scene, the first line of the play is Duncan's "What bloody man is that?" The man in question is the sergeant who reports brave Macbeth's bloody deeds. And immediately we are on the way to a definition of *man* as Bellona's bridegroom, a being who is valiant, courageous, and essentially a person committed to direct, unreflective physical action. Just as immediately, however, this simple definition is undermined as Macbeth and Banquo meet the witches, who "should be women" (1.3.45) but whose beards belie their sex. It is further undermined a few moments later as Macbeth, yielding to the suggestion that he actively try to bring about his accession to the kingship, finds "my seated heart knock at my ribs, / Against the use of nature." The thought shakes his "single state of man" (134-140). *Single* here is glossed by most modern editors as "weak," but Kenneth Muir notes "Grierson [in his 1914 edition]—I think rightly—says that *single* here means 'indivisible' and the phrase as a whole 'my composite nature—body, spirits, etc., made one by the soul.'"[2] Though either sense can be correct—and possibly both are—my sense of the lines accords with that of Muir and Grierson. *Integrity* is the word that the entire phrase "single state of man" suggests. (This is precisely the contention of Richard Horwich in "Integrity in *Macbeth*: The Search for the 'Single State of Man.'"[3])

Oddly, though *Macbeth* is ostensibly concerned with regicide and kingship, with the fate of a kingdom, the play proceeds on the values of a domestic tragedy. Whereas the history plays and the Roman plays enact their public values in public spaces, several of the tragedies—this one especially—seem to take place indoors and to focus on the values that are defined by and embodied in personal and familial relationships. Certainly the play begins on the battlefield where the integrity of the nation is called into question, and it ends there also, even if the final scene is staged in Macbeth's castle. But the scenes we remember most—those in the great middle of the play—are indoor scenes, dependent upon the relationship of husband and wife, of man and woman.

The word *man* first appears near the end of 1.4, as Macbeth tells Duncan that "I'll be myself the harbinger, and make joyful / The hearing of my wife with your approach" (45-46). The Folio opening stage direction for the next scene reads "*Enter Macbeths Wife with a Letter.*" Though it is true that Lady Macbeth's speech prefix is consistently *Lady,* and that several other stage directions (e.g., 1.6.10 and 1.7.28) read *enter Lady,* Lady Macbeth is not initially defined in her own right but regarded as an extension of her husband.

Likewise, the first appearance of *husband* is Lady Macbeth's anxious breaking off from "Had he not resembled / My father as he slept, I had done't" to greet "My husband!" (2.2.13) as Macbeth enters to announce "I have done the deed." But the word has ironically been anticipated by Banquo's statement at the beginning of the preceding scene that "There's husbandry in heaven, / Their candles are all out" (4-5). There is husbandry on earth also, and the snuffing of Duncan is its product.

As Macbeth's wife, Lady Macbeth is perceived and judged according to the roles and functions that a proper wife fulfills and performs. Given her station, there are two: to provide heirs to her lord, and to be his hostess. It is in the latter capacity that Duncan regards her as he arrives at Inverness: "See, see, our honor'd hostess!" (1.6.10). Surely it is no accident that Duncan's exclamation completes a speech of Banquo's that alludes to the child-bearing role:

> This guest of summer,
> The temple-haunting marlet, does approve,
> By his lov'd mansionry, that the heaven's breath
> Smell wooingly here; no jutty, frieze,
> Buttress, nor coign of vantage, but this bird
> Hath made his pendant bed and procreant cradle.
> Where they most breed and haunt, I have observ'd
> The air is delicate.
>
> (3-10)

The scene concludes with subtle but nevertheless insistent emphasis on the role of both the hostess and the host, Duncan asserting "Fair and noble hostess, / We are your guest to-night" (24-25), and finally going off with—

> Give me your hand.
> Conduct me to mine host, we love him highly,
> And shall continue our graces towards him.
> By your leave, hostess.

Host and *hostess* appear only once more each, in the immediately succeeding scenes. As Macbeth contemplates the murder of Duncan—"If it were done," etc.—he pauses to consider arguments against the murder.

> He's here in double trust:
> First, as I am his kinsman and his subject,
> Strong both against the deed; then, as his host.
>
> (1.7.12-14)

The crime of regicide is in Macbeth's mind, but not prominently. He is conscious of Duncan's "great office" (18) and of his own subjection to that office, but much more conscious of the domestic demands imposed upon kinsmen and hosts.

In the following scene, shortly after he notes the "husbandry in heaven," Banquo informs Macbeth that

> the King's a-bed.
> He hath been in unusual pleasure, and
> Sent forth great largess to your offices.
> This diamond he greets your wife withal,
> By the name of most kind hostess.
>
> (2.1.12-16)

In this apparently simple statement, just moments before the murder, the offices of host and hostess, the roles of wife, and nature—alluded to in *kind*—are all mentioned, casually; and all are about to be violated.

That Lady Macbeth is ambitious is unquestioned. But what is she ambitious for? She first appears in 1.5, reading Macbeth's letter, and chills us as she starts to lay the plans that will culminate in Duncan's death after his fatal entrance "Under my battlements," the instrument being "my keen knife." Yet nowhere, neither here nor elsewhere, does she ask for anything for herself, in her own right. She apostrophically addresses Macbeth with,

> Hie thee hither,
> That I may pour my spirits in thine ear,
> And chastise with the valor of my tongue
> All that impedes thee from the golden round,
> Which fate and metaphysical aid doth seem
> To have thee crown'd withal.
>
> (25-30)

At the end of the scene, but not before, she finally includes herself in the profit to be gained from the enterprise, and then only in general terms:

> and you shall put
> This night's great business into my dispatch,
> Which shall to all our nights and days to come
> Give solely soverign sway and masterdom.
>
> (67-70)

The terms of simple domestic relationships dominate 4.2, in which Lady Macduff and her son are murdered. In this scene, the great world is in the distance, but not forgotten.

Seana McKenna as Lady Macbeth in the Stratford Festival's 1995 production of Macbeth.

What we are concerned with here is *father, mother, husband, wife, babes,* and, as always, *natural,* as well as *man* and *woman*. The point of the scene comes to focus in Lady Macduff's speech immediately after she is warned of the approaching danger by the "homely man":

> Whither should I fly?
> I have done no harm. But I remember now
> I am in this earthly world—where to do harm
> Is often laudable, to do good sometime
> Accounted dangerous folly. Why then, alas,
> Do I put up that womanly defense,
> To say I have done no harm?
>
> (73-79)

Perversely, "womanly defense" should be "manly defense." Her defense—that only those who have done wrong need fear danger—is perfect logic, ideal logic: the kind of logic that reasonable men, rather than emotional women, supposedly use. But Macbeth has so perverted "this earthly world" that logic no longer obtains, and a reasonable defense, a "womanly defense," is absurd. The innocent, and innocence, are destroyed in such a world.

Not a particularly attractive scene in performance (one wonders if Shakespeare had ever seen or heard a real child) because so much of it is dominated by Macduff's "witty" child playing straight-man to his mother, this scene more than any other concentrates on the familial relationships and the disruption of these bonds and relationships.

An equally difficult scene, both in reading and performance, immediately follows; it is an almost actionless scene likely to bore both a reader and a spectator, and yet it brings together all the values and concerns of the play. The scene divides into two halves, Malcolm's testing of Macduff's loyalty, and Macduff's responses (and reactions) upon being informed of the slaughter of his family. These scenic beats are separated by lines concerned with the king's evil (140-159).

In his testing of Macduff, Malcolm accuses himself in general terms of being as bad as Macbeth. Finally, he focuses on "The cestern of my lust" (63) as the defining sin of his viciousness. Macduff's reply—"Boundless intemperance / In nature is a tyranny" (66-67)—is as good a statement of the theme of the play as can be found, and yet it seems almost a throw-away line, hardly noticed. Scotland can absorb such intemperance: "We have willing dames enough." The simplicity and honesty of *women* has given way to the pretentious *dames* in this debasing context.

Malcolm goes on to claim other vices such as avarice, but still Macduff raises no serious objection: "All these are portable" (89). Malcolm then disclaims all virtues, asserting—

> Nay, had I pow'r, I should
> Pour the sweet milk of concord into hell,
> Uproar the universal peace, confound
> All unity on earth.
>
> (97-100)

And at this point Macduff proves his loyalty to Malcolm and to virtue in rejecting Malcolm as unfit to govern.

Is it the word *milk* that affects Macduff so strongly? The word has been used thrice earlier in the play, always by Lady Macbeth ("th' milk of human kindness" [1.5.17]; "take my milk for gall" [1.5.48]; and "the babe that milks me" [1.7.55]), and in every case the image has amounted to a perversion of nature. Here, for the fourth time in the play—more than in any other Shakespearean play—the word appears again, and the equation is made through the image that peace is a feminine function and concern. Certainly the chief concern of Macduff's wife was peace.

Having convinced himself of Macduff's virtue, Malcolm denies all the intemperate desires of which he had accused himself as "strangers to my nature," and goes on to assure Macduff that "I am yet / Unknown to woman" (125-26). Ludicrous as this statement seems to be in equating ignorance (or innocence—both words reverberate throughout the play) of woman with manly goodness and virtue, it cannot be ignored. Does it mean that sexual knowledge is the knowledge of good and evil? This is a simplistic answer, especially in this play, which aims at a much richer definition of *man*, but no better answer suggests itself.

As Ellen J. O'Brien says in an article on teaching Shakespeare, Macduff's "understanding of the ambiguity of things intensifies in this scene"; Malcolm's testing of him amounts to a development of the "fair is foul" theme.[4] Following the clarification of his misconceptions regarding Malcolm, he is informed of the savage slaughter of his wife and babes, and the familiar terms of familial relationships come to the fore again, as do the terms of gender.

Momentarily reduced almost to inarticulateness and broken lines—in fact, after trying to forget the humanness of his wife and children by referring to them as chickens and their dam (218)—Macduff is urged by Malcolm to "Dispute it like a man." His reply—"I shall do so; / But I must also feel it as a man" (220-21)—signals the broader definition of *man* as someone capable of sympathy usually conceived of as feminine. Macduff goes on to say that "I could play the woman with mine eyes" (230), countenancing tears as a legitimate part of a warrior's psyche. When, a moment later, upon Macduff's resolution to pursue Macbeth at once, Malcolm approvingly states "This tune goes manly," he is of course referring to Macduff's warlike determination; but we sense also a larger and more encompassing definition of *manly* than had been present earlier in the play, even if Malcolm is not aware of the full implications of what he says. It is easy to agree with Robert Kimbrough, who says, "I would like to think that Malcom [*sic*] has understood the full significance of what he has seen and heard and intends 'manly' to mean more than bravely—but I doubt it."[5]

Though the play belongs to the Macbeths, the assertion of the fuller and more complex values of peace and family and humanity are stated and dramatized most positively in the Macduffs, despite Lady Macduff's complaint that in leaving her and their children Macduff "wants the natural touch" (4.2.9). Macduff's willingness to regard as natural to man the possession and even the expression of emotion posits a richer definition of *man* than merely that of a male capable of unflinching courage in battle and in the face of death. This definition counters that implied by the First Murderer—"We are men, my liege" (3.1.90)—as beings capable of killing remorselessly out of mere envy and resentment. Lady Macduff's instinctive resort to the procreant birds in her desperate plight—

> the poor wren,
> The most diminutive of birds, will fight,
> Her young ones in her nest—
>
> (4.2.9-11)

alludes to the barren and unnatural Lady Macbeth whose castle bears the outward signs of a pleasant seat in providing safety for the marlet but no protection for humanity: indeed harbors no humanity.

In short, the norm against which *Macbeth* works is a traditional definition of *man* as valorous, firm, commanding, humane, and limited; and a traditional definition of *woman* as soft, maternal, nourishing, a help meet to her husband, humane, and limited. The proper man and the proper woman are both richer than the simplistic stereotype even in the fairly restricted world of this play; but essential to full humanity is limitation within that defined role.[6]

Notes

1. *The Riverside Shakespeare,* ed. G. Blakemore Evans (Boston: Houghton, 1974). All quotations are from this edition unless otherwise specified.

2. *Macbeth,* Arden Edition (London: Methuen, 1962).

3. *Shakespeare Quarterly* 29 (1978): 366.

4. "Inside Shakespeare: Using Performance Techniques To Achieve Traditional Goals," *Shakespeare Quarterly* 35 (1984): 629.

5. "Macbeth: The Prisoner of Gender," *Shakespeare Studies* 16 (1983): 178.

6. After sending this paper off for publication, I read Laurence Olivier's autobiography, *Confessions of an Actor* (1982; New York: Penguin, 1984), in which, after telling us that he and his wife Vivien Leigh promised during the summer of 1954 to play *Macbeth* at the Shakespeare Memorial Theatre, he adds the comment that "as Sybil Thorndike always said, 'You must be married to play the Macbeths'" (198).

This paper had its genesis in a Seminar on Shakespearean Tragedy and Gender organized by Shirley Nelson Garner for the 1987 meeting of the Shakespeare Association of America, and profited from the criticism of that group.

PSYCHOLOGICAL APPROACHES

Robert L. Reid (essay date 1991)

SOURCE: "Macbeth's Three Murders: Shakespearean Psychology and Tragic Form," in *Renaissance Papers 1991,* edited by George Walton Williams and Barbara J. Baines, The Southeastern Renaissance Conference, 1992, pp. 75-92.

[*In the following essay, originally delivered in 1991, Reid contends that the three murders committed by Macbeth are representative of the three distinctive stages of evil that evolve in his psyche.*]

> *Macbeth* is a milestone in man's exploration of . . . this "depth of things" which our age calls the unconscious.
>
> Harold Goddard, *The Meaning of Shakespeare*

Interpreters of *Macbeth* have focused almost exclusively on the first murder, the killing of a king in Acts I-II, as the basis for understanding the play—its social, psychological, and metaphysical meanings. Macbeth's subsequent two assassinations, of Banquo in Act III, and of Macduff's wife and children in Acts IV-V, are either ignored, or are treated simply as efforts to secure the usurped crown, or perhaps as a kind of Freudian "repetition compulsion"—the blooded man's first heinous kill engendering serial slayings.[1] Neither of the subsequent murders has been accorded its own distinctive meaning and psychological motivation; they are seen as mere shadowy reenactments of the Oedipal complex which is presumed to underlie the one essential crime, the slaying of the patriarchal king.[2]

As R. A. Foakes puts it, "the murder of Duncan was the equivalent in mountaineering terms of scaling Everest, and after this [Macbeth] has no trouble with lower hills."[3] This exclusive highlighting of the regicide (as the "be-all and end-all" of the play) entails, however, that the final three acts must dwindle from real theatrical power to melodramatic spectacle[4]—a result of the victims' shrinking symbolic import and, correspondingly, the shrinking spiritual grandeur of the protagonists, who deliver fewer and fewer eloquent soliloquies, consign their villainies to hired thugs, and finally are swept aside by the nobler (but less charismatic) avengers, Macduff and Malcolm. Many astute critics of the play—including Bradley, Rossiter, Heilman, Sanders, Jorgensen, Mack, Kirsch, and Muir—have struggled with this central conundrum: can the playwright sustain great tragedy if the only true kingly spirit is dispatched at the outset?[5]

Like most of these critics, I believe that Macbeth's capacious mind, despite its moral degeneration, remains at center stage, showing the horrific consequences of a truly heroic spirit embracing evil. But instead of conceiving the tragedy as one great cosmos-shaking act of regicide followed by two subordinate aftershocks, I would characterize the Macbeths' journey into darkness as three equally significant stages of spiritual catastrophe, three distinctive and theatrically-potent dimensions of evil as it evolves and festers in the human psyche. Macbeth murders first a *parental ruler,* then a *brotherly friend* (his "chiefest friend" according to Holinshed), and finally a *mother and her children.*[6] His victims thus represent the three fundamental human bonds, together comprising (in reverse order) the three basic stages of human maturation, or the three essential cathexes of the human psyche. Thus, in the course of the three murders Macbeth deconstructs the entire psychological infrastructure of human identity. Shakespeare's awareness of this pattern is underscored by its earlier prototypical appearance in *Richard III,* where that villain-hero similarly kills a king (Henry VI), then a brother (Clarence), then children (the Princes).[7] In *Macbeth,* however, the playwright is much more fully apprised of the scheme's psychological implications, which he methodically exploits.

The dramaturgical design of *Macbeth* precisely emphasizes this three-phase pattern: Acts I and II present, in a continuous sequence, the regicide and its immediate consequences; Act III shows the murder of Banquo and then its impact on Macbeth at the banquet; Acts IV and V, another continuous cycle of action, presents the slaughter of Macduff's family, then its social and psychological consequences.[8] This 2-1-2 structure, the dramaturgic pattern of all of Shakespeare's mature tragedies, perfectly accommodates his treatment of Macbeth's three murders.

To attain this neatly coherent pattern of psychological devolution, Shakespeare has drastically altered Holinshed's *Chronicles*[9]—first, by condensing all the major crises of Duncan's six-year reign and of Macbeth's seventeen-year reign into the two-hour traffic of the stage. The entire battery of wars and assassinations seems to transpire in a matter of days, rather than a quarter of a century, making the three murders (as well as the broader framework of political violence in Acts I and V) seem closely and causally connected.

Equally striking is Shakespeare's moral reshaping of the victims, casting them as iconically benevolent members of the human family, in order to accommodate his three-fold tragic pattern. Instead of the chronicles' portrait of a weak, cowardly, and greedy king, about the same age as his cousin Macbeth, Shakespeare portrays Duncan as aged, humble, and generous—an ideal, almost saintly monarch.[10] Similarly Banquo, in the chronicles a co-conspirator in regicide, is recast as a devoted friend in life's warfare, modestly resisting each temptation to which his colleague falls prey.[11] Likewise Macduff, who in the chronicles enters the story belatedly, mainly seeking personal revenge, is transmuted into an ever-present touchstone of charitable social compassion—the Man of Feeling who best embodies what his wife and babes, those "strong knots of love," represent: the most primitive human bond. It is Macduff's horrified response to Duncan's murder that initiates the knocking of conscience in the Macbeths; and it is his patriotic opposition to the usurper that galvanizes Scotland and England into a retributive force.[12] Shakespeare's radical reconstruction of the chronicles, especially his amelioration of the victims' moral character, thus emphasizes the destruction of three primordial human bonds. This three-phase sequence of psychological disintegration (and implicit affirmation of the values destroyed) provides a paradigm of Shakespeare's mature tragic form.

I

In presenting an initial assault on regal or parental authority in Acts I-II, *Macbeth* is comparable to all the tragedies from *Hamlet* to *Coriolanus*. The murder of a parent-like king, reflecting the Macbeths' aspiration to God-like greatness and power, is an Oedipal repudiation of superego (as commentators since Freud and Jekels have acknowledged). Yet the gender implications of Duncan's rule have been too reductively construed by Oedipal-oriented psychoanalysts. For centuries it has been assumed that Duncan's *fatherliness* forms the basis of his comprehensive social identity (Scotland) and of his Christ-like spiritual identity ("The Lord's anointed temple," II.iii.70)—that as *patriarch* he, like Lear and Cymbeline, represents the acme of psychological development, the mature conscience of the race, or in Freudian terms, "superego."[13] Critics persistently construe the regicidal motive as an Oedipal antagonism, citing Lady Macbeth's distress at Duncan's fatherly appearance during the assault (II.ii.12-13), to which one might add Macbeth's condemnation of the murder as a "parricide," projecting his own Oedipal urges onto Malcolm and Donalbain (III.i.31).

Yet the Macbeths envision Duncan not just as a *father* (who "hath been / So clear in his great office," I.vii.17-18), but also as a *mother* (who vies with Lady Macbeth in expressing love for her husband and for the other thanes, and who is cast as Lucrece to Macbeth's "ravishing Tarquin" with his phallic dagger). In addition, both Macbeths at critical moments in their soliloquies envision the monarch as a vulnerable and soul-like *child* (the heavenly infant which Lady Macbeth would deny the chance to "peep through the blanket of the dark, / To cry, 'Hold, hold!'"; and which Macbeth projects apocalyptically as a "naked new-born babe" of Pity). Thus, in psychoanalytic (or "object relational") terms Duncan is not just the father, but all aspects of the human family—perhaps most poignantly, mother and child.[14] By their own gender obsessions, the Macbeths have promoted the erroneous and reductive conception of kingship as a pure patriarchy. As recent critics have noted, the Macbeths' urge for kingly greatness is expressed as a fantasy of becoming exclusively "manly" by taking up phallic weaponry to eliminate womanly and childlike characteristics.[15]

The Macbeths' notable series of monologues in Acts I-II is fueled by willful hyperbole, which accommodates their male-oriented aspiration to "*greatness*" (a word whose variants appear 17 times in Act I, more than in the other four acts combined). To the extent that we as audience identify with the Macbeths' grand speechmaking, hypnotic role-playing, and cosmic aspiration for greatness in these acts, we must also experience the ironies that emerge in the actual performance of the murder: pettiness, furtiveness, cowardice, and utter deceit.

As the hyperbolic fantasy of these early soliloquies reveals, the type of ego functioning that informs this regicidal-parenticidal stage of Macbeth's career in villainy is *sublimation* but in its most perverted form. Anna Freud describes sublimation as the highest phase of psychic functioning in the construction of selfhood, the ultimate means of enriching the ego.[16] Ideally, sublimation resolves the ongoing Oedipal struggle (a struggle for the final, genital stage of sexual maturation), not by evading bodily consummation of sexual energies, nor by suppressing the female aspect of those energies, but by promoting comprehensive and free interplay between gender-components of the self. Thus the Macbeths' brutish rape of kingly greatness works exactly contrary to authentic sublimation. By furtively killing the king they not only destroy the bond with this androgynous parent, but they also violate the illuminating and consolidating powers of their own superego or conscience, thus inducing a deeper regression into self-divisive and annihilative ego defenses.

II

The murder of Macbeth's "chiefest friend" in Act III is motivated not by further aspiration to greatness, but by rivalrous envy of a brotherly alter-ego.[17] According to Aquinas, "After the sin of pride [whereby Lucifer aspired to be a deity] there followed the evil of envy . . . whereby he grieved over man's good."[18] Envy, and the rivalrous doubling and splitting which necessitates confronting distasteful mirror-images of the self at the center of each of the tragedies, is secondary to that earlier violent effort to displace divine-regal-parental authority. The regicide-parenticide thus leads to fratricide-amiticide, a chronologically secondary but equally universal phenomenon, which carries its own momentous psychological implications.

This assault on a warrior-friend who is virtually the mirror-image or double of Macbeth ("all hail, Macbeth and Banquo! / Banquo and Macbeth, all hail!" I.iii.68-69) is a direct violation of ego, involving a psychological "splitting" into self and shadow-self, as Macbeth perversely identifies with the darker, more illusory component. Though he rationalizes the murder of Banquo in only one soliloquy, far less grandiose than the monologues of Acts I-II, Macbeth throughout Act III continues the fiery expression of his inner powers by a number of intense dialogues in which he no longer effectively communicates his deeper meaning either to his auditors or to himself.[19] They can only guess at the dark nuances in his spate of bestial images: serpents and scorpions (III.ii.13-5, 36; III.iv.28-30); bat, "shard-bound beetle," and crow (III.ii.40-2, 50-3); "greyhounds, mongrels, spaniels, curs" (III.i.92-4); "Russian bear, arm'd rhinoceros, or th'Hyrcan tiger" (III.iv.99-100); "magot-pies, and choughs, and rooks" (III.iv.121-4). If Acts I-II show a perverse mode of hyperbolic aspiration (appropriating sublimation as a means of overthrowing the superego or conscience), this furtive imagery of Act III shows Macbeth's regression to the prior psychic function of *projection,* the defensive externalization of his depraved and problematic qualities onto others, which enforces a general process of "decomposition" and "splitting" of the ego.[20] At its best, projection (an expulsive psychic function deriving from the anal stage of infancy) plays a key role in the development of selfhood, enabling one to influence others by projecting onto them one's own ego ideals and inadequacies, and also enabling one thereby to experiment with and test those values and identities. But at its worst, as in malicious rituals of murder and scapegoating, projection revises reality so drastically that "nothing is, / But what is not," and the murderer's own selfhood, his "single state of man," is increasingly shaken and disjoined (I.iii.134-42).

Envy, and the resultant splitting of selfhood, dictates the entire sequence of Act III: Macbeth's spiteful soliloquy in which he feels "rebuked" by Banquo's "royalty of nature"; his strange ranking of dogs in the abusive hiring of the assassins, humiliating them, even as he claims to raise and "make love" to them; his furtive insecurity even with his wife (rehearsing her part while concealing his full intent); his "half-participation" in the murder itself, perhaps as the third murderer;[21] and of course the self-division which builds to a climax during the banquet. Macbeth's schizoid vacillation between noblemen and assassins, between true and feigned selves, gradually gives way to a deeper vacillation between conscious and unconscious realities. His obscene praise of the missing guest ("And to our dear friend Banquo, whom we miss") serves the psychic function of invoking his double's macabre presence, filling the central seat to which Macbeth himself is inexorably drawn.[22]

Throughout Act III Macbeth's insecurity focuses no longer on the proud aspiration for kingly greatness, but on envious rivalry with his antithetical friend Banquo, who is to him what Edgar is to Edmund, Hal to Hotspur, Orlando to Oliver: the child favored with a loving heart, who thus calls into question the unloving self's entire "being" and must be utterly eliminated:

> every minute of his being thrusts
> Against my near'st of life: and though I could
> With bare-faced power sweep him from my sight,
> And bid my will avouch it, yet I must not,
> For certain friends that are both his and mine,
> Whose loves I may not drop.
>
> (III.i.116-21)

Instinctively Macbeth envisions the bond with his "chiefest friend" in the context of a universal siblinghood, making the murder of Banquo as broadly symbolic as that of Duncan: first he eliminates the universal parent or greater-self, then the archetypal sibling or mirror-self. In each of the mature Shakespearean tragedies, this shattering confrontation with an antithetical self-image occurs at the play's center, the middle of Act III: Othello's temptation by Iago (III.iii), Lear's discovery of "Poor Tom" (III.iv), Macbeth's spectral encounter with Banquo (III.iv), Antony's battle with Octavius (III.vii). As in Lear's meeting with the mad beggar, Macbeth's rencontre with his mutilated alter-ego engages him in full awareness of fraternal Otherness; but while this stunning encounter leads the kingly Lear instinctively to affirm the oneness of human souls, it provokes the usurper Macbeth to repudiate "that great bond" (III.ii.49).[23] In discarding Banquo, Macbeth thus divests himself of brother-love, the homoerotic bond, the second crucial cathexis forming the normative identity of the human psyche.

III

In Acts IV and V, focusing on the slaughter of a mother and children (and the immediate social and psychological consequences of that deed), Macbeth eliminates the third and most fundamental human bond, as he violates the primitive core of selfhood, what Freud called the id. Most critics treat this third assault as mere "fourth-act pathos," as a dim echo of the previous kills, or as a hasty and illogical afterthought testifying to a kind of madness in the tyrant, since these victims offer neither militant opposition nor patrilineal threat to Macbeth's royal claim.[24]

But Macbeth's essential motive for the third murder is not a reenactment of the Oedipal struggle (casting Macduff as the new parent-power to be deposed); nor is it another envious rivalry with a mirroring sibling (seeing Macduff's goodness, like Banquo's, as a galling comparison to his own evil). Rather, building upon and blossoming out of those two previous modes of aggression, Macbeth's "black and deep desires" now enter a third and culminating phase: scornful annihilative hatred of the simple passional core, the mother-and-child matrix of selfhood—the healthy "oral-narcissist" bonding which contrasts the perverse narcissism now unfolding in Macbeth.[25] Macbeth's contemptuous repudiation and perversion of the affective-cognitive human core (the "id") informs this final sequence of psychic degradation in Acts IV and V. The ego function which dominates this earliest phase of psychic development (and which most pertinently informs the final two acts of Shakespeare's mature tragedies) is *introjection,* the ego's incorporation of desired aspects of the nurturant other in order to construct its own identity.[26] Introjection of the beloved, for the purpose of achieving (or re-achieving) total selfhood, is the psychological principle which is either violated or embraced in the final phase of each of Shakespeare's major tragedies. Acts IV and V invariably draw their cathartic and transforming energy, not from the killing of a king, but from the heroic male's reaction to the destruction of a *beloved maiden* (Ophelia, Desdemona, Cordelia) or, in the final tragedies, a *mother with children* (Lady Macduff and Lady Macbeth; Cleopatra; Virgilia and Volumnia).[27]

A wholesome mode of introjective bonding informs the poignant scene of Lady Macduff and her son (IV.ii), where in the father's absence she frets over the child's continued sustenance. But the boy's affirmation that Providential if not parental care will feed him, echoing Matthew 6.26, suggests the dignity of what he has thus far introjected from his parents. This humane and spiritual nurture contrasts with the strikingly perverse mode of introjection in the preceding scene: the witches' materialistic, cannibalistic ritual. Into their womb-like cauldron's mouth (the *vagina dentata*)[28] they fling fragments of poisonous and ravenous beasts (toad, snake, dragon, wolf, shark, tiger) and parts representing the erotic and sensory powers of non-Christians (Jew's liver, Turk's nose, Tartar's lips)—including those lower senses of smell and taste involved in feeding.

The final and focal object in the witches' catalog of dismembered parts is "Finger of birth-strangled babe, / Ditch-deliver'd by a drab" (IV.i.26-31). Thus, from the "pilot's thumb" of the witches' early scene (I.iii.28), symbolizing the perversion of parental guidance or superego,) Macbeth regresses inexorably to the aborted potency of the child (or id), as symbolized by the foetal "finger" or phallus, "strangled"-castrated-devoured by the cauldron-womb-mouth of the Voracious Mother, the "drab" or prostitute. Introjection (an incorporative mode of identification deriving from the experience of sucking and swallowing during the oral stage of infancy) is thus materialized and brutalized by the witches to secure worldly power.

From the vicious opening ritual of Act IV (which provokes the entire cycle of action in Acts IV-V), Macbeth embraces the witches' omnivorous perversion of the primal introjective principle. Each of his three murders has been associated with imagery of feasting, but it is particularly in his impulsive butchering of mother and babes that Macbeth has willingly and unhesitatingly "supp'd full with horrors" (V.v.13). Thus the third murderous assault, a Herod-like massacre of innocents from which Macbeth completely distances himself, but which Shakespeare exposes to the audience with the most excruciating intimacy, brings us to the peak of horror, the breaking of the deepest taboo, which violates the very rudiment of selfhood and of social bonding.

Far more than King Duncan and Banquo, whose entrammelment in political motivations partly cloaks their essential being, the intimacy of mother and child brings us closest to the core of human nature. In each of Shakespeare's mature tragedies, the final cathartic sequence of Acts IV-V jeopardizes the primal psychic ground of being, the inception of love: the drawing of woman, "fool," or child into the web of deceit and violence promotes in the male authority-figures not merely revulsion against evil, but clear and intense awareness of the rich essence of life which has been lost. Macbeth himself, in his finest show of inner light, envisioned the soul's greatest power in its early innocence and in its affective mode of "pity": "like a naked new-born babe, / Striding the blast" (I.vii.19-20). As he loses touch with that child-like and woman-nurtured essence in himself, Macbeth also loses his capacity for true kingship.

Notes

This study is indebted to Professor Arthur Kirsch and the members of his 1988 NEH Seminar at the University of Virginia.

1. Freud's argument for the second instinctual drive, the aggressive death-wish, grew out of his reflections on the "repetition compulsion"—obsessive reenacting of a pleasurable sensation, or of a painful and self-destructive behavior. The motive, he felt, was not simply to sustain pleasure or pain, but subconsciously to use it as a means of recovering primal experience, especially in the case of the aggressive and destructive obsession, which he attributed to a desire to return to peaceful nothingness. See "Remembering, Repeating, and Working-through" (1914), *Standard Edition of the Complete Psychological Works of Sigmund Freud* [hereafter *SE*], trans. and ed. James Strachey

(London: Hogarth, 1957) 24 vols., 12:147-56; "Beyond the Pleasure Principle (1920), *SE* 18:7-64; Edward Bibring, "The Conception of the Repetition Compulsion," *Psychoanalytic Quarterly* 12 (1941), 486-519; Hans W. Loewald, "Some Considerations on Repetition and Repetition Compulsion," *International Journal of Psychoanalysis* [hereafter *IJP*], 52 (1971), 59-65.

2. See especially Freud, "Those Who Are Wrecked by Success" (1916), *SE* 14:318-24; and Ludwig Jekels, "The Riddle of Shakespeare's *Macbeth*" (1917), *The Design Within: Psychoanalytic Approaches to Shakespeare*, ed. M. D. Faber (New York: Science House, 1970), pp. 235-49. A survey of such readings is provided by Norman N. Holland, *Psychoanalysis and Shakespeare* (New York: McGraw, 1964), pp. 219-30. Recent treatments of the Oedipal theme include Northrop Frye, "My Father as He Slept," *Fools of Time* (Toronto: University of Toronto Press, 1967), pp. 3-39; Norman Rabkin, *Shakespeare and the Problem of Meaning* (Chicago: University of Chicago Press, 1981), pp. 101-10; Janis Krohn, "Addressing the Oedipal Dilemma in *Macbeth*," *Psychoanalytic Review* 73 (1986), 333-47; Pierre Janton, "Sonship and Fatherhood in *Macbeth*," *Cahiers Élisabéthains* 35 (1989), 47-58.

Important revisionary studies of gender-psychology (either shifting attention from embattled father to devouring mother, or totally reevaluating the parental roles) include David Barron, "The Babe That Milks: An Organic Study of *Macbeth*," (1960), in *The Design Within*, pp. 251-79; D. W. Harding, "Women's Fantasy of Manhood: A Shakespearean Theme," *Shakespeare Quarterly* 20 (1969), 245-53; Robert Kimbrough, "Macbeth: Prisoner of Gender," *Shakespeare Studies* 6 (1972), 175-90; Marilyn French, *Shakespeare's Division of Experience* (New York: Ballantine, 1981), pp. 242-53; Coppélia Kahn, *Man's Estate: Masculine Identity in Shakespeare* (Berkeley: University of California Press, 1981), pp. 151-5, 172-92; Carolyn Asp, "'Be bloody, bold, and resolute': Tragic Action and Sexual Stereotyping in *Macbeth*," *Studies in Philology* 78 (1981), 153-69; Patrick Colm Hogan, "*Macbeth*: Authority and Progenitorship," *American Imago* 40 (1983), 385-95; James J. Greene, "Macbeth: Masculinity as Murder," *American Imago* 41 (1984), 155-80; Arthur Kirsch, "Macbeth's Suicide," *ELH* 51 (1984), 269-96, esp. 276-80; C. L. Barber and Richard P. Wheeler, *The Whole Journey: Shakespeare's Power of Development* (Berkeley: University of California Press, 1986), pp. 11-13, 242, 266-9; Janet Adelman, "'Born of Woman': Fantasies of Maternal Power in *Macbeth*," in *Cannibals, Witches, and Divorce: Estranging the Renaissance*, ed. Marjorie Garber (Baltimore: Johns Hopkins Press, 1987), pp. 90-121; Dianne Hunter, "Doubling, Mythic Difference, and the Scapegoating of Female Power in *Macbeth*," *Psychoanalytic Review* 75 (1988), 129-52.

3. Foakes, "Images of Death: Ambition in *Macbeth*," *Focus on Macbeth*, ed. John Russell Brown (London: Routledge and Kegan Paul, 1982), p. 18.

4. Julian Markels, "The Spectacle of Deterioration: Macbeth and the 'Manner' of Tragic Deterioration," *Shakespeare Quarterly* 12 (1961), 293-303.

5. Heilman, Sanders, Mack, Muir insist on Macbeth's greatness of spirit, but also on the sordid depths of his degradation. Cf. A. C. Bradley, *Shakespearean Tragedies*, 2nd ed. (1905; rpt. New York: Macmillan, 1949), pp. 349-65; A. P. Rossiter, *Angel with Horns*, ed. Graham Storey (New York: Theatre Arts, 1961), pp. 209-34; Robert B. Heilman, "The Criminal as Tragic Hero: Dramatic Methods," *Shakespeare Survey* 19 (1966), 12-24; Wilbur Sanders, *The Dramatist and the Received Idea* (Cambridge: Cambridge University Press, Eng., 1968), pp. 253-316; Paul A. Jorgensen, *Our Naked Frailties: Sensational Art and Meaning in Macbeth* (Berkeley: University of California Press, 1971), pp. 185-216; Maynard Mack, Jr., *Killing the King* (New Haven: Yale University Press, 1973), pp. 138-85; Kirsch, "Macbeth's Suicide"; Kenneth Muir, introduction, *Macbeth*, New Arden Edition (London: Methuen, 1987), pp. xliii-liii, lxv.

6. This "object relations" pattern was (in slightly different form) first noted by L. Veszy-Wagner, "*Macbeth*: 'Fair is Foul and Foul is Fair,'" *American Imago* 25 (1968), 242-57. In her brief discussion of the pattern's implications, she subordinates each victim to a patriarchal version of the Oedipal struggle; but she acutely observes that Macbeth's "main problem is . . . uncertain identity" with regard to gender.

7. Cf. Emrys Jones, *Scenic Form in Shakespeare* (Oxford: Clarendon Press, 1971), pp. 195-224.

8. For detailed treatment of this three-part structure of *Macbeth*, see Jones, *Scenic Form*, pp. 195-224. On Shakespearean tragic structure as three stages of self-discovery, see Maynard Mack, Jr., "The Jacobean Shakespeare: Some Observations of the Construction of the Tragedies," *Stratford upon Avon Studies: Jacobean Theatre*, ed. John R. Brown and Bernard Harris (London: St. Martin's Press, 1960), pp. 11-42. Arguments for both a three-part and a five-part structure of Shakespearean tragedy are debated by Ruth Nevo, *Shakespeare's Tragic Form* (Princeton: Princeton University Press, 1972), pp. 3-30, 314-57.

My interpretation of the structure of mature Shakespearean tragedy is as follows: Acts I-II, like Acts IV-V, each work as a cyclical unit, in which the latter act "answers" the former. In *King Lear*, e.g., the lengthy opening scene of Act I, in which Lear divests, humiliates, and exiles Cordelia, is answered by the lengthy concluding scene of Act II, in which Lear himself is, in precisely analogous manner, stripped, humiliated, and exiled—thus completing a cycle of *worldly* empowerment and divestiture. Acts IV and V of the play similarly work as a unit, the latter "answering" the former, but now enforcing a cycle of *spiritual* empowerment and divestiture. Act III is always a coherent unit in itself, its action revolving around a climatic central encounter which is the axis of the entire play.

9. See Muir, pp. xxxvi-xliii; Muriel C. Bradbrook, "The Sources of *Macbeth,*" *Shakespeare Survey* 4 (1951), 35-48; David Norbrook, "*Macbeth* and the Politics of Historiography," *Politics of Discourse: The Literature and History of 17th-Century England,* ed. Kevin Sharpe and Steven N. Zavicker (Berkeley: University of California Press, 1987), pp. 78-116.

10. Though some recent critics, in the radically revisionist spirit of New Historicism, interpret Duncan's "womanliness" as Shakespeare's indication of his unkingly impotence, I believe Norman Sanders' view is correct: Duncan's nurturing, fertile, self-mortifying traits contribute positively to Shakespeare's portrait of "a most sainted king" (IV.iii.109). Duncan begins where Lear and Cymbeline end, as a king who can "see feelingly." Cf. Harry Berger Jr., "The Early Scenes of *Macbeth:* Preface to a New Interpretation," *ELH* 47 (1980), 1-31; James L. Calderwood, *If It Were Done: Macbeth and Tragic Action* (Amherst: University of Massachusetts Press, 1986), pp. 119-21; Graham Bradshaw, *Shakespeare's Skepticism* (New York: St. Martin's Press, 1987), pp. 244-50; Adelman, "'Born of Woman,'" pp. 93 ff.

11. Banquo's probity, even more than Duncan's, has been subjected to repeated questioning and qualification: see, e.g., A. C. Bradley, pp. 379-87; Roy Walker, *The Time Is Free* (London: Andrew Dakers, 1949), pp. 89 ff; Richard J. Jaarsma, "The Tragedy of Banquo," *Literature and Psychology* 17 (1967), 87-94. Berger's and Calderwood's subtle criticism of Duncan's "aggressive giving" (n. 10) would similarly qualify Banquo's lavish praise of his warrior-colleague (I.iv.54-58). Yet that Duncan's and Banquo's compliments are benevolent is underscored not only by their repeated association with "royalty" and "grace," but also by the contrast with Macbeth's deceitful, murderous mode of "aggressive giving"—especially his forceful invitation of Banquo to the feast (III.i.11-39) and flattery of the missing guest (III.ii.30-31, iv.41-44, 91-92). Though Shakespeare implies political shortcomings in Duncan's aged weakness and in Banquo's Hamlet-like inertia after the regicide (thus qualifying the playwright's compliment to James I), nevertheless in revising the chronicles Shakespeare has taken pains to idealize the moral character of both victims; their frailties, like Hamlet's, derive more from warring evils of the world than from their own innate urges.

12. Adelman and Hunter (n. 2) devalue Macduff's moral probity by taking seriously Lady Macduff's anxious but wittily-exaggerated accusations of her husband (IV.ii.6-14, 44-45); yet even the child appreciates the irony of her remarks. In spite of the pointed criticisms levelled at Macduff by his wife, by Malcolm (IV.iii.26-8), and, most emphatically, by himself (IV.iii.224-7), it is clear that he is moved by generous compassion for Scotland as a whole, and that his compassion grows out of the intense family feeling manifested by his wife and child.

13. In Acts I-II of each mature tragedy, Shakespeare portrays an assault on conscience or synteresis [Freudian superego], not merely as a fatherly or kingly power, but increasingly as a consolidating, androgynous figure of authority: Othello-Desdemona, Lear (whose initial attempt to arrogate female nurture confirms the flaw in his sovereignty), the bi-gendered Duncan, Antony-Cleopatra. On the nature and symbolization of superego, see S. Freud, "The Ego and the Id" (1923), *SE* 19:3-66; Manuel Furer, "The History of the Superego Concept in Psychoanalysis," in *Moral Value and the Superego Concept in Psychoanalysis,* ed. Seymour C. Post (New York: International Universities Press, 1972), pp. 11-62; Alex Holder, "Preoedipal Contributions to the Formation of the Superego," *Psychoanalytic Study of the Child* [hereafter *PSOC*] 37 (1982), 245-72.

On the Renaissance view of conscience or synteresis as a means of consolidating mental powers and gender-components of human nature, see Pierre de la Primaudaye, *The French Academie* (London, 1618), Part 2, pp. 364-511, especially on restoring of the Edenic communion between heart's affective powers (pp. 437-511) and head's intellective powers (pp. 364-436).

Both Elizabeth I and James I exploited the idea of monarchy as an androgynous consolidation of paternal authority and maternal nurture, as noted by Stephen Orgel and Louis A. Montrose in *Rewriting the Renaissance: The Discourses of Sexual Difference in Early Modern Europe,* ed. Margaret W. Ferguson, Maureen Quilligan, and Nancy J. Vickers (Chicago: University of Chicago Press, 1986), pp. 58-9, 65-87.

14. Cf. David Willbern, "Phantasmagoric Macbeth," *English Literary Renaissance* 16, (1986), esp. pp. 520-27.

15. See, e.g., Harding, Kimbrough, French, Kahn, Adelman, Hunter in note 2.

16. "Some Remarks on Infant Observation" (1952) in *The Writings of Anna Freud,* 8 vols. (New York: International Universities Press, 1968), 4:509-85. In her most important work, *The Ego and the Mechanisms of Defense,* 1936, Anna Freud began to establish that ego-functions serve not only defensive but constructive purposes. In much current Ego Psychology, "sublimation" is no longer a fashionable

term, being displaced by "neutralization" and "desexualization." These latter terms, however, emphasize the *defensive* nature of the ego's workings (especially its pacifying of the ever-clamorous libido) rather than identifying the essentially *constructive* purpose of this ultimate ego function, particularly its contribution to the Kohutian struggle for "grandiose selfhood" (the evident goal of the Macbeths). On the ego's defensive postures and mechanisms, see Willi Hoffer, "Defensive Process and Defensive Organization: Their Place in Psychoanalytic Technique," *IJP* 35 (1954), 194-8; and Heinz Hartmann, "The Development of the Ego Concept in Freud's Work," *IJP* 37 (1956), 425-38. On the ego's constructive functioning (especially in the closely-related processes of sublimation, superego formation, and therapeutic transference), see Hans W. Loewald, *Sublimation* (New Haven: Yale University Press, 1988), ch. 1-2; Heinz Kohut, *The Analysis of the Self* (New York: International Universities Press, 1971), pp. 309-24.

17. Rivalrous envy becomes Macbeth's *dominant* motivation only during Act III, in the deliberations over murdering Banquo. In Acts I-II Macbeth's basic motivation is not envy, either for Duncan, Banquo, or Malcolm (though the basis for later envy is obviously established): in spite of anxiety at Duncan's appointing of his son as Prince of Cumberland, Macbeth never considers killing Malcolm along with Duncan (leaving the unappointed Donalbain to shoulder the guilt). In his initial embracing of evil Macbeth is preoccupied with the sublime fantasy of regicide as the "be-all and end-all," conferring inviolable supremacy; only on discovering its failure to provide such aggrandizement does he turn to bitter envy of "fraternal" rivals.

18. Aquinas, *Summa Theologica* (Chicago: Encyclopedia Britannica, 1952), 2 vols., 1.63.2. Macbeth's rivalrous fury toward the fraternal Banquo is thus a second stage of evil, resulting from the failure to satisfy the hunger for greatness, just as Cain's envious fratricide stemmed from his parents' frustrated desire to emulate God. For a different perspective on the analogy between Cain and Macbeth, see Jorgensen, pp. 47-51, 190-5, 200, 213.

On the pervasiveness of envy in human motivation, see Melanie Klein, *Envy and Gratitude* (New York: Basic Books, 1957); and René Girard, *Violence and the Sacred,* trans. Patrick Gregory (1972; rpt. Baltimore: Johns Hopkins University Press, 1977), especially pp. 56-168. On the persistent use of this envy principle in Shakespeare's "enemy twins," see Joel Fineman, "Fratricide and Cuckoldry: Shakespeare's Doubles," *Representing Shakespeare: New Psychoanalytic Essays,* ed. Murray W. Schwartz and Coppélia Kahn (Baltimore: Johns Hopkins University Press, 1980), pp. 70-109.

19. Jorgensen (p. 194) calls these speeches (like the similar ravings of Lear in Act III) "soliloquys made public." Equally important, they are soliloquys made obscure through intense repression, so that neither Macbeth and Lear, nor their auditors, can easily fathom their speeches' profound self-reflections. Cf. Barry Weller, "Identity and Representation in Shakespeare," *ELH* 49 (1982), 356 ff; Robert Weimann, *Shakespeare and the Popular Tradition in the Theater,* ed. Robert Schwartz (Baltimore: Johns Hopkins University Press, 1978), pp. 218 ff.

20. On the key role of projection in developmental psychology see *The Writings of Anna Freud* 4:509-85; and Darius Ornston, "On Projection," *PSOC* 33 (1978), 117-66. Melanie Klein, in "Notes on Some Schizoid Mechanisms," *IJP* 27 (1946), 99-110, and in *The Psychoanalysis of Children,* trans. Alix Strachey (1932; rev. ed., New York: Delacorte Press, 1975), pp. 142-8, 178, observed a pattern in childhood development of *introjection-projection-reintrojection*. But I believe that the "reintrojection" occurs on a higher level, as in sublimation, and that this higher level is made possible by the stimulating effect of projection. Thus reintrojection, like Wordsworth's "recollection in tranquillity," is a culminating mode of psychic internalization and identity-construction occurring on a more comprehensive, controlled, and "sublime" level. Cf. Robert P. Knight, "Introjection, Projection, and Identification," *Psychoanalytic Quarterly* 9 (1940), 334-41; A. Freud, *The Ego and the Mechanisms of Defense* (New York: International Universities Press, 1966), pp. 50-53.

21. In spite of Macbeth's show of surprise at Fleance's survival (III.iv.20-24), it is tempting to believe that Macbeth is the "third murderer" [first advanced by Allan Park Paton, *Notes and Queries* (1869), and lucidly reformulated by Harold C. Goddard, *The Meaning of Shakespeare* (Chicago: Chicago University Press, 1960), 2 vols., 2:122-6]—so that he only "half-participates" in the second murder. That Macbeth can hardly admit (even to himself) his involvement suggests the extent of his splitting psyche: for if he *is* the third murderer, it reveals both a deepening insecurity and a growing obsession with rational control (utter self-repression, anal attentiveness to detail, and a host of other defensive mechanisms aimed at sustaining to others and to himself the illusion of kingship, including the pretense of shock on learning of Fleance's escape—which resembles his extravagant show of dismay on learning of Duncan's death). Macbeth's furtive pretense of uninvolvement even for his own cutthroats would thus demonstrate his increasing cowardice, alienation, and lack of a stable central self. Hence, for the second murder Macbeth both is and is not an active participant, owing to his descent into psychic bifurcation.

George Walton Williams, however, in "The Third Murderer in *Macbeth,*" *Shakespeare Quarterly* 23

(1972), 261, observes that "The supposition that Macbeth is the third murderer . . . necessitates a staging that twice violates the 'Law of Reentry.'" Thus, though the third murderer clearly indicates Macbeth's growing anxiety, and may vicariously represent his grasping for control (attending more closely than the others to the usurper's crucial purposes), stage convention would seem to argue against Macbeth's schizoid reappearance as monarch-cutthroat-monarch in such rapid sequence. Yet if we consider the extraordinary liberties and experimentation in the staging of other Shakespearean plays of this period (e.g., the Dover cliff scene in *King Lear*), one wonders at the theatrical ingenuity of having Macbeth immediately reenter, perhaps with a dark cape only thinly disguising his kingly garments, so that the audience would actually be *aware* of his devious schizophrenic "doubling." If so, it is the most stunningly purposeful violation of the Law of Reentry in the Shakespearean canon.

22. In "*Macbeth:* King James's Play," *South Atlantic Review* 47 (1982), 12-21, George Walton Williams astutely observes that the ghost of Banquo, rather than of Duncan, holds sway in the drama's central scene, thus heightening the compliment to King James I, even though it subverts decorum. Williams (pp. 20-21, fn. 12) notes the symbolic suggestiveness of the seating which underlies the doppelgänger effect at the banquet: "Macbeth does not sit in his throne [the "state" where Lady Macbeth remains]—to which he has no spiritual right; he does expect to sit at the table—a level to which he does have a right." The "place reserved" for Banquo, to which Macbeth is drawn as to his own natural place, is centrally located: "Both sides are even: here I'll sit i' th' midst" (III.iv.11). Almost exactly the same event occurs in Dostoyevsky's *The Double,* and similar psychic displacements occur in James' *The Turn of the Screw* and Conrad's "The Secret Sharer"; but only Macbeth confronts a double who represents not his sinister shadow, but the ruination of his better self.

No critic has fully considered Banquo as Macbeth's "double." Robert N. Watson briefly mentions Banquo as "doppelgänger," in "'Thriftless Ambition,' Foolish Wishes, and the Tragedy of *Macbeth*," *William Shakespeare's Macbeth,* ed. Harold Bloom (New York: Chelsea House, 1987), pp. 142-7; James Kirsch, in *Shakespeare's Royal Self* (New York: G. P. Putnam, 1965), pp. 331 ff, comments on the "participation mystique" of the two men (Macbeth being more attuned to the unconscious, but the weaker ego); Matthew N. Proser, *The Heroic Image in Five Shakespearean Tragedies* (Princeton: Princeton University Press, 1965), pp. 76-78, describes the good Banquo's ghost "as a kind of analogy for Macbeth's mutilated soul."

On literary uses of the "double" and the general process of "decomposition," see Doris L. Eder, "The Idea of the Double," *Psychoanalytic Review* 65 (1978), 579-614, esp. 587-9; and Robert Rogers, *A Psychoanalytic Study of the Double in Literature* (Detroit: Wayne State University Press, 1970), including a provocative but misleading identification of Macbeth and Lady Macbeth as doubles. Rogers does not distinguish between the *homoerotic* phenomenon of mirror-transference (between close friends, sibling rivals, or hero and alter-ego), and the more complex psychic transference between *heterosexual* partners, especially in marriage.

23. The positing of an "indissoluble tie" (*Macbeth* III.i.15-18) between self and shadow-self (or alter-ego) occurs at the exact center of *Othello* and *Macbeth* (and, with more benevolent implications, at the center of *King Lear*). At this moment each protagonist confronts the darkest possibilities of selfhood (the imputed treachery of Desdemona, the feigned sins of Poor Tom, the butchery inflicted by Macbeth himself).

24. See, e.g., Hogan (n. 2), who interprets the slaughter as a transference of the on-going Oedipal struggle, an indirect blow at Macduff as threatening authority and as fertile progenitor.

25. We must carefully distinguish Macbeth's tyrannous infantilism (culminating in narcissistic rage) from the healthy oral-narcissicistic bond, involving mutual recognition and respect between parent and child during the sucking stage. For the potentially negative aspects of infantile narcissism, see S. Freud, "On Narcissism: An Introduction," *SE* 14: 69-102; Otto F. Kernberg, *Borderline Conditions and Pathological Narcissism* (New York: International Universities Press, 1975); and the important Shakespearean studies of aberrant narcissism by Kirsch, "Macbeth's Suicide," and Adelman, "'Born of Woman'" (n. 2), and "'Anger's My Meat': Feeding, Dependency, and Aggression in *Coriolanus*," *Representing Shakespeare*, pp. 129-49. On the positive mode of narcissism and of maternal oral-narcissistic bonding, see Kohut, "Forms and Transformations of Narcissism," *JAPA* 14 (1966), 243-72; and Jessica Benjamin, *The Bonds of Love* (New York: Pantheon Books, 1988), pp. 11-50. Shakespeare seems particularly attuned to this primitive cathexis which forms the core of human identity, emphasizing not just negative but positive aspects of motherly nurture in the cathartic sequence of each of his mature tragedies, most strikingly in Cleopatra's death-scene ("Dost thou not see the baby at my breast / That sucks the nurse asleep?").

26. On "introjection" (as well as the related functions of "incorporation," "internalization," and "identification"), see, in addition to the writings of A. Freud and M. Klein cited in note 20, S. Freud, "Mourning and Melancholia" (1917), *SE* 14: 237-58; Hans W. Loewald, "Internalization, Separation,

Mourning, and the Superego," *Psychoanalytic Quarterly* 31 (1962), 483-504, and "On Internalization," *IJP* 54 (1973), 9-17; Roy Schafer, *Aspects of Internalization* (New York: International Universities Press, 1968); William W. Meissner, "Internalization and Object Relations," *Journal of the American Psychoanalytic Association* 27 (1979), 345-60, and *Internalization in Psychoanalysis* (New York: International Universities Press, 1981); Rebecca Smith Behrends and Sidney J. Blatt, "Internalization and Psychological Development throughout the Life Cycle," *PSOC* 40 (1985), 11-39.

27. Though the cathartic valuation of womanly/matronly nurture in Acts IV-V holds true for all of Shakespeare's major tragedies, *Hamlet* requires qualification. Never fully reunited with Ophelia or Gertrude, Hamlet only incipiently comprehends the meaning of a grave holding his "fool" and his beloved. The play's final focus on the killing of a false parent-king, of an inadequate sibling-double (Laertes), and of a disloyal nurturing mother, suggests unresolved Oedipal (and pre-Oedipal) anxieties and an incomplete quest for identity.

28. On the castration threat as a *vagina dentata* fantasy, see Otto Rank, *The Trauma of Birth* (New York: Robert Brunner, 1952; orig. 1924), pp. 48-49; Sandor F. Ferenczi, *The Theory and Technique of Psychoanalysis* (New York: Basic Books, 1925), pp. 278-81; Leonard Shengold, "The Effects of Overstimulation," *IJP* 48 (1967), 403-15; C. Philip Wilson, "Stone as a Symbol of Teeth," *Psychoanalytic Quarterly* 36 (1967), 418-27; Daniel B. Schuster, "Bisexuality and Body as Phallus," *Psychoanalytic Quarterly* 38 (1969), 72-80; and especially Roy Schafer, *Language and Insight* (New Haven: Yale University Press, 1978), pp. 153-60, who provides the context of a broad gender analysis.

Note, however, that the demoniac symbolism in *Macbeth* IV.i is an alliance of male and female perversions: the witches' devouring cauldron (*vagina dentata*) is shortly joined by their demon masters' "armed head" (*penis dentata*) which similarly tempts Macbeth to annihilate children (IV.i.69-86). This satanic collusion of perverted gender components, a marital travesty which promotes mutual deception and annihilation rather than mutual support and procreation, evolves throughout the play.

FURTHER READING

Criticism

Baldo, Jonathan. "The Politics of Aloofness in *Macbeth*." *English Literary Renaissance* 26, No. 3 (Autumn 1996): 531-60.

Discusses *Macbeth* in the context of Jacobean politics.

Berryman, John. "On *Macbeth*." In *Berryman's Shakespeare*, edited by John Haffenden, pp. 319-34. New York: Farrar, Straus, and Giroux, 1999.

Analyzes *Macbeth* in the context of Elizabethan and Jacobean cultures, including an overview of the play's major themes and action.

Callaghan, Dympna. "Wicked Women in *Macbeth:* A Study of Power, Ideology, and the Production of Motherhood." In *Reconsidering the Renaissance: Papers from the Twenty-First Annual Conference,* edited by Mario A. Di Cesare, pp. 355-69. Binghamton, NY: Medieval and Renaissance Texts and Studies, 1992.

Explores the cultural conflict between patriarchy and the rule of mothers, as well as skepticism surrounding witchcraft as it is portrayed in *Macbeth.*

Fox, Alice. "Obstetrics and Gynecology in *Macbeth*." *Shakespeare Studies* 12 (1979): 127-42.

Focuses on the frequent use of the vocabulary of obstetrics and gynecology in the language used by Macbeth and Lady Macbeth.

Guj, Luisa. "*Macbeth* and the Seeds of Time." *Shakespeare Studies* 18 (1986): 175-88.

Explores Shakespeare's treatment of the theme of time in *Macbeth,* tracing its origins in Renaissance myths, icons, and emblems.

Helms, Lorraine. "The Weyward Sisters: Towards a Feminist Staging of *Macbeth*." *New Theatre Quarterly* 8, No. 30 (May 1992): 167-77.

Studies the role of the witches in *Macbeth,* exploring the difficulty in staging the play in the absence of theater conventions that were prevalent in Shakespeare's day.

Janton, Pierre. "Sonship and Fatherhood in *Macbeth*." *Cahiers Elisabethains* 35 (April 1989): pp. 47-58.

Explores the theory that fear of assuming manhood is Macbeth's tragic flaw, leading him to annihilate all the potential and virtual father figures in the play.

Love, H. W. "Seeing the Difference: Good and Evil in the World of *Macbeth*." *Australasian Universities Language and Literature Association Journal (AUMLA)* 72 (1989): 203-28.

Examines *Macbeth* as a morality play, with special focus on the use of supernatural elements and vice figures.

Lynch, Kathryn L. "'What Hands Are Here?': The Hand as Generative Symbol in *Macbeth*." *Review of English Studies* 39, No. 153 (February 1988): 29-38.

Explores the significance of the hand motif in *Macbeth.*

Richardson, Brian. "'Hours Dreadful and Things Strange': Inversions of Chronology and Causality in *Macbeth*." *Philological Quarterly* 68, No. 3 (Summer 1989): 283-94.

    Suggests that the inversions of chronology in *Macbeth* are designed to mirror the central concerns of the play and that Shakespeare uses time as an integral part of his narrative technique.

Waters, D. Douglas. "Catharsis as Clarification." In *Christian Settings in Shakespeare's Tragedies,* pp. 79-118. Cranbury, NJ: Associated University Press, 1994.

    Discusses Shakespeare's tragic plays, and proposes that catharsis as clarification is the reader's main response to Shakespearean tragedies in Christian settings.

Willbern, David. "Phantasmagoric *Macbeth*." *English Literary Renaissance* 16, No. 3 (Autumn 1986): 520-49.

    Sketches a three-dimensional map of *Macbeth* in a visceral, psychoanalytic, and phantasmagoric context.

Wintle, Sarah and René Weis. "Macbeth and the Barren Sceptre." *Essays in Criticism* 41, No. 2 (April 1991): 128-46.

    Explores the topical nature of the action recreated in *Macbeth,* including references to such contemporary incidents as the Gunpowder Plot and other Jacobean political concerns.

The Winter's Tale

For further information on the critical and stage history of *The Winter's Tale,* see *SC,* Volumes 7, 15, 36, and 45.

INTRODUCTION

Scholars concur that *The Winter's Tale* was written in 1610 or early 1611 and that its earliest known performance was at the Globe Theatre on May 15th, 1611. Historians know that the play, a romance, was performed in 1613 as part of Princess Elizabeth's marriage celebrations, and that Shakespeare's main source for the play was Robert Green's *Pandosto* (1588). From its inception the play has attracted critical attention, although there is little or no consensus about its quality or theme. Many seventeenth- and eighteenth-century scholars found the play implausible, faulting Leontes's irrational rage and jealousy, the unaccounted sixteen year gap in the plot, and factual inaccuracies such as the mixing of time periods and the reference to a coastline in landlocked Bohemia. Today, scholars agree that the characteristics of the play typify the final period of Shakespeare's writing. However, instead of maintaining that this period represents a decline in Shakespeare's skill, many critics have reexamined the opinion that Shakespeare's final plays are morose and disjointed. Some critics now argue that Shakespeare was at his most innovative during his final period, creating new forms and perfecting themes that had shadowed him throughout his career. As this period has been redefined and gained greater appreciation, literary critics have applied these more positive views to *The Winter's Tale.* In addition, literary scholars have applied new concepts about feminism and emerging historical theories to *The Winter's Tale* in order to gain a better understanding of the play.

In his 1964 essay, Edward W. Tayler reflects upon the critical history of *The Winter's Tale,* arguing that while early critics such as Lytton Strachey doubted Shakespeare's ability in his final period, later scholars such as G. Wilson Knight and E. M. W. Tillyard have been more favorable. Tayler indicates that many modern critics concur that the improbable plot is meant to be symbolic, but they disagree over its meaning. He believes that Shakespeare was concerned ultimately with the relationship between art and nature, a topic which he focused on in his earlier plays and poems, such as *As You Like It* and *Venus and Adonis.* Additionally, Tayler discusses the importance of the pattern of integration and disruption in *The Winter's Tale,* a topic dealt with by Russ McDonald (1985) as well. McDonald states that the language and syntax of the play is difficult, complicated, and irregular. He posits that this tempo reflects the meaning within the plot, and that the plot and linguistic style are tightly intertwined. The critic argues that the marriage of plot and style is a distinctive characteristic of Shakespeare's final works and that both are built on his lifelong study of human nature.

Another topic which has drawn the attention of recent scholars is the sources, influences, and ideologies that shape *The Winter's Tale.* Literary critics agree that the play is based mainly upon Robert Greene's prose romance *Pandosto* (1588). Shakespeare made several key alterations that changed the focus of the play, but the early influence of Greene is still apparent. In addition, scholars note the influence of Ovid's *Metamorphoses* (1-8 A.D.), particularly on the statue scene in act five of *The Winter's Tale.* Scott F. Crider (1999) investigates the influence of Ovid's Pygmalian tale on this scene, and argues that by making Hermione become flesh again Shakespeare deviates from earlier versions of the story, reflecting a growing Renaissance conviction in the power of love, art, and faith over death. In his 1993 article, Robert Henke traces the influence of the Italian dramatist Battista Guarini on Shakespeare's later plays, arguing that in *The Winter's Tale* Shakespeare created an innovative new dramatic form—the pastoral tragi-comedy. Henke maintains that Shakespeare revolutionized the theater by skillfully bridging tragedy and comedy through the pastoral aspects of the play. Mary Ellen Lamb (1998) considers the influence of traditional women's tales in three of Shakespeare's plays. In her discussion, she examines the gender conflicts that arise from male anxiety over the influence that these women's tales had over children. In conclusion, the critic states that the very title of *The Winter's Tale* refers to the practice of telling folk tales, and maintains that Shakespeare's play suggests the "acceptance rather than rejection of old wives' tales."

Modern critics have applied new feminist theories to inform their analysis of *The Winter's Tale* as well. Specifically, they are interested in questions about the nature and function of Leontes's fury and the significance of the statue scene at the conclusion of the play in which Hermione is transformed from a statue to woman again. Critics such as David McCandless, M. Lindsay Kaplan, Katherine Eggert, and Lynn Enterline believe that the answers can be found in the interrelation between the patriarchal society and emerging fears of the power of women. McCandless (1990) describes the prevailing beliefs of the time in which women were blamed for original sin and the fall of man, as well as feared for their sexual power and ability to corrupt man. He argues that in the same way that the modern pornographer seeks to destroy the image of the women that he has created, Leontes is filled with a desire to destroy his view of Hermione as a sexually corrupt temptress. Lynn Enterline (1997) states that Hermione's and Paulina's strong rhetorical skills mark their threat against the authority of Leontes. In the end, Hermione learns to maintain her silence and thus preserve her status. In their 1994 article, M. Lindsey Kaplan and Katherine Eggert place the discussion of women's voice and power within the historical context of women's legal rights during the Elizabethan period. They maintain that *The Winter's Tale* was a means of reevaluating the power of Queen Elizabeth within a patriarchal society in which women were allotted neither a voice nor authority.

LANGUAGE, STRUCTURE, AND PLOT

Edward W. Tayler (essay date 1964)

SOURCE: "Nature and Art in Renaissance Literature: Shakespeare's *The Winter's Tale*," in *The Winter's Tale: Critical Essays,* edited by Maurice Hunt, Garland Publishing, 1995, pp. 119-38.

[*In the following essay, originally published in 1964, Tayler analyzes the underlying structure of* The Winter's Tale *and identifies the relationship between nature and art as a central concern.*]

The Winter's Tale, like Book VI of *The Faerie Queene,* exhibits a specialized use of the traditional materials of pastoral in conjunction with an explicit interest in the philosophical problem of Nature versus Art. Discussion must involve, at least initially and briefly, some reference to Shakespeare's earlier work and then to *Cymbeline* and *The Tempest,* both from his last period; for these later works, in particular, share many of the same intellectual concerns as well as the romance form. The last plays suffered a period of criticism in which, like Spenser's Legend of Courtesy, they were dismissed because they resembled insufficiently the work of The Poet's Serious Period. After the sentimental pleasure nineteenth-century critics like Dowden took in visualizing Shakespeare On The Heights in his last years at Stratford, the reaction, led by Lytton Strachey, took the romances in one way or another as evidence of senile decay. Shakespeare's powers were declining; like Spenser he was being bored to death by life and art. In the past twenty years, however, the last plays have received favorable attention from such writers as G. Wilson Knight and E. M. W. Tillyard, who have come to regard the romances as organic extensions of Shakespeare's earlier preoccupations, as complementary to his earlier tragic concerns.

In one way or another the writers of recent criticism have endeavored to lend the last plays dignity by arguing that Shakespeare had more on his mind than cranking out remunerative romances. The verse, in its range and intensity, seems to support the idea that these plays have depths beyond what is usually allowed to the genre of romance. In *Cymbeline,* for example, the generally wooden Posthumus, at long last united to Imogen, exclaims in the moment of their embrace:

> Hang there like fruit, my soul,
> Till the tree die!
>
> (V.v.263-64)[1]

The sudden power of lines such as these appears to point to a degree of seriousness that seems incompatible with the form of dramatic romance, and in *The Winter's Tale* and *The Tempest* the percentage of such lines increases.

A convenient example of the kind of intensity of which Shakespeare was capable at this time occurs in *The Winter's Tale* when Leontes describes his state of mind at discovering his wife's supposed infidelity:

> How blest am I
> In my just censure, in my true opinion!
> Alack for lesser knowledge! how accurs'd
> In being so blest! There may be in the cup
> A spider steep'd, and one may drink, depart,
> And yet partake no venom, for his knowledge
> Is not infected; but if one present
> Th' abhorr'd ingredient to his eye, make known
> How he hath drunk, he cracks his gorge, his sides,
> With violent hefts. I have drunk, and seen the spider.
>
> (II.i.36-45)

We are of course at liberty to see the rhetorical mastery and violent strength of verse like this as melodramatic; what is harder is to see it as appropriate to romance. Accordingly, recent criticism has quite properly tried to find "symbolic" and "mythic" undercurrents beneath a "superficial" surface of romance and pastoral elements. D. A. Traversi, for example, maintains that the "plot of *The Winter's Tale* is a perfect example of the symbolic technique perfected by Shakespeare in his last plays. It is the story of the division created in love and friendship by the passage of time and by the action of 'blood,' and of the healing of those divisions through penitence and renewed personal devotion."[2]

Granting it seems unwise to dismiss the genre of romance without having scrutinized it at all closely, most of us will nevertheless sympathize with such attempts to lend the last plays a serious purpose, if only because we are dissatisfied with the picture of Shakespeare as an elderly romanticist yawning his way through imitations of Beaumont and Fletcher. The tendency is to seek this serious purpose at some "mythic" or "symbolic" level because the romantic and pastoral elements are generally regarded as merely entertaining.

Putting aside for a moment the knowledge that pastoral does not preclude philosophy, the fact remains that the improbable plots of the last plays invite symbolic interpretation. In each of the plays a royal father loses his offspring through his own passionate excess, so that an initial atmosphere of prosperity and tranquillity precedes a time of confusion and suffering. In each the lost child is restored after living for a time among shepherds or in the wilderness, so that after the period of suffering, and out of the green world, emerges a new atmosphere of prosperity and tranquillity. This symbolic pattern is, however, so overlaid with the highly stylized elements of traditional romance—sublimely faithful love and excessive jealousy, complex incident and intrigue, puppet characterization, mistaken identity, disguisings, coincidence, innocuous poisons, white magic, amiable savages, and the like, that the pattern is hard to discern and harder still to exhibit as part of Shakespeare's conscious or unconscious intention.[3]

Although *The Winter's Tale* reveals a particularly complete and intense formulation of the "mythic" or "symbolic" pattern that critics suppose to be characteristic of the last plays, this underlying configuration is of such a comprehensive type that it has proved susceptible of translation into a variety of different terms: it may be a derivative pattern of a quasi-psychological kind, as in Tillyard's theory that the last plays represent a vital extension of concerns revealed by Shakespeare during his tragic phase; or it may be an anthropological pattern, a sophisticated vegetation myth, its ultimate meanings looking back on folk ritual;[4] or it may even be, despite the elements of romance, a theological pattern of sin, atonement, and redemption.[5] So far as *The Winter's Tale* is concerned, the problem is not so much whether the underlying pattern exists, but how it is to be theorized about.

The language and the imagery of the play, remarkably rich in allusions, seem to offer justification for psychological, theological, anthropological, and other interpretations, but my own conviction is that we are not likely to settle anything through appeals to different systems of abstraction; all such systems appear to be so comprehensive as to include the fundamental story elements of which the romances are compounded. My own contribution, in any case, is not to offer a new system of abstractions (for I intend to describe the underlying pattern in as neutral language as possible), but to point out that a fundamental part of the pattern reveals Shakespeare's literary and philosophical concern with Nature and Art. In other words, the "symbolic" pattern of *The Winter's Tale,* turning on images of the seasons, of birth and death, of the sea as destroyer and savior, works together with the conceptual pattern of Nature and Art.

The division between Nature and Art occupied Shakespeare throughout his career. It is implicit in the pastoral episodes of *As You Like It,* and even as early as *Venus and Adonis* he is toying with the conventional notion of strife between Nature and Art in painting:

> Look, when a painter would surpass the life
> In limning out a well-proportioned steed,
> His art with nature's workmanship at strife,
> As if the dead the living should exceed.
>
> (ll. 289-92)

And in reference to a painting of the siege of Troy in *The Rape of Lucrece*:

> A thousand lamentable objects there,
> In scorn of nature, art gave lifeless life.
>
> (ll. 1373-74)

The association of "art" with death and "nature" with life persists even so far as the "dead likeness" of Hermione in *The Winter's Tale*; and the commonplace pairing of Nature and Art is alluded to in play after play, reappearing at some length in *Timon of Athens,* shortly before the writing of the last romances. In the opening scene that advertises the main concerns of that play, the Poet and the Painter are discussing an example of the Painter's work, and the Poet is amiably self-important in traditional terms:

> I will say of it,
> It tutors nature. Artificial strife
> Lives in these touches, livelier than life.
>
> (I.i.36-38)

Such statements are commonplace, and despite some attempt at variation the similarity of wording implies that Shakespeare produced such literary detritus from his memory on demand, without thought and without effort, as the appropriate occasion presented itself.

Although Shakespeare's use of the division in his allusions to the fine arts is entirely traditional, Nature and Art represented a vital and living problem for him in the ethical speculations of the last plays. In *Cymbeline* the beginnings of what is to be an intense preoccupation may be glimpsed in one of the major ethical contrasts of the play—between the King's stepson, Cloten, and his real sons, Guiderius and Arviragus. Cloten is the product of the "art o' th' court" that Belarius, the guardian of the real sons, continually disparages. Guiderius and Arviragus, having been brought up in savage surroundings apart from the court, represent the triumph of Nature untutored by Art. As Belarius explains it:

> O thou goddess,
> Thou divine Nature, how thyself thou blazon'st
> In these two princely boys! They are as gentle
> As zephyrs blowing below the violet,
> Not wagging his sweet head; and yet as rough,
> (Their royal blood enchaf'd) as the rud'st wind
> That by the top doth take the mountain pine
> And make him stoop to th' vale. 'Tis wonder
> That an invisible instinct should frame them
> To royalty unlearn'd, honour untaught,
> Civility not seen from other, valour
> That wildly grows in them but yields a crop
> As if it had been sow'd.
>
> (IV.ii.169-81)

The opposition between Nature and Art is not absolute for Shakespeare—he allows the Princes to express an awareness that courts may be in many respects superior to caves—but throughout the terms have been manipulated in such a way as to provide a main theme of the romance. As far as the Princes are concerned, Shakespeare agrees with Spenser and the courtesy books in making Nature more powerful than nurture; and thus it is appropriate that Nature unaided by Art should figure in the reconciliation scene at the end of the play. Granted the thematic value of the terms, remarks like those of Belarius' attain in context a force beyond that which may be assigned to a commonplace. In *Cymbeline* statements about Nature and Art have become part of the dramatic design, so that they function, perhaps a little creakily, as part of the plot and not merely as isolated allusions.

By the time of *The Tempest* the process has been developed and intensified, passing from the relatively derivative use of the division to a more subtle and skillfully articulated study of the traditional opposition of Nature to Art. Frank Kermode's elegant Introduction to *The Tempest* takes full account of Nature and Art and there is no need to rehearse his arguments here; although one may grow restive at his identification of Caliban as the central figure of the play, against which all the other characters are measured, it nevertheless seems clear that Kermode is right in contending that the "main opposition is between the worlds of Prospero's Art and Caliban's Nature."[6] Hence there is little to be gained by pursuing this survey: enough has been said to establish Shakespeare's interest, early and late, in Nature and Art and to provide a context for detailed consideration of *The Winter's Tale,* the play that exploits most fully the relationship between the philosophical division and the pastoral genre.

Beneath the romance trappings of *The Winter's Tale* the critics have seen a pattern that, reduced to its essentials and stated in relatively neutral language, is based on cycles or alternations of harmony and alienation, of integration and disruption.[7] Harmony, symbolized in the friendship of Leontes and Polixenes, receives initial emphasis in the first scene as Camillo remarks, perhaps a little ambiguously: "They were train'd together in their childhoods; and there rooted betwixt them then such an affection which cannot choose but branch now." In the next scene Polixenes sounds the same note as he recalls for Hermione what it was like to be "boy eternal" with her husband, Leontes.

> We were as twinn'd lambs that did frisk i' th' sun
> And bleat the one at th' other. What we chang'd
> Was innocence for innocence; we knew not
> The doctrine of ill-doing, nor dream'd
> That any did. Had we pursu'd that life,
> And our weak spirits ne'er been higher rear'd
> With stronger blood, we should have answer'd heaven
> Boldly, "Not guilty," the imposition clear'd
> Hereditary ours.
>
> (I.ii.67-75)

The idea of carefree harmony and the connotations of spring and birth are in this particular passage subordinated to the theological terms. The harmony recalled by Polixenes is a vision of the integrity of man in Eden, free of the taint of original sin—an association reinforced by the wit of the following lines as he and Hermione joke about the boys having "first sinn'd with" the queens, the implication being that the innocence of former days was lost because of woman.

This is not allegory, of course, nor is *The Winter's Tale* a covert recapitulation of the Fall of Man. But the web of allusion in these lines provides a frame of reference within which the main events of the play can receive meaning: the speech introduces the vision of the green world, the ideal of past harmony, and associates it with birth, innocence, spring, even with the garden of Eden. To speak technically, this is the "integrity" of Nature before the Fall.

The vision of the Garden, however, is brief and not easily sustained. As Shakespeare's audience was well aware, the harmony of Eden had been lost to man so that his "stronger blood" was no longer free from the hereditary "imposition." Consequently the Elizabethan audience was better prepared than Shakespeare's modern critics for Leontes' sudden and unmotivated jealousy, the towering excess of passion that, appearing in the same scene as Polixenes' speech of remembered bliss, obliterates the initial mood of harmony and introduces chaos and death for which Leontes is finally to do penance.

Leontes is a man, his Nature impaired by the Fall, so that he is *non posse non peccare,* not able not to err. The terrible consequences of Leontes' passion—alienation from Polixenes and Camillo, the death of his son, the death of Antigonus, the apparent deaths of his daughter and wife—form the main burden of the play until the Chorus of Time that introduces Act IV. Meanwhile the members of Shakespeare's audience have seen the result of an excess of passion and have been able to judge the action in the terms, moral and theological, most meaningful to them. The first phase of the cycle is complete; harmony and integration have been replaced by alienation and disruption.

The pivotal point of the play lies where it should, toward the end of Act III; as in *Pericles* and *The Tempest* it involves a storm at sea, the archetypal image of birth and death. The young shepherd (the clown) witnesses the destruction of the ship and the death of Antigonus, but at the same time the old shepherd comes across the living babe whose restoration figures in the fulfillment of the oracle. The scene thus recalls the disruption and chaos of the earlier action and at the same time anticipates the restoration of harmony in the last act. As the old shepherd puts it, saying more than he understands: "Now bless thyself! thou met'st with things dying, I with things new-born" (III.iii.116-18).

Act IV includes the pastoral interlude and, as we have come to expect, the main references to the controversy over Nature and Art. Florizel, the son of Polixenes, has fallen in love with the shepherdess Perdita whom we know to be the daughter of Leontes, marooned by his order during a transport of jealousy. The child has grown up without the benefit of Art, and yet her demeanor, like that of the Princes in *Cymbeline,* reflects the irrefragable excellence of royal blood. Throughout the word "queen" is applied to her, for as Florizel says:

> Each your doing,
> So singular in each particular,
> Crowns what you are doing in the present deed,
> That all your acts are queens.
>
> (IV.iv.143-46)

Both royal children are for the moment disguised as shepherds, the difference being that Florizel knows his true birth whereas Perdita does not. And while they masquerade as pastoral figures, Shakespeare takes care to have us associate the children with more than purity of blood.

Florizel's name—it does not appear in Shakespeare's source—is clearly allegorical, and the association with Flora receives further emphasis in the Prince's description of Perdita in her role as queen of the sheep-shearing:

> These your unusual weeds to each part of you
> Do give a life—no shepherdess, but Flora
> Peering in April's front! This your sheep-shearing
> Is as a meeting of the petty gods,
> And you the queen on't.
>
> (IV.iv.1-5)

Despite the wide difference in (apparent) birth, Shakespeare makes it clear that there is no intention of exercising *droit du seigneur;* Florizel's "youth" and "blood" are as idyllic and pure as his pastoral surroundings, as Perdita herself recognizes even when his praise of her is so extravagant as to seem suspicious:

> Your praises are too large. But that your youth,
> And the true blood which peeps so fairly through't,
> Do plainly give you out an unstain'd shepherd,
> With wisdom I might fear, my Doricles [i.e., Florizel],
> You woo'd me the false way.
>
> (IV.iv.147-51)

Florizel makes it explicit:

> my desires
> Run not before mine honour, nor my lusts
> Burn hotter than my faith.
>
> (IV.iv. 33-35)

In short, Shakespeare has taken care to lend Florizel and Perdita the qualities that his audience associated with pastoral figures—idyllic innocence and artless Nature.

The value of Perdita's artlessness is particularly emphasized. Her intellectual simplicity cleaves directly to the heart of a problem, a quality that leads Camillo to acknowledge that he

> cannot say 'tis pity
> She lacks instructions, for she seems a mistress
> To most that teach.
>
> (IV.iv.592-94)

And her modest demeanor does not prevent her from making the pastoral comparison between country and court explicit in referring to Polixenes' rage at discovering his son in love with a "shepherdess":

> I was not much afeard: for once or twice
> I was about to speak, and tell him plainly
> The selfsame sun that shines upon his court
> Hides not his visage from our cottage, but
> Looks on alike.
>
> (IV.iv.453-57)

Even this satiric cut—it is in no sense "democratic"[8]—is of the kind common in pastoral. So far in Shakespeare there is no more than what may be expected from the bucolic tradition: spring, youth, innocence, idyllic love, and the assumption that Nature is superior to Art. But when we have understood the exact function of the pastoral episode in relation to the play as a whole, in relation to its dramatic structure and to its underlying alternation of harmony and disintegration, we will be in a better position to see the individual uses to which Shakespeare has put the traditional materials of Nature and Art.

The pastoral episode immediately precedes the last act, the time of reconciliation and reintegration. The court of Sicily—where the action of the play began—is now the scene of an elaborate series of discoveries in which poetic and other justice is rendered all around. A number of exchanges between Paulina and Leontes have assured the audience that the king is truly repentant; the theological note, sounded so persistently and quietly throughout the play, once more assumes a prominent function, as in the words of Cleomenes:

> Sir, you have done enough, and have perform'd
> A saint like sorrow. No fault could you make
> Which you have not redeem'd; indeed, paid down
> More penitence than done trespass. At the last,
> Do as the heavens have done: forget your evil;
> With them, forgive yourself.
>
> (V.i.1-6)

Redemption is indeed at hand.

Florizel and Perdita, fleeing Bohemia and the anger of Polixenes, appear at the Sicilian court; and Leontes, in words that recall the pastoral interlude, welcomes the lovers as a change from the winter of his discontent: "Welcome hither / As is the spring to th' earth" (V.i.151-52). The "unstain'd" youth of Florizel and Perdita, their "true blood," symbolizes the restoration of harmony, the coming of spring to the wasteland, and the purification of the "stronger blood" of their fathers that is impaired by the stain of original sin. Perdita, she who was lost, is found, and discovered to be the daughter of the King; Leontes and Polixenes are once more united in friendship; the way is cleared for the young lovers; Hermione is restored to Leontes during the famous (or notorious) statue scene; and the extraordinary network of repeated words and phrases—youth and age, spring and winter, Nature and Art, birth and death, innocence and sin, Nature and Grace, blood and infection, and so on—is resolved in a series of brilliant puns, in the paradoxical wit of the last scenes. The second phase of the cycle of alienation and harmony, of disruption and reintegration, has been completed.

Enough has been said so that the function of the pastoral scenes in this cycle of—to put it theologically—Fall and Redemption is perhaps obvious. Without these scenes the play would be structurally and symbolically defective, for they reflect, at the appropriate point in the action, the harmony with which the play began: the qualities that Leontes and Polixenes were said to have had as boys are those which Shakespeare gives in turn to Perdita and Florizel. And even the imagery of "twinn'd lambs," together with the assumption of innocence unimpaired by original sin, that Shakespeare uses in describing the young princes accurately reflects pastoral conventions; Shakespeare chose appropriately if not "originally" in this respect.

The imaginative force of the paradisiacal intimacy that once existed between Polixenes and Leontes is therefore essentially similar to the pastoral harmony that is now associated with Perdita and Florizel, and it is therefore proper that the two moments in the Garden balance each other structurally, the one preceding disruption and the other preceding integration. Moreover, the two moments serve a similar moral function in the play. In the cycle of disruption and integration the moments of childhood innocence and pastoral integrity provide the audience, in essentially similar ways, with visions of ideal order in terms of which the rest of the action may be meaningfully understood. The pastoral episode is consequently not merely a decorative interlude but the structural and symbolic prelude to the restoration of harmony in the last act.

Shakespeare's use of pastoral as the expression of an ethical ideal, of a simple world by which the more complex one might be judged, is strictly traditional, and yet it is a little more complicated than my statements so far might imply. Shakespeare's idealization of shepherd life, for example, does not extend much beyond Perdita who is, like Pastorella in *The Faerie Queene,* of shepherd nurture but not of shepherd nature. And while the old shepherd, that "weather-bitten conduit of many kings' reigns" (V.ii.61-62), is allowed to display a certain amount of rude dignity, the Mopsas and Dorcases of Shakespeare's pastoral world are bumpkins, foils for that snapper-up of unconsidered trifles, Autolycus. Perdita's royal blood manifests itself despite her surroundings and not because of them. For Shakespeare, then, shepherds may serve as exemplars of virtue if they are royal shepherds, and Nature may do without the civilizing influence of Art if it is royal Nature. Toward ordinary shepherds Shakespeare's attitude is realistic and gently satirical; his tolerant humor recalls Theocritus but is a long way from Vergil's delicate enthusiasms.

Shakespeare's attitude toward the division between Nature and Art is at least as complicated, but analysis begins most conveniently with his knowledge of traditional materials. Certainly he was aware of the long-standing association of pastoral with Nature and Art, for his pastoral episode includes a fairly thorough debate on the subject. Camillo and Polixenes, disguised, appear at the sheepshearing to investigate the truth of the rumored liaison between Florizel and some humble shepherdess. Polixenes and Perdita discuss flowers, but matters of cultural propriety are always near the surface of what is ostensibly a horticultural argument.

These speeches are worth quoting at length because of their explicit relevance to my thesis, their complex character, and their importance as conceptual statements of the ethical concerns of the play. Perdita begins by apologizing for presenting these men of "middle age" with winter flowers; she has no fall flowers because she will not grow "nature's bastards," and the discussion immediately turns into a highly technical debate on Nature and Art.

> *Per.* Sir, the year growing ancient,
> Not yet on summer's death nor on the birth
> Of trembling winter, the fairest flow'rs o' th' season
> Are our carnations and streak'd gillyvors,
> Which some call nature's bastards. Of that kind
> Our rustic garden's barren, and I care not
> To get slips of them.
> *Pol.* Wherefore, gentle maiden,
> Do you neglect them?
> *Per.* For I have heard it said
> There is an art which in their piedness shares
> With great creating nature.
> *Pol.* Say there be.
> Yet nature is made better by no mean
> But nature makes that mean. So, over that art
> Which you say adds to nature, is an art
> That nature makes. You see, sweet maid, we marry
> A gentler scion to the wildest stock
> And make conceive a bark of baser kind
> By bud of nobler race. This is an art
> Which does mend nature—change it rather; but
> The art itself is nature.
> *Per.* So it is.
> *Pol.* Then make your garden rich in gillyvors,
> And do not call them bastards.
> *Per.* I'll not put
> The dibble in earth to set one slip of them;
> No more than, were I painted, I would wish
> This youth should say 'twere well, and only therefore
> Desire to breed by me.
>
> (IV.iv.79-103)

The speeches are obviously meant to be significant in relation to the entire action of the play; they are not merely decorative commonplaces, but their function has never been fully explained.

There is a possibility that Shakespeare intended the actor portraying Polixenes to speak his lines in such a way that the audience will take the horticultural reasoning as a trap, as a device by which Polixenes hopes to expose Perdita as a scheming wench who is after that "bud of nobler race,"

Florizel. But it is Perdita who first commits herself against "nature's bastards," and Polixenes' tone, now deliberative, now authoritative, does not appear to support such an interpretation. The King seems pretty clearly to be reasoning in earnest.

Admittedly, the contention that an Art that changes Nature is in fact Nature may seem at first blush sophistical, calculated to make a young girl betray her desires for the "gentler scion." Yet Polixenes' stand is perhaps the most dignified and carefully argued in the whole history of possible opposition between Nature and Art. Like Aristotle and Plato, Polixenes points out that the "art itself is nature." Aristotle had argued in the *Physics* that when we claim that Art perfects Nature we do in fact mean in the last analysis that Nature perfects herself: "The best illustration is a doctor doctoring himself: nature is like that."[9] And Plato in the tenth book of the *Laws* had maintained that the good legislator "ought to support the law and also art, and acknowledge that both alike exist by nature, and no less than nature."[10] Although Polixenes' argument may appear sophistical, it is in fact an orthodox statement of the "real" significance of the ancient opposition.

There is of course nothing new in the mixture of horticultural and social vocabularies either, but the implications of the mixture in Polixenes' argument are shockingly unorthodox:

> You see, sweet maid, we marry
> A gentler scion to the wildest stock
> And make conceive a bark of baser kind
> By bud of nobler race.

Translated into purely social terms—Shakespeare's equivocal vocabulary forces the audience to consider the social implications—the argument of Polixenes seems to call for a program of egalitarian eugenics, a program equally shocking, one suspects, to Polixenes and to the Elizabethan audience. Especially in the given dramatic situation, for the King is at this moment disguised as a shepherd expressly to prevent his "gentler scion" from marrying a "bark of baser kind."

Perdita has throughout revealed a Spenserian appreciation of "degree," and now her reply to Polixenes rejects his (implied) social radicalism along with his horticultural orthodoxy:

> I'll not put
> The dibble in earth to set one slip of them;
> No more than, were I painted, I would wish
> This youth [Florizel] should say 'twere well, and only therefore
> Desire to breed by me.

Perdita's uneasiness in her "borrowed flaunts" (IV.iv.23), her modest conviction that she is, "poor lowly maid, / Most goddess-like prank'd up" (IV.iv.9-10), has culminated in her final identification of Art with deceit, with false imitation, with "painted" womanhood—a kind of Art morally and otherwise inferior to Nature. Her position is, indeed, as venerable as that of Polixenes, appearing in such diverse places as Plato's concept of imitation in the fine arts, in Castiglione's view of cosmetics,[11] and in virtually the whole of the pastoral tradition. Yet neither Polixenes nor Perdita may be taken to represent Shakespeare's final word on the division between Nature and Art.[12] The two traditions are both philosophically "respectable"; dramatic propriety alone requires that Polixenes maintain the court position and Perdita hold to the pastoral belief in the absolute dichotomy between the two terms.

If Shakespeare's "own" position must remain for the moment conjectural, it is at least possible to understand what he is doing with the ancient division between Nature and Art. Clearly he is using it *dramatically,* as an oblique commentary on the action of the play. Less obvious is his use of the conceptual terms of the division to reflect the major ethical concerns of the play, using them to sum up with dramatic irony the ethical and social questions of *The Winter's Tale.*

With Perdita, for example, the debate becomes a comment on the way Shakespeare has characterized her. She is given to us as the creation of Nature who, despite her lack of Art, is "mistress / To most that teach"; she is completely incapable of deceit, and her charming sensuousness is tempered by a clear perception of decorum, of her proper place in the order of things. At the same time her role in the sheepshearing is the creation of Art; her "unusual weeds" make her a "goddess," a "queen," but since these "borrowed flaunts" are deceitful, she resolves finally to "queen it no inch farther" (IV.iv.460). Thus Perdita's stand on the ancient debate accurately reflects her character; it is perfectly consistent with the manner in which she is dramatized. It is this and more. In addition it anticipates ironically the discoveries of the last act, for although Perdita at this point appears to be arguing (in horticultural terms) against a marriage with Florizel, her words describe unwittingly but exactly the final situation of the two lovers: in the last act it will be revealed that Perdita is a "queen" by Nature rather than by Art, that her "borrowed flaunts" are hers by right. At the time when she takes her stand on the question of Nature versus Art, she is by Nature what she conceives herself to be by Art.

Her speech to Polixenes is therefore effective in two main ways: on the one hand it accents her pastoral status as a figure of Nature, free of the corruption and taint of Art, suggesting the Nature of Eden; on the other hand the speech anticipates obliquely the last act of the play in which she and the other characters (the spectator is of course already aware of the dramatic irony of her speech) will understand that Florizel's metaphorical praise—"all your acts are queens"—represents truth on the literal as well as the figurative level.

Polixenes' argument similarly sets up reverberations far beyond the limits of his speech and the immediate context.

Polixenes, like Perdita, seemingly argues against his own best interests, for his resolution of the opposition between Nature and Art apparently sanctions the marriage of a noble to a commoner, the "bud of nobler race" to a "bark of baser kind." Thus, as far as Shakespeare and the audience are concerned, it is still another opportunity for dramatic irony; again the spectator is aware of more in a character's words than the character himself. Polixenes appears conscious only of the horticultural application of his words while the spectator is in a position to see that, in the case of Perdita, the "art itself *is* nature." Thus, Polixenes is also "right," even in the social sense of his words, though he cannot yet see the queenliness of Perdita's "nature is made better by no mean / But nature makes that mean." It is only in the last act that the disagreement between Perdita and Polixenes is transcended and resolved in the general restoration of harmony.

The last act is worth looking at in connection with Nature and Art because Shakespeare returns to the subject, this time in the sphere of the fine arts, in an attempt to resolve the paradoxical contrarieties generated out of the debate between Perdita and Polixenes. That which was lost has been found in the person of Perdita, and the two kings are reunited. All that remains is for the dead to rise as in *Pericles*: the "dead" Hermione is still lost to Leontes. Her improbable restoration in the statue scene has been condemned as a vulgar concession to popular taste and cited as an example of the triviality of the romance form. Such criticism quite misses the point, for it ignores the ground swell of harmony and alienation that informs the play and, even more pertinently, it neglects Shakespeare's preoccupation with Nature and Art.

Properly assessed, the "unrealistic" quality of the statue scene is beside the point. Here as elsewhere in the last romances Shakespeare's respect for "truth" lies in the intensity of his verse and in the underlying pattern of the plays. If the statue scene is improbable, it nevertheless conforms with fidelity to the cycle of alienation and harmony, and the verse of this scene possesses a rare imaginative integrity. All the crucial words of the play—summer and winter, "infancy and grace," Nature and Art, life and death—come together in the last scenes in a series of reckless paradoxes. Paulina speaks to the statue:

> Bequeath to death your numbness, for from him
> Dear life redeems you.
>
> (V.iii.102-3)

The time of Hermione's "better grace" has arrived; her stepping down from the pedestal means harmony, forgiveness, restoration, redemption.

The role played by Nature and Art in this larger resolution is perhaps obvious. Clearly a statue represents Art, and in this case the statue represents living Art,[13] or Nature. Such distinctions were equally clear to Shakespeare, and his language shows that he also expected his audience to have in mind the traditional opposition between the terms. We first hear of the statue from the Third Gentleman, whose description is marked by the ancient division and avails itself of the ancient analogy:

> . . . a piece many years in doing, and now newly perform'd, by that rare Italian master, Julio Romano, who, had he himself eternity and could put breath into his work, would beguile Nature of her custom, so perfectly he is her ape.
>
> (V.ii.103-8)

The artist is the ape of Nature, his imitation practiced so perfectly that he almost outdoes Nature, his final aim being *naturam vincere*. We have already seen the same notion in *Venus and Adonis*, the *Rape of Lucrece*, and *Timon*; it is the cliché of iconic poetry of the period, summed up in Cardinal Bembo's epitaph on Raphael: "Nature feared that she would be conquered while he lived, and would die when he died."[14] It is in this tradition of friendly contest between Art and Nature that Paulina invites praise of her "statue":

> Prepare
> To see the life as lively mock'd as ever
> Still sleep mock'd death,
>
> (V.iii.18-20)

and it is in this tradition that Leontes praises it:

> The fixture of her eye has motion in't,
> As we are mock'd with art.
>
> (V.iii.67-68)

Art has successfully imitated Nature, or so it seems to those who do not know that Paulina has preserved Hermione alive.

The symbolic value of the scene is clear: as with Perdita, the imitation or "mock" of Nature turns out finally to be Nature after all. What seems to be Art is in fact Nature, fulfilling Polixenes' assertion that the "art itself is nature" and confirming Perdita's belief in the supremacy of "great creating nature." The statue scene is with all its improbability a dramatic embodiment of Shakespeare's preoccupation with Nature and Art; it transcends the earlier disagreement between Perdita and Polixenes, for the opposition between Nature and Art dissolves in the pageantry of the statue's descent.

The traditional division lies at the center of *The Winter's Tale*. It is used conceptually and as an instrument of dramatic irony in the pastoral episode, and it appears symbolically as part of the total resolution of Act V. Nevertheless, Shakespeare does not seem to be as far committed to the division as Spenser. Although both poets take full advantage of the association of the literary genre with the philosophical division and although both use the pastoral as "an element in the harmonious solution of a longer story"[15] about the court, in Shakespeare the division lacks much of the didactic immediacy it possesses in Spenser. The virtue of courtesy must be placed properly in the order of nature, and Spenser uses Nature and Art to achieve this didactic end; he is thinking *with* the established terms more than he is *about* them. Perhaps because *The Winter's Tale* is less obtrusively didactic, Shakespeare thinks *about* the terms more than he does *with* them, finding in Nature and Art opportunities for witty debate and verbal paradox; perhaps because of his lack of absolute commitment he can afford to extract from various and conflicting interpretations the full dramatic value of the philosophical division. In *The Winter's Tale* the traditional terms represent, through dramatic irony, a conceptual summation of the ethical and social interests of the play, and in the last act they form a main part of the elaborate series of paradoxes culminating in the statue scene—the pun made flesh.

Notes

1. References will be to the accessible one-volume *Complete Works of Shakespeare,* ed. George Lyman Kittredge (Boston, 1936).
2. "The Last Plays," *An Approach to Shakespeare* (2d ed., rev.; Doubleday Anchor Books; New York, 1956), p. 261.
3. This is particularly true of the more obviously experimental romances, *Pericles* and *Cymbeline*.
4. See F. C. Tinkler's ingenious article on *The Winter's Tale, Scrutiny,* V (1937), 344-64.
5. See S. L. Bethell, *The Winter's Tale: A Study* (New York, 1947).
6. Since Kermode has discussed the matter so thoroughly and admirably in his introduction to the play (Arden Shakespeare; 5th ed., rev.; Cambridge, Mass., 1954), I merely allude to his work here. The quotation appears on p. xxiv.
7. I am aware that my language is not entirely neutral. "Harmony and alienation" may, as a pair, have for some readers theological associations, and "harmony," in particular, has musical connotations. My main effort is simply to avoid forcing the reader to choose between, say, the theological interpretation of S. L. Bethell and the anthropological interpretation of F. C. Tinkler; my own argument does not require the acceptance of either.
8. It seems appropriate to remark that Shakespeare, like Spenser, satirizes the "art o' th' court" without actually questioning the status quo: Nature that is admirable without benefit of Art almost invariably turns out to be royal or at least noble Nature.
9. *Physics* 199b.30-31, *The Basic Works of Aristotle,* ed. Richard McKeon (New York, 1941), p. 251.
10. *Laws* x.890, *The Dialogues of Plato,* trans. Benjamin Jowett (New York, 1937), II, 632. See also John of Salisbury's *Metalogicon* i.8, ed. Clement C. J. Webb (Oxford, 1929), pp. 29ff.
11. See *The Book of the Courtier,* trans. Charles S. Singleton (Anchor Books; New York, 1959), pp. 65f.
12. There is no warrant in the play for ascribing either position to Shakespeare. But despite the uncertainties arising from the dramatic form, it seems possible to determine Shakespeare's "own" position by seeking what he assumed rather than gave to characters, and by correlating generalizations about Nature and Art with his own artistic practice and with the conduct of "normative" characters. This, however, demands a thorough study of all the plays and is clearly beyond the scope of this chapter.
13. Generally Shakespeare associates Nature with life, Art with death; see the citations from *Venus and Adonis* and the *Rape of Lucrece* at the beginning of this chapter.
14. As quoted by Jean H. Hagstrum, *The Sister Arts: The Tradition of Literary Pictorialism and English Poetry from Dryden to Gray* (Chicago, 1958), in his discussion of Nature and Art in the Renaissance, pp. 81-88. Hagstrum emphasizes the idea of contest or competition between the artist and nature, seeing *The Winter's Tale* as the "negation of one element in the pictorialist and iconic tradition."
15. C. H. Herford, Introduction to *The Winter's Tale, The Works of William Shakespeare* (Eversley Shakespeare; 10 vols.; New York, 1899), IV, 268; the phrase is used without the specific application it has in my argument. Cf. Samuel L. Wolff, *The Greek Romances in Elizabethan Prose Fiction* (New York, 1912), p. 432. Wolff associates this use of pastoral, perhaps a little vaguely, with the long tradition of "escapes" from the "life active" to the "life contemplative" of the Lower World or the Fortunate Islands. He also points out that pastoral is not so used in Sannazaro, Tasso, or Guarini, all of whom lack the "urban enveloping action," which leads him to hazard, I believe correctly, that "this employment of pastoral is distinctive of Elizabethan fiction." There is some precedent, however slight, in Longus, but it seems that the Elizabethans were the only ones to exploit fully this social use of pastoral.

Russ McDonald (essay date 1985)

SOURCE: "Poetry and Plot in *The Winter's Tale,*" in *Shakespeare Quarterly,* Vol. 36, No. 3, Autumn, 1985, pp. 315-29.

[*In the following essay, McDonald focuses on the distinct linguistic form employed in* The Winter's Tale, *stating that its more complex style is connected with the intricate plot.*]

The Winter's Tale, it is generally agreed, is difficult to read. To move from *Macbeth* or *Antony and Cleopatra* into the world of Sicilia is to enter strange territory where a peculiar dialect is spoken. When Leontes steps apart from Hermione and Polixenes, turns to the audience, and utters his meditation beginning "Too hot, too hot," listeners and readers alike are apt to be mystified. We ought to be disturbed, of course, by the king's logic and conclusions; but more to the point, we are immediately confused by his language, and the trouble encountered in these early speeches is characteristic of the play as a whole and of the romances in general. Shakespeare's late verse is different from his earlier poetry—more complicated, elliptical, and irregular. J. M. Nosworthy, referring particularly to *Cymbeline,* describes the late style as follows: "Blank verse is handled with the utmost freedom, and run-on lines, light, weak, and double endings are marked characteristics. Ellipsis and elision contribute greatly to stylistic economy, and short speeches are so concentrated as to be perplexing. . . ."[1] The complexity of the late verse is a critical commonplace; the sources and functions of its syntactic and prosodic complexity are less well known.[2]

I wish to propose a correspondence between Shakespeare's command of a new kind of blank verse in *The Winter's Tale* and his treatment of dramatic action and theatrical effects. Moreover, I think I can demonstrate that the structure of the late style is, like the shape of the plots, determined by Shakespeare's tragicomic conception of the structure of human experience. The relation between verse and character has long been acknowledged; the agitation of Leontes' speech attests to the disorder of his mind. Yet to say this does not take us very far toward defining the particular stylistic qualities of this or the other romances. That connection, after all, is obvious in a host of other works, notably *Othello.* What distinguishes *The Winter's Tale* is that much of the poetic language is organized periodically: convoluted sentences or difficult speeches become coherent and meaningful only in their final clauses or movements. A similar principle governs the arrangement of dramatic action: the shape and meaning of events become apparent only in the final moments of the tragicomedy. Obviously every sentence is to some extent periodic. So, too, every play needs an ending to give it meaning.[3] In both respects, however, the late plays are distinctive. Shakespeare has exaggerated the grammatical means of suspension so that sentences or passages in these plays gain momentum and then "discharge" powerfully or unexpectedly.[4] Likewise, in each case the significance of complex actions is altered and clarified by a surprise ending. In other words, we find a parallel between syntactical and narrative satisfaction, between small and large units of dramatic structure, and such consistency is a function of the tragicomic vision that has generated both story and style. The late plays present a world that is not immediately comprehensible, but one that eventually rewards bewildered characters and spectators with understanding and happiness. By analyzing the words used to create that world, I will try, in the pages that follow, to demonstrate the truth of Derek Traversi's observation that in the plays of the final period "Shakespeare's power of uniting poetry and drama is now such that the plot has become simply an extension, an extra vehicle of the poetry."[5]

The reader will recognize here a fundamentally structuralist argument, an attempt at "locating and analyzing relationships between . . . one part of a text and another."[6] In identifying these relationships and exploring their artistic implications I have followed the lead of Tzvetan Todorov, who has written persuasively on structural unity—the identity of narrative and style—in the fantastic tales of Henry James:

> The Jamesian narrative is always based on *the quest for an absolute and absent cause.* Let us consider the terms of this phrase one by one. There exists a cause: this word must here be taken in a very broad sense; it is often a character but sometimes, too, an event or an object. The effect of this cause is the narrative, the story we are told. It is absolute: for everything in this narrative ultimately owes its presence to this cause. But the cause is absent and must be sought: it is not only absent but for the most part unknown; what is suspected is its existence, not its nature. The quest proceeds; the tale consists of the search for, the pursuit of, this initial cause, this primal essence. The narrative stops when it is attained. On one hand there is an absence (of the cause, of the essence, of the truth), but this absence determines everything; on the other hand there is a presence (of the quest), which is only the search for an absence. Thus the secret of Jamesian narrative is precisely the existence of an essential secret, of something not named, of an absent and superpowerful force which sets the whole machinery of the narrative in motion.[7]

Having firmly established the presence of this absence in tale after tale, Todorov goes on to show that "the complexity of James's style derives entirely from this principle of construction and not from a referential (for instance, psychological) complexity. 'Style,' 'feelings,' 'form,' and 'content' all say the same thing, all repeat the same figure in the carpet."[8] Todorov's argument moves from narrative cause to stylistic effect. I prefer, in treating *The Winter's Tale,* to reverse the process, to offer a descriptive survey of some major stylistic traits and then to relate them to the vision informing Shakespearean tragicomedy, the dramatist's confidence in the Providential ordination of human affairs. It must be significant that the poet's creation of a new style coincides with the playwright's mastery of a new mode and with the imaginist's revised conception of experience. In *The Winter's Tale,* even the syntax is tragicomic.

I

> Inch-thick, knee-deep; o'er head and ears a fork'd one.
> Go, play, boy, play: thy mother plays, and I
> Play too; but so disgrac'd a part, whose issue
> Will hiss me to my grave: contempt and clamour
> Will be my knell. Go, play, boy, play. . . .
>
> (I.ii.186-90)[9]

The most immediately striking feature of Leontes' poetry is its unpoetic sound. The crucial early speeches are rough, harsh, even cacophonous. In this passage consonants assault the ear, especially *k*'s, *d*'s, *p*'s, and *t*'s, letters that stop the line and compel the speaker to start over, as in

"Inch-thick." Sounds normally euphonious here create the opposite effect: in the clause "whose issue / Will hiss me to my grave," the sibilants and internal rhyme produce a decidedly sinister mood. The choppy rhythms are characteristic of the liberal approach to meter in Shakespeare's late style. Caesurae intrude repeatedly to disrupt the flow, as the heavy punctuation implies.[10] Although the lines submit to ordinary scansion, their harsh music arises from a disjunction between the familiar beat of the blank verse and the violent irregularity of the spoken rhythms, so that the chief impression they convey is one of turbulence and strife. And the cacophony of the lines I have quoted is typical. Consider such other instances as "be it concluded, / No barricado for a belly"; or "Come, captain, / We must be neat; not neat, but cleanly, captain"; or "any flax-wench that puts to / Before her troth plight."

Leontes' discordant music owes much to Shakespeare's metrical liberties. It is well established that in the early dramatic poetry the rhetorical unit tends to coincide with the poetic unit—the thought ceases with the line—and that as the poet gains experience with iambic pentameter his use of stops becomes much more liberal and varied.[11] By the time of the romances, Shakespeare uses the caesura to achieve a wide range of effects. Unwilling to wait for the end of the line, he stops early and stops often. A distinctive trick of the late style is Shakespeare's devotion to the pause in mid-foot:

> Why, he that wears her like her medal, hanging
> About his neck, Bohemia; who . . .
>
> They're here with me already; whisp'ring . . .
>
> Make that thy question, and go rot!
>
> Is goads, thorns, nettles, tails of wasps . . .

Such freedom with pauses is consistent with the increase in feminine endings and with an evident fondness for trochees (points to be taken up later), and it permits immense rhythmic variation; Shakespeare exploits such possibilities, especially at the beginning of *The Winter's Tale*, to suggest agitation and tension.

The pursuit of violent and unexpected effects extends beyond individual sounds to the placement of words and phrases within sentences. Jonathan Smith has identified two distinct languages in the king's early speeches: first, a courtly dialect based in Latinate polysyllables, and second, the language of blood, a simpler style consisting mainly of Anglo-Saxon monosyllables.[12] Smith demonstrates that the fierce diction of the second type quickly overpowers the more formal style, and we may extend his analysis to show that the basic language of blood is spiked with unusual and arresting nouns and verbs. Many of Leontes' celebrated passages consist almost exclusively of flat, workaday words that serve as foils to set off a shocking verb or a memorable image:

> There have been,
> (Or I am much deceiv'd) cuckolds ere now,
> And many a man there is (even at this present,
> Now, while I speak this) holds his wife by th'arm,
> That little thinks she has been sluic'd in's absence
> And his pond fish'd by his next neighbour, by
> Sir Smile, his neighbour. . . .
>
> (I.ii.190-96)

Everybody remembers this speech, thanks mainly to the uncommon images—"sluic'd," "fish'd," and the smarmy Sir Smile—words that stand out in relief against a background of homogeneous monosyllables. Those words that bear the pressure of the prosody also bear the pressure of meaning. For five lines the actor finds very little to emphasize except "cuckolds," and thus Shakespeare encourages him to pounce upon the nasty-sounding "sluic'd."

Even more striking than particular sounds or words is the architecture of the king's sentences, which manifest these same principles of harshness and variety. Leontes' syntax is, for the most part, choppy and complex. Clauses pile upon clauses, sentences run to uncommonly great length, verbs may lag behind their subjects by several lines, and often long sentences refuse to yield up their meanings until the last possible moment. A glance at the text reveals, in addition to the commas and verbal arresters already mentioned, an abundance of dashes, parentheses, and other such grammatical interrupters. The passage just quoted illustrates this feature, but there are still more impressive instances:

> Ha' not you seen, Camillo?
> (But that's past doubt: you have, or your eye-glass
> Is thicker than a cuckold's horn) or heard?
> (For to a vision so apparent rumour
> Cannot be mute) or thought? (for cogitation
> Resides not in that man that does not think)
> My wife is slippery?
>
> (I.ii.267-73)[13]

We might backtrack briefly to observe that "slippery" functions as does "sluic'd," as the odd word in the critical spot. But the important point now is that Shakespeare has controlled the grammar of the sentence to augment the effect of the final clause. Without it the sentence is meaningless, and yet getting to it is no easy matter. Leontes begins by posing a question for Camillo, but before disclosing its substance he leads the auditor through a maze of parenthetical elements and qualifying material: a series of three verbs, "seen," "heard," and "thought," alternates with a corresponding series of lengthy phrases asserting that Camillo must have seen, heard, and thought. The effect is that of a grammatical labyrinth in which we make our way through a series of baffles, then turn a corner, and find ourselves faced with the beast—"My wife is slippery."

Another way of putting it is to say that we are suspended in air, left dangling through six circumlocutory lines, until we land with a jolt on the final clause; and this tactic of suspension may be the most revealing stylistic trait of *The Winter's Tale*. The very first sentence of the play is just such a conditional—"If you shall chance, Camillo, to visit

Bohemia"—and Shakespeare repeats the construction again and again. According to the familiar form of such suspensions, the ear requires that the conditional beginning be resolved, but Shakespeare often elaborates and protracts the first term to such a degree that we may lose our way before receiving syntactical satisfaction. In addition to the strict "if-then" constructions, of which there are many, Shakespeare also includes a host of sentences that in one way or another delay their completions until the very end:

> This entertainment
> May a free face put on, derive a liberty
> From heartiness, from bounty, fertile bosom,
> And well become the agent: 't may, I grant:
> But to be paddling palms, and pinching fingers,
> As now they are, and making practis'd smiles
> As in a looking-glass; and then to sigh, as 'twere
> The mort o'th' deer—O, that is entertainment
> My bosom likes not, nor my brows....
>
> (I.ii.111-19)

Such a construction, although a strict Latinist might object to the designation, is periodic, if not in fact certainly in effect, and its operation is representative of Shakespeare's syntactic choices throughout the play. As Carol Thomas Neely points out, "The referents of the speech are not clear until its end, and even then [Leontes] refers to his guest and his wife only by the pronoun, 'they.'"[14] Leontes begins with a possibility (that such behavior might be innocent), enumerates in a string of verbal and prepositional phrases the ways in which it might be construed as proper, summarizes this interpretation in a conditional clause calculated to prepare for its rejection, then demolishes the case for purity in the massive infinitive phrase beginning with "But," and finally recapitulates his conclusion in the appended clause altering the sense of "entertainment." Technically speaking, the sentence owes its effect to the rhetorical device known as anacoluthon, a statement that begins in one direction, shifts in the center, and concludes in the opposite direction. Here the conjunction "But" signifies the reversal.

My use of the term "periodic" demands some explanation, especially since it is here applied to poetry, and not only to sentences but also to whole speeches. The poetic sentences I consider here lack the tight grammatical organization normally characteristic of periodic sentences in prose. In fact, the syntactical arrangement of most sentences in Shakespeare's late verse is discursive; they are made up of loosely connected phrases and clauses which are often interrupted by parentheses, dashes, and changes of direction.[15] The practical effect of this complication is to postpone the full disclosure of meaning until the end of the sentence. For example:

> Dost think I am so muddy, so unsettled,
> To appoint myself in this vexation; sully
> The purity and whiteness of my sheets,
> (Which to preserve is sleep, which being spotted
> Is goads, thorns, nettles, tails of wasps)
> Give scandal to the blood o'th' prince, my son,
> (Who I do think is mine and love as mine)
> Without ripe moving to't? Would I do this?
>
> (I.ii.325-32)

This passage captures the mutual effect of digressive and periodic strategies found throughout the first three acts. An instructive variation occurring more than once is the sentence which is finished, and completely revised, by another character. When Leontes summons the lords to follow him with the words "We are to speak in public; for this business / Will raise us all," Antigonus adds privately, "To laughter, as I take it, / If the good truth were known" (II.i. 197-99). Antigonus not only reverses the meaning of Leontes' words but also radically alters the tone at the end of the scene. Numerous passages take this general form, in which the speaker changes direction or moves back and forth through a series of qualifying phrases; and often the meaning of the passage depends entirely upon the shape of the very last phrase.

Leontes is not the only speaker who employs such loose periods. One of the most stunning suspensions comes from Paulina, in one of the most crucial scenes of the play, after the trial when she announces the death of the queen:

> What studied torments, tyrant, hast for me?
> What wheels? racks? fires? what flaying? boiling?
> In leads or oils? What old or newer torture
> Must I receive, whose every word deserves
> To taste of thy most worst? Thy tyranny,
> Together working with thy jealousies
> (Fancies too weak for boys, too green and idle
> For girls of nine), O think what they have done,
> And then run mad indeed: stark mad! for all
> Thy by-gone fooleries were but spices of it.
> That thou betray'dst Polixenes, 'twas nothing;
> That did but show thee, of a fool, inconstant
> And damnable ingrateful; nor was't much,
> Thou would'st have poison'd good Camillo's honour,
> To have him kill a king; poor trespasses,
> More monstrous standing by: whereof I reckon
> The casting forth to crows thy baby daughter
> To be or none or little; though a devil
> Would have shed water out of fire, ere done 't:
> Nor is't directly laid to thee the death
> Of the young prince, whose honourable thoughts
> (Thoughts high for one so tender) cleft the heart
> That could conceive a gross and foolish sire
> Blemish'd his gracious dam: this is not, no,
> Laid to thy answer: but the last—O lords,
> When I have said, cry 'woe!'—the queen, the queen,
> The sweet'st, dear'st creature's dead: and vengeance for't
> Not dropp'd down yet.
>
> (III.ii.175-202)

Paulina's obloquy is a masterpiece of calculation, for the speech throws all its force upon the fact of death. The beginning is, to say the least, indirect: Paulina utters a string of questions about how Leontes plans to torture her. Although this gambit is initially confusing, it coheres logically with the remainder of the passage it introduces, for torturing the faithful Paulina would be yet another of the errors and harms that the king's "Fancies" have visited upon those who love and serve him. Moreover, the extreme images with which she begins indicate the damage that Leontes has already inflicted. As the tirade unfolds, we perceive that Paulina's joint purposes are intertwined: she will simultaneously condemn Leontes and reveal his most appalling crime. The first objective waits upon the second, which remains unknown until the conclusion. Every line looks forward explicitly or implicitly to the climax, for every folly and act of cruelty must be compared with Leontes' last incomparable outrage. Thus not only is the tirade constructed periodically, but it also declares its periodic form early, just after the initial questions. Paulina insists, as she ticks off the specific harms done so far, that each must pale in light of what she will announce. It might be said also that the shape of her revelation is fundamentally theatrical. The plaint is obviously arranged to create a powerful effect upon the main member of her audience, Leontes, and is tailored for and addressed directly to him. But it works similarly upon the stage spectators, acknowledged in "O lords," and upon the theatre audience. The auditor is made to wait, to lean forward in anticipation of horror. This affective aim is consistent with Paulina's theatrical manner elsewhere. Pafford speaks of "the calculated tactlessness which is her favourite weapon,"[16] and her directorial style in the final scene is an expansion of her strategy in this crisis.

The emotion and energy of her condemnation make themselves felt in the violent music Shakespeare has composed. The syncopated effect of one rhythm superimposed upon another is especially noticeable here. The lines teem with spondees: "what wheels," "most worst," "stark mad," "'cry woe!'" Another kind of syncopation is discerned by F. E. Halliday, who asserts that "Shakespeare, particularly in his later plays, imposes a secondary rhythm on the primary iambics" by integrating "natural trochees" into the basic iambic pattern. Halliday illustrates the method with a well-known line of Alonso's in *The Tempest*: "I'll seek him deeper than e're plummet sounded." This same practice accounts for the richly polyphonic texture of Paulina's oration. A third of the lines contain at least two such falling disyllables, and many of these are connected, as Halliday shows they are in the passage from *The Tempest*, by alliteration and assonance: "newer torture," "monstrous standing," "little . . . devil," "Blemish'd . . . gracious." In each case the rhetorical movement of the sentence strains against the fundamental beat of the verse, and the tension creates a rich kind of music.[17]

Pace is important also, for it accelerates markedly. After the broken rhythms of the opening interrogatives, the passage gathers speed through the recitation of the king's crimes and moves purposefully toward its horrifying end. This swift pace is not easily or immediately achieved: for example, the general attack on Leontes' "tyranny" and "Fancies" (ll. 179-84), with its halts and jerks, its repetitions and appositives and interjections, necessarily retards the speaker. But the specific catalogue of crimes that fol-

Engraving from Galerie des Personnages de Shakespeare *(1844)*.

lows unfolds in a sentence that extends over seventeen lines. Of course the quickening pace is impeded by brief stops and a set of obstacles just prior to the conclusion: "but the last—O lords, / When I have said, cry 'woe!'— the queen. . . ." Paradoxically, however, the collision of such intrusive clauses with the established momentum of the sentence propels the listener even more rapidly toward the revelatory end. Paulina delays slightly with the repetition of "the queen," and the sibilants and elisions of the penultimate line thrust us toward the ugly monosyllable, "dead." But what about the remainder, that anti-climactic final clause? It records a fitting conclusion that has not occurred, and so the words "drop down" with a monosyllabic flatness, alliteration and assonance echoing the hollowness denoted. It is significant that the queen's death is neither the end of the sentence nor the end of the play.

Paulina bewails disorder in poetry that threatens to burst out of its formal limits. By a variety of means Shakespeare sees to it that the speech is crowded with words. Syntactical complexity tends to elongate the lines, as in the repeated questions needing a pause after each: "What wheels? racks? fires? what flaying? boiling?" Extra syllables abound: ten of the twenty-seven lines end with a soft syllable. One line, "Thy by-gone fooleries were but spices of it," contains twelve syllables, and even though *fooleries* is compressed into two, the end of the line is loaded with an additional beat, in *spices of,* thus throwing the emphasis on the still-nebulous *it*. Elision is frequently demanded: "That thou betray'dst Polixenes, 'twas nothing"; "The sweet'st, dear'st creature's dead." Order in the lines is barely maintained.[18] Generally speaking, the crowded lines and weak endings dominate the beginning of the passage. As Paulina moves more swiftly toward her end, the line endings become more regular and the iambic beat more audibly insistent. "More regular" is a relative term, to be sure: there are plenty of interruptions and metrical kinks. But it is fair to say that Paulina's creation of an ordered whole from a mysterious and chaotic beginning is mirrored in the increasing regularity of the verse.

Shakespeare embellishes this poetic structure with musical devices that reinforce the hearer's sense of its complexity. The introductory lines create a mood of incantation, particularly with the repetition of *l* sounds in lines 177 and 178. Indeed, the entire passage seems unusually alliterative: "What wheels?"; "To taste of thy most worst"; "green and idle / For girls of nine"; "kill a king"; "More monstrous standing by"; "casting forth to crows"; "thee the death"; "could conceive a gross and foolish sire / Blemish'd his gracious dam"; "sweet'st dear'st creature's dead." Similarly, internal rhymes create color: "newer torture"; "every word deserves . . . worst"; "Together working"; "damnable ingrateful." Sometimes these tactics are combined to create extraordinary aural effects: "O, think what they have done / And then run mad indeed. . . ." I may appear to have wandered far from the main issue, the periodic structure of Paulina's announcement, but all these poetic tricks contribute to the power of the verbal construction, adding a weight and difficulty that makes the resolution all the more impressive.

The supreme example of syntactic and prosodic complexity is also one of the most memorable speeches in the play:

> Is whispering nothing?
> Is leaning cheek to cheek? is meeting noses?
> Kissing with inside lip? stopping the career
> Of laughter with a sigh (a note infallible
> Of breaking honesty)? horsing foot on foot?
> Skulking in corners? wishing clocks more swift?
> Hours, minutes? noon, midnight? and all eyes
> Blind with the pin and web, but theirs; theirs only,
> That would unseen be wicked? is this nothing?
> Why then the world, and all that's in't, is nothing,
> The covering sky is nothing, Bohemia nothing,
> My wife is nothing, nor nothing have these nothings,
> If this be nothing.
>
> (I.ii.284-96)

This astonishing passage is a compendium of all the stylistic traits I have mentioned. Its dissonant music is made of assonance ("Is whispering," "leaning cheek . . . cheek . . . meeting," "wishing . . . swift," "If this"), alliteration ("skulking . . . corners . . . clocks," "then the . . . that's . . . nothing"), and the incantatory repetition of "nothing." Trochaic and iambic rhythms compete so violently that some lines seem to create their own unique rhythm. A majority of the lines end weakly, and caesurae are numerous and random. Ellipsis contributes to the artfully manipulated pace, particularly the dropped gerund ("wishing") in line 291. Although the first two-thirds of the speech consists of a series of rhetorical questions, the effect is of one amplified suspension in which the actor's voice must rise repeatedly to indicate the question and the listener expects some kind of descent, some turn that will clarify the purpose of the endless interrogatives. When the rejoinder does finally come, it is strong enough to balance the beginning—if this is unreal, then reality does not exist—and the strength of the answering term is fortified by the repetition of "nothing." Worth noting here, as in Paulina's great suspension, is the contribution of the additional clause tacked onto the end of the sentence so that the periodic effect is qualified: in this case the redundant but forceful "if this be nothing" returns us to the list of conditions, insisting ironically that this is something indeed. Most important, of course, is the double irony: we understand what Leontes will not or cannot, that this is nothing. As a number of critics have pointed out, Anne Barton most clearly, Shakespeare throughout the last plays affords the audience a superior understanding of the speaker's words, asks the audience to look beyond the specific speech and situation to the larger meaning.[19] For all the difficulty of the style, we penetrate to the essential truth of the words.

Such complicated periodicity seems to me prominent and frequent enough to be considered a major stylistic feature of *The Winter's Tale*. The reader who is hospitable to the argument thus far will find plenty of additional proof, but a couple of further examples are worth citing. Polixenes threatens Perdita in this style:

> And you, enchantment,—
> Worthy enough a herdsman; yea, him too,
> That makes himself, but for our honour therein,
> Unworthy thee. If ever henceforth thou
> These rural latches to his entrance open,
> Or hoop his body more with thy embraces,
> I will devise a death as cruel for thee
> As thou art tender to 't.
>
> (IV.iv.435-42)

The obstructions and convolutions leading to the final main clause—and even the conclusion is internally periodic—echo the language of Leontes, whose tyrannical place Polixenes has taken in the fourth act. At one time or another, virtually all the characters look to the future in language that propels us forward—Florizel, Camillo, even Hermione, whose innocence is usually expressed in uncommonly plain language. When Antigonus, recounting his dream, quotes the ghost's instructions to him, "Hermione's" style becomes complex and periodic:

> "Good Antigonus,
> Since fate, against thy better disposition,
> Hath made thy person for the thrower-out

Of my poor babe, according to thine oath,
Places remote enough are in Bohemia,
There weep, and leave it crying: and, for the babe
Is counted lost for ever, Perdita,
I prithee, call't. . . ."

(III.iii.27-34)

Although there are exceptions, periodic verbal structures appear most obviously in the first half of the play, when the conflict is most intense. But this distribution may itself be significant. As it is in particular sentences, so it is in the play as a whole: complexity yields to simplicity and clarity.

II

These distinctive periodic forms are intimately related to the dramatic structure in which they appear: the shape of language and action proceeds from Shakespeare's tragicomic understanding of human experience. In other words, the playwright has devised a distinctive language for the distinctive form of his last works. Such a correspondence of style and structure has been discerned in other areas of Shakespearean drama: "the argumentative character of the prose, its tendency to stick close to its syllogistic basis and to acknowledge this openly through the abundance of logical links—these one might relate to the network of causality that composes the intrigue plot."[20] So it is with the poetry of *The Winter's Tale* and of the tragicomedies in general. The organization of the verse recapitulates the arrangement of event, and both kinds of structure correspond to Shakespeare's conception of the course of human life.

Putting the matter as simply as possible, we may say that the shape of the verse reflects the shape of the plot. In general terms, this is self-evident. The constricted poetry of the first three acts yields to the lyricism and simplicity of the last two, just as the setting takes us from the confined madness of Sicilia to the pastoral liberty of Bohemia. But it is possible to be still more specific, to identify a formal parallel between important speeches, even individual sentences, and the tragicomic movement of the action as a whole.[21] The shocking and mystifying revelation of Leontes' suspicions is set forth in harsh and confusing poetry. The arresting, ugly nouns and verbs standing in relief against a neutral background—"and little think she has been sluic'd in's absence"—are represented on the stage by the solitary figure of Leontes set apart from and disrupting the concord of the great second scene. The king's words are at first opaque and disorienting because the universe into which Shakespeare thrusts us is initially puzzling. The difficulty of the verse attests to the complexity of the action it is used to portray, and this is not to say only that the disorder of Leontes' language signifies the chaos of his mind, but that the initial, apparent confusion of the verse represents the apparent disorder of mortal affairs in general.

For the listener, to come to terms with the language spoken is to apprehend the world depicted, and in neither case is this an easy undertaking. Modern interest in structural linguistics has focused attention on the temporal and linear quality of all speech. As Robert Scholes puts it in discussing the theories of Ferdinand de Saussure, "not only is each sign linear, each utterance is even more obviously so. Unlike the picture, which can display various significant elements simultaneously, the elements of a verbal narrative must be delivered in an order which is itself significant. The sign, then, as well as the sentence and all larger units of discourse, is primarily narrative. . . ."[22] The linearity of speech causes understanding to occur gradually, as the syntagmatic structure establishes itself: units of language modify one another, meaning is altered, until completion is finally achieved. Just as the massive periods of *The Winter's Tale* are founded upon devices of delay and surprise, so Shakespeare extends the narrative potentialities of sentences; and he does so in a manner approximating his protraction of the entire narrative. The auditor is drawn into complex verbal structures without being able to predict their destination, propelled in one direction and then another by unexpected, contradictory clauses, and finally delivered to clarity by a conclusion that makes sense of all that has gone before. And much the same is true of the plot of *The Winter's Tale*. The great syntactical suspensions approximate the suspensions in the action, the withholding of information that would complete and explicate an imperfect pattern. As listeners and spectators, we are forced to wait, left suspended, denied immediate understanding of a jarring phrase or a surprising event until the end of the sentence or the end of the play.

Other properties of Shakespeare's late style may be regarded as parallel to the larger elements of structure. The binary form of numerous sentences, such as the "if-then" construction, is equivalent to the tragicomic structure of the entire work. The second half modifies and illuminates the opening, which would be incomprehensible without the final segment. Dramatically and grammatically, the conflicts of the first unit are not canceled by the resolution of the second; rather, each term qualifies the other, and the meaning of the conclusion is enriched by the difficulties preceding it. Moreover, the choppy and hypotactic properties of the syntax are consistent with the shape of the action. The plot begins in one direction, with Leontes' jealousy; becomes more complex with the flight of Camillo and Polixenes, the illness of Mamillius, and the banishment of Perdita; reverses itself with Hermione's divine vindication and Leontes' epiphany; is intruded upon unexpectedly by the entrance of Time; begins afresh with the pastoral romance of Florizel and Perdita; changes course when Polixenes interferes (in a conversation with a surprise ending, [*Discovering himself*]); and is finally given coherence by the return of the young lovers to Sicilia, the reunion of the kings, and the restoration of the queen. Even more specifically, just as prosodic devices such as alliteration and internal rhyme give music to the language, so elements of action and character create emotional discord and harmony in the progress of the story. Ellipsis in the style corresponds to omissions in the plot: the gap of sixteen years, the reported deaths, the described reunion. The plot itself might be considered an enormous dramatic anacoluthon: its initial movement is negative, Time is the dash signifying a shift in direction, and the final movement is favorable.

The auditor's mixed response to the style—puzzlement and ironic confidence—is related to the spectator's response to the telling of the tale. Suspense and irony can often be mutually exclusive, as Wayne Booth has demonstrated in his study of narrative technique: the author who wishes to create suspense must suppress information, and this tactic is incompatible with irony, which gives the reader superior insight.[23] But Shakespeare has contrived to partake of the advantages of both. We are aware, as Leontes is not, that Perdita is alive and will serve as the means of his regeneration. And yet the play also surprises us, denying us knowledge of Hermione's survival until the very end of the work, challenging our confidence in our superior understanding and thus transforming our comprehension of the world we thought we knew.

Shakespeare has arranged the verse so that it illuminates and comments on two central themes of *The Winter's Tale,* the complexities of perception and the importance of time in the process of perception. Todorov, in commenting on James's supernatural stories, argues that "the fantastic text is not characterized by the simple presence of supernatural phenomena or beings, but by the hesitation which is established in the reader's perception of the events represented. Throughout the tale, the reader wonders (in the same way that a character often does, within the work) if the facts reported are to be explained by a natural or a supernatural cause, if they are illusions or realities."[24] The subtleties of the Jamesian style, then, contribute to the reader's bewilderment, and it strikes me that something similar occurs to those who witness—or, in seventeenth-century parlance, "hear"—a performance of *The Winter's Tale.* There is a sense in which perception is the central problem of the play. The agon arises from Leontes' "Fancies," and in the statue scene Paulina plays with the problem of illusion in her warning to Leontes: "No longer shall you gaze on't, lest your fancy / May think anon it moves" (V.iii.60-61). When "*Hermione comes down,*" we "perceive she stirs" (V.iii.103), but we are uncertain what to make of this perception. It is appropriate, therefore, that for much of the play Shakespeare devised a poetic style that engages us directly in the activity of perception and makes us aware of the difficulty. The combination of hypotaxis and parataxis, the violent rhythms, the false endings, and the withholding of syntactical and referential satisfaction allow us to participate at all times in the problems of comprehension.

Shakespeare's manipulation of the diachronic potentialities of the poetic sentence or speech contributes to his revelation of the importance of time in human affairs. As Time, the Chorus, puts it, "I that please some, try all"; he goes on to claim that he "makes and unfolds error" (IV.i.1-2). Leontes' self-inflicted miseries, which seem inexplicable and intolerable at the end of the third act, are assuaged and almost mended by the revelations and satisfactions of the ending. The words of Paulina's namesake are pertinent in this context: "we see through a glass, darkly." And the implied principles of patience and faith apply to the style as well. Clauses and sentences can be trying, even incomprehensible, while one is lost in their midst; but they finally cohere into a pleasing and meaningful pattern.

This correspondence of language, form, and dramatic universe suggests an identification among speaker, dramatist, and Providence that clarifies the meaning not only of the play in question but of the tragicomic universe as well.[25] If Leontes' verse does not immediately make itself clear, neither does Shakespeare's construction of events, nor does the divine architect's disposition of man's experience. An event the characters regard as a disaster may in fact be the prelude to unexpected joy. The grammatical delays and obstacles that temporarily obscure meaning in the middle of a protracted sentence are parts of a larger whole that is eventually elucidated. Something similar may be said of particular happenings in the action of *The Winter's Tale.* And Shakespeare implies that our world, of which the play is the mimetic instrument, should be interpreted likewise. For the mariners in *The Tempest,* the storm that interferes with their journey is catastrophic; for Alonso it is a dead end from which there is no escape. But as soon as the second scene opens, the spectator understands the storm, in the grammatical terms I have been using, as nothing more than an introductory element, a subordinate clause leading to heightened understanding and fulfillment.

The method set forth here might be extended to other sections of *The Winter's Tale* and to other plays. The great penultimate scene, in which three unfamiliar gentlemen announce and annotate the numerous happy reunions, is fertile territory for such work. The prose they speak contains delays and indirections similar to those that mark Leontes' poetry, and again we are suspended, made to wait for and to wonder about the final phase of the action. Indeed, the entire scene is a grand hesitation. A figure who shares Leontes' verbal style is Posthumus in *Cymbeline,* notably in his mad aria concluding the second act. Attention to Prospero's narrative in the second scene of *The Tempest* reveals the same stylistic traits: although the rhythm is less wild and the diction less violent, the verse displays a host of intrusive clauses, suspensions, broken phrases, and periodic conclusions. And I am persuaded that these same correspondences of style and structure appear in most of *Pericles,* in *Cymbeline,* and in *The Tempest.*

One of the leading ideas in the last plays is that an understanding of the world requires patience, flexibility, and perspective. An understanding of the style demands these same qualities. In the last act of *Cymbeline,* when Jupiter descends to explain to the Leonati his apparent mistreatment of their son, the god reveals that misfortune is part of a larger scheme: "Whom best I love, I cross; to make my gift, / The more delayed, delighted." It is a principle that applies as well to style as to action.

Notes

1. Introduction to *Cymbeline* (London: Methuen, 1955), p. lxii.

2. As late as 1975, Carol Thomas Neely remarked on the neglect of the poetry of this play: "there has been no detailed examination of the nature and variety of the language of *The Winter's Tale,* nor has there been any consideration of the thematic importance of language in the play." See "*The Winter's Tale:* The Triumph of Speech," *Studies in English Literature,* 15 (1975), 321. Critics who have contributed to our understanding of the late verse include F. E. Halliday, *The Poetry of Shakespeare's Plays* (London: Gerald Duckworth & Co., 1954), esp. pp. 28-33, 49-52, 167-87; B. Ifor Evans, *The Language of Shakespeare's Plays* (London: Methuen, 1952), pp. 189-212; James Sutherland, "The Language of the Last Plays," in *More Talking of Shakespeare,* ed. John Garrett (London: Longmans, 1959), pp. 144-58; and Frank Kermode, Introduction to the Arden edition of *The Tempest* (London: Methuen, 1954), pp. lxxvii-lxxxi. Percy Simpson's "Shakespeare's Versification: A Study of Development," *Studies in Elizabethan Drama* (Oxford: Clarendon, 1955), pp. 64-88, despite its promising title, is disappointing. At present the most stimulating work on Shakespeare's verse is being done by George T. Wright. See his splendid essay, "The Play of Phrase and Line in Shakespeare's Iambic Pentameter," *Shakespeare Quarterly,* 34 (1983), 147-58.

3. My attempt to connect language with action rather than character finds support from a recent article by Anne Barton, "Leontes and the spider: language and speaker in Shakespeare's Last Plays," in *Shakespeare's Styles: Essays in Honour of Kenneth Muir,* ed. Philip Edwards, Inga-Stina Ewbank, and G. K. Hunter (Cambridge: Cambridge Univ. Press, 1980), pp. 131-50: "Shakespeare not only does not try to conceal, he positively emphasises the fact that his material is the archetypal stuff of legend and fairy-tale. That we respond to it as something far more powerful and engaging than 'Cinderella' or 'Beauty and the Beast' testifies to the subtlety with which Shakespeare has adjusted his language and dramatic art to the demands of a new mode: one in which plot, on the whole, has become more vivid and emotionally charged than character" (p. 149). Also see Marion Trousdale, "Style in *The Winter's Tale,*" *Critical Quarterly,* 18 (1976), 25-32.

4. For a discussion of the way that sentences can "discharge," see Eric S. Rabkin, *Narrative Suspense* (Ann Arbor: Univ. of Michigan Press, 1973), pp. 85-89. My use of the term is somewhat less specific and complex than his; although his comments are revealing, they seem unnecessarily dependent on jargon.

5. *Shakespeare: The Last Phase* (London: Hollis and Carter, 1954), p. 3.

6. Robert Scholes, *Structuralism in Literature* (New Haven: Yale Univ. Press, 1974), p. 146.

7. "The Secret of Narrative," in *The Poetics of Prose,* tr. Richard Howard (Ithaca: Cornell Univ. Press, 1977), p. 145. I am grateful to Professor Jean Howard of Syracuse University, whose response to an early version of this argument led me to Todorov.

8. Ibid., p. 154.

9. I quote throughout from the Arden edition of *The Winter's Tale,* ed. J. H. P. Pafford (London: Methuen, 1963).

10. This passage is printed in the Folio thus:

    Ynch-thick, knee-deepe; ore head and eares a fork'd one.
    Goe play (Boy) play: thy Mother playes, and I
    Play too; but so disgrac'd a part, whose issue
    Will hisse me to my Graue: Contempt and Clamor
    Will be my Knell. Goe play (Boy) play, . . .

    Although the stops and starts are indicated by different (and less explicit) means than in modern texts, the jerkiness and vocal complexity of the lines are still apparent.

11. George T. Wright's discussion of the dynamics of the late verse is pertinent here: "The line is more and more cast into structural doubt, first by late-line pauses and free enjambment, . . . by sentences that flow freely over the margins, and by rashes of short-line exchanges that hover between verse and prose; later by a rhetoric that virtually abandons the flowing sentence for brief and abrupt bursts of staccato phrases that seem almost, at times, in their jagged discourse, to mock both line and phrase." ("The Play of Phrase and Line in Shakespeare's Iambic Pentameter," p. 155).

12. "The Language of Leontes," *SQ,* 19 (1968), 317-27.

13. Frank Kermode, in his edition of *The Winter's Tale* (New York: Signet, 1963), prints this speech with dashes instead of parentheses, thus making the disjunctive quality all the more evident.

14. "The Triumph of Speech," p. 327.

15. James Sutherland, who notices the abundance of parentheses and syntactical obstacles in the verse of the late plays, disputes the common notion that these are calculated to suggest spontaneity and naturalism in the characters' speech; instead, he attributes these stops and starts to Shakespeare's haste and willingness to content himself with a vague "impressionism" ("The Language of the Last Plays," pp. 146-47). It strikes me that neither explanation is adequate. Hesitation, revision, and reversal manifest themselves not only in Shakespeare's creation of language but also in his characterization and arrangement of action.

16. Introduction, pp. lxxiv-v.

17. *The Poetry of Shakespeare's Plays,* pp. 31-32: "This combination of rhythm and assonance, each emphasizing the other, adds another quality to the later poetry, in which whole speeches are integrated and harmonized by the complex contrapuntal interweaving of a double rhythm with a melodic theme." The general survey of Shakespearean verse that constitutes Halliday's introductory chapter is extremely suggestive. When he turns to each stage of Shakespeare's career in successive chapters, however, his application of his general observations does not fulfill the promise of the introduction. Still, Halliday's book is one of the few critical attempts to study particular characteristics of Shakespeare's dramatic poetry in different periods of its development.

18. Dorothy L. Sipe, *Shakespeare's Metrics,* Yale Studies in English 166 (New Haven: Yale Univ. Press, 1968), objects to the critical emphasis on irregularity in Shakespeare's verse, particularly to the study of contrapuntal rhythm suggested by Halliday and others. Her unshakable purpose is to establish "that Shakespeare was in fact greatly concerned about preserving the regularity of his verse" (p. 6). This aim deafens her to the subtlety of Shakespeare's rhythmic experiments.

19. "Leontes and the spider: language and speaker in Shakespeare's Last Plays," pp. 147-49. "People are constantly expressing the truth of the situation without grasping what, for us, is the primary meaning of their own words—as in the reiterated description of the lowly Perdita as a 'queen'" (p. 147).

20. Jonas A. Barish, *Ben Jonson and the Language of Prose Comedy* (Cambridge, Mass.: Harvard Univ. Press, 1960; rpt. New York: Norton, 1970), p. 38. Coburn Freer, *The Poetics of Jacobean Drama* (Baltimore: Johns Hopkins Univ. Press, 1981), p. 24, notices a similar principle in *Hamlet*: "The rhythm of Hamlet's 'To be, or not to be, that is the question' contains in itself the hesitant moves and final plunge that typify his speeches and actions throughout the whole play. . . ."

21. The sort of stylistic and narrative correspondence I am suggesting here has been discerned in a number of authors by a number of critics. Apart from Todorov, some of the most lucid such analysis has been performed by Eric S. Rabkin. Quoting a long sentence from *Absalom, Absalom!,* he shows how the syntax reflects narrative structure: "This interlocking, overlapping principle in fact is reflected in the method of multiple, overlayed narrative that Faulkner employs in *Absalom, Absalom!* and the constant effort to get to the heart of the thought behind the sentence is much like the constant effort of the narrators to get to heart of their tale, the central, untold story of Thomas Sutpen. The structural similarities between the manner of multiple narration and the style may be called, in opposition to image-structure, syntax-structure. Both image-structure and syntax-structure cooperate to foist the fictional reality subliminally on the reader" *(Narrative Suspense,* p. 56). Rabkin also illustrates a different brand of syntax-structure at work in *Tristram Shandy.* Virtually all such analyses of which I am aware are confined to prose fiction. It seems reasonable and fruitful to attempt such a study of dramatic poetry, as long as we are aware of its conventions and special requirements. The particular problems associated with iambic pentameter created for oral delivery are addressed by O. B. Hardison, Jr., "Blank Verse before Milton," *Studies in Philology,* 81 (1984), 253-74.

22. *Structuralism in Literature,* p. 17.

23. *The Rhetoric of Fiction* (Chicago: Univ. of Chicago Press, 1961), p. 255.

24. "The Secret of Narrative," p. 156.

25. Wright makes some brief but fascinating suggestions about this sort of correspondence: see "The Play of Phrase and Line," pp. 157-58.

SEXUALITY AND AUTHORITY

David McCandless (essay date 1990)

SOURCE: "'Verily Bearing Blood': Pornography, Sexual Love, and the Reclaimed Feminine in *The Winter's Tale,*" in *Essays in Theatre,* Vol. 9, No. 1, November, 1990, pp. 61-81.

[*In the following essay, McCandless posits that Leontes's persecution of Hermione represents his attempt to cast away his source of sexual shame.*]

Early in Shakespeare's *The Winter's Tale,* Polixenes recalls the boyhood paradise he shared with Leontes and attributes its end to the intrusion of "blood"—here a synonym for man's "sensual, animal appetite" *(OED* 1: 929).

> We were as twinn'd lambs that did frisk i' th' sun,
> And bleat the one at th' other. What we chang'd
> Was innocence for innocence; we knew not
> The doctrine of ill-doing, nor dream'd
> That any did. Had we pursu'd that life,
> And our weak spirits ne'er been higher rear'd
> With stronger blood, we should have answer'd heaven
> Boldly, "not guilty"; the imposition clear'd,
> Hereditary ours.
>
> (1.1.67-75)

Not only were the two future kings unacquainted with evil ("knew not the doctrine of ill-doing"), they were effectively exempt from original sin itself, the "hereditary imposition" of guilt they would have "cleared" had they remained unaroused by "blood"—the animal appetite of sexual passion. The agent of that corruption, Polixenes implies, the snake in the garden, is woman:

> Temptations have since then been born to 's: for
> In those unfledg'd days was my wife a girl;
> Your precious self had then not cross'd the eyes
> Of my young playfellow.
>
> (1.1.77-80)

Hermione, in rebuttal, chides Polixenes, "Of this make no conclusion, lest you say / Your queen and I are devils" (1.1.81-82). Yet Polixenes's portrait of paradise lost accords precisely with the medieval view, still alive in Shakespeare's age, that women were indeed devils, or at least daughters of Eve, the alluring devil's accomplice who seduced man into sin.[1]

This patriarchal myth, a projection of male dread of female sexuality, is no sooner invoked than it is mysteriously re-enacted, as Leontes, in some way newly aroused by "blood," inexplicably imagines his innocent wife to be a conniving whore and falls apart before our eyes. I would like, in this paper, to employ Susan Griffin's definition of pornography in order to discuss Leontes's fatal delusion as a kind of pornographic fantasy, in which he degrades Hermione in order to punish her for having afflicted him with a shaming sexual knowledge, for having affronted a false ideal of incorruptibility to which he ruinously clings. True to Griffin's definition of the pornographer, Leontes defends masculine culture against feminine nature, enforcing the subjugation of women by enacting a fantasy of archetypal female treachery—a kind of revision of The Fall, in which Adam defeats Eve's attempts to corrupt and enslave him.

Pornography is an exceptionally complex subject. Even within feminist ranks attitudes towards it differ sharply. For instance, Linda Williams, who calls herself an "anti-censorship feminist" finds Griffin's position—and those of other "anti-pornography feminists" like Andrea Dworkin and Susanne Kappeler—needlessly prosecutorial and untenably utopian. She argues, in essence, that nature cannot conquer culture, that the notion of "a whole and natural sexuality that stands outside history and free of power" (23) is purely mythical, and that power is an ineradicable part of human sexuality. Indeed, Williams finds in as unlikely a place as hard-core sadomasochistic film an affirmation of female subjectivity.

Moreover, two of Griffin's targets—Sade and Sacher-Masoch, whose names are synonymous with pornographic sexual violence—inspire Roland Barthes and Gilles Deleuze not to eloquent rage but to philosophical exegesis. Indeed, Barthes calls Sade "a founder of language" (3) and Deleuze considers Sacher-Masoch "a pornologist" (18). The line between pornography and art begins to seem confoundingly blurry.

Though Griffin's view is but one among many, she does offer a particularly powerful dissection of the kind of culture that Leontes defends, as well as the sort of sadistic fantasy that he enacts. She also very poetically evokes a nature not far removed from that which the play unleashes as a liberating force. Griffin's vision may be utopian. But so, in this play, I think, is Shakespeare's.

For Griffin, culture is to nature as mind is to body, form to material, myth to experience, constraint to license, masculine to feminine—but not, it must emphasized, male to female. In fact, the feminine image so extravagantly demeaned in pornography represents the pornographer's disowned feminine self. He disclaims the feminine because he wishes to disclaim his own materiality, his creatureliness, his bodily vulnerability:

> He would let his body speak; he would let the knowledge of the body in himself live; and yet this is also precisely the knowledge of which he is terrified. And so he tries to separate culture from nature. He would have what is natural in him be mute. But what is natural speaks in him. Therefore he gives "woman" a voice in pornography, but he gives her this voice only in order to silence her.
>
> (40)

I will argue that, by ruthlessly persecuting and scheming to eliminate a Hermione re-made in the image of whore, Leontes similarly seeks to expel a demonized feminine self and so remain innocent of the bodily knowledge it compels. If Leontes lethally implements the constraints of culture in the play's first part, however, Florizel and Perdita turn the licenses of nature into a revitalizing force in its second part, reconciling the innocence and "blood" that Leontes so destructively polarizes. Not only do they hasten Leontes's recovery by bringing regenerative nature to his moribund culture, but Leontes himself atones for his crime of banishing the feminine and objectifying Hermione, first by submitting to feminization at Paulina's hands, and second by rejecting the image of Hermione-as-object in favor of Hermione-as-person, effectively summoning her off the pedestal at the play's end.

The opening scene sets up the image of Hermione as female intruder: two men, Camillo and Archidamus, make no mention of her but speak exclusively of the long-standing friendship between Leontes and Polixenes and of the great hopes residing in the gallant child Mamillius. The stage is set for the entrance of three male figures. The fourth who enters, unannounced and female, is therefore something of an alien presence.

Moreover, Polixenes's verbal evocation of the "boy eternal" paradise could receive visual support from the image of Leontes at play with Mamillius, a key piece of stage business that the text strongly hints at. Leontes clearly does not attend to the conversation of Polixenes and Hermione ("Is he won yet?" [1.1.86]), the young prince should not be ignored for 120 lines, and the juxtaposition of word and image allows Polixenes to speak of his former "young playfellow" while Leontes disports himself with a current one, as if aiming to preserve the lost paradise.² Indeed, Leontes's play with Mamillius could be taken as his attempt to recreate (and perhaps re-create) himself in the image of "boy eternal."

This re-conjuring of the boyhood Eden extends the affirmations of Camillo and Archidamus, dramatizing the abiding friendship of Leontes and Polixenes and making of Mamillius a symbol for the continuity of its values. The return to paradise also has the effect of portending a second fall and of thus enhancing Hermione's status as suspicious outsider, potential snake in the garden. Can this intrinsically dangerous woman be safely integrated into male society? Can she possibly live up to male standards of purity and constancy? Leontes introduces doubt as he recalls the occasion of their betrothal:

> Three crabbed months had sour'd themselves to death,
> Ere I could make thee open thy white hand,
> And clap thyself my love; then didst thou utter,
> "I am yours for ever."
>
> (1.2.100-05)

Leontes yokes Hermione's vow of "forever" to a conception of time—a sour corrupting unto death—that denies the possibility of "forever" and thus seems to forecast a betrayal or at least to estrange her from the changeless innocence of the "boy eternal" world. In his essay "Of friendship," Montaigne promotes the constancy of "brotherly affection" over the violent variability of sexual love. The latter

> is more active, more scorching, and more intense. But it is an impetuous and fickle flame, undulating and variable, a fever flame, subject to fits and lulls, that holds us only by one corner. In friendship, it is a general and universal warmth, moderate and even, besides, a constant and settled warmth, all gentleness and smoothness, with nothing bitter and stinging about it.
>
> (Frame 137)

When Hermione presents her hand to Polixenes, that fever flame—in the form of violent sexual jealousy—engulfs Leontes, and the much-anticipated fall takes place. "Too hot, too hot," he cries, "To mingle friendship far is mingling bloods" (1.2.108-09). Woman's stirring of "stronger blood" once more assaults the tranquility of male friendship, once more destroys a vision of paradise. Having just recalled the occasion when Hermione's offering of her hand confirmed his selection as sexual partner, Leontes misreads Hermione's gesture as the choice of a new one.

Hermione unwittingly enacts the role of devilish seductress and precipitates a second fall. The notion of a "second fall" implies, however, that Hermione has somehow managed, at least until the moment of her alleged betrayal, to achieve integration into the "boy eternal" world—or that Leontes has managed to assimilate female sexuality to male myths of innocence. The sign of this assimilation is purely visual, for it is not once alluded to in the opening act: her pregnancy, her status as nurturing mother. As Coppelia Kahn says, "as mother and only as mother, woman is exonerated of Eve's crime . . . her pain in childbirth, her self-sacrifice in childraising, purify her sexuality" (78). Hermione can enter the "boy eternal" world solely in the guise of idealized madonna. Leontes's desire for her remains free of sexual taint so long as she remains an untainted mother-figure.

Her "entertainment" of Polixenes, however, immediately and irrevocably taints her. Her pregnancy ceases to be a sign of purity and becomes instead a mark of rank corruption, proof of infidelity. The ease with which Hermione moves, in Leontes's eyes, from madonna to whore suggests the extent to which he subjects her complex humanity to dehumanizing myth. He trades the myth of "boy eternal," in which woman as sacred nurturer palliates sexual guilt, for the myth of "the fall," in which woman as cunning seductress absorbs sexual shame. As Griffin observes, the pornographic mind "attempts to solve the problems of the psyche precisely by creating a world of illusion" (39).

The content of Leontes's fantasy obviously owes something to the patriarchal myth of woman as mysterious "other" who must be either exalted or reviled. He seems, however, to take that myth to its pornographic extreme, according to which woman is exalted precisely in order that she may be reviled. As Griffin explains, the pornographer's central project is to de-mystify his own mystified image of woman as beguiling, unattainable goddess, to expose her as pure flesh, to affirm her essential sordidness (29-35). Thus Leontes later salves his humiliation by savoring the fact that the wantonness of woman is all-pervasive, unmanageable, a "bawdy planet that will strike / Where 'tis predominant," an elemental force that comes from all directions and penetrates all barriers (1.2.200-04).³

While there can be little doubt that Leontes is horrifically deluded, Howard Felperin makes a provocative point: it is highly problematic to assert that Leontes "misreads" Hermione's actions when those actions are available to us only through Leontes's mediations: "Unless we are ready to suppose a positively hallucinatory Leontes, gestures in some degree susceptible of such descriptions must take place in front of us" (7). True enough. Such gestures as we may infer from Leontes's commentary—Hermione's taking Polixenes by the hand, sighing and smiling, looking up at him as they walk arm-in-arm toward the garden (1.2.115, 125-26, 116-117, 183-85)—are certain to be sensually charged, since Hermione asserts from her first appearance an unapologetic—perhaps even unconscious—sensuality. Once encouraged to assist in detaining Polixenes, she casts off imposed standards of feminine modesty, steps boldly forward and works her will on him with entreaties as warm, witty, and expansive as Leontes's were spare (1.2.27-57). Moreover, while protesting against the devil's role that Polixenes assigns her, Hermione also shows herself utterly unthreatened by it, implicitly affirming the wholesomeness of marital sexuality:

Th' offenses we have made you do we'll answer,
If you first sinn'd with us, and that with us
You did continue fault, and that you slipp'd not
With any but with us.

(1.2.83-86)

Hermione's unself-conscious sensuality may also be discerned in her erotically-charged solicitation of Leontes's flattery: "cram's with praise, and make's / As fat as tame things. . . . You may ride 's / With one soft kiss a thousand furlongs ere / With spur we heat an acre. . . . Nay, let me have't; I long" (1.2.91-2, 94-6, 101).

Thus, Hermione's friendly intimacy with Polixenes may indeed appear transgressive of feminine modesty. It undoubtedly should. Indeed, a director might be well-advised to make Hermione's displays of affection for Polixenes exuberant enough to afflict the audience with doubt, to attract a measure of sympathy for Leontes or at least to check a willingness to conclude unequivocally that his distress is unwarranted. Such a staging thus subjects Hermione's sexual charisma not only to Leontes's determining gaze but to the audience's as well, exploiting a prejudice against female sexuality, the prevailing notion that "nice girls don't," that warmth and sensuality too liberally dispersed convict a woman of lascivious intentions. In this manner audience members become implicated in Leontes's dementia and can only extricate themselves by questioning their instinctive stigmatizing of female sexuality.

Hermione's behavior appears so provocative because she combines the chastity and sexuality that Leontes (and patriarchy) insists on polarizing. She demonstrates that a woman may be a loyal and loving wife without requiring idealization as a madonna, that she can be a sexual being without meriting censure as a whore. Ironically, Leontes himself supplies the correct interpretation of her "entertainment" of Polixenes: it "derive[s] a liberty / From heartiness, from bounty, fertile bosom" (1.2.112-13). It discloses a forwardness ("liberty") derived not from wantonness but from a prodigal graciousness and generous affection constitutive of a more human version of woman as nurturer ("fertile bosom").

Unfortunately, Leontes harbors an "affection" of sexual jealousy that defeats this sound intuition. Indeed, rather than rest in his own assurance that affection "fellow'st nothing," he concludes instead that this one "co-joins with something" and delivers himself to illusion (1.2.138-46). Leontes fatally confuses cause and effect, construing his violent jealousy as proof of his wife's guilt when, in fact, her guilt is a fiction that his violent jealousy creates. Leontes's precipitous progression from suspicion to belief—"thou may'st . . . thou dost . . . and I find it" (1.2.143-44)—suggests an eagerness to debase his wife, a readiness to enact a vindictive pornographic fantasy. In this context, his feverish punning and quibbling, the voyeuristic fervor with which he fixes on the physical interplay of Polixenes and Hermione, give an impression of autoerotic stimulation. He appears to be aroused by the very image that repels him, another experience common to pornographers.

Indeed, Leontes thinks himself infected by the corruption that he has uncovered:

There may be in the cup
A spider steep'd, and one may drink; depart,
And yet partake no venom (for his knowledge
Is not infected), but if one present
Th' abhorr'd ingredient to his eye, make known
How he hath drunk, he cracks his gorge, his sides,
With violent hefts. I have drunk, and seen the spider.

(2.1.39-45)

He has, he feels, imbibed poison from Hermione. The previously unglimpsed spider of female lewdness taints the elixir of conjugal love, infects Leontes with knowledge of his own depravity, incites him to ghastly spasms of violence in an attempt to expel the poison. Hermione is made to bear the burden of Leontes's own sexual guilt. Afflicted with fleshly shame, he will mortify the flesh by mortifying Hermione whom he reduces to pure flesh. He must deprive her of a soul in order to save his. He must protect himself from sin by eliminating its imagined source.

In a key passage, Leontes testifies to a hyperconsciousness of sin and a need to be cleansed:

I have trusted thee, Camillo,
With all the nearest things to my heart, as well
My chamber-councils, wherein, priest-like, thou
Hast cleans'd my bosom: I from thee departed
Thy penitent reform'd.

(1.2.235-38)

This speech offers proof of Leontes's fragile conscience and explains his desperate attempt to dissociate himself from a corruption to which he feels dangerously susceptible. In urging Camillo to be Polixenes's cupbearer, Leontes appears to transform him from priest to assassin. In fact, he asks him to perform the same service as before: to cleanse his soul. Indeed, Leontes's recovery of a purified self requires the elimination of Polixenes, the impure self, the evil "twin" or bad "brother" whose sexual dereliction threatens Leontes with knowledge of his own.

If Polixenes, the adult embodiment of the "boy eternal" myth, fails as a mirror of Leontes's purity, then Mamillius, the childish image, must succeed. Leontes thus maniacally scrutinizes his son for evidence of bastardy, for traces of contamination. "We must be neat; not neat, but cleanly," Leontes declares while cleaning Mamillius's "smutch'd" nose—"a copy out of mine" (1.2.121-23). Leontes seeks to merge with an unblemished image of an innocent self, to move through Mamillius's looking-glass into the realm of "boy eternal." "Looking on the lines of my boy's face," he later tells Hermione and Polixenes,

methoughts I did recoil
Twenty-three years, and saw myself unbreech'd
In my green velvet coat, my dagger muzzled,

Lest it should bite its master, and so prove
(As ornament oft does) too dangerous.

(1.2.153-58)

Leontes adds a new detail to the boyhood dream: he owned a dangerous "dagger" that he kept "muzzled"—an image not of innocence but of repression, a symptom of sexual dread. Mamillius cannot bear the burden of Leontes's pathological need for purity. He cannot survive in actuality the expulsion of Hermione dictated by fantasy: separated from his mother, he sickens and dies.

In sum, Leontes's mistreatment of Hermione is a pornographer's mission of revenge: he punishes her for recalling him to his own fleshliness and frailty. The master of culture abhors exposure as a vulnerable creature of nature. Hermione's supposed sexual perfidy is but the sexual power that enforces knowledge of Leontes's essential powerlessness. He moves decisively to counter that power, which she so unthinkingly unleashes in her "entertainment" of Polixenes. With an entourage of guards, a male force, he violently invades a female space—presumably the queen's chamber (2.1.). This brutal male intrusion thus becomes emblematic of a rape, the violation of a woman's most private quarters. He arrests her, binds her, imprisons her, and threatens her with torture. He puts her on trial, adding trumped-up charges of treason to her supposed crime of adultery. In short, he brings the full power of the state to bear against this woman whose power he so fears, turning the instruments of male-centered authority into devices of subjugation, suppressing a potentially subversive female force. As Griffin observes, "when the pornographic mind creates an object, it prepares the stage for the enactment of its rage against that object. It is inevitable that this object must be rejected, humiliated, punished, tortured, bound up, silenced, even murdered" (46).

Ironically—as Peter Stallybrass says of Desdemona (141)—the more Hermione is persecuted, the more she appears to become the ideal wife: devoted, long-suffering, self-sacrificing. When first berated and arrested, she proclaims, "There's some ill planet reigns; / I must be patient, till the heavens look / With an aspect more favorable" and concludes, "The King's will be performed!" (2.1.105-07, 115). At her trial, she calls his favor "the crown and comfort of my life" which, since lost, makes death trifling (3.2.90-96) and protests that she loved Polixenes as Leontes himself "commanded; / Which not to have done I think had been in me / Both disobedience and ingratitude / To you and toward your friend" (3.2.66-69). Hermione seems compelled to create an alternative, idealized image of herself as faithful wife. Death fixes her in that martyred image, makes of her a monument of Patience smiling at grief. Leontes gets his wish: Hermione as statue, as lifeless icon of wifely devotion, may now be "his forever." Like Browning's Duke of Ferrara, he transforms a human being into an aesthetic object, bringing an independent woman under his firm control—but only by putting her to death. The Bohemian romance of Florizel and Perdita corrects Leontes's destructive dramatization of

"The Fall." These lovers, as in the "boy eternal" fantasy, are "two lambs frisking in the sun," innocent playmates in a pastoral world. Their innocence is not, however, of the pre-sexual sort celebrated in the boyhood dream but is mature and sexually aware, dispelling the dream's dark shadow of misogyny and sexual dread. In Leontes's vision of "paradise lost," woman destroys man's innocence and sexually defiles him. In Florizel's and Perdita's version of "paradise regained," man joins with woman in a wholesome sexual partnership.

Indeed, in effecting a release from the strangulated court to the vibrant countryside, in setting nature against culture, Bohemia initiates the rectification of Leontes's wrongs. Certainly it accommodates the sexual experience that so bedeviled him. The Old Shepherd regards Perdita precisely as Leontes did: as the product of some illicit sexual liaison—"some stair-work, some trunk-work, some behind-door-work" (3.3.74-75). Yet he unfussily, good-heartedly resolves to take care of her, accepting fleshly weakness as the way of the world. Similarly, sixteen years later when he exhorts Perdita, a reluctant "mistress of the feast," to emulate the livelier ways of his lusty wife who "welcom'd all, serv'd all," drank and sang, and danced with multiple partners (4.4.57), he seems to encourage the same sort of generous sensuality that in Hermione struck Leontes as shameless lust.

The sheep-shearing festival reinforces the naturalness of sexuality, depicting a whole pastoral society at earthy play. Autolycus sings randy songs and sells seductive trinkets, twelve "men of hair" perform a leaping, lusty satyr dance, and the shepherd's son, a bumpkin Don Juan, finds himself mediating an immodest squabble between two frisky mistresses, Mopsa and Dorcas. The festival sanctions the release of revitalizing libidinal energy, of the "red blood" that "reigns in the winter's pale" about which Autolycus sings (4.3.4). "Blood" here retains its sexual significance but adds connotations of "life-force," of the "vital fluid upon which life depends" (OED, 1: 929). Like the may-games of Whitsuntide (to which Perdita refers at 4.4.134), the sheep-shearing festival is essentially a fertility rite, celebrating nature's powers of renewal. Revelers dress themselves in garlands of flowers, affirming a connectedness to nature that exalts their licentious antics, as C. L. Barber observes: "May-game wantonness has a reverence about it because it is a realization of a power of life larger than the individual, crescent both in men and in their green surroundings" (24). By clothing themselves in nature's foliage, celebrants relate "the emotions of love to its fructifying function" (24).

Thus Shakespeare's play enacts, at least until Polixenes's violent intrusion, the ancient comic mythos of seasonal renewal: summer defeats winter, fertility overcomes sterility and, in Griffin's terms, nature revitalizes culture. The flower-dispersing Perdita, costumed as Flora, resembling Persephone, functions as goddess of fertility. Cast out by culture, she becomes the embodiment of nature and, because uncorrupted by culture's fear of the body, generates precisely the healthful sexuality necessary for culture's recovery.

Indeed, Perdita and Florizel together reconcile the teeming sexuality of the festival with the purity that so obsessed Leontes. These pastoral lovers do not use festivity as a license for looseness. Florizel rejects the role of royal debaucher he might conceivably have played and which Perdita invokes when claiming that his outsized oaths resemble a seducer's tactical flatteries (4.4.146-51). Neither do they retreat into bloodless amorous warbling. Though their desire for each other is disciplined by chaste regard and marital design, it is not prettily abstract but potently sexual. Florizel makes his sexual passion perfectly clear. When Perdita chides him for humbling his royalty with a shepherd's robes, he compares himself favorably to those gods who assumed lower forms for love's sake:

> Jupiter
> Became a bull and bellow'd; the green Neptune
> A ram and bleated; and the fire-rob'd god,
> Golden Apollo, a poor humble swain,
> As I seem now. Their transformations
> Were never for a piece of beauty rarer,
> Nor in a way so chaste, since my desires
> Run not before mine honor, nor my lusts
> Burn hotter than my faith.
>
> (4.4.27-35)

Florizel makes no attempt to hide his "lusts" and "desires"—indeed, he likens them to those appetites that made beasts of gods—but resolves to sanctify them in marriage, to reconcile passion and chastity, to harmonize the bleating of the lusty ram with that of the innocent lambs of Polixenes's Edenic vision.

Perdita, for her part, invokes Florizel's "desire to breed by me" with ingenuous frankness and evinces a longing for sexual satisfaction in wishing to bedeck Florizel with flowers and transform him into a "bank for love to lie and play on: / Not like a corpse; or if—not to be buried, / But quick, and in mine arms" (4.4.130-32). Perdita's sense of "play" combines the innocence and sexuality that Leontes insisted on polarizing. Indeed, Leontes's most telling pun is on the word "play": "Go play, boy, play. Thy mother plays" (1.2.187), insinuating a contrast between the innocent childish play of Mamillius—which is also the pastoral "boy eternal" play of himself and Polixenes—and the wicked sexual play of the corruptress Hermione. For Florizel and Perdita, sexual passion is not a corruptive force but the indispensable physical component to a fully generative love. Indeed, Florizel and Perdita are perhaps close to attaining the integration of body and soul that Montaigne considered the only means by which heterosexual love could surpass "brotherly affection":

> if such a relationship, free and voluntary, could be built up, in which not only would the souls have . . . complete enjoyment, but the bodies would also share in the alliance, so that the entire man would be engaged, it is certain that the resulting friend-ship would be fuller and more complete.
>
> (Frame 138)

In surpassing the pastoral friendship of Leontes and Polixenes, in wedding innocence to sexual experience, Florizel and Perdita do indeed turn Bohemia into a kind of paradise regained. They soon meet a second snake-in-the-garden, however, a stand-in for the man whose misdeeds they are redressing: Polixenes, whose sexually-laced fulminations are very nearly as cataclysmic as Leontes's. He undertakes to control his son's sexuality as strictly as Leontes sought to control his wife's. He similarly employs patriarchal sanctions as instruments of domination, threatening to disinherit Florizel if he persists in courting this lowly shepherdess. Also like Leontes, he forces an innocent woman into the role of wicked seductress and threatens her in terms that suggest he is susceptible to the very "affection" he seeks to suppress:

> if ever, henceforth, thou
> These rural latches to his entrance open,
> Or hoop his body more with thy embraces,
> I will devise a death as cruel for thee
> As thou art tender to't.
>
> (4.4.437-41)

In short, he too manifests a pornographic consciousness. He calls her "enchantment" and "fresh piece / Of excellent witchcraft" (4.4.434, 422-23), linking her with the earliest victims of pornographic violence—the "witches," the multitude of women tortured and murdered for their supposedly demonic sexual powers. Polixenes seems prepared to mete out a similar punishment. His promise to "have thy beauty scratched with briars" takes us back to Griffin's portrayal of the pornographer as desiring beauty in order to violate it. His threat to "devise a death as cruel for thee as thou art tender to 't" parallels the pornographer's sadistic focus on the female's physical vulnerability. Polixenes means for Perdita to feel her "tenderness" and to cower before his power to hurt her.

Like Leontes, Polixenes appears to lord his authority over those who threaten it and to avenge himself on a force that bewitches him. That Perdita has such an effect on him seems evident: the very accusations of witchcraft are covert tributes to her sexual allure and twice he openly extols her beauty (4.4.78, 156-57). Yet Perdita, youthful queen of the feast, implicitly disqualifies this king from the ranks of amorous swains and suitors, welcoming him with flowers that signify—at least to Polixenes—his status as "man of winter" at a summer frolic (4.4.73-79). Florizel later seconds this characterization of Polixenes as a man past his prime, addressing his disguised father as "ancient sir who . . . hath sometime loved" (4.4.361-62) and enlisting him as a witness to the betrothal from which he has, in actuality, been excluded. Polixenes, however, seems unreconciled to his position as impotent observer of potent youthful revels. He not only sardonically commends Perdita for her choice of "winter" flowers but, while still disguised, warms up for his brutal tirade against the lovers with a scathingly exaggerated portrait of himself as "stupid with age and alt'ring rheums," victim of a dreadfully incapacitating senility that makes him unfit for his own son's betrothal (4.4.397-402). The ferocity of the outburst that ensues may well owe something to a jealousy triggered by the sight of this perturbingly unattainable young woman's making amorous sport with a son seemingly intent on discarding him.

Polixenes could be considered a Pentheus-like character, adopting disguise for a mission of spying that discloses an almost prurient interest in the licentious proceedings he wishes to oppose, a craving for nature that culture demands he repel. The director could make clear the extent to which Polixenes not only passively witnesses the festival's mating rituals but is voyeuristically aroused by them. Indeed, the director might even play up the Polixenes-Leontes parallel by staging a moment of intimacy between Florizel and Perdita that moves Polixenes to Leontes-like excitation. Whatever sexual feeling is stirred in Polixenes can only cause frustration. In a festival brimming with sexual vigor, he is consigned to sexlessness. His response is to strike back against those who have neutered him—a son seemingly bent on overthrowing him and a woman whose untouchable youthful beauty is an insuperable provocation. Like Leontes, Polixenes explodes with sexual violence, prepared to destroy that which he lacks full power to possess.

Florizel's disregard of his father's interdictions, his determination to marry Perdita at the expense of his princely status, provides instructive contrast to Leontes's power-mad vendetta. If Leontes invests himself with the state's full power in order to destroy Hermione, Florizel renounces such power out of love for Perdita. In declaring himself "heir to my affection" rather than heir to the throne (4.4.481), Florizel chooses nature over culture, identifies with that vulnerable, feeling "feminine" self that Leontes so feverishly opposed. He gives himself to Perdita as Hermione gave herself to Leontes: "I cannot be / Mine own, nor any thing to any, if / I be not thine" (4.4.43-45). At the same time, his single-minded devotion to "affection," his obsessive pursuit of a personal vision, his ready embrace of "madness" (4.4.484) make him as determined a lover as Leontes is intractable a lunatic. He is thus indispensable to Perdita's revitalization of Leontes's court.

The cocksure cony-catcher Autolycus also assists in the symbolic defeat of Leontes, exuberantly lampooning—whether intentionally or not—Polixenes's re-enactment of Leontes's despotic cruelty. Posing as a preposterously swaggering courtier, he reprises Polixenes's ranting denunciation of Florizel's and Perdita's betrothal, heaping abuse not on the absent lovers but on the terrified yokels he pretends not to recognize. "Draw our throne into a sheepcote!" he cries (4.4.79-80), echoing Polixenes's censure of Florizel, a "sceptre's heir / That thus affects a sheephook" (4.4.419-20). His loving recital of the gruesome tortures that await the clown translate Polixenes's brutal threats into unthreatening comic grotesquery. By so farcically and irreverently standing in for Leontes's stand-in, Autolycus helps dispel the spectre of tragedy and preserve the spirit of festivity that he first bumptiously introduced.

Indeed, throughout the Bohemian idyll, Autolycus stands in for Leontes himself, removing, by means of comic parody, much of the sting from the crazed king's depredations. Like Leontes, he addresses the audience directly with conspiratorial asides and soliloquies, unveiling an "angling" mind intent on entrapping people. Unlike Leontes, however, he wins our allegiance, secures our admiration for his expert deceptions and pilferies. Our delight in this con-man's virtuosity stirs none of the unnerving moral qualms of our attraction to the seductive cunning of an Iago or Richard III. Autolycus is mostly a figure of fun, a crowd-pleasing prankster. Like Leontes, he traffics in illusion, but the stooges of his confidence game fare far better than the pawns of Leontes's pornographic theater.

He may seem as remorselessly submerged in selfhood as Leontes, as devoted to a self-serving mission that estranges him from an entire community. Yet, unlike Leontes's, Autolycus's predaciousness and self-absorption are assimilable—indeed indispensable—to his society. Bohemia derives much of its lifelikeness from Autolycus's zestful cynicism, his hearty trouncing of honesty and trust, his cheerful contempt for his gullible victims. He ensures that the idealized love of Florizel and Perdita unfolds in a world sufficiently infused by a force resistant to idealization. He keeps Arcadia grounded in reality.

Finally, Autolycus, like Leontes, is his world's version of "fallen man," the embodiment of a corrupt sexuality. He consorts with "doxies," "aunts," and "drabs" (4.3.2, 11, 27)—in other words, whores—and peddles songs full of "dildos and fadings" (4.4.195), the singing of which lulls celebrants into a collective stupor that Autolycus equates with desexualization: "You might have pinched a placket, it was senseless; 'twas nothing to geld a codpiece of a purse; I would have fil'd keys off that hung in chains" (4.4.609-12).

But Autolycus happily accepts the sexual passion that Leontes so passionately resisted. He is not so much a carrier of corruption as a bearer of "blood," an embodiment of that pulsating life-force that revivifies a world deadened by Leontes's misdeeds. He contributes mightily to Bohemia's effect of festive release. He not only accepts, as Leontes does not, his creaturely status. He absolutely revels in it.

Of course the play ultimately accents the insufficiencies of Autolycus's creaturely life. Indeed, one measure of Perdita's and Florizel's triumph is their transcendence of his pure materiality. Autolycus embodies a kind of nature rather different from the one that Griffin imagines: animal nature, amorally predacious, invincibly self-involved. It is the same nature embodied by the hungry bear who makes a meal of Antigonus or, in a very different context, the nature that is Edmund's goddess. From another angle, however, Autolycus does not represent nature but marauding, despoiling culture. A refugee from court who picks on gullible rustics, Autolycus exploits nature in order to gratify a culture-bound greediness for profit and power. Thus, although Autolycus defeats Leontes through parodic doubling, he must also himself suffer defeat. He has no share in the happiness that reigns at the play's end and is left ruefully to acknowledge the limitations of his roguery (5.2.113-23). In the last analysis, his failure to find redemption provides contrast for Leontes's achievement of it.

Leontes has positioned himself for redemption by undergoing a superhuman sixteen-year penance which, to an important degree, takes the form of feminization, of submission to a woman he had previously abhorred. Indeed, Paulina's domination of Leontes effects a shift in the play from female subjugation to female empowerment. In appointing herself Hermione's champion, Paulina avenges Leontes's invasion of female space by penetrating a male bastion of power—presumably the king's chamber (2.3.)—and by maintaining a determination to talk even in the face of physical threats and scurrilous slander. Words are Paulina's weapons. She denounces the king's "dangerous, unsafe lunes" and resolves, "He must be told on't," adding, "If I prove honey-mouthed, let my tongue blister" (2.2.29, 31). For Paulina, militant speech serves as the substitute for manly combat, a means of vindicating the queen's honor (2.3.59-61). Her headstrong remonstrances naturally earn her the epithet of shrew. Leontes calls her "Lady Margery" and berates Antigonus for his inability to control her, declaring him "woman-tired; unroosted / By thy Dame Partlet," a victim of beatings at her hands (2.3.160, 75-76, 92). Yet it is Leontes who takes a beating here. He yells at her, shrinks from her, implores his men to eject her and only succeeds in confirming his own impotence and cowardice.

Leontes's fear and attempted suppression of Paulina parallel his fear and attempted suppression of Hermione. The woman who is too free with her tongue is as threatening to male authority as the woman who is too free with her body. Indeed, in Shakespeare's era, a woman's verbal freedom was as strictly constrained as her sexual freedom. Patriarchy imposed on women a figurative veil of silence and the overly-talkative woman could be legitimately scorned as a whore. As Stallybrass explains, "silence, the closed mouth, is made a symbol of chastity" (127).

Since Paulina's unrestrained speech makes her as promiscuous and mutinous as Leontes imagines Hermione to be, his submission to chastisement at her hands is fitting atonement for his chastisement of Hermione. Since his need to control Hermione proved fatal to his marriage, he accepts as penance a metaphorical marriage to the uncontrollable Paulina, upon whom he confers full verbal freedom and authority. "Go on, go on; / Thou can'st not speak too much," he says, submitting to her excoriative censure in the wake of Hermione's apparent death. "Thou didst speak but well / When most the truth; which I receive much better / Than to be pitied of thee" (3.2.214-15, 232-34). The heretofore blustering, misogynist tyrant puts himself under a woman's power. He voluntarily accepts what he had previously feared: unbridled femaleness. He submits to that "callat / Of boundless tongue" (2.3.91-92) who steps in for that wife of seemingly boundless sexuality.[4]

Although she may seem to shift from shrew to saint, although she may profess, as Carol Thomas Neely contends, "to drop her loquaciousness" and "identify herself as a woman subordinate to Leontes" (200), Paulina continues her fearless, recriminatory talk and holds the upper hand over Leontes to the end. Even when his first wave of penitence moves her to lament her rashness and retract her words, even after a lord has urged "say no more" and rebuked the "boldness of your speech" (2.3.216-18), she cannot refrain from reminding Leontes of his catastrophic misdeeds:

> Sir, royal sir, forgive a foolish woman.
> The love I bore your queen—lo, fool again!—
> I'll speak of her no more, nor of your children;
> I'll not remember you of my own lord,
> Who is lost too. Take your patience to you,
> And I'll say nothing.
>
> (3.2.227-32)

Similarly, sixteen years later when contesting Cleomenes's and Dion's case for Leontes's re-marriage, Paulina's reference to Hermione as "she you killed" draws an anguished protest from the grief-stricken king: "thou strik'st me / Sorely to say I did." He implores her, "say so but seldom," to which Cleomenes rejoins, "not at all, good lady" (5.1.15, 17-18, 20). Once more Paulina is urged to hold her tongue, to curb her wounding words. Her penchant for unpleasant truth-telling confirms her status as untameable shrew.

Yet this untameable shrew amasses an impressive amount of political power. She alone adjudicates the urgent matter of the king's succession. The unwaveringly deferential Leontes overrules the persuasive appeals of his political advisers and sides with Paulina, promising never to re-marry without her permission (5.1.71, 82).

In asking Leontes to re-marry, Cleomenes and Dion essentially ask him to end his "marriage" to Paulina, to free himself from her dominance and resume his rightful place as unmediated male authority. That Paulina so easily prevails, so readily retains Leontes's allegiance, implies a radical ascension of feminine influence within male-centered society, a startling alteration of the power structure.[5]

Shakespeare thus ingeniously elevates the stock role of the man-baiting shrew. Indeed, Paulina plays a role in relation to the ravaged king that is, in some ways, analogous to that of Lear's Fool. This unsilenceable shrew is, like Lear's Fool, an unsilenceable conscience, a relentless voice of truth who spurns the subordinate's proper role of mollifying the distressed and distracted monarch. Like Lear's

Fool, she is a marginalized figure within the political order who becomes the king's soulmate. Just as Lear's kinship with the Fool represents a conscious flouting of hierarchical relations, an act of atonement for his kingly neglect of the outcast and unprivileged, so Leontes's submission to Paulina sweeps aside hierarchical imperatives and helps atone for his vilification of women. If, as Enid Welsford suggests, *King Lear* depicts the coronation of the Fool and the investment of the King with motley (269), then *The Winter's Tale* depicts the empowering of the shrew and the taming of the tyrant.

Leontes's "taming," his metaphorical marriage to Paulina, is not merely a penance. Indeed, its penitential aspects—subordination to a dominant "wife," acceptance of the sexlessness seemingly wished for in the crazed project of self-cleansing—make it a poor model for actual marriage. But it is also an intimate friendship, marked by mutual respect and understanding. Both Leontes and Paulina have lost a spouse, so each becomes the other's "mate" in an intense, sixteen-year alliance. Leontes does not simply do penance for his past error of depreciating the feminine but, by appreciating Paulina, corrects it in preparation for his future reconciliation with Hermione. Indeed, the path of feminization on which Paulina leads Leontes, the path to health and wholeness, is also the path back to Hermione.

Paulina's spectacular charade of animating a statue consummates the curing of Leontes's habit of objectification, the rehabilitation of his pornographic consciousness. Mesmerized by the statue's uncanny resemblance to the queen, Leontes once more elects to believe in an illusion—in this case a constructed, theatrical illusion—that, under the influence of a disarranging "affection," impresses him as true. The "affection" is his profound remorse and yearning for Hermione's return, for the recovery not simply of the image but of the woman. This longing for the whole person redeems his past crime of imprisoning her in nonpersonhood. If Leontes originally accedes to the outlandish fiction of Hermione's infidelity and proceeds to coerce her into an iconic posture of wifely subservience—thus turning her into a statue—his final acceptance of the outlandish fiction of Hermione's metamorphosis from statue to woman signals his reception of her as a living, breathing, fully independent being. Hermione's stature as venerated icon has seemingly grown in accordance with Leontes's exorbitant penance and Paulina's project of preserving her memory. In his own recollections Leontes idealizes Hermione as "the sweet'st companion that e'er man / Bred his hopes out of" (5.1.11-12). Paulina takes the superlatives even further:

> If, one by one, you wedded all the world,
> Or, from the all that are, took something good
> To make a perfect woman, she you kill'd
> Would be unparallel'd.
>
> (5.1.13-16)

Indeed, Paulina elicits Leontes's promise not to re-marry by activating a specific memory, riveting his mind on the image of her eyes. The eyes, we know, are the birthplace of fancy, of swooning infatuation and idealization (as well as pornographic depersonalization). Moved by the memory, Leontes himself spouts superlatives: "Stars, stars, / And all eyes else dead coals!" (5.1.67-68). He has passed from the extreme of pornographically degrading Hermione to that of rapturously idolizing her. Yet he still objectifies her.[6] Impelled by his own immense grief and Paulina's injunctions to remember, Leontes holds Hermione captive to memory's romanticized gaze, putting her forever on a pedestal.

In the final scene, then, when Leontes confronts Hermione's statue, he is, in effect, confronting his own idolatrous image of her. Her physical position perpetuates the posture of exhibited object to which he has recurrently consigned her. In 1.2., he stands aside, "frames" and tremulously narrates her supposedly salacious behavior, presenting her intimacy with Polixenes as a kind of lurid peepshow (2.115-18, 83-85). In 2.1., he urges his male entourage to "look on her, mark her well," displaying her as a woman whose beauty must be "seen through" to the harlotry that it hides (2.1.64-77). In 3.2., he turns her trial into a virtual sadomasochistic spectacle, showcasing her as a madonna-turned-whore, a degraded object, a shamed adulteress. He preys on the powerlessness to which he has sadistically reduced her, a powerlessness greatly aggravated by her physical weakness. While it would seem far-fetched to call Hermione a masochist, she does express love for her tormentor and assume a posture of martyred faithfulness, foreshadowing her statue's pose. Once pornographically displayed as sordid flesh, she is, in the final scene, idolatrously unveiled as sainted icon.

This final scene effects a reversal of Hermione's trial. Now Leontes is utterly powerless, a dazed participant in proceedings that he only imperfectly grasps, a pawn in the maneuverings of powerful women. Perdita, not Leontes, ends Hermione's cloistered withdrawal. Paulina, not Leontes, commands her to come to life. Hermione, not Leontes, holds the key to reconciliation: she may take him back or not. In one sense, Paulina and Hermione sadistically collude to sharpen Leontes's comeuppance. The already massively grieving king confronts, in the most wrenchingly vivid way, the consequences of his deranged objectification of his wife. "Here is the kind of wife that you wanted!" the statue seems mockingly to say. Its unveiling has the predictable effect of plunging him into new paroxysms of grief and guilt. Leontes is next made to suffer the exquisite torment of Paulina's teasing encouragement of his impossible, delirious longing for Hermione's recovery. Paulina acknowledges her sadistic manipulations: "I could afflict you further," she promises. "Do, Paulina," Leontes begs, "for this affliction has a taste as sweet / As any cordial comfort" (5.3.75-77). The scene salubriously re-works the pornographic sadomasochism of Hermione's trial: Leontes savors his ecstasy of distress, Paulina hurts him in order to please him. This time Leontes is put on trial, made to undergo a final penitential ritual in which Hermione may consent to return if the force of his grief-ridden longing compels her.

The detection of life in Hermione transforms Leontes from worshipful penitent to desiring husband. "Would you not deem it breathed?" he asks Polixenes, "and that those veins / Did verily bear blood?" (5.3.64-65). He ceases adoring a venerated icon and begins to covet a living being. To an important degree, that coveting draws on sheer physical longing. The dizzying excitement with which Leontes awaits his wife's return has a sexual charge. His detection of "blood" in her stirs "stronger blood" in him. Discerning motion in her eye and "breath" about her, he boldly resolves to kiss her (5.3.67, 78, 80). His red-blooded passion "reigns in winter's pale," melting away frozen idealization. His physical desire for Hermione helps elicit her physical reanimation. His wholesome assimilation of "blood" assists in releasing her from the limbo of objectification to which abhorrence of "blood" had consigned her.

The subtext of Leontes's longing might thus be imagined as "wife, I come," or—as he means to stimulate her, to elicit an arousal that betokens her satisfaction by him—"wife, please come," inviting Hermione to consummate their marriage in life even as Cleopatra aims to consummate hers with Antony in death. As Stanley Cavell explains, a woman's satisfaction—which encompasses but surpasses sexual satisfaction—lies beyond a man's capacity to enforce or determine. It is not a matter of proof but of faith. It is, in fact, an aspect of the faith that Paulina makes requisite for Hermione's revival (5.3.94-95), a faith he had once so signally lacked.

Indeed, in the play's first part, Leontes punishes Hermione for afflicting him with the uncertainty of her satisfaction, for inciting the fear that not he but Polixenes satisfies her—hence his extreme agitation when Camillo attributes Polixenes's delayed departure to his wish to "satisfy" the queen's entreaties: "Satisfy? / Th' entreaties of your mistress? Satisfy?" (1.2.233-34). As Cavell observes, assurance of satisfaction is a gift: "to elicit this gift, the extreme claim of male activeness, thus requires the man's acceptance of his absolute passiveness" (35). Leontes initially rejects this passiveness. He refuses to submit to the power she commands as judge of his sufficiency. He takes action. He asserts his own power. He converts the uncertainty of her satisfaction into the certainty of her dissatisfaction and brutally enacts a retributive dissatisfaction with her.

In the final scene, he amends his mistake, accepting a passive, submissive posture from which, insofar as he is able, he attempts to "elicit the gift" of Hermione's satisfaction. The sexually-charged longing is thus, in fact, a passionately chaste courtship. Leontes must woo and win Hermione once more. The scene functions as a second wedding, a theatrically extravagant renewal of vows. "O, thus she stood," Leontes exclaims upon beholding the statue, "when I first wooed her" (5.3.34-36). Her descent from the pedestal brings about a second betrothal. "Nay, present your hand," Paulina instructs an awestruck Leontes. "When she was young, you woo'd her; now, in age, / Is she become the suitor?" (5.3.107-109). This second joining of hands, this second betrothal, decisively ends the ill effects of that mock-betrothal that Leontes had perversely perceived in Hermione's presentation of her hand to Polixenes. The battle cry of "too hot, too hot" with which Leontes greeted that gesture gives way here to the joyous exclamation "Oh, she's warm!" (5.3.109) as he takes Hermione's hand, perhaps the first time in the entire play that he touches her. The "too hot" fever flame of obsessive sexual "affection" gives way to the "constant and settled warmth" of loving devotion—possibly even to that harmonization of spiritual and physical satisfaction that Montaigne identified as the ideal of sexual love.

After joining hands, the two hold each other in a long, silent embrace (5.3.110-120), creating a second statue, or at least a piece of living sculpture, a *tableau vivant* of reconciliation and intimacy that replaces the image of the solitary frozen queen and all the pornographic displays and idolatrous images of her that have preceded it. Indeed, Camillo and Polixenes narrate and frame this moment of intimacy in a manner reminiscent of Leontes's demented commentary on Hermione's interplay with Polixenes. "She embraces him," Camillo exclaims. "She hangs about his neck," Polixenes adds (5.3.111-12).

The embrace could be staged as a further instance of dominance-and-submission: Hermione might collapse into Leontes's enfolding arms or, by contrast, draw her kneeling husband to her bosom in the manner of a mother comforting a distressed child. It ought instead, I think, to provide an image of mutuality, of reciprocally offered love and comfort. Neither party assumes a dominant position. Each submits and is submitted to. Each nurtures and receives nurturance. Each confesses neediness and consents to meet the other's needs.

To the extent that Hermione nurtures Leontes, she gratifies his wish to be "boy eternal." To the extent, however, that he nurtures her, he allows her to be "girl eternal." The "eternal childhood" thus affirmed differs radically from Leontes's previous regressive fantasy, permitting not only mutuality but sexuality as well. This accommodation of sexuality accords with Griffin's portrayal of childhood as a period not of sexlessness but of pre-sexual eros:

> Isn't it eros we rediscover in the child's world? The beauty of the child's body. The child's closeness to the natural world. The child's heart. Her love. Touch never divided from meaning. Her trust. Her ignorance of culture. The knowledge she has of her own body. That she eats when she is hungry. Sleeps when she is tired. Believes what she sees. That no part of her body has been forbidden to her. No part of this body is shamed, numbed, or denied. That anger, fear, love, and desire pass freely through this body. And for her, meaning is never separate from feeling.
>
> (254)

Leontes's previous attempt to be "boy eternal" manifested adult terrors and constrictions utterly destructive of the child's trust and instinctuality and thus destructive of Mamillius, image of "boy eternal" and Hermione, preserver of "girl eternal." Florizel and Perdita successfully assimilate the eros of childhood to the sexuality of adulthood, and Leontes and Hermione follow their lead. They stand together not only as nurturer and nurtured but as lover and beloved. The embrace represents a passionately chaste love-making, the climax of Leontes's fervent wooing and arousing, an experience of mutual satisfaction. They do not speak to each other. There are no idealized vows of "I am yours forever," only the "speechless dialect" of a shared physical love, the silence of a savored, enveloping feeling. The two move, as it were, beyond speech, beyond the constructs of culture and into the sensations of nature, into a realm of pure feeling where simply to touch is to express love, a love that "doth verily bear blood."

It might reasonably be objected that the nature I invoke, following Griffin, is itself a cultural construct and that even sensations—or rather our experience of them—are culturally regulated. (Does not one's experience of bodily harm or bliss depend upon culturally-instilled attitudes toward pain and pleasure?) The objection begs a philosophical debate beyond the purview of the present essay. My point is simply that I imagine in the embrace of Hermione and Leontes the consummation of a mutual need to touch and be touched—a need that each of us brings into this world—so physically powerful that it submerges them momentarily in pure sensation and rends the protective coverings of their "culturalized" selves. Indeed, to a crucial extent, the meaning of this moment lies in sensation, not only in the characters' (and, on the characters' behalf, the actors') but in the audience's as well. The audience too must allow itself to be "touched."

More exacting feminist critics have discerned in the play's ending a revival of patriarchy and a re-subordination of women. They note that Hermione seems to return to Leontes exactly as she left him: a devoted, forgiving, long-suffering human icon, lacking the wit and feistiness that characterized her earlier displays of independence. Her return seems important mainly for its effect on Leontes, for the rapt experience of deliverance and achievement of wholeness that it affords him. From this angle, the recovered Hermione symbolizes Leontes's recovered feminine self. From another angle, Hermione returns precisely because Leontes has already integrated his feminine self and therefore no longer requires her to personify its sinister double. In that sense she returns as a person in her own right, not as an extension of Leontes. In addition, the implication that things have not changed all that much seems odd in light of Leontes's radical transformation and the utterly new mutuality that he and Hermione affirm through their embrace. It might also be added that exhibitions of wit and feistiness would seem out of keeping with the final scene's effect of sublime reconciliation. As Janet Adelman observes, Shakespeare's characters are sometimes shaped by "psychological pressures not their own" (140).

The revival of patriarchy does not seem to me, then, to be explicit in the play's action. Leontes does not—at least not unambiguously—reassert power or re-enslave women. True, the "open silence" of Paulina's response to his offer of Camillo as husband permits a mimed resistance on her part that could portray him as autocratically thwarting her. The open silence also lends itself, however, to a speechless happy compliance. Leontes's line "I partly know his mind" (5.3.142) suggests that Camillo might well present himself as a willing suitor. Certainly Paulina has little to fear from the institution of marriage itself. As Marianne Novy observes, "she has already demonstrated unambiguously how little marriage subordinates her" (177). Also, the words with which Paulina excludes herself from the "precious winners" celebration that she has overseen sound suspiciously like a death sentence (5.3.130-35) and could be taken as a self-martyring cue for precisely the invitation to the party that they elicit.

One could of course argue, as does Marilyn Williamson (149-153), that the revival of patriarchy and subordination of women is implicit rather than explicit, that regenerative female powers—Perdita's revitalizing youth, Hermione's loving forgiveness, Paulina's feminine guidance—work to "re-center" Leontes, to restore him fully to the status of husband, father and king. In preserving Leontes, the individual, that is, the women also necessarily preserve Leontes, the patriarch, and thus preserve patriarchy itself. Their gift of nurturance sustains a system that enforces their subjugation. Or, as Erickson less gloomily puts it, the play's female figures "are a powerful force for transforming the men, yet their power as facilitators is used to reform rather than to transcend the patriarchal framework" (167). The point is well-made, but to my mind under-appreciative of the implications of that "reform." As a living work of art, as a play frequently performed in the present age, when the increased participation and influence of women have been accompanied by the increased assimilation of pornographic images and the increased incidence of violent sexual crimes, *The Winter's Tale* offers itself as a testament to the power and worth of women, affirming the feminine as an essential component of human wholeness, depicting the rehabilitation of a pornographic consciousness and dramatizing the transformation of a sadistic would-be wife-murderer to a deeply grieving man who repairs his life through integration of his "woman's part." Indeed, if some ideologically-minded critics find that the play's fantasy does not go far enough, hard-headed realists might well find the fantasy untenable. In real life, violent, women-fearing men are seldom so amenable to reform. But, if *The Winter's Tale* demonstrates anything, it is the power and appeal of beautiful dreaming.

Notes

1. As Linda Woodbridge points out, the formal defenders of womanhood during the English Renaissance were at pains to downplay Eve's perfidy, either by ingeniously inventing excuses for her or by portraying her as the indispensable anti-type of the chaste Mary, whose devout obedience was thought to have redeemed

womankind from Eve's sin as surely as Christ's had redeemed mankind from Adam's, a medieval formulation that recurs regularly in the formalist debate. Although Woodbridge emphasizes that this debate should not be taken as too exact a reflection of contemporaneous attitudes toward women, the image of Eve as seductress was a fixture of Renaissance anti-feminist mythology and her inevitable pairing with Mary promoted the perilous madonna/whore polarity that persists, in one form or another, to the present day.

2. See Pyle for a more extended consideration of the merits of this choice (14).

3. Woodbridge suggests that the plenitude of slandered women in Renaissance drama may point to actual male anxiety about the assertive, liberated women—most especially the notorious cross-dressers—who were increasingly visible in the second decade of the seventeenth century (177-81).

4. I do not mean to minimize the difference between "whores" and "shrews" or to imply that they are interchangeable. My point is that both belong to the species of "female-who-is-too-open," both deviate from partriarchy's "normative woman." Thus there seems to be a kind of poetic justice in Leontes's penance: having sought to dominate one unruly woman, he now submits to another.

5. Given the duration and political import of Paulina's "insubordination," Erickson's assertion that "her domineering role is only temporary" seems a curious slighting of her achievement (163).

6. Neely believes that Leontes not only conceives of Hermione as "peerless" but as "sexual," "human," and "flawed" (205). It is indeed important to note that, in longing to kiss Hermione (5.1.54), the idealizing Leontes evinces a physical desire that foreshadows his intense yearning for her in the final scene. It seems to me, however, that the emphasis in this scene is overwhelmingly on idealization. When Leontes imagines Hermione "soul-vex'd," for instance (5.1.58), he is imagining her not as a woman but as a vengeful spirit.

Works Cited

Adelman, Janet. "'This Is and Is Not Cressid': The Characterization of Cressida." Garner 119-141.

Barber, C. L. *Shakespeare's Festive Comedy: A Study of Dramatic Form and its Relation to Social Custom.* Princeton: Princeton UP, 1959.

Barthes, Roland. *Sade Fourier Loyola.* Trans. Richard Miller. New York: Hill and Wang, 1976.

Cavell, Stanley. *Disowning Knowledge in Six Plays of Shakespeare.* Cambridge: Cambridge UP, 1987.

The Compact Edition of the Oxford English Dictionary. 2 vols. New York: Oxford UP, 1971.

Deleuze, Gilles. "Coldness and Cruelty." Trans. Jean McNeil. *Masochism.* New York: Zone, 1989.

Dworkin, Andrea. *Pornography: Men Possessing Women.* London: Women's Press, 1982.

Erickson, Peter. *Patriarchal Structures in Shakespeare's Drama.* Berkeley: U of California P, 1985.

Felperin, Howard. "'Tongue-Tied Our Queen?': The Deconstruction of Presence in *The Winter's Tale.*" *Shakespeare and the Question of Theory.* Ed. Patricia Parker and Geoffrey Hartman. New York: Methuen, 1985.

Frame, Donald M., ed. *The Complete Essays of Montaigne.* Stanford: Stanford UP, 1943.

Garner, Shirley Nelson, Claire Kahane, and Madelon Sprengnether, eds. *The (M)other Tongue: Essays in Feminist Psychoanalytic Interpretation.* Ithaca: Cornell UP, 1985.

Griffin, Susan. *Pornography and Silence: Culture's Revenge Against Nature.* New York: Harper, 1981.

Kahn, Coppelia. "The Hand That Rocks the Cradle: Recent Gender Theories and Their Implications." Garner 72-88.

Kappeler, Susanne. *The Pornography of Representation.* Minneapolis: U of Minnesota P, 1986.

Neely, Carol Thomas. *Broken Nuptials in Shakespeare's Plays.* New Haven: Yale UP, 1985.

Novy, Marianne. *Love's Argument: Gender Relations in Shakespeare.* Chapel Hill: U of North Carolina P, 1984.

Pyle, Fitzroy. The Winter's Tale: *A Commentary on the Structure.* London: Routledge, 1968.

Shakespeare, William. *The Riverside Shakespeare.* Ed. G. Blakemore Evans. Boston: Houghton, 1974.

Stallybrass, Peter. "Patriarchal Territories: The Body Enclosed." *Rewriting the Renaissance: The Discourse of Sexual Difference in Early Modern Europe.* Ed. Margaret W. W. Ferguson, Maureen Quilligan, and Nancy J. Vickers. Chicago: U of Chicago P, 1986. 123-142.

Welsford, Enid. *The Fool.* 1935. Gloucester, MA: Smith, 1966.

Williams, Linda. *Hard Core: Power, Pleasure, and the "Frenzy of the Visible".* Berkeley: U of California P, 1989.

Williamson, Marilyn. *The Patriarchy of Shakespeare's Comedies.* Detroit: Wayne State UP, 1986.

Woodbridge, Linda. *Women and the English Renaissance: Literature and the Nature of Womankind, 1540-1620.* Urbana: U of Illinois P, 1984.

M. Lindsay Kaplan and Katherine Eggert (essay date 1994)

SOURCE: "'Good queen, my lord, good queen': Sexual Slander and the Trials of Female Authority in *The Winter's Tale*," in *Renaissance Drama,* Vol. 25, 1994, pp. 89-118.

[*In the following essay, Kaplan and Eggert examine* The Winter's Tale*'s relation to questions of female sexuality and authority during Queen Elizabeth's reign.*]

The legal history of early modern Englishwomen has not yet been written, though recent contributions suggest that scholars are beginning to rectify this oversight.[1] One productive point of entry into this important field is presented by defamation, generally defined in early modern England as an injury inflicted by the false and malicious imputation of a crime. The popularity of this charge and its redresses is registered in the records for both common law and ecclesiastical courts in this period, both of which evidence dramatic increases in slander cases. The value of slander for the exploration of early modern women's legal concerns is multiple. First, defamation gives us an indication—albeit more reflective, perhaps, of public opinion than actual indictment rates—of the types of crimes women were thought to commit. After all, slanderous accusations have to have some plausibility in order to be damaging. Second, defamation is an injury that women both commit and complain about in significant numbers. Finally, the form of and redress for defamation are, for the most part, gendered. Imputations of bankruptcy, for example, which could have damaged a merchant and thus were actionable for a man, would probably have had little effect if directed toward a woman. In contrast, allegations of whoredom—which, while occasionally leveled at men, were not usually thought to injure male reputations—were overwhelmingly cited by women in the slander suits they brought.[2]

In this essay, we would like to make a foray into a gendered legal history of early modern England through the problem of slander as experienced by contemporary women and as represented and commented upon in Shakespeare's play *The Winter's Tale*. Not only does the play concern itself with slanders to women's reputations, it also engages a series of other transgressions particularly associated with women: adultery, petty treason, bastardy, infanticide, scolding, and witchcraft.[3] All the female offenses aired in the play thus reveal a pairing of common concerns about women in the period, their sexuality and their authority (a circumstance discussed by early modern commentators never as autonomy *from* men, but always as power *over* men). Female criminality was on the whole popularly defined in terms of either inverting gender hierarchy, as in petty treason or scolding, or transgressing sexual mores, as in bastardy or prostitution, or both, as in adultery or witchcraft. In fact, anxiety about female sexuality might be considered a displaced version of anxiety about female authority, insofar as a causative relation between these two can ever be established. Accusations of sexual impropriety often were unsubtly coded attacks on women's perceived dominance over men in a nonsexual sphere. In a period when a woman's reputation rested largely on her sexual behavior, there was insufficient language, besides that of promiscuity, to classify and to discourage the exercise of female authority. The next best category of opprobrium would be to characterize her behavior as male (Amussen 119-20).

England's ongoing concern with female dominance and female sexuality was only highlighted and exacerbated, in the second half of the sixteenth century, by the peculiar status of its monarch. Although Elizabeth Tudor preferred to promote herself as a singular woman, one whose sexual and legal autonomy was available to no one else, in fact her position as sole monarch and *femme sole* posed a significant challenge, as many critics have pointed out, to contemporary assumptions about the subordination of women. In her recent book on Elizabeth's multivalent presentations and representations, Carole Levin outlines Elizabeth's complex restructuring of gender hierarchies and the anxiety over an unfettered feminine sexuality she thus elicited. Far from simply categorizing the queen's monarchical persona as masculine, as some critics have tended to argue,[4] Elizabeth and her subjects also considered her rule to be precisely that of a woman over a kingdom of men; as a result, as Levin puts it, although "[h]er people might regard her body politic as both pure and virginal, and the incarnation of the sacred principle of male monarchy, . . . the rumors and seditious words so carefully gathered [by Elizabeth's detractors] suggest a perception of her body natural as potentially corrupt in a manifestly female way" (147). As critics such as Levin, Susan Frye, and Leah Marcus (*Puzzling* 59-73) have contended and as we discuss below, Elizabeth's queenship elicited her subjects' fantasies and fears that she was, as Shakespeare's Cleopatra puts it, "no more but e'en a woman," and that a woman ruling over men would necessarily subject her entire realm to unbridled feminine sexual desire. Those fantasies and fears were expressed and repeated in a number of different venues, including the courts of law, which during Elizabeth's reign heard cases that, had the female reputation at issue been not the queen's but a mere woman's, would have been considered under the rubric not of treason but of sexual slander.

Our discussion of a Jacobean play depends, however, on considering not what Elizabeth's sexual reputation underscored while she lived, but how her sexuality might have been remembered. Although Elizabeth's cherished virginity remained the topic of both idle curiosity and scurrilous attack well into the Stuart era (if not, indeed, into our own), the death of the queen tended to polarize the discussion of her sexual nature into clearer terms than the ones in circulation while she was alive. Elizabeth's disturbing presentation of herself as both virginal and sexual bifurcated after her death into opinion about whether she was virginal *or* sexual, so that on the one hand Elizabeth was apotheosized as the saint who through her refusal to marry had kept England Protestant and free,[5] while on the other hand she was still the object of detraction by persons such as "one Sheapheard, a barrister of Lincolns Inn, [and] a base Jesuited papist," who during James I's reign uttered "base and scandalous" words regarding the late queen's honor.[6] It is perhaps the case, then, that Elizabeth's passing offered a respite in which the late queen's sexuality could be named, codified, and contained. At the same time, however, Elizabeth's new status as a remembered personage gave England a neutral arena in which the debate over female sexuality and female authority, issues of increasing public anxiety as the seventeenth century wore on, could be creatively explored. That is, the threat posed by the desire and authority of real women is discussed in terms of the late queen so that it may be discussed at all. For these reasons, we contend, Shakespeare's *Winter's Tale* constructs its considerations of female sexuality around representations that remember and reevaluate Elizabeth. That reevaluation, we shall presently argue, in fact requires reaching back even farther in history, to Elizabeth's mother, Anne Boleyn, whose career provides a kind of prototype and a warning for all subsequent slandered women in positions of authority. Shakespeare's seventeenth-century recasting of sixteenth-century queens therefore serves as a larger commentary on the misrepresentations, if not defamations, that the law perpetrated against women in the early modern period in attempting to name and contain their behavior.

An account of how the law of defamation functioned for English women in the sixteenth and seventeenth centuries provides a necessary foundation for our argument. As we have already suggested, gender affected both the content of and the redress for defamation, due to a large extent to differences in the way male and female reputation was constructed. Susan Amussen observes:

> The defamation cases [suggest] that "honesty" had one meaning for women and another for men. Women's honesty was determined and judged by their sexual behavior; men's honesty was judged in a wide variety of contexts with their neighbours, and bore a closer relation to our notion of honesty as "truthful." Reputation was a gendered concept in early modern England.
>
> (104)

The development of defamation law in sixteenth-century England indicates how the courts reflected and reinforced gender distinctions in rectifying damage to reputation. At the beginning of the century, the only redress for defamation was to be found at the ecclesiastical courts. The offense was defined as the malicious imputation of a crime; the punishment was excommunication, which could be revoked upon the guilty party's doing public penance (Helmholz xiv). However, as the century progressed, the common law began offering a remedy for defamation, based on the same definition of the offense, which understood its effects as financial and offered as punishment and redress damages paid by the offender to the victim. The two jurisdictions were distinguished by the content of the defamations spoken: the church courts handled imputations of "spiritual" crimes (i.e., offenses against ecclesiastical law) while the common-law courts offered redress for imputations of "temporal" crimes (offenses actionable in secular law). Hence, a defamation alleging sexual impropriety by either sex would go to ecclesiastical court while a slander imputing theft, for example, would be heard in a court of common law (Helmholz xli-xlvii).[7]

J. A. Sharpe speculates that the gendered nature of defamation reflects the differences in social roles for men and women:

> . . . it is difficult not to see the wider types of defamation against which men litigated as a consequence of their more varied involvement in the affairs of the world. Women . . . were allowed free access to everyday activities, but their role within them was limited. The rarity with which they were slandered as perjurers, cheats and usurers, for example, suggests that they were not allowed to participate very fully in business or legal matters.
>
> (*Defamation* 28-29)

The conception of women in terms of their sexuality reflects the limitations of their economic autonomy: the early modern English husband not only took control over his wife's property upon marriage, he also acquired property in her body. The children she produced belonged to him, and for middling and upper classes, the family's very continuity depended on her bearing a legitimate male heir to carry on the family name and control its financial holdings. Anxiety about female promiscuity thus fixates on the possibility that the wife's children might not be her husband's, and that his property might be transmitted to another man's son. A woman's assertion of independent sexuality in this way belies the important fiction that her husband owns her body, and the children she bears, by demonstrating that her sexual choices are beyond her husband's control. Thus sexual slander, while perceived as a problem by its victims, nevertheless performed a valuable patriarchal function: the threat of public humiliation and rejection, or even of disciplinary prosecution for the imputed behavior, served as a deterrent against sexual misbehavior both for victims of slander themselves and for either chaste or promiscuous bystanders (Ingram 305-07, 311-13). In fact, as Laura Gowing suggests, slanders against women's sexual reputations drew on directives for female chastity expressed in canonical and noncanonical sources: conduct and household manuals, sermons and ballads (9-10). Hence, defamation could function as a valuable force for policing female sexuality, not just as an action disruptive of the social order.[8]

It is, then, not surprising that Elizabeth, the self-styled Virgin Queen, repeatedly found herself the victim of sexual slander in the context of attempts either to rein her into an acceptable marriage or to unseat her. Rumors alleging Elizabeth's sexual misconduct circulated repeatedly throughout her reign, revealing that even the queen was not protected from her gender. Early in her reign, such rumors tended to emerge around discussions of the queen's marriage plans and England's concomitant fears over either foreign entanglements or subjection to a powerful domestic peer. Her affection for Robert Dudley (later earl of Leicester), for example, caused such a flurry of scandal in England and on the Continent that the representative for one of her wooers felt it necessary to inquire if Elizabeth were still a virgin (Neale 79-83). Outside of court, stories circulated to the effect that she had borne Dudley at least one illegitimate child. Such slanders regarding the queen and Dudley returned in the 1570s, 1580s, and 1590s, long after the end of her childbearing years and the earl's death (Samaha 69); as Levin explains, when Elizabeth's ability to marry and bear children was no longer an issue, "the rumors [of Elizabeth's sexual misconduct] served as a focus for discontent and fear for the succession" (67), and particularly as a focus for England's increasing desire to end female rule and institute normative male rule instead (Levin 100-20; Eggert, "Nostalgia" 524-26). In this way slanders against Elizabeth from late in her reign revived debates from early in her reign over the very possibility of a woman's public status. As a female ruler in her own right, she—like Mary Tudor and Mary Queen of Scots—contradicted the conventional wisdom that women could not rule over, and hence be superior to, men (Jordan 116-33). The general weakness and inferiority of women were cited by authors of treatises against queenship; one serious concern voiced was that once freed from male control, female lust would know no bounds.

In turn, the sexual scandals surrounding Elizabeth's own lineage also generated slander during her reign, slander that vented discontent against Elizabeth in the context of England's bitter religious controversies. In its belief that Henry VIII's divorce from Catherine of Aragon was invalid, the Roman Catholic church viewed his subsequent marriage with Anne Boleyn as adulterous and considered Henry and Anne's daughter Elizabeth a bastard. Charges against Elizabeth and Anne continued to surface well into her reign, as Catholic propaganda alluding to Elizabeth's adulterous origins and linking them with her own alleged promiscuity circulated with increasing frequency and virulence as the sixteenth century wore on. In 1588 William Allen, expatriate Catholic Cardinal of England, published in Antwerp his *Admonition . . . Concerning the Present Warres,* which not only charges Elizabeth with being the product of an incestuous union, asserting that Anne Boleyn was Henry VIII's daughter as well as his wife (Levin 80-81), but conflates that attack with vicious allegations against Elizabeth's own sexual conduct:

> With [Leicester] . . . and diuers others she hathe abused her bodie, against Gods lawes, to the disgrace of princely maiestie & the whole nations reproche, by vnspeakable and incredible variety of luste, which modesty suffereth not to be remembred, neyther were it to chaste eares to be vttered how shamefully she hath defiled and infamed her person and cuntry, and made her Courte as a trappe, by this damnable and detestable arte, to intangle in sinne and ouerthrowe the yonger sorte of the nobilitye and gentlemen of the lande, whereby she is become notorious to the worlde, & in other cuntryes a comon fable for this her turpitude, which in so highe degre, namely in a woman and a Queene, deseruethe not onelie deposition, but all vengeaunce bothe of God and man, and cannot be tollerated without the eternal infamie of our whole cuntrie. . . .
>
> (xix, B2r)[9]

The illegitimacy of her birth and of her capacity to rule merge in this diatribe, which imagines Elizabeth's nymphomania transforming her realm into an effeminate "cuntry," emasculating and debauching its youth, and bringing infamy to England. Elizabeth's attackers hence transform the victim of slander into a source of defamation.

The treatment of Elizabeth's parentage in fact provides a paradigm for the ways in which sexual slander was used to control a woman's assertion of authority. It is now assumed by most historians of the period that Anne Boleyn was innocent of the charges that brought about her 1536 execution, a view apparently available in the Elizabethan period as well, since John Foxe styles her in his *Actes and Monuments* (1563) as a martyr whom he suspects was brought down by "some secret practising of the papists" (5: 136). However, popular stories of Anne as a treasonous witch and incestuous adulteress circulated from the time of her death well into the eighteenth century and are still current today (Warnicke 247). Henry VIII himself provided the basis for these slanders when, three years after his marriage to Anne, he charged her with adultery, incest, and treason, and had her executed and Elizabeth declared illegitimate. Foxe cites Anne's commitment to true religion as having provoked slander against her: "By reason whereof it may be easily considered, that this christian and devout Deborah could lack no enemies amongst such a number of Philistines, both within the realm, and without" (5: 136). Yet as the Second Act of Succession (1536) makes clear, it was Henry himself who removed the injunction against slanders of Anne and Elizabeth he had legislated earlier in the wake of criticisms over his divorce from Catherine of Aragon, in effect confirming and legalizing Catholic opinion in pardoning slanders against his second wife and her daughter:

> . . . the kings most roiall maiestie, most gratiouslie considering, that diuers and manie of thi most louing and obedient subiects now latelie afore the begining of the present parlement, haue spoken [etc.] . . . against the said vnlawfull mariage, solemnized betweene his highnesse and the said ladie Anne, and to the preiudice, slander disturbance and derogation thereof, but also to the perill, slander and disherison of the ladie Elizabeth the kings daughter illegitimat borne vnder the same mariage, and to the let, disturbance and interruption of the said ladie Elizabeth to the title of the crowne. . . . Which words, dooings, [etc.] albeit they proceeded of no malice, but vpon true and iust grounds, . . . yet neuerthelesse the kings said subiects might heereafter happen to be impeached, troubled and vexed for such their words, dooings, acts, [etc.] . . . The kings highnesse therefore of his most bountifull mercie and benignitie is pleased and contented that it be enacted . . . that all and singular his louing subiects, which haue spoken, . . . [etc.] against [the marriage, Anne, or Elizabeth], or to anie of their slanders, perils, or disherison: . . . shall be freelie and cleerelie pardoned, discharged, and released by authoritie of this act, of all those and such treasons and misprisions of treasons aboue mentioned.
>
> (28 Hen. VIII c. 7)

While Henry apparently believed the charges to be true, a sense still lingered that imputations against Anne and

Elizabeth had been considered defamatory in the past and might continue to be. Foxe tries to right this score by noting Henry's later change of mind as manifested in his last will, "wherein, expressly and by name, he did accept, and by plain ratification did allow, the succession of his marriage to stand good and lawful" (5: 136). Nevertheless, the Second Act of Succession remained on the statute books throughout Elizabeth's reign, licensing critics of her rule to deploy imputations of sexual impropriety against both Elizabeth and her mother.

The case of a king who falsely charges his wife with adultery, seeks to execute her, and bastardizes his daughter resonates strongly with the plot of *The Winter's Tale*, and in fact suggests a reading of the play as an allegory of Anne's downfall and Elizabeth's bastardization, seventy-five years after the fact. Horace Walpole expressed this opinion in 1769 in a digression from the main topic of his essay "Historic Doubts on the Life and Reign of King Richard the Third":

> . . . there is another of Shakespeare's plays, that may be ranked among the historic, though not one of his numerous critics and commentators have discovered the drift of it; I mean *The Winter Evening's Tale*, which was certainly intended (in compliment to queen Elizabeth) as an indirect apology for her mother Anne Boleyn. . . . The subject was too delicate to be exhibited on the stage without a veil; and it was too recent, and touched the queen too nearly, for the bard to have ventured so home an allusion on any other ground than compliment. The unreasonable jealousy of Leontes, and his violent conduct in consequence, form a true portrait of Henry the Eighth, who generally made the law the engine of his boisterous passions. . . . The Winter's Evening Tale was therefore in reality a second part of Henry the Eighth.
>
> (108-09)

Walpole's comments obviously contain inaccuracies, from the title of the play, to the date of its composition (he imagines it written during Elizabeth's lifetime), to its place in the Shakespearean chronology. Nonetheless, we find Walpole's reading of the play intriguing, and we propose to consider it at some length in the following pages. In the end, though, we mean not to suggest that Hermione's family and fatal career precisely correspond at every point to Anne Boleyn's, but to argue that *The Winter's Tale* entertains reminiscences both of the long-dead Anne and of her lately deceased daughter Elizabeth in order to expand consideration of the plight of the sexually slandered woman outside these defunct episodes. We are, then, precisely not making a "topical" argument regarding Anne Boleyn and *The Winter's Tale*; rather, we are arguing that while the historical issues the play engages are still current enough in the early seventeenth century to be familiar and thus useful, their use lies in their presenting a concluded and thus less controversial episode through which difficult contemporary problems surrounding gender might be explored.[10] Charges in the play that initially seem utterly specific to Hermione, and that seem uniquely to resonate with Anne Boleyn's case, begin to attach themselves to different female characters, including women of different generations and stations than Hermione's. In this regard we find it significant that *The Winter's Tale* glosses its own ostentatious historical gap of sixteen years as a matter of comparison and substitution. Just as Time promises both to measure and to obliterate the distinctions between past and present—"so shall I do / To th' freshest things now reigning, and make stale / The glistering of this present, as my tale / Now seems to it" (4.1.12-15)—so, too, do the play's female characters interchangeably occupy the slandered or slanderable positions occupied in turn by Anne Boleyn, Elizabeth Tudor, and their successors in both royal and non-royal positions: adulteress, witch, scold, virgin, bastard, bride.

One might argue, to concur for the moment with Walpole, that Leontes's apparently unmotivated jealousy begins to cohere only as a recollection of Henry VIII's rejection of Anne Boleyn. Not that Leontes is unreasonable because Henry was unreasonable (as Walpole argues), but rather that the play's bizarre accumulation of details around Leontes's suspicions recapitulates the bizarre accusations of adultery, incest, and treason through which Henry and his counselors, in the wake of Anne's failure to bear him a son, tried to make retrospective sense of Henry's wrecked lineal ambitions. For example, Leontes's reading of Hermione's hospitable reception of Polixenes—"But to be paddling palms, and pinching fingers, / As now they are, and making practis'd smiles / As in a looking-glass; and then to sigh, as 'twere / The mort o' th' deer" (1.2.115-18)—reiterates Henry's *ex post facto* conversion of Anne's Petrarchan flirtations with male courtiers into sexual, rather than social, intercourse. Although the five men charged with committing adultery with Anne represented the whole gamut of male positions at court (one musician, two grooms of the privy chamber, one former page of the king, and Anne's own brother George Boleyn, Viscount Rochford), all of them had attempted to advance their ambitions by playing the queen's courtly lovers, subscribing to what Eric Ives calls "the common currency of courtly dalliance" by claiming to love their sovereign's wife (366).[11] In the context of Anne's indictment, however, these interchanges became described as her "inciting . . . five men to have sexual relations with her by the use of touches and kisses that involved thrusting her tongue into their mouths and theirs in hers" (Warnicke 203). At issue seemed to be Anne's initiation of many of these mock flirtations as a way of consolidating her command of the royal household: Ives describes a conversation between Anne and one of the men later accused, Henry Norris, as her eliciting his political loyalty in the guise of his pledge of love (366). The same technique of the courtly lady commanding, rather than passively accepting, her lovers' pledges would later be used to great effect by Anne's daughter Elizabeth; but in Anne's case, this inversion of gender hierarchy came to be interpreted as a prelude to sexual malfeasance. As with Hermione and Leontes, it is a short step from the queen declaring "a lady's Verily's / As potent as a lord's" (1.1.50-51) to the king surmising that she "arms her with the boldness of a wife / To her allowing husband!" (1.2.184-85).

Like Anne Boleyn, Hermione is accused of adultery, treason, and conspiracy to murder the king, but hovering around those charges is another, stranger imputation that also haunted Anne: the imputation of witchcraft. Retha Warnicke has recently argued, suggestively if not conclusively, that Henry's horror of witchcraft was the primary reason he initiated proceedings to rid himself of Anne. On 29 January 1536, Anne was delivered of a stillborn male fetus whom the midwives probably thought deformed (Warnicke 201-03); witches were believed to give birth to deformed children. This circumstance, Warnicke contends, explains the care taken in the indictments of Anne to describe her as preternaturally seductive of both Henry and her adulterous lovers, initiating those "mortally sinful" tongue-thrusting kisses (Warnicke 203). Leontes is similarly disturbed by what he perceives as "[k]issing with inside lip" (1.2.286); witchcraft statutes cite "the intent to provoke any person to unlawful love" as actionable (5 Eliz. c. 16, qtd. in Rosen 56). At issue was not only the witch's provocation of men to desire, an action of course not unique to witches, but her intent to engage them thereby in unlawful, unnatural sexual acts that might in turn bring down God's punishment of a monstrous child. As well, Henry's concern that he had been bewitched might have moved him to declare himself a cuckold not only once, but five times over, since if Henry had fathered a child stillborn through witchcraft, then he himself might have been tainted through sexual contact with the witch's womb. On the other hand, sexual concourse with a witch was commonly thought to induce male impotence, a malady from which Henry evidently suffered, according to evidence given by Anne's brother George at his trial. The fact that George Boleyn's evidence was allowed to stand in the record is taken by Warnicke as evidence that Henry wanted his impotence with Anne to be made known, so that he could not possibly have fathered her monstrous son (216). Paradoxically, then, Henry's conversion of himself into a cuckold, and an impotent cuckold at that, allowed him to inoculate his patrilineage against the witch's sexual influence.

We are not qualified to assess whether Warnicke is right to hinge Anne's downfall on Henry's belief in her witchcraft. However, the rumors of witchery that sprang up against Anne and that persisted in the popular literature do bear reading in connection with *The Winter's Tale*'s treatment of uncertain paternity. Although witchcraft is a charge leveled not against Hermione but rather against Paulina, as we will discuss below, witchcraft's presumed effects on paternity—presumptions that distill and warp a whole constellation of early modern phobias about women's sexuality and women's authority—nevertheless haunt the margins of Leontes's irrational suspicions about Mamillius's parentage. Janet Adelman has described Leontes's contradictory responses to his son as gyrating attempts to purge himself of contact with feminine sexuality; while at one moment Leontes envisions Mamillius as his duplicate,

a product of fantasized parthenogenesis, at another moment Mamillius's resemblance to Hermione ("Though he does bear some signs of me, yet you / Have too much blood in him" [2.1.57-58]) causes Leontes further to recoil from Hermione's sexual desire and his own acquiescence to it (Adelman 224-28). Leontes ignores similar evidence of resemblance in the case of his baby daughter ("Although the print be little, the whole matter / And copy of the father" [2.3.98-99]) in order to declare her a bastard; one assumes that he discounts this evidence because of its source, Paulina, whose own forthrightness brings on her the charge of witchcraft that had never been elucidated against Hermione. But once the word "witch" has been uttered in connection with Paulina's refusal to keep silence, then Hermione's eloquent defense of herself, too, carries the tinge of female witchery—not solely, as Karen Newman has noted, because the witch's speech is heard in public, but because her speech coopts vehicles of hegemonic language: for early modern witches, prayers and the liturgy (66-70); for Hermione, the Oracle. But Hermione's speech, like that of the early modern witches who came to trial, and like that of Anne Boleyn at her own trial, falls on ears not prone to be seduced again. Like Anne, who pleaded her innocence with "so wise and discreet answers to all things laid against her, excusing herself with her words so clearly as though she had never been faulty to the same" (Ives 387),[12] Hermione is nonetheless ignored by her accuser, as is the Oracle that affirms her case.

Ignored, that is, until Leontes receives news that his son, "with mere conceit and fear / Of the queen's speed" (3.2.144-45), is dead. Here, then, is where Leontes begins to part company from Henry VIII, and where we have to gauge the effects of the play's slippage from a strict reproduction of 1530s events. Mamillius's resemblance to his father, along with the fact that he is a well-formed boy, not a monstrous fetus, bars Leontes from Henry's strategy of declaring that his son could not possibly be his. Thus, whereas for Henry the death of his unborn son constituted evidence for condemning the witch and her offspring, for Leontes the death of his son is, at last, convincing evidence of his own tyranny (3.2.146-47). *The Winter's Tale* thus airs Henry's warped reasoning only to expose it as precisely that, warped: "I have too much believ'd mine own suspicion" (3.2.151). Unlike Henry, who at the time of Anne's trial had already made preparations to further his patrilineal ambitions with a new wife, Leontes admits the Oracle's judgment that "the king shall live without an heir, if that which is lost be not found" (3.2.134-36), and accepts Paulina's stricture that he not remarry. In this way *The Winter's Tale* shifts its topical perspective from a Henrician era to a Jacobean stance. In a post-Elizabethan light Leontes's family seems in fact to revise and reverse Henry's, so that Mamillius begins to resemble not Anne's malformed, stillborn son, but the lamented Edward VI, cut down in his youth; and the baby, presumed dead, whose recovery saves the nation, resembles Elizabeth herself, who underwent a kind of internal exile and near-martyrdom (as Foxe reminded his readers) in her years of waiting to assume the throne from her sister Mary Tudor.

This displacement of historical judgment forward in time, called attention to by Time's own displacement of events in act 4, accounts in part for the possibility of reading the play's treatment of queenly reputation in multiple layers: Hermione's plight is replicated and redeemed in her daughter's, just as Anne Boleyn's reputation came to be absorbed and recuperated in Elizabeth's, and subsequently shadowed in the next Elizabeth, the Stuart princess. We wish briefly to consider the consequences of reading the second half of *The Winter's Tale* in light of Elizabethan and Jacobean reconstructions of Anne's downfall, with the aim of suggesting that the play's refracted treatments of the case of the slandered queen eventually unmoor the play from concerns specific only to royal women.

At first blush, the sixteen-year-old Perdita seems to continue to recollect Elizabeth Tudor, this time as an adult seeking to reform her mother's reputation. Perdita's concern for her chastity—to whose loss she seems to be darkly alluding when she avers that, faced with the wrath of his father, Florizel "must change this purpose" of marrying her "[o]r I my life" (4.4.39-40)—coalesces with her hatred for the grafted flowers she calls "nature's bastards" (4.4.83); and her refusal to plant these artificed and hence whorelike flowers demonstrates her desire to mend, in her own childbearing, any hint of bastardy: "No more than, were I painted, I would wish / This youth should say 'twere well, and only therefore / Desire to breed by me" (4.4.101-03). In this fashion, Perdita recalls Queen Elizabeth's steadfast maintenance of her virginity, which, many historians surmise, may have been motivated in part by her wish to expunge the nation's memory of Anne Boleyn's disastrous childbearing career as well as her own sporadic illegitimacy. As Frye describes her, Elizabeth early in her reign in fact sounded a great deal like Perdita: her coronation entry symbolically promised a queen who would be both fertile and wise, while at the same time it emphasized Elizabeth as the legitimate product of a legitimate royal marriage (33-36).[13] Later, of course, as it became clear that Elizabeth would not marry, the prospect of her fertility was dropped in favor of her sexual purity—and that virginity became a figure, as Peter Stallybrass has argued, for an inviolable England, an island nation defending its embattled borders against all comers. In the years leading up to and following the 1588 threat of Spanish invasion, Elizabeth's chastity admonished England to preserve its Protestantism and its sovereignty; together, England's religion and England's nationhood substituted for a child of Elizabeth's body as Elizabeth's "issue" (Sandler 164). And that admonition includes reminiscences of Anne Boleyn, converted (largely by means of Foxe's widely read *Actes and Monuments*) into a Protestant saint.[14]

In this regard even a slight romance like Robert Greene's *Pandosto*, Shakespeare's source for the plot of *The Winter's Tale*, might be read as a recuperation of Anne's reputation, and in turn Elizabeth's. Indeed, *Pandosto* provides an interesting initial case for our suggestion that Anne's story might be revived and revised to fit changing historical circumstances. Published in 1588, the year of the Armada and one year after the execution of Mary Queen of Scots, *Pandosto* capitalized on a historical moment in which the sexual status of queens was under intense scrutiny: even while English propagandists continued to publish accounts of Mary Queen of Scots as not only treasonous but also licentious, Catholic propagandists responded by describing Elizabeth as positively wolfish in her sexual appetites. Moreover, these Catholic accounts hurry to refer to Anne Boleyn as a means of further muddying Elizabeth's reputation.[15] *Pandosto*'s plot, in this milieu, seems to gather up English anxiety about the possibility of a sexual queen only to clear the queen's name.[16]

Pandosto's continued popularity—it went through six editions before *The Winter's Tale*'s first recorded performance in 1611 (Greene, *Perymedes* xxx-xxxii)—might be attributable, at least in part, to the continued resonance of the issue of queenly sexuality even after Elizabeth's death. As Barry Weller and Margaret Ferguson have recently argued, in the second decade of the seventeenth century Anne Boleyn's reputation was still a matter of religious and literary controversy.[17] Catholic polemicist Nicholas Sander's *De origine et progressu schismatis Anglicani*, first published in 1585, had gone through its sixth European edition in 1610: this work promotes a perception of Anne as witchlike, detailing her prodigious promiscuity as well as her physical disfigurements (Warnicke 247). On the other hand, historian and Protestant apologist John Speed asserts in his 1611 *History of Great Britaine*—a work Shakespeare consulted before writing *Henry VIII* circa 1611-13 (*Henry VIII* xxxv) and thus may have had to hand as he was writing or revising *The Winter's Tale*—that Anne Boleyn's "adulteries," like Hermione's, were merely a matter of misread queenly benevolence: "I haue heard it reported that [George Boleyn, Viscount] *Rochford* the Queenes brother comming to her bed side to solicite a suite, leaned thereupon to whisper her in the eare; which the Spials gaue forth that hee did so, to kisse the Queen" (771).[18] Placing *The Winter's Tale*'s plot in conjunction with a writer like Speed suggests a further displacement and revision of the slanderable queen in order to suit Jacobean circumstances. If the anticipated marriage of *The Winter's Tale*'s Perdita indeed refers, as David Bergeron has argued, to the 1613 wedding of Elizabeth Stuart to the Protestant Elector Palatine (*Shakespeare's Romances* 157, 160), then we might see Shakespeare's play as part of a national effort to recuperate Elizabeth Tudor as a new, less threatening Elizabeth, one who safeguards her chastity so that she may eventually deliver it into her husband's keeping.[19] This reading metamorphoses Perdita into James's daughter Elizabeth Stuart, and Hermione into an amalgamated and purified Anne Boleyn and Elizabeth Tudor. Hermione's reputation is so thoroughly cleared that her own sexuality, upon her revival, entirely disappears: like Elizabeth Tudor the Protestant martyr, her concern is only for the welfare of her daughter, the future of the nation.

In the end, though, *The Winter's Tale*'s centrifugal movement away from Anne Boleyn's historically limited case also moves the play beyond merely a study of queens' susceptibility to sexual slander. A focus solely on royal women past and present would allow *The Winter's Tale* to be a play more like *Henry VIII*—that is, a play whose final emphasis is on England's unsullied national lineage and national reputation, in which "when / The bird of wonder dies, the maiden phoenix, / Her ashes new create another heir / As great in admiration as herself" (5.4.39-42). And admittedly *Pandosto,* which contains all of the plot elements of *The Winter's Tale* that we have discussed so far, would be a sufficient text for our consideration of reputation in connection to queens. However, *The Winter's Tale* does not restrict its representation of slander and female criminality to a creative reworking of Anne's and Elizabeth's sexual and reproductive careers. As queens, these women experienced lives quite different from those of other women in the early modern period. Yet queens were also considered exemplary, just as the accusations that Hermione, Perdita, and even Paulina suffer are versions of those which many women had to face. *The Winter's Tale*'s two departures from *Pandosto*'s plot—the voice of Paulina, and the revival of the queen—prove crucial to our consideration here. Particularly in the context of these two original additions to Greene, Shakespeare's play pointedly returns its female characters to circumstances familiar to slandered early modern women of all classes; in other words, the play departs from allegories of queens into fictions of law. But in the process, the play also radically reinvents early modern legal culture in order to reread positively the nexus of female sexuality and authority that is so troubling to the patriarchal order, both of the play and of early modern England.

David Underdown explores the "crisis of order" in early modern England in terms of gender strains resulting from women's economic independence, suggesting that public anxieties about scolds, witches, and physically or sexually rebellious women, increasingly expressed between 1560 and 1660, are different manifestations of a similar response to opportunities for female economic autonomy (121, 135-36). Interestingly, Underdown does not consider Elizabeth's rule as a potentially contributing factor to this phenomenon. As a woman authorized to rule over men, she is the scold *par excellence,* and capable of obliquely but emphatically asserting her superiority to a male Parliament, as in her 1566 speech on marriage and succession, where she twice exclaimed that "it is monstrous that the feet should direct the head" (Rice 79, 81). It was precisely this specter of female regiment that was punished when scolds were "enthroned" on cucking stools, or "cuckqueans," and ducked in water (Boose 190, 195). Lynda Boose's remarks on the scold's nexus of verbal and sexual transgression are useful to contrast with our current discussion:

> . . . the talkative woman is frequently imagined as synonymous with the sexually available woman, her open mouth the signifier for invited entrance elsewhere. Hence the dictum that associates "silent" with "chaste" and stigmatizes women's public speech as a behavior fraught with cultural signs resonating with a distinctly sexual kind of shame.
>
> (196)

The Winter's Tale explicitly counters this nexus, within the context of a recuperation of Elizabeth's heritage and authority, by showing female outspokenness as compatible with and appropriate to female virtue and chastity, linking instead male speech with shame and the disruption of patriarchal succession.

Breaking the link between women's authority and their sexual malfeasance, however, requires *The Winter's Tale* to represent slanders against women, such as the imputation of scolding, as crimes with negative consequences for the social order, a representation that runs counter to most legal understandings of the problem in early modern England. First, it would be difficult to imagine that a king's accusations, regardless of their veracity or his motivations, could ever have been construed as constituting defamation. And even if this were possible, Leontes's words against Hermione would probably not have constituted defamation according to the ecclesiastical definition, because he believes the truth of his statements; he apparently does not speak them out of malice, and he pursues his allegations against her through legal channels (Ingram 295).[20] In only one limited and anomalous legal arena would sexual slanders against early modern Englishwomen have been understood as resulting in monetary loss or social unrest: the court of Star Chamber, in which a husband might complain that he, his wife, and the community at large were damaged by sexual slanders against her. Although the Star Chamber apparently takes cognizance only of a threat to a husband's reputation, it nevertheless registers that, since his reputation substantially depends on his wife's, sexual slander against her has a serious impact.[21] Only the court of Star Chamber, then, acknowledges the dilemma sexual slander poses for the patriarchy: even while it may circumscribe a woman's sexual behavior, it may also dismantle the family name.

The Winter's Tale raises this legal exception to the status of legal commonplace. In the world of the play, the horns of this patriarchal dilemma are exposed in the king's desire to protect his own honor while exposing the queen's dishonor. He asks Camillo,

> Dost think I am so muddy, so unsettled,
> To appoint myself in this vexation; sully
> The purity and whiteness of my sheets,
> (Which to preserve is sleep, which being spotted
> Is goads, thorns, nettles, tails of wasps)
> Give scandal to the blood o' th' prince, my son,
> . . . . .
> Without ripe moving to 't?
>
> (1.2.325-32)

The answer to this question, given Leontes's dislike of his wife's persuasive power over Polixenes, is yes: his accusations against her immediately defuse her influence in court.

But despite his status as king and his belief in his own allegations, Leontes's imputations against Hermione are clearly marked as slander causing widespread social damage. Paulina most evidently articulates the harm caused by threats to female reputation:

> . . . for he,
> The sacred honour of himself, his queen's,
> His hopeful son's, his babe's, betrays to slander,
> Whose sting is sharper than the sword's. . . .
>
> (2.3.83-86)

Strikingly, she focuses on the fact that his accusations harm not only his wife and children, but his own honor. The slander against Hermione transforms into a self-slander: "this most cruel usage of your queen / . . . will ignoble make you, / Yea, scandalous to the world" (2.3.116, 119-20). Even the king acknowledges early in the proceedings, if for the wrong reasons, that his animus against Hermione and her alleged co-conspirators only serves to damage him: "The very thought of my revenges . . . / Recoil upon me" (2.3.19-20). Later, Leontes is indeed shown that his slanders have serious consequences for his own reputation, his happiness, and the stability of his rule (3.2.185-202). Similarly, the false imputation of sexual impropriety that Polixenes makes against Perdita, and that threatens to replay the tragedy of her mother, is shown to wreak damage on the speaker, not the victim. Responding to his father's violent rebuke and sexual slander of Perdita, Florizel resolves to himself,

> . . . then
> Let nature crush the sides o' th' earth together,
> And mar the seeds within! . . .
> From my succession wipe me, father. . . .
>
> (4.4.478-81)

Polixenes will face the same loss of an heir and the same uncertain succession that Leontes is grappling with; in both cases, sexual slanders against women are shown to pose dangerous national consequences. But they also endanger, if on a higher social register, the legitimacy and respectability on which even middling classes depended for credit relations and for securing property transfer through inheritance.[22]

The play's rereading and transformation of the process of contemporary slander law for women is similarly employed in its representation of female criminality generally. Hermione, Paulina, and Perdita all are essentially defamed to the extent that they are falsely accused of a considerable number of transgressions; their manifest innocence serves not only to discredit the speakers of the imputations, but also to call into question the construction of commonly defined popular notions of women and crime. Paulina's role in particular broadens the play's scope to consider a number of slanders commonly directed toward women. Leontes consistently deploys the rhetoric used to describe scolds in his attempts to delegitimate and silence Paulina's speech. She is a "callat / Of boundless tongue, who late hath beat her husband, / And now baits me!" (2.3.90-92); her rebelliousness moves beyond her husband and threatens her king. He asks Antigonus, "canst not rule her?" (46), and charges he is "woman-tir'd, unroosted / By thy Dame Parlet here" (74-75), a "lozel, . . . worthy to be hang'd / That wilt not stay her tongue" (108-09). Antigonus, however, rejects the charges by responding in kind, but with a difference: "When she will take the rein I let her run; / But she'll not stumble" (51-52). The punishment of "bridling" was often imagined as a fit fate for early modern scolds (see Boose); Antigonus invokes this punishment only to demonstrate its inapplicability to the current circumstances. Paulina is also called a witch (67), a bawd (either a prostitute or a purveyor of prostitutes) (68), a traitor (81), and, by implication, a heretic (113-15); these, or similar charges of sexual or hierarchical transgression (including bastardy), are also laid at the feet of Hermione and/or Perdita. But these accusations are already defused before they are spoken, since not only the play's audience but also the other characters within the play are aware of their baselessness.

The irrationality of these imputations begins to put pressure on the logic of patriarchy itself. When Leontes remarks disparagingly that Antigonus "dreads his wife," again evoking the specter of the scold, Paulina retorts, "So I would you did; then 'twere past all doubt / You'd call your children yours" (2.3.79-81). The popular ideology that held women physically, intellectually, and morally inferior to men depends on the proposition that wives are more susceptible to sinning and cannot be trusted. In *The Winter's Tale,* in contrast, a husband who looks up to rather than down on his wife can trust that her integrity will keep her faithful to him. Paulina emphasizes the stupidity of Leontes's jealousy, by way of insisting on the legitimacy of his second child, in her catalogue of his similarities to his newborn daughter. She concludes:

> And thou, good goddess Nature, which hast made it
> So like to him that got it, if thou hast
> The ordering of the mind too, 'mongst all colours
> No yellow in 't, lest she suspect, as he does,
> Her children not her husband's!
>
> (2.3.103-07)

J. H. P. Pafford, the editor of the New Arden edition of the play, brings in a Leontesian note on these lines by suggesting that Paulina says the opposite of what she means here, "i.e., that it is the deliberate expression by Shakespeare of the kind of mistake which an excited woman might easily make" (49n106-07). But the absurdity here is not Paulina's, but Leontes's: as Pafford alternatively glosses, Perdita's doubting the fatherhood of her own children would be just as irrational as her father's baseless fears.

It is interesting to note that while slanders against women were relegated to the less powerful and the less lucrative jurisdiction of the ecclesiastical courts, slanders by women (often against men) were given the separate category of

*Act II, scene iii. By W.M. Craig.
Leontes, Antigonus, Lords, servants,
Paulina, and Perdita.*

scolding that received disproportionate attention in popular literature and vigorous initiative in the means of communal punishment (see Boose, Underdown). Strikingly, the play also departs from social and legal practice in vindicating Paulina's "scolding." At the moment when her charges appear to cross the line dividing truth and slander, when she comes closest to fitting the stereotype of a scold, Leontes justifies her speech. "Go on, go on: / Thou canst not speak too much; I have deserv'd / All tongues to talk their bitt'rest" (3.2.214-16). In contrast to Henry VIII's licensing defamations against Anne and Elizabeth to deflect infamy from himself, here the king licenses, in effect, defamations against himself as punishment for the infamy he has brought on his wife. While a bystanding lord chastises Paulina, and she remorsefully berates herself for showing "too much / The rashness of a woman" (220-21), Leontes insists on the validity of her words: "Thou didst speak but well / When most the truth: which I receive much better / Than to be pitied of thee" (232-34). Paulina's speaking is recuperated at its most radical and potentially most criminal moment, suggesting the need to reevaluate the category of scolding and the motivations behind its punishment.

Similarly, the charges of witchcraft leveled at Paulina in act 2 are dismissed at the play's end precisely when they are most credible. Leontes invokes the dangerous discourse of witchcraft in remarking on the astonishingly lifelike figure of Hermione:

> . . . O royal piece!
> There's magic in thy majesty, which has
> My evils conjur'd to remembrance, and
> From thy admiring daughter took the spirits,
> Standing like stone with thee.
>
> (5.3.38-42)

All of the statutes legislated against witchcraft in the sixteenth century particularly forbid the invocation of evil spirits; here, in contrast, the conjuration is marvelous and cathartic, reminding Leontes of his past deeds and uniting the spirits of Perdita with those of her mother. Leontes's licensing of the magic that here commences is all the more remarkable considering that Paulina, again the focus of anxiety over female authority, again expresses that anxiety herself, anticipating that others will make the charge of witchcraft against her:

> I'll make the statue move indeed; descend,
> And take you by the hand: but then you'll think
> (Which I protest against) I am assisted
> By wicked powers.
>
> (5.3.88-91)

She refers twice more to the possibility that some will suspect "it is unlawful business / I am about" (96-97, 105), even while making use of language associated with witches' practices as she addresses the statue: "Come! / I'll fill your grave up . . . / Bequeath to death your numbness; for from him / Dear life redeems you" (100-103). The witchcraft act passed by Parliament in 1604 forbids anyone to

> use practise or exercise any invocation or conjuration of any evil and wicked spirit . . . ; or take up any dead man, woman, or child out of his, her, or their grave, or any other place where the dead body resteth, . . . to be employed or used in any manner of witchcraft, sorcery, charm, or enchantment.
>
> (1 Jac. I c. 12, qtd. in Rosen 57)

With the threat of female transgression once more hanging in the air, Leontes steps in to validate the transgression itself: "If this be magic, let it be an art / Lawful as eating" (110-11). He is still not sure if magic is behind the revivification of his wife, but even so, he insists on the legitimacy of Paulina's actions.

The slanders spoken against Hermione, Perdita, and Paulina in the course of *The Winter's Tale* give a sense of how female criminality was understood at the time, but these accusations are shown, ultimately, to be constructs of male anxiety without basis in reality. The qualities associated with female transgression in early modern society are instead presented as valuable; rather than destabilizing the social order, Paulina's "offenses" serve, ultimately, to restore order and succession to Leontes's realm. This is not to say that disruptions to the social order do not occur in the play; damage is done, however, not by the women accused but by their male accusers. All three women suffer losses as a result of masculine defamations in the play, but perhaps the biggest loser, from a patriarchal perspective, is Leontes himself. If early modern patriarchal wisdom finds value in a less than vigorous redress of slanders against women, the play insists on the severity of those slanders' damages, not only to Hermione, Paulina, and Perdita, but especially to Leontes and his entire kingdom in the loss of a male heir.[23] The danger here lies not in female criminal behavior but in criminalizing female behavior.

We are suggesting that *The Winter's Tale* takes a feminist stance in relation to early modern law, though by "feminist" we do not mean the kind of thoroughgoing overthrow of patriarchal principles that would be indicated in a late twentieth-century use of the term. Rather, the play proposes women as integral and morally reliable caretakers of the patriarchal project of lineal inheritance; proposes that women's sexual reputations are to be treated as equal before the law to men's economic livelihoods; and, perhaps most audaciously, proposes that women have the authority to define those sexual reputations for themselves. However, Paulina's repeated, almost anxious iteration of the lawfulness of her actions serves as a reminder of women's tenuous stance before the law in early modern English society. After all, the radical claims that we argue *The Winter's Tale* advances are made within a play whose title suggests its very fictionality as well as its superannuation.[24] This improbability is further stressed by the play's disruption of the classical unities of action, place, and, most self-consciously, time. Time's choric appearance draws attention to the artificiality of his role, but also to its legality:

> I that please some, try all: both joy and terror
> Of good and bad, that makes and unfolds error,
> Now take upon me, in the name of Time,
> To use my wings. Impute it not a crime
> To me, or my swift passage, that I slide
> O'er sixteen years, and leave the growth untried
> Of that wide gap, since it is in my power
> To o'erthrow law, and in one self-born hour
> To plant and o'erwhelm custom.
>
> (4.1.1-9)

The strange self-referentiality of this speech (3-4) intensifies its implausibility even as Time authorizes his capacity to make or break law. His ability to judge (with the pun on "trial" in line 1) is indicated, yet he also expresses the fear of slander (4). He has the power to determine or dismiss law, but he must ask permission of the audience to skip these years and apologizes for the inconvenience (15, 29-32). The ambivalence Time voices in this speech articulates the difficult project of the play. Shakespeare stages a tale "stale [to] / The glistering of this present" (4.1.13-14), the bygone gender controversies embedded in the lives and deaths of Anne Boleyn and Elizabeth Tudor, as a vehicle for the very lively and disruptive current debates over women in early seventeenth-century England. In cautiously revivifying dead queens—and Time's appearance suggests that this recuperation is dependent on the hiatus—the play opens up a space, if an uncertain space, within which to begin a critique of current gender politics. Whether this fantastical tale found fertile ground in the legal culture of the seventeenth century is a question that future scholars of women's legal history will need to explore and answer.

Notes

The authors wish to thank Frances Dolan for her comments on an earlier draft of this essay; the members of Lindsay Kaplan's graduate and honors seminars in Women in Renaissance Law and Drama for their stimulating discussions of the essay's issues; and Laura Deal, Margaret Ferguson, Ralph Hexter, and Marjorie McIntosh for crucial scholarly advice.

1. As J. A. Sharpe notes, "Female crime, except for witchcraft, perhaps, is a subject which has so far attracted surprisingly little attention, one facet of the regrettably undeveloped nature of the study of women's history in the early modern period" (*Crime* 108); he cites Carol Wiener's and J. M. Beattie's articles as exceptions. Since the appearance of these essays, some important inroads have been made into this field, such as the work by Boose, Cioni, Dolan, Erickson, Ingram, and Spring, to mention just a few studies pertinent to the sixteenth and seventeenth centuries. For a consideration of defamation and gender that often parallels the views of our essay, see Jardine.

2. The content of the words spoken and their results also determined the jurisdiction for redress, as the common-law and ecclesiastical courts divided responsibility for remedying this wrong. For a rigorous account of the historical development of defamation in both the ecclesiastical and common-law courts in England, see Helmholz.

3. In her chapter "Finding What Has Been 'Lost': Representations of Infanticide and *The Winter's Tale*" Frances Dolan points out that this crime usually associated with mothers is linked in Shakespeare's play to a father, who is then excused of the crime (159-70). Because it is not explicitly linked with female criminality in the play, we omit consideration of infanticide in our essay.

4. Treatments of Elizabeth as successfully wielding a masculine persona depend upon unskeptically accepting that the legal doctrine of the King's Two Bodies served to expunge the monarch's political persona of all perceived weakness, including the weakness of being a woman. Such a belief has marred otherwise fine readings of, for example, Shakespeare's comedies (Marcus, "Shakespeare's Comic Heroines") and Spenser's *Faerie Queene* (Miller); for more complex analyses, see Marcus's revised account of Elizabeth's "composite" identity (*Puzzling* 51-105); Eggert, "Ravishment" (3-16);

Frye (12-19); and especially Levin's chapter "Elizabeth as King and Queen" (121-48).

5. Such a representation of Elizabeth as defender of the faith could be used both for and against James I and Charles I; see Woolf.

6. *The Diary of Sir Simonds D'Ewes, 1622-1624,* ed. E. Bourcier (Paris, 1974), 142, qtd. in Woolf 179.

7. One of the defining "incidents" determining redress of defamation in an ecclesiastical court was that the suit be "merely 'for the soul's health': in no circumstances could cash damages be awarded" (Ingram 296). Although in special circumstances offenders could request that their penance be commuted to a fine, these monies were paid to "poor relief and other pious objects," not to the victims (Ingram 336-37). While women were allowed to sue in common law for defamation if they could prove damages (Ingram 296; see the case of Davyes v. Gardiner, in which the competing jurisdictions are discussed [Baker and Milsom 627-28]), the vast majority of common-law slander cases list male plaintiffs. It should, however, be pointed out that most married women in the period did not have separate legal and, therefore, financial identities from those of their husbands (Baker 550-57).

8. Gowing claims that defamers "twisted [these materials] towards other ends than the original intention" (10). However, we would argue that both unauthorized and authorized commentators on female behavior, both slanderers and tract-writers, share the common aim of circumscribing female sexual behavior. See Kaplan for an exploration of slander's employment in general as a tool for punishment and humiliation. While the punishment for defamation in the ecclesiastical courts called for a humiliating public penance, it is clear from the small percentage of final sentences that many slanderers did not endure the same public embarrassment experienced by their victims (Ingram 336-37, 317-18).

9. As Bruce Boehrer explains, the charges of incest leveled against Elizabeth's parentage were by no means consistent: the same Catholic polemicist might call Elizabeth both the product of Henry's and Anne's incestuous marriage, and the product of Anne's incest with her brother George (47-48).

10. Richard Wilson also briefly notes the analogies between Hermione and Anne Boleyn in his discussion of early modern medical discourse and its shift toward male scrutiny and control of gynecological and obstetrical study and practice (134-35).

11. However, two of the five men charged were also suspected of sodomy. Buggery was also popularly implicated in early modern English discourses of incest and witchcraft, two of the charges against Anne (Warnicke 191-95). The homosexual transgression underlying accusations of the queen's "lovers" may be echoed by homoerotic tensions between Leontes and Polixenes in act 1 of *The Winter's Tale.*

12. The speaker is contemporary chronicler Charles Wriothesley, whose sympathy toward Anne is remarkable considering that he argued Catherine of Aragon's divorce to be unjust (Ives 387).

13. This was one emphasis made in Elizabeth's coronation procession through London; at Gracechurch, she was presented with "a stage of three tiers. . . . In the lowest were Henry VII and his Queen; in the next—happy sight after twenty-two years!—Henry VIII and Anne Boleyn; in the highest, Elizabeth" (Neale 61).

14. The 1587 edition of Holinshed's *Chronicles,* for example, after referring the reader to Foxe for a refutation of "the sinister iudgements, opinions and obiections of backebiters against that vertuous queene," digresses into Christopher Ocland's 1582 poem Ειρηναρχια Siue Elizabetha (miscited as another 1580s poem by Ocland, *Anglorum prælia*), which describes Anne as having a prophetic vision of her death and its ultimately triumphant Elizabethan consequences:

> Anglorum prælia saith, that this good queene was forwarned of hir death in a dreame, wherein Morpheus the god of sleepe (in the likenesse of hir grandfather) appeared vnto hir, and after a long narration of the vanities of this world (how enuie reigneth in the courts of princes, maligning the fortunate estate of the vertuous, how king Henrie the eight and his issue should be the vtter ouerthrow and expulsion of poperie out of England, and that the gouernment of queene Elizabeth should be established in tranquillitie & peace) he saith vnto hir in conclusion by waie of prophesie, as our poet hath recorded:
>
> Forti sis animo, tristis si nuncius adsum,
> Insperata tuæ velox necis aduenit hora,
> Intra triginta spacium moriere dierum:
> Hoc magnum mortis solamen habeto futuræ,
> Elizabetha suis præclarè filia gestis
> Nomen ad astra feret patris, matrísque, suúmque.
>
> (3: 797)

J. Sharrock's 1585 translation of Ocland's poem renders these lines as follows:

> Be not in minde dismayde, though mestiue message I foreshow,
> The houre vnlookt for of thine end, with swift course on doth draw,
> For within thirtie dayes, thou shalt outgasp thys vitall breath.
> Howbeit this solace great, of me receaue, before thy death:
> *Elizabeth* through wondrous actes, to starrs shall lift the name,

Both of her selfe, and mightie Sier, and most renowmed dame.

(B4v-C1r)

Anne's vision of Elizabeth's stellification of her parentage helps to carry out, in the 1580s, the cultural work of national self-defense: even as the Armada approaches England, Elizabeth's reign is imagined as one of "tranquillitie & peace." Small wonder that Ocland's poem was reprinted in 1589, just after the Armada year.

15. Adam Blackwood, in his 1587 *Martyre de la Royne d'Escosse,* declared that Anne "had buck teeth, six fingers on her left hand, and a large lump under her double chin; she was used as a whore by the principal courtiers of England and France, and was a Lutheran" (Phillips 174).

16. To our knowledge, *Pandosto* has not been given a topical reading in regard to events of the late 1580s, even though Greene was more than capable of capitalizing upon current events for the plots of his fiction: his *Spanish Masquerado,* for example, published the year after the Armada defeat, issues broadsides against the entire Spanish monarchy and military command, finally to conclude that England and its queen have been blest among nations. For Greene's canny expansion of his audience base for *Pandosto* via its combination of elite and popular literary forms, see Newcomb.

17. In their recent edition of Elizabeth Cary's *Tragedy of Mariam,* a play published in 1613 and probably composed at some time in the preceding decade, Weller and Ferguson argue that Anne Boleyn's story is a subtext both for Salome, the lascivious female villain of the piece, and Mariam, the virtuous and martyred second wife of the tyrant Herod (Cary 30-35); this refraction of the slandered queen into several personae is similar to the one we are describing in *The Winter's Tale.* The fact that a Jacobean writer like Cary, who eventually converted to Catholicism, might be ambivalent about Anne's moral status indicates, we think, the urgency of England's continuing cultural need to fix the queen's sexual reputation, even in the aftermath of queenship.

18. Suggestively, Speed marginally cites "Robert Greene" for his account of Anne's scaffold speech; however, we have been unable to discover a work in which Greene described Anne's death, or a speech from one of Greene's fictional imperiled women that would match the words Speed gives to Anne.

19. Katherine Eggert has argued the point of Hermione's desexualization of Elizabeth in an unpublished paper, "'The Statue Is But Newly Fix'd': Remembering Queenship in *The Winter's Tale* (Or, the Queen's No Body)." Glynne Wickham suggests that Hermione's statue would have reminded the play's original audience of Elizabeth's and Mary Queen of Scots's recently installed effigies in Westminster Abbey; Bergeron further postulates that the statue would have evoked memories of both Elizabeth's funeral effigy of 1603 and Henry Stuart's of 1612 ("Restoration" 132).

20. It should be emphasized here that, in all likelihood, Henry VIII also believed the charges he leveled against Anne (Warnicke 235), and like Leontes, pursued his accusations through a court proceeding. But although Henry won his case, the sense of the potential similarity of his claims and the slanders spoken against Anne earlier in her marriage to him registers obliquely in the Second Succession Act quoted above.

21. A definition of criminal defamation or libel, usually a written detraction either of a prominent figure or of someone else whose slandering led to a breach of the peace, developed in Star Chamber in the sixteenth and seventeenth centuries; the court meted out damages and punishments in passing sentence (Holdsworth 5: 201-12; Baker 137). In a sampling of Star Chamber defamation cases litigated around the turn of the sixteenth century, five of the twenty-four cases Lindsay Kaplan examined included men complaining about sexual slanders against wives: P.R.O. STAC 243/26, STAC 172/6, STAC 88/11, STAC 304/36, and STAC 5/18.

22. According to common law, a bastard could not inherit property from his parents (Baker 558). David Harris Sacks has remarked in conversation with Lindsay Kaplan that in early modern England, a man's reputation for controlling his wife was taken in the community as a measure of his ability to manage his household economy. If this reputation or credit suffered, it was difficult for him to convince tradespeople to extend the credit necessary to run that household.

23. For the intense love the people bear toward Mamillius, see Camillo's conversation with Archidamus (1.1.33-45). Oddly, the death of Mamillius suggests the enduring life of his subjects, who would desire to live until the king has another son, something that the conclusion of the play suggests is unlikely to happen.

24. Coleridge remarks that "on the whole, this play is exquisitely respondent to its title" (217). Several other uses of the phrase in Shakespeare's works help piece together a definition of the winter's tale. In *Macbeth* it is synonymous with an old wives' tale: "O! these flaws and starts / (Impostors to true fear), would well become / A woman's story at a winter's fire, / Authoris'd by her grandam" (3.4.62-65). Richard II sees it as a tragic story of bygone times: "In winter's tedious nights sit by the fire / With good old folks, and let them tell thee tales / Of woeful ages long ago betid; / And ere thou bid good night, to quite their griefs / Tell thou

the lamentable tale of me, / And send the hearers weeping to their beds" (5.1.40-45). In *3 Henry VI*, Prince Edward dismisses the validity of Richard's taunting remarks about his parents by retorting: "Let Aesop fable in a winter's night; / His currish riddles sorts not with this place" (5.5.25-26). Mamillius offers his view on the matter in *The Winter's Tale*: "A sad tale's best for winter: I have one / Of sprites and goblins" (2.1.25-26). He proceeds to tell what promises to be a classic ghost story: "There was a man . . . / Dwelt by a churchyard" (29-30). The play itself incorporates all these elements in its tragedy, its suggestions of raising the dead, and its radical improbability.

Works Cited

Adelman, Janet. *Suffocating Mothers: Fantasies of Maternal Origin in Shakespeare's Plays,* Hamlet *to* The Tempest. New York: Routledge, 1992.

Allen, William. *An Admonition . . . Concerninge the Present Warres.* Antwerp, 1588.

Amussen, Susan Dwyer. *An Ordered Society: Gender and Class in Early Modern England.* Oxford: Blackwell, 1988.

Baker, J. H. *An Introduction to English Legal History.* 3rd ed. London: Butterworths, 1990.

Baker, J. H., and S. F. C. Milsom. *Sources of English Legal History: Private Law to 1750.* London: Butterworths, 1986.

Beattie, J. M. "The Criminality of Women in Eighteenth-Century England." *Journal of Social History* 8 (1975): 80-116.

Bergeron, David M. "The Restoration of Hermione in *The Winter's Tale.*" *Shakespeare's Romances Reconsidered.* Ed. Carol McGinnis Kay and Henry E. Jacobs. Lincoln: U of Nebraska P, 1978. 125-33.

———. *Shakespeare's Romances and the Royal Family.* Lawrence: UP of Kansas, 1985.

Boehrer, Bruce Thomas. *Monarchy and Incest in Renaissance England: Literature, Culture, Kinship, and Kingship.* Philadelphia: U of Pennsylvania P, 1992.

Boose, Lynda E. "Scolding Brides and Bridling Scolds: Taming the Woman's Unruly Member." *Shakespeare Quarterly* 42 (1991): 179-213.

Cary, Elizabeth. *The Tragedy of Mariam, The Fair Queen of Jewry.* Ed. Barry Weller and Margaret W. Ferguson. Berkeley: U of California P, 1994.

Cioni, Maria L. *Women and Law in Elizabethan England, with Particular Reference to the Court of Chancery.* New York: Garland, 1985.

Coleridge, Samuel. *Coleridge's Literary Criticism.* London: Frowde, 1908.

Dolan, Frances E. *Dangerous Familiars: Representations of Domestic Crime in England, 1550-1700.* Ithaca: Cornell UP, 1994.

Eggert, Katherine. "Nostalgia and the Not Yet Late Queen: Refusing Female Rule in *Henry V.*" *ELH* 61 (1994): 523-50.

———. "Ravishment and Remembrance: Responses to Female Authority in Spenser and Shakespeare." Diss. U of California, Berkeley, 1991.

Erickson, Amy Louise. *Women and Property in Early Modern England.* London: Routledge, 1993.

Foxe, John. *Actes and Monuments.* 8 vols. New York: AMS, 1965.

Frye, Susan. *Elizabeth I: The Competition for Representation.* New York: Oxford UP, 1993.

Gowing, Laura. "Gender and the Language of Insult in Early Modern London." *History Workshop* 35 (1993): 1-21.

Greene, Robert. Perymedes the Blacksmith *and* Pandosto *by Robert Greene: A Critical Edition.* Ed. Stanley Wells. New York: Garland, 1988.

———. *The Spanish Masquerado. The Life and Complete Works in Prose and Verse of Robert Greene.* Ed. Alexander B. Grosart. 15 vols. 1881-86. New York: Russell, 1964. 5: 235-88.

Helmholz, R. H., ed. *Select Cases on Defamation to 1600.* Selden Soc. 101. London: Selden Soc., 1985.

Holdsworth, W. S. *A History of English Law.* 16 vols. Boston: Little, Brown-Methuen, 1927-66.

Holinshed, Raphael. *Holinshed's Chronicles of England, Scotland, and Ireland.* Ed. Henry Ellis. 6 vols. 1807-08. New York: AMS, 1965.

Ingram, Martin. *Church Courts, Sex, and Marriage in England, 1570-1640.* Cambridge: Cambridge UP, 1990.

Ives, E. W. *Anne Boleyn.* Oxford: Blackwell, 1986.

Jardine, Lisa. "'Why should he call her whore?': Defamation and Desdemona's Case." *Addressing Frank Kermode: Essays in Criticism and Interpretation.* Ed. Margaret Tudeau-Clayton and Martin Warner. Urbana: U of Illinois P, 1991. 124-53.

Jordan, Constance. *Renaissance Feminism: Literary Texts and Political Models.* Ithaca: Cornell UP, 1990.

Kaplan, M. Lindsay. "Slander for Slander in *Measure for Measure.*" *Renaissance Drama* ns 21 (1990): 23-54.

Levin, Carole. *"The Heart and Stomach of a King": Elizabeth I and the Politics of Sex and Power.* Philadelphia: U of Pennsylvania P, 1994.

Marcus, Leah S. *Puzzling Shakespeare: Local Reading and Its Discontents.* Berkeley: U of California P, 1988.

———. "Shakespeare's Comic Heroines, Elizabeth I, and the Political Uses of Androgyny." *Women in the Middle Ages and the Renaissance: Literary and Historical Perspectives.* Ed. Mary Beth Rose. Syracuse: Syracuse UP, 1986. 135-53.

Miller, David Lee. *The Poem's Two Bodies: The Poetics of the 1590* Faerie Queene. Princeton: Princeton UP, 1988.

Neale, J. E. *Queen Elizabeth I: A Biography.* 1934. New York: Anchor-Doubleday, 1960.

Newcomb, Lori Humphrey. "'Social Things': The Production of Popular Culture in the Reception of Robert Greene's *Pandosto.*" *ELH* 61 (1994): 753-81.

Newman, Karen. *Fashioning Femininity and English Renaissance Drama.* Chicago: U of Chicago P, 1991.

Ocland, Christopher. Ειρηναρχια Siue Elizabetha. London, 1582.

———. *The Valiant Actes and victorious Battailes of the English nation. . . . Also, of the peaceable and quiet state of England.* Trans. J. Sharrock. London, 1585.

Phillips, James Emerson. *Images of a Queen: Mary Stuart in Sixteenth-Century Literature.* Berkeley: U of California P, 1964.

Rice, George P., Jr. *The Public Speaking of Queen Elizabeth: Selections from Her Official Addresses.* New York: Columbia UP, 1951.

Rosen, Barbara. *Witchcraft in England, 1558-1618.* Amherst: U of Massachusetts P, 1991.

Samaha, Joel. "Gleanings from Local Criminal-Court Records: Sedition amongst the 'Inarticulate' in Elizabethan Essex." *Journal of Social History* 8 (1975): 61-79.

Sandler, Florence. "*The Faerie Queene:* An Elizabethan Apocalypse." *The Apocalypse in English Renaissance Thought and Literature: Patterns, Antecedents, and Repercussions.* Ed. C. A. Patrides and Joseph Wittreich. Ithaca: Cornell UP, 1984. 148-74.

Shakespeare, William. *King Henry VI Part 3.* Ed. Andrew S. Cairncross. London: Methuen, 1964.

———. *King Henry VIII.* Ed. R. A. Foakes. London: Methuen, 1957.

———. *King Richard II.* Ed. Peter Ure. London: Methuen, 1961.

———. *Macbeth.* Ed. Kenneth Muir. London: Methuen, 1984.

———. *The Winter's Tale.* Ed. J. H. P. Pafford. London: Methuen, 1963.

Sharpe, J. A. *Crime in Early Modern England, 1550-1750.* London: Longman, 1984.

———. *Defamation and Sexual Slander in Early Modern England: The Church Courts at York.* Borthwick Papers 58. York: Borthwick Institute of Historical Research, 1980.

Speed, John. *The History of Great Britaine.* London, 1611.

Spring, Eileen. *Law, Land and Family: Aristocratic Inheritance in England, 1300 to 1800.* Chapel Hill: U of North Carolina P, 1993.

Stallybrass, Peter. "Patriarchal Territories: The Body Enclosed." *Rewriting the Renaissance: The Discourses of Sexual Difference in Early Modern Europe.* Ed. Margaret W. Ferguson, Maureen Quilligan, and Nancy J. Vickers. Chicago: U of Chicago P, 1986. 123-42.

Statutes of the Realm. London, 1587.

Underdown, David E. "The Taming of the Scold: The Enforcement of Patriarchal Authority in Early Modern England." *Order and Disorder in Early Modern England.* Ed. Anthony Fletcher and John Stevenson. Cambridge: Cambridge UP, 1985. 116-36.

Walpole, Horace. *Historic Doubts on the Life and Reign of King Richard III.* Ed. P. W. Hammond. Gloucester: Sutton, 1987.

Warnicke, Retha M. *The Rise and Fall of Anne Boleyn: Family Politics at the Court of Henry VIII.* Cambridge: Cambridge UP, 1989.

Wickham, Glynne. "Romance and Emblem: A Study in the Dramatic Structure of *The Winter's Tale.*" *Elizabethan Theatre III.* Ed. David Galloway. Toronto: Macmillan, 1973. 82-99.

Wiener, Carol Z. "Sex Roles and Crime in Late Elizabethan Hertfordshire." *Journal of Social History* 8 (1975): 38-60.

Wilson, Richard. "Observations on English Bodies: Licensing Maternity in Shakespeare's Late Plays." *Enclosure Acts: Sexuality, Property, and Culture in Early Modern England.* Ed. Richard Burt and John Archer. Ithaca: Cornell UP, 1994. 121-50.

Woolf, D. R. "Two Elizabeths? James I and the Late Queen's Famous Memory." *Canadian Journal of History* 20 (1985): 167-91.

Lynn Enterline (essay date 1997)

SOURCE: "'You speak a language that I understand not': The Rhetoric of Animation in *The Winter's Tale,*" in *Shakespeare Quarterly,* Vol. 48, No. 1, Spring, 1997, pp. 17-44.

[*In the essay that follows, Enterline examines Shakespeare's interpretation of Ovidian and Petrarchan rhetoric as a means of discussing the role of power and the female voice in* The Winter's Tale.]

Between Leontes's opening imperative, "Tongue-tied our queen? Speak you" (1.2.28), and the final act, where Hermione as living statue returns to her husband yet says nothing directly to him, *The Winter's Tale* traces a

This aspect of Ovid's poem—in which female voices such as Daphne's are betrayed by the very words they speak—helps us to understand Hermione's courtroom protest that she stands somehow outside the restrictive terms of Leontes's accusation: "Sir, / You speak a language that I understand not" (3.2.79-80). To the woman who will later be restored to life as a version of Pygmalion's statue, her husband's "language," like his jealousy, violates her sense of herself. Hermione's ensuing remark about the deadly effects of fantasy—"My life stands in the level of your dreams, / Which I'll lay down"—then provokes Leontes's most concise statement of his Pygmalionlike revision of womankind: "Your actions are my dreams" (ll. 81-82). As both Apollo's desire and figurative language ensnare Daphne yet give her voice an unforeseen efficacy, so the collusion between language and male fantasy frames Hermione yet does not utterly deprive her voice of power. *The Winter's Tale* may mark her words as insufficient to tell the truth or command belief, yet it also gives her voice the power to unhinge her husband's sense of the world itself: "Is this nothing? / Why then the world and all that's in't is nothing" (1.2.292-93).

And the corollary aspect of Ovid's poem—in which female voices suggest that male voices are not so powerful as the stories of rape or of animation might lead one to believe—illuminates why Leontes, once he has lost the rhetorical competition with his wife, spends much of the play trying (and failing) to control his own language and the language of others. For Leontes the fact that tongues other than his own can speak becomes an increasing source of irritation. When his lords voice their initial opposition to his accusation of adultery, Leontes snaps: "Hold your peaces" (2.1.139). He then dismisses their comments as an infringement of his power:

> Why, what need we
> Commune with you of this, but rather follow
> Our forceful instigation? Our prerogative
> Calls not your counsels . . .
> We need no more of your advice. The matter,
> The loss, the gain, the ord'ring on't, is all
> Properly ours.
>
> (ll. 161-70)

Leontes always speaks as if his voice alone should be heard. When accusing Hermione, he leans on the implicit power of his own voice: "*I have said* / She's an adult'ress, *I have said* with whom" (ll. 87-88, my emphasis). The mere existence of a king's saying, he believes, should be enough to establish facts. Where Orpheus tried and failed to use his voice to master death, Leontes tries and fails to use the power of his tongue to master truth.[25] In both cases women's bodies become the signifiers of that desire. Leontes, moreover, pairs his sense of his own linguistic prerogative with a declaration designed to preempt all other voices whatsoever: "He who shall speak for her is afar off guilty / *But that he speak*" (ll. 104-5, my emphasis). To Leontes anyone else's discourse is but a further sign of guilt. This is so, I submit, because Leontes, like an Orpheus singing alone in the woods, can bear to hear only the sound of his own tongue.

The king aspires to order all linguistic exchanges in Sicily, but Hermione's voice teaches him that any such ordering properly belongs to no one. Just as she obeys his command, "Speak you," in Act 1 only to challenge Leontes's sense of authority over acts of persuasion, so in Act 2, scene 1, Hermione speaks in obedience to his command with words that prompt Leontes to assert that his voice has again been eclipsed. Although Leontes has just ordered "Away with her, to prison" (l. 103) and his order is obeyed, by the end of Hermione's speech, Leontes protests that he has somehow gone unheard. Hermione addresses herself to the attendant lords in words that obey the king's command and yet seem to him to undermine it:

> HERMIONE . . . Beseech you all, my lords,
> With thoughts so qualified as your charities
> Shall best instruct you, measure me; and so
> The King's will be perform'd!
> LEONTES   *Shall I be heard?*
> HERMIONE *Who is't that goes with me?*
>
> (ll. 112-16, my emphasis)

Hermione cedes the power of action to Leontes's word, but her token of obedience makes that word ring hollow. The act of "go[ing]"—an act that follows the letter of the king's order—begins, in her mouth, to sound like a declaration of alliance: "Who is't that goes with me?" To counter her question, Leontes can do no more than repeat himself as he tries to reassert power over one word: "Go, do our bidding; hence!" (l. 125).

Indeed the play as a whole instructs Leontes that the linguistic marketplace he hopes to master cannot be negotiated by the careful parsing out of what he calls "the loss, the gain." He finds that it cannot be ordered by the logic of equivalence at all: language, in this play, repeatedly exceeds Leontes's demand. Certain that the oracle will prove him right, Leontes finds himself instead proclaimed a "jealous tyrant" (3.2.133-34). Responding to the charge with "this is mere falsehood" (l. 141), Leontes is confronted with the news of Mamillius's death, a death that results from Leontes's having doubted oracular speech. Or so Leontes understands it: "Apollo's angry, and the heavens themselves / Do strike at my injustice" (ll. 146-47). And so Leontes finds himself, like Ovid's Orpheus, brought low by the clamorous noise of a crowd. In Shakespeare's interrogation of the fear of losing one's rhetorical power, however, Leontes's distrust of other voices turns into an imaginary scene in which he is encircled by "whisp'ring" gossip rather than Bacchic cries: "They're here with me already, whisp'ring, rounding: / 'Sicilia is a so-forth.' 'Tis far gone, / When I shall gust it last" (1.2.217-19).

It is the tongues of Hermione and Paulina together, however, that most distinctly instruct Leontes in what I take to be the lesson of Orpheus: that power resides only complex, fascinated, and uneasy relation to female speech.[1] A play much noted for interrogating the "myriad forms of human narration"[2]—old tales, reports, ballads, oracles—*The Winter's Tale* begins its investigation of language when Hermione tellingly jests to Polixenes, "Verily, / You shall not go; a lady's 'verily' is / As potent as a lord's" (ll. 49-51), for Leontes's swift turn to suspicion hinges on the power of his wife's speech. Unable to persuade Polixenes to stay, he first expresses annoyance when Hermione is able to do so. Polixenes has just assured his boyhood friend "There is no tongue that moves, none, none i' th' world, / So soon as yours could win me" (ll. 20-21). Nonetheless, it is Hermione's tongue, not her husband's, that wins Polixenes. "You, sir, / Charge him too coldly," she chides Leontes before persuading their friend to stay (ll. 29-30). Leontes therefore shifts quickly from "Well said, Hermione" (l. 33), to churlish acknowledgment of her rhetorical power. He understands her persuasive speech not as obedience to his desire—since he is the one who commanded "Speak you"—but as a force that eclipses his own:

> LEONTES   Is he won yet?
> HERMIONE He'll stay, my lord.
> LEONTES   At my request he would not.
>
> (ll. 86-87)

From Hermione's success, jealous deductions quickly follow. Indeed, the first hint that something is amiss in this marriage is this seemingly minor quibble over who speaks to better purpose and who is the better rhetorician. When he later broaches with Camillo Polixenes's decision to stay, Leontes confirms his suspicions on the basis of his own earlier failure to persuade:

> CAMILLO You had much ado to make his anchor hold,
> When you cast out, it still came home.
> LEONTES   Didst note it?
> CAMILLO He would not stay at your petitions, made
> His business more material.
> LEONTES   Didst perceive it?
>
> (ll. 213-16)

Outdone in rhetorical power by his wife, Leontes makes two interpretive moves to reassert control over her language. First, he reminds Hermione of her answer to his proposal of marriage—in fact, he quotes her words of assent, "'I am yours for ever'" (l. 105)—and calls those words a "better" speech than the one to which Polixenes has yielded. And, second, he reads as evidence of infidelity the conversation he has himself induced between Hermione and his friend: "Too hot, too hot!" (l. 108). Making himself arbiter of Hermione's language, Leontes approvingly quotes the words he prefers while giving a fixed, suspicious meaning to the ones he does not. The scene's pronounced interest in acts of persuasion, one failed and the other successful, produces an odd effect: plunging into Leontes's jealousy, the scene makes his unreasonable emotion appear to be the consequence of this rivalry between male and female speech. As the drama quickly unfolds, we watch the king turn a rhetorical anxiety—why do her words achieve the desired effect where mine do not?—into a sexual one, minimizing his wife's superior rhetorical skill by interpreting it narrowly as the consequence of her erotic power. In Act 5, however, Hermione returns as a theatrical version of Pygmalion's silent statue to the husband who was once so jealous of her tongue. Almost but not quite "tongue-tied," she addresses herself to her lost daughter only. (I will return to her words to Perdita at the end of this essay.) After her theatrical metamorphosis, Hermione does not address the man who doubted her to the brink of annihilation. Having once triggered a terrible response with her voice, she now evades the problem by saying nothing to Leontes.[3]

I am tempted to say Hermione has learned her lesson. But as I hope to show, *The Winter's Tale* defies an intuitive understanding of the difference between speech and silence—or, for that matter, the difference between agency and impotence, male and female, often allied with it. The elaborate Pygmalion fantasy offered in the last scene as a way to resolve the problems inaugurated by Hermione's initially "potent" tongue tells us that before we can begin to hear the full resonance of her concluding silence, we must consider the relationship between, on the one hand, the trope of the female voice in the Ovidian-Petrarchan tradition that Shakespeare inherits and transforms in this play and, on the other, the quite specific rhetorical concerns through which *The Winter's Tale* reads that tradition, turning it into theatrical metacommentary. Any reading of the play's uneasy fascination with the female voice, that is, must take account of the complex literary legacy of Pygmalion's obsession with his mute *simulacrum*. As this silent figure passes from Ovid to Petrarch to Shakespeare, it criticizes even as it perpetuates a mysterious tie between love of art and hatred for women. Narratives of rape and misogyny frame the figure of the animated statue, tarnishing the luster of a story that otherwise seems to be about love for beautiful form, visual as well as verbal. The literary legacy of Pygmalion's statue asks readers, therefore, to think again about the consequences of the many kinds, and discourses, of love.

I should preface this analysis by noting that when I speak of a "female voice" in this play, I mean to designate a pervasive and seductive trope—a discursive effect, not a prediscursive fact. Through the sound of the very "female" voice that inaugurates Leontes's jealousy, I will argue, the play distances itself from the king's essentializing effort to dismiss Hermione's rhetorical power by understanding it as erotic power only. Of course the arbitrary force of Leontes's jealous interpretation of his wife's tongue raises troubling questions about the violence latent in such culturally pervasive ideas as those of "male" speech and "female" silence. Because *The Winter's Tale* was written for a transvestite theater, moreover, I do not presume a given—or, more important, an intelligible—phenomenon anterior to the language that gives it shape (for instance, "woman" or "the female subject"). Reading the way in which the voices of Hermione and Leontes affect and implicate each other, I hope to show, tells us that—like

Echo and Narcissus or Salmacis and Hermaphroditus—female and male voices in this very Ovidian play are locked in a mutually defining, differential embrace. An analysis of the "female voice" in *The Winter's Tale* is important precisely because it must change our understanding of that term.

Renaissance revisers of the *Metamorphoses* routinely adopt such stories as Ovid's Pygmalion as a way to comment on the medium of their appearance; Shakespeare is no exception. Ovid's own generic experimentation, his rhetorical and poetic self-reflexivity, and his habit of linking oral/aural dilemmas to visual ones encouraged in Renaissance imitators a highly self-conscious practice of borrowing.[4] Erotic stories from the *Metamorphoses* became highly charged reflections on the power (and dangers) of the story's very medium—whether painting, poetry, music, or drama. Such self-conscious visitations prepare us for Shakespeare's much noted—and celebrated—effort to turn Ovid's story of Pygmalion into one about the transforming powers of theatrical representation, about a theater that succeeds where even Orpheus failed: "I'll fill your grave up" (5.3.101). Because the idea of the living statue plays a crucial role in Shakespeare's claims for the theater and in our own critical reception of those claims, it becomes vital that we understand the epistemological and ethical consequences of the rhetoric of animation. For Shakespeare's final invocation of the living statue's "magic" draws on a story that self-consciously proposes a close yet opaque alliance between aesthetics and misogyny. I will suggest that, in silence as in speech, the female voice in *The Winter's Tale* allows us to interrogate the terms and the limits of that alliance.

I. "Shall I Be Heard?"

To apprehend the burden Shakespeare assumes when he has Paulina tell Hermione to "bequeath to death" her "numbness," we must remember the symbolic and libidinal economy that informs the Pygmalion story in the two chief texts that gave it such tenacity as a fiction about voice, masculinity, and desire: Ovid's *Metamorphoses* and Petrarch's *Rime Sparse*. As Leonard Barkan writes, Hermione's metamorphosis enacts "a kind of marriage of Pygmalion and Petrarchanism."[5] In the *Rime Sparse*, Petrarch draws on numerous Ovidian characters to represent his own situation of unfulfilled desire; and in a pair of sonnets that praise Simone Martini's portrait of Laura, he brings Ovid's story of Pygmalion into the cycle as a particularly compelling analogue for his own predicament.[6] Two rhetorical issues are central to both Petrarch's and Shakespeare's versions of Ovid's Pygmalion: the trope of apostrophe and the language of praise or epideixis. By lamenting the picture's silence—"if only she could reply to my words!" ("*se risponder savesse a' detti miei!*")—Petrarch's apostrophe creates the fiction of his own voice; a second apostrophe accentuates the fiction of a voice and the language of epideixis at once: "Pygmalion, how much you must praise yourself for your image ("*quanto lodar ti dei*") if you received a thousand times what I yearn to have just once!" (78.11, 12-14).[7] In these concluding lines Petrarch rewrites Ovid's story according to one of the *Rime Sparse*'s controlling signifiers: *lodare*. He thereby refashions Ovid's Pygmalion in his own image, reading him as an artist devoted to *praising* himself for the excellence of his *simulacrum*. Petrarch derives the name Laura from the Latin *laudare* and, according to the *Secretum*, loves the name just as much as he loves the lady herself.[8]

In *The Winter's Tale*, Shakespeare reads the tradition Petrarch's poetry inaugurated in precise rhetorical terms—in terms, that is, of the power of address and of epideixis. Long before staging his own kinds of address to a composite Ovidian-Petrarchan statue ("Chide me, dear stone" or "descend; be stone no more; approach" [5.3.24, 99]), Shakespeare fits the representation of Hermione (and Leontes's relation to her) into a meditation on epideictic speech. Where *The Rape of Lucrece* explores the violent consequences of Petrarchan epideixis—because "Collatine unwisely did not let / To praise" Lucrece to other men (ll. 10-11), rape is the consequence[9]—*The Winter's Tale* gives us a Hermione who, in jest, offers herself as the beloved object of praise:

> What? have I twice said well? When was't before?
> I prithee tell me; cram's with praise, and make's
> As fat as tame things. One good deed dying tongueless
> Slaughters a thousand waiting upon that.
> Our praises are our wages.
>
> (1.2.90-94)

Understood in light of Shakespeare's critique of praise in *The Rape of Lucrece*, Hermione's pose as epideictic object for her husband while in the presence of another man should alert us that the rhetorical competition between Hermione and Leontes may already have entered the troubled world of Petrarchan verbal exchanges gone awry. Indeed, Hermione's very participation in a rhetorical competition with one man to vie for another man's ear alerts us that culturally dominant alignments of gender and rhetoric do not pertain. Her "potent" rhetoric disrupts received expectations for epideictic speech. And so in this play, terrible consequences attend *Hermione*'s speaking, even though Leontes is the character whom her playful remarks about praise might lead us to believe will follow Collatine as ill-fated epideictic rhetorician. Instead of hearing more from Leontes, however, we hear from Hermione; and what she speaks about is her own power of speech. Her balanced syntax hints to the jealous ear that, just as they are matched in her discourse, the two men may be equivalent objects for her exchange: "I have spoke to th' purpose twice: / The one for ever earn'd a royal husband; / Th' other for some while a friend" (ll. 106-8). As if following her lead into the language of payment and exchange, Leontes begins to angle for proof by changing Hermione's equation of the two men into a marketplace where she is *their* commodity: "Hermione, / How thou lov'st us, show in our brother's welcome; / Let what is dear in Sicily be cheap" (ll. 173-75). While the rest of the play may seem to return to expected discursive convention by making Hermione (and her fidelity) the enigmatic object of others' discourse—in praise and in slander—that predicament, we should remember, is initiated in Act 1 by the unexpected power of her persuasive tongue.

The play's most striking debt to the Petrarchan tradition, of course, emerges in the final scene when a stony lady comes to life. Both Ovid and Petrarch use what Kenneth Gross aptly calls "the dream of the moving statue" as an erotic, synesthetic investigation of the status of the human voice and the consequences of rhetorical speech. In both, as in Shakespeare's play, this investigation occurs by way of a meditation on the success or failure of an *address*. In each of the three texts, this address draws our attention to the way that all parties present are implicated in and defined by the verbal event. Before looking more carefully at Petrarch's version of Pygmalion, however, we must first understand the complex connections between rhetoric, voice, and sexuality which he inherited from Ovid's poem.

In the *Metamorphoses*, Pygmalion's wishes come true because he addresses words of prayer to Venus. The story of animation, the event of the statue's motion, offers an erotic version of a rhetorician's dream. The scene's action and considerable dramatic effect (waiting for a statue to move) derives from a pun on the desired end of rhetorical speech. Drawing on the contemporary word for rhetorical power—the power, that is, to "move" (*movere*)—the narrator tells us that in his statue, Pygmalion believes he has an audience who "*wants* to be moved" (X.251).[10] And because the narrator of the story is the grieving Orpheus, yet another compelling fantasy about the voice's power informs the ivory maiden's animation. Shakespeare, too, connects the stories of Orpheus and Pygmalion. After the "statue" moves, Paulina warns Leontes: "Do not shun her / Until you see her die again, for then / You kill her double" (5.3.105-7). Paulina's imperative deftly combines the story of Pygmalion's statue with that of Orpheus's Eurydice by implying two things: like the statue, Hermione has come to life; and because of this animation, she may, like Eurydice, die twice. Indeed, Golding's translation of Ovid's text may have suggested Paulina's wording. For Ovid's version of Eurydice's "twin" death—"*stupuit gemina nece coniugis Orpheus*" (X.69)—Golding renders, "This double dying of his wyfe set Orphye in a stound."[11]

The interwoven stories of Orpheus and Pygmalion seem, at first glance, to propose a familiar hierarchy between male verbal agency on the one hand and female silence and death on the other. Where the sculptor's prayer succeeds, the statue says nothing and has no name; where Orpheus's song momentarily takes over the narrative of the poem—thus predicating Book X of the *Metamorphoses* itself on Eurydice's absence—Eurydice utters a barely audible "*vale*" before "falling back again to the place whence she had come" (X.63). As Petrarch realized, the first (male verbal agency) seems to depend on the second (female silence and death). But trouble soon disturbs this too-sanguine version of male vocal power. Once able to move the inanimate world by "moving his voice in song" ("*hoc vocem carmine movit*" [l. 147]), Orpheus dies because Bacchic (female) noise drowns out his voice: the "huge uproar" of discordant flutes, horns, drums, "and howlings of the Bacchanals" overwhelms the sound of Orpheus's lyre ("*ingens / clamor . . . et Bacchei ululatus*" [XI.15-18]). Once-listening stones turn to weapons, stones now "reddened with the blood of the bard whose voice was unheard" ("*saxa / non exauditi rubuerunt sanguine vatis*" [ll. 18-19]). And where Pygmalion succeeds in animating his beloved, his narrator fails. Having won Eurydice only to lose her again through his own action, Orpheus then sings a song in which we hear the story of yet another beloved woman given life through art. Orpheus's *failure* underwrites the story he tells, making the fantasy of the statue's animation part of the wishful *fort-da* game of his impossible desire. These interwoven narratives therefore tell us that power is fleetingly, intermittently, and only phantasmatically granted the male voice. And they tell us, moreover, that his voice may not be the only sound that matters.

Still, we must acknowledge that Eurydice's death and the unnamed statue's silence in the Orpheus-Pygmalion sequence conform to a larger fantasy, first proposed in Book I of the *Metamorphoses*, in which male vocal triumph requires female absence or resistance. Two stories of attempted rape—Apollo's pursuit of Daphne and Pan's of Syrinx—tell the origins of epideictic and pastoral poetry by presenting a rigid sexual division of labor in the production of song. Close on Daphne's heels, the god of poetry fails to persuade and so becomes himself *because* she eludes his grasp.[12] And hard on the heels of that encounter follows Pan's pursuit of Syrinx, an attempted rape that repeats and intensifies the first. Where Apollo's breathing down Daphne's neck becomes the breath of poetry, Pan's breath turns into music as he sighs through the newly immobilized body of Syrinx: "the soft air stirring in the reeds gave forth a low and complaining sound" ("*sonum tenuem similemque querenti*" [I.708]). In the context of this violence, remember that yet other forms of misogyny underwrite the Orpheus-Pygmalion sequence. Grieving for Eurydice, Orpheus "shunned all love of womankind," becoming the "author" in Thrace of "giving his love to tender boys" ("*omnemque refugerat Orpheus / femineam Venerem . . . ille etiam Thracum populis fuit auctor amorem / in teneros*" [X.79-84]).[13] Pygmalion's "disgust" for female sexual behavior repeats his narrator's aversion: having seen the prostitution of the Propoetides, he creates a statue "better than any woman born" ("*qua femina nasci / nulla potest*" [ll. 248-49]) to eradicate the "faults that nature had so liberally given the female mind" ("*vitiis, quae plurima menti / femineae natura dedit*" [ll. 244-45]). For rejecting women, Orpheus will soon die at the hands of the Bacchantes. Ovid thus twice qualifies Pygmalion's seeming aesthetic triumph, suggesting that it is rooted in misogyny; aversion to women is its inaugural gesture.[14] The Bacchic cry upon seeing Orpheus—"here is the man who scorns us!" ("*hic est nostri contemptor!*" [XI.7])—claims that revenge is the best this erotic-symbolic economy can expect.[15]

Such misogyny was not lost on later writers. In "The Metamorphosis of Pigmalions Image" (1598), John Marston summarizes his reading of Pygmalion concisely:

> Pigmalion, whose hie love-hating minde
> Disdain'd to yeeld servile affection,
> Or amorous sute to any woman-kinde,
> Knowing their wants, and mens perfection.
> Yet Love at length forc'd him to know his fate,
> And love the shade, whose substance he did hate.[16]

As Shakespeare's only other direct reference to the story suggests, he is more than familiar with this "love-hating" tradition. In *Measure for Measure* the phrase "Pygmalion's image" means "prostitute," exactly recalling the reason for Pygmalion's creative act. "What, is there none of Pygmalion's images newly made woman to be had now, for putting the hand in the pocket and extracting [it] clutch'd?" (3.2.44-47).[17] In this version of the story, the fantasy of animation *is* the moment of sexual penetration (i.e., "to make a woman" is to deflower a virgin). Both Shakespeare and his audience were well aware of the sexual and misogynist aspects of the story that are omitted in order to achieve closure in *The Winter's Tale*. If we ignore the negative aspects of the Pygmalion tradition, we foreclose the possibility of thinking about the work and effects of repression in the play's last scene—or, for that matter, about the problem that Ovid's narrative so memorably posed: what, precisely, *is* the relationship between misogyny and art?[18]

In the first three acts Leontes's skepticism places the "truth" of Hermione's body (her innocence or her guilt) beyond the reach of words—beyond the reach, even, of oracular speech. Similarly, the final scene turns to a story in which evasion of the female body is representation's foundational premise: Pygmalion's statue is *not* mimetic; it is "better than any woman born." From this disquieting gap between language and the world, Shakespeare aspires to a mode of representation that can move beyond the impasse. If, as most critics agree, the spectacle of Hermione's pregnancy troubles the play's language from the start (most obviously in Polixenes's opening reference to "nine months"), this spectacle works together with her potent tongue to spark her husband's suspicions. The final scene of animation therefore works to reclaim another, "better" mode of generation than the one that so disturbs Leontes's understanding of the world. In constructing this scene, Shakespeare tries to replace the animating power of the maternal body with the language and visual spectacle of the theater.[19]

The play's implied claim for theatrical power, then, derives from a literary history of aversion to female flesh. But this is not the only story the play tells about its own fiction. I want to suggest not only that Hermione's concluding silence criticizes the symbolic-erotic economy inaugurated in Book I of the *Metamorphoses* and developed in the Orpheus-Pygmalion sequence, but that this economy itself tells us something important about why Hermione's speech is so unexpectedly powerful. It is as if the first half of The *Winter's Tale* were asking of this legacy, what would happen if the stony lady actually did speak back? To understand the play's question, we need only remember that Pygmalion's statue is both nameless and speechless. Or that Eurydice, lost again, says only "farewell" before finally disappearing in death. Although the first book of the *Metamorphoses* initially proposes a sexual division of labor in the creation of poetry and the Orpheus segment adds death to rape as one of the possible roles for women in the process of inventing poetic song, readers may have heard the murmur of a story different from the one that emerges from a focus on the activities of Apollo, Pan, or Orpheus. For in the line I quoted about Pan's music, Ovid leaves unclear exactly *whose* voice is audible in these pipes: "Instead of [Syrinx] he held nothing but marsh reeds . . . and while he sighed in disappointment, the soft air stirring in the reeds gave forth a low and complaining sound" (I.708). Ovid lets us wonder, whose sound is this? The complaint seems as much Syrinx's as Pan's. The female voice troubles the Apollo-Daphne story, too, thus disturbing one of the *Metamorphoses*'s most prominent narratives about the origins of poetry. Where Apollo's "imperfect" rhetoric ("*verba imperfecta*") fails to persuade her to stay, Daphne's prayer to lose the "figure" that provokes such violence convinces her father to change her shape. Her words possess a persuasive force that Apollo's do not; they inaugurate one of the metamorphoses that are the subject of Ovid's poem. If Book I creates the expectation that the poem will focus on male vocal power, that expectation is soon thwarted. In a series of influential stories, Ovid ventriloquizes numerous women, obliquely yet consistently hinting that these female characters are violated by the very mode of representation available to them. Echo's mimicking voice, Syrinx's complaining reed, Philomela's severed tongue, and, I would argue, Medusa's fearsome face mark female experience in the *Metamorphoses* as a struggle against the restrictive conditions within which they must represent themselves.[20] To return to the case in point: Daphne's metapoetic plea—that she lose her "*figura*"—tells us that the figural quality of language betrays her just as surely as her bodily form makes her vulnerable to Apollo's violence.[21] For when Daphne prays to lose her figure and is turned into a tree, she may not have meant to lose her human form: when used to signify the body rather than language, *figura* designates not only general shape but also a person's beauty.[22] What Daphne means to ask is to become less attractive, but what she actually *says* prompts her father to alter her human figure altogether. The relief brought her by the unintended power of her prayer is just as constricting as the figural language with which she must speak—language that departs "from the straightforward and obvious"[23] and whose obliquity therefore condemns her to be "immobilized" or "stuck fast" with "sluggish roots" ("*pigris radicibus haeret*" [1. 551]). Her voice may *do* more than Apollo's, her words may achieve greater effects, but their action eclipses her intention. And this sense of violation by language, I believe, forms the basis of Ovid's insistent alliance of the origin of poetry with rape.[24]

fleetingly in one's voice, even if it be the voice of a poet or a king. In the scene of Hermione's arrest (2.1), the queen notifies her husband, as she did indirectly in the first act, that he cannot bring all language—even his own—under control. Though Leontes may claim that "the matter" and "the ord'ring" of his accusation of adultery is "all / Properly ours," she teaches him otherwise. Once published, Hermione reminds him, a text will go its own way. It can be controlled by no mere speaking:

> How will this grieve you,
> When you shall come to clearer knowledge, that
> You thus have publish'd me! Gentle my lord,
> You scarce can right me thoroughly, then, to say
> You did mistake.
>
> (ll. 96-100)

Unable to master the truth by mastering other voices, Shakespeare's Orpheus/Leontes soon finds himself heavily beset by the tongue of Paulina. In her, Leontes contends with a voice that resists all ordering:

> LEONTES [What] noise there, ho?
> PAULINA No noise, my lord, but needful conference
> About some gossips for your Highness.
> LEONTES   How?
> Away with that audacious lady! Antigonus,
> I charg'd thee that she should not come about me:
> I knew she would.
>
> (2.3.39-44)

Like an Ovidian bad penny, Paulina returns to avenge her mistress. "A callat / Of boundless tongue, who," Leontes claims, "late hath beat her husband" (ll. 91-92), Paulina plagues Leontes with her "noise." A domestic version of the Bacchic horde, Paulina has a tongue that no man controls. Thus the harassed Leontes rebukes her husband, "What? canst not rule her?" (l. 46). Paulina, the somewhat softened spirit of a revenging Ovidian woman, goes about her work with a tongue that will, after sixteen years, cure Leontes rather than kill him.

II. "NOT GUILTY"

We have seen that when Shakespeare adopts the imagined scene of speaking to a stony lady as a way to repair the devastation caused by Leontes's jealousy, he turns the conflict between male and female verbal power into a meditation on Ovidian and Petrarchan rhetoric in general and on the role of the female voice in that literary legacy in particular. Before looking more closely at the telling role female voices play in *The Winter's Tale,* however, we must examine the vicissitudes of the voice in the *Rime Sparse,* particularly for those Ovidian characters whom Petrarch borrows as so many figures for his own situation. Like many of his literary contemporaries, Shakespeare frequently juxtaposes Ovidian rhetoric with Petrarchan in order to derive a flexible lexicon of figures for sexual experience, whether erotic or violent. Recall, for instance, that Marcus greets the mutilated Lavinia, Shakespeare's Philomela, with the conventional language of a *blason* in praise of her beauty and talent (*Titus Andronicus,* 2.4.22-47). Similarly, the narrator of *The Rape of Lucrece* sets his critique of Petrarchan epideixis in an explicitly Ovidian context, rewriting the story of Lucretia from the *Fasti* in terms of several other Ovidian characters: most notably, Philomela, Orpheus, and Hecuba. Understanding the *Rime Sparse* and Ovid's presence in it will help clarify why the female voice occasionally exercises such disruptive force in a play that ends with yet another version of Pygmalion's address to his statue.

In Sonnet 78 Petrarch's apostrophe to Ovid's Pygmalion epitomizes the rhetorical and erotic concerns of the *Rime Sparse,* bequeathing strategies, tropes, and effects to one of the most influential modes of Renaissance self-representation, and allowing the poet ample room to compare the relative merits of visual and verbal figuration. Because Petrarch, as a second Pygmalion, cannot make the picture speak, the speaker's desire for words replaces Ovid's scene of desire for a new and improved woman. Words, not sex, become the focus of the poet's longing: "if only she could reply to my words!" From Petrarch's repression of Ovid's bluntly sexual scene, verbal fetishism is born.[26] And so, too, is an imaginary conversation—not between Petrarch and Laura but between Petrarch and Pygmalion ("Pygmalion, how much you must praise yourself for your image . . ."). Laura's muteness, of course, is the necessary condition for this all-male conversation about aesthetic merit. And her silence deeply influenced English Petrarchanism: Barkan recalls Daniel's figure of the "marble brest" and "stony heart" and Marston's distinctly lascivious use of the metaphor. Indeed, the power relations implicit in the convention of the poet pleading with his silent mistress fuel Marston's satire of Petrarchanism: "O that my Mistres were an Image too, / That I might blameles her perfections view."[27]

Despite Marston's telling barb about the erotic advantages of female silence, however, and despite Petrarch's rhetorical turn in Sonnet 78 to speak to another male artist about her silence, the distinctions of power implied by such figures as Pygmalion's statue are not absolute in the *Rime Sparse.* The seemingly silenced female voice does, on occasion, interrupt Petrarchan self-reflection. First, the persona who takes Apollo's story as his own also represents himself as "Echo," exiled by the very language in which he represents his fate. Like Echo or Daphne, the poem's speaker is betrayed by his own speech; in canzone 23 his echoing song angers Laura as Diana, who imprisons the poet in stone (ll. 13, 64-66, 138-40). As with both Ovid's and Shakespeare's reflections on male and female voices, Petrarch's trope of echo implicates the fate of one voice in that of another. The male voice leans on various female voices from Ovid's text in order to define itself.[28] Echo's may not seem the kind of verbal power an aspiring Apollo would want to claim, since it disrupts any sure sense of intention or origin; yet it remains a kind of power nonetheless. Like Echo, the poet is never able to make his pain "resound" sweetly or softly enough so as to persuade ("*né mai in sì dolci o in sì soavi tempre* / risonar *seppi gli amorosi guai / che 'l cor s'umiliasse aspro et feroce*" [23.64-66]). But such failure finds its Apollonian solace in the aesthetic pleasures of Petrarchan autobiography: "every valley echoes to the sound of heavy sighs which prove how painful my life is" ("*et quasi in ogni valle / rimbombi il suon de' miei gravi sospiri, / ch' acquistan fede a la penosa vita*" [23.12-14]).

Second, though Laura rarely speaks in the *Rime Sparse*, her few words wield authority. As Diana, she utters the taboo against speaking that subtends the cycle: "make no word of this" ("'*Di ciò non far parola*'" [23.74]). Her prohibition enables Petrarch to portray himself as one driven by compulsion to write about what is forbidden. Laura's sentence against his speech becomes, paradoxically, the positive condition for Petrarch's appearance as the speaking subject in exile. Like the undertone in the complaining sound that issues from Syrinx's reed, Laura's spoken taboo is that without which we would not hear Petrarch's voice. Indeed, in the *Rime Sparse* as a whole, Laura's voice, when heard, carries the force of prohibition or revelation. "Soft, angelic," and "divine" ("*in voce . . . soave, angelica, divina*" [167.3-4]), it attracts her lover like "the sound of the sirens" ("*di sirene al suono*" [207.82]). I therefore understand the seeming polarity between male speech and female silence in Petrarch's rendition of the Pygmalion story in light of the larger fantasies about the poet's own symbolic and erotic condition, which give the female voice, though infrequently heard, an unsettling power.[29]

This voice articulates the specific rhetorical concerns that preoccupy Shakespeare as he transforms this Ovidian-Petrarchan legacy into a figure for the theater. Act 1, scene 2, the scene of rhetorical competition, opens with a brief meditation on the power and limits of a particular speech act: Polixenes complains of the imbalance between "thank you" and the time it takes to say it.

> Nine changes of the wat'ry star hath been
> The shepherd's note since we have left our throne
> Without a burthen. Time as long again
> Would be fill'd up, my brother, with our thanks,
> And yet we should, for perpetuity,
> Go hence in debt. And therefore, like a cipher
> (Yet standing in rich place), I multiply
> With one "We thank you" many thousands moe
> That go before it.
>
> (1.2.1-9)

Leontes's reply, however, only reopens the debt that Polixenes's "I multiply" was meant to close: "Stay your thanks a while, / And pay them when you part" (ll. 9-10). Polixenes's verbal maneuvers open a rhetorically self-conscious play in which Shakespeare continues to test language's power as a mode of action rather than mere vehicle of representation, to search for a kind of voice that can effect the changes of which it speaks. Moreover, the verbal power that Polixenes desires in this scene and Paulina finally stages in the last raises the same question—the question of language's ability to transcend time.

As the concluding scene's greater success suggests, Shakespeare asks this question most pointedly through the sound of the female voice—Leontes's less than "tongue-tied" queen and the "boundless tongue" of her faithful Paulina. He does so in such a way, I submit, that the (barely) suppressed undercurrent of illicit sexuality in Polixenes's opening references to nine months and "standing in rich place" comes to define the very notion of time.

Let us examine exactly how this happens. Beginning with Polixenes's desire for words that can discharge a debt—for some kind of verbal action—the play's rhetorical concern is precisely delimited by its often-repeated doublet, "to say" and "to swear." Preoccupied with the inability of any statement to prove Hermione innocent and the concomitant failure of all speech to persuade Leontes of the truth, the first three acts of *The Winter's Tale* continually present us with this pair, "to say" and "to swear." The doublet appears early: in the first scene of rhetorical and sexual competition, Hermione says of Polixenes, "To tell he longs to see his son were strong; / But let him say so then, and let him go; / But let him swear so, and he shall not stay, / We'll thwack him hence with distaffs" (ll. 34-37). Similarly, when Leontes charges Hermione directly, "'tis Polixenes / Has made thee swell thus," she responds: "But I'd say he had not; / And I'll be sworn you would believe my saying, / Howe'er you lean to th' nayward" (2.1.61-64). This iterated pair of verbs draws a distinction similar to the one made by J. L. Austin in his theory of the difference between constative and performative utterances, between *saying*—words that "'describe' some state of affairs . . . either truly or falsely"—and *swearing*—words in which to say something is "to do it."[30] In *The Winter's Tale* oath-taking and swearing faith take on the peculiar urgency of futility, since neither utterances that aspire to state the truth nor words conventionally designated as actions exercise any force.

Indeed we might say that this pair, saying and swearing, precisely distinguishes the two halves of the play. In Act 3, Paulina is the first woman whose spoken words command belief: "I say she's dead; I'll swear't. If word nor oath / Prevail not, go and see" (3.2.203-4). Before Paulina's oath no proof or belief attended woman's word. For women, according to Leontes, "will say anything" (1.2.131). After Paulina's oath Leontes views female speaking differently: "Go on, go on," he says to her, "Thou canst not speak too much" (3.2.214-15). But just as Leontes invokes the evidence of sight without ever having visual proof—Hermione's adultery "lack'd sight only" (2.1.177)—Paulina's imperative makes the "fact" of Hermione's death, like the "fact" of her innocence, a kind of metatheatrical crime: the one thing the audience *cannot* do is "go and see." The truth of Hermione's body—its innocence and its death—is always held from view; all that remains is the evidence of "word" and "oath." Where neither "word nor oath" allow Hermione to testify to the truth of her innocence, Paulina's oath marks the moment when a woman's words do finally work—but only to testify to a lie. Only a lie—Hermione is dead—establishes the trust in Leontes necessary for her to live as innocent. Only this lie to the audience, moreover, allows Shakespeare the surprise ending of the living statue that claims such powers for the theater.[31] Between Hermione's vain though truthful swearing of innocence and Paulina's successful yet false swearing of death, *The Winter's Tale* uses the female voice to point beyond truth or falsehood, beyond a conception of language as transparent description. Instead it asks us to consider the *effects* of language—particularly female language but also theatrical language—in relation to the fugitive truth of the female body and the "old tale" it tells.[32]

In the courtroom scene, saying and swearing come together at the moment of their failing. The oracle, for instance, is truth-telling's last chance. That telling is supposed to be secured by another performative, for the officers, swearing "upon this sword of justice" that they have been "at Delphos, and from thence have brought / This seal'd-up oracle," open it and read: "'Hermione is chaste, Polixenes blameless, . . . Leontes a jealous tyrant,'" and so on (3.2.124, 126-27, 132-34). Leontes merely declares, "There is no truth at all i' th' oracle" (l. 140). But in this scene, it is Hermione's voice in particular that puts performative language on trial by stressing its failure and, at the same time, connecting that failure to the central problem of the play. For her commentary on her own speaking, like Paulina's false oath that Hermione is dead, connects the transformation of language into action with the play's two chief preoccupations: the "truth" of the female body and the effects of theatrical representation. Brought forward to testify, Hermione declares her innocence by commenting on her own lack of vocal power. She quotes the one performative for which she longs but which, in this context, will not work:

> Since what I am to say must be but that
> Which contradicts my accusation, and
> The testimony on my part no other
> But what comes from myself, it shall scarce boot me
> To say, "Not guilty."
>
> (ll. 22-26)

Quoting the performative that in her mouth and in this place must misfire, Hermione's meditation on the inefficacy of saying "Not guilty" does two things. First, it constructs Leontes as tyrant for bringing her forth in a courtroom where no words can acquit her. Commenting on her own inability to speak, Hermione claims that her predicament, viewed by a higher, divine witness, "shall make / False accusation blush, and tyranny / Tremble at patience" (ll. 30-32). The necessary misfiring of Hermione's "Not guilty" becomes the verbal event that marks Leontes, against his hopes, as "tyrannous" (l. 5). Second, Hermione's meditation on the necessary failure of her "Not guilty" recalls an earlier "Not guilty." This one is first spoken offstage, but it defines the time of the play as the fallen time of sexuality. In Act 1, Polixenes remembers a prelapsarian idyll of male bonding. Of his boyhood friendship with Leontes he remarks,

> We were as twinn'd lambs that did frisk i' th' sun,
> And bleat the one at th' other. What we chang'd
> Was innocence for innocence; we knew not
> The doctrine of ill-doing, nor dream'd
> That any did.
>
> (1.2.67-71)

Had this edenic state continued, he claims, "we should have answer'd heaven / Boldly, 'Not guilty'; the imposition clear'd, / Hereditary ours" (ll. 73-75). In the decidedly less than innocent time of the play, "Not guilty," though boldly declared, will *not* clear "the imposition." Instead the immediate action of a prelapsarian performative is nullified by the sight of the female body:

> HERMIONE   By this we gather
> You have tripp'd since.
> POLIXENES   O my most sacred lady,
> Temptations have since then been born to 's: for
> In those unfledg'd days was my wife a girl;
> Your precious self had then not cross'd the eyes
> Of my young playfellow.
>
> (ll. 75-80)

Like Leontes's suspicious interpretation of her pregnancy, of course, Polixenes's comments on Leontes's fall from innocence mark Hermione's body as a sign of transgression. But the echoing of "Not guilty" across the play turns the female *voice*, too, into another mark of transgression. For the possibility of saying a "Not guilty" that performs the action of absolution belonged to a world without women. When young men answered to heaven, there was no human convention to be violated and so deprive these words of efficacious action. With a language so natural as that of lambs bleating, heaven automatically witnesses and ratifies all performatives; the one who enters a plea simultaneously delivers his own verdict. Between the two very different circumstances for saying "Not guilty," Shakespeare defines the play's time as one of broken linguistic conventions—conventions broken, moreover, around the question of sexual guilt. Turning what Shoshana Felman calls the scandal of the "*speaking body*" into the scandal of the speaking *maternal* body, Shakespeare sets *The Winter's Tale* in a time when woman's performative "Not guilty" cannot act.[33]

The failure of Hermione's "Not guilty" is implicit in Austin's definition of the performative. As Felman demonstrates of Austin's work, the performative is "defined only through the dimension of failure."[34] That failure is, however, not simple; it produces further effects. If the conventional rules governing a performative utterance are not in effect—if, as Austin writes, when we say "I do" in a marriage ceremony, "we are not in a position to do the act because we are, say, married already"—that does not mean that "I do" will be "void or without effect." Instead, "lots of things will have been done": for instance, "we shall most interestingly have committed the act of bigamy."[35] What other effects, then, follow from Hermione's meditation on the impossibility of saying "Not guilty"? As we have already seen, the inevitable misfiring of her "Not guilty" turns Leontes's court into a mockery, the ruse of a tyrant who has already determined the verdict. Within the fictions of the play and of Leontes's justice, Hermione's refusal to enter a plea defines, by rhetorical means, the extent of the king's tyranny.

But more radically still, the self-reflexivity that defines all performatives reminds us, suddenly, that we are not only in the mock courtroom of a tyrant. We are also in the mock courtroom of a play. Of such a fictive situation, Austin observes that "a performative utterance will . . . be *in a peculiar way* hollow or void if said by an actor on the stage."[36] I do not cite Austin's observation here in order to endorse his distinction between a "non-serious" theatrical use of language and a "serious" or "ordinary" use of language. Jacques Derrida, Barbara Johnson, and Shoshana Felman have amply demonstrated that such a distinction is untenable. But each of these critics argues, as well, that Austin's failed distinction is extremely revealing. When Austin writes that something "peculiar" is at work onstage or in a poem, his choice of words reminds us that his work is "often more fruitful in the acknowledgment of its impasses than in its positions."[37] I recall Austin's unsuccessful distinction, rather, because of the considerable theoretical work on the status of the speaking subject which it has enabled. For Derrida, Austin's attempt to exclude "non-ordinary" poetic or theatrical language from his theory of performative action turns on a foundational belief in consciousness or intention: "the conscious presence of the intention of the speaking subject in the totality of his speech act." Derrida argues that this exclusion allows Austin to avoid acknowledging the "general citationality" or "general iterability" that is the "risk" or "failure" internal to all performative intentions—their "positive condition of possibility." It is not that the "category of intention will disappear," only that intention will no longer "govern the entire scene and system of utterance": "the intention animating the utterance will never be through and through present to itself and its content."[38] Derrida therefore argues that an "absence of intention" is "essential" to performative utterances; and he calls such absence the performative's "structural unconscious."[39] In *The Literary Speech Act,* Felman elaborates the full psychoanalytic resonance of such a phrase, discussing the consequences of the performative's "structural unconscious" for her understanding of the condition of the speaking subject. Reading Austin together with Lacan, she rephrases Lacan's "deliberately superficial" notion of the unconscious in terms of a poststructuralist theory of the failure necessary to performatives. "It is precisely from the *breach in knowledge* . . . that the act takes its performative *power*: it is the very *knowledge that cannot know itself,* that [in the speaking subject] *acts.*"[40]

In order to specify what such a definition of the "structural unconscious" of performative utterances means for Hermione's courtroom speech, we must remember one further comment about what Austin finds so "peculiar" in a performative uttered onstage. As Barbara Johnson succinctly puts it, when Austin tries to distinguish between ordinary language and theatrical language for the purposes of his theory, he is "objecting not to the use of the verb but to the status of its subject." For in a poem or on the stage, "the speaking subject is only a persona, an actor, not a person." A theatrical performative is "peculiar" insofar as it reveals how all performatives put personae in place of persons. It reminds us that the necessity of speaking *in persona*—intrinsic to the conventionality of all performatives—opens up a difference *within* the speaker.[41] Johnson evokes *Hamlet* to illustrate her point: "the nonseriousness of a performative utterance 'said by an actor on the stage' results, then, not from his fictional status but *from his duality,* from the spectator's consciousness that although the character in the play is swearing to avenge his dead father's ghost, the actor's own performative commitments lie elsewhere."[42]

In the case of the trial scene in *The Winter's Tale,* Shakespeare presents us with an escalating succession of performatives. The series opens with the somber tones of an indictment that, because it is uttered in a play, divides its speaker from himself: "'Hermione, queen to the worthy Leontes, . . . thou art here accused and arraigned of high treason, in committing adultery,'" and so on (3.2.12-14); the messengers follow suit, swearing that they have fetched the oracle and left it unopened ("All this we swear" [l. 130]). And it culminates in an oracular message that should provide the last word by enacting the verdict it announces. In the case of Hermione, who explains why she can and will not utter the words "Not guilty," the play's rhetorical move here is pointedly and internally citational: she repeats Polixenes's phrase, thereby reminding us that he, in turn, was quoting a conventional utterance despite the fantasy of his youth as an originary moment prior to language. Hermione's quotation, then, makes us uncertain of the status of the subject who is giving her voice to these deeply conventional words by elaborately refusing to say them. The conceit of her impossible "Not guilty" tells us that "Hermione" is at once a (persuasive) character terribly wronged by her doubting husband *and* an actor "whose own performative commitments lie elsewhere." Hermione evanescently evokes the action her words cannot achieve if uttered, reminding us that this is so, in part, because we are listening to an actor speak in a play. Hermione's words do pass into action but not the act she intended and certainly not the one that the character "Hermione" could know. What she knows—that these words will fail—and what she does—reveal herself through these words as an actor playing a falsely accused Hermione—do not coincide.

Hermione protests that she has been "proclaim'd a strumpet" and "hurried / *Here to this place, i' th' open air*" to proclaim innocence in vain (ll. 104-5, my emphasis). It is "here" in "this place" that Hermione puts "Not guilty" in quotation marks. Her deictics refer us, within the fiction, to Leontes's mock courtroom. As if underlining the self-reflexive nature of performative utterances, however, they also refer us to the story's frame—to the "here" and now of "this" stage on which Hermione speaks.[43] The disjunction or misfiring that happens in "this place" of the theater is what Felman might call the unconscious action of *The Winter's Tale*, a "knowledge that cannot know itself" and therefore hollows out the speaking subject, Hermione, from within her own voice. Further still, Felman's psychoanalytic view of the import of theatrical performatives suggests that we must examine the relation between the play's unsettling rhetorical performance and its story of sexuality. I have argued that Hermione's "Not guilty," echoing Polixenes's "Not guilty," colors the entire question of performative misfiring through Leontes's obsession with female sexual guilt; only in the prelapsarian world inhabited by male twins do plea and verdict coincide. But if we read Hermione's rhetoric in light of the material conditions of the theater for which her lines were written—the here and now of the English transvestite theater—we are confronted with a division within the speaking subject called Hermione that is peculiar indeed. We are reminded not merely that Hermione is an actor, but that the voice speaking these lines was that of a *boy*-actor playing a falsely accused wife and mother. Leontes's suspicions may reduce Hermione's tongue to her body; similarly, the story attached to the two versions of "Not guilty" may define Hermione's voice through a story about the necessary link between the female body and sexual guilt. But the material practice of the English Renaissance stage, to which the rhetoric of Hermione's speech also refers, would tell a far different story about Hermione's body, one in which the alleged difference between two sexes is in fact a difference within one. The hollowness or duality of "her" voice, then, mirrors a division internal to the play's representation of gender. That is, the metatheatrical echo implicit in the performative and Hermione's deictics reminds us, as I suggested at the opening of this essay, that Shakespeare's representation of a "female" voice—what it can or cannot say and what effects it achieves—is a dramatic trope. It is, quite literally, a "travesty" of womanhood, a femininity-effect rather than a revelation of anything essential to what it continues to call the "female" tongue.

We might understand the tropological status of what counts as female in this play in one further way. As we have seen, what Felman calls an unconscious "breach in knowledge" is marked by the misfiring of "Not guilty." The precise content of this phrase will not let us forget that for Shakespeare a specific sexual story deeply informs what might otherwise seem a strictly rhetorical failure. Indeed, Felman's discussion of the affinities between Austin and Lacan suggests something further about the mysterious female body in *The Winter's Tale*. Through its constant meditation on the failures of its own language to reveal the truth or to act as intended, the play turns the secret of "female" sexuality—the question raised by Hermione's pregnancy—into what Lacan calls the missed encounter. Disjunction defines the subject's mediated, eccentric relation to "the real." One might say of the play's relation to Hermione what Lacan says of the speaking subject's relation to the real: "Misfiring *is* the object."[44] On such an understanding of the discursive limits to knowledge, we might comprehend what Stanley Cavell aptly calls Leontes's skeptical "annihilation of the world" in other terms—as the vanishing of the maternal body before the joint pressure of language and of fantasy. That is, Shakespeare is exploring the (Cartesian) problem of radical doubt by representing a specific body—the maternal body—as the privileged object that resists the play's knowledge and its verbal action.[45] A psychoanalytic perspective, moreover, reminds us that it is not a philosopher's idea about a deceptive, malignant deity but a husband's idea about a deceptive, pregnant wife which sets the process of skeptical annihilation in motion. Foundational to the way the play rhetorically defines the limits of knowledge, the female body remains, nonetheless, forever fugitive.

III. "Be Stone No More"

The literary figure to whom Shakespeare turns to explore such a vexed relation to the world is Ovid's Pygmalion.[46] For both skepticism *and* projection join hands to fashion Leontes's misery (e.g., "Your actions are my dreams"). On David Ward's persuasive argument for retaining the punctuation of the First Folio and for remembering the contemporary meaning of "co-active" as "coercive" or "compulsory" (and not merely "acting in concert"), Leontes's speech about "affection" is stressing "the *coercive* nature of affection," its "action upon the 'nothing' it generates in the imagination" (as Ward parses it, "Affection . . . Thou . . . Communicat'st with dreams . . . With what's unreal: thou co-active art, / And fellow'st nothing" [1.2.138-42]).[47] In addition, it is through Ovid's Orpheus-Pygmalion sequence—particularly as given the influential contours of Petrarchan linguistic self-consciousness—that Shakespeare can explore the subject's missed relation to that (maternal) object not as a process of doubting alone but as a meditation on the simultaneously productive and aberrant effects of rhetoric—on language conceived not merely as a representation *of* the world but as a mode of action *in* the world. As I suggested above concerning Hermione's vain yet truthful swearing of innocence and Paulina's successful yet false swearing of death, such action, precisely by distinguishing the two halves of the play, turns the relation between the subject and the world of which it speaks into a recurrent misfiring. On the one hand, neither saying nor swearing reestablishes the faith in Leontes required for Hermione to live as herself, outside Leontes's "dreams" or beyond the "language" of male fantasy she "understands not." And on the other, when Paulina's words do have effect, they do their work through a lie. That such misfirings as these or Hermione's impossible "Not guilty" are inaugurated by the mere sight of her pregnant body or the sound of her voice I understand as the symptom of a deeply entrenched—though not necessary or inevitable—collusion between the representational and libidinal economies of patriarchal culture.

When the truth of Hermione is the object of representation, representation fails, drawing attention to the opacity of language rather than the clarity of truth.[48] And when

Hermione speaks, something happens that she does not intend: though she intends to persuade Polixenes to stay, her words trigger Leontes's jealousy; though she intends to speak of her innocence, her speech about the failure of "Not guilty" in her case declares her an actor and the scene the space of the theater. That a failed performative still has power to act despite having dislocated language's action from intention becomes vividly clear when the scene ends. For this self-reflexively theatrical trial produces further unintended effects. We hear that Mamillius, "with mere conceit and fear / Of the Queen's speed" in this staged trial, has died (3.2.144-45). And the report of his death becomes, in turn, words with the power to kill: "This news is mortal to the Queen" (l. 148). Hermione's unintended act—the "Not guilty" that produces the effect of theatricality—and the lethal effects that attend the play's reflection on its own fictive enactment darkly underline Shakespeare's attempt to evoke consciously and artistically controlled theatrical effects through Paulina's staging of Pygmalion's statue. That story works through yet another woman's voice to rein in the action of a now-benign theater in which language appears to perform the act it intends: "Music! awake her! . . . descend; be stone no more" (5.3.98-99).

Paulina's imperative to the statue, we should note, is not literally a performative utterance. Rather, her command represents an *idea* about language as performance. Shakespeare inherits this idea from Ovid's Orpheus and calls it "magic": the dream of a voice so persuasive that it can effect the changes of which it speaks.[49] It is the dream of a language that, when it acts, "fills up" the grave, makes good our debt to time. Paulina's spectacle of Hermione-as-statue offers more than a meditation on the desire to see in the theater: it becomes a visual analogue for the play's desire for a truly performative language. The long-awaited verbal event—signaled by such performatives as "Not guilty," the incessant taking of oaths, and the search for oracular truth—finds its culminating visual icon in the event of Hermione's "animation." Drawing on verbal and visual fictions, Shakespeare nonetheless accentuates the power of the voice in Paulina's heavily weighted moment of invocation and, eventually, in the much-desired event of Hermione's speech. Although Leontes declares himself content to be a "looker-on" (l. 85), thus inscribing the audience in the theatrical circuit of his desire, and though Paulina apologizes for the effects of the "sight of my poor image" (l. 57), what everyone waits to hear is Hermione's voice. As the doubters in Paulina's audience demand, "If she pertain to life let her speak too" (l. 113) and "Ay, and make it manifest where she has liv'd, / Or how stol'n from the dead" (ll. 114-15). The scene, however, both claims and disavows the Orphic power for which it longs. Availing itself of a language at once oral and visual, this theater seems to "steal" Hermione, like Eurydice, "from the dead." At the same time, we hear a warning, through Paulina, that the Orphic story of life, were it "told . . . should be hooted at / Like an old tale" (ll. 116-17).

The acts that words do in the courtroom scene exceed intention and, by so doing, turn the theater into the space of these unpredictable effects. The final scene attempts to control verbal action through Paulina's careful stage management, her magically effective voice. Yet such an attempt may all too easily recall Leontes's disastrous desire to master the world by controlling all language. It therefore does not go unqualified. On the one hand, when Paulina proclaims "descend; be stone no more," a woman's successful voice in *The Winter's Tale* appears to replace Pygmalion's successful prayer to Venus in the *Metamorphoses*. On the other, just as Hermione once reminded her husband that even his own language exceeds his control, so now her voice is the one to remind us that the play's seeming animation is only a fiction. Despite the ruse of death, she has "preserv'd" herself somewhere else (l. 127). Hermione, moreover, says nothing to the man who now longs to hear her speak. She seems poised to speak to him—"Still methinks / There is an air comes from her. What fine chisel / Could ever yet cut breath?" (ll. 77-79)—but does not. Leontes's lines should remind us that throughout the *Metamorphoses* "breath" is the etymological root for Ovid's interest in speaking voices and poetry as "song": Apollo's "breath," the "wind" streaming through Daphne's hair, and the Orphic "*vox*" telling the story of the statue's animation all derive from the narrator's fascination with the vicissitudes of speech, with the uneasy relationship between voice and mind. For the *anima* in animation—meaning "the mind," "consciousness," and "breath"—is derived from the Greek *anemos* for "wind" internal and external to the body.[50] In this image of the chisel that can "cut breath," Leontes signals his, and the play's, desire for a rhetoric of animation, for a theatrical version of the "*l'aura*" or "breeze" that blows through the figures of the *Rime Sparse* or the "breath" that Ovid asks the gods to bestow on his song (I. 1-3).

What Hermione does and does not say in this scene tells us something about the cost of that desire. Given the gendered relations of power passed down through literary history as the "air" that seems to "come from her," very much indeed hangs on Hermione's voice. I take the fact of Hermione's silence toward Leontes—and the fact that, after she moves, Leontes never asks her a direct question—to be Shakespeare's way of acknowledging the problems raised by her voice in the first three acts. Nothing she says to Leontes diminishes the force of his projections; the language she "understand[s] not" limits the field of her possible responses; and any answer she makes must still be read by him, a reading she cannot control. This awareness of the limits that Leontes's fantasy places on the stony lady's possible reply stems, in part, from Shakespeare's understanding that, in Ovid as in Petrarch, the stories of Pygmalion and Narcissus are deeply intertwined.[51] Leontes has, of course, always viewed others through the mediating screen of his own form. Observing his son in Act 1, he begins testing his theory about his wife's guilt according to whether or not Mamillius is his mirror: "Looking on the lines / Of my boy's face, methoughts I did recoil / Twenty-three years, and saw myself unbreech'd" (1.2.153-55). Even Leontes's admission of culpability in the final scene, prompted when he gazes on the "statue," surreptitiously imports Narcissus's story into Pygmalion's. Repentant though he may be, Leontes still reads Hermione as a version of himself: "does not the stone rebuke me / For being more stone than it?" (5.3.37-38). To Leontes even her stoniness is not "hers." If anything of the world is to return to Leontes that does not stand at the level of his dreams, it cannot do so within the reflexively binary terms proposed by Petrarchan rhetoric. Rather, Paulina's intervention tells us that if Hermione is to be restored to Leontes and not fade away again before the force of fantasy and doubt, it is on the condition that she *not* respond to his words only, that she not conform utterly to his language and his desire. Therefore a third party (Paulina) must manage this meeting from outside the restrictive frame of Pygmalion's desirous yet annihilating address.

And finally, what Hermione *does* say—precisely not to Leontes but to her lost daughter—offers a telling index of how constraining have been the terms of that address. What Pygmalion loathes, what his phantasmatic love for his *simulacrum* pushes aside, Ovid tells us, is not simply female sexuality but "the female *mind*" ("*menti / femineae*" [X.244-45]). So one final allusion to the *Metamorphoses* tells us something about that mind. Hermione's allusion prompts a question that seems never to occur to Petrarch: what does *she* want? The shift from Petrarchan autobiography to Shakespearean ventriloquism marks a subtly but crucially different return to Ovidian narrative. In *The Winter's Tale*, Shakespeare animates Petrarchan tropes in order to perform an ethical critique of them, particularly the animating rhetoric of address and its role in Petrarch's story of love and the self. When Shakespeare listens once more to Ovid's female voices, he shifts the emphasis away from the otherness within the self (Petrarch's "exile" of blindness, obsession, and forgetting) to pose, instead, a question: the question of the other's desire. And for a moment that "other"—the Petrarchan stony lady—has something else in mind than "responding" to the speaker whose apostrophe restricts them both ("*se risponder savesse a' detti miei!*"). What "moved" Hermione, her last words tell us, were thoughts of Perdita. Turning to a daughter who has already coded herself as Proserpina at the moment of dropping her flowers, Hermione models herself on Ceres as a mother unable to forget her lost, though still living, daughter:

> Tell me, mine own,
> Where hast thou been preserv'd? where liv'd? how found
> Thy father's court? for thou shalt hear that I,
> Knowing by Paulina that the oracle
> Gave hope thou wast in being, have preserv'd
> Myself to see the issue.
>
> (5.3.123-28)

Hermione's question to Perdita—"Where hast thou been preserv'd? where liv'd?"—obliquely recalls Ovid's story of violent rape and maternal grief by making her reason for living the hope of reunion with her daughter.

Where the suspicion of female sexual guilt defines the relation between time and language's action in the first half of the play, in this final scene both are redefined by another story—that of rape and maternal grief. Hermione's allusion to Book V of the *Metamorphoses*, of course, echoes the title, place, and time of *The Winter's Tale*. For Ceres's grief over Proserpina's rape brought winter into the world. Golding's translation of that grief brings the story of Ceres closer still to that of the animated statue in Act 5. When the nymph Arethusa tells Ceres why her daughter has vanished, Golding renders Ovid's lines as follows: "Hir mother stoode as starke as stone . . . And long she was like one that in another worlde had beene."[52] It is left to Shakespeare's Hermione to return from that "other world" of stone in order to be reunited with her Proserpina. Alongside Pygmalion's prayer and Orpheus's suppliant song, then, we must also remember Ceres's curse. In Ovid's text we find yet another story, often less well remembered, about a voice that can bring about the changes of which it speaks. Orpheus's mother, the muse Calliope, tells us that when Ceres saw Proserpina's girdle floating on the surface of the pool, she "reproached all the lands loudly, calling them ungrateful . . . but *Sicily above all other lands,* where she had found the traces of her loss. . . . She ordered the plowed fields to fail in their trust and spoiled the seed" (ll. 474-80). Setting his "old tale" of Leontes's winter in Sicily, Shakespeare invokes but finally turns attention away from the fantasy of the animated statue.[53] He thereby suggests that Pygmalion's self-reflexive fantasy so narrowly constricts female speech that there is, quite literally, *nothing* Hermione can say. Yet by recalling Proserpina's rape and Ceres's powerful reproach, he grants her voice a different authority. Her last words to Perdita fleetingly testify to the violence against the female body that subtends such "old" and "sad" tales as that of an animated statue or the first appearance of winter.

Female voices in *The Winter's Tale* acquire an oblique but telling power: the power to point out that, in the Ovidian tradition, stories about poetic authority, creativity, or "voice," however purely "poetic" their claims may seem, nonetheless entail violence against the female body. Not necessarily conscious, that violence continues to emerge in the unlikely circumstance of metapoetic or metatheatrical reflection. Challenging Ovidian-Petrarchan tropes for male vocal power when they thwart Leontes's desire to control speech, the tongues of Hermione and Paulina recall Ovid's rhetorically self-conscious narratives of rape, misogyny, and female vengeance that form the background for Orpheus's descent into the underworld. When Shakespeare returns to Ovidian narrative in this play, therefore, he reminds us that if we isolate Pygmalion's story from Orpheus's, or Proserpina's from Ceres's, we fail to notice the ethical dilemmas woven into the very fabric of Ovid's rhetorical self-consciousness in the *Metamorphoses*. Investigating the causes and effects of rhetorical speech through these seemingly disparate figures, and inviting reflection on the connections between language and sexuality proposed by their interwoven stories, Shakespeare reveals the cost to women of Ovid's foundational tropes for poetic authority. It is in the voices of Hermione and

Paulina that we catch something of the sound of that cost. In their voices *The Winter's Tale* stages a cautionary story about the uncanny returns of cultural inheritance, one that attests to the often unconscious—yet no less lethal—consequences of representing such things as love, voice, and beauty in the Ovidian tradition.

Notes

A number of colleagues read and commented on this essay with care and acuity. I would like to thank them here: Ian Duncan, Kevin Dunn, Richard Halpern, William Jewett, Wayne Koestenbaum, Larry Manley, Jeff Nunokawa, Patricia Rosenmeyer, and Katherine Rowe. I owe the inaugural idea for this essay to a conversation several years ago with David Marshall.

1. Quotations of Shakespeare's plays follow *The Riverside Shakespeare,* ed. G. Blakemore Evans (Boston: Houghton Mifflin, 1974).

2. William R. Morse, "Metacriticism and Materiality: The Case of Shakespeare's *The Winter's Tale,*" *ELH* 58 (1991): 283-304, esp. 297.

3. How to read Hermione's silence has been an important question in much criticism of *The Winter's Tale*. I am particularly indebted to Kenneth Gross, *The Dream of the Moving Statue* (Ithaca, NY, and London: Cornell UP, 1992), 105-9; and Leonard Barkan, "'Living Sculptures': Ovid, Michelangelo, and *The Winter's Tale,*" *ELH* 48 (1981): 639-67.

4. For an overview, see Barkan, *The Gods Made Flesh: Metamorphosis & the Pursuit of Paganism* (New Haven, CT, and London: Yale UP, 1986). As Barkan comments of "Diana and Actaeon," Titian turns Ovid's story of Actaeon's visual transgression into a painting that comments on the act of looking at a painting. Actaeon, poised "on the threshold," lifts a curtain to gaze on Diana; therefore "the bath almost becomes a picture within a picture. The result is a powerful identification between the viewer and Actaeon as both participate in the visual, the voyeuristic, and the visionary" (200-201). One could make similar comments about the resonance between Petrarch's many allusions to Ovid's stories about the human voice and the characteristic fiction that a lyric poem is a spoken utterance—particularly in light of its favored trope, apostrophe. Such aesthetically self-reflexive allusions to Ovid's *Metamorphoses* are not a purely "Renaissance" phenomenon. On Dante's poetically self-conscious appropriations of Ovidian narrative, for example, see Rachel Jacoff and Jeffrey T. Schnapp, eds., *The Poetry of Allusion: Virgil and Ovid in Dante's "Commedia"* (Stanford, CA: Stanford UP, 1991).

5. Barkan, "'Living Sculptures,'" 660.

6. Sonnets 77 and 78. For further discussion of the relationship between Ovid's version of Pygmalion and Petrarch's, see my "Embodied Voices: Petrarch Reading (Himself Reading) Ovid" in *Desire in the Renaissance: Psychoanalysis and Literature,* Valeria Finucci and Regina Schwartz, eds. (Princeton, NJ: Princeton UP, 1994), 120-45.

7. I have here modified the translation of Robert M. Durling in *Petrarch's Lyric Poems: The Rime sparse and Other Lyrics* (Cambridge, MA, and London: Harvard UP, 1976) to capture the rhetorically specific sense of the verb *lodare,* "to praise." Elsewhere in this essay translations of Petrarch are Durling's. Barbara Johnson distinguishes between the two apostrophes in Shelley's "Ode to the West Wind" in a way that is useful for reading Petrarch's two sonnets: the first, emotive "if only" lays stress on the first person, and the second, vocative "Pygmalion" on the second person. The typography of Shelley's poem marks this difference as one between "oh" and "O," a difference Johnson allies with the one between Roman Jakobson's emotive function, or "pure presencing of the first person," and his conative function, or "the pure presencing of the second person" (Johnson, *A World of Difference* [Baltimore and London: Johns Hopkins UP, 1987], 187).

8. "[N]on minus nominis quam ipsius corporis splendore captus" (Petrarch, *Prose,* ed. G. Martellotti, P. G. Ricci, E. Carrara, and E. Bianchi [Milan and Naples: Riccardo Riccardi Editore, 1955], 158). Petrarch's anagrams and puns on *laurel* derive from Ovid's own verbal wit in the story of Apollo and Daphne (*Metamorphoses,* I.451ff).

9. On epideixis and gender in Petrarchanism, see Joel Fineman, "Shakespeare's *Will*: The Temporality of Rape" in *The Subjectivity Effect in Western Literary Tradition: Essays Toward the Release of Shakespeare's Will* (Cambridge, MA, and London: MIT Press, 1991), 165-221; and Nancy Vickers, "'The blazon of sweet beauty's best': Shakespeare's *Lucrece*" in *Shakespeare and the Question of Theory,* Patricia Parker and Geoffrey Hartman, eds. (New York and London: Methuen, 1985), 95-115.

10. Quotations of the *Metamorphoses* follow the text translated and edited by Frank Justus Miller (Cambridge, MA: Harvard UP, 1927), though I have made a few silent emendations to Miller's translations.

11. *The. xv. Bookes of P. Ouidius Naso; entytuled Metamorphosis, translated oute of Latin into English meeter, by Arthur Golding Gentleman* (London, 1567), 123[r].

12. The association between the stories of Orpheus and Eurydice and Apollo and Daphne is commonplace. The most influential Renaissance commentator on Ovid's poem, Raphael Regius, claims that Orpheus is Apollo's son, adding that the singer received his lyre from Apollo as a gift (*Metamorphoses* [Venice, 1556], X.1). The first edition of Regius's commentary appeared in 1492.

13. Despite the frequent representation of polymorphous desires in the *Metamorphoses,* Ovid's narrative almost always brings homoerotic moments such as this one back into the orbit of a controlling heterosexual imperative. Thus Iphis's love for Ianthe, which immediately precedes the story of Orpheus, is refracted through a missing penis; the phallus becomes the sign, therefore, that the love of one woman for another is "more mad" than the love of a woman for a bull (IX.668-797). Similarly, although Orpheus may be the "author" of love for boys, that love is represented as the effect of, and only in relation to, his love for his dead wife; the jury of avenging Bacchic women in Book XI then judge his love again as merely the sign of his feelings about women. Because of this frame (and its repetition in the hands of Pygmalion, Orpheus's surrogate), the song in Book X about the many kinds of transgressive love has little to say about male-male eroticism on its own terms.

14. Harry Berger Jr. recently argued that a gynophobic and misogynist discourse informs Book X ("Actaeon at the Hinder Gate: The Stag Party in Spenser's Gardens of Adonis" in Finucci and Schwartz, eds., 91-119).

15. Leontes signals an awareness of this punitive possibility. But he does so in the domestic register, containing the threat no sooner than uttered: "Chide me, dear stone, that I may say indeed / Thou art Hermione; or rather, thou art she / In thy not chiding; for she was as tender / As infancy and grace" (5.3.24-27).

16. John Marston, "The Metamorphosis of Pigmalions Image" in *Elizabethan Minor Epics,* ed. Elizabeth Story Donno (London: Routledge and Kegan Paul, 1963), 244-52, esp. 244. Citations of Marston follow this edition. On Marston's satire of the language of erotic idealism, particularly in the Petrarchan mode, see William Keach, *Elizabethan Erotic Narratives: Irony and Pathos in the Ovidian Poetry of Shakespeare, Marlowe, and Their Contemporaries* (New Brunswick, NJ: Rutgers UP, 1977), 134-61.

17. For a history of this misogynist tradition, see Barbara Rico's "From 'Speechless Dialect' to 'Prosperous Art': Shakespeare's Recasting of the Pygmalion Image," *Huntington Library Quarterly* 48 (1985): 285-95. Except for the two works I discuss here—the last act of *The Winter's Tale* and Petrarch's paired sonnets (77 and 78)—the Pygmalion story is generally not a positive one in the Middle Ages or the Renaissance. Misogynist diatribes inform it, and the story of prostitution, too, clings to it: John Marston uses Pygmalion to adjudicate between the "wanton" and the "obsceane" (252), and George Pettie's *A Petite Pallace* (London, 1586) alludes to the story of the statue in overtly misogynist ways. Jonathan Bate, in a book otherwise dedicated to tracing the minutiae of Ovid's *presence* in Shakespeare's poetry, oddly dismisses the relevance to *The Winter's Tale* of the misogynist genealogy in Ovid (*Shakespeare and Ovid* [Oxford: Clarendon Press, 1993]).

18. It seems to me no accident that the artist Shakespeare chose for his Pygmalion, Giulio Romano, was known not only as a painter but as a pornographer. The nature of Shakespeare's reference to Romano has been much debated. For a useful summary of the debate as well as an account of a contemporary English conduct book for young women which refers to the excellent work of "Iules Romain," see Georgianna Ziegler, "Parents, Daughters, and 'That Rare Italian Master': A New Source for *The Winter's Tale,*" *Shakespeare Quarterly* 36 (1985): 204-12. For Romano's notorious, if rarely seen, collaboration with Aretino (the so-called *posizioni*), see David O. Frantz, *Festum Voluptatis: A Study of Renaissance Erotica* (Columbus: Ohio State UP, 1989), 46-48 and 119-23; and Frederick Hartt, *Giulio Romano* (New Haven, CT: Yale UP, 1958), 29. As Hartt points out, Romano's prints, though suppressed, were also widely copied and widely destroyed; Frantz notes that when Perino del Vaga and Agostino Carracci imitated Romano, they did so in an Ovidian vein, calling their own versions of the "*posizioni*" the "loves of the gods" (123). It is the rumor of Romano's work, rather than an actual copy in England, that seems to me important to Shakespeare's reference.

19. See Janet Adelman's account of dreams of male parthenogenesis and the problem of the maternal body in this play in *Suffocating Mothers: Fantasies of Maternal Origin in Shakespeare's Plays,* Hamlet *to* The Tempest (New York and London: Routledge, 1992).

20. For a persuasive reading of the way language violates Philomela as surely as her rape—particularly Ovid's meditation on the severed "*lingua*" (both tongue and language more generally)—see Elissa Marder's recent "Disarticulated Voices: Feminism and Philomela," *Hypatia* 7 (Spring 1992): 148-66. My claim about Medusa lies outside the scope of this essay; I take up her story in greater detail in my next book, *The Rhetoric of the Body in Renaissance Ovidian Poetry.*

21. *Figura* signifies in both grammatical and rhetorical registers and designates the material aspects of writing as well. It can specify a written symbol or character or refer to the form, spelling, or grammatical inflection of a Latin word; it is also a rhetorical term for trope.

22. [F]*igura*, definition 3; see *Oxford Latin Dictionary,* 3 vols. (Oxford: Clarendon Press, 1968), 1:700.

23. [F]*igura*, definition 11, *OLD,* 1:700.

24. Here we should remember that, according to Ovid, Medusa became the Gorgon because she was raped,

and her beheading produced the fountain of poetry. Pegasus arose from the Gorgon's blood, and the Heliconian fountain, in turn, arose from the "beating of his feet" (both the horse's feet and the feet of poetic meter). The origin of poetry's fountain is therefore "the blood of the mother," the raped Medusa ("*vidi ipsum materno sanguine nasci . . . est Pegasus huius origo / fontis*" [V.259-63]).

25. For an analysis of the role that bodies—especially female bodies—play in the relationship between desire and "the drive to know" in modern narrative, see Peter Brooks, *Body Work: Objects of Desire in Modern Narrative* (Cambridge, MA, and London: Harvard UP, 1993). Leontes's devotion to speaking about the fantasized "truth" of Hermione's body might usefully be considered part of what Brooks calls "epistemophilia," a project in which we tell stories "about the body in the effort to know and to have it" and which results "in making the body a site of signification—the place for the inscription of stories—and itself a signifier, a prime agent in narrative plot and meaning" (5-6).

26. I adapt the phrase "verbal fetishism" from John Freccero ("The Fig Tree and the Laurel: Petrarch's Poetics" in *Literary Theory/Renaissance Texts*, Patricia Parker and David Quint, eds. [Baltimore and London: Johns Hopkins UP, 1986], 20-32, esp. 22). My understanding of the nature of fetishism in Petrarch and the literary filiation from which it derives differs from Freccero's and is outlined in my "Embodied Voices."

27. Marston, 246.

28. Petrarch uses both female and male Ovidian characters to suggest that he is alienated from his own tongue; the story of Actaeon, as well as of Echo and Daphne, appears in canzone 23 for this purpose. For further comment on Actaeon, see my "Embodied Voices." As we have seen, Ovid no sooner proposes the story of male poetic control over language than he dissolves it; this dissolution subtends Petrarch's poetic self-portrait. Although Ovid and Petrarch after him suggest that alienation from one's own tongue is the condition of having a voice—male or female—in both poets the trope of a female voice appears strategically, as the place in the text where one can hear the greatest strain on such cherished illusions about artistic vocal power as those proposed by Apollo, Pan, Pygmalion, and Orpheus. It is the diacritical function of the female voice, its ironic juxtaposition to such ostensibly "male" fantasies, that is important for understanding Shakespeare's representation of the tongues of Hermione and Paulina.

29. Heather Dubrow has recently argued that we must attend carefully to the complex and often contradictory role of Laura's voice if we are to understand the "relationship among speech, power, and gender" in the *Rime Sparse* and beyond; see her *Echoes of Desire: English Petrarchism and its Counterdiscourses* (Ithaca, NY, and London: Cornell UP, 1995), 40-48, esp. 42.

30. J. L. Austin, *How to do things with Words,* ed. J. O. Urmson (Oxford: Clarendon Press, 1962), 1 and 6. Austin lists *swear* (along with such other verbs as *promise, give my word, pledge myself*) as part of a class of "commissive" performatives in which conventional phrases are deployed to "commit the speaker to a certain course of action" (156-57). Over the course of his lectures, Austin renders problematic his "provisional" performative/constative distinction; he eventually rejects any absolute dichotomy between the two, finding that constatives may well have a performative aspect (91). My point here is simply to note that in *The Winter's Tale,* Shakespeare is exploring a distinction analogous to Austin's provisional one—between statements that report some state of affairs truly or falsely (in this case, the "state of affairs" in question being Hermione's fidelity) and other, conventional statements (such as "I swear") in which saying and doing explicitly converge. For a study of performatives in Shakespeare with an emphasis on cultural and institutional authority, see Susanne L. Wofford, "'To You I Give Myself, For I Am Yours': Erotic Performance and Theatrical Performatives in *As You Like It*" in *Shakespeare Reread: The Texts in New Contexts,* Russ McDonald, ed. (Ithaca, NY, and London: Cornell UP, 1994), 147-69.

31. Since, unlike the audience, the characters in the story *can* "go and see" the dead body of Hermione, Paulina's lie is dramaturgically more complicated than my presentation of it. Leontes describes scenes that the audience does not observe, and his words give playgoers every reason to believe that he will verify for us the fact of Hermione's death: "Prithee bring me / To the dead bodies of my queen and son. / One grave shall be for both. . . . Once a day I'll visit / The chapel where they lie, and tears shed there / Shall be my recreation. . . . Come, and lead me / To these sorrows" (3.2.234-43). Critics have argued that these lines, coupled with Antigonus's report in 3.3 of the appearance of Hermione's spirit, suggest that when Shakespeare wrote Act 3, he still intended to follow his source, in which the dead wife does not return. Whatever Shakespeare's intentions, the play's refusal to clear up ambiguities about Hermione's possible death and resurrection provides a compelling link between the play and the Orpheus/Eurydice story.

For a discussion of critical responses to the problem of Hermione's death and unexpected revival, see Barbara A. Mowat, *The Dramaturgy of Shakespeare's Romances* (Athens: U of Georgia P, 1976), 77ff and 145, n. 18.

32. In thinking about the relationship between performativity and sexuality, I have drawn on

several important discussions: Judith Butler, *Bodies That Matter: On the Discursive Limits of "Sex"* (New York and London: Routledge, 1993); Shoshana Felman, *The Literary Speech Act: Don Juan with J. L. Austin, or Seduction in Two Languages* (Ithaca, NY: Cornell UP, 1983); Lynne Huffer, "Luce et veritas: Toward an Ethics of Performance," *Yale French Studies* (1995): 20-41; and Johnson, *The Critical Difference: Essays in the Contemporary Rhetoric of Reading* (Baltimore and London: Johns Hopkins UP, 1980).

33. Felman, 94-96, esp. 94. Analyzing performative language in relation to the stories of Don Juan and of Oedipus, Felman's work is equally telling for the central dilemma of *The Winter's Tale*: the relationship between theatrical representation and the female body or, more generally in Ovidian narrative, between body and voice. Felman writes that "the problem of the human act," in psychoanalysis as well as performative analysis, "consists in the relation between language and body . . . because the act is conceived . . . as that which problematizes at one and the same time the separation and the opposition between the two. The act, an enigmatic and problematic production of the *speaking body* . . . , breaks down the opposition between body and spirit, between matter and language" (94). She reminds us of Austin's comment that "in the last analysis, doing an action must come down to the making of physical movements with parts of the body; but this is about as true as . . . saying something must . . . come down to making movements of the tongue" (as quoted in Felman, 94).

34. Felman, 82. Austin explores the contingent and context-bound nature of any speech act in "the doctrine of Infelicities" (14-24). Jacques Derrida's critique of Austin constitutes a sustained analysis of "the failure" that is an "essential" risk of performative utterances; see Derrida, "Signature Event Context," first published in *Glyph* 1 (1977) and translated by Samuel Weber and Jeffrey Mehlman in *Limited Inc* (Evanston, IL: Northwestern UP, 1988), 1-24.

35. Austin, 16-17.

36. Austin, 22.

37. Derrida, 10.

38. Derrida, 14 and 17.

39. Derrida, 18.

40. Felman, 96.

41. "If one considers the conventionality of all performative utterances (on which Austin often insists), can it really be said that the chairman who opens a discussion or the priest who baptizes a baby or the judge who pronounces a verdict are persons rather than personae? . . . The performative utterance thus automatically fictionalizes its utterer when it makes him the mouthpiece of a conventionalized authority" (Johnson, *The Critical Difference,* 60). Or one could say, as well, that read rhetorically, the performative utterance may uncover the *theatrical* nature of such "ordinary" social actions.

42. Johnson, *The Critical Difference,* 60 (my emphasis).

43. In light of the duality of Hermione's deictics, we might read the specification "i' th' open air" within historical context as well. The stage in London's earliest commercial theaters projected into a yard and therefore placed actors "i' th' open air." On the physical conditions of London's public amphitheaters and private halls, see Andrew Gurr, *Playgoing in Shakespeare's London* (Cambridge: Cambridge UP, 1987), 13-48. Most critics believe the play to have been written for the closed theater of Blackfriars. But a note on the play by Simon Forman tells us that at least one contemporary remembers having seen *The Winter's Tale* performed at the Globe (on 15 May 1611).

44. Jacques Lacan, *Encore* (Paris: Seuil, 1975), 55. On the important difference between the usual misprision of the Lacanian "lack" and the productive process of misfiring, see Felman, 82-84.

45. Stanley Cavell, *Disowning Knowledge in Six Plays of Shakespeare* (Cambridge: Cambridge UP, 1987), 193-221, esp. 214. Cavell is, of course, most concerned with Leontes's doubts about his son and his paternity. But in light of Janet Adelman's work on the play, one is led to wonder, when poised between these two powerful essays, why it is the *maternal* body that sparks Leontes's radical doubt. I would add to Adelman's analysis only that it is Hermione's language—the effects of her voice—as well as her body that unsettle her husband's sense of himself. To Cavell's approach, similarly, I would add only that the play explores the action of Leontes's doubt through the action of both language and thought. For the scandal of what cannot be known—the truth about Hermione—turns, as we have seen, into an interrogation of the power and the limits of theatrical representation as well as of two kinds of discourse: saying and swearing.

46. It is perhaps worth remembering, as Jonathan Bate points out, that Shakespeare's contemporaries understood him to be the inheritor of Ovid. Drawing on the very rhetoric of animation at issue here, Francis Meres observed that "the sweete wittie soule of Ouid liues in mellifluous and hony-tongued Shakespeare" (*Palladis Tamia* [1598], as quoted in *Elizabethan Critical Essays,* G. Gregory Smith, ed. [Oxford: Clarendon Press, 1904], 317). For further comment on Renaissance Ovidianism, see Bate, 1-47; and *Ovid Renewed: Ovidian influences on literature and art from the Middle Ages to the twentieth century,* Charles Martindale, ed. (Cambridge: Cambridge UP, 1988).

47. David Ward, "Affection, Intention, and Dreams in *The Winter's Tale*," *Modern Language Review* 82 (1987): 545-54, esp. 552. Ward offers a precise discussion of Leontes's "affection" in relation to sixteenth-century faculty psychology, particularly in medical discourse. Looking at discussions in Hooker and Burton, Ward suggests that with this word Leontes is designating a "disease of the mind" linked to the faculty of the appetite rather than to the will or to reason; for Hooker, affection is both involuntary ("Wherefore it is not altogether in our power") and a desire for the impossible, for "any thing which seemeth good, be it never so impossible" (as quoted in Ward, 546). For Shakespeare, Ovid's combined stories of Pygmalion and Orpheus give a distinctive mythographic and erotic turn to the involuntary aspect of affection (revulsion from womankind out of grief or disgust) and its connotation of a desire for the impossible (for art to conquer death).

48. See Howard Felperin, "'Tongue-tied our queen?': the deconstruction of presence in *The Winter's Tale*" in Parker and Hartman, eds., 3-18. Although I clearly agree with Felperin's emphasis on the play's consciousness of its own failure to refer, it seems to me that, by framing the question in terms of the possibility that Hermione may be guilty, Felperin participates in the very logic he critiques; his reading repeats what it might otherwise analyze—the question of *why* language's misfiring should be represented in cognitive terms as the truth or falsity of the maternal body.

49. Ovid, of course, shared this dream: the final lines of the *Metamorphoses* claim that the poet will live ("*vivam*"), his name survive the "gnawing tooth of time" though his body does not ("*nec edax abolere vetustas*"), if his poem is "read on the lips of the people" ("*perque omnia saecula fama*" [XV.871-79]). For my understanding of this scene, I am indebted to conversations with Thomas M. Greene on the relationship between poetry and magic. See his essays "The Balance of Power in Marvell's 'Horatian Ode,'" *ELH* 60 (1993): 379-96; and "Poetry as Invocation," *New Literary History* 24 (1993): 495-517.

50. Henry George Liddell and Robert Scott cite Hippocrates for the sense of wind in the body: derived from "ανε-, 'blow, breathe', cf. [Sanskrit], *áni-ti*, 'breathes'" (*Greek-English Lexicon*, 2 vols. [Oxford: Clarendon Press, 1951], 1:132). The primary meaning of *anima* is "breath" or "breathing as the characteristic manifestation of life," and it thus connotes "the characteristic or quality whose loss constitutes death" (*OLD*, 1:132-34). It can also designate "a disembodied spirit, soul, ghost" (132), a hint of which meaning appears, perhaps, when Polixenes asks Paulina to "make it manifest where she has liv'd, / Or how stol'n from the dead" (5.3.114-15). For interesting comments on the ghostly undertone here and at other moments in this scene, see Gross.

51. Since Ovid handled the scene, the link became one of the mainstays of the tradition. The subjective and objective genitive in Marston's title, "The Metamorphosis of Pigmalions Image," for instance, derives its power from this connection. Thus his Pygmalion is enamored less of the statue than of his own reflection in that statue: "Hee was amazed at the wondrous rarenesse / Of his owne workmanships perfection. . . . And thus admiring, was enamored / On that fayre Image *himselfe portraied*" (245, my emphasis). Pygmalion's resemblance to Narcissus was also central to the representation of the lover in the *Roman de la Rose*; for an overview, see Louise Vinge, *The Narcissus Theme in Western European Literature up to the Early 19th Century* (Lund: Gleerups, 1967). I learned to attend to the crucial role that Pygmalion and Narcissus play in the *Rime Sparse* from Giuseppe Mazzotta (*The Worlds of Petrarch* [Durham, NC, and London: Duke UP, 1993]).

52. Golding, 64ᵛ. Ovid uses the simile of turning to stone but says nothing of "another worlde": "*Mater ad auditas stupuit ceu saxea voces / attonitaeque diu similis fuit, utque dolore / pulsa gravi gravis est amentia*" (V.509-11). For another reading of the import of Ceres's grief for the play, see T. G. Bishop, *Shakespeare and the theatre of wonder* (Cambridge: Cambridge UP, 1996), 125-75.

53. Golding, too, preserves the detail of Sicily in his translation: "But bitterly aboue the rest she banned *Sicilie,* / In which the mention of hir losse she plainely did espie" (64ʳ). Understanding Hermione as a second Ceres may tell us why Shakespeare makes an otherwise puzzling change of location. Where Greene begins *Pandosto* in Bohemia and later moves to Sicily, Shakespeare *opens* the story of winter in Sicily only to move, in Act 4, to Bohemia's pastoral landscape.

SOURCES, INFLUENCES, AND IDEOLOGIES

William R. Morse (essay date 1991)

SOURCE: "Metacriticism and Materiality: The Case of Shakespeare's *The Winter's Tale*," in *ELH,* Vol. 58, No. 2, Summer, 1991, pp. 283-304.

[*In the essay below, Morse examines* The Winter's Tale *in order to reveal the shortcomings of New Historical criti-*

cism, and finds the ideology of the New Historicist conception to be "simplistic" and "misconceived."]

New Historical criticism of Renaissance literature over the past decade has not only effected a revolution in the way that critics read the literature and its relation to the culture that produces it, but has helped us to reconceive the nature of culture itself. Nevertheless, if the great strength of the school's approach has been the fertility and subtlety of its analyses of the cultural density which produces and is produced by literature, the theoretical models by which it has organized its reading have at times seemed inadequate, and thus misleading. The prevalent New Historicist conception of a dominant absolutist ideology centered in the court, in particular, seems in some ways simplistic, in others misconceived, and has generally tended towards a hegemonic conception of the nature of "dominant ideologies" that misrepresents in its totalizing impetus the inevitably multiform pressures of any culture understood not as historical object but rather as evolving process. There is a critical *aporia,* a hidden teleological hindsight at work, for instance, in the elaboration of a theory of cultural containment, the appropriation of all discourse by a unitary dominant ideology, that progressively rejects the autonomy, and thus ultimately the reality, of all subversion. More significantly, the prevalent New Historicist analysis of the dominant Renaissance ideology, the absolutist court of Elizabeth and James, is certainly oversimplified, and perhaps misconceived in historical terms. Given the comments by Anthony Easthope on the ideological implications of the rise of iambic pentameter, the analyses by Jonathan Dollimore and Catherine Belsey of the inscription in Renaissance drama of the liberal subject, and most especially the analysis of the emergence of "the discourse of modernism" by Timothy Reiss,[1] the whole question of the degree to which absolutist ideology was dominant, and indeed of whether it is best conceived as a residual element of an older discourse, or the first articulation of an emergent modern one, remains open.[2]

Beyond this specific problem lies a larger question, for the totalizing tendencies of the New Historicism could be seen to follow from a synchronic hypostatization of historical process. As Raymond Williams puts the issue:

> In what I have called "epochal" analysis, a cultural process is seized as a cultural system, with determinate dominant features. . . . This emphasis on dominant and definitive lineaments and features is important and often, in practice, effective. But it then often happens that its methodology is preserved for the very different function of historical analysis, in which a sense of movement within what is ordinarily abstracted as a system is crucially necessary, especially if it is to connect with the future as well as with the past. . . . Such errors are avoidable if, while retaining the epochal hypothesis, we can find terms which recognize not only "stages" and "variations" but the internal dynamic relations of any actual process.
>
> (121-22)

Exactly insofar as the New Historicism fails to address these dynamics of culture, and begins to totalize the "dominant feature" of its "epochal analysis"—the hegenomy of the court—thus far it is actually ahistorical in an important sense.

Related to this confusion is a certain imprecision in the use of the key term "ideology" itself. A number of recent critics, including Williams, have followed Louis Althusser's lead in complicating and extending the conception of ideology in response to the question of its relation to culture.[3] Althusser develops the argument that, since "ideology has a material existence," we must distinguish between on the one hand the traditional understanding of particular ideologies, implemented "by a 'clique' . . . who are the authors of the great ideological mystification" (165) and on the other "ideology in general . . . omnipotent and transhistorical" (160-61), of which it can be said that "there is no practice except by and in an ideology" (170). Although Williams uses the distinct terms "ideology" and "hegemony" in discussing these two senses of ideology, he develops a similar understanding based on Gramsci's distinction between "rule" and "hegemony":

> "Rule" is expressed in directly political forms and in times of crisis by direct or effective coercion. But the more normal situation is a complex interlocking of political, social, and cultural forces, and "hegemony" . . . is either this or the active social and cultural forces which are its necessary elements. . . . Hegemony is a concept which at once includes and goes beyond two powerful earlier concepts: that of "culture" as a "whole social process" [shaped by individuals] . . . and that of "ideology" [as] the projection of a particular class interest.
>
> (108)

From this distinction he comments that "it is in just this recognition of the *wholeness* of the process that the concept of 'hegemony' goes beyond 'ideology'" (108-9).

It is on the basis of Williams's work that Dollimore distinguishes between the "cognitive view" of ideology, "the view of ideology as a process of conspiracy on the part of the rulers and misrecognition on the part of the ruled," and a "materialist view," which identifies the incompleteness of the cognitive view by stressing "the extent to which ideology has a material existence; that is, ideology exists in, and as, the social practices which constitute people's lives. . . . Ideology becomes . . . the very terms in which we perceive the world, almost . . . the condition and grounds of consciousness itself" (9). Dollimore, following Williams, makes the valuable argument that the two articulations are "inextricably related" (10), and both are necessary to a full understanding of Renaissance culture. Nevertheless, he emphasizes the broader definition in his own analysis. This "materialist" analysis of ideology is at the heart of his reading of Renaissance drama as "radical tragedy," and at the heart, too, of the materialist disagreement with New Historical readings of the "dominant ideology" of Renaissance England. A good deal of the recent debate can be traced to a confusion of these two distinct senses of the term, for a focus on cognitive rather than material ideology is the source of the emphasis on the hegemony (using the term now in the New Historical rather than in Williams's sense) of the absolutist court.

A consideration of even so seemingly apolitical a play as Shakespeare's *The Winter's Tale* can help in representing the openness, the contingency, the play of culture and its inscription in the literary text, that are at work in this particular historical moment; not only does the text raise questions about the dominance of the court ideology in relation to the emergent modern discourse (this new discourse is itself clearly inscribed in the play), but it suggests ways in which the playwright is, if himself shaped by the culture's discourse, also consciously critical of it.[4] We may accept Fredric Jameson's dictum that we must "always historicize!"—that we must respect "the priority of the political interpretation of literary texts [and] the political perspective not as some supplementary method, not as an optional auxiliary to other interpretive methods current today . . . but rather as the absolute horizon of all reading and all interpretation."[5] It doesn't necessarily follow, however, that the drama can be reduced to the monolithic organ of Jacobean court ideology described by Leonard Tennenhouse[6] or to Stephen Greenblatt's radically contained "voice of subversion" that is actually "produced by the affirmations of order," nor that every aesthetic text addresses itself to the ideological in explicit, overt ways.[7] We must attend as well to the more fundamental epistemological grounds or ideological *structures* interrogated by these texts.

Language is the most obvious such structure. Reiss, for instance, carefully elaborates the complex ways in which discursive practices in the sixteenth century generally inscribe themselves within the consciousness of their particular practitioners. He comments nevertheless that at this historical moment the culture "teetered in the gap between an old discourse of analogies and a new one of analysis. But no longer were these presented as contradictory elements within a single class of discourse, or even as a class and a 'subclass' of emergent elements . . . a *choice was possible*" (168).[8] In the moment between the rising discourse's emergence from occlusion and its subsequent domination and suppression of the older orthodoxy, contradictions were briefly visible within the culture which both stimulated and authorized dissension. From this perspective Dollimore is correct to speak of "the period's developing awareness of ideology" (11).

Reiss argues that the distinction between an older analogical discourse of "patterning" and the modern "analytico-referential" discourse is to be found in "a passage from what one might call a discursive *exchange within* the world to the expression of knowledge as a reasoning *practice upon* the world" (30).[9] This suggests that absolutist culture itself, which deploys older, residual cultural elements in quite self-conscious ways, might more fruitfully be considered a preliminary manifestation of the newer discourse rather than the residual defender and champion of "custom and antiquity." As Stephen Orgel puts it, courtly mythology "was a mythology consciously designed to validate and legitimate an authority that must have seemed, to what was left of the old aristocracy, dangerously *arriviste*."[10]

From another perspective, Dollimore's insistence that Shakespeare's work be related to the skepticism of such figures as Machiavelli and Montaigne is especially promising because it emphasizes Shakespeare's self-conscious alienation from the absolutist discourse of the court; in raising the possibility that subversive tendencies of the Shakespearean drama might only be incompletely contained, he restores to the text a radical political openness. In particular, Dollimore cites the possibility of "the appropriation of dominant discourses" (27) by dissident elements within the culture, and his theoretical framework can clearly be applied not only to particular performances and texts but to forms of thought and expression as well.[11] I would argue that at least the later Shakespearean romances provide a perfect example: the appropriation of a genre closely associated with the older metaphysical discourse in order to interrogate and recast that discourse. As in his earlier experiments with both comic and tragic form, Shakespeare's self-conscious and artificial use of romance produces a disengagement within his audience that works toward the demystification of authority through the deconstruction of the transcendent conceptions of metaphysics and rationality that privilege and sustain it. Indeed, the relevance of romance itself could be conceived of as a structural subversion of the dominant discourse, bringing to fruition in Paulina's and Prospero's art the ironic challenge discernible as early as *A Midsummer Night's Dream* to all that "cool reason comprehends."

At the same time, however, because Shakespearean drama enacts a materialist critique of metaphysics, it is equally antagonistic to the emergent analytico-referential discourse. While Franco Moretti has persuasively argued that Shakespearean tragedy actively participates in the historic deconsecration of the absolutist monarch that eventuates in the execution of Charles I in 1649, the subversive implications of these works reach well beyond the status of the monarchy in itself. Moretti suggests that Renaissance tragedy defines the absolute monarch precisely in terms of an absolute disjunction between reason and will, will expressed in the *power* to act free of all rational restraint (11-12), thus effectually demystifying the monarch's metaphysical authority. But Shakespearean drama is preoccupied quite generally with that power of the human will subversive of all discursive reason, the power of the body of desire that is anterior to all rational purposing, and Shakespeare's critique of essentialist rationalism cannot but be equally subversive of an emergent culture whose fundamental empowering assumption remains, if reconstituted, human rationality.[12] The appropriation throughout the corpus of a dominant terminology of imagination, dream, and fantasy that inverts the normative schemes of psychic hierarchy works insistently to bring into question the grounds of the emergent discourse.[13]

Not only in *King Lear,* but in *Hamlet, Troilus and Cressida, Macbeth* and *Antony and Cleopatra* as well, discursive rationality is cast in the role of self-serving and self-deceiving mask. The plays consistently invoke the medieval image of "right reason," Aquinas's *ratio superior,* dramatizing its absence as the context for their staging of the *ratio inferior* or discursive reason, the political policy and calculation that pass for reason in the emergent discourse of the Renaissance political world.[14] Thus they insistently demystify not only the motives but the vocabulary of this political landscape. The widespread current critical habit of reading Shakespeare as a proleptic deconstructionist could be seen as a recognition of his recurrent staging of this will-ful ideological world. If, in *The Winter's Tale* for example, the Bohemian pastoral of act 4 draws its energy from a complex interplay of the audience's attraction to and awareness of the pastoral vision, the earlier acts are equally involved in eliciting a dual response to the more overtly political activity of Leontes.

From this perspective we might immediately note that the romances evolve within an ideological landscape where the old regime has already been consigned to a residual position: far from addressing the absolutist culture of the court as a dominant ideology to be subverted, *The Winter's Tale* works on a theater audience's evolving, if as yet unarticulated, sense of absolutism's tangential status as it proceeds to other issues. So far from inscribing the mystifications of royalist idolatry within its presentation, the play actively assumes the typicality of the royal family and its psychic drama.[15] Leontes, the heir of Othello and Lear, is in need of no deconsecration before he can play his role of jealous husband: as Moretti implies in his discussion of "the birth of (the audience from the structure of) tragedy" (19-20), Renaissance tragedy has already created an audience sufficiently self-assured in its ability to discriminate and judge that such strategies would be superfluous. To read Leontes as an example of Moretti's tyrant is exactly to articulate the single most conventional aspect of the entire play, a founding assumption rather than a vital issue.[16]

This distance or disengagement of the audience from the character and fate of the stage monarch marks the degree to which the culture's emergent subjectivity in both its materialist and essentialist manifestations has already progressed. Whatever the commitment of the court faction around James I to the ideology of absolutism, whatever their estimate of the hegemony of their position in 1610, the evidence of the drama suggests that the emergent ideology is already achieving cultural dominance, consigning the absolutist culture of the court to a residual status thirty years before political events confirm the shift. Indeed, Leontes can be read much more coherently as a "man" than as a king, as a representation of the new essentialist individual inscribed as a subject within a new discursive practice. Whatever emotional claims Leontes makes on an audience stem not from his metaphysical confrontation with fortune or destiny, but quite distinctly from the character's confrontation with his own self-representation as a subject. The impetus to jealousy is coincident with the impetus to self-representation, and the need to particularize and denote that self within a rational field of knowledge is the underlying motivation of the king's dementia. Belsey observes that "the subject of liberal humanism is required to know . . . [and this] knowledge is knowledge of things and people" (55). This observation coincides with the characterization of Leontes (as we shall see) and marks the play's participation in the emergent discourse.

Criticism of the play has traditionally been vexed by a divergence in Leontes's characterization between the emblematic and the realistic, most usually associated with a tension in the play between the demands of an archaic genre and a realistic psychology. But if we conceive of the unrealistic aspects of Leontes's characterization—the abrupt onset and, later, rejection, of jealousy, the absoluteness of his positions, his blindness to the coherence of opposing arguments—as conventional romance elements that serve the playwright's purposes, effecting the disengagement of a more sophisticated audience, we are left with a characterization that seems to a modern sensibility psychologically acute exactly because it embodies the modern essentialist conception of an autonomous, independent consciousness. In particular, the characterization of Leontes is carefully grounded in habits of self-contained self-representation, a positivist appropriation of unproblematic and external "nature," and most centrally in the valorizing of discursive rationality itself.

If the representation of the self is to be fixed or centered in the new ideology, independent of the medieval order of the world inscribed within a divine *logos,* external reality must be hypostatized within the domain of consciousness, and this is accomplished by the promulgation of a nature fixed and essential beyond the vagaries of mutability and metamorphosis. Leontes, like the new man, assumes the coincidence of the logical field of discourse and the natural order of the world.[17] Speaking now of his self-perception rather than the dramatic reality, his characteristic mode of address to the world in the opening acts is both "realistic" and rational: he is realistic in his disposition to judge of events within the framework of a preconceived conception of nature and the natural in human nature, and he is rational in the course of deductions which issue from this realism. The evaluation of his position proceeds in the context of a worldly common sense ("there have been . . . cuckolds ere now, and many a man there is . . ." [1.2.190-91]), and his most characteristic rhetorical formula is the logical dichotomy: "I have trusted thee, Camillo, . . . but" either "thou art not honest; or, if thou inclin'st that way, thou art a coward . . ." (1.2.235-43).[18]

Leontes's preoccupation with rationality is a particular effect of the character's place in a discourse of essentialist individualism: reason becomes a crucial concept within the play because it represents an authorizing ground for the individualism that Leontes pursues, fixing the play of significance within language and culture in order to stabilize the position of unified subject. In the romances more generally reason is revealed as a key ideological concept in the occlusion or suppression of those elements of cognition and self-knowledge resistant to the articulation of the essentialist subject. On the one hand the property of individuals, the locus of self-consciousness and a prime source of the stability and authority of the individual, on the other it serves to demonize and peripheralize other elements in the individual's consciousness such as fantasy and desire that would blur or undermine the sense of coherence. As a species of Galilean lens it distances the individual consciousness from the world of observable phenomena, thus resisting the metamorphic play of language that would work to draw the self into the world.

Leontes's madness—his surrender to the delusions of his sexual jealousy—is best understood in the context of this rationalist ideology. Because the basis of the rationalist project is a thoroughgoing hypostatization of primal reality, a transformation of mutable nature into conceptual field, change or flux is itself not merely inaccessible to reason, but fundamentally antipathetic to it. The power of Polixenes's edenic recollection in act 1, scene 2 grows not only from its asexuality, but from its evocation of unending constancy:

> Two lads that thought there was no more behind
> But such a day to-morrow as to-day,
> And to be boy eternal.
>
> (1.2.63-65)

At the first onset of doubt Leontes contains the possibility of inconstancy by reconceiving inconstancy itself as the unchanging rule of reality: "all's true that is mistrusted" (2.1.48) follows immediately upon his curse "Alack, for lesser knowledge!" Since mutability can only be accepted by fixing it through conceptualization, Leontes is driven to reinvent his world: "Physic for't there's none. / It is a bawdy planet, that will strike / Where 'tis predominant" (1.2.200-202). Rejecting all belief at the first qualm of doubt (and here we recall that the new discourse elaborates itself from within the vacuum of a crisis in belief), Leontes recreates his world on a parodic ideal of "nothing." His fundamental question to Camillo, "Is this nothing?" (1.2.284), echoes Lear's materialist confusion over the slippery complexity of the negation; as with Cordelia's love, so is this affair "no-thing." But whereas Lear's question is carefully inscribed within a medieval metaphysic implicitly delimiting Lear's materiality by emphasizing the reality of that no-thing, *The Winter's Tale* works quite otherwise. From Leontes's perspective as centered subject this no-thing of the phenomenal world becomes real in the moment of conception. Of course, this recreative invocation is carefully juxtaposed to the external reality that contradicts it, thus foregrounding cognitive representation as the central issue of the play:

> Is this nothing?
> Why then the world and all that's in't is nothing,
> The covering sky is nothing, Bohemia nothing,
> My wife is nothing, nor nothing have these nothings,
> If this be nothing.
>
> (1.2.292-96)

The paradox of a rational identity based on "nothing" is, of course, richly ironic, and provides the tensive power of the first three acts: while Leontes's mistake is self-evident to others, within the conceptual frame of his own world his conception remains absolute:

> Swear his thought over
> By each particular star in heaven, and
> By all their influences, you may as well
> Forbid the sea for to obey the moon
> As or by oath remove or counsel shake
> The fabric of his folly, whose foundation
> Is pil'd upon his faith, and will continue
> The standing of his body.
>
> (1.2.424-31)

Nevertheless, the omnipresence of mutability makes any mastery of it ephemeral; so fearful of metamorphic reality, Leontes is pursued, like an Actaeon, by metaphor itself—the vital, aggressive insistence of his own supposedly rational language to metamorphose even as he speaks it.

> Come, captain,
> We must be neat; not neat, but cleanly, captain:
> And yet the steer, the heckfer, and the calf are all call'd neat
>
> . . . . .
>
> —How now, you wanton calf,
> Art thou my calf?
>
> . . . . .
>
> Thou want'st a rough pash and the shoots that I have,
> To be full like me.
>
> (1.2.122-29)

Thus Leontes's subjectivity (in all its senses) is the fulcrum on which the drama decenters the emergent ideology of the subject: having deconstructed the metaphysical ground of its rationality, the dramatic action leaves exposed the occluded ground of affection that motivates such rationalizing, and Leontes becomes the effect of desire and fantasy:

> Affection! thy intention stabs the centre.
> Thou dost make possible things not so held,
> Communicat'st with dreams (how can this be?),
> With what's unreal thou co-active art,
> And fellow'st nothing. Then 'tis very credent
> Thou mayst co-join with something, and thou dost
> (And that beyond commission), and I find it
> (And that to the infection of my brains
> And hard'ning of my brows).
>
> (1.2.138-46)

The celebrated difficulty of this passage is entirely appropriate, for the pseudological character of the soliloquy starkly reveals to the audience Leontes's self-representation, his own impulse to rational subjectivity. If we apply Thomas Cartelli's conception of subversive self-presentation in the Shakespearean set speech, "the foregrounding of orthodox ideological content in dramatic contexts that reveal the speakers' self-investment in the positions they advance and undermine the validity of their pronouncements," we have a very precise articulation of the effect of the audience alienation of which I have been speaking.[19] Here it is the formal discursive properties of the speech rather than its content which is foregrounded, of course, for it appears in the midst of Leontes's passion, but the speech patently reveals the way in which reason panders will.[20] And, as Cartelli concludes about Ulysses and *Troilus and Cressida,* the effect of the alienation is to further "a habit of subversion that serves to demystify each of the drama's competing ideologies . . . which are revealed, in the end, to be equally imaginary, equally self-referential" (14).

At the same time, if taken ironically, that is, with Leontes's own rather than Hermione's presumed affection in mind, the passage brilliantly reveals both the state of Leontes's mind and the ideological implications of such a misordered representation of reality.[21] His opening line invokes, via the cosmological metaphor of "the centre," an ordered macrocosmic frame by which to judge the lack of such a dimension in Leontes's own psyche. Hearing in "centre" the premonition of the centered subjectivity we associate with modern discourse only emphasizes the illusory nature of such a self-conception. "Intention"—meaning both "tendency" and "intensity"—simultaneously reminds us of the fancy's roots in passion, and the extremity of Leontes's own case. Thus the line's overall impact is to reveal, even as Leontes turns his mind to analyzing his wife and friend, his impending self-destruction. The revelation that "thou [affection] dost make possible things not so held," following as it does upon the destruction of his present world, inaugurates a new one, manifestly built upon Leontes's own affection. Ostensibly imputing lust to Hermione's dreams, "unreal," and "nothing," and thence to the "something" of Polixenes's person, Leontes of course now more clearly reveals the role of his own affection in the generation of a very world of nothing, an anti-world of unreality not merely detached from, but actively antithetical to, any more generative representation. The faulty logic is so dramatically manifest that, at the critical point where he reasons from "thou may'st" to "thou dost," the move is marked by the utterly alogical connective "and."

Thus, if the first three acts function especially to reveal Leontes's complete conquest by his own affection, the particular thrust of this conquest's representation is its ground in an essentialist discourse. And the thematic import of the instance will be emphasized by its doubling later in the play, when Polixenes, originally a victim himself of Leontes's self-delusion, repeats Leontes's experience. Polixenes reveals his rationality in a sound, if slightly trite, argument, only to be overcome by passion at the prospect of applying his logical dicta to his own affairs, in the person of his son. The parallel to Leontes is made explicit: Camillo first validates the lovers' natural inclination with his comment to Florizel that "this shows a sound affection" (4.4.380), and then casts the split between father and son in terms of reason. Polixenes's reason is as partial as was Leontes's:

> Reason my son
> Should choose himself a wife, but as good reason
> The father (all whose joy is nothing else
> But fair posterity) should hold some counsel
> In such a business.
>
> (4.4.406-10)

And Florizel emphasizes this by reminding us how partial Polixenes's reasons are:

> I yield all this;
> But for some other reasons, my grave sir,
> Which 'tis not fit you know, I not acquaint
> My father of this business.
>
> (410-13)

Such self-delusion is no different from Claudius's, from Lear's, from Macbeth's. The romances are tragicomedies, distinguished from the earlier comic world because we see in them not simply the heart's desire of the green world, but the emergent discourse's rational perversion of that desire by what Friar Lawrence termed "rude will" (*Romeo and Juliet,* 2.3.28).

But if our response to the tragic drama of Sicily is founded on the progressive deconstruction of an essentialist discourse, with the move to Bohemia and the advent of the chorus we clearly enter into the experience of a different discourse; indeed, the dramatic shift (in particular both its pastoral tone and spaciousness) is created largely by means of this distinct discourse. But while this second mode has many of the attributes of a residual orthodoxy, it deploys these elements in a highly self-conscious counterpoint to the analytical discourse of Sicily, producing a coherent critique of that discourse rather than merely constructing an alternative model for its own sake.

The antithetical modes of *The Winter's Tale,* if not this reading of their significance, have of course been not just a commonplace, but the basis of the humanist critical tradition's approach to the play, for which the orthodoxy of its metaphysical elements has represented its ultimate meaning. This critical tradition would have no reservations about reading the play in terms of Reiss's description of the residual discourse of patterning, in which "patterns . . . suggest an *essence* that escapes its enunciator as a whole must its parts . . . the greater the accumulation of such meanings, the nearer the approach to a wisdom conceived as knowing participation in a totality" (32).

Thus medieval discourse has an analogical-mythic structure foreign to analytico-referential discourse. The liberal tradition seizes upon just this mythical aspect of the older discourse in order to mark its alterity, its otherness, thus containing any challenge to its own hegemony. On the one hand, Francis Barker is correct in his judgment that a primary ideological function of modern literary criticism has been to maintain "the sign of the literary greatness of Shakespeare [which] has played a major part in remaking the late feudal world in the image of the bourgeois settlement that grew up inside it."[22] But an equally prominent strategy of containment has been to colonize the older discourse, identifying it as related but inferior, the primitive or imperfect forerunner of modern discourse, thus simultaneously drawing on its "religious" (that is, metaphorical or mythic) qualities to validate essentialist ideology even as it is denied the status of analytico-referential knowledge. This is possible because, as Dollimore makes clear, both discourses share an essentialist outlook on the human condition, each occluding the material conditions of human existence and centering "man" in its own way. If in its first stance humanist criticism has modernized and recuperated Shakespeare, most obviously by representing his characters as centered subjects, a complementary approach has been to impose on the text a "conservative Shakespeare," archaized, mythic, and metaphysical in outline.

Any clear recognition of the ideological boundary represented by the historical rise of modern discourse immediately foregrounds the inconsistency of these two strategies, thus tending to reveal their ideological premises; the Shakespearean text itself provides the best ground on which to trace these ideological inconsistencies. If in *The Winter's Tale* we have addressed the question of a centered subject in discussing Leontes, it remains to juxtapose to it the mythic Shakespeare, the romance Shakespeare, the conservative Shakespeare. This strategy of colonization has worked so well because the play is indeed demonstrably constructed from elements of the residual analogical discourse.

The play's most immediate appropriation of the older discourse is the evocation in a variety of ways of totality—a metaphysical universe. A Christian terminology of belief, redemption, and providence is prominent, most obviously in the final scene, where the requirement that "you do awake your faith" (5.3.95) is a precondition to the miracle of the final revelation or resurrection of Hermione. The Bohemian pastoral draws heavily upon both Greek mythology and English folk custom, with the two married in the figure of Autolycus. Humanist critics find in Paulina a Prospero-like figure of the Renaissance mage, and all these elements are drawn into a powerful seasonal rhythm shepherded by Time himself as chorus, and presided over by "great creating Nature" (4.4.88) as the centered and authorizing deistic presence. If eclectic and patched, this bricolage has nevertheless been comfortably inscribed for three hundred years within, first, the mediation of the genre of Shakespearean romance itself, and ultimately the essentialist idealism (if not the literal orthodoxy) of traditional theocratic culture.

Nowhere has the covert ideological agenda of Shakespearean criticism, however, been more at odds with its text than in this struggle to totalize such heterogeneous materials within *The Winter's Tale*. On the other hand, relocating the play within the epistemic rupture (to use Foucault's term) of two discourses helps to unveil this agenda by foregrounding rather than suppressing the play's heterogeneity, which is now revealed as the sign of an ordering of discourse alien to the older tradition, the sign of an authorial stance self-consciously manipulative of it. The development of metacritical theory in the past twenty years has conclusively documented that texts like *The Winter's Tale* are explicitly self-reflective, consciously engaged in exploring the form-imposing and thus world-constructing nature of all human cognition; if materialist critics have rightly objected that such metacriticism remains uncritically inscribed within the ideology of the liberal humanist subject, it is nonetheless true that such a theory of self-conscious metaphoricity has important ideological implications.[23] For in appropriating and inverting the culture's peripheralized discourse of imagination, the text articulates an individual imaginatively and not rationally constituted; a discourse grounded in desire rather than thought; the opacity and density of a language that re-presents rather than the clarity of a language assumed to represent; and thus the decenteredness of the individual. Such a dramatic project corresponds exactly to the skepticism of the historical moment of Renaissance disorder when custom fails, revealing its constructedness and thus the contingency of cultural truth.[24]

This play that is also a tale draws our attention throughout to the contingency and artifice of all human action. The romance genre makes natural the references to oracles, defenses, dreams, reports, ballads, old tales, statues, and plays, but can't in itself explain the careful development Shakespeare gives to their appearances. Over against Mamillius's tale in the second act that, presumably, gives the play its name—the naivete of which does not preclude its immediately coming to life when Leontes enters following the opening words, "There was a man . . . dwelt by a churchyard" (2.1.29-30)—we find a careful orchestration of myriad forms of human narration, the stories in all their forms that cultures tell about themselves and their world. Antigonus ponders the truth of dream, Autolycus manipulates the truth of report, the clowns question Autolycus concerning the truth of ballads, gentlemen question the truth of news, and Leontes himself, that of the Oracle—the list seems endless.

Of course, from the perspective of analytico-referentiality this multiplication of narratives can be conceived of as merely a generic vice, typical of all romance in its pandering to popular culture, although in *The Winter's Tale* the play at least is credited with refusing to take itself too seriously, and shows a playful self-deprecation, especially in its last scenes:

> Ballad makers cannot be able to express . . . such a deal of wonder. . . . This news . . . is so like an old tale, that the verity of it is in strong suspicion. . . . I never heard of such another encounter, which lames

Engraving from Galerie des Personnages de Shakespeare *(1844).*

report to follow it. . . . Like an old tale still, which will have matter to rehearse, though credit be asleep.

(5.2.23-62)

But such a reading must carefully suppress the way in which narrative structure rounds on the rational perspective that would try to reduce it to benign similitude: "That she is living, / Were it but told you, should be hooted at / Like an old tale; but it appears she lives" (5.3.115-17). Within the rising incidence of encapsulated narratives, the instances that stand out are self-conscious. In opposition to the parodic world-destroying narratives of Leontes, Camillo and Paulina both submit themselves to the power of language and imagination, and from this submission gain the power to manipulate and direct this human habit of shaping towards satisfactory ends. The aggressively fictive narrations play against "a [modern] relation of narration . . . assuming some commented exterior whose existence as a knowable reality is taken as prior to that of discourse (the discourse of analysis and reference, of historicism, of experimentalism)" (Reiss, 29-30). Language itself, in its re-presentative function, insists on the resolution of the multiple actions that are revealed to be multiple narrations. What else is represented by the self-conscious manipulation of "antic fable" (*A Midsummer Night's Dream,* 5.1.3) that is Shakespearean romance than the reinscription of subjective analysis and reference within a culturally generated mythic realm of which it is, in reality, only an effect? Within the fiction that is the *Tale,* all narration is represented as "an ordering of the mind by the world" (Reiss, 30) rather than the reverse.

What are we to make, finally, of the last scene, one of the most compelling in drama? Certainly anomalous, it relies heavily on a participative engagement within the audience that dramatically contrasts with the disengagement or alienation that most of the play has sought to maintain. Although modern discourse will readily place the scene's wonder within an analysis of the conservative Shakespeare—the author is said to use spectacle to confirm the orthodox effects of the play—this is clearly inadequate, for realistic elements of explanation are carefully deployed simultaneously to complicate and even undercut the engagement already mentioned, provoking a conscious awareness of wonder in the audience even as it experiences this wonder. It would be an oversimplification to say that the playwright has language confront spectacle here. For instance, the conversation of the previous scene, in relating events offstage, clearly contributes to the "wondrous" engagement of the audience in several ways, while the spectacle of Hermione "like a statue" (5.3.20, s.d.) is initially subordinated to a discussion of the representational realism of the art of "Julio Romano" (5.2.97). Nevertheless, insofar as the spectacular is indigenous to a discourse of patterning that exists "within the world," and conversely foreign to a discourse of analysis and reference situating itself beyond the world, the scene firmly participates in the critical project that informs *The Winter's Tale* from the first; while the vital engagement of the audience, almost against its will, strikingly dramatizes the poverty and shrunkenness of the emergent discourse of modernism, the simultaneous demystification of such spectacle precludes any simple identification with a discourse as irretrievably decayed as the world of Hamlet's father's "antiquity forgot" (4.5.105). In other words, the metacritical effects of the scene insist on the cultural production of meaning, denying alike the older discourse's mystification of custom and the emergent discourse's reductive knowledge.

Thus the play confirms its relative emancipation from the constraints of a dominant ideology even as it also diverges from an emergent one. The complexity of Shakespearean drama, then, testifies in a vital way to the seminal significance of the Renaissance as a scene of epistemic rupture which reveals the omnipresence of ideology via particularly acute disjunctions in it. Situated in a moment when the analogic universe of medieval discourse is already in decline, and the emergent discourse of analysis and referentiality has clearly, if incompletely, begun to emerge, Shakespearean drama reveals these epochal shifts in the dynamic tensions and energies of its own conflicting modes of representation. Far from being hegemonic, English Renaissance culture is only dominated to a relative degree by the Elizabethan-Jacobean court, and the play of signification, as the play of power, is far more open than some New Historical criticism would suggest.

The important work of New Historical criticism in elaborating the complex relationships of literature to culture is far from complete, but to realize its radical potential it must evaluate its founding assumptions more carefully, and in particular its fascination with totalizing, hypostatized forms of the concept of hegemony. If it testifies to the hegemony of culture itself as the absolute horizon of all literary production, that is quite different from supposing culture ever to be coincident with any one historically determined structure within it. We need to return our attention to the historical contingency of all such dominations, the relativity of hegemony itself, and the unending play of power across the fissures and multiplicities that constitute the reality beyond any concept of culture.

Notes

1. Anthony Easthope, in *Poetry as Discourse* (New York: Methuen, 1983), discusses the ideological impetus of the instauration of iambic pentameter as the regulative norm of Tudor culture, implicitly raising the issue of the ways in which that culture already manifests elements of the emergent discourse; the texts featured by both Catherine Belsey in *The Subject of Tragedy* (Chicago: Univ. of Chicago Press, 1984) firmly root the discursive developments they address in Elizabethan culture. Timothy Reiss's *The Discourse of Modernism* (Ithaca: Cornell Univ. Press, 1982) is the single most thoroughly researched and carefully articulated investigation now available of Foucault's concept of "epistemic rupture" as it applies to the Renaissance; his project is an examination of

   > aspects of the emergence and development, of the consolidation and growth to dominance, of modern Western discourse. . . . The book sets up a model to describe how one dominant discourse gives way to another. In particular, it shows the creation and development of the various elements fundamental to analytico-referential discourse, and it demonstrates at the same time the necessary occultation of other elements whose visible presence in discourse would subvert its overt aims. (9)

   Reiss's elaboration of the development, over a period of almost two centuries, of a series of elements that eventuate in modern "analytico-referential discourse" greatly complicates any attempt to totalize the Tudor-Stuart political regime.

2. Dollimore (note 1) develops his concept of residual, emergent, and dominant cultural elements from Raymond Williams's discussion in *Marxism and Literature* (Oxford: Oxford Univ. Press, 1977), 121-27. Reiss's vocabulary of the "elements" of discourse corresponds exactly to Williams's perception, and his discussion of "emergent" elements is thus generally compatible with Williams's thinking.

3. See Louis Althusser's "Ideology and Ideological State Apparatuses," in *Lenin and Philosophy and Other Essays* (New York: Monthly Review Press, 1971), 127-86.

4. The single fullest account of the play in recent criticism is Charles Frey's excellent *Shakespeare's Vast Romance: A Study of "The Winter's Tale"* (Columbia: Univ. of Missouri Press, 1980); Frey is especially important for his analysis of the "affective structure" of the play. C. L. Barber and Richard P. Wheeler's *The Whole Journey: Shakespeare's Power of Development* (Berkeley: Univ. of California Press, 1986) provides a complex psychoanalytic approach to the play; Barber's associates, Coppelia Kahn (*Man's Estate: Masculine Identity in Shakespeare* [Berkeley: Univ. of California Press, 1981]) and Peter Erickson (*Patriarchal Structures in Shakespeare's Drama* [Berkeley: Univ. of California Press, 1985]), make recognizably cognate readings from a feminist perspective. With Frey, Howard Felperin carefully surveys the tradition that informs Shakespearean romance in his *Shakespearean Romance* (Princeton: Princeton Univ. Press, 1972). More recently, Felperin has authored an impressive deconstructive treatment of the play in his "'Tongue-Tied Our Queen?': The Deconstruction of Presence in *The Winter's Tale*," in *Shakespeare and the Question of Theory,* ed. Patricia Parker and Geoffrey Hartman (New York: Methuen, 1985). David P. Young's *The Heart's Forest: A Study of Shakespeare's Pastoral Plays* (New Haven: Yale Univ. Press, 1972) perceptively explores the play from the perspective of pastoral; for a rejoinder to such a "pastoral" approach, see Richard Studing's "Shakespeare's Bohemia Revisited: A Caveat," *Shakespeare Studies* 15 (1982): 217-226.

5. Fredric Jameson, *The Political Unconscious* (Ithaca: Cornell Univ. Press, 1981), 9, 17.

6. Leonard Tennenhouse, *Power on Display: The Politics of Shakespeare's Genres* (New York: Methuen, 1986). Tennenhouse, in his introduction, first makes the astute comment that "political conflict does not exist somewhere outside of these texts, for it concerns itself with the struggle among competing ways of representing power," but then immediately goes on to expel such "struggle" from the drama: "Mine is, in other words, an account of a hegemonic process. . . . The strategies of theater resembled those of the scaffold, as well as court performance . . . in observing a common logic of figuration that both sustained and testified to the

monarch's power" (15). The sudden move of this line of thought from the multiplicity of "competing ways of representing power" to a "hegemonic process" is difficult to accept, as is the assumption that a single mode of figuration can comprehend the cultural practice of the time.

7. Stephen Greenblatt, "Invisible Bullets: Renaissance Authority and Its Subversion, *Henry IV* and *Henry V*," in *Political Shakespeare*, ed. Jonathan Dollimore and Alan Sinfield (Ithaca: Cornell Univ. Press, 1985), 18-47. Greenblatt's brilliant argument for the ideological containment of subversion seems to recognize the possibility that the absolutist state is modern rather than medieval: in regards to the *Henriad* he comments that "the founding of the modern state . . . is shown to be based upon acts of calculation, intimidation, and deceit" (39). However, his totalizing tendency in arguing for the hegemony of the dominant discourse becomes clear in a statement such as "all kings are 'decked' out by the imaginary forces of the spectators, and a sense of the limitations of king or theatre only excites a more compelling exercise of those forces" (44).

Clark Hulse, in "Spenser, Bacon, and the Myth of Power," *The Historical Renaissance*, ed. Heather Dubrow and Richard Strier (Chicago: Univ. of Chicago Press, 1988), adapting a Bakhtinian model of "heteroglossia" to his discussion of the English Renaissance court, terms this adaptation only a "partial solution" exactly because it

> tends toward a paradox dominated by the polar terms of authority and subversion, echoing perhaps a simplistic myth of modern politics and creating a duality that is almost as flattering to the central authority as an acknowledgment of total sway. . . . One must look beyond heterodox language to heterodox power. . . . One must move, that is, to a view of the power structure that gets behind the totalizing picture of the political myth to the network of local forces operating in any particular situation.
>
> (317)

Franco Moretti's argument advancing tragedy's role in the subversion of absolutism, "'A Huge Eclipse': Tragic Form and the Deconsecration of Sovereignty," in *The Power of Forms in the English Renaissance*, ed. Stephen Greenblatt (Norman, Ok.: Pilgrim Books, 1982), 11-39, likewise seems explicitly to contradict a simple conception of hegemony by placing it within an ongoing historical process.

8. James H. Kavanagh, in "Shakespeare in Ideology," *Alternative Shakespeares*, ed. John Drakakis (New York: Methuen, 1985) recognizes the same rupture:

> Shakespeare occupied a unique proto-professional position of economic semi-independence between patronage and the market, while still under severe ideological compulsion . . . caught in an ideological space between modified absolutism and insurgent Puritanism. This position of relative economic independence combined with relative ideological constraint was itself the effect of a transitional alignment of classes.
>
> (149-50)

From his Marxist position Kavanagh is reluctant to grant the corollary that ideological consciousness might be a byproduct of this situation, but his own analysis implies at several points an authorial consciousness about the political alternatives inherent in such a position.

9. The discourse of "patterning" is based on Michel Foucault's "episteme of resemblance":

> Resemblance . . . largely guided exegesis and the interpretation of texts; it was resemblance that organized the play of symbols, made possible knowledge of things visible and invisible, and controlled the art of representing them. The universe was folded in upon itself: the earth echoing the sky, faces seeing themselves reflected in the stars, and plants holding within their stems the secrets that were of use to man.
>
> (*The Order of Things: An Archaeology of the Human Sciences,* trans. A. M. Sheridan-Smith [New York: Random House, 1970], 17)

Reiss (note 1) prefers "discursive classes" to "episteme" because he sees that although "one class is dominant, there may well be others that are contemporaneous with it," though these others may consist in "activities . . . that escape analysis by the dominant model, that do not acquire 'meaningfulness' in its terms" (11). In effect, Reiss (as will Foucault himself in *The History of Sexuality*) detotalizes the earlier Foucauldian concept in order to address the multifarious forces at play within discourse.

10. Stephen Orgel, "Making Greatness Familiar," in Greenblatt, *The Power of Forms* (note 7), 41.

11. Orgel (note 10) posits a distinctly similar understanding of the relation between the two sites of figuration:

> The relationships I have been describing [between court and theater performance] sound fairly cosy; but in fact they are distinctly uneasy and involve a good deal of tension. Theatrical pageantry, the miming of greatness, is highly charged because it employs precisely the same methods the crown was using to assert and validate its authority. To mime the monarch was a potentially revolutionary act—as both Essex and Elizabeth were well aware.
>
> (45)

12. Dollimore's use of the term "essentialist" clarifies the idealist continuities in the transition from a medieval theocratic to a modern liberal-humanist discourse. From the perspective of a materialist criticism, Dollimore finds modern discourse, that is

the humanist and liberal discourse of the individual subject that has defined Western culture since the Renaissance, to be as idealist in its authorizing assumptions as was medieval analogical discourse. If the older is essentialist in Christian terms, conceiving of a human soul defined by its relation to God, the seventeenth century turn towards a conception of the individual as "self-determining, free, and rational by nature" is founded upon "the idea that 'man' possesses some given, unalterable essence which is what makes 'him' human, which is the source and *essential* determinant of 'his' culture and its priority over [the material] conditions of existence" (250). In other words, in the face of an emergent Renaissance materialist subjectivity, modern discourse comes to dominance in part by reestablishing an essentialist metaphysic now suitably reinscribed within the subject himself. See Dollimore (note 1), especially 155-69 and chap. 16.

13. The best single treatment of the Shakespearean appropriation of this terminology remains that of David P. Young in *Something of Great Constancy: The Art of "A Midsummer Night's Dream"* (New Haven: Yale Univ. Press, 1966); see also Marjorie B. Garber's *Dream in Shakespeare* (New Haven: Yale Univ. Press, 1974). Luiz Costa Lima, in *Control of the Imaginary: Reason and Imagination in Modern Times*, trans. Ronald W. Sousa (Minneapolis: Univ. of Minnesota Press, 1988) provides a critique of the progressive containment by bourgeois culture of this disruptive inversion.

14. On the relevance of the scholastic tradition of reason see Terence Hawkes, *Shakespeare and the Reason* (London: Routledge & Kegan Paul, 1964), and Robert Hoopes, *Right Reason in the English Renaissance* (Cambridge: Harvard Univ. Press, 1962). See also my development of the details of Shakespeare's appropriation of the tradition in *Hamlet*, "Shakespearian Self-Knowledge: The Synthesizing Imagination and the Limits of Reason," in *Themes in Drama* 12 (1990): 47-59.

15. Certainly New Historical criticism is correct in focusing on the political dimension of the Shakespearean family. But the implications of the comment by Orgel quoted in note 11 are important here: if the metaphoric association of the crown with the head of the household is a prominent absolutist strategy, the significatory force of the association is always open to appropriation, and within the theater the crown must be domesticated even as it lends majesty to the patriarch.

16. In using *Gorboduc* to establish the paradigm, Moretti (note 7) comments that

> precisely what makes Gorboduc a sovereign—universality and self-determination—also proclaim him . . . a *tyrant*. The key to the metamorphosis comes early in the play, when Gorboduc expresses his intention of abdicating to his counsellors. Though the latter attempt to dissuade him with various "rational" arguments . . . Gorboduc never bothers in the least to confute them. He is king not because he can reason and persuade, but simply by virtue of the fact that he *decides*.
>
> (10)

The comment applies exactly to the most conventional elements of the representation of Leontes in the opening acts.

17. Reiss comments that

> during the period of which I will be speaking, a discursive order is achieved on the premise that the "syntactic" order of semiotic systems (particularly language) is coincident both with the logical ordering of "reason" and with the structural organization of a world given as exterior to both these orders. This relation is not taken to be simply one of analogy, but one of identity.
>
> (31)

18. All quotations of Shakespeare's plays are from *The Riverside Shakespeare*, ed. G. Blakemore Evans (Boston: Houghton Mifflin, 1974).

19. Thomas Cartelli, "Ideology and Subversion in the Shakespearean Set Speech," *ELH* 53 (1986): 2.

20. So too we might apply Cartelli's comment that the set speech is often "an extremely stylized mode of expression that tends to direct itself to subjects that presumably mean as much to its auditors as to its speaker" (3), where here we see that the subject in question is discursive rationality itself, and thus the "mode of expression" is coincident with the discursive "subject."

21. I assume here the legitimacy of both major interpretive traditions concerning the passage, which emphasize a reading of "affection" in relation either to Hermione's supposed lust, or Leontes's own psychic involvement with that supposition. The importance of the speech, of course, resides precisely in its linguistic indeterminacy, and our consequent awareness of both references. See the discussion by J. H. P. Pafford in the Arden edition of *The Winter's Tale* (London: Methuen, 1963), 165-67.

22. Francis Barker, *The Tremulous Private Body: Essays on Subjection* (New York: Methuen, 1984), 14.

23. Since the publication of the seminal *Shakespearean Metadrama* (Minneapolis: Univ. of Minnesota Press, 1969), James L. Calderwood has remained the most prominent exponent of the metacritical approach. Jackson Cope's *The Theater and the Dream: From Metaphor to Form in Renaissance Drama* (Baltimore: Johns Hopkins Univ. Press, 1973) carefully pursues the development in the Renaissance neoplatonic tradition of "structural metaphor" eventuating in "the theater of the dream" (211). Young (note 4) provides perhaps the best

metadramatic reading of *The Winter's Tale*. Michael Shapiro provides a convenient overview of the main strains of the practice in "Role-Playing, Reflexivity, and Metadrama in Recent Shakespearean Criticism," *Renaissance Drama*, n.s. 12 (1981): 145-61.

24. Thus Dollimore: "When epistemological and ethical truth was recognised to be relative to custom and social practice, then ideological considerations were inevitably foregrounded. Machiavelli, Montaigne and Hobbes all testify unambiguously to such recognition" (11).

Robert Henke (essay date 1993)

SOURCE: "*The Winter's Tale* and Guarinian Dramaturgy," in *Comparative Drama*, Vol. 27, No. 2, Summer, 1993, pp. 197-217.

[*In the essay below, Henke examines the relationship between Battista Guarini's tragicomic theory and Shakespeare's drama, particularly focusing on* The Winter's Tale.]

Genre concepts significantly affect our understanding of Shakespeare's *The Winter's Tale*. The play not only repeatedly calls attention to itself as fiction, but its tripartite tragical-pastoral-comical arrangement focuses our attention on three important dramatic genres of the late sixteenth and early seventeenth centuries and the dialogic relationships between them. In *Pericles*, Shakespeare emphasizes the romance source by dramatizing John Gower and narrative itself, the radical of presentation most congenial to romance. "Romance" also aptly describes the story of *The Winter's Tale:* a more schematic, typological presentation of character than obtains in the tragedies, the (apparent) suspension of the laws of cause and effect, marvelous recognitions over large expanses of space and time, and an overall trajectory from woe to weal. But Shakespeare takes the romance material available to him in Robert Greene's *Pandosto* and separates it into the three dramatic genres that constituted an important new Renaissance form, the avant-garde Italian pastoral tragicomedy. The non-dramatic term 'romance,' used first in the late nineteenth-century by Edward Dowden in what we would now call a modal sense to convey the serene, beneficent attitude of the last plays,[1] neither gets to the quick of *The Winter's Tale* as experienced by the theater audience nor speaks to our increasing sense of the conflicts between comic and tragic and pastoral visions in the play. 'Tragicomedy,' understood in the historical context of late Cinquecento dramatic theory and practice, better explains the dramaturgy (involving the transposition from romance story to staged play) and audience experience (mediated by genre concepts) of *The Winter's Tale*.

At the time of the composition of *The Winter's Tale*, few other Renaissance kinds had received so much recent theoretical and practical attention as had the controversial genre of Italian tragicomedy. In an acrimonious quarrel that eventually produced five documents between them, Battista Guarini defended and Giason Denores challenged the feasibility of tragicomic and pastoral drama.[2] Taken together, Guarini's responses to Denores reveal one of the most detailed and sophisticated dramaturgies in Renaissance drama, one acutely conscious of the ways in which genre signals mediate between playwright and audience by organizing various systems of signification, creating horizons of expectations, and eliciting various rhetorical effects in the audience. In the course of the entire quarrel, Guarini considers the technology of dramatic composition; the style, tone, set, action, and characters of his mixed genre; and its rhetorical performances. Although Guarini says that pastoral is incidental, not essential to tragicomedy, his account of the many ways in which pastoral may function as a bridge between tragedy and comedy is richly suggestive for *The Winter's Tale* as well as for *Cymbeline* and *The Tempest*. The middle style of pastoral, its flexible emotional register, the capacity of the pastoral set to range from the pleasance of the meadow to the harshness of the *selva* (forest) or mountains, its typical actions, and the indeterminacy of social status in bucolic literature, all make it possible for pastoral to function both as a "theater" of genre experimentation and as a means of transforming tragedy into comedy. The tensions and potential harmonies between tragedy, comedy, and pastoral become the material of tragicomedy, which stages debate and interaction between its constituent kinds.

Interest in the latest theatrical theories and experiments was far from beneath Shakespeare. Although Shakespeare's direct knowledge of the drama of Tasso and Guarini can be demonstrated (and, through Marston and Fletcher, his indirect awareness of theories of tragicomedy), the most convincing evidence of international cross-fertilization can be mustered from a comparative examination of the Italian and Shakespearean plays themselves, which demonstrates the persistent appearance of common theatrical structures: character typology, *topoi*, actions, and genre systems.[3] In particular, *Cymbeline, The Winter's Tale,* and *The Tempest* share with the late Cinquecento Italian hybrids a high degree of generic self-consciousness and a similar genre system constituted by tragedy, comedy, and pastoral. Although Shakespeare's direct knowledge of tragicomic theory was probably scanty, the Italian dramaturgical theory is so closely tied to actual theatrical practice that it should illuminate the "unwritten poetics" operative in Shakespeare's work, a work that shares with the late Cinquecento Italian drama similar generic alignments and some of the same dramaturgical strategies.[4]

The contexts in which the Italian and Shakespearean plays were performed reveal other important analogies. Although the differences between the situations of Guarini's amateur courtly theater and Shakespeare's professional, largely popular theater are more striking than the similarities, the new sophisticated audience of the Blackfriars theater, which most critics agree exerted some influence on the last plays of Shakespeare, resembles the kinds of learned audiences out of which the generically self-conscious form of Italian tragicomedy emerged: it is an audience of high "dramatic competence" that would have recognized, more quickly than the Globe theatergoers, the codes of genre variously manipulated in the last plays.[5] To a greater degree than the outdoor Globe, the intimate, candlelit Blackfriars theater would have accommodated the fine nuancing of style and emotion upon which, as we shall see, Guarinian tragicomedy is based.[6] Furthermore, the courtly Guarini's attempt to appropriate but severely control the bawdy popular theatrical energies of the newly emerging professional theater can be contrasted with the professional actor-playwright-shareholder Shakespeare's more fluid blending of learned and popular strains in plays performed at the Globe, the Blackfriars, and the court. Denores justifiably associates Guarini's generic experiments with those of the emerging *commedia dell' arte,* a theater from which Guarini was anxious to distance himself but which shared many of his assumptions about the flexible combinatory nature of genre. A professional actor himself, Shakespeare shared none of Guarini's disdain for the mercenary theater. But the fact that each of the *commedia*-like entertainers of the last plays—Stephano, Trinculo, and especially Autolycus—are chastened and diminished at the end of the play may reflect the changing and uncertain status of popular entertainment in the new environment of the Blackfriars and the Stuart court. In both Guarinian and late Shakespearean tragicomedy, the extremes of tragic horror and comic bawdry are "tempered" (this is Guarini's term), and the fortunes of the marginal figures are rendered particularly precarious.

Most Anglo-American critics who have examined the relation of Guarini's tragicomic theory to Shakespeare's drama have limited their reading of Guarini to *Il pastor fido* and an abridged translation of the last of the five documents in the Guarini-Denores quarrel, the *Compendio della poesia tragicomica.*[7] Critics tend even to repeat the same passage in which Guarini enumerates the rules for the composition of tragicomedy.[8] Because it lacks the tension of debate (Denores was dead by the time of its composition), the *Compendio* is in many ways the least interesting of the five documents. We need to consider the four earlier documents—Denores' *Discorso,* Guarini's first *Verato,* Denores' *Apologia,* and Guarini's second *Verato*—in order to understand more about Guarinian tragicomic dramaturgy. With the formulas and rules of the *Compendio,* Guarini parades his Aristotelian orthodoxy before his neo-classical critics. The arc of the entire debate, however, suggests a more capacious, innovative genre and dramaturgy than has often been associated with Guarini. Via the dramaturgical *idea* of tragicomedy to be explored in these pages which can generate several kinds of tragicomedies, it is possible (and fruitful) to compare late Cinquecento pastoral tragicomedy with English experiments unlike it externally—experiments that we consider to be rather more dramatically successful.

Both Guarini and Denores are extremely self-conscious of generic codes and of the signifying and performative capacities of genre. Although they may disagree with the meaning or function of a given genre, Guarini and Denores share the assumption that literary genres are not just sets of rules but powerful and effective semiotic systems that produce certain effects upon their readers or audiences. Considering poetry to derive its principles from ethics, Denores claims that his three canonical genres—tragedy, comedy, and epic—are inherently political and concentrates on the didactic effects of poetry. Epic, according to Denores, presents images of virtue and teaches the nature of monarchy; tragedy warns against the dangers of tyranny and is governed by the principles of oligarchy; comedy is regulated by the principles of democracy and is designed to "disponergli alla vita populare" ("prepare [man] for democratic life" [*Discorso* II, 155-56]).[9] In contesting Denores' claim that pastoral is of no moral utility for city dwellers, Guarini does appear to make didactic claims for the genre: pastoral can depict the better nature of man, free from the corruption of city or court. Usually, however, Guarini counters Denores' didacticism with an audience-centered rhetorical notion of genre that stresses the role of the emotions. For Guarini, poetry is a branch not of politics or civil philosophy but of rhetoric and cannot be said to have a primarily didactic function. Tragedy and comedy as well as other kinds of poetry may, however, indirectly adapt their audiences to the habit of virtue by their purgative, emotional capacities.[10] The tragic purgation of fear, for example, does not eradicate fear but adjusts and moderates it. The fear of the "morte dell'animâ" ("death of the soul") produced by tragedy checks an excessive fear of bodily death (*I Verato* II, 251). The laughter and relaxation of comedy frees its audiences from melancholy and thus disposes them to the duties of public life (*I Verato* II, 262). The "instrumental," or formal end of drama is to elicit delight by verisimilar and lively imitation; its "architectonic" or final end is to purge the audience of melancholy (the end of comedy and, according to Guarini, tragicomedy) or to purge the audience of pity and fear (the end of tragedy; *I Verato* II, 247). The differences, however, between Guarini and Denores may obscure what as a working hypothesis they share: an audience-centered theory of genre by which genres signify, create horizons of expectations, and affect their audiences in didactic or emotional ways.

An individual genre, then, constitutes for these theorists a distinctive semiotic framework (comprehensible by a reasonably competent audience) and performs a discreet rhetorical (be it didactic or emotional) operation. Furthermore, as in a linguistic system, a genre acquires meaning in relation to other genres as part of a genre system. Guarini defends a much more extensive genre system than Denores' ternary epic-tragedy-comedy both in his account of ancient genres (the dithyramb, argues Guarini, was a distinctive genre [*II Verato* III, 57-70]) and in the new, modern genres he is willing to allow.[11] If genres were forms by which one organized experience, "moderns" like Guarini believed that new genres like tragicomedy were needed to account for increasingly diverse and complicated experience even as the book revolution produced new texts and explorers discovered new lands.¹² Mixed genres, in particular, constituted the *nova reperta* of literature according to the principle that "a large, inclusive utterance may require mixture of the kinds."¹³ Now even in the reduced genre system of Denores we can see that genre systems provoke comparisons between genres: epic, tragedy, and comedy, for Denores, generate different political comparisons, based as they are on different forms of government (*Discorso* II, 155-57). To combine various genres in one work, as Guarini proposes, allows one genre to be viewed from the perspective of another; tragedy, for example, can be gauged from the perspective of pastoral. If genres constituted different interpretive frames on the world, mixed genres enabled "dialogues," as it were, between genres and the different points of view they represent. Several late Cinquecento and Jacobean plays, in fact, began with actual debates between figures representing "Tragedy" and "Comedy," and Guarini's own *Il pastor fido* begins with what amounts to a debate between tragic Seneca and comic Terence.¹⁴

The frequently excerpted passages from the *Compendio* appear to fix the genre by rules and definitions, but a reading of the two *Verati* reveals Guarini's openness to a great range of hybrid possibilities worthy of Polonius' notorious list. (Denores, indeed, taunts Guarini with Polonian litanies of dramatic hybrids [*Discorso* II, 348-49].) The amount of "tragicity" or "comicity" in a given play, in Guarini's view, can be adjusted according to an almost infinitely variable spectrum: "nella Tragedia il terrore più e men temperato costitiusce i gradi del più, e meno Tragico; così il riso, più e meno dissoluto fa la favola più, e men Comica" ("in tragedy, terror that is more and less tempered constitutes degrees of more and less tragic quality; similarly laughter that is more and less dissolute renders the play more and less comic" [*I Verato* II, 260-61]). If the Aristotelian tradition establishes the emotions as a centrally defining feature of genre (pity, fear, etc.), such emotional nuancing as Guarini proposes can hypothetically generate an almost infinite number of genres. Furthermore, Guarini argues that new audiences shape the creation of new genres. Generic flexibility arises out of the need to respond to the changing nature of audiences: "E questa è la vera cagione delle differenze, e dei gradi, che sono nelle favole più, e men Tragiche, perciocchè i poeti vedendo i gusti diversi degli ascoltanti, alcuna volta componevano favole co'l fin lieto per rimettere in parte quella acrimonia" ("And this is the true reason for the differences and the degrees of more tragic and less tragic plays, because the poets, seeing the various tastes of their audiences, sometimes wrote plays with a happy ending in order to make them less harsh" [*I Verato* II, 260]). Now the mutual responsivity of genre and audience characterized, as Denores was quick to point out, the emerging and suspect *commedia dell' arte*; the *comici* were selling theatrical wares to the public, and the public responded to variety and mixture. Throughout the *Discorso* and *Apologia* Denores attempts to condemn Guarini's generic experimentation by associating it with the genre mixtures of the *commedia dell'arte*. Guarini, of course, vehemently rejected such company. As learned *comici* themselves did under attack from post-Tridentine ecclesiastics, Guarini claimed for his art a high degree of authorial control. According to Guarini, the playwright creates new genres like tragicomedy by combining existing genres in various ways just as the metallurgist produces new compounds, as the painter mixes new colors from his palette, or as the politician or political philosopher creates a republic of mixed constitution such as Venice (*Il Verato* III, 158-65). Such assertion of authorial control, however, may register Guarini's anxiety (and Denores' belief) that he has unleashed a Pandora's box of dramatic experimentation.

The most important interaction in Guarinian tragicomedy occurs between pastoral and tragedy. In order to establish a more flexible and interactive genre system, it is crucial for Guarini to demonstrate points of contact between the traditionally low genre of pastoral and the higher genres of tragedy and epic just as Tasso and many other late Cinquecento playwrights had done.¹⁵ For Denores, pastoral is a genre that cannot traffic with tragedy or epic. It is a humble, homogeneous, and circumscribed genre, pure in its portrayal of virtuous shepherds, not subject to the principles of civic and moral philosophy as are his three principal politically based kinds (*Discorso* II, 201-02). Citing many examples of high action and tragic experience in non-dramatic pastoral literature, Guarini argues that shepherds are capable of tragic errors and vulnerable to tragic suffering (*I Verato* II, 293). In its style, emotions, set, actions, and social organization, Guarini's pastoral is much more capacious than the soft pastoral of Denores and is thus comparable to the pastoral of Shakespeare's last plays.

"Happy is your grace," says Amiens to the exiled Duke Senior of *As You Like It*, "That can translate the stubbornness of fortune / Into so quiet and so sweet a style" (II.i.18-20).¹⁶ Now the harshly pastoral winter and rough weather described in *As You Like It* elsewhere takes the form, in *King Lear*, of actual tragic experience. *King Lear* even repeats the images and language of Duke Senior's speech: Gloucester's "I see it feelingly" (IV.vi. 147) echoes Duke Senior's "feelingly persuade" (I.i.11). According to Amiens, however, Duke Senior's sweet pastoral style transforms potentially tragic pain. So it is in Guarini's dramaturgy: the sweet (*dolce*) style proper but not unique to the pastoral mode tempers tragic experience. As Guarini puts it, "il dolce . . . tempera quella grandezza, e sublimità, che è propria del puro Tragico" ("the sweet style tempers that grandeur and sublimity which are proper to the pure tragic style" [*I Verato* II, 274]). One literary kind, then, interacts with and transforms another. If the principle of generic decorum attaches a style to a genre, Guarini establishes a middle style for his hybrid, created by the careful mixing of the "politô," or polished style, and the "grave," or solemn style. For Guarini, the extreme "dimessô" (low) and the "magnificô" (magnificent) styles cannot be mixed together, as they were in the *commedia dell' arte* hybrids from which he was so concerned to distance himself (*Il Verato* II, 274). But unlike what

Guarini perceived (incorrectly) as the random stylistic juxtapositions of the mercenary theater, the technically sophisticated playwright of tragicomedy, in his view, consciously and carefully creates his style. As long as one avoids extreme mixtures, however, the playwright can create almost infinite stylistic gradations "a uso non di campane, ma di corde musicali" ("in the manner not of bells, but of musical chords" [*Il Verato* III, 226]), or as the painter mixes colors and creates shades of difference. Tragicomic dramaturgy, then, explores various and finely nuanced shades of style.

According to Guarini, the emotional tonalities of pastoral temper the extremes of tragedy and generate a range of emotional experience as broad as the range of style. With dramatic genres, in the tradition of Aristotle, partially defined by the kinds of emotion they elicit in the audience, Guarini explores new emotional terrain for his genre. If the violence of tragic actions elicits terror and if the buffooneries of the emerging professional comedy generate dissolute relaxation, Guarini explores shades of feeling between terror and laughter. Tragicomic dramaturgy explores this intermediate tonal range in several ways. First of all, the passive suffering of pastoral figures in the face of meteorological, occupational, political, and amatory misfortunes elicits the emotion of pity without extreme terror—the right kind of emotion for the new genre, according to Guarini. The shepherd of pastoral is not essential to tragicomedy but can stand as a representative figure for the new hybrid because his strength relative to his world is inferior to figures of epic or tragedy. In most versions of Renaissance pastoral the shepherd's or countryman's strength consists in his passive endurance—as Denores puts it, the capacity "tollerar le fatiche con pacienza, il sofferrir il caldo, ed il freddo" ("to tolerate hard labor with patience, to endure heat and cold" [*Apologia* II, 364]). Secondly, the playwright elicits intermediate tragicomic emotion by carefully controlling and diminishing terror. Whereas, in the *Compendio*, Guarini proscribes any version of terror for his hybrid, in the *Verati* he accepts a greater complexity in the way the playwright may exploit terror: "E siccome ogni cosa terribile non purga il terrore . . . così ogni rassomiglianza del terribile non produce Tragedia, s'ella non vien condotta con l'altre necessarie parti, che ci concorrono" ("And just as every terrible thing does not purge terror . . . so every likeness of the terrible does not produce tragedy, if it is not accompanied by the other necessary and converging parts" [*I Verato* II, 259]). Like Prospero manipulating his audience with the terror of an illusory storm, the tragicomic playwright produces "rassomiglianze del terribile," simulacra of terror, often diminished for being framed by the awareness of illusion. For Guarini, tragicomedy mutes terror because it contains a higher degree of fictionality than does tragedy: "Dunque la verità, che aiuta il verisimile, s'appartiene al poema Tragico, se noi crediamo ad Aristotile, e non al Tragicomico, che non ha bisogno di storia, per formar la sua favola, ma se la finge esso a suo modo, e talora con nomi noti, e talora con finti, secondo che più gli piace" ("Therefore truth, which contributes to the verisimilar, belongs to the tragic poem, if we believe Aristotle, and not to the tragicomic poem, which has no need of history to formulate its story but rather fabricates its story in its own way, sometimes with familiar names and sometimes with fictional names, according to its pleasure" [*Il Verato* III, 189]). Late Cinquecento tragicomedies frequently stage fictional deaths that are meant to transform the internal audience of the play. In Tasso's *Aminta*, the false deaths of Aminta and Silvia are not gratuitously theatrical but are important for the rhetorical effects elicited in the lovers. In *The Winter's Tale*, Paulina stages the fictional "death" and "resurrection" of Hermione in order to transform her audience Leontes. The oneiric fictions of *Il pastor fido*, other Italian pastoral tragicomedies, and *The Winter's Tale* also diminish tragic terror. Denores argues that terror admits of no degree and claims that the terror induced by dreams is inferior to real terror. For Guarini, however, the terror of dreams constitutes a unique, diminished emotion appropriate for the new genre (*Il Verato* III, 190-92). The terror of Montano's dream in *Il pastor fido* I.iv is tempered by a comforting prophecy.[17] In *The Winter's Tale*, the dream that Antigonus recounts before he relinquishes Perdita on the Bohemian sea coast similarly tempers terror with hope (*The Winter's Tale* III.iii.15-41).

In the two *Verati*, Guarini proposes for the third genre a generically flexible set capable of depicting experience of a greater range than that normally associated with the pleasance of the pastoral greensward. The pastoral set, as described by Sebastiano Serlio in *De Architettura* (and as realized in many late Cinquecento pastorals), can include not only pleasant meadows and woods, but also mountains, rocks, deserts, and dark, labyrinthine woods reminiscent of the landscapes of Dante and Ariosto.[18] For the titular heroine in Giovanni Battista Leoni's *Roselmina, favola tragisatiricomica* (1595) who wanders through Ireland, it is the confusion and discomfort of the *selva* (forest) and not the pleasance of the *prato* (meadow) that marks the landscape: "queste strane habitazioni di fiere e di gente selvaggia" ("these strange dwellings of beasts and savage people" [I.i]).[19] At the beginning of *Il pastor fido*, Guarini's Arcadia suffers from a Sophoclean blight. The generically liminal pastoral set of *The Winter's Tale* III.iii—the stark, stormy Bohemian sea-coast in which men are mauled by bears and "things new born" are discovered—is then very like the late Cinquecento pastoral set in the polyvalence of its generic codes.

The "scena satyrica" as described by Sebastiano Serlio adds to its natural elements temples which incorporate the columns, marble, and classical sculpture of the court-based scenic architecture of tragedy (*Il Verato* III, 268-71). Anticipating the expected objection of Denores that the inclusion of such architecture constitutes a monstrous pastiche of different genres, Guarini argues for the possibility of shifting elements of one genre onto another generic frame. Whereas the royal palaces and sumptuous edifices of tragedy signal the splendor and ambition of courtly life, pastoral transforms classical magnificence into a religious decorum—in Guarini's imagination, shepherds built temples not for ostentation, but for primarily religious reasons. The most significant counterpoint to Leontes' court tragedy of Acts I-III, the description by Cleomenes and Dion of the solemn temple and reverent religious ceremony they had witnessed on the "fertile" and "sweet" isle (sic) of Delphos, can then be understood in terms of the communicative power of place codes in tragicomic dramaturgy. The account of the temple lends a religious, reverent cast to the high decorum and prefigures the play's movement from tragedy to pastoral to what the Italians would call *commedia grave*. One could plausibly argue that, more so than the psychologically realistic development of character, the generically coded set itself (largely verbally invoked in Shakespeare's theater) performs the transformative work of the *The Winter's Tale*.

Guarini's pastoral transforms tragic actions. Insisting, against Denores, that tragedy tells not just the political stories of the falls of tyrants (the narrowest, most conventional Renaissance notion of tragedy), but the unfortunate stories of misaligned, often incestuous eros, Guarini establishes points of contact between tragedy and pastoral. Pastoral, whose precedent in the classical genre system as the "third genre" which Cinquecento theorists thought to be the libidinous satyr play, charts the eventually felicitous realignment of erotic energies. As is the case in the paradigmatic *Oedipus the King,* at the beginning of *Il pastor fido* unhappy eros has cast a blight on the land. Lucrina's rejection of Aminta has led to his suicide and the yearly sacrifice due to Diana. It is the new generation of lovers, Amarilli, Mirtillo, Silvio, and Dorinda, who must transform potentially tragic eros, reforming the erotic energies into a comic outcome. For Guarini, tragicomedy contains potential tragedy ("[tragedia] in potenza") but does not actualize tragedy ("non [tragedia] in atto" [*Il Verato* III, 184]). Both *Il pastor fido* and its precursor *Aminta* present the rhetoric and possibility of tragedy (frequent references to pity and fear, the continual possibility of suicide, violence, and death) only to deflect towards tragicomedy. The new generation of lovers recapitulates but reforms the tragic eros of the earlier generation. Silvio begins the play casting himself as a hero in the high style of epic or tragedy, quoting Hippolytus from Seneca's *Phaedra,* and referring to the heroic itinerary of his ancestor Hercules as a generic paradigm (I.i). The play forces him, however to modulate in respect to both genre and gender. In the play's opening debate, Linco argues to Silvio that the genre-flexible Hercules also dressed in women's clothes and worked at the loom. Silvio's transformative moment comes to be not his slaying of the boar but his falling in love with Dorinda. Similarly, *The Winter's Tale*'s Florizel and Perdita, as the new generation, reprise and revise the actions of the previous generation, which had produced tragic issue.

For Guarini, the social and political range of shepherds allows pastoral to function as a bridge between comedy and tragedy. Guarini usually understands pastoral as what we would call a mode, not a genre; pastoral is used adjectivally, as in "pastoral tragicomedy," and means that shepherds are the principal actors. A pastoral play is a "favola di pastori in forma o Comica o Tragica o Tragicomica" ("a story of shepherds in the form of comedy or tragedy or tragicomedy" [*Il Verato* III, 265]). Like Denores in his discussion of the politics of the various genres, many Cinquecento theorists interpreted Aristotle's remark that "[comedy] sets out to represent men as worse than they are, [tragedy] as better"[20] in a social, not moral sense. Guarini shared Denores' assumption about the social referentiality of genre, but the more complicated genre system he proposes, in which the politics of pastoral plays a significant role, corresponds to more complicated political structures than those treated by Denores. Tragicomedy, argues Guarini, is like the Venetian republic of his day, a capacious, mixed form that synthesizes the apparently contradictory forms of democracy and oligarchy (*Il Verato* III, 159-65). Guarini's tragicomedy, in the mode of pastoral, can respond to both oligarchic (tragic) and democratic (comic) claims because there is social difference in his Arcadia. Unlike Denores, Guarini distinguishes between shepherds and farmers, the latter with a more uniformly low social status. Among shepherds, there are not only servants but also owners (*padroni*) whose responsibility over their flock and their inferiors could represent the responsibilities of the Renaissance ruler. Shepherds, Guarini points out, have been priests and prophets, as in the Bible, and by what William Empson calls the fiction of a "beautiful relation between rich and poor," disguised courtiers.[21] The dramatized failures and successes of the courtiers Florizel, Polixenes, and Camillo, who cross social boundaries by disguising themselves as shepherds, Autolycus' social baiting of the naive shepherds after he suddenly receives Florizel's clothes, and the social passage of *The Winter's Tale*'s shepherds to gentlemanly status (with a kind of revenge on the social vagabond Autolycus) in the final, synthetic part of the play should all be seen in the social-dramaturgical context of Italian pastoral tragicomedy.

The frequently noted fictional self-awareness of *The Winter's Tale* includes the consciousness of dramatic genre produced by the tripartite structure—an awareness of kind reminiscent of Guarinian tragicomedy. Shakespeare's analysis of the Greene romance story into the three genres of Italian tragicomedy yields a fundamentally *comparative* play. If Renaissance genres could provide interpretive perspectives on the world,[22] *The Winter's Tale* invites its audiences to consider, for example, tragic problems of state and sexuality from a pastoral point of view. With *place* an important constituent element of Renaissance dramatic genres, the play generates comparisons by changing places (as the Italian tragicomedies normally do not do) and thus genres. The play begins in a court that soon becomes claustrophobically tragic, narratively evokes the serene, beneficent "isle" of Delphos in tonal opposition to Leontes' tragedy, moves to the generically liminal and pivotal "sea coast" of Bohemia, shifts to the less terrifying but not escapist greensward next to the shepherd's cottage for the long pastoral scene, and ends in a Sicilia transformed into comedy less festive than *grave,* solemnized by echoes of the masque in Paulina's "chapel." The notorious geographical errors for the two important places alternative to the Sicilian court—the "isle" of Delphos and the "seacoast" of Bohemia—might be thought to reflect less Shakespeare's carelessness than their status as places of the imagination—"landscapes of the mind"[23] that transform the original tragedy for both the internal and external audience.

Rosalie L. Colie has argued that the Polixenes-Perdita debate regarding natural purity and artificial mixture addresses the same issues taken up in the continental debate, with Polixenes (ironically) taking the Guarinian, and Perdita (against her wishes) assuming the Denorian points of view.[24] It is not only Florizel the gentler scion and Perdita the apparently wilder stock that must be joined to restore the Bohemia-Sicilia bond but also the various genres and points of view in the play that must be mixed, with pastoral playing an important mediatory role. The purity and isolation of something like Denorian pastoral is invoked by Polixenes shortly before the tragedy begins; it is far less capacious and variegated than the pastoral actually enacted later on in the play:

> Pol. We were, fair queen,
> Two lads that thought there was no more behind,
> But such a day to-morrow as to-day,
> And to be boy eternal.
> . . . . .
>
> We were as twinn'd lambs that did frisk i' th' sun,
> And bleat the one at th'other: what we chang'd
> Was innocence for innocence: we knew not
> The doctrine of ill-doing, nor dream'd
> That any did. Had we pursu'd that life,
> And our weak spirits ne'er been higher rear'd
> With stronger blood, we should have answer'd heaven
> Boldly 'not guilty', the imposition clear'd
> Hereditary ours.
>
> (I.ii.62-65, 67-75)[25]

With Denores and against Guarini, Polixenes remembers a pastoral of complete innocence, altogether bounded from the world of city and court and unable to converse with the "stronger blood" of sexuality and its potentially tragic consequences.[26] The purity of such soft pastoral yields, as its dark side, the pure tragedy of jealousy, conspiracy, and revenge that Leontes—Othello without need of a Iago—attempts to impose on his court.

Paulina soon opposes Leontes' pure tragedy. She resembles the Guarinian tragicomic playwright in her use of a variety of genre-like rhetorical strategies aimed at transforming Leontes, her audience. Paulina opposes Leontes' tragic projections with biting satiric language and with the less dangerous perspective of comic typology, attempting to cast Leontes into the role of a comic tyrant and Antigonus into that of a hen-pecked husband.[27] When, like Creon of *Antigone,* Leontes disobeys the oracle and completes the externalization of a tragedy which began as fantastical and unreal (I.ii.138-46), Paulina becomes, at III.ii.175-202, a tragic *nuncio* delivering a highly rhetorical (but none the less effective) account of Hermione's "death." Paulina's "tragedy" is important not for its referential content (which is false) but for the emotional effect that her speech immediately elicits in Leontes in the manner of Guarinian tragicomedy. She stages Leontes' sixteen-year penitence. Finally, adjusting herself and her audience to a very different generic decorum in Act V, Paulina carefully prepares and moves her audience (principally Leontes) in the solemn masque-like statue scene in her "chapel."

Leontes' conspiratorial sexual tragedy, then, is not unalterable form but is affected by other genres or points of view in the play. Genres are dialogic and interactive, as Mikhail Bakhtin argues: they are developed in relation and dialogue with other genres.[28] Neither the theater audience nor Leontes is bound to any single generic perspective. The complex, fluid generic system of *The Winter's Tale* tempers the two extremes Guarini was attempting to avoid in tragicomedy: tragic terror, and comic bawdry of the kind practiced by the *commedia dell'arte.* At the end of the play, Leontes' tragedy is over (though not forgotten), and Autolycus, a figure reminiscent of the itinerant professional entertainer, is a diminished thing.

The most important genre interaction in *The Winter's Tale* is that between pastoral and tragedy. In its style, emotional tone, symbolism of place, revisionary action, and social politics, the pastoral section of *The Winter's Tale* provides a reprise of matters that have had tragic issue in the first section and replays them through a different prism. The pastoral of Bohemia is a much tougher, more porous, and more heterogeneous genre than Polixenes' retrospective soft pastoral, and it is one that may converse with tragedy.

The old shepherd's "thou met'st with things dying, I with things new-born" announces the pivotal generic shift with a symmetrical balance befitting this tragical-pastoral-comical play. The sea coast of III.iii is especially liminal in regard to genre, well calibrated to intermediate stylistic and emotional registers; it is an eery, deserted place of storms, comically savage beasts,[29] and death without terror. The popular, homespun style of the shepherds differs from Guarini's intermediate "sweet" style but follows the idea of Guarinian dramaturgy in that it tempers tragedy. The style of the pastoral speakers places sexuality in a new generic framework. The sight of the infant Perdita signifies illicit sexuality for the old shepherd, as it did for Leontes, but his homely compound formulations reinterpret what had been a horribly particular sin for the Sicilian king into a new perspective, that of comic generality:[30]

> Though I am not bookish, yet I can read waiting-gentlewoman in the scape. This has been some stair-work, some trunk-work, some behind-door-work: they were warmer that got this than the poor thing is here.
>
> (III.iii.72-76)

The style and emotional register of the young clown also adjusts generic decorum in his account of the storm, the

wreck, and the mauling of Antigonus. Guarini, we remember, carefully distinguishes observed tragicomic terror from participated tragic terror, whereas Denores argues for only one emotional register. Just as Prospero tempers Miranda's tragically coded reaction to the initial storm in *The Tempest* (she claims to experience fear and pity for figures of high station),[31] the clown both registers an Aristotelian response (the poor souls utter a "piteous cry"; Antigonus is a nobleman) and compromises generic purity with the homeliness and humor of words like "corks," "hogsheads," and "flap-dragoning." Every event and speech in the scene mark it as a no man's land between engagement and detachment, a place of diminished terror. Elevated diction, echoes of encounters in the epic underworld ("thrice bow'd before me"), and ritual patterning serve to link Antigonus' strange dream (III.iii.16-41) with epic and tragedy. And yet it is grave and sorrowful, not terrifying like the dreams and apparitions in *Richard III, Hamlet, Julius Caesar,* and other tragedies; tonally it is very like the enabling dream Montano has of his son in *Il pastor fido* (I.iv), the memory of which at the fateful moment of sacrifice deflects his sacrificial sword (V.v). As Guarini argues against Denores, a dream of a terrifying event need not reproduce terror *tout court* but can modulate terror into a different emotional and generic register.

The actions of the entire pastoral episode transform the actions of the first section of the play by both resembling them and differing from them. In both the tragic and pastoral sections of the play, dangerous kings, violently disrupting placid situations, break or threaten a male-female bond. Leontes opposes the mixing of Polixenes and Hermione ("To mingle friendship far, is mingling bloods" [I.ii.109]), and Polixenes, despite his official position in the debate, opposes the mixing of the "gentler scion" and the "wilder stock." Both Paulina and Perdita ("The selfsame sun that shines upon his court / . . . / Looks on all alike" [IV.iv.445-47]) subversively undermine the kings, at least in word. In both sections Camillo "serves his master's highest interests by betraying him,"[32] and the victims of both outbursts must traverse the dangerous but providential sea. However, although Leontes, driven by a misogynist fear of sexual impurity, had desperately wanted Mamillius to be "a copy" (I.ii.119-56), the new generation is not altogether identical to the older generation. Florizel does resemble the older generation in a Denorian pastoral idyllism that hides the dark side of Arcadia. His "Apprehend / Nothing but jollity" (IV.iv.24-25) stands in contrast to Perdita's more realistic reservations about their pastoral disguises, and his confident enlistment of the gods themselves as theatrical-sexual exemplars (IV.iv.24-35) ignores the reality of their rapes. On the other hand, if Leontes had conflated and condemned both sexual and theatrical play ("Go play, boy, play: thy mother plays and I / Play too; but so disgrac'd a part, whose issue / Will hiss me to my grave" [I.ii.187-89]), Florizel with Perdita redeems sexuality and theatricality. After Polixenes discovers him, Florizel first launches into tragic, Lear-like diction inappropriate to the pastoral decorum: "Let nature crush the sides o' th' earth together, / And mar the seeds within!" (IV.iv.479-80). More like a "faithful shepherd" than like a tragic hero, however, Florizel shows himself flexible enough to submit to Camillo's plan, trusting the waters of providence and Camillo's vision (IV.iv.548-54) of a comic outcome.

Perdita's debate with Florizel about the viability of his pastoral disguise anticipates the more familiar debate she has with Polixenes about the possibility of mixing a "gentler scion" and a "wilder stock"; these exchanges about the possibility of social mixtures echo the Guarini-Denores debates about the mixture of socially coded genres. In response to Florizel's breezy confidence in the social flexibility of pastoral, by which princes may become shepherds and shepherdesses goddesses, Perdita reaffirms social and generic boundaries:

> To me the difference forges dread (your greatness
> Hath not been us'd to fear): even now I tremble
> To think your father, by some accident
> Should pass this way, as you did: O the Fates!
> How would he look, to see his work, so noble,
> Vilely bound up? What would he say? Or how
> Should I, in these my borrowed flaunts, behold
> The sternness of his presence?
>
> (IV.iv.17-24)

Perdita here affirms, as did Denores, the principle of theatrical, social, and sexual difference, in language proper to tragic discourse. The "stern" presence of the superior Polixenes and the awareness of the social differences that not even festival license erases elicit the emotions of tragedy: "dread," "fear," and "trembling." Perdita maintains a horizon of tragic rather than providentially tragicomic expectations with her invocation of the "Fates." But of course Perdita's own career as a royal foundling as well as the plot and dramaturgy of the entire play affirm not Denores' position in the debate but rather the social fluidity of Guarinian tragicomedy. The theatrical-sexual license of the pastoral festival centers on the freedom to explore various levels of social station; despite her verbal protestations, Perdita *does* mix with the gentler scion. Autolycus, the real hero of social metamorphosis in Act IV, plays a vagabond writhing in the road and, after the windfall of Florizel's costume, "a most rare courtier." And Polixenes' royal suspension of the festive license of social disguise delays but does not forestall the marriage of Perdita and Florizel. Although the trick of pastoral romance may reaffirm aristocratic privilege (the shepherdess really has royal blood), the gentling of the shepherds after the first recognition really does constitute a social mixture following the lines of Guarinian dramaturgy. The young shepherd marvels at the new kinship relations of the pastoral-royal family: "I was a gentleman born before my father; for the king's son took me by the hand, and called me brother; and then the two kings called my father brother; and then the prince, my brother, and the princess, my sister, called my father father; and so we wept; and there was the first gentleman-like tears that ever we shed" (V.ii.139-45). The translation of the shepherds from Bohemia to the Sicilian court heightens the generic status of pastoral—the very project of Tasso, Guarini, and other late Cinquecento dramatists. Autolycus, earlier the genius of social transformation in the subversive style of *commedia dell' arte,* now is humbled before the new gentlemen. The emotional responses elicited by *commedia dell' arte,* the relaxation and the laughter of farce, give way to the pathos-filled tonalities of Guarinian tragicomedy: "gentleman-like tears." The status of Autolycus is diminished, with the result that not only the extreme of tragic terror but also that of farcical comedy is "tempered."

In its implicit focus on dramatic genre, its genre dialogism, and its use of pastoral style, tone, set, actions, and social relationships to modify the extremes of tragedy and comedy, *The Winter's Tale* exemplifies the "unwritten poetics" of tragicomic dramaturgy as most thoroughly articulated by Guarini but also as practiced by many contemporary Italian playwrights. Probably independently of direct influence, *The Winter's Tale* realizes many of the dramaturgical possibilities articulated in Guarini's work, especially in the two *Verati*. The relationships between the constituent genres, of course, involves much more conflict in Shakespearean tragicomedy than in Guarinian and in most other late Cinquecento tragicomedy. Although the status of the rough and tumble *commedia*-like Autolycus diminishes in relation to the newly-gentled shepherds and their more refined sentiments, he resists integration into the new order and maintains strong audience appeal. To "temper" or reformulate tragedy, to begin to heal its wounds, as Shakespeare surely does beginning with the liminal pastoral scene of III.iii, is not to defuse it entirely. The transformative power effected by Hermione's fictional death does not efface the real deaths of Mamillius and Antigonus and the fact that the "wide gap of time" has sadly diminished the royal marriage, rendering Hermione disturbingly silent in the last scene. That Shakespeare handles tragicomic dramaturgy with innovation and complexity, however, is hardly surprising.

Notes

1. Edward Dowden, *Shakspere* (New York: American Book Company, n.d.), pp. 55-56. For the distinction between mode and genre, see Alastair Fowler, *Kinds of Literature: An Introduction to the Theory of Genre and Modes* (Cambridge: Harvard Univ. Press, 1982), pp. 106-11.

2. Guarini's extremely popular and influential pastoral tragicomedy, *Il pastor fido,* was written between 1580 and 1585 and circulated in manuscript before its publication in 1590. In 1586, Giason Denores presented his theories of genre and criticized tragicomedy and pastoral, without explicitly naming Guarini, in his *Discorso di Iason Denores intorno à que' principii, cause, et accrescimenti, che la comedia, la tragedia, et il poema heroico ricevono dalla philosophia morale, e civile, e da' governatori delle republiche* (Padua, 1586). Guarini responded, anonymously, in his *Il verrato ovvero difesa di quanto ha scritto M. Giason Denores contra le tragicomedie, et le pastorali, in un suo discorso di poesia* (Ferrara, 1588). Denores sallied back in his *Apologia contra l'auttor del Verato di Iason De Nores di quanto ha egli detto in un suo discorso delle tragicomedie, e delle pastorali* (Padua, 1590). Guarini countered with *Il verato secondo ovvero replica dell' attizzato accademico ferrarese in difesa del pastorfido,* completed by 1591 but not published until 1593 (Florence, 1593). Finally, in 1601 Guarini published a work incorporating the major points of his two earlier treatises, the *Compendio della poesia tragicomica, tratto dai duo verati, per opera dell' autore del pastor fido, colla giunta di molte cose spettanti all' arte* (Venice, 1601). A good account of the quarrel has been given by Bernard Weinberg, *A History of Literary Criticism in the Italian Renaissance* (Chicago: Chicago Univ. Press, 1961), II, 1074-1105. The five exchanges of the quarrel, treatises relevant to the quarrel by Angelo Ingegneri, Faustino Summo, Giovani Pietro Malacreta, Paolo Beni, and Giovanni Savio, and Guarini's principal literary works are collected together in a four-volume eighteenth-century edition: *Delle opere del cavalier Battista Guarini,* ed. Giovanni Alberto Timermani (Verona, 1738). All citations to the documents of the quarrel will refer to this edition; I list the treatise from which the citation is taken, followed by the volume and page reference in the Timermani edition.

3. Recently, the most thorough and convincing comparison of Cinquecento and Shakespearean drama has been made by Louise George Clubb in *Italian Drama in Shakespeare's Time* (New Haven: Yale Univ. Press, 1989). G. K. Hunter has made the best case for the direct influence of Guarini on Shakespeare and Marston in his "Italian Tragicomedy on the English Stage," *Renaissance Drama,* 6 (1973), 123-48. Tasso's *Aminta* and Guarini's *Il pastor fido,* printed together in London by John Wolfe in 1591, were well known among a select but important circle in London, and verbal echoes of the 1602 "Dymock" translation of *Il pastor fido* can be found, argues Hunter, in Marston's *The Malcontent* and in Shakespeare's *All's Well That Ends Well* and *Measure for Measure.* Several English dramatists contemporary with Shakespeare demonstrated a keen interest in both the theory and practice of the new genre: Samuel Daniel, who attempted a close imitation of Guarini's pastoral tragicomedy in *The Queene's Arcadia* (1605); John Marston, whose 1604 *The Malcontent* (entered as "Tragicomoedia" in the Stationer's Register) was appropriated by Shakespeare's company and performed at the Globe; and John Fletcher, new playwright of the King's Men as they began performing plays at the Blackfriars theater, future collaborator with Shakespeare, whose 1609 prologue to *The Faithful Shepherdess* demonstrates knowledge of Guarini's theories.

4. For the concept of "unwritten poetics" and a discussion of the close relationship between theory and practice in the Cinquecento, see Claudio Guillen, *Literature as System: Essays Toward the Theory of Literary History* (Princeton: Princeton Univ. Press, 1971), pp. 107-34.

5. The concept of "dramatic competence" is discussed in Keir Elam, *The Semiotics of Theatre and Drama* (London: Methuen, 1980), pp. 98-99.

6. Harley Granville-Barker has argued that the Blackfriars theater would have encouraged a more refined style of acting than that practiced in the outdoor theaters, by which "sentiment [would] become as telling as passion" (*Prefaces to Shakespeare* [1930; rpt. Princeton: Princeton Univ. Press, 1946], I, 470).

7. The standard version of Guarini that many critics use is that of Allan H. Gilbert's abridged translation of the *Compendio*, found in his *Literary Criticism: Plato to Dryden* (1940; rpt. Detroit: Wayne State Univ. Press, 1962), pp. 504-33. Some useful studies of Guarini and Renaissance English drama are Marvin T. Herrick, *Tragicomedy: Its Origin and Development in Italy, France, and England* (Urbana: Univ. of Illinois Press, 1955), pp. 34-45; Madeleine Doran, *Endeavors of Art: A Study of Form in Elizabethan Drama* (Madison: Univ. of Wisconsin Press, 1963), pp. 186-215; Arthur C. Kirsch, *Jacobean Dramatic Perspectives* (Charlottesville: Univ. Press of Virginia, 1972), pp. 7-15; Hunter, "Italian Tragicomedy on the English Stage," pp. 123-48; and David L. Hirst, *Tragicomedy* (London: Methuen, 1984), pp. 3-8, 18-21. Herrick does use the Timermani edition, although he concentrates on the *Compendio* and on passages in Gilbert's abridged edition. Some critics, like Kirsch, refer also to Weinberg's many quotations from Guarini, some indeed taken from the *Verati*. (Weinberg himself has read all of the quarrel documents in detail.) Hirst and Doran do refer to the complete *Compendio*, which they have consulted in Italian. The excellent essays by John T. Shawcross, Joseph Loewenstein, Barbara A. Mowat, Verna Foster, and James J. Yoch (*Renaissance Tragicomedy: Explorations in Genre and Politics,* ed. Nancy Klein Maguire [New York: AMS Press, 1987]) probably constitute the best recent work on Guarini and tragicomedy, but do not refer to the *Verati*.

8. The passage most commonly quoted is the following: "He who composes tragicomedy takes from tragedy its great persons but not its great action, its verisimilar plot but not its true one, its movement of the feelings but not its disturbance of them, its pleasure but not its sadness, its danger but not its death; from comedy it takes laughter that is not excessive, modest amusement, feigned difficulty, happy reversal, and above all the comic order of which we shall speak in its place" (*Literary Criticism,* ed. Gilbert, p. 511).

9. All translations of the Italian texts are my own.

10. Weinberg, *A History of Literary Criticism in the Italian Renaissance,* II, 658.

11. Denores, of course, could not but acknowledge ancient genres such as pastoral and lyric. Believing, however, that they were not governed by political and philosophical principles, he considered them much less important than the three major genres.

12. For the relationship between new nixed genres and the cultural changes of the sixteenth century, see Rosalie L. Colie, *The Resources of Kind: Genre-Theory in the Renaissance,* ed. Barbara K. Lewalski (Berkeley: Univ. of California Press, 1973), pp. 3, 28, 76-102.

13. Ibid., p. 28.

14. Alessandro Piccolomini's *L'Ortensio* begins with a debate between *Comedia* and *Tragedia* (*Commedie del Cinquecento,* ed. Aldo Borlenghi [Milan: Rizzoli, 1959], pp. 1041-45). A very similar debate begins Sforza Oddi's *Prigione d'amore* (*Il teatro italiano: la commedia del Cinquecento,* ed. Guido Davico Bonino [Turin: Einaudi, 1978], pp. 444-48). In England, the popular play *Mucedorus,* revived in 1610 by The King's Men, begins with a prologue that pits Comedy against Envy, the latter essentially representing tragedy. In the first scene of *Il pastor fido,* Silvio quotes from Seneca's *Phaedra* and Linco from Terence's *Heauton Timorumenos*.

15. Officially, however, Tasso stood on the side of the ancients on the question of genre mixture, for which see the discussion of Weinberg, *A History of Literary Criticism in the Italian Renaissance,* II, 1077. Concentrating on playwrights other than Tasso and Guarini, Clubb discusses the wide generic range of Cinquecento pastoral (*Italian Drama in Shakespeare's Time,* pp. 153-87).

16. *As You Like It,* Agnes Latham, ed. (London: Methuen, 1975). I am indebted to Paul Alpers for calling my attention to this passage.

17. All *Il pastor fido* citations refer to *Opere di Battista Guarini,* ed. Marziano Guglielminetti (1955; rpt. Turin: UTET, 1971).

18. See Sebastiano Serlio's description of the "scena satyrica" in *Il secondo libro, di prospettiva* (1545); see *I sette libri dell' architettura* (1584; facs. rprt. Bologna: A. Forni, 1978], I, 49^v-51.

19. *Roselmina, favola tragisatiricomica* (Venice, 1595).

20. Aristotle, *The Poetics,* trans. W. Hamilton Fyfe, Loeb Classical Library (1927; rpt. London: William Heinemann, 1932), XXIII.11.

21. William Empson, *Some Versions of Pastoral* (1935; rpt. New York: New Directions, 1974), p. 11.

22. Colie, *The Resources of Kind,* pp. 1-31.

23. The phrase is from Richard Cody, *The Landscape of the Mind: Pastoralism and Platonic Theory in*

Tasso's *Aminta and Shakespeare's Early Comedies* (Oxford: Clarendon Press, 1969).

24. Rosalie L. Colie, *Shakespeare's Living Art* (Princeton: Princeton Univ. Press, 1974), pp. 275-76.

25. All citations refer to *The Winter's Tale*, ed. J. H. P. Pafford (London: Methuen, 1963).

26. Arguing against Denores' narrow notion of tragedy as exclusively political, Guarini points out the many domestic sexual tragedies in the Greek corpus—e.g., *Medea, Hippolytus, Alcestis*. See *I Verato* II, 242.

27. Joan Hartwig makes this point in *Shakespeare's Tragicomic Vision* (Baton Rouge: Louisiana State Univ. Press, 1972), pp. 105-16.

28. M. M. Bakhtin and P. N. Medvedev, *The Formal Method in Literary Scholarship*, trans. Albert J. Wehrle (Cambridge: Harvard Univ. Press, 1978), pp. 129-37.

29. In a fascinating analysis of the genre-coded semiotics of animals in Cinquecento pastoral drama, Louise George Clubb argues that the generic ambivalence of the bear makes it appropriate for this liminal scene of the play (*Italian Drama in Shakespeare's Time*, pp. 140-52).

30. At one point in the tragic section of the play Leontes does, however, interject a note of comic generality that offsets his predominantly tragic rhetoric: "There have been, / (Or I am much deceiv'd) cuckolds ere now . . ." (I.ii.190-91).

31. Stephen Orgel draws attention to this in his edition of *The Tempest* (Oxford: Oxford Univ. Press, 1987), p. 102.

32. James Edward Siemon, "'But it Appears She Lives'; Iteration in *The Winter's Tale*," *PMLA*, 74 (1974), 13.

Mary Ellen Lamb (essay date 1998)

SOURCE: "Engendering the Narrative Act: Old Wives' Tales in *The Winter's Tale, Macbeth,* and *The Tempest*," in *Criticism*, Vol. XL, No. 4, Fall, 1998, pp. 529-53.

[*In the following essay, Lamb analyzes the role of women's folk tales and their influence in* The Winter's Tale, Macbeth, *and* The Tempest.]

As Macbeth stares in terror at Banquo's ghost during a banquet for the Scottish lords, Lady Macbeth contemptuously compares his hallucination to oral narratives circulated among women:

> O proper stuff!
> This the very painting of your fear;
> This the air-drawn dagger which you said
> Led you to Duncan. O, these flaws and starts
> (Imposters to true fear) would well become
> A woman's story at a winter's fire,
> Authoriz'd by her grandam. Shame itself,
> Why do you make such faces?[1]

Framing her criticism with attacks against his masculinity—"Are you a man?" and "What, quite unmanned in folly?"—Lady Macbeth represents Macbeth's fearfulness as a degrading regression to the androgyny of childhood. Her anxious allusion to women's tales in this context suggests their continuing and threatening power, and the effeminizing attraction of the early bonds with women they signify. Paradoxically, Lady Macbeth's accusation becomes self-reflexive to the play which includes it. The "air-drawn dagger" which Lady Macbeth denigrates as appropriate only to women's tales places *Macbeth* squarely within this devalued oral tradition; so do its ghosts and its witches. *Macbeth* is not alone in its self-reflexive allusions to this early scene of narration. Passages within *The Winter's Tale* and *The Tempest* also invoke this oral tradition as originary to their art. Together, these allusions expose the power of childhood tales as prototypes for the fictions of the stage.

From this distance in time, it is impossible to judge whether these stories were primarily "authoriz'd" by "grandams" or also composed and performed by men. The gender of their authors was, however, largely irrelevant to the reception of these tales by young children at the knees of the women who told them. Whatever the point of origin, the location of fiction within the special space shared between young children and the women who raised them contributed to what the narrative act meant. This space contained meanings specific to the early modern period. As Stephen Orgel has pointed out, within almost every early modern male there would have lurked a childhood memory of a self not fully distinguished from women.[2] Whether male or female, babies and children at the breast were thought to imbibe femaleness along with their nurses' other qualities.[3] Gender was especially blurred through the custom of dressing little boys in coats until they were "breech'd," sometime around the age of five.[4] Within a one-sex gender system distinguishing gender by social markers, gender differences were not yet fully present in young boys dominated as well as nurtured by women.[5] Not yet old enough to assume the social power defining their masculinity, boys younger than the age of seven were not yet considered fully rational, either; and so, much like women, young boys were perceived as creatures more of their bodies than their minds.[6] Shared with the seemingly large female bodies surrounding them, this sense of bodiliness served as a primary marker of an early effeminacy which invested the narrative act with gendered meanings specific to the early modern period.

The gendered meanings of this early female-dominated environment, implicit within the narratives it circulated, may not have become apparent to a boy until, sometime between seven and thirteen, he was given to male tutors or schoolmasters to learn Latin in what has been characterized by Walter Ong as a male puberty rite.[7] While scholars have recently debated the severity of humanist pedagogy, there remains little doubt that the standard exercises of intellect—the attainment of fluency in Latin, the ability to reason abstractly and to present logical arguments, the knowledge of classical cultures—created gender differences reinforcing the physiological differences between the sexes.[8] According to Keith Thomas, further gender distinctions were created through the process of learning Latin—the rigorous routines and disciplines—which required of boys an "instinctual renunciation" through which they were to master their bodily passions as a condition of their future privilege.[9] Underlying this version of masculinity was an analogical system which naturalized the subordination of the feminized body to the masculine mind.[10] Reinforced by the masculinizing aura of the humanist schoolroom, the flight from the feminine became a flight from corporeality itself.[11]

Nostalgia for this childhood period of effeminacy and its pleasures, including its narrative pleasures, could not be easily reconciled with a self built upon the rejection of the feminine and the corporeal. Humanist sentiment suggests that the highly intellectual form of masculinity achieved through the translation of classical texts within this literate culture did not easily accommodate the oral tradition of tales circulated among women at a winter's fire. Lady Macbeth's implicit opposition of the authority of grandams and pedagogues in her contemptuous juxtaposition of the words "grandam" and "authoriz'd" appears even more forcefully in Erasmus's similarly contemptuous dismissal of this vernacular oral tradition: "A boy (may) learn a pretty story from the ancient poets, or a memorable tale from history, just as readily as the stupid and vulgar ballad, or the old wives' fairy rubbish such as most children are steeped in nowadays by nurses and serving women."[12] Erasmus's expression of anxiety over these narratives as a source of female influence, and especially lower-class female influence, over children, was not isolated. It appears as well in childrearing manuals, which warned against the widespread existence of this oral tradition and its harmful potential as a means by which women—whether mothers or lower-class wet nurses—could exert permanent influence over young minds.[13]

The often abrupt removal of boys from a feminine space to a masculinizing schoolroom environment posed a form of gender trouble to many early modern males of the middle or upper classes. Individual boys undoubtedly experienced the conflict between these contradictory cultures, as well as their own differently gendered selves formed within them, with differing intensities, and they chose from a range of strategies available to manage these conflicts. While Erasmus dismissed this early environment and its narratives with contempt, John Aubrey expressed nostalgia for the vernacular tales of his own early seventeenth century childhood, when he had heard "old women and mayds" telling "fabulous stories nightimes, of Sprights and walking of Ghosts."[14] In several of Shakespeare's plays, the oral tradition shared between women and children implicates the narrative act composing the play itself. The responses to this form of female influence staged within these plays are complex and ambivalent, embracing nostalgia, horror, resignation, and perhaps even celebration. These gender conflicts arising from this sudden juxtaposition of highly gendered cultures remain central, I will argue, to the act of narration as represented in *The Winter's Tale, Macbeth,* and *The Tempest.*[15]

1. THE WINTER'S TALE

With its title explicitly identifying itself as a part of this oral tradition, *The Winter's Tale* provides an obvious starting point for an exploration of the continuing powers of these tales. Tales told in winter were commonly attributed to women not only because many middle-or upper-class children experienced woman as their first storyteller. Represented as simple entertainment to pass away long evenings when the cold and darkness prevented other chores or distractions, tales told in winter also became a trope for tales without serious purpose. In this period before fiction had become sufficiently theorized, tales told on long evenings before a fire required a woman storyteller because, presumably, a man would have had something more useful to do.[16] Stories told by women were of necessity without purpose; stories without purpose were most appropriately told by women. This sense emerges, for example, from Boccaccio's *Genealogy of the Gods*: "A maundering old woman, sitting with others late of a winter's night at the home fireside, making up tales of Hell, the fates, Ghosts and the like . . . to scare the little ones, or divert the young ladies, or amuse the old, or at least show the power of fortune."[17] In this context, Shakespeare's titling of the *Winter's Tale* reopens the question, circulating within his culture, not only of the power of this devalued tradition, but of the deeper purposes of writing fiction for pleasure.

As Mamillius tells his mother, "A sad tale's best for winter. I have one / Of sprites and goblins" (II.i.25-26), his creation of his own winter's tale makes the self-identification of *The Winter's Tale* with these oral tales of childhood explicit. The gender reversal of the expected audience and narrator further connects Mamillius' winter tale with the male-authored *Winter's Tale,* by showing their mutual appropriation of a tradition of "old wives' tales" usually gendered as female. Mamillius' tale demonstrates a debt to the easy intimacy staged in this play for the primarily female environment of childhood, as one of the queen's ladies offers to be his "playfellow" while another lets Mamillius tease her about her blue-painted eyebrows. This scene between Hermione and Mamillius suggests the centrality of this affective bond for the creation of Mamillius' own winter's tale, and by extension, of the play *Winter's Tale* itself. In her active role as audience, Hermione elicits his story, as she invites him to "Pray you, sit by us, / And tell 's a tale" (21-22). As she invites him again to sit down beside her, her praise for his ability reveals that this scene of narration has been enacted many times: "Come on, sit down, come on, and do your best / To fright me with your sprites: you're pow'rful at it" (27-28). This physical closeness to his mother forms a condition of his narration. As he offers to tell her his story so softly that "yond crickets shall not hear it" (30), Hermione asks him to "give't me in mine ear" (II.i.32). In this scene, Hermione is more than a receptive audience; as he whispers the first words, "There was a man . . . Dwelt by a churchyard" (28, 30), Mamillius is composing not only a story but a self defined in terms of an intimate and very physical bond with his visibly pregnant mother as well as with her surrounding ladies, who care for him.

The Winter's Tale also reveals the threat posed by this bond which in some sense forms its source. The dangerous centrality of this relationship between mother and son is amply demonstrated by Mamillius' response to his mother's imprisonment. Removed from her presence, in "mere conceit and fear / Of the Queen's speed" (III.ii.144-45), Mamillius dies. Leontes's sudden separation of Mamillius from his mother replicates the potentially traumatic entry of boys into a masculine environment. Like the traditional removal of boys from their early female-dominated environment, this sudden separation expresses rejection not only of the female, but of the female in Mamillius, as Leontes explains: "Though he does bear some signs of me, yet you / Have too much blood in him" (II.i.56-57). The business is completed in a few lines, as Leontes orders, "Give me the boy," and "Bear the boy hence, he shall not come about her. / Away with him!" (59-60). Yet the rejection of Mamillius' inner femininity is not so easily accomplished for a boy whose name is derived from the Latin word for "breasts."[18] While, as Leontes notes, Hermione had not actually nursed Mamillius, her physical closeness is as important as that of any nurse to an infant. Mamillius' illness duplicates the classic symptoms of depression as he "threw off his spirit, his appetite, his sleep / And downright languish'd" (II.iii.16-17). The one grave in which both Hermione and Mamillius are allegedly buried signifies this symbiotic union and continues it beyond death.[19]

Mamillius' death expresses the danger or even the impossibility of a complete transition from androgynous boyhood to adult masculinity. Even Leontes mourns the loss of his early effeminacy as, looking at Mamillius, Leontes succumbs to nostalgia, remembering himself at that age:

> Looking on the lines
> Of my boy's face, methought I did recoil
> Twenty-three years, and saw myself unbreech'd
> In my green velvet coat, my dagger muzzled,
> Lest it should bite its master, and so prove
> (As ornament oft does) too dangerous.
>
> (I.ii.153-58)

Leontes's regressive identification with Mamillius conveys more than a conventionally Freudian desire to unite with the mother.[20] Instead (or in addition), Leontes's reminiscences provide a window into a historically specific practice of childrearing now defunct. In representing that time when he still wore the coat also worn by girls, Leontes adds a detail unrecorded in histories of children's clothing: he remembers that he also wore a dagger, and that the dagger was muzzled.

If Leontes's memory reflects widespread early modern practice, then boys may have been somewhat differentiated from girls before breeching: perhaps even small boys displayed this highly visible sign of their masculinity. This instrument of aggression and / or sexuality was, however, muzzled and thus unavailable for their present use; it remained a promise of future potency. Leontes's description of his muzzled dagger as an ornament conveys a sense of its detachability, of its exteriority, of its nonessentiality. As an ornament, it could be laid aside, rendering the boy-Leontes again undifferentiated from girls. This passage raises questions critical to an understanding of early modern gender construction. If the dagger was in fact worn by young boys still in coats, when was it unmuzzled? During the breeching ceremony? If so, then the breeching ceremony itself constructed a boy's masculinity in terms of overt and possibly deadly aggression. While this passage points to the necessity of further research in children's clothing and the customs surrounding breeching, it seems clear that the term "muzzled," appropriate to a dangerous beast, reinforces a sense of aggression implicit in early modern masculinity. Leontes's representation of his muzzled dagger of early boyhood implies that since that time, his masculinity, as represented by his now unmuzzled dagger/phallus, has become able to bite its master, to become an instrument of self-aggression rather than of love for another. The dangerous potential of his muzzled dagger has been irrevocably released. No longer only an ornament, his adult dagger/phallus has made the easy intimacy of boyhood no longer possible.

The destructiveness of Leontes's phallic masculinity is borne out as the first two acts of *The Winter's Tale* follow a conventional tragic plot. It is the miraculous unlikelihood of the last three acts in which *The Winter's Tale* most resembles the oral narratives of childhood, as it points to its own profound implausibility by twice referring to itself as an "old tale." Relating the offstage reunion of Leontes and his daughter Perdita, the second Gentleman exclaims that "this news, which is call'd true, is so like an old tale, that the verity of it is in strong suspicion" (V.ii.27-29). Similarly, the third Gentleman describes the bear's fatal mauling of Antigonus as "like an old tale still, which will have matter to rehearse, though credit be asleep and not an ear open" (V.ii.61-63). While neither gentleman designates the probable gender of the teller of such old tales, the evocation of garrulity unimpeded by disbelief, indifference, or even sleepiness draws on a stereotype of talkative old women.[21] In their apologetic references to "old tales," first and second Gentleman call on their listeners and by extension the audience, to move beyond the critical judgment of adulthood to be filled with the wonder of children again.

In *The Winter's Tale*, this wonder characterizes not only children, but country folk gullible enough to buy the absurd ballads sold by Autolycus. Like Mamillius, like the first and second Gentleman, perhaps like the playwright of *The Winter's Tale* himself, Autolycus becomes yet another male purveyor of improbable tales associated with women. While his given name derives from classical literature, his self-representation reveals his own androgynous identification with the female tradition of narratives. In his self-defense, "Why should I carry lies abroad?" he describes himself by an expanded version of the name he had improvised as the supposed author, a Mistress Taleporter (or "carrier of tales/lies"). "Her" story of the usurer's wife who gave birth to twenty moneybags derives its point from the astonishing capacities of the female reproductive body, used in this tale as an analogue of capitalistic profits, much as Autolycus performs the capitalistic miracle of making money from such women's tales/tails. This supposed Mistress Taleporter, who signed her name to verify the truth of this story, gains her authority from her role as midwife. In selling "her" story, Autolycus appropriates not only the tradition, but the physicality of women's narratives as the sign of their power over the life and death of infants and children. In this ballad, however, women's very physical powers are parodied rather than rejected; rather than eliciting horror, they promote sales.[22]

Like Autolycus, Shakespeare appropriates the power of the female body to compose the miraculous conclusion of *The Winter's Tale*. As Hermione steps down from her pedestal, Shakespeare's stagecraft merges with Paulina's, for his audience is as ignorant as hers that Hermione still lives. Hermione's continuing love for Leontes represents perhaps the most wonderful implausiblity of the play; and it is this statue scene, often associated with the power of the playwright, which makes of this play a "winter's tale." Moreover, it is in this scene that a woman directly takes on a creative role. Like Mistress Taleporter's ballad, Paulina's stagecraft is also inseparable from the female body. Like the stories of early childhood, her "play" represents the culmination of her faithful attending to physical needs; for Paulina's visits to the statue "twice or thrice a day" (V.ii.105) were clearly designed to feed Hermione. In this sense, Leontes's representation of Paulina's art as "lawful as eating" (V.iii.111) has special point. Paulina's stagecraft is finally inseparable from acts of feeding and eating. Her art is also inseparable from the lives of those she cares for. Paulina cannot conclude her sixteen-year play until Perdita, the fruit of Hermione's visible pregnancy in Act I, is recovered.

Various critics have noted the psychoanalytic implications of Paulina's play, culminating in the statue scene. Murray Schwartz has read this final scene as expressing Shakespeare's acceptance and then renunciation of the "wish for fusion with the creative and destructive mother of infancy."[23] Adelman has pointed out that this scene figures "the loss and recovery of the world in the mother's body."[24] Erickson claims that "the play's final scene reenacts the symbiotic unity that Leontes now mourns."[25] These insights gain validity from a historical grounding of Paulina's play in childrearing practices. Overseeing Leontes's grief and enforcing his refusal to wed again until the oracle is fulfilled, Paulina uses her powers as playwright to return Leontes to the female dominance of boyhood. As Leontes puts himself in the hands of a woman he has called a "mankind witch" (II.iii.68), arguably both a nurse and a playwright, *The Winter's Tale* reenacts Macbeth's regressive receptivity to women's narratives with a difference. For Leontes, Paulina's narrative is redemptive. Under her direction, Leontes is in a sense permitted what was forbidden to early modern males: an extended period of mourning for "what was lost" in the transition away from the female environment of early childhood. And "what is found" is not only Perdita, not only Hermione, not only the Mother, but the bond with women inseparable from the "winter's tales" of childhood.

If the statue scene can be taken as a self-reflexive exploration of the playwright's art, what are its implications for *The Winter's Tale*? Does the gender of Paulina blur the outlines of the male playwright with a female caregiver of early childhood to reveal her influence even at the cost of exposing a humiliating dependency at the core of narrative? Or does it, as Abbe Blum argues, reveal a desire to "partake of an originary or originating moment" identified with the "preoedipal and the power of the mother," only to circumscribe that "maternal power with that of the male playwright?"[26] Either way this scene is read, the imagery of witchcraft in *The Winter's Tale* reveals that anxiety about women's influence over men, including male playwrights, is far from resolved. Paulina must draw careful lines around her stagecraft to distinguish it from demonic art. Cautiously placing her scene in a chapel, Paulina voices the fear that onlookers will "think (which I protest against) I am assisted by wicked powers" (V.iii.90-91). When Hermione steps down from her pedestal, Leontes expresses his sense of the miraculous by carefully marking off the differences between this magic from the unlawful kind (V.iii.109-11). These deliberate distinctions between sacred and demonic magic, designed to separate and contain the demonic powers of the witch-narrator, disclose the presence of the continuing threat of the power of women's tales. The nature of this threat is best explored in *Macbeth*, which collapses such distinctions to portray women's narratives as purely demonic.

2. MACBETH

In her contempt for "a woman's story at a winter's fire," Lady Macbeth shows her attempt to unsex herself, as she identifies with a critical perspective outside this oral tradition. Paradoxically, Lady Macbeth's contempt for women's narratives participates in the same cultural imperative expressed by Erasmus: to become fully masculine, males were to leave marks of female influence behind them. In this respect, the warrior culture of Macbeth was not unlike the humanist culture of the early modern period. In their strong constructions of masculinity, neither culture tolerated signs of boyhood androgyny in adult males. But in the circular doublethink of this play, Lady Macbeth herself authors a narrative of a murdered baby which profoundly motivates Macbeth to murder Duncan. Thus, Lady Macbeth's scorn for women's narratives within a play largely driven by women's narratives, including her own, dramatizes the impossibility of eradicating their power, or the power of the women who told them.

This power which could not be eradicated could, however, be demonized. As critics have noted, in their absolute power over the lives especially of male infants, Lady Macbeth and the witches enact a subjectivity lying outside the boundaries of patriarchy: they become demonic. It has not yet been noted that they become authors as well. While they themselves perform no murders, they achieve their will through the effect of these narratives—and the constructions of gender within them—on Macbeth. It is through women's stories that *Macbeth* stages the fantasy of maternal power which Macbeth cannot escape, which can only be escaped, in Adelman's memorable argument, by one "not of woman born."[27] It is through their compelling *narratives* that Lady Macbeth and the witches create their absolute authority over the infant that Macbeth in some sense becomes. Fleeing the effeminacy of his childhood, Macbeth acts out not only the desires, but also the magical narratives told by women who dominate him.

Participating in their patriarchal culture's dark fantasy of the overwhelming power and the demonic nature of the reproductive female body, these narratives told by women are, like Paulina's play in the *Winter's Tale*, inseparable from the female body. In their sheer corporeality, these narrative acts create *Macbeth* as a "woman's story" in their saturation with imagery of nursing, menstruation, and bloody births.[28] The extent to which women's authorship is empowered by their dangerous biological functions is especially evident in Lady Macbeth's imagined murder of an infant nursing at her breast, which makes it chillingly apparent that women's power to nurture also bestows upon them the power to destroy (I.vii.54-59). Critics have noted the infantilizing effect of this speech on Macbeth in its recreation of his own vulnerability to a murderous mother now represented by his wife.[29] He responds obediently by killing Duncan. But it has not been noted that Lady Macbeth is no more able than her husband to escape the power of her own maternal body. Her imagined divestment of her femininity paradoxically only makes her reproductive body more rather than less abundantly present to the audience. As she asks her blood to be thickened, her menstruation or "visitings of Nature"[30] to be stopped, her milk to become gall, her invocation confirms rather than denies her identification with the flesh (gendered female) rather than the mind (gendered male). Far from masculinized, her imagination invokes Night as performing the function of a sinister mother/nurse, pulling a blanket over Duncan's murder to prevent heaven from seeing the deed. This blanket of smoke is one of several images which make of Scotland a claustrophobic womb:

> Come, thick night,
> And pall thee in the dunnest smoke of hell,
> That my keen knife see not the wound it makes,
> Nor heaven peep through the blanket of the dark
> To cry, 'Hold, hold!'
>
> (I.v.50-54)

While Lady Macbeth and the witches never meet, their narratives share a form of dangerous authorship permeated by female functions, especially nursing. Adelman has noted that the distinctions between Lady Macbeth and the witches blur in a common "image of perverse nursery" (135). Willis and Callagan have ably explored the ways in which the witchcraft persecutions manifested not only women's victimization but their symbolic power as mothers as well.[31] This power was also invested in the lower-class nurses whose care of upper-class infants sometimes proved lethal.[32] According to a larger patriarchal plot of the culture, the act of nursing opened up one strategy for exposing witches, as authorities searched even old women's bodies for signs of the "devil's teat," the mark left anywhere on their skin to show where they provided suck to the devil or his familiars.[33] This life-and-death authority demonizing mothers/nurses is evoked by a very physical form of authorship: the recipe of body parts included in the witches' womb-like cauldron. A smaller version of the "pilot's thumb" (I.iii.28), the "finger of birth-strangled babe / Ditch-deliver'd by a drab" gathers into the play a contemporary horror over infanticides committed primarily by desperate single mothers.[34] The blood of the sow "that hath eaten / Her nine farrow" enacts a blurring of human and animal in a gruesome transformation of nursing into cannibalism (IV.i.30-31, 64-65).

This double capacity to destroy and create is especially displayed in the witches' authorship of the bloody babe script to the anxious Macbeth.[35] In their staging of this scene, the witches have authored a highly equivocal play identified with the body. The blood (if it is his) signifies the baby's own vulnerability to physical injury and/or (if the blood is his mother's) his maternal origin. Both of these remain at odds with his advice to Macbeth, to "be bloody, bold, and resolute: laugh to scorn / The pow'r of man; for none of woman born / Shall harm Macbeth" (IV.i.79-81). Interpreted in terms of the blood on the babe, the injunction to "be bloody" becomes multivalent: it can mean at the same time to be cruel (as Macbeth takes it), to be wounded, and to memorialize his abject dependence upon his mother.[36] In its ability to "mean" in various ways, the apparition of the bloody babe resembles nothing so much as a Shakespeare play.

It has not yet been observed, however, that the witches' incantations draw their power from another very physical connection to the bodies of the women of childhood. Verging on nonsense, the "magic" of spells is performed through their sounds, as in the hypnotic incantation "Double, double, toil and trouble, / Fire burn, and cauldron bubble" (IV.i.10-11). In their form and sound—their alliteration, emphatic tetrameters, frequent rhymes—these incantations present a striking resemblance to early modern nursery rhymes.[37] In their exaggerated reliance on sound to make language "mean," the witches' spells, like nursery rhymes, recapitulate a young child's early and very physical bond with nurses and/or mothers who rocked and bounced them to their sounds. This insistent linkage between bodily power and narrative gains further support from the writings of Julia Kristeva, who theorizes that poetry's nonsignifying practices, such as rhythm, rhyme, and alliteration, derive their "meaning" from what she calls the semiotic: the pulsations, rhythms, and tones which orient the preoedipal self to the mother's body.[38] While Kristeva's theory applies with special intensity to witches' spells and nursery rhymes as archaic forms of poetry, it is not essential to an understanding of how the rhythm of the heart and the repetition of the sounds in the mouth create a nonlogical assent for a couplet such as "Fair is foul, and foul is fair, / Hover through the fog and filthy air" (I.i.11-12). As Adelman notes, Macbeth's echo of the witches' rhyme in his first words, "So fair and foul a day I have not seen" casts doubts on "the very possibility of autonomous identity" of Macbeth from the witches.[39] This echo also casts doubts on the autonomy of Shakespeare's play from childhood nursery rhymes and from the women's bodies which gave them their primal meanings.

If this infantilizing and possibly even preoedipal material, closely tied to the female body experienced in childhood, forms the content of the cultural fantasy of the witches, what then is its function? Peter Stallybrass has explored the way *Macbeth* uses the witches to validate their antithesis, the godly rule of Banquo's heirs, including of course James I himself.[40] *Macbeth* undoubtedly functions in this way; this cleansing of Scotland of demonic female powers also reflects a liberating sense of James's rule in Great Britain after so many decades of the rules of his "mothers" Mary Stuart and Elizabeth.[41] But this use of the witches to legitimate a godly masculine alternative is not so clear-cut. Macduff's identity as "not of woman born" rests on a technicality.[42] No less than any other human, Macduff required his mother's body to conceive him, and a wet nurse's body to feed him. The meaning of his status as "not of woman born" is derived, finally, from an apparition staged by witches; and this women's narrative is as equivocal as *Macbeth* itself. Within *Macbeth* there is no clear escape from women's power, even in the political arena. James's own sovereignty, and even his life, remain contingent on the uninterrupted lineage staged in the witches' show of the eight kings descended from Banquo. The survival of Banquo's heirs still depends upon the terrifying and uncontrollable powers invested in the female reproductive body.

As a demonic version of women's authority experienced in childhood, the witches' narratives perform a yet more central function. In *Macbeth,* horror serves as an antidote to nostalgia. The sheer excess of the nightmare world of *Macbeth* suggests its defensive role as over-compensation, deriving from desire rather than revulsion for the childhood world of female dominance. This yearning for the closeness of childhood relationships with women surfaces in the heart-rending sweetness of the scene between Lady Macduff and her son, which radiates the same comfortable and comforting intimacy as the mother-son scene in *Winter's Tale*. The presence of this relationship between a mother and an actual child points to the emptiness of the cultural fantasy of regression staged in *Macbeth.*

Rather than nightmare horrors, the brief scene between Lady Macduff and her son provides the few moments of genuine intimacy the play affords. Theirs is a female-dominated environment; having joined Malcolm's forces, the father is noticeably absent, and Lady Macduff even pretends he is dead. Their interactions are marked by mutuality rather than dominance, so that the son can assertively answer his mother's question, "How will you do for a father?" with his own question, "Nay, how will you do for a husband?" (IV.ii.39-40). In easy collaboration, they author a fantasy, beginning with Lady Macduff's announcement of her husband's death, which her son does not believe, and ending with the son's humorous if morbid vision of the outnumbered honest men foolishly attempting to hang all the liars and swearers. Instead of the procreative functions permeating the narratives of Lady Macbeth and the witches, this fantasy touchingly evokes a sense of vulnerability and loss. But this scene of mutual and creative playfulness ends with the horrifying murder of the boy. Enacting a sudden and forced separation from his mother, his death, like that of Mamillius, recapitulates a potentially traumatic entry of boys into a masculine environment. While counterdiscourses also arose, the *ethos* of a warrior/humanist culture required androgynous boys to die into a newly formed masculine self.

3. THE TEMPEST

The subject of women's demonic authorship reappears in the *Tempest,* where the witchcraft of Sycorax defines, by opposition, the magic of Prospero. Prospero's allegation that Sycorax engaged in intercourse with the devil invests her bodily functions, like those of Shakespeare's other witches, with a power dangerously outside patriarchal control. Sycorax's demonic maternity, like theirs, also permeates her art. The one magical act reported for this witch, dead before the play begins, was her confinement of Ariel in a "cloven pine" because he was "Too delicate / To act her earthy and abhorr'd commands" (I.ii.273-74). Her imprisonment of Ariel in a tree trunk, especially one "cloven" like a vagina, suggests a forced return to the womb. In the context of the anxieties about maternal dominance staged, for example, in *Macbeth,* Sycorax's punishment of Ariel was particularly horrifying; for this entrapment in the denigrated female body was precisely his object, and the object of any male in the early modern system, to escape. The twelve years of Ariel's suffering before he was rescued by Prospero points to this imprisonment as a misogynistic version of the early female environment; for boys were removed (or, from a humanist perspective, *freed*) sometime between the ages of seven and thirteen.

This demonic physicality of Sycorax's magic provides her with a dramatic function accounting for the otherwise puzzling prominence of her memorialization in *The Tempest*; for she is, to a much greater extent than Prospero's wife, given a name, a history, and a presence forcefully remembered by her survivors.[43] The debasement of Sycorax's female black magic exalts Prospero's magic, and the theatrical spectacles he stages, as white and masculine. Deriving from an elaborate Neoplatonic system, the distinctions between Sycorax's black magic or "goety" and Prospero's white magic or "theurgy" articulate the split between body and mind organizing the Neoplatonic system.[44] As described by Curry, the Neoplatonic cosmos was highly vertical, stretching from base matter at the bottom to Absolute Light at the top. Between these floated three forms of daemons classified by spiritual levels: the intellectual substances, the rational or "aereal" substances, and the irrational substances (175). The human soul was similarly verticalized between a higher or transcendent soul, able to unite mystically with the divine, and the lower or sensual soul, unable to survive separation from the body (176-77). Through the development of his upper soul, the theurgist could move beyond his body and its passions to participate harmoniously in the intellectual or divine spheres, which granted him the power to command the higher daemons. Motivated by the selfish passions of the lower soul, the geotist, on the other hand, disturbed the order of the cosmos with an inferior magic dependent on the lowest or irrational daemons. This magic further debased the geotist to the control of passion (180).

The plausibility of this Neoplatonic system depended on its rehearsal of the gendered relationships to the body accepted as "true" by early modern gender ideology. This ideology rendered legible, even predictable, the power of Prospero's theurgic art to transcend or deny the material body through the refinement of his higher spirit and the reading of learned books. The qualities empowering his magic also characterize the masculinity inculcated in boys in the humanist classroom: the transcendence of the body and the lower passions to engage in the exercise of reason and intellect.[45] Sycorax's "earthy and abhorr'd commands," on the other hand, identify her as a geotist, whose physicality is only exacerbated by her function as sinister Maternal.[46] While Sycorax left little magic behind her beyond her punishment of Ariel, she did give birth to Caliban, "a freckled whelp, hag-born, not honor'd with / A human shape" whom she "littered" on the island (I.ii.282-83). Like his mother, Caliban is closely associated with his body and "brutish" passions. He is marginally human; Trinculo at first mistakes him for a fish (II.ii.24). Never proceeding farther than Miranda's elementary language instruction, Caliban presents a monitory example of a male too base to be inducted into schoolroom masculinity. While Caliban is hardly androgynous by modern definitions, his identity as "hag-seed" (I.ii.368) legitimates Prospero's domination, at least to Prospero. According to this system, Caliban's "female" bodiliness justifies his subjection to Prospero, just as Prospero's own body remains subjected to the rule of his masculine mind.[47]

Demonstrating the masculinity as well as the sublimity of his art, Prospero's masterful transcendence of the material body is thoroughly exhibited by his successful use of Ariel, whose name identifies him with the rational substances inhabiting the "aerial" sphere. According to Agrippa, an ariel spirit was composed of pure intelligence, "free from all gross and putrefying mass of a body."[48] The plays Prospero produces through this daemon of intelligence, as Kermode notes, are designed to "liberate the soul from the passions."[49] Addressing the court party as "three men of sin" (III.iii.52), Ariel makes clear that his performance as a harpy is intended not to amuse but to reform. The spirit-hounds Prospero and Ariel set on Caliban, Stephano, and Trinculo replicate the punishment for passion in Golding's moralization of Ovid's Actaeon myth.[50] Prospero's graceful masque of Ceres forbids the presence of Venus or her "blind boy's scandall'd company" (IV.i.90). These classical references display an ideological connection between the goal of subjecting passions and Prospero's masculine attainment of a classical education. These characteristics inform *The Tempest* as a whole, with its allusions to Virgil's *Aeneid* and its conformity to the classical unities of time and place.[51] In marked contrast to *Macbeth* and *The Winter's Tale*, *The Tempest* may be called, in a humanist sense, one of Shakespeare's most "masculine" works.

Paradoxically, the very rigidity of these divisions between masculine and feminine, mind and body, white and black magic presage their collapse by the end of *The Tempest*. These distinctions begin to weaken where they seem strongest: in Ariel's performances. Kermode has discussed the attributes Ariel shares with English fairies: he is small enough to couch in a cowslip's bell; he abhors unchastity; and like Puck, he leads mortals into standing pools.[52] These similarities link Ariel, the "airy spirit" of Neoplatonic philosophy, to the diminutive creatures of childhood stories. Even more striking are the noises of beasts—the "bow-wow" of dogs, the "cock-a-diddle-dow" of a rooster (I.ii.382, 384, 386)—in the songs of this "spirit of pure intelligence." Like the incantations of the witches in *Macbeth*, the "magic" of Ariel's songs bears striking resemblances to the nursery rhymes of early modern childhood in which these noises also appeared, such as "Bow, wow, wow, / Whose dog art thou? / Little Tom Tinker's Dog, / Bow, wow, wow" or the ancient "onomatoplasm" of "Cock a doodle doo, / My Dame has lost her shoe." The "ding dong bell" of his ethereal song "Full fathom five" echoes the rhyme "Ding dong Bell, / The Cat is in the Well."[53] In these rhymes, Ariel's art perhaps reveals its debt to his twelve years in Sycorax's tree/womb.

Caliban's sensitivity to music also blurs the otherwise exaggerated distinctions between the ethereal Ariel and this bestial "hag-seed" of Sycorax. Caliban's moving description of these "sounds and sweet airs, that give delight and hurt not" evoke a child's intense response to a lullaby:

> And then in dreaming,
> The clouds methought would open, and show riches
> Ready to drop upon me, that when I wak'd
> cried to dream again.
>
> (III.ii.139-42)

Like Ariel's songs, Caliban's song shows the influence of nursery rhymes. Caliban's composition, however, contributes a specifically political angle: his jingle, "''Ban, 'Ban, Ca-Caliban / Has a new master, get a new man" (II.ii.184-85), adapts a common derivation of numerous nursery rhymes as expressions of popular protest.[54]

This blurring of the initially clear differences between Ariel and Caliban, between classical myth and nursery rhyme, implicitly weakens Prospero's claim as ruler of this island. Demonstrated in the rational control of the body and its passions, the masculinity instilled in the schoolroom was to legitimate authority over others. As various critics have pointed out, however, Prospero is not always rational. He becomes irritated at Miranda on little pretext and he apparently desires vengeance on the court party. Most destructive to these gendered distinctions, however, is his vengeful threat to Ariel to enact the same form of punishment inflicted by Sycorax for resistance to his commands: to "rend an oak, / And peg thee in his knotty entrails" (I.ii.295-96). It is surely no coincidence that this image blurs the differences between male and female bodies. The pronoun "his" describing the tree's entrails reveals that Prospero's trunk, like that of Sycorax, has a human interior. The placement of a creature inside the entrails of a male, to form a kind of male womb, expresses the early modern sense of the essential physiological similarity of the genitalia of men and women.[55]

Prospero's earlier description of his own body as a trunk in the process of destruction by Antonio prepares for this dissolution of distinctions based on gender. In addition to identifying the similarities of genitalia, this image expresses what for Prospero is perhaps an even more radical identification of himself as a "trunk," or a physical body apart from soul or mind:

> He was
> The ivy which hid my princely trunk,
> And suck'd my verdure out on't.
>
> (I.ii.85-87)

In this representation of Antonio's sucking, an image of oral sexuality merges with that of maternal nursing. Prospero has become a lactating male who nourishes his parasite/child through the loss of his own semen/milk. He is effeminized, not by a homoerotic act, but by the power relationship it inscribes.[56]

The circumstances leading up to Antonio's sucking out of Prospero's strength call into question the humanist version of masculinity structuring *The Tempest*. Prospero lost his power over Antonio as well as Milan by engaging precisely in those practices upon which he based his magic: by reading learned books. "Rapt in secret studies" (I.ii.77), Prospero gave Antonio the "manage" of his state. Prospero chose his library as "dukedom large enough," while Antonio thought him "incapable" of "temporal royalties" (I.ii.110-11). Like Sycorax, he was banished from his realm. The image of fantasized pregnancy he uses to describe his care of his three-year-old daughter stresses its effeminizing effect. As Adelman notes, "he 'groan'd' under his 'burthen': her smiles 'rais'd in [him] / An undergoing stomach, to bear up / Against what should ensue'" (I.ii.156-58).[57] The intellectual mastery empowering Prospero's control of his island did not work in Milan. Precisely because of his "trunk," his bodiliness, Prospero was vulnerable to physical force. Faced with naked political power, men of intellect—including magicians/playwrights—become as powerless as women.

Perhaps because of this failure of Prospero's learned magic, and the form of masculinity it implied, Prospero renounces his art as he prepares to return to Milan. Various critics have noted that the lines between white and black magic begin to blur in Prospero's renunciation, especially in his claim that "graves at my command / Have wak'd their sleepers, op'd, and let 'em forth / By my so potent art" (V.i.48-50).[58] The intertextual meanings of this speech within early modern culture further blur these lines, so that the differences between male magus and female witch collapse entirely; so do the differences between magus and playwright. Surpassing Golding's popular translation from which it draws, Prospero's speech displays Shakespeare's virtuoso ability to render the Latin of Ovid's *Metamorphoses* into excellent English poetry.[59] In the experience of privileged early modern males, this fluency in Latin was itself a marker of masculinity. But the actual lines translated were spoken by Medea, an enchantress often represented as a witch in the early modern period.[60] A few years later, Sandys's 1632 commentary on this passage makes this conflation explicit: like a witch, Medea had no powers of her own, but acted as the dupe of demonic powers: "These wonders were not effected by the vertue of words, or skill of *Medea*; but rather by wicked Angels, who seem to subject themselves, the better to delude, to the art of the Inchantresse."[61]

Shakespeare's choice to translate this specific passage gains further force from its status in contemporary knowledges of witches. Shortly after *The Tempest,* a perception of Prospero's speech as an act of ventriloquism of the words of a female witch appears in Middleton's choice to give the Latin form of Medea's speech to Hecate in his play *The Witch* (1614).[62] According to Jean Bodin's influential *Demonomanie des sorciers,* these lines composed an actual witch's incantation which the devil had seduced Ovid into including in his work.[63] So who was the actual author of Medea's words? As he concludes his discussion of Medea's lines with the warning that the Devil has deceived men in all languages, including Latin, Bodin represents the poet as no more in control of his text than his character Medea. Ovid was only an intermediary; the real author was the Devil. With this claim, Ovid's mastery of Medea is no longer so clear. In Bodin's reading, this learned Latin text collapses into the demonic incantation it contains. And so, by implication, does Shakespeare's rendering of Prospero's renunciation, a translation of Ovid's lines spoken by Medea. Latin poet, classical enchantress, female witch, male magus, and even male playwright: all become indistinguishable in a whirling witch's brew.[64]

The issue at stake in Shakespeare's use of a witch's incantation is not so much literal belief as the identification of the male playwright with the very real powers attributed to female narratives through the staging of witches. As Prospero stands forward on the stage to speak the forbidden incantation of a witch, he not only renounces his art, but also the gender distinctions which that art rehearsed. With Prospero's renunciation, Shakespeare, in a sense, returns his own writing to the androgynous period dominated by women when narratives really were magic. This return is signified by the fairy tale lore embedded within his translation from Ovid. Like Golding, Shakespeare translates "di" as "elves" in the line, "Ye elves of hills, brooks, standing lakes, and groves" (V.i.32), but he has no apparent source for the invocation to "demi-puppets that / By moonshine do the green sour ringlets make, / Whereof the ewe not bites" (36-38) or to "you whose pastime / Is to make midnight mushrumps, that rejoice / To hear the solemn curfew" (38-40). It is through the aid of these local deities, "weak masters" though they be, that Prospero, and Shakespeare as well, "bedimm'd / The noontide sun" and even, like Paulina, seemed to open graves. Is there a connection between Prospero's renunciation of his art and this passage which is simultaneously a Latin poem, a witch's incantation, and fairy tale lore? Does this connection imply a parallel renunciation by the playwright of an art indebted to childhood narratives told by women?

There is another possibility, however, which suggests an acceptance rather than a rejection of old wives' tales. In the face of death, the mortal meanings of the physical body cannot be denied; and under the pressure of mortality, Prospero returns to his body. Soon after his renunciation speech, Prospero expresses his vulnerability to death, to foresee that in his retirement in Milan, "every third thought shall be my grave" (V.i.311). Enacting a return of the repressed, a series of womb images enscribes this movement towards death as a full-circle return to the comfort of women's bodies, represented as the locus of mortality as well as life. In Act III, Alonzo believes that his son "i' th' ooze is bedded" (III.iii.101); later he repeats this image in his desire to lie "mudded in that oozy bed / Where my son lies" (V.i.151-52). These repeated images of drowning as lying "bedded" in "ooze" imagine death by drowning as a return to the womb. Ariel's song, "Full fathom five," strikingly enacts the miraculous power of the art of birth/death practiced by this sea womb upon the body, capable of turning bones to coral and eyes to pearls. It is to this sea womb that Prospero returns his book, drowning it "deeper than did ever plummet sound" (V.i.55). In drowning his book, Prospero renounces not only his art, but the form of learned masculinity it signifies.

As Prospero perceives himself in terms of his mortal bodiliness, the power of his learning to elevate him above the flesh and the feminine loses its relevance. Stepping forward to ask the prayers of the audience, Prospero enacts a new and moving dependence. Freed from the authoritative presence of the learned *magus*, Prospero returns to the wise vulnerability of a child as he embarks on his longer journey towards the womb of death.

Notes

My thanks to Barbara Hodgdon for reading an earlier draft of this essay.

1. Macbeth, III.iv.60-68; this and other quotations are taken from *The Complete Works of Shakespeare*, ed. David Bevington (New York: HarperCollins, 1992).

2. Stephen Orgel, "Nobody's Perfect: Or Why Did the English Stage Take Boys for Women?" *South Atlantic Quarterly* 88 (1989): 14.

3. Gail Kern Paster, *The Body Embarrassed: Drama and the Disciplines of Shame in Early Modern England* (Ithaca: Cornell University Press, 1993), 200; Janet Adelman, *Suffocating Mothers: Fantasies of Maternal Origin in Shakespeare's Plays, Hamlet to the Tempest* (New York: Routledge, 1992), 7; Patricia Crawford, "The Construction and Experience of Maternity in Seventeenth-Century England," in *Women as Mothers in Pre-industrial England,* ed. Valerie Fildes (London: Routledge, 1990), 8.

4. The age of breeching appears to have varied from about five until eight, according to Susan Snyder, "Mamillius and Gender Polarization in *The Winter's Tale*," paper delivered at Shakespeare Association, April 1998; my thanks to Professor Snyder for providing me a copy of her meticulously researched paper. See *English Family Life, 1576-1716: An Anthology from Diaries,* ed. Ralph Houlbrooke (Oxford: Blackwell, 1988), 150, 147, 164. For ages somewhat later in the seventeenth century, see Ralph Josselin, *The Diary of Ralph Josselin,* ed. Alan Macfarlane (London: Oxford University Press, 1976), 407 and Roger North, *The Lives of the Norths,* ed. Augustus Jessopp (London: George Bell, 1890), 216. See also Randolph Trumbach, *The Rise of the Egalitarian Family* (New York: Academic Press, 1978), 251; Philippe Aries, *Centuries of Childhood: A Social History of Family Life* (New York: Vintage, 1962), 58-59.

5. Thomas Laqueur, *Making Sex: Body and Gender from the Greeks to Freud* (Cambridge: Harvard University Press, 1990), 123-27.

6. Phyllis Rackin, "Foreign Country: The Place of Women and Sexuality in Shakespeare's Historical World," in *Enclosure Acts: Sexuality, Property, and Culture in Early Modern England,* ed. Richard Burt and John Archer (Ithaca: Cornell University Press, 1994), 74; Leah Marcus, *Childhood and Cultural Despair* (Pittsburgh: University of Pittsburgh Press, 1978), 10.

7. Walter Ong, *Rhetoric, Romance, and Technology* (Ithaca: Cornell University Press, 1971), 113-41. Sometimes children were also sent away as servants in other households: see Alan Macfarlane, *Marriage and Love in England: Modes of Reproduction, 1300-1840* (Oxford: Blackwell, 1986), 83.

8. Rebecca W. Bushnell, *A Culture of Teaching: Early Modern Humanism in Theory and Practice* (Ithaca: Cornell University Press, 1996), 28; Richard Halpern, *The Poetics of Primitive Accumulation* (Ithaca: Cornell University Press, 1991), 27; Mary Ellen Lamb, "Apologizing for Pleasure in Sidney's *Apology for Poetry*: The Nurse of Abuse Meets the Tudor Grammar School," *Criticism* 36 (1994): 505-6. Gendered implications are traced ably by Jonathan Goldberg, *Writing Matter: From the Hands of the English Renaissance* (Stanford: Stanford University Press, 1990), esp. 141-46 on the "woman's hand"; Anthony Grafton and Lisa Jardine, *From Humanism to the Humanities: Education and the Liberal Arts in Fifteenth- and Sixteenth-Century Europe* (Cambridge: Harvard University Press, 1986), 55-57, *passim* on issues facing humanist women. Bushnell represents humanist education as kinder than have Goldberg and Grafton and Jardine.

9. Keith Thomas, *Rule and Misrule in the Schools of Early Modern England* (Reading: University of Reading, 1976), 8; Bushnell, 62. Routines and punishments are detailed in T. W. Baldwin, *William Shakspere's Small Latine & Lesse Greeke* (Urbana: University of Illinois Press, 1944), 1:353-72. These revived a classical technique of the self designed for the ruling class, as described by Michel Foucault, *The History of Sexuality,* Vol. 2: *The Use of Pleasure* (New York: Methuen, 1986), 84-85, 173.

10. Rackin, 76; this early modern commonplace was publicized from, for example, the homily on marriage, cited in Lawrence Stone, *The Family, Sex, and Marriage in England, 1500-1800* (New York: Harper and Row), 198.

11. This flight was not limited to early modern schoolrooms: see R. Howard Bloch, "Medieval Misogyny," *Representations* 20 (1987): 15, who defines misogyny as "the desire to escape the sense, perception, the corporeal"; he also associates the literary with the feminine, although for different reasons from mine.

12. Erasmus, *De pueris instituendis,* in William Harrison Woodward, *Desiderius Erasmus Concerning the Aim and Method of Education* (New York: Columbia University Teacher's College, 1964), 214; also cited Halpern, 25.

13. Bartholomeus Battus, *De Oeconomia Christiana,* trans. J. William Lowth as *The Christian Mans Closet* (London, 1581), 02; John Dod and Robert Cleaver, *A Godly Forme of Householde Government* (London: 1612), Q6v.

14. John Aubrey, "The Life and Times of John Aubrey," prefatory to *Brief Lives,* ed. Oliver Lawson Dick (London: Secker and Warburg, 1950), xxix, xxxiii; see also Stone, 170.

15. This issue is posed in partial answer to the seminal essay by Mary Beth Rose, "Where Are the Mothers in Shakespeare? Options for Gender Representation in the English Renaissance," *Shakespeare Quarterly* 42 (1991): 307. The effeminizing potential of fictions for other authors has recently been explored by Juliet Fleming, "The Ladies' Man and the Age of Elizabeth," in *Sexuality and Gender in Early Modern Europe,* ed. James Grantham Turner (Cambridge: Cambridge University Press, 1993), 158-81, Lamb, "Apologizing for Pleasure," and Richard Helgerson, *The Elizabethan Prodigals* (Berkeley: University of California Press, 1975), 32-36.

16. Fleming, 158, notes that since "the category of the aesthetic" was "absent" in early modern England, fictions written primarily to entertain were often represented as only "trifles" or "toys" suitable only to reading by women. George Peele's *Old Wives' Tales* conveys the delight possible to a late night tale told by a lower-class woman to three young pages.

17. Giovanni Boccaccio, *Boccaccio on Poetry,* ed. Charles Osgood (New York: Liberal Arts Press, 1956), 54.

18. The implications of Mamillius' name are discussed well by Paster, 265; her discussion of the forceful removal of an infant through wet-nursing prefigures and exaggerates the later trauma of a boy's separation from the women who raised him.

19. Peter Erickson, *Patriarchal Structures in Shakespeare's Drama* (Berkeley: University of California Press, 1985), 158, discusses this symbiotic union in the grave.

20. This regressive identification is discussed well by Paster, 265; Adelman, 224-25; and Coppelia Kahn, *Man's Estate: Masculine Identity in Shakespeare* (Berkeley: University of California Press, 1981), 216, who notes that Leontes is emotionally stuck in the symbiotic stage of development.

21. The stereotype of talkative old women is ably discussed by Patricia Parker, "Literary Fat Ladies and the Generation of Text," in *Literary Fat Ladies* (London: Methuen, 1987), 8-35.

22. This argument extends my discussion on the self-reflexive nature of these ballads in "Ovid and *The Winter's Tale*: Conflicting Views toward Art," in *Shakespeare and the Dramatic Tradition: Essays in Honor of S. F. Johnson,* ed. W. R. Elton and William B. Long (Newark: University of Delaware Press, 1989), 78-79.

23. Murray Schwartz, "*The Winter's Tale*: Loss and Transformation," *American Imago* 32 (1975): 198.

24. Adelman, 235.
25. Erickson, 158.
26. Abbe Blum, "'Strike all that look upon with mar(b)le': Monumentalizing Women in Shakespeare's Plays," in *The Renaissance Englishwoman in Print,* ed. Anne M. Haselkorn and Betty S. Travitsky (Amherst: University of Massachusetts Press, 1990), 112-13.
27. Adelman, 131-47. An early influential study is David B. Barron, "The Babe that Milks: An Organic Study of *Macbeth,*" in *The Design Within,* ed. M. D. Faber (New York: Science House, 1970), 251-80. See also Kahn, 151-91; David Willbern, "Phantasmagoric *Macbeth,*" *English Literary Renaissance* 16 (1986): 520-49; Paster, 220.
28. Alice Fox, "Obstetrics and Gynecology in *Macbeth,*" *Shakespeare Studies* 12 (1979): 127-42.
29. Baron, 265; Kahn, 153-54; Willbern, 522-30.
30. Fox, 129.
31. Deborah Willis, *Malevolent Nurture: Witch-Hunting and Maternal Power in Early Modern England* (Ithaca: Cornell University Press, 1995); Dympna Callagan, "Wicked Women in *Macbeth*: A Study of Power, Ideology, and the Production of Motherhood," in *Reconsidering the Renaissance,* ed. Mario Di Cesare (Binghamton, NY: MRTS, 1992), 355, 367; see also Karen Newman, *Fashioning Femininity* (Princeton: Princeton University Press, 1991), 58.
32. For association of witches and nurses, see Willis, 36-37; Paster, 248-60; Stone, 65; Adelman, 4; Karen Newman, 58. Dorothy McLaren, "Marital Fertility and Lactation, 1570-1720," in *Women in English Society, 1500-1800,* ed. Mary Prior (London: Methuen, 1985), 32 suggests the actual infant mortality rate for wet-nursed infants may be exaggerated. However, see also Keith Wrightson, "Infanticide in European History," *Criminal Justice History* 3 (1982): 12, who discusses the apparently deliberate role of certain wet nurses who "tacitly guaranteed" an "early death" for unwanted babies.
33. Willis, 64.
34. Wrightson, "Infanticide," 6-7, discusses cultural forces motivating infanticide by single mothers; see also Deborah A. Symonds, *Weep Not for Me: Women, Ballads, and Infanticide in Early Modern Scotland* (University Park: Pennsylvania State University Press, 1997), 69-94.
35. Kahn, 181; for slightly different readings see Adelman, 140 and Callagan, 361.
36. This double meaning of blood relates to the paradoxical significances of wounds as at once attesting to "a (feminine) vulnerability" and serving as "a cultural marker of manly virtue," as ably discussed by Coppelia Kahn, *Roman Shakespeare: Warriors, Wounds, and Women* (New York: Routeldge, 1997), 18.
37. William S. Baring-Gould and Ceil Baring-Gould, *The Annotated Mother Goose* (New York: Clarkson N. Potter, 1962), 56; this book contains many examples of forcefully alliterative tetrameter nursery rhymes.
38. Julia Kristeva, "Revolution in Poetic Language," *The Kristeva Reader,* ed. Toril Moi (New York: Columbia University Press, 1986), 89-136; also pertinent is her *Powers of Horror: An Essay on Abjection* (New York: Columbia University Press, 1982), 75.
39. Adelman, 131.
40. Peter Stallybrass, "*Macbeth* and Witchcraft," in *Focus on Macbeth* (London: Routeldge and Kegan Paul, 1982), 189-209.
41. Jonathan Goldberg, *James I and the Politics of Literature* (Baltimore: Johns Hopkins University Press, 1983).
42. Adelman, 140, further notes that "the play curiously enacts the fantasy that it seems to deny."
43. The near-absence of Prospero's wife is discussed in Stephen Orgel, "Prospero's Wife," in *Rewriting the Renaissance: Discourses of Sexual Difference in Early Modern Europe,* ed. Margaret W. Ferguson, Maureen Quilligan, and Nancy Vickers (Chicago: Chicago University Press, 1986), 50-64.
44. W. C. Curry, *Shakespeare's Philosophical Patterns* (Baton Rouge: Louisiana State University Press, 1936), 144-95; Wayne Shumaker, *The Occult Sciences in the Renaissance* (Berkeley: University of California Press, 1972), 108-59; K. M. Briggs, *Pale Hecate's Team* (London: Routledge and Kegan Paul, 1962), 56-57, 83; Frances Yates, *The Occult Philosophy in the Elizabethan Age* (London: Routledge and Kegan Paul, 1979), 44-47, 159-60; Frank Kermode, ed., Shakespeare's *The Tempest*. The Arden Shakespeare (1954; rpt. London: Routledge, 1990), xlvii-li, 143-47.
45. Adelman, 237, suggests the connection between the intellectuality of Prospero's art and his banishment of the mother in the form of Sycorax as Prospero reshapes "the world in the image of his own mind."
46. The horror (or the even more frightening nostalgia) for this period of female domination is perhaps the source of the "dread potential within Shakespeare's imagination of women" discerned in the representation of Sycorax's art by C. L. Barber and Richard P. Wheeler, *The Whole Journey: Shakespeare's Power of Development* (Berkeley: University of California Press, 1986), 336.
47. This naturalization of Prospero's rule over Caliban connects a gendered reading of *The Tempest* with recent colonialist readings to confirm Klaus Theweleit's claim that "the imperialist drives of the

European world against 'primitive' peoples" formed one aspect of an "inner imperialism that took as its territories lands formed from the subjugated nature of female bodies" (*Male Fantasies,* trans. Stephen Conway [Minneapolis: University of Minneapolis Press, 1987], 322).

48. As quoted and discussed by Kermode, 143.

49. Kermode, xlvii.

50. Golding moralizes the hounds of the Acteon myth to represent punishment for excesses of the flesh including drunkenness in *Shakespeare's Ovid* (London, Centaur Press, 1961), 3.

51. One of many such discussions of *The Tempest's* debt to Virgil is Donna B. Hamilton, "Defiguring Virgil in *The Tempest,*" *Style* 23 (1989): 352-75.

52. Kermode, 142-45.

53. *The Annotated Mother Goose,* 65; "bow wow" was also the conclusion to "Old Mother Hubbard," written in the early nineteenth century from much earlier, undated sources, 56, 58.

54. Albert Mason Stevens, *The Nursery Rhyme: Remnant of Popular Protest* (Lawrence: Coronado Press, 1968); *The Annotated Mother Goose;* Martin W. Walsh, "'Get a New Man': Caliban's Son and Autumnal Hiring Customs," *Cashiers Elisabethains* 43 (1993): 57-60.

55. Laqueur, 123, 267.

56. Power relations in early modern homoeroticism are well discussed by Bruce Smith, *Homosexual Desire in Shakespeare's England: A Cultural Poetics* (Chicago: University of Chicago Press, 1991), 185-95, *passim.*

57. Adelman, 237.

58. Cosmo Corfield, "Why Does Prospero Abjure His 'Rough Magic'?" *Shakespeare Quarterly* 36 (1985): 32-33, ably summarizes the extended debate on the relative whiteness or blackness of Shakespeare's magic, concluding that the impurities introduced into his theurgy by his renunciation created him as more human. I would claim they also create him as more feminine. Numerous contemporary thinkers, such as Bodin and Sandys, did not admit even a theoretical difference between any white magic and black magic.

59. Perhaps the most learned discussion of the relationship between these translations is T. W. Bald- win, 2:443-53; Baldwin, 445, relates Shakespeare's translation to the "school mode of translating."

60. Philip Stubbes, *Anatomie of Abuses,* pt. 1 (London, 1583), F5v; Robert Greene, "Debate between Follie and Love" in *Works,* ed. Alexander Grosart, 4:202; Francesco Maria Guazzo, *Compendium Maleficarum,* trans. E. A. Ashwin (New York: Dover, 1988), 92. Orgel, "Prospero's Wife," 61, also notes the collapse of black and white magic as Prospero speaks the words of Medea.

61. Kermode, 149; and see *Compendium Maleficarum,* 17, on the witch as devil's dupe.

62. In Thomas Middleton's play *The Witch* (c.1614), Hecate speaks this speech, untranslated from Latin; ed W. W. Greg (Oxford: Oxford University Press for Malone Society, 1948), 2:5.

63. Jean Bodin, *La Demonomanie des Sorciers* (Paris, 1579), G2. Reginald Scot, *The Discovery of Witchcraft* (London, 1584), N8, R3, remained skeptical about the efficacy of this and other spells.

64. Any discussion of the relationship between magic and Shakespeare's stagecraft must be indebted to Stephen Greenblatt, "Shakespeare and the Exorcists," in *Shakespeare and the Question of Theory,* ed. Patricia Parker and Geoffrey Hartman (New York: Methuen, 1985): 163-87.

Scott F. Crider (essay date 1999)

SOURCE: "Weeping in the Upper World: The Orphic Frame in 5.3 of *The Winter's Tale* and the Archive of Poetry," in *Studies in the Literary Imagination,* Vol. 32, No. 2, Spring, 1999, pp. 153-72.

[*In the essay below, Crider contends that the "mythic" and "theatrical" readings of Hermione are not mutually exclusive—that Hermione can be read as being both "dead and alive"—and provides textual evidence for both readings by examining Ovid's* Metamorphoses.]

> When there is poetry,
> it is Orpheus singing.
>
> —Rilke, *Sonnets to Orpheus* (1.5)

It is now a critical commonplace that Hermione is merely pretending to be a statue in the last act of Shakespeare's *The Winter's Tale* and that, as a consequence, there is no actual animation represented there. As Stephen Orgel explains in his introduction to the Oxford edition of the play, "Hermione is not, after all, a statue" (60). The evidence of the play, however, is rather less conclusive than Orgel's confidence would suggest. Using Jonathan Bate's fine distinction in *Shakespeare and Ovid,* we can say that Orgel has decided against the "mythic" reading of the scene and in favor of the "theatrical": A mythic reading would allow that, within the mimetic world of the play, Hermione is a statue and then becomes, in the mythic mode, a woman; a theatrical reading assumes that she is pretending to be a statue and performs, in the theatrical mode, the animation. Bate's reading of the play is characteristically fine, but he too precludes a "mythic" reading, and he too assumes rather than argues the case:

> [T]his is not really an animation or a resurrection. Paulina is staging a theatrical coup. Shakespeare has

Act V, scene iii. By William Hamilton. Leontes, Polixenes, Florizel, Perdita, Camillo, Paulina, Lords, Attendants, and Hermione.

triumphantly moved from Ovid's key of myth into his own of drama. . . . As the preserved Hermione pretends to be a statue coming to life, so does the boy actor. When we realize that Paulina and Harmione are staging a performance and when we see the correspondence between character and actor, we recognize that the magic which Paulina claims to be lawful is that of theater.

(237-8)

Throughout, Bate assumes that theater and myth are mutually exclusive. This assumption cannot do justice to the play's ambiguity, because there is textual evidence for both the theatrical and the mythic readings. The question is this: Is the animation actual, or is it a representation of an animation? Both Orgel and Bate assume that, without a doubt, we may not say that a statue of Hermione becomes Hermione herself. Hermione must never have been dead. Again, the play does not share their confidence. In fact, its very ambiguity denies that the two modes—theatrical and mythic—are exclusive, enacting a tension between the two which is itself mythic, demanding as it does that the audience experience the moment as simultaneously both. As Jean-Pierre Vernant explains in *Myth and Society in Ancient Greece,* "[M]yth brings into operation a form of logic that we may describe, in contrast to the logic of non-contradiction of the philosophers, as a logic of the ambiguous, the equivocal, a logic of polarity" (260). This "logic of the ambiguous" is the mythic logic of the statue scene in 5.3 of *The Winter's Tale,* yet Bate's humane skepticism would preclude our discernment of that mythic logic, a logic which allows Shakespearean mimesis to have two objects at once: a mythic *praxis* and a theatrical.[1]

Why does Shakespeare do this? To answer the question, I would like first to examine the intertextual relationship in the scene between Shakespeare and Ovid, the trace within 5.3 of both the Pygmalion tale and the Orphic frame of that tale in the tenth book of the *Metamorphoses.* I know of only two discussions of this point.[2] My provisional argument is that the play demands a double-reading, one in which Hermione is both dead and alive, and the statue scene is both mythic animation and theatrical performance. No reading of the play can perform the scene one way without suppressing the other. We begin to discern Shakespeare's intention when we remember that the Pygmalion tale, so often recognized as a source for the scene,[3] is actually told by Orpheus in Ovid's epic poem, one of the many tales he tells after Eurydice's death and before his own at the hands of the Thracian women. The Pygmalion tale *per se* is not a source for the scene; the tale *as told by Orpheus* is. Once we recognize that we must attend, not simply to the tale, but to the tale-within-the-tale, we can begin to explore the play's central ambiguity. There are three parts to my full discussion: The first examines Ovid; the second, Shakespeare's appropriation of Ovid; the third, that appropriation as a figure for literary history itself, the archive of the poetic tradition. The Orphic frame of the Pygmalion tale in Ovid's *Metamorphoses* suggests that the particular tale is a romance Orpheus fashions to make his own tragic circumstances intelligible to himself, a romance which, because of the frame, enacts Orpheus' desire for a *mimesis* which can transform the real. This Orphic romance, including both the animation of Pygmalion's statue and the death of Eurydice, is a classical, pagan mystery, a mystery for which death is an absolute horizon because both faith and love, though not art, fail before the ultimate givenness of mortality. When Shakespeare appropriates and transforms the tale of Pygmalion, he also appropriates and transforms the Orphic frame, disclosing an Orphic presence in the statue scene which will not allow us to preclude Hermione's actual animation. Shakespeare's revision of Ovid will allow the possibility that art, faith, and love might be able to triumph, if only briefly, over death; this is a Renaissance, pagan mystery in which *mimesis* can transform the real.[4] For Shakespearean romance, art, faith, and love are not completely powerless before death. Indeed, Shakespeare's poetic friendship with Ovid, a friendship Bate has gone a long way to illuminate, reveals that the literary tradition is itself a series of reanimations in which the living bestow life on the dead.

The archive of poetry is the temple of Orpheus: We examine now only its historicized ruins, the pieces of stone we can see and measure; what such an examination fails to sense is the music which animates stone, a music

at once both ancient and present. Shakespeare is not only an early modern, but also a late ancient. His lyre is Orpheus'. Ovid gave it to him.

I

[S]tories . . . make endurable our losses.
—George Steiner, "Two Cocks" (384)

The story is worth the telling. Orpheus' bride Eurydice dies on their wedding day, bitten in the heel by a snake (10.1-10), and Orpheus descends into the underworld to restore her, singing there a song (11-39) which persuades Pluto and Proserpina to release Eurydice on one condition: as Orpheus leads her up and out to the upper world, he is not to look back at her (40-52). Leading her out, he does just that, losing her again. After mourning for her in the underworld itself, he returns to the upper world where he forsakes the love of woman for that of young men (52-85). On a hill in Thrace where the trees have gathered to him (86-142), Orpheus sings five songs to himself: After his invocation and designated subject (148-54), he sings of Jupiter and Ganimede (155-61), Apollo and Hyacinthus (162-219), Pygmalion and Galatea (220-97), Cinyras and Myrra (298-502), and Venus and Adonis (503-739). (Venus herself tells the tale of Atalanta and Hippomenes to Adonis [566-707]). After singing his songs, Orpheus is dismembered by the Thracian women and reunited with Eurydice in the underworld, where the two play their game of "follow-the-leader" (11.1-85). All the tales must be understood metafictionally within the context of Orpheus' own tragic circumstances, especially the tale of the misogynist Pygmalion, the sculptor who, disgusted by the Propoetides, fashions through his own art an ideal woman he then desires and, after Venus' intervention, animates and marries. Interestingly, this is the one tale which does not enact the subject Orpheus earlier announced:

> But now I need a milder style to tell of pretty boys
> That were the darlings of the Gods: and of unlawful joys
> That burned in the breasts of Girls, who for their wicked lust
> According as they did deserve, received penance just.
>
> (152-4; 157-10)[5]

The "pretty boys" are Ganymede, Hyacinthus and Adonis; the "Girls" of "unlawful joys" are Myrra and Venus. (The tale of Venus and Adonis combines both subjects.) What of the tale of Pygmalion, though? The tales before it enact the first subject; those after, the second. Because the Pygmalion tale itself does not fit the announced subjects, I would suggest that it is a tale the teller had not planned on telling, a tale whose catalyst is Apollo's mourning for Hyacinthus. Apollo accidentally kills his pretty boy, remember, because the disc he threw takes a bad bounce and strikes him dead. As Orpheus has Apollo lament,

> Thou fad'st away, my Hyacinth, defrauded of thy prime
> Of youth (quoth Phoebus) and I see thy would my heinous crime.
> Thou art my sorrow and my fault: this hand of mine hath wrought
> Thy death: I like a murtherer have to thy grave thee brought.
>
> (196-9; 207-10)

Orpheus, aware of the parallel between Apollo's responsibility for Hyacinthus' death and his own for Eurydice's, then fashions a romance calibrated to make endurable his loss.

If one reads the Pygmalion tale with reference to its Orphic frame, one discovers that it is a more serious narrative than it appears in isolation. In *Orpheus: The Myth of the Poet*, Charles Segal reads Orpheus as Pygmalion's double in the tale (85-9), a doubling which reveals Ovid's poetic purpose: "By enclosing the story of Pygmalion within that of Orpheus, Ovid reflects on both the power and the limitations of art" (89). For Segal, Pygmalion's capacity, with Venus' divine assistance, to animate the statue comments upon Orpheus' inability to have brought Eurydice back from the dead; because the Pygmalion tale concerns only love and art, though—and not love, art and *death*—it is not a serious tale (88-9). For Segal, the power of Pygmalion's art to triumph over lifelessness, figured in Ovid's poem as stone, is diminished by the fact of Orphic art's failure before death.

This interpretation is true if one isolates the two narratives, then compares them as independent tales. This isolation diminishes the nature of the two stories, though; Ovid chooses to tell the one inside the other. Strictly speaking, there are not two narratives; instead, there is one narrative within another. Ovidian narrative is a *perpetuum . . . carmen* (1.5), remember; its "course" will run "directly" (1.4), according to Golding. The poem is ultimately one tale, all the tales within it versions of a single human action: the narrative of metamorphosis, "shapes transformed to bodies strange" (1.1-2; 1.1).[6] Ovid wants us to see one, continually changing story. Granted, one can separate the tales. In the case of Orpheus' songs, however, such a separation is not a good idea. One should not isolate the Pygmalion narrative from its Orphic frame because the *mimesis* Orpheus fashions represents his own *praxis* in order to make it intelligible to himself. Romance is not simply mystification; it is also clarification. Romance clarifies for us our desire to transcend our own mortality and to help others transcend theirs. Romance clarifies the fact that the beloved's death is often the result of the lover's inadequate love, not his or her inadequate art. In the Ovidian account, after all, Orpheus' failure is not a failure of art. His song to Pluto and Proserpina succeeds in reclaiming Eurydice from death: "And neither Pluto nor his Lady were so strong / And hard of stomach to withhold his just petition long" (46-7; 50-1). Orpheus' art saves her; his ethical weakness, his incapacity to keep the terms of her release, loses her. What, exactly, is that ethical weakness? The text is ambiguous. As they are ascending, he does indeed look back:

> They took a path that steep upright
> Rose dark and full of foggy mist. And now they were within
> A kenning of the upper earth, when Orpheus did begin
> To doubt him lest she followed not, and through an eager love
> Desirous for to see her his eyes did backward move.
> Immediately she slipped back.
>
> (53-7; 56-60)

Ovid provides two tragic errors, both of which indicate ethical failure: First, Orpheus fails because he is eager to see her; second, he fails because he begins to doubt that she is following him. The first weakness is incontinence. What is the second? The Ovidian narrator passes by the doubt silently, saying only—and sarcastically—"For why what had she to complain, unless it were of love / which made her husband back again his eyes upon her move?" (61; 65-6). The reader, remembering as he or she will how Orpheus lost her again—it has only been ten lines—cannot fail to notice that the narrator stresses only Orpheus' incontinence, not at all his doubt. What is the nature of Orphic doubt? Who is its object, the gods or his wife? Does he believe that Pluto and Proserpina have failed to stand by their word, or does he believe that Eurydice has failed to make the journey? The text is indeterminate: How, after all, is one to translate "*ne . . . deficeret*" (56)?[7] Orphic doubt may be either erotic or metaphysical or both, and the Ovidian indeterminacy may disclose an affinity between piety and love.

What we can say with certainty is this: Orpheus' failure is not artistic. If the arts of our poet and our sculptor are triumphs, then, Orpheus' faith is not as strong as Pygmalion's, and Orpheus recognizes as much in his romance by emphasizing Pygmalion's faith in Venus. Pygmalion's art is necessary for Galatea's metamorphosis, but it is insufficient. Prayer is required. At Venus' festival, Pygmalion prays for a woman like the statue he loves (250-76). Having fashioned a mimesis of an ideal woman, he now desires a real woman like her (276), a real simulation of his imaginary simulation of a real ideal. Pygmalion reveals piety, humility and—given his earlier autoerotic activities with the statue (251-69)—a portion of foolishness here. He is not in the least skeptical about his beloved or his gods. Orpheus was. If examined alone, the romance Orpheus fashions is ridiculous; if examined as *his* tale, it is quite serious indeed, although not without Ovidian humor. Ovid indicates that Orpheus' desire to transform the real by means of mimesis fails through doubt. It is no accident that the presiding deity in Orpheus' own tragic life is Death, but that the presiding deity in his story is Love. Depending on the nature of his doubt, Orpheus either fails to love Eurydice enough or doubted the gods too much. Pygmalion's miracle is Orpheus' comment upon both. In the middle of a series of tales of erotic "deviancy," Orpheus makes his own tragic error intelligible to himself, an intelligibility which, in the Aristotelian understanding, is what poetry is *for*. The Pygmalion tale, then, is not, as Segal would have it, "pure indulgence" (88-9); instead, it allows the reader to see that Orpheus is capable of educating himself through poetry. The tales within the Orphic frame constitute an inseparable whole, and—in the metafictional relation between Pygmalion and Orpheus—the Ovidian object of representation turns out to be art's limited capacity, when activated by the faith of love, to suspend death, if only for a short time. Of course, even romance has its limits.

After all, Galatea will eventually die, and, even had Orpheus achieved Eurydice's life, she too would have eventually died. He concedes as much in the song he sings in the underworld, a song which I believe is more moving than is often recognized. Orpheus' song appeals to Pluto and Proserpina by highlighting the necessity of death, even if—in this one case—it is postponed. Orphic transcendence is limited:

> All things to you belong.
> And though we lingering for a while our pageants do prolong,
> Yet soon or late we all to one abiding place do roam:
> We haste us hither all: this place becomes our latest home:
> And you do over human kind reign longest time. Now when
> This woman shall have lived full her time, she shall again
> Become your own.
>
> (31-7; 33-9)

Pagan reanimation, unlike Christian resurrection, still operates within the horizon of death, and there are other than Christian miracles. The gods themselves were moved enough by Orpheus' concession to them that death remains an ultimate limit for human beings to lend her to him, if he can meet their condition. Ovidian irony does not undermine this concession; without Virgilian sentiment, Ovid moves us. Orpheus' tales are indeed a fusion of the serious and the ridiculous, neither element a repudiation of the other.[8] Like Ovid, Orpheus is both mythographer and ironist.

Indeed, Orpheus operates in the *Metamorphoses* as a figure for Ovid himself. If William Anderson is right in "The Orpheus of Virgil and Ovid" that Orpheus is "a performer, egotistic, calculating, self-dramatizing" (47), so too is Ovid, yet neither *vates* is simply that.[9] Ovid is the poet who dwells inside the archive of his own poem, both animating others and awaiting animation, both Orpheus and Eurydice, Pygmalion and Galatea. He awaits a lover capable of leading him out into the upper world, and in the final lines of Ovid's own cosmos, even as he is reanimating Horace through the Horation formula of poetic immortality,[10] he himself awaits reanimation: "And time without all end / (If poets as by prophesy about the truth may aim) / My life shall everlastingly be lengthened by fame" (878-9; 993-5). Ovid believes that he will live *vivam*, that his presence will endure as does the presence of other poets, those he himself ironizes and honors. Ovid waits inside his poem for his own lover.

II

[F]or her to return to him is for him to recognize her; and for him to recognize her is for him to recognize his relation to her; in particular what his denial of her has done to her, hence to him. So Leontes recognizes the fate of stone to be the consequence of his particular skepticism.

—Stanley Cavell, *The Claim of Reason* (481)

When Shakespeare reanimates Ovid in *The Winter's Tale*, he does so by appropriating and metamorphosizing not only the Pygmalion tale, but also its Orphic frame. The statue scene interrogates the essence of aesthetics, of course, the relationship between art and nature, between the mimetic and the real.[11] If the scene is "theatrical," then Hermione performs *as* a statue who comes to life; if it is "mythic," she *is* one who does so. The metafictional narrative of Ovid's poem, including as it does the tale-within-the-tale, assists us in a reading of the scene and the play. Though I will concede the scene may be read either theatrically or mythically, I will read it mythically first, only allowing the theatrical reading later. That is, I will assume for now that Hermione has actually died.

The Pygmalion tale will often obscure the sequence unless the Orphic frame is called upon for assistance. Leontes and Perdita have come to see "the statue of our Queen" in Paulina's gallery (5.3.10), and, when Paulina exhibits it to them, they are silent (21). Leontes' response indicates that Giulio Romano is a kind of Pygmalion, one able to represent with such mimetic force that one might imagine the stone has human being:

> Chide me, dear stone, that I may say indeed
> Thou art Hermione—or rather, thou art she
> In not chiding; for she was as tender
> As infancy and grace.
>
> (24-7)

"Thou *art* Hermione": Unlike Pygmalion's statue, this is not a statue of an ideal woman; it is a statue of Leontes' wife, a woman whose death he himself caused through faithlessness. Though 5.3 often employs the ridiculousness of the Pygmalion sequence in Ovid—Hermione's wrinkles (28), for example, or the prospect that Leontes will smear the statue's paint, not yet dry, were he to kiss it (42-48)—the Orphic frame reminds us that Leontes is standing before a representation not only of his dead wife, but also of his own tragic error or *hamartia* in destroying her. It is he who destroyed her, death figured as the hard stillness of stone. After Paulina explains "Hermione's" age by pointing out that the sculptor made her, not as she *was*, but as she *might have been*, had she lived,[12] Leontes begins a meditation upon his own Orphic failure:

> O, thus she stood,
> Even with such life of majesty—warm life
> As now it coldly stands—when first I wooed her.
> I am ashamed. Does not the stone rebuke me
> For being more stone that it? O royal piece!
> There's magic in thy majesty, which has
> My evils conjured to remembrance. . . .
>
> (34-40)

Pygmalion's statue is only an actual person once Venus animates her, but the statue of Hermione is a representation of a person now dead, whose very death was this observer's responsibility. Leontes is both Pygmalion and Orpheus in the sequence; or, drawing upon my reading of Ovid, he is Orpheus as Orpheus imagines himself as Pygmalion. Leontes' "evil" was doubt, here a more specific doubt than Orpheus'—doubt concerning Hermione's fidelity—but doubt nonetheless; essentially, it was the doubt concerning the presence of the other. Both Orpheus and Leontes doubted female presence and destroyed the women they loved through such doubt. Only by means of a form of mimetic madness both Orphic and Pygmalionist—Orpheus' madness in descending to the underworld, Pygmalion's in imagining that his statue is an actual woman—can Leontes repair history: Art can conquer death only through the faith of love. This scene appropriates both the ridiculousness of Pygmalion and the seriousness of Orpheus in order to transform the source into a moment that reads Orpheus' understanding of his own tale: Belief in the presence of the other is an act of faith; we are all stone before the loveless gaze, all animated by the glance of love. Our contemporary conversation concerning desire has obscured the madness of love, a madness which compels Orpheus to pass over to the dark side of being in search of his dead beloved:

> PAULINA: I'll draw the curtain.
> My lord's so far transported that
> He'll think anon it lives.
> LEONTES: O sweet Paulina,
> Make me to think so twenty years together!
> No settled senses of the world can match
> The pleasure of that madness.
>
> (68-73)

Mimetic madness is necessary for reanimation, but it is not, however, sufficient. Only faith can animate stone. As Paulina instructs him, "It is required / You do awake your faith" (94-5). It is, of course, at this moment that music begins and "Hermione" the statue becomes Hermione, "[b]equeth[ing] to Death [her] numbness, for from him / Dear life redeems [her]" (102-3). The romance of *The Winter's Tale* is Orphic: Leontes is both Orpheus and Pygmalion; Hermione is Eurydice. Without the Orphic frame, one might assume that the scene is moving because it rejects Ovidian irony; with the frame, though, we see that it moves us because it transforms Ovidian irony by actualizing a sentiment potential within Ovid which Ovid did not himself, however, actualize, leaving only implicit the relation between tale and frame. The Ovidian frame augments our understanding of Shakespearean romance, animated as that romance is by the desire to conquer death. The scene certainly enacts, as Leonard Barkin puts it in *The Gods Made Flesh*, "a pagan mystery" (287), one which concerns the animating principle of human recognition of the presence of the other, a principle which Orpheus doubts, but Leontes by 5.3 believes.

This reading has all along assumed that Hermione did in fact die and that the statue *of* her *is* not Hermione pretending to be a statue *of* herself, yet the play is no more unambiguously "mythic" than it is unambiguously "dramatic." Ultimately, I am trying to qualify, not refute the theatrical reading of the play. I count seven moments in the play where one must choose a reading either mythical or theatrical: First, Paulina's announcement that Hermione is dead (3.2.170-241); second, Antigonus' relation of Hermione's visitation (3.3.15-45); third, Paulina's suggestion to Leontes that he remarry when Hermione is alive again (5.1.77-84); fourth, the Third Gentleman's relation of the existence of the statue (5.2.102-6); fifth, the Second Gentleman's report of Paulina's daily visits to the chapel (125-30); sixth, Hermione's explanation of events in the chapel (5.3.125-30); and, seventh, Leontes' statement that he saw Hermione dead (139-41). All seven moments will allow either reading, but some are easier to perform one way rather than the other. The "theatrical" reading would interpret each piece of evidence something like this: Paulina lies when she announces Hermione's death in order to preserve her until Perdita returns (1), as Hermione herself explains after her performance of animation (6); Antigonus' vision is only a dream (2); Paulina, knowing that Hermione is really alive, can offer Leontes the possibility that she will return (3); the statue Romano fashioned (4), either from a living Hermione or from some idea or image of her, is still around somewhere, Hermione having imitated it during the chapel scene, or it was a fiction all along; Paulina visited the chapel twice a day to feed Hermione (5); and Leontes only thought he saw her dead (7). This reading works, but I hope my reader will allow that it is less than fully persuasive concerning Antigonus' dream (2) and Romano's statue (4). The "mythical" reading, on the other hand, would interpret each of the six pieces of evidence something rather like this: Paulina announces an actual death (1); Antigonus has a genuine vision of Hermione's ghost (2); Paulina believes that Leontes will be able to reanimate the statue, so she offers him the hope that she will return (3); Romano's statue, the one others have seen and spoken of, is what all in 5.3 actually see before it becomes Hermione herself (4); Paulina's magic, whatever its exact nature, requires that she be in the chapel twice a day to prepare the lawful miracle (5); Hermione's report that she "preserved" herself (5.3.127-8) is a lie to preclude questions about the reanimation, which is why Paulina cuts her off (6); and Leontes did, in fact, see her dead (7). This reading too works, but I concede that it is less than fully persuasive concerning Paulina's visits (5) and Hermione's explanations (6). Each reading accommodates five of the seven moments. The play will allow, then, either reading, yet neither reading will be fully persuasive. If my reading of the evidence has been at all adequate, no critic should ever be allowed to assume uncritically the theatrical reading now so dominant that it simply goes without saying that Hermione is not, after all, a statue.

Why does Shakespeare design into the play this central ambiguity?[13] Or, rather, why does he design the ambiguity in such a way that no full performance will ever fully persuade an audience of the governing interpretation? Because he wants the mythic logic of the play experienced as such. Its plot or *muthos* is double, and a performance of that plot precludes the viewer from dwelling comfortably within either a skeptical or an enchanted mimetic world. Why, then, does he desire this doubleness? Because the human action represented is double. We are beings who, through an art motivated by love and faith, both can and cannot save the dead from death. The theatrical reading reminds one of Hermione's death; the mythical, of her reanimation. After all, we who weep in the upper world long for souls who have passed from bodies, and—in our most inspired moments—fashion new bodies for them, mimetic vessels we hope somehow will contain and carry their presences. Do such vessels *really* contain them? Can the lyre of Orpheus *really* raise the dead? A just representation of such a question must be double, both theatrical and mythic simultaneously. If the theatrical dominates, as it now does, death overwhelms art; if the mythical were to dominate, art would overwhelm death. In the late plays, Shakespeare's paganism precludes a single response, yet only in *The Winter's Tale* does he succeed in holding that doubleness in so fine a tension that a mature performance of the play requires that those involved, on the stage and in the audience, must descend into the ambiguity of (im)mortality. For some, Hermione does not die, so she is not reanimated; for others, she dies, so she is. Both responses are inadequate. Ultimately, the play discloses to us the character of our own faith, compelling us to live a question about ourselves: Can we awaken our faith in the presence of death? In Ovid's poem, Orpheus fails; in the first three acts of Shakespeare's play, Leontes too fails. In the last act, though, Leontes does not fail. How fully he succeeds is the question the play enacts. About the fact of the death of the beloved, we experience the logic of polarity in silent wonder. Any other response would make death unintelligible.

III

There is neither friendship nor justice toward soulless things.

—Aristotle, *Nicomachean Ethics* (1161b2)

STRANGER, if you passing meet me and desire to speak to me, why should you not speak to me?
And why should I not speak to you?

—Whitman, *Leaves of Grass* (175)

Shakespeare's appropriation and transformation of Ovid offers a figure for literary history itself, the nature of the archive of poetry. To see how, one may begin with what is now a mythic moment in Shakespearean studies, Steven Greenblatt's failed "desire to speak with the dead":

> If I never believed that the dead could hear me, and if I knew that the dead could not speak, I was nonetheless certain that I could re-create a conversation with them. Even when I came to understand that in my most intense moments of straining to listen all I could hear was my own voice, even then I did not abandon my desire. It was true that I could hear only my own voice, but my own voice was the voice of the dead, for the dead had contrived to leave textual traces of themselves, and those traces make themselves heard in the voices of the living. (1)

Though he assumes both that he is hearing only his own voice and that his voice has been fashioned by the voices of History, he does not forsake listening to simulated voices, "for simulations are undertaken in full awareness of the absence of the life they contrive to represent, and hence they may skillfully anticipate and compensate for the vanishing of the actual life that has empowered them" (1). I admire this author for expressing the desire to speak with the dead, but I want to question his assumption that this desire must fail. As one of his own chosen authors, Michel Foucault, cautions us, "It is not enough . . . to repeat the empty affirmation that the author has disappeared" (105).[14] I would like to argue that the author may, perhaps *must,* reappear if we are to fashion an understanding of the nature not only of literary history, but also of human association, if we are to discern, in effect, an ethics of historiography.[15] I do not believe that we ought to efface the "illuminating conversations" Steven had with Michel in Berkeley when Foucault was present there (viii). On the contrary, we ought to realize both that the intertextual relation was, in fact, a personal one and that such an association would have been ethical; by doing so, we would discover our own ethical responsibilities to that friendship. I no more doubt the human presence of Foucault than I do that of Greenblatt. I simply ask that we accord the dead the respect that we accord the living, that we imagine for the moment, in order to see if it is possibly true, that our cultural ancestors still do have presence, and that the voice-in-the-text we hear is neither a mere simulation of the imagination, nor a mere projection of historical narcissism, but the actual voice of the other. The archive of poetry is the temple of Orpheus, and it is full of voices. Those voices are more difficult to hear than the voices of the living, yet we may be forgetting how difficult it is to hear the living and how quickly the living become the dead. As Joyce puts it in "The Dead," "One by one, [we are] all becoming shades" (222). Indeed, perhaps the friendship and justice which Aristotle argues are impossible toward the "soulless," if practiced properly toward the dead, could be better practiced toward the living.

Present within Greenblatt's myth is the myth of Orpheus: Reader attempts to reanimate the voice of the dead, only to discover that the voice he hears is, all along, only *his.* Let us imagine that Orpheus figures both intertextuality itself, an author's desire to bring the dead poet back to life within a new poem, and at least one form of historiography, a critic's desire to write the story of such intertextuality. Orpheus' song might also figure poetry's power to reanimate dead poetry; his turning back, historiography's failure to trust the presence almost retrieved from absence. Must historiography fail thus? Or is it possible that, with a certain disposition toward the dead, their actual voices might be heard? An ethics of historiography will have to become mythographical.

I imagine that I am not supposed to say these things, that to do so puts me outside the academic discourse community. Yet I must confess that I find the theoretical stories I hear insufficient before my own experiences, imaginary and real. Shakespeare introduced me to Ovid, and I am grateful to him for having done so. I do not know how else to put it. The purpose of the following speculations is to discern conceptually how such an introduction is possible and how gratitude might then be called for.[16] My argument is composed of eight propositions: First, a text discloses the presence of a person; second, an intertextual relation discloses a mediated association between persons, either one of whom is dead, the other alive, or both of whom are living or both of whom are dead; third, intertextual relations are, by their associative nature, ethical; fourth, a literary historiographer may, perhaps must, not only recognize intertextual association as ethical, but also participate him/herself in that association, often the living historiographer reflecting upon a relation between two dead people, one of whom, however, was alive during the relation; fifth, that association is not synchronic, but diachronic, made possible by, but not limited to, historical time; sixth, in extraordinary intertextual relations—poet-to-poet or historiographer-to-poet(s)—the living animate the dead, recognizing and actualizing the living presence of the persons) in the text(s); seventh, that recognition and actualization are essentially Orphic, revealing both the possibility of reanimation and an inherent tendency toward failure, failure due to doubt concerning presence, the hesitancy to believe that the dead have presence; eight, that doubt is now the ideology of literary studies, the convention that the author is dead now an article of faith, so the literary historiographer may, perhaps must, question that convention in order to understand the ethics of the intertextual, becoming in the process a literary mythographer. Let me take these speculative points up one at a time.

A text discloses the presence of a person. Multiple authorship, whether in the form of co-authorship or in the form of compositional traditions, does not at all refute authorship. It certainly attenuates authorship, and makes it much more difficult, perhaps even impossible, to identify all the individuals and their respective contributions. That simply means that in such instances, and they are surprisingly rare in the literary traditions of the West, one cannot extricate the voices from one another, individualize one's relationship to a presence in the text, the presence of the dead author. The death of the human body is certainly a death, but it need not preclude the presence of the author within a new, textual body, one which is immortal, though not eternal.[17] This is, in fact, Ovid's own conception. *The Metamorphoses* ends, remember, with Ovid's boast to his gods and his ruler that, having fashioned a textual body for himself, he is free of their terror (15.871-9). When Shakespeare read both Ovid and Golding's translation of him, Ovid's text argued that Shakespeare was, in fact, holding the new, textualized presence Ovid was himself able to construct through his poetic craft and his regime's imperial power. Whatever human presence is, we assume that it either dies with the physiological body or that, if immortal, it is not so within the text itself. I am suggesting that we take, in good pagan fashion, the metaphor of the text-as-body quite seriously. I concede that this first principle is undemonstratable. The presence or "soul" of the other certainly can be denied, the consequences ranging all the way from loneliness to genocide; even so, that denial is no more firm than my affirmation. We do not know what *exactly* human presence is; even so, one either does or does not wager on presence.[18] I do not quite see how one wagers on absence without (re)living, in some fashion, Leontes' tragedy.

An intertextual relation discloses a mediated association between persons, then, often one of whom is dead, the other alive. Given that the new, textual body has as its medium language, often enough poetic language which can literally be voiced, why do we assume that the voice performed has no trace of the dead within it? Shakespeare's plays, for example, are representations of fictional voices, and I certainly concede that voicing *him* voicing them is difficult, yet this is one of the distinct pleasures of reading/performing Shakespeare: the sense of a presence, one quite near, playing all the parts and inviting "STRANGER, why should I not speak to you?"—us into his company. Is voicing Shakespeare voicing them impossible? Is there any reader/performer who imagines that Shakespeare admires Leontes' mad jealousy? If so, would we not agree that such a reading/performance is tone-deaf?[19] Intertextual relations are associations, the mediation subtlizing the relationship, but not making it impossible. Perhaps we might imagine intertextual relations as Dante does in *The Divine Comedy,* when Dante the character sees Virgil on the horizon, "one whose voice seemed weak from long silence" (1.63). In the poem, Dante is reading Virgil, and he figures this reading as the living being led by the dead: Somewhere within the imaginative experience of reading, Dante meets with Virgil's soul. I grant that the association is *imagined,* but deny that it is *imaginary,* after all, we must, in fact, imagine the living, as well, but that does not for a moment deny their real presence. Once one concedes my first principle, the second follows.

Such intertextual relations are, by their very associative nature, ethical. Reading is an associative activity and, as such, it is ethical. Let me explain. In Aristotelian ethics, one begins with human association, the fact that we are essentially social; sociality entails a shared form of life and any form of life assumes human goods *as* goods, including the good of human virtue itself. Virtue ethics does not demand Kantian, transcendental speculation; instead, it begins where we actually are, within a form of life with flexible rules of human conduct.[20] If a literary text is a new, textualized body for the soul of the poet, then reading is associative. As Whitman would have it, one is his associate when reading his poem; one is his Camerado. This entails certain intellectual and moral virtues. Because intertextuality is ethical, the same ethical principles that shape one's practical form of life ought to inform one's reading and writing. Harold Bloom's *The Anxiety of Influence* goes a long way to personalize intertextual relations: "In ways that need not be doctrinal, strong poems are omens of resurrection" (xxiv). Now, I would desire a greater number of descriptive possibilities than anxiety alone. I suggest that we consider the descriptive possibilities of Aristotelian virtue ethics, in great part because his categories of the virtues are those we employ within our own form of life. Their very prosaic character makes them useful. Even if we were not to agree that *his* ethics ought to govern our personal and textual lives, however, we would still require *an* ethics; even if we were to agree that we needed more than one ethics, we would still need to be able to assume one of them at any moment within a designated context.

A literary historiographer may, perhaps must, then, not only recognize intertextual association as ethical, but also participate him/herself in that association, often the living historiographer reflecting upon a relation between two dead people, one of whom, however, was alive during the relation. Once one recognizes such intertextual associations as ethical, one must respond to them as such, employing an ethical vocabulary to define the relationships. The metaphor here is an introduction: A friend introduces you to someone; his or her disposition toward the other disposes you, as well, though it does not determine your response. I have friends who do not like one another; their perceptions of one another have to be questioned. I am not myself persuaded by Bate's argument concerning Ovid in Shakespeare's *The Winter's Tale*; even so, I am grateful for an introduction some of whose details I have come to question. This association is a great deal more complicated than we acknowledge.

This is true in great part because that association is not synchronic, but diachronic, made possible by, but not limited to, historical time. Time is not a constant, but we treat it as such in our investigations. Because we are separated by time from the historical contexts of our texts, we imagine they are other; they are, but not as we imagine it. As Levinas explains in *Time and the Other,* time is itself the result of ethical association: "[T]ime is not the achievement of an isolated and lone subject, but . . . the very relationship of the subject with the Other" (39). We imagine that the association is attenuated to such an extent that it obscures presence. Why? It may very well be true that the text is available because of History. Shakespeare, after all, was a reader of Ovid because of the nature of English Renaissance education. Even so, he then became a reader of Ovid. If the poem is a new, textualized body, then History carries that text to one, it does not determine what one does once one has it, though. Poets continually speak as if there is another order of time, one in which they can speak with the dead. If temporal orders must be imagined to be experienced, then we might imagine a temporal order that can provide the space for such ethical associations. Perhaps the presence of the other, carried in the new, textualized body, can only be recognized through the power of our imagination. This is impossible to demonstrate, of course, but no more so than when considering living human beings. All follows from the first principle.

In extraordinary intertextual relations—poet-to-poet or historiographer-to-poet(s)—the living animate the dead, recognizing and actualizing the living presence of the persons in the text(s). This means that our recognition of presence actualizes what is only potential within the text; that is, without recognition, the presence is faint, but with it the presence grows stronger. Being is associative. Discursive practices do not merely see objects of discourse; they make possible the object's appearance. If there is a presence in the text, it is not imaginary, even if it must be imaginatively fulfilled by the reader. That recognition and actualization are essentially Orphic, revealing both the possibility of reanimation and an inherent tendency toward failure. Orpheus' failure to believe that Eurydice is present results in her loss. In my reading, the tragedy of the myth of Orpheus is doubt concerning the presence of the dead. If that reading is adequate, then the turn of this desirous glance reveals doubt, the doubt concerning her presence; the doubt then destroys her presence, Eurydice slipping into absence. The Ovidian myth, then, figures the consequences of the very refutational doubt I have been responding to; in fact, that doubt is self-confirming since, once he turns, he loses her again. My argument is that he is not destined to fail; his agency is qualified, but not extinguished, by the extraordinary circumstances of his journey. This is, in fact, one of his own discoveries in the myth of Pygmalion, the tale Ovid has Orpheus tell. Pygmalion's slightly mad desire for stone to become animate, for dead matter to be infused with life, attended as it is by the prayer to Venus, animates such stone. Doubt concerning presence stones people into absence. The framing here is crucial: The Pygmalion tale is the romance of presence Orpheus tells himself in order to make intelligible to himself his own tragedy of absence. Leontes is Orpheus and Pygmalion, the man who can—by means of Romano's art and Paulina's guidance—bring Hermione back from absence into presence. We are now ready to see that Shakespeare's own friendship with Ovid is Orphic: He brings him up out of the underworld into the upper, where he then introduces him to us. I have myself met Ovid because Shakespeare introduced him to me; indeed, I met Ovid because Bate introduced me to Shakespeare's introduction of him. Bate's own father appears to have introduced him to Ovid (xii). We are reluctant to put it this way, of course, because of the very doubt of skepticism Shakespeare enacts in Acts 1-3 of *The Winter's Tale*.

That doubt is now the ideology of literary studies, the convention that the author is dead now an article of faith.

Even so sensitive a reader as Greenblatt, one whose Orphic desire is both perceptive and admirable, turns back in doubt: "It was true that I could hear only my own voice. . . ." It certainly became true, yet did it need to? We nod—knowingly, sadly—that, of course, the recognition of presence must always fail. The myth of Orpheus in *The Winter's Tale* suggests it need not, even though it so often does. Pygmalion's prayer is Orpheus' own response to his doubt, and it is only with such a mimetic prayer that he is himself prepared for reunion with his wife. Without the prayer that itself signals to and responds to the other, there will be no ethics of historiography. Aristotle is right: "There is neither friendship nor justice towards soulless things." That the soul is itself a myth, a presence whose *presence* must be imagined to be activated, need not disturb us. Literary historiographers must become literary mythographers if we are to be ethicists. We have been all along, of course, postmodernity having proven that there are only myths. Perhaps, reader, you do not find my myth persuasive. What shall our myth of the other in the text be?[21] Please do not respond with *the myth of absence*. STRANGER, we need a new myth. Concerning both archive and city, I suggest the myth in *The Winter's Tale*, the myth of Orpheus, singing.[22]

Notes

1. The understanding of *mimesis* here is thoroughly Aristotelian: For Aristotle in the *Poetics,* emplotment [*muthos*], the arrangement of episodes, is the essence of the dramatic art, making intelligible to the audience as it does the nature of human action [*praxis*]. See Chapter 6 of the *Poetics* (1449b21-50b20). For fine readings of the *Poetics* in this regard, see the following: Stephen Halliwell, *Aristotle's Poetics,* especially Chapter 4, "Mimesis," 109-137 and his article, "Aristotelian Mimesis Reevaluated"; Paul Ricoeur, *Time and Narrative,* especially Volumes 1 (52-87) and 2 (7-28). An Aristotelian aesthetic is assumed throughout.

2. In his reading of the Romances, "The Dismemberment of Orpheus," David Armitage argues that "[a] suggestively Ovidian metamorphosis marks the presence of Orpheus in the statue scene (5.3), in which Shakespeare, like Ovid, combines the myths of Orpheus and Pygmalion" (130). His discussion is suggestive, but brief. In Lynn Enterline's fine reading of the play, "'You speak a language that I understand not,'" she argues that the scene "both claims and disavows the Orphic power for which it longs"; that power is "the rhetoric of animation" (41), a rhetoric which she sees as essentially patriarchal. Hers is a brilliant discussion, one which qualifies my own idealization of the scene. I cannot, however, see why the rhetoric of animation she examines so sensitively must by necessity be patriarchal.

3. In *Narrative and Dramatic Sources of Shakespeare,* Geoffrey Bullough excerpts the Pygmalion tale (10.243-97) without the Orphic frame. Brooks Otis

in *Ovid as Epic Poet* mistakenly argues that Orpheus' tales are only "nominally" his (190).

4. Though this understanding is very likely to have been made possible by the idea of Christian resurrection, Shakespeare's romance here is not that romance. Pagan reanimation does not deny death; it only postpones it. Shakespeare often distinguishes between and among three horizons of life, two of which are temporal, one eternal: The life of a human being is limited; the life of human history is less so, but is still finite, nonetheless; eternity is infinite. Here, as in the *Sonnets*, Shakespeare's focus is on the second horizon: "So till the judgment that yourself arise, / You live in this, and dwell in lovers' eyes" (55.13-4). Of course, within the first horizon—that of a human life—one might renimate someone who will, even so, still die within that first horizon. For discussions of paganism's presence in the Renaissance, see Leonard Barkan's *The Gods Made Flesh: Metamorphosis and the Pursuit of Paganism*. I am indebted to Barkan throughout, especially the chapters on Ovid (19-93) and Shakespeare (243-88). For a marvelous reading of both Ovid and Shakespeare, see Kenneth Gross's *The Dream of the Moving Statue* (72-9 and 99-109). Neither Barkan nor Gross notice the Orphic frame.

5. The translation here is Golding's, spelling modernized. When I refer to text without citation, line numbers refer to the Loeb edition; when I cite, I provide two references, the first to the Loeb, the second to Golding. As Bate points out, even though Shakespeare's Latin was certainly good enough that he did not need to rely upon Golding, he would no doubt have used it "for speed and convenience" (7-8). Bate himself shows that Shakespeare is often revising Golding's translation within his own intertextual relationship with Ovid. Even so, Golding remains Shakespeare's Ovid-in-English, so I cite his translation.

6. On the question of the relationship between narrative and metamorphosis, see Joseph Solodow's *The World of Ovid's Metamorphoses*. Ovid's unifying action may very well be his own narrative act, the *praxis* of a dramatized narrator fashioning a narrative cosmos for himself.

7. See William Anderson's note on the passage (479-80) in his commentary, where he explains that Ovid, unlike Virgil in the fourth *Georgic*, keeps the focus throughout on Orpheus. For a discussion of both poets in Shakespeare's education, see *William Baldwin's William Shakspere's Small Latine and Lesse Greeke*, vol. 2 (417-97).

8. The Ovidian aesthetic is akin, then, to the Shakespearean, which fuses what the Aristotelian separates, tragic seriousness and comic ridiculousness, as Johnson himself explains so well: "Shakespeare's plays [or Ovid's poem] are not in the rigorous and critical sense either tragedies or comedies, but compositions of a distinct kind; exhibiting the real state of sublunary nature, which partakes of good and evil, joy and sorrow, mingled with endless variety of proportion and innumerable modes of combination; and expressing the course of the world . . ." (266-7).

9. William Anderson argues in his essay on Ovid and Virgil that Ovid's parody of Virgil makes Orpheus "a cheap orator-poet" (47). 1 grant that Ovid's Orpheus is often more ridiculous that Virgil's, but Ovidian irony is not as deconstructive as is often thought: Like Shakespeare, who may very well have learned to mix generic tones from him, Ovid fuses the serious and the ridiculous. Ovid cannot abide Virgil's relentless seriousness and often treats moving moments with greater distance than Virgil, without, I would argue, turning the whole into mere parody.

10. See Horace's *Ode* 3: "I shall not altogether die, but a mighty part of me shall escape the death-goddess" (quoted from the Loeb translation by Booth, 227-8). For a discussion of the historical awareness such "immortality" discloses within the Renaissance, see Thomas M. Greene's *The Light in Troy* (1-80).

11. For a fine reading of the issues, see Mary Ellen Lamb's "Ovid and *The Winter's Tale*" and her bibliography of the relevant readings (84).

12. Her point is Aristotle's about poetry: It represents not the actual, but the hypothetical (1451a36-9): "[I]t is not the poet's function to relate actual events, but the *kinds* of things that might occur and are possible in terms of probability or necessity." Had Hermione lived, she would have looked like the statue, the sculptor having made "her / As [if] she lived now" (31-2). It is an Aristotelian commonplace that art can actualize natural potentialities that nature itself cannot and that art can, as a consequence, augment the given.

13. In *Appropriating Shakespeare,* Brian Vickers has made a compelling case that authorial intention is a legitimate object of literary study. His chapter on "Creator and Interpreters" (92-162) is persuasive that intertextuality is itself one way of discerning such intention. That the statue scene is, as is often noted, Shakespeare's own transformation of *Pandosto, or the Triumph of Tine* indicates the importance of 5.3 for understanding the whole of the play's enactment of the limited defeat of time.

14. Foucault's discursive project does not, as far as I have yet to ascertain, explain whether or not there is human agency within a discursive practice; if so, that would make possible my project, though I am quite aware that this is not a Foucauldian ethics. Again, it is thoroughly Aristotelian. If Foucault's argument is that there is no agency, then our projects would be incommensurate.

15. The modal auxiliary here will, I suspect, frighten some readers with its Kantian timber of an

imperative; I employ it in a deliberative, I hope not an authoritarian, manner. Tolerance need not preclude persuasion, and this essay hopes to be persuasive.

16. Christopher Ricks presented a moving reading of Beckett's gratitude to Shakespeare at the World Congress of International Shakespeare Association Meeting in Los Angeles (April 1996).

17. Again, the frame of reference is the second horizon of human comprehension: neither individual, human time nor divine eternity, but collective human time, the order of culture, an order which will last, but not forever.

18. For a brilliant discussion of this issue, see George Steiner's *Real Presences,* especially Chapter 3 (135-232).

19. See Howard Felperin's. Tongue-Tied Our Queen?" for such an ingenious, yet tone-deaf, reading of Leontes' suspicion as sensible.

20. See Book I of the *Nicomachean Ethics* for Aristotle's method; Books 2 and 3.1-4, for his conception of "virtue ethics." Nussbaum's superb *Fragility of Goodness* emphasizes just these prosaic limitations within the Aristotelian method (240-63) and offers an excellent reading of his ethical thought (264-372). Useful as well is Wayne Booth's *The Company We Keep* (168-373). Both Nussbaum's and Booth's discussions of ethics and literature concern only narrative, though their perceptions are, with attentive qualification, most enabling with regard to drama.

21. For a fine discussion of the general question of "literary history," see David Perkins' *Is Literary History Possible?*

22. I would like to thank the editors of *Studies in the Literary Imagination* for their editorial assistance. The following people have also provided generous assistance, correction and/or support: John Briggs. Lowell Gallagher, Theresa Kenney, Bob Miola, Martha Nussbaum, Lance Simmons, Stanley Stewart, Glen Thurow, Gerard Wegemer, Grace West, Deborah Willis, and the students in Studies in Myth (Mayterm 1996). As well, I would like to thank both Kyle Lemieux and Bryant Mason, whose production of *The Winter's Tale* at the University of Dallas (Spring 1998) demonstrated that a "mythic" reading of 5.3 can, in fact, be performed. This essay is dedicated to my father, Hollis M. Crider.

Works Cited

Anderson, W. S. "The Orpheus of Virgil and Ovid: *flebile nescio quid.*" *Orpheus: The Metamorphoses of a Myth.* Ed. John Warden. Toronto: U of Toronto P, 1982. 25-50.

Aristotle. *Nicomachean Ethics.* Trans. Terence Irwin. Indianapolis: Hackett, 1985.

———. *Poetics.* Ed. and trans. Stephen Halliwell. Cambridge: Harvard UP, 1995.

Armitage, David. "The Dismemberment of Orpheus: Mythic Elements in Shakespeare's Romances." *Shakespeare Survey* 39 (1987): 123-33.

Baldwin, T. W. *William Shakpere's Small Latine and Lesse Greeke.* 2 vols. Urbana: U of Illinois P, 1944.

Barkan, Leonard. *The Gods Made Flesh: Metamorphosis and the Pursuit of Paganism.* New Haven: Yale UP, 1986.

Bate, Jonathan. *Shakespeare and Ovid.* Oxford: Clarendon P, 1993.

Bloom, Harold. *The Anxiety of Influence: A Theory of Poetry.* Second ed. New York: Oxford UP, 1997.

Booth, Wayne. *The Company We Keep: An Ethics of Fiction.* Berkeley: U of California P, 1988.

Bullough, Geoffrey. Narrative and Dramatic Sources of Shakespeare. 8 volumes. London: Methuen, 1957-75.

Cavell, Stanley. *The Claim of Reason: Wittgenstein, Skepticism, Morality, and Tragedy.* Oxford: Oxford UP, 1979.

Dante. *The Divine Comedy.* Trans. and comm. John D. Sinclair. New York: Oxford UP, 1939.

Enterline, Lynn. "'You speak a language I know not': The Rhetoric of Animation in *The Winter's Tale.*" *Shakespeare Quarterly* 48 (1997): 17-44.

Felperin, Howard. "'Tongue-Tied Our Queen?': The Deconstruction of Presence in *The Winter's Tale.*" *Shakespeare and the Question of Theory.* Ed. Patricia Parker and Geoffrey Hartman. New York: Methuen, 1985. 1-18.

Foucault, Michel. "What Is an Author?" *The Foucault Reader.* Ed. Paul Rabinow. New York: Penguin, 1984. 101-120.

Greenblatt, Stephen. *Shakespearean Negotiations: The Circulation of Social Energy in Renaissance England.* Berkeley: U of California P, 1988.

Greene, Thomas M. *The Light in Troy: Imitation and Discovery in Renaissance Poetry.* New Haven: Yale UP, 1982.

Gross, Kenneth. *The Dream of the Moving Statue.* Ithaca: Cornell UP, 1992.

Halliwell, Stephen. *Aristotle's Poetics.* London: Duckworth, 1986.

———. "Aristotelian Mimesis Reevaluated." *Journal of the History of Philosophy* 28 (1990): 487-510.

Johnson, Samuel. "Preface to Shakespeare." *Samuel Johnson: Rasselas, Poems, and Selected Prose.* Ed. Bertrand H. Bronson. New York: Holt, Rinehart and Winston. 1971. 261-307.

Joyce, James. "The Dead." *Dubliners*. New York: Penguin, 1967. 175-223.

Lamb, Mary Ellen. "Ovid and *The Winter's Tale*: Conflicting Views toward Art." *Shakespeare and the Dramatic Tradition*. Ed. W. R. Elton and William B. Long. Newark: U of Delaware P, 1989. 69-87.

Levinas, Emmanuel. *Time and the Other*. Trans. Richard A. Cohen. Pittsburgh: Duquesne UP, 1987.

Nussbaum, Martha. *The Fragility of Goodness: Luck and Ethics in Greek Tragedy and Philosophy*. Cambridge: Cambridge UP, 1986.

Otis, Brooks. Ovid as Epic Poet. Cambridge: Cambridge UP, 1966.

Ovid. *The Metamorphoses*. Trans. Frank Justus Miller. Revised G. P. Goold. 2 vols. Cambridge: Harvard UP, 1977.

———. *Ovid's Metamorphoses: The Arthur Golding Translation (1567)*. Ed. John Fredrick Nims. New York: Macmillan Company, 1965.

———. *Ovid's Metamorphoses, Books 6-10*. Ed. William S. Anderson. Norman: U of Oklahoma P, 1972.

Perkins, David. *Is Literary History Possible?* Baltimore: Johns Hopkins UP, 1992.

Ricoeur, Paul. *Time and Narrative*. Trans. Kathleen McLaughlin and David Pellauer. Vols 1 and 2. Chicago: U of Chicago P, 1984-85.

Rilke. *Sonnets to Orpheus. The Selected Poetry of Rainer Maria Rilke*. Ed. and trans. Stephen Mitchell. New York: Random House, 1989. 225-55.

Segal, Charles. *Orpheus: The Myth of the Poet*. Baltimore: Johns Hopkins UP. 1989.

Shakespeare. *The Winter's Tale*. Ed. Stephen Orgel. Oxford: Oxford UP, 1996.

———. *Shakespeare's Sonnets*. Ed. Stephen Booth. New Haven: Yale UP, 1977.

Solodow, Joseph B. *The World of Ovid's Metamorphoses*. Chapel Hill: U of North Carolina P, 1988.

Steiner, George. *Real Presences*. Chicago: U of Chicago P, 1989.

———. "Two Cocks." *No Passion Spent: Essays, 1978-1995*. New Haven: Yale UP, 1996. 361-89.

Vernant, Jean-Pierre. *Myth and Society in Ancient Greece*. Trans. Janet Lloyd. New York: Zone Books, 1990.

Vickers, Brian. *Appropriating Shakespeare: Contemporary Quarrels*. New Haven: Yale UP, 1993.

Whitman, Walt. *Leaves of Grass. Complete Poetry and Collected Prose*. Library of America. New York: Viking P, 1982. 147-672.

FURTHER READING

Criticism

Bennett, Kenneth C. "Constructing *The Winter's Tale*." *Shakespeare Survey* 46 (1993): 81-90.
  Examines the relationship between unity and deconstruction in the play.

Cooley, Ronald W. "Speech Versus Spectacle: Autolycus, Class and Containment in *The Winter's Tale*." *Renaissance and Reformation* 21, No. 3 (Summer 1997): 5-23.
  Focuses on the character Autolycus as a representation of the Jacobeans and argues that through Autolycus, Shakespeare explores themes of social instability and assimilation.

Gallagher, Lowell. "'This seal'd-up Oracle': Ambivalent Nostalgia in *The Winter's Tale*." *Exemplaria* 7, No. 2 (Fall 1995): 465-98.
  Considers the concepts of nostalgia and belatedness as they relate to Leontes and Hermione.

Girard, René. "The Crime and Conversion of Leontes in *The Winter's Tale*." *Religion and Literature* 22, Nos. 2-3 (Summer/Autumn 1990): 193-219.
  Focuses on Leontes's transformation and argues that *The Winter's Tale* is Shakespeare's most moving play.

Horwitz, Eve. "'The Truth of Your Own Seeming': Women and Language in *The Winter's Tale*." *Unisa English Studies* 26, No. 2 (September 1988): 7-14.
  Considers language and time as they relate to femininity in *The Winter's Tale*.

Johnson, Nora. "Ganymedes and Kings: Staging Male Homosexual Desire in *The Winter's Tale*." *Shakespeare Studies* 26 (1998): 187-217.
  Explores the relationship between theater, identity, and homosexual desire in *The Winter's Tale*.

Jordan, Constance. "*The Winter's Tale*." In *Shakespeare's Monarchies: Ruler and Subject in the Romances*, pp. 107-46. Ithaca, NY: Cornell University Press, 1997.
  Argues that Shakespeare employed pastoral themes and conventions in *The Winter's Tale* in order to explore the generation and demise of political authority.

Mazzola, Elizabeth. "'Slippery Wives' and Other Missing Persons: Disappearing Acts in *The Winter's Tale*." *Women's Studies* 24, No. 3 (January 1995): 219-27.
  Explores feminist theory and romance while considering the ease with which some characters in *The Winter's Tale* "seem to slip in and out of view."

Platt, Peter G. "Reason Diminished: Wonder in *The Winter's Tale*." In *Reason Diminished: Shakespeare and the Marvelous*, pp. 153-68. Lincoln: University of Nebraska Press, 1997.

Contends that Shakespeare pits the rational against the marvelous in *The Winter's Tale.*

Robinson, Randal. "Family by Death: Stage Images in *Titus Andronicus* and *The Winter's Tale.*" In *From Page to Performance: Essays in Early English Drama,* edited by John A. Alford, pp. 221-33. East Lansing: Michigan State University Press, 1995.

Analyzes the underlying meaning of the visual links between *The Winter's Tale* and *Titus Andronicus.*

Snyder, Susan. "Mamillius and Gender Polarization in *The Winter's Tale.*" *Shakespeare Quarterly* 50, No. 1 (Spring 1999): 1-8.

Considers the metaphoric role of the child Mamillius.

Watterson, William Collins. "Shakespeare's Confidence Man." *Sewanee Review* 101, No. 4 (Fall 1993): 536-48.

Considers the autobiographical link between Shakespeare and the character Autolycus.

Cumulative Character Index

The Cumulative Character Index identifies the principal characters of discussion in the criticism of each play and non-dramatic poem. The characters are arranged alphabetically. Page references indicate the beginning page number of each essay containing substantial commentary on that character.

Aaron
Titus Andronicus **4**: 632, 637, 650, 651, 653, 668, 672, 675; **27**: 255; **28**: 249, 330; **43**: 176; **53**: 86, 92

Adonis
Venus and Adonis **10**: 411, 420, 424, 427, 429, 434, 439, 442, 451, 454, 459, 466, 473, 489; **25**: 305, 328; **28**: 355; **33**: 309, 321, 330, 347, 352, 357, 363, 370, 377; **51**: 345, 377

Adriana
The Comedy of Errors **16**: 3; **34**: 211, 220, 238; **54**: 189

Albany
King Lear **32**: 308

Alcibiades
Timon of Athens **25**: 198; **27**: 191

Angelo
Measure for Measure
  anxiety **16**: 114
  authoritarian portrayal of **23**: 307; **49**: 274
  characterization **2**: 388, 390, 397, 402, 418, 427, 432, 434, 463, 484, 495, 503, 511; **13**: 84; **23**: 297; **32**: 81; **33**: 77; **49**: 274, 293, 379
  hypocrisy **2**: 396, 399, 402, 406, 414, 421; **23**: 345, 358, 362
  repentance or pardon **2**: 388, 390, 397, 402, 434, 463, 511, 524

Anne (Anne Boleyn)
Henry VIII See **Boleyn**

Anne (Anne Page)
The Merry Wives of Windsor See **Page**

Anne (Lady Anne)
Richard III **52**: 223, 227, 239, 249, 280

Antigonus
The Winter's Tale
  characterization **7**: 394, 451, 464
  death (Act III, scene iii) **7**: 377, 414, 464, 483; **15**: 518, 532; **19**: 366

Antonio
The Merchant of Venice
  excessive or destructive love **4**: 279, 284, 336, 344; **12**: 54; **37**: 86
  love for Bassanio **40**: 156
  melancholy **4**: 221, 238, 279, 284, 300, 321, 328; **22**: 69; **25**: 22
  pitiless **4**: 254
  as pivotal figure **12**: 25, 129;
  versus Shylock **53**: 187
Twelfth Night **22**: 69

Antonio and Sebastian
The Tempest **8**: 295, 299, 304, 328, 370, 396, 429, 454; **13**: 440; **29**: 278, 297, 343, 362, 368, 377; **45**: 200

Antony
Antony and Cleopatra
  characterization **6**: 22, 23, 24, 31, 38, 41, 172, 181, 211; **16**: 342; **19**: 270; **22**: 217; **27**: 117; **47**: 77, 124, 142
  Caesar, relationship with **48**: 206
  Cleopatra, relationship with **6**: 25, 27, 37, 39, 48, 52, 53, 62, 67, 71, 76, 85, 100, 125, 131, 133, 136, 142, 151, 161, 163, 165, 180, 192; **27**: 82; **47**: 107, 124, 165, 174
  death scene **25**: 245; **47**: 142
  dotage **6**: 22, 23, 38, 41, 48, 52, 62, 107, 136, 146, 175; **17**: 28
  nobility **6**: 22, 24, 33, 48, 94, 103, 136, 142, 159, 172, 202; **25**: 245
  political conduct **6**: 33, 38, 53, 107, 111, 146, 181
  public vs. private personae **6**: 165; **47**: 107
  self-knowledge **6**: 120, 131, 175, 181, 192; **47**: 77
  as superhuman figure **6**: 37, 51, 71, 92, 94, 178, 192; **27**: 110; **47**: 71
  as tragic hero **6**: 38, 39, 52, 53, 60, 104, 120, 151, 155, 165, 178, 192, 202, 211; **22**: 217; **27**: 90
Julius Caesar
  characterization **7**: 160, 179, 189, 221, 233, 284, 320, 333; **17**: 269, 271, 272, 284, 298, 306, 313, 315, 358, 398; **25**: 272; **30**: 316
  funeral oration **7**: 148, 154, 159, 204, 210, 221, 238, 259, 350; **25**: 280; **30**: 316, 333, 362

Apemantus
Timon of Athens **1**: 453, 467, 483; **20**: 476, 493; **25**: 198; **27**: 166, 223, 235

Arcite
The Two Noble Kinsmen See **Palamon and Arcite**

Ariel
The Tempest **8**: 289, 293, 294, 295, 297, 304, 307, 315, 320, 326, 328, 336, 340, 345, 356, 364, 420, 458; **22**: 302; **29**: 278, 297, 362, 368, 377

Armado
Love's Labour's Lost **23**: 207

Arthur
   King John **9:** 215, 216, 218, 219, 229, 240, 267, 275; **22:** 120; **25:** 98; **41:** 251, 277; **56:** 345, 357

Arviragus
   Cymbeline See **Guiderius and Arviragus**

Audrey
   As You Like It **46:** 122

Aufidius
   Coriolanus **9:** 9, 12, 17, 19, 53, 121, 148, 153, 157, 169, 180, 193; **19:** 287; **25:** 263, 296; **30:** 58, 67, 89, 96, 133; **50:** 99

Autolycus
   The Winter's Tale **7:** 375, 380, 382, 387, 389, 395, 396, 414; **15:** 524; **22:** 302; **37:** 31; **45:** 333; **46:** 14, 33; **50:** 45

Banquo
   Macbeth **3:** 183, 199, 208, 213, 278, 289; **20:** 279, 283, 406, 413; **25:** 235; **28:** 339

Baptista
   The Taming of the Shrew **9:** 325, 344, 345, 375, 386, 393, 413; **55:** 334

Barnardine
   Measure for Measure **13:** 112

Bassanio
   The Merchant of Venice **25:** 257; **37:** 86; **40:** 156

the Bastard
   King John See **Faulconbridge (Philip) the Bastard**

Beatrice and Benedick
   Much Ado about Nothing
      Beatrice's femininity **8:** 14, 16, 17, 24, 29, 38, 41, 91; **31:** 222, 245; **55:** 221
      Beatrice's request to "kill Claudio" (Act IV, scene i) **8:** 14, 17, 33, 41, 55, 63, 75, 79, 91, 108, 115; **18:** 119, 120, 136, 161, 245, 257; **55:** 268
      Benedick's challenge of Claudio (Act V, scene i) **8:** 48, 63, 79, 91; **31:** 231
      Claudio and Hero, compared with **8:** 19, 28, 29, 75, 82, 115; **31:** 171, 216; **55:** 189
      marriage and the opposite sex, attitudes toward **8:** 9, 13, 14, 16, 19, 29, 36, 48, 63, 77, 91, 95, 115, 121; **16:** 45; **31:** 216; **48:** 14
      mutual attraction **8:** 13, 14, 19, 24, 29, 33, 41, 75; **48:** 14
      nobility **8:** 13, 19, 24, 29, 36, 39, 41, 47, 82, 91, 108
      popularity **8:** 13, 38, 41, 53, 79
      transformed by love **8:** 19, 29, 36, 48, 75, 91, 95, 115; **31:** 209, 216; **55:** 236
      unconventionality **8:** 48, 91, 95, 108, 115, 121; **55:** 221, 249, 268
      vulgarity **8:** 11, 12, 33, 38, 41, 47

      wit and charm **8:** 9, 12, 13, 14, 19, 24, 27, 28, 29, 33, 36, 38, 41, 47, 55, 69, 95, 108, 115; **31:** 241; **55:** 199

Belarius
   Cymbeline **4:** 48, 89, 141

Benedick
   Much Ado about Nothing See **Beatrice and Benedick**

Berowne
   Love's Labour's Lost **2:** 308, 324, 327; **22:** 12; **23:** 184, 187; **38:** 194; **47:** 35

Bertram
   All's Well That Ends Well
      characterization **7:** 15, 27, 29, 32, 39, 41, 43, 98, 113; **26:** 48; **26:** 117; **48:** 65; **55:** 90
      conduct **7:** 9, 10, 12, 16, 19, 21, 51, 62, 104; **50:** 59; **55:** 143, 154
      physical desire **22:** 78
      transformation or redemption **7:** 10, 19, 21, 26, 29, 32, 54, 62, 81, 90, 93, 98, 109, 113, 116, 126; **13:** 84

Bianca
   The Taming of the Shrew **9:** 325, 342, 344, 345, 360, 362, 370, 375
   Bianca-Lucentio subplot **9:** 365, 370, 375, 390, 393, 401, 407, 413, 430; **16:** 13; **31:** 339

the boar
   Venus and Adonis **10:** 416, 451, 454, 466, 473; **33:** 339, 347, 370

Boleyn (Anne Boleyn)
   Henry VIII **2:** 21, 24, 31; **41:** 180

Bolingbroke
   Richard II See **Henry (King Henry IV, previously known as Bolingbroke)**

Borachio and Conrade
   Much Ado about Nothing **8:** 24, 69, 82, 88, 111, 115

Bottom
   A Midsummer Night's Dream
      awakening speech (Act IV, scene i) **3:** 406, 412, 450, 457, 486, 516; **16:** 34
      folly of **46:** 1, 14, 29, 60
      imagination **3:** 376, 393, 406, 432, 486; **29:** 175, 190; **45:** 147
      self-possession **3:** 365, 376, 395, 402, 406, 480; **45:** 158
      Titania, relationship with **3:** 377, 406, 441, 445, 450, 457, 491, 497; **16:** 34; **19:** 21; **22:** 93; **29:** 216; **45:** 160
      transformation **3:** 365, 377, 432; **13:** 27; **22:** 93; **29:** 216; **45:** 147, 160

Brabantio
   Othello **25:** 189

Brutus
   Coriolanus See **the tribunes**
   Julius Caesar **50:** 194, 258
      arrogance **7:** 160, 169, 204, 207, 264, 277, 292, 350; **25:** 280; **30:** 351
      as chief protagonist or tragic hero **7:** 152, 159, 189, 191, 200, 204, 242, 250, 253, 264, 268, 279, 284, 298, 333; **17:** 272, 372, 387
      citizenship **25:** 272
      funeral oration **7:** 154, 155, 204, 210, 350
      motives **7:** 150, 156, 161, 179, 191, 200, 221, 227, 233, 245, 292, 303, 310, 320, 333, 350; **25:** 272; **30:** 321, 358
      nobility or idealism **7:** 150, 152, 156, 159, 161, 179, 189, 191, 200, 221, 242, 250, 253, 259, 264, 277, 303, 320; **17:** 269, 271, 273, 279, 280, 284, 306, 308, 321, 323, 324, 345, 358; **25:** 272, 280; **30:** 351, 362
      political ineptitude or lack of judgment **7:** 169, 188, 200, 205, 221, 245, 252, 264, 277, 282, 310, 316, 331, 333, 343; **17:** 323, 358, 375, 380; **50:** 13
      self-knowledge or self-deception **7:** 191, 200, 221, 242, 259, 264, 268, 279, 310, 333, 336, 350; **25:** 272; **30:** 316
      soliloquy (Act II, scene i) **7:** 156, 160, 161, 191, 221, 245, 250, 253, 264, 268, 279, 282, 292, 303, 343, 350; **25:** 280; **30:** 333
   The Rape of Lucrece **10:** 96, 106, 109, 116, 121, 125, 128, 135

Buckingham
   Henry VIII **22:** 182; **24:** 129, 140; **37:** 109

Cade (Jack Cade)
   Henry VI, Parts 1, 2, and 3 **3:** 35, 67, 92, 97, 109; **16:** 183; **22:** 156; **25:** 102; **28:** 112; **37:** 97; **39:** 160, 196, 205

Caesar
   Antony and Cleopatra
      Antony, relationship with as leader **48:** 206
   Julius Caesar **50:** 189, 230, 234
      ambiguous nature **7:** 191, 233, 242, 250, 272, 298, 316, 320
      ambitious nature **50:** 234
      arrogance **7:** 160, 207, 218, 253, 272, 279, 298; **25:** 280
      idolatry **22:** 137
      leadership qualities **7:** 161, 179, 189, 191, 200, 207, 233, 245, 253, 257, 264, 272, 279, 284, 298, 310, 333; **17:** 317, 358; **22:** 280; **30:** 316, 326; **50:** 234
      as tragic hero **7:** 152, 200, 221, 279; **17:** 321, 377, 384
      weakness **7:** 161, 167, 169, 179, 187, 188, 191, 207, 218, 221, 233, 250, 253, 298; **17:** 358; **25:** 280

Caius, Doctor
   The Merry Wives of Windsor **47:** 354

Caliban
   The Tempest **8:** 286, 287, 289, 292, 294, 295, 297, 302, 304, 307, 309, 315, 326, 328, 336, 353, 364, 370, 380, 390, 396, 401,

414, 420, 423, 429, 435, 454; **13:** 424, 440; **15:** 189, 312, 322, 374, 379; **22:** 302; **25:** 382; **28:** 249; **29:** 278, 292, 297, 343, 368, 377, 396; **32:** 367; **45:** 211, 219, 226, 259; **53:** 45, 64

Calphurnia
Julius Caesar
Calphurnia's dream **45:** 10

Cambridge
Henry V See **traitors**

Canterbury and the churchmen
Henry V **5:** 193, 203, 205, 213, 219, 225, 252, 260; **22:** 137; **30:** 215, 262

Cardinal Wolsey
Henry VIII See **Wolsey**

Casca
Julius Caesar
as Cynic **50:** 249
as proto-Christian **50:** 249

Cassio
Othello **25:** 189

Cassius
Julius Caesar **7:** 156, 159, 160, 161, 169, 179, 189, 221, 233, 303, 310, 320, 333, 343; **17:** 272, 282, 284, 344, 345, 358; **25:** 272, 280; **30:** 351; **37:** 203

Celia
As You Like It **46:** 94

Chorus
Henry V
role of **5:** 186, 192, 226, 228, 230, 252, 264, 269, 281, 293; **14:** 301, 319, 336; **19:** 133; **25:** 116, 131; **30:** 163, 202, 220

the churchmen
Henry V See **Canterbury and the churchmen**

Cinna
Julius Caesar
as poet **48:** 240

Claudio
Much Ado about Nothing
boorish behavior **8:** 9, 24, 33, 36, 39, 44, 48, 63, 79, 82, 95, 100, 111, 115; **31:** 209
credulity **8:** 9, 17, 19, 24, 29, 36, 41, 47, 58, 63, 75, 77, 82, 95, 100, 104, 111, 115, 121; **31:** 241; **47:** 25
mercenary traits **8:** 24, 44, 58, 82, 91, 95
noble qualities **8:** 17, 19, 29, 41, 44, 58, 75; **55:** 232
reconciliation with Hero **8:** 33, 36, 39, 44, 47, 82, 95, 100, 111, 115, 121; **55:** 236
repentance **8:** 33, 63, 82, 95, 100, 111, 115, 121; **31:** 245

sexual insecurities **8:** 75, 100, 111, 115, 121

Claudius
Hamlet **13:** 502; **16** 246; **21:** 259, 347, 361, 371; **28:** 232, 290; **35:** 104, 182; **44:** 119, 241

Cleopatra
Antony and Cleopatra
Antony, relationship with **6:** 25, 27, 37, 39, 48, 52, 53, 62, 67, 71, 76, 85, 100, 125, 131, 133, 136, 142, 151, 161, 163, 165, 180, 192; **25:** 257; **27:** 82; **47:** 107, 124, 165, 174
characterization **47:** 77, 96, 113, 124
contradictory or inconsistent nature **6:** 23, 24, 27, 67, 76, 100, 104, 115, 136, 151, 159, 202; **17:** 94, 113; **27:** 135
costume **17:** 94
creativity **6:** 197; **47:** 96, 113
death **6:** 23, 25, 27, 41, 43, 52, 60, 64, 76, 94, 100, 103, 120, 131, 133, 136, 140, 146, 161, 165, 180, 181, 192, 197, 208; **13:** 383; **17:** 48, 94; **25:** 245; **27:** 135; **47:** 71
personal attraction of **6:** 24, 38, 40, 43, 48, 53, 76, 104, 115, 155; **17:** 113
self-knowledge **47:** 77, 96
staging issues **17:** 94, 113
as subverter of social order **6:** 146, 165; **47:** 113
as superhuman figure **6:** 37, 51, 71, 92, 94, 178, 192; **27:** 110; **47:** 71, 174, 192
as tragic heroine **6:** 53, 120, 151, 192, 208; **27:** 144
as voluptuary or courtesan **6:** 21, 22, 25, 41, 43, 52, 53, 62, 64, 67, 76, 146, 161; **47:** 107, 174

Cloten
Cymbeline **4:** 20, 116, 127, 155; **22:** 302, 365; **25:** 245; **36:** 99, 125, 142, 155; **47:** 228

Collatine
The Rape of Lucrece **10:** 98, 131; **43:** 102; **48:** 291

Cominius
Coriolanus **25:** 245

Conrade
Much Ado about Nothing See **Borachio and Conrade**

Constance
King John **9:** 208, 210, 211, 215, 219, 220, 224, 229, 240, 251, 254; **16:** 161; **24:** 177, 184, 196

Cordelia
King Lear
attack on Britain **25:** 202
characterization **2:** 110, 116, 125, 170; **16:** 311; **25:** 218; **28:** 223, 325; **31:** 117, 149, 155, 162; **46:** 218, 225, 231, 242
as Christ figure **2:** 116, 170, 179, 188, 222, 286
gender identity **48:** 222
rebelliousness **13:** 352; **25:** 202

on stage **11:** 158
transcendent power **2:** 137, 207, 218, 265, 269, 273
women, the Christian ideal of **48:** 222

Corin
As You Like It See **pastoral characters**

Coriolanus
Coriolanus
anger or passion **9:** 19, 26, 45, 80, 92, 157, 164, 177, 189; **30:** 79, 96
as complementary figure to Aufidius **19:** 287
death scene (Act V, scene vi) **9:** 12, 80, 100, 117, 125, 144, 164, 198; **25:** 245, 263; **50:** 110
as epic hero **9:** 130, 164, 177; **25:** 245; **50:** 119
immaturity **9:** 62, 80, 84, 110, 117, 142; **30:** 140
inhuman attributes **9:** 65, 73, 139, 157, 164, 169, 189, 198; **25:** 263
internal struggle **9:** 31, 43, 45, 53, 72, 117, 121, 130; **44:** 93
introspection or self-knowledge, lack of **9:** 53, 80, 84, 112, 117, 130; **25:** 296; **30:** 133
isolation or autonomy **9:** 53, 65, 142, 144, 153, 157, 164, 180, 183, 189, 198; **30:** 58, 89, 111;**50:** 128
manipulation by others **9:** 33, 45, 62, 80; **25:** 296
as military leader **48:** 230
modesty **9:** 8, 12, 19, 26, 53, 78, 92, 117, 121, 144, 183; **25:** 296; **30:** 79, 96, 129, 133, 149
narcissism **30:** 111
noble or aristocratic attributes **9:** 15, 18, 19, 26, 31, 33, 52, 53, 62, 65, 84, 92, 100, 121, 148, 157, 169; **25:** 263; **30:** 67, 74, 96; **50:** 13
pride or arrogance **9:** 8, 11, 12, 19, 26, 31, 33, 43, 45, 65, 78, 92, 121, 148, 153, 177; **30:** 58, 67, 74, 89, 96, 129
punishment of **48:** 230
reconciliation with society **9:** 33, 43, 45, 65, 139, 169; **25:** 296
as socially destructive force **9:** 62, 65, 73, 78, 110, 142, 144, 153; **25:** 296
soliloquy (Act IV, scene iv) **9:** 84, 112, 117, 130
as tragic figure **9:** 8, 12, 13, 18, 25, 45, 52, 53, 72, 80, 92, 106, 112, 117, 130, 148, 164, 169, 177; **25:** 296; **30:** 67, 74, 79, 96, 111, 129; **37:** 283; **50:** 99
traitorous actions **9:** 9, 12, 19, 45, 84, 92, 148; **25:** 296; **30:** 133
as unsympathetic character **9:** 12, 13, 62, 78, 80, 84, 112, 130, 157

the courser and the jennet
Venus and Adonis **10:** 418, 439, 466; **33:** 309, 339, 347, 352

Cranmer
Henry VIII
prophesy of **2:** 25, 31, 46, 56, 64, 68, 72; **24:** 146; **32:** 148; **41:** 120, 190; **56:** 196, 230, 248, 273

Cressida
Troilus and Cressida
- as ambiguous figure **43**: 305
- inconsistency **3**: 538; **13**: 53; **16**: 70; **22**: 339; **27**: 362
- individual will vs. social values **3**: 549, 561, 571, 590, 604, 617, 626; **13**: 53; **27**: 396
- infidelity **3**: 536, 537, 544, 554, 555; **18**: 277, 284, 286; **22**: 58, 339; **27**: 400; **43**: 298
- lack of punishment **3**: 536, 537
- as mother figure **22**: 339
- objectification of **43**: 329
- as sympathetic figure **3**: 557, 560, 604, 609; **18**: 284, 423; **22**: 58; **27**: 396, 400; **43**: 305

Dark Lady
Sonnets **10**: 161, 167, 176, 216, 217, 218, 226, 240, 302, 342, 377, 394; **25**: 374; **37**: 374; **40**: 273; **48**: 346; **51**: 284, 288, 292, 321

the Dauphin
Henry V See **French aristocrats and the Dauphin**

Desdemona
Othello
- as Christ figure **4**: 506, 525, 573; **35**: 360
- culpability **4**: 408, 415, 422, 427; **13**: 313; **19**: 253, 276; **35**: 265, 352, 380
- innocence **35**: 360; **43**: 32; **47**: 25; **53**: 310, 333
- as mother figure **22**: 339; **35**: 282; **53**: 324
- passivity **4**: 402, 406, 421, 440, 457, 470, 582, 587; **25**: 189; **35**: 380
- spiritual nature of her love **4**: 462, 530, 559
- staging issues **11**: 350, 354, 359; **13**: 327; **32**: 201

Diana
Pericles
- as symbol of nature **22**: 315; **36**: 233; **51**: 71

Dogberry and the Watch
Much Ado about Nothing **8**: 9, 12, 13, 17, 24, 28, 29, 33, 39, 48, 55, 69, 79, 82, 88, 95, 104, 108, 115; **18**: 138, 152, 205, 208, 210, 213, 231; **22**: 85; **31**: 171, 229; **46**: 60; **55**: 189, 241

Don John
Much Ado about Nothing See **John (Don John)**

Don Pedro
Much Ado about Nothing See **Pedro (Don Pedro)**

Dromio Brothers
Comedy of Errors **42**: 80; **54**: 136, 152

Duke
Measure for Measure
- as authoritarian figure **23**: 314, 317, 347; **33**: 85; **49**: 274, 300, 358
- characterization **2**: 388, 395, 402, 406, 411, 421, 429, 456, 466, 470, 498, 511; **13**: 84, 94, 104; **23**: 363, 416; **32**: 81; **42**: 1; **44**: 89; **49**: 274, 293, 300, 358
- as dramatic failure **2**: 420, 429, 441, 479, 495, 505, 514, 522
- godlike portrayal of **23**: 320
- noble portrayal of **23**: 301
- speech on death (Act III, scene i) **2**: 390, 391, 395
Othello **25**: 189

Duncan
Macbeth **57**: 194, 236

Edgar
King Lear **28**: 223; **32**: 212; **32**: 308; **37**: 295; **47**: 9; **50**: 24, 45
- Edgar-Edmund duel **22**: 365

Edmund
King Lear **25**: 218; **28**: 223
- Edmund's forged letter **16**: 372

Edmund of Langley, Duke of York
Richard II See **York**

Elbow
Measure for Measure **22**: 85; **25**: 12

Elbow (Mistress Elbow)
Measure for Measure **33**: 90

elder characters
All's Well That Ends Well **7**: 9, 37, 39, 43, 45, 54, 62, 104

Elizabeth I
Love's Labour's Lost **38**: 239

Emilia
Othello **4**: 386, 391, 392, 415, 587; **35**: 352, 380; **43**: 32
The Two Noble Kinsmen **9**: 460, 470, 471, 479, 481; **19**: 394; **41**: 372, 385; **42**: 361

Enobarbus
Antony and Cleopatra **6**: 22, 23, 27, 43, 94, 120, 142; **16**: 342; **17**: 36; **22**: 217; **27**: 135

Evans, Sir Hugh
The Merry Wives of Windsor **47**: 354

fairies
A Midsummer Night's Dream **3**: 361, 362, 372, 377, 395, 400, 423, 450, 459, 486; **12**: 287, 291, 294, 295; **19**: 21; **29**: 183, 190; **45**: 147

Falstaff
Henry IV, Parts 1 and 2
- characterization **1**: 287, 298, 312, 333; **25**: 245; **28**: 203; **39**: 72, 134, 137, 143; **48**: 117, 151; **57**: 120, 156
- as comic figure **1**: 287, 311, 327, 344, 351, 354, 357, 410, 434; **39**: 89; **46**: 1, 48, 52; **57**: 120
- as comic versus tragic figure **49**: 178
- as coward or rogue **1**: 285, 290, 296, 298, 306, 307, 313, 317, 323, 336, 337, 338, 342, 354, 366, 374, 391, 396, 401, 433; **14**: 7, 111, 125, 130, 133; **32**: 166
- as deceiver deceived **47**: 308
- diminishing powers of **47**: 363
- dual personality **1**: 397, 401, 406, 434; **49**: 162
- female attributes **13**: 183; **44**: 44; **47**: 325
- Iago, compared with **1**: 341, 351
- as Jack-a-Lent **47**: 363
- Marxist interpretation **1**: 358, 361
- as outlaw **49**: 133
- as parody of the historical plot **1**: 314, 354, 359; **39**: 143
- as positive character **1**: 286, 287, 290, 296, 298, 311, 312, 321, 325, 333, 344, 355, 357, 389, 401, 408, 434
- rejection by Hal **1**: 286, 287, 290, 312, 314, 317, 324, 333, 338, 344, 357, 366, 372, 374, 379, 380, 389, 414; **13**: 183; **25**: 109; **39**: 72, 89; **48**: 95; **57**: 147
- as satire of feudal society **1**: 314, 328, 361; **32**: 103
- as scapegoat **1**: 389, 414; **47**: 358, 363, 375; **57**: 156
- stage interpretations **14**: 4, 6, 7, 9, 15, 116, 130, 146; **47**: 1
- as subversive figure **16**: 183; **25**: 109
Henry V **5**: 185, 186, 187, 189, 192, 195, 198, 210, 226, 257, 269, 271, 276, 293, 299; **28**: 146; **46**: 48
The Merry Wives of Windsor
- characterization in 1 and 2 Henry IV, compared with **5**: 333, 335, 336, 337, 339, 346, 347, 348, 350, 373, 400; **18**: 5, 7, 75, 86; **22**: 93
- diminishing powers **5**: 337, 339, 343, 347, 350, 351, 392
- as Herne the Hunter **38**: 256, 286; **47**: 358
- incapability of love **5**: 335, 336, 339, 346, 348; **22**: 93
- personification of comic principle or as Vice figure **1**: 342, 361, 366, 374; **5**: 332, 338, 369, 400; **38**: 273
- recognition and repentance of follies **5**: 338, 341, 343, 348, 369, 374, 376, 397
- sensuality **5**: 339, 343, 353, 369, 392
- shrewdness **5**: 332, 336, 346, 355
- threat to community **5**: 343, 369, 379, 392, 395, 400; **38**: 297
- as unifying force **47**: 358
- vanity **5**: 332, 339
- victimization **5**: 336, 338, 341, 347, 348, 353, 355, 360, 369, 373, 374, 376, 392, 397, 400
- as villain **47**: 358

Faulconbridge, (Philip) the Bastard
King John **41**: 205, 228, 251, 260, 277; **48**: 132; **56**: 306
- as chorus or commentator **9**: 212, 218, 229, 248, 251, 260, 271, 284, 297, 300; **22**: 120
- as comic figure **9**: 219, 271, 297; **56**: 365

development **9:** 216, 224, 229, 248, 263, 271, 275, 280, 297; **13:** 158, 163; **56:** 335
as embodiment of England **9:** 222, 224, 240, 244, 248, 271
heroic qualities **9:** 208, 245, 248, 254, 263, 271, 275; **25:** 98; **56:** 348
political conduct **9:** 224, 240, 250, 260, 280, 297; **13:** 147, 158; **22:** 120; **56:** 314

Fenton
The Merry Wives of Windsor
Anne Page-Fenton plot **5:** 334, 336, 343, 353, 376, 390, 395, 402; **22:** 93

Ferdinand
The Tempest **8:** 328, 336, 359, 454; **19:** 357; **22:** 302; **29:** 362, 339, 377

Feste
Twelfth Night
characterization **1:** 558, 655, 658; **26:** 233, 364; **46:** 1, 14, 18, 33, 52, 60, 303, 310
role in play **1:** 546, 551, 553, 566, 570, 571, 579, 635, 658; **46:** 297, 303, 310
song **1:** 543, 548, 561, 563, 566, 570, 572, 603, 620, 642; **46:** 297
gender issues **19:** 78; **34:** 344; **37:** 59

Flavius and Murellus
Julius Caesar **50:** 64

Fluellen
Henry V **30:** 278; **37:** 105

Fool
King Lear **2:** 108, 112, 125, 156, 162, 245, 278, 284; **11:** 17, 158, 169; **22:** 227; **25:** 202; **28:** 223; **46:** 1, 14, 18, 24, 33, 52, 191, 205, 210, 218, 225

Ford, Francis
The Merry Wives of Windsor **5:** 332, 334, 343, 355, 363, 374, 379, 390; **38:** 273; **47:** 321

Ford, Mistress Alice
The Merry Wives of Windsor **47:** 321

Fortinbras
Hamlet **21:** 136, 347; **28:** 290

French aristocrats and the Dauphin
Henry V **5:** 188, 191, 199, 205, 213, 281; **22:** 137; **28:** 121

Friar
Much Ado about Nothing **8:** 24, 29, 41, 55, 63, 79, 111; **55:** 249

Friar John
Romeo and Juliet See **John (Friar John)**

Friar Lawrence
Romeo and Juliet See **Lawrence (Friar Lawrence)**

the Friend
Sonnets **10:** 279, 302, 309, 379, 385, 391, 394; **51:** 284, 292, 300, 304, 316, 321

Ganymede
A Winter's Tale **48:** 309

Gardiner (Stephen Gardiner)
Henry VIII **24:** 129

Gaunt
Richard II **6:** 255, 287, 374, 388, 402, 414; **24:** 274, 322, 325, 414, 423; **37:** 222; **52:** 174, 183

Gertrude
Hamlet **21:** 259, 347, 392; **28:** 311; **32:** 238; **35:** 182, 204, 229; **43:** 12; **44:** 119, 160, 189, 195, 237, 247
death monologue **48:** 255

Ghost
Hamlet **1:** 75, 76, 84, 85, 128, 134, 138, 154, 171, 218, 231, 254; **16:** 246; **21:** 17, 44, 112, 151, 334, 371, 377, 392; **25:** 288; **35:** 152, 157, 174, 237; **44:** 119

Gloucester
King Lear **46:** 254

Gobbo, Launcelot
The Merchant of Venice **46:** 24, 60; **53:** 187, 214

Goneril
King Lear **31:** 151; **46:** 231, 242

Gonzalo
The Tempest **22:** 302; **29:** 278, 343, 362, 368; **45:** 280

Gower chorus
Pericles **2:** 548, 575; **15:** 134, 141, 143, 145, 149, 152, 177; **36:** 279; **42:** 352

Grey
Henry V See **traitors**

Guiderius and Arviragus
Cymbeline **4:** 21, 22, 89, 129, 141, 148; **25:** 319; **36:** 125, 158

Hal
See **Henry (King Henry V, formerly known as Prince Henry of Wales)**

Hamlet
Hamlet
as a fool **46:** 1, 29, 52, 74
delay **1:** 76, 83, 88, 90, 94, 98, 102, 103, 106, 114, 115, 116, 119, 120, 148, 151, 166, 171, 179, 188, 191, 194, 198, 221, 268; **13:** 296, 502; **21:** 81; **25:** 209, 288; **28:** 223; **35:** 82, 174, 212, 215, 237; **44:** 180, 209, 219, 229
divided nature **16:** 246; **28:** 223; **32:** 288; **35:** 182, 215; **37:** 241
elocution of the character's speeches **21:** 96, 104, 112, 127, 132, 172, 177, 179, 194, 245, 254, 257
madness **1:** 76, 81, 83, 95, 102, 106, 128, 144, 154, 160, 234; **21:** 35, 50, 72, 81, 99, 112, 311, 339, 355, 361, 371, 377, 384; **35:** 117, 132, 134, 140, 144, 212; **44:** 107, 119, 152, 209, 219, 229
melancholy **21:** 99, 112, 177, 194; **35:** 82, 95, 117; **44:** 209, 219
as negative character **1:** 86, 92, 111, 171, 218; **21:** 386; **25:** 209; **35:** 167
reaction to his father's death **22:** 339; **35:** 104, 174; **44:** 133, 160, 180, 189
reaction to Gertrude's marriage **1:** 74, 120, 154, 179; **16:** 259; **21:** 371; **22:** 339; **35:** 104, 117; **44:** 133, 160, 189, 195
religion **48:** 195
romantic aspects of the character **21:** 96; **44:** 198
as scourge or purifying figure **1:** 144, 209, 242; **25:** 288; **35:** 157
sentimentality vs. intellectuality **1:** 75, 83, 88, 91, 93, 94, 96, 102, 103, 115, 116, 120, 166, 191; **13:** 296; **21:** 35, 41, 44, 72, 81, 89, 99, 129, 132, 136, 172, 213, 225, 339, 355, 361, 371, 377, 379, 381, 386; **25:** 209; **44:** 198
soliloquies **1:** 76, 82, 83, 148, 166, 169, 176, 191; **21:** 17, 31, 44, 53, 89, 112, 268, 311, 334, 347, 361, 384, 392; **25:** 209; **28:** 223; **44:** 107, 119, 229
as a stoic at the end **54:** 96
theatrical interpretations **21:** 11, 31, 78, 101, 104, 107, 160, 177, 179, 182, 183, 192, 194, 197, 202, 203, 208, 213, 225, 232, 237, 249, 253, 254, 257, 259, 274, 311, 339, 347, 355, 361, 371, 377, 380; **44:** 198
virility **21:** 213, 301, 355

Helena
All's Well That Ends Well
as agent of reconciliation, renewal, or grace **7:** 67, 76, 81, 90, 93, 98, 109, 116; **55:** 176
as dualistic or enigmatic character **7:** 15, 27, 29, 39, 54, 58, 62, 67, 76, 81, 98, 113, 126; **13:** 66; **22:** 78; **26:** 117; **48:** 65; **54:** 30; **55:** 90, 170, 176
desire **38:** 96; **44:** 35; **55:** 109, 170
as "female achiever" **19:** 113; **38:** 89; **55:** 90, 101, 109, 122, 164
pursuit of Bertram **7:** 9, 12, 15, 16, 19, 21, 26, 27, 29, 32, 43, 54, 76, 116; **13:** 77; **22:** 78; **49:** 46; **55:** 90
virginity **38:** 65; **55:** 131, 176
virtue and nobility **7:** 9, 10, 12, 16, 19, 21, 27, 32, 41, 51, 58, 67, 76, 86, 126; **13:** 77; **50:** 59; **55:** 122
A Midsummer Night's Dream **29:** 269

Henry (King Henry IV, previously known as Bolingbroke)
Henry IV, Parts 1 and 2 **39:** 123, 137
effectiveness as ruler **49:** 116
guilt **49:** 112
historical context **49:** 139
illegitimacy of rule **49:** 112, 133, 137
power **49:** 139
as tragic figure **49:** 186
as usurper **49:** 116, 137

Richard II
Bolingbroke and Richard as opposites **24:** 423
Bolingbroke-Mowbray dispute **22:** 137
comic elements **28:** 134
guilt **24:** 423; **39:** 279
language and imagery **6:** 310, 315, 331, 347, 374, 381, 397; **32:** 189
as Machiavellian figure **6:** 305, 307, 315, 331, 347, 388, 393, 397; **24:** 428
as politician **6:** 255, 263, 264, 272, 277, 294, 364, 368, 391; **24:** 330, 333, 405, 414, 423, 428; **39:** 256; **52:** 124
Richard, compared with **6:** 307, 315, 347, 374, 391, 393, 409; **24:** 346, 349, 351, 352, 356, 395, 419, 423, 428; **52:** 108, 124
seizure of Gaunt's estate **49:** 60
his silence **24:** 423
structure, compared with **39:** 235
usurpation of crown, nature of **6:** 255, 272, 289, 307, 310, 347, 354, 359, 381, 385, 393; **13:** 172; **24:** 322, 356, 383, 419; **28:** 178; **52:** 108, 124

Henry (King Henry V, formerly known as Prince Henry of Wales)
Henry IV, Parts 1 and 2
and betrayal **49:** 123
as the central character **1:** 286, 290, 314, 317, 326, 338, 354, 366, 374, 396; **39:** 72, 100
dual personality **1:** 397, 406; **25:** 109, 151; **48:** 95; **49:** 112, 139, 153, 162; **57:** 130
as Everyman **1:** 342, 366, 374
from audience's perspective **49:** 153; **57:** 116
from Henry's perspective **49:** 153
fall from humanity **1:** 379, 380, 383
general assessment **1:** 286, 287, 289, 290, 314, 317, 326, 327, 332, 357, 397; **25:** 245; **32:** 212; **39:** 134; **48:** 151; **57:** 116, 130
as ideal ruler **1:** 289, 309, 317, 321, 326, 337, 342, 344, 374, 389, 391, 434; **25:** 109; **39:** 123; **47:** 60
as Machiavellian ruler **47:** 60
as negative character **1:** 312, 332, 333, 357; **32:** 212
as outlaw **49:** 112
preparation for rule **49:** 112; **57:** 116, 130
reformation **57:** 160
as restorer of law **49:** 133
Richard II, compared with **1:** 332, 337; **39:** 72
Henry V
brutality and cunning **5:** 193, 203, 209, 210, 213, 219, 233, 239, 252, 260, 271, 287, 293, 302, 304; **30:** 159; **43:** 24
characterization in 1 and 2 Henry IV contrasted **5:** 189, 190, 241, 304, 310; **19:** 133; **25:** 131; **32:** 157
chivalry **37:** 187
courage **5:** 191, 195, 210, 213, 228, 246, 257, 267
disguise **30:** 169, 259
education **5:** 246, 267, 271, 289; **14:** 297, 328, 342; **30:** 259
emotion, lack of **5:** 209, 212, 233, 244, 264, 267, 287, 293, 310

as heroic figure **5:** 192, 205, 209, 223, 244, 252, 257, 260, 269, 271, 299, 304; **28:** 121, 146; **30:** 237, 244, 252; **37:** 187; **49:** 194, 200, 236, 247
humor **5:** 189, 191, 212, 217, 239, 240, 276
intellectual and social limitations **5:** 189, 191, 203, 209, 210, 225, 226, 230, 293; **30:** 220
interpersonal relations **5:** 209, 233, 267, 269, 276, 287, 293, 302, 318; **19:** 133; **28:** 146
mercy **5:** 213, 267, 289, 293
mixture of good and bad qualities **5:** 199, 205, 209, 210, 213, 244, 260, 304, 314; **30:** 262, 273; **49:** 211
piety **5:** 191, 199, 209, 217, 223, 239, 257, 260, 271, 289, 310, 318; **30:** 244; **32:** 126
public vs. private selves **22:** 137; **30:** 169, 207
self-doubt **5:** 281, 310
slaughter of prisoners **5:** 189, 205, 246, 293, 318; **28:** 146
speech **5:** 212, 230, 233, 246, 264, 276, 287, 302; **28:** 146; **30:** 163, 227

Henry (King Henry VI)
Henry VI, Parts 1, 2, and 3
characterization **3:** 64, 77, 151; **39:** 160, 177; **47:** 32
source of social disorder **3:** 25, 31, 41, 115; **39:** 154, 187
as sympathetic figure **3:** 73, 143, 154; **24:** 32

Henry (King Henry VIII)
Henry VIII
as agent of divine retribution **2:** 49
characterization **2:** 23, 39, 51, 58, 60, 65, 66, 75; **28:** 184; **37:** 109; **56:** 242
incomplete portrait **2:** 15, 16, 19, 35; **41:** 120; **56:** 209
as realistic figure **2:** 21, 22, 23, 25, 32

Henry (Prince Henry)
King John **41:** 277; **56:** 348

Hermia
A Midsummer Night's Dream **29:** 225, 269; **45:** 117

Hermione
The Winter's Tale
characterization **7:** 385, 395, 402, 412, 414, 506; **15:** 495, 532; **22:** 302, 324; **25:** 347; **32:** 388; **36:** 311; **47:** 25; **49:** 18; **57:** 319
restoration (Act V, scene iii) **7:** 377, 379, 384, 385, 387, 389, 394, 396, 412, 425, 436, 451, 452, 456, 464, 483, 501; **15:** 411, 412, 413, 518, 528, 532; **49:** 18; **57:** 294, 367
sex as identity **48:** 309
supposed death **25:** 339; **47:** 25
trial of **49:** 18

Hero
Much Ado about Nothing **8:** 13, 14, 16, 19, 28, 29, 44, 48, 53, 55, 82, 95, 104, 111, 115, 121; **31:** 231, 245; **47:** 25; **55:** 209

Hippolyta
A Midsummer Night's Dream **48:** 23

Holofernes
Love's Labour's Lost **23:** 207

Horatio
Hamlet **44:** 189
stoic perfection, example of **48:** 195

Hotspur
Henry IV, Parts 1 and 2 **25:** 151; **28:** 101; **39:** 72, 134, 137; **42:** 99
and prisoners of war **49:** 137
versus Henry **49:** 137
Henry V **5:** 189, 199, 228, 271, 302

Humphrey
Henry VI, Parts 1, 2, and 3 **13:** 131; **56:** 187

Iachimo
Cymbeline **25:** 245, 319; **36:** 166; **47:** 274

Iago
Othello
affinity with Othello **4:** 400, 427, 468, 470, 477, 500, 506; **25:** 189; **44:** 57
as conventional dramatic villain **4:** 440, 527, 545, 582; **53:** 238
as homosexual **4:** 503; **53:** 275
Machiavellian elements **4:** 440, 455, 457, 517, 545; **35:** 336, 347
motives **4:** 389, 390, 397, 399, 402, 409, 423, 424, 427, 434, 451, 462, 545, 564; **13:** 304; **25:** 189; **28:** 344; **32:** 201; **35:** 265, 276, 310, 336, 347; **42:** 273; **53:** 246, 275, 324
revenge scheme **4:** 392, 409, 424, 451
as scapegoat **4:** 506
as victim **4:** 402, 409, 434, 451, 457, 470

Imogen
Cymbeline **4:** 21, 22, 24, 29, 37, 45, 46, 52, 56, 78, 89, 108; **15:** 23, 32, 105, 121; **19:** 411; **25:** 245, 319; **28:** 398; **32:** 373; **36:** 129, 142, 148; **47:** 25, 205, 228, 245, 274, 277
reawakening of (Act IV, scene ii) **4:** 37, 56, 89, 103, 108, 116, 150; **15:** 23; **25:** 245; **47:** 252

Isabella
Measure for Measure **2:** 388, 390, 395, 396, 397, 401, 402, 406, 409, 410, 411, 418, 420, 421, 432, 437, 441, 466, 475, 491, 495, 524; **16:** 114; **23:** 278, 279, 280, 281, 282, 296, 344, 357, 363, 405; **28:** 102; **33:** 77, 85

Jack Cade
Henry VI, Parts 1, 2, and 3 See **Cade**

the jailer's daughter
The Two Noble Kinsmen **9:** 457, 460, 479, 481, 486, 502; **41:** 340; **50:** 295, 305, 310, 348, 361

Jaques
As You Like It

love-theme, relation to **5:** 103; **23:** 7, 37, 118, 128
as malcontent **5:** 59, 70, 84
melancholy **5:** 20, 28, 32, 36, 39, 43, 50, 59, 63, 68, 77, 82, 86, 135; **23:** 20, 26, 103, 104, 107, 109; **34:** 85; **46:** 88, 94; **57:** 31
pastoral convention, relation to **5:** 61, 63, 65, 79, 93, 98, 114, 118
Seven Ages of Man speech (Act II, scene vii) **5:** 28, 52, 156; **23:** 48, 103, 105, 126, 138, 152; **46:** 88, 156, 164, 169
Shakespeare, relation to **5:** 35, 50, 154; **48:** 42
as superficial critic **5:** 28, 30, 43, 54, 55, 63, 65, 68, 75, 77, 82, 86, 88, 98, 138; **34:** 85

the jennet
Venus and Adonis See **the courser and the jennet**

Jessica
The Merchant of Venice **4:** 196, 200, 228, 293, 342; **48:** 54, 77; **53:** 159, 211

Joan of Arc
Henry VI, Parts 1, 2, and 3 **16:** 131; **32:** 212

John (Don John)
Much Ado about Nothing **8:** 9, 12, 16, 17, 19, 28, 29, 36, 39, 41, 47, 48, 55, 58, 63, 82, 104, 108, 111, 121

John (Friar John)
Romeo and Juliet
detention of **5:** 448, 467, 470

John (King John)
King John **41:** 205, 260
death **9:** 212, 215, 216, 240; **56:** 345
decline **9:** 224, 235, 240, 263, 275
Hubert, scene with (Act III, scene iii) **9:** 210, 212, 216, 218, 219, 280
moral insensibility **13:** 147, 163
negative qualities **9:** 209, 212, 218, 219, 229, 234, 235, 244, 245, 246, 250, 254, 275, 280, 297; **56:** 325
positive qualities **9:** 209, 224, 235, 240, 244, 245, 263

John of Lancaster, Prince
Henry IV **49:** 123
and betrayal **49:** 123

Julia
The Two Gentlemen of Verona **6:** 450, 453, 458, 476, 494, 499, 516, 519, 549, 564; **40:** 312, 327, 374; **54:** 325, 332

Juliet
Romeo and Juliet See **Romeo and Juliet**

Launcelot Gobbo
The Merchant of Venice See **Gobbo**

Kate
The Taming of the Shrew
characterization **32:** 1; **43:** 61
final speech (Act V, scene ii) **9:** 318, 319, 329, 330, 338, 340, 341, 345, 347, 353, 355, 360, 365, 381, 386, 401, 404, 413, 426, 430; **19:** 3; **22:** 48; **54:** 65; **55:** 299, 331
love for Petruchio **9:** 338, 340, 353, 430; **12:** 435; **55:** 294
portrayals of **31:** 282
shrewishness **9:** 322, 323, 325, 332, 344, 345, 360, 365, 370, 375, 386, 393, 398, 404, 413
transformation **9:** 323, 341, 355, 370, 386, 393, 401, 404, 407, 419, 424, 426, 430; **16:** 13; **19:** 34; **22:** 48; **31:** 288, 295, 339, 351; **55:** 294, 315

Katherine
Henry V **5:** 186, 188, 189, 190, 192, 260, 269, 299, 302; **13:** 183; **19:** 217; **30:** 278; **44:** 44
Henry VIII
characterization **2:** 18, 19, 23, 24, 38; **24:** 129; **37:** 109; **41:** 180
Hermione, compared with **2:** 24, 51, 58, 76
politeness strategies **22:** 182; **56:** 262
religious discourse **22:** 182
as tragic figure **2:** 16, 18

Kent
King Lear **25:** 202; **28:** 223; **32:** 212; **47:** 9

King
All's Well That Ends Well **38:** 150; **55:** 148

King Richard II
Richard II See **Richard**

King Richard III, formerly Richard, Duke of Gloucester
Richard III See **Richard**

Lady Macbeth
Macbeth See **Macbeth (Lady Macbeth)**

Laertes
Hamlet **21:** 347, 386; **28:** 290; **35:** 182

Launce and Speed
The Two Gentlemen of Verona
comic function of **6:** 438, 439, 442, 456, 458, 460, 462, 472, 476, 478, 484, 502, 504, 507, 509, 516, 519, 549; **40:** 312, 320

Lavatch
All's Well That Ends Well **26:** 64; **46:** 33, 52, 68; **55:** 143

Lavinia
Titus Andronicus **27:** 266; **28:** 249; **32:** 212; **43:** 1, 170, 239, 247, 255, 262

Lawrence (Friar Lawrence)
Romeo and Juliet
contribution to catastrophe **5:** 437, 444, 470; **33:** 300; **51:** 253
philosophy of moderation **5:** 427, 431, 437, 438, 443, 444, 445, 458, 467, 479, 505, 538
as Shakespeare's spokesman **5:** 427, 431, 437, 458, 467

Lear
King Lear
curse on Goneril **11:** 5, 7, 12, 114, 116
love-test and division of kingdom **2:** 100, 106, 111, 124, 131, 137, 147, 149, 151, 168, 186, 208, 216, 281; **16:** 351; **25:** 202; **31:** 84, 92, 107, 117, 149, 155; **46:** 231, 242
madness **2:** 94, 95, 98, 99, 100, 101, 102, 103, 111, 116, 120, 124, 125, 149, 156, 191, 208, 216, 281; **46:** 264
as scapegoat **2:** 241, 253
self-knowledge **2:** 103, 151, 188, 191, 213, 218, 222, 241, 249, 262; **25:** 218; **37:** 213; **46:** 191, 205, 225, 254, 264; **54:** 103
spiritual regeneration **54:** 103

Leontes
The Winter's Tale
characterization **19:** 431; **43:** 39; **45:** 366
jealousy **7:** 377, 379, 382, 383, 384, 387, 389, 394, 395, 402, 407, 412, 414, 425, 429, 432, 436, 464, 480, 483, 497; **15:** 514, 518, 532; **22:** 324; **25:** 339; **36:** 334, 344, 349; **44:** 66; **45:** 295, 297, 344, 358; **47:** 25; **57:** 294
Othello, compared with **7:** 383, 390, 412; **15:** 514; **36:** 334; **44:** 66; **47:** 25
repentance **7:** 381, 389, 394, 396, 402, 414, 497; **36:** 318, 362; **44:** 66; **57:** 294

Lord Chief Justice
Henry IV
as keeper of law and justice **49:** 133

Lucentio
The Taming of the Shrew **9:** 325, 342, 362, 375, 393

Lucio
Measure for Measure **13:** 104; **49:** 379

Lucrece
The Rape of Lucrece
chastity **33:** 131, 138; **43:** 92
as example of Renaissance virt[0097] **22:** 289; **43:** 148
heroic **10:** 84, 93, 109, 121, 128
patriarchal woman, model of **10:** 109, 131; **33:** 169, 200
self-perception **48:** 291
self-responsibility **10:** 89, 96, 98, 106, 125; **33:** 195; **43:** 85, 92, 158
unrealistic **10:** 64, 65, 66, 121
verbose **10:** 64, 81, 116; **25:** 305; **33:** 169
as victim **22:** 294; **25:** 305; **32:** 321; **33:** 131, 195; **43:** 102, 158

Macbeth
Macbeth
ambition **44:** 284, 324; **57:** 256
characterization **20:** 20, 42, 73, 107, 113, 130, 146, 151, 279, 283, 312, 338, 343, 379, 406, 413; **29:** 139, 152, 155, 165; **44:** 289; **57:** 189, 194, 236, 263, 267

courage **3:** 172, 177, 181, 182, 183, 186, 234, 312, 333; **20:** 107; **44:** 315
disposition **3:** 173, 175, 177, 182, 186; **20:** 245, 376
imagination **3:** 196, 208, 213, 250, 312, 345; **20:** 245, 376; **44:** 351
as "inauthentic" king **3:** 245, 302, 321, 345
inconsistencies **3:** 202
as Machiavellian villain **3:** 280; **57:** 236
manliness **20:** 113; **29:** 127, 133; **44:** 315; **57:** 256
psychoanalytic interpretations **20:** 42, 73, 238, 376; **44:** 284, 289, 297, 324; **45:** 48, 58; **57:** 267
Richard III, compared with **3:** 177, 182, 186, 345; **20:** 86, 92; **22:** 365; **44:** 269
as Satan figure **3:** 229, 269, 275, 289, 318
self-awareness **3:** 312, 329, 338; **16:** 317; **44:** 361; **57:** 256
as sympathetic figure **3:** 229, 306, 314, 338; **29:** 139, 152; **44:** 269, 306, 337
as tragic hero **44:** 269, 306, 315, 324, 337; **57:** 267

Macbeth (Lady Macbeth)
Macbeth
ambition **3:** 185, 219; **20:** 279, 345
characterization **20:** 56, 60, 65, 73, 140, 148, 151, 241, 279, 283, 338, 350, 406, 413; **29:** 109, 146; **57:** 256, 263
childlessness **3:** 219, 223; **48:** 214
good and evil, combined traits of **3:** 173, 191, 213; **20:** 60, 107
inconsistencies **3:** 202; **20:** 54, 137
influence on Macbeth **3:** 171, 185, 191, 193, 199, 262, 289, 312, 318; **13:** 502; **20:** 345; **25:** 235; **29:** 133; **57:** 263
psychoanalytic interpretations **20:** 345; **44:** 289, 297; **45:** 58
sleepwalking scene **44:** 261
as sympathetic figure **3:** 191, 193, 203

Macduff
Macbeth **3:** 226, 231, 253, 262; **25:** 235; **29:** 127, 133, 155; **57:** 194

MacMorris
Henry V **22:** 103; **28:** 159; **30:** 278

Malcolm
Macbeth **25:** 235
fatherhood **48:** 214

Malvolio
Twelfth Night
characterization **1:** 540, 544, 545, 548, 550, 554, 558, 567, 575, 577, 615; **26:** 207, 233, 273; **46:** 286
forged letter **16:** 372; **28:** 1
punishment **1:** 539, 544, 548, 549, 554, 555, 558, 563, 577, 590, 632, 645; **46:** 291, 297, 338
as Puritan **1:** 549, 551, 555, 558, 561, 563; **25:** 47
role in play **1:** 545, 548, 549, 553, 555, 563, 567, 575, 577, 588, 610, 615, 632, 645; **26:** 337, 374; **46:** 347

Mamillius
The Winter's Tale **7:** 394, 396, 451; **22:** 324

Margaret
Henry VI, Parts 1, 2, and 3
characterization **3:** 18, 26, 35, 51, 103, 109, 140, 157; **24:** 48
Suffolk, relationship with **3:** 18, 24, 26, 157; **39:** 213
Richard III **8:** 153, 154, 159, 162, 163, 170, 193, 201, 206, 210, 218, 223, 228, 243, 248, 262; **39:** 345

Marina
Pericles **37:** 361; **51:** 118

Menenius
Coriolanus **9:** 8, 9, 11, 14, 19, 26, 78, 80, 106, 148, 157; **25:** 263, 296; **30:** 67, 79, 89, 96, 111, 133

Mercutio
Romeo and Juliet
bawdy **5:** 463, 525, 550, 575
death **5:** 415, 418, 419, 547; **33:** 290
as worldly counterpart to Romeo **5:** 425, 464, 542; **33:** 290; **51:** 195

minor characters
Richard III **8:** 154, 159, 162, 163, 168, 170, 177, 184, 186, 201, 206, 210, 218, 223, 228, 232, 239, 248, 262, 267

Miranda
The Tempest **8:** 289, 301, 304, 328, 336, 370, 454; **19:** 357; **22:** 302; **28:** 249; **29:** 278, 297, 362, 368, 377, 396; **53:** 64

Mistress Elbow
Measure for Measure See **Elbow (Mistress Elbow)**

Mistress Quickly
Henry V See **Quickly**

Mortimer
Henry IV, Parts 1 and 2 **25:** 151

Norfolk
Henry VIII **22:** 182

Northumberland
Richard II **24:** 423

Nurse
Romeo and Juliet **5:** 419, 425, 463, 464, 575; **33:** 294

Oberon
A Midsummer Night's Dream
as controlling force **3:** 434, 459, 477, 502; **29:** 175

Octavius
Antony and Cleopatra **6:** 22, 24, 31, 38, 43, 53, 62, 107, 125, 146, 178, 181, 219; **25:** 257
Julius Caesar **30:** 316

Olivia
Twelfth Night **1:** 540, 543, 545; **46:** 286, 324, 369; **47:** 45

Ophelia
Hamlet **1:** 73, 76, 81, 82, 91, 96, 97, 154, 166, 169, 171, 218, 270; **13:** 268; **16:** 246; **19:** 330; **21:** 17, 41, 44, 72, 81, 101, 104, 107, 112, 136, 203, 259, 347, 381, 386, 392, 416; **28:** 232, 325; **35:** 104, 126, 140, 144, 182, 238; **44:** 189, 195, 248
in art **48:** 255
death **48:** 255
as icon **48:** 255
influence on popular culture **48:** 255

Orlando
As You Like It
as ideal man **5:** 32, 36, 39, 162; **34:** 161; **46:** 94
as younger brother **5:** 66, 158; **46:** 94

Orsino
Twelfth Night **46:** 286, 333; **47:** 45

Othello
Othello
affinity with Iago **4:** 400, 427, 468, 470, 477, 500, 506; **25:** 189; **35:** 276, 320, 327
as conventional "blameless hero" **4:** 445, 486, 500; **53:** 233, 238, 298, 304
credulity **4:** 384, 385, 388, 390, 396, 402, 434, 440, 455; **13:** 327; **32:** 302; **47:** 25, 51
Desdemona, relationship with **22:** 339; **35:** 301, 317; **37:** 269; **43:** 32; **53:** 315
divided nature **4:** 400, 412, 462, 470, 477, 493, 500, 582, 592; **16:** 293; **19:** 276; **25:** 189; **35:** 320; **53:** 268, 289, 343
egotism **4:** 427, 470, 477, 493, 522, 536, 541, 573, 597; **13:** 304; **35:** 247, 253
self-destructive anger **16:** 283; **53:** 324
self-dramatizing or self-deluding **4:** 454, 457, 477, 592; **13:** 313; **16:** 293; **35:** 317
self-knowledge **4:** 462, 470, 477, 483, 508, 522, 530, 564, 580, 591, 596; **13:** 304; **16:** 283; **28:** 243; **35:** 253, 317; **53:** 233, 343
spiritual state **4:** 483, 488, 517, 525, 527, 544, 559, 564, 573; **28:** 243; **35:** 253; **54:** 119

Page, Anne
The Merry Wives of Windsor **47:** 321
Anne Page-Fenton plot **5:** 334, 336, 343, 353, 376, 390, 395, 402; **22:** 93; **47:** 308

Page, Mistress Margaret
The Merry Wives of Windsor **47:** 321

Painter
Timon of Athens See **Poet and Painter**

Palamon and Arcite
The Two Noble Kinsmen **9:** 474, 481, 490, 492, 502; **50:** 295, 305, 348, 361

Parolles
All's Well That Ends Well
  characterization **7**: 8, 9, 43, 76, 81, 98, 109, 113, 116, 126; **22**: 78; **26**: 48, 73, 97; **26**: 117; **46**: 68; **55**: 90, 154
  exposure **7**: 9, 27, 81, 98, 109, 113, 116, 121, 126
  Falstaff, compared with **7**: 8, 9, 16

pastoral characters (Silvius, Phebe, and Corin)
As You Like It **23**: 37, 97, 98, 99, 108, 110, 118, 122, 138; **34**: 147

Paulina
The Winter's Tale **7**: 385, 412, 506; **15**: 528; **22**: 324; **25**: 339; **36**: 311; **57**: 319

Pedro (Don Pedro)
Much Ado about Nothing **8**: 17, 19, 48, 58, 63, 82, 111, 121

Perdita
The Winter's Tale
  characterization **7**: 395, 412, 414, 419, 429, 432, 452, 506; **22**: 324; **25**: 339; **36**: 328; **43**: 39
  reunion with Leontes (Act V, scene ii) **7**: 377, 379, 381, 390, 432, 464, 480

Pericles
Pericles
  characterization **36**: 251; **37**: 361
  patience **2**: 572, 573, 578, 579
  suit of Antiochus's daughter **2**: 547, 565, 578, 579; **51**: 126
  Ulysses, compared with **2**: 551

Petruchio
The Taming of the Shrew
  admirable qualities **9**: 320, 332, 341, 344, 345, 370, 375, 386; **55**: 294
  audacity or vigor **9**: 325, 337, 355, 375, 386, 404
  characterization **32**: 1
  coarseness or brutality **9**: 325, 329, 365, 390, 393, 398, 407; **19**: 122; **43**: 61
  as lord of misrule **9**: 393; **50**: 64; **55**: 322
  love for Kate **9**: 338, 340, 343, 344, 386; **12**: 435
  portrayals of **31**: 282
  pragmatism **9**: 329, 334, 375, 398, 424; **13**: 3; **31**: 345, 351
  taming method **9**: 320, 323, 329, 340, 341, 343, 345, 355, 369, 370, 375, 390, 398, 407, 413, 419, 424; **19**: 3, 12, 21 **31**: 269, 295, 326, 335, 339; **55**: 334

Phebe
As You Like It See **pastoral characters**

Pistol
Henry V **28**: 146

plebeians
Coriolanus **9**: 8, 9, 11, 12, 15, 18, 19, 26, 33, 39, 53, 92, 125, 153, 183, 189; **25**: 296; **30**: 58, 79, 96, 111

Poet and Painter
Timon of Athens **25**: 198

the poets
Julius Caesar **7**: 179, 320, 350

Polixenes
The Winter's Tale
  Leontes, relationship with **48**: 309

Polonius
Hamlet **21**: 259, 334, 347, 386, 416; **35**: 182

Porter
Henry VIII **24**: 155
Macbeth **3**: 173, 175, 184, 190, 196, 203, 205, 225, 260, 271, 297, 300; **20**: 283

Portia
The Merchant of Venice **4**: 194, 195, 196, 215, 254, 263, 336, 356; **12**: 104, 107, 114; **13**: 37; **22**: 3, 69; **25**: 22; **32**: 294; **37**: 86; **40**: 142, 156, 197, 208; **49**: 27

Posthumus
Cymbeline **4**: 24, 30, 53, 78, 116, 127, 141, 155, 159, 167; **15**: 89; **19**: 411; **25**: 245, 319; **36**: 142; **44**: 28; **45**: 67, 75; **47**: 25, 205, 228

Prince Henry
King John See **Henry (Prince Henry)**

Prospero
The Tempest
  characterization **8**: 312, 348, 370, 458; **16**: 442; **22**: 302; **45**: 188, 272
  as God or Providence **8**: 311, 328, 364, 380, 429, 435
  magic, nature of **8**: 301, 340, 356, 396, 414, 423, 458; **25**: 382; **28**: 391; **29**: 278, 292, 368, 377, 396; **32**: 338, 343
  psychoanalytic interpretation **45**: 259
  redemptive powers **8**: 302, 320, 353, 370, 390, 429, 439, 447; **29**: 297
  as ruler **8**: 304, 308, 309, 420, 423; **13**: 424; **22**: 302; **29**: 278, 362, 377, 396
  self-control **8**: 312, 414, 420; **22**: 302; **44**: 11
  self-knowledge **16**: 442; **22**: 302; **29**: 278, 292, 362, 377, 396
  as Shakespeare or creative artist **8**: 299, 302, 308, 312, 320, 324, 353, 364, 435, 447
  as tragic hero **8**: 359, 370, 464; **29**: 292

Proteus
The Two Gentlemen of Verona **6**: 439, 450, 458, 480, 490, 511; **40**: 312, 327, 330, 335, 359; **42**: 18; **54**: 325, 332

Puck
A Midsummer Night's Dream **45**: 96, 158

Quickly (Mistress Quickly)
Henry V **5**: 186, 187, 210, 276, 293; **30**: 278

Regan
King Lear **31**: 151; **46**: 231, 242

Richard (King Richard II)
Richard II
  artistic temperament **6**: 264, 267, 270, 272, 277, 292, 294, 298, 315, 331, 334, 347, 368, 374, 393, 409; **24**: 298, 301, 304, 315, 322, 390, 405, 408, 411, 414, 419; **39**: 289
  Bolingbroke, compared with **24**: 346, 349, 351, 352, 356, 419; **39**: 256; **52**: 108, 124
  characterization **6**: 250, 252, 253, 254, 255, 258, 262, 263, 267, 270, 272, 282, 283, 304, 343, 347, 364, 368; **24**: 262, 263, 267, 269, 270, 271, 272, 273, 274, 278, 280, 315, 322, 325, 330, 333, 390, 395, 402, 405, 423; **28**: 134; **39**: 279, 289; **52**: 169
  dangerous aspects **24**: 405
  delusion **6**: 267, 298, 334, 368, 409; **24**: 329, 336, 405
  homosexuality **24**: 405
  kingship **6**: 253, 254, 263, 272, 327, 331, 334, 338, 364, 402, 414; **24**: 278, 295, 336, 337, 339, 356, 419; **28**: 134, 178; **39**: 256, 263; **52**: 169
  loss of identity **6**: 267, 338, 368, 374, 381, 388, 391, 409; **24**: 298, 414, 428
  as martyr-king **6**: 289, 307, 321; **19**: 209; **24**: 289, 291; **28**: 134
  nobility **6**: 255, 258, 259, 262, 263, 391; **24**: 260, 263, 274, 280, 289, 291, 402, 408, 411
  political acumen **6**: 263, 264, 272, 292, 310, 327, 334, 364, 368, 374, 388, 391, 397, 402, 409; **24**: 405; **39**: 256
  private vs. public persona **6**: 317, 327, 364, 368, 391, 409; **24**: 428
  role in Gloucester's death **52**: 108, 124
  role-playing **24**: 419, 423; **28**: 178
  seizure of Gaunt's estate **6**: 250, 338, 388
  self-dramatization **6**: 264, 267, 307, 310, 315, 317, 331, 334, 368, 393, 409; **24**: 339; **28**: 178
  self-hatred **13**: 172; **24**: 383; **39**: 289
  self-knowledge **6**: 255, 267, 331, 334, 338, 352, 354, 368, 388, 391; **24**: 273, 289, 411, 414; **39**: 263, 289
  spiritual redemption **6**: 255, 267, 331, 334, 338, 352, 354, 368, 388, 391; **24**: 273, 289, 411, 414; **52**: 124

Richard (King Richard III, formerly Richard, Duke of Gloucester)
Henry VI, Parts 1, 2, and 3
  characterization **3**: 35, 48, 57, 64, 77, 143, 151; **22**: 193; **39**: 160, 177
  as revenger **22**: 193
  soliloquy (3 Henry VI, Act III, scene ii) **3**: 17, 48
Richard III
  ambition **8**: 148, 154, 165, 168, 170, 177, 182, 213, 218, 228, 232, 239, 252, 258, 267; **39**: 308, 341, 360, 370, 383; **52**: 201, 223
  attractive qualities **8**: 145, 148, 152, 154, 159, 161, 162, 165, 168, 170, 181, 182, 184, 185, 197, 201, 206, 213, 228, 243, 252, 258; **16**: 150; **39**: 370, 383; **52**: 272, 280
  credibility, question of **8**: 145, 147, 154, 159, 165, 193; **13**: 142

death **8:** 145, 148, 154, 159, 165, 168, 170, 177, 182, 197, 210, 223, 228, 232, 243, 248, 252, 258, 267
deformity as symbol **8:** 146, 147, 148, 152, 154, 159, 161, 165, 170, 177, 184, 185, 193, 218, 248, 252, 267; **19:** 164
inversion of moral order **8:** 159, 168, 177, 182, 184, 185, 197, 201, 213, 218, 223, 232, 239, 243, 248, 252, 258, 262, 267; **39:** 360; **52:** 205, 214
as Machiavellian villain **8:** 165, 182, 190, 201, 218, 232, 239, 243, 248; **39:** 308, 326, 360, 387; **52:** 201, 205, 257, 280, 285
as monster or symbol of diabolic **8:** 145, 147, 159, 162, 168, 170, 177, 182, 193, 197, 201, 228, 239, 248, 258; **13:** 142; **37:** 144; **39:** 326, 349; **52:** 227, 272
other literary villains, compared with **8:** 148, 161, 162, 165, 181, 182, 206, 213, 239, 267
role-playing, hypocrisy, and dissimulation **8:** 145, 148, 154, 159, 162, 165, 168, 170, 182, 190, 206, 213, 218, 228, 239, 243, 252, 258, 267; **25:** 141, 164, 245; **39:** 335, 341, 387 **52:** 257, 267
as scourge or instrument of God **8:** 163, 177, 193, 201, 218, 228, 248, 267; **39:** 308
as seducer **52:** 223, 227
as Vice figure **8:** 190, 201, 213, 228, 243, 248, 252; **16:** 150; **39:** 383, 387; **52:** 223, 267

Richard Plantagenet, Duke of York
Henry VI, Parts 1, 2, and 3 See **York**

Richmond
Richard III **8:** 154, 158, 163, 168, 177, 182, 193, 210, 218, 223, 228, 243, 248, 252; **13:** 142; **25:** 141; **39:** 349; **52:** 214, 257, 285

the Rival Poet
Sonnets **10:** 169, 233, 334, 337, 385; **48:** 352

Roman citizenry
Julius Caesar
portrayal of **7:** 169, 179, 210, 221, 245, 279, 282, 310, 320, 333; **17:** 271, 279, 288, 291, 292, 298, 323, 334, 351, 367, 374, 375, 378; **22:** 280; **30:** 285, 297, 316, 321, 374, 379; **37:** 229

Romeo and Juliet
Romeo and Juliet
death-wish **5:** 431, 489, 505, 528, 530, 538, 542, 550, 566, 571, 575; **32:** 212
first meeting (Act I scene v) **51:** 212
immortality **5:** 536
Juliet's epithalamium speech (Act III, scene ii) **5:** 431, 477, 492
Juliet's innocence **5:** 421, 423, 450, 454; **33:** 257
maturation **5:** 437, 454, 467, 493, 498, 509, 520, 565; **33:** 249, 257
rebellion **25:** 257
reckless passion **5:** 419, 427, 431, 438, 443, 444, 448, 467, 479, 485, 505, 533, 538, 542; **33:** 241
Romeo's dream (Act V, scene i) **5:** 513, 536, 556; **45:** 40; **51:** 203

Rosaline, Romeo's relationship with **5:** 419, 423, 425, 427, 438, 498, 542, 575

Rosalind
As You Like It **46:** 94, 122
Beatrice, compared with **5:** 26, 36, 50, 75
charm **5:** 55, 75; **23:** 17, 18, 20, 41, 89, 111
disguise, role of **5:** 75, 107, 118, 122, 128, 130, 133, 138, 141, 146, 148, 164, 168; **13:** 502; **23:** 35, 42, 106, 119, 123, 146; **34:** 130; **46:** 127, 134, 142; **57:** 23, 40
femininity **5:** 26, 36, 52, 75; **23:** 24, 29, 46, 54, 103, 108, 121, 146
love-theme, relation to **5:** 79, 88, 103, 116, 122, 138, 141; **23:** 114, 115; **34:** 85, 177

rustic characters
As You Like It **5:** 24, 60, 72, 84; **23:** 127; **34:** 78, 161
A Midsummer Night's Dream **3:** 376, 397, 432; **12:** 291, 293; **45:** 147, 160

Scroop
Henry V See **traitors**

Sebastian
The Tempest See **Antonio and Sebastian**

Shylock
The Merchant of Venice
alienation **4:** 279, 312; **40:** 175; **48:** 77; **49:** 23, 37
ambiguity **4:** 247, 254, 315, 319, 331; **12:** 31, 35, 36, 50, 51, 52, 56, 81, 124; **40:** 175; **53:** 111
ghettoization of **53:** 127
forced conversion **4:** 209, 252, 268, 282, 289, 321
Jewishness **4:** 193, 194, 195, 200, 201, 213, 214, 279; **22:** 69; **25:** 257; **40:** 142, 175, 181; **48:** 65, 77
master-slave relationship **53:** 136
motives in making the bond **4:** 252, 263, 266, 268; **22:** 69; **25:** 22
as outsider **53:** 127, 224
as Puritan **40:** 127, 166
as scapegoat figure **4:** 254, 300; **40:** 166; **49:** 27
as traditional comic villain **4:** 230, 243, 261, 263, 315; **12:** 40, 62, 124; **40:** 175
as tragic figure **12:** 6, 9, 10, 16, 21, 23, 25, 40, 44, 66, 67, 81, 97; **40:** 175

Sicinius
Coriolanus See **the tribunes**

Silvia
The Two Gentlemen of Verona **6:** 450, 453, 458, 476, 494, 499, 516, 519, 549, 564; **40:** 312, 327, 374; **54:** 325, 332

Silvius
As You Like It See **pastoral characters**

Sly
The Taming of the Shrew **9:** 320, 322, 350, 370, 381, 390, 398, 430; **12:** 316, 335, 416, 427, 441; **16:** 13; **19:** 34, 122; **22:** 48; **37:** 31; **50:** 74

soldiers
Henry V **5:** 203, 239, 267, 276, 281, 287, 293, 318; **28:** 146; **30:** 169,

Speed
The Two Gentlemen of Verona See **Launce and Speed**

Stephano and Trinculo
The Tempest
comic subplot of **8:** 292, 297, 299, 304, 309, 324, 328, 353, 370; **25:** 382; **29:** 377; **46:** 14, 33

Stephen Gardiner
Henry VIII See **Gardiner**

Talbot
Henry VI, Parts 1, 2, and 3 **39:** 160, 213, 222; **56:** 85, 145

Tamora
Titus Andronicus **4:** 632, 662, 672, 675; **27:** 266; **43:** 170

Tarquin
The Rape of Lucrece **10:** 80, 93, 98, 116, 125; **22:** 294; **25:** 305; **32:** 321; **33:** 190; **43:** 102
Petrarchan lover **48:** 291
platonic tyrant **48:** 291
Satan role **48:** 291

Thersites
Troilus and Cressida **13:** 53; **25:** 56; **27:** 381

Theseus
A Midsummer Night's Dream
characterization **3:** 363
Hippolyta, relationship with **3:** 381, 412, 421, 423, 450, 468, 520; **29:** 175, 216, 243, 256; **45:** 84
as ideal **3:** 379, 391
"lovers, lunatics, and poets" speech (Act V, scene i) **3:** 365, 371, 379, 381, 391, 402, 411, 412, 421, 423, 441, 498, 506; **29:** 175
as representative of institutional life **3:** 381, 403; **51:** 1

Time-Chorus
The Winter's Tale **7:** 377, 380, 412, 464, 476, 501; **15:** 518

Timon
Timon of Athens
comic traits **25:** 198
as flawed hero **1:** 456, 459, 462, 472, 495, 503, 507, 515; **16:** 351; **20:** 429, 433, 476; **25:** 198; **27:** 157, 161
misanthropy **13:** 392; **20:** 431, 464, 476, 481, 491, 492, 493; **27:** 161, 175, 184, 196; **37:** 222; **52:** 296, 301

as noble figure **1:** 467, 473, 483, 499; **20:** 493; **27:** 212

Titania
A Midsummer Night's Dream **29:** 243

Titus
Titus Andronicus **4:** 632, 637, 640, 644, 647, 653, 656, 662; **25:** 245; **27:** 255

Touchstone
As You Like It
callousness **5:** 88
comic and farcical elements **46:** 117
as philosopher-fool **5:** 24, 28, 30, 32, 36, 63, 75, 98; **23:** 152; **34:** 85; **46:** 1, 14, 18, 24, 33, 52, 60, 88, 105
relation to pastoral convention **5:** 54, 61, 63, 72, 75, 77, 79, 84, 86, 93, 98, 114, 118, 135, 138, 166; **34:** 72, 147, 161
satire or parody of pastoral conventions **46:** 122
selflessness **5:** 30, 36, 39, 76

traitors (Scroop, Grey, and Cambridge)
Henry V **16:** 202; **30:** 220, 278

the tribunes (Brutus and Sicinius)
Coriolanus **9:** 9, 11, 14, 19, 33, 169, 180

Trinculo
The Tempest   See **Stephano and Trinculo**

Troilus
Troilus and Cressida
contradictory behavior **3:** 596, 602, 635; **27:** 362
Cressida, relationship with **3:** 594, 596, 606; **22:** 58
integrity **3:** 617

opposition to Ulysses **3:** 561, 584, 590
as unsympathetic figure **18:** 423; **22:** 58, 339; **43:** 317
as warrior **3:** 596; **22:** 339

Ulysses
Troilus and Cressida
speech on degree (Act I, scene iii) **3:** 549, 599, 609, 642; **27:** 396

Valentine
The Two Gentlemen of Verona **54:** 325, 332

Venetians
The Merchant of Venice **4:** 195, 200, 228, 254, 273, 300, 321, 331

Venus
Venus and Adonis **10:** 427, 429, 434, 439, 442, 448, 449, 451, 454, 466, 473, 480, 486, 489; **16:** 452; **25:** 305, 328; **28:** 355; **33:** 309, 321, 330, 347, 352, 357, 363, 370, 377; **51:** 335, 352, 377, 388

Viola
Twelfth Night **26:** 308; **46:** 286, 324, 347, 369

Virgilia
Coriolanus **9:** 11, 19, 26, 33, 58, 100, 121, 125; **25:** 263; **30:** 79, 96, 133; **50:** 99

Volumnia
Coriolanus
Coriolanus's subservience to **9:** 16, 26, 33, 53, 62, 80, 92, 100, 117, 125, 142, 177, 183; **30:** 140, 149; **44:** 79
influence on Coriolanus **9:** 45, 62, 65, 78, 92, 100, 110, 117, 121, 125, 130, 148, 157, 183, 189, 193; **25:** 263, 296; **30:** 79, 96, 125, 133, 140, 142, 149; **44:** 93
as noble Roman matron **9:** 16, 19, 26, 31, 33
personification of Rome **9:** 125, 183; **50:** 119

Wat the hare
Venus and Adonis **10:** 424, 451

the Watch
Much Ado about Nothing   See **Dogberry and the Watch**

Williams
Henry V **13:** 502; **16:** 183; **28:** 146; **30:** 169, 259, 278

Witches
Macbeth
and supernaturalism **3:** 171, 172, 173, 175, 177, 182, 183, 184, 185, 194, 196, 198, 202, 207, 208, 213, 219, 229, 239; **16:** 317; **19:** 245; **20:** 92, 175, 213, 279, 283, 374, 387, 406, 413; **25:** 235; **28:** 339; **29:** 91, 101, 109, 120

Wolsey (Cardinal Wolsey)
Henry VIII **2:** 15, 18, 19, 23, 24, 38; **22:** 182; **24:** 80, 91, 112, 113, 129, 140; **37:** 109; **41:** 129; **56:** 248, 262

York (Edmund of Langley, Duke of York)
Richard II **6:** 287, 364, 368, 388, 402, 414; **24:** 263, 320, 322, 364, 395, 414; **39:** 243, 279

York (Richard Plantagenet, Duke of York)
Henry VI, Parts 1, 2, and 3
death of **13:** 131

Cumulative Topic Index

The Cumulative Topic Index indentifies the principal topics of discussion in the criticism of each play and non-dramatic poem. The topics are arranged alphabetically. Page references indicate the beginning page number of each essay containing substantial commentary on that topic. A parenthetical reference after a topic indicates that the topic is extensively discussed in that volume.

absurdities, inconsistencies, and shortcomings
The Two Gentlemen of Verona **6:** 435, 436, 437, 439, 464, 507, 541, 560; **54:** 295, 311

accident or chance
Romeo and Juliet **5:** 418, 444, 448, 467, 470, 487, 573

acting and dissimulation
Richard II **6:** 264, 267, 307, 310, 315, 368, 393, 409; **24:** 339, 345, 346, 349, 352, 356

adolescence
Romeo and Juliet **33:** 249, 255, 257

adultery
The Comedy of Errors **34:** 215

aggression
Coriolanus **9:** 112, 142, 174, 183, 189, 198; **30:** 79, 111, 125, 142; **44:** 11, 79

alienation
Timon of Athens **1:** 523; **27:** 161

allegorical elements
Antony and Cleopatra **52:** 5
King Lear **16:** 311
Measure for Measure **52:** 69
The Merchant of Venice **4:** 224, 250, 261, 268, 270, 273, 282, 289, 324, 336, 344, 350
The Phoenix and Turtle **10:** 7, 8, 9, 16, 17, 48; **38:** 334, 378; **51:** 138, 188
The Rape of Lucrece **10:** 89, 93
Richard II **6:** 264, 283, 323, 385

Richard III **52:** 5
The Tempest **8:** 294, 295, 302, 307, 308, 312, 326, 328, 336, 345, 364; **42:** 320
Troilus and Cressida **52:** 5
Venus and Adonis **10:** 427, 434, 439, 449, 454, 462, 480; **28:** 355; **33:** 309, 330

ambiguity
Antony and Cleopatra **6:** 53, 111, 161, 163, 180, 189, 208, 211, 228; **13:** 368
Hamlet **1:** 92, 160, 198, 227, 230, 234, 247, 249; **21:** 72; **35:** 241
King John **13:** 152; **41:** 243
Measure for Measure **2:** 417, 420, 432, 446, 449, 452, 474, 479, 482, 486, 495, 505
A Midsummer Night's Dream **3:** 401, 459, 486; **45:** 169
Richard III **44:** 11; **47:** 15
10: 251, 256; **28:** 385; **40:** 221, 228, 268
Troilus and Cressida **3:** 544, 568, 583, 587, 589, 599, 611, 621; **27:** 400; **43:** 305
Twelfth Night **1:** 554, 639; **34:** 287, 316
Venus and Adonis **10:** 434, 454, 459, 462, 466, 473, 480, 486, 489; **33:** 352; **51:** 368, 377, 388

ambition or pride
Henry IV, Parts 1 and 2 **57:** 94
Henry VIII **2:** 15, 38, 67
Macbeth **44:** 284, 324;
Richard III **52:** 201, 223

ambivalent or ironic elements
Henry VI, Parts 1, 2, and 3 **3:** 69, 151, 154; **39:** 160; **56:** 131
Richard III **44:** 11
Troilus and Cressida **43:** 340

amorality, question of
The Two Noble Kinsmen **9:** 447, 460, 492

amour-passion or Liebestod myth
Romeo and Juliet **5:** 484, 489, 528, 530, 542, 550, 575; **32:** 256; **51:** 195, 219, 236

amputations, significance of
Titus Andronicus **48:** 264

anachronisms
Julius Caesar **7:** 331

androgyny
Antony and Cleopatra **13:** 530
As You Like It **23:** 98, 100, 122, 138, 143, 144; **34:** 172, 177; **46:** 134; **57:** 13
Romeo and Juliet **13:** 530

anti-Catholic rhetoric
King John **22:** 120; **25:** 98

anti-romantic elements
As You Like It **34:** 72

antithetical or contradictory elements
Macbeth **3:** 185, 213, 271, 302; **25:** 235; **29:** 76, 127; **47:** 41

anxiety
Romeo and Juliet **13:** 235

appearance, perception, and illusion
A Midsummer Night's Dream **3:** 368, 411, 425, 427, 434, 447, 459, 466, 474, 477, 486, 497, 516; **19:** 21; **22:** 39; **28:** 15; **29:** 175, 190; **45:** 136

Appearance versus Reality (Volume 34: 1, 5, 12, 23, 45, 54)
   All's Well That Ends Well **7:** 37, 76, 93; **26:** 117
   As You Like It **34:** 130, 131; **46:** 105; **57:** 35, 40
   The Comedy of Errors **34:** 194, 201
   Coriolanus **30:** 142
   Cymbeline **4:** 87, 93, 103, 162; **36:** 99; **47:** 228, 286
   Hamlet **1:** 95, 116, 166, 169, 198; **35:** 82, 126, 132, 144, 238; **44:** 248; **45:** 28
   Macbeth **3:** 241, 248; **25:** 235
   The Merchant of Venice **4:** 209, 261, 344; **12:** 65; **22:** 69
   Much Ado about Nothing **8:** 17, 18, 48, 63, 69, 73, 75, 79, 88, 95, 115; **31:** 198, 209; **55:** 259, 268
   The Taming of the Shrew **9:** 343, 350, 353, 365, 369, 370, 381, 390, 430; **12:** 416; **31:** 326; **55:** 278, 299, 334
   Timon of Athens **1:** 495, 500, 515, 523; **52:** 311, 329
   The Two Gentlemen of Verona **6:** 494, 502, 511, 519, 529, 532, 549, 560
   Twelfth Night **34:** 293, 301, 311, 316
   The Winter's Tale **7:** 429, 446, 479; **57:** 336

appetite
   Twelfth Night **1:** 563, 596, 609, 615; **52:** 57

archetypal or mythic elements
   Macbeth **16:** 317

archetypal structure
   Pericles **2:** 570, 580, 582, 584, 588; **25:** 365; **51:** 71, 79

aristocracy and aristocratic values
   As You Like It **34:** 120
   Hamlet **42:** 212
   Julius Caesar **16:** 231; **22:** 280; **30:** 379; **50:** 194, 196, 211

art and nature
   See also **nature**
   Pericles **22:** 315; **36:** 233
   The Phoenix and Turtle **10:** 7, 42

art versus nature
   See also **nature**
   As You Like It **5:** 128, 130, 148; **34:** 147; **57:** 35, 75
   The Tempest **8:** 396, 404; **29:** 278, 297, 362
   The Winter's Tale **7:** 377, 381, 397, 419, 452; **36:** 289, 318; **45:** 329; **57:** 278

artificial nature
   Love's Labour's Lost **2:** 315, 317, 324, 330; **23:** 207, 233; **54:** 234, 248, 257, 263

Athens
   Timon of Athens **27:** 223, 230

Athens and the forest, contrast between
   A Midsummer Night's Dream **3:** 381, 427, 459, 466, 497, 502; **29:** 175

assassination
   Julius Caesar **7:** 156, 161, 179, 191, 200, 221, 264, 272, 279, 284, 350; **25:** 272; **30:** 326

audience interpretation
   Julius Caesar **48:** 240

audience perception
   The Comedy of Errors **1:** 37, 50, 56; **19:** 54; **34:** 258; **54:** 136, 144
   King Lear **19:** 295; **28:** 325
   Richard II **24:** 414, 423; **39:** 295
   Pericles **42:** 352; **48:** 364

audience perception, Shakespeare's manipulation of
   The Winter's Tale **7:** 394, 429, 456, 483, 501; **13:** 417; **19:** 401, 431, 441; **25:** 339; **45:** 374

audience perspective
   All's Well That Ends Well **7:** 81, 104, 109, 116, 121

audience response
   Antony and Cleopatra **48:** 206
   Hamlet **28:** 325; **32:** 238; **35:** 167; **44:** 107
   Julius Caesar **7:** 179, 238, 253, 255, 272, 316, 320, 336, 350; **19:** 321; **48:** 240
   Macbeth **20:** 17, 400, 406; **29:** 139, 146, 155, 165; **44:** 306
   Measure for Measure **48:** 1

audience versus character perceptions
   The Two Gentlemen of Verona **6:** 499, 519, 524

authenticity
   The Phoenix and Turtle **10:** 7, 8, 16
   Sonnets **10:** 153, 154, 230, 243; **48:** 325

Authorship Controversy (Volume 41: 2, 5, 18, 32, 42, 48, 57, 61, 63, 66, 76, 81, 85, 98, 110)
   Cymbeline **4:** 17, 21, 35, 48, 56, 78
   Henry VI, Parts 1, 2, and 3 **3:** 16, 18, 19, 20, 21, 26, 27, 29, 31, 35, 39, 41, 55, 66; **24:** 51; **56:** 77
   Henry VIII **2:** 16, 18, 19, 22, 23, 27, 28, 31, 35, 36, 42, 43, 44, 46, 48, 51, 58, 64, 68; **41:** 129, 146, 158, 171
   Love's Labour's Lost **2:** 299, 300; **32:** 308
   Pericles **2:** 538, 540, 543, 544, 545, 546, 548, 550, 551, 553, 556, 558, 564, 565, 568, 576, 586; **15:** 132, 141, 148, 152; **16:** 391, 399; **25:** 365; **36:** 198, 244
   Timon of Athens **1:** 464, 466, 467, 469, 474, 477, 478, 480, 490, 499, 507, 518; **16:** 351; **20:** 433
   Titus Andronicus **4:** 613, 614, 615, 616, 617, 619, 623, 624, 625, 626, 628, 631, 632, 635, 642
   The Two Gentlemen of Verona **6:** 435, 436, 437, 438, 439, 449, 466, 476
   The Two Noble Kinsmen
     Shakespeare not a co-author **9:** 445, 447, 455, 461
     Shakespearean portions of the text **9:** 446, 447, 448, 455, 456, 457, 460, 462, 463, 471, 479, 486; **41:** 308, 317, 355

     Shakespeare's part in the overall conception or design **9:** 444, 446, 448, 456, 457, 460, 480, 481, 486, 490; **37:** 313; **41:** 326; **50:** 326

autobiographical elements
   As You Like It **5:** 25, 35, 43, 50, 55, 61
   The Comedy of Errors **1:** 16, 18
   Cymbeline **4:** 43, 46; **36:** 134
   Hamlet **1:** 98, 115, 119; **13:** 487
   Henry VI, Parts 1, 2, and 3 **3:** 41, 55
   King John **9:** 209, 218, 245, 248, 260, 292
   King Lear **2:** 131, 136, 149, 165
   Measure for Measure **2:** 406, 410, 414, 431, 434, 437
   A Midsummer Night's Dream **3:** 365, 371, 379, 381, 389, 391, 396, 402, 432
   Othello **4:** 440, 444
   Pericles **2:** 551, 554, 555, 563, 581
   The Phoenix and Turtle **10:** 14, 18, 42, 48; **51:** 155
   Sonnets **10:** 159, 160, 166, 167, 175, 176, 182, 196, 205, 213, 215, 226, 233, 238, 240, 251, 279, 283, 302, 309, 325, 337, 377; **13:** 487; **16:** 461; **28:** 363, 385; **42:** 296; **48:** 325
   The Tempest **8:** 302, 308, 312, 324, 326, 345, 348, 353, 364, 380
   Timon of Athens **1:** 462, 467, 470, 473, 474, 478, 480; **27:** 166, 175
   Titus Andronicus **4:** 619, 624, 625, 664
   Troilus and Cressida **3:** 548, 554, 557, 558, 574, 606, 630
   Twelfth Night **1:** 557, 561, 599; **34:** 338
   The Winter's Tale **7:** 395, 397, 410, 419

avarice
   The Merry Wives of Windsor **5:** 335, 353, 369, 376, 390, 395, 402

battle of Agincourt
   Henry V **5:** 197, 199, 213, 246, 257, 281, 287, 289, 293, 310, 318; **19:** 217; **30:** 181

battle of the sexes
   Much Ado about Nothing **8:** 14, 16, 19, 48, 91, 95, 111, 121, 125; **31:** 231, 245; **55:** 199

bawdy elements
   As You Like It **46:** 122
   Cymbeline **36:** 155

bear-baiting
   Twelfth Night **19:** 42

beauty
   Sonnets **10:** 247; **51:** 288
   Venus and Adonis **10:** 420, 423, 427, 434, 454, 480; **33:** 330, 352

bed-trick
   All's Well That Ends Well **7:** 8, 26, 27, 29, 32, 41, 86, 93, 98, 113, 116, 126; **13:** 84; **26:** 117; **28:** 38; **38:** 65, 118; **49:** 46; **54:** 52; **55:** 109, 131, 176
   Measure for Measure **13:** 84; **49:** 313; **54:** 52

Beginnings and Endings in Shakespeare's Works (Volume **54**: 2, 6, 19, 24, 30, 35, 39, 43, 52, 58, 65, 75, 84, 96, 103, 110, 114, 119, 125)
 All's Well That Ends Well **54**: 30, 52
 Antony and Cleopatra **54**: 6
 Coriolanus **54**: 6
 Hamlet **54**: 2, 6, 19, 96
 Henry VIII **54**: 35
 Julius Caesar **54**: 6
 King Lear **54**: 2, 6, 103, 110, 114
 Love's Labour's Lost **54**: 58
 Macbeth **54**: 2, 6, 84
 Measure for Measure **54**: 52, 65
 The Merchant of Venice **54**: 52, 65
 Othello **54**: 2, 6, 119
 Pericles **54**: 35
 Romeo and Juliet **54**: 6, 125
 Richard III **54**: 84
 The Taming of the Shrew **54**: 58, 65
 The Tempest **54**: 19
 Troilus and Cressida **54**: 84
 Twelfth Night **54**: 19
 The Two Gentlemen of Verona **54**:
 The Two Noble Kinsmen **54**: 35

Biblical references
 Henry IV, Parts 1 and 2 **57**: 147

bird imagery
 The Phoenix and Turtle **10**: 21, 27; **38**: 329, 350, 367; **51**: 145, 181, 184

body, role of
 Troilus and Cressida **42**: 66

body politic, metaphor of
 Coriolanus **22**: 248; **30**: 67, 96, 105, 125; **50**: 105, 110, 119, 140, 145, 152

bonding
 The Merchant of Venice **4**: 293, 317, 336; **13**: 37

British nationalism
 See also **nationalism and patriotism**
 Cymbeline **4**: 19, 78, 89, 93, 129, 141, 159, 167; **32**: 373; **36**: 129; **45**: 6; **47**: 219, 265

brutal elements
 A Midsummer Night's Dream **3**: 445, 491, 497, 511; **12**: 259, 262, 298; **16**: 34; **19**: 21; **29**: 183, 225, 263, 269; **45**: 169

Cade scenes
 Henry VI, Parts 1, 2, and 3 **50**: 45, 51; **56**: 117, 122, 131, 180

Caesarism
 Julius Caesar **7**: 159, 160, 161, 167, 169, 174, 191, 205, 218, 253, 310; **30**: 316, 321; **50**: 196, 234

Calvinist implications
 Hamlet **48**: 195

capriciousness of the young lovers
 A Midsummer Night's Dream **3**: 372, 395, 402, 411, 423, 437, 441, 450, 497, 498; **29**: 175, 269; **45**: 107

caricature
 The Merry Wives of Windsor **5**: 343, 347, 348, 350, 385, 397

carnival elements
 Henry IV, Parts 1 and 2 **28**: 203; **32**: 103
 Henry VI, Parts 1, 2, and 3 **22**: 156
 Richard II **19**: 151; **39**: 273

casket scenes
 The Merchant of Venice **49**: 27

Catholic components
 Henry IV, Parts 1 and 2 **57**: 167

censorship
 Richard II **24**: 260, 261, 262, 263, 386; **42**: 118; **52**: 141, 144

ceremonies, rites, and rituals, importance of
 See also **pageantry**
 Coriolanus **9**: 139, 148, 169
 Hamlet **13**: 268; **28**: 232
 Julius Caesar **7**: 150, 210, 255, 259, 268, 284, 316, 331, 339, 356; **13**: 260; **22**: 137; **30**: 374; **50**: 258, 269,
 Richard II **6**: 270, 294, 315, 368, 381, 397, 409, 414; **24**: 274, 356, 411, 414, 419
 Titus Andronicus **27**: 261; **32**: 265; **48**: 264
 The Two Noble Kinsmen **9**: 492, 498

change
 Henry VIII **2**: 27, 65, 72, 81

characterization
 As You Like It **5**: 19, 24, 25, 36, 39, 54, 82, 86, 116, 148; **34**: 72; **48**: 42
 The Comedy of Errors **1**: 13, 21, 31, 34, 46, 49, 50, 55, 56; **19**: 54; **25**: 63; **34**: 194, 201, 208, 245; **54**: 144, 176
 Henry IV, Parts 1 and 2 **1**: 321, 328, 332, 333, 336, 344, 365, 383, 385, 389, 391, 397, 401; **19**: 195; **39**: 123, 137; **42**: 99, 162; **49**: 93; **57**: 88, 120, 156, 167, 181
 Henry V **5**: 186, 189, 192, 193, 199, 219, 230, 233, 252, 276, 293; **30**: 227, 278; **42**: 162
 Henry VI, Parts 1, 2, and 3 **3**: 18, 20, 24, 25, 31, 57, 64, 73, 77, 109, 119, 151; **24**: 22, 28, 38, 42, 45, 47; **39**: 160; **47**: 32;
 Henry VIII **2**: 17, 23, 25, 32, 35, 39; **24**: 106
 King John **9**: 222, 224, 229, 240, 250, 292; **41**: 205, 215; **56**: 365
 King Lear **2**: 108, 125, 145, 162, 191; **16**: 311; **28**: 223; **46**: 177, 210
 Love's Labour's Lost **2**: 303, 310, 317, 322, 328, 342; **23**: 237, 250, 252; **38**: 232; **47**: 35
 Macbeth **20**: 12, 318, 324, 329, 353, 363, 367, 374, 387; **28**: 339; **29**: 101, 109, 146, 155, 165; **45**: 67; **47**: 41; **57**: 189, 194, 236, 256, 263, 267
 Measure for Measure **2**: 388, 390, 391, 396, 406, 420, 421, 446, 466, 475, 484, 505, 516, 524; **23**: 299, 405; **33**:
 The Merry Wives of Windsor **5**: 332, 334, 335, 337, 338, 351, 360, 363, 366, 374, 379, 392; **18**: 74, 75; **38**: 264, 273, 313, 319
 The Tempest **8**: 287, 289, 292, 294, 295, 308, 326, 334, 336; **28**: 415; **42**: 332; **45**: 219
 Titus Andronicus **4**: 613, 628, 632, 635, 640, 644, 647, 650, 675; **27**: 293; **43**: 170, 176,;
 Troilus and Cressida **3**: 538, 539, 540, 541, 548, 566, 571, 604, 611, 621; **27**: 381, 391
 Twelfth Night **1**: 539, 540, 543, 545, 550, 554, 581, 594; **26**: 257, 337, 342, 346, 364, 366, 371, 374; **34**: 281, 293, 311, 338; **46**: 286, 324
 The Two Gentlemen of Verona **6**: 438, 442, 445, 447, 449, 458, 462, 560; **12**: 458; **40**: 312, 327, 330, 365; **54**: 338
 The Two Noble Kinsmen **9**: 457, 461, 471, 474; **41**: 340, 385; **50**: 305, 326
 The Winter's Tale **47**: 25

chastity
 A Midsummer Night's Dream **45**: 143

Chaucer's Criseyde, compared with
 Troilus and Cressida **43**: 305

chivalry
 Troilus and Cressida **16**: 84; **27**: 370, 374
 The Two Noble Kinsmen **50**: 305, 348

Christian elements
 See also **religious, mythic, or spiritual content**
 As You Like It **5**: 39, 98, 162; **57**: 31
 Coriolanus **30**: 111
 King Lear **2**: 137, 170, 179, 188, 191, 197, 207, 218, 222, 226, 229, 238, 249, 265, 286; **22**: 233, 271; **25**: 218; **46**: 276; **52**: 95
 Macbeth **3**: 194, 239, 260, 269, 275, 286, 293, 297, 318; **20**: 203, 206, 210, 256, 262, 289, 291, 294; **44**: 341, 366; **47**: 41; **57**: 236
 Measure for Measure **2**: 391, 394, 399, 421, 437, 449, 466, 479, 491, 511, 522; **48**: 1; **49**: 325
 The Merchant of Venice **52**: 89
 Much Ado about Nothing **8**: 17, 19, 29, 55, 95, 104, 111, 115; **31**: 209; **55**: 228
 The Phoenix and Turtle **10**: 21, 24, 31; **38**: 326; **51**: 162, 171, 181
 The Rape of Lucrece **10**: 77, 80, 89, 96, 98, 109
 Sonnets **10**: 191, 256
 Titus Andronicus **4**: 656, 680
 Twelfth Night **46**: 338
 The Two Gentlemen of Verona **6**: 438, 494, 514, 532, 555, 564
 The Winter's Tale **7**: 381, 387, 402, 410, 417, 419, 425, 429, 436, 452, 460, 501; **36**: 318

as Christian play
 King Lear **48**: 222

Chorus, role of
 Henry V **49**: 194, 200, 211, 219, 260

church versus state
   King John **9:** 209, 212, 222, 235, 240; **22:** 120

civilization versus barbarism
   Titus Andronicus **4:** 653; **27:** 293; **28:** 249; **32:** 265

Clarissa, (Samuel Richardson), compared with
   King Lear **48:** 277
   Measure for Measure **48:** 277
   Othello **48:** 277
   Titus Andronicus **48:** 277

class distinctions, conflict, and relations
   General Commentary **50:** 1, 34
   Henry V **28:** 146
   Henry VI, Parts 1, 2, and 3 **37:** 97; **39:** 187; **50:** 45, 51; **56:** 117, 131
   The Merry Wives of Windsor **5:** 338, 343, 346, 347, 366, 390, 395, 400, 402; **22:** 93; **28:** 69
   A Midsummer Night's Dream **22:** 23; **25:** 36; **45:** 160; **50:** 74, 86
   The Taming of the Shrew **31:** 300, 351; **50:** 64, 74; **55:** 342
   The Two Noble Kinsmen **50:** 295, 305, 310

classical influence and sources
   The Comedy of Errors **1:** 13, 14, 16, 31, 32, 43, 61; **54:** 169
   The Tempest **29:** 278, 343, 362, 368

Clowns and Fools in Shakespeare's Works (Volume **46:** 1, 14, 18, 24, 29, 33, 48, 52, 60)
   As You Like It **5:** 24, 28, 30, 32, 36, 39, 54, 61, 63, 72, 75, 76, 77, 79, 84, 86, 93, 98, 114, 118, 135, 138, 166; **23:**; **152;** **34:** 72, 85, 147, 161; **46:** 88, 105, 117, 122
   King Lear **2:** 108, 112, 125, 156, 162, 245, 278, 284; **11:** 17, 158, 169; **22:** 227; **25:** 202; **28:** 223; **46:** 191, 205, 210, 218, 225
   Twelfth Night **1:** 543, 548, 558, 561, 563, 566, 570, 572, 603, 620, 642, 655, 658; **26:** 233, 364; **46:** 297, 303, 310

colonialism
   Henry V **22:** 103
   A Midsummer Night's Dream **53:** 32
   The Tempest **13:** 424, 440; **15:** 228, 268, 269, 270, 271, 272, 273; **19:** 421; **25:** 357, 382; **28:** 249; **29:** 343, 368; **32:** 338, 367, 400; **42:** 320; **45:** 200, 280; **53:** 11, 21, 45, 67

combat
   King Lear **22:** 365
   Macbeth **22:** 365

comedy of affectation
   Love's Labour's Lost **2:** 302, 303, 304; **23:** 191, 224, 226, 228, 233

comic and tragic elements, combination of
   King Lear **2:** 108, 110, 112, 125, 156, 162, 245, 278, 284; **46:** 191
   Measure for Measure **16:** 102
   Romeo and Juliet **5:** 496, 524, 528, 547, 559; **46:** 78
   Troilus and Cressida **43:** 351

comic and farcical elements
   All's Well That Ends Well **26:** 97, 114; **48:** 65; **55:** 148, 154, 164
   Antony and Cleopatra **6:** 52, 85, 104, 125, 131, 151, 192, 202, 219; **47:** 77, 124, 149, 165
   The Comedy of Errors **1:** 14, 16, 19, 23, 30, 34, 35, 43, 46, 50, 55, 56, 59, 61; **19:** 54; **26:** 183, 186, 188, 190; **34:** 190, 245; **54:** 136, 144, 189
   Coriolanus **9:** 8, 9, 14, 53, 80, 106
   Cymbeline **4:** 35, 56, 113, 141; **15:** 111, 122; **47:** 296
   Henry IV, Parts 1 and 2 **1:** 286, 290, 314, 327, 328, 336, 353; **19:** 195; **25:** 109; **39:** 72; **57:** 120
   Henry V **5:** 185, 188, 191, 192, 217, 230, 233, 241, 252, 260, 276; **19:** 217; **28:** 121; **30:** 193, 202
   The Merry Wives of Windsor **5:** 336, 338, 346, 350, 360, 369, 373; **18:** 74, 75, 84
   Richard II **24:** 262, 263, 395; **39:** 243
   Twelfth Night **26:** 233, 257, 337, 342, 371; **51:** 1; **52:** 57
   Venus and Adonis **10:** 429, 434, 439, 442, 459, 462, 489; **33:** 352; **51:** 377

comic form
   As You Like It **46:** 105; **51:** 1; **57:** 2
   Love's Labour' Lost **54:** 257, 263
   Measure for Measure **2:** 456, 460, 479, 482, 491, 514, 516; **13:** 94, 104; **23:** 309, 326, 327; **49:** 349

comic resolution
   As You Like It **52:** 63
   Love's Labour's Lost **2:** 335, 340; **16:** 17; **19:** 92; **38:** 209; **51:** 1; **54:** 240, 248, 274

comic, tragic, and romantic elements, fusion of
   The Winter's Tale **7:** 390, 394, 396, 399, 410, 412, 414, 429, 436, 479, 483, 490, 501; **13:** 417; **15:** 514, 524, 532; **25:** 339; **36:** 295, 380; **57:** 347

commodity
   King John **9:** 224, 229, 245, 260, 275, 280, 297; **19:** 182; **25:** 98; **41:** 228, 269; **56:** 335

communication, failure of
   Troilus and Cressida **43:** 277

compassion, theme of
   The Tempest **42:** 339

complex or enigmatic nature
   The Phoenix and Turtle **10:** 7, 14, 35, 42; **38:** 326, 357; **51:** 145, 162

composition date
   The Comedy of Errors **1:** 18, 23, 34, 55
   Henry VIII **2:** 19, 22, 35; **24:** 129
   Pericles **2:** 537, 544

Sonnets **10:** 153, 154, 161, 166, 196, 217, 226, 270, 277; **28:** 363, 385
   Twelfth Night **37:** 78

conclusion
   All's Well That Ends Well **38:** 123, 132, 142; **55:** 148, 154, 170
   Love's Labour's Lost **38:** 172; **54:** 240, 248, 274
   Troilus and Cressida **3:** 538, 549, 558, 566, 574, 583, 594
   comedy vs. tragedy **43:** 351

conflict between Christianity and Judaism
   The Merchant of Venice **4:** 224, 250, 268, 289, 324, 344; **12:** 67, 70, 72, 76; **22:** 69; **25:** 257; **40:** 117, 127, 166, 181; **48:** 54, 77; **53:** 105, 159, 214

conscience
   Macbeth **52:** 15
   Richard III **8:** 148, 152, 162, 165, 190, 197, 201, 206, 210, 228, 232, 239, 243, 252, 258; **39:** 341; **52:** 5, 196, 205

as consciously philosophical
   The Phoenix and Turtle **10:** 7, 21, 24, 31, 48; **38:** 342, 378

conspiracy or treason
   The Tempest **16:** 426; **19:** 357; **25:** 382; **29:** 377
   Henry V **49:** 223

constancy and faithfulness
   The Phoenix and Turtle **10:** 18, 20, 21, 48; **38:** 329

construing the truth
   Julius Caesar **7:** 320, 336, 343, 350; **37:** 229

consummation of marriage
   Othello **22:** 207

contemptus mundi
   Antony and Cleopatra **6:** 85, 133

contractual and economic relations
   Henry IV, Parts 1 and 2 **13:** 213
   Richard II **13:** 213; **49:** 602

contradiction, paradox, and opposition
   As You Like It **46:** 105
   Romeo and Juliet **5:** 421, 427, 431, 496, 509, 513, 516, 520, 525, 528, 538; **33:** 287; **44:** 11
   Troilus and Cressida **43:** 377

contrasting dramatic worlds
   Henry IV, Parts 1 and 2 **14:** 56, 60, 61, 84, 105; **48:** 95; **49:** 162; **57:** 183
   The Merchant of Venice **44:** 11

contrasts and oppositions
   Othello **4:** 421, 455, 457, 462, 508; **25:** 189

corruption in society
   As You Like It **46:** 94; **57:** 35
   King John **9:** 222, 234, 280, 297

costume
As You Like It **46**: 117
Hamlet **21**: 81
Henry VIII **24**: 82, 87; **28**: 184
Richard II **24**: 274, 278, 291, 304, 325, 356, 364, 423
Romeo and Juliet **11**: 505, 509
Troilus and Cressida **18**: 289, 371, 406, 419

counsel
The Winter's Tale **19**: 401

Court of Love
The Phoenix and Turtle **10**: 9, 24, 50

court society
The Winter's Tale **16**: 410; **57**: 305, 336

courtly love
Troilus and Cressida **22**: 58

courtly love tradition, influence of
Romeo and Juliet **5**: 505, 542, 575; **33**: 233

courtship and marriage
See also **marriage**
As You Like It **34**: 109, 177; **48**: 32; **51**: 44
Much Ado about Nothing **8**: 29, 44, 48, 95, 115, 121, 125; **31**: 191, 231; **51**: 33, 44; **55**: 209

credibility
Twelfth Night **1**: 540, 542, 543, 554, 562, 581, 587

critical history
Henry IV, Parts 1 and 2 **42**: 185; **48**: 167

cynicism
Troilus and Cressida **43**: 298

dance
Henry VI, Parts 1, 2, and 3 **22**: 156

dance and patterned action
Love's Labour's Lost **2**: 308, 342; **23**: 191, 237

dark elements
All's Well That Ends Well **7**: 27, 37, 39, 43, 54, 109, 113, 116; **26**: 85; **48**: 65; **50**: 59; **54**: 30; **55**: 164, 170
Twelfth Night **46**: 310

death, decay, nature's destructiveness
Antony and Cleopatra **47**: 71
As You Like It **46**: 169
Hamlet **1**: 144, 153, 188, 198, 221, 242; **13**: 502; **28**: 280, 311; **35**: 241; **42**: 279
King Lear **2**: 93, 94, 101, 104, 106, 109, 112, 116, 129, 131, 137, 143, 147, 149, 156, 160, 170, 179, 188, 197, 207, 218, 222, 226, 231, 238, 241, 245, 249, 253, 265, 269, 273; **16**: 301; **25**: 202, 218; **31**: 77, 117, 137, 142; **46**: 264
Love's Labour's Lost **2**: 305, 331, 344, 348
Measure for Measure **2**: 394, 452, 516; **25**: 12; **49**: 370
Venus and Adonis **10**: 419, 427, 434, 451, 454, 462, 466, 473, 480, 489; **25**: 305; **33**: 309, 321, 347, 352, 363, 370

decay of heroic ideals
Henry VI, Parts 1, 2, and 3 **3**: 119, 126; **56**: 95

deception, disguise, and duplicity
As You Like It **46**: 134; **57**: 40, 45
Henry IV, Parts 1 and 2 **1**: 397, 406, 425; **42**: 99; **47**: 1, 60; **48**: 95
The Merry Wives of Windsor **5**: 332, 334, 336, 354, 355, 379; **22**: 93; **47**: 308, 314, 321, 325, 344
Much Ado about Nothing **8**: 29, 55, 63, 69, 79, 82, 88, 108, 115; **31**: 191, 198; **55**: 236
Sonnets **25**: 374; **40**: 221
The Taming of the Shrew **12**: 416

Deconstructionist interpretation of
Pericles **48**: 364

deposition scene
Richard II **42**: 118

Desire (Volume 38: 1, 19, 31, 40, 48, 56)
All's Well That Ends Well **38**: 96, 99, 109, 118; **55**: 122
As You Like It **37**: 43; **52**: 63
Love's Labour's Lost **38**: 185, 194, 200, 209
The Merchant of Venice **22**: 3; **40**: 142; **45**: 17
The Merry Wives of Windsor **38**: 286, 297, 300
Romeo and Juliet **51**: 227, 236
Troilus and Cressida **43**: 317, 329, 340

disappointment, theme of
The Merchant of Venice **53**: 211

discrepancy between prophetic ending and preceding action
Henry VIII **2**: 22, 25, 31, 46, 49, 56, 60, 65, 68, 75, 81; **32**: 148; **41**: 190; **56**: 273

disillusioned or cynical tone
Troilus and Cressida **3**: 544, 548, 554, 557, 558, 571, 574, 630, 642; **18**: 284, 332, 403, 406, 423; **27**: 376

disorder
Troilus and Cressida **3**: 578, 589, 599, 604, 609; **18**: 332, 406, 412, 423; **27**: 366; **54**: 84; **55**: 48

disorder and civil dissension
Henry VI, Parts 1, 2, and 3 **3**: 59, 67, 76, 92, 103, 126; **13**: 131; **16**: 183; **24**: 11, 17, 28, 31, 47; **25**: 102; **28**: 112; **39**: 154, 177, 187, 196, 205; **56**: 80, 110

displacement
All's Well That Ends Well **22**: 78
Measure for Measure **22**: 78

divine right versus justice
Henry IV **49**: 116; **57**: 88, 130

divine vs. worldly
King Lear **49**: 1

divine will, role of
Romeo and Juliet **5**: 485, 493, 505, 533, 573

domestic elements
As You Like It **46**: 142
Coriolanus **42**: 218; **50**: 145
Venus and Adonis **51**: 359

double-plot
King Lear **2**: 94, 95, 100, 101, 104, 112, 116, 124, 131, 133, 156, 253, 257; **46**: 254
Troilus and Cressida **3**: 569, 613

doubling of roles
Pericles **15**: 150, 152, 167, 173, 180

dramatic elements
Sonnets **10**: 155, 182, 240, 251, 283, 367
Venus and Adonis **10**: 459, 462, 486

dramatic shortcomings or failure
As You Like It **5**: 19, 42, 52, 61, 65
Love's Labour's Lost **2**: 299, 301, 303, 322; **54**: 240, 248
Romeo and Juliet **5**: 416, 418, 420, 426, 436, 437, 448, 464, 467, 469, 480, 487, 524, 562

dramatic structure
The Comedy of Errors **1**: 19, 27, 40, 43, 46, 50; **26**: 186, 190; **34**: 190, 229, 233; **37**: 12 **54**: 136, 155, 189
Cymbeline **4**: 17, 18, 19, 20, 21, 22, 24, 38, 43, 48, 53, 64, 68, 89, 116, 129, 141; **22**: 302, 365; **25**: 319; **36**: 115, 125
Othello **4**: 370, 390, 399, 427, 488, 506, 517, 569; **22**: 207; **28**: 243; **53**: 261
The Winter's Tale **7**: 382, 390, 396, 399, 402, 407, 414, 429, 432, 473, 479, 493, 497, 501; **15**: 528; **25**: 339; **36**: 289, 295, 362, 380; **45**: 297, 344, 358, 366; **57**: 278, 285, 347,

as dream-play
A Midsummer Night's Dream **3**: 365, 370, 372, 377, 389, 391; **29**: 190; **45**: 117

Dreams in Shakespeare (Volume 45: 1, 10, 17, 28, 40, 48, 58, 67, 75)
Antony and Cleopatra **45**: 28
Cymbeline **4**: 162, 167; **44**: 28; **45**: 67, 75
Hamlet **45**: 28
Julius Caesar **45**: 10
A Midsummer Night's Dream **45**: 96, 107, 117
Romeo and Juliet **45**: 40
The Tempest **45**: 236, 247, 259

dualisms
Antony and Cleopatra **19**: 304; **27**: 82
Cymbeline **4**: 29, 64, 73

duration of time
As You Like It **5**: 44, 45
A Midsummer Night's Dream **3**: 362, 370, 380, 386, 494; **45**: 175

economic relations
  Henry V **13:** 213

economics and exchange
  Coriolanus **50:** 152
  The Merchant of Venice **40:** 197, 208; **53:** 116

editorial and textual issues
  Sonnets **28:** 363; **40:** 273; **42:** 296

education
  All's Well That Ends Well **7:** 62, 86, 90, 93, 98, 104, 116, 126
  The Two Gentlemen of Verona **6:** 490, 494, 504, 526, 532, 555, 568

education or nurturing
  The Tempest **8:** 353, 370, 384, 396; **29:** 292, 368, 377

egotism or narcissism
  Much Ado about Nothing **8:** 19, 24, 28, 29, 55, 69, 95, 115; **55:** 209

Elizabeth, audience of
  Sonnets **48:** 325

Elizabeth's influence
  The Merry Wives of Windsor **5:** 333, 334, 335, 336, 339, 346, 355, 366, 402; **18:** 5, 86; **38:** 278; **47:** 344

Elizabethan and Jacobean politics, relation to
  Hamlet **28:** 232; **28:** 290, 311; **35:** 140

Elizabethan attitudes, influence of
  Richard II **6:** 287, 292, 294, 305, 321, 327, 364, 402, 414; **13:** 494; **24:** 325; **28:** 188; **39:** 273; **42:** 118; **52:** 141, 144

Elizabethan betrothal and marriage customs
  Measure for Measure **2:** 429, 437, 443, 503; **49:** 286

Elizabethan culture, relation to
  General Commentary **50:** 34; **53:** 169; **56:** 2, 3, 15, 47
  Antony and Cleopatra **47:** 103
  As You Like It **5:** 21, 59, 66, 68, 70, 158; **16:** 53; **28:** 46; **34:** 120; **37:** 1; **46:** 142; **57:** 23, 31, 64, 75
  The Comedy of Errors **26:** 138, 142; **34:** 201, 215, 233, 238, 258; **42:** 80; **54:** 169, 200
  Hamlet **1:** 76, 148, 151, 154, 160, 166, 169, 171, 176, 184, 202, 209, 254; **13:** 282, 494; **19:** 330; **21:** 407, 416; **22:** 258
  Henry IV, Parts 1 and 2 **19:** 195; **48:** 117, 143, 151, 175
  Henry V **5:** 210, 213, 217, 223, 257, 299, 310; **16:** 202; **19:** 133, 233; **28:** 121, 159; **30:** 215, 262; **37:** 187; **49:** 260
  Julius Caesar **16:** 231; **30:** 342, 379; **50:** 13, 211, 269, 280
  King Lear **2:** 168, 174, 177, 183, 226, 241; **19:** 330; **22:** 227, 233, 365; **25:** 218; **46:** 276; **47:** 9; **49:** 67

Measure for Measure **2:** 394, 418, 429, 432, 437, 460, 470, 482, 503
The Merchant of Venice **32:** 66; **40:** 117, 127, 142, 166, 181, 197, 208; **48:** 54, 77; **49:** 37; **53:** 105, 111, 116, 127, 159
A Midsummer Night's Dream **50:** 86
Much Ado about Nothing **8:** 23, 33, 44, 55, 58, 79, 88, 104, 111, 115; **51:** 15; **55:** 209, 241, 259
The Rape of Lucrece **33:** 195; **43:** 77
The Taming of the Shrew **31:** 288, 295, 300, 315, 326, 345, 351; **55:** 315, 322, 334
Timon of Athens **1:** 487, 489, 495, 500; **20:** 433; **27:** 203, 212, 230; **50:** 13; **52:** 320, 354
Titus Andronicus **27:** 282
Troilus and Cressida **3:** 560, 574, 606; **25:** 56
Twelfth Night **1:** 549, 553, 555, 563, 581, 587, 620; **16:** 53; **19:** 42, 78; **26:** 357; **28:** 1; **34:** 323, 330; **46:** 291; **51:** 15

Elizabethan dramatic conventions
  Cymbeline **4:** 53, 124
  Henry VIII **24:** 155; **56:** 196, 248

Elizabethan literary influences
  Henry VI, Parts 1, 2, and 3 **3:** 75, 97, 100, 119, 143; **22:** 156; **28:** 112; **37:** 97; **56:** 162, 180

Elizabethan love poetry
  Love's Labour's Lost **38:** 232

Elizabethan poetics, influence of
  Romeo and Juliet **5:** 416, 520, 522, 528, 550, 559, 575

Elizabethan politics, relation to
  Henry IV, Parts 1 and 2 **22:** 395; **28:** 203; **47:** 60; **48:** 117, 143, 167, 175; **57:** 88, 94
  Henry VIII **22:** 395; **24:** 115, 129, 140; **32:** 148; **56:** 201, 248
  King John **48:** 132; **56:** 306, 314, 325
  Richard III **22:** 395; **25:** 141; **37:** 144; **39:** 345, 349; **42:** 130; **52:** 201, 214, 257

Elizabethan setting
  The Two Gentlemen of Verona **12:** 463, 485

Elizabethan society
  The Merry Wives of Windsor **47:** 331

Epicureanism 50: 249

emulation or rivalry
  Julius Caesar **16:** 231; **50:** 211

England and Rome, parallels between
  Coriolanus **9:** 39, 43, 106, 148, 180, 193; **25:** 296; **30:** 67, 105

English language and colonialism
  Henry V **22:** 103; **28:** 159

English Reformation, influence of
  Henry VIII **2:** 25, 35, 39, 51, 67; **24:** 89; **56:** 201

epic elements
  Henry V **5:** 192, 197, 246, 257, 314; **30:** 181, 220, 237, 252

erotic elements
  A Midsummer Night's Dream **3:** 445, 491, 497, 511; **12:** 259, 262, 298; **16:** 34; **19:** 21; **29:** 183, 225, 269
  Venus and Adonis **10:** 410, 411, 418, 419, 427, 428, 429, 442, 448, 454, 459, 466, 473; **25:** 305, 328; **28:** 355; **33:** 321, 339, 347, 352, 363, 370; **51:** 345, 352, 359, 368

as experimental play
  Romeo and Juliet **5:** 464, 509, 528

Essex Rebellion, relation to
  Richard II **6:** 249, 250; **24:** 356

ethical or moral issues
  King John **9:** 212, 222, 224, 229, 235, 240, 263, 275, 280; **56:** 335
  King Lear **52:** 1, 95;
  Measure for Measure **52:** 69
  Twelfth Night **52:** 57

ethnicity
  The Winter's Tale **37:** 306

Euripides, influence of
  Titus Andronicus **27:** 285

evil
  See also **good versus evil**
  Macbeth **3:** 194, 208, 231, 234, 239, 241, 267, 289; **20:** 203, 206, 210, 374; **52:** 23; **57:** 267
  Othello **52:** 78
  Richard III **52:** 78
  Romeo and Juliet **5:** 485, 493, 505
  Titus Andronicus **53:** 86, 92

excess
  King John **9:** 251

fable of the belly
  Coriolanus **50:** 13, 110, 140

fame
  Coriolanus **30:** 58

family honor, structure, and inheritance
  Richard II **6:** 338, 368, 388, 397, 414; **39:** 263, 279
  Richard III **8:** 177, 248, 252, 263, 267; **25:** 141; **39:** 335, 341, 349, 370

family, theme of
  Cymbeline **44:** 28

fancy
  Twelfth Night **1:** 543, 546

as farce
  The Taming of the Shrew **9:** 330, 337, 338, 341, 342, 365, 381, 386, 413, 426; **55:** 357

farcical elements
See **comic and farcical elements**

fate
Richard II **6:** 289, 294, 304, 352, 354, 385
Romeo and Juliet **5:** 431, 444, 464, 469, 470, 479, 480, 485, 487, 493, 509, 530, 533, 562, 565, 571, 573; **33:** 249; **54:** 125

Fathers and Daughters (Volume 36: 1, 12, 25, 32, 37, 45, 70, 78)
As You Like It **46:** 94
Cymbeline **34:** 134
King Lear **34:** 51, 54, 60
  cruelty of daughters **2:** 101, 102, 106; **31:** 84, 123, 137, 142
Pericles **34:** 226, 233
The Winter's Tale **34:** 311, 318, 328

Feast of the Lupercal
Julius Caesar **50:** 269

female identity
See also **Gender Identity and Issues**
Macbeth **57:** 256

feminine power, role of
Macbeth **57:** 242

Feminist Criticism (Volume 55: 1, 16, 27, 37, 48, 56, 68, 78)
General Commentary **55:** 1, 16, 27, 56, 68, 78
As You Like It **23:** 107, 108;
Comedy of Errors **42:** 93
Hamlet **55:** 56
King Lear **55:** 68
Love's Labour's Lost **42:** 93
Measure for Measure **23:** 320; **55:** 16, 68
Merchant of Venice **55:** 27
A Midsummer Night's Dream **48:** 23
Troilus and Cressida **55:** 37, 48

feminism
As You Like It **57:** 2, 13

festive or folklore elements
Twelfth Night **46:** 338; **51:** 15

feud
Romeo and Juliet **5:** 415, 419, 425, 447, 458, 464, 469, 479, 480, 493, 509, 522, 556, 565, 566, 571, 575; **25:** 181; **51:** 245

fire and water
Coriolanus **25:** 263

flattery
Coriolanus **9:** 26, 45, 92, 100, 110, 121, 130, 144, 157, 183, 193; **25:** 296
Henry IV, Parts 1 and 2 **22:** 395
Henry VIII **22:** 395
Richard III **22:** 395

folk drama, relation to
The Winter's Tale **7:** 420, 451; **57:** 356

folk elements
The Taming of the Shrew **9:** 381, 393, 404, 426

folk rituals, elements and influence of
Henry VI, Parts 1, 2, and 3 **39:** 205
The Merry Wives of Windsor **5:** 353, 369, 376, 392, 397, 400; **38:** 256, 300

food, meaning of
The Comedy of Errors **34:** 220
Troilus and Cressida **43:** 298

forest
The Two Gentlemen of Verona **6:** 450, 456, 492, 514, 547, 555, 564, 568

Forest of Arden
As You Like It
  as "bitter" Arcadia **5:** 98, 118, 162; **23:** 97, 98, 99, 100, 122, 139
  Duke Frederick's court, contrast with **5:** 46, 102, 103, 112, 130, 156; **16:** 53; **23:** 126, 128, 129, 131, 134; **34:** 78, 102, 131; **46:** 164; **57:** 64
  pastoral elements **5:** 18, 20, 24, 32, 35, 47, 50, 54, 55, 57, 60, 77, 128, 135, 156; **23:** 17, 20, 27, 46, 137; **34:** 78, 147; **46:** 88
  as patriarchal society **5:** 168; **23:** 150; **34:** 177; **57:** 2
  as source of self-knowledge **5:** 98, 102, 103, 128, 130, 135, 148, 158, 162; **23:** 17; **34:** 102; **57:** 35
  as timeless, mythical world **5:** 112, 130, 141; **23:** 132; **34:** 78; **37:** 43; **46:** 88
  theme of play **46:** 88

forgiveness or redemption
Henry IV, Parts 1 and 2 **57:** 116
Venus and Adonis **51:** 377
The Winter's Tale **7:** 381, 389, 395, 402, 407, 436, 456, 460, 483; **36:** 318

free will versus fate
Macbeth **3:** 177, 183, 184, 190, 196, 198, 202, 207, 208, 213; **13:** 361; **44:** 351, 361, 366, 373; **54:** 6
The Two Noble Kinsmen **9:** 474, 481, 486, 492, 498

freedom and servitude
The Tempest **8:** 304, 307, 312, 429; **22:** 302; **29:** 278, 368, 377; **37:** 336

French language, Shakespeare's use of
Henry V **5:** 186, 188, 190; **25:** 131

Freudian analysis
A Midsummer Night's Dream **44:** 1

friendship
See also **love and friendship** and **love versus friendship**
Coriolanus **30:** 125, 142
Sonnets **10:** 185, 279; **28:** 380; **51:** 284, 288
The Two Noble Kinsmen **9:** 448, 463, 470, 474, 479, 481, 486, 490; **19:** 394; **41:** 363, 372; **42:** 361

Gender Identity and Issues (Volume 40: 1, 9, 15, 27, 33, 51, 61, 65, 75, 90, 99)
All's Well That Ends Well **7:** 9, 10, 67, 126; **13:** 77, 84; **19:** 113; **26:** 128; **38:** 89, 99, 118; **44:** 35; **55:** 101, 109, 122, 164
Antony and Cleopatra **13:** 368; **25:** 257; **27:** 144; **47:** 174, 192; **53:** 67, 77
As You Like It **46:** 127, 134; **57:** 13, 23, 45
The Comedy of Errors **34:** 215, 220
Coriolanus **30:** 79, 125, 142; **44:** 93; **50:** 128
Hamlet **35:** 144; **44:** 189, 195, 198
Henry IV, Parts 1 and 2 **13:** 183; **25:** 151; **44:** 44; **48:** 175
Henry V **13:** 183; **28:** 121, 146, 159; **44:** 44
Julius Caesar **13:** 260
Macbeth **57:** 256
The Merchant of Venice **40:** 142, 151, 156
Othello **32:** 294; **35:** 327
A Midsummer Night's Dream **53:** 1
Othello **53:** 255, 268, 310
The Rape of Lucrece **53:** 1
Richard II **25:** 89; **39:** 295
Richard III **25:** 141; **37:** 144; **39:** 345; **52:** 223, 239,
Romeo and Juliet **32:** 256; **51:** 253
Sonnets **37:** 374; **40:** 238, 247, 254, 264, 268, 273; **53:** 1
The Taming of the Shrew **28:** 24; **31:** 261, 268, 276, 282, 288, 295, 300, 335, 351; **55:** 278, 299, 305, 315, 322, 357
The Tempest **53:** 64, 67
Twelfth Night **19:** 78; **34:** 344; **37:** 59; **42:** 32; **46:** 347, 362, 369
The Two Gentlemen of Verona **40:** 374
The Two Noble Kinsmen **42:** 361

genre
All's Well That Ends Well **48:** 65
As You Like It **5:** 46, 55, 79
The Comedy of Errors **34:** 251, 258
Coriolanus **9:** 42, 43, 53, 80, 106, 112, 117, 130, 164, 177; **30:** 67, 74, 79, 89, 111, 125; **50:** 99
Hamlet **1:** 176, 212, 237
Love's Labour's Lost **38:** 163
The Merchant of Venice **4:** 191, 200, 201, 209, 215, 221, 232, 238, 247; **12:** 48, 54, 62; **54:** 65
Much Ado about Nothing **8:** 9, 18, 19, 28, 29, 39, 44, 53, 63, 69, 73, 79, 82, 95, 100, 104; **48:** 14; **55:** 232, 268
Richard III **8:** 181, 182, 197, 206, 218, 228, 239, 243, 252, 258; **13:** 142; **39:** 383; **52:** 239
The Taming of the Shrew **9:** 329, 334, 362, 375; **22:** 48; **31:** 261, 269, 276; **55:** 278
Timon of Athens **1:** 454, 456, 459, 460, 462, 483, 492, 499, 503, 509, 511, 512, 515, 518, 525, 531; **27:** 203
Troilus and Cressida **3:** 541, 542, 549, 558, 566, 571, 574, 587, 594, 604, 630, 642; **27:** 366
The Two Gentlemen of Verona **6:** 460, 468, 472, 516; **40:** 320

genres, mixture of
Timon of Athens **16:** 351; **25:** 198

gift exchange
Love's Labour's Lost **25:** 1

good versus evil
See also **evil**
Measure for Measure **2:** 432, 452, 524; **33:** 52, 61; **52:** 69
The Tempest **8:** 302, 311, 315, 370, 423, 439; **29:** 278; 297

grace
The Winter's Tale **7:** 420, 425, 460, 493; **36:** 328

grace and civility
Love's Labour's Lost **2:** 351

Greece
Troilus and Cressida **43:** 287

grotesque or absurd elements
Hamlet **42:** 279
King Lear **2:** 136, 156, 245; **13:** 343; **52:** 1

handkerchief, significance of
Othello **4:** 370, 384, 385, 396, 503, 530, 562; **35:** 265, 282, 380

Hercules Furens (Seneca) as source
Othello **16:** 283

heroism
Henry V **49:** 194, 200, 211, 236

Hippolytus, myth of
A Midsummer Night's Dream **29:** 216; **45:** 84

historical accuracy
Henry VI, Parts 1, 2, and 3 **3:** 18, 21, 35, 46, 51; **16:** 217; **24:** 16, 18, 25, 31, 45, 48
Richard III **8:** 144, 145, 153, 159, 163, 165, 168, 213, 223, 228, 232; **39:** 305, 308, 326, 383

historical allegory
The Winter's Tale **7:** 381; **15:** 528
The Merchant of Venice **53:** 179, 187

historical elements
Cymbeline **47:** 260

historical and dramatic elements
Henry IV **49:** 93

historical and romantic elements, combination of
Henry VIII **2:** 46, 49, 51, 75, 76, 78; **24:** 71, 80, 146; **41:** 129, 146, 180; **56:** 196, 201

historical content
Henry IV, Parts 1 and 2 **1:** 310, 328, 365, 366, 370, 374, 380, 387, 421, 424, 427, 431; **16:** 172; **19:** 157; **25:** 151; **32:** 136; **39:** 143; **48:** 143, 167; **57:** 137
Henry V **5:** 185, 188, 190, 192, 193, 198, 246, 314; **13:** 201; **19:** 133; **25:** 131; **30:** 193, 202, 207, 215, 252

King John **9:** 216, 219, 220, 222, 235, 240, 254, 284, 290, 292, 297, 300, 303; **13:** 163; **32:** 93, 114; **41:** 234, 243; **56:** 286, 296, 306, 357
The Tempest **8:** 364, 408, 420; **16:** 426; **25:** 382; **29:** 278, 339, 343, 368; **45:** 226; **53:** 21, 53

historical determinism versus free will
Julius Caesar **7:** 160, 298, 316, 333, 346, 356; **13:** 252

historical epic, as epilogue to Shakespeare's
Henry VIII **2:** 22, 25, 27, 39, 51, 60, 65

historical epic, place in or relation to Shakespeare's
Henry IV, Parts 1 and 2 **1:** 309, 314, 328, 374, 379, 424, 427
Henry V **5:** 195, 198, 205, 212, 225, 241, 244, 287, 304, 310; **14:** 337, 342; **30:** 215
Henry VI, Parts 1, 2, and 3 **3:** 24, 59; **24:** 51; **48:** 167; **56:** 95

historical principles
Richard III **39:** 308, 326, 387

historical relativity, theme of 41: 146;
Henry VIII **56:** 220

historical revisionism 56: 85, 110, 122, 131, 145

historical sources, compared with
Richard II **6:** 252, 279, 343; **28:** 134; **39:** 235; **49:** 60

historiography
General Commentary **56:** 3, 15, 25, 47, 53, 60
Henry IV, Parts 1 and 2 **56:** 2, 15, 25
Henry V **56:** 2, 15
Henry VI, Parts 1, 2, and 3 **56:** 2, 25
Henry VIII **37:** 109, 201, 209, 230
Richard II **56:** 2, 15
Richard III **56:** 2

homoerotic elements
As You Like It **46:** 127, 142; **57:** 23
Henry V **16:** 202
Sonnets **10:** 155, 156, 159, 161, 175, 213, 391; **16:** 461; **28:** 363, 380; **37:** 347; **40:** 254, 264, 273; **51:** 270, 284

homosexuality
As You Like It **46:** 127, 142; **57:** 13
Measure for Measure **42:** 1
The Merchant of Venice **22:** 3, 69; **37:** 86; **40:** 142, 156, 197
Twelfth Night **22:** 69; **42:** 32; **46:** 362
The Winter's Tale **48:** 309

honor or integrity
Coriolanus **9:** 43, 65, 73, 92, 106, 110, 121, 144, 153, 157, 164, 177, 183, 189; **30:** 89, 96, 133

hospitality
The Winter's Tale **19:** 366

as humanistic play
Henry VI, Parts 1, 2, and 3 **3:** 83, 92, 109, 115, 119, 131, 136, 143

hunt motif
Venus and Adonis **10:** 434, 451, 466, 473; **33:** 357, 370

hypocrisy
Henry V **5:** 203, 213, 219, 223, 233, 260, 271, 302

ideal love
See also **love**
Romeo and Juliet **5:** 421, 427, 431, 436, 437, 450, 463, 469, 498, 505, 575; **25:** 257; **33:** 210, 225, 272; **51:** 25; **51:** 44, 195, 203, 219

idealism versus pragmatism
Hamlet **16:** 246; **28:** 325

idealism versus realism
See also **realism**
Love's Labour's Lost **38:** 163
Othello **4:** 457, 508, 517; **13:** 313; **25:** 189; **53:** 350

identities of persons
Sonnets **10:** 154, 155, 156, 161, 166, 167, 169, 173, 174, 175, 185, 190, 191, 196, 218, 226, 230, 233, 240; **40:** 238

identity
The Comedy of Errors **34:** 201, 208, 211; **54:** 155, 169, 200
Coriolanus **42:** 243; **50:** 128
A Midsummer Night's Dream **29:** 269
The Two Gentlemen of Verona **6:** 494, 511, 529, 532, 547, 560, 564, 568; **19:** 34

illusion
The Comedy of Errors **1:** 13, 14, 27, 37, 40, 45, 59, 63; **26:** 188; **34:** 194, 211; **54:** 169, 200

illusion versus reality
Love's Labour's Lost **2:** 303, 308, 331, 340, 344, 348, 356, 359, 367, 371, 375; **23:** 230, 231

imagery
Venus and Adonis **10:** 414, 415, 416, 420, 429, 434, 449, 459, 466, 473, 480; **25:** 328; **28:** 355; **33:** 321, 339, 352, 363, 370, 377; **42:** 347; **51:** 335, 388

imagination and art
A Midsummer Night's Dream **3:** 365, 371, 381, 402, 412, 417, 421, 423, 441, 459, 468, 506, 516, 520; **22:** 39; **45:** 96, 126, 136, 147

immortality
Measure for Measure **16:** 102

imperialism
Antony and Cleopatra **53:** 67, 77
Henry V **22:** 103; **28:** 159

The Merchant of Venice **53**: 116

implausibility of plot, characters, or events
All's Well That Ends Well **7**: 8, 45
King Lear **2**: 100, 136, 145, 278; **13**: 343
The Merchant of Venice **4**: 191, 192, 193; **12**: 52, 56, 76, 119
Much Ado about Nothing **8**: 9, 12, 16, 19, 33, 36, 39, 44, 53, 100, 104
Othello **4**: 370, 380, 391, 442, 444; **47**: 51

inaction
Troilus and Cressida **3**: 587, 621; **27**: 347

incest, motif of
Pericles **2**: 582, 588; **22**: 315; **36**: 257, 264; **51**: 97, 110

inconsistencies
Henry VIII **2**: 16, 27, 28, 31, 60

inconsistency between first and second halves
Measure for Measure **2**: 474, 475, 505, 514, 524; **49**: 349, 358

induction
The Taming of the Shrew **9**: 320, 322, 332, 337, 345, 350, 362, 365, 369, 370, 381, 390, 393, 407, 419, 424, 430; **12**: 416, 427, 430, 431, 441; **19**: 34, 122; **22**: 48; **31**: 269, 315, 351; **55**: 331, 357

as inferior or flawed play
Henry VI, Parts 1, 2, and 3 **3**: 20, 21, 25, 26, 35
Pericles **2**: 537, 546, 553, 563, 564; **15**: 139, 143, 156, 167, 176; **36**: 198; **51**: 79
Timon of Athens **1**: 476, 481, 489, 499, 520; **20**: 433, 439, 491; **25**: 198; **27**: 157, 175; **52**: 338, 349

infidelity
Troilus and Cressida **43**: 298; **55**: 37, 48

innocence
Macbeth **3**: 234, 241, 327; **57**: 267
Othello **47**: 25
Pericles **36**: 226, 274

innocence to experience
The Two Noble Kinsmen **9**: 481, 502; **19**: 394

Ireland, William Henry, forgeries of
Sonnets **48**: 325

Irish affairs
Henry V **22**: 103; **28**: 159

ironic or parodic elements
The Two Gentlemen of Verona **6**: 447, 472, 478, 484, 502, 504, 509, 516, 529, 549; **13**: 12; **54**: 295, 307
Henry VIII **41**: 129; **56**: 220

irony
All's Well That Ends Well **7**: 27, 32, 58, 62, 67, 81, 86, 109, 116

Antony and Cleopatra **6**: 53, 136, 146, 151, 159, 161, 189, 192, 211, 224
As You Like It **5**: 30, 32, 154
Coriolanus **9**: 65, 73, 80, 92, 106, 153, 157, 164, 193; **30**: 67, 89, 133
Cymbeline **4**: 64, 77, 103
Henry V **5**: 192, 210, 213, 219, 223, 226, 233, 252, 260, 269, 281, 299, 304; **14**: 336; **30**: 159, 193
Julius Caesar **7**: 167, 257, 259, 262, 268, 282, 316, 320, 333, 336, 346, 350
The Merchant of Venice **4**: 254, 300, 321, 331, 350; **28**: 63
Much Ado about Nothing **8**: 14, 63, 79, 82; **28**: 63
The Rape of Lucrece **10**: 93, 98, 128
Richard II **6**: 270, 307, 364, 368, 391; **24**: 383; **28**: 188
Sonnets **10**: 256, 293, 334, 337, 346; **51**: 300
The Taming of the Shrew **9**: 340, 375, 398, 407, 413; **13**: 3; **19**: 122; **55**: 278, 299, 322
The Two Noble Kinsmen **9**: 463, 481, 486; **41**: 301; **50**: 348
The Winter's Tale **7**: 419, 420

the island
The Tempest **8**: 308, 315, 447; **25**: 357, 382; **29**: 278, 343

Italian influences
Sonnets **28**: 407

Jacobean culture, relation to
Coriolanus **22**: 248
Macbeth **19**: 330; **22**: 365; **57**: 218, 256
Pericles **37**: 361; **51**: 86, 110
The Winter's Tale **19**: 366, 401, 431; **25**: 347; **32**: 388; **37**: 306; **57**: 305, 336, 356

jealousy
The Merry Wives of Windsor **5**: 334, 339, 343, 353, 355, 363; **22**: 93; **38**: 273, 307
Othello **4**: 384, 488, 527; **35**: 253, 265, 282, 301, 310; **44**: 57, 66; **51**: 30
The Winter's Tale **44**: 66; **47**: 25

Jonsonian humors comedy, influence of
The Merry Wives of Windsor **38**: 319

judicial versus natural law
Measure for Measure **2**: 446, 507, 516, 519; **22**: 85; **33**: 58, 117; **49**: 1, 293

justice
As You Like It **46**: 94
Henry IV **49**: 112, 123; **57**: 137
King Lear **49**: 1
Othello **35**: 247

justice and mercy
Measure for Measure **2**: 391, 395, 399, 402, 406, 409, 411, 416, 421, 437, 443, 463, 466, 470, 491, 495, 522, 524; **22**: 85; **33**: 52, 61, 101; **49**: 1, 274, 293, 300
The Merchant of Venice **4**: 213, 214, 224, 250, 261, 273, 282, 289, 336; **12**: 80, 129; **40**: 127; **49**: 1, 23, 27, 37
Much Ado about Nothing **22**: 85

justice, divine vs. worldly
King Lear **49**: 67, 73

juxtaposition of opposing perspectives
As You Like It **5**: 86, 93, 98, 141; **16**: 53; **23**: 119; **34**: 72, 78, 131

Kingship (Volume 39: 1, 16, 20, 34, 45, 62)
Henry IV, Parts 1 and 2 **1**: 314, 318, 337, 366, 370, 374, 379, 380, 383, 424; **16**: 172; **19**: 195; **28**: 101; **39**: 100, 116, 123, 130; **42**: 141; **48**: 143; **57**: 88, 94, 108, 137, 160
Henry V **5**: 205, 223, 225, 233, 239, 244, 257, 264, 267, 271, 287, 289, 299, 302, 304, 314, 318; **16**: 202; **22**: 137; **30**: 169, 202, 259, 273; **42**: 141; **49**: 200
Henry VI, Parts 1, 2, and 3 **3**: 69, 73, 77, 109, 115, 136, 143; **24**: 32; **39**: 154, 177, 187; **47**: 32
Henry VIII **2**: 49, 58, 60, 65, 75, 78; **24**: 113; **41**: 129, 171; **56**: 242
King John **9**: 235, 254, 263, 275, 297; **13**: 158; **19**: 182; **22**: 120; **56**: 314
Richard II **6**: 263, 264, 272, 277, 289, 294, 327, 354, 364, 381, 388, 391, 402, 409, 414; **19**: 151, 209; **24**: 260, 289, 291, 322, 325, 333, 339, 345, 346, 349, 351, 352, 356, 395, 408, 419, 428; **28**: 134; **39**: 235, 243, 256, 263, 273, 279, 289; **42**: 173
Richard III **39**: 335, 341, 345, 349

knighthood
The Merry Wives of Windsor **5**: 338, 343, 390, 397, 402; **47**: 354

knowledge
Love's Labour's Lost **22**: 12; **47**: 35

language and imagery
All's Well That Ends Well **7**: 12, 29, 45, 104, 109, 121; **38**: 132, 65
Antony and Cleopatra **6**: 21, 25, 39, 64, 80, 85, 92, 94, 100, 104, 142, 146, 155, 159, 161, 165, 189, 192, 202, 211; **13**: 374, 383; **25**: 245, 257; **27**: 96, 105, 135
As You Like It **5**: 19, 21, 35, 52, 75, 82, 92, 138; **23**: 15, 21, 26; **28**: 9; **34**: 131; **37**: 43; **48**: 42; **57**: 35, 56
The Comedy of Errors **1**: 16, 25, 39, 40, 43, 57, 59; **34**: 233; **54**: 152, 162
Coriolanus **9**: 8, 9, 13, 53, 64, 65, 73, 78, 84, 100, 112, 121, 136, 139, 142, 144, 153, 157, 174, 183, 193, 198; **22**: 248; **25**: 245, 263; **30**: 111, 125, 142; **37**: 283; **44**: 79
Cymbeline **4**: 43, 48, 61, 64, 70, 73, 93, 108; **13**: 401; **25**: 245; **28**: 373, 398; **36**: 115, 158, 166, 186; **47**: 205, 286, 296
Hamlet **1**: 95, 144, 153, 154, 160, 188, 198, 221, 227, 249, 259, 270; **22**: 258, 378; **28**: 311; **35**: 144, 152, 238, 241; **42**: 212; **44**: 248; **52**: 35
Henry IV, Parts 1 and 2 **13**: 213; **16**: 172; **25**: 245; **28**: 101; **39**: 116, 130; **42**: 153; **47**: 1; **57**: 137
Henry V **5**: 188, 230, 233, 241, 264, 276; **9**: 203; **19**: 203; **25**: 131; **30**: 159, 181, 207, 234; **30**: 159, 181, 207, 234

Henry VI, Parts 1, 2, and 3 **3**: 21, 50, 52, 55, 57, 66, 67, 71, 75, 76, 97, 105, 109, 119, 126, 131; **24**: 28; **37**: 157; **39**: 213, 222; **56**: 154, 162, 172, 180

Henry VIII **41**: 180, 190; **56**: 262, 273

Julius Caesar **7**: 148, 155, 159, 188, 204, 207, 227, 242, 250, 277, 296, 303, 324, 346, 350; **13**: 260; **17**: 347, 348, 350, 356, 358; **19**: 321; **22**: 280; **25**: 280; **30**: 333, 342; **50**: 196, 258

King John **9**: 212, 215, 220, 246, 251, 254, 267, 280, 284, 292, 297, 300; **13**: 147, 158; **22**: 120; **37**: 132; **48**: 132; **56**: 286

King Lear **2**: 129, 137, 161, 191, 199, 237, 257, 271; **16**: 301; **19**: 344; **22**: 233; **46**: 177

Love's Labour's Lost **2**: 301, 302, 303, 306, 307, 308, 315, 319, 320, 330, 335, 344, 345, 348, 356, 359, 362, 365, 371, 374, 375; **19**: 92; **22**: 12, 378; **23**: 184, 187, 196, 197, 202, 207, 211, 221, 227, 231, 233, 237, 252; **28**: 9, 63; **38**: 219, 226; **54**: 225, 274

Macbeth **3**: 170, 193, 213, 231, 234, 241, 245, 250, 253, 256, 263, 271, 283, 300, 302, 306, 323, 327, 338, 340, 349; **13**: 476; **16**: 317; **20**: 241, 279, 283, 367, 379, 400; **25**: 235; **28**: 339; **29**: 76, 91; **42**: 258; **44**: 366; **45**: 58

Measure for Measure **2**: 394, 421, 431, 466, 486, 505; **13**: 112; **28**: 9; **33**: 69; **49**: 370

The Merry Wives of Windsor **5**: 335, 337, 343, 347, 351, 363, 374, 379; **19**: 101; **22**: 93, 378; **28**: 9, 69; **38**: 313, 319

The Merchant of Venice **4**: 241, 267, 293; **22**: 3; **25**: 257; **28**: 9, 63; **32**: 41; **40**: 106; **53**: 169

A Midsummer Night's Dream **3**: 397, 401, 410, 412, 415, 432, 453, 459, 468, 494; **22**: 23, 39, 93, 378; **28**: 9; **29**: 263; **45**: 143, 169, 175; **48**: 23, 32

Much Ado about Nothing **8**: 9, 38, 43, 46, 55, 69, 73, 88, 95, 100, 115, 125; **19**: 68; **25**: 77; **28**: 63; **31**: 178, 184, 222, 241, 245; **48**: 14; **55**: 199, 259

Othello **4**: 433, 442, 445, 462, 493, 508, 517, 552, 587, 596; **13**: 304; **16**: 272; **22**: 378; **25**: 189, 257; **28**: 243, 344; **42**: 273; **47**: 51; **53**: 261

Pericles **2**: 559, 560, 565, 583; **16**: 391; **19**: 387; **22**: 315; **36**: 198, 214, 233, 244, 251, 264; **51**: 86, 99

The Rape of Lucrece **10**: 64, 65, 66, 71, 78, 80, 89, 93, 116, 109, 125, 131; **22**: 289, 294; **25**: 305; **32**: 321; **33**: 144, 155, 179, 200; **43**: 102, 113, 141

Richard II **6**: 252, 282, 283, 294, 298, 315, 323, 331, 347, 368, 374, 381, 385, 397, 409; **13**: 213, 494; **24**: 269, 270, 298, 301, 304, 315, 325, 329, 333, 339, 356, 364, 395, 405, 408, 411, 414, 419; **28**: 134, 188; **39**: 243, 273, 289, 295; **42**: 173; **52**: 154, 157, 169, 174, 183

Richard III **8**: 159, 161, 165, 167, 168, 170, 177, 182, 184, 186, 193, 197, 201, 206, 218, 223, 243, 248, 252, 258, 262, 267; **16**: 150; **25**: 141, 245; **39**: 360, 370, 383; **47**: 15; **52**: 285, 290

Romeo and Juliet **5**: 420, 426, 431, 436, 437, 456, 477, 479, 489, 492, 496, 509, 520, 522, 528, 538, 542, 550, 559; **25**: 181, 245, 257; **32**: 276; **33**: 210, 272, 274, 287; **42**: 266; **51**: 203, 212, 227

Sonnets **10**: 247, 251, 255, 256, 290, 353, 372, 385; **13**: 445; **28**: 380, 385; **32**: 327, 352; **40**: 228, 247, 284, 292, 303; **51**: 270, 304

The Taming of the Shrew **9**: 336, 338, 393, 401, 404, 407, 413; **22**: 378; **28**: 9; **31**: 261, 288, 300, 326, 335, 339; **32**: 56

The Tempest **8**: 324, 348, 384, 390, 404, 454; **19**: 421; **29**: 278; **29**: 297, 343, 368, 377

Timon of Athens **1**: 488; **13**: 392; **25**: 198; **27**: 166, 184, 235; **52**: 329, 345, 354

Titus Andronicus **4**: 617, 624, 635, 642, 644, 646, 659, 664, 668, 672, 675; **13**: 225; **16**: 225; **25**: 245; **27**: 246, 293, 313, 318, 325; **43**: 186, 222, 227, 239, 247, 262

Troilus and Cressida **3**: 561, 569, 596, 599, 606, 624, 630, 635; **22**: 58, 339; **27**: 332, 366; **42**: 66

Twelfth Night **1**: 570, 650, 664; **22**: 12; **28**: 9; **34**: 293; **37**: 59

The Two Gentlemen of Verona **6**: 437, 438, 439, 445, 449, 490, 504, 519, 529, 541; **28**: 9; **40**: 343

The Two Noble Kinsmen **9**: 445, 446, 447, 448, 456, 461, 462, 463, 469, 471, 498, 502; **41**: 289, 301, 308, 317, 326; **50**: 310

The Winter's Tale **7**: 382, 384, 417, 418, 420, 425, 460, 506; **13**: 409; **19**: 431; **22**: 324; **25**: 347; **36**: 295; **42**: 301; **45**: 297, 344, 333; **50**: 45; **57**: 278, 285, 319, 347

language versus action
Titus Andronicus **4**: 642, 644, 647, 664, 668; **13**: 225; **27**: 293, 313, 325; **43**: 186

Law and Justice (Volume 49: 1, 18, 23, 27, 37, 46, 60, 67, 73)
Henry IV **49**: 112, 116, 123, 133, 137
Henry V **49**: 223, 236, 260
Measure for Measure **49**: 274, 286, 293
The Merchant of Venice **53**: 169
Othello **53**: 288, 350

law versus passion for freedom
Much Ado about Nothing **22**: 85

laws of nature, violation of
Macbeth **3**: 234, 241, 280, 323; **29**: 120; **57**: 242, 263

legal issues
King Lear **46**: 276

legitimacy
Henry VI, Parts 1, 2, and 3 **3**: 89, 157; **39**: 154,
Henry VIII **37**: 109; **56**: 209, 220, 230

legitimacy or inheritance
King John **9**: 224, 235, 254, 303; **13**: 147; **19**: 182; **37**: 132; **41**: 215; **56**: 325, 335

liberty versus tyranny
Julius Caesar **7**: 158, 179, 189, 205, 221, 253; **25**: 272

love
See also **ideal love**
All's Well That Ends Well **7**: 12, 15, 16, 51, 58, 67, 90, 93, 116; **38**: 80; **51**: 33, 44
As You Like It **5**: 24, 44, 46, 57, 79, 88, 103, 116, 122, 138, 141, 162; **28**: 46, 82; **34**: 85
King Lear **2**: 109, 112, 131, 160, 162, 170, 179, 188, 197, 218, 222, 238, 265; **25**: 202; **31**: 77, 149, 151, 155, 162
Love's Labour's Lost **2**: 312, 315, 340, 344; **22**: 12; **23**: 252; **38**: 194; **51**: 44
The Merchant of Venice **4**: 221, 226, 270, 284, 312, 344; **22**: 3, 69; **25**: 257; **40**: 156; **51**: 1, 44
sacrificial love **13**: 43; **22**: 69; **40**: 142
A Midsummer Night's Dream
passionate or romantic love **3**: 372, 389, 395, 396, 402, 408, 411, 423, 441, 450, 480, 497, 498, 511; **29**: 175, 225, 263, 269; **45**: 126, 136; **51**: 44
Much Ado about Nothing **8**: 24, 55, 75, 95, 111, 115; **28**: 56; **51**: 30
Othello **4**: 412, 493, 506, 512, 530, 545, 552, 569, 570, 575, 580, 591; **19**: 253; **22**: 207; **25**: 257; **28**: 243, 344; **32**: 201; **35**: 261, 317; **51**: 25, 30; **53**: 315; **54**: 119
The Phoenix and Turtle **10**: 31, 37, 40, 50; **38**: 342, 345, 367; **51**: 145, 151, 155
Sonnets **10**: 173, 247, 287, 290, 293, 302, 309, 322, 325, 329, 394; **28**: 380; **37**: 347; **51**: 270, 284, 288, 292
The Tempest **8**: 435, 439; **29**: 297, 339, 377, 396
Twelfth Night **1**: 543, 546, 573, 580, 587, 595, 600, 603, 610, 660; **19**: 78; **26**: 257, 364; **34**: 270, 293, 323; **46**: 291, 333, 347, 362; **51**: 30; **52**: 57
The Two Gentlemen of Verona **6**: 442, 445, 456, 479, 488, 492, 494, 502, 509, 516, 519, 549; **13**: 12; **40**: 327, 335, 343, 354, 365; **51**: 30, 44
The Two Noble Kinsmen **9**: 479, 481, 490, 498; **41**: 289, 301, 355, 363, 372, 385; **50**: 295, 361
The Winter's Tale **7**: 417, 425, 469, 490; **51**: 30, 33, 44

love and friendship
See also **friendship**
Julius Caesar **7**: 233, 262, 268; **25**: 272

love and honor
Troilus and Cressida **3**: 555, 604; **27**: 370, 374

love and passion
Antony and Cleopatra **6**: 51, 64, 71, 80, 85, 100, 115, 159, 165, 180; **25**: 257; **27**: 126; **47**: 71, 124,, 174, 192; **51**: 25, 33, 44

love and reason
See also **reason**
Othello **4**: 512, 530, 580; **19**: 253

Love and Romance (Volume 51: 1, 15, 25, 30, 33, 44)
Pericles topic:locators
51: 71
The Phoenix and Turtle **51**: 145, 151, 155

Romeo and Juliet **51**: 195, 203, 212
Sonnets **51**: 284, 288, 292
Venus and Adonis
    The Rhetoric of Desire **51**: 345, 352, 359, 368

love, lechery, or rape
Troilus and Cressida **43**: 357

love versus fate
Romeo and Juliet **5**: 421, 437, 438, 443, 445, 458; **33**: 249

love versus friendship
See also **friendship**
The Two Gentlemen of Verona **6**: 439, 449, 450, 458, 460, 465, 468, 471, 476, 480; **40**: 354, 365; **54**: 295, 307, 325, 344

love versus lust
Venus and Adonis **10**: 418, 420, 427, 434, 439, 448, 449, 454, 462, 466, 473, 480, 489; **25**: 305; **28**: 355; **33**: 309, 330, 339, 347, 357, 363, 370; **51**: 359

love versus reason
See also **reason**
Love's Labour's Lost **54**: 225, 234
Sonnets **10**: 329

love versus war
Troilus and Cressida **18**: 332, 371, 406, 423; **22**: 339; **27**: 376

Machiavellianism
Henry V **5**: 203, 225, 233, 252, 287, 304; **25**: 131; **30**: 273
Henry VI, Parts 1, 2, and 3 **22**: 193
Macbeth **52**: 29; **57**: 236

Madness (Volume **35**: 1, 7, 8, 24, 34, 49, 54, 62, 68)
Hamlet **19**: 330; **35**: 104, 117, 126, 132, 134, 140, 144
King Lear **19**: 330
Macbeth **19**: 330
Othello **35**: 265, 276, 282
Twelfth Night **1**: 554, 639, 656; **26**: 371

Magic and the Supernatural (Volume **29**: 1, 12, 28, 46, 53, 65)
The Comedy of Errors **1**: 27, 30; **54**: 215
Macbeth
    supernatural grace versus evil or chaos **3**: 241, 286, 323
    witchcraft and supernaturalism **3**: 171, 172, 173, 175, 177, 182, 183, 184, 185, 194, 196, 198, 202, 207, 208, 213, 219, 229, 239; **16**: 317; **19**: 245; **20**: 92, 175, 213, 279, 283, 374, 387, 406, 413; **25**: 235; **28**: 339; **29**: 91, 101, 109, 120; **44**: 351, 373; **57**: 194, 242
A Midsummer Night's Dream **29**: 190, 201, 210, 216
The Tempest **8**: 287, 293, 304, 315, 340, 356, 396, 401, 404, 408, 435, 458; **28**: 391, 415; **29**: 297, 343, 377; **45**: 272
Sonnets
    occult **48**: 346
The Winter's Tale
    witchcraft **22**: 324

male discontent
The Merry Wives of Windsor **5**: 392, 402

male domination
Love's Labour's Lost **22**: 12
A Midsummer Night's Dream **3**: 483, 520; **13**: 19; **25**: 36; **29**: 216, 225, 243, 256, 269; **42**: 46; **45**: 84

male/female relationships
As You Like It **46**: 134
The Comedy of Errors **16**: 3
Love's Labour's Lost **54**: 284
The Rape of Lucrece **10**: 109, 121, 131; **22**: 289; **25**: 305; **43**: 113, 141,
Troilus and Cressida **16**: 70; **22**: 339; **27**: 362

male sexual anxiety
Love's Labour's Lost **16**: 17

manhood
Macbeth **3**: 262, 309, 333; **29**: 127, 133; **57**: 242, 256, 263

Marlowe's works, compared with
Richard II **42**: 173

marriage
See also **courtship and marriage**
The Comedy of Errors **34**: 251
Hamlet **22**: 339; **51**: 44; **54**: 215
Love's Labour's Lost **2**: 335, 340; **19**: 92; **38**: 209, 232; **51**: 1, 44
Measure for Measure **2**: 443, 507, 516, 519, 524, 528; **25**: 12; **33**: 61, 90; **49**: 286; **51**: 44
The Merry Wives of Windsor **5**: 343, 369, 376, 390, 392, 400; **22**: 93; **38**: 297; **51**: 44
A Midsummer Night's Dream **3**: 402, 423, 450, 483, 520; **29**: 243, 256; **45**: 136, 143; **48**: 32; **51**: 1, 30, 44
Othello **35**: 369; **51**: 44;
The Taming of the Shrew **9**: 322, 325, 329, 332, 329, 332, 334, 341, 342, 343, 344, 345, 347, 353, 360, 362, 375, 381, 390, 398, 401, 404, 413, 426, 430; **13**: 3; **19**: 3; **28**: 24; **31**: 288; **51**: 44; **55**: 315, 331
Titus Andronicus
    marriage as political tyranny **48**: 264
Troilus and Cressida **22**: 339; **51**: 44
The Two Gentlemen of Verona **48**: 32

martial vs. civil law
Coriolanus **48**: 230

Marxist criticism
Hamlet **42**: 229
King Lear **42**: 229; **55**: 16
Macbeth **42**: 229; **55**: 16
Othello **42**: 229

masque elements
The Two Noble Kinsmen **9**: 490
The Tempest **42**: 332

master-slave relationship
Troilus and Cressida **22**: 58

mediation
The Merry Wives of Windsor **5**: 343, 392

as medieval allegory or morality play
Henry IV, Parts 1 and 2 **1**: 323, 324, 342, 361, 366, 373, 374; **32**: 166; **39**: 89; **47**: 60
Measure for Measure **2**: 409, 421, 443, 466, 475, 491, 505, 511, 522; **13**: 94
Timon of Athens **1**: 492, 511, 518; **27**: 155

medieval chivalry
Richard II **6**: 258, 277, 294, 327, 338, 388, 397, 414; **24**: 274, 278, 279, 280, 283; **39**: 256
Troilus and Cressida **3**: 539, 543, 544, 555, 606; **27**: 376

medieval dramatic influence
All's Well That Ends Well **7**: 29, 41, 51, 98, 113; **13**: 66
King Lear **2**: 177, 188, 201; **25**: 218
Othello **4**: 440, 527, 545, 559, 582

medieval homilies, influence of
The Merchant of Venice **4**: 224, 250, 289

medieval influence
Romeo and Juliet **5**: 480, 505, 509, 573

medieval literary influence
Henry VI, Parts 1, 2, and 3 **3**: 59, 67, 75, 100, 109, 136, 151; **13**: 131
Titus Andronicus **4**: 646, 650; **27**: 299

medieval mystery plays, relation to
Macbeth **44**: 341; **57**: 194

medieval physiology
Julius Caesar **13**: 260

mercantilism and feudalism
Richard II **13**: 213

merit versus rank
All's Well That Ends Well **7**: 9, 10, 19, 37, 51, 76; **38**: 155; **50**: 59

Messina
Much Ado about Nothing **8**: 19, 29, 48, 69, 82, 91, 95, 108, 111, 121, 125; **31**: 191, 209, 229, 241, 245

metadramatic elements
As You Like It **5**: 128, 130, 146; **34**: 130
Henry V **13**: 194; **30**: 181; **49**: 200, 211
Love's Labour's Lost **2**: 356, 359, 362
Measure for Measure **13**: 104
A Midsummer Night's Dream **3**: 427, 468, 477, 516, 520; **29**: 190, 225, 243; **50**: 86
The Taming of the Shrew **9**: 350, 419, 424; **31**: 300, 315
The Winter's Tale **16**: 410

metamorphosis or transformation
The Merry Wives of Windsor **47:** 314
Much Ado about Nothing **8:** 88, 104, 111, 115; **55:** 209, 228
The Taming of the Shrew **9:** 370, 430

metaphysical poem
The Phoenix and Turtle **10:** 7, 8, 9, 20, 31, 35, 37, 40, 45, 50; **51:** 143, 171, 184

Midlands Revolt, influence of
Coriolanus **22:** 248; **30:** 79; **50:** 140, 172

military and sexual hierarchies
Othello **16:** 272

mimetic rivalry
The Two Gentlemen of Verona **13:** 12; **40:** 335; **54:** 332

as "mingled yarn"
All's Well That Ends Well **7:** 62, 93, 109, 126; **38:** 65

Minotaur, myth of
A Midsummer Night's Dream **3:** 497, 498; **29:** 216

as miracle play
Pericles **2:** 569, 581; **36:** 205; **51:** 97

misgovernment
Measure for Measure **2:** 401, 432, 511; **22:** 85
Much Ado about Nothing **22:** 85; **55:** 241

misogyny
King Lear **31:** 123
Measure for Measure **23:** 358

misperception
Cymbeline **19:** 411; **36:** 99, 115; **47:** 228, 237, 252, 277, 286, 296

mistaken identity
The Comedy of Errors **1:** 13, 14, 27, 37, 40, 45, 49, 55, 57, 61, 63; **19:** 34, 54; **25:** 63; **34:** 194; **54:** 162, 176, 189, 215

modernization
Richard III **14:** 523

Montaigne's Essais, relation to
Sonnets **42:** 375
The Tempest **42:** 339

moral choice
Hamlet **52:** 35
Julius Caesar **7:** 179, 264, 279, 343

moral corruption
Macbeth **52:** 15, 23, 78
Othello **52:** 78
Troilus and Cressida **3:** 578, 589, 599, 604, 609; **18:** 332, 406, 412, 423; **27:** 366; **54:** 84

moral corruption of English society
Richard III **8:** 154, 163, 165, 177, 193, 201, 218, 228, 232, 243, 248, 252, 267; **39:** 308; **52:** 201

moral inheritance
Henry VI, Parts 1, 2, and 3 **3:** 89, 126

moral intent
Henry VIII **2:** 15, 19, 25; **24:** 140; **54:** 35

moral lesson
Macbeth **20:** 23

moral relativism
Antony and Cleopatra **22:** 217; **27:** 121

moral seriousness, question of
Measure for Measure **2:** 387, 388, 396, 409, 417, 421, 452, 460, 495; **23:** 316, 321

Morality in Shakespeare's Works (Volume 52: 1, 5, 15, 23, 29, 35, 43, 57, 63, 69, 78, 89, 95)
Antony and Cleopatra **52:** 5
As You Like It **52:** 63; **57:** 13
Henry V **5:** 195, 203, 213, 223, 225, 239, 246, 260, 271, 293
Macbeth **52:** 29
The Merchant of Venice **52:** 89
The Merry Wives of Windsor **5:** 335, 339, 347, 349, 353, 397
Richard III **52:** 5
The Tempest **52:** 43
Troilus and Cressida **52:** 5
The Two Gentlemen of Verona **6:** 438, 492, 494, 514, 532, 555, 564
Venus and Adonis **10:** 411, 412, 414, 416, 418, 419, 420, 423, 427, 428, 439, 442, 448, 449, 454, 459, 466; **33:** 330

multiple endings
Henry IV **49:** 102

multiple perspectives of characters
Henry VI, Parts 1, 2, and 3 **3:** 69, 154; **56:** 131

music
The Tempest **8:** 390, 404; **29:** 292; **37:** 321; **42:** 332
Twelfth Night **1:** 543, 566, 596

music and dance
A Midsummer Night's Dream **3:** 397, 400, 418, 513; **12:** 287, 289; **25:** 36
Much Ado about Nothing **19:** 68; **31:** 222

mutability, theme of
Sonnets **42:** 375

mythic or mythological elements
See also **religious, mythic, or spiritual content**
Richard II **52:** 154, 157, 169

mythological allusions
As You Like It **46:** 142
Antony and Cleopatra **16:** 342; **19:** 304; **27:** 110, 117; **47:** 71, 192

naming, significance of
Coriolanus **30:** 58, 96, 111, 125

narrative strategies
The Rape of Lucrece **22:** 294

nationalism and patriotism
See also **British nationalism**
Henry V **5:** 198, 205, 209, 210, 213, 219, 223, 233, 246, 252, 257, 269, 299; **19:** 133, 217; **30:** 227, 262; **49:** 219, 247
Henry VI, Parts 1, 2, and 3 **24:** 25, 45, 47; **56:** 80
King John **9:** 209, 218, 222, 224, 235, 240, 244, 275; **25:** 98; **37:** 132
The Merry Wives of Windsor **47:** 344
The Winter's Tale **32:** 388

nature
See also **art and nature** *and* **art versus nature**
As You Like It **46:** 94
The Tempest **8:** 315, 370, 390, 408, 414; **29:** 343, 362, 368, 377
The Winter's Tale **7:** 397, 418, 419, 420, 425, 432, 436, 451, 452, 473, 479; **19:** 366; **45:** 329

nature as book
Pericles **22:** 315; **36:** 233

nature, philosophy of
Coriolanus **30:** 74

negative appraisals
Cymbeline **4:** 20, 35, 43, 45, 48, 53, 56, 68; **15:** 32, 105, 121
Richard II **6:** 250, 252, 253, 255, 282, 307, 317, 343, 359
Venus and Adonis **10:** 410, 411, 415, 418, 419, 424, 429

Neoclassical rules
As You Like It **5:** 19, 20
Henry IV, Parts 1 and 2 **1:** 286, 287, 290, 293
Henry VI, Parts 1, 2, and 3 **3:** 17, 18
King John **9:** 208, 209, 210, 212; **56:** 365
Love's Labour's Lost **2:** 299, 300
Macbeth **3:** 170, 171, 173, 175; **20:** 17
Measure for Measure **2:** 387, 388, 390, 394; **23:** 269
The Merry Wives of Windsor **5:** 332, 334
Romeo and Juliet **5:** 416, 418, 426
The Tempest **8:** 287, 292, 293, 334; **25:** 357; **29:** 292; **45:** 200
Troilus and Cressida **3:** 537, 538; **18:** 276, 278, 281
The Winter's Tale **7:** 376, 377, 379, 380, 383, 410; **15:** 397

Neoplatonism
The Phoenix and Turtle **10:** 7, 9, 21, 24, 40, 45, 50; **38:** 345, 350, 367; **51:** 184
Sonnets **10:** 191, 205

nightmarish quality
Macbeth **3:** 231, 309; **20:** 210, 242; **44:** 261

nihilistic elements
King Lear **2:** 130, 143, 149, 156, 165, 231, 238, 245, 253; **22:** 271; **25:** 218; **28:** 325
Timon of Athens **1:** 481, 513, 529; **13:** 392; **20:** 481
Troilus and Cressida **27:** 354

nihilistic or pessimistic vision
King Lear **49:** 67

"nothing," significance of
Much Ado about Nothing **8:** 17, 18, 23, 55, 73, 95; **19:** 68; **55:** 259

nurturing or feeding
Coriolanus **9:** 65, 73, 136, 183, 189; **30:** 111; **44:** 79; **50:** 110

oaths, importance of
Love's Labour's Lost **54:** 257, 284
Pericles **19:** 387

obscenity
Henry V **5:** 188, 190, 260

Oldcastle, references to
Henry IV, Parts 1 and 2 **48:** 117

omens
Julius Caesar **22:** 137; **45:** 10; **50:** 265, 280

oppositions or dualisms
King John **9:** 224, 240, 263, 275, 284, 290, 300

order
Henry V **5:** 205, 257, 264, 310, 314; **30:** 193,
Twelfth Night **1:** 563, 596; **34:** 330; **46:** 291, 347

order versus disintegration
Titus Andronicus **4:** 618, 647; **43:** 186, 195

other sonnet writers, Shakespeare compared with
Sonnets **42:** 296

Ovid, compared with
Venus and Adonis **51:** 335, 352

Ovid, influence of
A Midsummer Night's Dream **3:** 362, 427, 497, 498; **22:** 23; **29:** 175, 190, 216
Titus Andronicus **4:** 647, 659, 664, 668; **13:** 225; **27:** 246, 275, 285, 293, 299, 306; **28:** 249; **43:** 195, 203, 206

Ovid's Metamorphoses, relation to
The Winter's Tale **42:** 301; **57:** 319, 367
Venus and Adonis **42:** 347

pagan elements
King Lear **25:** 218

pageantry
See also **ceremonies, rites, and rituals, importance of**
Henry VIII **2:** 14, 15, 18, 51, 58; **24:** 77, 83, 84, 85, 89, 91, 106, 113, 118, 120, 126, 127, 140, 146, 150; **41:** 120, 129, 190

paradoxical elements
Coriolanus **9:** 73, 92, 106, 121, 153, 157, 164, 169, 193

parent-child relations
A Midsummer Night's Dream **13:** 19; **29:** 216, 225, 243

pastoral convention, parodies of
As You Like It **5:** 54, 57, 72

pastoral convention, relation to
As You Like It **5:** 72, 77, 122; **34:** 161; **37:** 1

pastoral tradition, compared with
A Lover's Complaint **48:** 336

patience
Henry VIII **2:** 58, 76, 78
Pericles **2:** 572, 573, 578, 579; **36:** 251

patriarchal claims
Henry VI, Parts 1, 2, and 3 **16:** 131; **25:** 102

patriarchal or monarchical order
King Lear **13:** 353, 457; **16:** 351; **22:** 227, 233; **25:** 218; **31:** 84, 92, 107, 117, 123, 137, 142; **46:** 269

patriarchy
General Commentary **55:** 78
Cymbeline **32:** 373; **36:** 134; **47:** 237; **51:** 25
Henry V **37:** 105; **44:** 44
Titus Andronicus **50:** 13
Troilus and Cressida **22:** 58

patriotism
See **nationalism and patriotism**

Pattern of Painful Adventures (Lawrence Twine), compared with
Pericles **48:** 364

Pauline doctrine
A Midsummer Night's Dream **3:** 457, 486, 506

pedagogy
Sonnets **37:** 374
The Taming of the Shrew **19:** 122

perception
Othello **19:** 276; **25:** 189, 257; **53:** 246, 289

performance history
The Taming of the Shrew **31:** 282; **55:** 357

performance issues
See also **staging issues**
Julius Caesar **50:** 186

King Lear **2:** 106, 137, 154, 160; **11:** 10, 20, 27, 56, 57, 132, 136, 137, 145, 150, 154; **19:** 295, 344; **25:** 218
Much Ado about Nothing **18:** 173, 174, 183, 184, 185, 186, 187, 188, 189, 190, 191, 192, 193, 195, 197, 199, 201, 204, 206, 207, 208, 209, 210, 254; **55:** 221
Sonnets **48:** 352
The Taming of the Shrew **12:** 313, 314, 316, 317, 337, 338; **31:** 315; **55:** 357

pessimistic elements
Timon of Athens **1:** 462, 467, 470, 473, 478, 480; **20:** 433, 481; **27:** 155, 191

Petrarchan poetics, influence of
Romeo and Juliet **5:** 416, 520, 522, 528, 550, 559, 575; **32:** 276; **51:** 212, 236

philosophical elements
Julius Caesar **7:** 310, 324; **37:** 203
Twelfth Night **1:** 560, 563, 596; **34:** 301, 316; **46:** 297

physical versus intellectual world
Love's Labour's Lost **2:** 331, 348, 367

pictorial elements
Venus and Adonis **10:** 414, 415, 419, 420, 423, 480; **33:** 339

Platonic elements
A Midsummer Night's Dream **3:** 368, 437, 450, 497; **45:** 126

play-within-the-play, convention of
Henry VI, Parts 1, 2, and 3 **3:** 75, 149
The Merry Wives of Windsor **5:** 354, 355, 369, 402
The Taming of the Shrew **12:** 416; **22:** 48

plebians
Coriolanus **50:** 13, 105; **50:** 189, 196, 230

plot
Love's Labur's Lost **54:** 225
The Winter's Tale **7:** 376, 377, 379, 382, 387, 390, 396, 452; **13:** 417; **15:** 518; **45:** 374; **57:** 285

plot and incident
Richard III **8:** 146, 152, 159; **25:** 164

Plutarch and historical sources
Coriolanus **9:** 8, 9, 13, 14, 16, 26, 39, 92, 106, 130, 142, 164; **30:** 74, 79, 105; **50:** 99

poet-patron relationship
Sonnets **48:** 352

poetic justice, question of
King Lear **2:** 92, 93, 94, 101, 129, 137, 231, 245; **49:** 73
Othello **4:** 370, 412, 415, 427

poetic style
Sonnets **10:** 153, 155, 156, 158, 159, 160, 161, 173, 175, 182, 214, 247, 251, 255, 260, 265, 283, 287, 296, 302, 315, 322, 325, 337, 346, 349, 360, 367, 385; **16:** 472; **40:** 221, 228; **51:** 270

political and social disintegration
Antony and Cleopatra **6:** 31, 43, 53, 60, 71, 80, 100, 107, 111, 146; 180, 197, 219; **22:** 217; **25:** 257; **27:** 121

political content
Titus Andronicus **43:** 262

Politics (Volume 30: 1, 4, 11, 22, 29, 39, 42, 46, 49)
General Commentary **56:** 3
Coriolanus **9:** 15, 17, 18, 19, 26, 33, 43, 53, 62, 65, 73, 80, 92, 106, 110, 112, 121, 144, 153, 157, 164, 180; **22:** 248; **25:** 296; **30:** 58, 67, 79, 89, 96, 105, 111, 125; **37:** 283; **42:** 218; **48:** 230; **50:** 13, 140, 172
Hamlet **44:** 241
Henry IV, Parts 1 and 2 **28:** 101; **39:** 130; **42:** 141; **48:** 143, 175; **57:** 108
Henry V **49:** 219, 247, 260
Henry VIII **2:** 39, 49, 51, 58, 60, 65, 67, 71, 72, 75, 78, 81; **24:** 74, 121, 124; **41:** 146; **56:** 242
Julius Caesar **7:** 161, 169, 191, 205, 218, 221, 245, 262, 264, 279, 282, 310, 324, 333, 346; **17:** 317, 318, 321, 323, 334, 350, 351, 358, 378, 382, 394, 406; **22:** 137, 280; **25:** 272, 280; **30:** 285, 297, 316, 321, 342, 374, 379; **37:** 203; **50:** 13
King John **9:** 218, 224, 260, 280; **13:** 163; **22:** 120; **37:** 132; **41:** 221, 228; **56:** 314, 325
King Lear **46:** 269; **50:** 45
Macbeth **52:** 29; **57:** 218, 228
Measure for Measure **23:** 379; **49:** 274
A Midsummer Night's Dream **29:** 243
Pericles **37:** 361
The Tempest **8:** 304, 307, 315, 353, 359, 364, 401, 408; **16:** 426; **19:** 421; **29:** 339; **37:** 336; **42:** 320; **45:** 272, 280; **52:** 43
Timon of Athens **27:** 223, 230; **50:** 13
Titus Andronicus **27:** 282; **48:** 264
Troilus and Cressida **3:** 536, 560, 606; **16:** 84

popularity
Pericles **2:** 536, 538, 546; **37:** 361
Richard III **8:** 144, 146, 154, 158, 159, 162, 181, 228; **39:** 383
The Taming of the Shrew **9:** 318, 338, 404
Venus and Adonis **10:** 410, 412, 418, 427; **25:** 328

power
Henry IV **57:** 108
Henry V **37:** 175
Measure for Measure **13:** 112; **22:** 85; **23:** 327, 330, 339, 352; **33:** 85
The Merchant of Venice **53:** 136
A Midsummer Night's Dream **42:** 46; **45:** 84
Much Ado about Nothing **22:** 85; **25:** 77; **31:** 231, 245

pride and rightful self-esteem
Othello **4:** 522, 536, 541; **35:** 352

primitivism
Macbeth **20:** 206, 213; **45:** 48

primogeniture
As You Like It **5:** 66, 158; **34:** 109, 120
Titus Andronicus **50:** 13

as "problem" plays
The Comedy of Errors **34:** 251
Julius Caesar **7:** 272, 320
Measure for Measure **2:** 416, 429, 434, 474, 475, 503, 514, 519; **16:** 102; **23:** 313, 328, 351; **49:** 358, 370
Troilus and Cressida **3:** 555, 566
lack of resolution **43:** 277

procreation
Sonnets **10:** 379, 385; **16:** 461
Venus and Adonis **10:** 439, 449, 466; **33:** 321, 377

Protestant components
Henry IV, Parts 1 and 2 **57:** 167

providential order
General Commentary **56:** 15, 25
Henry IV, Parts 1 and 2 **56:** 15
Henry V **56:** 15
King Lear **2:** 112, 116, 137, 168, 170, 174, 177, 218, 226, 241, 253; **22:** 271; **49:** 1, 73; **56:** 25
Macbeth **3:** 208, 289, 329, 336; **57:** 218
Measure for Measure **48:** 1;
Richard II **56:** 15
Tempest **52:** 43

Psychoanalytic Interpretations of Shakespeare's Works (Volume 44: 1, 11, 18, 28, 35, 44, 57, 66, 79, 89, 93)
As You Like It **5:** 146, 158; **23:** 141, 142; **34:** 109; **48:** 42
Coriolanus **44:** 93
Cymbeline **45:** 67, 75
Hamlet **1:** 119, 148, 154, 179, 202; **21:** 197, 213, 361; **25:** 209; **28:** 223; **35:** 95, 104, 134, 237; **37:** 241; **44:** 133, 152, 160, 180, 209, 219
Henry IV, Parts 1 and 2 **13:** 457; **28:** 101; **42:** 185; **44:** 44
Henry V **13:** 457; **44:** 44
Julius Caesar **45:** 10
Macbeth **3:** 219, 223, 226; **44:** 11, 284, 289, 297; **45:** 48, 58
Measure for Measure **23:** 331, 332, 333, 334, 335, 340, 355, 356, 359, 379, 395; **44:** 89
Merchant of Venice **45:** 17
A Midsummer Night's Dream **3:** 440, 483; **28:** 15; **29:** 225; **44:** 1; **45:** 107, 117
Othello **4:** 468, 503; **35:** 265, 276, 282, 301, 317, 320, 347; **42:** 198; **44:** 57
Romeo and Juliet **5:** 513, 556; **51:** 253
The Tempest **45:** 259
Troilus and Cressida **43:** 287
Twelfth Night **46:** 333

psychological elements
Cymbeline **36:** 134; **44:** 28

public versus private principles
Julius Caesar **7:** 161, 179, 252, 262, 268, 284, 298; **13:** 252

public versus private speech
Love's Labour's Lost **2:** 356, 362, 371

public versus private worlds
As You Like It **46:** 164
Coriolanus **37:** 283; **42:** 218
Romeo and Juliet **5:** 520, 550; **25:** 181; **33:** 274

as "pure" poetry
The Phoenix and Turtle **10:** 14, 31, 35; **38:** 329

Puritanism
Measure for Measure **2:** 414, 418, 434; **49:** 325
Twelfth Night **1:** 549, 553, 555, 632; **16:** 53; **25:** 47; **46:** 338

Pyramus and Thisbe interlude
A Midsummer Night's Dream **50:** 74

Race (Volume 53: 1, 11, 21, 32, 45, 53, 64, 67, 77, 86, 92)
Antony and Cleopatra **53:** 67, 77
The Merchant of Venice **53:** 111, 116, 127, 136, 159, 169; **55:** 27
A Midsummer Night's Dream **53:** 1, 32
Othello **4:** 370, 380, 384, 385, 392, 399, 401, 402, 408, 427, 564; **13:** 327; **16:** 293; **25:** 189, 257; **28:** 249, 330; **35:** 369; **42:** 198; **53:** 1, 233, 238, 246, 255, 261, 268, 275, 289, 298, 304; **55:** 27
The Rape of Lucrece **53:** 1
Sonnets **53:** 1
The Tempest **53:** 1, 21, 45, 64, 67
Titus Andronicus **53:** 86, 92

rape
Titus Andronicus **43:** 227, 255; **48:** 277

realism
See also idealism versus realism
The Merry Wives of Windsor **38:** 313
The Tempest **8:** 340, 359, 464
Troilus and Cressida **43:** 357

reality and illusion
The Tempest **8:** 287, 315, 359, 401, 435, 439, 447, 454; **22:** 302; **45:** 236, 247

reason
See also love and reason and love versus reason
Venus and Adonis **10:** 427, 439, 449, 459, 462, 466; **28:** 355; **33:** 309, 330

reason versus imagination
Antony and Cleopatra **6:** 107, 115, 142, 197, 228; **45:** 28
A Midsummer Night's Dream **3:** 381, 389, 423, 441, 466, 506; **22:** 23; **29:** 190; **45:** 96

rebellion
See also **usurpation**
Henry IV, Parts 1 and 2 **22**: 395; **28**: 101
Henry VIII **22**: 395; **56**: 230
King John **9**: 218, 254, 263, 280, 297
Richard III **22**: 395

rebirth, regeneration, resurrection, or immortality
All's Well That Ends Well **7**: 90, 93, 98
Antony and Cleopatra **6**: 100, 103, 125, 131, 159, 181
Cymbeline **4**: 38, 64, 73, 93, 105, 113, 116, 129, 138, 141, 162, 170
Measure for Measure **13**: 84; **16**: 102, 114; **23**: 321, 327, 335, 340, 352; **25**: 12
Pericles **2**: 555, 564, 584, 586, 588; **36**: 205
The Tempest **8**: 302, 312, 320, 334, 348, 359, 370, 384, 401, 404, 414, 429, 439, 447, 454; **16**: 442; **22**: 302; **29**: 297; **37**: 336
The Winter's Tale **7**: 397, 414, 417, 419, 429, 436, 451, 452, 456, 480, 490, 497, 506; **25**: 339 452, 480, 490, 497, 506; **45**: 366

reconciliation
As You Like It **46**: 156
All's Well That Ends Well **7**: 90, 93, 98; **51**: 33
Antony and Cleopatra **6**: 100, 103, 125, 131, 159, 181
Cymbeline **4**: 38, 64, 73, 93, 105, 113, 116, 129, 138, 141, 162, 170
The Merry Wives of Windsor **5**: 343, 369, 374, 397, 402
A Midsummer Night's Dream **3**: 412, 418, 437, 459, 468, 491, 497, 502, 513; **13**: 27; **29**: 190
Romeo and Juliet **5**: 415, 419, 427, 439, 447, 480, 487, 493, 505, 533, 536, 562
The Tempest **8**: 302, 312, 320, 334, 348, 359, 370, 384, 401, 404, 414, 429, 439, 447, 454; **16**: 442; **22**: 302; **29**: 297; **37**: 336; **45**: 236

reconciliation of opposites
As You Like It **5**: 79, 88, 103, 116, 122, 138; **23**: 127, 143; **34**: 161, 172; **46**: 156

redemption
The Comedy of Errors **19**: 54; **26**: 188; **54**: 152, 189

regicide
Macbeth **3**: 248, 275, 312; **16**: 317, 328

relation to tetralogy
Henry V **49**: 223

relationship to other Shakespearean plays
Twelfth Night **46**: 303
Henry IV, Parts 1 and 2 **42**: 99, 153; **48**: 167; **49**: 93, 186

relationship between Parts 1 and 2
Henry IV, Parts 1 and 2 **32**: 136; **39**: 100; **49**: 178

religious and theological issues
Macbeth **44**: 324, 341, 351, 361, 366, 373
Measure for Measure **48**: 1

religious, mythic, or spiritual content
See also **Christian elements**
All's Well That Ends Well **7**: 15, 45, 54, 67, 76, 98, 109, 116
Antony and Cleopatra **6**: 53, 94, 111, 115, 178, 192, 224; **47**: 71
Cymbeline **4**: 22, 29, 78, 93, 105, 108, 115, 116, 127, 134, 138, 141, 159; **28**: 373; **36**: 142, 158, 186; **47**: 219, 260, 274
Hamlet **1**: 98, 102, 130, 184, 191, 209, 212, 231, 234, 254; **21**: 361; **22**: 258; **28**: 280; **32**: 238; **35**: 134
Henry IV, Parts 1 and 2 **1**: 314, 374, 414, 421, 429, 431, 434; **32**: 103; **48**: 151; **57**: 147, 156, 167
Henry V **25**: 116; **32**: 126
King Lear **49**: 67
Macbeth **3**: 208, 269, 275, 318; **29**: 109
Measure for Measure **48**: 1
Othello **4**: 483, 517, 522, 525, 559, 573; **22**: 207; **28**: 330
Pericles **2**: 559, 561, 565, 570, 580, 584, 588; **22**: 315; **25**: 365; **51**: 97
The Tempest **8**: 328, 390, 423, 429, 435; **45**: 211, 247
Timon of Athens **1**: 505, 512, 513, 523; **20**: 493

repentance and forgiveness
Much Ado about Nothing **8**: 24, 29, 111; **55**: 228
The Two Gentlemen of Verona **6**: 450, 514, 516, 555, 564
The Winter's Tale **44**: 66

resolution
Measure for Measure **2**: 449, 475, 495, 514, 516; **16**: 102, 114; **54**: 65
The Merchant of Venice **4**: 263, 266, 300, 319, 321; **13**: 37; **51**: 1
The Two Gentlemen of Verona **6**: 435, 436, 439, 445, 449, 453, 458, 460, 462, 465, 466, 468, 471, 476, 480, 486, 494, 509, 514, 516, 519, 529, 532, 541, 549; **19**: 34; **54**: 307, 311, 338

retribution
Henry VI, Parts 1, 2, and 3 **3**: 27, 42, 51, 59, 77, 83, 92, 100, 109, 115, 119, 131, 136, 151
Julius Caesar **7**: 160, 167, 200
Macbeth **3**: 194, 208, 318; **48**: 214
Richard III **8**: 163, 170, 177, 182, 184, 193, 197, 201, 206, 210, 218, 223, 228, 243, 248, 267

revenge
Hamlet **1**: 74, 194, 209, 224, 234, 254; **16**: 246; **22**: 258; **25**: 288; **28**: 280; **35**: 152, 157, 167, 174, 212; **44**: 180, 209, 219, 229; **54**: 96
The Merry Wives of Windsor **5**: 349, 350, 392; **38**: 264, 307
Othello **35**: 261

revenge tragedy elements
Julius Caesar **7**: 316
Titus Andronicus **4**: 618, 627, 628, 636, 639, 644, 646, 664, 672, 680; **16**: 225; **27**: 275, 318

reversals
A Midsummer Night's Dream **29**: 225;
The Two Gentlemen of Verona **54**: 338

rhetoric
Venus and Adonis **33**: 377; **51**: 335, 345, 352
Romeo and Juliet **42**: 266

rhetoric of consolation
Sonnets **42**: 375

rhetoric of politeness
Henry VIII **22**: 182; **56**: 262

rhetorical style
King Lear **16**: 301; **47**: 9

riddle motif
Pericles **22**: 315; **36**: 205, 214

rightful succession
Titus Andronicus **4**: 638

rings episode
The Merchant of Venice **22**: 3; **40**: 106, 151, 156

role-playing
Julius Caesar **7**: 356; **37**: 229
The Taming of the Shrew **9**: 322, 353, 355, 360, 369, 370, 398, 401, 407, 413, 419, 424; **13**: 3; **31**: 288, 295, 315

as romance play
As You Like It **5**: 55, 79; **23**: 27, 28, 40, 43

romance or chivalric tradition, influence of
Much Ado about Nothing **8**: 53, 125; **51**: 15

romance or folktale elements
All's Well That Ends Well **7**: 32, 41, 43, 45, 54, 76, 104, 116, 121; **26**: 117

romance or pastoral tradition, influence of
The Tempest **8**: 336, 348, 396, 404; **37**: 336

Roman citizenry, portrayal of
Julius Caesar **50**: 64, 230

romantic and courtly conventions
The Two Gentlemen of Verona **6**: 438, 460, 472, 478, 484, 486, 488, 502, 507, 509, 529, 541, 549, 560, 568; **12**: 460, 462; **40**: 354, 374; **54**: 344

romantic elements
The Comedy of Errors **1**: 13, 16, 19, 23, 25, 30, 31, 36, 39, 53
Cymbeline **4**: 17, 20, 46, 68, 77, 141, 148, 172; **15**: 111; **25**: 319; **28**: 373
King Lear **31**: 77, 84
The Taming of the Shrew **9**: 334, 342, 362, 375, 407

royalty
Antony and Cleopatra **6**: 94

Salic Law
   Henry V **5:** 219, 252, 260; **28:** 121

as satire or parody
   Love's Labour's Lost **2:** 300, 302, 303, 307, 308, 315, 321, 324, 327; **23:** 237, 252; **54:** 234
   The Merry Wives of Windsor **5:** 338, 350, 360, 385; **38:** 278, 319; **47:** 354, 363,

satire or parody of pastoral conventions
   As You Like It **5:** 46, 55, 60, 72, 77, 79, 84, 114, 118, 128, 130, 154

satirical elements
   The Phoenix and Turtle **10:** 8, 16, 17, 27, 35, 40, 45, 48
   Timon of Athens **27:** 155, 235
   Troilus and Cressida **3:** 539, 543, 544, 555, 558, 574; **27:** 341

Saturnalian elements
   Twelfth Night **1:** 554, 571, 603, 620, 642; **16:** 53

schemes and intrigues
   The Merry Wives of Windsor **5:** 334, 336, 339, 341, 343, 349, 355, 379

Scholasticism
   Macbeth **52:** 23
   The Phoenix and Turtle **10:** 21, 24, 31; **51:** 188

School of Night, allusions to
   Love's Labour's Lost **2:** 321, 327, 328

self-conscious or artificial nature of play
   Cymbeline **4:** 43, 52, 56, 68, 124, 134, 138; **36:** 99

self-deception
   Twelfth Night **1:** 554, 561, 591, 625; **47:** 45

self-indulgence
   Twelfth Night **1:** 563, 615, 635

self-interest or expediency
   Henry V **5:** 189, 193, 205, 213, 217, 233, 260, 287, 302, 304; **30:** 273; **49:** 223

self-knowledge
   As You Like It **5:** 32, 82, 102, 116, 122, 133, 164; **57:** 45
   Much Ado about Nothing **8:** 69, 95, 100
   Timon of Athens **1:** 456, 459, 462, 495, 503, 507, 515, 518, 526; **20:** 493; **27:** 166

self-love
   Sonnets **10:** 372; **25:** 374; **51:** 270, 300, 304

Senecan or revenge tragedy elements
   Timon of Athens **27:** 235
   Titus Andronicus **4:** 618, 627, 628, 636, 639, 644, 646, 664, 672, 680; **16:** 225; **27:** 275, 318; **43:** 170, 206, 227

servitude
   See also **freedom and servitude**
   Comedy of Errors **42:** 80

setting
   The Merry Wives of Windsor **47:** 375
   Much Ado about Nothing **18:** 173, 174, 183, 184, 185, 186, 187, 188, 189, 190, 191, 192, 193, 195, 197, 199, 201, 204, 206, 207, 208, 209, 210, 254
   Richard III **14:** 516, 528; **52:** 263
   The Two Gentlemen of Verona **12:** 463, 465, 485

sexual ambiguity and sexual deception
   As You Like It **46:** 134, 142; **57:** 23, 40, 45
   Twelfth Night **1:** 540, 562, 620, 621, 639, 645; **22:** 69; **34:** 311, 344; **37:** 59; **42:** 32
   Troilus and Cressida **43:** 365

sexual anxiety
   Macbeth **16:** 328; **20:** 283

sexual politics
   General Commentary **55:** 68
   King Lear **55:** 68
   Measure for Measure **55:** 68
   The Merchant of Venice **22:** 3; **51:** 44
   The Merry Wives of Windsor **19:** 101; **38:** 307

Sexuality in Shakespeare (Volume 33: 1, 12, 18, 28, 39)
   As You Like It **46:** 122, 127, 134, 142
   All's Well That Ends Well **7:** 67, 86, 90, 93, 98, 126; **13:** 84; **19:** 113; **22:** 78; **28:** 38; **44:** 35; **49:** 46; **51:** 44; **55:** 109, 131, 143, 176
   Coriolanus **9:** 112, 142, 174, 183, 189, 198; **30:** 79, 111, 125, 142
   Cymbeline **4:** 170, 172; **25:** 319; **32:** 373; **47:** 245
   Hamlet **55:** 56
   King Lear **25:** 202; **31:** 133, 137, 142
   Love's Labour's Lost **22:** 12; **51:** 44
   Measure for Measure **13:** 84; **16:** 102, 114; **23:** 321, 327, 335, 340, 352; **25:** 12; **33:** 85, 90, 112; **49:** 286, 338; **51:** 44
   A Midsummer Night's Dream **22:** 23, 93; **29:** 225, 243, 256, 269; **42:** 46; **45:** 107; **53:** 45
   Othello **22:** 339; **28:** 330, 344; **35:** 352, 360; **37:** 269; **44:** 57, 66; **51:** 44; **53:** 275, 310, 315
   Romeo and Juliet **25:** 181; **33:** 225, 233, 241, 246, 274, 300; **51:** 227, 236
   Sonnets **25:** 374; **48:** 325
   The Tempest **53:** 45
   Troilus and Cressida **22:** 58, 339; **25:** 56; **27:** 362; **43:** 365

Shakespeare and Classical Civilization (Volume 27: 1, 9, 15, 21, 30, 35, 39, 46, 56, 60, 67)
   Antony and Cleopatra
     Egyptian versus Roman values **6:** 31, 33, 43, 53, 104, 111, 115, 125, 142, 155, 159, 178, 181, 211, 219; **17:** 48; **19:** 270; **27:** 82, 121, 126; **28:** 249; **47:** 96, 103, 113, 149
   The Rape of Lucrece
     Roman history, relation to **10:** 84, 89, 93, 96, 98, 109, 116, 125, 135; **22:** 289; **25:** 305; **33:** 155, 190
   Timon of Athens **27:** 223, 230, 325
   Titus Andronicus **27:** 275, 282, 293, 299, 306
     Roman elements **43:** 206, 222
   Troilus and Cressida
     Trojan versus Greek values **3:** 541, 561, 574, 584, 590, 596, 621, 638; **27:** 370

Shakespeare's artistic growth, Richard III's contribution to
   Richard III **8:** 165, 167, 182, 193, 197, 206, 210, 228, 239, 267; **25:** 164; **39:** 305, 326, 370

Shakespeare's canon, place in
   Titus Andronicus **4:** 614, 616, 618, 619, 637, 639, 646, 659, 664, 668; **43:** 195
   Twelfth Night **1:** 543, 548, 557, 569, 575, 580, 621, 635, 638

Shakespeare's dramas, compared with
   The Phoenix and Turtle **51:** 151, 155
   The Rape of Lucrece **43:** 92

Shakespeare's moral judgment
   Antony and Cleopatra **6:** 33, 37, 38, 41, 48, 51, 64, 76, 111, 125, 136, 140, 146, 163, 175, 189, 202, 211, 228; **13:** 368, 523; **25:** 257

Shakespeare's other plays, compared with
   King John **56:** 306, 348, 357
   The Merchant of Venice: **53:** 74
   Much Ado about Nothing **55:** 189, 209, 232, 241, 249
   The Taming of the Shrew **50:** 74; **55:** 331

Shakespeare's political sympathies
   Coriolanus **9:** 8, 11, 15, 17, 19, 26, 39, 52, 53, 62, 80, 92, 142; **25:** 296; **30:** 74, 79, 89, 96, 105, 133; **50:** 172
   Richard II **6:** 277, 279, 287, 347, 359, 364, 391, 393, 402
   Richard III **8:** 147, 163, 177, 193, 197, 201, 223, 228, 232, 243, 248, 267; **39:** 349; **42:** 130

Shakespeare's Representation of History (Volume 56: 2, 3, 15, 25, 47, 53, 60, 95, 196, 286)
   Henry VI **56:** 95, 110, 122, 131, 145
   Henry VIII **56:** 196, 201, 209, 220, 230
   King John **56:** 286, 296, 306, 348, 357

Shakespeare's Representation of Women (Volume 31: 1, 3, 8, 12, 16, 21, 29, 34, 35, 41, 43, 48, 53, 60, 68)
   Henry VI, Parts 1, 2, and 3 **3:** 103, 109, 126, 140, 157; **16:** 183; **39:** 196
   King John **9:** 222, 303; **16:** 161; **19:** 182; **41:** 215, 221
   King Lear **31:** 117, 123, 133
   Love's Labour's Lost **19:** 92; **22:** 12; **23:** 215; **25:** 1
   The Merry Wives of Windsor **5:** 335, 341, 343, 349, 369, 379, 390, 392, 402; **19:** 101; **38:** 307
   Much Ado about Nothing **31:** 222, 231, 241, 245

Othello **19:** 253; **28:** 344
The Taming of the Shrew **31:** 288, 300, 307, 315
The Winter's Tale **22:** 324; **36:** 311; **42:** 301; **51:** 30; **57:** 294, 305, 356

Shakespeare's romances, compared with
  Henry VIII **41:** 171; **54:** 35; **56:** 273
  Pericles **54:** 35
  The Two Noble Kinsmen **54:** 35

shame
  Coriolanus **42:** 243

sibling rivalry
  As You Like It **34:** 109
  Henry VI, Parts 1, 2, and 3 **22:** 193

slander or hearsay, importance of
  Coriolanus **48:** 230
  Much Ado about Nothing **8:** 58, 69, 82, 95, 104; **55:** 249

social action
  Sonnets **48:** 352

social and moral corruption
  King Lear **2:** 116, 133, 174, 177, 241, 271; **22:** 227; **31:** 84, 92; **46:** 269

social and political context
  All's Well That Ends Well **13:** 66; **22:** 78; **38:** 99, 109, 150, 155; **49:** 46

social aspects
  Measure for Measure **23:** 316, 375, 379, 395
  The Merchant of Venice **53:** 214

Social Class (**Volume 50:** 1, 13, 24, 34, 45, 51, 59, 64, 74, 86)
  General Commentary **50:** 1, 34
  Coriolanus **50:** 105, 110, 119
  Julius Caesar **50:** 189, 194, 196, 211, 230
  Timon of Athens **1:** 466, 487, 495; **25:** 198; **27:** 184, 196, 212
  The Two Noble Kinsmen **50:** 295, 305, 310

social milieu
  The Merry Wives of Windsor **18:** 75, 84; **38:** 297, 300

social order
  As You Like It **37:** 1; **46:** 94; **57:** 2
  The Comedy of Errors **34:** 238; **54:** 155, 215

society
  Coriolanus **9:** 15, 17, 18, 19, 26, 33, 43, 53, 62, 65, 73, 80, 92, 106, 110, 112, 121, 144, 153, 157, 164, 180; **22:** 248; **25:** 296; **30:** 58, 67, 79, 89, 96, 105, 111, 125; **50:** 13, 105, 119, 152
  Troilus and Cressida **43:** 298

soldiers
  Henry V **49:** 194

songs, role of
  Love's Labour's Lost **2:** 303, 304, 316, 326, 335, 362, 367, 371, 375; **54:** 240

sonnet arrangement
  Sonnets **10:** 174, 176, 182, 205, 226, 230, 236, 315, 353; **28:** 363; **40:** 238

sonnet form
  Sonnets **10:** 255, 325, 367; **37:** 347; **40:** 284, 303; **51:** 270

sonnets, compared with
  A Lover's Complaint **48:** 336

source of tragic catastrophe
  Romeo and Juliet **5:** 418, 427, 431, 448, 458, 469, 479, 480, 485, 487, 493, 509, 522, 528, 530, 533, 542, 565, 571, 573; **33:** 210; **51:** 245

sources
  General Commentary **56:** 25
  Antony and Cleopatra **6:** 20, 39; **19:** 304; **27:** 96, 126; **28:** 249
  As You Like It **5:** 18, 32, 54, 59, 66, 84; **34:** 155; **46:** 117
  The Comedy of Errors **1:** 13, 14, 16, 19, 31, 32, 39; **16:** 3; **34:** 190, 215, 258; **54:** 155, 176
  Cymbeline **4:** 17, 18; **13:** 401; **28:** 373; **47:** 245, 265, 277
  Hamlet **1:** 76, 81, 113, 125, 128, 130, 151, 191, 202, 224, 259
  Henry IV, Parts 1 and 2 **56:** 2
  Henry V **56:** 2
  Henry VI, Parts 1, 2, and 3 **3:** 18, 21, 29, 31, 35, 39, 46, 51; **13:** 131; **16:** 217; **39:** 196; **56:** 2, 122, 131, 187
  Henry VIII **2:** 16, 17; **24:** 71, 80
  Julius Caesar **7:** 149, 150, 156, 187, 200, 264, 272, 282, 284, 320; **30:** 285, 297, 326, 358
  King John **9:** 216, 222, 300; **32:** 93, 114; **41:** 234, 243, 251; **56:** 296, 357
  King Lear **2:** 94, 100, 143, 145, 170, 186; **13:** 352; **16:** 351; **28:** 301
  Love's Labour's Lost **16:** 17
  Measure for Measure **2:** 388, 393, 427, 429, 437, 475; **13:** 94; **49:** 349
  The Merry Wives of Windsor **5:** 332, 350, 360, 366, 385; **32:** 31; **52:** 69
  A Midsummer Night's Dream **29:** 216
  Much Ado about Nothing **8:** 9, 19, 53, 58, 104
  Othello **28:** 330
  Pericles **2:** 538, 568, 572, 575; **25:** 365; **36:** 198, 205; **51:** 118, 126,
  The Phoenix and Turtle **10:** 7, 9, 18, 24, 45; **38:** 326, 334, 350, 367; **51:** 138
  The Rape of Lucrece **10:** 63, 64, 65, 66, 68, 74, 77, 78, 89, 98, 109, 121, 125; **25:** 305; **33:** 155, 190; **43:** 77, 92, 148
  Richard II **56:** 2
  Richard III **52:** 263, 290; **56:** 2
    chronicles **8:** 145, 165, 193, 197, 201, 206, 210, 213, 228, 232
    Marlowe, Christopher **8:** 167, 168, 182, 201, 206, 218
    morality plays **8:** 182, 190, 201, 213, 239
    Seneca, other classical writers **8:** 165, 190, 201, 206, 228, 248
  Romeo and Juliet **5:** 416, 419, 423, 450; **32:** 222; **33:** 210; **45:** 40; **54:** 125

  Sonnets **10:** 153, 154, 156, 158, 233, 251, 255, 293, 353; **16:** 472; **28:** 407; **42:** 375
  The Taming of the Shrew
    folk tales **9:** 332, 390, 393
    Old and New Comedy **9:** 419
    Ovid **9:** 318, 370, 430
    Plautus **9:** 334, 341, 342
    shrew tradition **9:** 355; **19:** 3; **32:** 1, 56; **55:** 342
    text and sources **55:** 334, 357
  The Tempest **45:** 226
  Timon of Athens **16:** 351; **27:** 191; **52:** 301
  Troilus and Cressida **3:** 537, 539, 540, 541, 544, 549, 558, 566, 574, 587; **27:** 376, 381, 391, 400
  Twelfth Night **1:** 539, 540, 603; **34:** 301, 323, 344; **46:** 291
  The Two Gentlemen of Verona **6:** 436, 460, 462, 468, 476, 480, 490, 511, 547; **19:** 34; **40:** 320; **54:** 295
  The Two Noble Kinsmen **19:** 394; **41:** 289, 301, 363, 385; **50:** 326, 348
  Venus and Adonis **10:** 410, 412, 420, 424, 429, 434, 439, 451, 454, 466, 473, 480, 486, 489; **16:** 452; **25:** 305; **28:** 355; **33:** 309, 321, 330, 339, 347, 352, 357, 370, 377; **42:** 347

spectacle
  Love's Labour's Lost **38:** 226
  Macbeth **42:** 258
  Pericles **42:** 352

spectacle versus simple staging
  The Tempest **15:** 206, 207, 208, 210, 217, 219, 222, 223, 224, 225, 227, 228, 305, 352; **28:** 415

stage history
  As You Like It **46:** 117; **57:** 56
  Antony and Cleopatra **17:** 84, 94, 101
  The Merry Wives of Windsor **18:** 66, 67, 68, 70, 71

staging issues
  See also performance issues
  All's Well That Ends Well **19:** 113; **26:** 15, 19, 48, 52, 64, 73, 85, 92, 93, 94, 95, 97, 114, 117, 128; **54:** 30
  Antony and Cleopatra **17:** 6, 12, 84, 94, 101, 104, 110; **27:** 90; **47:** 142
  As You Like It **13:** 502; **23:** 7, 17, 19, 22, 58, 96, 97, 98, 99, 101, 110, 137; **28:** 82; **32:** 212; **57:** 56, 75
  The Comedy of Errors **26:** 182, 183, 186, 188, 190; **54:** 136
  Coriolanus **17:** 172, 242, 248
  Cymbeline **15:** 6, 23, 75, 105, 111, 121, 122; **22:** 365
  Hamlet **13:** 494, 502; **21:** 11, 17, 31, 35, 41, 44, 50, 53, 78, 81, 89, 101, 112, 127, 139, 142, 145, 148, 151, 157, 160, 172, 182, 183, 202, 203, 208, 225, 232, 237, 242, 245, 249, 251, 259, 268, 270, 274, 283, 284, 301, 311, 334, 347, 355, 361, 371, 377, 379, 380, 381, 384, 386, 392, 407, 410, 416; **44:** 198
  Henry IV, Parts 1 and 2 **32:** 212; **47:** 1; **49:** 102

Henry V **5:** 186, 189, 192, 193, 198, 205, 226, 230, 241, 281, 314; **13:** 194, 502; **14:** 293, 295, 297, 301, 310, 319, 328, 334, 336, 342; **19:** 217; **32:** 185
Henry VI, Parts 1, 2, and 3 **24:** 21, 22, 27, 31, 32, 36, 38, 41, 45, 48, 55; **32:** 212; **56:** 154, 172, 180, 187
Henry VIII **24:** 67, 70, 71, 75, 77, 83, 84, 85, 87, 89, 91, 101, 106, 113, 120, 127, 129, 136, 140, 146, 150, 152, 155; **28:** 184; **56:** 220, 248
Julius Caesar **48:** 240; **50:** 186
King John **16:** 161; **19:** 182; **24:** 171, 187, 203, 206, 211, 225, 228, 241, 245, 249; **56:** 286, 365
King Lear **11:** 136, 137, 142, 145, 150, 151, 154, 158, 161, 165, 169; **32:** 212; **46:** 205, 218
Love's Labour's Lost **23:** 184, 187, 191, 196, 198, 200, 201, 202, 207, 212, 215, 216, 217, 229, 230, 232, 233, 237, 252
Macbeth **13:** 502; **20:** 12, 17, 32, 64, 65, 70, 73, 107, 113, 151, 175, 203, 206, 210, 213, 245, 279, 283, 312, 318, 324, 329, 343, 345, 350, 353, 363, 367, 374, 376, 379, 382, 387, 400, 406, 413; **22:** 365; **32:** 212
Measure for Measure **2:** 427, 429, 437, 441, 443, 456, 460, 482, 491, 519; **23:** 283, 284, 285, 286, 287, 291, 293, 294, 298, 299, 311, 315, 327, 338, 339, 340, 342, 344, 347, 363, 372, 375, 395, 400, 405, 406, 413; **32:** 16
The Merchant of Venice **12:** 111, 114, 115, 117, 119, 124, 129, 131
The Merry Wives of Windsor **18:** 74, 75, 84, 86, 90, 95
A Midsummer Night's Dream **3:** 364, 365, 371, 372, 377; **12:** 151, 152, 154, 158, 159, 280, 284, 291, 295; **16:** 34; **19:** 21; **29:** 183, 256; **48:** 23
Much Ado about Nothing **8:** 18, 33, 41, 75, 79, 82, 108; **16:** 45; **18:** 245, 247, 249, 252, 254, 257, 261, 264; **28:** 63; **55:** 221
Othello **11:** 273, 334, 335, 339, 342, 350,354, 359, 362
Pericles **16:** 399; **48:** 364; **51:** 99; **53:** 233, 304
Richard II **13:** 494; **24:** 273, 274, 278, 279, 280, 283, 291, 295, 296, 301, 303, 304, 310, 315, 317, 320, 325, 333, 338, 346, 351, 352, 356, 364, 383, 386, 395, 402, 405, 411, 414, 419, 423, 428; **25:** 89
Richard III **14:** 515, 527, 528, 537; **16:** 137; **52:** 263, 272
Romeo and Juliet **11:** 499, 505, 507, 514, 517; **13:** 243; **25:** 181; **32:** 212
The Tempest **15:** 343, 346, 352, 361, 364, 366, 368, 371, 385; **28:** 391, 415; **29:** 339; **32:** 338, 343; **42:** 332; **45:** 200; **54:** 19
Timon of Athens **20:** 445, 446, 481, 491, 492, 493
Titus Andronicus **17:** 449, 452, 456, 487; **25:** 245; **32:** 212, 249
Troilus and Cressida **16:** 70; **18:** 289, 332, 371, 395, 403, 406, 412, 419, 423, 442, 447, 451
Twelfth Night **26:** 219, 233, 257, 337, 342, 346, 357, 359, 360, 364, 366, 371, 374; **46:** 310, 369; **54:** 19
The Two Gentlemen of Verona **12:** 457, 464; **42:** 18
The Winter's Tale **7:** 414, 425, 429, 446, 464, 480, 483, 497; **13:** 409; **15:** 518; **48:** 309

Stoicism
Hamlet **48:** 195
Julius Caesar **50:** 249

strategic analysis
Antony and Cleopatra **48:** 206

structure
All's Well That Ends Well **7:** 21, 29, 32, 45, 51, 76, 81, 93, 98, 116; **22:** 78; **26:** 128; **38:** 72, 123, 142
As You Like It **5:** 19, 24, 25, 35, 44, 45, 46, 86, 93, 116, 138, 158; **23:** 7, 8, 9, 10, 11; **34:** 72, 78, 131, 147, 155
Coriolanus **9:** 8, 9, 11, 12, 13, 14, 16, 26, 33, 45, 53, 58, 72, 78, 80, 84, 92, 112, 139, 148; **25:** 263; **30:** 79, 96
Hamlet **22:** 378; **28:** 280, 325; **35:** 82, 104, 215; **44:** 152
Henry IV, Parts 1 and 2 **49:** 93 **56:** 53, 60; **57:** 181
Henry V **5:** 186, 189, 205, 213, 230, 241, 264, 289, 310, 314; **30:** 220, 227, 234, 244
Henry VI, Parts 1, 2, and 3 **3:** 31, 43, 46, 69, 83, 103, 109, 119, 136, 149, 154; **39:** 213; **56:** 77, 80, 85
Henry VIII **2:** 16, 25, 27, 28, 31, 36, 44, 46, 51, 56, 68, 75; **24:** 106, 112, 113, 120; **56:** 209
Julius Caesar **7:** 152, 155, 159, 160, 179, 200, 210, 238, 264, 284, 298, 316, 346; **13:** 252; **30:** 374
King John **9:** 208, 212, 222, 224, 229, 240, 244, 245, 254, 260, 263, 275, 284, 290, 292, 300; **24:** 228, 241; **41:** 260, 269, 277
King Lear **28:** 325; **32:** 308; **46:** 177
Love's Labour's Lost **22:** 378; **23:** 191, 237, 252; **38:** 163, 172
Macbeth **16:** 317; **20:** 12, 245
Measure for Measure **2:** 390, 411, 449, 456, 466, 474, 482, 490, 491; **33:** 69; **49:** 379
The Merchant of Venice **4:** 201, 215, 230, 232, 243, 247, 254, 261, 263, 308, 321; **12:** 115; **28:** 63
The Merry Wives of Windsor **5:** 332, 333, 334, 335, 343, 349, 355, 369, 374; **18:** 86; **22:** 378
A Midsummer Night's Dream **3:** 364, 368, 381, 402, 406, 427, 450, 513; **13:** 19; **22:** 378; **29:** 175; **45:** 126, 175
Much Ado about Nothing **8:** 9, 16, 17, 19, 28, 29, 33, 39, 48, 63, 69, 73, 75, 79, 82, 115; **31:** 178, 184, 198, 231; **55:** 189
Othello **22:** 378; **28:** 325
The Phoenix and Turtle **10:** 27, 31, 37, 45, 50; **38:** 342, 345, 357; **51:** 138, 143
The Rape of Lucrece **10:** 84, 89, 93, 98, 135; **22:** 294; **25:** 305; **43:** 102, 141
Richard II **6:** 282, 304, 317, 343, 352, 359, 364, 39; **24:** 307, 322, 325, 356, 395
Richard III **8:** 154, 161, 163, 167, 168, 170, 177, 184, 193, 197, 201, 206, 210, 218, 223, 228, 232, 243, 252, 262, 267; **16:** 150

Romeo and Juliet **5:** 438, 448, 464, 469, 470, 477, 480, 496, 518, 524, 525, 528, 547, 559; **33:** 210, 246
Sonnets **10:** 175, 176, 182, 205, 230, 260, 296, 302, 309, 315, 337, 349, 353; **40:** 238
The Taming of the Shrew **9:** 318, 322, 325, 332, 334, 341, 362, 370, 390, 426; **22:** 48, 378; **31:** 269; **55:** 278, 342, 371
The Tempest **8:** 294, 295, 299, 320, 384, 439; **28:** 391, 415; **29:** 292, 297; **45:** 188
Timon of Athens **27:** 157, 175, 235; **52:** 338, 345, 349 375
Titus Andronicus **4:** 618, 619, 624, 631, 635, 640, 644, 646, 647, 653, 656, 659, 662, 664, 668, 672; **27:** 246, 285
Troilus and Cressida **3:** 536, 538, 549, 568, 569, 578, 583, 589, 611, 613; **27:** 341, 347, 354, 391
Twelfth Night **1:** 539, 542, 543, 546, 551, 553, 563, 570, 571, 590, 600, 660; **26:** 374; **34:** 281, 287; **46:** 286
The Two Gentlemen of Verona **6:** 445, 450, 460, 462, 504, 526
The Two Noble Kinsmen **37:** 313; **50:** 326, 361
Venus and Adonis **10:** 434, 442, 480, 486, 489; **33:** 357, 377

style
Henry VIII **41:** 158
The Phoenix and Turtle **10:** 8, 20, 24, 27, 31, 35, 45, 50; **38:** 334, 345, 357; **51:** 171, 188
The Rape of Lucrece **10:** 64, 65, 66, 68, 69, 70, 71, 73, 74, 77, 78, 81, 84, 98, 116, 131, 135; **43:** 113, 158
Venus and Adonis **10:** 411, 412, 414, 415, 416, 418, 419, 420, 423, 424, 428, 429, 439, 442, 480, 486, 489; **16:** 452

subjectivity
Hamlet **45:** 28
Sonnets **37:** 374

substitution of identities
Measure for Measure **2:** 507, 511, 519; **13:** 112; **49:** 313, 325

subversiveness
Cymbeline **22:** 302
The Tempest **22:** 302
The Winter's Tale **22:** 302

supernatural grace versus evil or chaos
Measure for Measure **48:** 1

suffering
King Lear **2:** 137, 160, 188, 201, 218, 222, 226, 231, 238, 241, 249, 265; **13:** 343; **22:** 271; **25:** 218; **50:** 24
Pericles **2:** 546, 573, 578, 579; **25:** 365; **36:** 279

symbolism
The Winter's Tale **7:** 425, 429, 436, 452, 456, 469, 490, 493

textual arrangement
Henry VI, Parts 1, 2, and 3 **24:** 3, 4, 6, 12, 17, 18, 19, 20, 21, 24, 27, 42, 45; **37:** 165
Richard II **24:** 260, 261, 262, 263, 271, 273, 291, 296, 356, 390

textual issues
Henry IV, Parts 1 and 2 **22:** 114
King Lear **22:** 271; **37:** 295; **49:** 73
A Midsummer Night's Dream **16:** 34; **29:** 216
The Taming of the Shrew **22:** 48; **31:** 261, 276; **31:** 276; **55:** 342, 371
The Winter's Tale **19:** 441; **45:** 333; **57:** 278, 285, 356

textual problems
Henry V **5:** 187, 189, 190; **13:** 201

textual revisions
Pericles **15:** 129, 130, 132, 134, 135, 136, 138, 152, 155, 167, 181; **16:** 399; **25:** 365; **51:** 99

textual variants
Hamlet **13:** 282; **16:** 259; **21:** 11, 23, 72, 101, 127, 129, 139, 140, 142, 145, 202, 208, 259, 270, 284, 347, 361, 384; **22:** 258; **32:** 238

theatrical viability
Henry VI, Parts 1, 2, and 3 **24:** 31, 32, 34; **56:** 80, 172

theatricality
Antony and Cleopatra **47:** 96, 103, 107, 113
Macbeth **16:** 328
Measure for Measure **23:** 285, 286, 294, 372, 406; **49:** 358
The Merry Wives of Windsor **47:** 325

thematic disparity
Henry VIII **2:** 25, 31, 56, 68, 75; **41:** 146

time
As You Like It **5:** 18, 82, 112, 141; **23:** 146, 150; **34:** 102; **46:** 88, 156, 164, 169
Macbeth **3:** 234, 246, 283, 293; **20:** 245; **57:** 218
Richard II **22:** 137
Sonnets **10:** 265, 302, 309, 322, 329, 337, 360, 379; **13:** 445; **40:** 292
The Tempest **8:** 401, 439, 464; **25:** 357; **29:** 278, 292; **45:** 236
Troilus and Cressida **3:** 561, 571, 583, 584, 613, 621, 626, 634
Twelfth Night **37:** 78; **46:** 297
The Winter's Tale **7:** 397, 425, 436, 476, 490; **19:** 366; **36:** 301, 349; **45:** 297, 329, 366, 374

time and change, motif of
Henry IV, Parts 1 and 2 **1:** 372, 393, 411; **39:** 89; **48:** 143
As You Like It **46:** 156, 164, 169

time scheme
Othello **4:** 370, 384, 390, 488; **22:** 207; **35:** 310; **47:** 51

topical allusions or content
Hamlet **13:** 282
Henry V **5:** 185, 186; **13:** 201
Love's Labour's Lost **2:** 300, 303, 307, 315, 316, 317, 319, 321, 327, 328; **23:** 187, 191, 197, 203, 221, 233, 237, 252; **25:** 1
Macbeth **13:** 361; **20:** 17, 350; **29:** 101

traditional values
Richard III **39:** 335

tragedies of major characters
Henry VIII **2:** 16, 39, 46, 48, 49, 51, 56, 58, 68, 81; **41:** 120

tragic elements
The Comedy of Errors **1:** 16, 25, 27, 45, 50, 59; **34:** 229; **54:** 144
Cymbeline **25:** 319; **28:** 373; **36:** 129; **47:** 296
Hamlet **55:** 78
Henry V **5:** 228, 233, 267, 269, 271
Julius Caesar **50:** 258, 265
King John **9:** 208, 209, 244
King Lear **55:** 78
Macbeth **52:** 15; **55:** 78; **57:** 189
A Midsummer Night's Dream **3:** 393, 400, 401, 410, 445, 474, 480, 491, 498, 511; **29:** 175; **45:** 169
Othello **55:** 78
The Rape of Lucrece **10:** 78, 80, 81, 84, 98, 109; **43:** 85, 148
Romeo and Juliet **55:** 78
The Tempest **8:** 324, 348, 359, 370, 380, 408, 414, 439, 458, 464
Twelfth Night **1:** 557, 569, 572, 575, 580, 599, 621, 635, 638, 639, 645, 654, 656; **26:** 342

treachery
Coriolanus **30:** 89
King John **9:** 245

treason and punishment
Macbeth **13:** 361; **16:** 328

trial scene
The Merchant of Venice **49:** 1, 23, 37

trickster, motif of
Cymbeline **22:** 302
The Tempest **22:** 302; **29:** 297
The Winter's Tale **22:** 302; **45:** 333

triumph over death or fate
Romeo and Juliet **5:** 421, 423, 427, 505, 509, 520, 530, 536, 565, 566; **51:** 219

Trojan War
Troilus and Cressida as myth **43:** 293

The Troublesome Reign (anonymous), compared with
King John **41:** 205, 221, 260, 269; **48:** 132; **56:** 357

Troy
Troilus and Cressida **43:** 287

Troy passage
The Rape of Lucrece **43:** 77, 85

Tudor doctrine
King John **9:** 254, 284, 297; **41:** 221; **56:** 345

Tudor myth
Henry VI, Parts 1, 2, and 3 **3:** 51, 59, 77, 92, 100, 109, 115, 119, 131; **39:** 222
Richard III **8:** 163, 165, 177, 184, 193, 201, 218, 228, 232, 243, 248, 252, 267; **39:** 305, 308, 326, 387; **42:** 130

Turkish elements
Henry IV, Parts 1 and 2 **19:** 170
Henry V **19:** 170

two fathers
Henry IV, Parts 1 and 2 **14:** 86, 101, 105, 108; **39:** 89, 100; **49:** 102

tyranny
King John **9:** 218

unity
Antony and Cleopatra **6:** 20, 21, 22, 24, 25, 32, 33, 39, 43, 53, 60, 67, 111, 125, 146, 151, 165, 208, 211, 219; **13:** 374; **27:** 82, 90, 135
Hamlet **1:** 75, 76, 87, 103, 113, 125, 128, 142, 148, 160, 184, 188, 198, 264; **16:** 259; **35:** 82, 215
Henry VI, Parts 1, 2, and 3 **39:** 177, 222
A Midsummer Night's Dream **3:** 364, 368, 381, 402, 406, 427, 450, 513; **13:** 19; **22:** 378; **29:** 175, 263

unity of double plot
The Merchant of Venice **4:** 193, 194, 201, 232; **12:** 16, 67, 80, 115; **40:** 151

unnatural ordering
Hamlet **22:** 378
Love's Labour's Lost **22:** 378
The Merry Wives of Windsor **22:** 378
A Midsummer Night's Dream **22:** 378
Othello **22:** 378

as unsuccessful play
Measure for Measure **2:** 397, 441, 474, 482; **23:** 287

usurpation
See also **rebellion**
Richard II **6:** 263, 264, 272, 287, 289, 315, 323, 331, 343, 354, 364, 381, 388, 393, 397; **24:** 383; **52:** 108, 141, 154
The Tempest **8:** 304, 370, 408, 420; **25:** 357, 382; **29:** 278, 362, 377; **37:** 336

utopia
The Tempest **45:** 280

value systems
Troilus and Cressida **3:** 578, 583, 589, 602, 613, 617; **13:** 53; **27:** 370, 396, 400

Venetian politics
Othello **32:** 294

Venice, Elizabethan perceptions of
The Merchant of Venice **28:** 249; **32:** 294; **40:** 127

Venus and Adonis
The Rape of Lucrece **43:** 148

Vergil, influence of
Titus Andronicus **27:** 306; **28:** 249

verisimilitude
As You Like It **5:** 18, 23, 28, 30, 32, 39, 125; **23:** 107

Verona society
Romeo and Juliet **5:** 556, 566; **13:** 235; **33:** 255; **51:** 245

Violence in Shakespeare's Works (Volume 43: 1, 12, 24, 32, 39, 61)
Henry IV, Parts 1 and 2 **25:** 109
Henry VI, Parts 1, 2, and 3 **24:** 25, 31; **37:** 157
Julius Caesar **48:** 240
Love's Labour's Lost **22:** 12
Macbeth **20:** 273, 279, 283; **45:** 58; **57:** 228, 267
Othello **22:** 12
The Rape of Lucrece **43:** 148, 158
The Taming of the Shrew **55:** 322
Titus Andronicus **13:** 225; **25:** 245; **27:** 255; **28:** 249; **32:** 249, 265; **43:** 186, 203, 227, 239, 247, 255, 262
Troilus and Cressida **43:** 329, 340, 351, 357, 365, 377

virginity or chastity, importance of
Much Ado about Nothing **8:** 44, 75, 95, 111, 121, 125; **31:** 222; **55:** 268

Virgo vs. Virago
King Lear **48:** 222

visual arts, relation to
Sonnets **28:** 407

visual humor
Love's Labour's Lost **23:** 207, 217

war
Coriolanus **25:** 263; **30:** 79, 96, 125, 149
Henry V **5:** 193, 195, 197, 198, 210, 213, 219, 230, 233, 246, 281, 293; **28:** 121, 146; **30:** 262; **32:** 126; **37:** 175, 187; **42:** 141; **49:** 194, 236, 247, 260

Wars of the Roses
Richard III **8:** 163, 165, 177, 184, 193, 201, 218, 228, 232, 243, 248, 252, 267; **39:** 308

Watteau, influence on staging
Love's Labour's Lost **23:** 184, 186

wealth
The Merchant of Venice **4:** 209, 261, 270, 273, 317; **12:** 80, 117; **22:** 69; **25:** 22; **28:** 249; **40:** 117, 197, 208; **45:** 17; **49:** 1; **51:** 15

wealth and social class
Timon of Athens **1:** 466, 487, 495; **25:** 198; **27:** 184, 196, 212; **50:** 13

wheel of fortune, motif of
Antony and Cleopatra **6:** 25, 178; **19:** 304
Hamlet **52:** 35
Henry VIII **2:** 27, 65, 72, 81

widowhood and remarriage, themes of
Hamlet **32:** 238

wisdom
King Lear **37:** 213; **46:** 210
Love's Labour's Lost **54:** 257

wit
The Merry Wives of Windsor **5:** 335, 336, 337, 339, 343, 351
Much Ado about Nothing **8:** 27, 29, 38, 69, 79, 91, 95; **31:** 178, 191; **55:** 228

witchcraft
See **Magic and the Supernatural**

women, role of
See **Shakespeare's Representation of Women**

wonder, dynamic of
The Comedy of Errors **37:** 12

wordplay
As You Like It **46:** 105
Romeo and Juliet **32:** 256

written versus oral communication
Love's Labour's Lost **2:** 359, 365; **28:** 63

youth
The Two Gentlemen of Verona **6:** 439, 450, 464, 514, 568

youth versus age
All's Well That Ends Well **7:** 9, 45, 58, 62, 76, 81, 86, 93, 98, 104, 116, 126; **26:** 117; **38:** 109

Cumulative Topic Index, by Play

The Cumulative Topic Index, by Play identifies the principal topics of discussion in the criticism of each play and non-dramatic poem. The topics are arranged alphabetically by play. Page references indicate the beginning page number of each essay containing substantial commentary on that topic. A parenthetical reference after a play indicates which volumes discuss the play extensively.

All's Well That Ends Well (**Volumes 7, 26, 38, 55**)

    appearance versus reality **7:** 37, 76, 93; **26:** 117
    audience perspective **7:** 81, 104, 109, 116, 121
    bed-trick **7:** 8, 26, 27, 29, 32, 41, 86, 93, 98, 113, 116, 126; **13:** 84; **26:** 117; **28:** 38; **38:** 65, 118; **49:** 46; **54:** 52; **55:** 109, 131, 176
    Bertram
        characterization **7:** 15, 27, 29, 32, 39, 41, 43, 98, 113; **26:** 48; **26:** 117; **55:** 90
        conduct **7:** 9, 10, 12, 16, 19, 21, 51, 62, 104; **50:** 59; **55:** 143, 154
        desire **22:** 78
        transformation or redemption **7:** 10, 19, 21, 26, 29, 32, 54, 62, 81, 90, 93, 98, 109, 113, 116, 126; **13:** 84
    comic elements **26:** 97, 114; **48:** 65; **55:** 148, 154, 164
    conclusion **38:** 123, 132, 142; **54:** 52 **55:** 148, 154, 170
    dark elements **7:** 27, 37, 39, 43, 54, 109, 113, 116; **26:** 85; **48:** 65; **50:** 59; **54:** 30; **55:** 164, 170
    Decameron (Boccaccio), compared with **7:** 29, 43
    desire **38:** 99, 109, 118; **55:** 122
    displacement **22:** 78
    education **7:** 62, 86, 90, 93, 98, 104, 116, 126
    elder characters **7:** 9, 37, 39, 43, 45, 54, 62, 104
    gender issues **7:** 9, 10, 67, 126; **13:** 77, 84; **19:** 113; **26:** 128; **38:** 89, 99, 118; **44:** 35; **55:** 101, 109, 122, 164
    genre **48:** 65
    Helena
        as agent of reconciliation, renewal, or grace **7:** 67, 76, 81, 90, 93, 98, 109, 116; **55:** 176
        as dualistic or enigmatic character **7:** 15, 27, 29, 39, 54, 58, 62, 67, 76, 81, 98, 113, 126; **13:** 66; **22:** 78; **26:** 117; **54:** 30; **55:** 90, 170, 176
        as "female achiever" **19:** 113; **38:** 89; **55:** 90, 101, 109, 122, 164
        desire **38:** 96; **44:** 35; **55:** 109, 170
        pursuit of Bertram **7:** 9, 12, 15, 16, 19, 21, 26, 27, 29, 32, 43, 54, 76, 116; **13:** 77; **22:** 78; **49:** 46; **55:** 90
        virginity **38:** 65; **55:** 131, 176
        virtue and nobility **7:** 9, 10, 12, 16, 19, 21, 27, 32, 41, 51, 58, 67, 76, 86, 126; **13:** 77; **50:** 59; **55:** 122
    implausibility of plot, characters, or events **7:** 8, 45
    irony, paradox, and ambiguity **7:** 27, 32, 58, 62, 67, 81, 86, 109, 116
    King **38:** 150; **55:** 148
    language and imagery **7:** 12, 29, 45, 104, 109, 121; **38:** 132; **48:** 65
    Lavatch **26:** 64; **46:** 33, 52, 68; **55:** 143
    love **7:** 12, 15, 16, 51, 58, 67, 90, 93, 116; **38:** 80; **51:** 33, 44
    merit versus rank **7:** 9, 10, 19, 37, 51, 76; **38:** 155; **50:** 59
    "mingled yarn" **7:** 62, 93, 109, 126; **38:** 65
    morality plays, influence of **7:** 29, 41, 51, 98, 113; **13:** 66
    opening scene **54:** 30
    Parolles
        characterization **7:** 8, 9, 43, 76, 81, 98, 109, 113, 116, 126; **22:** 78; **26:** 48, 73, 97; **26:** 117; **46:** 68; **55:** 90, 154
        exposure **7:** 9, 27, 81, 98, 109, 113, 116, 121, 126
        Falstaff, compared with **7:** 8, 9, 16
    reconciliation **7:** 90, 93, 98; **51:** 33
    religious, mythic, or spiritual content **7:** 15, 45, 54, 67, 76, 98, 109, 116
    romance or folktale elements **7:** 32, 41, 43, 45, 54, 76, 104, 116, 121; **26:** 117
    sexuality **7:** 67, 86, 90, 93, 98, 126; **13:** 84; **19:** 113; **22:** 78; **28:** 38; **44:** 35; **49:** 46; **51:** 44; **55:** 109, 131, 143, 176
    social and political context **13:** 66; **22:** 78; **38:** 99, 109, 150, 155; **49:** 46
    staging issues **19:** 113; **26:** 15, 19, 48, 52, 64, 73, 85, 92, 93, 94, 95, 97, 114, 117, 128; **54:** 30
    structure **7:** 21, 29, 32, 45, 51, 76, 81, 93, 98, 116; **22:** 78; **26:** 128; **38:** 72, 123, 142
    youth versus age **7:** 9, 45, 58, 62, 76, 81, 86, 93, 98, 104, 116, 126; **26:** 117; **38:** 109

Antony and Cleopatra (**Volumes 6, 17, 27, 47**)

    allegorical elements **52:** 5
    All for Love (John Dryden), compared with **6:** 20, 21; **17:** 12, 94, 101
    ambiguity **6:** 53, 111, 161, 163, 180, 189, 208, 211, 228; **13:** 368
    androgyny **13:** 530
    Antony
        characterization **6:** 22, 23, 24, 31, 38, 41, 172, 181, 211; **16:** 342; **19:** 270; **22:** 217; **27:** 117; **47:** 77, 124, 142
        Cleopatra, relationship with **6:** 25, 27, 37, 39, 48, 52, 53, 62, 67, 71, 76, 85, 100, 125, 131, 133, 136, 142, 151, 161, 163, 165, 180, 192; **27:** 82; **47:** 107, 124, 165, 174
        death scene **25:** 245; **47:** 142
        dotage **6:** 22, 23, 38, 41, 48, 52, 62, 107, 136, 146, 175; **17:** 28
        nobility **6:** 22, 24, 33, 48, 94, 103, 136, 142, 159, 172, 202; **25:** 245

political conduct **6:** 33, 38, 53, 107, 111, 146, 181
public versus private personae **6:** 165; **47:** 107
self-knowledge **6:** 120, 131, 175, 181, 192; **47:** 77
as superhuman figure **6:** 37, 51, 71, 92, 94, 178, 192; **27:** 110; **47:** 71
as tragic hero **6:** 38, 39, 52, 53, 60, 104, 120, 151, 155, 165, 178, 192, 202, 211; **22:** 217; **27:** 90
audience response **48:** 206
Cleopatra
  Antony, relationship with **6:** 25, 27, 37, 39, 48, 52, 53, 62, 67, 71, 76, 85, 100, 125, 131, 133, 136, 142, 151, 161, 163, 165, 180, 192; **25:** 257; **27:** 82; **47:** 107, 124, 165, 174
  characterization **47:** 77, 96, 113, 124
  contradictory or inconsistent nature **6:** 23, 24, 27, 67, 76, 100, 104, 115, 136, 151, 159, 202; **17:** 94, 113; **27:** 135
  costume **17:** 94
  creativity **6:** 197; **47:** 96, 113
  death, decay, and nature's destructiveness **6:** 23, 25, 27, 41, 43, 52, 60, 64, 76, 94, 100, 103, 120, 131, 133, 136, 140, 146, 161, 165, 180, 181, 192, 197, 208; **13:** 383; **17:** 48, 94; **25:** 245; **27:** 135; **47:** 71
  personal attraction of **6:** 24, 38, 40, 43, 48, 53, 76, 104, 115, 155; **17:** 113
  self-knowledge **47:** 77, 96
  staging issues **17:** 94, 113
  as subverter of social order **6:** 146, 165; **47:** 113
  as superhuman figure **6:** 37, 51, 71, 92, 94, 178, 192; **27:** 110; **47:** 71, 174, 192
  as tragic heroine **6:** 53, 120, 151, 192, 208; **27:** 144
  as voluptuary or courtesan **6:** 21, 22, 25, 41, 43, 52, 53, 62, 64, 67, 76, 146, 161; **47:** 107, 174
comic elements **6:** 52, 85, 104, 125, 131, 151, 192, 202, 219; **47:** 77, 124, 149, 165
contemptus mundi **6:** 85, 133
dreams **45:** 28
dualisms **19:** 304; **27:** 82
Egyptian versus Roman values **6:** 31, 33, 43, 53, 104, 111, 115, 125, 142, 155, 159, 178, 181, 211, 219; **17:** 48; **19:** 270; **27:** 82, 121, 126; **28:** 249; **47:** 96, 103, 113, 149
Elizabethan culture, relation to **47:** 103
Enobarbus **6:** 22, 23, 27, 43, 94, 120, 142; **16:** 342; **17:** 36; **22:** 217; **27:** 135
gender issues **13:** 368; **25:** 257; **27:** 144; **47:** 174, 192; **53:** 67, 77
imperialism **53:** 67, 77
irony or paradox **6:** 53, 136, 146, 151, 159, 161, 189, 192, 211, 224
language and imagery **6:** 21, 25, 39, 64, 80, 85, 92, 94, 100, 104, 142, 146, 155, 159, 161, 165, 189, 192, 202, 211; **13:** 374, 383; **25:** 245, 257; **27:** 96, 105, 135
love and passion **6:** 51, 64, 71, 80, 85, 100, 115, 159, 165, 180; **25:** 257; **27:** 126; **47:** 71, 124, 174, 192; **51:** 25, 33, 44
monument scene **13:** 374; **16:** 342; **17:** 104, 110; **22:** 217; **47:** 142, 165
morality **52:** 5
moral relativism **22:** 217; **27:** 121
mythological allusions **16:** 342; **19:** 304; **27:** 110, 117; **47:** 71, 192
Octavius **6:** 22, 24, 31, 38, 43, 53, 62, 107, 125, 146, 178, 181, 219; **25:** 257
opening scene **54:** 6
political and social disintegration **6:** 31, 43, 53, 60, 71, 80, 100, 107, 111, 146, 180, 197, 219; **22:** 217; **25:** 257; **27:** 121
race **53:** 67, 77
reason versus imagination **6:** 107, 115, 142, 197, 228; **45:** 28
reconciliation **6:** 100, 103, 125, 131, 159, 181
religious, mythic, or spiritual content **6:** 53, 94, 111, 115, 178, 192, 224; **47:** 71
royalty **6:** 94
Seleucus episode (Act V, scene ii) **6:** 39, 41, 62, 133, 140, 151; **27:** 135
Shakespeare's major tragedies, compared with **6:** 25, 53, 60, 71, 120, 181, 189, 202; **22:** 217; **47:** 77
Shakespeare's moral judgment **6:** 33, 37, 38, 41, 48, 51, 64, 76, 111, 125, 136, 140, 146, 163, 175, 189, 202, 211, 228; **13:** 368, 523; **25:** 257
sources **6:** 20, 39; **19:** 304; **27:** 96, 126; **28:** 249
stage history **17:** 84, 94, 101
staging issues **17:** 6, 12, 84, 94, 101, 104, 110; **27:** 90; **47:** 142
strategic analysis **48:** 206
theatricality and role-playing **47:** 96, 103, 107, 113
unity **6:** 20, 21, 22, 24, 25, 32, 33, 39, 43, 53, 60, 67, 111, 125, 146, 151, 165, 208, 211, 219; **13:** 374; **27:** 82, 90, 135
wheel of fortune, motif of **6:** 25, 178; **19:** 304

As You Like It (Volumes 5, 23, 34, 46, 57)

Appearance versus Reality **46:** 105 **57:** 35, 40
androgyny **23:** 98, 100, 122, 138, 143, 144; **34:** 172, 177; **46:** 134; **57:** 13
anti-romantic elements **34:** 72
aristocracy **34:** 120
art versus nature **5:** 128, 130, 148; **34:** 147; **57:** 35, 75
Audrey **46:** 122
autobiographical elements **5:** 25, 35, 43, 50, 55, 61
bawdy elements **46:** 122
Celia **46:** 94
characterization **5:** 19, 24, 25, 36, 39, 54, 82, 86, 116, 148; **34:** 72; **48:** 42
Christian elements **5:** 39, 98, 162; **57:** 31
contradiction, paradox, and opposition **46:** 105
comic form **46:** 105; **51:** 1; **57:** 2
comic resolution **52:** 63
corruption in society **46:** 94; **57:** 35
costume **46:** 117
courtship and marriage **34:** 109, 177; **48:** 32; **51:** 44
death, decay, nature's destructiveness **46:** 169
deception, disguise, and duplicity **46:** 134; **57:** 40
desire **37:** 43; **52:** 63
domestic elements **46:** 142
dramatic shortcomings or failure **5:** 19, 42, 52, 61, 65
duration of time **5:** 44, 45
Elizabethan culture, relation to **5:** 21, 59, 66, 68, 70, 158; **16:** 53; **28:** 46; **34:** 120; **37:** 1; **46:** 142; **57:** 23, 31, 64, 75
Fathers and Daughters **46:** 94
feminism **23:** 107, 108; **57:** 2, 13
Forest of Arden
  as "bitter" Arcadia **5:** 98, 118, 162; **23:** 97, 98, 99, 100, 122, 139
  Duke Frederick's court, contrast with **5:** 46, 102, 103, 112, 130, 156; **16:** 53; **23:** 126, 128, 129, 131, 134; **34:** 78, 102, 131; **46:** 164; **57:** 64
  pastoral elements **5:** 18, 20, 24, 32, 35, 47, 50, 54, 55, 57, 60, 77, 128, 135, 156; **23:** 17, 20, 27, 46, 137; **34:** 78, 147; **46:** 88
  as patriarchal society **5:** 168; **23:** 150; **34:** 177; **57:** 2
  as source of self-knowledge **5:** 98, 102, 103, 128, 130, 135, 148, 158, 162; **23:** 17; **34:** 102; **57:** 35
  as timeless, mythical world **5:** 112, 130, 141; **23:** 132; **34:** 78; **37:** 43; **46:** 88
  theme of play **46:** 88
gender identity **46:** 127, 134; **57:** 13, 23, 45
genre **5:** 46, 55, 79
homoerotic elements **46:** 127, 142; **57:** 23
homosexuality **46:** 127, 142; **57:** 13
Hymen episode **5:** 61, 116, 130; **23:** 22, 48, 54, 109, 111, 112, 113, 115, 146, 147; **57:** 40
irony **5:** 30, 32, 154
Jaques
  love-theme, relation to **5:** 103; **23:** 7, 118, 128
  as malcontent **5:** 59, 70, 84
  melancholy **5:** 20, 28, 32, 36, 39, 43, 50, 59, 63, 68, 77, 82, 86, 135; **23:** 20, 26, 103, 104, 107, 109; **34:** 85; **46:** 88, 94
  pastoral convention, relation to **5:** 61, 63, 65, 79, 93, 98, 114, 118
  Seven Ages of Man speech (Act II, scene vii) **5:** 28, 52, 156; **23:** 48, 103, 105, 126, 138, 152; **46:** 88, 156, 164, 169
  Shakespeare, relation to **5:** 35, 50, 154
  as superficial critic **5:** 28, 30, 43, 54, 55, 63, 65, 68, 75, 77, 82, 86, 88, 98, 138; **34:** 85
justice **46:** 94
juxtaposition of opposing perspectives **5:** 86, 93, 98, 141; **16:** 53; **23:** 119; **34:** 72, 78, 131
language and imagery **5:** 19, 21, 35, 52, 75, 82, 92, 138; **23:** 15, 21, 26; **28:** 9; **34:** 131; **37:** 43; **48:** 42; **57:** 35, 56
love **5:** 24, 44, 46, 57, 79, 88, 103, 116, 122, 138, 141, 162; **28:** 46, 82; **34:** 85
Love in a Forest (Charles Johnson adaptation) **23:** 7
metadramatic elements **5:** 128, 130, 146; **34:** 130
morality **52:** 63; **57:** 13
mythological allusions **46:** 142
nature **46:** 94
Neoclassical rules **5:** 19, 20
Orlando
  as ideal man **5:** 32, 36, 39, 162; **34:** 161; **46:** 94
  as younger brother **5:** 66, 158; **46:** 94
pastoral characters (Silvius, Phebe, and Corin) **23:** 37, 97, 98, 99, 108, 110, 118, 122, 138; **34:** 147
pastoral convention, parodies of **5:** 54, 57, 72

pastoral convention, relation to **5:** 72, 77, 122; **34:** 161; **37:** 1
primogeniture **5:** 66, 158; **34:** 109, 120
psychoanalytic interpretation **5:** 146, 158; **23:** 141, 142; **34:** 109; **48:** 42
public versus private worlds **46:** 164
reconciliation of opposites **5:** 79, 88, 103, 116, 122, 138; **23:** 127, 143; **34:** 161, 172; **46:** 156
as romance **5:** 55, 79; **23:** 27, 28, 40, 43
Rosalind **46:** 94, 122,
    Beatrice, compared with **5:** 26, 36, 50, 75
    charm **5:** 55, 75; **23:** 17, 18, 20, 41, 89, 111
    disguise, role of **5:** 75, 107, 118, 122, 128, 130, 133, 138, 141, 146, 148, 164, 168; **13:** 502; **23:** 35, 42, 106, 119, 123, 146; **34:** 130; **46:** 134
    femininity **5:** 26, 36, 52, 75; **23:** 24, 29, 46, 54, 103, 108, 121, 146
    as Ganymede **46:** 127, 142
    love-theme, relation to **5:** 79, 88, 103, 116, 122, 138, 141; **23:** 114, 115; **34:** 85, 177
rustic characters **5:** 24, 60, 72, 84; **23:** 127; **34:** 78, 161
sexual ambiguity and sexual deception **46:** 134, 142; **57:** 23, 40, 45
Sexuality in Shakespeare **46:** 122, 127, 134, 142
as satire or parody of pastoral conventions **5:** 46, 55, 60, 72, 77, 79, 84, 114, 118, 128, 130, 154
self-knowledge **5:** 32, 82, 102, 116, 122, 133, 164; **57:** 45
sibling rivalry **34:** 109
social order **37:** 1; **46:** 94; **57:** 2
sources **5:** 18, 32, 54, 59, 66, 84; **34:** 155; **46:** 117
stage history **46:** 117; **57:** 56
staging issues **13:** 502; **23:** 7, 17, 19, 22, 58, 96, 97, 98, 99, 101, 110, 137; **28:** 82; **32:** 212; **57:** 56, 75
structure **5:** 19, 24, 25, 35, 44, 45, 46, 86, 93, 116, 138, 158; **23:** 7, 8, 9, 10, 11; **34:** 72, 78, 131, 147, 155
time **5:** 18, 82, 112, 141; **23:** 146, 150; **34:** 102; **46:** 88, 156, 164, 169
Touchstone
    callousness **5:** 88
    comic and farcical elements **46:** 117
    as philosopher-fool **5:** 24, 28, 30, 32, 36, 63, 75, 98; **23:** 152; **34:** 85; **46:** 1, 14, 18, 24, 33, 52, 60, 88, 105,
    relation to pastoral convention **5:** 54, 61, 63, 72, 75, 77, 79, 84, 86, 93, 98, 114, 118, 135, 138, 166; **34:** 72, 147, 161
selflessness **5:** 30, 36, 39, 76
verisimilitude **5:** 18, 23, 28, 30, 32, 39, 125; **23:** 107
wordplay **46:** 105

The Comedy of Errors (Volumes 1, 26, 34, 54)

Adriana **16:** 3; **34:** 211, 220, 238; **54:** 189
adultery **34:** 215
audience perception **1:** 37, 50, 56; **19:** 54; **34:** 258; **54:** 136, 144
autobiographical elements **1:** 16, 18
characterization **1:** 13, 21, 31, 34, 46, 49, 50, 55, 56; **19:** 54; **25:** 63; **34:** 194, 201, 208, 245 **54:** 144, 176

classical influence and sources **1:** 13, 14, 16, 31, 32, 43, 61; **54:** 169
comic elements **1:** 43, 46, 55, 56, 59; **26:** 183, 186, 188, 190; **34:** 190, 245
composition date **1:** 18, 23, 34, 55
dramatic structure **1:** 19, 27, 40, 43, 46, 50; **26:** 186, 190; **34:** 190, 229, 233; **37:** 12; **54:** 136, 155, 189
Dromio brothers **42:** 80; **54:** 136, 152
Elizabethan culture, relation to **26:** 138, 142; **34:** 201, 215, 233, 238, 258; **42:** 80; **54:** 169, 200
farcical elements **1:** 14, 16, 19, 23, 30, 34, 35, 46, 50, 59, 61; **19:** 54; **26:** 188, 190; **34:** 245; **54:** 136, 144, 189
feminist criticism **42:** 93
food, meaning of **34:** 220
gender issues **34:** 215, 220
genre **34:** 251, 258
identity **34:** 201, 208, 211; **54:** 155, 169, 200
illusion **1:** 13, 14, 27, 37, 40, 45, 59, 63; **26:** 188; **34:** 194, 211; **54:** 169, 200
language and imagery **1:** 16, 25, 39, 40, 43, 57, 59; **34:** 233; **54:** 152, 162
male/female relationships **16:** 3
marriage **34:** 251; **54:** 215
mistaken identity **1:** 13, 14, 27, 37, 40, 45, 49, 55, 57, 61, 63; **19:** 34, 54; **25:** 63; **34:** 194; **54:** 176, 162, 189, 215
Plautus's works, compared with **1:** 13, 14, 16, 53, 61; **16:** 3; **19:** 34; **54:** 162, 176
problem comedy **34:** 251
redemption **19:** 54; **26:** 188; **54:** 152, 189
romantic elements **1:** 13, 16, 19, 23, 25, 30, 31, 36, 39, 53
servitude **42:** 80
social order **34:** 238; **54:** 155, 215
sources **1:** 13, 14, 16, 19, 31, 32, 39; **16:** 3; **34:** 190, 215, 258; **54:** 155, 176,
staging issues **26:** 182, 183, 186, 188, 190; **54:** 136
supernatural, role of **1:** 27, 30; **54:** 215
tragic elements **1:** 16, 25, 27, 45, 50, 59; **34:** 229; **54:** 144
wonder, dynamic of **37:** 12

Coriolanus (Volumes 9, 17, 30, 50)

aggression **9:** 112, 142, 174, 183, 189, 198; **30:** 79, 111, 125, 142; **44:** 11, 79
Anthony and Cleopatra, compared with **30:** 79, 96; **50:** 105
appearance versus reality **30:** 142
Aufidius **9:** 9, 12, 17, 19, 53, 121, 148, 153, 157, 169, 180, 193; **19:** 287; **25:** 263, 296; **30:** 58, 67, 89, 96, 133; **50:** 99
body politic, metaphor of **22:** 248; **30:** 67, 96, 105, 125; **50:** 105, 110, 119, 140, 145, 152
butterfly episode (Act I, scene iii) **9:** 19, 45, 62, 65, 73, 100, 125, 153, 157
capitulation scene (Act V, scene iii) **9:** 19, 26, 53, 65, 100, 117, 125, 130, 157, 164, 183
ceremonies, rites, and rituals, importance of **9:** 139, 148, 169
Christian elements **30:** 111
comic elements **9:** 8, 9, 14, 53, 80, 106
Cominius **25:** 245
Cominius's tribute (Act II, scene ii) **9:** 80, 100. 117, 125, 144, 164, 198; **25:** 296
Coriolanus

anger or passion **9:** 19, 26, 45, 80, 92, 157, 164, 177, 189; **30:** 79, 96
as complementary figure to Aufidius **19:** 287
death scene (Act V, scene vi) **9:** 12, 80, 100, 117, 125, 144, 164, 198; **25:** 245, 263; **50:** 110
as epic hero **9:** 130, 164, 177; **25:** 245; **50:** 119
immaturity **9:** 62, 80, 84, 110, 117, 142; **30:** 140
inhuman attributes **9:** 65, 73, 139, 157, 164, 169, 189, 198; **25:** 263
internal struggle **9:** 31, 43, 45, 53, 72, 117, 121, 130; **44:** 93
introspection or self-knowledge, lack of **9:** 53, 80, 84, 112, 117, 130; **25:** 296; **30:** 133
isolation or autonomy **9:** 53, 65, 142, 144, 153, 157, 164, 180, 183, 189, 198; **30:** 58, 89, 111; **50:** 128
manipulation by others **9:** 33, 45, 62, 80; **25:** 296
modesty **9:** 8, 12, 19, 26, 53, 78, 92, 117, 121, 144, 183; **25:** 296; **30:** 79, 96, 129, 133, 149
narcissism **30:** 111
noble or aristocratic attributes **9:** 15, 18, 19, 26, 31, 33, 52, 53, 62, 65, 84, 92, 100, 121, 148, 157, 169; **25:** 263; **30:** 67, 74, 96; **50:** 13
pride or arrogance **9:** 8, 11, 12, 19, 26, 31, 33, 43, 45, 65, 78, 92, 121, 148, 153, 177; **30:** 58, 67, 74, 89, 96, 129
reconciliation with society **9:** 33, 43, 45, 65, 139, 169; **25:** 296
as socially destructive force **9:** 62, 65, 73, 78, 110, 142, 144, 153; **25:** 296
soliloquy (Act IV, scene iv) **9:** 84, 112, 117, 130
as tragic figure **9:** 8, 12, 13, 18, 25, 45, 52, 53, 72, 80, 92, 106, 112, 117, 130, 148, 164, 169, 177; **25:** 296; **30:** 67, 74, 79, 96, 111, 129; **37:** 283; **50:** 99
traitorous actions **9:** 9, 12, 19, 45, 84, 92, 148; **25:** 296; **30:** 133
as unsympathetic character **9:** 12, 13, 62, 78, 80, 84, 112, 130, 157
domestic elements **42:** 223; **50:** 145
economics **50:** 152
England and Rome, parallels between **9:** 39, 43, 106, 148, 180, 193; **25:** 296; **30:** 67, 105; **50:** 172
fable of the belly (Act I, scene i) **9:** 8, 65, 73, 80, 136, 153, 157, 164, 180, 183, 189; **25:** 296; **30:** 79, 105, 111; **50:** 13, 110, 140
fame **30:** 58
fire and water **25:** 263
flattery or dissimulation **9:** 26, 45, 92, 100, 110, 121, 130, 144, 157, 183, 193; **25:** 296
friendship **30:** 125, 142
gender issues **30:** 79, 125, 142; **44:** 93; **50:** 128
genre **9:** 42, 43, 53, 80, 106, 112, 117, 130, 164, 177; **30:** 67, 74, 79, 89, 111, 125; **50:** 99
honor or integrity **9:** 43, 65, 73, 92, 106, 110, 121, 144, 153, 157, 164, 177, 183, 189; **30:** 89, 96, 133
identity **42:** 248; **50:** 128
irony or satire **9:** 65, 73, 92, 106, 153, 157, 164, 193; **30:** 67, 89, 133

Jacobean culture, relation to **22:** 248
language and imagery **9:** 8, 9, 13, 53, 64, 65, 73, 78, 84, 100, 112, 121, 136, 139, 142, 144, 153, 157, 174, 183, 193, 198; **22:** 248; **25:** 245, 263; **30:** 111, 125, 142; **37:** 283; **44:** 79
Macbeth, compared with **30:** 79
martial vs. civil law **48:** 230
Menenius **9:** 8, 9, 11, 14, 19, 26, 78, 80, 106, 148, 157; **25:** 263, 296; **30:** 67, 79, 89, 96, 111, 133
Midlands Revolt, influence of **22:** 248; **30:** 79; **50:** 140, 172
naming, significance of **30:** 58, 96, 111, 125
nature, philosophy of **30:** 74
nurturing or feeding **9:** 65, 73, 136, 183, 189; **30:** 111; **44:** 79; **50:** 110
opening scene **54:** 6
paradoxical elements **9:** 73, 92, 106, 121, 153, 157, 164, 169, 193
plebeians **9:** 8, 9, 11, 12, 15, 18, 19, 26, 33, 39, 53, 92, 125, 153, 183, 189; **25:** 296; **30:** 58, 79, 96, 111; **50:** 13, 105
Plutarch and historical sources **9:** 8, 9, 13, 14, 16, 26, 39, 92, 106, 130, 142, 164; **30:** 74, 79, 105; **50:** 99
politics **9:** 15, 17, 18, 19, 26, 33, 43, 53, 62, 65, 73, 80, 92, 106, 110, 112, 121, 144, 153, 157, 164, 180; **22:** 248; **25:** 296; **30:** 58, 67, 79, 89, 96, 105, 111, 125; **37:** 283; **42:** 223; **48:** 230; **50:** 13, 140, 172
psychoanalytic interpretations **44:** 93
public versus private worlds **37:** 283; **42:** 223
sexuality **9:** 112, 142, 174, 183, 189, 198; **30:** 79, 111, 125, 142
shame **42:** 248
Shakespeare's political sympathies **9:** 8, 11, 15, 17, 19, 26, 39, 52, 53, 62, 80, 92, 142; **25:** 296; **30:** 74, 79, 89, 96, 105, 133; **50:** 145, 172
slander **48:** 230
society **9:** 15, 17, 18, 19, 26, 33, 43, 53, 62, 65, 73, 80, 92, 106, 110, 112, 121, 144, 153, 157, 164, 180; **22:** 248; **25:** 296; **30:** 58, 67, 79, 89, 96, 105, 111, 125; **50:** 13, 105, 119, 152
staging issues **17:** 172, 242, 248
structure **9:** 8, 9, 11, 12, 13, 14, 16, 26, 33, 45, 53, 58, 72, 78, 80, 84, 92, 112, 139, 148; **25:** 263; **30:** 79, 96
treachery **30:** 89
the tribunes (Brutus and Sicinius) **9:** 9, 11, 14, 19, 33, 169, 180
Virgilia **9:** 11, 19, 26, 33, 58, 100, 121, 125; **25:** 263; **30:** 79, 96, 133; **50:** 99
Volumnia
   Coriolanus's subservience to **9:** 16, 26, 33, 53, 62, 80, 92, 100, 117, 125, 142, 177, 183; **30:** 140, 149; **44:** 79
   influence on Coriolanus **9:** 45, 62, 65, 78, 92, 100, 110, 117, 121, 125, 130, 148, 157, 183, 189, 193; **25:** 263, 296; **30:** 79, 96, 125, 133, 140, 142, 149; **44:** 93
   as noble Roman matron **9:** 16, 19, 26, 31, 33
   personification of Rome **9:** 125, 183; **50:** 119
war **25:** 263; **30:** 79, 96, 125, 149

Cymbeline (Volumes 4, 15, 36, 47)

appearance versus reality **4:** 87, 93, 103, 162; **36:** 99; **47:** 228, 286
authorship controversy **4:** 17, 21, 35, 48, 56, 78
autobiographical elements **4:** 43, 46; **36:** 134
bawdy elements **36:** 155
Beaumont and Fletcher's romances, compared with **4:** 46, 52, 138
Belarius **4:** 48, 89, 141
British nationalism **4:** 19, 78, 89, 93, 129, 141, 159, 167; **32:** 373; **36:** 129; **45:** 67; **47:** 219, 265
Cloten **4:** 20, 116, 127, 155; **22:** 302, 365; **25:** 245; **36:** 99, 125, 142, 155; **47:** 228
combat scenes **22:** 365
comic elements **4:** 35, 56, 113, 141; **15:** 111, 122; **47:** 296
dramatic structure **4:** 17, 18, 19, 20, 21, 22, 24, 38, 43, 48, 53, 64, 68, 89, 116, 129, 141; **22:** 302, 365; **25:** 319; **36:** 115, 125
dreams **4:** 162, 167; **44:** 28; **45:** 67, 75
dualisms **4:** 29, 64, 73
Elizabethan dramatic conventions **4:** 53, 124
family, theme of **44:** 28
Guiderius and Arviragus **4:** 21, 22, 89, 129, 141, 148; **25:** 319; **36:** 125, 158
historical elements **47:** 260
Iachimo **25:** 245, 319; **36:** 166
Imogen **4:** 21, 22, 24, 29, 37, 45, 46, 52, 56, 78, 89, 108; **15:** 23, 32, 105, 121; **19:** 411; **25:** 245, 319; **28:** 398; **32:** 373; **36:** 129, 142, 148; **47:** 25, 205, 228, 245, 274, 277
Imogen's reawakening (Act IV, scene ii) **4:** 37, 56, 89, 103, 108, 116, 150; **15:** 23; **25:** 245; **47:** 252
irony **4:** 64, 77, 103
language and imagery **4:** 43, 48, 61, 64, 70, 73, 93, 108; **13:** 401; **25:** 245; **28:** 373, 398; **36:** 115, 158, 166, 186; **47:** 205, 286, 296
Lucretia, analogies to **36:** 148
misperception **19:** 411; **36:** 99, 115; **47:** 228, 237, 252, 277, 286, 296,
negative appraisals **4:** 20, 35, 43, 45, 48, 53, 56, 68; **15:** 32, 105, 121
patriarchy **32:** 373; **36:** 134; **47:** 237; **51:** 30
Posthumus **4:** 24, 30, 53, 78, 116, 127, 141, 155, 159, 167; **15:** 89; **19:** 411; **25:** 245, 319; **36:** 142; **44:** 28; **45:** 67, 75; **47:** 25, 205, 228,
psychological elements **36:** 134; **44:** 28; **45:** 67, 75
reconciliation **4:** 38, 64, 73, 93, 105, 113, 116, 129, 138, 141, 162, 170
religious, mythical, or spiritual content **4:** 22, 29, 78, 93, 105, 108, 115, 116, 127, 134, 138, 141, 159; **28:** 373; **36:** 142, 158, 186; **47:** 219, 260, 274
romantic elements **4:** 17, 20, 46, 68, 77, 141, 148, 172; **15:** 111; **25:** 319; **28:** 373
self-conscious or artificial nature of play **4:** 43, 52, 56, 68, 124, 134, 138; **36:** 99
sexuality **4:** 170, 172; **25:** 319; **32:** 373; **47:** 245
Shakespeare's lyric poetry, compared with **13:** 401
sources **4:** 17, 18; **13:** 401; **28:** 373; **47:** 245, 265, 277
staging issues **15:** 6, 23, 75, 105, 111, 121, 122; **22:** 365

subversiveness **22:** 302
tragic elements **25:** 319; **28:** 373; **36:** 129; **47:** 296
trickster, motif of **22:** 302
vision scene (Act V, scene iv) **4:** 17, 21, 28, 29, 35, 38, 78, 105, 108, 134, 150, 167; **47:** 205
wager plot **4:** 18, 24, 29, 53, 78, 155; **22:** 365; **25:** 319; **47:** 205, 277

Hamlet (Volumes 1, 21, 35, 44)

ambiguity **1:** 92, 160, 198, 227, 230, 234, 247, 249; **21:** 72; **35:** 167
appearance versus reality **1:** 95, 116, 166, 169, 198; **35:** 82, 126, 132, 144, 238; **44:** 248; **45:** 28
aristocracy **42:** 217
audience response **28:** 325; **32:** 238; **35:** 167; **44:** 107
autobiographical elements **1:** 98, 115, 119; **13:** 487
beginning **54:** 19
Calvinist implications **48:** 195
classical Greek tragedies, compared with **1:** 74, 75, 130, 184, 212; **13:** 296; **22:** 339
Claudius **13:** 502; **16** 246; **21:** 259, 347, 361, 371; **28:** 232, 290; **35:** 104, 182; **44:** 119, 241
closet scene (Act III, scene iv) **16:** 259; **21:** 151, 334, 392; **35:** 204, 229; **44:** 119, 237
costume **21:** 81
death, decay, and nature's destructiveness **1:** 144, 153, 188, 198, 221, 242; **13:** 502; **28:** 280, 311; **35:** 241; **42:** 284
dreams **45:** 28
dumbshow and play scene (Act III, scene ii) **1:** 76, 86, 134, 138, 154, 160, 207; **13:** 502; **21:** 392; **35:** 82; **44:** 241; **46:** 74
Elizabethan culture, relation to **1:** 76, 148, 151, 154, 160, 166, 169, 171, 184, 202, 209, 254; **13:** 282, 494; **19:** 330; **21:** 407, 416; **22:** 258
Elizabethan and Jacobean politics, relation to **28:** 232; **28:** 290, 311; **35:** 140
ending **54:** 96
feminist criticism **55:** 56
fencing scene (Act V, scene ii) **21:** 392; **54:** 96
Fortinbras **21:** 136, 347; **28:** 290
gender issues **35:** 144; **44:** 189, 195, 198,
genre **1:** 176, 212, 237
Gertrude **21:** 259, 347, 392; **28:** 311; **32:** 238; **35:** 182, 204, 229; **44:** 119, 160, 189, 195, 237, 248
Ghost **1:** 75, 76, 84, 85, 128, 134, 138, 154, 171, 218, 231, 254; **16:** 246; **21:** 17, 44, 112, 151, 334, 371, 377, 392; **25:** 288; **35:** 152, 157, 174, 237; **44:** 119
gravedigger scene (Act V, scene i) **21:** 392; **28:** 280; **46:** 74
grotesque elements **42:** 284
Hamlet
   delay **1:** 76, 83, 88, 90, 94, 98, 102, 103, 106, 114, 115, 116, 119, 120, 148, 151, 166, 171, 179, 188, 191, 194, 198, 221, 268; **13:** 296, 502; **21:** 81; **25:** 209, 288; **28:** 223; **35:** 82, 174, 212, 215, 237; **44:** 180, 209, 219, 229
   divided nature **16:** 246; **28:** 223; **32:** 288; **35:** 182, 215; **37:** 241

elocution of the character's speeches **21:** 96, 104, 112, 127, 132, 172, 177, 179, 194, 245, 254, 257
as a fool **46:** 1, 29, 52, 74
madness **1:** 76, 81, 83, 95, 102, 106, 128, 144, 154, 160, 234; **21:** 35, 50, 72, 81, 99, 112, 311, 339, 355, 361, 371, 377, 384; **35:** 117, 132, 134, 140, 144, 212; **44:** 107, 119, 152, 209, 219, 229
melancholy **21:** 99, 112, 177, 194; **35:** 82, 95, 117; **44:** 209, 219
as negative character **1:** 86, 92, 111, 171, 218; **21:** 386; **25:** 209; **35:** 167
reaction to his father's death **22:** 339; **35:** 104, 174; **44:** 133, 160, 180, 189
reaction to Gertrude's marriage **1:** 74, 120, 154, 179; **16:** 259; **21:** 371; **22:** 339; **35:** 104, 117; **44:** 133, 160, 189, 195
romantic aspects of the character **21:** 96; **44:** 198
as scourge or purifying figure **1:** 144, 209, 242; **25:** 288; **35:** 157
sentimentality versus intellectuality **1:** 75, 83, 88, 91, 93, 94, 96, 102, 103, 115, 116, 120, 166, 191; **13:** 296; **21:** 35, 41, 44, 72, 81, 89, 99, 129, 132, 136, 172, 213, 225, 339, 355, 361, 371, 377, 379, 381, 386; **25:** 209; **44:** 198
soliloquies **1:** 76, 82, 83, 148, 166, 169, 176, 191; **21:** 17, 31, 44, 53, 89, 112, 268, 311, 334, 347, 361, 384, 392; **25:** 209; **28:** 223; **44:** 107, 119, 229
as a stoic at the end **54:** 96
theatrical interpretations **21:** 11, 31, 78, 101, 104, 107, 160, 177, 179, 182, 183, 192, 194, 197, 202, 203, 208, 213, 225, 232, 237, 249, 253, 254, 257, 259, 274, 311, 339, 347, 355, 361, 371, 377, 380
virility **21:** 213, 301, 355; **44:** 198
Hamlet with Alterations (David Garrick adaptation) **21:** 23, 334, 347
Horatio **44:** 189
idealism versus pragmatism **16** 246; **28:** 325
Laertes **21:** 347, 386; **28:** 290; **35:** 182
language and imagery **1:** 95, 144, 153, 154, 160, 188, 198, 221, 227, 249, 259, 270; **22:** 258, 378; **28:** 311; **35:** 144, 152, 238, 241; **42:** 217; **44:** 248; **52:** 35
madness **19:** 330; **35:** 104, 126, 134, 140, 144; **44:** 107, 119, 152, 209, 219, 229
marriage **22:** 339; **51:** 44
Marxist criticism **42:** 234
moral choice **52:** 35
nunnery scene (Act III, scene i) **21:** 157, 381, 410
opening scene **54:** 2, 6, 19
Ophelia **1:** 73, 76, 81, 82, 91, 96, 97, 154, 166, 169, 171, 218, 270; **13:** 268; **16:** 246; **19:** 330; **21:** 17, 41, 44, 72, 81, 101, 104, 107, 112, 136, 203, 259, 347, 381, 386, 392, 416; **28:** 232, 325; **35:** 104, 126, 140, 144, 182, 238; **44:** 189, 195, 248
Polonius **21:** 259, 334, 347, 386, 416; **35:** 182
prayer scene (Act III, scene iii) **1:** 76, 106, 160, 212, 231; **44:** 119
psychoanalytic interpretations **1:** 119, 148, 154, 179, 202; **21:** 197, 213, 361; **25:** 209; **28:** 223; **35:** 95, 104, 134, 237; **37:** 241; **44:** 133, 152, 160, 180, 209, 219

religious, mythic, or spiritual content **1:** 98, 102, 130, 184, 191, 209, 212, 231, 234, 254; **21:** 361; **22:** 258; **28:** 280; **32:** 238; **35:** 134
revenge **1:** 74, 194, 209, 224, 234, 254; **16:** 246; **22:** 258; **25:** 288; **28:** 280; **35:** 152, 157, 167, 174, 212; **44:** 180, 209, 219, 229; **54:** 96
Richard II, compared with **1:** 264
rites, rituals, and ceremonies, importance of **13:** 268; **28:** 232
sexuality **55:** 56
sources **1:** 76, 81, 113, 125, 128, 130, 151, 191, 202, 224, 259
staging issues **13:** 494, 502; **21:** 11, 17, 31, 35, 41, 44, 50, 53, 78, 81, 89, 101, 112, 127, 139, 142, 145, 148, 151, 157, 160, 172, 182, 183, 202, 203, 208, 225, 232, 237, 242, 245, 249, 251, 259, 268, 270, 274, 283, 284, 301, 311, 334, 347, 355, 361, 371, 377, 379, 380, 381, 384, 386, 392, 407, 410, 416; **44:** 198; **54:** 19
Stoicism **48:** 195
structure **22:** 378; **28:** 280, 325; **35:** 82, 104, 215; **44:** 152
subjectivity **45:** 28
textual variants **13:** 282; **16:** 259; **21:** 11, 23, 72, 101, 127, 129, 139, 140, 142, 145, 202, 208, 259, 270, 284, 347, 361, 384; **22:** 258; **32:** 238
topical allusions or content **13:** 282
tragic elements **13:** 78
unity **1:** 75, 76, 87, 103, 113, 125, 128, 142, 148, 160, 184, 188, 198, 264; **16:** 259; **35:** 82, 215
unnatural ordering **22:** 378
wheel of fortune, motif of **52:** 35
widowhood and remarriage, themes of **32:** 238

Henry IV, Parts 1 and 2 (Volumes 1, 14, 39, 49, 57)

ambition **57:** 94
Biblical references **57:** 147
carnival elements **28:** 203; **32:** 103
Catholic components **57:** 167
characterization **1:** 321, 328, 332, 333, 336, 344, 365, 383, 385, 389, 391, 397, 401; **19:** 195; **39:** 123, 137; **42:** 101, 164; **49:** 93; **57:** 88, 167, 181
comic elements **1:** 286, 290, 314, 327, 328, 336, 353; **19:** 195; **25:** 109; **39:** 72; **57:** 120
contractual and economic relations **13:** 213
contrasting dramatic worlds **14:** 56, 60, 61, 84, 105; **48:** 95; **49:** 162; **57:** 183
critical history **42:** 187; **48:** 167
deception, disguise, and duplicity **1:** 397, 406, 425; **42:** 101; **47:** 1, 60; **48:** 95
divine right versus justice **49:** 116; **57:** 88, 130
Elizabethan culture, relation to **19:** 195; **48:** 117, 143, 151, 175
Elizabethan politics, relation to **22:** 395; **28:** 203; **47:** 60; **48:** 117, 143, 167, 175; **57:** 88, 94
Falstaff
characterization **1:** 287, 298, 312, 333; **25:** 245; **28:** 203; **39:** 72, 134, 137, 143; **57:** 120, 156

as comic figure **1:** 287, 311, 327, 344, 351, 354, 357, 410, 434; **39:** 89; **46:** 1, 48, 52; **49:** 178; **57:** 120
as coward or rogue **1:** 285, 290, 296, 298, 306, 307, 313, 317, 323, 336, 337, 338, 342, 354, 366, 374, 391, 396, 401, 433; **14:** 7, 111, 125, 130, 133; **32:** 166
dual personality **1:** 397, 401, 406, 434; **49:** 162
female attributes **13:** 183; **44:** 44
Iago, compared with **1:** 341, 351
Marxist interpretation **1:** 358, 361
as outlaw **49:** 133
as parody of the historical plot **1:** 314, 354, 359; **39:** 143
as positive character **1:** 286, 287, 290, 296, 298, 311, 312, 321, 325, 333, 344, 355, 357, 389, 401, 408, 434
rejection by Hal **1:** 286, 287, 290, 312, 314, 317, 324, 333, 338, 344, 357, 366, 372, 374, 379, 380, 389, 414; **13:** 183; **25:** 109; **39:** 72, 89; **57:** 147
as satire of feudal society **1:** 314, 328, 361; **32:** 103
as scapegoat **1:** 389, 414; **57:** 156
stage interpretations **14:** 4, 6, 7, 9, 15, 116, 130, 146; **47:** 1
as subversive figure **16:** 183; **25:** 109
as Vice figure **1:** 342, 361, 366, 374
flattery **22:** 395
gender issues **13:** 183; **25:** 151; **44:** 44; **48:** 175
Hal
audience's perspective of **49:** 153; **57:** 116
and betrayal **49:** 123
as the central character **1:** 286, 290, 314, 317, 326, 338, 354, 366, 374, 396; **39:** 72, 100
dual personality **1:** 397, 406; **25:** 109, 151; **49:** 112, 139, 153, 162; **57:** 130
as Everyman **1:** 342, 366, 374
fall from humanity **1:** 379, 380, 383
general assessment **1:** 286, 287, 289, 290, 314, 317, 326, 327, 332, 357, 397; **25:** 245; **32:** 212; **39:** 134; **57:** 116, 130
Henry's perspective of **49:** 153
as ideal ruler **1:** 289, 309, 317, 321, 326, 337, 342, 344, 374, 389, 391, 434; **25:** 109; **39:** 123; **47:** 60
as Machiavellian ruler **47:** 60
as negative character **1:** 312, 332, 333, 357; **32:** 212
as outlaw **49:** 112
preparation for rule **49:** 112; **57:** 116, 130
reformation **57:** 160
Richard II, compared with **1:** 332, 337; **39:** 72
as restorer of law **49:** 133
Henry **39:** 123, 137; **49:** 139
effectiveness as ruler **49:** 116
guilt **49:** 112
illegitimacy of rule **49:** 112, 133, 137
as tragic figure **49:** 186
as usurper **49:** 116, 137
historical content **1:** 310, 328, 365, 366, 370, 374, 380, 387, 421, 424, 427, 431; **16:** 172; **19:** 157; **25:** 151; **32:** 136; **39:** 143; **48:** 143, 167; **49:** 139; **57:** 137
historical and dramatic elements **49:** 93
historical epic, place in or relation to Shakespeare's **1:** 309, 314, 328, 374, 379, 424, 427; **48:** 167

historiography **56:** 2, 15, 25
Hotspur **25:** 151; **28:** 101; **39:** 72, 134, 137; **42:** 101; **49:** 137
    and prisoners of war **49:** 137
    versus Henry **49:** 137
John of Lancaster, Prince
    and betrayal **49:** 123
justice **49:** 112, 123; **57:** 137
kingship **1:** 314, 318, 337, 366, 370, 374, 379, 380, 383, 424; **16:** 172; **19:** 195; **28:** 101; **39:** 100, 116, 123, 130; **42:** 143; **48:** 143; **57:** 88, 94, 108, 137, 160
language and imagery **13:** 213; **16:** 172; **25:** 245; **28:** 101; **39:** 116, 130; **42:** 155; **47:** 1; **57:** 137
Lord Chief Justice
    as keeper of law and justice **49:** 133
    as medieval allegory or morality play **1:** 323, 324, 342, 361, 366, 373, 374; **32:** 166; **39:** 89; **47:** 60
Mortimer **25:** 151
multiple endings **49:** 102
Neoclassical rules **1:** 286, 287, 290, 29
politics **28:** 101; **39:** 130; **42:** 143; **48:** 143, 175; **57:** 108
power **49:** 139; **57:** 108
Protestant components **57:** 167
providential order **56:** 15
psychoanalytic interpretations **13:** 457; **28:** 101; **42:** 187; **44:** 44
rebellion **22:** 395; **28:** 101
redemption **57:** 116
references to **22:** 114; **32:** 166; **48:** 117
relationship to other Shakespeare plays **1:** 286, 290, 309, 329, 365, 396; **28:** 101; **42:** 101, 155; **48:** 167; **49:** 93, 186
relationship of Parts 1 and 2 **32:** 136; **39:** 100; **49:** 178; **57:** 160, 181
religious, mythic, or spiritual content **1:** 314, 374, 414, 421, 429, 431, 434; **32:** 103; **48:** 151; **57:** 147, 156, 167
    as autonomous works **1:** 289, 337, 338, 347, 348, 373, 387, 393, 411, 418, 424
    comparison **1:** 290, 295, 329, 348, 358, 393, 411, 419, 429, 431, 441
    unity of both parts **1:** 286, 290, 309, 314, 317, 329, 365, 373, 374, 396, 402, 404, 419
sources **56:** 2
sovereignty **57:** 94
staging issues **32:** 212; **47:** 1; **49:** 102
structure **49:** 93; **56:** 53, 60; **57:** 181
textual issues **22:** 114
time and change, motif of **1:** 372, 393, 411; **39:** 89; **48:** 143
Turkish elements **19:** 170
two fathers **14:** 86, 101, 105, 108; **39:** 89, 100; **49:** 102
violence **25:** 109

Henry V (Volumes 5, 14, 30, 49)

battle of Agincourt **5:** 197, 199, 213, 246, 257, 281, 287, 289, 293, 310, 318; **19:** 217; **30:** 181
Canterbury and churchmen **5:** 193, 203, 205, 213, 219, 225, 252, 260; **22:** 137; **30:** 215, 262
characterization **5:** 186, 189, 192, 193, 199, 219, 230, 233, 252, 276, 293; **30:** 227, 278
Chorus, role of **5:** 186, 192, 226, 228, 230, 252, 264, 269, 281, 293; **14:** 301, 319, 336; **19:** 133; **25:** 116, 131; **30:** 163, 202, 220; **49:** 194, 200, 211, 219, 260
class distinctions, conflict, and relations **28:** 146
colonialism **22:** 103
comic elements **5:** 185, 188, 191, 192, 217, 230, 233, 241, 252, 260, 276; **19:** 217; **28:** 121; **30:** 193, 202,
economic relations **13:** 213
Elizabethan culture, relation to **5:** 210, 213, 217, 223, 257, 299, 310; **16:** 202; **19:** 133, 233; **28:** 121, 159; **30:** 215, 262; **37:** 187; **49:** 260
English language and colonialism **22:** 103; **28:** 159
epic elements **5:** 192, 197, 246, 257, 314; **30:** 181, 220, 237, 252
Falstaff **5:** 185, 186, 187, 189, 192, 195, 198, 210, 226, 257, 269, 271, 276, 293, 299; **28:** 146; **46:** 48
Fluellen **30:** 278; **37:** 105
French aristocrats and the Dauphin **5:** 188, 191, 199, 205, 213, 281; **22:** 137; **28:** 121
French language, Shakespeare's use of **5:** 186, 188, 190; **25:** 131
gender issues **13:** 183; **28:** 121, 146, 159; **44:** 44
Henry
    brutality and cunning **5:** 193, 203, 209, 210, 213, 219, 233, 239, 252, 260, 271, 287, 293, 302, 304; **30:** 159,
    characterization in 1 and 2 Henry IV contrasted **5:** 189, 190, 241, 304, 310; **19:** 133; **25:** 131; **32:** 157
    chivalry **37:** 187
    courage **5:** 191, 195, 210, 213, 228, 246, 257, 267
    disguise **30:** 169, 259
    education **5:** 246, 267, 271, 289; **14:** 297, 328, 342; **30:** 259
    emotion, lack of **5:** 209, 212, 233, 244, 264, 267, 287, 293, 310
    as heroic figure **5:** 192, 205, 209, 223, 244, 252, 257, 260, 269, 271, 299, 304; **28:** 121, 146; **30:** 237, 244, 252; **37:** 187; **49:** 194, 200, 236, 247
    humor **5:** 189, 191, 212, 217, 239, 240, 276
    intellectual and social limitations **5:** 189, 191, 203, 209, 210, 225, 226, 230, 293; **30:** 220
    interpersonal relations **5:** 209, 233, 267, 269, 276, 287, 293, 302, 318; **19:** 133; **28:** 146
    mercy **5:** 213, 267, 289, 293
    mixture of good and bad qualities **5:** 199, 205, 209, 210, 213, 244, 260, 304, 314; **30:** 262, 273; **49:** 211
    piety **5:** 191, 199, 209, 217, 223, 239, 257, 260, 271, 289, 310, 318; **30:** 244; **32:** 126
    public versus private selves **22:** 137; **30:** 169, 207
    self-doubt **5:** 281, 310
    slaughter of prisoners **5:** 189, 205, 246, 293, 318; **28:** 146
    speech **5:** 212, 230, 233, 246, 264, 276, 287, 302; **28:** 146; **30:** 163, 227
heroism **49:** 194, 200, 211, 236

historical content **5:** 185, 188, 190, 192, 193, 198, 246, 314; **13:** 201; **19:** 133; **25:** 131; **30:** 193, 202, 207, 215, 252; **49:** 223
historical epic, place in or relation to Shakespeare's **5:** 195, 198, 205, 212, 225, 241, 244, 287, 304, 310; **14:** 337, 342; **30:** 215
historiography **56:** 2, 15
homoerotic elements **16:** 202
Hotspur **5:** 189, 199, 228, 271, 302
hypocrisy **5:** 203, 213, 219, 223, 233, 260, 271, 302
imperialism **22:** 103; **28:** 159
Irish affairs **22:** 103; **28:** 159
irony **5:** 192, 210, 213, 219, 223, 226, 233, 252, 260, 269, 281, 299, 304; **14:** 336; **30:** 159, 193,
Katherine **5:** 186, 188, 189, 190, 192, 260, 269, 299, 302; **13:** 183; **19:** 217; **30:** 278; **44:** 44
kingship **5:** 205, 223, 225, 233, 239, 244, 257, 264, 267, 271, 287, 289, 299, 302, 304, 314, 318; **16:** 202; **22:** 137; **30:** 169, 202, 259, 273; **49:** 200
language and imagery **5:** 188, 230, 233, 241, 264, 276; **19:** 203; **25:** 131; **30:** 159, 181, 207, 234
law and justice **49:** 223, 226, 260
Machiavellianism **5:** 203, 225, 233, 252, 287, 304; **25:** 131; **30:** 273
MacMorris **22:** 103; **28:** 159; **30:** 278
Marlowe's works, compared with **19:** 233
metadramatic elements **13:** 194; **30:** 181; **49:** 200, 211
Mistress Quickly **5:** 186, 187, 210, 276, 293; **30:** 278
morality **5:** 195, 203, 213, 223, 225, 239, 246, 260, 271, 293
obscenity **5:** 188, 190, 260
order **5:** 205, 257, 264, 310, 314; **30:** 193
patriarchy **37:** 105; **44:** 44
politics and ideology **49:** 219, 247, 260
providential order **56:** 15
nationalism and patriotism **5:** 198, 205, 209, 210, 213, 219, 223, 233, 246, 252, 257, 269, 299; **19:** 133, 217; **30:** 227, 262; **49:** 219, 247
Pistol **28:** 146
power **37:** 175
psychoanalytic interpretations **13:** 457; **44:** 44
religious, mythic, or religious content **25:** 116; **32:** 126
Salic Law **5:** 219, 252, 260; **28:** 121
self-interest or expediency **5:** 189, 193, 205, 213, 217, 233, 260, 287, 302, 304; **30:** 273; **49:** 223
soldiers **5:** 203, 239, 267, 276, 281, 287, 293, 318; **28:** 146; **30:** 169; **49:** 194
sources **56:** 2
staging issues **5:** 186, 189, 192, 193, 198, 205, 226, 230, 241, 281, 314; **13:** 194, 502; **14:** 293, 295, 297, 301, 310, 319, 328, 334, 336, 342; **19:** 217; **32:** 185
structure **5:** 186, 189, 205, 213, 230, 241, 264, 289, 310, 314; **30:** 220, 227, 234, 244
tetralogy, relation to **49:** 223
textual problems **5:** 187, 189, 190; **13:** 201
topical allusions or content **5:** 185, 186; **13:** 201
tragic elements **5:** 228, 233, 267, 269, 271

traitors (Scroop, Grey, and Cambridge) **16:** 202; **30:** 220, 278
    Southampton conspiracy **49:** 223
Turkish elements **19:** 170
violence **43:** 24
war **5:** 193, 195, 197, 198, 210, 213, 219, 230, 233, 246, 281, 293; **28:** 121, 146; **30:** 262; **32:** 126; **37:** 175, 187; **42:** 143; **49:** 194, 236, 247, 260
Williams **13:** 502; **16:** 183; **28:** 146; **30:** 169, 259, 278
wooing scene (Act V, scene ii) **5:** 186, 188, 189, 191, 193, 195, 260, 276, 299, 302; **14:** 297; **28:** 121, 159; **30:** 163, 207

Henry VI, Parts 1, 2, and 3 (Volumes 3, 24, 39, 56)

ambivalent or ironic elements **3:** 69, 151, 154; **39:** 160; **56:** 131
authorship controversy **3:** 16, 18, 19, 20, 21, 26, 27, 29, 31, 35, 39, 41, 55, 66; **24:** 51; **56:** 77
autobiographical elements **3:** 41, 55
Bordeaux sequence **37:** 165
Cade scenes **3:** 35, 67, 92, 97, 109; **16:** 183; **22:** 156; **25:** 102; **28:** 112; **37:** 97; **39:** 160, 196, 205; **50:** 45, 51; **56:** 117, 122, 131, 180
carnival elements **22:** 156
characterization **3:** 18, 20, 24, 25, 31, 57, 64, 73, 77, 109, 119, 151; **24:** 22, 28, 38, 42, 45, 47; **39:** 160
class distinctions, conflict, and relations **37:** 97; **39:** 187; **50:** 45, 51; **56:** 117, 131
dance **22:** 156
decay of heroic ideals **3:** 119, 126; **56:** 95
disorder and civil dissension **3:** 59, 67, 76, 92, 103, 126; **13:** 131; **16:** 183; **24:** 11, 17, 28, 31, 47; **25:** 102; **28:** 112; **39:** 154, 177, 187, 196, 205; **56:** 80, 85, 110
Elizabethan literary and cultural influences **3:** 75, 97, 100, 119, 143; **22:** 156; **28:** 112; **37:** 97; **56:** 162, 180
Folk rituals, elements and influence of **39:** 205
Henry
    characterization **3:** 64, 77, 151; **39:** 160, 177; **47:** 32
    source of social disorder **3:** 25, 31, 41, 115; **39:** 154, 187
    as sympathetic figure **3:** 73, 143, 154; **24:** 32
historical accuracy or revisionism **3:** 18, 21, 35, 46, 51; **16:** 217; **24:** 16, 18, 25, 31, 45, 48; **56:** 85, 110, 122, 131, 145
historical epic, place in or relation to Shakespeare's **3:** 24, 59; **24:** 51; **56:** 95
historiography **56:** 2, 25
as humanistic play **3:** 83, 92, 109, 115, 119, 131, 136, 143
Humphrey **13:** 131; **56:** 187
as inferior or flawed plays **3:** 20, 21, 25, 26, 35
Joan of Arc **16:** 131; **32:** 212
kingship **3:** 69, 73, 77, 109, 115, 136, 143; **24:** 32; **39:** 154, 177, 187; **47:** 32
language and imagery **3:** 21, 50, 52, 55, 57, 66, 67, 71, 75, 76, 97, 105, 109, 119, 126, 131; **24:** 28; **37:** 157; **39:** 213, 222; **56:** 154, 162, 172, 180
legitimacy **3:** 89, 157; **39:** 154,

Machiavellianism **22:** 193
Margaret
    characterization **3:** 18, 26, 35, 51, 103, 109, 140, 157; **24:** 48
    Suffolk, relationship with **3:** 18, 24, 26, 157; **39:** 213
Marlowe's works, compared with **19:** 233
medieval literary influence **3:** 59, 67, 75, 100, 109, 136, 151; **13:** 131
molehill scene (3 Henry VI, Act III, scene ii) **3:** 75, 97, 126, 149; **56:** 154
moral inheritance **3:** 89, 126
multiple perspectives of characters **3:** 69, 154; **56:** 131
nationalism and patriotism **24:** 25, 45, 47; **56:** 80 25, 45, 47
Neoclassical rules **3:** 17, 18
patriarchal claims **16:** 131 **25:** 102
play-within-the-play, convention of **3:** 75, 149
retribution **3:** 27, 42, 51, 59, 77, 83, 92, 100, 109, 115, 119, 131, 136, 151
Richard of Gloucester
    characterization **3:** 35, 48, 57, 64, 77, 143, 151; **22:** 193; **39:** 160, 177
    as revenger **22:** 193
    soliloquy (3 Henry VI, Act III, scene ii) **3:** 17, 48
sibling rivalry **22:** 193
sources **3:** 18, 21, 29, 31, 35, 39, 46, 51; **13:** 131; **16:** 217; **39:** 196; **56:** 2, 122, 131, 187
staging issues **24:** 21, 22, 27, 31, 32, 36, 38, 41, 45, 48, 55; **32:** 212; **56:** 154, 172, 180, 187
structure **3:** 31, 43, 46, 69, 83, 103, 109, 119, 136, 149, 154; **39:** 213; **56:** 77, 80, 85
Talbot **39:** 160, 213, 222; **56:** 85, 145
textual arrangement **24:** 3, 4, 6, 12, 17, 18, 19, 20, 21, 24, 27, 42, 45; **37:** 165
theatrical viability **24:** 31, 32, 34; **56:** 80, 172
Tudor myth **3:** 51, 59, 77, 92, 100, 109, 115, 119, 131; **39:** 222
Unity **39:** 177, 222
violence **24:** 25, 31; **37:** 157
women, role of **3:** 103, 109, 126, 140, 157; **16:** 183; **39:** 196
York's death **13:** 131

Henry VIII (Volumes 2, 24, 41, 56)

ambition or pride **2:** 15, 38, 67
authorship controversy **2:** 16, 18, 19, 22, 23, 27, 28, 31, 35, 36, 42, 43, 44, 46, 48, 51, 58, 64, 68; **41:** 129, 146, 158, 171,
Anne Boleyn **2:** 21, 24, 31; **41:** 180
Buckingham **22:** 182; **24:** 129, 140; **37:** 109
change **2:** 27, 65, 72, 81
characterization **2:** 17, 23, 25, 32, 35, 39; **24:** 106
composition date **2:** 19, 22, 35; **24:** 129
costumes **24:** 82, 87; **28:** 184
Cranmer's prophecy **2:** 25, 31, 46, 56, 64, 68, 72; **24:** 146; **32:** 148; **41:** 120, 190; **56:** 196, 230, 248, 273
Cymbeline, compared with **2:** 67, 71
discrepancy between prophetic ending and preceding action **2:** 22, 25, 31, 46, 49, 56, 60, 65, 68, 75, 81; **32:** 148; **41:** 190; **56:** 273
Elizabethan dramatic conventions **24:** 155; **56:** 196, 248

Elizabethan politics, relation to **22:** 395; **24:** 115, 129, 140; **32:** 148; **56:** 201, 248
English Reformation, influence of **2:** 25, 35, 39, 51, 67; **24:** 89; **56:** 201
flattery **22:** 395
historical and romantic elements, combination of **2:** 46, 49, 51, 75, 76, 78; **24:** 71, 80, 146; **41:** 129, 146, 180; **56:** 196, 201
historical epic, as epilogue to Shakespeare's **2:** 22, 25, 27, 39, 51, 60, 65
historical relativity, theme of **41:** 146; **56:** 220
historiography **37:** 109 **56:** 201, 209, 230
inconsistencies **2:** 16, 27, 28, 31, 60
ironic aspects **41:** 129; **56:** 220
Katherine
    characterization **2:** 18, 19, 23, 24, 38; **24:** 129; **37:** 109; **41:** 180
    Hermione, compared with **2:** 24, 51, 58, 76
    politeness strategies **22:** 182; **56:** 262
    religious discourse **22:** 182
    as tragic figure **2:** 16, 18
King Henry
    as agent of divine retribution **2:** 49
    characterization **2:** 23, 39, 51, 58, 60, 65, 66, 75; **28:** 184; **37:** 109; **56:** 242
    incomplete portrait **2:** 15, 16, 19, 35; **41:** 120; **56:** 209
    as realistic figure **2:** 21, 22, 23, 25, 32
kingship **2:** 49, 58, 60, 65, 75, 78; **24:** 113; **41:** 129, 171; **56:** 242
language and imagery **41:** 180, 190; **56:** 262, 273
legitimacy **37:** 109; **56:** 209, 220, 230
moral intent **2:** 15, 19, 25; **24:** 140; **54:** 35
Norfolk **22:** 182
pageantry **2:** 14, 15, 18, 51, 58; **24:** 77, 83, 84, 85, 89, 91, 106, 113, 118, 120, 126, 127, 140, 146, 150; **41:** 120, 129, 190
patience **2:** 58, 76, 78
politics **2:** 39, 49, 51, 58, 60, 65, 67, 71, 72, 75, 78, 81; **24:** 74, 121, 124; **41:** 146; **56:** 242
Porter **24:** 155
Prologue **54:** 35
rebellion **22:** 395; **56:** 230
rhetoric of politeness **22:** 182; **56:** 262
Shakespeare's romances, compared with **2:** 46, 51, 58, 66, 67, 71, 76; **41:** 171; **54:** 35; **56:** 273
sources **2:** 16, 17; **24:** 71, 80
staging issues **24:** 67, 70, 71, 75, 77, 83, 84, 85, 87, 89, 91, 101, 106, 113, 120, 127, 129, 136, 140, 146, 150, 152, 155; **28:** 184; **56:** 220, 248
Stephen Gardiner **24:** 129
structure **2:** 16, 25, 27, 28, 31, 36, 44, 46, 51, 56, 68, 75; **24:** 106, 112, 113, 120; **56:** 209
style **41:** 158
thematic disparity **2:** 25, 31, 56, 68, 75; **41:** 146
tragedies of major characters **2:** 16, 39, 46, 48, 49, 51, 56, 58, 68, 81; **41:** 120
wheel of fortune, motif of **2:** 27, 65, 72, 81
Wolsey (Cardinal Wolsey) **2:** 15, 18, 19, 23, 24, 38; **22:** 182; **24:** 80, 91, 112, 113, 129, 140; **37:** 109; **41:** 129; **56:** 248, 262

Julius Caesar (Volumes 7, 17, 30, 50)

anachronisms **7:** 331
Antony
    characterization **7:** 160, 179, 189, 221, 233, 284, 320, 333; **17:** 269, 271, 272, 284, 298, 306, 313, 315, 358, 398; **25:** 272; **30:** 316
    funeral oration **7:** 148, 154, 159, 204, 210, 221, 238, 259, 350; **25:** 280; **30:** 316, 333, 362
aristocratic values **16:** 231; **22:** 280; **30:** 379; **50:** 194, 196, 211
the assassination **7:** 156, 161, 179, 191, 200, 221, 264, 272, 279, 284, 350; **25:** 272; **30:** 326
audience interpretation **48:** 240
audience response **7:** 179, 238, 253, 255, 272, 316, 320, 336, 350; **19:** 321; **48:** 240
Brutus **50:** 194, 258
    arrogance **7:** 160, 169, 204, 207, 264, 277, 292, 350; **25:** 280; **30:** 351
    as chief protagonist or tragic hero **7:** 152, 159, 189, 191, 200, 204, 242, 250, 253, 264, 268, 279, 284, 298, 333; **17:** 272, 372, 387
    citizenship **25:** 272
    funeral oration **7:** 154, 155, 204, 210, 350
    motives **7:** 150, 156, 161, 179, 191, 200, 221, 227, 233, 245, 292, 303, 310, 320, 333, 350; **25:** 272; **30:** 321, 358
    nobility or idealism **7:** 150, 152, 156, 159, 161, 179, 189, 191, 200, 221, 242, 250, 253, 259, 264, 277, 303, 320; **17:** 269, 271, 273, 279, 280, 284, 306, 308, 321, 323, 324, 345, 358; **25:** 272, 280; **30:** 351, 362; **50:** 194
    political ineptitude or lack of judgment **7:** 169, 188, 200, 205, 221, 245, 252, 264, 277, 282, 310, 316, 331, 333, 343; **17:** 323, 358, 375, 380; **50:** 13
    self-knowledge or self-deception **7:** 191, 200, 221, 242, 259, 264, 268, 279, 310, 333, 336, 350; **25:** 272; **30:** 316
    soliloquy (Act II, scene i) **7:** 156, 160, 161, 191, 221, 245, 250, 253, 264, 268, 279, 282, 292, 303, 343, 350; **25:** 280; **30:** 333
Caesar **50:** 189, 230, 234
    ambiguous nature **7:** 191, 233, 242, 250, 272, 298, 316, 320
    ambitious nature **50:** 234
    arrogance **7:** 160, 207, 218, 253, 272, 279, 298; **25:** 280
    idolatry **22:** 137
    leadership qualities **7:** 161, 179, 189, 191, 200, 207, 233, 245, 253, 257, 264, 272, 279, 284, 298, 310, 333; **17:** 317, 358; **22:** 280; **30:** 316, 326; **50:** 234
    as tragic hero **7:** 152, 200, 221, 279; **17:** 321, 377, 384
    weakness **7:** 161, 167, 169, 179, 187, 188, 191, 207, 218, 221, 233, 250, 253, 298; **17:** 358; **25:** 280
Caesarism **7:** 159, 160, 161, 167, 169, 174, 191, 205, 218, 253, 310; **30:** 316, 321; **50:** 196, 234
Calphurnia
    dream **45:** 10
Casca
    as Cynic **50:** 249
    as proto-Christian **50:** 249

Cassius **7:** 156, 159, 160, 161, 169, 179, 189, 221, 233, 303, 310, 320, 333, 343; **17:** 272, 282, 284, 344, 345, 358; **25:** 272, 280; **30:** 351; **37:** 203
ceremonies, rites, and rituals, importance of **7:** 150, 210, 255, 259, 268, 284, 316, 331, 339, 356; **13:** 260; **22:** 137; **30:** 374; **50:** 258, 269
construing the truth **7:** 320, 336, 343, 350; **37:** 229
Elizabethan culture, relation to **16:** 231; **30:** 342, 379; **50:** 13, 211, 269, 280
emulation or rivalry **16:** 231
Epicureanism **50:** 249
Flavius and Murellus **50:** 64
gender issues **13:** 260
historical determinism versus free will **7:** 160, 298, 316, 333, 346, 356; **13:** 252
irony or ambiguity **7:** 167, 257, 259, 262, 268, 282, 316, 320, 333, 336, 346, 350
language and imagery **7:** 148, 155, 159, 188, 204, 207, 227, 242, 250, 277, 296, 303, 324, 346, 350; **13:** 260; **17:** 347, 348, 350, 356, 358; **19:** 321; **22:** 280; **25:** 280; **30:** 333, 342; **50:** 196, 258
liberty versus tyranny **7:** 158, 179, 189, 205, 221, 253; **25:** 272
love and friendship **7:** 233, 262, 268; **25:** 272
medieval physiology **13:** 260
moral choice **7:** 179, 264, 279, 343
Octavius **30:** 316
omens **22:** 137; **45:** 10; **50:** 265, 280
opening scene **54:** 6
patricians versus plebeians **50:** 189, 196
philosophical elements **7:** 310, 324; **37:** 203
plebeians versus tribunes **50:** 230
the poets **7:** 179, 320, 350
politics **7:** 161, 169, 191, 205, 218, 221, 245, 262, 264, 279, 282, 310, 324, 333, 346; **17:** 317, 318, 321, 323, 334, 350, 351, 358, 378, 382, 394, 406; **22:** 137, 280; **25:** 272, 280; **30:** 285, 297, 316, 321, 342, 374, 379; **37:** 203; **50:** 13
as "problem play" **7:** 272, 320
psychoanalytic interpretation **45:** 10
public versus private principles **7:** 161, 179, 252, 262, 268, 284, 298; **13:** 252
quarrel scene (Act IV, scene iii) **7:** 149, 150, 152, 153, 155, 160, 169, 188, 191, 204, 268, 296, 303, 310
retribution **7:** 160, 167, 200
revenge tragedy elements **7:** 316
role-playing **7:** 356; **37:** 229
Roman citizenry, portrayal of **7:** 169, 179, 210, 221, 245, 279, 282, 310, 320, 333; **17:** 271, 279, 288, 291, 292, 298, 323, 334, 351, 367, 374, 375, 378; **22:** 280; **30:** 285, 297, 316, 321, 374, 379; **37:** 229; **50:** 230
Senecan elements **37:** 229
Shakespeare's English history plays, compared with **7:** 161, 189, 218, 221, 252; **22:** 137; **30:** 369
Shakespeare's major tragedies, compared with **7:** 161, 188, 227, 242, 264, 268
sources **7:** 149, 150, 156, 187, 200, 264, 272, 282, 284, 320; **30:** 285, 297, 326, 358
staging **48:** 240; **50:** 186
Stoicism **50:** 249
structure **7:** 152, 155, 159, 160, 179, 200, 210, 238, 264, 284, 298, 316, 346; **13:** 252; **30:** 374
tragic elements **50:** 258, 265

violence **48:** 240

King John (Volumes 9, 24, 41, 56)

ambiguity **13:** 152; **41:** 243
anti-catholic rhetoric **22:** 120; **25:** 98
Arthur **9:** 215, 216, 218, 219, 229, 240, 267, 275; **22:** 120; **25:** 98; **41:** 251, 277; **56:** 345, 357
autobiographical elements **9:** 209, 218, 245, 248, 260, 292
characterization **9:** 222, 224, 229, 240, 250, 292; **41:** 205, 215; **56:** 365
church versus state **9:** 209, 212, 222, 235, 240; **22:** 120
commodity or self-interest **9:** 224, 229, 245, 260, 275, 280, 297; **19:** 182; **25:** 98; **41:** 228; **56:** 335
commodity versus honor **41:** 269
Constance **9:** 208, 210, 211, 215, 219, 220, 224, 229, 240, 251, 254; **16:** 161; **24:** 177, 184, 196
corruption in society **9:** 222, 234, 280, 297
Elizabethan politics, relation to **48:** 132; **56:** 306, 314, 325
ethical or moral issues **9:** 212, 222, 224, 229, 235, 240, 263, 275, 280 **56:** 335
excess **9:** 251
Faulconbridge, the Bastard **41:** 205, 228, 251, 260, 277; **56:** 306, 314, 335, 348, 365
    as chorus or commentator **9:** 212, 218, 229, 248, 251, 260, 271, 284, 297, 300; **22:** 120
    as comic figure **9:** 219, 271, 297; **56:** 365
    development **9:** 216, 224, 229, 248, 263, 271, 275, 280, 297; **13:** 158, 163; **56:** 335
    as embodiment of England **9:** 222, 224, 240, 244, 248, 271
    heroic qualities **9:** 208, 245, 248, 254, 263, 271, 275; **25:** 98; **56:** 348
    political conduct **9:** 224, 240, 250, 260, 280, 297; **13:** 147, 158; **22:** 120; **56:** 314
Henry **41:** 277; **56:** 348
historical content **9:** 216, 219, 220, 222, 235, 240, 254, 284, 290, 292, 297, 300, 303; **13:** 163; **32:** 93, 114; **41:** 234, 243; **56:** 286, 296, 357
John **41:** 205, 260; **56:** 325, 345
    death, decay, and nature's destructiveness **9:** 212, 215, 216, 240; **56:** 345
    decline **9:** 224, 235, 240, 263, 275
    Hubert, scene with (Act III, scene iii) **9:** 210, 212, 216, 218, 219, 280
    moral insensibility **13:** 147, 163
    negative qualities **9:** 209, 212, 218, 219, 229, 234, 235, 244, 245, 246, 250, 254, 275, 280, 297; **56:** 325
    positive qualities **9:** 209, 224, 235, 240, 244, 245, 263
kingship **9:** 235, 254, 263, 275, 297; **13:** 158; **19:** 182; **22:** 120; **56:** 314
language and imagery **9:** 212, 215, 220, 246, 251, 254, 267, 280, 284, 292, 297, 300; **13:** 147, 158; **22:** 120; **37:** 132; **48:** 132; **56:** 286
legitimacy or inheritance **9:** 224, 235, 254, 303; **13:** 147; **19:** 182; **37:** 132; **41:** 215; **56:** 325, 335
Neoclassical rules **9:** 208, 209, 210, 212; **56:** 365

oppositions or dualisms **9:** 224, 240, 263, 275, 284, 290, 300
Papal Tyranny in the Reign of King John (Colley Cibber adaptation) **24:** 162, 163, 165
nationalism and patriotism **9:** 209, 218, 222, 224, 235, 240, 244, 275; **25:** 98; **37:** 132
politics **9:** 218, 224, 260, 280; **13:** 163; **22:** 120; **37:** 132; **41:** 221, 228; **56:** 314, 325
rebellion **9:** 218, 254, 263, 280, 297
Roman citizenry, portrayal of **50:** 64
Shakespeare's other history plays, compared with **9:** 218, 254; **13:** 152, 158; **25:** 98; **56:** 306, 348, 357
sources **9:** 216, 222, 300; **32:** 93, 114; **41:** 234, 243, 251; **56:** 296, 357
staging issues **16:** 161; **19:** 182; **24:** 171, 187, 203, 206, 211, 225, 228, 241, 245, 249; **56:** 286, 365
structure **9:** 208, 212, 222, 224, 229, 240, 244, 245, 254, 260, 263, 275, 284, 290, 292, 300; **24:** 228, 241; **41:** 260, 269, 277
tragic elements **9:** 208, 209, 244
treachery **9:** 245
The Troublesome Reign (anonymous), compared with **9:** 216, 244, 260, 292; **22:** 120; **32:** 93; **41:** 205, 221, 260, 269; **48:** 132; **56:** 357
Tudor doctrine **9:** 254, 284, 297; **41:** 221; **56:** 345
tyranny **9:** 218
women, role of **9:** 222, 303; **16:** 161; **19:** 182; **41:** 205, 221

King Lear (Volumes 2, 11, 31, 46)

Albany **32:** 308
allegorical elements **16:** 311
audience perception **19:** 295; **28:** 325
autobiographical elements **2:** 131, 136, 149, 165
characterization **2:** 108, 125, 145, 162, 191; **16:** 311; **28:** 223; **46:** 177, 210
Christian elements **2:** 137, 170, 179, 188, 191, 197, 207, 218, 222, 226, 229, 238, 249, 265, 286; **22:** 233, 271; **25:** 218; **46:** 276; **49:** 67; **52:** 95
as Christian play **48:** 222
Clarissa (Samuel Richardson), compared with **48:** 277
combat scenes **22:** 365
comic and tragic elements, combination of **2:** 108, 110, 112, 125, 156, 162, 245, 278, 284; **46:** 191
Cordelia
 attack on Britain **25:** 202
 characterization **2:** 110, 116, 125, 170; **16:** 311; **25:** 218; **28:** 223, 325; **31:** 117, 149, 155, 162; **46:** 225, 231, 242
 as Christ figure **2:** 116, 170, 179, 188, 222, 286
 rebelliousness **13:** 352; **25:** 202
 self-knowledge **46:** 218
 on stage **11:** 158
 transcendent power **2:** 137, 207, 218, 265, 269, 273
Cornwall's servants (III.vii) **54:** 114
cruelty of daughters **2:** 101, 102, 106; **31:** 84, 123, 137, 142
death, decay, and nature's destructiveness **2:** 93, 94, 101, 104, 106, 109, 112, 116, 129, 131, 137, 143, 147, 149, 156, 160, 170, 179, 188, 197, 207, 218, 222, 226, 231, 238, 241, 245, 249, 253, 265, 269, 273; **16:** 301; **25:** 202, 218; **31:** 77, 117, 137, 142; **46:** 264
deaths of Lear and Cordelia **54:** 103, 110, 114
double-plot **2:** 94, 95, 100, 101, 104, 112, 116, 124, 131, 133, 156, 253, 257; **46:** 254
Dover Cliff scene **2:** 156, 229, 255, 269; **11:** 8, 151; **54:** 103
Edgar **28:** 223; **32:** 212; **32:** 308; **37:** 295; **47:** 9; **50:** 24, 45
Edgar-Edmund duel **22:** 365
Edmund **25:** 218; **28:** 223
Edmund's forged letter **16:** 372
Elizabethan culture, relation to **2:** 168, 174, 177, 183, 226, 241; **19:** 330; **22:** 227, 233, 365; **25:** 218; **46:** 276; **47:** 9; **49:** 67
ending **54:** 103, 110, 114
ethical and moral issues **52:** 1
feminist criticism **55:** 68
Fool **2:** 108, 112, 125, 156, 162, 245, 278, 284; **11:** 17, 158, 169; **22:** 227; **25:** 202; **28:** 223; **46:** 1, 14, 18, 24, 33, 52, 191, 205, 210, 218, 225
Gloucester **46:** 254
Goneril **31:** 151; **46:** 231, 242
grotesque or absurd elements **2:** 136, 156, 245; **13:** 343; **52:** 1
implausibility or plot, characters, or events **2:** 100, 136, 145, 278; **13:** 343
Job, compared with **2:** 226, 241, 245; **25:** 218
justice, divine vs. worldly **49:** 1, 67, 73
Kent **25:** 202; **28:** 223; **32:** 212; **47:** 9
language and imagery **2:** 129, 137, 161, 191, 199, 237, 257, 271; **16:** 301; **19:** 344; **22:** 233; **46:** 177
Lear
 curse on Goneril **11:** 5, 7, 12, 114, 116
 love-test and division of kingdom **2:** 100, 106, 111, 124, 131, 137, 147, 149, 151, 168, 186, 208, 216, 281; **16:** 351; **25:** 202; **31:** 84, 92, 107, 117, 149, 155; **46:** 231, 242
 madness **2:** 94, 95, 98, 99, 100, 101, 102, 103, 111, 116, 120, 124, 125, 149, 156, 191, 208, 216, 281; **46:** 264
 as scapegoat **2:** 241, 253
 self-knowledge **2:** 103, 151, 188, 191, 213, 218, 222, 241, 249, 262; **25:** 218; **37:** 213; **46:** 191, 205, 225, 254, 264, **54:** 103
legal issues **46:** 276
love **2:** 109, 112, 131, 160, 162, 170, 179, 188, 197, 218, 222, 238, 265; **25:** 202; **31:** 77, 149, 151, 155, 162
madness **19:** 330
Marxist criticism **42:** 234; **55:** 16
medieval or morality drama, influence of **2:** 177, 188, 201; **25:** 218
misogyny **31:** 123
moral or ethical issues **52:** 95
nihilistic or pessimistic vision **2:** 130, 143, 149, 156, 165, 231, 238, 245, 253; **22:** 271; **25:** 218; **28:** 325; **49:** 67
opening scene **54:** 2, 6
order **56:** 25
pagan elements **25:** 218
patriarchal or monarchical order **13:** 353, 457; **16:** 351; **22:** 227, 233; **25:** 218; **31:** 84, 92, 107, 117, 123, 137, 142; **46:** 269
performance issues **2:** 106, 137, 154, 160; **11:** 10, 20, 27, 56, 57, 132, 136, 137, 145, **150, 154; 19:** 295, 344; **25:** 218
poetic justice, question of **2:** 92, 93, 94, 101, 129, 137, 231, 245; **49:** 73
politics **46:** 269; **50:** 45
providential order **2:** 112, 116, 137, 168, 170, 174, 177, 218, 226, 241, 253; **22:** 271; **49:** 1, 73
Regan **31:** 151; **46:** 231, 242
rhetorical style **16:** 301; **47:** 9
romantic elements **31:** 77, 84
sexuality **25:** 202; **31:** 133, 137, 142
sexual politics **55:** 68
social and moral corruption **2:** 116, 133, 174, 177, 241, 271; **22:** 227; **31:** 84, 92; **46:** 269
sources **2:** 94, 100, 143, 145, 170, 186; **13:** 352; **16:** 351; **28:** 301
spiritual regeneration **54:** 103
staging issues **11:** 1-178; **32:** 212; **46:** 205, 218; **54:** 103
structure **28:** 325; **32:** 308; **46:** 177
suffering **2:** 137, 160, 188, 201, 218, 222, 226, 231, 238, 241, 249, 265; **13:** 343; **22:** 271; **25:** 218; **50:** 24
Tate's adaptation **2:** 92, 93, 94, 101, 102, 104, 106, 110, 112, 116, 137; **11:** 10, 136; **25:** 218; **31:** 162
textual issues **22:** 271; **37:** 295; **49:** 73
Timon of Athens, relation to **16:** 351
tragic elements **55:** 78
Virgo vs. Virago **48:** 222
wisdom **37:** 213; **46:** 210

Love's Labour's Lost (Volumes 2, 23, 38, 54)

Armado **23:** 207
artificial nature **2:** 315, 317, 324, 330; **23:** 207, 233; **54:** 234, 248, 257, 263
authorship controversy **2:** 299, 300; **32:** 308
Berowne **2:** 308, 324, 327; **22:** 12; **23:** 184, 187; **38:** 194; **47:** 35
characterization **2:** 303, 310, 317, 322, 328, 342; **23:** 237, 250, 252; **38:** 232; **47:** 35
as comedy of affectation **2:** 302, 303, 304; **23:** 191, 224, 226, 228, 233
comic resolution **2:** 335, 340; **16:** 17; **19:** 92; **38:** 209; **51:** 1; **54:** 240, 248, 274
comic form **54:** 257, 263
conclusion **38:** 172; **54:** 240, 248, 274
dance and patterned action **2:** 308, 342; **23:** 191, 237
death, decay, and nature's destructiveness **2:** 305, 331, 344, 348
desire **38:** 185, 194, 200, 209
dramatic shortcomings or failure **2:** 299, 301, 303, 322; **54:** 240, 248
Elizabeth I **38:** 239
Elizabethan love poetry **38:** 232
ending **54:** 58
feminist criticism **42:** 93
genre **38:** 163
gift exchange **25:** 1
grace and civility **2:** 351
Holofernes **23:** 207

illusion versus reality **2**: 303, 308, 331, 340, 344, 348, 356, 359, 367, 371, 375; **23**: 230, 231
knowledge **22**: 12; **47**: 35
language and imagery **2**: 301, 302, 303, 306, 307, 308, 315, 319, 320, 330, 335, 344, 345, 348, 356, 359, 362, 365, 371, 374, 375; **19**: 92; **22**: 12, 378; **23**: 184, 187, 196, 197, 202, 207, 211, 221, 227, 231, 233, 237, 252; **28**: 9, 63; **38**: 219, 226; **54**: 225, 274
love **2**: 312, 315, 340, 344; **22**: 12; **23**: 252; **38**: 194; **51**: 44
love vs. reason **54**: 225, 234
male domination **22**: 12
male/female relationships **54**: 284
male sexual anxiety **16**: 17
marriage **2**: 335, 340; **19**: 92; **38**: 209, 232; **51**: 1, 44
metadramatic elements **2**: 356, 359, 362
Neoclassical rules **2**: 299, 300
oaths **54**: 257, 284
physical versus intellectual world **2**: 331, 348, 367
plot **54**: 225
public versus private speech **2**: 356, 362, 371
as satire or parody **2**: 300, 302, 303, 307, 308, 315, 321, 324, 327; **23**: 237, 252; **54**: 234
School of Night, allusions to **2**: 321, 327, 328
sexuality **22**: 12; **51**: 44
songs, role of **2**: 303, 304, 316, 326, 335, 362, 367, 371, 375; **54**: 240
sources **16**: 17
spectacle **38**: 226
staging issues **23**: 184, 187, 191, 196, 198, 200, 201, 202, 207, 212, 215, 216, 217, 229, 230, 232, 233, 237, 252
structure **22**: 378; **23**: 191, 237, 252; **38**: 163, 172
theme
    idealism versus realism **38**: 163
topical allusions or content **2**: 300, 303, 307, 315, 316, 317, 319, 321, 327, 328; **23**: 187, 191, 197, 203, 221, 233, 237, 252; **25**: 1
unnatural ordering **22**: 378
violence **22**: 12
visual humor **23**: 207, 217
Watteau, influence on staging **23**: 184, 186
women, role of **19**: 92; **22**: 12; **23**: 215; **25**: 1
wisdom and folly **54**: 257
written versus oral communication **2**: 359, 365; **28**: 63

Macbeth (Volumes 3, 20, 29, 44, 57)

antithetical or contradictory elements **3**: 185, 213, 271, 302; **25**: 235; **29**: 76, 127; **47**: 41
appearance versus reality **3**: 241, 248; **25**: 235
archetypal or mythic elements **16**: 317
audience response **20**: 17, 400, 406; **29**: 139, 146, 155, 165; **44**: 306
banquet scene (Act III, scene iv) **20**: 22, 32, 175
Banquo **3**: 183, 199, 208, 213, 278, 289; **20**: 279, 283, 406, 413; **25**: 235; **28**: 339
characterization **20**: 12, 318, 324, 329, 353, 363, 367, 374, 387; **28**: 339; **29**: 101, 109, 146, 155, 165; **44**: 289; **47**: 41; **57**: 267
Christian elements **3**: 194, 239, 260, 269, 275, 286, 293, 297, 318; **20**: 203, 206, 210, 256, 262, 289, 291, 294; **44**: 341, 366; **47**: 41; **57**: 236
combat scenes **22**: 365
conscience **52**: 15
dagger scene (Act III, scene i), staging of **20**: 406
Duncan **57**: 194, 236
ending **54**: 84
evil **3**: 194, 208, 231, 234, 239, 241, 267, 289; **20**: 203, 206, 210, 374; **52**: 23; **57**: 267
female identity **57**: 256
feminine power, role of **57**: 242
free will versus fate **3**: 177, 183, 184, 190, 196, 198, 202, 207, 208, 213; **13**: 361; **44**: 351, 361, 366, 373; **54**: 6
innocence **3**: 234, 241, 327; **57**: 267
Jacobean culture, relation to **19**: 330; **22**: 365; **57**: 218, 256
Lady Macbeth
    ambition **3**: 185, 219; **20**: 279, 345
    characterization **20**: 56, 60, 65, 73, 140, 148, 151, 241, 279, 283, 338, 350, 406, 413; **29**: 109, 146; **57**: 256, 263
    childlessness **3**: 219, 223
    good and evil, combined traits of **3**: 173, 191, 213; **20**: 60, 107
    inconsistencies **3**: 202; **20**: 54, 137
    influence on Macbeth **3**: 171, 185, 191, 193, 199, 262, 289, 312, 318; **13**: 502; **20**: 345; **25**: 235; **29**: 133; **57**: 263
    psychoanalytic interpretations **20**: 345; **44**: 289, 297, 324; **45**: 58
    as sympathetic figure **3**: 191, 193, 203
    language and imagery **3**: 170, 193, 213, 231, 234, 241, 245, 250, 253, 256, 263, 271, 283, 300, 302, 306, 323, 327, 338, 340, 349; **13**: 476; **16**: 317; **20**: 241, 279, 283, 367, 379, 400; **25**: 235; **28**: 339; **29**: 76, 91; **42**: 263; **44**: 366; **45**: 58
laws of nature, violation of **3**: 234, 241, 280, 323; **29**: 120; **57**: 242, 263
letter to Lady Macbeth **16**: 372; **20**: 345; **25**: 235
Macbeth
    ambition **44**: 284, 324; **57**: 256
    characterization **20**: 20, 42, 73, 107, 113, 130, 146, 151, 279, 283, 312, 338, 343, 379, 406, 413; **29**: 139, 152, 155, 165; **44**: 289; **57**: 189, 194, 236, 263, 267
    courage **3**: 172, 177, 181, 182, 183, 186, 234, 312, 333; **20**: 107; **44**: 315
    disposition **3**: 173, 175, 177, 182, 186; **20**: 245, 376
    imagination **3**: 196, 208, 213, 250, 312, 345; **20**: 245, 376; **44**: 351
    as "inauthentic" king **3**: 245, 302, 321, 345
    inconsistencies **3**: 202
    as Machiavellian villain **3**: 280; **57**: 236
    manliness **20**: 113; **29**: 127, 133; **44**: 315; **57**: 256
    psychoanalytic interpretations **20**: 42, 73, 238, 376; **44**: 284, 289, 297, 324; **45**: 48, 58; **57**: 267
    Richard III, compared with **3**: 177, 182, 186, 345; **20**: 86, 92; **22**: 365; **44**: 269
    as Satan figure **3**: 229, 269, 275, 289, 318
    self-awareness **3**: 312, 329, 338; **16**: 317; **44**: 361; **57**: 256
    as sympathetic figure **3**: 229, 306, 314, 338; **29**: 139, 152; **44**: 269, 306, 337
    as tragic hero **44**: 269, 306, 315, 324, 337; **57**: 267
Macduff **3**: 226, 231, 253, 262,; **25**: 235; **29**: 127, 133, 155; **57**: 194
Machiavellianism **52**: 29; **57**: 236
madness **19**: 330
major tragedies, relation to Shakespeare's other **3**: 171, 173, 213; **44**: 269; **57**: 189
Malcolm **25**: 235
manhood **3**: 262, 309, 333; **29**: 127, 133; **57**: 242, 263
Marxist criticism **42**: 234; **55**: 16
medieval mystery plays, relation to **44**: 341; **57**: 194
morality **52**: 15, 23, 29
moral lesson **20**: 23
murder scene (Act II, scene ii) **20**: 175
Neoclassical rules **3**: 170, 171, 173, 175; **20**: 17
nightmarish quality **3**: 231, 309; **20**: 210, 242; **44**: 261
opening scene **54**: 2, 6
politics **52**: 29; **57**: 218, 228
Porter scene (Act II, scene iii) **3**: 173, 175, 184, 190, 196, 203, 205, 225, 260, 271, 297, 300; **20**: 283; **44**: 261; **46**: 29, 78
primitivism **20**: 206, 213; **45**: 48
providential order **3**: 208, 289, 329, 336; **57**: 218
psychoanalytic interpretations **3**: 219, 223, 226; **44**: 11, 284, 289, 297
regicide **16**: 317, 328; **45**: 48 248, 275, 312
religious and theological issues **44**: 324, 341, 351, 361, 366, 373
religious, mythic, or spiritual content **3**: 208, 269, 275, 318; **29**: 109
retribution **3**: 194, 208, 318; **48**: 214
Scholasticism **52**: 23
sexual anxiety **16**: 328; **20**: 283
sleepwalking scene (Act V, scene i) **3**: 191, 203, 219; **20**: 175; **44**: 261
staging issues **13**: 502; **20**: 12, 17, 32, 64, 65, 70, 73, 107, 113, 151, 175, 203, 206, 210, 213, 245, 279, 283, 312, 318, 324, 329, 343, 345, 350, 353, 363, 367, 374, 376, 379, 382, 387, 400, 406, 413; **22**: 365; **32**: 212
structure **16**: 317; **20**: 12, 245
supernatural grace versus evil or chaos **3**: 241, 286, 323
theatricality **16**: 328
time **3**: 234, 246, 283, 293; **20**: 245; **57**: 218
topical allusions or content **13**: 361; **20**: 17, 350; **29**: 101
tragic elements **52**: 15; **55**: 78; **57**: 189
treason and punishment **13**: 361; **16**: 328
violence **20**: 273, 279, 283; **45**: 58; **57**: 228, 267
witches and supernaturalism **3**: 171, 172, 173, 175, 177, 182, 183, 184, 185, 194, 196, 198, 202, 207, 208, 213, 219, 229, 239; **16**: 317; **19**: 245; **20**: 92, 175, 213, 279, 283, 374, 387, 406, 413; **25**: 235; **28**: 339; **29**: 91, 101, 109, 120; **44**: 351, 373; **57**: 194, 242

Measure for Measure (Volumes 2, 23, 33, 49)

    allegorical elements **52**: 69
    ambiguity **2**: 417, 420, 432, 446, 449, 452, 474, 479, 482, 486, 495, 505
    Angelo
        anxiety **16**: 114
        authoritarian portrayal of **23**: 307; **49**: 274
        characterization **2**: 388, 390, 397, 402, 418, 427, 432, 434, 463, 484, 495, 503, 511; **13**: 84; **23**: 297; **32**: 81; **33**: 77; **49**: 274, 293, 379
        hypocrisy **2**: 396, 399, 402, 406, 414, 421; **23**: 345, 358, 362
        repentance or pardon **2**: 388, 390, 397, 402, 434, 463, 511, 524
    audience response **48**: 1
    autobiographical elements **2**: 406, 410, 414, 431, 434, 437
    Barnardine **13**: 112
    bed-trick **13**: 84; **49**: 313; **54**: 52
    characterization **2**: 388, 390, 391, 396, 406, 420, 421, 446, 466, 475, 484, 505, 516, 524; **23**: 299, 405; **33**: 77
    Christian elements **2**: 391, 394, 399, 421, 437, 449, 466, 479, 491, 511, 522; **48**: 1; **49**: 325
    Clarissa (Samuel Richardson), compared with **48**: 277
    comic form **2**: 456, 460, 479, 482, 491, 514, 516; **13**: 94, 104; **23**: 309, 326, 327; **49**: 349
    death, decay, and nature's destructiveness **2**: 394, 452, 516; **25**: 12; **49**: 370
    displacement **22**: 78
    Duke
        as authoritarian figure **23**: 314, 317, 347; **33**: 85; **49**: 274, 300, 358
        characterization **2**: 388, 395, 402, 406, 411, 421, 429, 456, 466, 470, 498, 511; **13**: 84, 94, 104; **23**: 363, 416; **32**: 81; **42**: 1; **44**: 89; **49**: 274, 293, 300, 358
        dramatic shortcomings or failure **2**: 420, 429, 441, 479, 495, 505, 514, 522
        godlike portrayal of **23**: 320
        noble portrayal of **23**: 301
        speech on death (Act III, scene i) **2**: 390, 391, 395
    Elbow **22**: 85; **25**: 12
    Elbow, Mistress **33**: 90
    Elizabethan betrothal and marriage customs **2**: 429, 437, 443, 503; **49**: 286
    Elizabethan culture, relation to **2**: 394, 418, 429, 432, 437, 460, 470, 482, 503
    ending **54**: 52, 65
    ethical or moral issues **52**: 69
    feminist criticism **55**: 16, 68
    feminist interpretation **23**: 320
    good and evil **2**: 432, 452, 524; **33**: 52, 61; **52**: 69
    homosexuality **42**: 1
    immortality **16**: 102
    inconsistency between first and second halves **2**: 474, 475, 505, 514, 524; **49**: 349, 358
    Isabella **2**: 388, 390, 395, 396, 397, 401, 402, 406, 409, 410, 411, 418, 420, 421, 432, 437, 441, 466, 475, 491, 495, 524; **16**: 114; **23**: 278, 279, 280, 281, 282, 296, 344, 357, 363, 405; **28**: 92; **33**: 77, 85
    judicial versus natural law **2**: 446, 507, 516, 519; **22**: 85; **33**: 58, 117; **49**: 293
    justice and mercy **2**: 391, 395, 399, 402, 406, 409, 411, 416, 421, 437, 443, 463, 466, 470, 491, 495, 522, 524; **22**: 85; **33**: 52, 61, 101; **49**: 274, 293, 300
    judicial vs. natural law **49**: 1
    justice and mercy **49**: 1
    language and imagery **2**: 394, 421, 431, 466, 486, 505; **13**: 112; **28**: 9; **33**: 69; **49**: 370
    Lucio **13**: 104; **49**: 379
    marriage **2**: 443, 507, 516, 519, 524, 528; **25**: 12; **33**: 61, 90; **49**: 286; **51**: 44
    as medieval allegory or morality play **2**: 409, 421, 443, 466, 475, 491, 505, 511, 522; **13**: 94
    metadramatic elements **13**: 104
    misgovernment **2**: 401, 432, 511; **22**: 85
    misogyny **33**: 358
    moral seriousness, question of **2**: 387, 388, 396, 409, 417, 421, 452, 460, 495; **23**: 316, 321
    Neoclassical rules **2**: 387, 388, 390, 394; **23**: 269
    politics **23**: 379; **49**: 274
    power **13**: 112; **22**: 85; **23**: 327, 330, 339, 352; **33**: 85
    as "problem play" **2**: 416, 429, 434, 474, 475, 503, 514, 519; **16**: 102; **23**: 313, 328, 351; **49**: 358, 370
    providential order **48**: 1
    psychoanalytic interpretations **23**: 331, 332, 333, 334, 335, 340, 355, 356, 359, 379, 395; **44**: 79
    Puritanism **2**: 414, 418, 434; **49**: 325
    rebirth, regeneration, resurrection, or immortality **13**: 84; **16**: 102, 114; **23**: 321, 327, 335, 340, 352; **25**: 12
    religious and theological issues **48**: 1
    religious, mythic, or spiritual content **48**: 1
    resolution **2**: 449, 475, 495, 514, 516; **16**: 102, 114; **54**: 65
    sexuality **13**: 84; **16**: 102, 114; **23**: 321, 327, 335, 340, 352; **25**: 12; **33**: 85, 90, 112; **49**: 286, 338; **51**: 44
    sexual politics **55**: 68
    social aspects **23**: 316, 375, 379, 395; **49**: 338
    sources **2**: 388, 393, 427, 429, 437, 475; **13**: 94; **49**: 349; **52**: 69
    staging issues **2**: 427, 429, 437, 441, 443, 456, 460, 482, 491, 519; **23**: 283, 284, 285, 286, 287, 291, 293, 294, 298, 299, 311, 315, 327, 338, 339, 340, 342, 344, 347, 363, 372, 375, 395, 400, 405, 406, 413; **32**: 16
    structure **2**: 390, 411, 449, 456, 466, 474, 482, 490, 491; **33**: 69; **49**: 379
    substitution of identities **2**: 507, 511, 519; **13**: 112; **49**: 313, 325
    supernatural grace vs. evil or chaos **48**: 1
    theatricality **23**: 285, 286, 294, 372, 406; **49**: 358
    comic and tragic elements, combination of **16**: 102
    as unsuccessful play **2**: 397, 441, 474, 482; **23**: 287

The Merchant of Venice (Volumes 4, 12, 40, 53)

    Act V, relation to Acts I through IV **4**: 193, 194, 195, 196, 204, 232, 270, 273, 289, 300, 319, 321, 326, 336, 356

    allegorical elements **4**: 224, 250, 261, 268, 270, 273, 282, 289, 324, 336, 344, 350; **53**: 179, 187
    Antonio
        excessive or destructive love **4**: 279, 284, 336, 344; **12**: 54; **37**: 86
        love for Bassanio **40**: 156
        melancholy **4**: 221, 238, 279, 284, 300, 321, 328; **22**: 69; **25**: 22
        pitiless **4**: 254
        as pivotal figure **12**: 25, 129
        versus Shylock **53**: 187
    appearance versus reality **4**: 209, 261, 344; **12**: 65; **22**: 69
    Bassanio **25**: 257; **37**: 86; **40**: 156
    bonding **4**: 293, 317, 336; **13**: 37
    casket scenes **4**: 226, 241, 308, 344; **12**: 23, 46, 47, 65, 117; **13**: 43; **22**: 3; **40**: 106; **49**: 27
    Christian elements **52**: 89
    comparison to other works of Shakespeare **53**: 105
    contrasting dramatic worlds **44**: 11
    conflict between Christianity and Judaism **4**: 224, 250, 268, 289, 324, 344; **12**: 67, 70, 72, 76; **22**: 69; **25**: 257; **40**: 117, 127, 166, 181; **48**: 54, 77; **53**: 105, 159, 214
    desire **22**: 3; **40**: 142; **45**: 17
    disappointment, theme of **53**: 211
    Economics and exchange **40**: 197, 208; **53**: 116
    Elizabethan culture, relation to **32**: 66; **40**: 117, 127, 142, 166, 181, 197, 208; **48**: 54, 77; **49**: 37; **53**: 105, 111, 127, 159, 169, 214, 224
    ending **54**: 52, 65
    feminist criticism **55**: 27
    genre **4**: 191, 200, 201, 209, 215, 221, 232, 238, 247; **12**: 48, 54, 62; **54**: 65
    homosexuality **22**: 3, 69; **37**: 86; **40**: 142, 156, 197
    imperialism **53**: 116
    implausibility of plot, characters, or events **4**: 191, 192, 193; **12**: 52, 56, 76, 119
    irony **4**: 254, 300, 321, 331, 350; **28**: 63
    Jessica **4**: 196, 200, 228, 293, 342; **53**: 159, 211
    justice and mercy **4**: 213, 214, 224, 250, 261, 273, 282, 289, 336; **12**: 80, 129; **40**: 127; **49**: 1, 23, 27, 37
    language and imagery **4**: 241, 267, 293; **22**: 3; **25**: 257; **28**: 9, 63; **32**: 41; **40**: 106; **53**: 169
    Launcelot Gobbo **46**: 24, 60; **50**: 64; **53**: 187, 214
    law and justice **53**: 169
    love **4**: 221, 226, 270, 284, 312, 344; **22**: 3, 69; **25**: 257; **40**: 156; **51**: 1, 44
    medieval homilies, influence of **4**: 224, 250, 289
    morality **52**: 89
    Portia **4**: 194, 195, 196, 215, 254, 263, 336, 356; **12**: 104, 107, 114; **13**: 37; **22**: 3, 69; **25**: 22; **32**: 294; **37**: 86; **40**: 142, 156, 197, 208; **49**: 27
    psychoanalytic interpretation **45**: 17
    race **53**: 111, 116, 127, 136, 159, 169; **55**: 27
    resolution **4**: 263, 266, 300, 319, 321; **13**: 37; **51**: 1
    rings episode **22**: 3; **40**: 106, 151, 156
    sacrificial love **13**: 43; **22**: 69; **40**: 142
    sexual politics **22**: 3; **51**: 44
    Shylock

alienation **4:** 279, 312; **40:** 175; **49:** 23, 37
ambiguity **4:** 247, 254, 315, 319, 331; **12:** 31, 35, 36, 50, 51, 52, 56, 81, 124; **40:** 175; **53:** 111
forced conversion **4:** 209, 252, 268, 282, 289, 321
ghettoization of **53:** 127
Jewishness **4:** 193, 194, 195, 200, 201, 213, 214, 279; **22:** 69; **25:** 257; **40:** 142, 175, 181
master-slave relationship **53:** 136
motives in making the bond **4:** 252, 263, 266, 268; **22:** 69; **25:** 22
as outsider **53:** 127, 224
as Puritan **40:** 127, 166
as scapegoat figure **4:** 254, 300; **40:** 166 **49:** 27
as traditional comic villain **4:** 230, 243, 261, 263, 315; **12:** 40, 62, 124; **40:** 175
as tragic figure **12:** 6, 9, 10, 16, 21, 23, 25, 40, 44, 66, 67, 81, 97; **40:** 175
social criticism **53:** 214
staging issues **12:** 111, 114, 115, 117, 119, 124, 129, 131
structure **4:** 201, 215, 230, 232, 243, 247, 254, 261, 263, 308, 321; **12:** 115; **28:** 63
trial scene **13:** 43; **25:** 22; **40:** 106, 156; **49:** 1, 23, 27, 37
unity of double plot **4:** 193, 194, 201, 232; **12:** 16, 67, 80, 115, **40:** 151
Venetians **4:** 195, 200, 228, 254, 273, 300, 321, 331
Venice, Elizabethan perceptions of **28:** 249; **32:** 294; **40:** 127
wealth **4:** 209, 261, 270, 273, 317; **12:** 80, 117; **22:** 69; **25:** 22; **28:** 249; **40:** 117, 197, 208; **45:** 17; **49:** 1; **51:** 15

The Merry Wives of Windsor (Volumes 5, 18, 38, 47)

Anne Page-Fenton plot **5:** 334, 336, 343, 353, 376, 390, 395, 402; **22:** 93; **47:** 308
avarice **5:** 335, 353, 369, 376, 390, 395, 402
Caius, Doctor **47:** 354
caricature **5:** 343, 347, 348, 350, 385, 397
characterization **5:** 332, 334, 335, 337, 338, 351, 360, 363, 366, 374, 379, 392; **18:** 74, 75; **38:** 264, 273, 313, 319
class distinctions, conflict, and relations **5:** 338, 343, 346, 347, 366, 390, 395, 400, 402; **22:** 93; **28:** 69
comic and farcical elements **5:** 336, 338, 346, 350, 360, 369, 373; **18:** 74, 75, 84
The Comical Gallant (John Dennis adaptation) **18:** 5, 7, 8, 9, 10
deception, disguise, and duplicity **5:** 332, 334, 336, 354, 355, 379; **22:** 93; **47:** 308, 314, 321, 325, 344
desire **38:** 286, 297, 300
Elizabethan society **47:** 331
Elizabeth's influence **5:** 333, 334, 335, 336, 339, 346, 355, 366, 402; **18:** 5, 86; **38:** 278; **47:** 344
Evans, Sir Hugh **47:** 354
Falstaff
characterization in 1 and 2 Henry IV, compared with **5:** 333, 335, 336, 337, 339, 346, 347, 348, 350, 373, 400; **18:** 5, 7, 75, 86; **22:** 93

diminishing powers **5:** 337, 339, 343, 347, 350, 351, 392; **28:** 373; **47:** 363
as Herne the Hunter **38:** 256, 286; **47:** 358
incapability of love **5:** 335, 336, 339, 346, 348; **22:** 93
as Jack-a-Lent **47:** 363
personification of comic principle or Vice figure **5:** 332, 338, 369, 400; **38:** 273
recognition and repentance of follies **5:** 338, 341, 343, 348, 369, 374, 376, 397
as scapegoat **47:** 358, 363, 375
sensuality **5:** 339, 343, 353, 369, 392
shrewdness **5:** 332, 336, 346, 355
threat to community **5:** 343, 369, 379, 392, 395, 400; **38:** 297
as unifying force **47:** 358
vanity **5:** 332, 339
victimization **5:** 336, 338, 341, 347, 348, 353, 355, 360, 369, 373, 374, 376, 392, 397, 400
as villain **47:** 358
as a woman **47:** 325
folk rituals, elements and influence of **5:** 353, 369, 376, 392, 397, 400; **38:** 256, 300
Ford, Francis **5:** 332, 334, 343, 355, 363, 374, 379, 390; **38:** 273; **47:** 321
Ford, Mistress Alice **47:** 321
insults **47:** 331
jealousy **5:** 334, 339, 343, 353, 355, 363; **22:** 93; **38:** 273, 307
Jonsonian humors comedy, influence of **38:** 319
knighthood **5:** 338, 343, 390, 397, 402; **47:** 354
language and imagery **5:** 335, 337, 343, 347, 351, 363, 374, 379; **19:** 101; **22:** 93, 378; **28:** 9, 69; **38:** 313, 319
male discontent **5:** 392, 402
marriage **5:** 343, 369, 376, 390, 392, 400; **22:** 93; **38:** 297; **51:** 44
mediation **5:** 343, 392
morality **5:** 335, 339, 347, 349, 353, 397
Neoclassical rules **5:** 332, 334
Page, Anne **47:** 321
Page, Mistress Margaret **47:** 321
play and theatricality **47:** 325
play-within-the-play, convention of **5:** 354, 355, 369, 402
realism **38:** 313
reconciliation **5:** 343, 369, 374, 397, 402
revenge **5:** 349, 350, 392; **38:** 264, 307
as satire or parody **5:** 338, 350, 360, 385; **38:** 278, 319; **47:** 354, 363
schemes and intrigues **5:** 334, 336, 339, 341, 343, 349, 355, 379
setting **47:** 375
sexual politics **19:** 101; **38:** 307
social milieu **18:** 75, 84; **38:** 297, 300
sources **5:** 332, 350, 360, 366, 385; **32:** 31
stage history **18:** 66, 67, 68, 70, 71
staging issues **18:** 74, 75, 84, 86, 90, 95
structure **5:** 332, 333, 334, 335, 343, 349, 355, 369, 374; **18:** 86; **22:** 378
unnatural ordering **22:** 378
wit **5:** 335, 336, 337, 339, 343, 351
women, role of **5:** 335, 341, 343, 349, 369, 379, 390, 392, 402; **19:** 101; **38:** 307

A Midsummer Night's Dream (Volumes 3, 12, 29, 45)

adaptations **12:** 144, 146, 147, 153, 280, 282

ambiguity **3:** 401, 459, 486; **45:** 169
appearance, perception, and illusion **3:** 368, 411, 425, 427, 434, 447, 459, 466, 474, 477, 486, 497, 516; **19:** 21; **22:** 39; **28:** 15; **29:** 175,190; **45:** 136
Athens and the forest, contrast between **3:** 381, 427, 459, 466, 497, 502; **29:** 175
autobiographical elements **3:** 365, 371, 379, 381, 389, 391, 396, 402, 432
Bottom
awakening speech (Act IV, scene i) **3:** 406, 412, 450, 457, 486, 516; **16:** 34
folly of **46:** 1, 14, 29, 60
imagination **3:** 376, 393, 406, 432, 486; **29:** 175, 190; **45:** 147
self-possession **3:** 365, 376, 395, 402, 406, 480; **45:** 158
Titania, relationship with **3:** 377, 406, 441, 445, 450, 457, 491, 497; **16:** 34; **19:** 21; **22:** 93; **29:** 216; **45:** 160
transformation **3:** 365, 377, 432; **13:** 27; **22:** 93; **29:** 216; **45:** 147, 160
brutal elements **3:** 445, 491, 497, 511; **12:** 259, 262, 298; **16:** 34; **19:** 21; **29:** 183, 225, 263, 269; **45:** 169
capriciousness of the young lovers **3:** 372, 395, 402, 411, 423, 437, 441, 450, 497, 498; **29:** 175, 269; **45:** 107
chastity **45:** 143
class distinctions, conflict, and relations **22:** 23; **25:** 36; **45:** 160; **50:** 74, 86
colonialism **53:** 32
as dream-play **3:** 365, 370, 372, 377, 389, 391; **29:** 190; **45:** 117
dreams **45:** 96, 107, 117
duration of time **3:** 362, 370, 380, 386, 494; **45:** 175
Elizabethan culture, relation to **50:** 86
erotic elements **3:** 445, 491, 497, 511; **12:** 259, 262, 298; **16:** 34; **19:** 21; **29:** 183, 225, 269
fairies **3:** 361, 362, 372, 377, 395, 400, 423, 450, 459, 486; **12:** 287, 291, 294, 295; **19:** 21; **29:** 183, 190; **45:** 147
feminist interpretation **48:** 23
gender **53:** 1
Helena **29:** 269
Hermia **29:** 225, 269; **45:** 117
Hippolytus, myth of **29:** 216; **45:** 84
identity **29:** 269
imagination and art **3:** 365, 371, 381, 402, 412, 417, 421, 423, 441, 459, 468, 506, 516, 520; **22:** 39
language and imagery **3:** 397, 401, 410, 412, 415, 432, 453, 459, 468, 494; **22:** 23, 39, 93, 378; **28:** 9; **29:** 263; **45:** 96, 126, 136, 147; **45:** 143, 169, 175; **48:** 23, 32
male domination **3:** 483, 520; **13:** 19; **25:** 36; **29:** 216, 225, 243, 256, 269; **42:** 46; **45:** 84
marriage **3:** 402, 423, 450, 483, 520; **29:** 243, 256; **45:** 136, 143; **48:** 32; **51:** 1, 30, 44
metadramatic elements **3:** 427, 468, 477, 516, 520; **29:** 190, 225, 243; **50:** 86
Metamorphoses (Golding translation of Ovid) **16:** 25
Minotaur, myth of **3:** 497, 498; **29:** 216
music and dance **3:** 397, 400, 418, 513; **12:** 287, 289; **25:** 36
Oberon as controlling force **3:** 434, 459, 477, 502; **29:** 175

Ovid, influence of **3**: 362, 427, 497, 498; **22**: 23; **29**: 175, 190, 216
parent-child relations **13**: 19; **29**: 216, 225, 243
passionate or romantic love **3**: 372, 389, 395, 396, 402, 408, 411, 423, 441, 450, 480, 497, 498, 511; **29**: 175, 225, 263, 269; **45**: 126, 136; **51**: 44
Pauline doctrine **3**: 457, 486, 506
Platonic elements **3**: 368, 437, 450, 497; **45**: 126
politics **29**: 243
power **42**: 46; **45**: 84
psychoanalytic interpretations **3**: 440, 483; **28**: 15; **29**: 225; **44**: 1; **45**: 107, 117
Puck **45**: 96, 158
Pyramus and Thisbe interlude **3**: 364, 368, 379, 381, 389, 391, 396, 408, 411, 412, 417, 425, 427, 433, 441, 447, 457, 468, 474, 511; **12**: 254; **13**: 27; **16**: 25; **22**: 23; **29**: 263; **45**: 107, 175; **50**: 74
race **53**: 1, 32
reason versus imagination **3**: 381, 389, 423, 441, 466, 506; **22**: 23; **29**: 190; **45**: 96
reconciliation **3**: 412, 418, 437, 459, 468, 491, 497, 502, 513; **13**: 27; **29**: 190
reversal **29**: 225
Romeo and Juliet, compared with 3: 396, 480
rustic characters **3**: 376, 397, 432; **12**: 291, 293; **45**: 147, 160
sexuality **22**: 23, 93; **29**: 225, 243, 256, 269; **42**: 46; **45**: 107 **53**: 32
sources **29**: 216
staging issues **3**: 364, 365, 371, 372, 377; **12**: 151, 152, 154, 158, 159, 280, 284, 291, 295; **16**: 34; **19**: 21; **29**: 183, 256; **48**: 23
structure **3**: 364, 368, 381, 402, 406, 427, 450, 513; **13**: 19; **22**: 378; **29**: 175; **45**: 126, 175
textual issues **16**: 34; **29**: 216
Theseus **51**: 1
    characterization **3**: 363
    Hippolyta, relationship with **3**: 381, 412, 421, 423, 450, 468, 520; **29**: 175, 216, 243, 256; **45**: 84
    as ideal **3**: 379, 391
    "lovers, lunatics, and poets" speech (Act V, scene i) **3**: 365, 371, 379, 381, 391, 402, 411, 412, 421, 423, 441, 498, 506; **29**: 175
    as representative of institutional life **3**: 381, 403
Titania **29**: 243
tragic elements **3**: 393, 400, 401, 410, 445, 474, 480, 491, 498, 511; **29**: 175; **45**: 169
unity **3**: 364, 368, 381, 402, 406, 427, 450, 513; **13**: 19; **22**: 378; **29**: 175, 263
unnatural ordering **22**: 378

Much Ado about Nothing (Volumes 8, 18, 31, 55)

appearance versus reality **8**: 17, 18, 48, 63, 69, 73, 75, 79, 88, 95, 115; **31**: 198, 209; **55**: 259, 268
battle of the sexes **8**: 14, 16, 19, 48, 91, 95, 111, 121, 125; **31**: 231, 245 **55**: 199
Beatrice and Benedick
    Beatrice's femininity **8**: 14, 16, 17, 24, 29, 38, 41, 91; **31**: 222, 245; **55**: 221
    Beatrice's request to "kill Claudio" (Act IV, scene i) **8**: 14, 17, 33, 41, 55, 63, 75, 79, 91, 108, 115; **18**: 119, 120, 136, 161, 245, 257; **55**: 268
    Benedick's challenge of Claudio (Act V, scene i) **8**: 48, 63, 79, 91; **31**: 231
    Claudio and Hero, compared with **8**: 19, 28, 29, 75, 82, 115; **31**: 171, 216; **55**: 189
    marriage and the opposite sex, attitudes toward **8**: 9, 13, 14, 16, 19, 29, 36, 48, 63, 77, 91, 95, 115, 121; **16**: 45; **31**: 216
    mutual attraction **8**: 13, 14, 19, 24, 29, 33, 41, 75
    nobility **8**: 13, 19, 24, 29, 36, 39, 41, 47, 82, 91, 108
    popularity **8**: 13, 38, 41, 53, 79
    transformed by love **8**: 19, 29, 36, 48, 75, 91, 95, 115; **31**: 209, 216; **55**: 236
    unconventionality **8**: 48, 91, 95, 108, 115, 121; **55**: 221, 249, 268
    vulgarity **8**: 11, 12, 33, 38, 41, 47
    wit and charm **8**: 9, 12, 13, 14, 19, 24, 27, 28, 29, 33, 36, 38, 41, 47, 55, 69, 95, 108, 115; **31**: 241; **55**: 199
Borachio and Conrade **8**: 24, 69, 82, 88, 111, 115
Christian elements **8**: 17, 19, 29, 55, 95, 104, 111, 115; **31**: 209 55: 228
church scene (Act IV, scene i) **8**: 13, 14, 16, 19, 33, 44, 47, 48, 58, 63, 69, 75, 79, 82, 91, 95, 100, 104, 111, 115; **18**: 120, 130, 138, 145, 146, 148, 192; **31**: 191, 198, 245; **55**: 236
Claudio
    boorish behavior **8**: 9, 24, 33, 36, 39, 44, 48, 63, 79, 82, 95, 100, 111, 115; **31**: 209
    credulity **8**: 9, 17, 19, 24, 29, 36, 41, 47, 58, 63, 75, 77, 82, 95, 100, 104, 111, 115, 121; **31**: 241; **47**: 25
    mercenary traits **8**: 24, 44, 58, 82, 91, 95
    noble qualities **8**: 17, 19, 29, 41, 44, 58, 75; **55**: 232
    reconciliation with Hero **8**: 33, 36, 39, 44, 47, 82, 95, 100, 111, 115; **55**: 236
    repentance **8**: 33, 63, 82, 95, 100, 111, 115, 121; **31**: 245
    sexual insecurities **8**: 75, 100, 111, 115, 121
courtship and marriage **8**: 29, 44, 48, 95, 115, 121, 125; **31**: 191, 231; **51**: 33, 44; **55**: 209
deception, disguise, and duplicity **8**: 29, 55, 63, 69, 79, 82, 88, 108, 115; **31**: 191, 198; **55**: 236
Dogberry and the Watch **8**: 9, 12, 13, 17, 24, 28, 29, 33, 39, 48, 55, 69, 79, 82, 88, 95, 104, 108, 115; **18**: 138, 152, 205, 208, 210, 213, 231; **22**: 85; **31**: 171, 229; **46**: 60; **55**: 189, 249
Don John **8**: 9, 12, 16, 17, 19, 28, 29, 36, 39, 41, 47, 48, 55, 58, 63, 82, 104, 108, 111, 121
Don Pedro **8**: 17, 19, 48, 58, 63, 82, 111, 121
eavesdropping scenes (Act II, scene iii and Act III, scene i) **8**: 12, 13, 17, 19, 28, 29, 33, 36, 48, 55, 63, 73, 75, 82, 121; **18**: 120, 138, 208, 215, 245, 264; **31**: 171, 184; **55**: 259
egotism or narcissism **8**: 19, 24, 28, 29, 55, 69, 95, 115; **55**: 209
Elizabethan culture, relation to **8**: 23, 33, 44, 55, 58, 79, 88, 104, 111, 115; **51**: 15; **55**: 209, 241, 259
Friar **8**: 24, 29, 41, 55, 63, 79, 111; **55**: 249
genre **8**: 9, 18, 19, 28, 29, 39, 41, 44, 53, 63, 69, 73, 79, 82, 95, 100, 104; **48**: 14; **55**: 232, 268
Hero **8**: 13, 14, 16, 19, 28, 29, 44, 48, 53, 55, 82, 95, 104, 111, 115, 121; **31**: 231, 245; **47**: 25; **55**: 209
implausibility of plot, characters, or events **8**: 9, 12, 16, 19, 33, 36, 39, 44, 53, 100, 104
irony **8**: 14, 63, 79, 82; **28**: 63
justice and mercy **22**: 85
language and imagery **8**: 9, 38, 43, 46, 55, 69, 73, 88, 95, 100, 115, 125; **19**: 68; **25**: 77; **28**: 63; **31**: 178, 184, 222, 241, 245; **48**: 14; **55**: 199, 259
law versus passion for freedom **22**: 85
love **8**: 24, 55, 75, 95, 111, 115; **28**: 56; **51**: 30
Messina **8**: 19, 29, 48, 69, 82, 91, 95, 108, 111, 121, 125; **31**: 191, 209, 229, 241, 245
misgovernment **22**: 85; **55**: 241
music and dance **19**: 68; **31**: 222
"nothing," significance of **8**: 17, 18, 23, 55, 73, 95; **19**: 68; **55**: 259
performance issues **18**: 173, 174, 183, 184, 185, 186, 187, 188, 189, 190, 191, 192, 193, 195, 197, 199, 201, 204, 206, 207, 208, 209, 210, 254; **55**: 221
power **22**: 85; **25**: 77; **31**: 231, 245
repentance or forgiveness **8**: 24, 29, 111; **55**: 228
resurrection, metamorphosis, or transformation **8**: 88, 104, 111, 115; **55**: 209
romance or chivalric tradition, influence of **8**: 53, 125; **51**: 15
self-knowledge **8**: 69, 95, 100
setting **18**: 173, 174, 183, 184, 185, 186, 187, 188, 189, 190, 191, 192, 193, 195, 197, 199, 201, 204, 206, 207, 208, 209, 210, 254
slander or hearsay, importance of **8**: 58, 69, 82, 95, 104; **55**: 249
sources **8**: 9, 19, 53, 58, 104
staging issues **8**: 18, 33, 41, 75, 79, 82, 108; **16**: 45; **18**: 245, 247, 249, 252, 254, 257, 261, 264; **28**: 63; **55**: 221
structure **8**: 9, 16, 17, 19, 28, 29, 33, 39, 48, 63, 69, 73, 75, 79, 82, 115; **31**: 178, 184, 198, 231; **55**: 189
virginity or chastity, importance of **8**: 44, 75, 95, 111, 121, 125; **31**: 222; **55**: 268
wit **8**: 27, 29, 38, 69, 79, 91, 95; **31**: 178, 191; **55**: 228
works by Shakespeare or other authors, compared with **8**: 16, 19, 27, 28, 33, 38, 39, 41, 53, 69, 79, 91, 104, 108; **31**: 231; **55**: 189, 209, 232, 241, 249

Othello (Volumes 4, 11, 35, 53)

autobiographical elements **4**: 440, 444; **53**: 324
Brabantio **25**: 189
Cassio **25**: 189
Clarissa (Samuel Richardson), compared with **48**: 277

consummation of marriage **22:** 207; **53:** 246, 333
contrasts and oppositions **4:** 421, 455, 457, 462, 508; **25:** 189; **53:** 268
Desdemona
    as Christ figure **4:** 506, 525, 573; **35:** 360
    culpability **4:** 408, 415, 422, 427; **13:** 313; **19:** 253, 276; **35:** 265, 352, 380
    innocence **35:** 360; **47:** 25; **53:** 310, 333
    as mother figure **22:** 339; **35:** 282; **53:** 324
    passivity **4:** 402, 406, 421, 440, 457, 470, 582, 587; **25:** 189; **35:** 380
    spiritual nature of her love **4:** 462, 530, 559
    staging issues **11:** 350, 354, 359; **13:** 327; **32:** 201
dramatic structure **4:** 370, 390, 399, 427, 488, 506, 517, 569; **22:** 207; **28:** 243; **53:** 261
Duke **25:** 189
Emilia **4:** 386, 391, 392, 415, 587; **35:** 352, 380
ending **54:** 119
evil **52:** 78
gender issues **32:** 294; **35:** 327; **53:** 255, 268, 310, 315, 324
handkerchief, significance of **4:** 370, 384, 385, 392, 396, 503, 530, 562; **35:** 265, 282, 380; **53:** 333
Hercules Furens (Seneca) as source **16:** 283
Iago
    affinity with Othello **4:** 400, 427, 468, 470, 477, 500, 506; **25:** 189; **44:** 57
    as conventional dramatic villain **4:** 440, 527, 545, 582; **53:** 288
    as homosexual **4:** 503; **53:** 275
    Machiavellian elements **4:** 440, 455, 457, 517, 545; **35:** 336, 347
    motives **4:** 389, 390, 397, 399, 402, 409, 423, 424, 427, 434, 451, 462, 545, 564; **13:** 304; **25:** 189; **28:** 344; **32:** 201; **35:** 265, 276, 310, 336, 347; **42:** 278; **53:** 246, 275, 324
    revenge scheme **4:** 392, 409, 424, 451
    as scapegoat **4:** 506
    as victim **4:** 402, 409, 434, 451, 457, 470
idealism versus realism **4:** 457, 508, 517; **13:** 313; **25:** 189; **53:** 350
implausibility of plot, characters, or events **4:** 370, 380, 391, 442, 444; **47:** 51
jealousy **4:** 384, 488, 527; **35:** 253, 265, 282, 301, 310; **44:** 57, 66; **51:** 30
justice **35:** 247; **53:** 288, 350
language and imagery **4:** 433, 442, 445, 462, 493, 508, 517, 552, 587, 596; **13:** 304; **16:** 272; **22:** 378; **25:** 189, 257; **28:** 243, 344; **42:** 278; **47:** 51; **53:** 261
love **4:** 412, 493, 506, 512, 530, 545, 552, 569, 570, 575, 580, 591; **19:** 253; **22:** 207; **25:** 257; **28:** 243, 344; **32:** 201; **35:** 261, 317; **51:** 25, 30; **53:** 315; **54:** 119
love and reason **4:** 512, 530, 580; **19:** 253
madness **35:** 265, 276, 282
marriage **35:** 369; **51:** 44; **53:** 315
Marxist criticism **42:** 234
Measure for Measure, compared with **25:** 189
medieval dramatic conventions, influence of **4:** 440, 527, 545, 559, 582
Merchant of Venice, compared with **53:** 288, 255, 268, 298

military and sexual hierarchies **16:** 272; **53:** 324
moral corruption **52:** 78
opening scene **54:** 2, 6
Othello
    affinity with Iago **4:** 400, 427, 468, 470, 477, 500, 506; **25:** 189; **35:** 276, 320, 327
    as conventional "blameless hero" **4:** 445, 486, 500; **53:** 233, 288, 298, 304
    credulity **4:** 384, 385, 388, 390, 396, 402, 434, 440, 455; **13:** 327; **32:** 302; **47:** 25, 51
    Desdemona, relationship with **22:** 339; **35:** 301, 317; **37:** 269; **53:** 315
    divided nature **4:** 400, 412, 462, 470, 477, 493, 500, 582, 592; **16:** 293; **19:** 276; **25:** 189; **35:** 320; **53:** 268, 289, 343
    egotism **4:** 427, 470, 477, 493, 522, 536, 541, 573, 597; **13:** 304; **35:** 247, 253
    self-destructive anger **16:** 283; **53:** 324
    self-dramatizing or self-deluding **4:** 454, 457, 477, 592; **13:** 313; **16:** 293; **35:** 317
    self-knowledge **4:** 462, 470, 477, 483, 508, 522, 530, 564, 580, 591, 596; **13:** 304, 313; **16:** 283; **28:** 243; **35:** 253, 317; **53:** 233, 343
    spiritual state **4:** 483, 488, 517, 525, 527, 544, 559, 564, 573; **28:** 243; **35:** 253; **53:** 298
perception **19:** 276; **25:** 189, 257; **53:** 246, 289
poetic justice, question of **4:** 370, 412, 415, 427
pride and rightful self-esteem **4:** 522, 536, 541; **35:** 352
psychoanalytic interpretations **4:** 468, 503; **35:** 265, 276, 282, 301, 317, 320, 347; **42:** 203; **44:** 57; **53:** 275, 343
racial issues **4:** 370, 380, 384, 385, 392, 399, 401, 402, 408, 427, 564; **13:** 327; **16:** 293; **25:** 189, 257; **28:** 249, 330; **35:** 369; **42:** 203 **37:** 336; **53:** 1, 233, 238, 246, 255, 261, 268, 275, 289, 298, 304; **55:** 27
religious, mythic, or spiritual content **4:** 483, 517, 522, 525, 559, 573; **22:** 207; **28:** 330; **53:** 289
revenge **35:** 261
Romeo and Juliet, compared with **32:** 302
sexuality **22:** 339; **28:** 330, 344; **35:** 352, 360; **37:** 269; **44:** 57, 66; **51:** 44; **53:** 275, 310, 315
sources **28:** 330
staging issues **11:** 273, 334, 335, 339, 342, 350,354, 359, 362; **53:** 233, 304
structure **22:** 378; **28:** 325
time scheme **4:** 370, 384, 390, 488; **22:** 207; **35:** 310; **47:** 51; **53:** 333
tragic elements **55:** 78
unnatural ordering **22:** 378
Venetian politics **32:** 294; **53:** 350
violence **22:** 12; **43:** 32
The Winter's Tale, compared with **35:** 310
women, role of **19:** 253; **28:** 344; **53:** 310

Pericles (Volumes 2, 15, 36, 51)

archetypal structure **2:** 570, 580, 582, 584, 588; **25:** 365; **51:** 71, 79
art and nature **22:** 315; **36:** 233
audience perception **42:** 359; **48:** 364

authorship controversy **2:** 538, 540, 543, 544, 545, 546, 548, 550, 551, 553, 556, 558, 564, 565, 568, 576, 586; **15:** 132, 141, 148, 152; **16:** 391, 399; **25:** 365; **36:** 198, 244
autobiographical elements **2:** 551, 554, 555, 563, 581
brothel scenes (Act IV, scenes ii and vi) **2:** 548, 550, 551, 553, 554, 586, 590; **15:** 134, 145, 154, 166, 172, 177; **36:** 274; **51:** 118
composition date **2:** 537, 544
Deconstructionist interpretation of **48:** 364
Diana, as symbol of nature **22:** 315; **36:** 233; **51:** 71
doubling of roles **15:** 150, 152, 167, 173, 180
Gower chorus **2:** 548, 575; **15:** 134, 141, 143, 145, 149, 152, 177; **36:** 279; **42:** 359
incest, motif of **2:** 582, 588; **22:** 315; **36:** 257, 264; **51:** 110, 97
as inferior or flawed plays **2:** 537, 546, 553, 563, 564; **15:** 139, 143, 156, 167, 176; **36:** 198; **51:** 79
innocence **36:** 226, 274
Jacobean culture, relation to **37:** 361; **51:** 110, 86
language and imagery **2:** 559, 560, 565, 583; **16:** 391; **19:** 387; **22:** 315; **36:** 198, 214, 233, 244, 251, 264; **51:** 86, 99
Marina **37:** 361; **51:** 118
as miracle play **2:** 569, 581; **36:** 205; **51:** 97
nature as book **22:** 315; **36:** 233
oaths, importance of **19:** 387
patience **2:** 572, 573, 578, 579; **36:** 251
Pericles
    characterization **36:** 251; **37:** 361
    patience **2:** 572, 573, 578, 579
    suit of Antiochus's daughter **2:** 547, 565, 578, 579; **51:** 126
    Ulysses, compared with **2:** 551
politics **37:** 361
popularity **2:** 536, 538, 546; **37:** 361
Prologue **54:** 35
recognition scene (Act V, scene i) **15:** 138, 139, 141, 145, 161, 162, 167, 172, 175
reconciliation **2:** 555, 564, 584, 586, 588; **36:** 205
religious, mythic, or spiritual content **2:** 559, 561, 565, 570, 580, 584, 588; **22:** 315; **25:** 365; **51:** 97
riddle motif **22:** 315; **36:** 205, 214
Shakespeare's other romances, relation to **2:** 547, 549, 551, 559, 564, 570, 571, 584, 585; **15:** 139; **16:** 391, 399; **36:** 226, 257; **51:** 71, 79 **54:** 35
spectacle **42:** 359
sources **2:** 538, 568, 572, 575; **25:** 365; **36:** 198, 205; **51:** 118, 126
staging issues **16:** 399; **48:** 364; **51:** 99
suffering **2:** 546, 573, 578, 579; **25:** 365; **36:** 279
textual revisions **15:** 129, 130, 132, 134, 135, 136, 138, 152, 155, 167, 181; **16:** 399; **25:** 365; **51:** 99

The Phoenix and Turtle (Volumes 10, 38, 51)

allegorical elements **10:** 7, 8, 9, 16, 17, 48; **38:** 334, 378; **51:** 138, 188
art and nature **10:** 7, 42
authenticity **10:** 7, 8, 16
autobiographical elements **10:** 14, 18, 42, 48; **51:** 155

bird imagery **10:** 21, 27; **38:** 329, 350, 367; **51:** 145, 181, 184
Christian elements **10:** 21, 24, 31; **38:** 326; **51:** 162, 171, 181
complex or enigmatic nature **10:** 7, 14, 35, 42; **38:** 326, 357; **51:** 145, 162
consciously philosophical **10:** 7, 21, 24, 31, 48; **38:** 342, 378
constancy and faithfulness **10:** 18, 20, 21, 48; **38:** 329
Court of Love **10:** 9, 24, 50
Donne, John, compared with **10:** 20, 31, 35, 37, 40; **51:** 143
satiric elements **10:** 8, 16, 17, 27, 35, 40, 45, 48
love **10:** 31, 37, 40, 50; **38:** 342, 345, 367; **51:** 145, 151, 155
as metaphysical poem **10:** 7, 8, 9, 20, 31, 35, 37, 40, 45, 50; **51:** 143, 171, 184
Neoplatonism **10:** 7, 9, 21, 24, 40, 45, 50; **38:** 345, 350, 367, 184
as "pure" poetry **10:** 14, 31, 35; **38:** 329
Scholasticism **10:** 21, 24, 31; **51:** 188
Shakespeare's dramas, compared with **10:** 9, 14, 17, 18, 20, 27, 37, 40, 42, 48; **38:** 342; **51:** 151, 155
sources **10:** 7, 9, 18, 24, 45; **38:** 326, 334, 350, 367; **51:** 138
structure **10:** 27, 31, 37, 45, 50; **38:** 342, 345, 357; **51:** 138, 143
style **10:** 8, 20, 24, 27, 31, 35, 45, 50; **38:** 334, 345, 357, 171; **51:** 188

The Rape of Lucrece (Volumes 10, 33, 43)

allegorical elements **10:** 89, 93
Brutus **10:** 96, 106, 109, 116, 121, 125, 128, 135
Christian elements **10:** 77, 80, 89, 96, 98, 109
Collatine **10:** 98, 131; **43:** 102
Elizabethan culture, relation to **33:** 195; **43:** 77;
gender **53:** 1
irony or paradox **10:** 93, 98, 128
language and imagery **10:** 64, 65, 66, 71, 78, 80, 89, 93, 116, 109, 125, 131; **22:** 289, 294; **25:** 305; **32:** 321; **33:** 144, 155, 179, 200; **43:** 102, 113, 141
Lucrece
  chastity **33:** 131, 138; **43:** 92
  as example of Renaissance virtù **22:** 289; **43:** 148
  heroic **10:** 84, 93, 109, 121, 128
  patriarchal woman, model of **10:** 109, 131; **33:** 169, 200
  self-responsibility **10:** 89, 96, 98, 106, 125; **33:** 195; **43:** 85, 92, 158
  unrealistic **10:** 64, 65, 66, 121
  verbose **10:** 64, 81, 116; **25:** 305; **33:** 169
  as victim **22:** 294; **25:** 305; **32:** 321; **33:** 131, 195; **43:** 102, 158
male/female relationships **10:** 109, 121, 131; **22:** 289; **25:** 305; **43:** 113, 141
narrative strategies **22:** 294
race **53:** 1
Roman history, relation to **10:** 84, 89, 93, 96, 98, 109, 116, 125, 135; **22:** 289; **25:** 305; **33:** 155, 190
Shakespeare's dramas, compared with **10:** 63, 64, 65, 66, 68, 71, 73, 74, 78, 80, 81, 84, 98, 116, 121, 125; **43:** 92
sources **10:** 63, 64, 65, 66, 68, 74, 77, 78, 89, 98, 109, 121, 125; **25:** 305; **33:** 155, 190; **43:** 77, 92, 148,
structure **10:** 84, 89, 93, 98, 135; **22:** 294; **25:** 305; **43:** 102, 141
style **10:** 64, 65, 66, 68, 69, 70, 71, 73, 74, 77, 78, 81, 84, 98, 116, 131, 135; **43:** 113, 158
Tarquin **10:** 80, 93, 98, 116, 125; **22:** 294; **25:** 305; **32:** 321; **33:** 190; **43:** 102
tragic elements **10:** 78, 80, 81, 84, 98, 109; **43:** 85, 148
the Troy passage **10:** 74, 89, 98, 116, 121, 128; **22:** 289; **32:** 321; **33:** 144, 179; **43:** 77, 85
Venus and Adonis, compared with **10:** 63, 66, 68, 69, 70, 73, 81; **22:** 294; **43:** 148
violence **43:** 148, 158

Richard II (Volumes 6, 24, 39, 52)

abdication scene (Act IV, scene i) **6:** 270, 307, 317, 327, 354, 359, 381, 393, 409; **13:** 172; **19:** 151; **24:** 274, 414; **52:** 141, 144
acting and dissimulation **6:** 264, 267, 307, 310, 315, 368, 393, 409; **24:** 339, 345, 346, 349, 352, 356
allegorical elements **6:** 264, 283, 323, 385
audience perception **24:** 414, 423; **39:** 295
Bolingbroke
  comic elements **28:** 134
  guilt **24:** 423; **39:** 279
  language and imagery **6:** 310, 315, 331, 347, 374, 381, 397; **32:** 189
  as Machiavellian figure **6:** 305, 307, 315, 331, 347, 388, 393, 397; **24:** 428
  as politician **6:** 255, 263, 264, 272, 277, 294, 364, 368, 391; **24:** 330, 333, 405, 414, 423, 428; **39:** 256; **52:** 124
  Richard, compared with **6:** 307, 315, 347, 374, 391, 393, 409; **24:** 346, 349, 351, 352, 356, 395, 419, 423, 428; **52:** 108, 124
  his silence **24:** 423
  structure, compared with **39:** 235
  usurpation of crown, nature of **6:** 255, 272, 289, 307, 310, 347, 354, 359, 381, 385, 393; **13:** 172; **24:** 322, 356, 383, 419; **28:** 178; **52:** 108, 124
Bolingbroke and Richard as opposites **24:** 423
Bolingbroke-Mowbray dispute **22:** 137
carnival elements **19:** 151; **39:** 273
censorship **24:** 260, 261, 262, 263, 386; **42:** 120; **52:** 141, 144
ceremonies, rites, and rituals, importance of **6:** 270, 294, 315, 368, 381, 397, 409, 414; **24:** 274, 356, 411, 414, 419
comic elements **24:** 262, 263, 395; **39:** 243
contractual and economic relations **13:** 213; **49:** 60
costumes **24:** 274, 278, 291, 304, 325, 356, 364, 423
deposition scene (Act III, scene iii) **24:** 298, 395, 423; **42:** 120
Elizabethan attitudes, influence of **6:** 287, 292, 294, 305, 321, 327, 364, 402, 414; **13:** 494; **24:** 325; **28:** 188; **39:** 273; **42:** 120; **52:** 141, 144
Essex Rebellion, relation to **6:** 249, 250; **24:** 356
family honor, structure, and inheritance **6:** 338, 368, 388, 397, 414; **39:** 263, 279
fate **6:** 289, 294, 304, 352, 354, 385
garden scene (Act III, scene iv) **6:** 264, 283, 323, 385; **24:** 307, 356, 414
Gaunt **6:** 255, 287, 374, 388, 402, 414; **24:** 274, 322, 325, 414, 423; **39:** 263, 279
gender issues **25:** 89; **39:** 295
historical sources, compared with **6:** 252, 279, 343; **28:** 134; **39:** 235; **49:** 60
historiography **56:** 2, 15
irony **6:** 270, 307, 364, 368, 391; **24:** 383; **28:** 188
King of Misrule **19:** 151; **39:** 273
kingship **6:** 263, 264, 272, 277, 289, 294, 327, 354, 364, 381, 388, 391, 402, 409, 414; **19:** 151, 209; **24:** 260, 289, 291, 322, 325, 333, 339, 345, 346, 349, 351, 352, 356, 395, 408, 419, 428; **28:** 134; **39:** 235, 243, 256, 273, 279, 289; **42:** 175
language and imagery **6:** 252, 282, 283, 294, 298, 315, 323, 331, 347, 368, 374, 381, 385, 397, 409; **13:** 213, 494; **24:** 269, 270, 298, 301, 304, 315, 325, 329, 333, 339, 356, 364, 395, 405, 408, 411, 414, 419; **28:** 134, 188; **39:** 243, 273, 289, 295; **42:** 175; **52:** 154, 157, 169, 174, 183
Marlowe's works, compared with **19:** 233; **24:** 307, 336; **42:** 175
medievalism and chivalry, presentation of **6:** 258, 277, 294, 327, 338, 388, 397, 414; **24:** 274, 278, 279, 280, 283; **39:** 256
mercantilism and feudalism **13:** 213
mirror scene (Act IV, scene i) **6:** 317, 327, 374, 381, 393, 409; **24:** 267, 356, 408, 414, 419, 423; **28:** 134, 178; **39:** 295
mythological elements **52:** 154, 157, 169
negative assessments **6:** 250, 252, 253, 255, 282, 307, 317, 343, 359
Northumberland **24:** 423
providential order **56:** 15
Richard
  artistic temperament **6:** 264, 267, 270, 272, 277, 292, 294, 298, 315, 331, 334, 347, 368, 374, 393, 409; **24:** 298, 301, 304, 315, 322, 390, 405, 408, 411, 414, 419; **39:** 289
  Bolingbroke, compared with **24:** 346, 349, 351, 352, 356, 419; **39:** 256; **52:** 108, 124
  characterization **6:** 250, 252, 253, 254, 255, 258, 262, 263, 267, 270, 272, 282, 283, 304, 343, 347, 364, 368; **24:** 262, 263, 267, 269, 270, 271, 272, 273, 274, 278, 280, 315, 322, 325, 330, 333, 390, 395, 402, 405, 423; **28:** 134; **39:** 279, 289; **52:** 169
  dangerous aspects **24:** 405
  delusion **6:** 267, 298, 334, 368, 409; **24:** 329, 336, 405
  homosexuality **24:** 405
  kingship **6:** 253, 254, 263, 272, 327, 331, 334, 338, 364, 402, 414; **24:** 278, 295, 336, 337, 339, 356, 419; **28:** 134, 178; **39:** 256, 263; **52:** 169
  loss of identity **6:** 267, 338, 368, 374, 381, 388, 391, 409; **24:** 298, 414, 428
  as martyr-king **6:** 289, 307, 321; **19:** 209; **24:** 289, 291; **28:** 134
  nobility **6:** 255, 258, 259, 262, 263, 391; **24:** 260, 263, 274, 280, 289, 291, 402, 408, 411

political acumen **6:** 263, 264, 272, 292, 310, 327, 334, 364, 368, 374, 388, 391, 397, 402, 409; **24:** 405; **39:** 256
private versus public persona **6:** 317, 327, 364, 368, 391, 409; **24:** 428
role-playing **24:** 419, 423; **28:** 178
role in Gloucester's death **52:** 108, 124
seizure of Gaunt's estate **6:** 250, 338, 388; **49:** 60
self-dramatization **6:** 264, 267, 307, 310, 315, 317, 331, 334, 368, 393, 409; **24:** 339; **28:** 178
self-hatred **13:** 172; **24:** 383; **39:** 289
self-knowledge **6:** 255, 267, 331, 334, 338, 352, 354, 368, 388, 391; **24:** 273, 289, 411, 414; **39:** 263, 289
spiritual redemption **6:** 255, 267, 331, 334, 338, 352, 354, 368, 388, 391; **24:** 273, 289, 411, 414; **52:** 124
Shakespeare's other histories, compared with **6:** 255, 264, 272, 294, 304, 310, 317, 343, 354, 359; **24:** 320, 325, 330, 331, 332, 333; **28:** 178
Shakespeare's sympathies, question of **6:** 277, 279, 287, 347, 359, 364, 391, 393, 402
Sicilian Usurper (Nahum Tate adaptation) **24:** 260, 261, 262, 263, 386, 390
sources **56:** 2
staging issues **13:** 494; **24:** 273, 274, 278, 279, 280, 283, 291, 295, 296, 301, 303, 304, 310, 315, 317, 320, 325, 333, 338, 346, 351, 352, 356, 364, 383, 386, 395, 402, 405, 411, 414, 419, 423, 428; **25:** 89
structure **6:** 282, 304, 317, 343, 352, 359, 364, 39; **24:** 307, 322, 325, 356, 395
textual arrangement **24:** 260, 261, 262, 263, 271, 273, 291, 296, 356, 390
time **22:** 137
usurpation **6:** 263, 264, 272, 287, 289, 315, 323, 331, 343, 354, 364, 381, 388, 393, 397; **24:** 383; **52:** 108, 141, 154
York **6:** 287, 364, 368, 388, 402, 414; **24:** 263, 320, 322, 364, 395, 414; **39:** 243, 279

Richard III (Volumes 8, 14, 39, 52)

allegorical elements **52:** 5
ambivalence and ambiguity **44:** 11; **47:** 15
conscience **8:** 148, 152, 162, 165, 190, 197, 201, 206, 210, 228, 232, 239, 243, 252, 258; **39:** 341; **52:** 5, 196, 205
Elizabethan politics, relation to **22:** 395; **25:** 141; **37:** 144; **39:** 345, 349; **42:** 132 **52:** 201, 214, 257
ending **54:** 84
evil **52:** 78
family honor, structure and inheritance **8:** 177, 248, 252, 263, 267; **25:** 141; **39:** 335, 341, 349, 370
flattery **22:** 395
gender issues **25:** 141; **37:** 144; **39:** 345; **52:** 223, 239
genre **8:** 181, 182, 197, 206, 218, 228, 239, 243, 252, 258; **13:** 142; **39:** 383; **52:** 239
ghost scene (Act V, scene iii) **8:** 152, 154, 159, 162, 163, 165, 170, 177, 193, 197, 210, 228, 239, 243, 252, 258, 267
Henry VI, relation to **8:** 159, 165, 177, 182, 193, 201, 210, 213, 218, 228, 243, 248, 252, 267; **25:** 164; **39:** 370

historical accuracy **8:** 144, 145, 153, 159, 163, 165, 168, 213, 223, 228, 232; **39:** 305, 308, 326, 383
historical principles **39:** 308, 326, 387
historiography **56:** 2
language and imagery **8:** 159, 161, 165, 167, 168, 170, 177, 182, 184, 186, 193, 197, 201, 206, 218, 223, 243, 248, 252, 258, 262, 267; **16:** 150; **25:** 141, 245; **39:** 360, 370, 383; **47:** 15; **52:** 285, 290
Margaret **8:** 153, 154, 159, 162, 163, 170, 193, 201, 206, 210, 218, 223, 228, 243, 248, 262; **39:** 345
Christopher Marlowe's works, compared with **19:** 233
minor characters **8:** 154, 159, 162, 163, 168, 170, 177, 184, 186, 201, 206, 210, 218, 223, 228, 232, 239, 248, 262, 267
modernization **14:** 523
moral corruption of English society **8:** 154, 163, 165, 177, 193, 201, 218, 228, 232, 243, 248, 252, 267; **39:** 308; **52:** 78, 201
morality **52:** 5, 78
plot and incident **8:** 146, 152, 159; **25:** 164
popularity **8:** 144, 146, 154, 158, 159, 162, 181, 228; **39:** 383
rebellion **22:** 395
retribution **8:** 163, 170, 177, 182, 184, 193, 197, 201, 206, 210, 218, 223, 228, 243, 248, 267
Richard III
ambition **8:** 148, 154, 165, 168, 170, 177, 182, 213, 218, 228, 232, 239, 252, 258, 267; **39:** 308, 341, 360, 370, 383; **52:** 201, 223
attractive qualities **8:** 145, 148, 152, 154, 159, 161, 162, 165, 168, 170, 181, 182, 184, 185, 197, 201, 206, 213, 228, 243, 252, 258; **16:** 150; **39:** 370, 383; **52:** 272, 280, 285
credibility, question of **8:** 145, 147, 154, 159, 165, 193; **13:** 142
death, decay, and nature's destructiveness **8:** 145, 148, 154, 159, 165, 168, 170, 177, 182, 197, 210, 223, 228, 232, 243, 248, 252, 258, 267
deformity as symbol **8:** 146, 147, 148, 152, 154, 159, 161, 165, 170, 177, 184, 185, 193, 218, 248, 252, 267; **19:** 164
inversion of moral order **8:** 159, 168, 177, 182, 184, 185, 197, 201, 213, 218, 223, 232, 239, 243, 248, 252, 258, 262, 267; **39:** 360; **52:** 205, 214
as Machiavellian villain **8:** 165, 182, 190, 201, 218, 232, 239, 243, 248; **39:** 308, 326, 360, 387; **52:** 201, 205, 257, 285
as monster or symbol of diabolic **8:** 145, 147, 159, 162, 168, 170, 177, 182, 193, 197, 201, 228, 239, 248, 258; **13:** 142; **37:** 144; **39:** 326, 349; **52:** 227, 272
other literary villains, compared with **8:** 148, 161, 162, 165, 181, 182, 206, 213, 239, 267
role-playing, hypocrisy, and dissimulation **8:** 145, 148, 154, 159, 162, 165, 168, 170, 182, 190, 206, 213, 218, 228, 239, 243, 252, 258, 267; **25:** 141, 164, 245; **39:** 335, 341, 387; **52:** 257, 267
as scourge or instrument of God **8:** 163, 177, 193, 201, 218, 228, 248, 267; **39:** 308
as seducer **52:** 223

self-esteem **52:** 196
shamelessness **52:** 196
as Vice figure **8:** 190, 201, 213, 228, 243, 248, 252; **16:** 150; **39:** 383, 387; **52:** 223, 267
Richmond **8:** 154, 158, 163, 168, 177, 182, 193, 210, 218, 223, 228, 243, 248, 252; **13:** 142; **25:** 141; **39:** 349; **52:** 214, 257, 285
settings **14:** 516, 528; **52:** 263
Shakespeare's artistic growth, Richard III's contribution to **8:** 165, 167, 182, 193, 197, 206, 210, 228, 239, 267; **25:** 164; **39:** 305, 326, 370
Shakespeare's political sympathies **8:** 147, 163, 177, 193, 197, 201, 223, 228, 232, 243, 248, 267; **39:** 349; **42:** 132
sources **52:** 263, 290; **56:** 2
chronicles **8:** 145, 165, 193, 197, 201, 206, 210, 213, 228, 232
Marlowe, Christopher **8:** 167, 168, 182, 201, 206, 218
morality plays **8:** 182, 190, 201, 213, 239
Seneca, other classical writers **8:** 165, 190, 201, 206, 228, 248
staging issues **14:** 515, 527, 528, 537; **16:** 137; **52:** 263, 272
structure **8:** 154, 161, 163, 167, 168, 170, 177, 184, 193, 197, 201, 206, 210, 218, 223, 228, 232, 243, 252, 262, 267; **16:** 150
The Tragical History of King Richard III (Colley Cibber adaptation), compared with **8:** 159, 161, 243
traditional values **39:** 335
Tudor myth **8:** 163, 165, 177, 184, 193, 201, 218, 228, 232, 243, 248, 252, 267; **39:** 305, 308, 326, 387; **42:** 132
Wars of the Roses **8:** 163, 165, 177, 184, 193, 201, 218, 228, 232, 243, 248, 252, 267; **39:** 308
wooing scenes (Act I, scene ii and Act IV, scene iv) **8:** 145, 147, 152, 153, 154, 159, 161, 164, 170, 190, 197, 206, 213, 218, 223, 232, 239, 243, 252, 258, 267; **16:** 150; **19:** 164; **25:** 141, 164; **39:** 308, 326, 360, 387; **52:** 227, 249, 280

Romeo and Juliet (Volumes 5, 11, 33, 51)

accident or chance **5:** 418, 444, 448, 467, 470, 487, 573
adolescence **33:** 249, 255, 257
amour-passion or Liebestod myth **5:** 484, 489, 528, 530, 542, 550, 575; **32:** 256; **51:** 195, 219, 236
androgyny **13:** 530
anxiety **13:** 235
balcony scene **32:** 276; **51:** 219
Caius Marius (Thomas Otway adaptation) **11:** 377, 378, 488, 495
comic and tragic elements, combination of **5:** 496, 524, 528, 547, 559 **46:** 78
contradiction, paradox, and opposition **5:** 421, 427, 431, 496, 509, 513, 516, 520, 525, 528, 538; **33:** 287; **44:** 11; **54:** 125
costuming **11:** 505, 509
courtly love tradition, influence of **5:** 505, 542, 575; **33:** 233
desire **51:** 227, 236
detention of Friar John **5:** 448, 467, 470

divine will, role of **5:** 485, 493, 505, 533, 573
double opening **54:** 6
dramatic shortcomings or failure **5:** 416, 418, 420, 426, 436, 437, 448, 464, 467, 469, 480, 487, 524, 562
Elizabethan poetics, influence of **5:** 416, 520, 522, 528, 550, 559, 575
ending **54:** 125
evil **5:** 485, 493, 505
as experimental play **5:** 464, 509, 528
fate **5:** 431, 444, 464, 469, 470, 479, 480, 485, 487, 493, 509, 530, 533, 562, 565, 571, 573; **33:** 249; **54:** 125
feud **5:** 415, 419, 425, 447, 458, 464, 469, 479, 480, 493, 509, 522, 556, 565, 566, 571, 575; **25:** 181; **51:** 245
Friar Lawrence
    contribution to catastrophe **5:** 437, 444, 470; **33:** 300; **51:** 253
    philosophy of moderation **5:** 427, 431, 437, 438, 443, 444, 445, 458, 467, 479, 505, 538
    as Shakespeare's spokesman **5:** 427, 431, 437, 458, 467
    ideal love **5:** 421, 427, 431, 436, 437, 450, 463, 469, 498, 505, 575; **25:** 257; **33:** 210, 225, 272; **51:** 25, 44, 195, 203, 219
gender issues **32:** 256; **51:** 253
lamentation scene (Act IV, scene v) **5:** 425, 492, 538
language and imagery **5:** 420, 426, 431, 436, 437, 456, 477, 479, 489, 492, 496, 509, 520, 522, 528, 538, 542, 550, 559; **25:** 181, 245, 257; **32:** 276; **33:** 210, 272, 274, 287; **42:** 271; **51:** 203, 212, 227
love versus fate **5:** 421, 437, 438, 443, 445, 458; **33:** 249; **54:** 125
medieval influence **5:** 480, 505, 509, 573
Mercutio
    bawdy **5:** 463, 525, 550, 575
    death, decay, and nature's destructiveness **5:** 415, 418, 419, 547; **33:** 290
    as worldly counterpoint to Romeo **5:** 425, 464, 542; **33:** 290; **51:** 195
Neoclassical rules **5:** 416, 418, 426
Nurse **5:** 419, 425, 463, 464, 575; **33:** 294
Othello, compared with **32:** 302
Petrarchian poetics, influence of **5:** 416, 520, 522, 528, 550, 559, 575; **32:** 276; **51:** 212, 236
prose adaptations of Juliet's character **19:** 261
psychoanalytic interpretation **5:** 513, 556; **51:** 253
public versus private worlds **5:** 520, 550; **25:** 181; **33:** 274
reconciliation **5:** 415, 419, 427, 439, 447, 480, 487, 493, 505, 533, 536, 562
rhetoric **42:** 271
rival productions **11:** 381, 382, 384, 385, 386, 487
Romeo and Juliet
    death-wish **5:** 431, 489, 505, 528, 530, 538, 542, 550, 566, 571, 575; **32:** 212
    first meeting (Act I, scene v) **51:** 212
    immortality **5:** 536
    Juliet's epithalamium speech (Act III, scene ii) **5:** 431, 477, 492
    Juliet's innocence **5:** 421, 423, 450, 454; **33:** 257
    maturation **5:** 437, 454, 467, 493, 498, 509, 520, 565; **33:** 249, 257

rebellion **25:** 257
reckless passion **5:** 419, 427, 431, 438, 443, 444, 448, 467, 479, 485, 505, 533, 538, 542; **33:** 241
Romeo's dream (Act V, scene i) **5:** 513, 536, 556; **45:** 40; **51:** 203
Rosaline, Romeo's relationship with **5:** 419, 423, 425, 427, 438, 498, 542, 575
sexuality **25:** 181; **33:** 225, 233, 241, 246, 274, 300; **51:** 227, 236
source of tragic catastrophe **5:** 418, 427, 431, 448, 458, 469, 479, 480, 485, 487, 493, 509, 522, 528, 530, 533, 542, 565, 571, 573; **33:** 210; **51:** 245
sources **5:** 416, 419, 423, 450; **32:** 222; **33:** 210; **45:** 40; **54:** 125
staging issues **11:** 499, 505, 507, 514, 517; **13:** 243; **25:** 181; **32:** 212
structure **5:** 438, 448, 464, 469, 470, 477, 480, 496, 518, 524, 525, 528, 547, 559; **33:** 210, 246
tomb scene (Act V, scene iii) **5:** 416, 419, 423; **13:** 243; **25:** 181, 245; **51:** 219; **54:** 125
triumph over death or fate **5:** 421, 423, 427, 505, 509, 520, 530, 536, 565, 566; **51:** 219
tragic elements **55:** 78
Verona society **5:** 556, 566; **13:** 235; **33:** 255; **51:** 245
wordplay **32:** 256

Sonnets (Volumes 10, 40, 51)

ambiguity **10:** 251, 256; **28:** 385; **40:** 221, 228, 268
audience **51:** 316
authenticity **10:** 153, 154, 230, 243; **48:** 325
autobiographical elements **10:** 159, 160, 166, 167, 175, 176, 182, 196, 205, 213, 215, 226, 233, 238, 240, 251, 279, 283, 302, 309, 325, 337, 377; **13:** 487; **16:** 461; **28:** 363, 385; **42:** 303; **48:** 325
beauty **10:** 247; **51:** 288
Christian elements **10:** 191, 256
composition date **10:** 153, 154, 161, 166, 196, 217, 226, 270, 277; **28:** 363, 385
Dark Lady **10:** 161, 167, 176, 216, 217, 218, 226, 240, 302, 342, 377, 394; **25:** 374; **37:** 374; **40:** 273; **48:** 346; **51:** 284, 288, 292, 321
deception, disguise, and duplicity **25:** 374; **40:** 221
dramatic elements **10:** 155, 182, 240, 251, 283, 367
editorial and textual issues **28:** 363; **40:** 273; **42:** 303
Elizabeth, audience of **48:** 325
the Friend **10:** 279, 302, 309, 379, 385, 391, 394; **51:** 284, 288, 292, 300, 304, 316, 321
friendship **10:** 185, 279; **28:** 380; **51:** 284
gender issues **37:** 374; **40:** 238, 247, 254, 264, 268, 273; **53:** 1
homoerotic elements **10:** 155, 156, 159, 161, 175, 213, 391; **16:** 461; **28:** 363, 380; **37:** 347; **40:** 254, 264, 273; **51:** 270, 284
identities of persons **10:** 154, 155, 156, 161, 166, 167, 169, 173, 174, 175, 185, 190, 191, 196, 218, 226, 230, 233, 240; **40:** 238
Ireland, William Henry, forgeries of **48:** 325

irony or satire **10:** 256, 293, 334, 337, 346; **51:** 300
Italian influences **28:** 407
language and imagery **10:** 247, 251, 255, 256, 290, 353, 372, 385; **13:** 445; **28:** 380, 385; **32:** 327, 352; **40:** 228, 247, 284, 292, 303; **51:** 270, 304
love **10:** 173, 247, 287, 290, 293, 302, 309, 322, 325, 329, 394; **28:** 380; **37:** 347; **51:** 270, 284, 288, 292
love versus reason **10:** 329
A Lover's Complaint (the Rival Poet) **10:** 243, 353
    gender issues **48:** 336
    pastoral tradition, compared with **48:** 336
    sonnets, compared with **48:** 336
lust **51:** 292
lust versus reason **51:** 288
magic **48:** 346
Mr. W. H. **10:** 153, 155, 161, 169, 174, 182, 190, 196, 217, 218, 377
Montaigne's Essais, relation to **42:** 382
mutability, theme of **42:** 382
Neoplatonism **10:** 191, 205
occult **48:** 346
other sonnet writers, Shakespeare compared with **10:** 247, 260, 265, 283, 290, 293, 309, 353, 367; **28:** 380, 385, 407; **37:** 374; **40:** 247, 264, 303; **42:** 303
pedagogy **37:** 374
performative issues **48:** 352
poet-patron relationship **48:** 352
poetic style **10:** 153, 155, 156, 158, 159, 160, 161, 173, 175, 182, 214, 247, 251, 255, 260, 265, 283, 287, 296, 302, 315, 322, 325, 337, 346, 349, 360, 367, 385; **16:** 472; **40:** 221, 228; **51:** 270
procreation **10:** 379, 385; **16:** 461;
race **53:** 1
rhetoric of consolation **42:** 382
the Rival Poet **10:** 169, 233, 334, 337, 385; **48:** 352
self-love **10:** 372; **25:** 374; **51:** 270, 300, 304
selfishness versus self-knowledge **51:** 292
sexuality **25:** 374
as social action **48:** 352
sonnet arrangement **10:** 174, 176, 182, 205, 226, 230, 236, 315, 353; **28:** 363; **40:** 238
sonnet form **10:** 255, 325, 367; **37:** 347; **40:** 284, 303; **51:** 270
sonnets (individual):
    3 **10:** 346
    12 **10:** 360
    15 **40:** 292
    18 **40:** 292
    20 **10:** 391; **13:** 530
    21 **32:** 352
    26 **10:** 161
    30 **10:** 296
    35 **10:** 251
    49 **10:** 296
    53 **10:** 349; **32:** 327, 352
    54 **32:** 352
    55 **13:** 445
    57 **10:** 296
    59 **16:** 472
    60 **10:** 296; **16:** 472
    64 **10:** 329, 360
    65 **10:** 296; **40:** 292
    66 **10:** 315
    68 **32:** 327
    71 **10:** 167
    73 **10:** 315, 353, 360

76 **10:** 334
79 **32:** 352
82 **32:** 352
86 **32:** 352
87 **10:** 296; **40:** 303
93 **13:** 487
94 **10:** 256, 296; **32:** 327
95 **32:** 327
98 **32:** 352
99 **32:** 352
104 **10:** 360
105 **32:** 327
107 **10:** 270, 277
116 **10:** 329, 379; **13:** 445
117 **10:** 337
119 **10:** 337
121 **10:** 346
123 **10:** 270
124 **10:** 265, 270, 329
126 **10:** 161
129 **10:** 353, 394; **22:** 12
130 **10:** 346
138 **10:** 296
144 **10:** 394
145 **10:** 358; **40:** 254
146 **10:** 353
sonnets (groups):
   1-17 **10:** 296, 315, 379, 385; **16:** 461; **40:** 228
   1-21 **40:** 268
   1-26 **10:** 176
   1-126 **10:** 161, 176, 185, 191, 196, 205, 213, 226, 236, 279, 309, 315, 372
   18-22 **10:** 315
   18-126 **10:** 379
   23-40 **10:** 315
   27-55 **10:** 176
   33-9 **10:** 329
   56-77 **10:** 176
   76-86 **10:** 315
   78-80 **10:** 334, 385
   78-101 **10:** 176
   82-6 **10:** 334
   100-12 **10:** 337
   102-26 **10:** 176
   123-25 **10:** 385
   127-52 **10:** 293, 385
   127-54 **10:** 161, 176, 185, 190, 196, 213, 226, 236, 309, 315, 342, 394
   151-52 **10:** 315
sources **10:** 153, 154, 156, 158, 233, 251, 255, 293, 353; **16:** 472; **28:** 407; **42:** 382
structure **10:** 175, 176, 182, 205, 230, 260, 296, 302, 309, 315, 337, 349, 353; **40:** 238
subjectivity **37:** 374
time **10:** 265, 302, 309, 322, 329, 337, 360, 379; **13:** 445; **40:** 292
visual arts, relation to **28:** 407
voice **51:** 316
   apparent inconsistencies in **51:** 321

The Taming of the Shrew (Volumes 9, 12, 31, 55)

appearance versus reality **9:** 343, 350, 353, 365, 369, 370, 381, 390. 430; **12:** 416; **31:** 326; **55:** 278, 299, 334
Baptista **9:** 325, 344, 345, 375, 386, 393, 413; **55:** 334
Bianca **9:** 325, 342, 344, 345, 360, 362, 370, 375

Bianca-Lucentio subplot **9:** 365, 370, 375, 390, 393, 401, 407, 413, 430; **16:** 13; **31:** 339
Catherine and Petruchio (David Garrick adaptation) **12:** 309, 310, 311, 416
class distinctions, conflict, and relations **31:** 300, 351; **50:** 64, 74; **55:** 342
deception, disguise, and duplicity **12:** 416
Elizabethan culture, relation to **31:** 288, 295, 300, 315, 326, 345, 351; **55:** 315, 322, 334
ending **54:** 58, 65
as farce **9:** 330, 337, 338, 341, 342, 365, 381, 386, 413, 426; **55:** 357
folk elements **9:** 381, 393, 404, 426
gender issues **28:** 24 **31:** 261, 268, 276, 282, 288, 295, 300, 335, 351; **55:** 278, 299, 305, 315, 322, 357
genre **9:** 329, 334, 362, 375; **22:** 48; **31:** 261, 269, 276; **55:** 278
induction **9:** 320, 322, 332, 337, 345, 350, 362, 365, 369, 370, 381, 390, 393, 407, 419, 424, 430; **12:** 416, 427, 430, 431, 441; **19:** 34, 122; **22:** 48; **31:** 269, 315, 351; **55:** 331, 357
irony or satire **9:** 340, 375, 398, 407, 413; **13:** 3; **19:** 122; **55:** 278, 299, 322
Kate
   characterization **32:** 1
   final speech (Act V, scene ii) **9:** 318, 319, 329, 330, 338, 340, 341, 345, 347, 353, 355, 360, 365, 381, 386, 401, 404, 413, 426, 430; **19:** 3; **22:** 48; **55:** 299, 331
   love for Petruchio **9:** 338, 340, 353, 430; **12:** 435; **55:** 294
   portrayals of **31:** 282
   shrewishness **9:** 322, 323, 325, 332, 344, 345, 360, 365, 370, 375, 386, 393, 398, 404, 413
   transformation **9:** 323, 341, 355, 370, 386, 393, 401, 404, 407, 419, 424, 426, 430; **16:** 13; **19:** 34; **22:** 48; **31:** 288, 295, 339, 351 **55:** 294, 315
Kiss Me, Kate (Cole Porter adaptation) **31:** 282
language and imagery **9:** 336, 338, 393, 401, 404, 407, 413; **22:** 378; **28:** 9; **31:** 261, 288, 300, 326, 335, 339; **32:** 56
Lucentio **9:** 325, 342, 362, 375, 393
marriage **9:** 322, 325, 329, 332, 329, 332, 334, 341, 342, 343, 344, 345, 347, 353, 360, 362, 375, 381, 390, 398, 401, 404, 413, 426, 430; **13:** 3; **19:** 3; **28:** 24; **31:** 288; **51:** 44; **55:** 315, 331
metadramatic elements **9:** 350, 419, 424; **31:** 300, 315
metamorphosis or transformation **9:** 370, 430
pedagogy **19:** 122
performance history **31:** 282; **55:** 357
performance issues **12:** 313, 314, 316, 317, 337, 338; **31:** 315; **55:** 357
Petruchio
   admirable qualities **9:** 320, 332, 341, 344, 345, 370, 375, 386; **55:** 294
   audacity or vigor **9:** 325, 337, 355, 375, 386, 404
   characterization **32:** 1
   coarseness or brutality **9:** 325, 329, 365, 390, 393, 398, 407; **19:** 122
   as lord of misrule **9:** 393; **50:** 64; **55:** 322
   love for Kate **9:** 338, 340, 343, 344, 386; **12:** 435

   portrayals of **31:** 282
   pragmatism **9:** 329, 334, 375, 398, 424; **13:** 3; **31:** 345, 351
   taming method **9:** 320, 323, 329, 340, 341, 343, 345, 355, 369, 370, 375, 390, 398, 407, 413, 419, 424; **19:** 3, 12, 21 **31:** 269, 295, 326, 335, 339; **55:** 334
popularity **9:** 318, 338, 404
role-playing **9:** 322, 353, 355, 360, 369, 370, 398, 401, 407, 413, 419, 424; **13:** 3; **31:** 288, 295, 315
romantic elements **9:** 334, 342, 362, 375, 407
Shakespeare's other plays, compared with **9:** 334, 342, 360, 393, 426, 430; **31:** 261; **50:** 74; **55:** 331
Sly **9:** 320, 322, 350, 370, 381, 390, 398, 430; **12:** 316, 335, 416, 427, 441; **16:** 13; **19:** 34, 122; **22:** 48; **37:** 31; **50:** 74
sources
   Ariosto **9:** 320, 334, 341, 342, 370
   folk tales **9:** 332, 390, 393
   Gascoigne **9:** 370, 390
   Old and New Comedy **9:** 419
   Ovid **9:** 318, 370, 430
   Plautus **9:** 334, 341, 342
   shrew tradition **9:** 355; **19:** 3; **32:** 1, 56; **55:** 342
structure **9:** 318, 322, 325, 332, 334, 341, 362, 370, 390, 426; **22:** 48, 378; **31:** 269; **55:** 278, 342, 371
play-within-a-play **12:** 416; **22:** 48
The Taming of a Shrew (anonymous), compared with **9:** 334, 350, 426; **12:** 312; **22:** 48; **31:** 261, 276, 339; **55:** 305, 371;
text and sources **55:** 334, 357
textual issues **22:** 48; **31:** 261, 276; **31:** 276; **55:** 342, 371
violence **43:** 61; **55:** 322

The Tempest (Volumes 8, 15, 29, 45)

allegorical elements **8:** 294, 295, 302, 307, 308, 312, 326, 328, 336, 345, 364; **42:** 327
Antonio and Sebastian **8:** 295, 299, 304, 328, 370, 396, 429, 454; **13:** 440; **29:** 278, 297, 343, 362, 368, 377
Ariel **8:** 289, 293, 294, 295, 297, 304, 307, 315, 320, 326, 328, 336, 340, 345, 356, 364, 420, 458; **22:** 302; **29:** 278, 297, 362, 368, 377
art versus nature **8:** 396, 404; **29:** 278, 297, 362
autobiographical elements **8:** 302, 308, 312, 324, 326, 345, 348, 353, 364, 380
beginning **54:** 19
Caliban **8:** 286, 287, 289, 292, 294, 295, 297, 302, 304, 307, 309, 315, 326, 328, 336, 353, 364, 370, 380, 390, 396, 401, 414, 420, 423, 429, 435, 454; **13:** 424, 440; **15:** 189, 312, 322, 374, 379; **22:** 302; **25:** 382; **28:** 249; **29:** 278, 292, 297, 343, 368, 377, 396; **32:** 367; **45:** 211, 219, 226, 259; **53:** 45, 64
characterization **8:** 287, 289, 292, 294, 295, 308, 326, 334, 336; **28:** 415; **42:** 339; **45:** 219
classical influence and sources **29:** 278, 343, 362, 368

colonialism **13:** 424, 440; **15:** 228, 268, 269, 270, 271, 272, 273; **19:** 421; **25:** 357, 382; **28:** 249; **29:** 343, 368; **32:** 338, 367, 400; **42:** 327; **45:** 200, 280; **53:** 11, 21, 45, 67
compassion, theme of **42:** 346
conspiracy or treason **16:** 426; **19:** 357; **25:** 382; **29:** 377
dreams **45:** 236, 247, 259
education or nurturing **8:** 353, 370, 384, 396; **29:** 292, 368, 377
exposition scene (Act I, scene ii) **8:** 287, 289, 293, 299, 334
Ferdinand **8:** 328, 336, 359, 454; **19:** 357; **22:** 302; **29:** 362, 339, 377
freedom and servitude **8:** 304, 307, 312, 429; **22:** 302; **29:** 278, 368, 377; **37:** 336
gender **53:** 64, 67
Gonzalo **22:** 302; **29:** 278, 343, 362, 368
Gonzalo's commonwealth **8:** 312, 336, 370, 390, 396, 404; **19:** 357; **29:** 368; **45:** 280
good versus evil **8:** 302, 311, 315, 370, 423, 439; **29:** 278; 297
historical content **8:** 364, 408, 420; **16:** 426; **25:** 382; **29:** 278, 339, 343, 368; **45:** 226; **53:** 21, 53
the island **8:** 308, 315, 447; **25:** 357, 382; **29:** 278, 343
language and imagery **8:** 324, 348, 384, 390, 404, 454; **19:** 421; **29:** 278; **29:** 297, 343, 368, 377
love **8:** 435, 439; **29:** 297, 339, 377, 396
magic or supernatural elements **8:** 287, 293, 304, 315, 340, 356, 396, 401, 404, 408, 435, 458; **28:** 391, 415; **29:** 297, 343, 377; **45:** 272
the masque (Act IV, scene i) **8:** 404, 414, 423, 435, 439; **25:** 357; **28:** 391, 415; **29:** 278, 292, 339, 343, 368; **42:** 339; **45:** 188
Miranda **8:** 289, 301, 304, 328, 336, 370, 454; **19:** 357; **22:** 302; **28:** 249; **29:** 278, 297, 362, 368, 377, 396; **53:** 64
Montaigne's Essais, relation to **42:** 346
morality **52:** 43
music **8:** 390, 404; **29:** 292; **37:** 321; **42:** 339
nature **8:** 315, 370, 390, 408, 414; **29:** 343, 362, 368, 377
Neoclassical rules **8:** 287, 292, 293, 334; **25:** 357; **29:** 292; **45:** 200
politics **8:** 304, 307, 315, 353, 359, 364, 401, 408; **16:** 426; **19:** 421; **29:** 339; **37:** 336; **42:** 327; **45:** 272, 280; **52:** 43
Prospero
  characterization **8:** 312, 348, 370, 458; **16:** 442; **22:** 302; **45:** 188, 272
  as God or Providence **8:** 311, 328, 364, 380, 429, 435
  magic, nature of **8:** 301, 340, 356, 396, 414, 423, 458; **25:** 382; **28:** 391; **29:** 278, 292, 368, 377, 396; **32:** 338, 343
  psychoanalytic interpretation **45:** 259
  redemptive powers **8:** 302, 320, 353, 370, 390, 429, 439, 447; **29:** 297
  as ruler **8:** 304, 308, 309, 420, 423; **13:** 424; **22:** 302; **29:** 278, 362, 377, 396
  self-control **8:** 312, 414, 420; **22:** 302; **44:** 11
  self-knowledge **16:** 442; **22:** 302; **29:** 278, 292, 362, 377, 396
  as Shakespeare or creative artist **8:** 299, 302, 308, 312, 320, 324, 353, 364, 435, 447

  as tragic hero **8:** 359, 370, 464; **29:** 292
providential order **52:** 43
race **53:** 11, 21, 45, 53, 64, 67
realism **8:** 340, 359, 464
reality and illusion **8:** 287, 315, 359, 401, 435, 439, 447, 454; **22:** 302; **45:** 236, 247
reconciliation **8:** 302, 312, 320, 334, 348, 359, 370, 384, 401, 404, 414, 429, 439, 447, 454; **16:** 442; **22:** 302; **29:** 297; **37:** 336; **45:** 236
religious, mythic, or spiritual content **8:** 328, 390, 423, 429, 435; **45:** 211, 247
romance or pastoral tradition, influence of **8:** 336, 348, 396, 404; **37:** 336
sexuality **53:** 45
Shakespeare's other plays, compared with **8:** 294, 302, 324, 326, 348, 353, 380, 401, 464; **13:** 424
spectacle versus simple staging **15:** 206, 207, 208, 210, 217, 219, 222, 223, 224, 225, 227, 228, 305, 352; **28:** 415
sources **45:** 226
staging issues **15:** 343, 346, 352, 361, 364, 366, 368, 371, 385; **28:** 391, 415; **29:** 339; **32:** 338, 343; **42:** 339; **45:** 200; **54:** 19
Stephano and Trinculo, comic subplot of **8:** 292, 297, 299, 304, 309, 324, 328, 353, 370; **25:** 382; **29:** 377; **46:** 14, 33
structure **8:** 294, 295, 299, 320, 384, 439; **28:** 391, 415; **29:** 292, 297; **45:** 188
subversiveness **22:** 302
The Tempest; or, The Enchanted Island (William Davenant/John Dryden adaptation) **15:** 189, 190, 192, 193
The Tempest; or, The Enchanted Island (Thomas Shadwell adaptation) **15:** 195, 196, 199
time **8:** 401, 439, 464; **25:** 357; **29:** 278, 292; **45:** 236
tragic elements **8:** 324, 348, 359, 370, 380, 408, 414, 439, 458, 464
trickster, motif of **22:** 302; **29:** 297
usurpation or rebellion **8:** 304, 370, 408, 420; **25:** 357, 382; **29:** 278, 362, 377; **37:** 336
utopia **45:** 280

Timon of Athens (Volumes 1, 20, 27, 52)

Alcibiades **25:** 198; **27:** 191
alienation **1:** 523; **27:** 161
Apemantus **1:** 453, 467, 483; **20:** 476, 493; **25:** 198; **27:** 166, 223, 235
appearance versus reality **1:** 495, 500, 515, 523; **52:** 311, 329
Athens **27:** 223, 230
authorship controversy **1:** 464, 466, 467, 469, 474, 477, 478, 480, 490, 499, 507, 518; **16:** 351; **20:** 433
autobiographical elements **1:** 462, 467, 470, 473, 474, 478, 480; **27:** 166, 175
Elizabethan culture, relation to **1:** 487, 489, 495, 500; **20:** 433; **27:** 203, 212, 230; **50:** 13; **52:** 320, 354
as inferior or flawed plays **1:** 476, 481, 489, 499, 520; **20:** 433, 439, 491; **25:** 198; **27:** 157, 175; **52:** 338, 349
genre **1:** 454, 456, 459, 460, 462, 483, 492, 499, 503, 509, 511, 512, 515, 518, 525, 531; **27:** 203

King Lear, relation to **1:** 453, 459, 511; **16:** 351; **27:** 161; **37:** 222
language and imagery **1:** 488; **13:** 392; **25:** 198; **27:** 166, 184, 235; **52:** 329, 345, 354
language and philosophy **52:** 311
as medieval allegory or morality play **1:** 492, 511, 518; **27:** 155
mixture of genres **16:** 351; **25:** 198
nihilistic elements **1:** 481, 513, 529; **13:** 392; **20:** 481
pessimistic elements **1:** 462, 467, 470, 473, 478, 480; **20:** 433, 481; **27:** 155, 191
Poet and Painter **25:** 198; **52:** 320
politics **27:** 223, 230; **50:** 13
religious, mythic, or spiritual content **1:** 505, 512, 513, 523; **20:** 493
satirical elements **27:** 155, 235
self-knowledge **1:** 456, 459, 462, 495, 503, 507, 515, 518, 526; **20:** 493; **27:** 166
Senecan elements **27:** 235
Shakespeare's other tragedies, compared with **27:** 166; **52:** 296
sources **16:** 351; **27:** 191; **52:** 301
staging issues **20:** 445, 446, 481, 491, 492, 493
structure **27:** 191; **52:** 338, 345, 349
Timon
  comic traits **25:** 198
  as flawed hero **1:** 456, 459, 462, 472, 495, 503, 507, 515; **16:** 351; **20:** 429, 433, 476; **25:** 198; **27:** 157, 161
  misanthropy **13:** 392; **20:** 431, 464, 476, 481, 491, 492, 493; **27:** 161, 175, 184, 196; **37:** 222; **52:** 296, 301
  as noble figure **1:** 467, 473, 483, 499; **20:** 493; **27:** 212
wealth and social class **1:** 466, 487, 495; **25:** 198; **27:** 184, 196, 212; **50:** 13

Titus Andronicus (Volumes 4, 17, 27, 43)

Aaron **4:** 632, 637, 650, 651, 653, 668, 672, 675; **27:** 255; **28:** 249, 330; **43:** 176; **53:** 86, 92
amputations, significance of **48:** 264
authorship controversy **4:** 613, 614, 615, 616, 617, 619, 623, 624, 625, 626, 628, 631, 632, 635, 642
autobiographical elements **4:** 619, 624, 625, 664
banquet scene **25:** 245; **27:** 255; **32:** 212
ceremonies, rites, and rituals, importance of **27:** 261; **32:** 265; **48:** 264
characterization **4:** 613, 628, 632, 635, 640, 644, 647, 650, 675; **27:** 293; **43:** 170, 176
Christian elements **4:** 656, 680
civilization versus barbarism **4:** 653; **27:** 293; **28:** 249; **32:** 265
Clarissa (Samuel Richardson), compared with **48:** 277
Elizabethan culture, relation to **27:** 282
Euripides, influence of **27:** 285
evil **53:** 86, 92
language and imagery **4:** 617, 624, 635, 642, 644, 646, 659, 664, 668, 672, 675; **13:** 225; **16:** 225; **25:** 245; **27:** 246, 293, 313, 318, 325; **43:** 186, 222, 227, 239, 247, 262,
language versus action **4:** 642, 644, 647, 664, 668; **13:** 225; **27:** 293, 313, 325; **43:** 186

Lavinia **27:** 266; **28:** 249; **32:** 212; **43:** 170, 239, 247, 255, 262
marriage as political tyranny **48:** 264
medieval literary influence **4:** 646, 650; **27:** 299
order versus disintegration **4:** 618, 647; **43:** 186, 195
Ovid, influence of **4:** 647, 659, 664, 668; **13:** 225; **27:** 246, 275, 285, 293, 299, 306; **28:** 249; **43:** 195, 203, 206
partiarchy **50:** 13
political content **43:** 262
politics **27:** 282; **48:** 264
primogeniture **50:** 13
race **53:** 86, 92
rape **43:** 227, 255; **48:** 277
rightful succession **4:** 638
Roman elements **43:** 206, 222
Romans versus Goths **27:** 282
Senecan or revenge tragedy elements **4:** 618, 627, 628, 636, 639, 644, 646, 664, 672, 680; **16:** 225; **27:** 275, 318; **43:** 170, 206, 227
Shakespeare's canon, place in **4:** 614, 616, 618, 619, 637, 639, 646, 659, 664, 668; **43:** 195
Shakespeare's other tragedies, compared with **16:** 225; **27:** 275, 325
staging issues **17:** 449, 452, 456, 487; **25:** 245; **32:** 212, 249
structure **4:** 618, 619, 624, 631, 635, 640, 644, 646, 647, 653, 656, 659, 662, 664, 668, 672; **27:** 246, 285
Tamora **4:** 632, 662, 672, 675; **27:** 266; **43:** 170
Titus **4:** 632, 637, 640, 644, 647, 653, 656, 662; **25:** 245; **27:** 255
Vergil, influence of **27:** 306; **28:** 249
violence **13:** 225; **25:** 245; **27:** 255; **28:** 249; **32:** 249, 265; **43:** 1, 186, 203, 227, 239, 247, 255, 262

Troilus and Cressida (Volumes 3, 18, 27, 43)

allegorical elements **52:** 5
ambiguity **3:** 544, 568, 583, 587, 589, 599, 611, 621; **27:** 400; **43:** 365
ambivalence **43:** 340
assignation scene (Act V, scene ii) **18:** 442, 451
autobiographical elements **3:** 548, 554, 557, 558, 574, 606, 630
body, role of **42:** 66
characterization **3:** 538, 539, 540, 541, 548, 566, 571, 604, 611, 621; **27:** 381, 391
Chaucer's Criseyde, compared with **43:** 305
chivalry, decline of **16:** 84; **27:** 370, 374
communication, failure of **43:** 277
conclusion **3:** 538, 549, 558, 566, 574, 583, 594
comedy vs. tragedy **43:** 351
contradictions **43:** 377
costumes **18:** 289, 371, 406, 419
courtly love **22:** 58
Cressida
as ambiguous figure **43:** 305
inconsistency **3:** 538; **13:** 53; **16:** 70; **22:** 339; **27:** 362
individual will versus social values **3:** 549, 551, 571, 590, 604, 617, 626; **13:** 53; **27:** 396
infidelity **3:** 536, 537, 544, 554, 555; **18:** 277, 284, 286; **22:** 58, 339; **27:** 400; **43:** 298
lack of punishment **3:** 536, 537
as mother figure **22:** 339
objectification of **43:** 329
as sympathetic figure **3:** 557, 560, 604, 609; **18:** 284, 423; **22:** 58; **27:** 396, 400; **43:** 305
cynicism **43:** 298
desire **43:** 317, 329, 340
disillusioned or cynical tone **3:** 544, 548, 554, 557, 558, 571, 574, 630, 642; **18:** 284, 332, 403, 406, 423; **27:** 376
disorder **3:** 578, 589, 599, 604, 609; **18:** 332, 406, 412, 423; **27:** 366; **54:** 84; **55:** 48
double plot **3:** 569, 613
Elizabeth I
waning power **43:** 365
Elizabethan culture, relation to **3:** 560, 574, 606; **25:** 56
ending **54:** 84
feminist criticism **55:** 37, 48
food imagery **43:** 298
genre **3:** 541, 542, 549, 558, 566, 571, 574, 587, 594, 604, 630, 642; **27:** 366
Greece **43:** 287
inaction **3:** 587, 621; **27:** 347
infidelity **55:** 37, 48
language and imagery **3:** 561, 569, 596, 599, 606, 624, 630, 635; **22:** 58, 339; **27:** 332; 366; **42:** 66
love and honor **3:** 555, 604; **27:** 370, 374
love versus war **18:** 332, 371, 406, 423; **22:** 339; **27:** 376; **43:** 377
male/female relationships **16:** 70; **22:** 339; **27:** 362
marriage **22:** 339; **51:** 44
master-slave relationship **22:** 58
medieval chivalry **3:** 539, 543, 544, 555, 606; **27:** 376
moral corruption **3:** 578, 589, 599, 604, 609; **18:** 332, 406, 412, 423; **27:** 366; **43:** 298; **54:** 84
morality **52:** 5
Neoclassical rules **3:** 537, 538; **18:** 276, 278, 281
nihilistic elements **27:** 354
patriarchy **22:** 58
politics **3:** 536, 560, 606; **16:** 84
as "problem play" **3:** 555, 566
lack of resolution **43:** 277
psychoanalytical criticism **43:** 287
rape **43:** 357
satirical elements **3:** 539, 543, 544, 555, 558, 574; **27:** 341
sexuality **22:** 58, 339; **25:** 56; **27:** 362; **43:** 365
sources **3:** 537, 539, 540, 541, 544, 549, 558, 566, 574, 587; **27:** 376, 381, 391, 400
staging issues **16:** 70; **18:** 289, 332, 371, 395, 403, 406, 412, 419, 423, 442, 447, 451
structure **3:** 536, 538, 549, 568, 569, 578, 583, 589, 611, 613; **27:** 341, 347, 354, 391
Thersites **13:** 53; **25:** 56; **27:** 381
time **3:** 561, 571, 583, 584, 613, 621, 626, 634
Troilus
contradictory behavior **3:** 596, 602, 635; **27:** 362
Cressida, relationship with **3:** 594, 596, 606; **22:** 58
integrity **3:** 617
opposition to Ulysses **3:** 561, 584, 590
as unsympathetic figure **18:** 423; **22:** 58, 339; **43:** 317
as warrior **3:** 596; **22:** 339
Troilus and Cressida, or Truth Found too late (John Dryden adaptation) **18:** 276, 277, 278, 280, 281, 283
Trojan versus Greek values **3:** 541, 561, 574, 584, 590, 596, 621, 638; **27:** 370
Trojan War
as myth **43:** 293
Troy **43:** 287
Ulysses's speech on degree (Act I, scene iii) **3:** 549, 599, 609, 642; **27:** 396
value systems **3:** 578, 583, 589, 602, 613, 617; **13:** 53; **27:** 370, 396, 400
violence **43:** 329, 351, 357, 365, 377
through satire **43:** 293

Twelfth Night (Volumes 1, 26, 34, 46)

ambiguity **1:** 554, 639; **34:** 287, 316
Antonio **22:** 69
appetite **1:** 563, 596, 609, 615; **52:** 57
autobiographical elements **1:** 557, 561, 599; **34:** 338
bear-baiting **19:** 42
beginning **54:** 19
characterization **1:** 539, 540, 543, 545, 550, 554, 581, 594; **26:** 257, 337, 342, 346, 364, 366, 371, 374; **34:** 281, 293, 311, 338; **46:** 286, 324
Christian elements **46:** 338
comic elements **26:** 233, 257, 337, 342, 371; **51:** 1; **52:** 57
composition date **37:** 78
credibility **1:** 540, 542, 543, 554, 562, 581, 587
dark or tragic elements **46:** 310
Elizabethan culture, relation to **1:** 549, 553, 555, 563, 581, 587, 620; **16:** 53; **19:** 42, 78; **26:** 357; **28:** 1; **34:** 323, 330; **46:** 291; **51:** 15
ethical or moral issues **52:** 57
fancy **1:** 543, 546
Feste
characterization **1:** 558, 655, 658; **26:** 233, 364; **46:** 1, 14, 18, 33, 52, 60, 303, 310
role in play **1:** 546, 551, 553, 566, 570, 571, 579, 635, 658; **46:** 297, 303, 310
song **1:** 543, 548, 561, 563, 566, 570, 572, 603, 620, 642; **46:** 297
festive or folklore elements **46:** 338; **51:** 15
gender issues **19:** 78; **34:** 344; **37:** 59; **42:** 32; **46:** 347, 362, 369
homosexuality **22:** 69; **42:** 32; **46:** 362
language and imagery **1:** 570, 650, 664; **22:** 12; **28:** 9; **34:** 293; **37:** 59
love **1:** 543, 546, 573, 580, 587, 595, 600, 603, 610, 660; **19:** 78; **26:** 257, 364; **34:** 270, 293, 323; **46:** 291, 333, 347, 362; **51:** 30; **52:** 57
madness **1:** 554, 639, 656; **26:** 371
Malvolio
characterization **1:** 540, 544, 545, 548, 550, 554, 558, 567, 575, 577, 615; **26:** 207, 233, 273; **46:** 286
forged letter **16:** 372; **28:** 1
punishment **1:** 539, 544, 548, 549, 554, 555, 558, 563, 577, 590, 632, 645; **46:** 291, 297, 338
as Puritan **1:** 549, 551, 555, 558, 561, 563; **25:** 47

role in play **1:** 545, 548, 549, 553, 555, 563, 567, 575, 577, 588, 610, 615, 632, 645; **26:** 337, 374; **46:** 347
music **1:** 543, 566, 596
Olivia **1:** 540, 543, 545; **46:** 286, 333, 369; **47:** 45
order **1:** 563, 596; **34:** 330; **46:** 291, 347
Orsino **46:** 286, 333; **47:** 45
philosophical elements **1:** 560, 563, 596; **34:** 301, 316; **46:** 297
Puritanism **1:** 549, 553, 555, 632; **16:** 53; **25:** 47; **46:** 338
psychoanalytic criticism **46:** 333
Saturnalian elements **1:** 554, 571, 603, 620, 642; **16:** 53
self-deception **1:** 554, 561, 591, 625; **47:** 45
self-indulgence **1:** 563, 615, 635
sexual ambiguity and sexual deception **1:** 540, 562, 620, 621, 639, 645; **22:** 69; **34:** 311, 344; **37:** 59; **42:** 32
Shakespeare's canon, place in **1:** 543, 548, 557, 569, 575, 580, 621, 635, 638
Shakespeare's other plays, relation to **34:** 270; **46:** 303
sources **1:** 539, 540, 603; **34:** 301, 323, 344; **46:** 291
staging issues **26:** 219, 233, 257, 337, 342, 346, 357, 359, 360, 364, 366, 371, 374; **46:** 310, 369; **54:** 19
structure **1:** 539, 542, 543, 546, 551, 553, 563, 570, 571, 590, 600, 660; **26:** 374; **34:** 281, 287; **46:** 286
time **37:** 78; **46:** 297
tragic elements **1:** 557, 569, 572, 575, 580, 599, 621, 635, 638, 639, 645, 654, 656; **26:** 342
Viola **26:** 308; **46:** 286, 324, 347, 369

The Two Gentlemen of Verona (Volumes 6, 12, 40, 54)

absurdities, inconsistencies, and shortcomings **6:** 435, 436, 437, 439, 464, 507, 541, 560; **54:** 295, 311
appearance versus reality **6:** 494, 502, 511, 519, 529, 532, 549, 560
audience versus character perceptions **6:** 499, 519, 524
authorship controversy **6:** 435, 436, 437, 438, 439, 449, 466, 476
characterization **6:** 438, 442, 445, 447, 449, 458, 462, 560; **12:** 458; **40:** 312, 327, 330, 365; **54:** 338
Christian elements **6:** 438, 494, 514, 532, 555, 564
education **6:** 490, 494, 504, 526, 532, 555, 568
Elizabethan setting **12:** 463, 485
forest **6:** 450, 456, 492, 514, 547, 555, 564, 568
genre **6:** 460, 468, 472, 516; **40:** 320
identity **6:** 494, 511, 529, 532, 547, 560, 564, 568; **19:** 34
ironic or parodic elements **6:** 447, 472, 478, 484, 502, 504, 509, 516, 529, 549; **13:** 12; **54:** 295, 307
Julia or Silvia **6:** 450, 453, 458, 476, 494, 499, 516, 519, 549, 564; **40:** 312, 327, 374; **54:** 325, 332
language and imagery **6:** 437, 438, 439, 445, 449, 490, 504, 519, 529, 541; **28:** 9; **40:** 343

Launce and Speed, comic function of **6:** 438, 439, 442, 456, 458, 460, 462, 472, 476, 478, 484, 502, 504, 507, 509, 516, 519, 549; **40:** 312, 320
love **6:** 442, 445, 456, 479, 488, 492, 494, 502, 509, 516, 519, 549; **13:** 12; **40:** 327, 335, 343, 354, 365; **51:** 30, 44
love versus friendship **6:** 439, 449, 450, 458, 460, 465, 468, 471, 476, 480; **40:** 354, 359, 365; **54:** 295, 307, 325, 344
marriage **48:** 32
mimetic rivalry **13:** 12; **40:** 335; **54:** 332
morality **6:** 438, 492, 494, 514, 532, 555, 564
Proteus **6:** 439, 450, 458, 480, 490, 511; **40:** 312, 327, 330, 335, 359; **42:** 18; **54:** 325, 332
repentance and forgiveness **6:** 450, 514, 516, 555, 564
resolution **6:** 435, 436, 439, 445, 449, 453, 458, 460, 462, 465, 466, 468, 471, 476, 480, 486, 494, 509, 514, 516, 519, 529, 532, 541, 549; **19:** 34; **54:** 307, 311, 338
reversals **54:** 338
romantic and courtly conventions **6:** 438, 460, 472, 478, 484, 486, 488, 502, 507, 509, 529, 541, 549, 560, 568; **12:** 460, 462; **40:** 354, 374; **54:** 344
setting **12:** 463, 465, 485
sources **6:** 436, 460, 462, 468, 476, 480, 490, 511, 547; **19:** 34; **40:** 320; **54:** 295
staging issues **12:** 457, 464; **42:** 18
structure **6:** 445, 450, 460, 462, 504, 526
youth **6:** 439, 450, 464, 514, 568
Valentine **54:** 325, 332

The Two Noble Kinsmen (Volumes 9, 41, 50)

amorality, question of **9:** 447, 460, 492
authorship controversy
 Shakespeare not a co-author **9:** 445, 447, 455, 461
 Shakespearean portions of the text **9:** 446, 447, 448, 455, 456, 457, 460, 462, 463, 471, 479, 486; **41:** 308, 317, 355
 Shakespeare's part in the overall conception or design **9:** 444, 446, 448, 456, 457, 460, 480, 481, 486, 490; **37:** 313; **41:** 326; **50:** 326
ceremonies, rites, and rituals, importance of **9:** 492, 498
characterization **9:** 457, 461, 471, 474; **41:** 340, 385; **50:** 305, 326
chivalry **50:** 305, 348
class distinctions, conflict and relations **50:** 295, 305, 310
Emilia **9:** 460, 470, 471, 479, 481; **19:** 394; **41:** 372, 385; **42:** 368
free will versus fate **9:** 474, 481, 486, 492, 498
friendship **9:** 448, 463, 470, 474, 479, 481, 486, 490; **19:** 394; **41:** 355, 363, 372; **42:** 368
gender issues **42:** 368; **50:** 310
innocence to experience **9:** 481, 502; **19:** 394
irony or satire **9:** 463, 481, 486; **41:** 301; **50:** 348
the jailer's daughter **9:** 457, 460, 479, 481, 486, 502; **41:** 340; **50:** 295, 305, 310, 348, 361
language and imagery **9:** 445, 446, 447, 448, 456, 461, 463, 469, 471, 498, 502; **41:** 289, 301, 308, 317, 326; **50:** 310
love **9:** 479, 481, 490, 498; **41:** 289, 301, 363, 372, 385; **50:** 295, 361
masque elements **9:** 490
Palamon and Arcite **9:** 474, 481, 490, 492, 502; **50:** 295, 305, 348, 361
Prologue **54:** 35
relation to Shakespeare's other romances **54:** 35
sexuality **50:** 361
sources **19:** 394; **41:** 289, 301, 363, 385; **50:** 326, 348
structure **37:** 313; **50:** 326, 361

Venus and Adonis (Volumes 10, 33, 51)

Adonis **10:** 411, 420, 424, 427, 429, 434, 439, 442, 451, 454, 459, 466, 473, 489; **25:** 305, 328; **28:** 355; **33:** 309, 321, 330, 347, 352, 357, 363, 370, 377; **51:** 345, 377
allegorical elements **10:** 427, 434, 439, 449, 454, 462, 480; **28:** 355; **33:** 309, 330
ambiguity **10:** 434, 454, 459, 462, 466, 473, 480, 486, 489; **33:** 352; **51:** 368, 377, 388
beauty **10:** 420, 423, 427, 434, 454, 480; **33:** 330, 352
the boar **10:** 416, 451, 454, 466, 473; **33:** 339, 347, 370; **51:** 359, 368
comic elements **51:** 377
the courser and the jennet **10:** 418, 439, 466; **33:** 309, 339, 347, 352
death, decay, and nature's destructiveness **10:** 419, 427, 434, 451, 454, 462, 466, 473, 480, 489; **25:** 305; **33:** 309, 321, 347, 352, 363, 370
dramatic elements **10:** 459, 462, 486
domesticity **51:** 359
eroticism or sensuality **10:** 410, 411, 418, 419, 427, 428, 429, 442, 448, 454, 459, 466, 473; **25:** 305, 328; **28:** 355; **33:** 321, 339, 347, 352, 363, 370; **51:** 345, 352, 359, 368
Faerie Queene (Edmund Spenser), compared with **33:** 339
forgiveness **51:** 377
Hero and Leander (Christopher Marlowe), compared with **10:** 419, 424, 429; **33:** 309, 357; **51:** 345, 377
comic elements **10:** 429, 434, 439, 442, 459, 462, 489; **33:** 352
hunt motif **10:** 434, 451, 466, 473; **33:** 357, 370
imagery **10:** 414, 415, 416, 420, 429, 434, 449, 459, 466, 473, 480; **25:** 328; **28:** 355; **33:** 321, 339, 352, 363, 370, 377; **42:** 348; **51:** 335, 388
love versus lust **10:** 418, 420, 427, 434, 439, 448, 449, 454, 462, 466, 473, 480, 489; **25:** 305; **28:** 355; **33:** 309, 330, 339, 347, 357, 363, 370; **51:** 359
morality **10:** 411, 412, 414, 416, 418, 419, 420, 423, 427, 428, 439, 442, 448, 449, 454, 459, 466; **33:** 330
negative appraisals **10:** 410, 411, 415, 418, 419, 424, 429
Ovid, compared with **32:** 352; **42:** 348; **51:** 335, 352
pictorial elements **10:** 414, 415, 419, 420, 423, 480; **33:** 339
popularity **10:** 410, 412, 418, 427; **25:** 328
procreation **10:** 439, 449, 466; **33:** 321, 377

reason **10:** 427, 439, 449, 459, 462, 466; **28:** 355; **33:** 309, 330
rhetoric **33:** 377; **51:** 335, 345, 352
Shakespeare's plays, compared with **10:** 412, 414, 415, 434, 459, 462
Shakespeare's sonnets, compared with **33:** 377
sources **10:** 410, 412, 420, 424, 429, 434, 439, 451, 454, 466, 473, 480, 486, 489; **16:** 452; **25:** 305; **28:** 355; **33:** 309, 321, 330, 339, 347, 352, 357, 370, 377; **42:** 348; **51:** 335
structure **10:** 434, 442, 480, 486, 489; **33:** 357, 377
style **10:** 411, 412, 414, 415, 416, 418, 419, 420, 423, 424, 428, 429, 439, 442, 480, 486, 489; **16:** 452
Venus **10:** 427, 429, 434, 439, 442, 448, 449, 451, 454, 466, 473, 480, 486, 489; **16:** 452; **25:** 305, 328; **28:** 355; **33:** 309, 321, 330, 347, 352, 357, 363, 370, 377; **51:** 335, 352, 377, 388
Wat the hare **10:** 424, 451

The Winter's Tale (Volumes 7, 15, 36, 45, 57)

Antigonus
  characterization **7:** 394, 451, 464
  death scene (Act III, scene iii) **7:** 377, 414, 464, 483; **15:** 518, 532; **19:** 366
appearance versus reality **7:** 429, 446, 479; **57:** 336
art versus nature **7:** 377, 381, 397, 419, 452; **36:** 289, 318; **45:** 329; **57:** 278
audience perception, Shakespeare's manipulation of **7:** 394, 429, 456, 483, 501; **13:** 417; **19:** 401, 431, 441; **25:** 339; **45:** 374
autobiographical elements **7:** 395, 397, 410, 419
Autolycus **7:** 375, 380, 382, 387, 389, 395, 396, 414; **15:** 524; **22:** 302; **37:** 31; **45:** 333; **46:** 14, 33; **50:** 45
Christian elements **7:** 381, 387, 402, 410, 417, 419, 425, 429, 436, 452, 460, 501; **36:** 318
counsel **19:** 401
court society **16:** 410; **57:** 305, 336
dramatic structure **7:** 382, 390, 396, 399, 402, 407, 414, 429, 432, 473, 479, 493, 497, 501; **15:** 528; **25:** 339; **36:** 289, 295, 362, 380; **45:** 297, 344, 358, 366; **57:** 278, 285, 347
ethnicity **37:** 306
folk drama, relation to **7:** 420, 451; **57:** 356
forgiveness or redemption **7:** 381, 389, 395, 402, 407, 436, 456, 460, 483; **36:** 318
fusion of comic, tragic, and romantic elements **7:** 390, 394, 396, 399, 410, 412, 414, 429, 436, 479, 483, 490, 501; **13:** 417; **15:** 514, 524, 532; **25:** 339; **36:** 295, 380; **45:** 295, 329; **57:** 347
grace **7:** 420, 425, 460, 493; **36:** 328
Hermione
  characterization **7:** 385, 395, 402, 412, 414, 506; **15:** 495, 532; **22:** 302, 324; **25:** 347; **32:** 388; **36:** 311; **47:** 25; **49:** 18; **57:** 319
  restoration (Act V, scene iii) **7:** 377, 379, 384, 385, 387, 389, 394, 396, 412, 425, 436, 451, 452, 456, 464, 483, 501; **15:** 411, 412, 413, 518, 528, 532; **49:** 18; **57:** 294, 367
  supposed death **25:** 339; **47:** 25
  trial of **49:** 18
as historical allegory **7:** 381; **15:** 528
homosexuality **48:** 309
hospitality **19:** 366
irony **7:** 419, 420
Jacobean culture, relation to **19:** 366, 401, 431; **25:** 347; **32:** 388; **37:** 306; **57:** 305, 336, 356
language and imagery **7:** 382, 384, 417, 418, 420, 425, 460, 506; **13:** 409; **19:** 431; **22:** 324; **25:** 347; **36:** 295; **42:** 308; **45:** 297, 333, 344; **50:** 45; **57:** 278, 285, 319, 347
Leontes
  characterization **19:** 431; **45:** 366
  jealousy **7:** 377, 379, 382, 383, 384, 387, 389, 394, 395, 402, 407, 412, 414, 425, 429, 432, 436, 464, 480, 483, 497; **15:** 514, 518, 532; **22:** 324; **25:** 339; **36:** 334, 344, 349; **44:** 66; **45:** 295, 297, 344, 358; **47:** 25; **57:** 294
  Othello, compared with **7:** 383, 390, 412; **15:** 514; **36:** 334; **44:** 66; **47:** 25
  repentance **7:** 381, 389, 394, 396, 402, 414, 497; **36:** 318, 362; **44:** 66; **57:** 294
love **7:** 417, 425, 469, 490; **51:** 30, 33, 44
Mamillius **7:** 394, 396, 451; **22:** 324
metadramatic elements **16:** 410
myth of Demeter and Persephone, relation to **7:** 397, 436
nationalism and patriotism **32:** 388
nature **7:** 397, 418, 419, 420, 425, 432, 436, 451, 452, 473, 479; **19:** 366; **45:** 329
Neoclassical rules **7:** 376, 377, 379, 380, 383, 410; **15:** 397
Ovid's Metamorphoses, relation to **42:** 308; **57:** 319, 367
Pandosto, compared with **7:** 376, 377, 390, 412, 446; **13:** 409; **25:** 347; **36:** 344, 374
Paulina **7:** 385, 412, 506; **15:** 528; **22:** 324; **25:** 339; **36:** 311; **57:** 319
Perdita
  characterization **7:** 395, 412, 414, 419, 429, 432, 452, 506; **22:** 324; **25:** 339; **36:** 328
  reunion with Leontes (Act V, scene ii) **7:** 377, 379, 381, 390, 432, 464, 480
plot **7:** 376, 377, 379, 382, 387, 390, 396, 452; **13:** 417; **15:** 518; **45:** 374; **57:** 285
rebirth, regeneration, resurrection, or immortality **7:** 397, 414, 417, 419, 429, 436, 451, 452, 456, 480, 490, 497, 506; **25:** 339 452, 480, 490, 497, 506; **45:** 366
sheep-shearing scene (Act IV, scene iv) **7:** 379, 387, 395, 396, 407, 410, 412, 419, 420, 429, 432, 436, 451, 479, 490; **16:** 410; **19:** 366; **25:** 339; **36:** 362, 374; **45:** 374
staging issues **7:** 414, 425, 429, 446, 464, 480, 483, 497; **13:** 409; **15:** 518; **48:** 309
statue scene (Act V, scene iii) **7:** 377, 379, 384, 385, 387, 389, 394, 396, 412, 425, 436, 451, 456, 464, 483, 501; **15:** 411, 412, 518, 528, 532; **25:** 339, 347; **36:** 301; **57:** 294, 367
subversiveness **22:** 302
symbolism **7:** 425, 429, 436, 452, 456, 469, 490, 493
textual issues **19:** 441; **45:** 333; **57:** 278, 285, 356
Time-Chorus **7:** 377, 380, 412, 464, 476, 501; **15:** 518
time **7:** 397, 425, 436, 476, 490; **19:** 366; **36:** 301, 349; **45:** 297, 329, 366, 374
trickster, motif of **22:** 302; **45:** 333
Union debate, relation to **25:** 347
violence **43:** 39
witchcraft **22:** 324
women, role of **22:** 324; **36:** 311; **42:** 308; **51:** 30; **57:** 294, 305, 319, 356

ISBN 0-7876-4695-4